SIXTH EDITION

Business:
Its Legal, Ethical,
and Global
Environment

65

SIXTH EDITION

Business: Its Legal, Ethical, and Global Environment

Marianne Moody Jennings
Arizona State University

THOMSON
™
SOUTH-WESTERN
WEST

Australia · Canada · Mexico · Singapore · Spain · United Kingdom · United States

THOMSON

SOUTH-WESTERN

WEST

Business: Its Legal, Ethical, and Global Environment, Sixth Edition

Marianne M. Jennings

Vice President, Team Director:
Michael P. Roche

Senior Acquisitions Editor:
Rob Dewey

Developmental Editor:
Bob Sandman

Marketing Manager:
Nicole Moore

Production Editor:
Tamborah Moore

Production House:
Shepherd, Inc.

Media Developmental Editor:
Peggy Buskey

Media Production Editor:
Mark Sears

Manufacturing Coordinator:
Rhonda Utley

Printer:
R.R. Donnelley & Sons Company
Willard Manufacturing Division

Design Project Manager:
Michelle Kunkler

Cover and Internal Design:
Jennifer Lambert, Jen2Design

Cover Image:
©Massimo Mastrorillo/
corbisstockmarket.com

Photography Manager:
Deanna Ettinger

Photo Researcher:
Susan Van Etten

Library of Congress Cataloging-in-Publication Data

Jennings, Marianne.
    Business: its legal, ethical, and
    global environment / Marianne
    Moody Jennings.—6th ed.
        p.   cm.
    Includes bibliographical
    references and index.
    ISBN 0-324-12185-7
    1. Business law—United States.
    2. Business ethics.   I. Title.
KF889.3.J46   2002
346.7307—dc21   2002017532

ISBN: 0-324-16485-8 (core text, InfoTrac, CD package)
ISBN: 0-324-18206-6 (core text and CD package)
ISBN: 0-324-12185-7 (core text only)
ISBN: 0-324-15850-5 (CD)

GET CONNECTED

Reader's Guide to

BUSINESS

Its Legal, Ethical, & Global Environment

Dear Reader:

Since the last edition of this book was published, the world has changed. We have witnessed a new economy, a resulting stock market bubble that burst and the tragic events of September 11, 2001. Many have said in reaction to these major events, "Things are different now."

While our business and personal lives may have changed dramatically, the issues of law and ethics have retained their role and importance. In fact, now more than ever we need to understand the legal and ethical issues that affect our businesses and our lives. The knowledge base and even the questions in law and ethics remain the same but the underlying facts have changed. For example, we still debate the social responsibility role of business. Now we raise that issue in the context of Bayer's patent on Cipro and its cost for selling its drug that cures anthrax. We still have the question of when a contract is formed. Now we face that question with "point and click" technology rather than faxes and letters. We are concerned about our privacy as consumers. But, we apply the law to our use of the Internet for our purchases and correspondence and wonder whether companies can use the information they find there. We still wonder about the extent of copyright law. Today we wonder if it applies when we use Napster to download music, free of charge.

The world is different, but law and ethics remain a constant framework into which we fit the issues of the day. In the materials that follow, you have the chance to understand the marvelous stability of this framework and the ease with which you can apply it to this very different world.

Please feel free to contact me (Marianne.Jennings@asu.edu) with thoughts, issues, questions and concerns.

Sincerely,

Marianne M. Jennings

Marianne Jennings
Professor of Legal and Ethical Studies
College of Business
Arizona State University
Tempe, AZ

A CLOSER LOOK AT THE
CONNECTIONS

COURT CASES

The **Case Headline** provides a memorable synopsis of the legal and ethical issues.

See more on pages 12, 281, and 729.

Facts summarize the issues and the **Judicial Opinion** provides the actual words of the court, edited for relevance.

CASE 1.2

A & M Records, Inc. v. Napster, Inc.
239 F.3d 1004 (9th Cir. 2001)

Downloading Music: Copyright Infringement or Peer-to-Peer File Sharing?

FACTS

A & M Records and others, including Geffen Records, Sony Music, MCA Records, Atlantic Recording, Motown Records and Capital Records (plaintiffs), are in the business of the commercial recording, distribution and sale of copyrighted musical compositions and sound recordings. They filed suit against Napster, Inc. (Napster) as a contributory and vicarious copyright infringer. Napster operates an online service for "peer-to-peer file sharing" (*www.Napster.com*) so that users can, free of charge, download recordings via the Internet through a process known as "ripping," which is the downloading of digital MP3 files. MP3 is the abbreviated term for audio recordings in a digital format known as MPEG-3. This compressed format allows for rapid transmission of digital audio files from one computer to another.

Napster's online service provides a search vehicle for files stored on others' computers and permits the downloading of the recordings from the hard drives of other Napster users. Napster provides

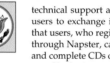

technical support as well as a chat room for users to exchange information. The result is that users, who register and have a password through Napster, can download single songs and complete CDs or albums, via the peer-to-peer file sharing.

The district court granted a preliminary injunction to the plaintiffs enjoining Napster from "engaging in, or facilitating others in copying, downloading, uploading, transmitting, or distributing plaintiffs' copyrighted musical compositions and sound recordings, protected by either federal or state law, without express permission of the rights owner."

The ninth circuit entered a temporary stay of the injunction in order to review the case.

JUDICIAL OPINION

BEEZER, Circuit Judge
Plaintiffs must satisfy two requirements to present a prima facie case of direct infringement: (1) they must show ownership of the allegedly infringed material

---

Case Questions test the understanding of the points of law in the cases and facilitate legal reasoning skills.

that the files are user named. In crafting the injunction on remand, the district court should recognize that Napster's system does not currently appear to allow Napster access to users' MP3 files.

AFFIRMED IN PART, REVERSED IN PART AND REMANDED.

NOTE AND AFTERMATH: On remand, the district court refashioned the injunction and ordered Napster to remove from its files all songs provided by the plaintiffs for which they held a copyright. The task of blocking the songs proved arduous because the downloading of a song under an inexact name permitted downloading to continue. For example, a song provided as "Down to You," by the record com-

pany could still be downloaded if carried by the file users as "Down 2 You" or "Down 2 U."

CASE QUESTIONS

1. Describe what Napster is and how it works.
2. Is Napster engaged in copyright infringement?
3. What factors does the court look at in examining fair use?
4. How does the court apply the *Sony* case?
5. Is Napster vicariously liable for the downloading of copyrighted songs by its users? What technological limitations exist in honoring the copyrights

Relative or alternative fact patterns, often from real court cases, follow legal or ethical concepts discussed in the text.

See more on pages 115, **436***, and 599.*

C O N S I D E R . . .

11.10 Firestone ATX, ATX II, and Wilderness tires have come under fire in the media because of complaints about the failure of those tires being linked to so many accidents. In May, following a report by a Houston television station on a correlation between the tires and accidents in that area, the National Highway Traffic Safety Administration (NHTSA) received a flurry of complaints about the tires.

The treads on the tires, about 48 million of them, found on many trucks and SUVs and used mostly on Ford Explorers, seem to suddenly separate, although no one yet understands why. One theory is heat and poor tire maintenance. A former Firestone tire engineer, however, theorizes that these particular tires lack nylon caps between their steel belts and the rubber to keep the belts from sawing through the tread. Such caps are common in other tires and cost about $1.00.

Does the company have any liability during the waiting period? What if customers wanted substitute transportation during the time they were waiting for tire replacements?

Most of the tires were on Ford Explorers, and Ford has distanced itself from the recall saying it did not know until the last few weeks of the tire problems and that it wants the recall accelerated. Why is Ford concerned?[3]

E T H I C A L   I S S U E S

The **Ethical Issues** present actual real-world ethical dilemmas involving individuals and businesses.

See more on pages **17***,* *434, and 892.*

ETHICAL ISSUES 11.2

A cell-phone controversy continues on several fronts. There are the vehicle safety issues surrounding the use of cell phones while driving with some cities prohibiting their use while operating a vehicle. The other controversy is whether the cell phones cause cancer.

Some studies conclude that they do not, but the Wireless Technology Research program, a program funded by the cellular-phone industry, has concluded that there are enough questions about their safety that no one should assure users that the phones are absolutely safe.

The FDA's Center for Devices and Radiological Health has concluded that there are no adverse health effects from cell phones and that no additional warn-ings are needed. Following a lawsuit filed by a cell-phone user in 1993 in which the allegation was made that the cell phone caused his cancer, the industry placed $27 million into a blind trust for research projects supported by the funding. The Wireless Technology Research program was one of the beneficiaries of the trust.

Review the findings on cell phone safety at http://www.medscape.com

If you were a cell-phone manufacturer, would you take any action? Would you provide warnings? What about those who drive with cell phones and cause accidents? Are cell-phone manufacturers liable to those who are injured by cell-phone-using drivers?

A CLOSER LOOK AT THE
CONNECTIONS

BUSINESS STRATEGY

new feature **Business Strategy** provides insights into the strategic aspects of the law, reinforcing the impacts on individuals and businesses.

See more on pages **288**, *504, and 850.*

BUSINESS STRATEGY

While cyberspace has presented many legal difficulties for courts and businesses, the technology that created cyberspace has also developed solutions. Many companies are incorporating systems that automatically destroy e-mails after a selected period of time. The idea is to destroy the electronic trail of e-mail messages. Companies offering such technology have their own Web sites:

> http://www.authentica.com
> http://www.disappearinginc.com
> http://www.qvtech.com

Microsoft has taken the consumer's desire for privacy over the Internet and developed the Platform for Privacy (P3P), a program that lets consumers choose the amount of privacy they want when they use various Internet sites. AOL, Time Warner, and IBM have all agreed to make their sites P3P compatible. The program would save these companies from the additional expense of steps in their programs that are required to allow consumers to choose their privacy protection. Such a program would, however— as competitors have noted to Congress, the Justice Department, and the Federal Trade Commission— give Microsoft a dominant position in the Internet market. Microsoft has used knowledge of technology and the law as it applies to privacy and consumers to develop a product and a potential market edge.

Source: Glenn R. Simpson, "The Battle Over Web Privacy," *Wall Street Journal*, 21 March 2001, B1, B4.

BUSINESS STRATEGY APPLICATION

new feature **Business Strategy Applications** require students to go one step further to answer questions on strategic issues related to the law and business.

See more on pages **76**, *679, and 903.*

BUSINESS STRATEGY APPLICATION

Business Ethics magazine has named its top 100 corporate citizens. Looking at the investment portfolios of socially responsible investment funds leads to creation of the list. Those funds focus on issues such as human rights, animal testing, diversity, non–weapon production, and impact on the environment. The top twenty corporate citizens are listed here:

1. Procter & Gamble
2. Hewlett-Packard
3. Fannie Mae
4. Motorola
5. IBM
6. Sun Microsystems
7. Herman Miller
8. Polaroid
9. St. Paul Cos.
10. Freddie Mac
11. Home Depot
12. State Street
13. QRS
14. Dime Bancorp
15. HB Fuller
16. Cummins Engine
17. Amgen
18. Intel
19. Cisco Systems
20. Avon Products

The CD-ROM exercise gives you the Web sites for the companies. You can view their codes of ethics and financial performance. You will be asked to note any differences between and among their codes of ethics. You will also be asked to find and compare their financial performances with their rankings. Finally, you can then discuss the issue of whether good ethics is good business. Is social responsibility the same as ethics?

In-depth readings show how businesses interrelate with law and ethics.

See more on pages 194, **567***, and 731.*

Re: ATM Fees and Other Creative Bank Charges

In California, there is a heated battle between banks and consumers over ATM fees. Consumers have been upset recently with ATM usage charges that can be as much as $3.50 for the withdrawal of $20. For example, a bank can charge $2.00 when a customer uses an ATM from a different bank. The bank the customer uses can also charge money, generally $1.50, for the foreign customer using its system. The result is a total charge for the consumer of $3.50.

When ATMs were first gaining popularity, banks waived such fees in order to encourage usage of the electronic forms of banking as opposed to the labor-intensive and costly physical tellers. In fact, the two major ATM systems had joined together to fight charging fees. However, legislatures in fifteen states passed statutes permitted the ATM surcharges.

Now states are swinging the other way, with Connecticut and Iowa being two examples of states that do not permit the surcharges. The litigation in the San Francisco area involves the issue of whether states can regulate banking surcharges. The issue of preemption has been raised with respect to state statutes on ATM fees.

Credit card holders have discovered new and creative fees being assessed to them by their credit card companies. The following is a list of the latest new forms of charges on credit card bills:

- Foreign transaction fees—foreign transaction fees have increased from 1 percent to 3 percent.
- Cash advance fees have increased from 1 percent to between 3 percent and 5 percent, and the minimum fee has increased from $1 to between $5 and $10.
- Balance transfer fees for transferring the balance from one credit card to another with lower interest is typically 3 percent of the balance, with minimum transfer fees ranging from $5 to $50.
- On some of the credit cards, cancellation of the card can lead to an accelerated interest rate such as the 26.99 percent charged by Fleet Financial.

The fees are in response to a new consumer trend to pay off their credit card balances. In 1991, 29 percent of consumers paid off their monthly credit card bills. In 1999, the figure had risen to 44 percent. With so little interest income from the cards, the cards are generating revenue in other ways, such as by the aforementioned new fees and charges.

Readings often are reprinted from major business publications such as *The Wall Street Journal.*

A CLOSER LOOK AT THE
CONNECTIONS

BUSINESS STRATEGY APPLICATION CD–ROM

new

Business Strategy Application CD–ROM: Every new copy of the text includes this new Business Strategy Application CD-ROM. From the end-of-chapter exercises, students are directed to the CD-ROM where they utilize various companies' public records and documents to analyze and apply the legal principles to real-world business situations. Students then see the significance of how the law affects real-life companies. Examples include Microsoft Case Arguments, Creating a Diversity Program, Name that Tort, and many more.

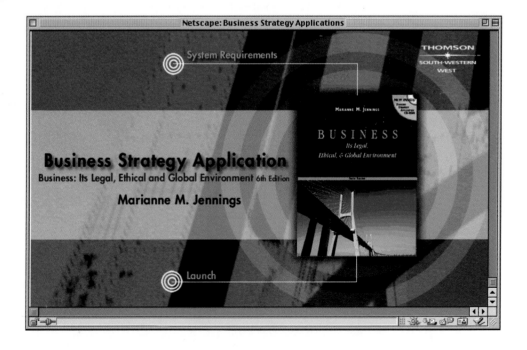

new

Every **Business Strategy Application** contains instructions, topics, and resources for this application, along with an overall chapter assignment. Each application provides a summary, objectives, key concepts, bridges to the text and tutorials to help identify the strategic issues involved in each application and assignment.

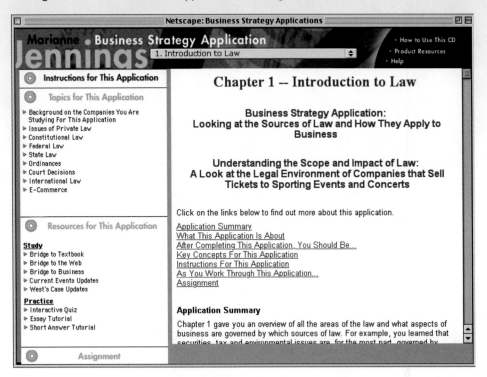

new

Business Application Assignments apply the chapter concepts, the online corporate documents and materials to a specific strategic issue or question. Using the email functionality, answers can be emailed directly to instructors for immediate review.

To the core of my global environment:
Terry, Sarah, Claire, Sam, and John

Brief Contents

Contents

PART TWO

BUSINESS: ITS REGULATORY ENVIRONMENT 159

CHAPTER SIX

ADMINISTRATIVE LAW 204

CHAPTER SEVEN

INTERNATIONAL LAW 246

CHAPTER EIGHT

CYBER LAW 278

PART THREE

BUSINESS COMPETITION AND SALES 487

PART FOUR

BUSINESS AND ITS EMPLOYEES 681

PART FIVE

BUSINESS FORMS AND CAPITALIZATION 819

Preface

A DIFFERENT WORLD, BUT THE SAME ISSUES

Since the last edition of this book was published, the world has changed. We have witnessed a new economy, a resulting stock market bubble that burst, and the tragic events of September 11, 2001. Many have said in reaction to these major events, "Things are different now."

While our business and personal lives may have changed dramatically, the issues of law and ethics have retained their role and importance. In fact, now more than ever we need to understand the legal and ethical issues that affect our businesses and our lives. The knowledge base and even the questions in law and ethics remain the same but the underlying facts have changed. For example, we still debate the social responsibility role of business. Now we raise that issue in the context of Bayer's patent on Cipro and its cost for selling its drug that cures anthrax. We still have the question of when a contract is formed. Now we face that question with "point and click" technology rather than faxes and letters. We are concerned about our privacy as consumers. But we apply the law to our use of the Internet for our purchases and correspondence and wonder whether companies can use the information they find there. We still wonder about the extent of copyright law. Today we wonder if it applies when we use Napster to download music, free of charge.

The world is different, but law and ethics remain a constant framework into which we fit the issues of the day. In the materials that follow, you have the chance to understand the marvelous stability of this framework and the ease with which you can apply it to this very different world. Be sure to look for descriptions of the exciting new features, **Business Strategy** and the **Business Strategy Application CD-ROM,** and of the new chapter, Cyber Law.

BUILDING THE BRIDGE: APPLYING LEGAL AND ETHICAL REASONING TO BUSINESS ANALYSIS

My students recently completed a project on the expansion of an Internet service provider (ISP) firm in South America. Because this project was their capstone experience for their degrees, their discussion of the strategic issues was phenomenal. The students offered classic SWOT analysis: Strengths, Weaknesses, Opportunities, and Threats. Should the company try cyber cafes? What about merging with cellular companies? How about working with cable firms? In came the students' economic analysis, factoring in the nature and importance of economic swings and the vulnerability of dot-coms. There was the cash burn rate, capital expenses and the advertising dollars. Their work demonstrated that we had trained very capable *business* students.

But with each presentation I found myself raising the same unanswered questions: What about copyright issues? What happens if the users download music on the ISP? What happens if digital technology allows circumvention of protections? What if the ISP is used for defamation? And what laws apply to disputes? Is it the law of Bolivia or the law of the United States? Will the ISP have to go to

Brazil to defend lawsuits? When does a subscriber agree to a contract for service? What happens if companies that advertise use the subscribers' names and information and sell them to others? Is this a breach of privacy? And what about the ethical and social responsibility issues when pornography sites seek subscribers via this company's ISP? Our capable business students, adept at complex business analysis, stumbled over basic legal and ethical issues.

Why couldn't these students competently discuss legal issues? It was not for lack of exposure to the law. I taught my course "by the book," so to speak. Students could recite the components of a valid contract, rattle off the requirements for bankruptcy, recall from memory the antitrust statutes. Yet, I was coming to realize, this rote knowledge was not enough. One of my best former students, who had gone on to medical school, came to me perplexed about her office lease. She said that the complex in which she wanted to open her practice had a "no advertising" policy. In fact, she said that when she toured the premises with a leasing agent, the leasing agent turned to her and said, "You're not one of those doctors who advertises, are you? Because if you are, we can't lease to you. We have a policy against it." One of my best students, who knew the antitrust statutes well, could not apply them to her everyday business. Worse, perhaps, she could not *recognize* when to apply these statutes: She did not see the antitrust implications of the agent's statements nor the problems with the physicians in the complex taking such an approach to screening tenants.

I reached the conclusion that there were shortcomings in the standard approach to teaching business students law and ethics. Students were not ignorant of the law; rather, they simply lacked the necessary skills to recognize legal and ethical issues and to apply their knowledge of law and ethics to business decision making. As instructors, we were not integrating legal and ethical reasoning with business analysis. My conclusion led me to develop my own materials for classroom use and eventually led to the publication of the first edition of this book. Now in its sixth edition, *Business: Its Legal, Ethical, and Global Environment* brings to the classroom the most integrated approach to learning law and ethics available in the market today. Throughout every chapter and in every feature, students and instructors are continually reminded of how various legal and ethical principles apply in business contexts. For all areas of law and ethics, this book answers the question: How does this concept affect a business? This book builds a bridge for the student between knowledge of law and ethics and application of both in business. In fact, new to this edition is the Business Strategy feature. Each chapter contains a discussion of how the legal issues covered in the chapter must be integrated into or affect business strategic planning and decisions.

STRENGTHENING THE BRIDGE: NEW CONTENT, BUSINESS APPLICATIONS, AND LEARNINGS AIDS

For the sixth edition, *Business: Its Legal, Ethical, and Global Environment* has undergone further refinement. New content has been added, new business applications integrated into every chapter, and the learning aids have been modified and refocused to help students understand and apply legal and ethical concepts.

New Content

The sixth edition of *Business: Its Legal, Ethical, and Global Environment* continues to meet its goal of helping students with their understanding of how law and ethics apply to the business world. The organizational structure continues from the fifth edition because the changes made then were well received. In general, each part begins with an overview that helps students see the importance of the various aspects of law in business management and operations. Part I offers the student an overview of the legal, ethical, and judicial environments of business. Part II covers the regulatory environments of business. New to this edition is a chapter on cyber law. Part III covers the law and ethics of competition and sales and has been reorganized to provide a more logical flow of material. Part IV covers the legal and ethical issues of business and employees. Part V covers the law and ethical dilemmas of business organization and capitalization.

Ethics

Business Ethics and Social Responsibility (Chapter 2) offers new examples and insights on the application of ethics to business decision making. Ethics coverage is also integrated throughout all chapters.

Property

While the chapter on business property still includes coverage of the latest issues affecting intellectual, tangible personal, and real property in business, the addition of the cyber law chapter has allowed for greater discussion of the intellectual property issues that have arisen because of new technologies and the Internet.

BUSINESS APPLICATIONS

Business Strategy

New to this edition is the Business Strategy feature. Each chapter contains an example and discussion of how the legal issues covered in the chapter must be integrated into or affect business strategic planning and decisions.

Biography

Each chapter contains at least one biography. Biographies (1- to 3-page features) provide students with business history through the study of individuals and companies involved with the area of law and ethics covered in the chapter. For example, Chapter 17, Antitrust Law, provides a look at the giant auction houses, Sotheby's and Christie's and how their chairmen and CEOs managed to violate the Sherman Act and end up with criminal trials, guilty pleas and ended careers. Students can also read the story of the 15-year-old pump-and-dump king, Jonathan Lebed, as well as the disastrous fall of William Aramony, the former head of United Way.

For the Manager's Desk

Each chapter also contains at least one For the Manager's Desk. These readings provide students with excerpts from various business publications, including *Forbes, Wall Street Journal, Fortune,* and *Business Week,* as well as other publications, including *National Law Journal, California Management Review, American Business*

Law Journal, and the *Real Estate Law Journal.* These readings, some short and others in-depth, offer students the opportunity to see how business interrelates with ethics and law.

LEARNING AIDS

Internet Margin Notes

For further student exploration, every chapter integrates World Wide Web addresses highlighting links to legal and business resources. At their option, students can review unedited cases and full statutes, visit governmental departments and international organizations, and examine relevant business materials. The text includes over 100 Web addresses.

Research Problems

Each chapter also contains a research problem for students to explore using both the Internet and other resources. The problems can be used in class or as assignments.

Case Headlines

Every court case has a case headline that summarizes what issues are involved in the case. In Business Torts (Chapter 9), students read *McClung* v. *Delta Square Limited Partnership* (384–387), a case addressing the liability of store and shopping-center owners to customers who are victims of crimes while shopping. Although students likely won't remember the name *McClung,* the headline, "Kidnapped at the Local Wal-Mart: High Noon and No One Was Watching," will keep the case and its holding fresh in their memories.

Chapter Openers

Chapters begin with an opening problem, titled "Consider . . . ," which presents a legal dilemma relevant to the chapter's discussion and similar to those business managers need to handle. These are revisited and answered in the body of the chapter. For example, Chapter 1's opening "Consider" involves Shawn Fanning and his Napster company and its program for downloading music via peer-to-peer file sharing. Students will not only read about the *Napster* copyright infringement case in Chapter 1, they will read it after they have studied the *Sony* case in which the courts grappled with a similar infringement issue when the new technology was the VCR. Moreover, these answers are referenced in the text and clearly marked. Next, opening statements discuss the major topics of the chapter and present the general goals for the chapter in the form of questions to be answered. Finally, quotations, often humorous, pique students' interest and focus the chapter to the major issues.

Chapter Summary

Each chapter concludes with a summary that reinforces the major concepts of the chapter. Each summary is constructed around the key questions introduced at the start of the chapter and key terms presented throughout the chapter.

Business Strategy Applications CD-ROM

New to the sixth edition are CD-ROM Business Strategy Applications. Each chapter has an exercise designed to teach the students how to use the materials they have learned in the chapter. The reference in the text directs students to the CD-ROM packaged with each new book. For example, for Chapter 1, the students have the chance to walk two new businesses through the laws that affect them. They read about two companies beginning businesses that will sell tickets to sporting and concert events over the Internet. They will see how these companies are affected by local laws, federal statutes and even international law. For Chapter 5, they take a look at freedom of speech for corporations in the context of political donations and how those speech rights are balanced with regulations on contributions and how companies use the donations strategically. For Chapter 2, they do an integration exercise in which they compare codes of ethics for companies with the companies' financial performance. In Chapter 20, they will have the chance to study various approaches to diversity and develop a good diversity plan for their own companies.

These exercises have questions to help them review the chapter materials, questions to help them understand the application materials and an assignment that they can do to bring knowledge, application and strategy together. These exercises help students understand the material in the book, but they also provide an understanding of why the material is important and how it fits in the strategic plans and decisions of a business.

THINKING, APPLYING, AND REASONING: ORGANIZATION AND FEATURES

In addition to the new features added to this edition, the classic features have been updated and strengthened. The organization has been retained to continue to meet student needs in the classroom.

ORGANIZATION

As noted above, there are five parts in the book, which serve to organize the materials around business operations. Every chapter integrates international and ethical topics.

Part I

In four chapters, Part I offers an introduction to law, an introduction to business ethics and the judicial system, and a discussion of litigation and alternative dispute resolution. Part I provides students with a foundation in law and ethics, as well as legal and ethical reasoning, necessary for the areas of law in the chapters that follow. By being brief (four chapters), Part I offers instructors an early and logical break for exams.

Part II

In seven chapters, Part II covers the regulatory environment of business, including the following topics: constitutional law, administrative and international law, cyber law, business crimes and business torts, product advertising and liability, and environmental regulation. With the completion of Parts I and II, students have a grasp of the legal system, ethical boundaries, and the laws that affect business operational decisions, even those in cyber space.

Part III

The five chapters in Part III present students with the legal and ethical issues surrounding competition and sales. Part III includes the following topics: real, tangible personal, and intellectual property; trade restraints and antitrust laws; contract and sales law; and financing of sales and leases, including credit disclosure and requirements. From the negotiation of price to the collection of accounts, this segment of the book covers all aspects of selling business products and services. This section has been reorganized so that contracts precede the complexities of property and competition.

Part IV

The three chapters in Part IV discuss the contractual and regulatory aspects of employer and employee relationships. Topics include agency law and employee conduct, management of employee welfare, and employment discrimination.

Part V

In Part V, students study the advantages and disadvantages of various business organizations and the regulation of the capital markets. The two chapters in Part V include the following topics: business organization, securities laws, and business combinations.

FEATURES

Court Cases

Edited court language cases provide in-depth points of law, and many cases include dissenting and concurring opinions. Case questions follow to help students understand the points of law in the case and think critically about the decision.

Consider . . .

Consider problems, along with Ethical Issues boxes and Business Planning Tips, have been a part of every chapter since the first edition. Considers, often based on real court cases, ask students to evaluate and analyze the legal and ethical issues discussed in the preceding text. By being integrated into the text, students must address and think critically about these issues as they encounter them. Through interactive problems, students learn to judge case facts and determine the consequences.

Ethical Issues

Ethical Issues boxes appear in every chapter and present students with real-world ethical problems for students to grapple with. Ethical Issues help integrate coverage of ethics into every chapter.

Business Planning Tips

Students are given sound business and legal advice through Business Planning Tips. With these tips, students not only know the law, they know how to anticipate issues and ensure compliance.

E-Commerce and the Law

Most chapters also include a segment on the law as it relates to e-commerce. While the cyber law chapter offers a good overview, these chapter-by-chapter materials give students the chance to see how the new technology fits into the existing legal framework.

Exhibits

Exhibits include charts, figures, and business and legal documents that help highlight or summarize legal and ethical issues from the chapter.

End of Chapter Problems

The end of the chapter problems have been updated and focus more on actual cases.

THE INFORMED MANAGER: WHO SHOULD USE THIS BOOK?

With its comprehensive treatment of the law, integrated business applications, and new full-color design, *Business: Its Legal, Ethical, and Global Environment* is well suited for both undergraduate and MBA students. The book is used extensively in undergraduate education programs around the country. In addition, this edition has been class-tested with MBA students, and it is appropriate for MBA and executive education programs.

A NOTE ON AACSB STANDARDS

The AACSB standards emphasize the need for students to have an understanding of ethical and global issues. The sixth edition continues with its separate chapter on ethics as well as ethical issues and dilemmas for student discussion and resolution in every chapter. The separate chapter on international law appears in expanded version in this edition, and each chapter has a segment devoted to international law issues. The sixth edition includes readings on language issues in contracts, women as executives in other cultures, the role of lawyers in other countries, and attitudes outside the United States on insider trading.

This edition presents students with the legal foundation necessary for business operations and sales, but also affords the students the opportunities to analyze critically the social and political environments in which the laws are made and in which businesses must operate. Just an examination of the lists of the companies and individuals covered in the biographies and of the publications from which the For the Manager's Desk readings are taken demonstrates the depth of background the sixth edition offers in those areas noted as critical by the AACSB. The materials provide a balanced look at regulation, free enterprise, and the new global economy.

This edition continues margin notes that direct the student to various tools and topics available on the Internet. These margin notes offer students the opportunity to browse for more information or undertake projects for additional research and class work.

SUPPLEMENTS

Business: Its Legal, Ethical, and Global Environment offers a comprehensive and well-crafted supplements package for both students and instructors. Contact your Thomson Learning/West Legal Studies in Business Sales Representative for more details, or visit the Jennings Business Web site at http://jennings.westbuslaw.com.

Weekly Law Updates. Available to instructors and students is the weekly update on the law at http://jennings.westbuslaw.com. The weekly updated contributed by the author offers current events for discussion and analysis. The update features new decisions, new statutes, new regulations, and cites to current periodicals.

Student Study Guide. (ISBN: 0-324-15799-1) Written under the guidance of the author, the Study Guide provides the following for each chapter: an outline; chapter outlines, key terms; and matching, fill-in-the-blank, and short answer questions.

Instructor's Manual. (ISBN: 0-324-15852-1) The Instructor's Manual, written by the author, provides the following for each chapter: a detailed outline; answers to Considers, Ethical Issues, and case problems; briefs of all cases; supplemental readings; and interactive/cooperative learning exercises.

Test Bank. (ISBN: 0-324-15853-X) Written by the author, the Test Bank includes more than 1,500 questions in true-false, multiple-choice, and essay questions. Answers to questions provide a subject word for easy identification and a classification indicating if they are intended for review of concepts or for analysis and application of concepts.

ExamView Testing Software—Computerized Testing Software. (ISBN: 0-324-16486-6) This testing software contains all of the questions in the printed test bank. This program is an easy-to-use test creation software compatible with Microsoft Windows. Instructors can add or edit questions, instructions, and answers; and select questions by previewing them on the screen, selecting them randomly, or selecting them by number. Instructors can also create and administer quizzes online, whether over the Internet, a local area network (LAN), or a wide area network (WAN).

Microsoft PowerPoint Lecture Review Slides. PowerPoint slides are available for use by students as an aid to note-taking, and by instructors for enhancing their lectures. Download these slides at http://jennings.westbuslaw.com.

Lesson Plans and Lectures. Lesson Plans and Lectures, available to download at http://jennings.westbuslaw.com, provides detailed lectures for each semester class period (32 lectures in all) plus sample syllabi, teaching tips, and content and reading quizzes.

InfoTrac College Edition. This online library contains hundreds of scholarly and popular periodicals, including *American Business Law Journal, Journal of International Business Studies, Environmental Law,* and *Ethics.* A package can be created that provides students free access to InfoTrac College Edition with this textbook. Contact your local Thomson Learning/West Legal Studies in Business Sales Representative to set up a package for your course.

Videos. Qualified adopters using this text have access to the entire library of West videos, a vast selection covering most business law issues. There are some restrictions, and if you have questions, please contact your local Thomson Learning/ West Legal Studies in Business sales representative or visit http://www.westbuslaw.com/video_library.html.

About the Author

Professor Marianne Jennings is a member of the legal studies in business area of the Department of Supply Chain Management in the College of Business at Arizona State University and a professor of legal and ethical studies in business. She served as director of the Joan and David Lincoln Center for Applied Ethics from 1995–1999. Professor Jennings earned her undergraduate degree in finance and her J. D. from Brigham Young University. She has worked with the Federal Public Defender and U.S. Attorney in Nevada and has done consulting work for law firms, businesses, and professional groups, including Dial Corporation, Motorola, the National Association of Credit Managers, Mesa Community College, Southern California Edison, the Arizona Auditor General, the Cities of Phoenix, Mesa, and Tucson, Midwest Energy Supply, Hy-Vee Foods, IBM, Bell Helicopter, Amgen, and VIAD.

She joined the faculty at ASU in 1977 as an assistant professor. She was promoted to associate professor in 1980 and to full professor in 1983. At ASU she teaches graduate courses in the MBA program in business ethics and the legal environment of business. She has authored more than 130 articles in academic, professional and trade journals. Currently she has six textbooks and monographs in circulation. The fourth edition of her textbook, *Business Ethics: Case Studies and Selected Readings,* will be published in early 2002. The sixth edition of her textbook, *Real Estate Law,* was published in July 2001. The sixth edition of her textbook, *Business: Its Legal, Ethical, and Global Environment* was published in March 2002. She was added as a co-author to *Anderson's Business Law and the Legal Environment in* 1997 for the 17th Edition. The 18th Edition is now available. The 15th Edition of *Anderson's Business and the Regulatory Environment* will be available in August 2003. Her book, *Business Strategy for the Political Arena,* was selected in 1985 by *Library Journal* as one of its recommended books in business/government relations. In 2000 her book on corporate governance was published by the *New York Times* MBA Pocket Series.

Her weekly columns are syndicated around the country, and her work has appeared in the *Wall Street Journal,* the *Chicago Tribune,* the *New York Times,* and the *Reader's Digest.* A collection of her essays, *Nobody Fixes Real Carrot Sticks Anymore,* was published in 1994. She was given an Arizona Press Club award in 1994 for her work as a feature columnist. She has been a commentator on business issues on *All Things Considered* for National Public Radio.

She has conducted more than 200 workshops and seminars in the areas of business, personal, and government, legal, academic and professional ethics. She has been named professor of the year in the College of Business in 1981, 1987 and 2000 and was the recipient of a Burlington Northern teaching excellence award. In 1999 she was given best article awards by the Academy of Legal Studies in Business and the Association for Government Accountants. She was named a Wakonse Fellow in 1994 and was named Distinguished Faculty Researcher for the College of Business that same year. She has been a Dean's Council of 100 Distinguished Scholars since 1995. In 2000 the Association of Government Accountants inducted her into its Speakers Hall of Fame.

She is a contributing editor for the *Real Estate Law Journal,* the *Corporate Finance Review,* and the articles editor for the *Journal of Legal Studies Education.* She has received nine research grants. In 1984, she served as then Governor Bruce Babbitt's appointee to the Arizona Corporation Commission. In 1999 she was appointed by Governor Jane Dee Hull to the Arizona Commission on Character. During 1986–1988, she served as Associate Dean in the College of Business. From 1986–87, she served as ASU's faculty athletic representative to the NCAA and PAC-10. In 1999 she was elected president of the Arizona Association of Scholars.

She is a member of twelve professional organizations, including the State Bar of Arizona, and has served on four boards of directors, including that of Arizona Public Service from 1987–2000. She served as chair of the Bonneville International Advisory Board for KHTC/KIDR from 1994–1997 and was a weekly commentator on KGLE during 1998. She has appeared on *CBS This Morning,* the *Today Show, CBS Evening News* and *Dateline NBC.*

She is married to Terry H. Jennings of the Maricopa County Attorney's office, and has four children: Sarah, Claire, Sam, and John.

Acknowledgments

By its sixth edition, a book has evolved to a point of trademark characteristics. This book is known for its hands-on examples and readings for business managers. That trademark evolves because of the efforts of many. There are the reviewers and adopters of the text who provide ideas, cases, and suggestions for improvement and inclusion. For this edition, the following colleagues offered their seasoned advice:

Richard Coffinberger, *George Mason University*
Deborah Lynn Bundy Ferry, *Marquette University*
Sherry Kaiser, *Keller Graduate School of Management*
Ann C. Morales, *University of Miami*
Catherine D. Weber, *Southern Methodist University*

Any edition of a book bears the mark of the editors who work to design, refine, market, and produce it. This book carries the insight of Rob Dewey, the work and inspiration of Bob Sandman, the steadiness, calm and eye for detail of Tamborah Moore, the production editor, and Mary Grivetti. The CD-ROM exercises for this book brought Peggy Buskey to help me learn to point, click, platform, and develop all manner of IT skills. The marvelous CD-ROM exercises reflect her talent and are proof of her patience with an author on a steep, high-tech learning curve.

This book also carries the unmistakable liveliness of an author who shares her life with four helpful children and one tolerant husband. Their vibrancy is found in the color and charm of these pages. I am grateful for their unanimous support for my work. I am finally grateful to my parents who taught me through their words and examples of the importance and rewards of ethics and hard work.

Marianne Moody Jennings

PART ONE

Business: Its Legal, Ethical, and Judicial Environment

Every business and businessperson needs parameters for operation. What is legal? Where can I find the laws I need to know? How do I make decisions about legal conduct that, personally, is morally or ethically troublesome to me? What if a disagreement occurs with a customer, employee, or shareholder? How can I resolve our differences? What forums are available for airing disputes?

This portion of the book explains what law is, where it can be found, how it is applied, and how legal disputes are resolved. Beyond the legal environment of a business, what is its ethical posture? Beyond operating a business within the bounds of the law, is the manager making ethical choices and behaving honorably in the conduct of business? Law and ethics are inextricably intertwined. A commitment to both is necessary and helpful in ensuring smooth operations and successful business performance.

CHAPTER ONE

Introduction to Law

Most people understand the law through their own experiences with it. More often than not, people are exposed to law through some personal problem. Some are exposed to law through traffic tickets. Others encounter the law when a problem arises with a landlord or lease. Their understanding of the law may be limited by the anger they feel about the landlord or traffic ticket. However, if there were no traffic laws, the roads would be a study in survival of the fittest; and, in the case of a troublesome landlord, the law provides a remedy when parties do not meet their agreed-upon obligations.

Types of laws and penalties for violating them vary from state to state and from city to city; but, however much they vary, laws exist everywhere and at every level of government. Indeed, law is a universal, necessary foundation of an orderly society; it helps maintain order and ensures that members of a society meet minimum standards of conduct or risk penalties. Law is made up of rules that control people's conduct and their interrelationships. Traffic laws control not only our conduct when we are driving but also our relationships with other drivers using the roads. In some instances, we owe them a right-of-way and are liable to them for any injuries we cause by not following the traffic laws.

This chapter offers an introduction to law. How is law defined? What types of laws are there? What are the purposes and characteristics of law? Where are laws found, and who enacts them?

It is the spirit and not the form of law that keeps justice alive.

EARL WARREN
Chief Justice, U.S. Supreme Court, 1953–1969

CONSIDER...

Shawn Fanning, a young college student, was able to develop a program that permitted the downloading of music from computer to computer over the Internet. Using MP3 digital technology, Shawn founded Napster, a site that permitted users to exchange their music. Users could download one song from a CD or entire albums. The service was free, and it was called "peer-to-peer file sharing." Recording artists and record companies called "peer-to-peer file sharing" nothing more than copyright infringement. "It's a technology no one anticipated and the law doesn't apply," was the observation of one legal expert. Don Henley, formerly of The Eagles, and Alanis Morrissette both testified before Congress that Napster deprived them of their royalty income and their rights in their intellectual property. Members of Congress wanted to know if existing laws could be applied or if Shawn Fanning had found a technological loophole. The record companies filed suit for copyright infringement, and Napster defended on the grounds that it was not copying any music and made no money from the program. How does the law determine the rights of the parties when there is a technological tidal wave like Napster?

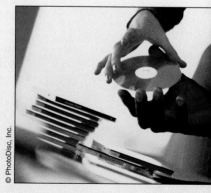

© PhotoDisc, Inc.

DEFINITION OF LAW

Philosophers and scholars throughout human history have offered definitions of law. Aristotle, the early Greek philosopher, wrote that "the law is reason unaffected by desire" and that "law is a form of order, and good law must necessarily mean good order." Oliver Wendell Holmes Jr., a U.S. Supreme Court justice of the early twentieth century, said that "law embodies the story of a nation's development through many centuries." Sir William Blackstone, the English philosopher and legal scholar, observed that law was "that rule of action which is prescribed by some superior and which the inferior is bound to obey." *Black's Law Dictionary* defines law as "a body of rules of action or conduct prescribed by the controlling authority, and having legal binding force." Law has been defined at least once by every philosopher, statesman, politician, and police officer.

Law is simply the body of rules governing individuals and their relationships. A society enacts most of those rules through a recognized governmental authority. It gives us basic freedoms, rights, and protections. Law offers a consistent model of conduct for members of society in their business and personal lives and gives them certainty of expectations. Plans, businesses, contracts, and property ownership are based on the expectation of the law's consistent protection of rights. Without such a consistent framework of legal boundaries, ours would be a society of chaos and confusion.

CLASSIFICATIONS OF LAW

Public versus Private Law

Public law includes laws that are enacted by some authorized governmental body. State and federal constitutions and statutes are all examples of public laws, as are the federal securities laws, state incorporation and partnership procedures, and zoning laws.

Private law, on the other hand, is developed between two individuals. For example, landlords usually have regulations for their tenants and these regulations are private laws. The terms of a contract are a form of private law for the parties to that contract. Although the requirements for forming and the means for enforcing that contract may be a matter of public law, the terms for performance are the private law created by the parties to that rental contract. Employer rules in a corporation are also examples of private law; so long as those rules do not infringe any public rights or violate any statutory protections, those rules are a private law relationship between employer and employee and constitute part of the employee's performance standards.

Criminal versus Civil Law

A violation of a **criminal law** is a wrong against society. A violation of a **civil law** is a wrong against another person or persons. Criminal violations have penalties such as fines and imprisonment. Running a red light is an example of a criminal violation and generally carries a fine as punishment. Violations of civil laws require restitution: The party who violated the civil law must compensate the harmed party. If you do run a red light and strike and injure a pedestrian, you have committed a civil wrong, and may be required to pay for that pedestrian's damages.

If you drive while intoxicated, you are breaking a criminal law and are subject to a fine, jail term, or license suspension. If you have an accident while driving intoxicated, you commit a civil wrong against anyone you injure. People who are injured as a result of your driving while intoxicated can file a civil suit against you to recover for injuries to their persons and property (cars).

There are other differences between civil and criminal laws and their enforcement. For example, there are different rights and procedures in the trials of criminal cases (see Chapter 9 for more details).

Substantive versus Procedural Law

Substantive laws are those that give rights and responsibilities. **Procedural laws** provide the means for enforcing substantive rights. For example, if Zeta Corporation has breached its contract to buy 3,000 microchips from Yerba Corporation, Yerba has the substantive right to expect performance and may be able to collect damages for breach of contract by bringing suit. The laws governing how Yerba's suit is brought and the trial process are procedural laws; the laws regarding subject matter and issues of the litigation are substantive laws.

Common versus Statutory Law

The term **common law** has been in existence since 1066, when the Normans conquered England and William the Conqueror sought one common set of laws governing a then very divided England. The various customs of each locality were compromised and conglomerated so that each locality would then operate under a "common" system of law. This common law was developed by the judges in each locality as they settled disputes. They consulted their fellow judges before making decisions so that their body of common law achieved consistency. This principle of following other decisions is referred to as *stare decisis,* meaning "let the decision stand" (see p. 25 and also Chapter 3); and, as a process of legal reasoning, it is still followed today. The courts use the judicial decisions of the past in making their judgments to provide for consistency or to serve as a basis for making a change in the law when circumstances are different.

As much of an improvement as it was, the common law was still just uncodified law. Because of increased trade, population, and complexities, the common law needed to be supplemented. Thus, **statutory law,** which is passed by some governmental body and written in some form, was created.

Today, in the United States, there is both common law and statutory law. Some of our common law still consists of principles from the original English common law. For example, how we own and pass title to real property is largely developed from English common law. There is, however, still a growing body of common law: The judicial system's decisions constitute a form of common law that is used in the process of *stare decisis.* Courts throughout the country look to other court decisions when confronted with similar cases. Statutory law exists at all levels of government—federal, state, county, city, and town.

Our statutory law varies throughout our nation because of the cultural heritages of various regions. For example, the southwestern states have marital property rights statutes—often referred to as community property laws—that were influenced by the Spanish legal system implemented in Mexico. The northeastern states have very different marital property laws that were influenced by English laws on property ownership. Louisiana's contract laws are based on French principles because of the early French settlements there.

Law versus Equity

Equity is a body of law that attempts to do justice when the law does not provide a remedy, or when the remedy is inadequate, or when the application of the law is terribly unfair. Equity originated in England because the technicalities of the common law often resulted in unresolved disputes or unfair resolutions. The monarchy allowed its chancellor to hear those cases that could not be resolved in the common law courts; and, eventually, a separate set of equity courts developed that were not bound by rigid common law rules. These courts could get more easily to the heart of a dispute; and, over time, they developed remedies not available under common law. Common law, for example, usually permitted only the recovery of monetary damages. Courts of equity, on the other hand, could issue orders, known as **injunctions,** prohibiting certain conduct or ordering certain acts. The equitable remedies available in the courts of chancery were gradually combined with the legal remedies of the common law courts so that now parties can have both their legal and equitable remedies determined by the same court.

Today's courts award equitable remedies when the legal remedy of money damages would be inadequate. For example, Walt Disney often brings suit against companies and individuals for infringement of its copyrighted characters. Disney cannot be adequately compensated with money because the continued use of the characters will cost Disney its exclusive rights. The remedy it seeks and is given is an injunction that orders the infringing party to stop the unauthorized use.

PURPOSES OF LAW

Keeping Order

Visit laws by subject matter:
http://www.law.indiana.
edu/v-lib

Laws carry some form of penalty for their violation. Traffic violations carry a fine or imprisonment or both. Violations of civil laws also carry sanctions. If your landlord breaches some part of your lease, you can seek money damages. A driver who injures another while driving intoxicated must pay for the damages and the costs of the injuries the other person experiences. These penalties for violations of laws prevent feuds and other methods of settling disputes—for example, methods based on force.

Influencing Conduct

Laws also influence the conduct of society's members. For example, securities laws require certain disclosures to be made about securities before they can be sold to the public. The antitrust laws of the early twentieth century prohibited some methods of competition while they controlled others. In effect, these laws changed the way businesses operated.

Honoring Expectations

Businesses commit resources, people, and time with the expectation that the contracts for those commitments will be honored and enforced according to existing law. Investors buy stock with the knowledge that they will enjoy some protection in that investment through the laws that regulate both the securities themselves and the firms in which they have invested. Laws allow prior planning based on the protections inherent in the law.

Promoting Equality

Laws have been used to achieve equality in those aspects of life and portions of the country in which equality is not a reality. For example, the equal right to employment acts (see Chapter 20) were passed to bring equality to the job market. The social welfare programs of state and federal governments were created to further the cause of economic justice. The antitrust laws attempt to provide equal access to the free enterprise system.

Law as the Great Compromiser

A final and very important purpose of law is to act as the great compromiser. Few people, groups, or businesses agree philosophically on how society, business, or government should be run. Law serves to mesh different views into one united view so that all parties are at least partially satisfied. When disputes occur, the courts impose the law upon the parties in an attempt to compromise their two opposing views. The U.S. Supreme Court has provided compromises for business and labor through its interpretation of the statutes relating to union organizations, strikes, and other economic weapons (see Chapter 19). In the relationship between labor and management, the law serves as the mediator.

CHARACTERISTICS OF LAW

Flexibility

As society changes, the law must change with it. When the United States was an agricultural nation, the issues of antitrust, employment discrimination, and securities fraud rarely arose. However, as the United States became an industrialized nation, those areas of law expanded and continue to expand today. As the United States evolves toward a technological and information-based society, still more areas of law will be created and developed. The area of computer fraud, for example, was unknown thirty years ago; today, most states have criminal statutes to cover such theft (see Chapter 9). The introduction of the fax machine has required courts to reexamine how offers and acceptances of contracts are made to take into account the speed with which contracts may now be formed (see Chapter 13).

Changing circumstances require courts to review and interpret laws. Circumstances change through technology, sociology, and even biology. In the chapter opening "Consider," those who benefit and those affected struggled with the newfound technology of "peer-to-peer file sharing" brought about by MP3 technology. Downloading quality music via the Internet was now possible, and the issues of copyright protection and infringement became confusing because of the manner in which songs were copied. Changing circumstances brought forward for judicial review a heretofore unaddressed issue.

Consistency

Although the law must be flexible, it still must be predictable. Law cannot change so suddenly that parties cannot rely on its existence or protection. Being able to predict the outcome of a course of conduct allows a party to rely on and enter into a contract or dissuades a party from the commission of a crime. For a contract, there is a judicial remedy for breach or nonperformance; for a crime, there is a prescribed punishment.

Pervasiveness

The law must be pervasive and cover all necessary areas; but, at the same time, it cannot infringe individual freedoms or become so complex that it is difficult to enforce. For example, laws cover the formation, operation, and dissolution of corporations. Laws govern corporate management decisions on expanding, developing, and changing the nature of the corporation. Laws also ensure that shareholders' rights are protected. The corporation has great flexibility in management, so long as it stays within these legal boundaries.

In the two following cases, the courts struggle as they try to honor law's purposes of keeping order and honoring expectations while also grappling with the unique issues modern technology and its applications and use raise in the context of balancing those purposes. The principle of *stare decisis* is at work in these two cases (see Chapter 3). The *Sony* case is briefed in Exhibit 1.1. A **brief** is a tool used by lawyers, law students, and judges to help them summarize a case and focus in on its facts and the key points of the decision by the court. The *Napster* case provides the answer for the chapter opening problem.

CASE 1.1

Sony Corporation of America v. *Universal City Studios, Inc.*
464 U.S. 417 (1984)

Tape Delay: Contributory Infringement or Fair Use?

FACTS

Sony Corporation (Petitioner) manufactures millions of Betamax video tape recorders (VTRs) and sells them through retail establishments (also included as petitioners in the case).
The Betamax can record a broadcast off one station while the TV set is tuned to another channel. Tapes can be erased and reused. A timer in the Betamax can be used to activate and deactivate the equipment at predetermined times so the viewer/owner can record programs while not at home.

Universal City Studios, Inc. and Walt Disney Productions (respondents) produce and hold the copyrights on a substantial number of motion pictures and other audiovisual works. They can earn additional returns on these works by licensing limited showings on cable and network television, by selling syndicated rights for repeated airings on local TV, and by marketing programs on prerecorded videotapes or videodiscs.

Universal and Walt Disney brought a copyright infringement action against Sony and its retailers in Federal District Court. Universal and Walt Disney claimed that Betamax consumers were using their machines to record copyrighted works from commercially sponsored television. Evidence submitted by both parties indicated that most Betamax owners used their machines for "time-shifting," which is the practice of recording a program to view it at a later time and then erase it. Consumers used time-shifting to see programs they would otherwise miss because they were not at home, were otherwise occupied, or were viewing another station.

Universal and Walt Disney requested money damages, an accounting for profits, and an injunction against the manufacture and marketing of Betamax.

The District Court found there was no infringement and denied relief. The Court of Appeals held that Universal and Walt Disney were entitled to enjoin the sales of Betamax VTRs or to collect a royalty on each sale. Sony appealed.

JUDICIAL OPINION

STEVENS, Justice

From its beginning, the law of copyright has developed in response to significant changes in technology. Indeed, it was the invention of a new form of copying equipment—the printing press—that gave rise to the original need for copyright protection. Repeatedly, as new developments have occurred in this country, it has been the Congress that has fashioned the new rules that new technology made necessary.

In a case like this, in which Congress has not plainly marked our course, we must be circumspect in construing the scope of rights created by a legislative enactment which never contemplated such a calculus of interests. In doing so, we are guided by Justice Stewart's exposition of the correct approach to ambiguities in the law of copyright: "The limited scope of the copyright holder's statutory monopoly, like the limited copyright duration required by the Constitution, reflects a balance of competing claims upon the public interest: Creative work is to be encouraged and rewarded, but private motivation must ultimately serve the cause of promoting broad public availability of literature, music, and the other arts. The immediate effect of our copyright law is to secure a fair return for an 'author's' creative labor. But the ultimate aim is, by this incentive, to stimulate artistic creativity for the general public good. 'The sole interest of the United States and the primary object in conferring the monopoly,' this court has said, 'lie in the general benefits derived by the public from the labors of authors.' When technological

change has rendered its literal terms ambiguous, the Copyright Act must be construed in light of this basic purpose."

The Copyright Act does not expressly render anyone liable for infringement committed by another. In contrast, the Patent Act expressly brands anyone who "actively induces infringement of a patent" as an infringer, 35 U.S.C. § 271(b), and further imposes liability on certain individuals labeled "contributory" infringers. . . . The absence of such express language in the copyright statute does not preclude the imposition of liability for copyright infringements on certain parties who have not themselves engaged in the infringing activity. For vicarious liability is imposed in virtually all areas of the law, and the concept of contributory infringement is merely a species of the broader problem of identifying the circumstances in which it is just to hold one individual accountable for the actions of another.

As the District Court correctly observed, however, "the lines between direct infringement, contributory infringement, and vicarious liability are not clearly drawn. . . ." The lack of clarity in this area may, in part, be attributable to the fact that an infringer is not merely one who uses a work without authorization by the copyright owner, but also one who authorizes the use of a copyrighted work without actual authority from the copyright owner.

Petitioners in the instant case do not supply Betamax consumers with respondents' works; respondents do. Petitioners supply a piece of equipment that is generally capable of copying the entire range of programs that may be televised: those that are uncopyrighted, those that are copyrighted but may be copied without objection from the copyright holder, and those that the copyright holder would prefer not to have copied. The Betamax can be used to make authorized or unauthorized uses of copyrighted works, but the range of its potential use is much broader.

The only contact between Sony and the users of the Betamax that is disclosed by this record occurred at the moment of sale. The District Court expressly found that "no employee of Sony had either direct involvement with the allegedly infringing activity or direct contact with purchasers of Betamax who recorded copyrighted works off-the-air."

If vicarious liability is to be imposed on petitioners in this case, it must rest on the fact that they have sold equipment with constructive knowledge of the fact that their customers may use that equipment to make unauthorized copies of copyrighted material.

(continued)

There is no precedent in the law of copyright for the imposition of vicarious liability on such a theory. The closest analogy is provided by the patent law cases to which it is appropriate to refer because of the historic kinship between patent law and copyright law. The two areas of the law, naturally, are not identical twins, and we exercise the caution which we have expressed in the past in applying doctrine formulated in one area to the other.

When a charge of contributory infringement is predicated entirely on the sale of an article of commerce that is used by the purchaser to infringe a patent, the public interest in access to that article of commerce is necessarily implicated. A finding of contributory infringement does not, of course, remove the article from the market altogether; it does, however, give the patentee effective control over the sale of that item. Indeed, a finding of contributory infringement is normally the functional equivalent of holding that the disputed article is within the monopoly granted to the patentee. For that reason, in contributory infringement cases arising under the patent laws the Court has always recognized the critical importance of not allowing the patentee to extend his monopoly beyond the limits of his specific grant.

We recognize there are substantial differences between the patent and copyright laws. But in both areas the contributory infringement doctrine is grounded on the recognition that adequate protection of a monopoly may require the courts to look beyond actual duplication of a device or publication to the products or activities that make such duplication possible. The staple article of commerce doctrine must strike a balance between a copyright holder's legitimate demand for effective—not merely symbolic—protection of the statutory monopoly, and the rights of others freely to engage in substantially unrelated areas of commerce. Accordingly, the sale of copying equipment, like the sale of other articles of commerce, does not constitute contributory infringement if the product is widely used for legitimate, unobjectionable purposes. Indeed, it need merely be capable of substantial noninfringing uses.

The question is thus whether the Betamax is capable of commercially significant noninfringing uses. In order to resolve that question, we need not explore all the different potential uses of the machine and determine whether or not they would constitute infringement. Rather, we need only consider whether on the basis of the facts as found by the district court a significant number of them would be non-infringing. Moreover, in order to resolve this case we need not give precise content to the question of how much use is commercially significant. For one potential use of the Betamax plainly satisfies this standard, however it is understood: private, non-commercial time-shifting in the home. It does so both (A) because respondents have no right to prevent other copyright holders from authorizing it for their programs, and (B) because the District Court's factual findings reveal that even the unauthorized home time-shifting of respondents' programs is legitimate fair use.

If there are millions of owners of VTR's who make copies of televised sports events, religious broadcasts, and educational programs such as Mister Rogers' Neighborhood, and if the proprietors of those programs welcome the practice, the business of supplying the equipment that makes such copying feasible should not be stifled simply because the equipment is used by some individuals to make unauthorized reproductions of respondents' works. The respondents do not represent a class composed of all copyright holders. Yet a finding of contributory infringement would inevitably frustrate the interests of broadcasters in reaching the portion of their audience that is available only through time-shifting.

Of course, the fact that other copyright holders may welcome the practice of time-shifting does not mean that respondents should be deemed to have granted a license to copy their programs. Third party conduct would be wholly irrelevant in an action for direct infringement of respondents' copyrights. But in an action for contributory infringement against the seller of copying equipment, the copyright holder may not prevail unless the relief that he seeks affects only his programs, or unless he speaks for virtually all copyright holders with an interest in the outcome. In this case, the record makes it perfectly clear that there are many important producers of national and local television programs who find nothing objectionable about the enlargement in the size of the television audience that results from the practice of time-shifting for private home use. The seller of the equipment that expands those producers' audiences cannot be a contributory infringer if, as is true in this case, it has had no direct involvement with any infringing activity.

Even unauthorized uses of a copyrighted work are not necessarily infringing. An unlicensed use of the copyright is not an infringement unless it conflicts with one of the specific exclusive rights conferred by the copyright statute.

If the Betamax were used to make copies for a commercial or profit-making purpose, such use would presumptively be unfair. The contrary presumption is appropriate here, however, because the District Court's findings plainly establish that time-shifting for private home use must be characterized as a noncommercial, nonprofit activity. Moreover, when one considers the nature of a televised copyrighted audiovisual work, and that timeshifting merely enables a viewer to see such a work which he had been invited to witness in its entirety free of charge, the fact that the entire work is reproduced does not have its ordinary effect of militating against a finding of fair use.

The timeshifter no more steals the program by watching it once than does the live viewer, and the live viewer is no more likely to buy pre-recorded videotapes than is the timeshifter. Indeed, no live viewer would buy a pre-recorded videotape if he did not have access to a VTR.

[A]lthough every commercial use of copyrighted material is presumptively an unfair exploitation of the monopoly privilege that belongs to the owner of the copyright, noncommercial uses are a different matter. A challenge to a noncommercial use of a copyrighted work requires proof either that the particular use is harmful, or that if it should become widespread, it would adversely affect the potential market for the copyrighted work. Actual present harm need not be shown; such a requirement would leave the copyright holder with no defense against predictable damage. Nor is it necessary to show with certainty that future harm will result. What is necessary is a showing by a preponderance of the evidence that some meaningful likelihood of future harm exists. If the intended use is for commercial gain, that likelihood may be presumed. But if it is for a noncommercial purpose, the likelihood must be demonstrated. In this case, respondents failed to carry their burden with regard to home time-shifting.

Today, the larger the audience for the original telecast, the higher the price plaintiffs can demand from broadcasters from rerun rights. There is no survey within the knowledge of this court to show that the rerun audience is comprised of persons who have not seen the program. In any event, if ratings can reflect Betamax recording, original audiences may increase and, given market practices, this should aid plaintiffs rather than harm them.

Of course, plaintiffs may fear that the Betamax will keep the tapes long enough to satisfy all their interest in the program and will, therefore, not patronize later theater exhibitions. It should also be noted that there is no evidence to suggest that the public interest in later theatrical exhibitions of motion pictures will be reduced any more by Betamax recording than it already is by the television broadcast of the film.

After completing that review, the District Court restated its overall conclusion several times, in several different ways. "Harm from time-shifting is speculative and, at best, minimal." "The audience benefits from the time-shifting capability have already been discussed. It is not implausible that benefits could also accrue to plaintiffs, broadcasters, and advertisers, as the Betamax makes it possible for more persons to view their broadcasts." "No likelihood of harm was shown at trial, and plaintiffs admitted that there had been no actual harm to date." "Testimony at trial suggested that Betamax may require adjustments in marketing strategy, but it did not establish even a likelihood of harm." "Television production by plaintiffs today is more profitable than it has ever been, and, in five weeks of trial, there was no concrete evidence to suggest that the Betamax will change the studios' financial picture."

The District Court's conclusions are buttressed by the fact that to the extent time-shifting expands public access to freely broadcast television programs, it yields societal benefits. When these factors are all weighed in the "equitable rule of reason" balance, we must conclude that this record amply supports the District Court's conclusion that home time-shifting is fair use. In light of the findings of the District Court regarding the state of the empirical data, it is clear that the Court of Appeals erred in holding that the statute as presently written bars such conduct.

Reversed.

CASE QUESTIONS

1. What is "time-shifting"?
2. What is the significance of the fair use doctrine in the court's decision?
3. What is the standard for imposing "vicarious liability for infringement"? What does the court examine in determining copyright vicarious infringement liability?
4. Has Sony infringed the rights of Universal and Walt Disney?

EXHIBIT 1.1 Sample Case Brief

Name of case:	*Sony Corporation of America* v. *Universal City Studios, Inc.*
Court:	U.S. Supreme Court
Citation:	464 U.S. 417 (1984)
Parties and their roles:	*Sony* Corporation (petitioner and defendant); Universal Studios, Inc., and Walt Disney Productions (plaintiffs and respondents)
Facts:	*Sony* manufactures video tape machines (VTRs) that can record programs in homes. Universal and Walt Disney produce movies. They claimed that Sony's VTRs were being used to copy their protected and copyrighted films and that they were therefore entitled to some payment for the type of machine use.
Issues:	Does *Sony's* VTR and its use by its customers infringe on the film makers' copyright?
Lower court decision:	The District Court found no infringement. The Court of Appeals found for Universal and Walt Disney and held that they were entitled to either halt the sales of the VTRs or collect a royalty on each.
Decision:	No infringement by *Sony.*
Reasoning:	Congress did not give absolute control over all uses of copyright materials. Some uses (fair uses) are permitted. Consumer uses of the machines for time-shifting to watch shows at another time were not only noncommercial, they were beneficial to those who produced and advertised on the shows because they permitted greater audience exposure. Further, Sony could not be held vicariously liable for infringement using its equipment when it was not a party to such activity and the equipment had valuable uses apart from infringement.

CASE 1.2

A & M Records, Inc. v. *Napster, Inc.*
239 F.3d 1004 (9th Cir. 2001)

Downloading Music: Copyright Infringement or Peer-to-Peer File Sharing?

FACTS

A & M Records and others, including Geffen Records, Sony Music, MCA Records, Atlantic Recording, Motown Records and Capital Records (plaintiffs), are in the business of the commercial recording, distribution and sale of copyrighted musical compositions and sound recordings. They filed suit against Napster, Inc. (Napster) as a contributory and vicarious copyright infringer. Napster operates an online service for "peer-to-peer file sharing" (*www.Napster.com*) so that users can, free of charge, download recordings via the Internet through a process known as "ripping," which is the downloading of digital MP3 files. MP3 is the abbreviated term for audio recordings in a digital format

known as MPEG-3. This compressed format allows for rapid transmission of digital audio files from one computer to another.

Napster's online service provides a search vehicle for files stored on others' computers and permits the downloading of the recordings from the hard drives of other Napster users. Napster provides technical support as well as a chat room for users to exchange information. The result is that users, who register and have a password through Napster, can download single songs and complete CDs or albums, via the peer-to-peer file sharing.

The district court granted a preliminary injunction to the plaintiffs enjoining Napster from "engaging in, or facilitating others in copying, downloading, uploading, transmitting, or distributing plaintiffs' copyrighted musical compositions and sound recordings, protected by either federal or state law, without express permission of the rights owner."

The ninth circuit entered a temporary stay of the injunction in order to review the case.

JUDICIAL OPINION

BEEZER, Circuit Judge

Plaintiffs must satisfy two requirements to present a prima facie case of direct infringement: (1) they must show ownership of the allegedly infringed material and (2) they must demonstrate that the alleged infringers violate at least one exclusive right granted to copyright holders under 17 U.S.C. § 106. Plaintiffs have sufficiently demonstrated ownership. The record supports the district court's determination that "as much as eighty-seven percent of the files available on Napster may be copyrighted and more than seventy percent may be owned or administered by plaintiffs."

The district court also noted that "it is pretty much acknowledged . . . by Napster that this is infringement."

Napster contends that its users do not directly infringe plaintiffs' copyrights because the users are engaged in fair use of the material. Napster identifies three specific alleged fair uses: sampling, where users make temporary copies of a work before purchasing; space-shifting, where users access a sound recording through the Napster system that they already own in audio CD format; and permissive distribution of recordings by both new and established artists.

The district court considered factors listed in 17 U.S.C. § 107, which guide a court's fair use determination. These factors are: (1) the purpose and character of the use; (2) the nature of the copyrighted work; (3) the "amount and substantiality of the portion used" in relation to the work as a whole; and (4) the effect of the use upon the potential market for the work or the value of the work.

1. Purpose and Character of the Use

This factor focuses on whether the new work merely replaces the object of the original creation or instead adds a further purpose or different character. In other words, this factor asks "whether and to what extent the new work is 'transformative.' "See *Campbell* v. *Acuff-Rose Music, Inc.*, 510 U.S. 569, 579, 114 S.Ct. 1164, 127 L.Ed.2d 500 (1994).

The district court first concluded that downloading MP3 files does not transform the copyrighted work. This conclusion is supportable. Courts have been reluctant to find fair use when an original work is merely retransmitted in a different medium.

This "purpose and character" element also requires the district court to determine whether the allegedly infringing use is commercial or noncommercial. A commercial use weighs against a finding of fair use but is not conclusive on the issue. The district court determined that Napster users engage in commercial use of the copyrighted materials largely because (1) "a host user sending a file cannot be said to engage in a personal use when distributing that file to an anonymous requester" and (2) "Napster users get for free something they would ordinarily have to buy."

Direct economic benefit is not required to demonstrate a commercial use. Rather, repeated and exploitative copying of copyrighted works, even if the copies are not offered for sale, may constitute a commercial use. In the record before us, commercial use is demonstrated by a showing that repeated and exploitative unauthorized copies of copyrighted works were made to save the expense of purchasing authorized copies.

2. The Nature of the Use

Works that are creative in nature are "closer to the core of intended copyright protection" than are more fact-based works. The district court determined that plaintiffs' "copyrighted musical compositions and sound recordings are creative in nature . . . which cuts against a finding of fair use under the second factor." We find no error in the district court's conclusion.

3. The Portion Used

"While 'wholesale copying does not preclude fair use per se,' copying an entire work 'militates against a finding of fair use.' " The district court determined that Napster users engage in "wholesale copying" of copyrighted work because file transfer necessarily "involves copying the entirety of the copyrighted work." We agree. [however], See, e.g., *Sony Corp.* v. *Universal City Studios, Inc.*, 464 U.S. 417, 449-50, 104 S.Ct. 774, 78 L.Ed.2d 574 (1984) (acknowledging that fair use of time-shifting necessarily involved making a full copy of a protected work).

4. Effect of Use on Market

"Fair use, when properly applied, is limited to copying by others which does not materially impair the marketability of the work which is copied." A

(continued)

challenge to a noncommercial use of a copyrighted work requires proof either that the particular use is harmful, or that if it should become widespread, it would adversely affect the potential market for the copyrighted work. . . . If the intended use is for commercial gain, that likelihood [of market harm] may be presumed. But if it is for a noncommercial purpose, the likelihood must be demonstrated.

Addressing this factor, the district court concluded that Napster harms the market in "at least" two ways: it reduces audio CD sales among college students and it "raises barriers to plaintiffs' entry into the market for the digital downloading of music." The district court relied on evidence plaintiffs submitted to show that Napster use harms the market for their copyrighted musical compositions and sound recordings.

As for defendant's experts, plaintiffs objected to the report of Dr. Peter S. Fader, in which the expert concluded that Napster is beneficial to the music industry because MP3 music file-sharing stimulates more audio CD sales than it displaces. The district court found problems in Dr. Fader's minimal role in overseeing the administration of the survey and the lack of objective data in his report. The court decided the generality of the report rendered it "of dubious reliability and value." The court did not exclude the report, however, but chose "not to rely on Fader's findings in determining the issues of fair use and irreparable harm."

Here the record supports the district court's finding that the "record company plaintiffs have already expended considerable funds and effort to commence Internet sales and licensing for digital downloads." Having digital downloads available for free on the Napster system necessarily harms the copyright holders' attempts to charge for the same downloads.
a. Sampling

Napster contends that its users download MP3 files to "sample" the music in order to decide whether to purchase the recording.

The district court determined that sampling remains a commercial use even if some users eventually purchase the music. We find no error in the district court's determination. The record supports a finding that free promotional downloads are highly regulated by the record company plaintiffs and that the companies collect royalties for song samples available on retail Internet sites. Evidence relied on by the district court demonstrates that the free downloads provided by the record companies consist of thirty-to-sixty second samples or are full songs programmed to "time out," that is, exist only for a short

time on the downloader's computer. In comparison, Napster users download a full, free and permanent copy of the recording.
b. Space-Shifting

Napster also maintains that space-shifting is a fair use. Space-shifting occurs when a Napster user downloads MP3 music files in order to listen to music he already owns on audio CD. Napster asserts that we have already held that space-shifting of musical compositions and sound recordings is a fair use. We conclude that the district court did not err when it refused to apply the "shifting" analyses of *Sony* . . . [w]here "the majority of VCR purchasers . . . did not distribute taped television broadcasts, but merely enjoyed them at home." Conversely, it is obvious that once a user lists a copy of music he already owns on the Napster system in order to access the music from another location, the song becomes "available to millions of other individuals," not just the original CD owner.

We first address plaintiffs' claim that Napster is liable for contributory copyright infringement. Traditionally, "one who, with knowledge of the infringing activity, induces, causes or materially contributes to the infringing conduct of another, may be held liable as a 'contributory'. Put differently, liability exists if the defendant engages in "personal conduct that encourages or assists the infringement."

Contributory liability requires that the secondary infringer "know or have reason to know" of direct infringement. The district court found that Napster had both actual and constructive knowledge that its users exchanged copyrighted music. The district court also concluded that the law does not require knowledge of "specific acts of infringement" and rejected Napster's contention that because the company cannot distinguish infringing from noninfringing files, it does not "know" of the direct infringement.

It is apparent from the record that Napster has knowledge, both actual and constructive, of direct infringement. Napster claims that it is nevertheless protected from contributory liability by the teaching of *Sony Corp.* v. *Universal City Studios, Inc.*, 464 U.S. 417, 104 S.Ct. 774, 78 L.Ed.2d 574 (1984). We disagree. We observe that Napster's actual, specific knowledge of direct infringement renders *Sony's* holding of limited assistance to Napster.

The district court found actual knowledge because: (1) a document authored by Napster co-founder Sean Parker mentioned "the need to remain ignorant of users' real names and IP addresses 'since they are exchanging pirated music'"; and (2) the Recording Industry Association of America

("RIAA") informed Napster of more than 12,000 infringing files, some of which are still available. The district court found constructive knowledge because: (a) Napster executives have recording industry experience; (b) they have enforced intellectual property rights in other instances; (c) Napster executives have downloaded copyrighted songs from the system; and (d) they have promoted the site with "screen shots listing infringing files."

The *Sony* Court refused to hold the manufacturer and retailers of video tape recorders liable for contributory infringement despite evidence that such machines could be and were used to infringe plaintiffs' copyrighted television shows. *Sony* stated that if liability "is to be imposed on petitioners in this case, it must rest on the fact that they have sold equipment with constructive knowledge of the fact that their customers may use that equipment to make unauthorized copies of copyrighted material." The *Sony* Court declined to impute the requisite level of knowledge where the defendants made and sold equipment capable of both infringing and "substantial noninfringing uses."

We are bound to follow *Sony,* and will not impute the requisite level of knowledge to Napster merely because peer-to-peer file sharing technology may be used to infringe plaintiffs' copyrights. We depart from the reasoning of the district court that Napster failed to demonstrate that its system is capable of commercially significant noninfringing uses. The district court improperly confined the use analysis to current uses, ignoring the system's capabilities. Consequently, the district court placed undue weight on the proportion of current infringing use as compared to current and future noninfringing use. Regardless of the number of Napster's infringing versus noninfringing uses, the evidentiary record here supported the district court's finding that plaintiffs would likely prevail in establishing that Napster knew or had reason to know of its users' infringement of plaintiffs' copyrights.

We agree that if a computer system operator learns of specific infringing material available on his system and fails to purge such material from the system, the operator knows of and contributes to direct infringement. Conversely, absent any specific information which identifies infringing activity, a computer system operator cannot be liable for contributory infringement merely because the structure of the system allows for the exchange of copyrighted material. See *Sony,* 464 U.S. at 436, 442-43, 104 S.Ct. 774. To enjoin simply because a computer network allows for infringing use would, in our opinion, violate *Sony* and potentially restrict activity unrelated to infringing use. We nevertheless conclude that sufficient knowledge exists to impose contributory liability when linked to demonstrated infringing use of the Napster system.

Under the facts as found by the district court, Napster materially contributes to the infringing activity.

We turn to the question whether Napster engages in vicarious copyright infringement. Vicarious copyright liability is an "outgrowth" of *respondeat superior.* In the context of copyright law, vicarious liability extends beyond an employer/employee relationship to cases in which a defendant "has the right and ability to supervise the infringing activity and also has a direct financial interest in such activities."

Before moving into this discussion, we note that *Sony*'s "staple article of commerce" analysis has no application to Napster's potential liability for vicarious copyright infringement. The issues of *Sony*'s liability under the "doctrines of 'direct infringement' and 'vicarious liability'" were not before the Supreme Court, although the Court recognized that the "lines between direct infringement, contributory infringement, and vicarious liability are not clearly drawn." Consequently, when the *Sony* Court used the term "vicarious liability," it did so broadly and outside of a technical analysis of the doctrine of vicarious copyright infringement.

Financial benefit exists where the availability of infringing material "acts as a 'draw' for customers." Ample evidence supports the district court's finding that Napster's future revenue is directly dependent upon "increases in userbase." More users register with the Napster system as the "quality and quantity of available music increases." We conclude that the district court did not err in determining that Napster financially benefits from the availability of protected works on its system.

The district court determined that Napster has the right and ability to supervise its users' conduct. The ability to block infringers' access to a particular environment for any reason whatsoever is evidence of the right and ability to supervise. Here, plaintiffs have demonstrated that Napster retains the right to control access to its system. Napster has an express reservation of rights policy, stating on its website that it expressly reserves the "right to refuse service and terminate accounts in [its] discretion, including, but not limited to, if Napster believes that user conduct violates applicable law . . . or for any reason in Napster's sole discretion, with or without cause."

(continued)

To escape imposition of vicarious liability, the reserved right to police must be exercised to its fullest extent. Turning a blind eye to detectable acts of infringement for the sake of profit gives rise to liability. The district court, however, failed to recognize that the boundaries of the premises that Napster "controls and patrols" are limited. Put differently, Napster's reserved "right and ability" to police is cabined by the system's current architecture. As shown by the record, the Napster system does not "read" the content of indexed files, other than to check that they are in the proper MP3 format.

Napster, however, has the ability to locate infringing material listed on its search indices, and the right to terminate users' access to the system. The file name indices, therefore, are within the "premises" that Napster has the ability to police. We recognize that the files are user-named and may not match copyrighted material exactly (for example, the artist or song could be spelled wrong). For Napster to function effectively, however, file names must reasonably or roughly correspond to the material contained in the files, otherwise no user could ever locate any desired music.

Napster's failure to police the system's "premises," combined with a showing that Napster financially benefits from the continuing availability of infringing files on its system, leads to the imposition of vicarious liability.

Napster alleges that two statutes insulate it from liability. First, Napster asserts that its users engage in actions protected by § 1008 of the Audio Home Recording Act of 1992, 17 U.S.C. § 1008. Second, Napster argues that its liability for contributory and vicarious infringement is limited by the Digital Millennium Copyright Act, 17 U.S.C. § 512.

Napster contends that MP3 file exchange is the type of "noncommercial use" protected from infringement actions by the statute. Napster asserts it cannot be secondarily liable for users' nonactionable exchange of copyrighted musical recordings.

We agree with the district court that the Audio Home Recording Act does not cover the downloading of MP3 files to computer hard drives. First, "[u]nder the plain meaning of the Act's definition of digital audio recording devices, computers (and their hard drives) are not digital audio recording devices because their 'primary purpose' is not to make digital audio copied recordings." Napster also interposes a statutory limitation on liability by asserting the protections of the "safe harbor" from copyright infringement suits for "Internet service providers" contained in the Digital Millennium Copyright Act,

17 U.S.C. § 512. We do not agree that Napster's potential liability for contributory and vicarious infringement renders the Digital Millennium Copyright Act inapplicable per se.

Napster may be vicariously liable when it fails to affirmatively use its ability to patrol its system and preclude access to potentially infringing files listed in its search index. Napster has both the ability to use its search function to identify infringing musical recordings and the right to bar participation of users who engage in the transmission of infringing files.

The preliminary injunction which we stayed is overbroad because it places on Napster the entire burden of ensuring that no "copying, downloading, uploading, transmitting, or distributing" of plaintiffs' works occur on the system.

As stated, we place the burden on plaintiffs to provide notice to Napster of copyrighted works and files containing such works available on the Napster system before Napster has the duty to disable access to the offending content. Napster, however, also bears the burden of policing the system within the limits of the system. Here, we recognize that this is not an exact science in that the files are user named. In crafting the injunction on remand, the district court should recognize that Napster's system does not currently appear to allow Napster access to users' MP3 files.

AFFIRMED IN PART, REVERSED IN PART AND REMANDED.

NOTE AND AFTERMATH: On remand, the district court refashioned the injunction and ordered Napster to remove from its files all songs provided by the plaintiffs for which they held a copyright. The task of blocking the songs proved arduous because the downloading of a song under an inexact name permitted downloading to continue. For example, a song provided as "Down to You," by the record company could still be downloaded if carried by the file users as "Down 2 You" or "Down 2 U."

CASE QUESTIONS

1. Describe what Napster is and how it works.
2. Is Napster engaged in copyright infringement?
3. What factors does the court look at in examining fair use?
4. How does the court apply the *Sony* case?
5. Is Napster vicariously liable for the downloading of copyrighted songs by its users? What technological limitations exist in honoring the copyrights?

What do you think of the ethics of peer-to-peer file sharing? Is peer-to-peer file sharing the same as copyright infringement? Who is harmed by the activity? Who is helped? Do you think the users of Napster should have had permission to download the copyrighted music?

CONSIDER...

1.1 Brief the *Napster* case in the same format as Exhibit 1.1 for the *Sony* case.

BUSINESS STRATEGY

Another important lesson of both the *Sony* and *Napster* cases is the importance of business strategy. The VTR was the beginning of *Blockbuster*, video rentals, and a

© AP/Wide World Photos

new revenue stream for Universal, Disney, and all other film makers. The possibilities still seem endless as the technology has evolved into DVD. DVD films include commentary from directors and additional scenes cut from the original film.

The same may be true for the capabilities of Napster. While the free downloading of songs may have ended, the music industry is just beginning its partnerships with Internet service providers to offer customers the ability to download music. America on Line (AOL) has already forged a partnership with Sony, one of the plaintiffs in the Napster case.

The law is one tool used to enforce rights and protect stability. However, sometimes the law is a stop-gap measure or even something that interferes with the strategic planning for technological changes. Litigation and decisions are often not the best resolution to a problem. Here, both industries needed to look at the technology's possibilities and use it, not try to stop it.

THE THEORY OF LAW: JURISPRUDENCE

Law is the compromise of conflicting ideas. Not only do people differ in their thinking on the types of specific laws, they also differ on the theory behind the law or the values a legal system should try to advance or encourage. Many can agree on the definition of law and its purposes but still differ on how those purposes are best accomplished. The incorporation of theories or values into the legal process is, perhaps, what makes each society's laws different and causes law to change as society changes its values. These different theories or value bases for law are found in an area of legal study called **jurisprudence,** a Latin term meaning "wisdom of the law." The "Manager's Desk" called "A Primer on Jurisprudence" provides a brief overview on the philosophy of law.

Justice Oliver Wendell Holmes, in "The Common Law," had a different view of the theory of law than that expressed in "A Primer on Jurisprudence." In his famous essay written in 1918, at the height of World War I, Holmes rejected the notion of natural law. His essay began with the famous phrase, "The life of the law has not been logic; it has been experience." Holmes's opinion is that our interactions with each other constitute the foundation of law.

Re: A Primer on Jurisprudence (Legal Philosophy in a Nutshell; Five Minutes of Legal Philosophy)

First Minute

"An order is an order," the soldier is told. "A law is a law," says the jurist. The soldier, however, is required neither by duty nor by law to obey an order that he knows to have been issued with a felony or misdemeanor in mind, while the jurists, since the last of the natural law theorists among them disappeared a hundred years ago, have recognized no such exceptions to the validity of a law or to the requirement of obedience by those subject to it. A law is valid because it is a law, and it is a law if in the general run of cases it has the power to prevail.

This view of the nature of a law and of its validity (we call it the positivistic theory) has rendered the jurist as well as the people defenseless against laws, however arbitrary, cruel, or criminal they may be. In the end the positivistic theory equates the law with power; there is law only where there is power.

Second Minute

There have been attempts to supplement or replace this tenet with another: Law is what benefits the people. That is, arbitrariness, breach of contract, and illegality, provided only that they benefit the people, are law. Practically speaking, that means that every whim and caprice of the despot, punishment without laws or judgment, lawless killing of the sick—whatever the state authorities deem to benefit the people—is law. That *can* mean that the private benefit of those in power is regarded as a public benefit. The equating of the law with supposed or ostensible benefits to the people thus transformed a *Rechtsstaat* into a state of lawlessness.

No, this tenet should not be read as: Whatever benefits the people is law. Rather, it is the other way around: Only what is law benefits the people.

Third Minute

Law is the will to justice, and justice means: To judge without regard to person, to treat everyone according to the same standard.

If one applauds the assassination of political opponents and orders the murder of those of another race while meting out the most cruel, degrading punishments for the same acts committed against those of one's own persuasion, that is neither justice nor law.

If laws consciously deny the will to justice, if, for example, they grant and deny human rights arbitrarily, then these laws lack validity, the people owe to them no obedience, and even the jurists must find the courage to deny their legal character.

Fourth Minute

Surely public benefit, along with justice, is an end of the law. Surely laws as such, even bad laws, have value nonetheless—the value of safety regarding the law against doubt. And surely, owing to human imperfection, the three values of law—public benefit, legal certainty, and justice—cannot always be united harmoniously in laws. It remains, then, only to consider whether validity is to be granted to bad, detrimental, or unjust laws for the sake of legal certainty or whether it is to be denied them because they are unjust or socially detrimental. One thing, however, must be indelibly impressed on the consciousness of the people and the jurists: There can be laws that are so unjust, so socially detrimental, that their validity, indeed their very character as laws, must be denied.

Fifth Minute

There are, therefore, principles of law that are stronger than any statute, so that a law conflicting with these principles is devoid of validity. One calls these principles the natural law or the law of reason. To be sure, their details remain somewhat doubtful, but the work of the centuries has established a solid core of them and they have come to enjoy such a far-reaching consensus in the declaration of human and civil rights that only the deliberate skeptic can still entertain doubts about some of them.

In religious language, the same thoughts have been recorded in Biblical passages. On the one hand it is written that you are to obey the authorities who have power over you. But then on the other, it is also written that you are to obey God before man—and this is not simply a pious wish, but a valid proposition of law. The tension between these two directives cannot, however, be relieved by appealing to a third—say, to the maxim: Render unto Caesar the things that are Caesar's and unto God the things that are God's. For this directive too, leaves the boundary in doubt. Rather, it leaves the solution to the voice of God, which speaks to the conscience of the individual only in the exceptional case.

Discussion Questions

1. What is the positivist's view of law? Does it matter to a positivist whether a law is just?

2. What type of law is stronger than any statute? What are its origins? Do you have an example of a principle today that would fit into this type of law?

3. If a law is unjust, is obedience to that law necessary? How should people respond or react to unjust laws? Is civil disobedience justified?

4. How does the author respond to the statement: Law is what benefits the people. Does he agree or disagree?

Source: "Funf Minuten Rechtsphilosophie," by Gustave Radbruch, translated by Stanley L. Paulson, in *Rechtsphilosophie,* and edited by Erik Wolf and Hans-Peter Schneider (Stuttgart: K. F. Koehler Verlag, 1973), pp. 327–29. Reprinted with permission of K. F. Koehler Verlag.

Roscoe Pound, another legal philosopher and dean of Harvard Law School for twenty years, had a very different view of jurisprudence from Justice Holmes. His view was that law exists as the result of those who happen to be in power. In 1941, Pound wrote his famous credo, called "My Philosophy of Law."

C O N S I D E R . . .

1.2   Apply the theories of jurisprudence to the following situations:

1. A supervisor has ordered an employee to inflate the company's earnings for the quarter so that their unit can meet their goals and attain their bonuses. Must the employee obey?

2. Is a businessperson who believes the tax system to be unconstitutional justified in refusing to pay taxes? How will society react to such a position?

There are many cases in which how the law should work is unclear. Conflicting philosophical views often come together in litigation. Judges and lawmakers must struggle to do the best good for the most members of society.

SOURCES OF LAW

Laws exist in different forms at every level of government. As discussed earlier, law exists not only in statutory form but also in its common law form through judicial decisions. Statutory law exists at all levels of government. Statutes are written laws that are enacted by some governmental body with the proper authority—legislatures, city governments, and counties—and that are published and made available for public use and knowledge. These written statutes are sometimes referred to as codified law, and their sources, as well as constitutions, are covered in the following sections.

Constitutional Law

Explore the U.S. Constitution:
http://www.law.emory.edu/ FEDERAL/usconst.html

The U.S. Constitution and the constitutions of the various states are unique forms of law. **Constitutions** are not statutes because they cannot be added to, amended, or repealed with the same ease as can statutes. Constitutions are the law of the

Re: The Common Law (Ideas and Doubts: Oliver Wendell Holmes)

It is not enough for the knights of romance that you agree that his lady is a very nice girl—if you do not admit that she is the best that God ever made or will make, you must fight. There is in all men a demand for the superlative, so much so that the poor devil who has no other way of reaching it attains it by getting drunk. It seems to me that this demand is at the bottom of the philosopher's effort to prove that truth is absolute and of the jurist's search for criteria of the universal validity which he collects under the head of natural law.

The jurists who believe in natural law seem to be in that naive state of mind that accepts what has been familiar and accepted by them and their neighbors as something that must be accepted by all men everywhere. No doubt it is true that, so far as we can see ahead, some arrangements and the rudiments of familiar institutions seem to be necessary elements in any society that may spring from our own and that would seem to us to be civilized—some form of permanent association between the sexes—some residue of property individually owned—some mode of binding oneself to a specified future conduct—at the bottom of it all, some protection for the person.

It is true that beliefs and wishes have a transcendental basis in the sense that their foundation is arbitrary. You cannot help entertaining and feeling them, and there is an end of it. As an arbitrary fact people wish to live, and we say with

various degrees of certainty that they can do so, only on certain conditions. To do it they must eat and drink. That necessity is absolute. It is a necessity of a lesser degree but practically general that they should live in society. If they live in society, so far as we can see, there are further conditions. If I do live with others they tell me what I must do if I wish to remain alive. If I do live with others they tell me what I must do and abstain from doing various things or they will put the screws to me.

Discussion Questions

1. According to Justice Holmes, what makes people obey certain laws and subscribe to certain standards?

2. Why does he see natural law as evidence of man's desire to deal in superlatives?

3. Does Justice Holmes feel that everyone's view of natural law is the same?

4. Another legal philosopher, John Austin, stated, "The matter of jurisprudence is positive law: law, simply and strictly so called: or law set by political superiors to political inferiors." Does Justice Holmes's philosophy agree or disagree with this position? Is there a different theory advanced with this statement?

Source: Essay by Oliver Wendell Holmes; reprinted with permission from 32 *Harvard Law Review* 40 (1918). Copyright © 1918 by The Harvard Law Review Association.

---

people and are changed only by lengthier and more demanding procedures than those used to repeal statutes.

Constitutions also tend to protect general rights, such as speech, religion, and property (see Chapter 5 for a more complete discussion). They also are a framework for all other forms of laws. The basic rights and protections afforded in them cannot be abridged or denied by the other sources of law. In other words, a statute's boundaries are formed by constitutionally protected rights. Exhibit 1.2 is an illustration of the sources of law; constitutional law is at the base of the pyramid diagram because of its inviolate status.

Statutory Law at the Federal Level

Explore the U.S. Code:
http://www.law.cornell.edu/
uscode

Congressional Law

Congress is responsible for statutory law at the federal level. The laws passed by Congress become part of the **United States Code (U.S.C.).** Examples of such laws

Re: My Philosophy of Law: Roscoe Pound

I think of law as in one sense a highly specialized form of social control in a developed politically organized society—a social control through the systematic and orderly application of the force of such a society. In this sense it is a regime—the regime which we call the legal order. But that regime operates in a systematic and orderly fashion because of a body of authoritative grounds for or guides to determination which may serve as rules of decision, as rules of or guides to conduct, and as bases of prediction of official action, or may be regarded by the bad man, whose attitude is suggested by Mr. Justice Holmes as a test, as threats of official action which he must take into account before he acts or refrains from action. Moreover, it operates through a judicial process and *an administrative process, which also go by the name of law. . . .*

Discussion Questions

1. Would it be fair to consider Dean Pound's view of the law as merely the rules of those in charge?

2. What is Dean Pound's view on how Holmes's "bad man" is controlled by law?

3. Does Dean Pound discount the theory of natural law?

4. Do you agree with Dean Pound's views?

Source: From *My Philosophy of Law* by Roscoe Pound. © 1941 West Publishing Corporation. Reprinted with permission of West Group.

---

are the 1933 and 1934 Securities Acts (see Chapter 22), the Sherman Act and other antitrust laws (see Chapter 17), the Equal Employment Opportunity Act (see Chapter 20), the National Labor Relations Act (see Chapter 19), the Truth-in-Lending Act (see Chapter 15), and the Internal Revenue Code (see Chapter 21).

Statutes from the U.S.C. are referenced or cited by a standard form of legal shorthand, often referred to as a **cite** or **citation.** The number of the title is put in front of "U.S.C." to tell which volume of the Code to go to. For example, "15 U.S.C." refers to Title 15 of the United States Code (Title 15 happens to cover securities). There may be more than one volume that is numbered "15," however. To enable you to find the volume you need, the reference or cite has a section (§) number following it. This section number is the particular statute referenced, and you must look for the volume of Title 15 that contains that section. For example, the first volume of Title 15 contains §§ 1–11. A full reference or cite to a United States Code statute looks like this: 15 U.S.C. § 77. When a U.S.C. cite is given, the law cited will be a federal law passed by Congress.

Administrative Regulations

Explore the Code of Federal Regulations:
http://www.access.gpo.gov/nara/cfr/cfr-table-search.html *or*
http://www.access.gpo.gov/su_docs/locators/coredocs/index.html

Another form of codified law exists at the federal level; it consists of regulations passed by administrative agencies. Called the **Code of Federal Regulations (C.F.R.),** the administrative regulations at the federal level are extensive and affect virtually every business. The details of compliance with federal statutes (found in the United States Code) are found in the C.F.R. For example, sample forms for disclosure of credit information are found in the C.F.R., as are the Security and Exchange Commission's requirements for financial disclosures in the periodic reports of a public company. The current debate on airbags in cars is over an administrative regulation of the Department of Transportation. A full discussion of regulation and administrative agencies is found in Chapter 6.

EXHIBIT 1.2
Sources of Law

Explore executive orders:
http://www.whitehouse.gov/
news/orders

Executive Orders

Executive orders are laws of the executive branch of the federal government and deal with those matters under the direct control of that branch. For example, when Richard Nixon was president, he issued an executive order governing the classification and release of "top secret" documents. During his presidency, Jimmy Carter issued executive orders that required government contractors to employ a certain percentage of minority workers in their businesses in order to qualify for federal projects (see Chapter 20). George Bush issued one executive order requiring federal agencies to use alternative dispute resolution before going to court and another requiring them to implement recycling programs. On his second day as president, Bill Clinton issued an executive order reversing George Bush's "gag rule" on abortion counseling. The same order also reversed a previous executive order banning the use of federal funds for research involving fetal tissue obtained from abortions. During his first 100 days in office, George W. Bush issued an executive order banning federal funds use for abortion in other countries receiving U.S. financial assistance.

Statutory Law at the State Level

Legislative Law and State Codes

Explore the Uniform Commercial Code:
http://www.law.cornell.edu/
ucc/ucc.table.html

Each state has its own code containing the laws passed by its legislature. **State codes** contain the states' criminal laws, laws for incorporation, laws governing partnerships, and contract laws. Much of the law that affects business is found in these state codes. Some of the laws passed by the states are **uniform laws,** which are drafted by groups of businesspeople, scholars, and lawyers in an effort to make interstate business less complicated. For example, the **Uniform Commercial Code,** which has been adopted in forty-nine states, governs contracts for the sale

BIOGRAPHY

GIVING, SPENDING AND EMBEZZLING THE UNITED WAY: WILLIAM ARAMONY'S FOLLY

The United Way, which evolved from the local community chests of the 1920s, is a national organization that funnels funding to charities through a payroll-deduction system. Ninety percent of all charitable deductions in 1991 were for the United Way.

United Way came under fire through the actions of William Aramony, president of the United Way from 1970 to 1992. During his tenure, United Way receipts grew from $787 million in 1970 to $3 billion in 1990; but some of Aramony's effects on the organization were less positive.

In early 1992, the *Washington Post* reported that Aramony

Was paid $463,000 per year.
Flew first class on commercial airlines.
Spent $20,000 in one year for limousines.
Used the Concorde for trans-Atlantic flights.

The article also revealed that one of the taxable spin-off companies Aramony had created to provide travel and bulk purchasing for United Way chapters had bought a $430,000 condominium in Manhattan and a $125,000 apartment in Coral Cables, Florida, for his use. Another spin-off had hired Aramony's son, Robert Aramony, as vice president. In addition, $80,000 of United Way funds were paid to Aramony's girlfriend, a 1986 high school graduate, for consulting, even though she did no work.

Aramony resigned after fifteen chapters of the United Way threatened to withhold their annual dues to the national office. Said Robert O. Bothwell, executive director of the National Committee for Responsive Philanthropy, "I think it is obscene that he is making that kind of salary and asking people who are making $10,000 a year to give 5 percent of their income."*

In August 1992, the United Way board of directors hired Elaine Chao, the Peace Corps director, to replace William Aramony at a salary of $195,000, with no perks.† She reduced staff from 275 to 185 and borrowed $1.5 million to compensate for a decline in donations. By 1995, United Way donations had still not returned to their 1991 level of $3.2 billion.

In September 1994, William Aramony and two other United Way officers, including the chief financial officer, were indicted by a federal grand jury for conspiracy, mail fraud, and tax fraud. The indictment alleged the three officers diverted more than $2.74 million of United Way funds to purchase the condominium in New York City, interior decorating for $72,000, an apartment, vacations, and a lifetime pass on American Airlines.

On April 3, 1995, Aramony was found guilty of twenty-five counts of fraud, conspiracy, and money laundering. Two other United Way executives were also convicted.

By April 1998, donation levels had still not been completely regained, and relationships between local chapters and the national organization were often strained. United Way's donations had fallen 11 percent since 1991, although overall charitable giving had risen by 10 percent.

ISSUES

1. What types of laws did Mr. Aramony violate?

2. Why do you think he engaged in illegal conduct? Provide some possible rationalizations.

3. What impact did Mr. Aramony's conduct have on United Way? Do you think corporate officers can produce equally harmful results to their companies through illegal conduct?

*Felicity Barringer, "United Way Head Is Forced Out in a Furor over His Lavish Style," *New York Times*, February 1992, A1.

†Desda Moss, "Peace Corps Director to Head United Way," *USA Today*, 27 August 1992, 6A; Sabra Chartrand, "Head of Peace Corps Named United Way President," *New York Times*, 27 August 1992, A8. Ms. Chao was named Labor Secretary by President Bush in 2001.

ETHICAL ISSUES 1.2

In late 1992 and early 1993, Bill Clinton, the newly elected president of the United States, began working to fill cabinet positions for his new administration. His first choice for position of attorney general was Zoë Baird, general counsel for Aetna Life Insurance Company. Ms. Baird's nomination was eventually withdrawn when it was revealed that she and her husband, a professor at Yale Law School, had hired a nanny and a chauffeur in the United States illegally and had failed to pay taxes on the pair's wages.

Following Ms. Baird's failed nomination, President Clinton began discussions with a federal judge, Kimba Wood. Judge Wood had also employed a nanny for the care of her child. The nanny was not an illegal alien, but Judge Wood and her husband, a writer for *Time* magazine, had also not paid taxes on her wages. Judge Wood's name, although appearing in news reports as a candidate for attorney general, was never formally sent forward as a nomination. Eventually, Janet Reno, a public attorney from Florida who had no children, was nominated and confirmed as attorney general.

After the issues surrounding household employee taxes in relation to Ms. Baird and Judge Wood arose, subsequent nominees and candidates for office were scrutinized for these wage tax problems. If the candidates or nominees had not paid their taxes, they were categorized as "having a Zoë Baird problem." "Having a Zoë Baird problem" was the end of many nominations and candidacies.

Since the time of her failed nomination, Ms. Baird first continued her work with Aetna and now heads up a nonprofit organization in New York City. She recently gave birth to a second child. Judge Wood continues her work on the federal bench; she fell victim to intense media scrutiny when the private diaries of a New York broker became public and revealed the judge's affair with him.

1. Would Judge Wood's and Ms. Baird's lives have been different if they had obeyed the law?

2. Did they limit their opportunities by not complying with the law?

3. At the time of their nominations, only 25 percent of all U.S. citizens with household help complied with the law. Shouldn't the two women have been given leniency since everybody else was doing what they were doing?

Explore the UCC and other uniform laws at the Commercial Law League of America:
www.clla.org

of goods, commercial paper, security interests, and other types of commercial transactions. Having this uniform law in the various states gives businesses the opportunity to deal across state lines with some certainty. Other uniform acts passed by many state legislatures include the Uniform Partnership Act, the Uniform Residential Landlord Tenant Act, the Model Business Corporation Act, and the Uniform Probate Code.

State Administrative Law

Visit hyperlinks to state legislation:
http://www.washlaw.edu/ uslaw/statelaw.html

Just as at the federal level, state governments have administrative agencies with the power to pass regulations dealing with the statutes and powers given by the state legislatures. For example, most states have an agency to handle incorporations and the status of corporations in the state. Most states also have a tax agency to handle income or sales taxes in the state.

Local Laws of Cities, Counties, and Townships

In addition to federal and state statutes, local governments can pass **ordinances** or statutes within their areas of power or control. For example, cities and counties have the authority to handle zoning issues, and the municipal code outlines the zoning system and whatever means of enforcement and specified penalties apply. These local laws govern lesser issues, such as dog licensing, curfews, and loitering.

```
                                              ┌─────────────────────────┐
                                              │ FOR THE MANAGER'S DESK  │
                                              └─────────────────────────┘
```

Re: Regulation is Everywhere

City	Ordinance
Ridgewood, N.J.	No "silly string" between May 15 and July 15 or during December
Weaverville, N.C.	No unleashed miniature pigs in public
Salt Lake City, Utah	No spitting on sidewalks
Los Angeles, Calif.	No gas-powered leaf blowers
South Padre Island, Tex.	No wearing of ties or socks
Jonesboro, Ga.	No profanity in front of children under 14
Manhattan, Kans.	No indoor furniture on outdoor porches
Topeka, Kans.	No alcohol in a teacup
Singapore	No chewing gum

Private Laws

Private laws are a final source of written law and are found in contracts and the regulations agreed to, for example, by employers and employees. These are laws limited in their application to the parties involved in a contractual relationship. However, these private laws are just as enforceable through lawsuits for breach of contract (see Chapters 3 and 4).

Court Decisions

Looking at Exhibit 1.2, you can see that all of the sources of law just covered are surrounded in the pyramid by the term "court decisions." Often the language in the statute is unclear or perhaps simply whether the statute or ordinance applies in a particular situation is unclear. When there are these ambiguities or omissions in the statutory language, a decision rendered by a court in a dispute brought by one party against another serves to provide an interpretation or clarification of the law. These court decisions are then read along with the statutory language in order to give a complete analysis of the scope and intent of the statute.

C O N S I D E R . . .

1.3   Often, business people must read statutes, regulations, and ordinances to determine whether their business operations are legal, require licenses, or are otherwise regulated. Ticket brokers and scalpers would be affected by the following three New York statutes. Read them and then answer the questions that follow.

§ 25.07. *Ticket prices*

1. Every operator of a place of entertainment shall, if a price be charged for admission thereto, print or endorse on the face of each such ticket the established price. Such operator shall likewise be required to print or endorse on each ticket the maximum premium price at which such ticket or other evidence of the right of entry may be resold or offered for resale.

2. Maximum premium price. It shall be unlawful for any person, firm or corporation to resell or offer to resell any ticket to any place of entertainment for more than the maximum premium price.

§ 25.09. Ticket speculators

1. Any person who in violation of subdivision two of section 25.07 of this article unlawfully resells or offers to resell or solicits the purchase of any ticket to any place of entertainment shall be guilty of ticket speculation.

2. Any person, firm, or corporation which in violation of subdivision two of section 25.07 of this article unlawfully resells, offers to resell, or purchases with the intent to resell five or more tickets to any place of entertainment shall be guilty of aggravated ticket speculation.

§ 25.11. Resales of tickets within one thousand feet of a place of entertainment having a permanent seating capacity in excess of five thousand persons

1. No person, firm, corporation, or not-for-profit organization shall resell, offer to resell or solicit the resale of any ticket to any place of entertainment having a permanent seating capacity in excess of five thousand persons within one thousand feet from the physical structure of such place of entertainment unless such person, firm, or corporation is lawfully reselling tickets from a location licensed pursuant to section 25.13 of this article.

2. Notwithstanding subdivision one of this section, an operator may designate an area within the property line of such place of entertainment having a permanent seating capacity in excess of five thousand persons for the lawful resale of tickets only to events at such place of entertainment by any person, firm, corporation, or not-for-profit organization which purchased the tickets for the purposes described in section 25.05 of this article and is no longer able to use them.

What is ticket speculation? Is it legal? Is it ethical? Are these statutes civil or criminal statutes? If you were a ticket broker, what would you need to do to be in compliance with the law? (Note: These statutes are suspended until June 1, 2003, and changes are under consideration.)

INTRODUCTION TO INTERNATIONAL LAW

Governmental changes in Germany and the former U.S.S.R., the evolution of the European Union, and the competitive skills of Japan and other nations have caused a dramatic change in the business marketplace. Businesses now operate in a global market. Companies headquartered in Japan have factories in the United States, and U.S. firms have manufacturing plants in South America. Trade and political barriers to economic development no longer exist. An international market requires businesses to understand laws beyond those of the United States.

International law is not a neat body of law like contract law or the Uniform Commercial Code. Rather, it is a combination of the laws of various countries, international trade customs, and international agreements. Article 38(1) of the Statute of the International Court of Justice (a court of the United Nations that countries consent to have resolve disputes) is a widely recognized statement of the sources of international law:

Ethical Issues 1.3

Does ticket scalping serve a purpose for some people? At the NCAA Final Four Basketball Tournament in 1992, midcourt seats were selling for $2,500. The late concert promoter Bill Graham once said, "If I wanted to, I could make more money scalping tickets than producing a show." Mr. Graham led a crusade for antiscalping legislation in California. Selling tickets at the event site is illegal in California, but ticket brokers are permitted to sell tickets at prices above the original cost so long as they operate away from the event.

Economist Steve Happel favors little or no regulation of scalping: "Look at the people on the Chicago Board of Trade. They buy wheat futures. Why are we so concerned about ticket scalpers?"

California state assemblyman Bill Lockyer, who has introduced antiscalping legislation, has stated, "The brokering of tickets confers an advantage to the wealthy and the well connected that the fan of average means does not have. I still believe we need a law to stop the practice."

Does scalping encourage unethical behavior? For example, in exchange for alcohol, drugs, or money, homeless people in Texas are recruited to stand in ticket lines to buy tickets when there are limits on purchases. In California, a lawsuit was filed accusing a ticket broker of bribing ticket agency employees to obtain more and better seats to concert events that would later be sold for between ten and twenty times their face value. Would you participate in scalping, either as a buyer or a seller? Why or why not?

Explore the Statute of the International Court of Justice:
http://www.un.org/Overview/Statute/contents.html

The Court, whose function is to decide in accordance with international law such disputes as are submitted to it, shall apply:
(a) international conventions, whether general or particular, establishing rules expressly recognized by the contesting states;
(b) international custom as evidence of a general practice accepted as law;
(c) the general principles of law recognized by civilized nations;
(d) judicial decisions and the teachings of the most highly qualified publicists of the various nations, as subsidiary means for the determination of rules of law.

Custom

Every country has its boundaries for allowable behavior, and these boundaries are unwritten but recognized laws. The standards of behavior are reflected in statements made by government officials. Among countries that have the same standards of acceptable behavior, there exists an international code of custom. Custom develops over time and through repeated conduct. For example, the continental shelf sea territorial standard came into existence in 1945 when President Harry S. Truman, in the Truman Declaration, established mileage boundary lines. Most countries accepted the declaration because it reflected their customary operations. By 1958, the standard became a part of the Geneva Convention.

Another example of international custom, though one not yet accepted by all nations, is the granting of diplomatic asylum. Some nations grant it, and others do not; it is an area of developing custom.

Explore foreign and international laws:
http://www.washlaw.edu/forint/forintmain.html

Each individual country will have its own customs peculiar to business trade. Businesses operating in various other countries must understand those customs in negotiating contracts and conducting operations within those countries. For example, unlike the United States, most countries do not offer a warranty protection on goods and instead follow a philosophy of *"Caveat emptor,"* "Let the buyer beware." Other countries also do not recognize the extensive rules of insurance and risk followed here with respect to the shipment of goods.

Multinational firms must make provisions for protection of shipments in those countries with different standards.

Recently, the customs of Mainland China with respect to intellectual property, most particularly computer software, lagged behind those of Europe and the United States. Chinese custom was to separate infringement into two categories: ordinary and serious acts. Ordinary infringement is not regarded as a legal issue and requires only that the party apologize, destroy the software, and not engage in infringement again. Courts were rarely involved in ordinary infringement cases. However, the U.S. government demanded more protection for its copyright holders by imposing trade sanctions, and China eventually agreed to revise its customs and laws to afford protection. In this case, China's customs had to be changed to provide protection similar to that afforded in other countries.

Treaties

Examine various treaties:
http://law.house.gov

A **treaty** is an agreement between or among nations on a subject of international law signed by the leaders of the nations and ratified by the nations' governing bodies. In the United States, treaties are ratified by the Senate and are included in the pyramid (Exhibit 1.2) as federal legislative enactments.

Treaties can be between two nations—**bilateral treaties**—or among several nations—**multilateral treaties.** There are also treaties that are recognized by almost all nations, which are called general or **universal treaties.** Universal treaties are a reflection of widely followed standards of behavior. For example, the Geneva Convention is a universal treaty covering the treatment of prisoners of war. The Vienna Convention is a universal treaty covering diplomatic relations. The Warsaw Convention is a treaty that provides international law on the issues of liability for injuries to passengers and property during international air travel.

Private Law in International Transactions

Those businesses involved in multinational trade and production rely heavily on private law to assure performance of contractual obligations. Even though each country has a different set of laws, all of them recognize the autonomy of parties in an international trade transaction and allow the parties to negotiate contract terms that suit their needs, so long as none of the terms is illegal. **Party autonomy** allows firms to operate uniformly throughout the world if their contracts are recognized as valid in most countries. For example, most international trade contracts have a choice-of-law clause whereby the parties decide which country's law will apply to their disputes under the contract.

International Organizations

Some international organizations offer additions to international law. For example, the United Nations General Assembly has the authority to adopt resolutions to govern international relations and to censure companies that create difficulties in the international marketplace because of unfair dealings.

Act of State Doctrine

The **act of state doctrine** is a theory that protects governments from reviews of their actions by courts in other countries. In any action in which the government of a country has taken steps to condemn or confiscate property, the courts of other countries will not interfere. For example, in many cases, foreign countries engage in **expropriation** (also called **appropriation**), or the taking of private property. Also referred to as **confiscation** or **nationalization,** the process is really one of eminent domain, and courts of other countries will not interfere in this governmental process.

Trade Law and Policies

The importance of trade laws, tariffs, and policies has increased directly with increases in international business transactions. For example, the U.S. trade representative, once a dignitary position, has been upgraded to a cabinet-level position. Although Congress is responsible for enacting trade laws and various federal agencies are responsible for their administration, the U.S. trade representative assumes responsibility for negotiating trade agreements with foreign countries. The laws passed by Congress include import restrictions, tariffs, and enactments such as the Buy American Act (41 U.S.C. §§ 10a–10d [1987]), which requires federal agencies to give preference to U.S. suppliers in their procurement of goods and services. Additional details on trade laws, tariffs, restrictions, and trade agreements are found in Chapter 7.

The United States and China used a trade agreement as the means for requiring the Chinese to afford greater intellectual property protections (patent, copyright, trademark) for U.S. businesses.

Explore GATT:
http://www.washlaw.edu/
forint/alpha/g/gatt.htm

Two important treaties to which the United States is a party have had a significant effect on our economy. The first is the Geneva-based General Agreement on Tariffs and Trade (GATT). GATT establishes uniform trade policies between the United States and the European Union nations. The goal of GATT has been called "borderless trade."

Explore NAFTA:
gopher://wiretap.spies.com/
11/Gov/NAFTA

The second treaty is the North American Free Trade Agreement (NAFTA), which is a trade agreement among the United States, Canada, and Mexico. This lengthy agreement was signed by then–president George Bush in 1992 and has been approved by the legislative bodies of all three nations. The agreement, now in the implementation stage, is designed to permit the free flow of goods, services, and capital among the three nations. Some have called the resulting trade from NAFTA a "borderless North America."

A new sort of treaty has arisen that requires those countries ratifying the treaty to change certain internal laws to achieve international uniformity. For example, the Kyoto Treaty requires the United States and other countries to substantially reduce their carbon dioxide emissions to address what some scientists believe is global warming. Not only do countries ratify the treaty, they also pass new laws within their countries for compliance. More and more of these behavior- and law-changing treaties are being passed. In 2000, the U.S. Congress passed its E-sign law so that it could become one of many nations now subscribing to the requirement that electronic signatures be recognized as valid for purposes of contract formation.

Uniform International Laws

Because trade barriers have been largely eliminated, contracts have been and are being formed between and among businesses from virtually all nations. However, not all nations have the same approach to contracts. Indeed, some nations have no

With NAFTA, 800,000 low-skill manufacturing jobs (such as those in the apparel, food-processing, and consumer-goods manufacturing industries) have been transferred to Mexico, where labor costs are lower. The effect of this transfer of labor is that U.S. blue-collar workers must retrain and retool. Economists also maintain that the agreement now permits efficient use of resources and may reduce costs. Some labor representatives in the United States opposed NAFTA because of disparity in the wage levels in Mexico and the U.S. minimum wage levels. Does NAFTA take advantage of a poorer economy and its workers? Should companies transfer their plants to Mexico to take advantage of the lower wages there? Who should pay the costs of retaining displaced U.S. workers?

contract laws or commercial codes. In an attempt to introduce uniformity in international contract law, the Vienna Convention adopted the UN convention on Contracts for the International Sale of Goods (CISG) which has been adopted widely. Similar to the UCC (see Chapter 13), the CISG has provisions on formation, performance, and damages. More information on the CISG can be found in Chapters 7, 13, and 14.

The European Union

Learn more about the European Union: http://europa.eu.int/ index.htm

Once referred to as the Common Market and the European Community (EC), the European Union (EU) is a tariff-free group of European countries that includes Austria, Belgium, Denmark, Finland, France, Germany, Greece, Ireland, Italy, Luxembourg, the Netherlands, Portugal, Spain, Sweden, and the United Kingdom. This group of fifteen countries has joined together to enjoy the benefits of barrier-free trade. Formed in 1992, the single economic community requires member nations to subscribe to the same monetary standard, the elimination of immigration and customs controls, universal product and job safety standards, uniform licensing of professionals, and unified taxation schedules. The EU continues to evolve to trade as one country with the introduction of the euro, its single currency, in January 1999. More details on the governance of the EU and its laws can be found in Chapter 7.

SUMMARY

How is law defined?

- Law is a form of order. Law is the body of rules of society governing individuals and their relationships.

What types of laws are there?

- Public law—codified law; statutes; law by government body

- Private law—rules created by individuals for their contracts, tenancy, and employment

- Civil law—laws regulating harms and carrying damage remedies

- Criminal law—laws regulating wrongful conduct and carrying sentences and fines

- Statutory law—codified law

- Common law—law developed historically and by judicial precedent

- Substantive laws—laws giving rights and responsibilities

- Procedural laws—laws that provide enforcement rights

What are the purposes of law?

- Keep order; influence conduct; honor expectations; promote equality; offer compromises

What are the characteristics of law?

- Flexibility; consistency; pervasiveness
- Jurisprudence—theory of law

Where are laws found and who enacts them?

- Constitution—document that establishes structure and authority of a government
- Federal statutes—laws passed by Congress: the United States Code

- State statutes—laws passed by state legislatures, including uniform laws on contracts and business organizations
- Ordinances—local laws passed by cities, counties, and townships

What are the sources of international law?

- Treaties—agreements between and among nations regarding their political and commercial relationships
- Act of state doctrine—immunity of governmental action from discipline by other countries; sanctity of government's right to govern
- European Union—group of fifteen nations working collectively for uniform laws and barrier-free trade
- Uniform laws—Contracts for International Sale of Goods (CISG)

QUESTIONS AND PROBLEMS

1. Bryant Gunderson is a sole proprietor with a successful bungee-jumping business. He is considering incorporating his business. What levels and sources of law would affect and govern the process of incorporation?

2. Jeffrey Stalwart has just been arrested for ticket scalping outside the Great Western Forum in Los Angeles. Jeffrey sold a ticket to an Alanis Morrissette concert to an intense fan for $1,200; the face value of the ticket was $48. Ticket scalping in Los Angeles is a misdemeanor. Will Jeffrey's court proceedings be civil or criminal? Suppose that the fan sued Jeffrey under a provision of the Consumer Protection Act that permits recovery of fees paid scalpers in excess of a ticket's face value. Would these court proceedings be civil or criminal?

3. In 1933, Walt Disney Company entered into a contract with Irving Berlin, Inc., assigning musical copyrights in exchange for a share of Berlin revenues. The agreement exempted from copyright protection Disney's use of the assigned music in motion pictures. The music was used in several Disney feature-length cartoons (*Snow White* and *Pinocchio*) that were later made available for sale on videocassette. Berlin's heirs brought suit, alleging infringement. Was this new technology an infringement? Could videocassettes have been anticipated? (*Bourne* v. *Walt Disney Co.*, 68 F.3d 621 [2d Cir. 1995])

4. Define and contrast the following:
a. Civil law and criminal law
b. Substantive law and procedural law
c. Common law and statutory law
d. Private law and public law

5. Why are there differences in types and extent of laws in various countries? How do countries reconcile their legal differences to facilitate international business?

6. Jane Pregulman leases a one-bedroom apartment at Desert Cove Apartments. One of the regulations listed in her lease prohibits tenants from parking bicycles on their balconies or patios. What type of law is this? Is it enforceable?

7. Randy Redmond is an engineer with a city utility. The city has adopted an employment policy that creates a smoke-free work environment. Randy has smoked for fifteen years and now can no longer smoke at his desk. Is this a form of law? What is it? Is it enforceable? (For more discussion of this issue, see Chapters 19 and 20.)

8. Classify the following subject matters as substantive or procedural laws:
a. Taxation
b. Corporation law
c. Evidence
d. Labor law
e. Securities

9. Mercury Corporation manufactures solar panels for residential use. Mercury is experiencing some sales resistance because homeowners fear that trees and buildings will block the sunlight from their solar panels. At this time there is no law in Mercury's state protecting light for solar panels. What can Mercury do? What bodies in government could pass protective legislation?

10. Jose Camilo-Torres is a cacao farmer in Guyana. He has operated a large, successful business for twenty-two years and has sold his chocolate base product to U.S. companies such as M&M/Mars and Hershey's. After a change in government, Camilo-Torres's farm is taken over by the new government's agriculture department. Camilo-Torres will operate the farm and be paid a salary, but the profits will belong to the new government. Camilo-Torres has turned to his U.S. buyers and requested their assistance in stopping the actions of his government. Can anything be done? Could the government's actions be set aside in a U.S. court? What if the government's takeover is unfair and does not provide Camilo-Torres with adequate compensation? What label is given to the government's takeover of the farm?

RESEARCH PROBLEM

The Cost of Corporate Wrongdoing Business Strategy

11. Read and analyze "Paying the Piper: An Empirical Examination of Longer-Term Financial Consequences of Illegal Corporate Behavior," 40 *Academy of Management Journal* 129 (1997), by Melissa S. Baucus and David A. Baucus, and answer the following questions:
a. What financial impact does illegal corporate behavior have on a company?
b. How long does a company feel the impact of illegal behavior?
c. How does the market react to illegal corporate behavior?
d. What strategic issues exist in making a decision to comply with the law?

BUSINESS STRATEGY APPLICATION

The CD-ROM exercise for Chapter 1 provides an opportunity to look at the legal issues two relatively new companies face as they begin operations in a new industry. You can see how many sources of law affect a business and how the law must be considered as part of a business's strategic plan.

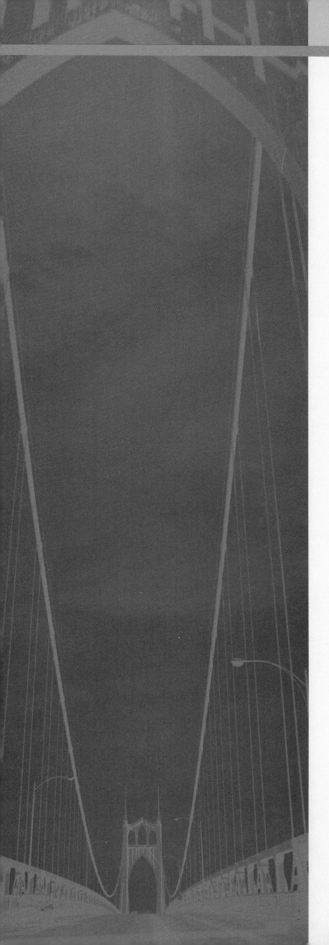

CHAPTER TWO

Business Ethics and Social Responsibility

Every business and every businessperson will at some time face an ethical dilemma. That dilemma may be deciding whether to hire a top marketing executive from your competitor's ranks. The dilemma may be one that offers a choice between survival and demise as when Yahoo faced whether to offer access to pornographic Web sites as a way to increase declining earnings. The dilemma may be like Finova's in the chapter opening "Consider . . .": Should I disclose the problems on the loan now or wait? An ethical dilemma could be as simple as whether to delay a product release date because there is a safety issue or whether to tell your employees that there may be some health consequences from long-term exposure to hazards in the workplace.

The old philosophy of "what's good for business is good for the country" is no longer adequate to ensure a business's long-term survival and earnings. Businesses today must answer not only to their shareholders but also to a myriad of constituents, often referred to as stakeholders, who demand responsibility and integrity if companies are to win their patronage. For example, Yahoo reversed its decision to offer access to pornographic sites within a matter of days because of customer objections. Both ethical and socially responsible behavior are demanded by shareholders to ensure long-term earnings growth, by customers in return for their loyalty, and by communities as a condition for incentives to locate and maintain business facilities in the area. In short, the shareholder is only one of many forces that work to shape the direction, goals, and conduct of a company. Other stakeholders, such as employees, customers, and communities, have an interest in the long-term success of a company. Ethics show in the attitudes of management and the responses of employees. This chapter answers the questions: What is business ethics? Why is business ethics important? What ethical standards should a business adopt? How do employees recognize ethical dilemmas? How are ethical dilemmas resolved? How does a business create an ethical atmosphere?

> **There is no pillow as soft as a clear conscience.**
>
> KENNETH BLANCHARD AND NORMAN VINCENT PEALE
> *The Power of Ethical Management*

> **Three people can keep a secret if two are dead.**
>
> HELL'S ANGELS

> **Goodness is the only investment that never fails.**
>
> HENRY D. THOREAU
> *Walden: "Higher Laws"*

> **A bad reputation is like a hangover. It takes a while to get rid of, and it makes everything else hurt.**
>
> JAMES PRESTON
> *Former CEO, Avon*

> **There is a big difference between what we have the right to do and what is right.**
>
> HON. JUSTICE POTTER STEWART
> *Associate Justice, U.S. Supreme Court, 1958–1981*

CONSIDER...

Finova Capital Corporation, based in Phoenix, Arizona, was ranked as one of the country's top ten employers. The firm's benefits, including everything from an on-site gym to college tuition for employees' children, were internationally known. Finova had also been a stellar Wall Street performer. By occupying a niche in the lending market of focusing on small- to mid-size firms, Finova had been able to achieve double-digit earnings growth for each of the five years from 1992 to 1997. But, one of Finova's loans to a California computer company in the amount of $70 million was in jeopardy. Officers in the company disagreed about whether the company should write off the loan and reflect the results in the financial reports. Some worried about the impact on the stock price. Some said there is flexibility when making a decision to write off a loan. Others said that shareholders should be told when a loan is likely to be bad. Others worried about harming employees because such a public disclosure would mean cutbacks. What should they do? Should they disclose that the loan is in jeopardy?

© CORBIS

WHY BUSINESS ETHICS?

Many people have referred to the term **business ethics** as an oxymoron: the words *business* and *ethics* seem to somehow contradict each other. Nonetheless, there are some compelling reasons for choosing ethical behavior. These reasons are discussed in the following sections.

Importance of Values in Business Success

As you learn in other disciplines, from economics to management, business is driven by the bottom line. Profits control whether the firm can obtain loans or gain investors and serve as the sole indicator of the firm's success—and, in most cases, its employees' success, as well. Indeed, business firms can be defined as groups of people working together to obtain maximum profits. The pursuit of the bottom line, however, can occasionally distort the perspective of even the most conscientious among us. The fear of losing business and, consequently, losing profits and capital support can persuade people to engage in conduct that, although not illegal, is unethical. But those who pursue only the bottom line fail to recognize that a successful business is more like a marathon than a sprint, requiring that ethical dilemmas be resolved with a long-term perspective in mind. Indeed, those firms that adhere to ethical standards perform better financially over the long run.

A 1997 study on the relationship between corporate behavior and financial performance concluded that firms involved in regulatory or criminal violations or product-liability litigation because of an unsafe product experience lower returns and slower sales growth even five years after their problems in these areas occur.[1]

Visit the Markkula Center for Applied Ethics of Santa Clara University:
http://www.scu.edu/ethics

The Tylenol tampering incident of 1982 offers one of the most telling examples of the rewards of being ethical. When Tylenol capsules were discovered to have been tainted with deadly poison, Tylenol's manufacturer, McNeil Consumer Products Company, a subsidiary of Johnson & Johnson, followed its code of ethics, which required it to put the interests of the consumer first. In what many financial analysts and economists considered to be a disastrous decision and a dreadful mistake, McNeil recalled all Tylenol capsules from the market—31 million bottles with a retail value of about $100 million. A new and safer form of a noncapsule Tylenol caplet was developed, and within a few months Tylenol regained its majority share of the market. The recall had turned out to be neither a poor decision nor a financial disaster. Rather, the company's actions enhanced its reputation and served to create a bond between Tylenol and its customers that was based largely on trust and respect for the integrity of the company and the product. (See "Leadership's Role . . ." for further discussion of this issue.)

Visit Beech-Nut:
http://www.beechnut.com

In contrast to the positive nature of ethical behavior is unethical behavior. For example, companies in the defense contracting business who were part of the spending and overcharging scandal several years ago are still reeling from the charges, struggling to regain credibility. Beech-Nut suffered tremendous earnings losses as a result of the discovery that its baby food "apple juice" did not in fact contain any real apple juice. Nestlé has endured many consumer boycotts since the early 1970s as a result of its intense—and what came to be perceived by the public as exploitative and unethical—marketing of infant formula in then–Third World nations, where the lack of sanitation, refrigeration, and education led to serious health problems in infants given the formula. In 1989, nearly twenty years after the infant formula crisis, Nestlé's new "Good Start" formula was slow in market infiltration and, because of continuing consumer resistance, did not perform as well as its quality and innovativeness would have predicted. Nestlé has never gained the market share or reputation its quality product deserves. As the Nestlé case illustrates, a firm's reputation for ethical behavior is the same as an individual's reputation: It takes a long time to gain, but it can be lost instantly as the result of one bad choice.

In 1992, Texaco was rocked by the disclosure of tape-recorded conversations among three executives about a racial discrimination suit pending against the company. The lawsuit involved 1,500 employees and alleged a pattern of discrimination by Texaco as well as a hostile environment. The tape-recorded conversations, although subsequently established as containing errors, quoted one executive as saying (accurately), "I'm still having trouble with Hanukkah. Now, we have Kwanza. (Laughter.)" A boycott against Texaco was declared, with a resulting $3 per share drop in the stock's value. Within days, Peter Bijur, Texaco's CEO, pledged to eliminate discrimination and settled the discrimination suit for $176 million. Mr. Bijur's pledge ended the boycott and restored both earnings and stock value.

Visit Salomon Brothers, Inc.:
**http://www.
salomonsmithbarney.com**

Salomon Brothers, Inc., became the target of an eleven-month probe after it was discovered that Salomon bond traders were controlling the U.S. Treasury bond market through prearranged transactions using major customers' names. Almost immediately after the news of Salomon's cornering of the bond market appeared in national papers, there was a $29 million drop in earnings for one quarter. Further, Salomon paid $122 million in fines, was given a two-month suspension from bond trading, and was required to establish a $100 million fund to compensate other firms hurt by the cornering of the bond market. Bausch & Lomb and Enron executives and employees overstated company earnings, which were subsequently revealed in audits as accounting irregularities. Both companies experienced drops in share prices, sales, and earnings.

*Visit the U.S. Securities and
Exchange Commission:*
http://sec.gov

During the early 1990s, the financial returns on investments in derivative securities were enticing. Many firms, from Procter & Gamble through Gibson Greetings to Barings Bank, joined the bandwagon to invest in these risky ventures, which offered high returns, but which, if leveraged, could bring disaster if the high stakes turned against the firm (see Chapter 22). The risk and high exposure of these investment mechanisms were not disclosed to shareholders or the public. When the markets turned, the investments went bad and the firms experienced large financial write-offs or even, in the case of Barings Bank, bankruptcy. The firms now face lawsuits from shareholders and customers, and the Securities and Exchange Commission (SEC) now strictly regulates derivatives through required, detailed disclosures (see Chapter 22 for more details).

*Visit Orange County,
California:*
http://www.oc.ca.gov

Orange County, California, had invested heavily in derivatives and was heavily leveraged when the derivatives market turned the wrong way for its portfolio. The result was a reorganization in bankruptcy for the county. A financial newsletter commented, "It was the biggest orgy of bond speculation in world history." A professional surfer from Huntington Beach offered his views on the county's bankruptcy: "It all comes down to greed."

The poor value choices of the aforementioned firms resulted in tremendous financial setbacks and, in the case of Orange County, destruction. The core values of a firm give it long-standing profitability. "The Tony Bennett Factor" offers some insight into longevity, profitability, and values.

Re: The Tony Bennett Factor

I had blocked out the background noise offered courtesy of MTV and my teenager, but I glanced up and saw Tony Bennett. My parents raised me on Tony Bennett LPs back in the '50s. "I Left My Heart in San Francisco" enjoyed hours of play in Tyrone, Pa. And here he was back, "Tony Bennett Unplugged."

Mr. Bennett has not changed. Yet his success has spanned generations. Suddenly my work with a colleague, Prof. Louis Grossman, had new meaning. We had been studying business longevity, trying to determine what makes some businesses survive so successfully for so long.

Prof. Grossman and I began our study when we spotted a 1982 full-page ad in this newspaper placed by Diamond Match Co. The ad touted the company's 100 years of consistent dividend payments. Today's standards tell us that 100 quarters of dividend payments would be stellar. What kind of company was this? Were there others?

We discovered seven other industrial firms that could boast of making at least an annual dividend payment for a string of 100 years or more: Scovill, Inc.; Ludlow Corp.; Stanley Works; Singer Co.; Pennwalt, Inc.; Pullman, Inc.; and Corning Glass Works. Pullman, Ludlow and Stanley had unbroken chains of a century of quarterly dividend payments as well.

Mr. Bennett and our eight companies have survival in common. These survivors' tools make management theories of today seem trite. They had no shifting paradigms. No buzzwords.

Mr. Bennett recognized his strength as a balladeer and stuck with it, through everything from the Beatles to Hootie and the Blowfish. Although each of our companies recognized the importance of diversification, they all held fast to a WBAWI—or "what business are we in?"—philosophy. They knew their strengths, developed strong market presences based on those strengths and never forgot their roots. Mr. Bennett never performed without singing "I Wanna Be Around." Singer never left its sewing machines. Pullman never deserted its train cars. Diamond held on to its matches.

The firms diversified only when their strengths allowed. Scovill began as a brass button

manufacturer and backed into brass manufacturing because it knew brass. Scovill bought Hamilton Beach because Hamilton Beach was a major brass purchaser. Scovill understood this customer's business.

Other companies have forgotten the WBAWI lesson and paid the price. Sears abandoned its catalog, insurance and real estate businesses and now struggles to find a retail presence. IBM has suffered for not understanding its business was the workplace, not mainframe computers. Its Lotus takeover shows it may recognize the PC as the workplace.

All Mr. Bennett needs are a microphone and a pianist to make music. All eight of our companies were low-cost producers. All eight were cost conscious. Scovill executive vice presidents with worldwide responsibilities shared a secretary. Spartan company headquarters were the rule for these firms. There were barely six-figure salaries for executives. By contrast, IBM's Louis Gerstner hired an executive chef at $120,000 just last month.

Mr. Bennett has used the same musical arranger for nearly 30 years. Our eight companies' management team histories are in direct contrast to the executive recruiting practices in vogue today. Scovill, founded during the Jefferson administration in 1803, had only 12 CEOs during its 100-year dividend run. Three of the companies (Singer, Stanley and Diamond) had CEOs who served for more than 40 years. Seven of the companies never had a CEO serve for fewer than 10 years. They were not afraid of home-grown management. Their officers and CEOs came up through the ranks. Management succession is found in all eight companies.

Perhaps this information demonstrates the importance of continuity and stability. The executives appreciated the tension between short-term results and long-term performance, but the short term did not control decision making. Donald Davis, chairman and CEO of Stanley Works, put it this way: "The tension is always there. One of the top management's toughest jobs really is to mediate between the two viewpoints—short-term profit results now versus investment for future development."

Mr. Bennett did and does spend time on the road in concert, in direct contact with audiences—no mega-tours, just constant gigs. And a full century before we heard of customer service, these firms sent their sales forces and vice presidents alike out on the road to talk directly with customers. They had interesting marketing studies: one-on-one feedback. Sales calls, follow-ups, replacements, and refunds allowed them to remain in the customers' minds and good graces.

One officer said it best: "Anyone can read the monthly financial reports: What we need to do is to interpret them so we can spot trends. We call on customers, on suppliers, we look at the bottom line of course, but we know how that line reached the bottom."

Mr. Bennett has never made a bad recording or disappointed during a live performance. Our eight firms had strong commitments to integrity. Their mantra was: "If there's integrity, there will be quality and profits." Their integrity manifested itself in more than just quality. Frederick T. Stanley, founder of Stanley Works, spoke of the intricate balance between automation and employees:

"Machines are no better than the skill, care, ingenuity and spirit of the men who operate them. We can achieve perfect harmony when shortening of an operation provides mutual advantages to the workman and the producers." Ethics before its time. Re-engineering done correctly in the 1800s. Nothing at the expense of the customer or the employee.

Our firms were no less remarkable than Mr. Bennett and his success with Generation X—his third generational conquest. The sad part of their stories is what happened following the takeover battles of the '80s. But that is a story for another time. For now, it is reassuring to realize that cost-consciousness, focus, customer service, home-grown management and integrity are keys to longevity. Today's management fads seem as shallow as Ice-T and Madonna. There is a simple Tony Bennett factor in success that makes today's fads much easier to debunk and infinitely easier to question.

In 1989, the Exxon oil tanker *Valdez* ran aground in Alaska's Prince William Sound, and 11 million gallons of crude oil leaked into Alaska's waters and onto its shores. Evidence of cutbacks in crews and maintenance levels for tankers dogged Exxon as the cleanup litigation continued through 1996. The Exxon name suffered because of its association with oil spills. Further, Congress permanently banned the *Valdez* from Prince William Sound.

Visit General Motors:
http://www.gm.com

As General Motors prepared to release its Chevrolet Malibu for production in 1976, an engineer drafted a memo about some issues with the placement of the car's gas tank and the likelihood of its explosion in the event of a rear-end collision. The memo discussed both the potential liability for such accidents and the costs of modifying the design. The Malibu went forward without production and design changes. By 1981, there was some litigation related to rear-end collisions involving the Malibu and gas tank explosions. A lawyer working the cases found the 1976 memo and explained the need to keep the engineer's thoughts and analysis from being disclosed. In December 1999, a jury awarded the victims of a Malibu rear-end collision and explosion over $107 million compensatory damages and $4.8 billion punitive damages (later reduced to $1.2 billion on appeal) and explained that its high damage verdict was directly attributable to the memo, the knowledge and the failure to disclose that information or take corrective action.

Ethics as a Strategy

Ethical behavior not only increases long-term earnings; it also enables businesses to plan ahead and anticipate social needs and cultural changes that require the firm or its product to evolve. One of the benefits of a firm's ethical behavior and participation in community concerns is the goodwill that such involvement fosters. Conversely, the absence of that goodwill and consequent loss of trust can mean the destruction of the firm.

When methyl isocyanate gas leaked from the Union Carbide plant in Bhopal, India, in 1984, the deadly gas left over 2,500 dead and 200,000 injured. It was later discovered that there had been problems in the plant with some of the equipment designed to prevent such leaks. While actual liability issues were hotly debated in court, many ethical questions were raised regarding the plant and Union Carbide. Was it a wise decision to build the plant in a country with little expertise in the relevant technology? Did the people in the town know of the potential dangers of the plant? Why was a city of shacks allowed to be erected so close to the plant?

According to the Indian government, the plant had been operated well within legal and regulatory requirements and Union Carbide's management had been cooperative in installing any additional equipment needed. Should Union Carbide have done more than was legally required? Did the plant operators need more training for such emergencies? Finally, the Bhopal incident raises many questions about the relationship between U.S. businesses and their operations in developing countries that may not be prepared to deal with the latest technologies and may not be fully informed about the associated risks.

Business Ethics for Personal Reasons

It would be misleading to say that every ethical business is a profitable business. First, not all ethical people are good managers or possess the necessary skills for making a business a success; but there are many competent businesspeople who have suffered for being ethical and many others who seem to survive despite their lack of ethics. Columnist Dave Barry has noted that every time there is an oil spill, the oil companies ready themselves for the higher prices and profits that come because all that oil is lost at sea. Despite his conviction and jail term related to junk bond sales in the 1980s, Michael Milken recently earned a $50 million fee for helping Ted Turner negotiate a merger with Time Warner.[2] There are many whistle-blowers who, although respected by many, have been unable to find employment in their industries. If ethical behavior does not guarantee success, then why have ethics? The answer has to do with personal ethics applied in a business context. Ivan Boesky was once described as follows: "He beguiled everybody about his exhaustive research and canny stock analysis when he really made money the old-fashioned way. He stole it." Business ethics is really nothing more than a standard of personal behavior applied to a group of people working together to make a profit. Some people are ethical because it enables them to sleep better at night. Some people are ethical because of the fear of getting caught. But being personally ethical is a justification for business ethics—it is simply the correct thing to do. The parable of the Sadhu focuses on business ethics for personal reasons.

Re: The Parable of the Sadhu

[In 1982], as the first participant in the new six-month sabbatical program that Morgan Stanley has adopted, I enjoyed a rare opportunity to collect my thoughts as well as do some traveling. I spent the first three months in Nepal, walking 600 miles through 200 villages in the Himalayas and climbing some 120,000 vertical feet. On the trip my sole Western companion was an anthropologist who shed light on the cultural patterns of the villages we passed through.

During the Nepal hike, something occurred that has had a powerful impact on my thinking about corporate ethics. Although some might argue that the experience has no relevance to business, it was a situation in which a basic ethical dilemma suddenly intruded into the lives of a group of individuals. How the group responded I think holds a lesson for all organizations no matter how defined.

The Sadhu

The Nepal experience was more rugged and adventuresome than I had anticipated. Most commercial treks last two or three weeks and cover a quarter of the distance we traveled.

My friend Stephen, the anthropologist, and I were halfway through the 60-day Himalayan part of the trip when we reached the highpoint, an 18,000-foot pass over a crest that we'd have to traverse to reach the village of Muklinath, an ancient holy place for pilgrims.

Six years earlier I had suffered pulmonary edema, an acute form of altitude sickness, at 16,500 feet in the vicinity of Everest base camp, so we were understandably concerned about what would happen at 18,000 feet. Moreover, the Himalayas were having their wettest spring in 20 years; hip-deep powder and ice had already driven us off one ridge. If we failed to cross the pass, I feared that the last half of our "once in a lifetime" trip would be ruined.

The night before we would try the pass, we camped at a hut at 14,500 feet. In the photos taken at the camp, my face appears wan. The last village we'd passed through was a sturdy two-day walk below us, and I was tired.

During the late afternoon, four backpackers from New Zealand joined us, and we spent most of the night awake, anticipating the climb. Below we could see the fires of two other parties, which turned out to be two Swiss couples and a Japanese hiking club.

To get over the steep part of the climb before the sun melted the steps cut in the ice, we departed at 3:30 A.M. The New Zealanders left first, followed by Stephen and myself, our porters and Sherpas, and then the Swiss. The Japanese lingered in their camp. The sky was clear, and we were confident that no spring storm would erupt that day to close the pass.

At 15,500 feet, it looked to me as if Stephen were shuffling and staggering a bit, which are symptoms of altitude sickness. (The initial stage of altitude sickness brings a headache and nausea. As the condition worsens, a climber may encounter difficult breathing, disorientation, aphasia, and paralysis.) I felt strong, my adrenaline was flowing, but I was very concerned about my ultimate ability to get across. A couple of our porters were also suffering from the height, and Pasang, our Sherpa sirdar (leader), was worried.

Just after daybreak, while we rested at 15,500 feet, one of the New Zealanders, who had gone ahead, came staggering down toward us with a body slung across his shoulders. He dumped the almost naked, barefoot body of an Indian holy man—a sadhu—at my feet. He had found the pilgrim lying on the ice, shivering and suffering from hypothermia. I cradled the sadhu's head and laid him out on the rocks. The New Zealander was angry. He wanted to get across the pass before the bright sun melted the snow. He said, "Look, I've done what I can. You have porters and Sherpa guides. You care for him. We're going on!" He turned and went back up the mountain to join his friends.

I took a carotid pulse and found that the sadhu was still alive. We figured he had probably visited the holy shrines at Muklinath and was on his way home. It was fruitless to question why he had chosen this desperately high route instead of the safe, heavily traveled caravan route through the kali Gandaki gorge. Or why he was almost naked and with no shoes, or how long he had been lying in the pass. The answers were not going to solve our problem.

Stephen and the four Swiss began stripping off outer clothing and opening their packs. The sadhu was soon clothed from head to foot. He was not

(continued)

able to walk, but he was very much alive. I looked down the mountain and spotted below the Japanese climbers marching up with a horse.

Without a great deal of thought, I told Stephen and Pasang that I was concerned about withstanding the heights to come and wanted to get over the pass. I took off after several of our porters who had gone ahead.

On the steep part of the ascent where, if the ice steps had given way, I would have slid down about 3,000 feet, I felt vertigo. I stopped for a breather, allowing the Swiss to catch up with me. I inquired about the sadhu and Stephen. They said that the sadhu was fine and that Stephen was just behind. I set off again for the summit.

Stephen arrived at the summit an hour after I did. Still exhilarated by victory, I ran down the snow slope to congratulate him. He was suffering from altitude sickness, walking fifteen steps, then stopping, walking fifteen steps, then stopping. When I reached them, Stephen glared at me and said: "How do you feel about contributing to the death of a fellow man?"

I did not fully comprehend what he meant.

"Is the sadhu dead?" I inquired.

"No," replied Stephen, "but he surely will be!"

After I had gone, and the Swiss had departed not long after, Stephen had remained with the sadhu. When the Japanese had arrived, Stephen had asked to use their horse to transport the sadhu down to the hut. They had refused. He had then asked Pasang to have a group of our porters carry the sadhu. Pasang had resisted the idea, saying that the porters would have to exert all their energy to get themselves over the pass. He had thought they could not carry a man down 1,000 feet to the hut, reclimb the slope, and get across safely before the snow melted. Pasang had pressed Stephen not to delay any longer.

The Sherpas had carried the sadhu down to a rock in the sun at about 15,000 feet and had pointed out the hut another 500 feet below. The Japanese had given him food and drink. When they had last seen him he was listlessly throwing rocks at the Japanese party's dog, which had frightened him.

We do not know if the sadhu lived or died.

For many of the following days and evenings Stephen and I discussed and debated our behavior toward the sadhu. Stephen is a committed Quaker with deep moral vision. He said, "I feel that what happened with the sadhu is a good example of the breakdown between the individual ethic and the corporate ethic. No one person was willing to assume ultimate responsibility for the sadhu. Each was willing to do his bit just so long as it was not too inconvenient. When it got to be a bother, everyone just passed the buck to someone else and took off. Jesus was relevant to a more individualist stage of society, and how do we interpret his teaching today in a world filled with large, impersonal organizations and groups?"

I defended the larger group, saying, "Look, we all cared. We all stopped and gave aid and comfort. Everyone did his bit. The New Zealander carried him down below the snow line. I took his pulse and suggested we treat him for hypothermia. You and the Swiss gave him clothing and got him warmed up. The Japanese gave him food and water. The Sherpas carried him down to the sun and pointed out the easy trail toward the hut. He was well enough to throw rocks at a dog. What more could we do?"

"You have just described the typical affluent Westerner's response to a problem. Throwing money—in this case food and sweaters—at it, but not solving the fundamentals!" Stephen retorted.

"What would satisfy you?" I said. "Here we are, a group of New Zealanders, Swiss, Americans, and Japanese who have never met before and who are at the apex of one of the most powerful experiences of our lives. Some years the pass is so bad no one gets over it. What right does an almost naked pilgrim who chooses the wrong trail have to disrupt our lives? Even the Sherpas had no interest in risking the trip to help him beyond a certain point."

Stephen calmly rebutted, "I wonder what the Sherpas would have done if the sadhu had been a well-dressed Nepali, or what the Japanese would have done if the sadhu had been a well-dressed Asian, or what you would of done, Buzz, if the sadhu had been a well-dressed Western woman?"

"Where, in your opinion," I asked instead, "is the limit of our responsibility in a situation like this? We had our own well-being to worry about. Our Sherpa guides were unwilling to jeopardize us or the porters for the sadhu. No one else on the mountain was willing to commit himself beyond certain self-imposed limits."

Stephen said, "As individual Christians or people with a Western ethical tradition, we can fulfill our obligations in such a situation only if (1) the sadhu dies in our care, (2) the sadhu demonstrates to us that he could undertake the two-day walk down to the village, or (3) we carry the sadhu for two days down to the village and convince someone there to care for him."

"Leaving the sadhu in the sun with food and clothing, while he demonstrated hand-eye coordination by throwing a rock at a dog, comes close to fulfilling items one and two," I answered. "And it wouldn't have made sense to take him to the village where the people appeared to be far less caring than the Sherpas, so the third condition is impractical. Are you really saying that, no matter what the implications, we should, at the drop of a hat, have changed our entire plan?"

The Individual versus the Group Ethic

Despite my arguments, I felt and continue to feel guilt about the sadhu. I had literally walked through a classic moral dilemma without fully thinking through the consequences. My excuses for my actions include a high adrenaline flow, a superordinate goal, and a once-in-a-lifetime opportunity—factors in the usual corporate situation, especially when one is under stress.

Real moral dilemmas are ambiguous, and many of us hike right through them, unaware that they exist. When, usually after the fact, someone makes an issue of them, we tend to resent his or her bringing it up. Often, when the full import of what we have done (or not done) falls on us, we dig into a defensive position from which it is very difficult to emerge. In rare circumstances we may contemplate what we have done from inside a prison.

Had we mountaineers been free of physical and mental stress caused by the effort and the high altitude, we might have treated the sadhu differently. Yet isn't stress the true test of personal and corporate values? The instant decisions executives make under pressure reveal the most about personal and corporate character.

Among the many questions that occur to me when pondering my experience are: What are the practical limits of moral imagination and vision? Is there a collective or institutional ethic beyond the ethics of the individual? At what level of effort or commitment can one discharge one's ethical responsibilities?

Not every ethical dilemma has a right solution. Reasonable people often disagree; otherwise there would be no dilemma. In a business context, however, it is essential that managers agree on a process for dealing with dilemmas.

The sadhu experience offers an interesting parallel to business situations. An immediate response was mandatory. Failure to act was a decision in itself. Up on the mountain we could not resign and submit our résumé to a headhunter. In contrast to philosophy, business involves action and implementation—getting things done. Managers must come up with answers to problems based on what they see and what they allow to influence their decision-making processes. On the mountain, none of us but Stephen realized the true dimensions of the situation we were facing.

One of our problems was that as a group we had no process for developing a consensus. We had no sense of purpose of plan. The difficulties of dealing with the sadhu were so complex that no one person could handle it. Because it did not have a set of preconditions that could guide its action to an acceptable resolution, the group reacted instinctively as individuals. The cross-cultural nature of the group added a further layer of complexity. We had no leader with whom we could identify and in whose purpose we believed. Only Stephen was willing to take charge, but he could not gain adequate support to care for the sadhu.

Some organizations do have a value system that transcends the personal values of the managers. Such values, which go beyond profitability, are usually revealed when the organization is under stress. People throughout the organization generally accept its values, which, because they are not presented as a rigid list of commandments, may be somewhat ambiguous. The stories people tell, rather than printed materials, transmit these conceptions of what is proper behavior.

For twenty years I have been exposed at senior levels to a variety of corporations and organizations. It is amazing how quickly an outsider can sense the tone and style of an organization and the degree of tolerated openness and freedom to challenge management.

Organizations that do not have a heritage of mutually accepted, shared values tend to become unhinged during stress, with each individual bailing out for himself. In the great takeover battles

(continued)

we have witnessed during past years, companies that had strong cultures drew the wagons around them and fought it out, while other companies saw executives, supported by their golden parachutes, bail out of the struggles.

Because corporations and their members are interdependent, for the corporation to be strong the members need to share a preconceived notion of what is correct behavior, a "business ethic," and think of it as a positive force, not a constraint.

As an investment banker I am continually warned by well-meaning lawyers, clients, and associates to be wary of conflicts of interest. Yet if I were to run away from every difficult situation, I wouldn't be an effective investment banker. I have to feel my way through conflicts. An effective manager can't run from risk either; he or she has to confront and deal with risk. To feel "safe" in doing this, managers need the guidelines of an agreed-on process and set of values within the organization.

After my three months in Nepal, I spent three months as an executive-in-residence at both Stanford Business School and the Center for Ethics and Social Policy at the Graduate Theological Union at Berkeley. These six months away from my job gave me time to assimilate twenty years of business experience. My thoughts turned often to the meaning of the leadership role in any large organization. Students at the seminary thought of themselves as antibusiness. But when I questioned them they agreed they distrusted all large organizations, including the church. They perceived all large organizations as impersonal and opposed to individual values and needs. Yet we all know of organizations where people's values and beliefs are respected and their expressions encouraged. What makes the difference? Can we identify the difference and, as a result, manage more effectively?

The word "ethics" turns off many and confuses more. Yet the notions of shared values and an agreed-on process for dealing with adversity and change—what many people mean when they talk about corporate culture—seem to be at the heart of the ethical issue. People who are in touch with their own core beliefs and the beliefs of others and are sustained by them can be more comfortable living on the cutting edge.

At times, taking a tough line or a decisive stand in a muddle of ambiguity is the only ethical thing to do.

If a manager is indecisive and spends time trying to figure out the "good" thing to do, the enterprise may be lost.

Business ethics, then, has to do with authenticity and integrity of the enterprise. To be ethical is to follow the business as well as the cultural goals of the corporation, its owners, its employees, and its customers. Those who cannot serve the corporate vision are not authentic business people and, therefore, are not ethical in the business sense.

At this stage of my own business experience I have a strong interest in organizational behavior. Sociologists are keenly studying what they call corporate stories, legends, and heroes as a way organizations have of transmitting the value system. Corporations such as Arco have even hired consultants to perform an audit of their corporate culture. In a company, the leader is the person who understands, interprets, and manages the corporate value system. Effective managers are then action-oriented people who resolve conflict, are tolerant of ambiguity, stress, and change, and have a strong sense of purpose for themselves and their organizations.

If all this is true, I wonder about the role of the professional manager who moves from company to company. How can he or she quickly absorb the values and culture of different organizations? Or is there, indeed, an art of management that is totally transportable? Assuming such fungible managers do exist, is it proper for them to manipulate the values of others?

What would have happened had Stephen and I carried the sadhu for two days back to the village and become involved with the villagers in his care? In four trips to Nepal my most interesting experiences occurred in 1975 when I lived in a Sherpa home in the Khumbu for five days recovering from altitude sickness. The high point of Stephen's trip was an invitation to participate in a family funeral ceremony in Manang. Neither experience had to do with climbing the high passes of the Himalayas. Why were we so reluctant to try the lower path, the ambiguous trail? Perhaps because we did not have a leader who could reveal the greater purpose of the trip to us.

Why didn't Stephen with his moral vision opt to take the sadhu under his personal care? The answer is because, in part, Stephen was hard-stressed physically himself, and because, in part, without some support system that involved our involuntary and episodic community on the mountain, it was beyond his individual capacity to do so.

I see the current interest in corporate culture and corporate value systems as a positive response to Stephen's pessimism about the decline of the role of the individual in large organizations. Individuals who operate from a thoughtful set of personal values provide the foundation of a corporate culture. A corporate tradition that encourages freedom of inquiry, supports personal values, and reinforces a focused sense of direction can fulfill the need for individuality along with the prosperity and success of the group. Without such corporate support, the individual is lost.

That is the lesson of the sadhu. In a complex corporate situation, the individual requires and deserves the support of the group. If people cannot find such support from their organization, they don't know how to act. If such support is forthcoming, a person has a stake in the success of the group, and can add much to the process of

establishing and maintaining a corporate culture. It is the management's challenge to be sensitive to individual needs, to shape them, and to direct and focus them for the benefit of the group as a whole.

For each of us the sadhu lives. Should we stop what we are doing and comfort him; or should we keep trudging up toward the high pass? Should I pause to help the derelict I pass on the street each night as I walk by the Yale Club en route to Grand Central Station? Am I his brother? What is the nature of our responsibility if we consider ourselves to be ethical persons? Perhaps it is to change the values of the group so that it can, with all its resources, take the other road.

Discussion Question

Consider the closing questions Mr. McCoy poses. How do they apply to you personally and to businesses?

Source: Reprinted by permission of *Harvard Business Review,* "The Parable of the Sadhu," by Bowen H. McCoy, May–June 1997. Copyright © 1997 by the Harvard Business School Publishing Corporation; all rights reserved.

The Value of a Good Reputation

A reputation, good or bad, stays with a business or individual for a long time. Richard Teerlink, the former CEO of Harley-Davidson, has said, "A reputation, good or bad, is tough to shake." Another executive, lamenting his chances to try again, commented, "Would anybody let Roseanne sing the national anthem again?" Once a company makes poor ethical choices, it carries the baggage of those choices despite successful and sincere efforts to reform. Salt Lake City struggled to regain its credibility as the trials from the bribery allegations surrounding its winning the bid for the 2002 Winter Olympics progressed and companies withdrew sponsorships. Businesses remain unsure about the reputations and trustworthiness of those running the Salt Lake City operations.

CONSIDER...

2.1 In the chapter opening "Consider . . . ," Finova's dilemma is representative of similar ones faced by many companies during 2000 as the reality of the financial positions of many of the dot-com firms became clear. Many executives and auditors were debating the issue of what to disclose and when to disclose it. In other words, they debated whether and when to release negative but accurate information that would have an impact on share prices and shareholders.

In the situation with the loan, Finova decided not to write down the $70 million loan. By the end of 1999, when it became clear that the loan was not collectible, the auditors for Finova insisted that the write-down be taken. Finova refused and fired its auditor. However, when a new auditor was hired, it insisted that the annual report be held up because the write-down needed to be taken. When news of the disagreement with the auditors broke, along with the fact that the $70 million loan had been in question, investors lost faith in the company and the disclosures. The value of Finova's shares dipped from a high of $46 to $0.88 before it declared bankruptcy in early 2001. Finova had squandered its reputational capital with the loan decision and was unable to regain investor confidence.

Leadership's Role in Ethical Choices

George Fisher, the former CEO of Motorola and Kodak, has defined leadership as the ability to see around corners. In other words, a leader sees a problem before it becomes a legal issue or liability and fixes it, thus saving company time and money. All social, regulatory, and litigation issues progress along a time line. As the issue is brought to the public's attention, either by stories or by the sheer magnitude of the problem, the momentum for remedies and reforms continues until behavior is changed and regulated. Ethical choices afford firms opportunities to take positions ahead of the curve. Firms can choose to go beyond the law and perhaps avoid regulation that might be costly or litigation that can be devastating. For example, the issues relating to the problems with asbestos dust in the lungs of asbestos workers and installers were clear in the 1930s. More studies needed to be done, but there was sufficient evidence to justify lung protection for workers and the development of alternative forms of insulation. However, the first litigation relating to asbestos and asbestos workers did not arise until 1968. For that thirty-year period, those in the business of producing and selling asbestos insulation products had the opportunity to take preventive actions. They chose to wait out the cycle. The result was a ban on asbestos and litigation at levels that forced the largest producer, Johns-Manville (now Manville), into bankruptcy. Leadership choices were available in the 1930s for offering warnings, providing masks, and developing alternative insulators. Johns-Manville chose to continue its posture of controlling information releases and studies. The liability issue progressed to a point of no choice other than that of bankruptcy and reorganization.

Visit the U.S. Federal Trade Commission:
http://www.ftc.gov

Every business regulation that exists today controls business conduct in an area where there was once no control but, rather, the opportunity for businesses to self-regulate by making good value choices. For credit disclosures (see Chapter 15) before requirements were imposed by Congress and the Federal Trade Commission, lenders and creditors had the option of designing their own disclosure forms and providing full information to buyers and debtors. That option was not chosen, and the result is a full scheme of regulation, including forms and advertising requirements. More recently, the problems resulting from a lack of candor in auto-leasing agreements have resulted in federal regulation of contracts in this consumer area. In the spring of 2001, all companies with credit cards began an expensive campaign to send all customers a right-to-privacy notice. Customers had to be given a choice as to when, how, and if they wanted information about them and their spending habits used or disclosed. This expensive regulatory compliance effort resulted from too many companies using information about their customers without permission. That information was sold to other companies so that the customers could be specifically and successfully target marketed based on their spending patterns. Protests by consumers and litigation resulted in complex compliance and disclosure requirements that, in turn, resulted in substantial costs

EXHIBIT 2.1
Leadership and
Ethics: Making
Choices before
Liability

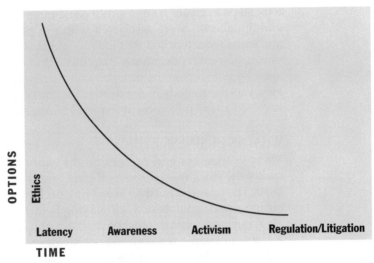

Source: Adapted from James Frierson's "Public Policy Forecasting: A New Approach," *SAM Advanced Management Journal,* Spring 1985, 18–23.

for doing business. Giving customers the right to protect their privacy from the outset would have eliminated the need for the substantial costs of compliance.

Ethical choices give businesses the freedom to make choices before regulators mandate them. Breaches of ethics bring about regulation and liability with few opportunities to choose and less flexibility. The notion of choices and leadership are diagrammed in Exhibit 2.1. Every issue progresses along a cycle that begins with a *latency* phase, in which the industry is aware of a problem. The use of private information about consumers' buying patterns was well known in the marketing industry, but few consumers were aware of that use of their personal buying histories. The *awareness* stage begins when the popular press reports on an issue and raises questions. Once the public has knowledge of a problem, it responds by demanding assurance that the problem either is resolved or is not really an issue—or by calling for reform. The *activism* stage is one in which members of the public ask for either voluntary or regulatory reform. If voluntary reform is not forthcoming, those affected may sue or lobby for reform, or both. For example, a group of parents, police officers, and shareholders protested Time Warner's production of "Cop Killer," a song by the rap music artist Ice-T. The public outcry was strong both in the press and at Time Warner's shareholder meeting. Congress was considering holding hearings on record labels and record content. Time Warner took the voluntary action of removing the song from the album. Time Warner eventually made a choice to withdraw the song, later in the regulatory cycle when public outcry was strong, but still averted regulation. It is important to understand that Time Warner could have made the choice not to publish the song of Ice-T initially.

One aspect of the Tylenol poisonings case (noted earlier in the chapter) that few realize is that the issue of tamper-proof packaging had been a concern in the industry long before the poisonings involving Tylenol occurred. Those in the industry were concerned that packaging that did not signal unauthorized entry so that a buyer could spot tampering could open the door to the tragedy that eventually occurred. However, no one in the industry, despite knowledge of this issue, took steps to create tamper-proof packaging. The law did not require such a step; additional costs were associated with the packaging and re-tooling production; and some were worried that they would be at a competitive disadvantage if their products were harder to use than those that did not have the tamper-proof packages. By not solving the problem voluntarily, companies faced unpleasant results. First was the tragedy of the deaths. Second, additional regulations and costs were imposed as the government required tamper-proof packaging.

WHAT IS BUSINESS ETHICS?

Many economists and professors of finance argue that insider trading actually makes the stock market more efficient and that such conduct should not be regulated. The purpose of ethics is to bring back into the purely quantitative models of business the elements of a fair playing field.

A business faces the special problem of having to develop moral standards for a group of people who will work together toward the common goal of profit for the firm. Individuals in the group will have personal moral standards, but employees may find that the moral standards imposed by those at the top in a business result in possible harm to those at the bottom or to others outside the firm. An employee may feel compelled to resolve the conflict between loyalty to an employer and the performance of an illegal or immoral act ordered by that employer by simply following the employer's direction. In other words, in developing standards of business ethics, an employee has personal economic interests in continuing employment that may compromise personal moral standards.

Moral standards can be derived from different sources, and ethicists often debate about the origins of these standards. One theory is that our moral standards are simply the same as actual or **positive law,** that our ethical decisions are made simply upon the basis of whether an activity is legal. Positive law, or codified law, establishes the standard for ethical behavior.

Others believe that our moral standards are derived from a higher source and that they are universal. Often labeled **natural law,** this school of ethical thought supports the notion that some standards do not exist because of law (and, indeed, may exist in spite of laws). For example, at one time the United States permitted slavery. Even though the positive law allowed the activity and the standard of positive law considered slave ownership ethical, natural law dictated that the deprivation of others' rights was unethical.

Moral relativism (also called *situational ethics*) establishes moral standards according to the situation in which the dilemma is faced. Violation of the law, for example, is permitted if you are stealing to provide food for your starving family. Under moral relativism, adultery is justified when you are caught in an unhappy marriage, as is the business situation in which you engage in lying to avoid offending a co-worker or a customer. Bribery is illegal in the United States, and most companies have firm policies against even accepting gifts as conflicts of interest; but, some companies still use a relativist approach and argue that to be competitive in international markets is different and they follow a philosophy of "When in Rome, do as the Romans do." They follow the standards and customs in a given country even though those same behaviors in the United States would be unacceptable and even illegal.

A final source of moral standards is religious beliefs or divine revelation. The source of standards can be the Bible or the Koran or any inspired book or writing someone believes has resulted from divine revelation.

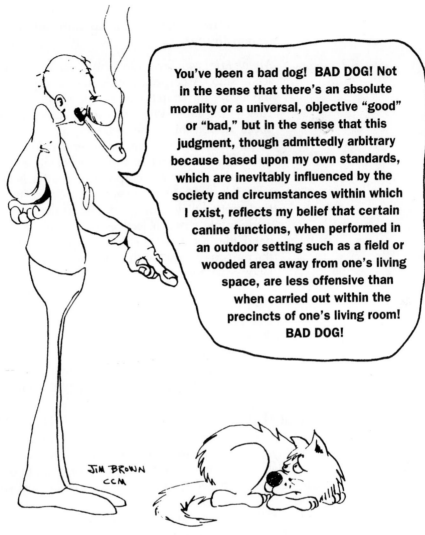

Source: Reprinted with permission of Jim Brown © 1991.

In some ethical dilemmas in business, conflicts arise among and between the interests of various stakeholders of the business. For example, shareholders are interested in earnings and dividends. The members of the community in which the business is located are interested in the jobs the business provides and are concerned about the environmental impact of the business. Suppose the business discovers that its air pollution–control equipment is not state-of-the-art technology and that, although no laws are being violated, more pollution is being released than is necessary. To correct the problem, its factory must be shut down for a minimum of three months. The pollution will harm the air and the community, but the shutdown will harm the workers and the shareholders. The business must consider the needs and interests of all its stakeholders in resolving the ethical dilemma it faces. There has been much discussion and disagreement about this particular issue. In the following interview excerpt, economist Milton Friedman offers a different perspective on this ethical dilemma:

Q: **Quite apart from emission standards and effluent taxes, shouldn't corporate officials take action to stop pollution out of a sense of social responsibility?**

Milton Friedman: I wouldn't buy stock in a company that hired that kind of leadership. A corporate executive's responsibility is to make as much money for the shareholders as possible, as long as he operates within the rules of the game. When an executive decides to take action for reasons of social responsibility, he is taking money from someone else—from the stockholders, in the form of lower dividends; from the employees, in the form of lower wages; or from the consumer, in the form of higher prices. The responsibility of a corporate executive is to fulfill the terms of his contract. If he can't do that in good conscience, then he should quit his job and find another way to do good. He has the right to promote what he regards as desirable moral objectives only with his own money. If, on the other hand, the executives of U.S. Steel undertake to reduce pollution in Gary for the purpose of making the town attractive to employees and thus lowering labor costs, then they are doing the stockholders' bidding. And everyone benefits: The stockholders get higher dividends; the customer gets cheaper steel; the workers get more in return for their labor. That's the beauty of free enterprise. . . . To the extent that pollution caused by the U.S. Steel plant there is confined to that city and the people there are truly concerned about the problem, it's to the company's advantage to do something about it. Why? Because if it doesn't, workers will prefer to live where there is less pollution, and U.S. Steel will have to pay them more to live in Gary, Indiana.[3]

ETHICAL POSTURES, SOCIAL RESPONSIBILITY, AND BUSINESS PRACTICE

The ethical perspective of a business often sets the tone for its operations and employees' choices. Historically, the philosophical debate over the role of business in society has evolved into four schools of thought on ethical behavior based on the responses to two questions: (1) Whose interest should a corporation serve? and (2) To whom should a corporation be responsive in order to best serve that interest? These questions have only two answers—"shareholders only" and "the larger society"—and the combination of those answers defines the school of thought. The following discussion is summarized in Exhibit 2.2.

EXHIBIT 2.2   Social Responsibility of Corporations

	MORAL QUESTION: WHOSE INTEREST SHOULD CORPORATION SERVE?	POLICY QUESTION: BEST WAY TO SERVE INTEREST IS IF THE CORPORATION IS RESPONSIVE TO:
Inherence	Shareholders only	Shareholders only
Enlightened self-interest	Shareholders only	Larger society
Invisible hand	Larger society	Shareholders only
Social resonsibility	Larger society	Larger society

Source: Adapted with permission of *American Business Law Journal*, from Daryl Hatano, "Should Corporations Exercise Their Freedom of Speech Rights?" 22 A.B.L.J. 165 (1984).

Inherence

According to the **inherence** school of thought, managers answer only to shareholders and act only with shareholders' interests in mind. This type of manager would not become involved in any political or social issues unless it was in the shareholders' best interests to do so and provided the involvement did not backfire and cost the firm sales. Milton Friedman's philosophy, as previously expressed, is an example of inherence. To understand how a business following the inherence school of thought would behave, consider the issue of a proposed increase in residential property taxes for school funding. A business that subscribes to the inherence school would support a school-tax increase only if the educational issue affected the company's performance and only if such a position did not offend those who opposed the tax increase.

Enlightened Self-Interest

According to this school of thought, the manager is responsible to the shareholders but serves them best by being responsive to the larger society. **Enlightened self-interest** is based on the view that, in the long run, business value is enhanced if business is responsive to the needs of society. In this school, managers are free to speak out on societal issues without the constraint of offending someone, as in inherence. Businesses would anticipate social changes and needs and be early advocates for change. For example, many corporations today have instituted job sharing, child-care facilities, and sick-child care in response to the changing structure of the American family and workforce. This responsiveness to the needs of the larger society should also be beneficial to shareholders, because it enables the business to retain a quality workforce.

The Invisible Hand

The **invisible hand** school of thought is the opposite of enlightened self-interest. According to this philosophy, business ought to serve the larger society and it does this best when it serves the shareholders only. Such businesses allow government to set the standards and boundaries for appropriate behavior and simply adhere to these governmental constraints as a way of maximizing benefits to their shareholders. They become involved in issues of social responsibility or in political issues only when society lacks sufficient information on an issue to make a decision. Even then, their involvement is limited to presenting data and does not extend to advocating a particular viewpoint or position. This school of thought holds that it is best for society to guide itself and that businesses work best when they serve shareholders within those constraints.

Social Responsibility

In the **social responsibility** school of thought, the role of business is to serve the larger society, which is best accomplished by being responsive to the larger society. This view is simply a reflection of the idea that businesses profit by being responsive to society and its needs. A business following this school of thought would advocate full disclosure of product information to consumers in its advertising and would encourage political activism on the part of its managers and employees on all issues, not just those that affect the corporation. These businesses adhere to the belief that their sense of social responsibility contributes to their long-term success.

C O N S I D E R . . .

2.2   Pepsico has an opportunity to expand into India. While Coca-Cola has had a presence in India, it has decided to pull out and this billion-customer market remains untapped. Pepsico would work with the government to help farmers in India develop better techniques for producing crops and would provide jobs and job training in its bottling plants there so that it could help with the country's lagging economic development and poor nutrition. Nutrition among India's slum children in the urban areas and among most children in the rural areas is poor. Both income and food are limited.

Pepsico's market research shows that only a small percentage of the population in India, primarily in the cities, would have sufficient income to buy Pepsi soft drinks and Frito-Lay snacks. The vast majority of the population would have to spend about 20 percent of its weekly income to buy two Pepsi snacks.

Should Pepsi enter India and sell its products there? Wouldn't Pepsi play an important role in economic development? Which school of thought applies here? Would Pepsi be socially responsible by entering India with its products and programs or socially responsible by staying out of India?

RECOGNIZING ETHICAL DILEMMAS

Despite having a strong value system, an individual facing the complexities of business needs help in recognizing ethical dilemmas. An ethical dilemma can be spotted in two ways: by language and by category.

The Language of Ethical Lapses

The first way to spot an ethical dilemma is by paying attention to the language those involved use. Key phrases of rationalization are employed in ethical dilemmas. Those phrases are listed in Exhibit 2.3.

"Everybody Else Does It"
When 15-year-old Jonathan Lebed was caught using many different screen names to post notices about the value of stocks he had purchased so that he could pump up their value and then sell them (pump and dump—see Chapter 8 for more details), he had made over $800,000 by taking advantage of others who believed the false notices posted. His father said that he was proud of his son because his son was doing what all the other analysts and investment firms on Wall Street were doing. "Everybody else does it" is a rationalization, but it is not an analysis of the ethical issues involved in conduct.

"If We Don't Do It, Someone Else Will"
The rationalization of competition is that since someone will do it and make money, it might as well be us. For Halloween 1994, O. J. Simpson masks and plastic knives and Nicole Brown Simpson masks and costumes complete with slashes and blood stains were offered for sale. When Nicole Simpson's family objected to

EXHIBIT 2.3 **The Language of Rationalization**

> "Everybody else does it."
> "If we don't do it, they'll get someone else to do it."
> "That's the way it's always been done."
> "We'll wait until the lawyers tell us it's wrong."
> "It doesn't really hurt anyone."
> "The system is unfair."
> "I was just following orders."

this violation of the basic standard of decency, a costume-shop owner commented that if he didn't sell the items, someone down the street would. While nothing about the marketing of the costumes was illegal, ethical issues abound surrounding earning a profit from an event as heinous as the brutal murder of a young mother.

C O N S I D E R . . .

2.3 Refer to the materials on companies on the CD-ROM exercise and read through their discussion of the issues, such as the environment, animal testing, and diversity. Do you see analysis of the ethical issues or do you see rationalization?

"That's the Way It Has Always Been Done"

Corporate or business history and business practices are not always sound. The fact that for years nothing has changed in a firm may indicate the need for change and an atmosphere that invites possible ethical violations. For example, until the Securities and Exchange Commission required corporate boards of directors compensation committees to make reports and to disclose the identities of their members, the sitting members of many of these committees had conflicts of interest. For example, a senior partner of a law firm who represented a given corporation often sat on that client's board and on its compensation committee. The result was that a lawyer whose firm was economically dependent on the corporation as a client was making salary determinations for the corporation's officers, who, of course, made the decisions about which law firm would represent their company. A conflict of interest existed, but everybody was doing it, and it was the way corporations had always been governed. Again, unquestioning adherence to a pattern of practice or behavior often indicates an underlying ethical dilemma.

Recently, with the failures of many dot-coms that did not follow time-tested guidelines for corporate structure, the issues of conflicts and sound practices have been raised. For example, Jeff Dachis, when questioned as to why he had no outsiders on the board of Razorfish, the company he founded, responded, "*I control 10 percent of the company. What's good for me is good for all shareholders. Management isn't screwing up. We've created enormous shareholder value.*" The company's stock premiered at $56 in June 1999 and by May 2001 was at $1.11 per share after revealing multi-million-dollar losses for 2000. Dachis was replaced as CEO in 2000, and the company added three outsiders to its board following the announcement of the losses. Razorfish and Dachis simply followed the patterns of the time, which included few or no outsiders on the board and a lack of independence on the board. While these practices may have been what everyone was doing and the way they had always done things, they were not the best practices in keeping conflicts in check and in managing the company. For more discussion of board independence, see Chapter 21.

"We'll Wait until the Lawyers Tell Us It's Wrong"

Lawyers are trained to provide only the parameters of the law. In many situations, they offer an opinion that is correct in that it does not violate the law. Whether the conduct they have passed judgment on as legal is ethical is a different question. Allowing law and lawyers to control a firm's destiny ignores the opportunity to make wise and ethical choices. For example, lawyers disagreed over whether the downloading of music over the Internet was a violation of copyright law. However, whether the downloading was legal does not answer the question of whether gaining access to and using someone's else's intellectual property without permission or compensation were ethical.

"It Doesn't Really Hurt Anyone"

When we are the sole rubberneckers on the freeway, traffic remains unaffected. But if everyone rubbernecks, we have a traffic jam. All of us making poor ethical choices would cause significant harm. A man interviewed after he was arrested for defrauding insurance companies through staged auto accidents remarked, "It didn't really hurt anyone. Insurance companies can afford it." The second part of his statement is accurate. The insurance companies can afford it—but not without cost to someone else. Such fraud harms all of us because we must pay higher premiums to allow insurers to absorb the costs of investigating and paying for fraudulent claims.

"The System Is Unfair"

Often touted by students as a justification for cheating on exams, this rationalization eases our consciences by telling us we are cheating only to make up for deficiencies in the system; yet, just one person cheating can send ripples through an entire system. The credibility of grades and the institution come into question as students obtain grades through means beyond the system's standards. As we see events unfold in China, Italy, and Brazil, with government employees awarding contracts and rights to do business on the basis of payments rather than on the merits of a given company or its proposal, we understand how such bribery only results in greater unfairness within and greater costs to those countries. Many economists have noted that a country's businesses and economy will not progress without some fundamental assurance of trust.

"I Was Just Following Orders"

In many criminal trials and disputes over responsibility and liability, managers will disclaim their responsibility by stating, "I was just following orders." There are times when individuals cannot follow the directions of supervisors, for they have been asked to do something illegal or immoral. Judges who preside over the criminal trials of war criminals often remind defendants that an order is not necessarily legal or moral. Values require us to question or depart from orders when others will be harmed or wronged.

ETHICAL ISSUES 2.1

Consider the following statistics and evaluate where you stand on the conduct described.

A survey by O'Neill Associates reveals:

- 75 percent of working adults overstate facts on their employment application.
- 70 percent of working adults have called in sick when they really were not sick.
- 6 percent of working adults have blamed a co-worker for a problem when it was truly their fault.
- 76 percent of working adults believe we do personal things during work time.
- 21 percent of working adults say that they have used company facilities or materials for personal tasks.

A study of resume fraud reveals the following:

- 22 percent of all resumes contain fraudulent information.

- That figure has doubled since 1998.

A study of workers' reactions to being asked to do something against their standards reveals the following:

- 25 percent of working adults were asked during the past year to do something that violated their personal ethical standards.
- 41 percent of those asked to do something that violated their personal ethical standards did it.
- 40 percent tried to resolve it without losing their jobs.
- 39 percent did talk to their bosses about it before doing anything.
- 5 percent quit.

The Categories of Ethical Dilemmas

The second method for spotting an ethical dilemma is to understand the categories of ethical dilemmas. The following twelve categories were developed and listed in *Exchange,* the magazine of the Brigham Young University School of Business.

Taking Things That Don't Belong to You

Everything from the unauthorized use of the Pitney-Bowes postage meter at your office for mailing personal letters to exaggerations on travel expenses belongs in this category of ethical violations. Regardless of size, motivation, or the presence of any of the preceding rationalizations, the unauthorized use of someone else's property or taking property under false pretenses still means taking something that does not belong to you. A chief financial officer of a large electric utility reported that, after taking a cab from LaGuardia International Airport to his midtown Manhattan hotel, he asked for a receipt. The cab driver handed him a full book of blank receipts and drove away. Apparently, the problem of accurately reporting travel expenses involves more than just employees.

Saying Things You Know Are Not True

Often, in their quest for promotion and advancement, fellow employees discredit their co-workers. Falsely assigning blame or inaccurately reporting conversations is lying. While "This is the way the game is played around here" is a common justification, saying things that are untrue is an ethical violation.

A Conde Nash survey on ethics has produced some interesting results:

ETHICAL ISSUES 2.2

- 64 percent of all women admitted that they had cheated in some way in their lives.

- 75 percent of all men admitted that they had cheated in some way in their lives.

- 25 percent of all the respondents in the survey believed that men are "bigger cheaters."

- 16 percent said that they had cheated with money matters or taxes.

- 59 percent said that they had cheated with money matters or taxes because they believed they could get away with it.

- 24 percent said that they had cheated with money matters or taxes because everyone else was doing it.

- For those who had not cheated, 98 percent of the women and 96 percent of the men said it was because of their individual sense of morals; 85 percent of the women and 72 percent of the men said it was because they did not want to hurt others; and 81 percent of the women and 72 percent of the men said cheating would cheapen the accomplishments they had achieved.

- Fear of getting caught was cited as the reason for not cheating among 19 percent of the women and 11 percent of the men.

Do you have any explanations for the data? Why do you think there are gender differences?

In developing your personal standards, consider the following dilemmas, answers, and analyses.

ETHICAL ISSUES 2.3

1. If my boss asked me to lie to cover up his mistake, I would:

   a. Quit

   b. Lie

   c. Say it made me uncomfortable

   d. Do it this time but refuse if it became a pattern

2. If a vendor who was also a personal friend offered me a free laptop, I would:

   a. Turn it down and report the vendor to our purchasing officer

   b. Accept the gift if it was personal rather than business-related

   c. Ask my supervisor if I should accept it

   d. Accept the gift but tell the vendor he will get no special consideration

ANSWER a—the nonconformist who is difficult to get along with

ANSWER b—the negotiator who makes up the rules as he goes along

ANSWER c—the navigator who has the sound moral compass

ANSWER d—the wiggler who dodges ethical issues to protect his own interests

Courtesy of Mark Pastin, The Council of Ethical Organizations.

Giving or Allowing False Impressions

The salesman who permits a potential customer to believe that his cardboard boxes will hold the customer's tomatoes for long-distance shipping when he knows the boxes are not strong enough has given a false impression. A car dealer who fails to disclose that a car has been in an accident is misleading potential customers. A co-worker or supervisor who takes credit for another employee's idea

ETHICAL ISSUES 2.4

Actress Demi Moore starred in the 1995 movie entitled *The Scarlet Letter,* which was based on Nathaniel Hawthorne's book of the same name. Hollywood Pictures ran the following quote from a *Time* magazine review: "`Scarlet Letter' Gets What It Always Needed: Demi Moore." The actual review by *Time* magazine read: "Stuffy old *Scarlet Letter* gets what it always needed: Demi Moore and a happier ending." A *Time* spokesman noted that the statement was clearly ironic. In the same review, the *Time* critic, Richard Corliss, referred to the movie as "revisionist slog" and gave it an "F."

An ad for the 1995 movie *Seven* quoted *Entertainment Weekly* as calling it a "masterpiece." The actual review read, "The credits sequence . . . is a small masterpiece of dementia."

Ads for the movie, "Thirteen Days" included the following descriptive phrases, "by-the-numbers recreation" and "Close to perfect," in order to reflect what the producers see as strength of the film—its historical accuracy.

However, the ads also included pictures of the Spruance-class destroyer and F-15 jet fighters. Neither of these defense systems was available in 1962, the time of the movie, which is a depiction of the 13-day Cuban missile crisis during the Kennedy administration. These systems were not developed until the 1970s.

The movie studios pulled the ads after they had run for one weekend.

Also, the movie ads showed the star, Kevin Costner, walking with the actors who played John and Robert Kennedy and that scene depicted in the ads is not part of the movie.

Ads by *Sony* studios had theater critic David Manning proclaim that *The Animal* (2001), starring Rob Scheider and ex-*Survivor* participant Colleen Haskell was "another winner." Mr. Manning also gave a favorable review of Sony's *A Knight's Tale.* However, David Manning is fictitious. He is a made-up critic created by marketing staff at Sony.

A movie industry observer stated in response to these examples, "The practice of fudging critics' quotes [in ads] is common."

Is the practice of fudging quotes ethical? Are some of these examples violations of any of the categories of ethical breaches?

---

has allowed a false impression. A company that does not accurately reflect its financial status, as when it does not write down loans, has given investors and shareholders a false impression.

Buying Influence or Engaging in Conflict of Interest

A company awards a construction contract to a firm owned by the father of the state attorney general while the state attorney general's office is investigating that company. A county administrator responsible for awarding the construction contract for a baseball stadium accepts from contractors interested in bidding on the project paid travel around the country to other stadiums that the contractors have built. The wife of a state attorney general accepts trading advice from the corporate attorney for a highly regulated company and subsequently earns, in her first foray into the market, over $100,000 in cattle futures.

All of these examples illustrate conflicts of interest. Those involved in situations such as these often protest, "But I would never allow that to influence me." The ethical violation is the conflict. Whether the conflict can or will influence those it touches is not the issue, for neither party can prove conclusively that a *quid pro quo* was not intended. The possibility exists, and it creates suspicion.

C O N S I D E R . . .

2.4   Barbara Walters, as part of a Friday evening ABC television *20/20* news program broadcast, did a profile of Sir Andrew Lloyd Webber as a timely review of his career on the eve of the opening of his then-new Broadway play, *Sunset Boulevard.* The piece was very flattering to Webber and his work. On Monday morning, one of the New York papers revealed that Ms. Walters had a $100,000 investment in *Sunset Boulevard.* ABC issued an apology for not disclosing the information. Why should the information have been disclosed? Do you think disclosure is enough or should Ms. Walters have removed herself from the story? Later, when *20/20* profiled Jerry Springer and *The Jerry Springer Show,* Ms. Walters announced that her daytime show, *The View,* competed with Mr. Springer's show but that she had no role in the production or content of the piece. Why did she make this disclosure?

Hiding or Divulging Information

Taking your firm's product development or trade secrets to a new place of employment constitutes an ethical violation: divulging proprietary information. Failing to disclose the results of medical studies that indicate that your firm's new drug has significant side effects is the ethical violation of hiding information that the product could be harmful to purchasers.

Taking Unfair Advantage

Many current consumer protection laws were passed because so many businesses took unfair advantage of those who were not educated or were unable to discern the nuances of complex contracts. Credit disclosure requirements, truth-in-lending provisions, and regulations on auto leasing all resulted because businesses misled consumers who could not easily follow the jargon of long and complex agreements.

Committing Acts of Personal Decadence

While many argue about the ethical notion of an employee's right to privacy, it has become increasingly clear that personal conduct outside the job can influence performance and company reputation. Thus, a company driver must abstain from substance abuse because of safety issues. Even the traditional company Christmas party and picnic have come under scrutiny as the behavior of employees at and following these events has brought harm to others in the form of alcohol-related accidents.

Perpetrating Interpersonal Abuse

A manager sexually harasses an employee. Another manager is verbally abusive to an employee. Still another manager subjects employees to humiliating correction in the presence of customers. In some cases, laws protect employees. However, many situations are simply ethical violations that constitute interpersonal abuse.

Permitting Organizational Abuse

Many U.S. firms with operations overseas, such as Levi Strauss & Co., The Gap, Nike, and Esprit, have faced issues of organizational abuse. The unfair treatment of workers in international operations appears in the form of child labor, demeaning wages, and too-long hours. While a business cannot change the culture of another country, it can perpetuate—or alleviate—abuse through its operations there.

Violating Rules

Review Stanford University's "Code of Conduct for Business Activities": http://adminguide. stanford.edu

Many rules, particularly those in large organizations that tend toward bureaucracy from a need to maintain internal controls or follow lines of authority, seem burdensome to employees trying to serve customers and other employees. Stanford University experienced difficulties in this area of ethics as it used funds from federal grants for miscellaneous university purposes. Questions arose about the propriety of the expenditures, which quite possibly could have been approved through proper channels but were not. The rules for the administration of federal grant monies used for overhead were not followed. The result was not only an ethical violation but also damage to Stanford's reputation and a new president for the university.

Condoning Unethical Actions

Visit Lockheed-Martin's Code of Ethics: http://www.lockheedmartin. com

In this breach of ethics, the wrong results from the failure to report the wrong. What if you witnessed a fellow employee embezzling company funds by forging his signature on a check that was to be voided? Would you report that violation? A winking tolerance of others' unethical behavior is in itself unethical. Suppose that as a product designer you were aware of a fundamental flaw in your company's new product—a product predicted to catapult your firm to record earnings. Would you pursue the problem to the point of halting the distribution of the product? Would you disclose what you know to the public if you could not get your company to act?

Balancing Ethical Dilemmas

Visit Levi Strauss & Co. http://www.levi.com

In these types of situations, there are no right or wrong answers; rather, there are dilemmas to be resolved. For example, Levi Strauss & Co. struggled with its decision about whether to do business in the People's Republic of China because of known human rights violations by the government there. Other companies debated doing business in South Africa when that country's government followed a policy of apartheid. In some respects, the presence of these companies would help by advancing human rights and, certainly, by improving the standard of living for at least some international operations workers. On the other hand, their ability to recruit businesses could help such governments sustain themselves by enabling them to point to economic successes despite human rights violations.

RESOLUTION OF BUSINESS ETHICAL DILEMMAS

The resolution of ethical dilemmas in business is often difficult, even in firms with a code of ethics and a culture committed to compliance with ethical models for decision making. Managers need guidelines for making ethical choices. Several prominent scholars in the field of business ethics have developed models for use in difficult situations.

Blanchard and Peale

The late Dr. Norman Vincent Peale and management expert Kenneth Blanchard offer three questions that managers should ponder in resolving ethical dilemmas: Is it legal? Is it balanced? How does it make me feel?

Browse antitrust cases at the U.S. Department of Justice: http://www.usdoj.gov

If the answer to the first question, "Is it legal?" is no, a manager should not proceed any further. An examination of the Justice Department's antitrust case against some of the country's best and largest universities demonstrates that managers still fail to ask the basic ethical question of whether they are in compliance with the law. In that case, twenty-two large private northeastern universities had agreed to offer the same financial aid packages to students, so that students' decisions on which institution to attend were based on factors other than the level of financial aid. This loan package arrangement was nothing more than an agreement on price; antitrust laws prohibit such agreements.

Answering the second question, "Is it balanced?" requires a manager to step back and view a problem from other perspectives—those of other parties, owners, shareholders, or the community. For example, an M&M/Mars cacao buyer was able to secure a very low price on cacao for his company because of pending government takeovers and political disruption. M&M/Mars officers decided to pay more for the cacao than the negotiated figure. Their reason was that some day their company would not have the upper hand, and then they would want to be treated fairly when the price became the seller's choice.

Answering "How does it make me feel?" requires a manager to do a self-examination of the comfort level of a decision. Some decisions, though they may be legal and may appear balanced, can still make a manager uncomfortable. For example, many managers feel uncomfortable about the "management" of earnings when inventory and shipments are controlled to maximize bonuses or to produce a particularly good result for a quarter. Although they have done nothing illegal, managers who engage in such practices often suffer such physical effects as insomnia and appetite problems. Known as the element of conscience, this test for ethics requires business people to find the source of their discomfort in a particular decision.

The Front-Page-of-the-Newspaper Test

One very simple ethical model requires only that a decision maker envision how a reporter would describe a decision on the front page of a local or national newspaper. For example, with regard to the NBC News report on the sidesaddle gas tanks in GM pickup trucks, the *USA TODAY* headline read: "GM Suit Attacks NBC Report: Says show faked fiery truck crash." Would NBC have made the same decisions about its staging of the truck crash if that headline had been foreseen? The execution of accused Oklahoma City bomber, Timothy McVeigh, had to be postponed when headlines revealed, "FBI Withheld Documents from McVeigh's Lawyers." Condensing conduct into a single phrase often gives a harsh dose of reality.

When Salomon Brothers illegally cornered the U.S. government's bond market, the *Business Week* headline read: "How Bad Will It Get?"; nearly two years later, a follow-up story on Salomon's crisis strategy was headlined "The Bomb Shelter That Salomon Built." During the aftermath of the bond market scandal, the interim chairman of Salomon, Warren Buffett, told employees, "Contemplating any business act, an employee should ask himself whether he would be willing to see it immediately described by an informed and critical reporter on the front page of his local paper, there to be read by his spouse, children, and friends. At Salomon we simply want no part of any activities that pass legal tests but that we, as citizens, would find offensive."

Laura Nash and Perspective

Business ethicist Laura Nash has developed a series of questions that business managers should ask themselves as they evaluate their ethical dilemmas. One of the questions is, "How would I view the issue if I stood on the other side of the fence?" For example, several large manufacturers produced a product called an infant baby walker. An infant as young as four months can be placed in the walker and enjoy upright movements long before motor skills have developed sufficiently to permit such movements unaided. The result was that many infants injured themselves; nearly 30,000 injuries were reported in 1992. The American Medical Association asked the federal Consumer Product Safety Commission to ban and recall the walkers because of the clear dangers they present; but, initially, the commission refused. The AMA has also expressed concern about possible long-term skeletal damage because infants who are not yet ready to stand unaided are standing in the walkers.

The industry continued to sell the walkers up to the time of the eventual ban in 1994, but what if you were a parent? Would you not want to have the information about the walker's safety? Would you bring suit against the company if there were an injury to your child while using the walker? Parents certainly see the walkers as something other than the high profit margins they offered.

Other questions in the Nash model include: "Am I able to discuss my decision with my family, friends, and those closest to me?" "What am I trying to accomplish with my decision?" "Will I feel as comfortable about my decision over time as I do today?" The Nash model forces managers to seek additional perspectives as decisions are evaluated and implemented. For example, when William Aramony served as the CEO of United Way (see Biography, Chapter 1), he enjoyed such perks as an annual salary of close to $400,000, flights on the Concorde, and limousine service. Even though these benefits were about the same as those of other CEOs managing comparable assets, it would still be difficult to justify such benefits to a donor who earns $12,000 a year and has pledged 5 percent of it to United Way.

The *Wall Street Journal* Model

The *Wall Street Journal* model for resolution of ethical dilemmas consists of compliance, contribution, and consequences. Like the Blanchard-Peale model, any proposed conduct must first be in compliance with the law. The next step requires an evaluation of a decision's contributions to the shareholders, the employees, the community, and the customers. For example, furniture manufacturer Herman Miller decided both to invest in equipment that would exceed the requirements for compliance with the 1990 Clean Air Act and to refrain from using rain forest woods in producing its signature Eames chair. The decision was costly to the shareholders at first, but ultimately they, the community, and customers enjoyed the benefits.

Explore the 1990 Clean Air Act:
http://www.law.cornell.edu/ uscode/42/ch85.html

Finally, managers are asked to envision the consequences of a decision, such as whether headlines that are unfavorable to the firm may result. The initial consequence for Miller's decisions was a reduction in profits because of the costs of the changes. However, the long-term consequences were the respect of environmental regulators, a responsive public committed to rain forest preservation, and Miller's recognition by *Business Ethics* as one of America's top twenty corporate citizens since 1992.

One of the misunderstandings of U.S.-based businesses is that ethical standards in the United States vary significantly from the ethical standards in other countries. Operating under this misconception can create a great deal of ethical confusion among employees. What is known as the "Golden Rule" in the United States actually has existed for some time in other religions and cultures and among philosophers. Following is a list of how this simple rule is phrased in different writings. The principle is the same even if the words vary slightly. Strategically, businesses and their employees are more comfortable when they operate under uniform standards. This simple rule may provide them with that standard.

Categorical Imperative: How would you want to be treated?

Are you comfortable with a world with your standards?

Christian principle: The Golden Rule
And as ye would that men should do to you, do ye also to them likewise. Luke 6:31
Thou shalt love . . . thy neighbor as thyself. Luke 10:27

Confucius:
What you do not want done to yourself, do not do to others.

Aristotle:
We should behave to our friends as we wish our friends to behave to us.

Judaism:
What you hate, do not do to anyone.

Buddhism:
Hurt not others with that which pains thyself.

Islam:
No one of you is a believer until he loves for his brother what he loves for himself.

Hinduism:
Do nothing to thy neighbor which thou wouldst not have him do to thee.

Sikhism:
Treat others as you would be treated yourself.

Plato:
May I do to others as I would that they should do unto me.

Other Models

Of course, there are much simpler models for making ethical business decisions. One stems from Immanuel Kant's categorical imperative, loosely similar to the Golden Rule, of "Do unto others as you would have them do unto you." Treating others or others' money as we would want to be treated is a powerful evaluation technique in ethical dilemmas.

CREATION OF AN ETHICAL ATMOSPHERE IN BUSINESS

The Tone at the Top

Ethics begins at the top of a company. A business must have from its board and its CEO a commitment to earning a profit *within ethical boundaries.* Employees work under the pressures of meeting quarterly and annual goals and can make poor choices if the company's priority with respect to values and ethics is not made clear. Evidence of that ethical commitment comes from a firm's adoption of a **code of ethics.**

C O N S I D E R . . .

2.5 Top management must continue to emphasize that, above all, employees must perform within the ethical boundaries established by the company's code of ethics. When the state of California revealed that its undercover investigation of Sears Auto Centers found repeated patterns of unnecessary repairs, then-CEO Ed Brennan stated that employees had made mistakes by making poor choices. The pay incentive systems in the auto centers were tied to the receipts from repairs and sales of parts, and such an incentive system conflicted with the values established by Sears. Somehow the employees failed to grasp that the ethical standards were to take priority. Top management's continued emphasis on ethics can take the form of ongoing training and seminars in ethics for all employees. How does Sears change?

Reporting Lines

Most companies have either an ombudsperson or a hot line, or both, to which employees can anonymously report ethical violations. Many firms have developed ethical news bulletins to offer employees examples of and guidelines on ethical dilemmas. Du Pont delivers an ethics bulletin to employees through its electronic mail system.

Developing an Ethics Stance

Both individuals and firms should decide up front what types of conduct they would never engage in and be certain that the rules are in writing, that everyone understands the rules, and that the rules will be enforced uniformly. Individuals can vary in their responses to various ethical dilemmas. For example, a woman who had taken $12,000 from her employer was terminated immediately upon the company's discovery of the embezzlement. At the company's next board meeting, the board members discussed the issue and had varying views. One director felt that taking something that does not belong to you is wrong and that termination was the appropriate action. Another director said that his remedy would be determined by whether the money was taken all at once or over a period of time. Another director said that his remedy would be determined according to why the employee took the money. Still

another director noted that perhaps the employee did not understand that this type of action is wrong. The directors varied in their views on ethics. One is pragmatic—it is simply wrong. Another applies a relative approach—why did she take the money? The ethical stances of the directors are diagrammed in Exhibit 2.4.

Knowing where you stand as a company sends clear signals to employees. Knowing where you stand as an individual sends clear signals for the behavior of those around you. Taking a position on a set of values helps a company avoid the either/or conundrum in which tough situations are boiled down to something such as, "Either we release this product now with its flaws and meet the deadline and start getting earnings or we don't and the company collapses." A value-based decision is one that says, "We as a company do not cheat our customers with poorly designed or manufacturered products and we don't hurt them with defective ones. Because of that value, we retool quickly and correct the problem and get the product out there as soon as possible." With this value-based decision, the company also makes a good business decision for it has chosen to avoid the often destructive costs of releasing a defective product when there is knowledge of that defect. The Malibu case discussed earlier represents the destructive costs of deciding not to take action based on values but, rather, taking action based only on immediate returns.

EXHIBIT 2.4
Your Ethics Stance:
The Embezzling
Employee

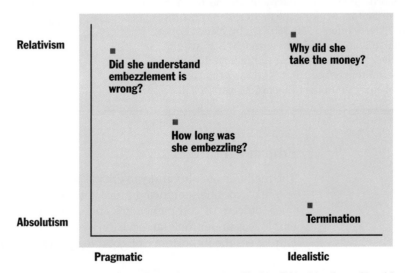

Source: Developed from Professor Patricia Pattison's presentation, "Teaching Ethics," Academy of Legal Studies in Business Annual Meeting, August 11–15, 1994, Dallas, Texas and adapted from "Teaching Ethics" by D. R. Forsych, Journal of Personality and Social Psychology.

BIOGRAPHY

THE ESPIONAGE AMONG THE DOT-COMS: LAWRENCE J. ELLISON AND ORACLE

The Association for Competitive Technology (ACT) is a trade group funded largely by Microsoft Corporation. During Microsoft's antitrust trial, ACT was active in public relations as it worked to convince everyone from the public to members of Congress that the antitrust case would thwart innovation in computers, software, and their uses.

Lawrence J. Ellison, chairman of Oracle Corporation, a software manufacturer and Microsoft competitor, was concerned that the public might not understand that ACT was funded by Microsoft and was not truly an independent group. Ellison and Bill Gates, the chairman of Microsoft, were known as fierce competitors and often referred to as each others' nemesis. Through Oracle, Ellison hired Group International, a private investigation firm headed by Terry Lenzner (who became famous for his work on the Watergate investigation during the Nixon administration and also for President Clinton's lawyers during the Paula Jones civil suit for sexual harassment). Group International was to find information tying Microsoft to ACT. Ellison described his hiring of Group International as his "civic duty."

Shortly after Group International was hired by Oracle, janitors working the night shift at the offices of ACT were offered $50–$60 each by Blanca Lopez, a woman who worked for Lenzner, if they would turn over ACT's trash to her rather than dumping it. The janitors refused and Ms. Lopez returned the next evening and offered them $500 each for the trash plus $200 extra to the supervisor if he could convince the janitors to cooperate. All of the staff declined and Ms. Lopez left them her card, explained that she was working on a criminal case, and asked them to call if they changed their minds.

When the janitors disclosed what had happened and the investigator was traced back to Mr. Ellison, he said, "All we did was to try to take information that was hidden and bring it into the light. I don't think that's arrogance. That's a public service."

Mr. Ellison also offered to box up all of Oracle's trash and send it to Mr. Gates in Redmond, Washington, noting, "We believe in full disclosure."

Do you think what Oracle did was legal? Do you think it was ethical? How do you evaluate Mr. Ellison's claim that he was performing a civic responsibility?

SOURCES

John Markoff, "Oracle Leader Calls Microsoft Spying 'Civic Duty,' " *New York Times,* 29 June 2000, C1, C8.

John Markoff and Matt Richtel, "Double Duty for Microsoft Investigator," *New York Times,* 27 June 2000, C1, C28.

Ted Bridis, Glen Simpson, and Mylene Mangalindan, "How Microsoft's Trash Became Latest Focus in Gates-Ellison Feud," *Wall Street Journal,* 29 June 2000, A1, A10.

Ethical Culture

The methods of cultivating an ethical environment became more crucial when the federal corporate sentencing guidelines went into effect in 1995. Under the guidelines, officers of companies are able to mitigate the sentences for violations by employees under their supervision by documenting their own efforts to clarify for employees the importance of good legal and ethical choices (see Chapter 9).

BUSINESS STRATEGY

Companies continue to have ethical challenges. A 2000 survey of 1,800 working adults by KPMG, the international accounting and consulting firm, revealed the following:

© Douglas Slone/CORBIS

- 76 percent of employees said that they observed violations of the law or company standards during the past year.
- 50 percent of employees said that their firms "would significantly lose public trust" if the information they knew found its way into the media.

However, companies continue to work to change their internal structures to emphasize the importance of ethics. In 1987, only 21 percent of corporate boards were involved in creating and enforcing their companies' codes of ethics. By the end of 2000, that number had increased to 78 percent.

More companies have ethics officers. Nearly one-third of these ethics officers are lawyers by training, and nearly 100 percent of them have been with their companies for fifteen years or more. Nearly all fellow employees describe their companies' ethics officers as "respected and trusted." All ethics officers report either to the board of directors, the CEO, or a senior vice president.

Of these ethics officers' investigations of complaints or allegations:

- 44 percent result in positive changes in the organization's policies.
- 18 percent result in conveying information about company policies to employees.
- 38 percent required no changes in policies or further action.

Having an ethics officer is a positive factor in the federal corporate sentencing guidelines. Most companies report reduced fines when their own ethics officers' internal investigations result in self-reporting of conduct.

Top management also needs to watch closely for practices and signals that are indications of a poor ethical environment. Here are a few signs of an atmosphere that is ripe for unethical behavior:

1. Competition is so intense that business survival is threatened.

   Example: An employee steals drawings of a competitor's product.

2. Managers make poor judgments.

   Example: Chrysler executives had the odometers from their company cars disconnected so that the cars could later be sold as new.

3. Employees have few or no personal values.

   Example: Personal ethics are left at the company door because, as ethicist Albert Carr says, "Business is business," just as poker is poker.

4. Employees respond only to earnings demands. No constraints are placed on how the earnings are achieved.

   Example: E. F. Hutton's 1986 check-kiting scheme was perpetuated by branch managers as a way to maximize interest on accounts without regard to the risk involved, particularly for small banks.

ETHICAL ISSUES IN INTERNATIONAL BUSINESS

The global market presents firms with more complex ethical issues than they would experience if operations were limited to one country and one culture. Moral standards vary across cultures. In some cases, cultures change and evolve to accept conduct that was not previously acceptable. For example, it is permissible in India for donors to sell body organs for transplantation. Residents of India have sold their kidneys to buy televisions or just to increase their standard of living. In the United States, the buying and selling of organs by donors is not permitted, but recently experts have called for such a system as a means of resolving the supply-and-demand dilemma that exists because of limited availability of donors and a relative excess of needy recipients.

In many executive training seminars for international business, executives are taught to honor customs in other countries and to "Do as the Romans do." Employees are often confused by this direction.

A manager for a U.S. title insurer provides a common example. He complained that if he tipped employees in the U.S. public-recording agencies for expediting property filings, the manager would not only be violating the company's code of ethics but could be charged with violations of the Real Estate Settlement Procedures Act and state and federal antibribery provisions. Yet, that same type of practice is permitted, recognized, and encouraged in other countries as a cost of doing business. Paying a regulatory agency in the United States to expedite a licensing process would be bribery of a public official. Yet, many businesses maintain that they cannot obtain such authorizations to do business in other countries unless such payments are made. So-called grease or facilitation payments are permitted under the Foreign Corrupt Practices Act (see Chapter 9), but legality does not necessarily make such payments ethical.

An inevitable question arises when custom and culture clash with ethical standards and moral values adopted by a firm. Should the national culture or the company code of ethics control?

Typical business responses to the question of whether cultural norms or company codes of ethics should control in international business operations are: Who am I to question the culture of another country? Who am I to impose U.S. standards on all the other nations of the world? Isn't legality the equivalent of ethical behavior? The attitude of businesses is one that permits ethical deviations in the name of cultural sensitivity. Many businesses fear that the risk of offending is far too high to impose U.S. ethical standards on the conduct of business in other countries.

The successful operation of commerce is dependent upon the ethical roots of business. A look at the three major parties in business explains this point. These parties are the risk-takers, the employees, and the customers. Risk-takers—those furnishing the capital necessary for production—are willing to take risks on the assumption that their products will be judged by customers' assessment of their value. Employees are willing to offer production input, skills, and ideas in exchange for wages, rewards, and other incentives. Consumers and customers are willing to purchase products and services so long as they receive value in exchange for their furnishing, through payment, costs and profits to the risk-takers and employers. To the extent that the interdependency of the parties in the system is affected by factors outside of their perceived roles and control, the intended business system does not function on its underlying assumptions.

C O N S I D E R . . .

2.6 Göttingen University, through Transparency International, published its annual corruption index. Business executives are asked to rank countries on a scale from 1 to 10, with 10 being the least corrupt. The results for 2001 are as follows:

Least Corrupt Countries		Most Corrupt Countries	
Finland	9.9	Russia	2.3
Denmark	9.5	Cameroon	2.0
New Zealand	9.4	Kenya	2.0
Iceland	9.2	Bolivia	2.0
Singapore	9.2	India	1.9
Sweden	9.0	Uganda	1.9
Canada	8.9	Nigeria	1.0
Netherlands	8.8	Bangladesh	0.4
Luxembourg	8.7		
Norway	8.6		
Australia	8.5		

The U.S. is at 7.6 (or 16th)

Why do you think the index appears as it does? Is there a correlation between economic development or its absence and corruption?

The business system is, in short, an economic system endorsed by society that allows risk-takers, employees, and customers to allocate scarce resources to competing ends.

Although the roots of business have been described as primarily economic, this economic system cannot survive without recognition of some fundamental values. Some of the inherent—indeed, universal—values built into our capitalistic economic system, as described here, are as follows: (1) the consumer is given value in exchange for the funds expended; (2) employees are rewarded according to their contribution to production; and (3) the risk-takers are rewarded for their investment in the form of a return on that investment.

To a large extent, all business is based on trust. The tenets for doing business are dissolved as an economy moves toward a system in which one individual can control the market in order to maximize personal income.

Suppose, for example, that the sale of a firm's product is determined not by perceived consumer value but, rather, by access to consumers, which is controlled by government officials. That is, your company's product cannot be sold to consumers in a particular country unless and until you are licensed within that country. Suppose further that the licensing procedures are controlled by government officials and that those officials demand personal payment in exchange for your company's right to even apply for a business license. Payment size may be arbitrarily determined by officials who withhold portions for themselves. The basic values of the system have been changed. Consumers no longer directly determine the demand.

> **BUSINESS PLANNING TIP**
>
> A new trend among international firms is to adopt international codes of ethics. For example, employees who are given gifts as part of cultural rituals must give them to the company. They are then donated to charity.

Beyond just the impact on the basic economic system, ethical breaches involving grease payments introduce an element beyond a now-recognized component in economic performance: consumer confidence in long-term economic performance. Economist Douglas Brown has described the differences between the United States and other countries in explaining why capitalism works here and not in all nations. His theory is that capitalism is dependent upon an interdependent system of production. For economic growth to proceed, consumers, risk-takers, and employees must all feel confident about the future, about the concept of a level playing field, and about the absence of corruption. To the extent that consumers, risk-takers, and employees feel comfortable about a market driven by the basic assumptions, the investment and commitments necessary for economic growth via capitalism will be made. Significant monetary costs are incurred by business systems based on factors other than customer value, as discussed earlier.

In developing countries where there are "speed" or grease payments and resulting corruption by government officials, the actual money involved may not be significant in terms of the nation's culture. Such activities and payments introduce an element of demoralization and cynicism that thwart entrepreneurial activity when these nations most need risk-takers to step forward.

Bribes and *guanxi* (gifts) in China given to establish connections with the Chinese government are estimated at 3 to 5 percent of operating costs for companies, totaling $3 billion to $5 billion of 1993's foreign investment. But China incurs costs from the choices government officials make in return for payments. For example, *guanxi* are often used to persuade government officials to transfer government assets to foreign investors for substantially less than their value. Chinese government assets have fallen over $50 billion in value over the same period of economic growth, primarily because of the large undervaluation by government officials in these transactions with foreign companies. China's economy is adrift because of this underlying corruption.

Perhaps Italy and Brazil provide the best examples of the long-term impact of foreign business corruption. While the United States, Japan, and Great Britain have scandals such as the savings and loan failures, political corruption, and insurance regulation, these forms of misconduct are not indicative of corruption that pervades entire economic systems. The same cannot be said about Italy. Elaborate connections between government officials, the Mafia, and business executives have been unearthed. As a result, half of Italy's cabinet has resigned, and hundreds of business executives have been indicted. It has been estimated that the interconnections of these three groups have cost the Italian government $200 billion, as well as compromising the completion of government projects.

In Brazil, the level of corruption has led to a climate of murder and espionage. Many foreign firms have elected not to do business in Brazil because of so much uncertainty and risk—beyond the normal financial risks of international investment. Why send an executive to a country where officials may use force when soliciting huge bribes?

The *Wall Street Journal* offered an example of how Brazil's corruption has damaged the country's economy despite growth and opportunity in surrounding nations. The governor of the northeastern state of Paraiba in Brazil, Ronaldo Cunha Lima, was angry because his predecessor, Tarcisio Burity, had accused Lima's son of corruption. Lima shot Burity twice in the chest while Burity was having lunch at a restaurant. The speaker of Brazil's Senate praised Lima for his courage in doing the shooting himself as opposed to sending someone else. Lima was given a medal by the local city council and granted immunity from prosecution by Paraiba's state legislature. No one spoke for the victim, and the lack of support was reflective of a culture controlled by self-interest that benefits those in control. Unfortunately, these self-interests preclude economic development.

Economists in Brazil document hyperinflation and systemic corruption. A Sao Paulo businessman observed, "The fundamental reason we can't get our act together is we're an amoral society." This businessperson probably understands capitalism. Privatization that has helped the economies of Chile, Argentina, and Mexico cannot take hold in Brazil because government officials enjoy the benefits of generous wages and returns from the businesses they control. The result is that workers are unable to earn enough even to clothe their families, 20 percent of the Brazilian population lives below the poverty line, and crime has reached levels of nightly firefights. Brazil's predicament has occurred over time, as graft, collusion, and fraud have become entrenched in the government-controlled economy.[4]

SUMMARY

What is business ethics?

- Moral standards—standards of behavior set by culture

- Moral obligations—standards of behavior set by natural law

- Moral relativism—moral standards by situation

Why is business ethics important?

- Profit

- Leadership

- Reputation

- Strategy

What ethical standard should a business adopt?

- Positive law—codified law

- Inherence—serves shareholders' interests

- Enlightened self-interest—serves shareholders' interest by serving larger society

- Invisible hand—serves larger society by serving shareholders' interests

- Social responsibility—serves larger society by serving larger society

How do employees recognize ethical dilemmas?

- Language

- Categories

How do employees resolve ethical dilemmas?

- Blanchard and Peale

- Front-page-of-the-newspaper test

- *Wall Street Journal* and stakeholders

- Laura Nash and perspective

- Categorical imperative

How does a business create an ethical atmosphere?

- Tone at the top

- Code of ethics

- Reporting lines

- Ethical posture

QUESTIONS AND PROBLEMS

1. E&J Gallo, the world's largest winery, has just announced that it will stop selling its Thunderbird and Night Train Express wines in the Tenderloin, the skid row of San Francisco, for six months. Gallo took the action after meeting with an activist group called Safe and Sober Streets, which has asked grocers to remove the high-alcohol wine from the district, where citizens say drunks create a menace. One retailer in the district said, "If I don't sell this, I will have to close my doors and go home."

Discuss the actions of Gallo and the dilemma of the retailers in the district. Be sure to discuss the type of philosophy each of them holds with respect to social responsibility and ethical dilemmas.

2. Paul Backman is the head of the purchasing department for L. A. East, one of the "Baby Bells" that came into existence after the divestiture of AT&T. Backman and his department purchase everything for the company, from napkins to wires for equipment lines.

S. C. Rydman is an electronics firm and a supplier for L. A. East. L. A. East has used Rydman as a major supplier since 1984. Rydman is also the cosponsor of an exhibit at Wonder World, a theme park in Florida.

Rydman's vice president and chief financial officer, Gunther Fromme, visited Backman in his office on April 3, 1993. Rydman had no bids pending at that time, and Fromme told Backman that he was there "for goodwill." Fromme explained that Rydman had a block of rooms at Wonder World because of its exhibit there and that Backman and his group could use the rooms at any time, free of charge.

Should Backman and his employees use the block of rooms? Why or why not?

3. During the height of the Cold War, the United States, Japan, and members of what was then called the European Common Market had imposed restrictions on the sales of high-tech equipment and armored vehicles to the Soviet Union. During that time, Toshiba Machine Company, a subsidiary of Toshiba Corporation of Japan, sold eight robotized milling machines to the Soviet Union. The machines were used in the production of propellers for Soviet submarines. In spite of the propellers' military use, sales of the milling machines to the Soviets were continued because such sales were not specifically prohibited under the guidelines.

Was Toshiba's choice to continue the sales ethical? Does it matter that the sales were legal under the multinational agreement? What if the end of the Cold War had come through combat? Would Toshiba have been responsible for aiding the Soviet Union?

4. Old Joe Camel, originally a member of a circus that passed through Winston-Salem, North Carolina, each year, was adopted by R. J. Reynolds (RJR) marketers in 1913 as the symbol for a brand being changed from "Red Kamel" to "Camel." In the late 1980s, RJR revived Old Joe with a new look in the form of a cartoon. He became the camel with a "Top Gun" flier jacket, sunglasses, a smirk, and a lot of appeal to young people.

In December 1991, the *Journal of the American Medical Association (JAMA)* published three surveys that found the cartoon character Joe Camel reached children very effectively. Of children between the ages of 3 and 6 who were surveyed, 51.1 percent of them recognized old Joe Camel as being associated with Camel cigarettes.[5] The 6-year-olds were as familiar with Joe Camel as they were with the Mickey Mouse logo for the Disney Channel. The surveys also established that 97.7 percent of students between the ages of 12 and 19 had seen Old Joe and 58 percent thought the ads he was used in were cool. Camel was identified by 33 percent of the students who smoked as their favorite brand.[6]

Before the survey results appeared in *JAMA*, the American Cancer Society, the American Heart Association, and the American Lung Association had petitioned the FTC to ban the ads as "one of the most egregious examples in recent history of tobacco advertising that targets children."[7]

In 1990, Camel shipments rose 11.3 percent. Joe Camel helped RJR take its Camel cigarettes from 2.7 percent to 3.1 percent of the market.

Michael Pertschuk, former FTC head and co-director of the Advocacy Institute, an antismoking group, said, "These are the first studies to give us hard evidence, proving what everybody already knows is true: These ads target kids. I think this will add impetus to the movement to further limit tobacco advertising." Joe Tye, founder of Stop Teenage Addictions to Tobacco, has stated, "There is a growing body of evidence that teen smoking is increasing. And it's 100 percent related to Camel."[8]

A researcher who worked on the December 1991 *JAMA* study, Dr. Joseph R. DiFranza, stated, "We're hoping this information leads to a complete ban of cigarette advertising." Dr. John Richards summarized the study as follows: "The fact is that the ad is reaching kids, and it is changing their behavior."[9]

RJR spokesman David Fishel responded to the allegations with sales evidence: "We can track 98 percent of Camel sales; and they're not going to youngsters. It's simply not in our best interest for young people to smoke, because that opens the door for the government to interfere with our product." At the time the survey results were published, RJR, along with the other manufacturers and the Tobacco Institute, began a multimillion-dollar campaign with billboards and bumper stickers to discourage children from smoking but announced it had no intention of abandoning Joe Camel. The Tobacco Institute publishes a free popular pamphlet called "Tobacco: Helping Youth Say No."

Former U.S. Surgeon General Antonia Novello was very vocal in her desire to change alcohol and cigarette advertising. In March 1992, she called for the withdrawal of the Joe Camel ad campaign: "In years past R. J. Reynolds would have us walk a mile for a Camel. Today its time we invite old Joe Camel himself to take a hike."[10] The AMA's executive vice president, Dr. James S. Todd, concurred:

> This is an industry that kills 400,000 per year, and they have got to pick up new customers. We believe the company is directing its ads to the children who are 3, 6, and 9 years old.

Cigarette sales are, in fact, declining 3 percent per year in the United States. The average Camel smoker is 35 years old, responded an RJR spokeswoman: "Just because children can identify our logo doesn't mean they will use our product." Since the introduction of Joe Camel, however, Camel's share of the under-18 market has climbed to 33 percent from 5 percent. Among 18- to 25-year-olds, Camel's market share has climbed to 7.9 percent from 4.4 percent. The Centers for Disease Control reported in March 1992 that smokers between the ages of 12 and 18 prefer Marlboro, Newport, or Camel cigarettes, the three brands with the most extensive advertising.[11]

Teenagers throughout the country were wearing Joe Camel T-shirts. Brown & Williamson, the producer of Kool cigarettes, began testing a cartoon character for its ads, a penguin wearing sunglasses and Day-Glo sneakers. Company spokesman Joseph Helewicz stated that the ads are geared to smokers between 21 and 35 years old. Helewicz added that cartoon advertisements for adults are not new and cited the Pillsbury Doughboy and the Pink Panther as effective advertising images.

In mid-1992, then–Surgeon General Novella, along with the American Medical Association, began a campaign called "Dump the Hump" to pressure the tobacco industry to stop ad campaigns that teach kids to smoke. In 1993, the FTC staff recommended a ban on the Joe Camel ads. In 1994, then–Surgeon General Joycelyn Elders blamed the tobacco industry's $4 billion in ads for increased smoking rates among teens. RJR's tobacco division chief, James W. Johnston, responded, "I'll be damned if I'll pull the ads." RJR put together a team of lawyers and others it referred to as in-house censors to control Joe's influence. A campaign to have Joe wear a bandana was nixed, as was one for a punker Joe with pink hair.

In 1994, RJR CEO James Johnston testified before a Congressional panel on the Joe Camel controversy and stated, "We do not market to children and will not," and added, "We do not survey anyone under the age of 18."

As health issues related to smokers continued to expand, along with product liability litigation and state attorneys' general pursuit of compensation for their states' health system costs of smokers, more information about the Joe Camel campaign was discovered. Lawyers in a California suit against RJR discovered charts from a presentation at a September 30, 1974, Hilton Head, South Carolina, retreat of RJR top executives and board. The charts offered the following information:

Company	Brand	Share of 14- to 24-year-old market
Philip Morris	Marlboro	33%
Brown & Williamson	Kool	17%
Reynolds	Winston	14%
Reynolds	Salem	9%

RJR's then–vice president of marketing, C. A. Tucker, said, "As this 14–24 age group matures, they will account for a key share of total cigarette volume for at least the next 25 years." The meeting then produced a plan for increasing RJR's presence among the under-35 age group, which included sponsoring NASCAR auto racing. Another memo described plans to study "the demographics and smoking behavior of 14-to-17 year olds." Internal documents about targeting young people were damaging. A 1981 RJR internal memo on marketing surveys cautioned research personnel to tally underage smokers as "age 18." A 1981 Philip Morris internal document indicated information about smoking habits in children as young as 15 was important because "today's teen-ager is tomorrow's potential regular customer." Other Philip Morris documents from the 1980s expressed concerns that Marlboro sales would soon decline because teen-age smoking rates were falling.

A 1987 marketing survey in France and Canada by RJR before it launched the Joe Camel campaign showed that the cartoon image with its fun and humor attracted attention. One 1987 internal document uses the phrase "young adult smokers" and notes a target campaign to the competition's "male Marlboro smokers ages 13–24."

A 1997 survey of 534 teens by *USA TODAY* revealed the following:

Ad	Have Seen Ad	Liked Ad
Joe Camel	95%	65%
Marlboro Man	94%	44%
Budweiser Frogs	99%	92%

Marlboro was the brand smoked by most teens in the survey. The survey found 28 percent of teens between ages 13 and 18 smoke—an increase of 4 percent since 1991. In 1987, Camels were the cigarette of choice for 3 percent of teenagers when Joe Camel debuted. By 1993, the figure had climbed to 16 percent.

In early 1990, the Federal Trade Commission (FTC) began an investigation of RJR and its Joe Camel ads to determine whether underage smokers were illegally targeted by the 10-year Joe Camel Campaign. The FTC had dismissed a complaint in 1994, but did not have the benefits of the newly discovered internal memos.

By late 1997, RJR began phasing out Joe Camel. New Camel ads featured men and women in their 20s, with a healthy look, in clubs and swimming pools, with just a dromedary logo somewhere in the ad. Joe continued as a youth icon. A "Save Joe Camel" web site developed and Joe Camel paraphernalia brought top dollar. A Joe Camel shower curtain sold for $200. RJR also vowed not to feature the Joe Camel character on non-tobacco items such as T-shirts. The cost of the abandonment was estimated at $250 million.

Philip Morris proposed its own plan to halt youth smoking in 1996, which includes no vending machine ads, no billboard ads, no tobacco ads in magazines with 15 percent or more of youth subscribers, and limits on sponsorships to events (rodeos, motor sports) where 75 percent or more of attendees are adults.

In 1998, combined pressure from Congress, the state attorneys general, and ongoing class action suits produced what came to be known as "the tobacco settlement." In addition to payment of $206 billion, the tobacco settlement in all of its various forms bars outdoor advertising, the use of human images (Marlboro man) and cartoon characters, and vending-machine sales. This portion of the settlement was advocated by those who were concerned about teen-agers and their attraction to cigarettes via these ads and their availability in machines.

Suppose you were the executive in charge of marketing for R.J. Reynolds. Would you have recommended an alternative to the Joe Camel character? What if RJR insisted on the Joe Camel ad?

Suppose you work with a pension fund that has a large investment in RJR. Would you consider selling your RJR holdings? Strategically, did R.J. Reynolds make a good business decision on Joe Camel ads?

5. Chateau Giscours, a French winemaker, has been charged by the French government with adding cheap wine to its chateau wine. The allegations state that wines from two different vintages were mixed together and then sold as the more expensive vintage. In addition, the charges from the French government allege that the winemaker added excess sugar to increase the wine's alcohol content and that wood chips were used to give the wine the taste and smell of wine that had been aged in oak barrels.

The charges followed a two-year undercover investigation that included wine experts who were used to determine whether the practices were a one-time event or part of an ongoing pattern. The investigation began following a tip on the use of oak chips, but the investigation of the oak chips led to other issues.

Currently, the market of Bordeaux wines is at a pace and level that no one could have predicted. Competition among the sixty-one chateaus that produce wine is intense.

Why did the winemaker add the chips and sugar? What ethical issues do you see in the allegations? In the chateau wine industry?

6. Burns & McCallister, an international management consulting firm, is listed by *Working Mother* magazine as one of the top fifty firms in the United States for employment of working mothers and is listed as one of the top ten firms for women by *Working Woman* magazine. Burns & McCallister has earned this reputation for several reasons. First, nearly 50 percent of its partners are women. Second, the firm has a menu of employee benefits that include such things as flexible hours, sabbaticals, family leave, home-based work, and part-time partner-track positions.

However, Burns & McCallister has recently been the subject of a series of reports by both the *Los Angeles Times* and the *New York Times* because its policy on female executives in certain nations has become public. Burns & McCallister has learned, through its fifty years of consulting, that in certain countries in which they negotiate for contracts, women cannot be used in the negotiation process. The culture of many of these countries is such that women are not permitted to speak in a meeting of men. Burns & McCallister has thus implemented a policy prohibiting female partners from being assigned these potential account negotiations and later from the accounts themselves. Clerical help in the offices can be female, but any contact with the client must be through a male partner or account executive only.

For example, Japan still has a two-track hiring system, with only 3 percent of professional positions open to women. The remainder of the women in the workforce become office workers who file, wear uniforms, and serve tea. Dentsu, Inc., a large Japanese advertising firm, recently had a picture of the typical Dentsu "Working Girl" in its recruiting brochure. Surrounding the photo were comments primarily about her physical appearance: "Her breasts are 'pretty large'; her bottom is 'rather soft.' "[12]

Burns & McCallister is being criticized for its posture. The head of Burns & McCallister's New York office has explained:

Look, we're about as progressive a firm as you'll find. But the reality of international business is that if we try to use women, we don't get the job. It's not a policy on all foreign accounts. We've just identified certain cultures in which women will not be able to successfully land or work on accounts. This restriction does not interfere with their career track. It does not apply in all countries.

The National Organization for Women (NOW) would like Burns & McCallister to take the position that its standards in the United States apply to all its operations. Because no restrictions are placed on women here, it contends that the other cultures should adapt to our standards; we should not change our standards to adapt to their culture. NOW maintains that without such a posture, change can never come about. Do you agree with Burns & McCallister's policy for certain cultures with regard to female partners? Is Burns & McCallister doing anything that violates federal employment discrimination laws? Given Burns & McCallister's record with regard to women, is the issue really relevant to women's advancement in the firm? If the cultures in which the prohibition of women traditionally applies bring in the accounts with the highest dollar values, would your opinion regarding the posture be different? Do you agree with the NOW position that change can never come about if Burns & McCallister does not take a stand? Would Burns & McCallister be sacrificing revenues in changing its policies? Is this an appropriate sacrifice?

Source: Case Studies in Business Ethics, 2d ed., by Marianne M. Jennings, 118. © 1995. Reprinted with permission of South-Western College Publishing, a division of International Thomson Publishing. Fax 800 730-2215.

7. Coca-Cola has withdrawn its advertising from the World Wrestling Federation (WWF). Others that preceded Coca-Cola in withdrawing their advertising include the U.S. Army, AT&T and Mars, Inc. WWF has promised to tone down its participants so that the sport can become more of a PG-rated program that parents can watch with their children.

The demographics of WWF show that its audience is primarily males between the ages of 12 and 24. This group is also a prime buying group, and ads on WWF will bring revenues. Do you think the corporations should have withdrawn their ads? Have they made a wise decision for their shareholders?

Source: Lionel Tiger, "Advertisers Finally Wrestle with Their Consciences," Wall Street Journal, 8 December 1999, A22.

8. Subway customers wrote to the executives of Subway and complained about Subway's sponsorship of the Howard Stern radio show, a nationally syndicated radio show. Stern, nicknamed the "Shock Jock," often has material of questionable taste on his program. Subway has a unique decision-making process for its ad placement. Because there are so many owners of Subway sandwich shops, a board of trustees elected by shop owners makes decisions on advertising policies for the entire chain of stores. The board met and recommended against advertising on Howard Stern's show, but some owners object because they have no other radio advertising that is as effective at bringing in customers. Would you, as a Subway shop owner, keep or dump Stern ads?

9. Heinz Ketchup holds 54 percent of the U.S. ketchup market, and nine of every ten restaurants feature Heinz ketchup. However, Heinz has learned that many restaurant owners simply refill Heinz bottles with cheaper ketchup, thereby capitalizing on the Heinz name without the cost. One restaurant owner explains, "It's just ketchup. The customers don't notice." There are no specific health regulations that apply, and owners are not breaking the law by refilling the bottles. Do you think this practice is ethical?

10. When you take a flight, the flight attendant will tell you, among all the other instructions, not to use your cell phone once the door on the plane is closed because the use of your cell phone during a flight "may interfere with the aircraft's communication and navigation systems."

However, the evidence to back the claim is simply not there. Boeing and Airbus have both bombarded their planes with cell-phone frequencies and found that there is no interference with communication, navigation, or any aircraft systems. Cellular phones do not operate on any of the frequencies used by the airlines. However, the FAA and the FCC continue to recommend the ban because they have anecdotal evidence of interference. However, the airlines exceed even FAA and FCC guidelines, often prohibiting the use of phones even while passengers are on the ground still boarding or deplaning.

If passengers cannot use their cell phones, they must use the phones on the aircraft, and the airlines receive a portion of the revenues from every call made on board their planes. The director of a National Transportation Safety Board study on the lack of cell-phone interference maintains that the decisions to ban phones are strictly revenue-motivated.

Is there a conflict of interest in those who enforce or apply the cell-phone rules? Should the airlines disclose this conflict?

11. In the fall of 2001, following the deadly attacks on the World Trade Center, the United States experienced the first cases of anthrax it had seen since 1978. The sources of the anthrax spores were letters sent to the American Media, Inc. building in Florida, Tom Brokaw of NBC News, Dan Rather of CBS News, and Senators Edward Kennedy, Tom Daschle, and Patrick Leahy in the United States Senate. There were a series of deaths, cutaneous infections and hundreds of employees at these organizations who tested positive for exposure to the anthrax spores.

As a result of these exposures, the most effective antibiotic for treating anthrax, Cipro, was in high demand. Bayer A.G., a German company, owns the patent for this antibiotic and a significant ramp-up in production was needed to meet the increasing demand for those who had been exposed to anthrax. Bayer A.G.'s United States unit went into 24-hour shifts following the anthrax breakouts. Mr. Brokaw held up a bottle of Cipro on his program, "NBC Nightly News," and calmed a jittery public by saying, "In Cipro we trust." Workers at one of Bayer's U.S. plants cheered with the coverage.

However, executives at headquarters for the company remained silent for weeks about the company's ability to manufacture sufficient amounts of the patented antibiotic. Executives indicated that the company was concerned that if it appeared in the media it would give the appearance of taking advantage of the dire circumstances. Bayer's history made it wary of any involvement in international battles. Bayer A.G. had to pay reparations following World War II and its patent for its world-famous aspirin, Bayer, was stripped from it and awarded to a U.S. company. It was not until 2000 that Bayer was once again permitted to use its name. The company's low profile during the anthrax scares was deliberate and explained by executives as a desire to avoid appearing "exploitive of the problem" of the infections and illnesses.

Frustrated with the lack of communication from Bayer, Canada suspended Bayer's patent in Canada and ordered other drug manufacturers to begin production of their pending generic formulas for Cipro. Other drug companies do have their own formulas developed and ready to go, but could not produce these generics so long as Bayer held its patent protection. One company, Apotex, indicated its production method would not infringe on Bayer's patent, but Bayer threatened litigation and indicated it would deliver all the Cipro needed and/or ordered by both the United States and Canadian governments. Health officials were skeptical and one stated, "There's no way you can tell me getting it from six companies is going to be slower than getting it from one company."

Professor John W. Dienhart, a business ethics professor at Seattle University, stated that Bayer should be a "good corporate citizen." He added, "This is not breaking a patent but adjusting a patent to meet a particular need."

The U.S. Congress was considering suspension of the Cipro patent in the U.S. in order to ramp-up production even more. The legislation would permit federal judges to suspend patents on the basis of public health issues.

In response to some panic in the United States, pharmacies in Mexico, permitted to sell Cipro without a doctor's prescription, as required in the United States, were ordering large amounts of Cipro, increasing their prices and doing a great deal of profitable business from U.S. orders. For example, the Zipp Pharmacy, located in Ciudad Juarez, a border town, says its orders for Cipro increased 15 times what they were before the 2001 anthrax infections. A nurse buying doses of Cipro for her entire family said, "What if there are mad runs on it? It's nice to have it around just in case."

Physicians at the Center for Disease Control (CDC) were concerned about the Mexico purchases and use of the drug without physician prescription. They note the following problems: (1) some people are allergic to Cipro and can become quite ill with just one dose; (2) Cipro has side effects for almost everyone including nausea, vomiting, and loss of appetite; (3) Cipro does have an effect on the brain including possible seizures and hallucinations or simple mood changes and insomnia; and (4) Cipro damages cartilage in the joints, especially when taken by children and is given to children only when there is the absolute need (i.e., there is an infection ongoing). The CDC has advised use of Cipro only upon determination of exposure or infection from anthrax.

Bayer continues to struggle with its position, promises, and public perception as the anthrax infections increased. Bayer's corporate policy is as follows:

We offer our customers a wide variety of products and services in areas ranging from health care and agriculture to plastics and specialty chemicals. Bayer is

RESEARCH PROBLEM

research-based and is aiming for technological leadership in its core activities.

Our goals are to steadily increase corporate value and generate a high value added for the benefit of our stockholders, our employees and the community in every country in which we operate. We believe that our technical and commercial expertise involves responsibility to work for the common good and contribute to sustainable development.

Bayer: Success through Expertise with Responsibility.

What decisions do you think Bayer should make in this situation? Should it suspend its patent voluntarily? What recommendations should it make on taking Cipro? Should it back the warning from the CDC? Is it wrong for Bayer to profit from this public health problem? Develop a memo that offers ethical guidelines for a Bayer executive.

For more information on anthrax, Cipro, and the ethical issues, visit the following Web sites:

http://www.bayer.com

http://www.cdc.com

http://www.cptech.org

The last Web site is one for Ralph Nader's Consumer Project on Technology and provides information on the patents and sale of Cipro.

NOTES

1. Melissa S. Baucus and David A. Baucus, "Paying the Piper: An Empirical Examination of Longer-Term Financial Consequences of Illegal Corporate Behavior," 40 *Academy of Management Journal* 129 (1997).

2. Mr. Milken was required by the Securities Exchange Commission (SEC) to pay fine for his involvement in the negotiations (see Chapter 22).

3. From "Interview: Milton Friedman," *Playboy*, February 1973. © 1973 *Playboy*.

4. This material was adapted from Larry Smeltzer and Marianne M. Jennings, "Why an International Code of Business Ethics Would Be Good for Business," 17 *Journal of Business Ethics* 57 (1998).

5. Kathleen Deveny, "Joe Camel Ads Reach Children, Research Finds," *Wall Street Journal*, 11 December 1991, B1.

6. Walecia Konrad, "I'd Toddle a Mile for a Camel," *Business Week*, 23 December 1991, 34. While the studies and their methodology have been questioned, their impact was made before the challenges and questions were raised.

7. Deveny, "Joe Camel Ads," B1.

8. Laura Bird, "Joe Smooth for President," *Adweek's Marketing Week*, 20 May 1991, 21.

9. "Camels for Kids," *Time*, 23 December 1991, 52.

10. William Chesire, "Don't Shoot: It's Only Joe Camel." *Arizona Republic*, 15 March 1992, C1.

11. "Selling Death," *Mesa Tribune*, 16 March 1992, A8.

12. Ted Holden and Jennifer Wiener, "Revenge of the 'Office Ladies,'" *Business Week*, 13 July 1992, 42–43.

BUSINESS STRATEGY APPLICATION

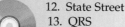

Business Ethics magazine has named its top 100 corporate citizens. Looking at the investment portfolios of socially responsible investment funds leads to creation of the list. Those funds focus on issues such as human rights, animal testing, diversity, non–weapon production, and impact on the environment. The top twenty corporate citizens are listed here:

1. Procter & Gamble
2. Hewlett-Packard
3. Fannie Mae
4. Motorola
5. IBM
6. Sun Microsystems
7. Herman Miller
8. Polaroid
9. St. Paul Cos.
10. Freddie Mac
11. Home Depot
12. State Street
13. QRS
14. Dime Bancorp
15. HB Fuller
16. Cummins Engine
17. Amgen
18. Intel
19. Cisco Systems
20. Avon Products

The CD-ROM exercise gives you the Web sites for the companies. You can view their codes of ethics and financial performance. You will be asked to note any differences between and among their codes of ethics. You will also be asked to find and compare their financial performances with their rankings. Finally, you can then discuss the issue of whether good ethics is good business. Is social responsibility the same as ethics?

CHAPTER THREE

The Judicial System

Our introduction to law included discussions of statutory law and common law. With all of the statutes at various levels, it may appear that statutory law is a complete source of law. However, sometimes statutes require interpretation. Someone must determine when, how, and to whom statutes apply. The law in statutory form is not even half of all the law, the bulk of which is found in judicial decisions. These contain both statutory interpretations and common law. This chapter covers the parties involved as well as the courts—what they decide, when they can decide, and how those decisions are made.

For as thou urgest justice, be assured thou shalt have justice, more than thou desirest.

PORTIA
The Merchant of Venice, *Act IV, Scene 1*

CONSIDER...

Bensusan Restaurant Corporation operates a jazz club in New York City known as "The Blue Note." "The Blue Note" is a federally registered trade name and trademark that belongs to Bensusan.

Richard B. King owns and operates a small jazz club in Columbia, Missouri, also called "The Blue Note." In April 1996, King posted an Internet site on the World Wide Web. The Web site has general information about the Missouri club, as well as a calendar of events and ticketing information.

Bensusan, upon pulling up King's "Blue Note" Web site, brought suit in New York for infringement. King maintains that the New York courts cannot require him to go to New York and appear in court there. Is he right?

© Kelley-Mooney/CORBIS

TYPES OF COURTS

In all U.S. court systems, there are two different types or levels of courts: trial courts and appellate courts.

Trial Courts

A **trial court** is the place in the judicial system where the facts of a case are presented. This court is where the jury will sit if the case is a jury trial. It is where the evidence and witnesses will be presented and where the first decision in the case is made, by either judge or jury. Courts at the trial level have the power to hear a case originally. The procedures for trials and trial courts are covered in Chapter 4.

Appellate Courts

There is always at least one other court, an **appellate court,** to review a trial court decision or to check the conduct of the judge, the trial, the lawyers, and the jury. This process of review helps assure a proper application of the law and proper use of procedural laws. Further, this system of review provides the legal system with uniformity. Reviews may result in published opinions, which can then be referred to and used for resources in deciding future cases.

HOW COURTS MAKE DECISIONS

The Process of Judicial Review

Appellate courts do not hold trials. Rather, they review what has been done by trial courts to determine whether the trial court, often referred to as the lower court, made an error in applying the substantive or procedural law in the case. This is the process of **judicial review.**

The appellate court atmosphere is very different from that of the trial court. There are no witnesses, no jury, and no testimony. No new evidence is considered; only the evidence presented at trial is reviewed. The court reviews a transcript of the trial along with all the evidence presented at trial to determine whether an error has been made.

In addition to the transcript and evidence, each of the parties to a case can present the appellate court with a **brief,** which is a summary of the case and the legal issues being challenged on appeal. The appellate brief is each side's summary of why the trial court decision or procedures were correct or incorrect. The parties make their arguments for their positions in the brief and support them with statutes and decisions from other cases. The brief serves as a summary of the major points of error the parties allege occurred during the trial. This type of brief is called an **appellate brief** and is very detailed. In fact, many refer to lawyers' "briefs" as a misnomer because they are generally quite lengthy. Note that these briefs differ from the case brief presented in Exhibit 1.1.

Many appellate courts permit the attorneys for the opposing parties to make timed **oral arguments** in their cases. An oral argument is a summary of the points that have been made in each party's brief. The judge can also ask questions of the attorneys at that time. At the trial level, one judge makes all decisions. At the appellate level, more than one judge reviews the actions of the lower court in a case. The typical number is three, but, in the case of state supreme courts and the

Listen to oral arguments made before the Supreme Court:
http://oyez.at.nwu.edu/ oyez.html

Learn more about the Supreme Court justices:
http://www.law.cornell.edu/supct/justices/fullcourt.html

U.S. Supreme Court, the full bench of judges on the court hears each case. For example, in U.S. Supreme Court decisions, all nine justices review the cases before the Court unless they have recused (disqualified) themselves because of some conflict.

The panel of appellate judges reviews the case and the briefs, hears the oral argument, and then renders a decision. The decision in the case could be unanimous or could be a split vote, such as 2 to 1. In the case of a split vote, the justice who is not in the majority will frequently draft a **dissenting opinion,** which is the judge's explanation for a vote different from that of the majority.

Checking for Error

A **reversible error** is one that might have affected the outcome of the case or would have influenced the decision made. Examples of reversible errors include the refusal to allow some evidence to be admitted that should have been admitted, the refusal to allow a particular witness to testify, and misapplication of the law.

When a reversible error is made, the appellate court **reverses** the lower court's decision. However, in some cases, the appellate court will also **remand** the case, which means the case is sent back to the trial court for further work. For example, if there is a reversal because some evidence should have been admitted that was not, the case is remanded for a new trial with that evidence admitted (i.e., allowed).

If there has not been an error, the appellate court simply **affirms** the decision of the lower court. An affirmed decision does not mean no mistakes were made; it means that none of the mistakes was a reversible error. The decision of the court is written by a member of the court who has voted with the majority. The decision explains the facts and the reasons for the court's reversal, remand, or affirmation.

In some appellate cases, the court will **modify** the decision of a lower court. The full case is neither reversed nor affirmed; instead, a portion or portions of the case are reversed or modified. For example, a trial court verdict finding a defendant negligent might be affirmed, but the appellate court could find that the damages awarded were excessive. In this type of decision, the case would be remanded for a redetermination of damages at the trial court level.

Statutory Interpretation

In addition to checking for error, appellate courts render interpretations of statutes. Often, statutes seem perfectly clear until a new factual situation not covered by the statute arises.

The Doctrine of *Stare Decisis*

Judicial review by appellate courts of lower court decisions provides the database for the doctrine of *stare decisis.* The decisions of the appellate courts are written and often published so that they may be analyzed, reviewed, and perhaps applied in the future.

Setting Precedent

When a court reviews the decisions of lower courts, that court's previous decisions, along with decisions of other courts on the same topic, are consulted. This process of examining other decisions for help in a new case uses case **precedent,**

Re: A Look at What Appellate Courts Do

The following chart, organized by federal circuits, shows the percentage of time the U.S. Supreme Court reverses the decisions of lower courts.

CATEGORY	NUMBER OF CASES	PERCENT REVERSED OR VACATED
Total	74	58%
1st Circuit	1	0%
2d Circuit	3	100%
3d Circuit	1	0%
4th Circuit	9	56%
5th Circuit	9	56%
6th Circuit	4	75%
7th Circuit	8	75%
8th Circuit	5	20%
9th Circuit	10	90%
10th Circuit	1	0%
11th Circuit	5	40%
Federal Circuit	2	100%
D.C. Circuit	3	0%
District Courts	2	0%
State appellate courts	11	64%

Source: "A Small, Potent Docket, and a Lot of Close Votes," *National Law Journal,* 7 August 2000, A1.

which is the doctrine of *stare decisis,* a Latin term meaning "let the decision stand." Such judicial thinking requires an examination of all related cases to determine whether the issue has already been decided and whether the same decision should apply again. Following case precedent does not mean similar cases will be decided identically; there are several factors that influence the weight given to precedent.

The Quality of the Precedent

Where the case originated is one of the factors that influences the application of precedent in a case. In federal courts, precedent from other federal courts is strongest when the case involves federal statutes.

In state courts, prior decisions within a particular state's own court system are given greater weight than decisions from courts of other states. One state's courts are not obliged to follow the precedent of another state's courts; they are free to examine it and use it, but, as with all precedent, there is no mandatory requirement to follow another state's decisions.

Purposes of Precedent

The purposes of precedent are the same as the purposes of law. Law offers some assurance of consistency and reliability. The judiciary recognizes these obligations in applying precedent. There must be stability and predictability in the way law functions. There is no exact formula for deciding a case, but consistency is a key element in applying precedent.

In addition to consistency, however, judges must incorporate into their legal thought the need for flexibility in the law. New twists in facts arise, and new technology develops; and the judiciary must be receptive to the need for change. For example, in Chapter 1, the *Sony* and *Napster* cases illustrated the need for a reexamination of the scope of a law based on a newly evolved technology and its role in copyright law and protections.

Interpretation of Precedent

There is more to precedent than just finding similar cases. Every case decision has two parts. One is the actual rule of law, which technically is the precedential part. However, judges never offer just a rule of law in a case. Their rule of law is given at the end of the case decision after there has been a full discussion of their reasons and other precedent. This discussion is called the ***dicta*** of the case, in which case precedents may be cited to the benefit of each party. In some instances, the rule of law may benefit one party while the *dicta* benefits the other party.

A dissenting opinion is *dicta* and is often quoted in subsequent cases to urge a court to change existing precedent. Application of precedent is not a scientific process; there is much room for interpretation and variation.

C O N S I D E R . . .

3.1 The following rule appears in State University's current catalog:

> *A course in which a grade of "C" or better has been earned may not be repeated. The second entry will not be counted in earned hours or grade point index for graduation.*

Rod took his business math course and earned a "C." Not satisfied with his grade but unaware of the catalog regulation, Rod took the math course again and this time earned a "D." The registrar has entered the "D" grade in Rod's cumulative average. Rod objects based on the catalog rule, but the registrar says the rule applies only if a higher grade is earned. What should Rod do? Should the grade count?

The purpose of the university regulation was to prevent students from retaking courses to earn a higher grade point average (GPA). In the factual situation, the student earned a lower grade. The registrar entered the grade with the idea that entering a lower grade would be a deterrent for students retaking courses when they had a "C" or better. However, it is clear that a second grade, whether higher or lower, should not be entered.

Suppose that the registrar has always counted the lower grades in the cumulative GPA. Does Rod still have an effective argument? Is the registrar using a strained interpretation of the regulation?

When Precedent Is Not Followed

Precedent may not be followed for several reasons. Some of those reasons have already been given: The precedent is from another state, or the precedent is interpreted differently because of the *dicta* in that precedent. Precedent is also not followed when the facts of cases can be "distinguished," which means that the context of the facts in one case is sufficiently different so that the precedent cannot be applied. For example, suppose that a court decided that using roadblocks to stop motorists to check for drunk drivers is constitutional. A subsequent case regarding roadblocks used to check for drivers' licenses may not be decided the same way. The distinguishing factor in the first case is the nature of the roadblocks: to prevent a hazardous highway condition. The court may not see the same urgency or safety issue in checking for drivers' licenses. The precedent is distinguishable.

The theories of law discussed in Chapter 1 may also control whether precedent is applied. For example, a court may not follow a precedent because of a moral reason or because of the need to change law on the basis of what is moral or what is right. A precedent may also be abandoned on an economic theory, in which the court changes the law to do the most good for the most people. For example, a factory may be a nuisance because of the noise and pollution it creates. There is probably ample case law to support the shutdown of the factory as a nuisance. However, the factory may also be the town's only economic support and shutting it down will mean unemployment for virtually the whole town. In balancing the economic factors, the nuisance precedent may not be followed or it may be followed in only a modified way.

Courts struggle with issues of fact and law and with changes in society as they apply precedent and consider modifications.

PARTIES IN THE JUDICIAL SYSTEM (CIVIL CASES)

Plaintiffs

Plaintiffs are the parties who initiate a lawsuit and are seeking some type of recovery. In some types of cases, they are called **petitioners** (such as in an action for divorce). The plaintiffs file their suit in the appropriate court, and this filing begins the process.

Defendants

Defendants are the ones from whom the plaintiffs want recovery. They are the ones charged with some violation of the civil rights of the plaintiff. In some cases, they are referred to as *respondents*.

Lawyers

BUSINESS PLANNING TIP
Business people should exercise caution in the protection of their lawyer-client privilege. Letters and memos to lawyers should be marked as privileged, and limitations should be placed on access to those letters and memos. Revealing to others your communications to your lawyer may cost you your privilege. Holding a conversation or meeting with your lawyer with others present may cost you your privilege, too. Privileged communications should be with your lawyer(s) only.

In most cases, each of the parties are represented by a lawyer. Lawyers have other functions besides representing clients in a lawsuit. Many lawyers offer "preventive" services. Lawyers draft contracts, wills, and other documents to prevent legal problems from arising. Clients are advised in advance so that they can minimize legal problems and costs.

The attorney-client relationship is a fiduciary one and one that carries privilege. The attorney is expected to act in the best interests of the client and can do so without the fear of having to disclose the client's thoughts and decisions. The **attorney-client privilege** keeps the relationship confidential and assures that others (even an adversary in a lawsuit) have limited access to lawyer-client conversations.

Under the American Bar Association's Model Rules for Professional Responsibility, attorneys are obligated to represent clients zealously. Once an attorney agrees to represent a client, that representation must

To whom does the attorney-client privilege belong? An attorney who is general counsel for a corporation or a lawyer who represents a corporation has but one client: the corporation. The privilege applies to her communication with that client. While officers and employees provide the attorney with the information about what the corporation did, the lawyer does not represent those officers and employees. In most situations, the interests of the officers and employees are the same as those of the corporations and a lawyer can work closely with the officers and employees to represent the corporation. However, there can be circumstances in which the corporation's interests are different from those of the employees. For example, suppose that a general counsel for a corporation learned that its officers had engaged in price-fixing. (See Chapter 9 for more discussion of criminal prosecutions of officers of a corporation and Chapter 17 for discussion of price-fixing and antitrust violations.) The general counsel would discuss the issue with the board (see Chapter 21) and perhaps conclude that it is best to disclose what has happened to the Justice Department. While the officers involved might object, they are not protected by any privilege with the corporation's attorney. The attorney is protecting her client, the company, by disclosing the misconduct and perhaps providing assurance that the board was unaware of the price-fixing, which would then reduce any penalties the company might be required to pay.

Visit the American Bar Association Center for Professional Responsibility: http://www.abanet.org/cpr/home.html

be given to the best of the lawyer's ability. Because of the privilege, many lawyers know that their clients actually did commit a crime or breach a contract. However, the client's confession to an attorney is confidential. Even with that knowledge, it is the attorney's obligation to represent the client and make certain that the client is given all rights and protections under the law. A criminal defense attorney may know that her client has committed a crime. But committing a crime and the required proof for conviction of that crime are two different things. It is the lawyer's job to see that the other side meets its burdens and responsibilities in proving a case against the client. Lawyers do represent guilty people. Their role is to make sure that the system operates fairly with guilty and innocent people alike.

Lawyers and their titles and roles vary from country to country. Great Britain and most of Canada have *solicitors* and *barristers*. Solicitors prepare legal documents, give legal advice, and represent clients in some of the lesser courts. Barristers are the only "lawyers" who can practice before higher courts and administrative agencies. Quebec and France have three types of lawyers: the *avocat*, who can practice before the higher courts and give legal advice; the *notaire*, who can handle real property transactions and estates and can prepare some legal documents; and the *juriste* (legal counselor), who can give advice and prepare legal documents. In Germany, a lawyer who litigates is called *Rechtsanwalt* and a lawyer who advises clients but does not appear in court is called *Rechtsbeistand*. Japan has but one class of lawyers, called *bengoshi*. In Italy, the two types of lawyers—whose roles are similar to the dual British system—are *avocati* and *procuratori*.

Judges

Judges control the proceedings in a case and, in some instances, the outcome. Trial judges control the trial of a case from the selection of a jury to ruling on evidence questions. (See Chapter 4 for more details on trial procedures.) **Appellate** judges review the work of trial court judges. They do not actually hear evidence but, rather, review transcripts. Their job is one of determining error but does not include conducting trials.

Judges are selected in various ways throughout the country. Some judges are elected to their offices. Some states have merit appointment systems, wherein judges are appointed on the basis of their qualifications. In some states, judges are appointed by elected officials subject to the approval of the legislature; and, in some states with appointed judges, the judges are put on the ballot every other year (or some other period) for retention; voters in these states do not decide whom they want as judges but do decide whether they want to keep them once they are in office. Federal judges are appointed by the president with Senate approval.

Name Changes on Appeal

The lawyers and the parties stay in the "game" even after a case is appealed. However, the names of the parties do change on appeal. The party appealing the case is called the **appellant.** Some courts also call the party appealing a case the **petitioner.** The other party (the one not appealing) is called the **appellee** or **respondent.**

Some states change the name of the case if the party appealing the case is the defendant. For example, suppose that Smith sues Jones for his damages in a car accident. The name of the case at trial is *Smith* v. *Jones.* Smith is the plaintiff, and Jones is the defendant. If Smith wins the case at trial and Jones decides to appeal, Jones is the appellant and Smith is the appellee. In some courts, the name of the case on appeal becomes *Jones* v. *Smith.* Other courts leave the case name the same but still label Jones the appellant and Smith the appellee.

THE CONCEPT OF JURISDICTION

There are courts at every level of government, and every court handles a different type of case. In order for a court to decide or try a particular case, both parties to the case and the subject matter of the case must be within the established powers of the court. The established powers of a court make up the court's **jurisdiction.** *Juris* means law, and *diction* means to speak.

Jurisdiction is the authority or power of a court to speak the law. Some courts can handle bankruptcies, whereas others may be limited to traffic violations. Some courts handle violations of criminal laws, whereas others deal only with civil matters. The subject matter of a case controls which court has jurisdiction. For example, a case involving a federal statute belongs in a federal district court by its subject matter. However, there are federal district courts in every state, and jurisdiction also involves the issue of which court. ***In personam* jurisdiction,** or jurisdiction over the person, controls which of the federal district courts will decide the case. Determining which court can be used is a two-step process; subject matter and *in personam* jurisdiction must fit in the same court.

SUBJECT MATTER JURISDICTION OF COURTS:
THE AUTHORITY OVER CONTENT

There are two general court systems in the United States: the federal court system (see Exhibit 3.1) and the state court system.

**EXHIBIT 3.1
The Federal Court
System**

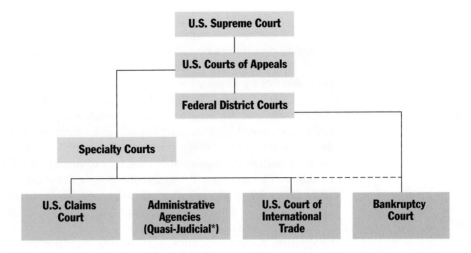

*For example, the Federal Trade Commission (FTC) or the National Labor Relations Bureau (NLRB).

The Federal Court System

The Trial Court of the Federal System

Learn more about the U.S. Federal Court system:
http://www.uscourts.gov/
or
http://www.fjc.gov

The **federal district court** is the general trial court of the federal system. However, federal district courts are limited in the types of cases they can hear; that is, their subject matter jurisdiction is limited. Federal district courts can hear three types of cases: those in which the United States is a party, those that involve a federal question, and those that involve diversity of citizenship.

Jurisdiction When the United States Is a Party

Anytime the U.S. government is a party in a lawsuit, it will want to be tried in its own court system—the federal system. The United States is a party when it brings suit or when it is the defendant named in a suit. For example, if the Navy must bring an action to enforce a contract against a supplier, the United States is the plaintiff and the federal court system has subject matter jurisdiction. If a victim of a plane crash names the Federal Aviation Administration (FAA) in a suit, the United States is a defendant and the federal system again has jurisdiction.

Federal Jurisdiction for a Federal Question

The federal district court has jurisdiction over cases involving federal questions. For example, if a business is suing for treble damages (a remedy of three times the amount of damages experienced) under the federal antitrust laws (see Chapter 17), there is a federal question and the case may be brought in federal district court. A suit charging a violation of the Equal Protection Clause of the U.S. Constitution (see Chapter 5 for more details) also involves a federal question and can be brought in federal district court. Prosecutions for federal crimes also involve federal questions, and the United States will be a party as the prosecutor; these criminal cases are tried in federal district court. When the United States is a party in a case, the federal district court has exclusive jurisdiction.

Many federal questions can also be heard by a state court. For example, most state constitutions include the same Fifth Amendment protections included in the U.S. Constitution. A plaintiff often has a choice between federal and state court, and the decision to proceed in one forum as opposed to the other may be a strategic one based on the nature of the case, rules of procedure, and other factors related to differences between the two court systems.

Jurisdiction by Diversity

Most of the civil cases in federal district court are not there because they are federal questions or because the United States is a party. Most civil cases are in federal district court because the plaintiff and defendant are from different states and their case involves damage claims in excess of $75,000. Cases in which the parties are from different states qualify them for **diversity of citizenship** status, and federal district courts have the authority to hear these diversity cases. That authority is not exclusive; a state court can also hear diversity cases so long as neither party chooses to exercise the right to a federal district court trial. In diversity cases, state and federal courts have *concurrent jurisdiction.* Concurrent jurisdiction means that two courts have the authority to hear a case. By contrast, *exclusive jurisdiction* means that only one court has the authority to hear the case. For example, federal district courts have exclusive jurisdiction over cases in which the United States has charged an individual or corporation with a federal crime.

It is logical that federal courts should decide controversies among citizens of different states. If the case is held in one side's state court, that side might have an unfair advantage or built-in prejudice because of the location of the court.

When corporations are parties to suits, the diversity issue is more complex. The citizenship of a corporation can be its state of incorporation or the state in which its principal office is located. This citizenship test is used for subject matter jurisdiction. The citizenship test for *in personam* jurisdiction has been greatly expanded.

It is important to understand that when a federal court tries a case on the basis of diversity, it is simply trying the case under the same state laws but without the local prejudice that might exist in a state court. In other words, federal courts do not rule under a different set of laws; they simply apply the state law in a different setting.

Limited Jurisdiction—The Special Trial Courts of the Federal System

Look for updates on federal courts:
http://www.federalcourts.com

Not all cases in which the United States is a party or in which there is a federal question are decided in federal district courts. The federal system also has specialized trial courts to handle limited matters. For example, there is a Tax Court in the federal system, the jurisdiction of which is limited to tax issues. If you should decide to challenge the Internal Revenue Service because it would not allow one of your deductions, your case would be heard in Tax Court. Bankruptcy Court is a well-used limited court in the federal system that has exclusive jurisdiction over all bankruptcies. No other court can handle a bankruptcy or bankruptcy issues. The Bankruptcy Court is limited to handling bankruptcies and does not handle any other type of trial or suit.

The U.S. Claims Court is another specialized federal court: It handles the claims of government contractors against the U.S. government and vice versa. This court is experienced in government contracts and claims and provides a faster forum for disposing of these issues without the longer process through federal district court.

The U.S. Court of International Trade is also a specialized court that focuses on international trade transactions regulated by federal agencies in various ways.

Another court that is often discussed along with the federal system is the Indian Tribal Court. These are courts of the Native American nations, and they have exclusive jurisdiction over criminal and civil matters on the reservations. They are unique courts because of both their limited jurisdiction and their exclusivity, arising from their sovereign nature.

The Structure of the Federal District Court System

There is at least one federal district per state. The number of federal districts in each state is determined by the state's population and caseload. States such as Arizona and Nevada have only one federal district each, whereas states such as Illinois and New York have many. The number of courts and judges in each federal district is also determined by the district's population and caseload. Even in those states in which there is just one district, there are several judges and multiple courtrooms for federal trials. There are ninety-four federal districts in the fifty states plus one each in the District of Columbia and Puerto Rico.

The Importance of Federal District Court Decisions

Review online recent U.S. Courts of Appeals decisions: http://www.law.emory.edu/ FEDCTS

The subject matter of cases qualifying for federal district court is important. Such cases involve the interpretation of federal statutes and, in many cases, the resolution of constitutional issues. Because of the importance of these decisions, the opinions of federal district judges are published in a reporter series called the *Federal Supplement,* which reprints most opinions issued by federal district judges in every federal district. (Decisions of the Court of International Trade are also found in the *Federal Supplement.*) Cases in the *Federal Supplement* provide excellent precedent for interpretation and application of federal statutes. Just as there is a system for citing statutes (see Chapter 1), there is a system for citing case opinions. Such a system is necessary so that precedent can be found easily for use in future cases.

All case cites consist of three elements: an abbreviation for the reporter, the volume number, and the page number. The abbreviation for the *Federal Supplement* is "F.Supp." or, for the second series, after volume 999, "F.Supp.2d." The volume number always appears in front of the abbreviation, and the page number appears after it. A formal cite includes in parentheses the federal district in which the case was decided and the year the case was decided. A sample federal district court cite of a case decided in the Eastern District of Michigan looks like this:

Gratz v. *Bollinger*
135 F.Supp.2d 790 (E.D. Mich. 2001)

This method of uniform citation not only helps ease the burden of research; it is an automatic way of knowing where a case came from and how it can be used. A number of systems available on the Internet offer copies of court opinions for a fee.

The Appellate Level in the Federal System

Cases decided in federal district court and the specialized trial courts of the federal system can be appealed. These cases are appealed to the U.S. courts of appeals (formerly called the U.S. circuit courts of appeals).

Structure All of the federal district courts are grouped into **federal circuits** according to their geographic location. Exhibit 3.2 is a map that shows the thirteen federal circuits. Note that eleven of the circuits are geographic groupings of states; the twelfth is the District of Columbia, and the thirteenth is a nongeographic

EXHIBIT 3.2 The Thirteen Federal Judicial Circuits

Source: Reprinted with permission and courtesy of West Publishing Company.

circuit created to handle special cases. A fourteenth circuit made by dividing the Ninth Circuit has been proposed.

Each circuit has its own court of appeals. The office of the court's clerk is located in the starred city shown in each of the federal circuits in Exhibit 3.2. The number of judges for each of the federal circuits varies according to caseload. However, most cases are heard by a panel of three of the circuit judges. It is rare for a case to be heard *en banc* (by the whole bench or all the judges in that circuit).

Procedures   The U.S. courts of appeals are appellate courts and operate by the same general procedures discussed earlier in the chapter. An appeal consists of a record of the trial in the court below (here, the federal district court), briefs, and possible oral argument. The standard for reversal is reversible error. Because the right of appeal is automatic, the appellate courts have tremendous caseloads. A full opinion is not given in every case. In the cases that are affirmed, the opinion may consist of that one word. Other decisions are issued as memorandum opinions for the benefit of the parties but not for publication.

Read about proposed changes in the federal court system:
http://app.com.uscourts.gov

Opinions The opinions of the U.S. courts of appeals are published in a series of reporters called the *Federal Reporter.* The system of citation for these cases is the same as for the federal district court opinions. The abbreviation for the *Federal Reporter* is "F." (or sometimes "F.2d" or "F.3d"; the "2d" means the second series, which was started after the first "F." series reached volume 300, and now there is a third series—"3d"). A formal cite includes in parentheses the federal circuit and date of the decision. A sample U.S. court of appeals cite would look like this:

> *A&M Records, Inc.* v. *Napster, Inc.*
> 239 F.3d 1004 (9th Cir. 2001)

The U.S. Supreme Court

A decision by a U.S. court of appeals is not necessarily the end of a case. There is one more appellate court in the federal system—the **U.S. Supreme Court.** However, the Supreme Court's procedures and jurisdiction are slightly different from those of other appellate courts.

Appellate Jurisdiction and Process The Supreme Court handles appeals from the U.S. courts of appeals. This appeal process, however, is not an automatic right. The Supreme Court must first decide whether a particular case merits review. That decision is announced when the Court issues a *writ of certiorari* for those cases it will review in full. The Supreme Court, in its writ, actually makes a preliminary determination about the case and whether it should be decided. Only a small number of cases appealed to the Supreme Court are actually heard. In 1945, 1,460 cases were appealed to the court. By 1960, that number had grown to 2,313. Now the number averages about 7,000 each year. The court grants *certiorari* in about 140 cases and hears oral arguments and issues written opinions in about 70 to 80 cases. For example, in the 2000 term, the Supreme Court reviewed 148 cases of the cases on its docket and issued 74 opinions. The opinions in total are about 5,000 pages in length including the majority, concurring, and dissenting opinions.

The court grants *writs of certiorari* on cases because there may be a conflict among the circuits about the law or because the case presents a major constitutional issue. This *writ of certiorari* procedure also applies to other sources of appellate cases. Although the appellate workload of the U.S. Supreme Court is great, it is only part of the Court's jurisdictional burden. Decisions from state supreme courts, for example, can be appealed to the U.S. Supreme Court. The Supreme Court also decides whether to review these cases. For example, in 2000, the U.S. Supreme Court granted *certiorari* on George W. Bush's appeal of a Florida Supreme Court decision on recounting the Florida ballots in the November 2000 presidential election. That case, because of its significance and its interpretation of statutory law and the role of judicial review, follows.

CASE 3.1

Bush v. *Gore*
531 U.S. 98 (2000)

The *Certiorari* That Decided a Presidential Election

FACTS

On November 8, 2000, the day following the Presidential election, the Florida Division of Elections reported that Governor George W. Bush (petitioner), had received 2,909,135 votes, and Vice President Albert Gore, Jr. (respondent) had received 2,907,351 votes, a margin of 1,784 for Governor Bush.

Because Governor Bush's margin of victory was less than "one-half of a percent . . . of the votes cast," an automatic machine recount was conducted under § 102.141(4) of the election code, the results of which showed Governor Bush still winning the race but by a diminished margin. Vice President Gore then sought manual recounts in Volusia, Palm Beach, Broward, and Miami-Dade Counties, under Florida's election protest provisions. A dispute arose concerning the deadline for local county canvassing boards to submit their returns to the Secretary of State (Secretary). The Secretary declined to waive the November 14 deadline imposed by statute. The Florida Supreme Court, however, set the deadline at November 26. We granted certiorari and vacated the Florida Supreme Court's decision, finding considerable uncertainty as to the grounds on which it was based. On December 11, the Florida Supreme Court issued a decision on remand reinstating that date.

On November 26, the Florida Elections Canvassing Commission certified the results of the election and declared Governor Bush the winner of Florida's 25 electoral votes. On November 27, Vice President Gore, pursuant to Florida's contest provisions, filed a complaint in Leon County Circuit Court contesting the certification. The Circuit Court denied relief, stating that Vice President Gore failed to meet his burden of proof. He appealed to the First District Court of Appeal, which certified the matter to the Florida Supreme Court.

Accepting jurisdiction, the Florida Supreme Court affirmed in part and reversed in part. On December 8, 2000, the Supreme Court of Florida ordered that the Circuit Court of Leon County tabulate by hand 9,000 ballots in Miami-Dade County. It also ordered the inclusion in the certified vote totals

of 215 votes identified in Palm Beach County and 168 votes identified in Miami-Dade County for Vice President Gore and Senator Joseph Lieberman, Democratic Candidates for President and Vice President. The Supreme Court noted that Governor Bush asserted that the net gain for Vice President Gore in Palm Beach County was 176 votes, and directed the Circuit Court to resolve that dispute on remand. The court further held that relief would require manual recounts in all Florida counties where so-called "undervotes" had not been subject to manual tabulation. The court ordered all manual recounts to begin at once. Governor Bush and Richard Cheney, Republican Candidates for the Presidency and Vice Presidency, filed an emergency application for a stay. On December 9, 2000, the U.S. Supreme Court granted *certiorari*.

JUDICIAL OPINION

PER CURIAM

The petition presents the following questions: whether the Florida Supreme Court established new standards for resolving Presidential election contests, thereby violating Art. II, § 1, cl. 2, of the United States Constitution and failing to comply with 3 U.S.C. § 5, and whether the use of standardless manual recounts violates the Equal Protection and Due Process Clauses. With respect to the equal protection question, we find a violation of the Equal Protection Clause.

The closeness of this election, and the multitude of legal challenges which have followed in its wake, have brought into sharp focus a common, if heretofore unnoticed, phenomenon. Nationwide statistics reveal that an estimated 2% of ballots cast do not register a vote for President for whatever reason, including deliberately choosing no candidate at all or some voter error, such as voting for two candidates or insufficiently marking a ballot. In certifying election results, the votes eligible for inclusion in the certification are the votes meeting the properly established legal requirements.

This case has shown that punch card balloting machines can produce an unfortunate number of ballots which are not punched in a clean, complete way by the voter. After the current counting, it is likely legislative bodies nationwide will examine ways to improve the mechanisms and machinery for voting.

The individual citizen has no federal constitutional right to vote for electors for the President of the United States unless and until the state legislature chooses a statewide election as the means to implement its power to appoint members of the Electoral College. History has now favored the voter, and in each of the several States the citizens themselves vote for Presidential electors. When the state legislature vests the right to vote for President in its people, the right to vote as the legislature has prescribed is fundamental; and one source of its fundamental nature lies in the equal weight accorded to each vote and the equal dignity owed to each voter.

The right to vote is protected in more than the initial allocation of the franchise. Equal protection applies as well to the manner of its exercise. Having once granted the right to vote on equal terms, the State may not, by later arbitrary and disparate treatment, value one person's vote over that of another.

There is no difference between the two sides of the present controversy on these basic propositions. Respondents say that the very purpose of vindicating the right to vote justifies the recount procedures now at issue. The question before us, however, is whether the recount procedures the Florida Supreme Court has adopted are consistent with its obligation to avoid arbitrary and disparate treatment of the members of its electorate.

Much of the controversy seems to revolve around ballot cards designed to be perforated by a stylus but which, either through error or deliberate omission, have not been perforated with sufficient precision for a machine to count them. In some cases a piece of the card—a chad—is hanging, say by two corners. In other cases there is no separation at all, just an indentation.

The Florida Supreme Court has ordered that the intent of the voter be discerned from such ballots. For purposes of resolving the equal protection challenge, it is not necessary to decide whether the Florida Supreme Court had the authority under the legislative scheme for resolving election disputes to define what a legal vote is and to mandate a manual recount implementing that definition. The recount mechanisms implemented in response to the decisions of the Florida Supreme Court do not satisfy the minimum requirement for nonarbitrary treatment of vot-

ers necessary to secure the fundamental right. Florida's basic command for the count of legally cast votes is to consider the "intent of the voter." This is unobjectionable as an abstract proposition and a starting principle. The problem inheres in the absence of specific standards to ensure its equal application. The formulation of uniform rules to determine intent based on these recurring circumstances is practicable and, we conclude, necessary.

The law does not refrain from searching for the intent of the actor in a multitude of circumstances; and in some cases the general command to ascertain intent is not susceptible to much further refinement. In this instance, however, the question is not whether to believe a witness but how to interpret the marks or holes or scratches on an inanimate object, a piece of cardboard or paper which, it is said, might not have registered as a vote during the machine count. The factfinder confronts a thing, not a person. The search for intent can be confined by specific rules designed to ensure uniform treatment.

The want of those rules here has led to unequal evaluation of ballots in various respects. As seems to have been acknowledged at oral argument, the standards for accepting or rejecting contested ballots might vary not only from county to county but indeed within a single county from one recount team to another.

The record provides some examples. A monitor in Miami-Dade County testified at trial that he observed that three members of the county canvassing board applied different standards in defining a legal vote. And testimony at trial also revealed that at least one county changed its evaluative standards during the counting process. Palm Beach County, for example, began the process with a 1990 guideline which precluded counting completely attached chads, switched to a rule that considered a vote to be legal if any light could be seen through a chad, changed back to the 1990 rule, and then abandoned any pretense of a per se rule, only to have a court order that the county consider dimpled chads legal. This is not a process with sufficient guarantees of equal treatment.

The State Supreme Court ratified this uneven treatment. It mandated that the recount totals from two counties, Miami-Dade and Palm Beach, be included in the certified total. The court also appeared to hold *sub silentio* that the recount totals from Broward County, which were not completed until after the original November 14 certification by the Secretary of State, were to be considered part of

(continued)

the new certified vote totals even though the county certification was not contested by Vice President Gore. Yet each of the counties used varying standards to determine what was a legal vote. Broward County used a more forgiving standard than Palm Beach County, and uncovered almost three times as many new votes, a result markedly disproportionate to the difference in population between the counties.

In addition, the recounts in these three counties were not limited to so-called undervotes but extended to all of the ballots. The distinction has real consequences. A manual recount of all ballots identifies not only those ballots which show no vote but also those which contain more than one, the so-called overvotes. Neither category will be counted by the machine. This is not a trivial concern. At oral argument, respondents estimated there are as many as 110,000 overvotes statewide. As a result, the citizen whose ballot was not read by a machine because he failed to vote for a candidate in a way readable by a machine may still have his vote counted in a manual recount; on the other hand, the citizen who marks two candidates in a way discernable by the machine will not have the same opportunity to have his vote count, even if a manual examination of the ballot would reveal the requisite indicia of intent.

Furthermore, the citizen who marks two candidates, only one of which is discernable by the machine, will have his vote counted even though it should have been read as an invalid ballot. The State Supreme Court's inclusion of vote counts based on these variant standards exemplifies concerns with the remedial processes that were under way.

In addition to these difficulties the actual process by which the votes were to be counted under the Florida Supreme Court's decision raises further concerns. That order did not specify who would recount the ballots. The county canvassing boards were forced to pull together ad hoc teams comprised of judges from various Circuits who had no previous training in handling and interpreting ballots. Furthermore, while others were permitted to observe, they were prohibited from objecting during the recount.

The recount process, in its features here described, is inconsistent with the minimum procedures necessary to protect the fundamental right of each voter in the special instance of a statewide recount under the authority of a single state judicial officer. Our consideration is limited to the present circumstances, for the problem of equal protection in election processes generally presents many complexities.

When a court orders a statewide remedy, there must be at least some assurance that the rudimentary requirements of equal treatment and fundamental fairness are satisfied.

Upon due consideration of the difficulties identified to this point, it is obvious that the recount cannot be conducted in compliance with the requirements of equal protection and due process without substantial additional work. It would require not only the adoption (after opportunity for argument) of adequate statewide standards for determining what is a legal vote, and practicable procedures to implement them, but also orderly judicial review of any disputed matters that might arise.

The Supreme Court of Florida has said that the legislature intended the State's electors to "participat[e] fully in the federal electoral process, . . .". That statute, in turn, requires that any controversy or contest that is designed to lead to a conclusive selection of electors be completed by December 12. That date is upon us, and there is no recount procedure in place under the State Supreme Court's order that comports with minimal constitutional standards. Because it is evident that any recount seeking to meet the December 12 date will be unconstitutional for the reasons we have discussed, we reverse the judgment of the Supreme Court of Florida ordering a recount to proceed.

Seven Justices of the Court agree that there are constitutional problems with the recount ordered by the Florida Supreme Court that demand a remedy. The only disagreement is as to the remedy.

None are more conscious of the vital limits on judicial authority than are the members of this Court, and none stand more in admiration of the Constitution's design to leave the selection of the President to the people, through their legislatures, and to the political sphere. When contending parties invoke the process of the courts, however, it becomes our unsought responsibility to resolve the federal and constitutional issues the judicial system has been forced to confront.

Reversed and remanded.

CHIEF JUSTICE REHNQUIST, with whom Justice SCALIA and Justice THOMAS join, concurring.
This inquiry does not imply a disrespect for state courts but rather a respect for the constitutionally prescribed role of state legislatures. To attach definitive weight to the pronouncement of a state court, when the very question at issue is whether the court has actually departed from the statutory meaning,

would be to abdicate our responsibility to enforce the explicit requirements of Article II.

Justice STEVENS, with whom Justice GINSBURG and Justice BREYER join, dissenting.

The Constitution assigns to the States the primary responsibility for determining the manner of selecting the Presidential electors. See Art. II, § 1, cl. 2. When questions arise about the meaning of state laws, including election laws, it is our settled practice to accept the opinions of the highest courts of the States as providing the final answers. On rare occasions, however, either federal statutes or the Federal Constitution may require federal judicial intervention in state elections. This is not such an occasion.

The legislative power in Florida is subject to judicial review pursuant to Article V of the Florida Constitution, and nothing in Article II of the Federal Constitution frees the state legislature from the constraints in the state constitution that created it. Moreover, the Florida Legislature's own decision to employ a unitary code for all elections indicates that it intended the Florida Supreme Court to play the same role in Presidential elections that it has historically played in resolving electoral disputes. The Florida Supreme Court's exercise of appellate jurisdiction therefore was wholly consistent with, and indeed contemplated by, the grant of authority in Article II.

Nor are petitioners correct in asserting that the failure of the Florida Supreme Court to specify in detail the precise manner in which the "intent of the voter," is to be determined rises to the level of a constitutional violation. We found such a violation when individual votes within the same State were weighted unequally, but we have never before called into question the substantive standard by which a State determines that a vote has been legally cast. And there is no reason to think that the guidance provided to the factfinders, specifically the various canvassing boards, by the "intent of the voter" standard is any less sufficient—or will lead to results any less uniform—than, for example, the "beyond a reasonable doubt" standard employed everyday by ordinary citizens in courtrooms across this country.

Admittedly, the use of differing substandards for determining voter intent in different counties employing similar voting systems may raise serious concerns. Those concerns are alleviated—if not eliminated—by the fact that a single impartial magistrate will ultimately adjudicate all objections arising from the recount process.

Even assuming that aspects of the remedial scheme might ultimately be found to violate the Equal Protection Clause, I could not subscribe to the majority's disposition of the case. As the majority explicitly holds, once a state legislature determines to select electors through a popular vote, the right to have one's vote counted is of constitutional stature. As the majority further acknowledges, Florida law holds that all ballots that reveal the intent of the voter constitute valid votes. Recognizing these principles, the majority nonetheless orders the termination of the contest proceeding before all such votes have been tabulated. Under their own reasoning, the appropriate course of action would be to remand to allow more specific procedures for implementing the legislature's uniform general standard to be established. In the interest of finality, however, the majority effectively orders the disenfranchisement of an unknown number of voters whose ballots reveal their intent—and are therefore legal votes under state law—but were for some reason rejected by ballot-counting machines. It does so on the basis of the deadlines set forth in Title 3 of the United States Code. But, as I have already noted, those provisions merely provide rules of decision for Congress to follow when selecting among conflicting slates of electors. They do not prohibit a State from counting what the majority concedes to be legal votes until a bona fide winner is determined.

Thus, nothing prevents the majority, even if it properly found an equal protection violation, from ordering relief appropriate to remedy that violation without depriving Florida voters of their right to have their votes counted. As the majority notes, "[a] desire for speed is not a general excuse for ignoring equal protection guarantees."

What must underlie petitioners' entire federal assault on the Florida election procedures is an unstated lack of confidence in the impartiality and capacity of the state judges who would make the critical decisions if the vote count were to proceed. Otherwise, their position is wholly without merit. The endorsement of that position by the majority of this Court can only lend credence to the most cynical appraisal of the work of judges throughout the land. It is confidence in the men and women who administer the judicial system that is the true backbone of the rule of law. Time will one day heal the wound to that confidence that will be inflicted by today's decision. One thing, however, is certain. Although we may never know with complete certainty the identity

(continued)

of the winner of this year's Presidential election, the identity of the loser is perfectly clear. It is the Nation's confidence in the judge as an impartial guardian of the rule of law.

I respectfully dissent.

Justice SOUTER, with whom Justice BREYER joins and with whom Justice STEVENS and Justice GINSBURG join with regard to all but Part C, dissenting.

The Court should not have reviewed either *Bush* v. *Palm Beach County Canvassing Bd.*, or this case, and should not have stopped Florida's attempt to recount all undervote ballots, by issuing a stay of the Florida Supreme Court's orders during the period of this review. If this Court had allowed the State to follow the course indicated by the opinions of its own Supreme Court, it is entirely possible that there would ultimately have been no issue requiring our review, and political tension could have worked itself out in the Congress following the procedure provided in 3 U.S.C. § 15.

CASE QUESTIONS

1. Describe the issues that the parties raised about the voting results and their tabulation in the Florida presidential election.

2. Describe which courts were involved prior to the U.S. Supreme Court and why.

3. Can you determine which judges decided what and who was part of the PER CURIAM opinion? Explain.

4. What does the court interpret in the case?

5. What does the U.S. Supreme Court decide to do about the recounts and the election? Why?

6. How will this case serve as precedent?

The U.S. Supreme Court also acts as a trial court or a court of **original jurisdiction** in certain cases. When one state is suing another state, the U.S. Supreme Court becomes the states' trial court. For example, the water dispute among California, Arizona, Colorado, and Nevada has been tried over a period of years by the U.S. Supreme Court. The Court also handles the trials (on an espionage charge, for example) of ambassadors and foreign consuls.

Structure   The U.S. Supreme Court consists of nine judges, who are nominated to the Court by the president and confirmed by the Senate. The appointment runs for a lifetime. A president who has the opportunity to appoint a Supreme Court justice is shaping the structure of the Court and the resulting decisions. For this reason, the U.S. Supreme Court is often labeled "conservative" or "liberal." The makeup of the bench controls the philosophy and decisions of the Court.

Review online Supreme Court cases:
http://supct.law.cornell.edu/supct/index.html
and
www.supremecourtus.gov

Opinions   Because the Court is the highest in the land, its opinions are precedent for every other court in the country. The importance of these opinions has resulted in three different volumes of reporters for U.S. Supreme Court opinions. The first is the ***United States Reports*** (abbreviated "U.S."). These reports are put out by the U.S. Government Printing Office and are the official reports of the Court. Because these reports are often slow to be published, two private companies publish opinions in the ***Supreme Court Reporter*** (abbreviated "S. Ct.") and the ***Lawyer's Edition*** (abbreviated "L. Ed." or "L. Ed.2d"). The three-part cite for *Bush* v. *Gore* follows:

531 U.S. 98 (2000)
148 L. Ed.2d 388 (2000)
121 S.Ct. 525 (2000)

BIOGRAPHY

SANDRA DAY O'CONNOR: FIRST WOMAN OF U.S. SUPREME COURT

During his 1980 presidential campaign, Ronald Reagan said, "One of the first Supreme Court vacancies in my administration will be filled by the most qualified woman I can find, one who meets the high standards I demand for all my appointments." When Justice Potter Stewart stepped down in July 1981, Mr. Reagan had the responsibility of nominating a justice for the Supreme Court bench.

Sandra Day O'Connor, who earned her undergraduate and law degrees at Stanford University, was recommended by the late Senator Barry Goldwater and, ultimately, was nominated by Mr. Reagan and confirmed by the Senate on September 15, 1981. Confirmed by a vote of 99–0, she became the first woman to occupy the bench of the Supreme Court.

Justice O'Connor had served as a senator in the Arizona State Senate and was serving as an Arizona Court of Appeals judge at the time of her nomination.

Judge O'Connor was raised on her family's ranch in Eastern Arizona. When she graduated from high school at age 16, she went immediately to Stanford, where she earned both her bachelor's and J. D. degrees in five years total. Chief Justice William Rehnquist was in her law school class, and they graduated number 1 and 2, respectively. She worked as a deputy county attorney for two years in San Mateo, California, before she married. She traveled with her husband in his role as a member of the Army Judge Advocate General Corps but also worked as a civilian lawyer on Army cases.

She had three sons and worked in private practice until she became an assistant attorney general in Arizona. From 1969 to 1974, she served in the Arizona State Senate and was the first woman to serve as majority leader there. From 1974 to 1980, she was a trial judge for Maricopa County Superior Court. From 1980 to 1981, she served on Arizona's Court of Appeals.

When Mr. Reagan nominated Judge O'Connor, he described her as "truly a 'person for all seasons,' possessing those unique qualities of temperament, fairness, intellectual capacity and devotion to the public good which have characterized the 101 'brethren' who have preceded her."

The American Bar Association gave Judge O'Connor a qualified endorsement. The ABA noted her judicial temperament and integrity but felt that she did not have sufficient experience as a judge or attorney and that her experience was not "as extensive or challenging as that of some other persons." Many commented that a man with O'Connor's record would not have been nominated.

Two years later, Justice O'Connor, in a speech to the American Law Institute, spoke of how one gets to be a justice on the U.S. Supreme Court:

While there are many supposed criteria for the selection of a justice, when the eventual decision is made as to who the nominee will be, that decision from the nominee's viewpoint is probably a classic example of being the right person in the right spot at the right time. Stated simply, you must be lucky. That certainly is how I view my nomination.

ISSUES

1. Do you think gender was the sole criterion?
2. Is Justice O'Connor right? Is it luck?

EXHIBIT 3.3
Typical State Court System

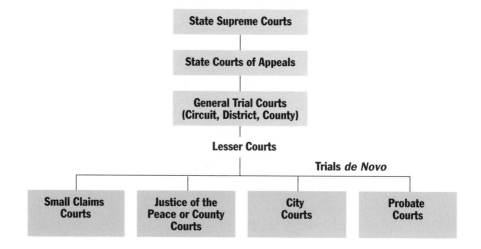

The State Court Systems

Learn more about the state court system:
http://www.ncsconline.org
Review state court decisions for selected states:
http://law.house.gov/17.htm

Although each state court has a different structure for its court system and the courts may have different names, there is a basic structure in each state that is similar to the federal system. Exhibit 3.3 is a diagram of a sample state court system.

State Trial Courts

Each state has its own general trial court. This court is usually called a circuit, district, county, or superior court. It is the court in which nondiversity civil cases are heard and state criminal cases are tried.

In addition to its general trial court, each state also has its own group of "lesser courts." These are courts with **limited jurisdiction;** they are comparable to the specialty courts of the federal system. For example, most states have a **small claims court** in which civil cases with minimal damage claims are tried. In a true small claims court, there are no attorneys. Parties represent themselves before a judge. Such a setting offers parties the chance to have a judge arrive at a solution without the expense of attorneys. The amount recoverable in small claims court is indeed very small: $200–$5,000 are the typical limits.

The records of the Maricopa County Superior Court can be found at
http://www.maricopa.gov

Most states also have a lesser court that allows the participation of lawyers but limits the amount that can be recovered. The idea is to take the burden of lesser cases away from the usually overburdened general trial courts. These courts are called **justice of the peace courts** or **county courts.**

Most cities also have their own trial courts, which are limited in their jurisdiction to the trial of lesser crimes, such as a violation of a city ordinance. Many states call these courts **traffic courts,** because city ordinances involve so many traffic regulations.

In addition to these courts, some states have very specialized courts to handle matters that are narrow in their application of law but frequent in occurrence. For example, although probating (processing) a will and an estate involves narrow issues of law, there is a constant supply of this type of case. Many states have a special court to handle this and such related matters as guardianships for incompetent persons.

EXHIBIT 3.4 **National Reporter System Regions**

Pacific (P. or P.2d)	Northwestern (N.W. or N.W.2d)	Northeastern (N.E. or N.E.2d)	Southeastern (S.E. or S.E.2d)
Alaska	Iowa	Illinois	Georgia
Arizona	Michigan	Indiana	North Carolina
(California)	Minnesota	Massachusetts	South Carolina
Colorado	Nebraska	(New York)	Virginia
Hawaii	North Dakota	Ohio	West Virginia
Idaho	South Dakota		
Kansas	Wisconsin	**Atlantic (A. or A.2d)**	**Southern (So. or So.2d)**
Montana		Connecticut	Alabama
Nevada	**Southwestern (S.W. or S.W.2d)**	Delaware	Florida
New Mexico	Arkansas	District of Columbia	Louisiana
Oklahoma	Kentucky	Maine	Mississippi
Oregon	Missouri	Maryland	
Utah	Tennessee	New Hampshire	
Washington	Texas	New Jersey	
Wyoming		Pennsylvania	
		Rhode Island	
		Vermont	

Note: California and New York each has its own reporter system.

Source: The national reporter system was developed by West Publishing Company. Reprinted with permission of West Publishing Company.

Many of the lesser courts allow appeals to a general state trial court for a new trial (trial *de novo*) because not all judges in these lesser courts are lawyers and constitutional protections require a right of *de novo* appeal.

State Appellate Courts

State appellate courts serve the same function as the U.S. courts of appeals. There is an automatic right of review in these courts. Some states have two appellate-level courts to handle the number of cases being appealed. The opinions of these courts are reported in the state's individual reporter, which contains the state's name and some indication that an appellate court decided the case. For example, state appellate decisions in Colorado are reported in *Colorado Appeals Reports* (abbreviated "Colo. App."). These opinions are also reported in a **regional reporter.** All of the states are grouped into regions, and opinions of state appellate courts are grouped into the reporter for that region. Exhibit 3.4 presents the various regions and state groupings. For example, Nevada is part of the Pacific region, and its appellate reports are found in the *Pacific Reporter* (abbreviated "P.," "P.2d," or "P.3d").

State Supreme Courts

State supreme courts are similar in their function and design to the U.S. Supreme Court. These courts do not hear every case, because the right of appeal is not automatic. There is some discretion in what these supreme courts will hear. State

BUSINESS STRATEGY

In May 2001, Boeing Company announced that it was moving its corporate headquarters from Seattle, Washington, to Chicago, Illinois. When the announcement was made, many plaintiffs' lawyers for airline crash victims cheered. Cook County courts traditionally have juries drawn from blue collar workers who tend to be very tough on business. One lawyer said, "Any case in Cook County is worth more than it would be in most places on earth." Cook County is home to a 1994 settlement for a US Air plane crash of $25.2 million for one family. The settlement remains the largest in aviation history.

Most airline crash suits are brought in federal district court because of the diversity of citizenship

©AFP/CORBIS

of the parties, the passengers, and the airlines. Which federal court remains a venue issue; and most courts will allow cases to be filed where the defendant is located; in the case of an airline that venue is where it is headquartered. So, plaintiffs in airline crashes can now file in Cook County, Boeing's new residency for purposes of federal district court diversity.

In choosing a business location, the common strategic factors are often taxes, workforce, education resources, transportation, and climate. Businesses should add one more strategic factor: litigation climate.

Source: Blake Morrison, "Crash Lawyers Like Boeing Move," *USA Today*, 16 May 2001, 1A.

Visit state courts online:
http://www.ljextra.com/courthouse/statelinks.html

Visit the state court locator:
http://www.clip.org/State-Ct

supreme courts also act as trial courts in certain types of cases and are courts of original as well as appellate jurisdiction. For example, if two counties within a state have a dispute, the state supreme court would take the trial to ensure fairness. After a state supreme court decides an issue, it is important to remember that there is still a possibility of appeal to the U.S. Supreme Court if the case involves a federal question or an issue of constitutional rights.

The opinions of state supreme courts are significant and are reported in the regional reporters discussed earlier. Many states also have their own reporters for state supreme court opinions. For example, California has the *California Reporter*. The state supreme court reporters are easily recognized because their abbreviations are the abbreviation of each state's name. The following cite is one of a state supreme court:

> *Padilla* v. *State*
> 273 Ga. 553, 544 S.E.2d 147 (Ga. 2001)

Judicial Opinions

Throughout the discussion of subject matter jurisdiction, published opinions of various courts have been mentioned. Although these opinions vary in their place of publication, the format is the same. Exhibit 3.5 is a sample page from a reporter, with each part of the excerpt identified. Opinions are reported consistently in this manner so that precedents can be found and used easily.

Venue

The concept of jurisdiction addresses the issue of which court system has the authority to try a case. The concept of **venue** addresses the issue of the location of the court in the system. For example, a criminal case in which a defendant is charged with a felony can be tried in any of a state's general trial courts. Heavy

STATE v. REMY

Cite as 711 A.2d 665 (Vt. 1998)

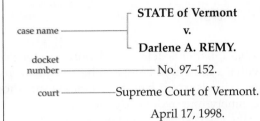

case name — STATE of Vermont
v.
Darlene A. REMY.

docket number — No. 97–152.

court — Supreme Court of Vermont.

April 17, 1998.

Defendant was convicted on a conditional guilty plea in the District Court, Unit No. 1, Bennington Circuit, Robert Grussing III, J., of driving under the influence (DUI). Defendant appealed. The Supreme Court, Morse, J., held that: (1) police officer had probable cause to believe an assault against a household member had occurred, and therefore was authorized to make a warrantless arrest after stopping the vehicle; and (2) officer was entitled to stop the vehicle to issue a citation and then investigate further regarding probable cause to arrest for DUI.

decision of the court — Affirmed

1. Arrest 63.4(11)

decision issue research tool — Police officer, who had been informed of report that occupants of particular vehicle had been drinking and had committed assault against one occupant's former husband, had probable cause to believe an assault against a household member had occurred, and therefore was authorized to make a warrantless arrest after stopping vehicle. Rules Crim. Proc., Rule 3(a).

2. Automobiles 349(7)

Police officer with authority to make warrantless arrest of occupant of vehicle for assault of household member was entitled to stop the vehicle to issue a citation, and, having detected clear signs of intoxication, the officer was then authorized to investigate further in order to confirm or negate his suspicions regarding probable cause to arrest for driving under the influence (DUI). Rules Crim.Proc., Rule 3(c).

William D. Wright, Bennington County State's Attorney, David R. Fenster, Deputy State's Attorney, and Mary Pat Murphy, Law Clerk (on the brief), Bennington, for Plaintiff–Appellee. — attorneys for parties
David A. Howard and Joyce Brennan, Law Clerk (on the brief), of Cormier & Howard, Bennington, for Defendant–Appellant.

Before AMESTOY, C.J., and GIBSON, DOOLEY, MORSE and JOHNSON, JJ.

MORSE, Justice. — judge deciding case

In these consolidated appeals defendant Darlene Remy challenges her conviction of driving under the influence of intoxicating liquor in violation of 23 V.S.A. § 1201(a)(2), and the related civil suspension of her license under 23 V.S.A. § 1205. She contends that the trial court erred in denying her motion to suppress all evidence relating to the DUI because the police: (1) lacked the statutory authority to stop and detain her under V.R.Cr.P. 3(c); and (2) lacked a reasonable suspicion of wrongdoing necessary to effectuate the stop. We affirm. — opinion

On February 1, 1997, at approximately 5:40 p.m., Officer Rowland of the Bennington Police Department responded to an assault complaint from Stephen Woodie. Woodie informed the officer that he had been on a service call for AAA in the parking lot of the Apple Valley Inn when a van driven by defendant approached. Woodie's former wife, Elaine Palmer, was a passenger in the van. Both women were yelling at Woodie. Palmer eventually got out of the van and punched Woodie in the mouth. At that point, Woodie left in his truck and returned to the service.

EXHIBIT 3.5 Sample Page of a Case in a National Reporter

media coverage, however, may result in a judge's changing the venue of a case from the place where the crime was committed to another trial court where the publicity is less and it is easier to obtain an impartial jury.

IN PERSONAM JURISDICTION OF COURTS: THE AUTHORITY OVER PERSONS

Once the proper court according to subject matter is determined, only half the job is done. For example, a case may involve a million-dollar claim between citizens of different states, in which case federal district court has subject matter jurisdiction over the parties. But there are ninety-four federal districts, so how is it decided which federal court will hear the case? The case will be heard by the federal district court with *in personam* jurisdiction over the parties. Subject matter jurisdiction only partly determines which trial court has jurisdiction; the other jurisdictional issue is power over the parties involved in the case.

The various criteria for determining *in personam* jurisdiction are examined here and are outlined in Exhibit 3.6.

Ownership of Property within the State

A party who owns real property in a state is subject to the jurisdiction of that state's courts for litigation related to that property. Actually, this type of jurisdiction gives the court authority over the person because the person owns a thing in the state. Technically, this type of jurisdiction is called ***in rem jurisdiction.***

**EXHIBIT 3.6
Personal
Jurisdiction**

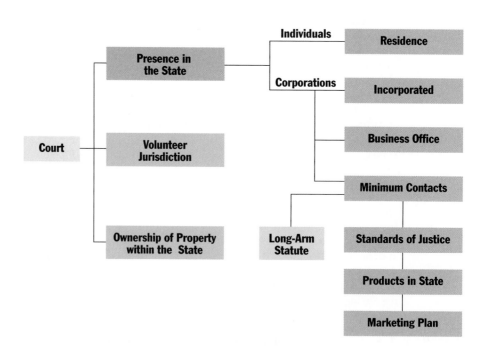

Volunteer Jurisdiction

A court has jurisdiction over a person who agrees to be subject to that court. In some contracts, for example, the parties agree that any lawsuits will be brought in the seller's state. The seller's state courts then have jurisdiction over that volunteer buyer. Most Internet contracts have a venue clause.

Presence in the State

The third and final way a state court can take jurisdiction is by the "presence" of a party in the state, which is determined by different factors.

Residence

Individuals are present in a state if they have a residence in that state. There are different definitions of residency for tax and election laws, but the requirement here is simply that the person live in the state some time during any given year.

Corporations are residents of the states in which they are incorporated. A corporation is also a resident of any state in which it has a business office with employees.

"Minimum Contacts"

Both corporations and residents can be subject to a state court's jurisdiction if they have "minimum contacts" in that state. The standard for **minimum contacts** is a fairness standard, which was established by the U.S. Supreme Court in *International Shoe* v. *Washington*, 326 U.S. 310 (1945). The Court basically required the states to notify out-of-state defendants of a suit and those defendants to have some contact with the state. Such contact can be simply the shipping of a product of the corporation into the state; or the contact can be advertising the firm's product or service in a magazine with national circulation. Fairness does not require an office or an employee in the state. A business is present if its products or ads make their way into the state. These standards for *in personam* jurisdiction are more liberal than the citizenship requirements for diversity actions.

Long Arm Statutes: The Tools of Minimum Contracts

Review a uniform long arm statute:
http://www.law.vill.edu/vls/ student_home/courses/ civpro/unilonga.htm

In order to follow the Supreme Court's ruling on fairness, all of the states have adopted **long arm statutes.** These statutes are appropriately named: They give courts the power to extend their arms of jurisdiction into other states. For example, suppose that Zeta Corporation is incorporated in Ohio and has its manufacturing plant there. Zeta ships its glass baking dishes to every state in the country, although it has no offices anywhere except in Ohio. Joan Berferd, who lives in Alabama, is injured when one of Zeta's baking dishes explodes. Can the Alabama courts allow Berferd to file suit there and require Zeta to come to Alabama to defend the suit? Yes, because a long arm statute is fair if it covers businesses shipping products to the state. Zeta entered the Alabama market voluntarily and must be subject to the Alabama courts. Long arm statutes generally cover businesses with offices in the state, businesses shipping products into the state, and businesses that cause a **tort** to be committed in that state.

The following case provides an answer for the chapter opening "Consider."

CASE 3.2

Bensusan Restaurant Corp. v. *King*
126 F.3d 25 (2d Cir. 1997)

The Long Arm Blues

FACTS

Since 1980, King (defendant) has operated a jazz club under the name "The Blue Note" in Columbia, Missouri. Bensusan (plaintiff) is "the creator of an enormously successful jazz club in New York City called 'The Blue Note,'" which name "was registered as a federal trademark for cabaret services on May 14, 1985." Around 1993, a Bensusan representative wrote to King demanding that he cease and desist from calling his club The Blue Note. King's attorney informed the writer that Bensusan had no legal right to make the demand.

Nothing further was heard from Bensusan until April 1996, when King, at the suggestion of a local Web-site design company, ThoughtPort Authority, Inc., permitted that company to create a Web-site or cyberspot on the Internet for King's cabaret. This work was done in Missouri. Bensusan then brought the instant action in the Southern District of New York, alleging violations of the Lanham Act, 15 U.S.C. §§ 1114(1) & 1125(a), and section 3(c) of the Federal Trademark Dilution Act of 1995 as well as common law unfair competition.

In addition to seeking trebled compensatory damages, punitive damages, costs and attorney's fees, Bensusan requests that King be enjoined from: using the mark "The Blue Note", or any other indicia of the Blue Note in any manner likely to cause confusion, or to cause mistake, or to deceive, or from otherwise representing to the public in any way that [King's club] is in any way sponsored, endorsed, approved, or authorized by, or affiliated or connected with, Plaintiff or its CABARET, by means of using any name, trademark, or service mark of Plaintiff or any other names whatsoever, including but not limited to removal of Defendant's website. . . .

The Web-site describes King's establishment as "Mid-Missouri's finest live entertainment venue, . . . [l]ocated in beautiful Columbia, Missouri," and it contains monthly calendars of future events and the Missouri telephone number of King's box office. Initially, it contained the following text:

The Blue Note's CyberSpot should not be confused with one of the world's finest jazz club Blue Note, located in the heart of New York's Greenwich Village. If you should ever find yourself in the big apple give them a visit.

This text was followed by a hyperlink that could be used to connect a reader's computer to a Web-site maintained by Bensusan. When Bensusan objected to the above-quoted language, King reworded the disclaimer and removed the hyperlink, substituting the following disclaimer that continues in use:

The Blue Note, Columbia, Missouri, should not be confused in any way, shape, or form with Blue Note Records or the jazz club, Blue Note, located in New York. The CyberSpot is created to provide information for Columbia, Missouri, area individuals only, any other assumptions are purely coincidental.

The district court dismissed the complaint in a scholarly opinion that was published in 937 F.Supp. 295 (1996). Bensusan appealed.

JUDICIAL OPINION

VAN GRAAFEILAND, Circuit Judge

Although we realize that attempting to apply established trademark law in the fast-developing world of the internet is somewhat like trying to board a moving bus, we believe that well-established doctrines of personal jurisdiction law support the result reached by the district court.

In diversity or federal question cases the court must look first to the long-arm statute of the forum state, in this instance, New York. If the exercise of jurisdiction is appropriate under that statute, the court then must decide whether such exercise comports with the requisites of due process. Because we believe that the exercise of personal jurisdiction in the instant case is proscribed by the law of New York, we do not address the issue of due process.

The New York law dealing with personal jurisdiction based upon tortious acts of a non-domiciliary who does not transact business in New York is contained in sub-paragraphs (a)(2) and (a)(3) of CPLR § 302, and Bensusan claims jurisdiction with some degree of inconsistency under both sub-paragraphs.

Because King does not transact business in New York State, Bensusan makes no claim under section 302(a)(1). The legislative intent behind the enactment of sub-paragraphs (a)(2) and (a)(3) best can be gleaned by reviewing their disparate backgrounds. Sub-paragraph (a)(2), enacted in 1962, provides in pertinent part that a New York court may exercise personal jurisdiction over a non-domiciliary who "in person or through an agent" commits a tortious act within the state. The New York Court of Appeals has construed this provision in several cases. In *Feathers* v. *McLucas*, 15 N.Y.2d 443, 458, 261 N.Y.S.2d 8, 209 N.E.2d 68 (1965), the Court held that the language "commits a tortious act within the state," as contained in sub-paragraph (a)(2), is "plain and precise" and confers personal jurisdiction over nonresidents "when they commit acts within the state." *Feathers* adopted the view that CPLR § 302(a)(2) reaches only tortious acts performed by a defendant who was physically present in New York when he performed the wrongful act. The official Practice Commentary to CPLR § 302 explains that "if a New Jersey domiciliary were to lob a bazooka shell across the Hudson River at Grant's tomb, *Feathers* would appear to bar the New York courts from asserting personal jurisdiction over the New Jersey domiciliary in an action by an injured New York plaintiff." C302:17. The comment goes on to conclude that:

> As construed by the *Feathers* decision, jurisdiction cannot be asserted over a nonresident under this provision unless the nonresident commits an act in this state. This is tantamount to a requirement that the defendant or his agent be physically present in New York. . . . In short, the failure to perform a duty in New York is not a tortious act in this state, under the cases, unless the defendant or his agent enters the state.

In 1990, Judge McLaughlin, who wrote the above-quoted commentary on section 302(a)(2), further evidenced his belief that the commentary correctly interpreted the statute when he quoted its substance in *Twine* v. *Levy*, 746 F.Supp. 1202, 1206 (E.D.N.Y.1990).

Applying these principles, we conclude that Bensusan has failed to allege that King or his agents committed a tortious act in New York as required for exercise of personal jurisdiction under CPLR § 302(a)(2). The acts giving rise to Bensusan's lawsuit—including the authorization and creation of King's web site, the use of the words "Blue Note" and the Blue Note logo on the site, and the creation of a hyperlink to Bensusan's web site—were performed by persons physically present in Missouri and not in New York. Even if Bensusan suffered injury in New York, that does not establish a tortious act in the state of New York within the meaning of § 302(a)(2).

Bensusan's claims under sub-paragraph (a)(3) can be quickly disposed of. Sub-paragraph (a)(2) left a substantial gap in New York's possible exercise of jurisdiction over non-residents because it did not cover the tort of a non-resident that took place outside of New York but caused injury inside the state. Accordingly, in 1966 the New York Legislature enacted sub-paragraph (a)(3), which provides in pertinent part that New York courts may exercise jurisdiction over a non-domiciliary who commits a tortious act without the state, causing injury to person or property within the state. However, once again the Legislature limited its exercise of jurisdictional largess. Insofar as is pertinent herein it restricted the exercise of jurisdiction under sub-paragraph (a)(3) to persons who expect or should reasonably expect the tortious act to have consequences in the state and in addition derive substantial revenue from interstate commerce. To satisfy the latter requirement, Bensusan relies on the arguments that King participated in interstate commerce by hiring bands of national stature and received revenue from customers—students of the University of Missouri—who, while residing in Missouri, were domiciliaries of other states. These alleged facts were not sufficient to establish that substantial revenues were derived from interstate commerce, a requirement that "is intended to exclude non-domiciliaries whose business operations are of a local character."

Affirmed.

CASE QUESTIONS

1. Describe the basis of Bensusan's claim against the Missouri Blue Note.

2. Did The Missouri Blue Note make a distinction on its Web site?

3. What does the New York statute require for long arm jurisdiction?

4. Was the Missouri Blue Note recruiting customers through its Web site?

5. Can Bensusan require King to come to New York and defend a lawsuit?

However, the following case reaches just the opposite result.

CASE 3.3

Alitalia-Linee Aeree Italiane v. *Casinoalitalia.com*
128 F.Supp.2d 340 (E.D. Va. 2001)

Clipping the Wings on Using "Alitalia"

FACTS

Alitalia-Linee Aeree Italiane (plaintiff) ("Alitalia"), an Italian airline, sued Casinoalitalia.com (defendant), the foreign registrant of an allegedly infringing domain name. The plaintiff filed a motion for summary judgment motion under the Anticybersquatting Consumer Protection Act ("ACPA" or the "Act") for determination of whether a mark owner may maintain *in personam* claims against a domain name registrant using Virginia's long arm statute to reach the foreign registrant.

JUDICIAL OPINION

ELLIS, District Judge

Plaintiff is Italy's national airline and is in the business of providing air cargo service and passenger transportation between Italy and the United States, among other foreign countries. Alitalia is the owner of a United States Trademark Registration issued on March 21, 1995, for the mark "Alitalia." Alitalia's founders coined the term "Alitalia," which has been used by the airline since 1957, by combining the words "Ali," which in Italian means "wings," and "d'Italia," which means "Italian"; the term "Alitalia," therefore, literally means "Italian wings."

Since Alitalia began operation in 1957, the airline has made continuous and widespread use of the mark "Alitalia" through extensive advertising and other means by which the carrier promotes and sells its services. In this regard, Alitalia spends approximately $60 million per year in advertising and promoting the "Alitalia" logo and mark. In addition, Alitalia maintains a website for its airline business at <www.alitalia.it> and has registered the Internet domain names <www.alitalia.com> and <www.alitalia.net>. A search of the Internet for the word "alitalia," however, returns not only Alitalia's website, but also an Internet site using the domain name <casinoalitalia.com>, which has no affiliation or connection whatever to Alitalia.

Defendant Technologia JPR, Inc., ("JPR") has registered the domain name <casinoalitalia.com> with registrar Network Solutions, Inc., ("NSI"). JPR is an entity established under the laws of the Dominican Republic, and JPR's NSI registration information lists JPR's place of business (including administrative, technical, and billing contacts) as located in Santo Domingo, Dominican Republic. JPR conducts its business entirely outside of the United States, and the company has no offices or other physical presence in the United States; it neither owns nor leases property in the United States and has no employees in the United States. Alitalia claims that JPR registered the domain name on or about October 13, 1999, although it appears from NSI's registration information that JPR registered the domain name with NSI in August 1998.

It is evident from a visit to <casinoalitalia.com> that the website exists for the purpose of conducting the business of online casino gambling. A visitor to the website can play one or more online casino games—e.g., blackjack, poker, keno, slots, craps, and roulette—by opening an account with <casinoalitalia.com> and purchasing casino "credits" that may be used to play individual games. Players can then win credits that can be redeemed for U.S. currency. In this regard, the website appears to be an attempt to simulate the experience of gambling at a conventional "brick and mortar" casino.

A visit to the website also reveals that the term "Alitalia" appears on the first page. Given this, Alitalia, which has not given JPR permission to use the mark "Alitalia" or any variation thereof for any purpose, claims that the domain name <casinoalitalia.com> and JPR's unauthorized use of the term "alitalia" create a false impression that Alitalia promotes the business of online gambling and/or any other enterprise pursued by defendants.

Indeed, Alitalia claims that the word "casino" means "brothel," so that a literal translation of "casinoalitalia" is "alitalia's brothel." Thus, argues Alitalia, the site appears in the minds of consumers familiar with the Italian language to offer the services of a brothel associated or affiliated with Alitalia. In this regard, plaintiff contends, the website <casinoalitalia.com> irreparably harms, tarnishes, and dilutes the goodwill, reputation, and image of the Alitalia mark.

It is well-settled that the resolution of a challenge to *in personam* jurisdiction involves a two-step inquiry. First, a court must determine whether the particular facts and circumstances of the case fall within the reach of Virginia's long-arm statute. Second, a court must decide whether the long-arm statute's reach in the case exceeds its constitutional grasp—namely, whether the exercise of personal jurisdiction in the matter is consistent with traditional notions of fair play and substantial justice under the Due Process Clause. [T]he plaintiff ultimately bears the burden of proving the existence of personal jurisdiction by a preponderance of the evidence. *America Online, Inc.* v. *Huang,* 106 F.Supp.2d 848, 853 (E.D.Va.2000).

These principles, applied here, compel the conclusion that Section 8.01-328.1(A)(4) of the Virginia long-arm statute reaches JPR's contacts with Virginia and that this reach is constitutional. Section 8.01-328.1(A)(4) provides for *in personam* jurisdiction over a person (i) who causes tortious injury (ii) in Virginia (iii) by an act or omission outside of Virginia if that person (a) regularly does or solicits business in Virginia, (b) engages in any other persistent course of conduct in Virginia, or (c) derives substantial revenue from goods used or consumed or services rendered in Virginia. Here, the requirement of a tortious injury is met; trademark infringement is a tort. And, "for domain name disputes based on federal or common law trademark infringement . . . , the relevant tortious act is the use of the domain name." Thus, insofar as JPR uses an allegedly infringing domain name by using <casinoalitalia.com> on its servers in the Dominican Republic, it commits a tortious act outside Virginia. This act, moreover, causes injury in Virginia, as it is alleged that JPR's use of <casinoalitalia.com> on the Internet (i) is likely to cause confusion, mistake, and deception of Virginia consumers and (ii) dilutes the distinctive quality of Alitalia's famous mark, and thereby damages Alitalia's business, reputation, and goodwill among Virginia consumers. Finally, JPR "engages in a persistent course of conduct in Virginia" through its maintenance of <casinoalitalia.com>, an interactive website accessible to Virginia consumers 24 hours a day. Accordingly, the Virginia long-arm statute, by its terms, reaches JPR, and the next question is whether this reach comports with due process.

The Due Process Clause requires that no defendant be haled into court unless he has "certain minimum contacts" with the forum state "such that the maintenance of the suit does not offend 'traditional notions of fair play and substantial justice.'" (*International Shoe Co.* v. *Washington,* 326 U.S. 310, 316, 66 S.Ct. 154, 90 L.Ed. 95 (1945)). Moreover, jurisdiction is only appropriate in circumstances where a defendant has purposefully directed his activities at residents of the forum, resulting in litigation that emanates from alleged injuries arising out of or relating to those activities. But merely because a defendant is aware "that the stream of commerce may or will sweep the product into the forum State does not convert the mere act of placing the product into the stream into an act purposefully directed toward the forum State." Rather, the defendant must have " 'purposely avail[ed] itself of the privilege of conducting activities within the forum state' . . . to ensure that a defendant will not be haled into a jurisdiction solely as a result of 'random,' 'fortuitous,' or 'attenuated' contacts."

No published Fourth Circuit opinion definitively addresses the exercise of personal jurisdiction in Internet domain name disputes. A majority of courts that have addressed the issue have examined "the nature and quality of activity that a defendant conducts over the Internet," and have applied the analytical "sliding scale" formulated in *Zippo Manufacturing Co.* v. *Zippo Dot Com, Inc.,* 952 F.Supp. 1119 (W.D.Pa.1997); see *Millennium Enters., Inc.* v. *Millennium Music, LP,* 33 F.Supp.2d 907, 916 (D.Or.1999). The district court in *Zippo* described a continuum of three principle [sic] types of Internet jurisdiction cases. At one end of the continuum lie businesses or persons who clearly conduct business over the Internet and have repeated contacts with the forum state such that the exercise of in personam jurisdiction is proper. Thus, for example, "[i]f the defendant enters into contracts with residents of a foreign jurisdiction that involve the knowing and repeated transmission of computer files over the Internet, personal jurisdiction is proper." At the other end of the continuum are defendants who have done nothing more than post information or advertising on a website that is

(continued)

accessible to users in the forum jurisdiction. In this regard, "[a] passive Web site that does little more than make information available to those who are interested in it is not grounds for the exercise of personal jurisdiction." The middle ground between the two poles "is occupied by interactive Web sites where a user can exchange information with the host computer," and, there, "the exercise of jurisdiction is determined by examining the level of interactivity and commercial nature of the exchange of information that occurs on the Web site." Simply put, as the level of interactivity of the website and the commercial nature of the exchange of information increase, the more reasonable it is to conclude that a defendant directed its activities purposefully at the forum state and should reasonably have foreseen being haled into court in the forum jurisdiction.

This analysis, applied here, points persuasively to the conclusion that JPR's contacts with Virginia constitute sufficient minimum contacts and purposeful availment to satisfy due process requirements. First, <casinoalitalia.com> provides intense real-time interactivity to its members; indeed, the product that JPR markets and provides through <casinoalitalia.com>—namely, online casino gambling—is an inherently interactive activity. Moreover, the provision of this product necessarily requires JPR to enter into contracts with <casinoalitalia.com> members, who must purchase "credits" in order to play individual games. This makes clear that JPR's website is not merely a passive website, placed into the stream of Internet commerce and not purposefully directed at Virginia

or its residents, but rather is a website that interacts with Virginia consumers to such degree as to put JPR on notice that it is purposefully directing its activities at Virginia and its residents. Second, the record discloses that Virginia residents have visited, joined, and played games on casinoalitalia.com. Of the 750 members of the online gambling website, five have provided billing addresses in Virginia. Defendants' contacts with these residents are sufficient to put JPR on notice that it is purposefully directing its activities at Virginia, and that it should therefore foresee being haled into court in this forum.

These Virginia members undoubtedly played the games in Virginia as if they were at a casino in Virginia, and any winnings earned would have been sent to Virginia. As in Thompson, therefore, the nature and extent of JPR's contacts with Virginia and its residents are sufficient to satisfy the requirements of due process.

Accordingly, JPR is subject to in personam jurisdiction in Virginia. . . .

CASE QUESTIONS

1. What infringement is alleged?
2. What is the purpose of the Web site at issue?
3. What does Virginia's long-arm statute require? How is it different from New York's statute?
4. How are the Web sites in the two cases different?
5. Can Virginia take jurisdiction over the defendant?

Do you think that Casinoalitalia.com has taken advantage of Alitalia's good- **ETHICAL ISSUES 3.1** will? Do you think it is ethical to do so?

CONSIDER...

3.2 Courts vary in their positions as to whether a Web site subjects a company to jurisdiction of the courts of all 50 states. How could this issue be finally resolved?

THE INTERNATIONAL COURTS

The decisions of international courts provide precedent for parties involved in international trade. However, one of the restrictions on international court decisions is that the decision binds only the immediate parties to the suit on the basis of their factual situation. International courts do not carry the enforcement power or authority carried by courts in the U.S. federal and state systems. They are consensual courts and are only used when the parties agree to use them.

There are several courts of international jurisdiction. The **International Court of Justice** (ICJ) is the most widely known court. It was first established as the Permanent Court of International Justice (PCIJ) in 1920 by the League of Nations. In 1945, the United Nations (UN) changed the name and structure of the court. The ICJ is made up of fifteen judges, no more than two of whom can be from the same nation, who are elected by the General Assembly of the UN. The court has been described as having *contentious jurisdiction*, which is to say that the court's jurisdiction is consensual: When there is a dispute, the parties can agree to submit the dispute to the ICJ.

There are other international courts in addition to the ICJ. The European Union has its **Court of Justice of European Communities** and the **European Court of Human Rights.** Jurisdiction in these courts is also consensual. Finally, there is the **Inter-American Court of Human Rights.**

The decisions of these courts and decisions from individual countries' courts dealing with international law issues can be found in *International Law Reports.*

In recent years, London's Commercial Court, established over 100 years ago, has become a popular forum for the resolution of international commercial disputes. Over half the cases in this court involve foreign enterprises. Some companies choose London's Commercial Court as the forum for their disputes for several reasons, even though neither they nor their transaction have any connection with England. First, the court has the advantage of being a neutral forum. Second, for U.S. firms, the use of the English language in the court is important. Third, the court has a wide range of experience in international disputes, from shipping contracts to joint trading ventures. Fourth, the judges on the court were all once commercial litigators themselves and bring their depth of experience to the cases. Fifth, the court is known for its rapid calendar, moving cases along quickly. Major cases are heard within one year from the service of summons. Finally, the court has used a variety of creative remedies. The Commercial Court has issued pretrial injunctions to freeze assets, and its ties to the English government afford the injunctions international recognition. Perhaps the most famous of the Commercial Court's cases is its handling of the twenty class actions against Lloyd's of London.

Jurisdictional Issues in International Law

The jurisdiction of courts within a particular country over businesses from other countries is a critical issue in international law. A common subject in international

---

Learn more about the International Court of Justice:
http://www.icj-cij.org

BUSINESS PLANNING TIP

With national and international business transactions becoming so frequent, many contracts now include "forum selection" clauses. These portions of a contract to which the parties agree stipulate that if litigation is required, a particular court in a particular state or country will have jurisdiction over both parties. For example, a franchisor might have the forum-selection clause provide that all litigation by franchisees would be in the state and city where the franchisor's principal office is located. Checking a contract carefully for these clauses will enable you to decide, before signing, whether you want to agree to travel to another state or country if litigation becomes necessary.

disputes is whether courts in the United States, for example, can require foreign companies to defend lawsuits within the United States.

Conflicts of Law in International Disputes

The courts and judicial systems of countries around the globe vary, as do the procedural aspects of litigation. For example, in Japan there is no discovery process that permits the parties to examine each others' documents and witnesses prior to trial (see Chapter 4 for more details on discovery and the Japanese court system); and the United States permits lawyers to collect contingency fees and also permits broader tort recovery than would be available in most other countries.

Because of liberal discovery and recovery rules in the United States, many plaintiffs injured in other countries by products manufactured by U.S.-based firms want to bring suit in the United States to take advantage of our judicial system's processes and rules. However, the California Supreme Court has ruled in *Stangvik* v. *Shiley, Inc.*, 819 P.2d 858 (Cal. 1991), that if a plaintiff's home country provides an adequate forum for a dispute, the case cannot be brought in the United States. The suit involved family members of various patients who had died when their heart valves, manufactured by Shiley of Irvine, California, failed. The decision of the California Supreme Court required the plaintiffs to return to their home countries, where the recovery would be substantially less. However, states do differ on their conclusions about international product liability litigation (for a different result see *Ison* v. *E.I. DuPont de Nemours and Co., Inc.*, 729 A.2d 832 (Del. 1999)).

SUMMARY

What is the judicial process?

- Judicial review—review of a trial court's decisions and verdict to determine whether any reversible error was made

- Appellate court—court responsible for review of trial court's decisions and verdict

- Brief—written summary of basis for appeal of trial court's decisions and verdict

- Reversible error—mistake by trial court that requires a retrial or modification of a trial court's decision

  Options for appellate court:

  - Reverse—change trial court's decision

  - Remand—return case to trial court for retrial or reexamination of issues

  - Affirm—uphold trial court's decisions and verdict

  - Modify—overturn a portion of the trial court's verdict

- *Stare decisis*—Latin for "let the decision stand"; doctrine of reviewing, applying, and/or distinguishing prior case decisions

- Case opinion—written court decision used as precedent; contains *dicta* or explanation of reasoning and, often, a minority view or dissenting opinion

Who are the parties in the judicial system?

- Plaintiffs/petitioners—initiators of litigation

- Defendants/respondents—parties named as those from whom plaintiff seeks relief

- Lawyers—officers of the court who speak for plaintiffs and defendants

- Attorney-client privilege—confidential protections for client conversations

- Appellant—party who appeals lower court's decision

- Appellee—party responding in an appeal

What courts can decide jurisdiction? The power of the court to hear cases

- Subject matter jurisdiction—authority of court over subject matter

- Jurisdiction over the parties: *in personam* jurisdiction

  - Voluntary

  - Through property

  - Presence in the state: minimum contacts

  - Residence

  - Business office

What are the courts and court systems?

Federal court system

- Federal district court—trial court in federal system; hears cases in which there is a federal question, the United States is a party, or the plaintiff and defendant are from different states (diversity of citizenship) and the case involves $75,000 or more; opinions reported in *Federal Supplement*

- Limited jurisdiction courts—bankruptcy court, court of claims

- U.S. Courts of Appeals—federal appellate courts in each of the circuits; opinions reported in *Federal Reporter*

- U.S. Supreme Court—highest court in United States; requires *writ of certiorari* for review; acts as trial court (original jurisdiction) for suits involving states and diplomats

State court system

- Lesser courts—small claims, traffic courts, justice of the peace courts

- State trial courts—general jurisdiction courts in each state

- State appellate courts—courts that review trial court decisions

- State supreme courts—courts that review appellate court decisions

International courts

- Voluntary jurisdiction

- International Court of Justice—UN court; contentious (consensual) jurisdiction; reported in *International Law Reports*

- London Commercial Court—voluntary court of arbitration

QUESTIONS AND PROBLEMS

1. The brokerage firm of E.F. Hutton was charged with federal criminal violations of interstate funds transfers. In reviewing the case, the lawyers for the government discovered internal memorands from and between branch managers in several states that outline a process for checking-kiting (a literal stringing together of checks and deposits) that enabled E.F. Hutton to earn interest on phantom deposits. Where will the case be tried? Which court system? Which court? Why?

What are the lawyer's obligations with respect to the document? What is the company's obligation? If you were a manager at Hutton, would you voluntarily disclose the document to the government?

2. Compare the procedures at the trial and appellate levels of the court system. Is additional evidence presented at the appellate level? Will a jury be present at both the trial and the appeal of the case? How many judges will hear the case at the trial and appellate levels?

3. Music Millennium is a business incorporated in Oregon (Oregon MM) with its principal place of business located in Portland, Oregon. It opened its first retail outlet under the name "Music Millennium" in 1969 and now operates two retail music stores in Portland and also sells products through mail and telephone orders and its Internet Web site.

Millennium Music, Inc., is a South Carolina corporation and general partner of defendant Millennium Music, L.P., a South Carolina limited partnership (LP). It operates retail music stores in South Carolina under the name "Millennium Music" and sells products through its retail outlets and its Internet Web site, although the vast majority of sales occur at its retail stores. From March 1998 through September 1998, the LP sold fifteen compact discs to nine separate customers in six states and one foreign country. The sales totaled approximately $225. During the same period, its retail sales were $2,180,000. LP offers franchising circulars through the Internet and has two franchised stores in North Carolina.

LP has also purchased a small amount of compact discs from Allegro Corporation ("Allegro"), a distributor located in Portland, Oregon. Total purchases from Allegro in 1994–1997 totaled approximately one-half of one percent of inventory purchases for those years.

On or about July 7, 1998, Oregon MM received a credit document from Allegro. The credit was mailed to Oregon MM in error; the document apparently was intended for LP. On August 21, 1998, an Oregon resident, Linda Lufkin, purchased a compact disc from LP through its Web site. An attorney at the law firm for which Ms. Lufkin works requested that she purchase a compact disc from LP. Apparently, the attorney is an acquaintance of Oregon MM's counsel.

Oregon MM filed suit against LP on Oregon for its use of the name "Millennium Music" in connection with common law trademark rights. LP says it cannot be forced to come to Oregon to defend the suit. Is LP correct? [*Millenium Enterprises, Inc. v. Millennium Music, LP,* 33 F.Supp.2d 907 (D.Or. 1999)]

4. Century Gas is a utility in Arizona. In 1989, Century applied to the Arizona Corporation Commission for a rate increase based on an expected increase in the price of natural gas during 1991. The commission ruled, and the appellate court affirmed, that rate decisions could not be based on future events. According to the judicial opinion, rate decisions and increases must be based on historical costs and financial information.

In 1992, Century had a takeover offer from Norwest Utility, a large electric utility from the Pacific Northwest. Century filed an application with the commission to have the takeover approved. If the takeover occurred, Century's costs would decrease nearly 35 percent. In approving the merger, the commission wished also to decrease Century's rates based on the anticipated decrease in costs once the merger took place. Based on precedent, could the commission take this action?

5. Determine which court(s) would have jurisdiction over the following matters:
a. Selling securities without first registering them with the Securities and Exchange Commission, as required under 15 U.S.C. § 77 *et seq.*;
b. A suit between a Hawaiian purchaser of sunscreen lotion and its California manufacturer for severe sunburn that resulted in $65,000 in medical bills.

6. Jeffrey Dawes, the comptroller for Umbrellas, Inc., a New York Stock Exchange company, has been charged with two violations of the federal Foreign Corrupt Practices Act. In which court will he be tried?

7. A Delaware banking corporation was named as trustee for the large estate of a wealthy individual in that individual's will. The beneficiaries of the trust are the deceased's two children, one of whom lives in Pennsylvania and the other in Florida. The bank does business in Delaware only. Can the beneficiary in Florida successfully require the bank to submit to the jurisdiction of Florida courts? [*Hanson v. Denckla,* 357 U.S. 235 (1958).]

8. Eulala Shute lived in Arlington, Washington, and through a local travel agent purchased a seven-day Carnival cruise. The cruise began in Los Angeles, went to Puerto Vallarta, Mexico, and then returned to Los Angeles. Carnival Cruise Lines, Inc., the owner of the ship and the firm responsible for the cruise, is a corporation based in Miami, Florida. While the cruise ship was in international waters off of Mexico, Shute tripped and fell on a deck mat during a guided tour of the ship's galley.

Shute filed suit in federal district court in the state of Washington against Carnival to recover for her injuries. Could the Washington court take *in personam* jurisdiction over Carnival? [*Carnival Cruise Lines, Inc. v. Shute,* 499 U.S. 585 (1991).]

9. Hicklin Engineering, Inc., is a Minnesota corporation that manufactures transmission testing stands for worldwide sales. Hicklin's only place of business is Iowa. Aidco, Inc., is a Michigan corporation with its principal place of business in Michigan. Aidco also manufactures transmission testing stands for worldwide sales. Aidco sent letters to several of Hicklin's customers, raising questions about Hicklin's products and expertise, and offering a promotion of its transmission stands. Aidco is not licensed to do business in Iowa and has no offices, employees, or agents there. Hicklin has filed suit in Iowa against Aidco for the tort of intentional interference with contractual relations. Can Aidco be required to come to Iowa to defend the suit? [*Hicklin Engineering, Inc. v. Aidco, Inc.,* 959 F.2d 738 (8th Cir. 1992).]

10. The words "I've fallen and I can't get up!" were part of a TV commercial for a device whose marketing was directed at the elderly and whose appeal was that the device was hooked to communication links with emergency care providers. In fact, the device provided a link, but not a direct link, to a "911" number; there would be some interlink delay in getting notification to emergency personnel. The devices, worn around the neck, were in fact a means of effecting communication when the wearer could not get to a phone. However, the device was not directly linked to a "911" number.

Officials in Arizona brought charges against the company for deceptive advertising. Standards in Arizona require proof only that someone could be misled by the commercials; actions against advertisers do not require proof that someone was actually misled. The devices have been a help to many people, bringing assistance to those who would otherwise, because of temporary or permanent mobility impairment, be unable to call for help. Officials in other states did not find the ads misleading. Does Arizona have jurisdiction?

If you were an official for the company, would you change all of your ads, or modify only those in Arizona? Were the ads unethical?

11. Read the following additional cases and provide a summary of where the courts stand on Web sites and long arm jurisdiction:

Inset Systems, Inc. v. Instruction Set, Inc., 937 F.Supp. 161 (D.Ct. 1996)

CompuServe, Inc. v. Patterson, 89 F.3d 1257 (6th Cir. 1996)

Edias Software Int'l, L.L.C. v. Basis International Ltd., Ison v. E.I. DuPont de Nemours and Co., Inc., 729 A.2d 832 (Del. 1999); *Edias software Int'l, L.L.C. v. Basis Int'l LTD.*, 947 F.Supp.413 (D.Ariz.1996)

Should there be a difference between a Web site with a toll-free number and a Web site from which goods can be ordered?

BUSINESS STRATEGY APPLICATION

In the Business Strategy exercise for the CD-ROM, you can walk through the *U.S.* v. *Microsoft* case from the federal district court decision to the petition for certiorari at the U.S. Supreme Court. You can view decisions, briefs and even excerpts from oral arguments at the appellate level. You will be able to see various decision points in the case as well as the risk companies take with litigation.

CHAPTER FOUR

Managing Disputes: Alternative Dispute Resolution and Litigation Strategies

The study of business regulation to this point has involved an overview of ethics, law, and the courts responsible for enforcing, interpreting, and applying the law. This chapter focuses on disputes and answers the following questions: How can businesses best resolve disputes? What strategies should a business follow if litigation is inevitable? How do courts proceed with litigation?

Everyone Makes Mistakes: Real Humor in the Court

The youngest son, the 20-year-old, how old is he?

How many times have you committed suicide?

Were you alone or by yourself?

Q: You were shot in the fracas?

A: No, I was shot midway between the fracas and the navel.

LAWYERS' COURTROOM BLOOPERS FROM THE COLLECTION OF WILLIAM LITANT, EDITOR
Massachusetts Bar Association Lawyers Journal

If I were asked where I place the American aristocracy, I should reply without hesitation that it occupies the judicial bench and bar.

ALEXIS DE TOCQUEVILLE (1805–1859)

CONSIDER...

Gateway Computers included the following provision in its contract for sale of computers to consumers:

10. Dispute Resolution. Any dispute or controversy arising out of or relating to this Agreement or its interpretation shall be settled exclusively and finally by arbitration. The arbitration shall be conducted in accordance with the Rules of Conciliation and Arbitration of the International Chamber of Commerce. The arbitration shall be conducted in Chicago, Illinois, U.S.A., before a sole arbitrator. Any award referenced in any such arbitration proceeding shall be final and binding on each of the parties, and judgment may be entered thereon in a court of competent jurisdiction.

What type of arbitration is required? Is this clause valid and enforceable?

WHAT IS ALTERNATIVE DISPUTE RESOLUTION?

Alternative dispute resolution (ADR) offers parties alternative means of resolving their differences outside actual courtroom litigation and the costly aspects of preparation for it. ADR ranges from very informal options, such as a negotiated settlement between the CEOs of companies, to the formal, written processes of the American Arbitration Association. These processes may be used along with litigation or in lieu of litigation.

TYPES OF ALTERNATIVE DISPUTE RESOLUTION

Arbitration

Nature of Arbitration

Arbitration is the oldest form of ADR and is the resolution of disputes in a less formal setting than a trial. Many contracts today have mandatory arbitration clauses in them that require, in the event of a dispute, that the parties submit to arbitration. Other contracts, including many consumer auto insurance contracts, offer voluntary arbitration for consumers involved in disputes over their coverage.

Arbitration can be binding or nonbinding. Binding arbitration means that the decision of the arbitrators is final. The parties cannot appeal the decision to any court. Nonbinding arbitration is a preliminary step to litigation. If one of the parties is not satisfied with the result in the arbitration, the case may still be litigated.

Arbitration Procedures

Arbitration can be agreed upon well in advance. A contract may contain a future arbitration clause so that the parties agree at the time of contracting that any disputes will be submitted to arbitration. The parties may also agree to submit to arbitration after their dispute arises even though they do not have such a clause in their contract. The issue of mandatory arbitration, particularly when there are consumers involved or employees who have statutory rights, has been a focus of litigation. The Federal Arbitration Act (FAA) was passed to stop some of the judicial decisions that were holding arbitration clauses, particularly in consumer contracts, invalid. In the following case, the U.S. Supreme Court provided its interpretation of the binding nature of arbitration clauses in contracts under the FAA.

Visit the American Arbitration Association: http://www.adr.org

---

CASE 4.1

Green Tree Financial Corp. v. *Randolph*
531 U.S. 79 (2000)

A Mandatory Arbitration Clause? I Dispute That!

FACTS

Larketta Randolph (Respondent) purchased a mobile home from Better Cents Home Builders, Inc., in Opelika, Alabama. She financed this purchase through Green Tree Financial Corporation and its subsidiary (Petitioners). The contract that Ms. Randolph signed, the Manufactured Home Retail Installment Contract and Security Agreement, required that Randolph buy Vendor's Single Interest insurance, which protects the seller (vendor) or lienholder (Green Tree) against the costs of repossession in the event of default. The agreement also provided that all disputes arising from, or relating to, the contract, whether arising under case law or statutory law, would be resolved by binding arbitration. The arbitration clause provides:

All disputes, claims, or controversies arising from or relating to this Contract or the relationships which result from this Contract, or the validity of this arbitration clause or the entire contract, shall be resolved by binding arbitration by one arbitrator selected by Assignee with consent of Buyer(s). This arbitration Contract is made pursuant to a transaction in interstate commerce, and shall be governed by the Federal Arbitration Act at 9 U.S.C. Section 1. Judgment upon the award rendered may be entered in any court having jurisdiction. The parties agree and understand that they choose arbitration instead of litigation to resolve disputes. The parties understand that they have a right or opportunity to litigate disputes through a court, but that they prefer to resolve their disputes through arbitration, except as provided herein. THE PARTIES VOLUNTARILY AND KNOWINGLY WAIVE ANY RIGHT THEY HAVE TO A JURY TRIAL EITHER PURSUANT TO ARBITRATION UNDER THIS CLAUSE OR PURSUANT TO A COURT ACTION BY ASSIGNEE (AS PROVIDED HEREIN). The parties agree and understand that all disputes arising under case law, statutory law, and all other laws, including, but not limited to, all contract, tort, and property disputes will be subject to binding arbitration in accord with this Contract. The parties agree and understand that the arbitrator shall have all powers provided by the law and the Contract.

Ms. Randolph sued Green Tree, as part of a class action lawsuit, alleging that they violated the Truth in Lending Act (TILA), 15 U.S.C. § 1601 et seq., [see Chapter 15 for more information on this statute] by failing to disclose as a finance charge the $15 annual fee she was required to pay for the Vendor's Single Interest insurance requirement. She later amended her complaint to add a claim that petitioners violated the Equal Credit Opportunity Act, 15 U.S.C. §§ 1691-1691f, [See Chapter 15] by requiring her to arbitrate her claims that arose under federal statutes. Green Tree filed a motion to compel arbitration which the District Court granted. Randolph appealed and the Court of Appeals held that the arbitration agreement failed to provide the minimum guarantees for protection of Randolph's statutory rights under the TILA. On that basis, the court held that the agree-

ment to arbitrate posed a risk to Randolph's statutory rights and was therefore unenforceable. Green Tree appealed and the U.S. Supreme court granted *certiorari.*

JUDICIAL OPINION

REHNQUIST, Chief Justice

We now turn to the question whether Randolph's agreement to arbitrate is unenforceable because it says nothing about the costs of arbitration, and thus fails to provide her protection from potentially substantial costs of pursuing her federal statutory claims in the arbitral forum. Section 2 of the FAA provides that "[a] written provision in any maritime transaction or a contract evidencing a transaction involving commerce to settle by arbitration a controversy thereafter arising out of such contract . . . shall be valid, irrevocable, and enforceable, save upon such grounds as exist at law or in equity for the revocation of any contract." In considering whether respondent's agreement to arbitrate is unenforceable, we are mindful of the FAA's purpose "to reverse the longstanding judicial hostility to arbitration agreements . . . and to place arbitration agreements upon the same footing as other contracts."

In light of that purpose, we have recognized that federal statutory claims can be appropriately resolved through arbitration, and we have enforced agreements to arbitrate that involve such claims. We have likewise rejected generalized attacks on arbitration that rest on "suspicion of arbitration as a method of weakening the protections afforded in the substantive law to would-be complainants." . . . [E]ven claims arising under a statute designed to further important social policies may be arbitrated because "'so long as the prospective litigant effectively may vindicate [his or her] statutory cause of action in the arbitral forum,'" the statute serves its functions.

In determining whether statutory claims may be arbitrated, we first ask whether the parties agreed to submit their claims to arbitration, and then ask whether Congress has evinced an intention to preclude a waiver of judicial remedies for the statutory rights at issue. In this case, it is undisputed that the parties agreed to arbitrate all claims relating to their contract, including claims involving statutory rights. Nor does Randolph contend that the TILA evinces an intention to preclude a waiver of judicial remedies. She contends instead that the arbitration agreement's silence with respect to costs and fees creates a "risk"

(continued)

that she will be required to bear prohibitive arbitration costs if she pursues her claims in an arbitral forum, and thereby forces her to forgo any claims she may have against petitioners. Therefore, she argues, she is unable to vindicate her statutory rights in arbitration.

It may well be that the existence of large arbitration costs could preclude a litigant such as Randolph from effectively vindicating her federal statutory rights in the arbitral forum. But the record does not show that Randolph will bear such costs if she goes to arbitration. Indeed, it contains hardly any information on the matter. The record reveals only the arbitration agreement's silence on the subject, and that fact alone is plainly insufficient to render it unenforceable. The "risk" that Randolph will be saddled with prohibitive costs is too speculative to justify the invalidation of an arbitration agreement.

In Randolph's Motion for Reconsideration in the District Court, she asserted that "[a]rbitration costs are high" and that she did not have the resources to arbitrate. But she failed to support this assertion. She first acknowledged that petitioners had not designated a particular arbitration association or arbitrator to resolve their dispute. Her subsequent discussion of costs relied entirely on unfounded assumptions. She stated "[f]or the purposes of this discussion, we will assume filing with the [American Arbitration Association], the filing fee is $500 for claims under $10,000 and this does not include the cost of the arbitrator or administrative fees." Randolph relied on, and attached as an exhibit what appears to be informational material from the American Arbitration Association that does not discuss the amount of filing fees. She then noted "[The American Arbitration Association] further cites $700 per day as the average arbitrator's fee." For this proposition she cited a [sic] article in the Daily Labor Report, February 15, 1996, published by the Bureau of National Affairs, entitled Labor Lawyers at ABA Session Debate Role of American Arbitration Association. The article contains a stray statement by an association executive that the average arbitral fee is $700 per day. Randolph plainly failed to make any factual showing that the American Arbitration Association

would conduct the arbitration, or that, if it did, she would be charged the filing fee or arbitrator's fee that she identified. These unsupported statements provide no basis on which to ascertain the actual costs and fees to which she would be subject in arbitration. In this Court, Randolph's brief lists fees incurred in cases involving other arbitrations as reflected in opinions of other Courts of Appeals, while petitioners' counsel states that arbitration fees are frequently waived by petitioners. None of this information affords a sufficient basis for concluding that Randolph would in fact have incurred substantial costs in the event her claim went to arbitration.

To invalidate the agreement on that basis would undermine the "liberal federal policy favoring arbitration agreements." It would also conflict with our prior holdings that the party resisting arbitration bears the burden of proving that the claims at issue are unsuitable for arbitration. We have held that the party seeking to avoid arbitration bears the burden of establishing that Congress intended to preclude arbitration of the statutory claims at issue. Similarly, we believe that where, as here, a party seeks to invalidate an arbitration agreement on the ground that arbitration would be prohibitively expensive, that party bears the burden of showing the likelihood of incurring such costs. Randolph did not meet that burden.

The judgment of the Court of Appeals is reversed on the issue of the validity of the arbitration clause.

CASE QUESTIONS

1. Describe the effect of the arbitration clause in the contract that Ms. Randolph signed.

2. What is the underlying dispute regarding her contract?

3. What is the relationship between the Truth-in-Lending Act and the FAA?

4. What problems did the court see with Ms. Randolph's arguments about costs of arbitration?

5. Is the arbitration clause valid and binding?

C O N S I D E R . . .

4.1 Review the arbitration clause in the chapter opening "Consider" from the Gateway Computer contract. Based on the *Randolph* case, do you think that this clause is valid and enforceable against the consumers who buy Gateway computers? Does it make a difference that they must travel to Chicago for their arbitration?

Once the parties agree to arbitrate, they usually notify the American Arbitration Association (AAA), which for a fee will handle all the steps in the arbitration. The AAA is the largest ADR provider in the country with an annual case load of 140,188 for 1999, which is a 50 percent increase from 1998. A tribunal administrator is appointed for each case, and this administrator communicates with the parties and helps move the arbitration along. The fee charged by the AAA depends upon the amount of the claim. For example, a claim between $75,000 and $150,000 has a fee of about $2,000 for filing, with the costs and expenses of the abritrator not included. The arbitrator is generally paid by the hour. A multimillion dollar arbitration case will have a $10,000–$15,000 fee plus arbitrator fees and expenses. Exhibit 4.1 is a sample AAA form of a demand for arbitration and the method for beginning arbitration. This document is the complaint form for arbitration.

Once a demand for arbitration is received, the tribunal administrator sends each of the parties a proposed list of arbitrators. Exhibit 4.2 is a sample of such a notice. The parties are given seven days to reject any of the proposed arbitrators and to rank the remaining named possibilities in the order of their preference. The tribunal tries to make a mutually agreeable choice but can submit a new list if necessary. If the parties cannot agree, the AAA appoints an arbitrator but will never appoint anyone rejected by one of the parties.

The hearing date is set at a mutually agreeable time. Between the time the date is set and the actual hearing, the parties have the responsibility of gathering together the evidence and witnesses necessary for their cases. The parties are, in effect, doing their preparation. The parties can also request that the other party bring certain documents to the hearing. Some arbitrators are given subpoena power in certain states; that is, they have the power to require the production of documents or to have a witness testify.

The parties need not have lawyers but have the right to use one under AAA rules. A rule requires that the AAA and other parties be notified if an attorney will be used and that the attorney be identified.

Although the atmosphere is more relaxed, an arbitration hearing parallels a trial. The parties are permitted brief opening statements, after which they discuss the remedy that is sought. Each of the parties then has the opportunity to present evidence and witnesses. There is a right of cross-examination, and closing statements are also given. Some of the emotion of a trial is missing because,

---

> ### BUSINESS PLANNING TIP
>
> The following statistics on medical malpractice cases* offer some compelling reasons for arbitration:
>
> | | Arbitration | Malpractice Lawsuits |
> |---|---|---|
> | Time for resolution | 19 months | 33 months |
> | Length of hearing/trial | 2–4 days | Several weeks |
> | Settlement prior to hearing/trial | 89% | 90% |
> | Decision for plaintiff | 52% | 33% |
> | Decision for defendant | 48% | 67% |
>
> *Source: U.S. General Accounting Office.

American Arbitration Association

MEDIATION   Please consult the Commercial Mediation Rules regarding mediation procedures. If you want the AAA to contact the other party and attempt to arrange a mediation, please check this box. ☐

COMMERCIAL ARBITRATION RULES
DEMAND FOR ARBITRATION

DATE: _____

TO: Name _____
(of the party upon whom the demand is made)

Address _____

City and State _____ ZIP Code _____

Telephone ( ) _____ Fax _____

Name of Representative _____
(if known)

Representative's Address _____

City and State _____ ZIP Code _____

Telephone ( ) _____ Fax _____

The named claimant, a party to an arbitration agreement contained in a written contract, dated _____ _____, providing for arbitration under the Commercial Arbitration Rules, hereby demands arbitration thereunder.

(Attach the arbitration clause or quote it hereunder.)

NATURE OF DISPUTE:

CLAIM OR RELIEF SOUGHT (amount, if any):

TYPE OF BUSINESS: Claimant _____ Respondent _____

HEARING LOCALE REQUESTED: _____
(City and State)

You are hereby notified that copies of our arbitration agreement and of this demand are being filed with the American Arbitration Association at its _____ office, with the request that it commence the administration of the arbitration. Under the rules, you may file an answering statement within ten days after notice from the administrator.

Signed _____ Title _____
(may be signed by a representative)

Name of Claimant _____

Address (to be used in connection with this case) _____

City and State _____ ZIP Code _____

Telephone ( ) _____ Fax _____

Name of Representative _____

Representative's Address _____

City and State _____ ZIP Code _____

Telephone ( ) _____ Fax _____

To institute proceedings, please send three copies of this demand with the administrative fee, as provided for in the rules, to the AAA. Send the original demand to the respondent.

Form C2–11/90

EXHIBIT 4.1   Sample Demand for Arbitration

Source: Form appears courtesy of the American Arbitration Association.

American Arbitration Association

Do not send this form to the other party.

CASE NUMBER: _____ DATE LIST SUBMITTED: _____

PARTIES: _____ AND _____

LIST FOR SELECTION OF ARBITRATOR(S)

After striking the name of any unacceptable arbitrator(s), please indicate your order of preference by number. We will try to appoint arbitrator(s) mutually acceptable who can hear your case promptly. Leave as many names as possible.

NOTE: Biographical information is attached. Unless your response is received by the Association by _____, all names submitted may be deemed acceptable.

REQUEST FOR DATES

To enable the arbitrator(s) to avoid fixing an inconvenient hearing date, please cross off the dates that are not acceptable for a hearing, but leave as many days as possible so that the first mutually agreeable date for hearing may be set. If a mutually agreeable date is not available for these two months, the arbitrator(s) is/are empowered under the rules to fix the time and place for each hearing. If this form is not returned by _____, it will be assumed that any open date is satisfactory to you. The hearing will then be scheduled for a date preferred by the other party.

NOTE: **Saturdays, Sundays, and other unavailable days have been marked off.**

Month of _____
1 2 3 4 5 6 7
8 9 10 11 12 13 14
15 16 17 18 19 20 21
22 23 24 25 26 27 28
29 30 31

Month of _____
1 2 3 4 5 6 7
8 9 10 11 12 13 14
15 16 17 18 19 20 21
22 23 24 25 26 27 28
29 30 31

Please note that hearings generally commence at _____ a.m./p.m.

I anticipate that my case will require _____ **hours/days of hearing.**

PARTY: _____

BY: _____ TITLE: _____

Your telephone or fax response to this inquiry will be appreciated and will expedite administration. Please refer to the telephone and fax numbers on the enclosed letterhead.   Form G4-4/89

EXHIBIT 4.2   Sample List for Selection of Arbitrators

Source: Form appears courtesy of the American Arbitration Association.

although emotional appeal influences juries, an expert arbitrator is not likely to be influenced by it. After the close of the hearing, the arbitrator has thirty days to make a decision.

In binding arbitration, the arbitrator's award is final. The award and decision cannot be changed, modified, or reversed. Only the parties can agree to have the case reopened; the arbitrator cannot do so.

Many state courts, in order to encourage alternative dispute resolution, now impose mandatory arbitration in all cases involving amounts less than $25,000 or $50,000, for example. In Arizona, these mandatory arbitration proceedings are arbitrated by lawyers in the state, who are required to accept such assignments on a rotating basis either for fee or as part of their *pro bono* activities. Such mandatory arbitration requirements have reduced the civil caseloads in many states by as much as 50 percent.

Mediation

Arbitration can be complex and expensive in spite of its self-imposed procedural limitations. However, other forms of alternative dispute resolution are readily available and relatively inexpensive. **Mediation** is one such alternative. In a 1999 survey by the *National Law Journal* and the American Arbitration Association, 88 percent of lawyers indicated mediation as their preferred method of dispute resolution, with most noting that arbitration did not save much money or work over a full-blown trial.[1] Mediation is a process in which both parties meet with a neutral mediator who listens to each side explain its position. The mediator is trained to get the parties to respond to each other and their concerns. The mediator helps break down impasses and works to have the parties arrive at a mutually agreeable solution. Unlike an arbitrator, the mediator does not issue a decision; the role of the mediator is to try to get the parties to agree on a solution. Mediation is completely confidential; what is said to the mediator cannot be used later by the parties or their lawyers in the event litigation becomes necessary. Mediation is less expensive than arbitration and does not require that the parties bring lawyers. Mediation is not binding unless the parties have agreed to be bound by the decision.

Mediation has been a popular form of dispute resolution among business-to-business (B2B) e-commerce companies. Amazon.com and Ebay have used mediation regularly in the resolution of disputes.

Medarb

Mediation arbitration is a recent creation in which the arbitrator begins by attempting to negotiate between the two parties. If he is unable to reach a settlement, the case proceeds to arbitration with the same party serving as arbitrator. One percent of the AAA's cases each year are decided by a medarb process.

The Minitrial

In a **minitrial,** the parties have their lawyers present the strongest aspects of their cases to senior officials from both companies in the presence of a neutral advisor or a judge with experience in the field. At the end of the presentations by both parties, the neutral advisor can provide several forms of input, which are controlled by the parties. The advisor may be asked to provide what his judgment would be

Visit a firm specializing in alternative dispute resolution, National Arbitration & Mediation (NAM):
http://www.nationaladr.com

For more information about mediation in B2B disputes, go to
www.spidr.org *or* www.dr.bbb.org
For more information about e-commerce dispute resolution, also see
http://www.adrworld.com

in the case, or the advisor may be asked to prepare a settlement proposal based on the concerns and issues presented by the parties. Minitrials are more adversarial than mediation, but they are confidential; and the input from a neutral but respected advisor may help to bring the parties together. A minitrial is not binding.

Rent-a-Judge

Many companies and individuals are discovering that the time that elapses between the filing of a lawsuit and its resolution is too great to afford much relief. As a result, a kind of private court system, known as **rent-a-judge,** is developing in which parties may have their case heard before someone with judicial experience without waiting for the slower process of public justice. These private courts are like *The People's Court* without the television cameras. The parties pay filing fees and pay for the judges and courtrooms. These private courts also offer less expensive settlement conferences to afford the parties a chance at mediation prior to their private hearing. This and the other methods of alternative dispute resolution previously discussed offer parties the chance to obtain final dispositions of their cases more quickly and at less cost.

Summary Jury Trials

Under this relatively new method of alternative dispute resolution, the parties are given the opportunity to present summaries of their evidence to judge and jurors. The jurors then give an advisory verdict to start the settlement process. If the parties are unable to agree on a settlement, a formal trial proceeds. The benefit of this means of resolution is that the parties have an idea of a jury's perception so that they are assisted in their guidelines for settlement. This type of resolution occurs late in the litigation process, after the costs of discovery have been incurred. It can, however, save the expense of a trial.

Early Neutral Evaluation

Early neutral evaluation requires another attorney to meet with the parties, receive an assessment of the case by both sides, and then provide an evaluation of the merits of the case. The attorney, who is either a paid consultant or a volunteer

---

BUSINESS PLANNING TIP

Employers considering an arbitration clause in employment agreements should provide employees with both internal and external means for dispute resolution.

Internal means of employment dispute resolution follow:

1. Peer review

2. Ombudspersons

3. Mediation (someone within the company but outside the employee's immediate area serves as mediator)

External means of employment dispute resolution follow:

1. Mediation (as done by an outsider)

2. Nonbinding arbitration

3. Final and binding arbitration

When developing an arbitration clause and policy for employees:

1. Decide the types of dispute included.

2. Decide who may serve as arbitrators.

3. Provide rules for fact-finding and discovery of evidence.

4. Give the same types of remedies employees would have under any statutory protections they have.

5. Give employees the same time frames for submitting claims that they have under a statute.

6. Do not preclude the right to file a complaint with an agency for violation of employment laws.

7. Notify all potential employees of the arbitration plan and its requirements and provisions.

8. Give disclosure on right of representation.

9. If it is a new plan being put into place, give employees notice and adequate time to make decisions and adjustments.

Re: Southwest Airlines and Creative Dispute Resolution

In 1991, Dallas-based Southwest Airlines began a marketing campaign, using the slogan, "Just Plane Smart." Greenville-based Stevens Aviation had been using the slogan "Plane Smart" to market its airline service business. Following posturing by lawyers, Kurt Herwald, the chairman of Stevens Aviation, called Herb Kelleher, the chairman of Southwest Airlines, and offered to arm wrestle for the rights to the slogan. Kelleher rented a wrestling auditorium, sold tickets to the event, and offered the proceeds to charity. Kelleher, then 61, lost to Herwald, then 38, who is also a weight lifter. Herwald said, "Just to show sympathy for the elderly and that there's no hard feelings, we've decided to allow Southwest Airlines to continue using our slogan." After the event, a commentator noted, "Not only did the companies save a court battle that would have taken years and cost several hundred thousand dollars, they gained loads of free publicity. They also made donations to charities."

through the state bar association, renders an opinion on the resolution of the case. The idea in this method of resolution is to encourage settlement. Because early neutral evaluation occurs before the discovery phase of the case, it can save time and money if the parties are able to settle.

Peer Review

A new form of dispute resolution, particularly for disputes between employers and employees, called peer review, has become a popular method of dispute resolution and is used by Darden Industries (Red Lobster, Olive Garden), TRW Inc., Rockwell International Corp., and Marriott International, Inc. Peer review, which is generally conducted within three weeks of demand, is a review by co-workers of the action taken against an employee (demotion, termination, discipline). These panels of fellow employees (one chosen by management, one chosen by the employee, and one chosen randomly) can take testimony, review documents, and make decisions that can include an award of damages.

Employers say that sometimes their decisions are reversed in peer review, but Darden Industries indicates that peer review has reduced employee litigation and legal fees. Of the 100 disputes handled each year in peer review, only 10 proceed to litigation.

Experiments in the use of peer review for customers, contractors, and physicians are ongoing around the country. The advantage many see in this new form of ADR is the perception by all involved of its fairness.

RESOLUTION OF INTERNATIONAL DISPUTES

Visit the International Chamber of Commerce:
http://www.iccwbo.org

Arbitration has been used in the international business arena since 1922. The **International Chamber of Commerce** (ICC) is a private organization that handles more than 280 arbitration cases each year. Most requests for ICC arbitration come from Western countries, and the typical subject matters are trade transactions, contracts, intellectual property, agency, and corporate law. The following statistics were taken from the ICC's annual report for 2000:

- 541 Requests for Arbitration were filed with ICC.
- Those Requests involved 1,398 parties from 120 different countries.

For a look at the types of awards made by the ICC, go to
http://www.iccwbo.org/
court/english/bulletin/
bulletin.asp

You can find the standard ICC arbitration clause in over seventy-five languages at
http://www.iccwbo.org/
court/english/arbitration/
model_clause.asp

Visit the ICC conciliation site and rules:
http://www.iccwbo.org
click on services and go to ICC International Court of Arbitration

Visit the ICSID:
http://www.worldbank.org/
icsid

Visit the UNCITRAL site:
http://www.uncitral.org/
en-index.htm

- State or para-statal entities represented 12.5 percent of the parties.
- Places of arbitration were fixed in forty-three different countries on five continents.
- Arbitrators of fifty-eight different nationalities were appointed or confirmed under the ICC Rules.
- The amount in dispute exceeded one million U.S. dollars in 54 percent of new cases.
- 334 awards were rendered.

The ICC process is very similar to that discussed earlier for the American Arbitration Association. A request for arbitration is submitted to the ICC Secretariat in Paris; the parties can nominate arbitrators and choose the location for the arbitration hearing. The award of the ICC is final, and payment must be made at the location of the hearing.

The ICC also provides mediation, referred to as conciliation, services. In conciliation, the court assigns an expert to work with the parties to try and achieve a settlement of the case.

In addition to the ICC, the World Bank has established the International Center for Settlement of Investment Disputes (ICSID). The ICSID is an arbitral organization created specifically to hear disputes between investors and the nations in which they have made investments. This arbitration forum was created because of investors' fears that the courts of the nation in which they have invested may favor the government of that nation. Again, investment contracts can provide for the submission of disputes to the ICSID. Decisions of the ICSID are final and are enforceable as if they were court orders.

The United Nations Commission on International Trade Law (UNCITRAL) adopted a Model Law for Arbitration in 1985 that deals with where arbitration should be held (the parties can decide) and which country's laws should apply.

> **BUSINESS PLANNING TIP**
>
> The ICC recommends the following clause for insertion in contracts:
>
> *All disputes arising out of or in connection with the present contract shall be finally settled under the Rules of Arbitration of the International Chamber of Commerce by one or more arbitrators appointed in accordance with the said Rules.*

LITIGATION VERSUS ADR: THE ISSUES AND COSTS

Speed and Cost

Speed and cost are two compelling reasons businesses turn to ADR to resolve disputes. Costs of ADR are frequently one-tenth of the cost of litigating a dispute.

Protection of Privacy

There are other reasons parties may choose ADR. Whatever matter is in dispute can be kept private if referred directly to ADR; there are then no public court documents available for examination. Even when a suit is filed, the negotiated settlement achieved through alternative means can be kept private to protect the interests of the parties. When Dillard's, a national department-store chain, and Joseph Horne Company, a department store based in Pittsburgh, were litigating over

Dillard's conduct in a Horne's takeover, the parties' dispute centered on whether Dillard's was conducting due diligence in obtaining access to Horne's facilities and records, or whether Dillard's was actually running the stores in an attempt to drive down the acquisition price. The business press reported on the litigation and the underlying dispute. The information was not flattering to either party. Dillard's was portrayed as a large firm taking advantage of a small chain and engaging in unethical conduct with respect to verifying financial information prior to acquisition. Horne's was portrayed as naive and inept. Dillard's and Horne's settled the dispute, and both agreed to keep the terms of the settlement confidential. The result was that not only was the very public litigation ended, but the focus on alleged misconduct changed because of the settlement and its private nature.

Creative Remedies

Visit Intel Corporation:
http://www.intel.com

Often, without the constraints of court jurisdiction and restraints of legal boundaries, a creative remedy can be crafted that helps both sides. For example, Intel, a computer chip manufacturer, experienced ongoing disputes with employees who left the company to begin their own businesses with products and in areas that would compete with Intel. Intel's concern was whether the departing employees were taking with them technology that had been developed at and belonged to Intel. Using only the courts, Intel would find itself in lengthy, expensive, and complex litigation over engineering and developmental issues. Such litigation is costly not only in a monetary sense but also for the morale of employees charged with product development. Constant legal battles with former employees is not healthy for a corporate image within a company or from the outside.

After filing suit against one group of employees, Intel agreed, along with the former employees, to have an expert oversee the former employees' work in their business. The expert would have knowledge of Intel's product development that the employees had been involved with and would agree to notify all sides if the new company of the former employees was infringing any of Intel's patents. The expert agreed to oversee the new company's work for one year, at which point technology would make obsolete anything developed by the former employees while they were still at Intel. This creative solution permitted the former employees to operate their business, but it also provided Intel officials with the reassurance that their intellectual property was not being taken.

BUSINESS PLANNING TIP

Businesses such as Intel have now taken litigation strategy to a prevention stage. Intel and other firms, particularly those in high-tech and product development fields, now offer departing employees a partnership if they are leaving to start their own firms. The company provides a sort of incubator for the departing employee to get started in business. The company is an investor and will share in the returns the new product brings. The strategy here is why try and beat them in litigation when you can join them with an investment?

Judge and Jury Unknowns

While a good case and preparation are often offered as explanations for victory in a lawsuit, there are many good cases that, despite excellent preparation, are lost. There are unknowns in all forms of litigation. The unknowns are judges and juries and their perceptions and abilities. Research shows that 80 percent of all jurors have made up their minds about a case after only the opening statements in a trial have been made. Further research has shown that juries use their predetermined ideas in reaching a verdict. Finally, research shows that juries employ hindsight bias in their deliberation processes; that is, juries view the outcome of a set of facts and conclude that one party should have done more. Knowing that someone was injured often clouds our ability to determine whether that person should have been able to prevent the injury. The following statistics on jurors are from a 1999 *National Law Journal* survey:[2]

- 81.3 percent of jurors believe that when companies do something wrong, CEOs try to cover it up.
- 48.8 percent feel they should ignore the judge's instructions in reaching a just verdict in a case.
- 75.8 percent of the adult population have served as jurors.
- 8 percent said they could not be fair if one of the parties were a corporate executive.
- 15 percent said they could not be fair if the defendant were a tobacco company or gun manufacturer.
- 45 percent believe jury awards are "out of control." 43 percent believe jury awards are "generally reasonable."

Based on information about juries, many businesses will opt for a trial to a court in which a judge renders a decision. However, research with judges has demonstrated that even they are affected in their judgments in cases by predetermined ideas and hindsight bias, although to a lesser extent than jurors. "The Wild Card in Complex Business Litigation: The Jury" provides background information on the risks that juries pose for businesses in litigation.

FOR THE MANAGER'S DESK

Re: The Wild Card in Complex Business Litigation: The Jury

Former Chief Justice Warren Burger was one of the most vocal critics on the issue of mandatory jury trials in complex civil cases with his feelings that juries waste time and are often incapable of understanding the issues presented to them and the application of the law to the case. England and a good part of the third world nations have abandoned the jury system as an inadequate way of resolving civil disputes, but the United States seems to hang on as a holdout because of the constitutional aura surrounding the jury trial. This right is Jeffersonian in its origin and resulted from the complaints the colonists had against King George III for his trials without juries. Yet, it is important to note that most criticisms regarding the use of juries in complex suits is focused on civil cases and not on criminal prosecutions.

In the 1978 IBM antitrust case, a jury heard five months of testimony on IBM's alleged monopolization of various market segments in the computer industry. Again, there was a deadlocked jury, and an interview with one of the jurors afterward gave some indication of the level of comprehension that resulted from the trial. The concept of "interface" was critical in the trial since the ability to interface would largely control whether there was ease of market entry and product compatibility.

Stephen J. Adler documents the following exchange in the case in *The Jury*:

Judge: "What is software?"

Juror: "That's the paper software."

Asked to define "interface," the juror said: "Well, if you take a blivet, turn it off one thing and drop it down, it's an interface change, right?"

The judge asked a second juror, "What about barriers to entry?"—to which she answered, "I would have to read about it."

A mistrial was declared.

In addition to the problems of complexity, there are additional difficulties with finding available jurors. Complex civil suits are quite lengthy, and this

---

(continued)

problem is only compounding. Trials are simply getting longer, as evidenced by the following statistics: in 1968, only 26 percent of the civil trials in federal district courts took one day; today that statistic is down to 14 percent; and in 1968, 75 cases lasted ten days or more and today that number is 359 cases. The question that arises about the jurors is, In cases like the five-month IBM trial, who were these people who were able to spend every day for five months sitting on a jury? Many critics noted that the result is an overabundance of retired individuals, housewives, and the unemployed. There is an absence of professionals and businesspeople who might have some experience with the issues. A cultural and financial gap is created when a jury has limited cross-sectional representation. The perceptions of individuals differ according to their circumstances. The late Peter Grace once noted that while he was working on the Grace Commission on government spending, he was dealing with billion-dollar deficits and it was difficult for him to return to his corporate life and get excited about million-dollar losses. He had adapted the standard of the federal government as a means of evaluating dollars. The same thing happens inversely with jurors. For example, the American Bar Association's study of juror deliberations indicated the verdict figures in a trade secret case ranged from $1 to $1.5 million, and one juror commented as follows:

"When you start talking millions, I can't relate to that. It doesn't mean anything to me. I have trouble paying $8 for parking every day."

Source: Adapted from Marianne Jennings and Chris P. Neck, "The Wild Card in Complex Business Litigation: The Jury." Reprinted with permission from the *Commercial Law Journal* 96, No. 1, 45. Copyright © 1991 by the Commercial Law League of America. All rights reserved.

Absence of Technicalities

Under ADR, the parties have the opportunity to tell their stories. The strict procedural rules and evidentiary exclusions do not apply in these forums, and many companies feel more comfortable because ADR seems to be more of a search for the truth than a battle of processes. A mediator can serve as a communication link between the parties and help them to focus on issues and concerns. As one mediator expressed the benefit of ADR, "If you've done your job, . . . everyone goes home with big smiles."

Exhibit 4.3 provides a list of the benefits of ADR versus litigation.

EXHIBIT 4.3   Benefits of ADR versus Litigation

LITIGATION	ALTERNATIVE DISPUTE RESOLUTION
Technical discovery rules	Open lines of communication
Judicial constraints of precedent	Parties can agree to anything
Remedies limited (by law and precedent)	Creative remedies permitted
Backlog	Parties set timetable
Public proceeding	Privacy
Control by lawyers	Control by parties (or mediator/arbitrator)
Expensive	Cheaper
Strict procedures/timing	More flexibility
Judge/jury unknowns	Parties select mediator/arbitrator
Those who can afford to stay in win	Positions examined for validity
Judicial enforcement tools	Enforcement by good faith

Re: A Checklist for When to Litigate

Costs

Every lawsuit costs time and money. Costs of litigation include but by no means end with attorneys' fees, and other significant costs are often not considered before a business decides to become embroiled in a legal battle.

Legal Costs

The total legal fee must be considered in every case of possible litigation. A lawyer should be required to give an estimate of fees for any suit before the suit begins. The estimate should always include discovery costs. . . .

Time Costs (Hidden Downtime)

Litigation costs time as well as money. Indeed, in many cases, the loss of time can be more devastating to a firm than the financial loss. If a firm takes part in major litigation, chances are that its officers and possibly its directors will be involved in depositions, other forms of pretrial discovery and paperwork, and eventually in the trial itself. This involvement inevitably diverts the attention of the officers from their normal duties. . . .

Image Costs

If a lawsuit attracts the attention of the media, a firm may incur money and time costs stemming from public relations. Someone must be available to explain the firm's position to reporters and perhaps initiate an affirmative campaign to minimize negative publicity about the suit.

Capital Costs

Many auditors require that pending litigation be listed in the financial reports of the company. Ongoing litigation that carries the potential for great financial loss to a business can have a negative effect on the firm's financial rating and the ability to raise capital.

Costs of Alternatives to Litigation

The costs of litigation should be compared with the costs of alternatives to litigation. For example, it may not add much to potential litigation costs to submit a case to arbitration before pursuing full litigation. Such arbitration may produce a settlement that makes the trip to court unnecessary.

Costs of Not Litigating

There are costs for litigating, but there are also costs for not litigating. If the stakes are high enough, litigation may be worth pursuing regardless of the expense. For example, if a suit challenges the land records and thus the title to the land on which the business is located, the cost of not responding to the suit may be the loss of the property and the expense of reestablishing the business at another site. In a trademark or trade name suit the cost may be a product or company name or label. In a patent infringement case, the failure to sue an infringer may undermine a company's sales and its exclusivity in the marketplace.

Sometimes the price of not litigating or of not responding vigorously to litigation can be a firm's very existence. For example, the product liability suits involving Johns-Manville and the other makers of asbestos threatened the lives of those firms because they involved the only product the firms made.

Public Relations Issues

Litigation is not a private matter. In every city, at least one reporter is assigned to the clerk's office in the state and federal courts for the purpose of checking on suits filed.

Many an electric bill goes unpaid simply because it is not good public relations for a utility company to appear in the newspapers and on television as the "bad guy" when a retired widow explains that the big power company has just filed suit because she has no money to pay her bill. . . .

Jury Appeal

When considering the effects of publicity on a case, a company should also consider the closely related matter of jury appeal. In some cases it will not matter how correct a business may be, how much of a remedy the law provides, or how wrong the other side is; the jury will simply side with the "little guy," and the business will have no chance of succeeding in the courtroom. For example, the Arthur Murray Dance Studios once fully litigated a case in which a man who had been severely injured in a car accident and was unable to complete the lessons in his contract with Arthur Murray (some 2,734 lessons, for which he had paid $24,812.40) sought to recover his payments on the grounds that performance had become impossible. It is really very difficult to build jury appeal into such a case.

Discussion Questions

1. List the factors you should consider as you make a decision to litigate.

2. At the awards show for the Academy of Motion Picture Arts and Sciences (Academy), a character dressed as Snow White appeared in the opening musical number and sang with

actor Rob Lowe. Walt Disney, Inc., had not given the Academy permission to use the Snow White likeness, a trademarked Disney character. If you were the Walt Disney Corporation, would you sue the Academy?

3. List concerns you would have as an employer litigating a sexual harassment case.

Source: Frank Shipper and Marianne Jennings. *Avoiding and Surviving Lawsuits: The Executive Guide to Strategic Legal Planning for Business*, Jossey-Bass Publishing, Inc., 59–73. © 1989. Excerpted and reprinted with permission of the authors.

WHEN YOU ARE IN LITIGATION . . .

There are times when a business must face litigation. In this portion of the chapter, the language, process, and strategies of civil litigation are explained.

How Does a Lawsuit Start?

A lawsuit begins because someone feels his rights have been violated. It is important to note that lawsuits are based on feelings. Whether rights have been violated and what damages were caused as a result of that violation are the issues that a trial determines. The only restriction on the filing of a suit is that the plaintiff's claim of right is based on some law, either statutory law or common law.

People begin lawsuits. The judicial system does not unilaterally begin the enforcement of civil rights. This means that each individual has the responsibility of protecting his rights. The role of the judicial system is to determine whether those rights have been violated.

Although procedures vary from state to state, the following sections offer a general discussion of the procedures involved in a civil lawsuit. Exhibit 4.4 is a summary of the trial process.

For a look at what state and federal court systems are doing to improve the litigation process, visit the American Bar Association Web site:
http://www.abanet.org/
justice

The Complaint (Petition)

The first step in a lawsuit is the filing of a document called a **complaint** or **petition.** The plaintiff must file the petition or complaint within certain time limits each state has for filing suit. These time limits are called *statutes of limitations.* They vary depending upon the type of rights involved in a suit. The typical statute of limitations for personal injuries is two years; the typical limitation for contracts is four years.

A complaint is a general statement of the plaintiff's claim of rights. For example, if a plaintiff is suing for a breach of contract, the complaint must describe the contract, when it was entered into, and what the defendant did that the plaintiff says is a breach. Exhibit 4.5 is a sample complaint in a suit over a car accident.

EXHIBIT 4.4
The Trial Process

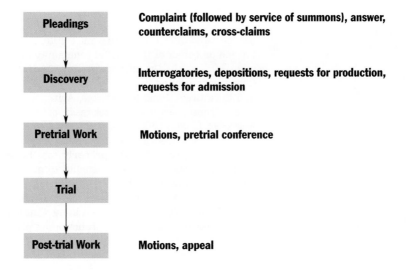

Pleadings	Complaint (followed by service of summons), answer, counterclaims, cross-claims
Discovery	Interrogatories, depositions, requests for production, requests for admission
Pretrial Work	Motions, pretrial conference
Trial	
Post-trial Work	Motions, appeal

EXHIBIT 4.5
Sample Complaint

Reed C. Tolman, Esq. (006502)
TOLMAN & OSBORNE, P.C.
1400 E. Southern, Suite 625
Tempe, Arizona 85282
Attorneys for Plaintiffs

SUPERIOR COURT OF ARIZONA

MARICOPA COUNTY

CRAIG CONNER and KATHY CONNER,) husband and wife, individually and on behalf of their minor son, CASEY CONNER,))))	**CV92-91319**
Plaintiffs,)	COMPLAINT (Tort-Motor Vehicle)
v.)	
CARMEN A. CHENAL and THOMAS K.) CHENAL, wife and husband,)	
Defendants,)	

For their complaint, plaintiffs allege:

    1. Plaintiffs and defendants are residents of Maricopa County, Arizona.

    2. This Court has jurisdiction over the subject matter under the Arizona Constitution, Art. 6, § 14.

    3. Casey Conner is the minor son of Craig and Kathy Conner.

EXHIBIT 4.5
(continued)

4. Carmen A. Chenal and Thomas K. Chenal are wife and husband. At all times relevant hereto, Carmen A. Chenal was acting for and on behalf of the marital community of which she is a member.

5. On or about July 20, 1990, defendant Carmen A. Chenal was driving her motor vehicle in the vicinity of Primrose Path and Cave Creek Road in Carefree, Arizona. At the time, Casey Conner was a passenger in the back seat of defendants' vehicle, a 1976 Mercedes, ID No.116033312051326.

6. At all times relevant hereto, defendant Carmen A. Chenal had a duty to care properly for the safety of Casey Conner. That duty included the responsibility to place Casey in an appropriate and functioning seatbelt.

7. Prior to the accident that resulted in injuries to Casey Conner, Carmen A. Chenal knew that the right rear door of her vehicle was damaged and not functioning properly.

8. Despite the duty Carmen A. Chenal had to care properly for the safety of Casey Conner, and despite her knowledge of a malfunctioning right rear door, Carmen A. Chenal negligently failed to place Casey in an appropriate and functioning seatbelt and negligently and carelessly operated her vehicle in such a way that the right rear door opened and allowed Casey to be ejected from the vehicle while the vehicle was in operation.

9. Carmen A. Chenal's failure to exercise reasonable care for the safety of Casey and the failure to operate her vehicle in a careful and safe manner proximately caused Casey to suffer personal injuries.

10. As a result of Casey Conner's injuries, he has experienced physical and psychological suffering, and his parents have incurred medical and other expenses, as well as lost earnings.

WHEREFORE, plaintiffs request judgment against defendants for compensatory damages in an amount to be determined at trial.

DATED: this _____ day of July, 1992.
TOLMAN & OSBORNE

By: _____
Reed C. Tolman
1400 E. Southern
Suite 625
Tempe, Arizona 85282

Source: Complaint appears courtesy of Tolman & Osborne, P.C., Tempe, AZ 85282.

The complaint need not have every detail described in it. The standard for a valid complaint is that it must be definite enough in its description of what happened for the defendant to understand why the suit has been brought.

In addition to describing the violation of rights, the complaint must establish the subject matter jurisdiction of the court. For example, for a federal district court action, the complaint would either have to show that there was diversity and a damage claim of more than $75,000 or that a federal question was involved.

Review current and concluded class action suits represented by The Alexander Law Firm:
http://www.alexanderlaw.com/class.html

Visit a Web site with information on airline class action litigation:
http://www.AirSafe.com

A Web site on silicone breast implant class actions can be found at:
http://www.pbs.org/wgbh/pages/frontline/implants

In some cases, the complaint is filed by a group of plaintiffs who have the same cause of action against one defendant. These types of suits are called **class action suits** and are typically filed in antitrust cases, shareholder actions against corporations, and employment discrimination cases. The class action suit enables a group of plaintiffs to share one lawyer and minimize litigation expenses while at the same time preserving their individual rights. Perhaps the most widely publicized type of class action lawsuit is the suit that results when a large jet airliner crashes and there are multiple deaths and injuries. All the plaintiffs were injured in the same event, and the defendant then litigates once with a group of plaintiffs (See Chapter 11 for more information on product liability class action litigation).

Another form of class action suit is the **derivative suit** in which shareholders sue a corporation to recover damages for actions taken by the corporation. (See Chapter 21 for more information.)

The final paragraphs of a complaint list the damages or remedies the plaintiff wants. The damages may be a **legal remedy** such as money, in which case a dollar amount is specified. The plaintiff may seek an **equitable remedy,** such as specific performance in the case of an action for breach of contract. **Specific performance** is an order of the court requiring a defendant to perform on a contract. In some cases, the plaintiff just wants the defendant to stop violating his rights. In those complaints, plaintiffs ask for **injunctions,** which are court orders requiring the defendant to stop doing the act complained of. In an action for nuisance, for example, an injunction orders the defendant to stop engaging in the conduct that causes the nuisance or orders the defendant to comply with a law or a previous decision; or, an injunction could order the construction of a fence to restrain animals that have become a nuisance.

The Summons

The complaint or petition of the plaintiffs is filed with the clerk of the appropriate court—that is, the court with subject matter jurisdiction, *in personam* jurisdiction, and venue. The defendant however, will not know of the suit just because it is filed. Thus, the second step in a lawsuit is serving the defendant with a copy of the complaint and a **summons,** which is a legal document that tells the defendant of the suit and explains the defendant's rights under the law. Those rights include the opportunity to respond and the grant of a limited amount of time for responding. Exhibit 4.6 is a sample summons.

A summons must be delivered to the defendant. Some states require that the defendant be given the papers personally. Other states allow the papers to be given to some member of the defendant's household or, in the case of a business, to an agent of that business (see Chapter 18 for a discussion of an agent's authority to receive the papers notifying the business of a lawsuit).

The summons is delivered by an officer of the court (such as a sheriff or magistrate) or by private firms licensed as **process servers.** Once the defendant is served, the server must file an affidavit with the court to indicate when and where the service was made. In rare circumstances, courts allow service of process by mail or by publishing the summons and complaint. These circumstances, however, are very limited and are carefully supervised by the courts.

The Answer

The parties' positions in a case are found in the **pleadings.** The complaint or petition is a pleading. The defendant's position is found in the **answer,** another

EXHIBIT 4.6
Sample Summons

Name:
Address:
City, State, Zip:
Telephone:
State Bar Code:
Client:

ARIZONA SUPERIOR COURT, County of

ACTION NO:

SUMMONS

THE STATE OF ARIZONA TO THE DEFENDANTS:

YOU ARE HEREBY SUMMONED and required to appear and defend, within the time applicable, in this action in this court. If served within Arizona, you appear and defend within 20 days after the service of the Summons and Complaint upon you, exclusive of the day of service. If served out of the State of Arizona - whether by direct service, by registered or certified mail, or by publication—you shall appear and defend within 30 days after the service of the Summons and Complaint upon you is complete, exclusive of the day of service. Where process is served upon the Arizona Director of Insurance as an insurer's attorney to receive service of legal process against it in this state, the insurer shall not be required to appear, answer or plead until expiration of 40 days after date of such service upon the Director. Service by registered or certified mail without the State of Arizona is complete 30 days after the date of receipt by the party being served. Service by publication is complete 30 days after the date of first publication. Direct service is complete when made. Service upon the Arizona Motor Vehicle Superintendent is complete 30 days after filing the Affidavit of Compliance and return receipt or Officer's Return. RCP 4; ARS §§ 20-222, 28-502, 28-503.

Copies of the pleadings filed herein may be obtained by contacting the Clerk of Superior Court, _____ County, located at _____,
Arizona. RCF 4.1(e).

SUMMONS
(Continued on Reverse Side)   1-1 ©LawForms 10-92 1-93

pleading in a case. The defendant must file an answer within the time limits allowed by the court or risk default. The time limits are typically twenty days for in-state defendants and thirty days for out-of-state defendants. A failure to answer, or a **default,** is like a forfeit in sports: The plaintiff wins because the defendant failed to show up. The plaintiff can then proceed to a judgment to collect damages.

The defendant's answer can do any or all of several different things. The defendant may admit certain facts in the answer. While it is rare for a defendant to admit the wrong alleged by the plaintiff, the defendant might admit parts of the plaintiff's complaint, such as those that establish jurisdiction and venue. If the plaintiff already has correct venue, fighting that issue is costly and admitting jurisdiction is a way to move on with the case. If, however, the court lacked *in personam*

EXHIBIT 4.6
(continued)

> YOU ARE HEREBY NOTIFIED that in case of your failure to appear and defend within the time applicable, judgment by default may be rendered against you for the relief demanded in the Complaint.
>
> YOU ARE CAUTIONED that in order to appear and defend, you must file an Answer or proper response in writing with the Clerk of this Court, accompanied by the necessary filing fee, within the time required, and you are required to serve a copy of any Answer or response upon the Plaintiff's' attorney. RCP l0(D); ARS 12-311; RCP5.
>
> The name and address of plaintiffs' attorney is:
>
> SIGNED AND SEALED this date :_____
>
> ....
> Clerk
>
> Method of Service:
> ☐ Private Process Service
> ☐ Sheriff or Marshall
> ☐ Personal Service
> ☐ Registered/Certified Mail (out of State)
>
> By ....
> Deputy Clerk
>
> SUMMONS   1-1© LawForms 11-67, 3-84, 1-93

Source: Form appears courtesy of National LawForms, Inc., Phoenix, Arizona.

jurisdiction over the defendant, the defendant could deny the jurisdiction. (See Chapter 3 for more discussion of *in personam* jurisidiction.)

A denial is a simple statement in the answer whereby the defendant indicates that the allegation is denied. An answer might also include a statement that the defendant does not know enough to admit or deny the allegations in the complaint and might include a demand for proof of those allegations.

An answer might also include a **counterclaim,** with which the defendant, in effect, countersues the plaintiff, alleging a violation of rights and damages against the plaintiff. The plaintiff must respond to the counterclaim using the same answer process of admitting and/or denying the alleged wrong. Exhibit 4.7 is a sample answer.

The answer must be filed with the clerk of the court and a copy sent to the plaintiff. With the exception of amendments to these documents, the pleadings are now complete.

Seeking Timely Resolution of the Case

The fact that a suit has been filed does not mean that the case will go to trial. A great majority of suits are disposed of before trial because of successful motions to end them. **Motions** are requests to the court that it take certain action. They are usually made in writing and include citations to precedent that support granting the motion. Often the judge will have the attorneys present oral arguments for and against the motion, after which the court then issues a ruling on the motion.

EXHIBIT 4.7
Sample Answer

Grand, Canyon & Rafts
12222 W. Camelback
Phoenix, Arizona
555-5555
Attorneys for Defendant

SUPERIOR COURT OF ARIZONA

MARICOPA COUNTY

CRAIG CONNER and KATHY CONNER,)
husband and wife, individually)
and on behalf of their minor)
son, CASEY CONNER,)
)
            Plaintiffs,)
)
             v.)
)
CARMEN A. CHENAL and THOMAS K.)
CHENAL, wife and husband,)
)
           Defendants,)
_____)

CV92-91319

ANSWER

        For their answer, defendants respond to plaintiffs'
complaint as follows:

          1. Admit paragraph one.

          2. Admit paragraph two.

          3. Have no knowledge to admit or deny paragraph three.

          4. Have no knowledge to admit or deny paragraph four.

          5. Admit paragraph five.

          6. As for paragraphs 6 through 10, inclusive of plaintiffs'
complaint, defendants have no knowledge of the statements alleged and
deny all statements made therein.

        Defendents deny any and all parts of plaintiffs' complaints
not specifically mentioned herein.

            DATED this _____ day of August, 1992.

                Grand, Canyon & Raft

    By: _____

            Robert C. Canyon
            12222 W. Camelback
            Phoenix, Arizona

Motion for Judgment on the Pleadings

Either in the answer or by separate motion, a defendant can move for judgment based just on the content of the pleadings. The theory behind a **motion for judgment on the pleadings** is that there is no cause of action even if everything the plaintiff alleges is true. For example, a plaintiff could file suit claiming the defendant is an annoying person; but unless the defendant is annoying to the extent of invading privacy or not honoring contracts, there is no right of recovery. The defendant in this case could win a motion for judgment on the pleadings because the law (perhaps unfortunately) does not provide a remedy for annoying people. A denial of a motion for judgment on the pleadings does not imply victory for the plaintiff. It simply means that the case will proceed with the next steps covered in this chapter.

Motion to Dismiss

A **motion to dismiss** can be filed any time during the proceedings but usually is part of the defendant's answer. Such a motion can be based on the court's lack of subject matter or *in personam* jurisdiction. Again, if the case is not dismissed, it does not mean that the plaintiff wins; it just means that the case will proceed to the next steps and possibly trial.

Motion for Summary Judgment

A **motion for summary judgment** has two requirements. Summary judgment is appropriate only when the moving party is entitled to a judgment under the law and when there are no issues of fact. Actions brought on the basis of motor vehicle accidents, for example, always involve different witnesses' testimonies and variations in facts. These types of cases cannot be decided by summary judgment. There are cases, however, in which the parties do not dispute the facts but differ on the applications of law. Consider, for example, a dispute involving a contract for the repair of a computer, including service and parts. Different laws govern contractual provisions for services and provisions for goods. The parties do not dispute the facts: They agree goods and services are covered in the contract. At issue is the question as to which law applies, and a summary judgment appropriately will resolve it. There may be other factual disputes about contract performance, but the partial summary judgment will determine which contract law will apply.

How a Lawsuit Progresses: Discovery

Trials in the United States are not conducted by ambush. Before the trial, the parties engage in a mandatory process of mutual disclosure of all relevant documents and other evidence. This court-supervised process of gathering evidence is called **discovery.** Under relatively recent changes to these procedural rules, the parties must offer to the other side lists of witnesses, all relevant documents, tangible evidence, and statements related to the case. Under the old discovery rules, the expense and difficulty of discovery techniques often meant the search for the truth was a cat-and-mouse game won by those with the most funds. Armed with the evidence in a case, the parties are more prepared, and perhaps more inclined, to negotiate a settlement. The new discovery rules provide for sanctions (penalties) for not turning over relevant documents at the start of a case. The following are the traditional tools of discovery.

Requests for Admissions

A **request for admissions** asks the other side to admit a certain fact. There is some incentive to admit the facts requested if they are true, because if these facts are denied and then proved at trial, attorney fees can be recovered for the costs of proving the facts that were denied. Requests for admissions sometimes merely request the other party to admit that a document is authentic. For example, the parties might have a dispute about the amount due under a contract but should be willing to admit that they signed the contract and that it is authentic. These requests for admission reduce the length of trials because an admission establishes a fact as true.

Depositions

Depositions are the oral testimony of parties or witnesses that are taken under oath but outside the courtroom and before the trial. They can be taken long before a trial and help preserve a witness's or party's recollection. Depositions are also helpful in determining just how strong a case is. It is far better to discover damaging information in a deposition than it is to spend all the time and money to go to trial and discover the damaging testimony there.

Limitations on Discovery

Discovery has the general limitation of relevance. Only things that are evidence or could lead to the discovery of evidence are discoverable. However, discovery also has a specific limitation. Discovery cannot require the production of **work product,** which consists of the attorney's research, thoughts, analysis, and strategy. Discovery allows the other side the right to know all the evidence (if it asks for it), but it does not give the other side the right to know how that evidence will be used or what legal precedent supports a party's position. Discovery cannot request the production of legal research, trial strategy, or an attorney's comments or reactions to a witness.

Certain evidence in cases is not discoverable. Communications between lawyers and their clients is protected by a privilege and, except in certain limited circumstances, cannot be discovered or used by the opposition.

Requests for Production

A **request for production** requires the other side to produce requested documents that have not already been given under the new discovery rules. For example, if a business is suing to recover lost profits, the defendant will probably want to request the income statements and perhaps income tax returns of that business so that he can prepare for damages issues. A request for production can include medical records as well as tangible evidence. In the following case, the failure to produce physical evidence that was part of an accident resulted in sanction for a store.

CASE 4.2

Wal-Mart Stores, Inc. v. *Johnson*
39 S.W.3d 729 (Tx. App. 2001)

"Reining" Deer at the Local Wal-Mart

FACTS

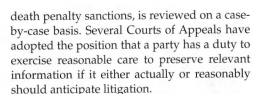

Monroe Johnson was injured when objects fell on him from on overhead shelf at Wal-Mart. A Wal-Mart employee arranging merchandise on a high shelf pushed several reindeer Christmas decorations onto Mr. Johnson, who was standing on the other side of the aisle. The record is unclear on the number of reindeer that dropped onto Mr. Johnson. However, there were fewer than eight reindeer.

Mr. Johnson and and his wife, Brandy Johnson, sued Wal-Mart Stores, Inc., for his resulting injuries. The judge included as a jury instruction [see p. 152 for more information on jury instructions] the following:

You are instructed that, when a party has possession of a piece of evidence at a time he knows or should have known it will be evidence in a controversy, and thereafter he disposes of it, makes it unavailable, or fails to produce it, there is a presumption in law that the piece of evidence, had it been produced, would have been unfavorable to the party who did not produce it. If you find by a preponderance of the evidence that Wal-Mart had possession of the reindeer at a time it knew or should have known they would be evidence in this controversy, then there is a presumption that the reindeer, if produced, would be unfavorable to Wal-Mart.

The jury found for Mr. and Mrs. Johnson and awarded damages. Wal-Mart did not appeal the award or the damages. Rather, Wal-Mart appealed the jury instruction.

JUDICIAL OPINION

WALKER, Chief Justice.

In an opinion declining the adoption of an independent tort for spoliation of evidence, the Texas Supreme Court recognized that when spoliation occurs, there must be adequate measures within the context of the lawsuit in which it is relevant to ensure that the destruction of evidence does not improperly impair a litigant's rights. As with any discovery abuse or evidentiary issue, the trial court's broad discretion in dealing with spoliation, ranging from a jury instruction on the spoliation presumption to death penalty sanctions, is reviewed on a case-by-case basis. Several Courts of Appeals have adopted the position that a party has a duty to exercise reasonable care to preserve relevant information if it either actually or reasonably should anticipate litigation.

The primary controversy developed in the course of the trial was whether the reindeer were substantial enough to have caused Johnson's injuries. According to Wal-Mart's store manager, Ron Wheeler, the reindeer retailed from $6.95 to $12.95, were made of papier mache, were twelve to fifteen inches high, hollow, and weighed from five to eight ounces. The stocker had no idea how much the reindeer weighed, but he agreed that they were made of papier mache. In contrast, Johnson and his wife both testified that the reindeer were made of wood, not papier mache. According to Johnson, the decorations weighed about ten pounds each. The falling reindeer were heavy enough to gash Johnson's arm. Wal-Mart failed to produce the reindeer in response to discovery. Wheeler did not profess to possession of personal knowledge of the fate of the reindeer, other than that they were either thrown away or sold.

Wheeler described the procedure followed by Wal-Mart when there is an accident involving a customer. The manager with firsthand knowledge of the incident fills in the report, then calls it in to the claims agent, who calls back and talks to the assistant who filed the report. Wal-Mart also refers its customer incident reports to claims management. Wheeler had no personal knowledge of how claims management handles matters.

The manager on duty at the time of the accident, Phyllis McLane, prepared an incident report a week after the accident. She incorrectly recorded Johnson's age on the form. Her report noted that Johnson suffered a cut to his right arm. Under the heading "What did alleged injured person say happened," the report stated, "Wal-Mart associate working on opposite side knocked paper mache reindeer and columns onto his head and left arm." Attached to the form is the stocker's statement, dated at the time of the accident but actually taken later that day. It states,

(continued)

"I was moving wall products to next riser, some fell back and knocked some reindeer off on customer." McLane took down Johnson's statement on a yellow legal pad, too, but that statement was not produced with the report. The notes McLane took the day of the accident were thrown away after the report was filled out. McLane used an instant camera to photograph the scene, but the quality of the photograph is too poor to reveal the composition of the reindeer. Wheeler admitted that the scene was altered before the photograph was taken. McLane also took two photographs of the cut on Johnson's arm, but those photographs were not produced by Wal-Mart. Wheeler admitted that it was unusual to take a picture of the injured arm. Wheeler admitted that he had no idea personally what Johnson said. McLane did not testify.

Wheeler was not present in the store the day of the accident. A week later Wheeler spoke with John Almaguer about the accident, but Almaguer could not recall whether they talked about having to go to court. Wheeler testified he had no idea that a lawsuit might be filed when the reindeer were thrown away or sold.

Johnson filed suit about six months after the accident. One of Johnson's interrogatories asked if Wal-Mart had in its possession any notes made during interviews of witnesses or employees. Wal-Mart objected on the grounds that the interrogatory sought information prepared in anticipation of litigation. The only notes were made on the day the accident occurred.

Johnson argues he was entitled to a spoliation instruction because Wal-Mart anticipated litigation on the day of the incident and failed to provide a reasonable explanation for its failure to preserve the evidence. The manager on duty noted that the customer had suffered an objective physical injury. The evidence-gathering actions taken by Wal-Mart employees, such as taking statements and photographs and submitting reports to claims management, indicate an anticipation of litigation. For other discovery purposes, Wal-Mart took the position that it anticipated litigation on the day of the accident. Given that Wal-Mart is a retail establishment, the store manager assumed the reindeer were sold, but Wal-Mart provided no inventory or other documentation to support its supposition. The person with personal knowledge of what happened to the reindeer and the other evidence did not provide an explanation for not preserving a reindeer because she did not testify.

Wal-Mart contends the trial court erred in instructing the jury on spoliation because it provided testimony regarding the reindeer's physical attributes and Johnson failed to establish that Wal-Mart intentionally destroyed the reindeer for the purpose of concealing evidence. Wal-Mart argues a presumption arises from the non-production of evidence under only two circumstances: the deliberate spoliation of relevant evidence and the failure of a party to produce relevant evidence or offer testimony to explain its non-production. Wheeler's explanation was not based on personal knowledge, however. Wal-Mart is a retailer and the reindeer were merchandise; so one could presume, as Wheeler did, that the reindeer may have been sold in the ordinary course of business. It is, however, more difficult to assume that the ordinary course of business includes "throwing" potential evidence away? What Wheeler did not explain, and could not explain because he was not there, is why Wal-Mart did not set aside a reindeer along with the other evidence it gathered. Although Wal-Mart explained the reindeer's disappearance, the trial court was not compelled to accept the explanation as reasonable, especially in view of the cavalier disposition of evidence of critical importance to this case.

Wal-Mart argues Johnson is not entitled to a spoliation instruction because Wal-Mart employees supplied testimony regarding the weight of the reindeer. In *Brewer v. Dowling*, 862 S.W.2d 156, 159 (Tex.App.—Fort Worth 1993, writ denied), the trial court did not abuse its discretion by refusing to instruct the jury on spoliation because the defendant produced the same information contained in the missing fetal monitor strip through hospital charts and nurse's notes prepared before the appellees knew of the infant's severe problems. In *Watson v. Brazos Elec. Power Co-op., Inc.*, 918 S.W.2d 639, 642-44 (Tex.App.—Waco 1996, writ denied), the trial court abused its discretion by refusing to include a spoliation instruction in the jury charge, where the defendant negligently destroyed a key piece of evidence, the condition of which was in controversy. There is nothing inherently reliable about the testimony offered by Wal-Mart as a substitute for the reindeer. The incident report was prepared in anticipation of litigation and Wheeler's testimony is both interested and partially based upon hearsay. Wal-Mart reduced the lawsuit to a swearing match by gathering evidence and then letting it disappear. Under these circumstances, we cannot say that the trial court's decision to include a spoliation instruction in the jury charge amounted to an abuse of its discretion. Issue one is overruled.

AFFIRMED.

GAULTNEY, Justice, dissenting.

Respectfully, I dissent. If spoliation occurred, the offense is serious. Spoliation constitutes obstruction of justice. However, there must be evidence that a breach of a duty to preserve evidence occurred before the trial court is vested with discretion on how to punish the bad conduct. The trial court serves as factfinder when spoliation is alleged. The trial court must determine whether the charged party is in fact a spoliator. Here, the trial court's conclusion is recorded as follows:

The Court: [Y]our proposed instruction says: Wal-Mart lost, sold or—[Plaintiff's counsel]: Discarded.

The Court:—discarded the reindeer, none of which I can—I don't think there's any evidence to support that any specific thing happened to it—well, the best evidence is that it was sold or that they were sold.

[Plaintiff's counsel]: Right.

The record supports the trial court's conclusion, agreed to by plaintiff's counsel, that the best evidence is that the reindeer were sold.

The store sold its merchandise. The circumstances surrounding the accident did not put the store on notice that a dispute would develop later over whether the fallen reindeer were made of wood or paper mache. Plaintiff suffered a cut on his left arm which a store employee cleaned and covered with a band-aid. Plaintiff admits he told the store employees he was not injured. Was the store then under a duty to remove its merchandise from the shelf and safe-keep the reindeer for a later lawsuit? What is wrong with a store selling its merchandise under these circumstances? No evidence was presented to prove that a breach of a duty to preserve this specific evidence occurred. Because I do not believe selling merchandise constitutes an obstruction of justice, I would hold that the trial court erred in giving the spoliation instruction and would reverse and remand this case for a new trial.

CASE QUESTIONS

1. What happened that resulted in the litigation against Wal-Mart?
2. What happened to the reindeer?
3. What is spoliation?
4. What does the dissenting judge think is required to prove spoliation?

C O N S I D E R . . .

4.2 How could the lawyers for the plaintiffs in the Wal-Mart case have obtained/preserved the reindeer?

Resolution of a Lawsuit: The Trial

If a case is not settled (and many are settled literally on the courthouse steps), the trial begins.

The Type of Trial—Jury or Nonjury

Occasionally, the parties agree not to have a jury trial and instead have a trial to the court. In these cases, the judge acts as both judge and jury—both running the trial and determining its outcome. In highly technical cases it is sometimes better for both sides to have a knowledgeable judge involved than to try to explain the complexities of the case to a jury of laypersons.

If the parties do not agree on a nonjury trial, there are certain types of cases that carry a constitutional right to a trial by jury. The Seventh Amendment to the U.S. Constitution covers the jury requirement in civil trials:

In suits at common law, where the value in controversy shall exceed twenty dollars, the right of trial by jury shall be preserved, and no fact tried by a jury, shall be

BUSINESS STRATEGY

Once a company has evidence regarding a product, a contract, or conduct of employees, it is costly to try and hide that information before or during litigation.

Wal-Mart has experienced sanctions and bad publicity from a number of lawsuits in which it is a defendant for its alleged failure to be forthcoming with discovery requests and documents. The cases in which Wal-Mart has had issues of discovery abuse and sanctions include:

© Susan Van Etten

Bergeron v. *Wal-Mart Stores*, No. 85405 (Dt. Ct. Laforche Par. La)

Christ v. *Wal-Mart Stores*, No. 55747 (Dist. Ct. Liberty Co. Texas)

In re Visa Check/Mastermoney Antitrust Litigation, No. 96-5283 (E.D.N.Y.)

Meissner v. *Wal-Mart Stores*, No. A-159-432 (Dist. Ct. Jefferson Co.)

Wal-Mart released the following data on its litigation:

1998—20 sanctions for discovery abuse

1999—22 sanctions for discovery abuse

2000—10 sanctions

In the *McClung* v. *Delta Square Limited Partnership,* 937 S.W.2d 891 (Tenn. 1996) case Wal-Mart's issues with regard to discovery began. After the case was tried, the husband of the woman killed after being abducted from the parking lot at a Wal-Mart store learned that Wal-Mart had conducted a study and pilot program showing that store parking lots could be made safer with relatively little cost just by adding safety patrols. The study was not released to the husband during the litigation. When the report surfaced in other cases, plaintiffs' lawyers had the report in hand even as Wal-Mart denied in discovery requests that the report existed. Wal-Mart was sanctioned $18 million in one case for its failure to reveal the report.*

*Bob Van Voris, "Wal-Mart Mending Its Ways?" *National Law Journal,* 22 January 2001, A1, A8.

---

otherwise re-examined in any court of the United States other than according to the rules of common law.

Although this right is limited to what existed at common law at the time the U.S. Constitution was adopted, many states have expanded the right under their state constitutions. The absolute right to a jury trial exists only in criminal cases as covered in Article III and the Fifth and Sixth Amendments of the U.S. Constitution.

The size of a jury varies; some states require only six jurors. A jury may have twelve to eighteen members, which includes alternates, particularly in long trials, to ensure that a panel of twelve participates fully in the trial.

The pool of potential jurors and the selection of those jurors are resolved before trial. Usually, voting lists alone or combined with other lists (of driver's license holders, for example) are used as pools for potential jurors. People on these lists are randomly notified of a period of time during which they should report for jury duty. Many states excuse from jury duty certain individuals, like doctors and emergency workers, because of the needs they serve in society. Students are often excused if they are summoned for duty during the semester because of their peculiar obligations and time limitations on completing classes. Judges also usually have the power to excuse certain individuals who would

ETHICAL ISSUES 4.2

Thomas Talcott was a Dow Corning materials engineer in 1976, when Dow was developing its silicone breast implant. Talcott had questions about the safety of the implants and raised his concerns, but product development, production, and marketing went forward anyway. In 1991 and 1992, concerns about the safety of the breast implants increased, and a number of women filed lawsuits alleging that the implants had leaked and/or ruptured and caused cancer, lupus, and other autoimmune disorders. Lawyers for the women sought access to the company records from the time of product development. Are the lawyers entitled to those records? If you had been Talcott and had strong feelings about the safety of a new product your employer was about to sell, what would you have done? Would it have done any good to bring it to the attention of all in the chain of command, from your supervisor up to the CEO? If you had been Talcott, would you have been able to continue to work for Dow Corning? Suppose that Talcott discussed his concerns about safety of the implants with everyone in the chain of command, but still the product was to enter the market. Would you notify a government agency or "leak" your information to the media? Why, or why not? Should Talcott say anything to the lawyers for the women?

Aftermath

Talcott left Dow Corning in 1976. He served as an expert witness for the women who brought implant suits and was paid $400 per hour.

experience hardship if they were required to serve. For example, a sole proprietor of a service business would have no income during the time of jury service and would probably be excused on a hardship basis.

Many more jurors than are needed are summoned to serve. These extra numbers are required because all the parties to a dispute participate in the selection of a jury. Once a pool is available, the court begins the process of *voir dire*, which determines whether a potential juror is qualified to serve. Most states have jurors complete a questionnaire on general topics so that the selection process can move quickly. The questionnaire covers personal information—age, occupation, and so on. The questionnaire might also ask whether one has ever been a juror, a party to a lawsuit, or a witness. Exhibit 4.8 provides some sample *voir dire* questions.

A juror can be removed from a jury panel for two reasons. First, a juror can be removed for cause, which means the juror is incapable of making an impartial decision in the case. If a juror is related to one of the attorneys in the case, for example, the juror would be excused for cause. Some jurors reveal their biases or prejudices, like racial prejudice, in the questionnaire they are required to complete. Others may express strong feelings of animosity toward the medical profession. Clearly, the removal of such jurors for cause in cases involving civil rights and malpractice suits, respectively, is an important part of trial strategy.

Sometimes a juror cannot be excused for cause but an attorney feels uncomfortable about the juror or the juror's attitudes. In these circumstances, the lawyer issues a **peremptory challenge,** which excuses the juror. The peremptory challenge is the attorney's private tool. However, the use of peremptory challenges is limited. All states have a statute or court rule limiting the number of peremptory challenges an attorney may use in a trial. In recent years, the U.S. Supreme Court has ruled that there are some limitations on the use of peremptory challenges. The

EXHIBIT 4.8 **Sample *Voir Dire* Questions**

1. Do you know any of the parties or lawyers in this case? (Asked after the judge introduces all parties and lawyers.)
2. What is your occupation?
3. Are you married?
4. What is your spouse's occupation?
5. Have you ever served on a jury?
6. Are you in favor of compensation for emotional injuries?
7. Do you believe in compensation for victims of police misconduct?
8. Do you support capital punishment?
9. What is your educational background?
10. Did you attend private or public school?
11. What is your spouse's educational background?
12. What seminars, courses, and workshops have you taken since you left school?
13. How old are you?
14. Do you have children? What are their ages and sexes?
15. How would people describe you?
16. Do you believe that people bring about their own misfortunes?
17. Do you do volunteer work? What type?
18. Do you have any relatives who are police officers?
19. Do you belong to a political party?
20. Did you serve in the armed forces?
21. Have you read about this case or heard TV/radio reports about it?
22. Have you formed an opinion about this case?
23. Do you equate laziness with black people?
24. Do you think there is any difference between black and white people?
25. Do you believe black people commit more crimes than white people?

Court has indicated that such a challenge cannot be based on either race or gender. If the trial judge suspects that either of these factors may have induced one of the lawyers to seek a peremptory challenge, the lawyer will be required to produce a plausible explanation for the use of the peremptory challenge that is unrelated to race or gender.

CONSIDER . . .

4.3 Jimmy Elem was convicted of second-degree robbery in a Missouri trial court. During *voir dire*, the prosecutor struck (dismissed) two black men, offering the following explanation:

I struck [juror] number twenty-two because of his long hair. He had long curly hair. He had the longest hair of anybody on the panel by far. He appeared to not be a good juror for that fact, the fact that he had long hair hanging down shoulder length, curly, unkempt hair. Also, he had a mustache and a goatee-type beard. And juror number twenty-four also has a mustache and goatee-type beard. Those are the only two people on the jury . . . with facial hair. . . . And I don't like the way they looked, with the way the hair is cut, both of them. And the mustaches and the beards look suspicious to me.

After his conviction, Elem challenged the prosecutor's use of the peremptory challenge on the two black men as racially motivated and demanded a new trial. Is the prosecutor's explanation race-neutral? [*Purkett* v. *Elem*, 514 U.S. 765 (1995)]

Re: The Stealth Juror

There are three principal methods for detecting stealth jurors: analyzing nonverbal behavior associated with deception; identifying discrepancies between written questionnaire responses and oral voir dire responses; and determining bias indirectly by uncovering "correlates" of bias.

The Eyes Have It

An emerging body of social science research focuses specifically on the issue of deceptive communication, one aspect of which is nonverbal behavior, or "body language," of lying. Relevant indicators in this area include blinking, higher speech tone or pitch, faster speech rate, changes in eye contact and postural cues, and delays in answering, known as "response latency."

Such indicators may be difficult to interpret accurately, however, without knowing an individual's normal, idiosyncratic behavior patterns. For example, failure to maintain eye contact—the old-wives'-tale method of lie detection—is actually a weak indicator of lying, because the characteristic level of eye contact varies widely among individuals. Deception cannot reliably be inferred from a potential juror's degree of eye contact unless his or her typical behavior is known. As an index, blinking is much more reliable.

Another key indicator is what experts in deceptive communication call adapters—unusual body movements designed to vent or relieve stress, such as rubbing hands together or running them through the hair, tapping fingers on the hand or knee, or adjusting clothes. Some social psychologists assert that people exercise considerably greater control over facial expressions than they do over peripheral parts of the body, and thus when they lie, stress "leaks" to the hands and feet in the form of such repetitive body movements.

Stress, however, is not exclusively a byproduct of lying; it is also a common, natural response to the high-pressure environment of a courtroom. Film and television depictions notwithstanding, the average potential juror is unaccustomed to this setting, and the *voir dire* process is likely to be his or her first exposure to it.

Being placed in such an alien environment generates a certain level of arousal among jurors,

and deceptive communication only enhances this already stimulated state. As a result, adapters deserve attention as promising indicators of misrepresentations during *voir dire*.

Speak No Evil

Discrepancies between written questionnaire and oral *voir dire* responses also may be telling. Prospective jurors are more candid in written answers, which have an anonymous quality, than in open-court questioning. Jurors commonly offer extemporaneous comments and verbal qualifiers in written responses, but tend to self-censor in *voir dire*, when—with attorneys, fellow jurors and perhaps a judge bearing down on them—they fear they may be held accountable for, or suffer negative repercussions from, their responses.

Social psychological studies are replete with findings supporting the conclusion that written questionnaires afford more intimate, candid and uncensored reflections of jurors' attitudes and opinions than do statements made in open court. Such research strongly suggests that statements made in public are associated with a greater degree of personal accountability than are other forms of communication.

Still other research reveals that people are less likely to divulge negative or critical opinions when in the presence of individuals who possess a high degree of power or status. An attorney who represents a high-profile corporate client—to whom the disclosure of such opinions is most critical—is perceived as just that sort of status figure. Consequently, such an attorney is ill-advised to rely exclusively on oral voir dire as the principal indicator of a juror's disposition.

A Slip of the Lip

Because stealth jurors rarely plan or contemplate consistency between their questionnaire and oral voir dire responses, they frequently "slip up" during oral questioning. For example, in an antitrust case against a large oil company, jurors who displayed pro-environmental biases were sought out. A woman in the jury pool wrote in her questionnaire that she joined the Sierra Club because of principles she held. During oral *voir dire*, when questioned by the oil company's attorney as

(continued)

to her reason for joining, she responded, "I like the hikes."

In another high-profile case, a prospective juror, in response to a questionnaire inquiry about his opinions of the various parties involved in the case, checked "somewhat favorable" for all but the defendant pharmaceutical company, for which he checked "somewhat unfavorable."

During oral *voir dire*, when asked by the defense attorney about the basis for his unfavorable opinion, he replied that he in fact held no such

opinion and had checked that response in error. Trial counsel did not strike this juror, who eventually became foreman and behaved very negatively during trial, refusing to look at defense counsel and turning away when defense witnesses were on the stand.

Source: Edward M. Bodaken and George R. Speckart, "To Down a Stealth Juror, Strike First," *National Law Journal*, Sept. 23, 1996, B1, B9. Reprinted with permission from the September 23, 1996, edition of the *National Law Journal*. © 1996 NLP IP Company.

Visit a jury consultant, Carolyn Robbins Jury Simulations, Inc.:
http://www.crjury.com

Jury selection is an art and a science. Jury consulting firms specialize in providing data to attorneys for jury selection. These firms do thorough checks of the potential jurors' backgrounds and offer statistics on the reactions of certain economic and social groups to trials and trial issues. There is much about a case at trial that is uncontrollable, but jury selection is a part of the process that, with thorough preparation, can increase the likelihood of favorable results by ensuring an optimally favorable jury panel.

Jury or trial consultants perform jury profiles, find surrogate juries, and often conduct mock trials. The use of trial consultants has increased dramatically since the 1970s, and membership in the American Society of Trial Consultants has grown from 19 members in 1983 to 250 members today. Jury consultants were used to assist in defense victories in the Sean "Puffy" Combs shooting trial and the O. J. Simpson double homicide trial.

Trial Language

It is often difficult to piece together all the witnesses and evidence in a trial. A lengthy trial may leave the jurors confused. The attorney for each party, therefore, is permitted to make an **opening statement** that summarizes what that party hopes to prove and how it will be proved. Most attorneys also mention the issue of **burden of proof,** which controls who has the responsibility for proving what facts. Although the plaintiff has the burden of proving a case, the defendant has the burden of proving the existence of any valid defenses. There are various standards for meeting the burden of proof. In criminal cases, the standard is proof beyond a reasonable doubt. In civil cases, the standard is proof by a preponderance of the evidence.

Because the plaintiff has the burden of proof, the plaintiff presents his case and evidence first. The attorney for the plaintiff decides the order of the witnesses; questioning of these witnesses under oath is called **direct examination.** Although the defense cannot present witnesses during this part of the trial, it can question the plaintiff's witnesses after their direct examination is through. The defense questioning of plaintiff witnesses is called **cross-examination,** after which the plaintiff may again pose questions to clarify under **redirect examination.**

Once the plaintiff has finished his case, there must be enough evidence to establish a *prima facie case,* one in which the plaintiff has offered some evidence on all the elements required to be established for recovery. Although the evidence may be subject to credibility questions and be challenged by defense evidence, there must be some proof for each part of the claim. If the plaintiff does not meet this standard, the defendant can and may make a motion for a **directed verdict.** This motion for a directed verdict is made outside the jury's hearing and argued to the judge. If it is not granted, the trial proceeds with the defendant's case.

If there is no directed verdict, the defendant has the same opportunity to present witnesses and evidence. Throughout the trial, the judge will apply the rules of evidence to determine what can and cannot be used as evidence. The typical evidence is a witness's testimony. However, there is also tangible evidence. In a contracts case, there is likely to be a great deal of paper evidence—letters, memos, and cost figures.

One of the evidentiary issues that has been debated and litigated over the past few years is the use of expert testimony in cases. The issue the courts face is determining whether the expert's testimony reflects scientific knowledge or whether the testimony is contrived for the trial (often called "junk science.") In *Daubert* v. *Merrell Dow Pharmaceuticals,* the U.S. Supreme Court was faced with the issue of which experts and experiments should be allowed as evidence in a case.

CASE 4.3

Daubert v. *Merrell Dow Pharmaceuticals, Inc.*
509 U.S. 579 (1993)

Birth Defects from Pills: Junk or Truth?

FACTS

Jason Daubert and Eric Schuller (petitioners) were born with serious birth defects. Through their parents, they filed suit against Merrell Dow Pharmaceuticals, Inc. (respondent), the manufacturer of the anti-nausea drug, Bendectin, which both their mothers had taken during the first trimester of their pregnancy.

One expert, Dr. Steven Lamm, has filed an affidavit in the case stating that the use of Bendectin during the first trimester has not been shown to be a risk factor for birth defects. Eight experts for the Dauberts and Schullers concluded, based on animal and epidemiological studies, that Bendectin can cause birth defects.

These experts had concluded that Bendectin can cause birth defects. Their conclusions were based upon "in vitro" (test tube) and "in vivo" (live) animal studies that found a link between Bendectin and malformations; pharmacological studies of the chemical structure of Bendectin that purported to show similarities between the structure of the drug and that of other substances known to cause birth defects; and the "reanalysis" of previously published epidemiological (human statistical) studies.

Merrell Dow moved for summary judgment, which the District Court granted, holding that the studies of the eight experts did not establish causation because the studies were recalculations of data previously published that established no causal link between the drug and birth defects. Further, the court ruled that the experts' work had not been published or subjected to peer review.

The court of appeals affirmed, and Daubert and Schuller appealed from that judgment.

(continued)

JUDICIAL OPINION

BLACKMUN, Justice

The *Frye* (*Frye* v. *United States*, 293 F. 1013 [1923]) test has its origin in a short and citation-free 1923 decision concerning the admissibility of evidence derived from a systolic blood pressure deception test, a crude precursor to the polygraph machine. In what has become a famous (perhaps infamous) passage, the then Court of Appeals for the District of Columbia described the device and its operation and declared:

Just when a scientific principle or discovery crosses the line between the experimental and demonstrable stages is difficult to define. Somewhere in this twilight zone the evidential force of the principle must be recognized, and while courts will go a long way in admitting expert testimony deduced from a well-recognized scientific principle or discovery, the thing from which the deduction is made must be sufficiently established to have gained general acceptance in the particular field in which it belongs. [emphasis added]

Because the deception test had "not yet gained such standing and scientific recognition among physiological and psychological authorities as would justify the courts in admitting expert testimony deduced from the discovery, development, and experiments thus far made," evidence of its results was ruled inadmissible.

The merits of the *Frye* test have been much debated, and scholarship on its proper scope and application is legion. Petitioners' primary attack, however, is not on the content but on the continuing authority of the rule. They contend that the *Frye* test was superseded by the adoption of the Federal Rules of Evidence. We agree.

"Relevant evidence" is defined as that which has "any tendency to make the existence of any fact that is of consequence to the determination of the action more probable or less probable than it would be without the evidence." Rule 401. The Rule's basic standard of relevance thus is a liberal one.

Here there is a specific Rule that speaks to the contested issue. Rule 702, governing expert testimony, provides:

If scientific, technical, or other specialized knowledge will assist the trier of fact to understand the evidence or to determine a fact in issue, a witness qualified as an expert by knowledge, skill, experience, training, or education, may testify thereto in the form of an opinion or otherwise.

Nothing in the text of this Rule establishes "general acceptance" as an absolute prerequisite to admissibility. Nor does respondent present any clear indication that Rule 702 or the Rules as a whole were intended to incorporate a "general acceptance" standard. The drafting history makes no mention of *Frye*, and a rigid "general acceptance" requirement would be at odds with the "liberal thrust" of the Federal Rules and their "general approach of relaxing the traditional barriers to 'opinion' testimony."

The primary locus of this obligation is Rule 702, which clearly contemplates some degree of regulation of the subjects and theories about which an expert may testify. "If *scientific*, technical, or other specialized *knowledge will assist the trier of fact* to understand the evidence or to determine a fact in issue" an expert "may testify *thereto*." The subject of an expert's testimony must be "scientific . . . knowledge." The adjective "scientific" implies a grounding in the methods and procedures of science. Similarly, the word "knowledge" connotes more than subjective belief or unsupported speculation. The term "applies to any body of known facts or to any body of ideas inferred from such facts or accepted as truths on good grounds."

Rule 702 further requires that the evidence or testimony "assist the trier of fact to understand the evidence or to determine a fact in issue." This condition goes primarily to relevance. "Expert testimony which does not relate to any issue in the case is not relevant and, ergo, non-helpful."

Faced with a proffer of expert scientific testimony, then, the trial judge must determine at the outset, pursuant to Rule 104(a), whether the expert is proposing to testify to (1) scientific knowledge that (2) will assist the trier of fact to understand or determine a fact in issue. This entails a preliminary assessment of whether the reasoning or methodology underlying the testimony is scientifically valid and of whether that reasoning or methodology properly can be applied to the facts in issue. We are confident that federal judges possess the capacity to undertake this review. Many factors will bear on the inquiry, and we do not presume to set out a definitive checklist or test. But some general observations are appropriate.

Ordinarily, a key question to be answered in determining whether a theory or technique is scientific knowledge that will assist the trier of fact will be whether it can be (and has been) tested. "Scientific methodology today is based on generating hypotheses and testing them to see if they can be falsified; indeed, this methodology is what distinguishes science from other fields of human inquiry."

Another pertinent consideration is whether the theory or technique has been subjected to peer review and publication. Publication (which is but one element of peer review) is not a *sine qua non* of admissibility; it does not necessarily correlate with reliability, see S. Jasanoff, The Fifth Branch: Science Advisors as Policymakers 61-76 (1990), and in some instances well-grounded but innovative theories will not have been published. Some propositions, moreover, are too particular, too new, or of too limited interest to be published. But submission to the scrutiny of the scientific community is a component of "good science," in part because it increases the likelihood that substantive flaws in methodology will be detected. The fact of publication (or lack thereof) in a peer-reviewed journal thus will be a relevant, though not dispositive, consideration in assessing the scientific validity of a particular technique or methodology on which an opinion is premised.

Finally, "general acceptance" can yet have a bearing on the inquiry. A "reliability assessment does not require, although it does permit, explicit identification of a relevant scientific community and an express determination of a particular degree of acceptance within that community." Widespread acceptance can be an important factor in ruling particular evidence admissible, and "a known technique that has been able to attract only minimal support within the community" may properly be viewed with skepticism.

The inquiry envisioned by Rule 702 is, we emphasize, a flexible one. Its overarching subject is the scientific validity—and thus the evidentiary relevance and reliability—of the principles that underlie a proposed submission. The focus, of course, must be solely on principles and methodology, not on the conclusions that they generate.

Throughout, a judge assessing a proffer of expert scientific testimony under Rule 702 should also be mindful of other applicable rules. Rule 703 provides that expert opinions based on otherwise inadmissible hearsay are to be admitted only if the facts or data are "of a type reasonably relied upon by experts in the particular field in forming opinions or inferences upon the subject." Rule 706 allows the court at its discretion to procure the assistance of an expert of its own choosing. Finally, Rule 403 permits the exclu-

sion of relevant evidence "if its probative value is substantially outweighed by the danger of unfair prejudice, confusion of the issues, or misleading the jury. . . ." Judge Weinstein has explained: "Expert evidence can be both powerful and quite misleading because of the difficulty in evaluating it. Because of this risk, the judge in weighing possible prejudice against probative force under Rule 403 of the present rules exercises more control over experts than over lay witnesses."

We conclude by briefly addressing what appear to be two underlying concerns of the parties and *amici* in this case. Respondent expresses apprehension that abandonment of "general acceptance" as the exclusive requirement for admission will result in a "free-for-all" in which befuddled juries are confounded by absurd and irrational pseudoscientific assertions. In this regard respondent seems to us to be overly pessimistic about the capabilities of the jury, and of the adversary system generally. Vigorous cross-examination, presentation of contrary evidence, and careful instruction on the burden of proof are the traditional and appropriate means of attacking shaky but admissible evidence. Additionally, in the event the trial court concludes that the scintilla of evidence presented supporting a position is insufficient to allow a reasonable juror to conclude that the position more likely than not is true, the court remains free to direct a judgment, Fed. Rule Civ. Proc. 50(a), and likewise to grant summary judgment. These conventional devices, rather than wholesale exclusion under an uncompromising "general acceptance" test, are the appropriate safeguards where the basis of scientific testimony meets the standards of Rule 702.

Petitioners and, to a greater extent, their *amici*, exhibit a different concern. They suggest that recognition of a screening role for the judge that allows for the exclusion of "invalid" evidence will sanction a stifling and repressive scientific orthodoxy and will be inimical to the search for truth. It is true that open debate is an essential part of both legal and scientific analyses. Yet there are important differences between the quest for truth in the courtroom and the quest for truth in the laboratory. Scientific conclusions are subject to perpetual revision. Law, on the other hand, must resolve disputes finally and quickly. The scientific project is advanced by broad and wide-ranging consideration of a multitude of hypotheses, for those that are incorrect will eventually be shown to be so, and that in itself is an advance. Conjectures that are

(continued)

probably wrong are of little use, however, in the project of reaching a quick, final, and binding legal judgment—often of great consequence—about a particular set of events in the past. We recognize that in practice, a gatekeeping role for the judge, no matter how flexible, inevitably on occasion will prevent the jury from learning of authentic insights and innovations. That, nevertheless, is the balance that is struck by Rules of Evidence designed not for the exhaustive search for cosmic understanding but for the particularized resolution of legal disputes.

To summarize: "general acceptance" is not a necessary precondition to the admissibility of scientific evidence under the Federal Rules of Evidence, but the Rules of Evidence—especially Rule 702—do assign to the trial judge the task of ensuring that an expert's testimony both rests on a reliable foundation and is relevant to the task at hand. Pertinent evidence based on scientifically valid principles will satisfy those demands.

The inquiries of the District Court and the Court of Appeals focused almost exclusively on "general acceptance," as gauged by publication and the decisions of other courts.

Reversed and remanded.

CASE QUESTIONS

1. What is the difference between Merrell Dow's expert and the Daubert/Schuller experts?

2. Without their experts, do Daubert and Schuller have a case?

3. What is the standard for admission of scientific evidence?

4. How does this decision affect medical product liability suits?

C O N S I D E R . . .

4.4 Karsten Manufacturing Corporation filed suit against the Professional Golf Association (PGA) because the PGA had proposed a ban of Karsten's U-groove Ping brand clubs from professional play. Karsten hired Richard Smith, then an Arizona State University finance professor, to develop an economic model to correlate professional and consumer usage. Smith's model showed that if pros play with Ping clubs, a proportionate number of duffers will play with them. If the pros cannot use Ping clubs, Karsten is out of business because amateur golfers will not purchase Karsten products. Professor Smith said he conducted valid regression analysis. The attorney for the PGA, Larry Hammond, called it "junk science" that interferes with the real issues in the case. Should the Smith model be admitted? Does it make a difference that the model was developed only for the case? Does it make a difference that Professor Smith's consulting firm was paid over $1 million for the model?

There are restrictions on the forms and types of evidence that can be used at trial. Most people are familiar with the hearsay rule of evidence. **Hearsay** is evidence offered by a witness who does not have personal knowledge of the information being given but just heard it from someone else. For example, suppose that Arkansas Sewing and Fit Fabric are involved in contract litigation. Fit says there was no contract. Arkansas has a witness who overheard the president of Fit Fabric talking to someone on a plane saying he had a contract with Arkansas but had no intention of performing on it. The witness's testimony of the airplane conversation is hearsay and cannot be used to prove the contract existed. The reason for

BIOGRAPHY

THE STORY OF THE LARGEST VERDICTS FOR 2000

Lawyers Weekly USA releases its study of jury verdicts for each year. What follows is a profile of jury verdicts in the United States for the year 2000.

- The amount of money awarded by juries fell by almost two-thirds for the year 2000 from 1999 levels.
- The 1999 total was $9 billion, but $4.6 billion of that was due to one family's verdict in a case against GM (see Chapter 11 for more information).
- The total amount of jury verdicts for 2000 was $2.6 billion.
- The largest single verdict went to former Guess model Anna Nicole Smith as a settlement for her interest in her late husband's estate ($474.7 million).
- The second largest verdict went to former Iranian hostage Terry Anderson who was held by the Iranians for nearly seven years after his capture in 1976 ($341.7 million from the government of Iran).

- The third largest verdict was also paid by the government of Iran for its role in planting a car bomb that resulted in the death of two children ($327 million).
- Both the Anderson and Smith verdicts were awarded by judges, and the remainder were jury verdicts.
- The only product liability case in the top ten verdicts for 2000 is a Firestone tire case for $105 million.
- There was one medical malpractice case in the top ten for $268.7 million awarded to the family of a teen who was killed when a physician prescribed a dose of drugs 40 times the recommended level.
- Disney, Inc., has appealed the seventh largest verdict, which was entered against it in favor of two businessmen who claim that Disney stole the idea for its sports complex at Disney World from them. The jury in Florida awarded the two men $240 million.

the hearsay rule is to keep evidence as reliable as possible. The person testifying about the hearsay may not know of the circumstances or background of the conversation and he is testifying only to what was said by another.

Once the evidence is presented and the parties are finished with their cases, there is one final "go" at the jury. The parties are permitted to make **closing arguments,** which review the evidence that was presented, highlight the important points for the jurors, and point out the defects in the other side's case. After the cases and closing arguments are presented, the jurors are given their **instructions.** These instructions tell the jurors what the law is and how to apply the law to the facts presented. The instructions are developed by the judge and all the attorneys in the case.

Jury deliberations are done privately; they cannot be recorded and no one can attend the deliberations except the jurors. Jurors can, but are not required to, discuss what happened during the deliberations after they are ended and a decision is returned to the court.

The U.S. Supreme Court has ruled that jury verdicts need not be unanimous. A state can adopt a rule that requires only a simple majority or three-fourths of the jury to agree on a verdict. In those states requiring unanimous verdicts, it is not unusual for juries to be unable to agree on a verdict. The jurors have then reached

EXHIBIT 4.9 Steps in Civil Litigation

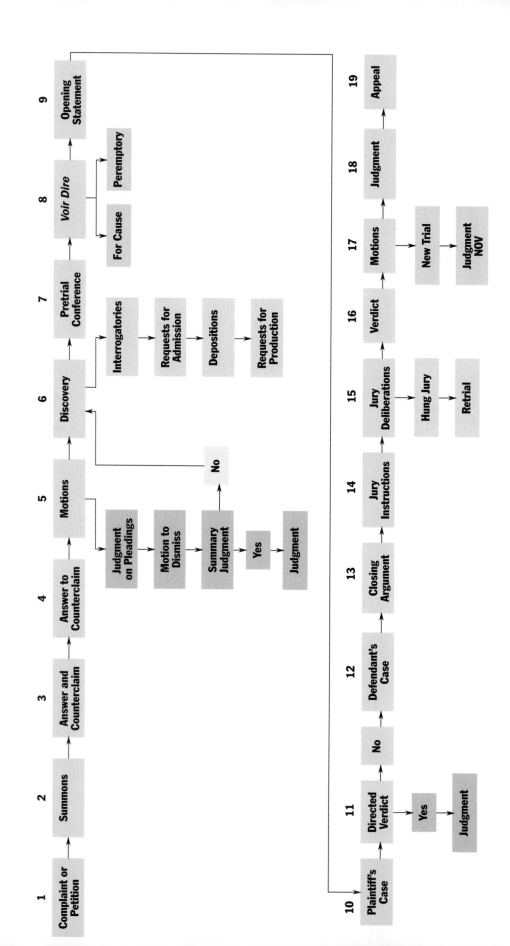

a deadlock, which is called a **hung jury.** If a trial results in a hung jury, the case can be retried. There is, however, the additional expense of retrying the case.

The result of jury deliberations is the **verdict.** The verdict is given to the judge and is usually read by the judge's clerk.

Even after the verdict, the case is not over. The losing party can make several motions to get around the verdict. One such motion is for a new trial, wherein the attorney argues the need and reason for a new trial to the judge.

Another motion after the verdict, one that a judge is less likely to grant, is a motion for a **judgment** NOV. *NOV* stands for *non obstante veredicto,* which means "notwithstanding the verdict." In other words, the moving attorney is asking the trial judge to reverse the decision of the jury. The basis for granting a judgment NOV is that the jury's verdict is clearly against the weight of the evidence. Occasionally, juries are swayed by the emotion of a case and do not apply the law properly. It is, however, a strong show of judicial authority for a judge to issue a judgment NOV, and they are rare.

Even if no motions are granted, the case still may not be over; it can go to an appellate court for review. Such an appeal must be done within a specified time limit in each state. Here the trial has come full cycle to the principle of judicial review and *stare decisis.* Exhibit 4.9 summarizes the steps in civil litigation.

ISSUES IN INTERNATIONAL LITIGATION

As noted earlier, international courts have no enforcement powers. They serve as avenues for voluntary mediation. However, courts in each nation in which a firm is doing business would have jurisdiction over that firm in the nation's court system. In a recent infringement dispute over Mattel's "Barbie" and the French doll "Sindy," the parties litigated in London, where both firms were doing business and the dolls were selling well.

Among the critical questions that arise in international litigation are, which set of laws applies? and What court is the appropriate forum for a lawsuit that involves citizens of different countries? For example, many non–U.S. citizens who are injured in their own countries by products made by U.S. firms will generally be able to recover more under the product liability and tort laws of the United States. In *Piper Aircraft Co.* v. *Reyno,* 454 U.S. 235 (1981), the pilot and five passengers were killed when a charter flight from Blackpool to Perth, Scotland, crashed in the Scottish highlands. The pilot and passengers were traveling in a twin-engine Piper Aztec, an aircraft manufactured in Pennsylvania by Piper Aircraft Co. The British Department of Trade conducted an investigation of the crash and determined that its cause was mechanical failure. The relatives and estates of the passengers brought suit in the United States against Piper Aircraft. Scottish law does not recognize strict tort liability (see Chapter 11), and U.S. laws on liability and damages are far more favorable than those of Scotland. The Supreme Court held that the case was properly heard in Scotland because the accident was in Scotland and all the parties in the case were either English or Scottish.

A similar ruling was made with respect to the 2,500 victims of the Union Carbide gas leak in Bhopal, India. Some of the victims filed suit in the United States because the law and damages provisions here afforded them much greater relief. Their suit was dismissed to India, and the court added that Union Carbide would be required to submit to the jurisdiction of Indian courts and to follow discovery rules of the United States.

Re: Following Japan in Reform

Japan's Reforms for Controlling Litigation

Many businesspeople have argued that too many lawyers and lawsuits hurt the United States in the competitive international market. The following curbs instituted in Japan have been cited as ways of controlling litigation:

Limits on the Number of Lawyers

To become a *bengoshi* (lawyer) in Japan, an individual must win a slot at the Legal Training & Research Institute. This government-run school accepts only 2 percent of the 35,000 annual applicants. Only 400 new *bengoshi* are added each year to Japan's 14,336 lawyers.

Limits on Recovery

No class actions or contingent fees are permitted in Japan.

Costs to Plaintiffs

Plaintiffs are required to pay money to their lawyers up front. The amount required is 8 percent of the recovery sought plus the nonrefundable filing fee.

Discovery Limitations

There is no discovery from either side. Parties go to trial not knowing the evidence the other side will present. The theory here is that plaintiffs must be certain about their evidence before a case goes to trial.

Limits on Damage Awards

Judges, not juries, determine damages, and even in wrongful death cases the damages may not exceed $150,000.

Encouragement of Settlement and Cultural Disdain for Confrontation

In Japan, a cultural pride exists in being able to resolve disputes outside the courtroom; those who must litigate are looked down upon.

Discussion Questions

1. If the United States adopted the Japanese litigation system, would you feel that your rights would be affected?

2. Is the United States beginning to adopt a cultural attitude to eliminate confrontation by embracing ADR?

3. In the English court system, the loser pays court costs and the costs of the other party involved in the litigation. Should such a rule be adopted in the United States? In all cases? Would you be less willing to pursue a case for yourself or your company if you knew that you would be required to pay if you lost the case?

Sources: Michele Galen et al., "Guilty," *Business Week*, April 13, 1992, 60–66; and ABA Report on International Lawyers (1990).

Some businesspeople feel the United States has too many lawyers and that too much legal activity leads to higher costs and a loss of our competitive edge in the international market.

Our legal system and its parties vary greatly from other countries' systems. "Following Japan in Reform" describes some of the limitations other countries use to control litigation.

SUMMARY

How can businesses resolve disputes?

- Alternative Dispute Resolution (ADR)—means of resolving disputes apart from court litigation

Types of ADR:

- Arbitration—hearing with relaxed rules of evidence

- Mediation—third party acts as go-between
- Conciliation–international term for mediation
- Medarb—combination of mediation and arbitration
- Minitrial—private judge and courtroom; shortened trial
- Rent-a-judge—hired judge resolves dispute
- Summary jury trial—advisory verdict by jurors in a mock trial
- Early neutral evaluation—third-party evaluation before litigation proceeds
- International Chamber of Commerce (ICC)—voluntary international court that offers arbitration in international disputes

What strategies should business follow if litigation is inevitable?

- *Voir dire*—jury selection method to screen bias
- Production—obtain and produce documents
- Deposition—questioning of witnesses under oath

How do courts proceed with litigation?

- Litigation—use of courts to resolve disputes
- Complaint—plaintiff's statement of a case
- Summons—document to serve defendant with lawsuit
- Answer—defendant's response in litigation
- Statute of limitations—time limit for filing suit
- Discovery—advance disclosure of evidence in case
- Deposition—testimony in advance of trial while under oath
- Reform—steps to limit suits and damage awards
- Trial—jury selection done through *voir dire*
- Opening statements
- Plaintiff's case
- Defendant's case
- Evidence consists of testimony, tangible evidence but not hearsay to prove the case

---

QUESTIONS AND PROBLEMS

1. Anna's Dresses, Inc., was delinquent in its payment to one of its suppliers. Anna's intended to pay them, but it had a cash-flow problem and chose to pay rent to its landlord so as not to be evicted from its store rather than make a payment to the supplier. Anna's president is served with a complaint for breach of contract and a summons. The complaint lists the supplier as the plaintiff. What has happened? What must Anna's do now?

2. In the Johns-Manville asbestos litigation, Samuel Greenstone, an attorney for eleven asbestos workers, settled their claims for $30,000 and a promise that he would not "directly or indirectly participate in the bringing of new actions against the Corporation." The 1933 case settlement was documented in the minutes of Johns-Manville's board meeting. Could the information in the minutes be used in later litigation against Johns-Manville? How could a plaintiff's attorney obtain the information?

3. In Question 2, do you feel Greenstone made an ethical decision in his agreement? Wasn't his loyalty to his eleven clients and his obligation to obtain compensation for them? Would you have agreed to the no-further-participation-in-a-lawsuit clause? Would

you, if you had been an executive at Johns-Manville, have supported the clause?

4. Whaler Manufacturing entered into a contract to buy seven lathes from Hooper, Inc. Hooper delivered the machines, and Whaler was to pay for them over a period of one year. Detroit Second National Bank came to repossess the machines from Whaler because Hooper had failed to make payment. To stop the repossession, Whaler paid Detroit the $5,000 due on Hooper's loan from Detroit. Because Whaler had only agreed to pay $4,000 for the machines to Hooper, it stopped its payments. Hooper sued for breach of contract. In answering Hooper's lawsuit, what does Whaler need to include?

5. A discrimination suit by a former flight attendant against Atlantic East Airlines is going to trial. Jury selection has begun. An executive from Atlantic East notices that a member of the potential juror panel was a flight attendant responsible for pregnancy leave reforms among airline flight attendants during the early 1980s. This potential juror is no longer a flight attendant and is raising two small children at home. The executive informs Atlantic East's lawyer. Can the lawyer do anything to prevent the woman from sitting on the jury?

6. Applegate is in litigation with Magnifium over a contract breach. Applegate has been approached by a former janitor for Magnifium who can testify regarding conversations about the contract between Magnifium executives. The janitor heard them when the executives had stayed late at work and he was doing his cleaning. Can Applegate use the statements at trial?

7. Robert Joiner began work as an electrician in the Water & Light Department of Thomasville, Georgia, in 1973. Joiner worked with and around electrical transformers that contained a fluid. In 1983, the city of Thomasville discovered that this fluid contained polychlorinated biphenyls (PCBs), a substance considered hazardous.

Joiner was diagnosed with lung cancer in 1991 and filed suit against General Electric, the manufacturer of the transformers, for negligence and product liability. Joiner had been a smoker, his parents were smokers, and there was a history of lung cancer in his family.

Joiner offered expert testimony on studies involving the injection of PCB into the stomachs of infant mice and resulting cancer. The experts had no epidemiological studies on PCB exposure. Should the expert testimony be admitted? [*General Electric Co.* v. *Joiner*, 522 U.S. 136 (1997)]

8. The ABC news program, *Day One,* ran two reports on February 28 and March 7, 1995, that left viewers with the impression that Philip Morris Company was spiking its cigarettes with nicotine to make them more addictive. Philip Morris filed a $10 billion defamation suit against Capital Cities/ABC, Inc., for defamation on March 24, 1995. The suit alleged that the "spiking" report was untrue. An ABC News spokesman said in response to the suit, "ABC News stands by its reporting on this issue."

Philip Morris is based in New York; the suit was filed in Richmond, Virginia; and a news conference to announce the suit was held in Washington, D.C., on the day hearings were to begin to determine whether the FDA should regulate nicotine as a drug. Philip Morris was not the primary target of the *Day One* report, but it was mentioned by name in the broadcasts. Philip Morris did not ask ABC for a retraction prior to filing suit.

J. D. Lee, a Knoxville, Tennessee, plaintiff's attorney who has had experience litigating against tobacco companies, noted that the prospect of getting his hands on Philip Morris's internal documents in such a suit made him gleeful: "I would have a field day with Philip Morris."

· By September 1995, ABC and Philip Morris had settled the suit. ABC issued the following public apology and agreed to pay attorneys' fees for Philip Morris:

> It is the policy of ABC News to make corrections where they are warranted. On February 28 and March 7, 1994, the ABC program, Day One, aired segments dealing with the tobacco industry. Philip Morris filed a defamation lawsuit alleging that the segments wrongly reported that, through the introduction of significant amounts of nicotine from outside sources, Philip Morris "artificially spikes" and "fortifies" its cigarettes with nicotine, and "carefully controls" and "manipulates" nicotine for the purpose of "addicting" smokers.
>
> Philip Morris states that it does not add nicotine in any measurable amount from any outside source for any purpose in the course of its manufacturing process, and that its finished cigarettes contain less nicotine than is found in the natural tobacco from which they are made.
>
> ABC does not take issue with those two statements. We now agree that we should not have reported that Philip Morris adds significant amounts of nicotine from outside sources. That was a mistake that was not deliberate on the part of ABC, but for which we accept responsibility and which requires correction. We apologize to our audience and Philip Morris.
>
> ABC and Philip Morris continue to disagree about whether the principal focus of the reports was on the use of nicotine from outside sources. Philip Morris believes that this was the main thrust of the programs. ABC believes that the principal focus of the reports was whether cigarette companies use the reconstituted tobacco process to control the levels of nicotine in cigarettes in order to keep people smoking. Philip Morris categorically denies that it does so. ABC thinks the reports speak for themselves on this issue and is prepared to have the issue resolved elsewhere.
>
> ABC and Philip Morris have agreed to discontinue the defamation action.

What do you think of Philip Morris's decision to litigate? Would you have made the same decision? Was it a public relations tactic as well as an enforcement of rights? What motivation did both sides have for settling the case? Evaluate the ethics of ABC News in running the story. Evaluate the ethics of Philip Morris in filing suit without first approaching ABC for a retraction.

9. Jared Neil is a U.S. citizen. He flew from New York City to Stockholm, Sweden, on a flight of Transnational Airways, a British corporation. The plane crashed as it was landing in Stockholm. Although no passengers were killed, Neil and others were severely injured. The crash was caused by the pilot's negligence. Could Neil sue Transnational? In which country? Are there any restrictions on his recovery? If so, what?

10. In October 1995, Saint Clair Adams applied for a job at Circuit City Stores, Inc., a national retailer of consumer electronics. Adams signed an employment application which included the following provision:

"I agree that I will settle any and all previously unasserted claims, disputes or controversies arising out of or relating to my application or candidacy for employment, employment and/or cessation of employment with Circuit City, exclusively by final and binding arbitration before a neutral Arbitrator. By way of example only, such claims include claims under federal, state, and local statutory or common law, such as the Age Discrimination in Employment Act, Title VII of the Civil Rights Act of 1964, as amended, including the amendments of the Civil Rights Act of 1991, the Americans with Disabilities Act, the law of contract and the law of tort."

Adams was hired as a sales counselor in Circuit City's store in Santa Rosa, California.

Two years later, Adams filed an employment discrimination lawsuit against Circuit City in state court, asserting claims under California's Fair Employment Act. Circuit City filed suit in the United States District Court seeking to stop the state-court action and to compel arbitration under the FAA. Adams says the arbitration clause violates his statutory rights for protection against employment discrimination and that he has the right to go to court, not arbitration. Who is correct? Can Adams be required to submit to arbitration? [*Circuit City Stores, Inc.* v. *Adams,* 532 U.S. 105 (2001)]

RESEARCH PROBLEM

Of Jurors, Stealth, and Grisham

11. Read John Grisham's novel *The Runaway Jury* and determine how lawyers might have detected the presence of a stealth juror.

NOTES

1. Lisa Brennan, "What Lawyers Like: Mediation," *National Law Journal,* Nov. 15, 1999, A1, A10.

2. Bob Van Voris, "Voir Dire Tip: Pick Former Juror," *National Law Journal,* 1 November 1999, A1, A6.

BUSINESS STRATEGY APPLICATION

The CD-ROM exercise for this chapter allows you to walk through the trial of a case, again *U.S.* v. *Microsoft.* However, now the focus is on the complaint, the answer and discovery. You will have the chance to see the pleadings in the case and also a chance to study depositions by reading Bill Gates's deposition in the case. Again you are asked to determine the strategies and risks for a company involved in such litigation. You also have a chance to study the settlement agreement for one of the private parties in the suit. This settlement shows you how ADR can work.

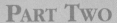

PART TWO

Business: Its Regulatory Environment

A business is regulated by everything from the U.S. Constitution to the guidelines of the Consumer Product Safety Commission. Managers must know codified law as well as the law that develops as cases are litigated and new issues of liability arise. The regulatory environment of business includes penalties for criminal conduct and punitive damages for knowing injuries to customers. Part II describes laws that regulate businesses and business operations, the sanctions that are imposed for violation of these laws, and the manner by which businesses can make compliance with the law a key part of their values.

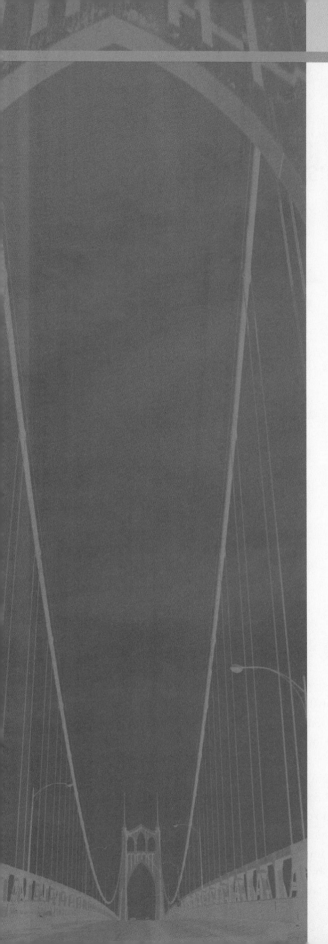

CHAPTER FIVE

Business and the Constitution

The U.S. Constitution is a remarkable document. It was drafted by a group of independent states two hundred years ago in an attempt to unify the states into one national government that could function smoothly and efficiently without depriving those independent states of their rights. The fact that it has survived so many years with so few changes is indicative of the flexibility and foresight built into the document.

This chapter covers the application of the U.S. Constitution to business. There are several questions answered in this chapter: What are the constitutional limitations on business regulation? Who has more power to regulate business—the states or the federal government? What individual freedoms granted under the Constitution apply to businesses?

Some men look at constitutions with sanctimonious reverence, and deem them like the ark of the covenant, too sacred to be touched. . . . I am certainly not an advocate for frequent and untried changes in laws and constitutions. . . . But . . . laws and institutions must go hand in hand with the progress of the human mind.

THOMAS JEFFERSON

The history of the United States has been written not merely in the halls of Congress, in the Executive offices and on the battlefields, but to a great extent in the chambers of the Supreme Court of the United States.

CHARLES WARREN

CONSIDER...

Alfonso Lopez, Jr., a twelfth-grade student at Edison High School in San Antonio, Texas, arrived at school on March 10, 1992, carrying a concealed .38 caliber handgun and five bullets. School officials, acting on an anonymous tip, confronted Lopez. He admitted that he had the gun. Lopez was arrested and charged with a violation of a Texas law that prohibits firearm possession on school premises. The next day these state criminal charges were dismissed after federal agents charged Lopez with violating the federal law called the Gun-Free School Zones Act of 1990. A federal grand jury indicted Lopez for knowing possession of a firearm in a school zone, a felony violation of the Gun-Free School Zones Act. The penalties for violation of the state law were much less and Lopez would probably be tried as a minor whereas the federal law carried mandatory prison time. Lopez asked his lawyer, "How is it that federal law applies to a high school in San Antonio? Shouldn't Texas law apply? What authority does the federal government have to run schools in Texas?"

© PhotoDisc, Inc.

THE U.S. CONSTITUTION

An Overview of the U.S. Constitution

Review the U.S. Constitution:
http://www.law.emory.edu/
FEDERAL/usconst.html

Although virtually every constitutional issue and every court decision on a constitutional issue are complicated and detailed, the **U.S. Constitution** itself is a simple and short document. Contained within it is the entire structure of the federal government, its powers, the powers of the states, and the rights of all citizens. The exact language of the U.S. Constitution is presented in Appendix A.

Articles I, II, and III—The Framework for Separation of Powers

The first three articles of the U.S. Constitution set up the three branches of the federal government. Article I establishes the **legislative branch** of the federal government. The two houses of Congress—the House of Representatives and the Senate—are created, their method of election of members is specified, and their powers are listed.

Article II creates the **executive branch** of the federal government. The office of president along with its qualifications, manner of election, term, and powers are specified.

Article III establishes the **judicial branch** of the federal government. This article creates only the U.S. Supreme Court and establishes its jurisdiction. Congress, however, is authorized to establish inferior courts, which it has done in the form of federal district courts, specialized federal courts, and U.S. courts of appeals (see Chapter 3, Exhibit 3.1).

The first three articles establish the nature of the federal government as involving the **separation of powers.** Each of these branches is given unique functions that the other branches cannot perform, but each branch also has curbing powers on the other branches of government through the exercise of its unique powers. For example, the judicial branch cannot pass laws, but it can prevent a law passed by Congress from taking effect by judicially interpreting the law as unconstitutional. The executive branch does not pass legislation but has veto power over legislation passed by Congress. The executive branch has responsibility for foreign relations and negotiating treaties. However, those treaties do not take effect until they are ratified by the Senate. This system of different powers that can be used to curb the other branches' exercise of power is called a system of **checks and balances.**

The drafters of the U.S. Constitution designed the federal government this way to avoid the accumulation of too much power in any one branch of government. In *Nixon* v. *Administrator of General Services*, 433 U.S. 425 (1977), the Supreme Court held that former President Nixon was required to turn over to Congress any records and materials of the executive branch that were relevant to the congressional inquiry into the Watergate scandal, a break-in at the Democratic Party's national headquarters that was masterminded by members of the Nixon administration. In *Department of Commerce* v. *U.S. House of Representatives*, 525 U.S. 316 (1999), the Supreme Court ruled that an administrative agency under the executive branch could not ignore either congressional statute or constitutional mandate and conduct the U.S. Census by statistical sampling. The Court ruled that the Department of Commerce had to do a physical count of all U.S. citizens as required by statute and the Constitution; and, in *Clinton* v. *Jones*, 520 U.S. 681 (1997), the U.S. Supreme Court ruled that even the president is subject to the laws of the land and is accountable for civil wrongs alleged by private citizens. In the case, Paula Corbin Jones alleged that she had been sexually harassed by Mr. Clinton while he was governor of Arkansas. The Court ruled that the president cannot be above the law or judicial process when he has violated the rights of a citizen in his private conduct. In the case, the Court quoted the federal district judge who wrote, "Nowhere in the Constitution, congressional acts, or the writings of any judge or scholar, may any credible support for such a proposition be found. It is contrary to our form of government, which asserts as did the English in the Magna Carta and the Petition of Right, that even the sovereign is subject to God and the law."

Other Articles

Article IV is the clause dealing with states' interrelationships. Article V provides the procedures for constitutional amendments. Article VI is the **Supremacy Clause** (discussed later in the chapter), and Article VII simply provides the method for state ratification of the Constitution.

The Bill of Rights

In addition to the three articles, the U.S. Constitution has twenty-seven amendments, the first ten of which are the **Bill of Rights.** Although these rights were originally applicable to federal procedures only, they were extended to apply to the states by the **Fourteenth Amendment.** These amendments cover rights from freedom of speech (First Amendment) to the right to a jury trial (Sixth Amendment) to protection of privacy from unlawful searches (Fourth Amendment) to due process before deprivation of property (Fifth Amendment). The amendments as they apply to businesses are covered later in this chapter and in Chapter 9.

THE ROLE OF JUDICIAL REVIEW AND THE CONSTITUTION

The Supreme Court and its decisions are often in the news because the cases decided by the Court are generally significant ones that provide interpretations of the U.S. Constitution and also define the extent of the rights we are afforded under it. The role of the U.S. Supreme Court is to decide what rights are provided by the general language of the U.S. Constitution. For example, the Fifth Amendment guarantees that we will not be deprived of our life, liberty, or property without "due process of law." Due process of law, interpreted by the courts many times now, includes such rights as the right to a hearing before a mortgage foreclosure or at least the right of notice before property is sold after repossession as a result of nonpayment of the debt on it.

The First Amendment protects the simple right to freedom of speech, but the Supreme Court has been faced with issues such as whether limits on campaign contributions are a violation of that right to be heard. The Fourth Amendment is the privacy amendment and protects us from warrantless searches. This general idea has been analyzed in the context of garbage taken from cans waiting for pickup on the street and unannounced inspections by OSHA regulators of company workplaces.

The U.S. Supreme Court has the responsibility of determining the extent and scope of the rights and protections afforded by the U.S. Constitution. In addition, the U.S. Supreme Court plays the unique role of reviewing the actions of the other branches of government. The Court is a crucial part of the checks-and-balances system set up in our Constitution. Recently, the Court reviewed the action of Congress for the constitutionality of its legislation granting the president line-item veto authority on the budget. The U.S. Supreme Court also reviews the constitutionality of actions taken by the other branches of government.

CONSTITUTIONAL LIMITATIONS OF ECONOMIC REGULATIONS

The Commerce Clause

The **Commerce Clause** is found in Article 1, Section 8, Part 3, of the U.S. Constitution and provides Congress with the power "[t]o regulate Commerce with foreign Nations, and among the several States, . . ." Although the language is short and simple, the phrase *among the several states* has created much controversy. The clause limits Congress to the regulation of interstate commerce. Local commerce and intrastate commerce is left to the states for regulation. Defining interstate commerce has been the task of the courts. The standards are defined from two perspectives: federal regulation of state and local commerce, and state and local regulation of interstate commerce.

Standards for Congressional Regulation
of State and Local Business Activity
The issue as defined by the Court is whether there is sufficient interstate contact or effects for the application of federal standards. The Constitution gives Congress authority to regulate "interstate" matters and vests all the remaining regulatory authority in the states.

The U.S. Supreme Court has defined the extent of interstate commerce. The Court initially gave a very narrow interpretation to the scope of the Commerce Clause. For activity to be subject to federal regulation, there had to be a "direct and immediate effect" on interstate commerce. In 1918, the Court ruled that manufacturing was not "commerce" (was solely intrastate) and struck down an act of Congress that attempted to regulate goods manufactured in plants using child labor [*Hammer* v. *Dagenhart,* 247 U.S. 251 (1918)]. During the 1930s, Congress and President Roosevelt bumped heads with the Court many times in their attempts to legislate a recovery from the depression. The Court consistently refused to validate federal legislation of manufacturing, operations, and labor [*Schechter Poultry* v. *United States,* 295 U.S. 495 (1935); *Carter* v. *Carter Coal,* 298 U.S. 238 (1936)]. Roosevelt refused to accept the roadblock to his legislation and initiated his court-packing plan to increase the number of members of the court with Roosevelt appointees.

The Court responded in *NLRB* v. *Laughlin Steel,* 336 U.S. 460 (1940), by ruling that intrastate activities, even though local in character, may still affect interstate commerce and thus be subject to federal regulation. The "affectation" doctrine thus expanded the authority of the federal government in regulating commerce. In the words of the Court, "If it is interstate commerce that feels the pinch, it does not matter how local the squeeze" (336 U.S. at 464). Today, judicial review of congressional action based on the Commerce Clause is perfunctory. Typically, there is always some connection between the legislation and congressional authority.

The Commerce Clause has had a critical role in the elimination of discrimination because the Court's liberal definition of what constitutes interstate commerce has permitted the application of federal civil rights laws to local activities.

The following case is a landmark one in which the U.S. Supreme Court defined the extent of the interstate commerce.

CONSIDER...

5.1   As you read through this decision, watch for information that helps you resolve the questions raised in the chapter opening "Consider."

CASE 5.1

U.S. v. *Morrison*
529 U.S. 598 (2000)

Economic Impact Is Not the Same as Commerce: Violence Is Intrastate Activity

FACTS

Christy Brzonkala (Petitioner) enrolled at Virginia Polytechnic Institute (Virginia Tech) in the fall of 1994. In September of that year, Brzonkala met Antonio Morrison and James Crawford (respondents), who were both students at Virginia Tech and members of its varsity football team. Brzonkala alleges that, within 30 minutes of meeting Morrison and Crawford, they assaulted and repeatedly raped her. After the attack, Morrison allegedly told Brzonkala, "You better not have any . . . diseases." In the months following the rape, Morrison also allegedly announced in the dormitory's dining room that he "like[d] to get girls drunk and. . . ." The court omitted portions of the quotes from the briefs in issuing its opinion stating only that they "consist of boasting, debased remarks about what Morrison would do to women, vulgar remarks that cannot fail to shock and offend."

Ms. Brzonkala became severely emotionally disturbed and depressed. She sought assistance from a university psychiatrist, who prescribed antidepressant medication. Shortly after the rape Brzonkala stopped attending classes and withdrew from the university.

In early 1995, Brzonkala filed a complaint against respondents under Virginia Tech's Sexual Assault Policy. During the school-conducted hearing on her complaint, Morrison admitted having sexual contact with her despite the fact that she had twice told him "no." After the hearing, Virginia Tech's Judicial Committee found insufficient evidence to punish Crawford, but found Morrison guilty of sexual assault and sentenced him to immediate suspension for two semesters.

Virginia Tech's dean of students upheld the judicial committee's sentence. However, in July 1995, Virginia Tech informed Brzonkala that Morrison intended to initiate a court challenge to his conviction under the Sexual Assault Policy. University officials told her that a second hearing would be necessary to remedy the school's error in prosecuting her complaint under that policy, which had not been widely circulated to students. The university therefore conducted a second hearing under its Abusive Conduct Policy, which was in force prior to the dissemination of the Sexual Assault Policy.

Following this second hearing the Judicial Committee again found Morrison guilty and sentenced him to an identical 2-semester suspension. This time, however, the description of Morrison's offense was, without explanation, changed from "sexual assault" to "using abusive language."

(continued)

Mr. Morrison appealed his second conviction through the university's administrative system. On August 21, 1995, Virginia Tech's senior vice president and provost set aside Mr. Morrison's punishment. She concluded that it was "'excessive when compared with other cases where there has been a finding of violation of the Abusive Conduct Policy,'" Virginia Tech did not inform Ms. Brzonkala of this decision. After learning from a newspaper that Morrison would be returning to Virginia Tech for the fall 1995 semester, she dropped out of the university.

In December 1995, Ms. Brzonkala sued Morrison, Crawford, and Virginia Tech in Federal District Court. Her complaint alleged that Morrison's and Crawford's attack violated 42 U.S.C. § 13981, the Violence Against Women Act, VAWA. Morrison and Crawford moved to dismiss this complaint on the grounds that it failed to state a claim and that § 13981's civil remedy is unconstitutional.

The district court held that Congress lacked authority for the enactment of VAWA and dismissed the complaint against Morrison and Crawford. The court of appeals affirmed the finding that VAWA was unconstitutional and Ms. Brzonkala appealed.

JUDICIAL OPINION

REHNQUIST, Chief Justice
[We] consider the constitutionality of 42 U.S.C. § 13981, which provides a federal civil remedy for the victims of gender-motivated violence.

Section 13981 was part of the Violence Against Women Act of 1994. It states that "[a]ll persons within the United States shall have the right to be free from crimes of violence motivated by gender."

42 U.S.C. § 13981(b). To enforce that right, subsection (c) declares:

"A person (including a person who acts under color of any statute, ordinance, regulation, custom, or usage of any State) who commits a crime of violence motivated by gender and thus deprives another of the right declared in subsection (b) of this section shall be liable to the party injured, in an action for the recovery of compensatory and punitive damages, injunctive and declaratory relief, and such other relief as a court may deem appropriate."

Every law enacted by Congress must be based on one or more of its powers enumerated in the Constitution. Due respect for the decisions of a coordinate branch of Government demands that we invalidate a congressional enactment only upon a plain showing that Congress has exceeded its constitutional

bounds. With this presumption of constitutionality in mind, we turn to the question whether § 13981 falls within Congress' power under Article I, § 8, of the Constitution. Brzonkala and the United States rely upon the third clause of the Article, which gives Congress power "[t]o regulate Commerce with foreign Nations, and among the several States, and with the Indian Tribes."

As we discussed at length in *Lopez*, our interpretation of the Commerce Clause has changed as our Nation has developed. We need not repeat that detailed review of the Commerce Clause's history here; it suffices to say that, in the years since *NLRB* v. *Jones & Laughlin Steel Corp.*, 301 U.S. 1, 57 S.Ct. 615, 81 L.Ed. 893 (1937), Congress has had considerably greater latitude in regulating conduct and transactions under the Commerce Clause than our previous case law permitted.

As we observed in *Lopez*, modern Commerce Clause jurisprudence has "identified three broad categories of activity that Congress may regulate under its commerce power." "First, Congress may regulate the use of the channels of interstate commerce." "Second, Congress is empowered to regulate and protect the instrumentalities of interstate commerce, or persons or things in interstate commerce, even though the threat may come only from intrastate activities." "Finally, Congress' commerce authority includes the power to regulate those activities having a substantial relation to interstate commerce, . . . i.e., those activities that substantially affect interstate commerce."

Petitioners do not contend that these cases fall within either of the first two of these categories of Commerce Clause regulation. They seek to sustain § 13981 as a regulation of activity that substantially affects interstate commerce.

Since *Lopez* most recently canvassed and clarified our case law governing this third category of Commerce Clause regulation, it provides the proper framework for conducting the required analysis of § 13981. In *Lopez*, we held that the Gun-Free School Zones Act of 1990, 18 U.S.C. § 922(q)(1)(A), which made it a federal crime to knowingly possess a firearm in a school zone, exceeded Congress' authority under the Commerce Clause.

First, we observed that § 922(q) was "a criminal statute that by its terms has nothing to do with 'commerce' or any sort of economic enterprise, however broadly one might define those terms." Reviewing our case law, we noted that "we have upheld a wide variety of congressional Acts regulating intrastate economic activity where we have concluded that the activity substantially affected interstate commerce." Although we cited only a few examples, including *Wickard* v. *Filburn*, 317 U.S. 111, 63 S.Ct. 82, 87 L.Ed. 122 (1942); *Katzenbach* v. *McClung*, 379 U.S. 294, 85 S.Ct. 377, 13 L.Ed.2d 290 (1964); and *Heart of Atlanta Motel*, we stated that the pattern of analysis is clear. "Where economic activity substantially affects interstate commerce, legislation regulating that activity will be sustained."

Both petitioners and Justice SOUTER's dissent downplay the role that the economic nature of the regulated activity plays in our Commerce Clause analysis. But a fair reading of *Lopez* shows that the noneconomic, criminal nature of the conduct at issue was central to our decision in that case. The possession of a gun in a local school zone is in no sense an economic activity that might, through repetition elsewhere, substantially affect any sort of interstate commerce. "[U]nlike the earlier cases to come before the Court here neither the actors nor their conduct has a commercial character, and neither the purposes nor the design of the statute has an evident commercial nexus. The statute makes the simple possession of a gun within 1,000 feet of the grounds of the school a criminal offense. In a sense any conduct in this interdependent world of ours has an ultimate commercial origin or consequence, but we have not yet said the commerce power may reach so far". *Lopez*'s review of Commerce Clause case law demonstrates that in those cases where we have sustained federal regulation of intrastate activity based upon the activity's substantial effects on interstate commerce, the activity in question has been some sort of economic endeavor.

. . . [w]e noted that neither § 922(q) " 'nor its legislative history contain[s] express congressional findings regarding the effects upon interstate commerce of gun possession in a school zone.' " While Congress normally is not required to make formal findings as to the substantial burdens that an activity has on interstate commerce, the existence of such findings may "enable us to evaluate the legislative judgment that the activity in question substantially affect[s] interstate commerce, even though no such substantial effect [is] visible to the naked eye."

Finally, our decision in *Lopez* rested in part on the fact that the link between gun possession and a substantial effect on interstate commerce was attenuated. The United States argued that the possession of guns may lead to violent crime, and that violent crime "can be expected to affect the functioning of the national economy. The Government also argued that the presence of guns at schools poses a threat to the educational process, which in turn threatens to produce a less efficient and productive workforce, which will negatively affect national productivity and thus interstate commerce.

We rejected these "costs of crime" and "national productivity" arguments because they would permit Congress to "regulate not only all violent crime, but all activities that might lead to violent crime, regardless of how tenuously they relate to interstate commerce."

With these principles underlying our Commerce Clause jurisprudence as reference points, the proper resolution of the present cases is clear. Gender-motivated crimes of violence are not, in any sense of the phrase, economic activity. While we need not adopt a categorical rule against aggregating the effects of any noneconomic activity in order to decide these cases, thus far in our Nation's history our cases have upheld Commerce Clause regulation of intrastate activity only where that activity is economic in nature.

In contrast with the lack of congressional findings that we faced in *Lopez*, § 13981 is supported by numerous findings regarding the serious impact that gender-motivated violence has on victims and their families. " '[S]imply because Congress may conclude that a particular activity substantially affects interstate commerce does not necessarily make it so.' " Rather, " '[w]hether particular operations affect interstate commerce sufficiently to come under the constitutional power of Congress to regulate them is ultimately a judicial rather than a legislative question, and can be settled finally only by this Court.' "

In these cases, Congress' findings are substantially weakened by the fact that they rely so heavily on a method of reasoning that we have already rejected as unworkable if we are to maintain the Constitution's enumeration of powers. Congress found that gender-motivated violence affects interstate commerce "by deterring potential victims from traveling interstate, from engaging in employment in interstate business, and from transacting with business, and in places involved in interstate commerce; . . . by diminishing national productivity, increasing medical and other costs, and decreasing the supply of and the demand for interstate products."

(continued)

Given these findings and petitioners' arguments, the concern that we expressed in *Lopez* that Congress might use the Commerce Clause to completely obliterate the Constitution's distinction between national and local authority seems well founded. The reasoning that petitioners advance seeks to follow the but-for causal chain from the initial occurrence of violent crime (the suppression of which has always been the prime object of the States' police power) to every attenuated effect upon interstate commerce. If accepted, petitioners' reasoning would allow Congress to regulate any crime as long as the nationwide, aggregated impact of that crime has substantial effects on employment, production, transit, or consumption. Indeed, if Congress may regulate gender-motivated violence, it would be able to regulate murder or any other type of violence since gender-motivated violence, as a subset of all violent crime, is certain to have lesser economic impacts than the larger class of which it is a part.

Petitioners' reasoning, moreover, will not limit Congress to regulating violence but may, as we suggested in *Lopez*, be applied equally as well to family law and other areas of traditional state regulation since the aggregate effect of marriage, divorce, and childrearing on the national economy is undoubtedly significant. Congress may have recognized this specter when it expressly precluded § 13981 from being used in the family law context. Under our written Constitution, however, the limitation of congressional authority is not solely a matter of legislative grace.

We accordingly reject the argument that Congress may regulate noneconomic, violent criminal conduct based solely on that conduct's aggregate effect on interstate commerce. The Constitution requires a distinction between what is truly national and what is truly local. In recognizing this fact we preserve one of the few principles that has been consistent since the Clause was adopted. The regulation and punishment of intrastate violence that is not directed at the instrumentalities, channels, or goods involved in interstate commerce has always been the province of the States.

Affirmed.

DISSENTING OPINION

Justice SOUTER, with whom Justice STEVENS, Justice GINSBURG, and Justice BREYER join, dissenting.

Our cases, which remain at least nominally undisturbed, stand for the following propositions.

Congress has the power to legislate with regard to activity that, in the aggregate, has a substantial effect on interstate commerce. The fact of such a substantial effect is not an issue for the courts in the first instance, but for the Congress, whose institutional capacity for gathering evidence and taking testimony far exceeds ours. By passing legislation, Congress indicates its conclusion, whether explicitly or not, that facts support its exercise of the commerce power. The business of the courts is to review the congressional assessment, not for soundness but simply for the rationality of concluding that a jurisdictional basis exists in fact. See ibid. Any explicit findings that Congress chooses to make, though not dispositive of the question of rationality, may advance judicial review by identifying factual authority on which Congress relied. Applying those propositions in these cases can lead to only one conclusion.

One obvious difference from *United States* v. *Lopez*, 514 U.S. 549, 115 S.Ct. 1624, 131 L.Ed.2d 626 (1995), is the mountain of data assembled by Congress, here showing the effects of violence against women on interstate commerce. Passage of the Act in 1994 was preceded by four years of hearings, which included testimony from physicians and law professors; from survivors of rape and domestic violence; and from representatives of state law enforcement and private business. The record includes reports on gender bias from task forces in 21 States, and we have the benefit of specific factual findings the eight separate Reports issued by Congress and its committees over the long course leading to enactment.

Indeed, the legislative record here is far more voluminous than the record compiled by Congress and found sufficient in two prior cases upholding Title II of the Civil Rights Act of 1964 against Commerce Clause challenges. In *Heart of Atlanta Motel, Inc.* v. *United States*, 379 U.S. 241, 85 S.Ct. 348, 13 L.Ed.2d 258 (1964), and *Katzenbach* v. *McClung*, 379 U.S. 294, 85 S.Ct. 377, 13 L.Ed.2d 290 (1964), the Court referred to evidence showing the consequences of racial discrimination by motels and restaurants on interstate commerce. Congress had relied on compelling anecdotal reports that individual instances of segregation cost thousands to millions of dollars. Congress also had evidence that the average black family spent substantially less than the average white family in the same income range on public accommodations, and that discrimination accounted for much of the difference.

If the analogy to the Civil Rights Act of 1964 is not plain enough, one can always look back a bit further. In *Wickard*, we upheld the application of the Agricultural Adjustment Act to the planting and consumption of homegrown wheat. The effect on interstate commerce in that case followed from the possibility that wheat grown at home for personal consumption could either be drawn into the market by rising prices, or relieve its grower of any need to purchase wheat in the market. The Commerce Clause predicate was simply the effect of the production of wheat for home consumption on supply and demand in interstate commerce. Supply and demand for goods in interstate commerce will also be affected by the deaths of 2,000 to 4,000 women annually at the hands of domestic abusers. . . . Violence against women may be found to affect interstate commerce and affect it substantially.

All of this convinces me that today's ebb of the commerce power rests on error, and at the same time leads me to doubt that the majority's view will prove to be enduring law. There is yet one more reason for doubt. Although we sense the presence of *Carter Coal*, *Schechter*, and *Usery* once again, the majority embraces them only at arm's-length. Where such decisions once stood for rules, today's opinion points to considerations by which substantial effects are discounted. Cases standing for the sufficiency of substantial effects are not overruled; cases overruled since 1937 are not quite revived. As our predecessors learned then, the practice of such *ad hoc* review cannot preserve the distinction between the judicial and the legislative, and this Court, in any event, lacks the institutional capacity to maintain such a regime for very long. This one will end when the majority realizes that the conception of the commerce power for which it entertains hopes would inevitably fail the test expressed in Justice Holmes's statement that "[t]he first call of a theory of law is that it should fit the facts." The facts that cannot be ignored today are the facts of integrated national commerce and a political relationship between States and Nation much affected by their respective treasuries and constitutional modifications adopted by the people. The federalism of some earlier time is no more adequate to account for those facts today than the theory of laissez-faire was able to govern the national economy 70 years ago.

CASE QUESTIONS

1. What does the Violence Against Women Act do?
2. What did Congress do to establish the connection of VAWA to commerce?
3. What does the majority opinion say the test is for the constitutionality of federal regulation under the Commerce Clause?
4. What does the dissenting opinion say the test for the constitutionality of federal regulation under the Commerce Clause should be?
5. Is VAWA constitutional?
6. What rights does Ms. Brzonkala have other than those afforded by VAWA?

CONSIDER . . .

5.2 Ollie's Barbecue is a family-owned restaurant in Birmingham, Alabama, specializing in barbecued meats and homemade pies, with a seating capacity of 220 customers. It is located on a state highway eleven blocks from an interstate highway and a somewhat greater distance from railroad and bus stations. The restaurant caters to a family and white-collar trade, with a take-out service for "Negroes." (Note: this term is used by the court in its opinion in the case.)

In the twelve months preceding the passage of the Civil Rights Act, the restaurant purchased locally approximately $150,000 worth of food, $69,683 or 46 percent of which was meat that it bought from a local supplier who had procured it from outside the state.

Ollie's has refused to serve Negroes in its dining accommodations since its original opening in 1927, and since July 2, 1964, it has been operating in violation of the Civil Rights Act. A lower court concluded that if it were required to serve Negroes, it would lose a substantial amount of business.

> The lower court found that the Civil Rights Act did not apply because Ollie's was not involved in "interstate commerce." Will the Commerce Clause permit application of the Civil Rights Act to Ollie's? [*Katzenbach* v. *McClung*, 379 U.S. 294 (1964)]

Standards for State Regulation of Interstate Commerce

The Commerce Clause does not deal only with the issue of federal power. The interpretation of the clause also involves how much commerce the states can regulate without interfering in the congressional domain of interstate commerce. In answering this question, the courts are concerned with two factors: (1) whether federal regulation supersedes state involvement and (2) whether the benefits achieved by the regulation outweigh the burden on interstate commerce. These two factors are meant to prevent states from passing laws that would give local industries and businesses an unfair advantage over interstate businesses. There are, however, some circumstances in which the states can regulate interstate commerce. Those circumstances occur when the state is properly exercising its **police power.**

What Is the Police Power?   The police power is the states' power to pass laws that promote the public welfare and protect public health and safety. Regulation of these primary concerns is within each state's domain. It is, however, inevitable that some of the laws dealing with public welfare and health and safety will burden interstate commerce. Many of the statutes that have been challenged constitutionally have regulated highway use. For example, there are cases that have tested a state's power to regulate the length of trucks on state highways [*Raymond Motor Transportation* v. *Rice*, 434 U.S. 429 (1978)]. In *Bibb* v. *Navajo Freight Lines, Inc.*, 359 US. 520 (1959), the Supreme Court analyzed an Illinois statute requiring all trucks using Illinois roads to be equipped with contour mudguards. These mudguards were supposed to reduce the amount of mud splattering the windshields of other drivers and preventing them from seeing. Both cases revolved around the public safety purpose of the statutes.

The Balancing Test   A statute is not entitled to constitutional protection just because it deals with public health, safety, or welfare. Although the courts try to protect the police power, that protection is not automatic. The police power is upheld only so long as the benefit achieved by the statute does not outweigh the burden imposed on interstate commerce. Each case is decided on its own facts. States present evidence of the safety benefits involved, and the interstate commerce interests present evidence of the costs and effects for interstate commerce. The question courts must answer in these constitutional cases is whether the state interest in public health, welfare, or safety outweighs the federal interest in preventing interstate commerce from being unduly burdened. In performing this balancing test, the courts of course examine the safety, welfare, and health issues. However, the courts also examine other factors, such as whether the regulation or law provides an unfair advantage to intrastate or local businesses. A prohibition on importing citrus into Florida would give in-state growers an undue advantage.

Courts also examine the degree of the effect on interstate commerce. State statutes limiting the length of commercial vehicles would require commercial truck lines to buy different trucks for certain routes or in some cases to stop at a state's border to remove one of the double trailers being pulled. Such stops can have a substantial effect on interstate travel. On the other hand, a state law that requires travelers to stop at the border for a fruit and plant check is not as burdensome: Only a stop is required, and the traveler would not be required to make any further adjustments. Also, the state's health interest is great; most fruit and plant checks are done to keep harmful insects from entering the state and destroying its crops. In the *Bibb* case, the courts found that the evidence of increased safety was not persuasive enough to outweigh the burden on interstate commerce.

Another question courts answer in their analysis is whether there is any way the state could accomplish its health, welfare, or safety goal with less of a burden on interstate commerce. Suppose a state has a health concern about having milk properly processed. One way to cover the concern is to require all milk to be processed in-state. Such a regulation clearly favors that state's businesses and imposes a great burden on out-of-state milk producers. The same result, however, could be produced by requiring all milk sellers to be licensed. The licensing procedure would allow the state to check the milk-processing procedures of all firms and accomplish the goal without imposing such a burden on out-of-state firms.

In recent years the most compelling police power issue has involved the states' authority to regulate hazardous waste disposal. The following case focuses on this issue and provides insights on evolving issues of waste disposal.

CASE 5.2

Fort Gratiot Sanitary Landfill, Inc. v. Michigan Dept. of Natural Resources
504 U.S. 353 (1992)

This Landfill Is Our Landfill

FACTS

In 1978 Michigan enacted its Solid Waste Management Act (SWMA), which required all Michigan counties to estimate the solid waste they would generate over the next 20 years and to develop plans for providing for its disposal.

St. Clair County adopted such a plan and required permits for the operation of solid waste landfills. Fort Gratiot (petitioner) held such a permit for operation.

On December 28, 1988, the Michigan legislature amended the SWMA by adopting two provisions concerning the "acceptance of waste or ash generated outside the county of disposal area." Those amendments (Waste Import Restrictions), which became effective immediately, provide:

A person shall not accept for disposal solid waste . . . that is not generated in the county in which the disposal area is located unless the acceptance of solid waste . . . that is not generated in the county is explicitly authorized in the approved county solid waste management plan. In order for a disposal area to serve the disposal needs of another county, state, or country, the service . . . must be explicitly authorized in the approved solid waste management plan of the receiving county.

On February 1, 1989, Fort Gratiot was denied a permit for operation because it accepted up to 1,750 tons per day of out-of-state waste. Fort Gratiot filed suit seeking a declaration that the Waste Import Restrictions were unconstitutional. The district court dismissed the complaint and the court of appeals affirmed. Fort Gratiot appealed.

(continued)

JUDICIAL OPINION

STEVENS, Justice

Before discussing the rather narrow issue that is contested, it is appropriate to identify certain matters that are not in dispute. Michigan's comprehensive program of regulating the collection, transportation, and disposal of solid waste, as it was enacted in 1978 and administered prior to the 1988 Waste Import Restrictions, is not challenged. No issue relating to hazardous waste is presented, and there is no claim that petitioner's operation violated any health, safety, or sanitation requirement. Nor does the case raise any question concerning policies that municipalities or other governmental agencies may pursue in the management of publicly owned facilities. The case involves only the validity of the Waste Import Restrictions as they apply to privately owned and operated landfills.

As we have long recognized, the "negative" or "dormant" aspect of the Commerce Clause prohibits States from "advanc[ing] their own commercial interests by curtailing the movement of articles of commerce, either into or out of the state." A state statute that clearly discriminates against interstate commerce is therefore unconstitutional "unless the discrimination is demonstrably justified by a valid factor unrelated to economic protectionism."

New Jersey's prohibition on the importation of solid waste failed this test. [T]he evil of protectionism can reside in legislative means as well as legislative ends. Thus, it does not matter whether that ultimate aim of [a law] is to reduce the waste disposal costs of New Jersey residents or to save remaining open lands from pollution, for we assume New Jersey has every right to protect its residents' pocketbooks as well as their environment. And it may be assumed as well that New Jersey may pursue those ends by slowing the flow of *all* waste into the State's remaining landfills, even though interstate commerce may incidentally be affected. But whatever New Jersey's ultimate purpose, it may not be accompanied by discriminating against articles of commerce coming from outside the State unless there is some reason, apart from their origin, to treat them differently. Both on its face and in its plain effect, [the law] violates this principle of nondiscrimination.

The Court has consistently found parochial legislation of this kind to be constitutionally invalid, . . .

The Waste Import Restrictions enacted by Michigan authorize each of its 83 counties to isolate itself from the national economy. Indeed, unless a county acts affirmatively to permit other waste to enter its jurisdiction, the statute affords local waste producers complete protection from competition from out-of-state waste producers who seek to use local waste disposal areas. In view of the fact that Michigan has not identified any reason, apart from its origin, why solid waste coming from outside the county should be treated differently from solid waste within the county, the foregoing reasoning would appear to control the disposition of this case.

Respondents Michigan and St. Clair County argue, however, that the Waste Import Restrictions—unlike the New Jersey prohibition on the importation of solid waste—do not discriminate against interstate commerce on their face or in effect because they treat waste from other Michigan counties no differently than waste from other States. Instead, respondents maintain, the statute regulates evenhandedly to effectuate local interests and should be upheld because the burden on interstate commerce is not clearly excessive in relation to the local benefits.

In *Dean Milk Co.* v. *Madison,* 340 U.S. 349, 71 S.Ct. 295, 95 L.Ed. 329 (1951), another Illinois litigant challenged a city ordinance that made it unlawful to sell any milk as pasteurized unless it had been processed at a plant "within a radius of five miles from the central square of Madison." We held the ordinance invalid, explaining:

[T]his regulation, like the provision invalidated in Baldwin v. Seelig, Inc., [294 U.S. 511, 5 S.Ct. 497, 79 L.Ed. 1032 (1935)], in practical effect excludes from distribution in Madison wholesome milk produced and pasteurized in Illinois. "The importer . . . may keep his milk or drink it, but sell it he may not." In thus erecting an economic barrier protecting a major local industry against competition from without the State, Madison plainly discriminates against interstate commerce.

The fact that the ordinance also discriminated against all Wisconsin producers whose facilities were more than five miles from the center of the city did not mitigate its burden on interstate commerce. As we noted, it was "immaterial that Wisconsin milk from outside the Madison area is subjected to the same proscription as that moving in interstate commerce."

In short, neither the fact that the Michigan statute purports to regulate intercounty commerce in waste nor the fact that some Michigan counties accept out-of-state waste provides an adequate basis for distinguishing this case. For the foregoing reasons, the Waste Import Restrictions unambiguously discriminate against interstate commerce and are appropriately characterized as protectionist measures that cannot withstand scrutiny under the Commerce Clause. The judgment of the Court of Appeals is therefore reversed.

DISSENTING OPINION

REHNQUIST, Chief Justice, and BLACKMUN, Justice

When confronted with a dormant Commerce Clause challenge "[t]he crucial inquiry . . . must be directed to determining whether [the challenged statute] is basically a protectionist measure, or whether it can fairly be viewed as a law directed to legitimate local concerns, with effects upon interstate commerce that are only incidental." Because I think the Michigan statute is at least arguably directed to legitimate local concerns, rather than improper economic protectionism, I would remand this case for further proceedings.

It is no secret why capacity is not expanding sufficiently to meet demand—the substantial risks attendant to waste sites make them extraordinarily unattractive neighbors. The result, of course, is that while many are willing to generate waste—indeed, it is a practical impossibility to solve the waste problem by banning waste production—few are willing to help dispose of it. Those locales that do provide disposal capacity to serve foreign waste effectively are affording reduced environmental and safety risks to the States that will not take charge of their own waste.

In adopting this legislation, the Michigan Legislature also appears to have concluded that, like the State, counties should reap as they have sown—hardly a novel proposition. It has required counties within the State to be responsible for the waste created within the county. It has accomplished this by prohibiting waste facilities from accepting waste generated from outside the county, unless special permits are obtained. In the process, of course, this facially neutral restriction (i.e., it applies equally to both interstate and intrastate waste) also works to ban disposal from out-of-state sources unless appropriate permits are procured. But I cannot agree that such a requirement, when imposed as one part of a comprehensive approach to regulating in this difficult field, is the stuff of which economic protectionism is made.

CASE QUESTIONS

1. What type of restrictions has Michigan placed on solid waste disposal?

2. Of what significance is it that the restrictions apply both to outside counties and to other states?

3. Is economic protectionism involved?

4. Does this decision on the Michigan restrictions exacerbate the problem of waste and its disposal?

5. Does the dissent support the restrictions? Why, or why not?

Congressional Regulation of Foreign Commerce

The Commerce Clause also grants Congress the power to regulate foreign commerce. The case of *Gibbons* v. *Ogden*, 9 Wheat. 1 (1824), defined foreign commerce as any "commercial intercourse between the United States and foreign nations." This power to regulate applies regardless of where the activity originates and where it ends. For example, many international trade transactions begin and end in the city of New York. Although the paperwork and delivery of the goods may be solely within one state (here within one city), the foreign commerce power is not restricted by intrastate standards. If there is foreign commerce, there can be congressional regulation regardless of the place of transaction.

ETHICAL ISSUES 5.1

Alabama is one of only sixteen states that have commercial hazardous waste landfills, and the Emelle, Alabama, facility is the largest of the twenty-one landfills of this kind located in these sixteen states.

The wastes and substances being disposed of at the Emelle facility "include substances that are inherently dangerous to human health and safety and to the environment. Such waste consists of ignitable, corrosive, toxic and reactive wastes which contain poisonous and cancer-causing chemicals and which can cause birth defects, genetic damage, blindness, crippling and death." Increasing amounts of out-of-state hazardous wastes are shipped to the Emelle facility for permanent storage each year. From 1985 through 1989, the annual tonnage of hazardous waste received has more than doubled, increasing from 341,000 tons in 1985 to 788,000 tons by 1989. Of this, up to 90 percent of the tonnage permanently buried each year is shipped in from other states.

Is it ethical for states to enjoy the economic benefits of production and dispose of waste elsewhere? Are the extra fees charged unconscionable? Couldn't states monopolize the "dumping" market and enjoy a robust economy?

Constitutional Standards for Taxation of Business

Article I, Section 8, Paragraph (1), gives Congress its powers of taxation: "The Congress shall have Power To lay and collect Taxes, Duties, Imposts and Excises, . . ." In addition, the Sixteenth Amendment to the Constitution gives this power: "The Congress shall have power to lay and collect taxes on income, from whatever source derived, without apportionment among the several States, and without regard to any census or enumeration."

It has been said that taxes are the price we pay for a civilized society. The U.S. Supreme Court has consistently upheld the ability of Congress, and local governments as well, to impose taxes. However, there is one area in taxation that still results in considerable litigation. This area involves state and local taxation of interstate commerce. Interstate businesses are not generally exempt from state and local taxes just because they are interstate businesses. However, the taxes imposed on these businesses must meet certain standards.

First, the tax cannot discriminate against interstate commerce. A tax on milk could not be higher for milk that is shipped in from out of state than for milk produced within the state.

Second, the tax cannot unduly burden interstate commerce. For example, a tax on interstate transportation companies that is based upon the weight of their trucks as measured upon entering and leaving the states would be a burdensome tax.

Third, there must be some connection—"a sufficient **nexus**"—between the state and the business being taxed. The business must have some activity in the state, such as offices, sales representatives, catalog purchasers, or distribution systems.

Finally, the tax must be apportioned fairly. This standard seeks to avoid having businesses taxed in all fifty states for their property. It also seeks to avoid having businesses pay state income tax on all their income in all fifty states. Their income and property taxes must be apportioned according to the amount of business revenues in each state and the amount of property located in that state. General Motors does not pay an inventory tax to all fifty states on all of its inventory, but it does pay an inventory tax on the inventory it holds in each state. Perhaps the most significant decision on state taxation in recent years is the following U.S. Supreme Court case on catalog sales.

CASE 5.3

Quill Corporation v. North Dakota
504 U.S. 298 (1992)

Is North Dakota a Taxing State?

FACTS

Quill is a Delaware corporation with offices and warehouses in Illinois, California, and Georgia. None of its employees works or lives in North Dakota, and it owns no property in North Dakota.

Quill sells office equipment and supplies; it solicits business through catalogs and flyers, advertisements in national periodicals, and telephone calls. Its annual national sales exceed $200 million, of which almost $1 million are made to about three thousand customers in North Dakota. The sixth largest vendor of office supplies in the state, it delivers all of its merchandise to its North Dakota customers by mail or common carriers from out-of-state locations.

As a corollary to its sales tax, North Dakota imposes a use tax upon property purchased for storage, use, or consumption within the state. North Dakota requires every "retailer maintaining a place of business in" the state to collect the tax from the consumer and remit it to the state. In 1987, North Dakota amended its statutory definition of the term "retailer" to include "every person who engages in regular or systematic solicitation of a consumer market in th[e] state." State regulations in turn define "regular or systematic solicitation" to mean three or more advertisements within a 12-month period. Thus, since 1987 mail-order companies that engage in such solicitation have been subject to the tax even if they maintain no property or personnel in North Dakota.

Quill has taken the position that North Dakota does not have the power to compel it to collect a use tax from its North Dakota customers. Consequently, the state, through its tax commissioner, filed this action to require Quill to pay taxes (as well as inter-

est and penalties) on all such sales made after July 1, 1987. The trial court ruled in Quill's favor.

The North Dakota Supreme Court reversed, and Quill appealed.

JUDICIAL OPINION

STEVENS, Justice

This case, like *National Bellas Hess, Inc. v. Department of Revenue of Ill.*, 386 U.S. 753, 87 S.Ct. 1389, 18 L.Ed.2d 505 (1967), involves a State's attempt to require an out-of-state mail-order house that has neither outlets nor sales representatives in the State to collect and pay a use tax on goods purchased for use within the State. In *Bellas Hess* we held that a similar Illinois statute violated the Due Process Clause of the Fourteenth Amendment and created an unconstitutional burden on interstate commerce. In particular, we ruled that a "seller whose only connection with customers in the State is by common carrier or the United States mail" lacked the requisite minimum contacts with the State.

In this case the Supreme Court of North Dakota declined to follow *Bellas Hess* because "the tremendous social, economic, commercial, and legal innovations" of the past quarter-century have rendered its holding "obsole[te]."

As in a number of other cases involving the application of state taxing statutes to out-of-state sellers, our holding in *Bellas Hess* relied on both the Due Process Clause and the Commerce Clause.

The Due Process Clause "requires some definite link, some minimum connection, between a state and the person, property or transaction it seeks to tax," and that the "income attributed to the State for tax purposes must be rationally related to 'values

(continued)

connected with the taxing State.'" Prior to *Bellas Hess,* we had held that that requirement was satisfied in a variety of circumstances involving use taxes. For example, the presence of sales personnel in the State, or the maintenance of local retail stores in the State, justified the exercise of that power because the seller's local activities were "plainly accorded the protection and services of the taxing State." We expressly declined to obliterate the "sharp distinction . . . between mail order sellers with retail outlets, solicitors, or property within a State, and those who do no more than communicate with customers in the State by mail or common carrier as a part of a general interstate business."

Our due process jurisprudence has evolved substantially in the 25 years since *Bellas Hess,* particularly in the area of judicial jurisdiction. Building on the seminal case of *International Shoe Co. v. Washington,* 326 U.S. 310, 66 S.Ct. 154, 90 L.Ed. 95 (1945), we have framed the relevant inquiry as whether a defendant had minimum contacts with the jurisdiction "such that the maintenance of the suit does not offend 'traditional notions of fair play and substantial justice.'"

Applying these principles, we have held that if a foreign corporation purposefully avails itself of the benefits of an economic market in the forum State, it may subject itself to the State's *in personam* jurisdiction even if it has no physical presence in the State.

Comparable reasoning justifies the imposition of the collection duty on a mail-order house that is engaged in continuous and widespread solicitation of business within a State. In "modern commercial life" it matters little that such solicitation is accomplished by a deluge of catalogs rather than a phalanx of drummers: the requirements of due process are met irrespective of a corporation's lack of physical presence in the taxing State. Thus, to the extent that our decisions have indicated that the Due Process Clause requires physical presence in a State for the imposition of duty to collect a use tax, we overrule those holdings as superseded by developments in the law of due process.

In this case, there is no question that Quill has purposefully directed its activities at North Dakota residents, that the magnitude of those contacts are more than sufficient for due process purposes, and that the use tax is related to the benefits Quill receives from access to the State. We therefore agree with the North Dakota Supreme Court's conclusion that the Due Process Clause does not bar enforcement of that State's use tax against Quill.

Affirmed.

CASE QUESTIONS

1. Did Quill Corporation own any property in North Dakota?

2. Were any Quill offices or personnel located in North Dakota?

3. How did Quill come to have customers in North Dakota?

4. Will Quill be subject to North Dakota's use tax?

5. Is there a jurisdictional difference between pamphlets being present in a state and the presence of salespeople in that state?

C O N S I D E R . . .

5.3 J.C. Penney, a retail merchandiser, has its principal place of business in Plano, Texas. It operates retail stores in all fifty states, including ten stores in Massachusetts, and a direct-mail catalog business.

In connection with its catalog business, each year Penney issued three major seasonal catalogs, as well as various small sale or specialty catalogs, that described and illustrated merchandise available for purchase by mail order. The planning, artwork, design, and layout for these catalogs were completed and paid for outside of Massachusetts, primarily in Texas, and Penney contracted with independent printing companies located outside Massachusetts to produce the catalogs. The three major catalogs were generally printed in Indiana, while the specialty catalogs were printed in South Carolina and Wisconsin. Penney supplies the printers with paper, shipping wrappers, and address labels for the catalogs; the printers supplied the ink, binding materials, and labor. None of these materials was purchased in Massachusetts.

Printed catalogs, with address labels and postage affixed, were transported by a common carrier from the printer to a U.S. Postal Service office located outside Massachusetts, where they were sent to Massachusetts addressees via third or fourth class mail. Any undeliverable catalogs were returned to Penney's distribution center in Connecticut.

The catalogs advertised a broader range of merchandise than was available for purchase in Penney's retail stores. The purpose for mailing these catalogs, free of charge, to residents of, among other places, Massachusetts, was to solicit mail order purchases from current and potential customers. Purchases of catalog merchandise were made by telephoning or returning an order form to Penney at a location outside Massachusetts, and the merchandise was shipped to customers from a Connecticut distribution center.

The Massachusetts Department of Revenue audited Penney's in 1995 and assessed a use tax, penalty, and interest on the catalogs that had been shipped into Massachusetts. The use tax is imposed in those circumstances "in which tangible personal property is sold inside or outside the Commonwealth for storage, use, or other consumption within the Commonwealth." The position of the Department was that there was a tax due of $314,674.62 on the catalogs that were used by Massachusetts customers of Penney. Penney's said such a tax was unconstitutional in that it had no control or contact with the catalogs in the state. Can the state impose the tax? [*Commissioner of Revenue* v. *J.C. Penney Co., Inc.*, 730 N.E.2d 266 (Mass. 2001)]

STATE VERSUS FEDERAL REGULATION OF BUSINESS—CONSTITUTIONAL CONFLICTS: PREEMPTION AND THE SUPREMACY CLAUSE

Although the Constitution has some specific sections dealing with the authority of the federal government and that of state and local governments, it is inevitable that there should be some crossovers in laws. For example, both state and federal governments regulate the sale of securities and have laws controlling the sale of real property. When there are crossover areas and those crossovers create conflicts, there is a constitutional issue of who has the power to regulate. This constitutional issue of conflict is governed by Article VI of the Constitution, sometimes called the **Supremacy Clause,** which provides: "This Constitution, and the Laws of the United States which shall be made in Pursuance thereof; and all Treaties made, or which shall be made, under the Authority of the United States, shall be the supreme Law of the Land; . . ."

This clause means that when state and local laws conflict with federal statutes or regulations or executive orders or treaties, the federal law, regulation, executive order, or treaty is superior to the state or local law. However, there are often cases in which a state law does not directly conflict with the federal law but the field to which the laws apply is largely regulated or preempted by the federal government. Occasionally, Congress actually specifies its intent in an act. For example, many credit laws on the federal level can be circumvented by state law so long as the state law is at least as protective as the federal law. In other words, Congress allows the states to regulate the field in some instances and sets the standards for doing so. Most statutes, however, do not specify congressional intent on **preemption.** Whether a field has been preempted is a question of fact, of interpretation, and of legislative history. The question of preemption is determined on a case-by-case basis. The questions examined in a preemption issue are:

1. What does the legislative history indicate? Some hearings offer clear statements of the effect and scope of a federal law.

2. How detailed is the federal regulation of the area? The more regulation there is, the more likely a court is to find preemption. Volume itself is indicative of congressional intent.

3. What benefits exist from having federal regulation of the area? Some matters are more easily regulated by one central government. Airlines fly across state lines, and if each state had different standards there would be no guarantee of uniform standards. The regulation of aircraft and their routes is clearly better handled by the federal government.

4. How much does a state law conflict with federal law? Is there any way that the two laws can coexist?

The following case deals with a preemption issue.

CASE 5.4

Geier v. American Honda Motor Co., Inc.
529 U.S. 861 (2000)

Explosive Preemption Issues: Honda and Airbag Liability

FACTS

In 1992, Alexis Geier (petitioner), driving a 1987 Honda Accord, collided with a tree and was seriously injured. The car was equipped with manual shoulder and lap belts which Geier had buckled up at the time. The car was not equipped with airbags or other passive restraint devices.

Geier and her parents (also petitioners), sued the car's manufacturer, American Honda Motor Company, Inc., and its affiliates (hereinafter American Honda), under District of Columbia tort law. They claimed, among other things, that American Honda had designed its car negligently and defectively because it lacked a driver's side airbag. The District Court dismissed the lawsuit. The court noted that FMVSS 208 gave car manufacturers a choice as to whether to install airbags. And the court concluded that petitioners' lawsuit, because it sought to establish a different safety standard—i.e., an airbag requirement—was expressly pre-empted by a provision of the Act which pre-empts "any safety standard" that is not identical to a federal safety standard

applicable to the same aspect of performance, 15 U.S.C. § 1392(d) (1988 ed.). The Court of Appeals agreed with the District Court.

JUDICIAL OPINION

BREYER, Justice

This case focuses on the 1984 version of a Federal Motor Vehicle Safety Standard promulgated by the Department of Transportation under the authority of the National Traffic and Motor Vehicle Safety Act of 1966, 80 Stat. 718, 15 U.S.C. § 1381 et seq. (1988 ed.). The standard, FMVSS 208, required auto manufacturers to equip some but not all of their 1987 vehicles with passive restraints. We ask whether the Act pre-empts a state common-law tort action in which the plaintiff claims that the defendant auto manufacturer, who was in compliance with the standard, should nonetheless have equipped a 1987 automobile with airbags. We conclude that the Act, taken together with FMVSS 208, pre-empts the lawsuit.

Several state courts have held to the contrary, namely, that neither the Act's express pre-emption nor FMVSS 208 pre-empts a "no airbag" tort suit. All of the Federal Circuit Courts that have considered the question, however, have found pre-emption. We now hold that this kind of "no airbag" lawsuit conflicts with the objectives of FMVSS 208, a standard authorized by the Act, and is therefore pre-empted by the Act.

In reaching our conclusion, we consider three subsidiary questions. First, does the Act's express pre-emption provision pre-empt this lawsuit? We think not. Second, do ordinary pre-emption principles nonetheless apply? We hold that they do. Third, does this lawsuit actually conflict with FMVSS 208, hence with the Act itself? We hold that it does.

We first ask whether the Safety Act's express pre-emption provision pre-empts this tort action. The provision reads as follows:

"*Whenever a Federal motor vehicle safety standard established under this subchapter is in effect, no State or political subdivision of a State shall have any authority either to establish, or to continue in effect, with respect to any motor vehicle or item of motor vehicle equipment[,] any safety standard applicable to the same aspect of performance of such vehicle or item of equipment which is not identical to the Federal standard.*" 15 U.S.C. § 1392(d) (1988 ed.).

American Honda points out that a majority of this Court has said that a somewhat similar statutory provision in a different federal statute—a provision that uses the word "requirements"—may well expressly pre-empt similar tort actions. Petitioners reply that this statute speaks of pre-empting a state-law "safety standard," not a "requirement," and that a tort action does not involve a safety standard. Hence, they conclude, the express pre-emption provision does not apply.

We need not determine the precise significance of the use of the word "standard," rather than "requirement," however, for the Act contains another provision, which resolves the disagreement. That provision, a " saving" clause, says that "[c]ompliance with" a federal safety standard "does not exempt any person from any liability under common law." 15 U.S.C. § 1397(k) (1988 ed.). The saving clause assumes that there are some significant number of common-law liability cases to save. And a reading of the express pre-emption provision that excludes common-law tort actions gives actual meaning to the saving clause's literal language, while leaving adequate room for state tort law to operate—for example, where federal law creates only a floor, i.e., a minimum safety standard. Without the saving clause, a broad reading of the express pre-emption provision arguably might pre-empt those actions, for, as we have just mentioned, it is possible to read the pre-emption provision, standing alone, as applying to standards imposed in common-law tort actions, as well as standards contained in state legislation or regulations. And if so, it would pre-empt all nonidentical state standards established in tort actions covering the same aspect of performance as an applicable federal standard, even if the federal standard merely established a minimum standard. On that broad reading of the pre-emption clause little, if any, potential "liability at common law" would remain. And few, if any, state tort actions would remain for the saving clause to save. We have found no convincing indication that Congress wanted to pre-empt, not only state statutes and regulations, but also common-law tort actions, in such circumstances. Hence the broad reading cannot be correct. The language of the pre-emption provision permits a narrow reading that excludes common-law actions. Given the presence of the saving clause, we conclude that the pre-emption clause must be so read.

We have just said that the saving clause at least removes tort actions from the scope of the express pre-emption clause. Does it do more? In particular, does it foreclose or limit the operation of ordinary pre-emption principles insofar as those principles instruct us to read statutes as pre-empting state laws (including common-law rules) that "actually conflict" with the statute or federal standards promulgated thereunder? Petitioners concede that the pre-emption provision, by itself, does not foreclose "any possibility of implied [conflict] pre-emption," . . . . But they argue that the saving clause has that very effect.

Nothing in the language of the saving clause suggests an intent to save state-law tort actions that conflict with federal regulations. The words "[c]ompliance" and "does not exempt," 15 U.S.C. § 1397(k) (1988 ed.), sound as if they simply bar a special kind of defense, namely, a defense that compliance with a federal standard automatically exempts a defendant from state law, whether the Federal Government meant that standard to be an absolute requirement or only a minimum one. It is difficult to understand why Congress would have insisted on a compliance-with-federal-regulation precondition to the provision's applicability had it wished the Act to "save" all state-law tort actions, regardless of their potential threat to the objectives of federal safety standards promulgated under that Act.

(continued)

Nor does our interpretation conflict with the purpose of the saving provision, say by rendering it ineffectual. As we have previously explained, the saving provision still makes clear that the express pre-emption provision does not of its own force pre-empt common-law tort actions. And it thereby preserves those actions that seek to establish greater safety than the minimum safety achieved by a federal regulation intended to provide a floor.

Neither do we believe that the pre-emption provision, the saving provision, or both together, create some kind of "special burden" beyond that inherent in ordinary pre-emption principles—which "special burden" would specially disfavor pre-emption here. The two provisions, read together, reflect a neutral policy, not a specially favorable or unfavorable policy, towards the application of ordinary conflict pre-emption principles. On the one hand, the pre-emption provision itself reflects a desire to subject the industry to a single, uniform set of federal safety standards. Its pre-emption of all state standards, even those that might stand in harmony with federal law, suggests an intent to avoid the conflict, uncertainty, cost, and occasional risk to safety itself that too many different safety-standard cooks might otherwise create. This policy by itself favors pre-emption of state tort suits, for the rules of law that judges and juries create or apply in such suits may themselves similarly create uncertainty and even conflict, say, when different juries in different States reach different decisions on similar facts.

Why, in any event, would Congress not have wanted ordinary pre-emption principles to apply where an actual conflict with a federal objective is at stake? Some such principle is needed. In its absence, state law could impose legal duties that would conflict directly with federal regulatory mandates, say, by premising liability upon the presence of the very windshield retention requirements that federal law requires.

The basic question, then, is whether a common-law "no airbag" action like the one before us actually conflicts with FMVSS 208. We hold that it does. In petitioners' and the dissent's view, FMVSS 208 sets a minimum airbag standard. As far as FMVSS 208 is concerned, the more airbags, and the sooner, the better. But that was not the Secretary's view. DOT's comments, which accompanied the promulgation of FMVSS 208, make clear that the standard deliberately provided the manufacturer with a range of choices among different passive restraint devices. Those choices would bring about a mix of different devices introduced gradually over time; and FMVSS 208 would thereby lower costs, overcome technical safety problems, encourage technological development, and win widespread consumer acceptance—all of which would promote FMVSS 208's safety objectives.

The history of FMVSS 208 helps explain why and how DOT sought these objectives. See generally *Motor Vehicle Mfrs. Assn. of United States, Inc.* v. *State Farm Mut. Automobile Ins. Co.,* 463 U.S. 29, 34–38, 103 S.Ct. 2856, 77 L.Ed.2d 443 (1983). [See Chapter 6 for this case.] In 1967, DOT, understanding that seatbelts would save many lives, required manufacturers to install manual seat belts in all automobiles. It became apparent, however, that most occupants simply would not buckle up their belts. DOT then began to investigate the feasibility of requiring "passive restraints," such as airbags and automatic seatbelts. In 1970, it amended FMVSS 208 to include some passive protection requirements, while making clear that airbags were one of several "equally acceptable" devices and that it neither " 'favored' [n]or expected the introduction of airbag systems." In 1971, it added an express provision permitting compliance through the use of nondetachable passive belts, and in 1972, it mandated full passive protection for all front seat occupants for vehicles manufactured after August 15, 1975, 37 Fed.Reg. 3911. Although the agency's focus was originally on airbags, FMVSS 208 was " 'a de facto airbag mandate' " because of the state of passive restraint technology, at no point did FMVSS 208 formally require the use of airbags. From the start, as in 1984, it permitted passive restraint options.

Read in light of this history, DOT's own contemporaneous explanation of FMVSS 208 makes clear that the 1984 version of FMVSS 208 reflected the following significant considerations. First, buckled up seatbelts are a vital ingredient of automobile safety. Second, despite the enormous and unnecessary risks that a passenger runs by not buckling up manual lap and shoulder belts, more than 80% of front seat passengers would leave their manual seatbelts unbuckled. Third, airbags could make up for the dangers caused by unbuckled manual belts, but they could not make up for them entirely. Fourth, passive restraint systems had their own disadvantages, for example, the dangers associated with, intrusiveness of, and corresponding public dislike for, nondetachable automatic belts. Fifth, airbags brought with them their own special risks to safety, such as the risk of danger to out-of-position occupants (usually children) in small cars. Sixth, airbags were expected to be significantly more expensive than other passive restraint devices, raising the average cost of a vehicle price $320 for full frontal airbags over the cost of a car with manual lap and shoulder seatbelts (and potentially much more if production volumes were low). And the agency worried that the high replacement cost—estimated to be $800—could lead car owners to refuse to replace them after deployment. Seventh, the public, for reasons of cost, fear, or physical intrusiveness, might resist installation or use of any of the then available passive restraint devices. . . .

DOT explained why FMVSS 208 sought the mix of devices that it expected its performance standard to produce. DOT wrote that it had rejected a proposed FMVSS 208 "all airbag" standard because of safety concerns (perceived or real) associated with airbags, which concerns threatened a "backlash" more easily overcome "if airbags" were "not the only way of complying." It added that a mix of devices would help develop data on comparative effectiveness, would allow the industry time to overcome the safety problems and the high production costs associated with airbags, and would facilitate the development of alternative, cheaper, and safer passive restraint systems. And it would thereby build public confidence necessary to avoid another interlock-type fiasco.

The 1984 FMVSS 208 standard also deliberately sought a gradual phase-in of passive restraints. And it explained that the phased-in requirement would allow more time for manufacturers to develop airbags or other, better, safer passive restraint systems. It would help develop information about the comparative effectiveness of different systems, would lead to a mix in which airbags and other nonseatbelt passive restraint systems played a more prominent role than would otherwise result, and would promote public acceptance.

Finally FMVSS 208's passive restraint requirement was conditional. DOT believed that ordinary manual lap and shoulder belts would produce about the same amount of safety as passive restraints, and at significantly lower costs—if only auto occupants would buckle up. Thus, FMVSS 208 provided for rescission of its passive restraint requirement if, by September 1, 1989, two-thirds of the States had laws in place that, like those of many other nations, required auto occupants to buckle up. The Secretary wrote that "coverage of a large percentage of the American people by seatbelt laws that are enforced would largely negate the incremental increase in safety to be expected from an automatic protection requirement." In the event, two-thirds of the States did not enact mandatory buckle-up laws, and the passive restraint requirement remained in effect.

In effect, petitioners' tort action depends upon its claim that manufacturers had a duty to install an airbag when they manufactured the 1987 Honda Accord. Such a state law—i.e., a rule of state tort law imposing such a duty—by its terms would have required manufacturers of all similar cars to install airbags rather than other passive restraint systems, such as automatic belts or passive interiors. It thereby would have presented an obstacle to the variety and mix of devices that the federal regulation sought. It would have required all manufacturers to have installed airbags in respect to the entire District-of-Columbia-related portion of their 1987 new car fleet, even though FMVSS 208 at that time required only that 10% of a manufacturer's nationwide fleet be equipped with any passive restraint device at all. It thereby also would have stood as an obstacle to the gradual passive restraint phase-in that the federal regulation deliberately imposed. In addition, it could have made less likely the adoption of a state mandatory buckle-up law. Because the rule of law for which petitioners contend would have stood "as an obstacle to the accomplishment and execution of" the important means-related federal objectives that we have just discussed, it is pre-empted.

The judgment of the Court of Appeals is affirmed.

CASE QUESTIONS

1. Why do you think the Supreme Court decided to grant *certiorari* and hear this case?

2. What in the history of the passive restraint system regulation supports a preemption finding?

3. What would happen if the states were permitted to set their own standards, via tort litigation, for auto safety devices?

4. Was there a duty to install an airbag at the time Geier purchased her Honda?

5. What standard did Honda meet in the design and safety devices of its car?

Would you have installed the airbags in your cars that you produce even though they are not required? Is it ethical not to do so? Volvo, Inc., installed airbags in its cars years

ETHICAL ISSUES 5.2

ahead of the federal mandate. Why would it choose to do so? Is there a business advantage in so doing?

CONSIDER...

5.4 Wolens and others (plaintiffs) are participants in American Airlines's frequent flyer program, AAdvantage. AAdvantage members earn mileage credits when they fly on American. The members can exchange those credits for flight tickets or class-of-service upgrades. Wolens complained that AAdvantage program modifications, instituted by American in 1988, devalued credits that AAdvantage members had already earned. The examples Wolens gave were American's imposition of capacity controls (limiting the number of seats per flight available to AAdvantage members) and blackout dates (restrictions on dates AAdvantage members could use their credits). Wolens brought suit alleging that these changes and cutbacks violated the Illinois Consumer Fraud and Deceptive Business Practices Act.

American Airlines challenged the suit on the grounds that the regulation of airlines was preempted by the Airline Deregulation Act (ADA) of 1978, which deregulated domestic air transportation but also included the following clause on preemption: "[N]o State . . . shall enact or enforce any law, rule, regulation, standard, or other provision having the force and effect of law relating to rates, routes, or services of any air carrier. . . ." [49 U.S.C. App. § 1305(a).] The Illinois Supreme Court found that the rules on the frequent flyer program were only tangentially related to rates, routes, and services and required American Airlines to defend the suit. American Airlines appealed. Who is correct? Is the litigation preempted? [*Frequent Flyer Programs: Advantage AirlinesAmerican Airlines, Inc.* v. *Wolens*, 513 U.S. 219 (1995)]

APPLICATION OF THE BILL OF RIGHTS TO BUSINESS

Certain of the amendments to the U.S. Constitution have particular significance for business. This is especially true for the First Amendment on freedom of speech and the Fourteenth Amendment for its issues of substantive and procedural due process and equal protection. The Fourth, Fifth, and Sixth Amendments on criminal procedures also have significance for business; those issues are covered in Chapter 9.

Commercial Speech and the First Amendment

Review recent legal actions taken by The Media Institute, a nonprofit research foundation for the media's right to free speech:
http://www.mediainst.org

The area of First Amendment rights and freedom of speech is complicated and full of significant cases. The discussion here is limited to First Amendment rights as they apply to businesses. The speech of business is referred to as **commercial speech,** which is communication that is used to further the economic interests of the speaker. Advertising is clearly a form of commercial speech.

First Amendment Protection for Advertising

Until the early 1970s, the U.S. Supreme Court held that commercial speech was different from the traditional speech afforded protection under the First Amendment. The result was that government regulation of commercial speech was virtually unlimited. The Court's position was refined in the 1970s, however, to a view that commercial speech was entitled to First Amendment protection but not on the same level as noncommercial speech. Commercial speech was not an absolute freedom; rather, the benefits of commercial speech were to be weighed against the benefits achieved by government regulation of that speech. Several factors are examined in performing this balancing test:

1. Is there a substantial government interest that is furthered by the restriction of the commercial speech?
2. Does the restriction directly accomplish the government interest?
3. Is there any other way of accomplishing the government interest? Can it be accomplished without regulating commercial speech? Are the restrictions no more extensive than necessary to serve that interest?

Under these standards, there is clearly authority for regulation of fraudulent advertising and advertising that violates the law. For example, if credit terms are advertised, Regulation Z requires full disclosure of all terms (see Chapter 15 for more details). This regulation is acceptable under the standards just listed. Further, restrictions on where and when advertisements are made are permissible. For example, cigarette ads are not permitted on television, and such a restriction is valid. In the following case, the court addresses an advertising prohibition.

CASE 5.5

44 Liquormart, Inc. v. *Rhode Island*
517 U.S. 484 (1996)

The Price Isn't Right: Banning Liquor Ads

FACTS

In 1956, the Rhode Island Legislature passed legislation that prohibits "advertising in any manner whatsoever" the price of any alcoholic beverage and also prohibited news media from carrying such ads. 44 Liquormart, Inc., and Peoples Super Liquor Stores, Inc. (petitioners), ran an ad in a Rhode Island newspaper in which they gave prices for peanuts, potato chips, and Schweppes mixers. Next to pictures of various brands of packaged liquor was the word "WOW!" in large letters. The ad also included the following phrase, "State law prohibits advertising liquor prices."

The Rhode Island Liquor Control Administrator found the ad in violation of the 1956 law and fined 44 Liquormart and Peoples $400. Both retailers paid the fine but brought suit challenging the ban on ads as a violation of the First Amendment freedom-of-speech rights.

The trial court concluded that the ban on price advertisements was an unconstitutional restriction on commercial speech. The Court of Appeals reversed. 44 Liquormart and Peoples appealed.

JUDICIAL OPINION

STEVENS, Justice

In accord with the role that commercial messages have long played, the law has developed to ensure

(continued)

that advertising provides consumers with accurate information about the availability of goods and services. In the early years, the common law, and later, statutes, served the consumers' interest in the receipt of accurate information in the commercial market by prohibiting fraudulent and misleading advertising. It was not until the 1970s, however, that this Court held that the First Amendment protected the dissemination of truthful and nonmisleading commercial messages about lawful products and services. . . .

In *Bigelow* v. *Virginia*, 421 U.S. 809, 95 S.Ct. 2222, 44 L.Ed.2d 600 (1975), we held that it was error to assume that commercial speech was entitled to no First Amendment protection or that it was without value in the marketplace of ideas. The following Term in *Virginia Bd. of Pharmacy* v. *Virginia Citizens Consumer Council, Inc.*, 425 U.S. 748, 96 S.Ct. 1817, 48 L.Ed.2d 346 (1976), we expanded on our holding in *Bigelow* and held that the State's blanket ban on advertising the price of prescription drugs violated the First Amendment.

. . . *Virginia Pharmacy Bd.* reflected the conclusion that the same interest that supports regulation of potentially misleading advertising, namely the public's interest in receiving accurate commercial information, also supports an interpretation of the First Amendment that provides constitutional protection for the dissemination of accurate and nonmisleading commercial messages.

We explained:

Advertising, however tasteless and excessive it sometimes may seem, is nonetheless dissemination of information as to who is producing and selling what product, for what reason, and at what price. So long as we preserve a predominantly free enterprise economy, the allocation of our resources in large measure will be made through numerous private economic decisions. It is a matter of public interest that those decisions, in the aggregate, be intelligent and well informed. To this end, the free flow of commercial information is indispensable.

The opinion further explained that a State's paternalistic assumption that the public will use truthful, nonmisleading commercial information unwisely cannot justify a decision to suppress it:

There is, of course, an alternative to this highly paternalistic approach. That alternative is to assume that this information is not in itself harmful, that people will perceive their own best interests if only they are well enough informed, and that the best means to that end is to open the channels of communication rather than to close them. If they are truly open, nothing prevents the "professional" pharmacist from marketing his own assertedly superior

product, and contrasting it with that of the low-cost, high-volume prescription drug retailer. But the choice among these alternative approaches is not ours to make or the Virginia General Assembly's. It is precisely this kind of choice, between the dangers of suppressing information, and the dangers of its misuse if it is freely available, that the First Amendment makes for us.

On the basis of these principles, our early cases uniformly struck down several broadly based bans on truthful, nonmisleading commercial speech, each of which served ends unrelated to consumer protection. Indeed, one of those cases expressly likened the rationale that *Virginia Pharmacy Bd.* employed to the one that Justice Brandeis adopted in his concurrence in *Whitney* v. *California*, 274 U.S. 357, 47 S.Ct. 641, 71 L.Ed. 1095 (1927). There, Justice Brandeis wrote, in explaining his objection to a prohibition of *political* speech, that "the remedy to be applied is more speech, not enforced silence. Only an emergency can justify repression." . . .

As our review of the case law reveals, Rhode Island errs in concluding that *all* commercial speech regulations are subject to a similar form of constitutional review simply because they target a similar category of expression. The mere fact that messages propose commercial transactions does not in and of itself dictate the constitutional analysis that should apply to decisions to supress them. See *Rubin* v. *Coors Brewing Co.*, 115 S.Ct., at 1587–1588.

When a State regulates commercial messages to protect consumers from misleading, deceptive, or aggressive sales practices, or requires the disclosure of beneficial consumer information, the purpose of its regulation is consistent with the reasons for according constitutional protection to commercial speech and therefore justifies less than strict review. However, when a State entirely prohibits the dissemination of truthful, nonmisleading commercial messages for reasons unrelated to the preservation of a fair bargaining process, there is far less reason to depart from the rigorous review that the First Amendment generally demands.

Sound reasons justify reviewing the latter type of commercial speech regulation more carefully. Most obviously, complete speech bans, unlike content-neutral restrictions on the time, place, or manner of expression, are particularly dangerous because they all but foreclose alternative means of disseminating certain information.

Our commercial speech cases have recognized the dangers that attend governmental attempts to single out certain messages for suppression. For example, in *Linmark,* 431 U.S., at 92–94, 97 S.Ct., at 1618–1619, we concluded that a ban on "For Sale" signs was "content based" and failed to leave open "satisfactory" alternative channels of communication. Moreover, last Term we upheld a 30-day prohibition against a certain form of legal solicitation largely because it left so many channels of communication open to Florida lawyers. *Florida Bar* v. *Went For It, Inc.,* 115 S.Ct. 2371, 2380–2381, 132 L.Ed.2d 541 (1995).

The special dangers that attend complete bans on truthful, nonmisleading commercial speech cannot be explained away by appeals to the "common sense distinctions" that exist between commercial and noncommercial speech. Regulations that suppress the truth are no less troubling because they target objectively verifiable information, nor are they less effective because they aim at durable messages. As a result, neither the "greater objectivity" nor the "greater hardiness" of truthful, nonmisleading commercial speech justifies reviewing its complete suppression with added deference. . . .

Precisely because bans against truthful, nonmisleading commercial speech rarely seek to protect consumers from either deception or overreaching, they usually rest solely on the offensive assumption that the public will respond "irrationally" to the truth. The First Amendment directs us to be especially skeptical of regulations that seek to keep people in the dark for what the government perceives to be their own good. That teaching applies equally to state attempts to deprive consumers of accurate information about their chosen products:

The commercial marketplace, like other spheres of our social and cultural life, provides a forum where ideas and information flourish. Some of the ideas and information are vital, some of slight worth. But the general rule is that the speaker and the audience, not the government, assess the value of the information presented. Thus, even a communication that does no more than propose a commercial transaction is entitled to the coverage of the First Amendment. . . .

In this case, there is no question that Rhode Island's price advertising ban constitutes a blanket prohibition against truthful, nonmisleading speech about a lawful product. There is also no question that the ban serves an end unrelated to consumer protection. Accordingly, we must review the price advertising ban with "special care," mindful that speech prohibitions of this type rarely survive constitutional review. The State argues that the price advertising prohibition should nevertheless be upheld because it

directly advances the State's substantial interest in promoting temperance, and because it is no more extensive than necessary. Although there is some confusion as to what Rhode Island means by temperance, we assume that the State asserts an interest in reducing alcohol consumption.

In evaluating the ban's effectiveness in advancing the State's interest, we note that a commercial speech regulation "may not be sustained if it provides only ineffective or remote support for the government's purpose." For that reason, the State bears the burden of showing not merely that its regulation will advance its interest, but also that it will do so "to a material degree." The need for the State to make such a showing is particularly great given the drastic nature of its chosen means—the wholesale suppression of truthful, nonmisleading information. Accordingly, we must determine whether the State has shown that the price advertising ban will *significantly* reduce alcohol consumption.

We can agree that common sense supports the conclusion that a prohibition against price advertising, like a collusive agreement among competitors to refrain from such advertising, will tend to mitigate competition and maintain prices at a higher level than would prevail in a completely free market. Despite the absence of proof on the point, we can even agree with the State's contention that it is reasonable to assume that demand, and hence consumption throughout the market, is somewhat lower whenever a higher, noncompetitive price level prevails. However, without any findings of fact, or indeed any evidentiary support whatsoever, we cannot agree with the assertion that the price advertising ban will significantly advance the State's interest in promoting temperance.

Although the record suggests that the price advertising ban may have some impact on the purchasing patterns of temperature drinkers of modest means, the State has presented no evidence to suggest that its speech prohibition will *significantly* reduce market-wide consumption. Indeed, the District Court's considered and uncontradicted finding on this point is directly to the contrary. Moreover, the evidence suggests that the abusive drinker will probably not be deterred by a marginal price increase, and that the true alcoholic may simply reduce his purchases of other necessities.

In addition, as the District Court noted, the State has not identified what price level would lead to a significant reduction in alcohol consumption, nor has it identified the amount that it believes prices would

(continued)

decrease without the ban. Thus, the State's own showing reveals that any connection between the ban and a significant change in alcohol consumption would be purely fortuitous.

As is evident, any conclusion that elimination of the ban would significantly increase alcohol consumption would require us to engage in the sort of "speculation or conjecture" that is an unacceptable means of demonstrating that a restriction on commercial speech directly advances the State's asserted interest. Such speculation certainly does not suffice when the State takes aim at accurate commercial information for paternalistic ends.

The State also cannot satisfy the requirement that its restriction on speech be no more extensive than necessary. It is perfectly obvious that alternative forms of regulation that would not involve any restriction on speech would be more likely to achieve the State's goal of promoting temperance. As the State's own expert conceded, higher prices can be maintained either by direct regulation or by increased taxation. Per capita purchases could be limited as is the case with prescription drugs. Even educational campaigns focused on the problems of excessive, or even moderate, drinking might prove to be more effective.

As a result, even under the less than strict standard that generally applies in commercial speech cases, the State has failed to establish a "reasonable fit" between its abridgment of speech and its temperance goal.

The State responds by arguing that it merely exercised appropriate "legislative judgment" in determining that a price advertising ban would best promote temperance.

. . . [I]n keeping with our prior holdings, we conclude that a state legislature does not have the broad discretion to suppress truthful, nonmisleading information for paternalistic purposes. As we explained in *Virginia Pharmacy Bd.*, "[i]t is precisely this kind of choice, between the dangers of suppressing information, and the dangers of its misuse if it is freely available, that the First Amendment makes for us."

We also cannot accept the State's second contention, which is premised entirely on the "greater-includes-the-lesser" reasoning.

In *Rubin* v. *Coors Brewing Co.*, 115 S.Ct. 1585, 131 L.Ed.2d 532 (1995), the United States advanced a similar argument as a basis for supporting a statutory prohibition against revealing the alcoholic content of malt beverages on product labels. We rejected the argument. Further consideration persuades us that the "greater-includes-the-lesser" argument should be rejected for the additional and more important reason that it is inconsistent with both logic and well-settled doctrine.

Although we do not dispute the proposition that greater powers include lesser ones, we fail to see how that syllogism requires the conclusion that the State's power to regulate commercial *activity* is "greater" than its power to ban truthful, nonmisleading commercial *speech*. We think it quite clear that banning speech may sometimes prove far more intrusive than banning conduct. As a venerable proverb teaches, it may prove more injurious to prevent people from teaching others how to fish than to prevent fish from being sold. Similarly, a local ordinance banning bicycle lessons may curtail freedom far more than one that prohibits bicycle riding within city limits. In short, we reject the assumption that words are necessarily less vital to freedom than actions, or that logic somehow proves that the power to prohibit an activity is necessarily "greater" than the power to suppress speech about it.

Because Rhode Island has failed to carry its heavy burden of justifying its complete ban on price advertising, we conclude that R.I. Gen. Laws § § 3-8-7 and 3-8-8.1, as well as Regulation 32 of the Rhode Island Liquor Control Administration, abridge speech in violation of the First Amendment as made applicable to the States by the Due Process Clause of the Fourteenth Amendment. The judgment of the Court of Appeals is therefore reversed.

CASE QUESTIONS

1. What was the prohibition and what justification was given for it?

2. Is the prohibition sufficiently related to the state's goal?

3. Is the prohibition constitutional?

4. What other forms of regulation could the State use to advance its goal of temperance?

CONSIDER...

5.5 Mrs. Margaret Gilleo owns a single-family home in the area of Willow Hill in Ladue, Missouri. Mrs. Gilleo placed a 24-inch by 36-inch sign on her lawn that read, "SAY NO TO WAR IN THE PERSIAN GULF. CALL CONGRESS NOW." A Ladue ordinance prohibited such signs in residential areas, and Mrs. Gilleo was asked to remove it. She filed suit, claiming the ordinance violated her free speech rights. She said that other residents were permitted to put signs up advertising their homes for sale. Should Mrs. Gilleo's rights be protected? Does it make a difference that her speech was political and not commercial speech? [*City of Ladue* v. *Gilleo*, 512 U.S. 43 (1994)]

Browse essays discussing the impact of the Internet on free speech:
http://www.scripting.com/twentyFour

Exhibit 5.1 illustrates the degrees of protection afforded business speech. The gray area represents those cases in which the need for information dissemination conflicts with regulations on ad content or form.

The shaded-area cases in the 1970s (noted in the Rhode Island case) that resulted in the reform of the commercial speech doctrine began with restrictions on professional advertising. In *Virginia State Board of Pharmacy* v. *Virginia Citizens Consumer Council, Inc.*, 425 U.S. 748 (1976), the Supreme Court dealt with the issue of the validity of a Virginia statute that made it a matter of "unprofessional conduct" for a pharmacist to advertise the price or any discount of prescription drugs. In holding the statute unconstitutional, the Court emphasized the need for the dissemination of information to the public. In a subsequent case, the Court applied the same reasoning to advertising by lawyers [*Bates* v. *State Bar of Arizona*, 433 U.S. 350 (1977)].

First Amendment Rights and Profits from Sensationalism

In the past few years, a number of book publishers and movie producers have pursued criminal figures for the rights to tell the stories of their crimes in books, television programs, and movies. Many of the victims of the crimes and their

EXHIBIT 5.1
Commercial Speech Rights and Limitations

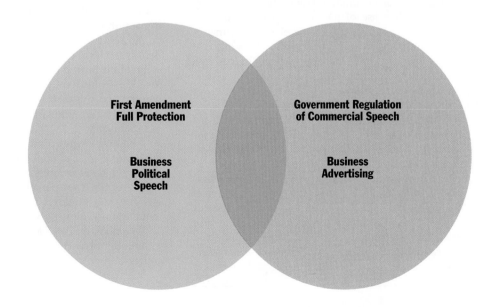

First Amendment
Full Protection

Government Regulation
of Commercial Speech

Business
Political
Speech

Business
Advertising

families have opposed such money-making ventures as benefits that encourage the commission of crimes. The state of New York, for example, has passed a statute requiring that earnings from sales of such stories be used first to compensate victims of the crimes. Statutes such as the one in New York create dilemmas between First Amendment rights and public policy issues concerning criminal activities. The following case deals with this First Amendment dilemma.

CASE 5.6

Simon & Schuster, Inc. v. *Members of the New York State Crime Victims Board*
502 U.S. 105 (1991)

Do the Crime, Make a Dime: Murderers Turned Authors

FACTS

In the summer of 1977, New York City was terrorized by a serial killer popularly known as the Son of Sam. The hunt for the Son of Sam received considerable publicity, and by the time David Berkowitz was identified as the killer and apprehended, the rights to his story were worth a substantial amount of money. Berkowitz's chance to profit from his notoriety while his victims and their families remained uncompensated did not escape the notice of New York State's legislature.

The legislature enacted what came to be known as its Son of Sam law, which provides that monies received by criminals in cases of notoriety will first be made available to crime victims. The author of the statute, Senator Emanual R. Gold, said, "It is abhorrent to one's sense of justice and decency that an individual . . . can expect to receive large sums of money for his story once he is captured—while five people are dead, [and] other people were injured as a result of his conduct."

The law is as follows:

Every person, firm, corporation, partnership, association or other legal entity contracting with any person or the representative or assignee of any person, accused or convicted of a crime in this state, with respect to the reenactment of such crime, by way of a movie, book, magazine article, tape recording, phonograph record, radio or television presentation, live entertainment of any kind, or from the expression of such accused or convicted person's thoughts, feelings, opinions or emotions regarding such crime, shall submit a copy of such contract to the board and pay over to the board any moneys which would otherwise, by terms of such contract, be owing to the person so

accused or convicted or his representatives. [N.Y. Exec. Law § 632-a(l) (McKinney 1982)]

The money is deposited in an escrow account and is payable to any victim of the crime who brings suit within five years from the establishment of the account.

Since its enactment in 1977, the Son of Sam law has been invoked only a handful of times. These include for Jean Harris, the convicted killer of "Scarsdale Diet" doctor Herman Tarnower; Mark David Chapman, the convicted assassin of John Lennon; and R. Foster Winans, the former *Wall Street Journal* columnist convicted of insider trading.

Simon & Schuster entered into a contract in 1981 with organized crime figure Henry Hill (who was arrested in 1980) and author Nicholas Pileggi for a book about Hill's life. Hill said, "At the age of twelve my ambition was to be a gangster. To be a wiseguy. To me being a wiseguy was better than being president of the United States." Hill admitted engineering some of the most daring crimes of his day, including the 1978–79 Boston College basketball point-shaving scandal and the theft of $6 million from Lufthansa Airlines in 1978, the largest successful cash robbery in U.S. history.

Hill and Pileggi produced *Wiseguy*, a book published in 1986. The book depicts, in colorful detail, the day-to-day workings of organized crime, primarily in Hill's first-person narrative. Throughout *Wiseguy*, Hill frankly admits to having participated in an astonishing variety of crimes.

The book was also a commercial success: Within 19 months of its publication, more than a million copies were in print. A few years later, the book was converted into a film called *Goodfellas,* which won a host of awards as the best film of 1990.

The Crime Victims Board requested that Simon & Schuster turn over all monies paid to Hill and that all future royalties be payable not to Hill but to the statutorily prescribed escrow account.

Simon & Schuster brought suit seeking both a declaration that the Son of Sam law violates the First Amendment and an injunction barring the statute's enforcement. The district court found the statute consistent with the First Amendment. A divided court of appeals affirmed. Simon & Schuster appealed.

JUDICIAL OPINION

O'CONNOR, Justice

A statute is presumptively inconsistent with the First Amendment if it imposes a financial burden on speakers because of the content of their speech.

"Regulations which permit the Government to discriminate on the basis of the content of the message cannot be tolerated under the First Amendment."

The Son of Sam law is such a content-based statute. It singles out income derived from expressive activity for a burden the State places on no other income, and it is directed only at works with a specified content. Whether the First Amendment "speaker" is considered to be Henry Hill, whose income the statute places in escrow because of the story he has told, or Simon & Schuster, which can publish books about crime with the assistance of only those criminals willing to forgo remuneration for at least five years, the statute plainly imposes a financial disincentive only on speech of a particular content.

The Son of Sam law establishes a financial disincentive to create or publish works with a particular content. In order to justify such differential treatment, "the State must show that its regulation is necessary to serve a compelling state interest and is narrowly drawn to achieve that end."

There can be little doubt, on the other hand, that the State has a compelling interest in ensuring that victims of crime are compensated by those who harm them. Every State has a body of tort law serving exactly this interest. The State's interest in preventing wrongdoers from dissipating their assets before victims can recover explains the existence of the State's statutory provisions for prejudgment remedies and orders of restitution.

The State likewise has an undisputed compelling interest in ensuring that criminals do not profit from their crimes. Like most if not all States, New York has long recognized the "fundamental equitable principle," that "[n]o one shall be permitted to profit by his own fraud, or to take advantage of his own wrong, or to found any claim upon his own iniquity, or to acquire property by his own crime."

As a means of ensuring that victims are compensated from the proceeds of crime, the Son of Sam law is significantly over inclusive. As counsel for the Board conceded at oral argument, the statute applies to works on *any* subject, provided that they express the author's thoughts or recollections about his crime, however tangentially or incidentally. In addition, the statute's broad definition of "person convicted of a crime" enables the Board to escrow the income of any author who admits in his work to having committed a crime, whether or not the author was ever actually accused or convicted.

These two provisions combine to encompass a potentially very large number of works. Had the Son of Sam law been in effect at the time and place of publication, it would have escrowed payment for such works as *The Autobiography of Malcolm X,* which describes crimes committed by the civil rights leader before he became a public figure; *Civil Disobedience,* in which Thoreau acknowledges his refusal to pay taxes and recalls his experience in jail; and even the *Confessions of Saint Augustine,* in which the author laments "my past foulness and the carnal corruptions of my soul," one instance of which involved the theft of pears from a neighboring vineyard. The argument that a statute like the Son of Sam law would prevent publication of all of these works is hyperbole—some would have been written without compensation—but the Son of Sam law clearly reaches a wide range of literature that does not enable a criminal to profit from his crime while a victim remains uncompensated.

Should a prominent figure write his autobiography at the end of his career, and include in an early chapter a brief recollection of having stolen (in New York) a nearly worthless item as a youthful prank, the Board would control his entire income from the book for five years, and would make that income available to all of the author's creditors, despite the fact that the statute of limitations for this minor incident had long since run.

The State's interest in compensating victims from the fruits of crime is a compelling one, but the Son of

(continued)

Sam law is not narrowly tailored to advance that objective. As a result, the statute is inconsistent with the First Amendment.

The judgment of the Court of Appeals is accordingly reversed.

CASE QUESTIONS

1. Why was the so-called Son of Sam law passed?

2. What happened to monies earned by criminals for "selling their stories"?

3. What book is at issue in this case?

4. Does the Son of Sam statute violate the First Amendment?

5. How can the statute be rewritten?

6. Does Hill keep his royalties?

Orenthal James (O. J.) Simpson was charged with murder in June 1994 in the double homicide of his ex-wife, Nicole Brown Simpson, and her friend Ronald Goldman.

Because Mr. Simpson was charged with a capital crime, he was incarcerated upon being charged. California's version of the Son of Sam law only prevents profits from crimes after there has been a conviction. Mr. Simpson authored a book, *I Want to Tell You*, while he was incarcerated and his nine-month trial progressed. Mr. Simpson also signed autographs and sports memorabilia and sold them from the Los Angeles County jail. Mr. Simpson's cottage industry from jail netted him in excess of $3 million. Could a law that passes constitutional muster be passed to prevent profits from crime like those Mr. Simpson was able to obtain?

Mr. Simpson was acquitted of the murders. Following his acquittal, prosecutors in the case, Christopher

ETHICAL ISSUES 5.3

Darden, Marcia Clark, and Hank Goldberg signed multimillion dollar book contracts to write about their experiences during the trial. Alan Dershowitz, Johnnie Cochran, and Robert Shapiro, members of the Simpson defense team, signed six-figure contracts to write books about the trial from the defense perspective. Daniel Petrocelli, the lawyer who represented the Goldmans in their civil suit against Simpson, also has a new book, *Triumph of Justice: The Final Judgment on the Simpson Saga*. Mr. Simpson has not yet signed for a new book but did make a video detailing his side of the story.

Is it moral to profit from a crime and a trial? Are these contracts a form of making money from the deaths of two people? Many TV stations have refused to carry advertisements for Mr. Simpson's video. Would you have declined this advertising revenue?

Corporate Political Speech

Not all commercial speech is advertising. Some businesses engage in **corporate political speech.** For example, many businesses will participate in advertising campaigns against certain propositions or resolutions—for example, tax resolutions going before the voters. However, many states once restricted the political advertising allowed corporations and other businesses. The rationale for such a restriction was that corporate assets and funds were great and that corporations might be able to exercise too much power in influencing voters.

In *First National Bank of Boston* v. *Bellotti*, the U.S. Supreme Court developed what has become known as the *Bellotti* doctrine, which gives corporations the same degree of First Amendment protection for their political speech that individuals enjoy in their political speech. Although commercial speech can be regulated, political speech enjoys full First Amendment rights.

CASE 5.7

First National Bank of Boston v. Bellotti
435 U.S. 765 (1978)

Banks Are People, Too: First Amendment Political Speech

FACTS

Massachusetts had passed a statute that prohibited businesses and banks from making contributions or expenditures "for the purpose of . . . influencing or affecting the vote on any question submitted to the voters, other than one materially affecting any of the property, business or assets of the corporation." The statute also provided that "no question submitted to the voters solely concerning the taxation of the income, property or transactions of individuals shall be deemed materially to affect the property, business or assets of the corporation." The statute carried a fine of up to $50,000 for the corporation and $10,000 and/or one year imprisonment for corporate officers.

First National Bank and other banks and corporations (appellants) wanted to spend money to publicize their views on an upcoming ballot proposition that would permit the legislature the right to impose a graduated tax on individual income. Frances X. Bellotti, the attorney general for Massachusetts (appellee), told First National and the others that he intended to enforce the statute against them. First National and the others brought suit to have the statute declared unconstitutional. The lower courts held the statute constitutional and First National appealed.

JUDICIAL OPINION

POWELL, Justice
"There is practically universal agreement that a major purpose of [the First] Amendment was to protect the free discussion of governmental affairs." If the speakers here were not corporations, no one would suggest that the State could silence their proposed speech. It is the type of speech indispensable to decision making in a democracy, and this is no less true because the speech comes from a corporation rather than an individual. The inherent worth of the speech in terms of its capacity for informing the public does not depend upon the identity of its source, whether corporation, association, union, or individual.

The court below nevertheless held that corporate speech is protected by the First Amendment only when it pertains directly to the corporation's interests. In deciding whether this novel and restrictive gloss on the First Amendment comports with the Constitution and the precedents of this Court, we need not survey the outer boundaries of the Amendment's protection of corporate speech, or address the abstract question whether corporations have the full measure of rights that individuals enjoy under the First Amendment. The question in this case, simply put, is whether the corporate identity of the speaker deprives this proposed speech of what otherwise would be its clear entitlement to protection.

Freedom of speech and the other freedoms encompassed by the First Amendment always have been viewed as fundamental components of the liberty safeguarded by the Due Process Clause, and the Court has not identified a separate source for the right when it has been asserted by corporations.

In the realm of protected speech, the legislature is constitutionally disqualified from dictating the subjects about which persons may speak and the speakers who may address a public issue. If a legislature may direct business corporations to "stick to business," it may also limit other corporations—religious, charitable, or civic—to their respective "business" when addressing the public. Such power

(continued)

in government to channel the expression of views is unacceptable under the First Amendment. Especially where, as here, the legislature's suppression of speech suggests an attempt to give one side of a debatable public question an advantage in expressing its views to people, the First Amendment is plainly offended. Yet the State contends that its action is necessitated by governmental interests of the highest order. We next consider these asserted interests.

Appellee . . . advances two principal justifications for the prohibition of corporate speech. The first is the State's interest in sustaining the active role of the individual citizen in the electoral process and thereby preventing diminution of the citizen's confidence in government. The second is the interest in protecting the rights of shareholders whose views differ from those expressed by management on behalf of the corporation.

Preserving the integrity of the electoral process, preventing corruption and "sustaining the active, alert responsibility of the individual citizen in a democracy for the wise conduct of government" are interests of the highest importance. Preservation of the individual citizen's confidence in government is equally important.

To be sure, corporate advertising may influence the outcome of the vote; this would be its purpose. But the fact that advocacy may persuade the electorate is hardly a reason to suppress it: The Constitution "protects expression which is eloquent no less than that which is unconvincing." We noted only recently that "the concept that government may restrict speech of some elements of our society in order to enhance the relative voice of others is wholly foreign to the First Amendment. . . ." Moreover, the people in our democracy are entrusted with the responsibility for judging and evaluating the relative merits of conflicting arguments. They may consider, in making their judgment, the source and credibility of the advocate. But if there be any danger that the

people cannot evaluate the information and arguments advanced by appellants, it is a danger contemplated by the Framers of the First Amendment.

The statute is said to . . . prevent the use of corporate resources in furtherance of views with which some shareholders may disagree. This purpose is belied, however, by the provisions of the statute, which are both under- and over-inclusive.

The under-inclusiveness of the statute is self-evident. Corporate expenditures with respect to a referendum are prohibited, while corporate activity with respect to the passage or defeat of legislation is permitted, even though corporations may engage in lobbying more often than they take positions on ballot questions submitted to voters.

The over-inclusiveness of the statute is demonstrated by the fact that [it] would prohibit a corporation from supporting or opposing a referendum even if its shareholders unanimously authorized the contribution or expenditure.

Assuming, arguendo, that protection of shareholders is a "compelling" interest under the circumstances of this case, we find "no substantially relevant correlation between the governmental interest asserted and the State's effort" to prohibit appellants from speaking.

Reversed.

CASE QUESTIONS

1. What did the Massachusetts statute regulate?
2. What justification did Massachusetts offer for the statute? What were its concerns in passing the statute?
3. Why does the Court discuss under-inclusiveness and over-inclusiveness?
4. How does the Court respond to the fact that corporate speech might be more persuasive?
5. Is the statute constitutional?

Eminent Domain—The Takings Clause

The right of a governmental body to take title to property for a public use is called **eminent domain.** This right is established in the Fifth Amendment to the Constitution and may also be established in various state constitutions. Private individuals cannot require property owners to sell their property, but governmental entities can require property owners to transfer title for public projects for the public

BUSINESS STRATEGY

The issue of corporate political donations became a central focus of the 2000 presidential elections with Senator John McCain running on a platform of controlling "special interest" money with his focus being on corporate donations.

© PhotoDisc, Inc.

Businesses do have an active voice in the political arena through political action committee donations (PAC money, also known as "hard dollars") and donations to political parties where there are no limits on the amounts that can be given (so-called "soft dollars"). A look at the following list of top corporate/trade PACs indicates that those businesses whose markets or prices are controlled by the government are the most active political voices.

Rank/Name
1. Realtors Political Action Committee
2. Association of Trial Lawyers of America Political Action Committee
3. American Federation of State, County, & Municipal Employees (AFSCME)
4. Dealers Election Action Committee of the National Automobile Dealers Association (NADA)
5. Democrat Republican Independent Voter Education
6. International Brotherhood of Electrical Workers Committee on Political Education
7. Machinists Nonpartisan Political League
8. UAW-V-CAP (UAW Voluntary Community Action Program)
9. American Medical Association Political Action Committee
10. Service Employees International Union Political Campaign Committee
11. National Beer Wholesalers' Association Political Action Committee (NBWA PAC)
12. Build Political Action Committee of the National Association of Home Builders
13. Laborers' Political League-Laborers' International Union of NA
14. United Parcel Service Inc Political Action Committee

good. The Fifth Amendment provides that "property shall not be taken for a public use without just compensation." Thus, for a governmental entity to exercise properly the right of eminent domain, three factors must be present: public purpose, taking (as opposed to regulating), and just compensation.

Public Purpose

To exercise eminent domain, the exercising governmental authority must establish that the taking is necessary for the accomplishment of a government or *public purpose*. When eminent domain is mentioned, use of property for highways and schools is thought of most frequently. However, the right of the government to eminent domain extends much further. For example, the following uses have been held to constitute public purposes: the condemnation of slum housing (for purposes of improving city areas), the limitation of mining and excavation within city limits, the declaration of property as a historic landmark, and the taking of property to provide a firm that is a town's economic base with a large enough tract for expansion.

According to the U. S. Supreme Court, the public purpose requirement for eminent domain is to be interpreted broadly, and "the role of the judiciary in determining whether that power is being exercised for a public purpose is an extremely narrow one" [*United States ex rel. TVA v. Welch*, 327 U.S. 546 (1946)].

Re: A Look at the Supreme Court

The court does not operate in a vacuum, nor is it composed of Olympians. It functions as a legal, governmental, and political institution under a basic document that stands in constant need of interpretation against the backdrop of what Holmes referred to as the "felt necessities of the times"—always provided the presence of explicit or implicit constitutional authority.

Our Founding Fathers created a magnificent Constitution. But they could hardly foresee some of the contemporary problems that have found their way to the Court for resolution. Indeed, whereas for most of our history we have made laws to help solve public issues, in recent years the byword has been "let's go to court." It is a regrettable development but one that is here to stay.

The nine Supreme Court justices who interpret the Constitution are steeped and trained in the law. But they respond to human situations: In Justice Cardozo's beautiful and telling words, "The great tides and currents which engulf the rest of mankind do not turn aside in their course and pass the judges idly by"; and in Justice Frankfurter's parlance, the judges are "[m]en . . . not disembodied spirits, they respond to human emotions."

Moreover, the justices are well aware of two important facts of life: ultimately they do not have the power to enforce their decisions, for the purse is in the hands of the legislature and the sword in those of the executive; and the Court may be reversed by legislative action or by constitutional amendment. We should recognize that much of our reaction to the Court's ruling is highly subjective. A "good" decision is one that pleases us; a "poor" one is one that does not. All too often our response depends on "whose ox is gored." Nor is that bit of wisdom confined to laypersons. It includes political leaders, such as presidents whose calls for strict constructionists on the bench may be but a thinly disguised synonym for justices who agree with their philosophy of government and politics.

There is, of course, nothing wrong in a president's attempt to staff the Court with jurists who read the Constitution his way. All presidents have tried to pack the Court, to mold it in their images. Nothing is wrong with this, provided, however, that the nominees are professionally, intellectually, and morally qualified to serve.

The Supreme Court of the United States is, indeed, engaged in the political process; but, in Justice Frankfurter's admonition, it is "the Nation's ultimate judicial tribunal, not a super-legal aid bureau." Neither is the Court, in the second Justice Harlan's admonition, "a panacea for every blot upon the public welfare, nor should this Court ordained as a judicial body, be thought of as a general haven for reform movements." In other words, the Constitution of the United States was simply not designed to provide judicial remedies for every social or political ill.

The Supreme Court is much better at saying yes or no to the government than in prescribing policy; indeed, it should resolutely shun *prescriptive* policymaking. It has quite enough to do in constitutional and statutory interpretation and application. The Court is much better at saying what the government may *not* do or what it *may* do than in prescribing what public policy the government ought to chart and how to go about doing it. Paraphrasing Professor Paul A. Freund, the question is not whether the Court can do everything, but whether it can do something in its proper sphere.

Of course, all judging involves decision making, and the Court can escape neither controversy nor criticism, nor should it. In Justice Holmes's oft-quoted words: "We are very quiet up there, but it is the quiet of a storm center, as we all know." As an institution at once legal, political, and human, it possesses both the assets and liabilities that attend these descriptive characteristics.

Yet, when all is said and done, the Court is the "living voice of the Constitution," as Lord Bryce once phrased it. As such it is both arbiter and educator and, in essence, represents the sole solution short of anarchy under the American system of government as we know it. Within the limits of procedure and deference to the presumption of the constitutionality of legislation, the Court—our sober second thought—is the natural forum in American society for the individual and small groups, what Madison, the father of the Bill of Rights, fervently hoped it would always be. The Court is infinitely more qualified to protect minority rights than the far more easily pressured, more impulsive, and more emotionally charged legislative and executive branches. All too readily do these two yield to the politically expedient and the popular, for they are close indeed to what Judge Learned Hand once called "the pressure of public panic, and public greed."

In general, if not unfailingly, the Supreme Court of the United States has evinced a remarkable degree of common constitutional sense in its striving, as a voice of reason, to maintain the blend of continuity and change that constitute the *sine qua non* for desirable stability in the basic governmental processes of a democracy. In that role it will—because it must—live in history.

Source: Henry J. Abraham, *Justices and Presidents: A Political History of Appointments to the Supreme Court*, 3rd ed. (New York: Oxford University Press), 1992, 370–373. Copyright © 1974, 1985, 1992 by Henry J. Abraham Used by permission of Oxford University Press, Inc.

Taking or Regulating

For a governmental entity to be required to pay a landowner compensation under the doctrine of eminent domain, that there has been a taking of the property must be established. Mere regulation of the property does not constitute a taking, as established by *Village of Euclid, Ohio* v. *Ambler Realty Co.*, 272 U.S. 365 (1926). Rather, a taking must go so far as to deprive the landowner of any use of the property. In the landmark case of *Pennsylvania Coal* v. *Mahon*, 260 U.S. 393 (1922), the Supreme Court established standards for determining a taking as opposed to mere regulation. At that time Pennsylvania had a statute that prohibited the mining of coal under any land surface where the result would be the subsidence of any structure used as a human habitation. The owners of the rights to mine subsurface coal brought suit challenging the regulation as a taking, and the Supreme Court ruled in their favor, holding that the statute was more than regulation and, in fact, was an actual taking of the subsurface property rights.

Because of the vast amount of technology that has developed since that case was decided, there are many new and subtly different issues in what constitutes a taking. For example, in some areas the regulation of cable television companies is an infringement on air rights. Such specialized areas of real estate rights are particularly difficult to resolve. In *Loretto* v. *Teleprompter Manhattan CATV Corp.*, 458 U.S. 100 (1982), the U.S. Supreme Court held that the small invasion of property by the placement of cable boxes and wires did constitute a taking, albeit very small, and required compensation of the property owners for this small, but permanent, occupation of their land. Recently, the courts have been faced with the issue of whether zoning or use regulations serve to limit the use of land so much that the result is a taking.

In recent years, the issue of taking has addressed local zoning restrictions on development. These restrictions focus on maintenance of beaches, wetlands, and other natural habitats. For example, in *Nollan* v. *California Coastal Commission*, 483 U.S. 825 (1987), the Nollans sought permission from the California Coastal Commission to construct a home on their coastal lot where they currently had only a small bungalow. The commission refused to grant permission to the Nollans for construction of their home unless they agreed to give a public easement across their lot for beach access. The Supreme Court held that the demand by the commission for an easement was a taking without compensation and, in effect,

BIOGRAPHY

A LOOK AT SUPREME COURT DECISION DYNAMICS

look at the most recent term of the U.S. Supreme Court

- The most common majority (in thirteen cases) consisted of Justices Rehnquist, O'Connor, Scalia, Kennedy, and Thomas.
- There were nineteen unanimous decisions. In 1998–99, there were eighteen; in 1997–98 there were twenty-nine.

DISSENTING OPINIONS

Justice	Number of Dissenting Opinions
Rehnquist	26
Stevens	18
O'Connor	28
Scalia	10
Kennedy	17
Souter	4
Thomas	20
Ginsburg	5
Breyer	14

- Justice Breyer agreed most often with Justice Stevens and least often with Justice Thomas.
- Justice Ginsburg agreed most often with Justice Souter and least often with Justice Scalia.
- Justice Thomas agreed most often with Justice Scalia and least often with Justice Ginsburg.
- Justice Kennedy agreed most often with Justice O'Connor and least often with Justice Ginsburg.
- Justice O'Connor agreed most often with Justice Rehnquist and least often with Justice Stevens.
- Justice Stevens agreed most often with Justice Ginsburg and least often with Justice Scalia.
- Chief Justice Rehnquist agreed most often with Justice O'Connor and least often with Justice Stevens.

THE MONEY

- Salary for supreme court associate justices: $173,600
- Salary for the chief justice: $181,400

prevented the Nollans from using their property until they surrendered their exclusive use.

Yet another issue that arises in taking occurs when regulations take effect after owners have acquired land but before it is developed. In *Lucas* v. *South Carolina Coastal Council*, 505 U.S. 1003 (1992), the U.S. Supreme Court declared that *ex post facto* legislation that prevents development of previously purchased land is a taking. In *Lucas*, David Lucas purchased for $975,000 two residential lots on the Isle of Palms in Charleston County, South Carolina. In 1988, the South Carolina legislature enacted the Beachfront Management Act, which barred any permanent habitable structures on coastal properties. The court held South Carolina was required to compensate Mr. Lucas because his land was rendered useless.

Just Compensation

The final requirement for the proper exercise by a governmental entity of the right of eminent domain is that the party from whom the property is being taken be given **just compensation.** The issue of just compensation is difficult to determine and is always a question of fact. Basic to this determination is that the owner is to be compensated for loss and that the compensation is not measured by the governmental entity's gain. In *United States* v. *Miller*, 317 U.S. 369 (1943), the Supreme Court held that in cases where it can be determined, fair market value is the measure of compensation; and, in *United States ex rel. TVA* v. *Powelson*, 319 U.S. 266

(1943), the Supreme Court defined fair market value to be "what a willing buyer would pay in cash to a willing seller."

Possible problems in applying these relatively simple standards include peculiar value to the owner, consequential damages, and greater value of the land because of the proposed governmental project. Basically, the issue of just compensation becomes an issue of appraisal, which is affected by all the various factors involved. Thus, in determining just compensation, the courts must consider such factors as surrounding property values and the owner's proposed use.

Procedural Due Process

Both the Fifth and the Fourteenth Amendments require state and federal governments to provide citizens (businesses included) due process under the law. **Procedural due process** is a right that requires notice and the opportunity to be heard before rights or properties are taken away from an individual or business. Most people are familiar with due process as it exists in the criminal justice system: the right to a lawyer, a trial, and so on (Chapter 9). However, procedural due process is also very much a part of civil law. Before an agency can take away a business license or suspend a license or impose a fine for a violation, there must be due process. This is true of both state and federal agencies.

Businesses encounter the constitutional protections of due process in their relationships with customers. For example, the eviction of a nonpaying tenant cannot be done unilaterally. The tenant has the right to be heard in the setting of a hearing. The landlord must file an action against the tenant, and the tenant will have the opportunity to present defenses for nonpayment of rent. The Due Process Clause of the U.S. Constitution provides protection for individuals before their property is taken. Property includes land (as in the case of eminent domain, see pgs. 193–196), rights of possession (tenants and leases), and even intangible property rights. For example, students cannot be expelled from schools, colleges, or universities without the right to be heard. Students must have some hearing before their property rights with respect to education are taken away.

All proceedings designed to satisfy due process requirements must provide notice and the right to be heard and present evidence (see Chapter 6 for more details). If these rights are not afforded, the constitutional right of due process has been denied and the action taken is rescinded until due process requirements are met. Suppose that OSHA charged a company with safety violations in its plants. Before a fine or order could be imposed, procedural due process requires that the company have the right to be heard and present evidence on the violation. In court cases, a matter reduced to a judgment entitles the victorious side to collect on that judgment. However, under due process, even the proceedings for collection allow the losing party or debtor to be notified of the proceedings and to be heard.

C O N S I D E R . . .

5.6 When the Crafts moved into their residence in October 1972, they noticed that there were two separate gas and electric meters and only one water meter serving the premises. The residence had been used previously as a duplex. The Crafts assumed, based on information from the seller, that the second set of meters was inoperative.

In 1973, the Crafts began receiving two bills: their regular bill and another with an account number in the name of Willie C. Craft, as opposed to Willie S. Craft. In October 1973, after learning from a Memphis Light, Gas & Water (MLG&W) meter reader that both sets of meters were running in their home, the Crafts hired a private plumber and electrical contractor to combine the meters into one gas and one electric meter. Because the contractor did not combine the meters properly, they continued to receive two bills until January 1974. During this time period, the Crafts' utility service was terminated five times for nonpayment.

Mrs. Craft missed work several times to go to MLG&W offices to resolve the "double billing" problem. She sought explanations on each occasion but was never given an answer.

In February 1974, the Crafts and other MLG&W customers filed suit for violation of the Due Process Clause. The district court dismissed the case. The court of appeals reversed and MLG&W appealed.

Have the Crafts been given due process? [*Memphis Light, Gas & Water Div.* v. *Craft*, 436 U.S. 1 (1978)]

Substantive Due Process

Procedural rules deal with how things are done. All rules on the adjudication of agency charges are procedural rules. Similarly, all rules for the trial of a civil case, from discovery to jury instructions, are also procedural. These rules exist to make sure the substantive law is upheld. Substantive law consists of rights, obligations, and behavior standards. Criminal laws are substantive laws, and criminal procedure rules are procedural laws. **Substantive due process** is the right to have laws that do not deprive businesses or citizens of property or other rights without justification and reason.

Most of the early court cases dealing with substantive due process centered around economic issues. During the late nineteenth and early twentieth centuries, there was as much expansion of business regulation as there was expansion of business. Many of these regulations were challenged on grounds they were depriving businesses of economic rights without justification and unreasonably. In the landmark case of *Lochner* v. *New York*, 198 U.S. 45 (1905), the U.S. Supreme Court invalidated a New York statute that prohibited bakery employees from working more than ten hours a day and sixty hours a week. The Court found that in balancing the economic rights of the business against the health of employees, there was not enough evidence to show that the law accomplished its purpose. In other words, the statute was an unjustified invasion of the rights of bakeries without some "substantial showing" of benefits achieved.

Since *Lochner* and other early twentieth-century cases, the Court has broadened its standards for substantive due process. Now the Court uses a test of "some (more or less) relation" to the achievement of a government goal. A substantial showing is not required, only a tenuous connection. So long as the law is reasonably designed to correct a harm, it is substantively valid.

CONSIDER . . .

5.7   Larry Collins was an employee in the sanitation department of Harker Heights, Texas (respondent). On October 21, 1988, he died of asphyxia after entering a manhole to unstop a sewer line. His widow, Myra Jo Collins (petitioner), brought suit alleging that Collins "had a constitutional right to be free from unreasonable risks of harm to his body, mind and emotions and a constitutional right to be protected from the city of Harker Heights's custom and policy of deliberate indifference toward the safety of its employees." Her complaint alleged that the city violated that right by following a custom and policy of not training its employees about the dangers of working in sewer lines and manholes, not providing safety equipment at job sites, and not providing safety warnings. The complaint also alleged that a prior incident had given the city notice of the risks of entering the sewer lines and that the city had systematically and intentionally failed to provide the equipment and training required by a Texas statute.

The district court dismissed the complaint, and the court of appeals affirmed. Collins appealed on the grounds that the city substantively deprived her husband of his life through its lack of training.

Did the city violate Collins's due process rights? [*Collins* v. *City of Harker Heights, Texas,* 503 U.S. 115 (1992)]

CONSIDER . . .

5.8   The Village of Hoffman passed an ordinance that requires a business to obtain a license if it sells any items that are "designed or marked for use with illegal cannabis or drugs." Guidelines define the items (such as "roach clips," "pipes," "paraphernalia"). Flipside is a merchant in the village selling, among other things, "roach clips" and pipes specially designed for smoking marijuana. Flipside filed suit challenging the ordinance as overly vague, broad, and violative of due process because of the inability to apply the ordinance consistently. Is the ordinance constitutional? [*Village of Hoffman Est.* v. *Flipside, Hoffman Est.,* 455 U.S. 191 (1982)]

Equal Protection Rights for Business

The Fourteenth Amendment grants citizens the right to the **equal protection** of the law. Lawmakers, however, are often required to make certain distinctions in legislating and regulating that result in classes of individuals being treated differently. Such different or **disparate treatment** is justified only if there is some rational basis for it. In other words, there must be a rational connection between the classifications and the achievement of some governmental objective. Most classifications survive the rational basis test. An example of a classification that would not survive is one requiring the manufacturers of soft drinks to use only nonbreakable bottles for their product but allowing juice manufacturers to use glass bottles; this is irrational. If there is a public safety concern about the glass, it must apply equally to all beverage manufacturers.

Browse constitutions from around the world:
http://www.urich.edu/
~jpjones/confinder/
const.html

THE ROLE OF CONSTITUTIONS IN INTERNATIONAL LAW

Although the U.S. Constitution is the basis for all law in the United States, not all countries follow a similar system of governance. The incorporation of other systems (such as a constitution or code) depends upon a nation's history, including its colonization by other countries and those countries' forms of law. The United States and England (and countries established through English colonization) tend to follow a pattern of establishing a general set of principles, as set forth in a constitution, and of reliance on custom, tradition, and precedent for the establishment of law in particular legal areas.

In countries such as France, Germany, and Spain (and nations colonized through their influences), a system of law that is dependent on code law exists. These countries have very specific codes of law that attempt to be all-inclusive and cover each circumstance that could arise under a particular provision. These nations do not depend on court decisions, and often there are inconsistent results in application of the law because of the lack of dependence on judicial precedent.

Approximately twenty-seven countries follow Islamic law in some way. When Islamic law is the dominant force in a country, it governs all aspects of personal and business life. The constitutions in these lands are the tenets of the nation's religion.

SUMMARY

What is the Constitution?

- U.S. Constitution—document detailing authority of U.S. government and rights of its citizens

What are the constitutional limitations on business regulations?

- Commerce Clause—portion of the U.S. Constitution that controls federal regulation of business; limits Congress to regulating of interstate and international commerce

- Intrastate commerce—business within state borders

- Interstate commerce—business across state lines

- Foreign commerce—business outside U.S. boundaries

Who has more power to regulate business—the states or the federal government?

- Supremacy Clause—portion of the U.S. Constitution that defines relationship between state and federal laws

What individual freedoms granted under the Constitution apply to businesses?

- Bill of Rights—first ten amendments to the U.S. Constitution, providing individual freedoms and protection of individual rights

- First Amendment—freedom-of-speech protection in U.S. Constitution

- Commercial speech—ads and other speech by businesses

- Corporate political speech—business ads or positions on candidates or referenda

- Due process—indicates constitutional guarantee against the taking of property or other governmental exercise of authority without an opportunity for a hearing

- Equal protection—indicates constitutional protection for U.S. citizens against disparate treatment

- Substantive due process—constitutional protection against taking of rights or property by statute

QUESTIONS AND PROBLEMS

1. Oklahoma statute Title 29, Section 4-115(B), provides in part: "No person may transport or ship minnows for sale outside the state which were seined or procured within the waters of this state." William Hughes holds a Texas license to operate a commercial minnow business near Wichita Falls, Texas. Hughes was arrested by an Oklahoma game warden for transporting from Oklahoma to Texas minnows purchased from a licensed Oklahoma dealer.

He was charged with a violation of § 4-115(B) and he challenged the charges on the grounds that the statute was repugnant to the Commerce Clause. The lower court convicted and fined him, and he appealed. Is the Oklahoma statute constitutional or an impermissible burden on interstate commerce? [*Hughes v. Oklahoma*, 441 U.S. 322 (1979)]

2. Mrs. Florence Dolan owned a plumbing and electric supply store on Main Street in Portland. Fanno Creek flows through the southeastern corner of Mrs. Dolan's lot on which her store is located. She applied to the city for a permit to redevelop her lot. Her plans included the addition of a second structure.

The City Planning Commission granted Mrs. Dolan's permit but included the following requirement:
Where landfill and/or development is allowed within and adjacent to the 100-year floodplain, the city shall require the dedication of sufficient open land area for greenway adjoining and within the floodplain. This area shall include portions at a suitable elevation for the construction of a pedestrian/bicycle pathway within the floodplain in accordance with the adopted pedestrian/bicycle plan.

Mrs. Dolan maintained that the requirements were a taking of her property because she would be required to reserve a portion of her property for the pedestrian/bike path, and her plans would have to be redone to accommodate the city's requirements. The city maintains that its requirements are all simply part of a redevelopment plan for the city and a means of working with the flood plain created by Fanno Creek. Mrs. Dolan says the city has imposed additional expense and forced her to dedicate a large portion of her lot to public use. Who is correct? Is Portland taking property from Mrs. Dolan? Is the city required to pay compensation to her? [*Dolan v. City of Tigard*, 512 U.S. 374 (1994)]

3. The Public Utility Regulatory Policies Act of 1978 (PURPA) was part of the federal legislation of the 1970s' energy crisis. PURPA gave the Federal Energy Regulatory Commission (FEBC) the power to regulate the development of small and cogeneration power facilities. The state of Mississippi has brought suit in federal district court to have that portion of PURPA declared unconstitutional. Mississippi maintains the federal government is regulating purely intrastate matters and that because there is no commerce involved, there can be no reliance on the federal government's commerce power. Is PURPA unconstitutional? Is the regulation of utilities the regulation of commerce? [*Federal Energy Regulatory Commission v. Mississippi*, 456 U.S. 742 (1982)]

4. Bruce Church, Inc., is a company engaged in extensive commercial farming in Arizona and California. A provision of the Arizona Fruit and Vegetable Standardization Act requires that all cantaloupes grown in Arizona "be packed in regular compact arrangement in closed standard containers approved by the supervisor." Arizona, through its agent Pike, issued an order prohibiting Bruce Church from transporting uncrated cantaloupes from its ranch in Parker, Arizona, to nearby Blythe, California, for packing and processing.

It would take many months and $200,000 for Bruce Church to construct a processing plant in Parker. Further, Church had $700,000 worth of cantaloupes ready for transportation. Church filed suit in federal district court challenging the constitutionality of the Arizona statutory provision on shipping cantaloupes. The court issued an injunction against the enforcement of the act on the grounds that it was an undue on interstate commerce. Will the regulation withstand Commerce Clause scrutiny? [*Pike v. Bruce Church, Inc.*, 397 U.S. 137 (1970)]

5. The International Longshoremen's Union refused to unload cargo shipped from the Soviet Union as a way of protesting the Soviet invasion of Afghanistan. Allied International, an importer of Soviet wood products, could not get its wood unloaded when it arrived in Boston. Allied sued on the basis of the National Labor Relations Act, claiming the conduct was an unlawful boycott. The union claims no commerce is involved and that federal law does not apply. Is there commerce? Does the National Labor Relations Act apply? [*International Longshoremen's Association v. Allied International, Inc.*, 456 U.S. 212 (1982)]

6. For the past sixty-two years, Pacific Gas & Electric (PG&E) has distributed a newsletter in its monthly billing envelopes. The newsletter, called Progress, reaches over 3 million customers and has contained tips on conservation, utility billing information, public interest information, and political editorials.

A group called TURN (Toward Utility Rate Normalization) asked the Public Utility Commission (PUC) of California to declare that the envelope space belonged to the ratepayers and that TURN was entitled to use the Progress space four times each year. The PUC ordered TURN's request, and PG&E appealed the order to the California Supreme Court. When the California Supreme Court denied review, PG&E appealed to the U.S. Supreme Court, alleging a violation of its First Amendment rights. Is PG&E correct? [*Pacific Gas & Electric* v. *Public Utility Commission of California,* 475 U.S. 1 (1986)]

7. The Minnesota legislature enacted a 1977 statute banning the retail sale of milk in plastic nonreturnable, nonrefillable containers, but permitting such sale in other nonrefillable containers, such as paperboard milk cartons. Clover Leaf Creamery brought suit challenging the constitutionality of the statute under the Equal Protection Clause, alleging that there was no rational basis for the statute. The Minnesota legislature's purpose in passing the statute was to control solid waste, arguing that plastic containers take up more space in solid waste disposal dumps. The Minnesota Supreme Court found evidence to the contrary: The jugs took up less space and required less energy to produce. On appeal to the U.S. Supreme Court, can the statute survive a constitutional challenge? Is there a "rational basis" for the statute? What effect does the evidence to the contrary have on the statute's constitutionality? [*Minnesota* v. *Clover Leaf Creamery,* 449 U.S. 456 (1981)]

8. Iowa passed a statute restricting the length of vehicles that could use its highways. The length chosen was 55 feet. Semi trailers are generally 55 feet long; double or twin tracks (one cab pulling two trailers) are 65 feet long. Other states in the Midwest have adopted the 65-foot standard. Consolidated Freightways brought suit, challenging the Iowa statute as an unconstitutional burden on interstate commerce. The Iowa statute meant Consolidated could not use its twins in Iowa. The Iowa legislature claims the 65-foot doubles are more dangerous than the 55-foot singles. However, the statute did provide a border exception: Towns and cities along Iowa borders could make an exception to the length requirements to allow trucks to use their city and town roads. Can Iowa's statute survive a constitutional challenge? Is the statute an impermissible burden on interstate commerce? [*Kassel* v. *Consolidated Freightways Corp.,* 450 U.S. 662 (1981)]

9. In 1989, the city of Cincinnati authorized Discovery Network, Inc., to place sixty-two free-standing newsracks on public property for distributing free magazines that consisted primarily of advertising for Discovery Network's service. In 1990, the city became concerned about the safety and attractive appearance of its streets and sidewalks and revoked Discovery Network's permit on the ground that the magazines were commercial handbills whose distribution was prohibited on public property by a preexisting ordinance. Discovery Network says the prohibition is an excessive regulation of its commercial speech and a violation of its rights. The city maintains the elimination of the newsracks decreases litter and increases safety. Is the ban on newsracks constitutional? [*City of Cincinnati* v. *Discovery Network, Inc.,* 507 U.S. 410 (1993)]

10. In 1988, the voters of Escondido, California, approved Proposition K, an ordinance that set rents at their 1986 levels and prohibited increases without city council approval. John and Irene Yee own several mobile home parks in Escondido and have filed suit alleging that "the rent control law has had the effect of depriving [them] of all use and occupancy of [their] real property and granting to tenants the right to physically permanently occupy their land." Is the rent ordinance constitutional? [*Yee* v. *City of Escondido, California,* 503 U.S. 519 (1992)]

RESEARCH PROBLEM

11. List the current justices of the Supreme Court, their ages, political affiliations, and number of years on the bench. Justice Stevens has written the most dissenting opinions for this court and is the most frequent lone dissenter. Why do you think his record is such?

BUSINESS STRATEGY APPLICATION

CD-ROM Exercise

In this exercise you will have a chance to study PAC contributions. You can study what groups gave the most, and study those groups with the greatest decline in giving. You will be able to deter- 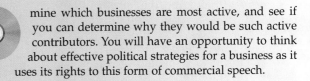 mine which businesses are most active, and see if you can determine why they would be such active contributors. You will have an opportunity to think about effective political strategies for a business as it uses its rights to this form of commercial speech.

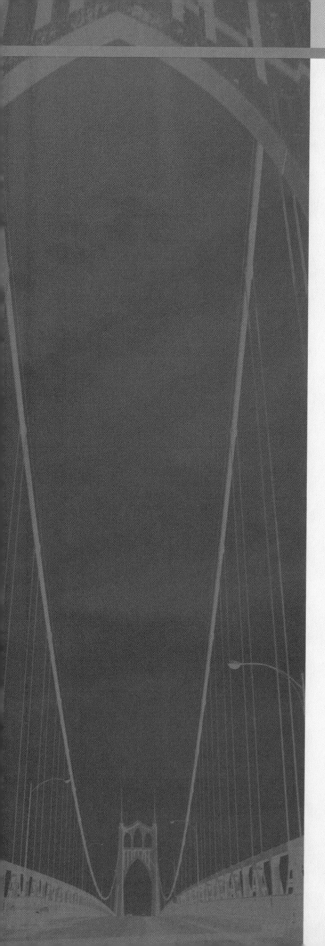

CHAPTER SIX

Administrative Law

The regulations of administrative agencies at the federal and state levels affect the day-to-day operations of all businesses. From permits to labor regulations, every business is affected. Agencies are the enforcement arm of governments. Created by one of the branches of government, they affect the way businesses operate. This chapter answers the following questions: What is an administrative agency? What does it do? What laws govern the operation of administrative agencies? How do agencies pass rules? How do agencies enforce the law?

Lord's Prayer	66 words
Gettysburg Address	286 words
Declaration of Independence	1,322 words
Federal regulations on the sale of cabbage	26,911 words
Internal Revenue Code	6,200,000 words

Grade A Fancy ketchup must flow no more than 9 centimeters in 30 seconds at 69 degrees Fahrenheit.

EXCERPT FROM A FOOD AND DRUG ADMINISTRATION REGULATION

Ninety percent of a 100-person panel, composed of people 50 to 70 years old, must be able to open and close the package within five minutes, then again within one minute.

CONSUMER PRODUCT SAFETY COMMISSION RULE ON CHILDPROOF CAPS

Because of the Veterans Day holiday next Wednesday, this release will be published on Friday, November 13, instead of on Thursday, November 12. It will be issued on Thursday, November 19, its usual publication date, but will be delayed the following week until Friday, November 17, because of the Thanksgiving Day holiday on Thursday, November 26.

FEDERAL RESERVE MEMO, 1992

DO NOT REMOVE UNDER PENALTY OF LAW.

WARNING PRINTED ON TAGS REQUIRED ON MATTRESSES SOLD IN THE UNITED STATES

THIS TAG NOT TO BE REMOVED EXCEPT BY THE CONSUMER

MODIFIED WARNING TAG REQUIRED ON MATTRESSES SO THAT AGENCY COULD REDUCE THE NUMBER OF CALLS FROM CITIZENS

ABOUT REMOVING THEIR MATTRESS TAGS

CONSIDER...

A. Duda & Sons, Inc., has a plaque posted in the lobby of its company headquarters that reads: "But seek ye first the Kingdom of God, and his righteousness and all these things shall be added unto you." An employee complained to the Equal Employment Opportunity Commission (EEOC) about the plaque, stating that it constituted religious harassment in the workplace.

At the Montgomery County Middle School, the name of its December music event was changed from "Christmas Concert" to "Winter Concert" when a teacher complained that the use of the word "Christmas" constituted religious harassment.

Based on these complaints and others (a total of 538 religious harassment complaints), the EEOC proposed rules on religious harassment that prohibited verbal or physical contact that "denigrates or shows hostility or aversion toward an individual because of his/her religion . . . or that of his/her relatives, friends or associates."

An executive in a Florida hospital asked, "These rules could prevent an employee from wearing a necklace with a crucifix to work. Would I have to control Bible reading by my employees when they're having a break? The rules are unmanageable. Where do I turn? How can I raise my concerns about them?"

© Douglas Peebles/CORBIS

WHAT ARE ADMINISTRATIVE AGENCIES?

An **administrative agency** is best defined by what it is not: It is not a legislative or judicial body. An administrative agency is a statutory creation within the executive branch with the power to make, interpret, and enforce laws. Such agencies exist at practically every level of government, and their names vary considerably. Exhibit 6.1 is a list of all the federal administrative agencies and their acronyms.

States also have administrative agencies that are responsible for such things as the licensing of professions and occupations. Architects, contractors, attorneys, accountants, cosmetologists, doctors, dentists, real estate agents, and nurses are all professionals whose occupations are regulated in most states by some administrative agency. Utility and securities regulation are also handled by administrative agencies in each of the states.

All these agencies at every level of government derive their authority from the particular legislature responsible for their creation. Congress creates federal agencies; state legislatures create state agencies; and city governments create their cities' administrative agencies.

The structures of agencies may differ significantly, but most have an organizational chart to show how different departments operate. Exhibit 6.2 is an organizational chart for the Securities and Exchange Commission.

Legislators begin the administrative process leading to the creation of an agency with the recognition of a problem and the passage of a law designed to remedy the problem. The enacted law gives the overview—what the legislature wants to accomplish and the penalties for noncompliance with the law. The law may also establish an administrative agency with the power to adopt rules to deal with the problems of enforcement of the statute. The law, referred to as an **enabling act,** gives the agency the power to deal with the issues and problems the act addresses.

ROLES OF ADMINISTRATIVE AGENCIES

Specialization

Administrative agencies are specialists in their particular areas of law, and this type of specialization is needed not only because of the complexities of law but also because of the complexities of the regulated areas. For example, environmental regulation is complex because of both the chemical analyses involved in determining pollution levels and the types of equipment and technology needed for controlling pollution.

Visit the Federal Communication Commission: http://www.fcc.gov *Visit the Commodity Futures Trading Commission:* http://www.cftc.gov

Similarly, neither Congress nor the judiciary has the necessary specialization or expertise to deal with the highly technical matters handled by administrative agencies, such as broadcast frequencies (Federal Communications Commission), commodities trading (Commodity Futures Trading Commission), and mining (Federal Mine Safety and Health Review Commission). The people staffing these agencies, therefore, can be chosen for their expertise, which helps ensure adequate protection for the public and the members of the regulated industries.

EXHIBIT 6.1   Major Federal Administrative Agencies

Executive Office of the President

Executive Departments

Department of Agriculture

Department of Commerce

Department of Defense

   Office of the Secretary of Defense

   Department of the Air Force

   Department of the Army

   Department of the Navy

Department of Education

Department of Energy

Department of Health and Human Services

Department of Housing and Urban Development (HUD)

Department of the Interior

Department of Justice

Department of Labor

Department of State

Department of Transportation

Department of the Treasury

Independent Agencies

ACTION

Administrative Committee of the Federal Register

Advisory Committee on Intergovernmental Relations

American Battle Monuments Commission

Appalachian Regional Council

Board for International Broadcasting

Civil Aeronautics Board (CAB)

Commission on Fine Arts (CFA)

Commodity Futures Trading Commission (CFTC)

Consumer Product Safety Commission (CPSC)

Environmental Protection Agency (EPA)

Equal Employment Opportunity Commission (EEOC)

Export-Import Bank of the United States

Federal Aviation Administration (FAA)

Farm Credit Administration (FCA)

Federal Communications Commission (FCC)

Federal Deposit Insurance Corporation (FDIC)

Federal Election Commission (FEC)

Federal Emergency Management Agency (FEMA)

Federal Labor Relations Authority (FLRA)

Federal Maritime Commission (FMC)

Federal Mediation and Conciliation Service

Federal Mine Safety and Health Review Commission

Federal Reserve System

Federal Trade Commission (FTC)

General Services Administration (GSA)

Inter-American Foundation

International Communications Agency (ICA)

International Development Cooperation Agency (IDCA)

Interstate Commerce Commission (ICC)

Merit Systems Protection Board

National Aeronautics and Space Administration (NASA)

National Credit Union Administration

National Foundation on the Arts and Humanities

National Highway Traffic Safety Administration

National Indian Gaming Commission

National Labor Relations Board (NLRB)

National Mediation Board

National Science Foundation (NSF)

National Transportation Safety Board (NTSB)

Nuclear Regulatory Commission (NRC)

Occupational Safety and Health Administration (OSHA)

Office of Personnel Management (OPM)

Overseas Private Investment Corporation

Patent and Trademark Office

Pension Benefit Guaranty Corporation

Pennsylvania Avenue Development Corporation

Railroad Retirement Board (RRB)

Securities and Exchange Commission (SEC)

Selective Service System (SSS)

Small Business Administration (SBA)

Tennessee Valley Authority (TVA)

U.S. Arms Control and Disarmament Agency

U.S. Commission on Civil Rights

U.S. International Trade Commission

U.S. Metric Board

U.S. Postal Service (USPS)

U.S. Water Resources Council

Veterans Administration (VA)

EXHIBIT 6.2 SEC Organizational Chart

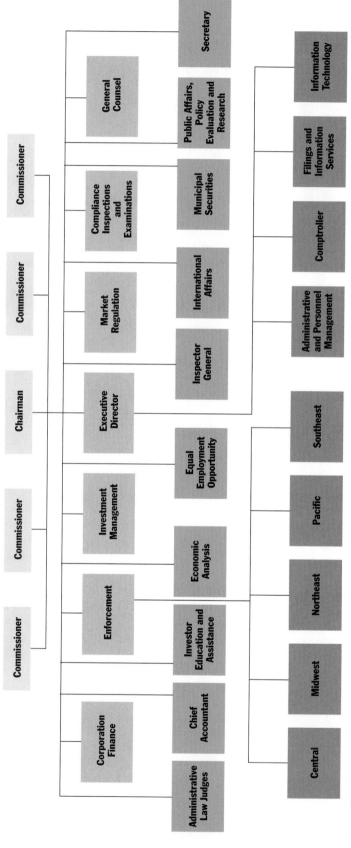

Protection for Small Business

Administrative agencies have traditionally been protectors of small interests. An individual or competitor who finds a false advertisement in a newspaper would probably not take the time or effort to bring a private suit to collect damages for the false advertisement. But an agency created to oversee truth in advertising would undertake routine enforcement against such advertisements, and so the small business competitor and the consumer are afforded protection and rights they might not otherwise have. An agency's enforcement authority has the effect of making others more aware of the need for compliance. Enforcement of one small claim creates an atmosphere of compliance.

Faster Relief

If enforcement of all government regulations were dependent upon court hearings, not only would there be a substantial increase in the caseload of the courts, but there would be a backlog for those hearings that would interfere with the goal of swift action and enforcement. Administrative agencies help to expedite the investigation and disposition of violations. In addition, administrative agencies serve as review boards for the granting of licenses. If such license applications required legislative hearings, license and permit applications would be delayed substantially and businesses would be left in limbo until a hearing could be held. An administrative agency provides an efficient way for fast licensing and timely enforcement.

Due Process

Administrative agencies provide the opportunity to be heard before any action to remove property, rights, or income can be taken. *Goldberg* v. *Kelly*, 397 U.S. 254 (1970), is often described as the judicial decision responsible for the creation of administrative agencies and procedures as we have them today. In *Goldberg*, the Supreme Court ruled that before a benefit (such as aid to dependent children) could be taken away, the agency must present its evidence and allow a response. Regulatory action thus requires due process, which includes the right to see the evidence and present your side of the story (see Chapter 5).

Social Goals

Visit the Environmental Protection Agency:
http://www.epa.gov

Some experts see administrative agencies as a means for accomplishing social goals that might otherwise be delayed or debated until no resolution could be reached. For example, the Environmental Protection Agency is assigned the goal of creating a cleaner environment. If every permit for a factory or rule on discharges were debated by Congress, the goal might be lost in the political arena. Further, having judicial review and determination of these issues would result in a delay that might make the goal moot. Administrative agencies can be created and then permitted to function as supervised by the judicial and legislative branches. Very often, these agencies are created in response to a pressing social issue. For example, the Federal Home Loan Bank Board was established to regulate home mortgages after all the difficulties with foreclosures in the Great Depression. The goal was a more equitable system for mortgage lending and mortgage foreclosure, and an agency was created to accomplish those goals.

LAWS GOVERNING ADMINISTRATIVE AGENCIES

Apart from their enabling acts, administrative agencies are also subject to some general laws on the functioning of agencies. This section covers those laws.

The Administrative Procedures Act

Review the Administrative Procedures Act:
http://www.law.cornell.edu/ uscode/5/ch5.html

This act was the first to deal with administrative agency procedures. It was passed in 1946 after some agencies had been in existence long enough for some standard procedures to be established. The **Administrative Procedures Act** (APA) requires agencies to follow certain uniform procedures in making rules (those procedures are covered later in this chapter). The APA has been amended a number of times—by the Freedom of Information Act, the Federal Privacy Act, and the Government in the Sunshine Act, among others.

The Freedom of Information Act

Review the Freedom of Information Act:
http://www.law.cornell.edu/ uscode/5/552a.html

The **Freedom of Information Act** (FOIA) is an APA amendment passed in 1966. It allows access to certain information federal agencies possess and requires that the agencies publicly disclose their procedures and decisions. The types of procedures that must be publicly disclosed relate to agencies' structures: where the central and regional offices are located and which office or office division will respond to requests for information. Agencies must also publish their rules, regulations, procedures, policy statements, and reports.

Some agency information need not be published, but it must be available to the public upon request. This information includes the orders resulting from a hearing, any interpretations of unpublished rules the agency follows, and in-house management tools such as staff policies and manuals.

This information, not published but available to the public, can be obtained by an **FOIA request,** which must be written and must describe the documents sought. A general request for all the agency's research would not be a sufficient description, but a request, say, for the results of the Federal Trade Commission's study of coaching programs for college entrance exams would be allowable. The agency can charge for time and for copying costs in processing the request, although these charges must be published and applied uniformly to all requests. One exception allows an agency to waive fees for nonprofit public interest groups.

If an agency wrongfully refuses to supply the information requested, the party requesting it can bring a court action to enforce the request, with all costs paid by the agency.

Some information is exempt from FOIA requests. There are nine categories of exemptions, including requests that would reveal trade secrets or information about government workers' personnel records.

Agencies can refuse to release information that is exempt, but they can also decide to release that information if they wish to waive an exemption. Some requests have resulted in court cases brought by the parties protected by the exemptions. For example, suppose that one cola company requests the patented formula for another company's cola from the Department of Commerce. The company with the formula could bring suit to stop the disclosure. Such suits are called "reverse FOIA suits." However, the U.S. Supreme Court has held in *Chrysler Corp.* v. *Brown,* 441 U.S. 281 (1979), that the right to stop or grant disclosure rests with the agency and not with the party who supplied the information to the agency.

Federal Privacy Act

Review the Federal Privacy Act:
http://www.law.cornell.edu/usecode/5/552a.html

By 1974, federal agencies had tremendous amounts of information about businesses and individuals. At least one, and usually more than one, agency could give an individual's name, occupation, address, Social Security number, and income. Furthermore, agencies were exchanging information among themselves to obtain more data for their files, all of which activity was going on without the knowledge of the individuals involved. In 1974, Congress passed the **Federal Privacy Act** (FPA) to reduce exchanges of information between agencies about individuals.

The FPA prohibits federal agencies from communicating any records to another agency or person without first obtaining the consent of the person whose record is being communicated. The FPA protects all records about individuals that might be in the possession of the agency, including medical and employment histories.

There are certain exemptions from the FPA. Because law enforcement agencies would have a difficult time trying to conduct investigations if they had to get permission from the individuals being investigated in order to obtain information, law enforcement agencies are exempt. Congress can also obtain information without consent. Routine agency tasks are also exempt from the prior permission requirement. For example, employees of the Securities and Exchange Commission (SEC) need constant access to information about stock sales by directors to perform their duties regarding the control of insider trading.

Government in the Sunshine Act

Review the Government in the Sunshine Act:
http://www.law.cornell.edu/uscode/5/552b.html

The **Government in the Sunshine Act** is a 1976 amendment to the APA and is often called an **open meeting law.** Its purpose is to require prior public notice of meetings of those agencies with heads appointed by the president. All the agencies with the word *commission* in their names have agency heads appointed by the president.

This open meeting law applies only to meetings between or among agency heads. For example, when the commissioners of the FTC meet together, that meeting must be public and held only after there has been prior notice. Staff members can hold meetings in private without giving notice. Most states also have sunshine laws for state administrative government operations.

As with the other statutes, there are exemptions under the open meeting law. If an agency meeting will cover national defense, foreign policy, trade secrets, personnel, or law enforcement issues, the meetings need not be public. The SEC commissioners could meet privately to discuss an enforcement program designed to curb insider trading (see Chapter 22).

ETHICAL ISSUES 6.2

In 1997, the Internal Revenue Service (IRS) disciplined employees who, out of curiosity, were looking up tax returns of famous people. The employees were not working on the taxpayers' returns; they were not obtaining information for investigations; they were simply checking to see who made how much income. The IRS fired 23 employees, disciplined 349, and provided counseling for 472.

During 1996 and 1997, the IRS investigated 1,515 cases of snooping among its 102,000 employees.

Is this practice so bad? What is wrong with just looking at data that are accessible at work? The IRS employees said they did not disclose the data and therefore didn't violate federal privacy laws. Are ethics and laws the same thing?

The Federal Register Act

Although the **Federal Register Act** (FRA) is not a part of the APA, its provisions are necessary for all the acts under the APA to work. The FRA created the **Federal Register System,** which oversees publication of federal agency information. This system provides the means for Sunshine Act notices and publication of agency rules and procedures.

Three publications make up the Federal Register System. The first is the *U.S. Government Manual.* This publication is reprinted each year and lists all federal agencies and their regional offices along with addresses. In addition, the *Manual* contains statistics about the agencies and their sizes.

Review the Code of Federal Regulations:
http://www.access.gpo.gov/nara/cfr/cfr-table-search.html

The second publication of the Federal Register Act is the *Code of Federal Regulations* (covered in Chapter 1). The *Code of Federal Regulations* contains all regulations of all the federal agencies. The volumes are in paperback, and the entire *Code* is republished each year because of tremendous changes in the regulations. Exhibit 6.3 is a sample excerpt from the *Code.*

The third publication under the Federal Register System serves to provide a daily update on changes in the regulations. This publication, called the *Federal Register,* is published every government working day and contains proposed regulations, notices of meetings (under the Government in the Sunshine Act), notices of hearings on proposed regulations, and the final versions of amended or new regulations. The *Federal Register* totals about 60,000 pages a year, or about 250 pages every working day. More than 7,000 regulations are published each year in the *Federal Register.*

Search the Federal Register *and the* U.S. Government Manual:
http://www.access.gpo.gov

THE FUNCTIONS OF ADMINISTRATIVE AGENCIES AND BUSINESS INTERACTION

Administrative agencies have three functions: promulgating regulations and enforcing and adjudicating rules. Businesses will find themselves interacting with agencies in all three areas of operation.

Providing Input on Regulations during Agency's Promulgation

Promulgating regulations is the legislative function of administrative agencies. It has two forms: **formal rulemaking** and **informal rulemaking.** Some agencies combine these into a rulemaking that is a cross between formal and informal—**hybrid rulemaking.**

EXHIBIT 6.3 **Federal Regulations on Post-Mortem Inspection of Cattle, Excerpted from 9 C.F.R. § 310.1 [2001]**

§310.1 Extent and time of post-mortem inspection; post-mortem inspection staffing standards.

(a) A careful post-mortem examination and inspection shall be made of the carcasses and parts thereof of all live-stock slaughtered at official establishments. Such inspection and examination shall be made at the time of slaughter unless, because of unusual circumstances, prior arrangements acceptable to the Administrator have been made in specific cases by the circuit supervisor for making such inspection and examination at a later time.

(b)(1) The staffing standards on the basis of the number of carcasses to be inspected per hour are outlined in the following tables. Standards for multiple inspector lines are based on inspectors rotating through the different types of inspection stations during each shift to equalize the workload. The inspector in charge shall have the authority to require the establishment to reduce slaughter line speeds where, in his judgment, the inspection procedure cannot be adequately performed at the current line speed because of particular deficiencies in carcass preparation and presentation by the plant at the higher speed, or because the health condition of the particular animals indicates a need for more extensive inspection.

(2) *Cattle inspection.* For all cattle staffing standards, an "a" in the "Number of Inspectors by Stations" column means that one inspector performs the entire inspection procedure and a "b" means that one inspector performs the head and lower carcass inspection and a second inspector performs the viscera and upper carcass inspection.[1]

[1] The "Maximum Slaughter Rates" figures listed in paragraph (b)(2)(i) of this section for one (a) and two (b) inspector kills are overstated because the time required to walk from one inspection station to another is not included. To determine the proper adjusted maximum slaughter line speed, paragraph (b)(2)(i)(A) of this section for one inspector kills or paragraph (b)(2)(i)(B) of this section for two inspector kills must be used along with their accompanying rules.

(i) Inspection Using the Viscera Truck.

STEERS AND HEIFERS

Maximum slaughter rates (head per hour)	Number of inspectors by stations		
	Head	Viscera	Carcass
1 to 27	a	a	a
28 to 56	b	b	b
57 to 84	1	1	1
85 to 86	1	2	1
87 to 143	2	2	1

COWS AND BULLS

Maximum slaughter rates (head per hour)	Number of inspectors by stations		
	Head	Viscera	Carcass
1 to 27	a	a	a
28 to 55	b	b	b
56 to 77	1	1	1
78 to 81	1	2	1
82 to 134	2	2	1

(A) Rules for determining adjusted maximum slaughter rates for single-inspector kills considering walking distance according to the table in this subdivision: Determine the distances the inspector actually walks between the points shown in columns 2 through 14 of the following table. For each column, determine the deduction figure opposite the appropriate number of feet in column 1. Compute the total of the deduction figures for columns 2 through 14. The adjusted maximum rate is the maximum rate in paragraph (b)(2)(i) of this section minus total of the deduction figures. If the resultant number is not a whole number, it must be rounded off to the next *lowest* whole number.

Formal Rulemaking
The steps involved in formal rulemaking are diagrammed in Exhibit 6.4.

Review the Truth-in-Lending Act:
http://www.law.cornell.edu/uscode/15/1601.html

Congressional Enabling Act Congress is responsible for passing statutes designed to remedy a perceived problem that is within federal jurisdiction. At the point of legislation, constituents have an opportunity to voice their views and concerns about problem areas. For example, many people saw a problem with the way credit transactions were being handled in the early 1970s. There were concerns about disclosures, billings, and advertisements. In response to these concerns and problems, Congress passed the Consumer Credit Protection Act, or Truth-in-Lending Act. In addition, Congress authorized the Federal Reserve Board to promulgate rules covering the specifics of disclosure and gave the board the responsibility to enforce this new credit regulation. The actual details of credit

EXHIBIT 6.4
Steps in Formal Rulemaking by Administrative Agencies

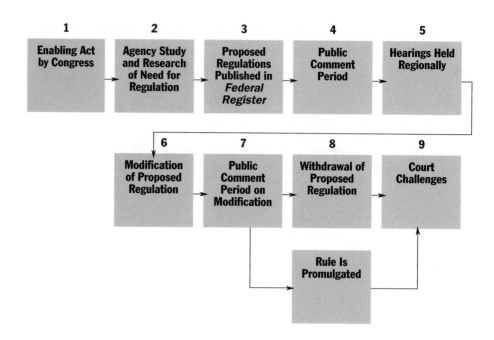

disclosures are found in the Federal Reserve Board's regulations (called, as a group, Regulation Z).

After the 1929 stock market crash, Congress perceived problems with the way securities were being sold and traded on the national exchanges. To correct some of the problems and abuses in the trading of securities, Congress passed the 1933 and 1934 Securities Acts (see Chapter 22 for more details), the first of which created the Securities and Exchange Commission (SEC) as the administrative agency responsible for the enforcement of the two acts. The following is an excerpt from the 1933 Securities Act, the enabling act for the SEC:

Explore the 1933 and 1934 Securities Acts:
http://www.law.uc.edu/CCL

> *(a) There is hereby established a Securities and Exchange Commission (hereinafter referred to as the "Commission") to be composed of five commissioners to be appointed by the President by and with the advice and consent of the Senate. Not more than three of such commissioners shall be members of the same political party and in making appointments members of different political parties shall be appointed alternately as nearly as may be practicable. . . .*
>
> *(b) The Commission is authorized to appoint and fix the compensation of such officers, attorneys, examiners, and other experts as may be necessary for carrying out its functions under this chapter. . . .*

Agency Research of the Problem Any regulation passed by an administrative agency must have some purpose and evidence to show that the regulation will accomplish the purpose. Rules passed without some study and evidence supporting their need or effectiveness could be challenged by the persons or industries affected as arbitrary and capricious (discussed later in this chapter).

The study can be done by the agency staff, or the agency can hire outside experts to conduct the study for it. The study examines issues such as whether the regulation will be cost-effective. Some regulations may cost billions of dollars for industries to follow. Regulation Z, for example, requires lenders to send out a substantial amount of paperwork; the preparation of the paperwork and the cost of mailing, along with personnel costs for the work involved, are tremendous. However, full knowledge of the cost of consumer debt is an important goal as specified by Congress in the Consumer Credit Protection Act. Although the study may reveal that the cost is great, it could also reveal that the cost outweighs the hazards to consumers. In other words, the study focuses not only on monetary costs but also on the problems the regulation is trying to correct and the cost of those problems to the individual and to society.

Proposed Regulations After the study, and based upon the needs and costs shown by the study, the agency publishes its proposed rules or rule changes in the *Federal Register.* By this time, the published form of the regulation has been through many departments and many hands. Legal counsel for the agency reviews the regulation for language problems. Other experts within the agency also review its content for problems and inaccuracies. Economists, financial analysts, and scientists are examples of experts used within an agency to review a regulation before publication.

To be valid, the notice in the *Federal Register* must contain certain information. If notice is not given or is given improperly, a court can set aside the action taken by the agency and require the rulemaking process to be repeated with proper notice. Requirements for a *Federal Register* notice include the following:

1. The name of the agency proposing the rules
2. The statutory authority the agency has for promulgating the rules (citing the enabling act)
3. Either the language of the proposed rule or an accurate summary or description of the proposed rules

Review the Regulatory Flexibility Act: http://www.law.cornell.edu/ uscode/5/601.html

Although not required to do so, some agencies provide background information in the notice so that some history and the function of the rule are given. In addition to publishing the notice of proposed rules in the *Federal Register,* an agency is required under the **Regulatory Flexibility Act** to publish a notice in the publications of those trades and industries that will be affected by the rule. For example, the regulation governing disclosures of sales of used vehicles was published in automobile dealers associations' publications. Exhibit 6.5 is a sample of a proposed rule publication from the Federal Trade Commission on proposed new rules on telemarketing practices.

The Public Comment Period One of the purposes for publication of proposed rules is to allow the public an opportunity to review and provide input on the proposed rules. The period during which the agency accepts comments on the rule is called the **public comment period.** Under the APA, the public comment period cannot be less than thirty days, but most agencies make the public comment period much longer.

Private citizens, government officials, industry representatives, businesspeople, and corporations can all send in their public comments. This is the opportunity business has to provide information and express concerns about proposals. There is no formal format for a public comment; most just appear in letter form. Because comments are generally made by those who do not like the rule, most comment letters are negative. Anyone who wishes to challenge later the validity

EXHIBIT 6.5   Sample Proposed Rule Notice from the *Federal Register*

FEDERAL TRADE COMMISSION

Telemarketing Sales Rule 16 CFR 310

AGENCY: Federal Trade Commission.

ACTION: Rule review, request for public comments, and announcement of public forums.

SUMMARY: The Federal Trade Commission ("the Commission" or "FTC") is requesting public comment on the Commission's Telemarketing Sales Rule ("TSR" or "the Rule"). The Telemarketing and Consumer Fraud and Abuse Prevention Act, 15 U.S.C. § 6101 *et seq.,* ("the Telemarketing Act" or "the Act") directed the Commission to promulgate rules to protect consumers from deceptive telemarketing practices and other abusive telemarketing activities. In response to this directive, the Commission adopted the TSR, which requires telemarketers to make specific disclosures of material information; prohibits misrepresentations; sets limits on the times telemarketers may call consumers; prohibits calls to a consumer who has asked not to be called again; and sets payment restrictions for the sale of certain goods and services.

The Act requires that no later than five years after its effective date of December 31, 1995, the Commission initiate a rule review to evaluate the Rule's operation and report the results of that review to Congress. Pursuant to this mandatory rule review requirement, the Commission now hereby seeks comment about the overall costs and benefits of the TSR, and its overall regulatory and economic impact since its adoption in 1995.

In addition to reviewing the Rule and its effect on deceptive and abusive telemarketing practices, the Commission intends to use this rule review to examine telemarketing generally over the past two decades, and to determine its impact on consumers. This broader review will result in a report addressing issues such as changes in technology, composition of the industry, telemarketers' efforts at self-regulation, the effectiveness of law enforcement and legislation, trends in telemarketing, and current consumer issues related to telemarketing. In order to initiate discussion of these and other issues, the Request for Comment invites written responses to the series of questions in Sections F and G, *infra,* which set forth with more specificity the type of information the Commission particularly desires related to the Rule and about telemarketing generally.

In addition, this document contains an invitation to participate in a series of public forums to be held in the future to afford the Commission staff and interested parties an opportunity to explore and discuss the issues underlying the list of questions and any other topics that emerge from the comments we receive in response to this notice. A public forum to discuss provisions of the TSR, other than the "do-not-call" provision, will be held on July 27–28, 2000.

DATES: Papers and written comments responding to the Request for Comment will be accepted until April 27, 2000. A public forum to discuss provisions of the TSR, other than the "do-not-call" provision, will be held on July 27–28, 2000, in Washington, D.C., from 8:30 A.M. until 5:30 P.M. Notification of interest in participating in this forum must be submitted in writing on or before June 16, 2000. The exact dates, location, and information about participation in future FTC forums held in connection with the TSR review will be announced later by *Federal Register* notice.

ADDRESSES: Six paper copies of each paper and/or written comment should be submitted to the Office of the Secretary, Federal Trade Commission, Room 159, 600 Pennsylvania Avenue, NW, Washington, DC 20580. Alternatively, the Commission will accept papers and comments submitted to the following e-mail

EXHIBIT 6.5 *(continued)*

address: tsr@ftc.gov, provided the content of any papers or comments submitted by e-mail is organized in sequentially numbered paragraphs. All submissions should be identified as "Telemarketing Review—Comment. FTC File No. P994414." Notification of interest in participating in the public forum scheduled for July 27–28, 2000, should be submitted in writing to Carole I. Danielson, Division of Marketing Practices, Federal Trade Commission, 600 Pennsylvania Avenue, NW, Room 238, Washington, DC 20580 on or before June 16, 2000. The public forum will be held at the Federal Trade Commission, 600 Pennsylvania Avenue, NW, Room 432, Washington, DC 20580.

Form and Availability of Comments: To encourage prompt and efficient review and dissemination of the comments to the public, all papers and comments should also be submitted, if possible, on either a 5-¼ or a 3-½ inch computer disk, with a label on the disk stating the name of the commenting party and the name and version of the word processing program used to create the document, as well as the identification "Telemarketing Review—Comment. FTC File No. P994414." (Programs based on DOS are preferred. Files from other operating systems must be submitted in ASCII text format to be accepted.) Individual members of the public filing comments need not submit multiple copies or comments in electronic form.

Papers and written comments will be available for public inspection in accordance with the Freedom of Information Act, 5 U.S.C. § 552, and Commission regulations, 16 C.F.R. Part 4.9, on normal business days between the hours of 8:30 A.M. and 5:00 P.M. in Room 130, Federal Trade Commission, 600 Pennsylvania Avenue, NW, Washington, DC 20580. The Commission will make this notice and, to the extent possible, all papers or comments received in response to this notice available to the public through the Internet at the following address: http://www.ftc.gov

Application to Participate in Public Forum: A public forum to discuss provisions of the TSR, other than the "do-not-call" provision, will be held on July 27–28, 2000, in Washington, DC, from 8:30 A.M. until 5:30 P.M. Notification of interest in participating in the public forum scheduled for July 27–28, 2000, should be submitted in writing to Carole I. Danielson, Division of Marketing Practices, Federal Trade Commission, 600 Pennsylvania Avenue, NW, Room 238, Washington, DC 20580, on or before June 16, 2000. The exact dates, location, and information about participation in future FTC forums held in connection with the TSR review will be announced later by *Federal Register* notice.

FOR FURTHER INFORMATION CONTACT: Catherine Harrington-McBride (202) 326-2452, e-mail cmcbride@ftc.gov; Karen Leonard (202) 326-3597, e-mail kleonard@ftc.gov; or Carole Danielson (202) 326-3115, e-mail cdanielson@ftc.gov, Division of Marketing Practices, Bureau of Consumer Protection, Federal Trade Commission, 600 Pennsylvania Avenue, NW, Washington, DC 20580.

of a federal regulation must participate in the comment period and voice his concerns at that time.

Some agencies allow members of the public (and others who would be entitled to make comments) to participate in public hearings. These hearings are not for the purpose of challenging the agency's study that resulted in the rule; they are not trial proceedings and are only informational in nature. The hearing officers or commissioners for the agency ask questions of witnesses, but no other parties can question those who appear to make comments. The purpose of the hearings is to

EXHIBIT 6.6 **Sample Consumer Letter on Proposed Telemarketing Sales Regulation**

From: Mary Bowman-Kruhm
To: FTC.SERIUS("tsr@ftc.gov")
Date: Sun, May 28, 2000 8:14 AM
Subject: Telemarkeeting [sic] Review—Comment. FTC File No. P994414

I do not feel that the current regulations protect the public from unethical telemarketing practices. I resent getting calls from people who tell me they are not selling me anything, just taking a survey or providing information, when in fact I know full well they are not.

My worst example is a recent call. The message was, "Hi, this message is for Mary. This is Jeffrey Colwall (sp?) with the National Consumer Council, 800-555-3991. I'm calling in regard to your consumer credit cards and the high interest rates that they carry. Your record is now in our database and we would be happy to assist and recommend consolidation, cutting your monthly payments in half in most cases. I encourage you to call us here at the NCC. We are a non-profit organization formed to help home owners just like yourself." He went on to add/repeat to this to encourage me to call.

My husband and I pay off our credit cards each month and, except for a house loan, are debt-free. When I called to ask what was in their database regarding my record, I found that I had reached a loan service (non-profit?). Jeffrey was on another line and the chap with whom I talked said that they did not, in fact, have my record in a database but, unless they make that statement, people do not return their calls. I indicated my displeasure at their calling and at their tactics and hung up.

To me, this is extremely fraudulent and I resent the telephone service for which I pay being used in this manner.

Mary Bowman-Kruhm
CC: "Kruhm, Carl"

take input on the proposals and consider additional evidence and factors relevant in promulgating the final version of the rule.

Exhibits 6.6, 6.7, and 6.8 are examples of letters sent to the SEC offering input on the proposed rules on telemarketing (see proposal in Exhibit 6.5).

One of the important distinctions between the legislative process and the regulatory rulemaking process is the nature of the role of those involved. Legislators, such as representatives and senators, can accept campaign contributions and lunches and dinners from lobbyists. However, those who work in administrative agencies fulfill both a rulemaking and enforcement role and cannot accept such gifts. The Mike Espy biography on p. 239 and the *Sun Diamond* case on p. 220 illustrate what can happen when businesses and regulators cross the fine line on influence.

The *Sun Diamond* case is a criminal prosecution for alleged bribery of officials in order to persuade them to abandon or change proposed regulations before the agency.

EXHIBIT 6.7   **Sample Business Letter on Proposed Telemarketing Sales Regulation**

From: "Dennis McGarry" dmcgarry@bellsouth.net
To: "ATA" tsr@ftc.gov
Date: Tue, May 23, 2000 2:14 PM
Subject: Telemarketing Sales Rule
DATE: May 23, 2000
TO: FTC Committee Members
FROM: Dennis McGarry, President
Personal Legal Plans, Inc.
5821 Fairview Road, Suite G-9
Charlotte, NC 28209
SUBJECT: Telemarketing Sales Rule Comments

As a small business owner, who has been in business since 1981, I would like to make the following comments in regards to the current Telemarketing Sales Rule:

1) Do not change the rule - it works. The public is becoming more aware of the Telemarketing Sales Rule as every day passes. My only suggestion is convince Congress to increase your budget for enforcement of the current rules.

2) I strongly support company specific do not call lists as you currently have it. Consumers should be empowered to make choices on who can call or not call. My company relies heavily on the telephone to generate clients for my services. The telephone is the most cost-effective means for my company and thousands of other companies to transact business. I have almost 200,000 clients. In my almost 20 years of conducting my business I have never had a complaint from the Better Business Bureau.

3) Millions of people prefer to buy over the telephone - it's easy and convenient. According to information I have read, the Teleservices industry generates over $500 billion to our economy and employs millions of people. Telemarketing is a viable and important part of our healthy economy. We create jobs and generate business.

4) Do not hurt small businesses - it is the backbone of our economy. My business relies on client referrals, we follow up on these referrals via the telephone.

Thank you for allowing me to provide you with my thoughts. Have a great day!

EXHIBIT 6.8   **Sample Consumer Letter**

To: HQ.DCMAIL3(TSR)
Date: Thu, Mar 2, 2000 1:50 PM
Subject: Telemarketing Review—Comment. FTC File No. P994414
Hello!

People should have a choice if they want to receive marketing calls or not. It is a nightmare when every other call is a sales call. Lets get some rules out there so that the consumer doesn't have to put up with this. And . . . please, please don't allow these machines that dial us & then half the time hang up on you after you wait to see who is there. The machines malfunction & keep recalling, then hanging up. . . and then we have no way to even know who is calling so we can get it to STOP. And, it should be absolutely illegal for a sales call to leave messages on answering machines.

Thanks so much!

Darcy Dawson

CASE 6.1

U.S. v. Sun-Diamond Growers of California
526 U.S. 398 (1999)

Gratitude Can't Be in Cash or Kind

FACTS

Sun-Diamond Growers (Respondent) is a trade association that engaged in marketing and lobbying activities on behalf of its member cooperatives, which were owned by approximately 5,000 individual growers of raisins, figs, walnuts, prunes, and hazelnuts. The United States (Petitioner) is represented by Independent Counsel Donald Smaltz, who, as a consequence of his investigation of former Secretary of Agriculture Michael Espy [see p. 239], charged Sun-Diamond with making illegal gifts to Espy in violation of § 201(c)(1)(A). That statute provides, in relevant part, that anyone who *"otherwise than as provided by law for the proper discharge of official duty . . . directly or indirectly gives, offers, or promises anything of value to any public official, former public official, or person selected to be a public official, for or because of any official act performed or to be performed by such public official, former public official, or person selected to be a public official . . . shall be fined under this title or imprisoned for not more than two years, or both."*

Count One of the indictment charged Sun-Diamond with giving Espy approximately $5,900 in illegal gratuities: tickets to the 1993 U.S. Open Tennis Tournament (worth $2,295), luggage ($2,427), meals ($665), and a framed print and crystal bowl ($524). The indictment alluded to two matters in which Sun-Diamond had an interest in favorable treatment from the Secretary at the time it bestowed the gratuities. First, Sun-Diamond's member cooperatives participated in the Market Promotion Plan (MPP), a grant program administered by the Department of Agriculture to promote the sale of U.S. farm commodities in foreign countries. The cooperatives belonged to trade organizations, such as the California Prune Board and the Raisin Administrative Committee, which submitted overseas marketing plans for their respective commodities. If their plans were approved by the Secretary of Agriculture, the trade organizations received funds to be used in defraying the foreign marketing expenses of their constituents.

Second, Sun-Diamond had an interest in the Federal Government's regulation of methyl bromide, a low-cost pesticide used by many individual growers. In 1992, the Environmental Protection Agency announced plans to promulgate a rule to phase out the use of methyl bromide in the United States. The indictment alleged that Sun-Diamond sought the Department of Agriculture's assistance in persuading EPA to abandon its proposed rule altogether, or at least to mitigate its impact. In the latter event, respondent wanted the Department to fund research efforts to develop reliable alternatives to methyl bromide.

The jury convicted Sun-Diamond and the District Court sentenced respondent on this count to pay a fine of $400,000. The Court of Appeals reversed the conviction on Count One and remanded for a new trial.

The Supreme Court granted certiorari.

JUDICIAL OPINION

SCALIA, Justice

Talmudic sages believed that judges who accepted bribes would be punished by eventually losing all knowledge of the divine law. The Federal Government, dealing with many public officials who are not judges, and with at least some judges for whom this sanction holds no terror, has constructed a framework of human laws and regulations defining various sorts of impermissible gifts, and punishing those who give or receive them with administrative sanctions, fines, and incarceration. One element of that framework is 18 U.S.C. § 201(c)(1)(A), the "illegal gratuity statute," which prohibits giving "anything of value" to a present, past, or future public official "for or because of any official act performed or to be performed by such public official." In this case, we consider whether conviction under the illegal gratuity statute requires any showing beyond the fact that a gratuity was given because of the recipient's official position.

The first crime, described in § 201(b)(1) as to the giver, and § 201(b)(2) as to the recipient, is bribery, which requires a showing that something of value was corruptly given, offered, or promised to a public official (as to the giver) or corruptly demanded, sought, received, accepted, or agreed to be received or accepted by a public official (as to the recipient) with intent, inter alia, "to influence any official act" (giver) or in return for "being influenced in the performance of any official act" (recipient). The second crime, defined in § 201(c)(1)(A) as to the giver, and § 201(c)(1)(B) as to the recipient, is illegal gratuity, which requires a showing that something of value was given, offered, or promised to a public official (as to the giver), or demanded, sought, received, accepted, or agreed to be received or accepted by a public official (as to the recipient), "for or because of any official act performed or to be performed by such public official."

The distinguishing feature of each crime is its intent element. Bribery requires intent "to influence" an official act or "to be influenced" in an official act, while illegal gratuity requires only that the gratuity be given or accepted "for or because of" an official act. In other words, for bribery there must be a *quid pro quo*—a specific intent to give or receive something of value in exchange for an official act. An illegal gratuity, on the other hand, may constitute merely a reward for some future act that the public official will take (and may already have determined to take), or for a past act that he has already taken. The punishments prescribed for the two offenses reflect their relative seriousness: Bribery may be punished by up to 15 years' imprisonment, a fine of $250,000 ($500,000 for organizations) or triple the value of the bribe, whichever is greater, and disqualification from holding government office. Violation of the illegal gratuity statute, on the other hand, may be punished by up to two years' imprisonment and a fine of $250,000 ($500,000 for organizations).

The District Court's instructions in this case, in differentiating between a bribe and an illegal gratuity, correctly noted that only a bribe requires proof of a *quid pro quo*. The point in controversy here is that the instructions went on to suggest that § 201(c)(1)(A), unlike the bribery statute, did not require any connection between respondent's intent and a specific official act. It would be satisfied, according to the instructions, merely by a showing that respondent gave Secretary Espy a gratuity because of his official position—perhaps, for example, to build a reservoir of goodwill that might ultimately affect one or more of a multitude of unspecified acts, now and in the future.

In our view, this interpretation does not fit comfortably with the statutory text, which prohibits only gratuities given or received "for or because of any official act performed or to be performed." It seems to us that this means "for or because of some particular official act of whatever identity"—just as the question "Do you like any composer?" normally means "Do you like some particular composer?" It is linguistically possible, of course, for the phrase to mean "for or because of official acts in general, without specification as to which one"—just as the question "Do you like any composer?" could mean "Do you like all composers, no matter what their names or music?" But the former seems to us the more natural meaning, especially given the complex structure of the provision before us here. Why go through the trouble of requiring that the gift be made "for or because of any official act performed or to be performed by such public official," and then defining "official act" (in § 201(a)(3)) to mean "any decision or action on any question, matter, cause, suit, proceeding or controversy, which may at any time be pending, or which may by law be brought before any public official, in such official's official capacity," when, if the Government's interpretation were correct, it would have sufficed to say "for or because of such official's ability to favor the donor in executing the functions of his office"? The insistence upon an "official act," carefully defined, seems pregnant with the requirement that some particular official act be identified and proved.

Besides thinking that this is the more natural meaning of § 201(c)(1)(A), we are inclined to believe it correct because of the peculiar results that the Government's alternative reading would produce. It would criminalize, for example, token gifts to the President based on his official position and not linked to any identifiable act—such as the replica jerseys given by championship sports teams each year during ceremonial White House visits. Similarly, it would criminalize a high school principal's gift of a school baseball cap to the Secretary of Education, by reason of his office, on the occasion of the latter's visit to the school. That these examples are not fanciful is demonstrated by the fact that counsel for the United States maintained at oral argument that a group of farmers would violate § 201(c)(1)(A) by providing a complimentary lunch for the Secretary of Agriculture in conjunction with his speech to the farmers concerning various matters of USDA policy—so long as the Secretary had before him, or had in prospect, matters affecting the farmers. Of course the Secretary of Agriculture always has before him or in prospect matters that affect farmers, just as the President

(continued)

always has before him or in prospect matters that affect college and professional sports, and the Secretary of Education matters that affect high schools.

And the criminal statutes are merely the tip of the regulatory iceberg. In 5 U.S.C. § 7353, which announces broadly that no "employee of the executive, legislative, or judicial branch shall solicit or accept anything of value from a person . . . whose interests may be substantially affected by the performance or nonperformance of the individual's official duties," Congress has authorized the promulgation of ethical rules for each branch of the Federal Government. Pursuant to that provision, each branch of Government regulates its employees' acceptance of gratuities in some fashion.

All of the regulations, and some of the statutes, contain exceptions for various kinds of gratuities given by various donors for various purposes. Many of those exceptions would be snares for the unwary, given that there are no exceptions to the broad prohibition that the Government claims is imposed by § 201(c)(1).

More important for present purposes, however, this regulation, and the numerous other regulations and statutes littering this field, demonstrate that this is an area where precisely targeted prohibitions are commonplace, and where more general prohibitions

have been qualified by numerous exceptions. Given that reality, a statute in this field that can linguistically be interpreted to be either a meat axe or a scalpel should reasonably be taken to be the latter. Absent a text that clearly requires it, we ought not expand this one piece of the regulatory puzzle so dramatically as to make many other pieces misfits.

We hold that, in order to establish a violation of 18 U.S.C. § 201(c)(1)(A), the Government must prove a link between a thing of value conferred upon a public official and a specific "official act" for or because of which it was given. We affirm the judgment of the Court of Appeals, which remanded the case to the District Court for a new trial on Count One.

Reversed and remanded.

CASE QUESTIONS

1. What violation is alleged?
2. Are administrative agency employees permitted to accept gifts from those affected by their regulations and policies?
3. What is required for proof of criminal wrongdoing in making a gift?
4. What happens with the conviction?

Deciding What to Do with the Proposed Regulation After the comment period is over, the agency has three choices about what to do with the proposed rules. The first choice is simply to adopt the rules. The second choice is to modify the proposed rules and go through the process of public comment again. If the modification is minor, however, the APA allows the agency to adopt a modified version of the rule without going through the public comment period again. The final choice of the proposing agency would be to withdraw the rule. Some rules have so many comments pointing out their impracticability, inflexibility, or prematurity that they are withdrawn from the promulgation process. For example, the Federal Trade Commission withdrew its proposed rules on regulating advertisements during children's programming hours because of strong industry opposition, the existence of a private industry code already controlling the area, and complicated legal issues involved in the regulation of commercial speech. Subsequently, modified rules were proposed and adopted.

C O N S I D E R . . .

6.1 This chapter's opening paragraphs described the EEOC's proposed guidelines on religious harassment in the workplace and the business concerns about those guidelines.

Ethical Issues 6.3

Three Chippewa Indian tribes submitted applications to the U.S. Department of the Interior seeking approval to convert a greyhound racing facility in Hudson, Wisconsin, to an off-reservation casino.

On June 8, 1995, the Indian Gaming staff in the department issued a draft report recommending approval of the Chippewa application.

While final decision on the application was pending in the agency, Harold Ickes (then White House Deputy Chief of Staff for Policy and Political Affairs) received a letter from Patrick O'Connor, a lobbyist for tribes that opposed the Chippewa application. The O'Connor letter explained the significance of the Chippewa decision, that the opposition tribes were important contributors to the Democratic party, and that the Chippewa tribes were Republican supporters. In addition, Donald Fowler, the Democratic

National Committee chairman, met with Ickes and discussed the basis for the opposition to creating another gaming casino." Further, there were faxes regarding the application between White House staff and Department of the Interior staff.

On June 27, 1995, the Chippewas' application was denied. The decision cited "community opposition" but did not incorporate or discuss the lengthy and detailed reports the staff had prepared for its June 8th recommendation of approval.

Interior Secretary Bruce Babbitt told Paul Eckstein, a lawyer of the Chippewas and a lifetime friend of Babbitt's, that Harold Ickes required him to issue the decision on June 27.

What ethical issues arise when political activities cross into administrative proceedings? How would the Chippewas perceive this series of events?

The U.S. Senate passed a resolution 94–0 urging the EEOC to drop the guidelines. The general public became actively involved in the rulemaking. Religious and business groups flooded the EEOC with more than 100,000 letters of protest.

Attorneys who examined the proposed rules issued opinions for their business clients that concluded the only way to avoid religious harassment lawsuits by employees or customers under the proposed rules was to ban all religious expression in the workplace, including the wearing or display of a yarmulke or a cross. The attorneys further concluded that banning such personal expression, a form of speech, would result in a flood of First Amendment suits.

The EEOC withdrew the proposed rules. EEOC spokesman Mike Widomski explained that "the public outcry and the number of comments that were received" triggered the reversal.

Public comments and input have an impact in the regulatory process. Is this a reasonable process? How do you feel about this particular rulemaking situation? Do you believe allowing comments is a fair process?

Court and Legislative Challenges to Proposed Rules Those parties who made comments on the rules during their proposal stage can challenge the validity of the rules in court. An administrative rule can be challenged on several different grounds.

The first ground on which to challenge an agency rule is that it is arbitrary, capricious, an abuse of discretion, or is in violation of some other law. This standard is generally applied to informal rulemaking and simply requires the agency to show that there is evidence to support the proposed rule. Without such evidence, the rule can be held to be **arbitrary and capricious.** The following case addresses the issue of whether an agency's action is arbitrary and capricious.

CASE 6.2

Motor Vehicles Manufacturers Ass'n. v. State Farm Mutual Insurance Co.
463 U.S. 29 (1983)

Fasten Your Seat Belts: Rulemaking Is a Rough Ride

FACTS

The Department of Transportation (DOT), charged with the enforcement of the National Traffic and Motor Vehicle Safety Act of 1966 and the task of reducing auto accidents, passed Standard 208 in 1967. Standard 208 is the seat belt requirement for motor vehicles, and its original form simply required that all cars be equipped with seat belts. It soon became clear to the DOT that people did not use the belts, so the department began a study of passive restraint systems, which do not require any action on the part of the occupant other than operating the vehicle. The two types considered were automatic seat belts and air bags. Studies showed that these devices could prevent approximately 12,000 deaths a year and over 100,000 serious injuries.

In 1972, after many hearings and comments, the Department of Transportation passed a regulation requiring some type of passive restraint system on all vehicles manufactured after 1975. The regulation allowed an ignition interlock system, which requires car occupants to have their seat belts fastened before a car could be started. Congress, however, revoked the requirement of the ignition interlock.

Because of changes in directors of the DOT and the unfavorable economic climate in the auto industry, the requirements for passive restraints were postponed. In 1981, the department proposed a rescission of the passive restraint rule. After receiving written comments and holding public hearings, the agency concluded there was no longer a basis for reliably predicting that passive restraints increased safety levels or decreased accidents. Further, the agency found it would cost $1 billion to implement the rule, and they were unwilling to impose such substantial costs on auto manufacturers.

State Farm filed suit on the rescission of the rule on the basis that it was arbitrary and capricious. The court of appeals held the rescission was, in fact, arbitrary and capricious. Auto manufacturers appealed.

JUDICIAL OPINION

WHITE, Justice

The ultimate question before us is whether NHTSA's (National Highway Traffic Safety Administration) rescission of the passive restraint requirement of Standard 208 was arbitrary and capricious. We conclude, as did the Court of Appeals, that it was.

The first and most obvious reason for finding the rescission arbitrary and capricious is that NHTSA apparently gave no consideration whatever to modifying the Standard to require that airbag technology be utilized. Standard 208 sought to achieve automatic crash protection by requiring automobile manufacturers to install either of two passive restraint devices: airbags or automatic seatbelts. There was no suggestion in the long rulemaking process that led to Standard 208 that if only one of these options were feasible, no passive restraint standard should be promulgated. Indeed, the agency's original proposed standard contemplated the installation of inflatable restraints in all cars. Automatic belts were added as a means of complying with the standard because they were believed to be as effective as airbags in achieving the goal of occupant crash protection.

The agency has now determined that the detachable automatic belts will not attain anticipated safety benefits because so many individuals will detach the mechanism. Even if this conclusion were acceptable in its entirety, standing alone it would not justify any more than an amendment of Standard 208 to disallow compliance by means of the only technology which will not provide effective passenger protection. It does not cast doubt on the need for a passive restraint standard or upon the efficacy of airbag technology. In its most recent rulemaking, the agency again acknowledged the life-saving potential of the airbag.

Given the effectiveness ascribed to airbag technology by the agency, the mandate of the Safety Act to achieve traffic safety would suggest that the logical response to the faults of detachable seatbelts would be to require the installation of airbags. At the very least this alternative way of achieving objectives of the Act should have been addressed and adequate reasons given for its abandonment. But the agency not only did not require compliance through airbags, it did not even consider the possibility in its 1981 rulemaking. Not one sentence of its rulemaking statement discusses the airbags-only option. We have frequently reiterated that an agency must cogently explain why it had exercised its discretion in a given manner.

For nearly a decade, the automobile industry waged the regulatory equivalent of war against the airbag and lost—the inflatable restraint was proven sufficiently effective. Now the automobile industry has decided to employ a seatbelt system which will not meet the safety objectives of Standard 208. This hardly constitutes cause to revoke the standard itself. Indeed the Motor Vehicle Safety Act was necessary because the industry was not sufficiently responsive to safety concerns. The Act intended that safety standards not depend on current technology and would be "technology-forcing" in the sense of inducing the development of superior safety design.

It is not infrequent that the available data does not settle a regulatory issue and the agency must then exercise its judgment in moving from the facts and probabilities on the record to a policy conclusion. Recognizing that policy making in a complex society must account for uncertainty, however, does not imply that it is sufficient for an agency to merely recite the terms "substantial uncertainty" as a justification for its actions. The agency must explain the evidence which is available, and must offer a "rational connection between the facts found and the choice made."

In this case, the agency's explanation for rescission of the passive restraint requirement is not sufficient to enable us to conclude that the rescission was the product of reasoned decision making. We start with the accepted ground that if used, seatbelts unquestionably would save many thousands of lives and would prevent tens of thousands of crippling injuries. Unlike recent regulations we have reviewed, the safety benefits of wearing seatbelts are not in doubt and it is not challenged that were those benefits to accrue, the monetary costs of implementing the standard would be easily justified.

Since 20 to 50 percent of motorists currently wear seatbelts on some occasions, there would seem to be grounds to believe that seatbelt use by occasional users will be substantially increased by the detachable passive belts. Whether this is the case is a matter for the agency to decide, but it must bring its expertise to bear on the question.

An agency's view of what is in the public interest may change, either with or without a change in circumstances. But an agency changing its course must supply a reasoned analysis. We do not accept all of the reasoning of the Court of Appeals but we do conclude that the agency has failed to supply the requisite "reasoned analysis" in this case. Accordingly, we remand the matter to the NHTSA for further consideration consistent with this opinion.

CASE QUESTIONS

1. What regulation is at issue in the case?
2. When was the regulation first adopted?
3. What changes has the regulation undergone over the years?
4. What was done with the regulation to result in this judicial decision?
5. Who challenged the agency's actions, and what were the reasons for this challenge?
6. Is the agency's action valid?

A second theory for challenging an agency's regulation is that the regulation is unsupported by substantial evidence. This **substantial evidence test** is applied in the review of formal and hybrid rulemaking. Where the arbitrary and capricious standard simply requires some proof or basis for the regulation, substantial evidence requires that more convincing evidence exist in support of the regulation than against it. Case 6.3 on p. 227 involves a business challenge to an administrative regulation based on the issue of whether substantial evidence was presented.

Re: The Airbag Issue That Does Not Go Away

The issue of passive restraints in vehicles and the Department of Transportation's rejection of them resurfaced in 1996. Following the **State Farm** *case, passive restraint systems, including airbags, were mandated in passenger vehicles. However, in 1996, evidence of a problem—noted by General Motors in a 1979 comment to DOT and in DOT studies in 1981—emerged: Children were killed in auto accidents when the airbags in the vehicles in which they were riding deployed.*

Engineers discovered that the force of an inflating bag (up to 200 mph) was sufficient to snap a child's neck or deform a child's head. In several of the accidents, chidren were decapitated by the inflated bags. Children involved in the accidents were properly restrained in their seat belts or carseats. The cause of the 50 injuries or deaths involving children between 1991 and 1996 was the passenger-side airbag.

Over a six-month period the National Highway Traffic Safety Administration (NHTSA) studied the issue and considered the following options:

1. Elimination of airbags
2. Installation of switches to turn off passenger-side airbags
3. Warning in vehicles on the dangers of passenger-side airbags
4. Recommending that all children ride in the back seat of vehicles

Insurers and auto manufacturers opposed elimination of airbags and switches for fear of liability and misuse of switches. Consumers favored switches. NHTSA, following input, required warnings in all vehicles about airbags but did not require switches. The warning labels (three in all new cars beginning in February 1998) must be posted on the dashboard as well as on each side of the car visor. The dashboard label reads as follows:

WARNING

Children may be KILLED *or* INJURED *by Passenger Airbag*

The back seat is the safest place for children 12 and under.

Make sure all children use seat belts or child seats.

NHTSA will continue to study cut-off switches and will allow vehicle owners, by petition, to have airbags disconnected.

In September 1998 the Department of Transportation began a rulemaking process for modifying airbag requirements. Under the proposed rules, airbags must pass safety tests using all sizes of crash dummies. The current rule requires only the use of adult-size dummies. Also under review are side airbags and their effect on child passengers.

The first lawsuits for the airbag deaths of children have begun going to trial. A court in New York awarded a family $750,000 for the death of their 5-year-old son when the airbag deployed on the passenger side in the family's 1995 Dodge Caravan. The child was not wearing a seat belt when the van was hit going 9–11 mph. Daimler Chrysler is appealing the verdict.

The airbag continues to be a lightning rod for discussion and controversy. One of the key researchers who testified of the need for airbags over twenty years ago testified that he was wrong and that passenger-side airbags do not save enough lives to justify their risk and expense. John Graham, the director of Harvard's Center for Risk Analysis, announced his change of heart at a National Transportation Safety Board hearing.

Side airbags have also been subject to safety questions because of their potential harm to children riding in back seats of cars. With the safety warnings against having children ride in the front passenger seat, their only place for riding is in the back, and side airbags now appear to be a safety threat there.

The jury verdicts continue in cases involving children with some of the latest cases involving testimony that the children would have lived had the airbags not deployed.

BUSINESS STRATEGY

In the *State Farm* case, an insurer—not an auto manufacturer—is challenging the proposed regulation (or lack thereof). Certainly the insurer does not carry the responsibility of implementing the safety designs or perfecting the technology. However, because the implementation of such safety features helps reduce claims for accident injuries and damages, the insurer has a business interest in seeing

© Spencer Grant/PhotoEdit

that the regulations are passed. Very often, businesses, like the insurers here, must become involved in regulatory proceedings for rules that might not regulate them directly but will benefit or cost them indirectly. In regulatory proceedings, businesses that will experience indirect impact often take a position and use the process to their business benefit.

CASE 6.3

Corn Products Co. and Derby Foods, Inc. v. Department of Health, Education, & Welfare and Food and Drug Administration
427 F.2d 511 (3d Cir. 1970)

Skippy and Peter Pan Take On the FDA

FACTS

Corn Products Company (petitioner) manufactures peanut butter known as "Skippy" brand and holds 22 percent of the peanut butter market. Derby (also a petitioner) holds 14 percent of the market with its product, "Peter Pan."

Peanut butter originally was made of ground peanuts, salt, and sometimes sugar. This combination had the disadvantages of oil separation, short shelf life, and stickiness. These deficiencies have been diminished, if not eliminated, by the addition of stabilizing ingredients, mainly hydrogenated vegetable oils. Today peanut butter is made of peanuts, an oil component, the stabilizer, and seasonings.

The Food and Drug Administration (FDA) adopted a regulation limiting the percentage (by weight) of optional ingredients that may be added to the peanut ingredients to 10 percent. The regulation allows for the addition or removal of peanut oil but limits the fat content to 55 percent.

Corn Products and Derby urged the adoption of a 13 percent as opposed to a 10 percent standard and challenged the regulation as not being supported by substantial evidence.

JUDICIAL OPINION

STALEY, Circuit Judge

Using an affirmative approach to the order under consideration, the issue becomes whether the findings upon which the 90 percent standard is based are supported by substantial evidence. Corn Products' argument that the standard should have designated partially hydrogenated peanut oil as peanut ingredient must be directed at those findings which equate them.

Skippy fails to comply with the standard because it contains 8½ percent of partially hydrogenated peanut oil and an amount of seasonings which together exceed the 10 percent limit on optional ingredients. No distintion is made in the standard between hydrogenated peanut oil and other hydrogenated vegetable oils.

Four expert witnesses, all chemists, testified to the dissimilarity between vegetable oil and hydrogenated oil. There was testimony that there is no nutritional variation between these oils. The basic function of the hydrogenated oil, to prevent oil separation in the product, is said to be served regardless of the source oil. The use of hydrogenated peanut oil does not add flavor to the product. From

(continued)

the foregoing, it is quite clear that there is substantial evidence to support a conclusion which makes no distinction between hydrogenated vegetable oils.

The standard reflects the practice of a number of manufacturers and to those not in compliance there will be no economic hardship in complying. The fact of exclusion of the leading producers does not make the regulation unreasonable. Skippy and Peter Pan will not be banned; merely a change in product formula will be required.

CASE QUESTIONS

1. What standard did the FDA pass for peanut butter?

2. Why didn't Corn Products and Derby meet the standard?

3. What arguments do they make in appealing the regulation?

4. Does it matter that the regulation excluded their substantial shares of the market?

5. Was there substantial evidence to support the rule changes?

A third ground on which to challenge an agency's regulation involves the rule that a regulation can be set aside if the agency did not comply with the APA requirements of notice, publication, and public comment or input. The procedures for rulemaking must be followed in order for the regulatory process and resulting rules to be valid. Thus, an agency that seeks public comment for the purposes of drafting legislation cannot then turn the legislation into rules after the comment period. The notice must specify that promulgated rules will be the result of the proceedings. The following case addresses an agency's attempt to change a rule without following the APA requirements.

CASE 6.4

San Diego Air Sports Center, Inc. v. *Federal Aviation Administration*
887 F.2d 966 (9th Cir. 1989)

Are Parachutes Air Traffic?

FACTS

San Diego Air Sports Center (SDAS) operates a sports parachuting business in Otay Mesa, California. SDAS offers training to beginning parachutists and facilitates recreational jumping for experienced parachutists. It indicates that the majority of SDAS jumps occur at altitudes in excess of 5,800 feet.

The jump zone used by SDAS overlaps the San Diego Traffic Control Area (TCA). Although the aircraft carrying the parachutists normally operate outside the TCA, the parachutists themselves are dropped through it. Thus, each jump must be approved by the air traffic controllers.

In July 1987, an air traffic controller in San Diego filed an Unsatisfactory Condition Report complaining of the strain that parachuting was putting on the controllers and raising safety concerns. The report led to a staff study of parachute jumping within the San Diego TCA. In October 1987, representatives of the San Diego Terminal Radar Approach Control (TRACON) facility met with SDAS operators. In December 1987, the San Diego TRACON sent to SDAS a draft letter of agreement outlining agreed-upon procedures and coordination requirements. Nonetheless, the San Diego TRACON conducted another study between January 14, 1988, and February 11, 1988, and about two months after the draft letter was sent, the San Diego TRACON withdrew it.

SDAS states that the air traffic manager of the San Diego TRACON assured SDAS that it would be invited to attend all meetings on parachuting in the San Diego TCA. However, SDAS was not informed of or invited to any meetings.

In March 1988, the FAA sent a letter to SDAS informing SDAS that "[e]ffective immediately parachute jumping within or into the San Diego TCA in the Otay Reservoir Jump Zone will not be authorized." The FAA stated that the letter was final and appealable.

SDAS challenged the letter in federal court on grounds that it constituted rulemaking without compliance with required APA procedures.

JUDICIAL OPINION

BEEZER, Circuit Judge

The Federal Aviation Act requires that rules affecting the use of navigable airspace be issued in accordance with the Administrative Procedure Act (APA). 49 U.S.C. App. § 1348(d). The "principal purpose" of section 553 of the APA is "to provide that the legislative functions of administrative agencies shall so far as possible be exercised only upon public participation." Section 553 of the APA requires agencies to adhere to three steps when promulgating rules: Notice of the proposed rule, opportunity to comment, and an explanation of the rule ultimately adopted. 5 U.S.C. § (b),(c). These three requirements have been referred to as "the statutory *minima*" imposed by Congress.

Not every decision made by administrative agencies requires citizen participation. The APA lists four instances when the statutory *minima* do not apply: When the agency is promulgating (1) interpretive rules, (2) general statements of policy, or (3) rules of agency organization, procedure, or practice, or (4) when the requirement of notice and participation are impractical or contrary to public interest.

Congress was concerned that the exceptions to section 553, though necessary, might be used too broadly. The Senate noted that the courts have a "duty . . . to prevent avoidance of the requirements of the [Act] by any manner or form of indirection." We have stated that "[t]he exceptions to section 533 will be 'narrowly construed and only reluctantly countenanced.'"

The FAA letter does not come within either of the first two exceptions. The letter creates an immediate, substantive rule, i.e., that no parachuting will be allowed in the San Diego TCA.

The FAA argues that parachuting created an emergency to which it responded in the letter at issue. It is further argued that a response to an immediate emergency is covered by the fourth exception. This argument is not persuasive. The only accident known to the FAA occurred two years before it issued its letter. Furthermore, the FAA itself claims to have extensively studied the situation before issuing the letter. The FAA does not explain why public participation as required by the APA could not be included in its study.

Finally, the FAA argues that the letter is not a rule at all; rather, the FAA characterizes the letter as an order to which the requirements set forth in section 553 of the APA does [sic] not apply. We find this argument somewhat mystifying, as there are equally stringent participation requirements for orders. Furthermore, the FAA is wrong; the letter is a rule.

A time-honored principle of administrative law is that the label an agency puts on its actions "is not necessarily conclusive." Equally true, however, is the fact that agencies can issue rules through adjudication (the process by which orders are normally issued) and orders through rulemaking.

In this case no record was kept of the "process" that resulted in the FAA letter; we can only scrutinize the letter itself. The letter clearly promulgates a rule. It states that *all* parachuting by any party will be prohibited in the San Diego TCA from the time it is issued. This comports with this court's statement that "[s]ubstantive rules are those which effect a change in existing law or policy."

The Federal Aviation Act requires that rules affecting the use of navigable airspace be issued in accordance with the APA, 49 U.S.C.App. § 1348(d). In issuing this substantive rule, the FAA failed to do so. A substantive rule is invalid if the issuing agency fails to comply with the APA. Therefore, the petition for review is granted.

(continued)

CASE QUESTIONS

1. What problem did the FAA have with SDAS?
2. How did the FAA attempt to control SDAS?
3. Was the letter an attempt to promulgate regulation?
4. Would the FAA letter shut down SDAS?
5. Was SDAS deprived of due process by the letter?

Another basis for challenging a regulation is that the regulation is unconstitutional. Many challenges based on constitutional grounds deal with regulations that give an agency authority to search records or that impose discriminatory requirements for licensing professionals. For example, a requirement of a minimum residency period before allowing an applicant to become licensed in a particular profession has been challenged successfully. Zoning board regulations that discriminate against certain classes or races as to the use of property have also been successfully challenged as unconstitutional. Further, broadcasters will often depend on freedom of speech—the First Amendment—to challenge new Federal Communication Commission (FCC) regulations.

In the following case, a business challenged a labeling rule on grounds that its First Amendment rights were violated and that the agency was exceeding its authority.

CASE 6.5

Rubin v. Coors Brewing Company
514 U.S. 476 (1995)

Rocky Mountain High: Alcohol Content on the Label

FACTS

Coors Brewing Company (respondent) brews beer. In 1987, it applied to the Bureau of Alcohol, Tobacco and Firearms (BATF) for approval of proposed labels and advertisements that disclosed the alcohol content of its beer. BATF refused to approve the disclosure under section 205(e)(2) of the Federal Alcohol Administration Act (FAAA), which prohibits the selling, shipping, or delivery of malt beverages, distilled spirits, or wines in bottles:

unless such products are bottled, packaged, and labeled in conformity with such regulations, to be prescribed by the Secretary of the Treasury, with respect to packaging, marking, branding, and labeling and size and fill of container . . . as will provide the consumer with adequate information as to the identity and quality of the products, the alcoholic content thereof (except that statements of, or

statements likely to be considered as statements of, alcoholic content of malt beverages are prohibited unless required by State law and except that, in case of wines, statements of alcoholic content shall be required only for wines containing more than 14 per centum of alcohol by volume), the net contents of the package, and the manufacturer or bottler or importer of the product.

Regulations related to this statutory restriction (27 C.F.R. § 7.26(a)) prohibit the disclosure of alcohol content on beer labels.

In addition to prohibiting numerical indications of alcohol content, the labeling regulations proscribe descriptive terms that suggest high content, such as "strong," "full strength," "extra strength," "high test," "high proof," "pre-war strength," and "full oldtime alcoholic strength" (27 C.F.R. § 7.29(f)). The prohibitions do not preclude labels from identifying a beer as "low alcohol," "reduced alcohol," "non-alcoholic," or "alcohol-free."

When BATF refused to approve the labels, Coors filed suit in federal district court challenging the regulation as violative of the First Amendment. BATF (the government) argued that the ban on alcohol content in labels was needed to prevent "strength wars" among brewers who would then compete in the marketplace on the potency of their beers.

The district court found for Coors, but the U.S. Court of Appeals for the Tenth Circuit reversed, finding that the government's interest in suppressing strength wars was substantial. It remanded the case to the trial court for determining whether the ban was an appropriate means of avoiding strength wars. The lower court found there was no evidence of any relationship between the disclosure on labels of alcohol content and competition on the basis of content. The court of appeals (on the second appeal) concluded that BATF's regulation violated the First Amendment.

JUDICIAL OPINION

THOMAS, Justice

Both the lower courts and the parties agree that respondent seeks to disclose only truthful, verifiable, and nonmisleading factual information about alcohol content on its beer labels. Thus, our analysis focuses on the substantiality of the interest behind § 205(e)(2) and on whether the labeling ban bears an acceptable fit with the Government's goal. A careful consideration of these factors indicates that § 205(e)(2) violates the First Amendment's protection of commercial speech.

According to the Government, the FAAA's restriction prevents a particular type of beer drinker—one who selects a beverage because of its high potency—from choosing beers solely for their alcohol content. In the Government's view, restricting disclosure of information regarding a particular product characteristic will decrease the extent to which consumers will select the product on the basis of that characteristic.

Respondent counters that Congress actually intended the FAAA to achieve the far different purpose of preventing brewers from making inaccurate claims concerning alcohol content. According to respondent, when Congress passed the FAAA in 1935, brewers did not have the technology to produce beer with alcohol levels within predictable tolerances—a skill that modern beer producers now

possess. Further, respondent argues that the true policy guiding federal alcohol regulation is not aimed at suppressing strength wars. If such were the goal, the Government would not pursue the opposite policy with respect to wines and distilled spirits.

Rather than suppressing the free flow of factual information in the wine and spirits markets, the Government seeks to control competition on the basis of strength by monitoring distillers' promotions and marketing. The respondent quite correctly notes that the general thrust of federal alcohol policy appears to favor greater disclosure of information, rather than less. This also seems to be the trend in federal regulation of other consumer products as well. See, *e.g.,* Nutrition Labeling and Education Act of 1990, Pub. L. 101-535, 104 Stat. 2353, as amended (requiring labels of food products sold in the United States to display nutritional information).

The Government carries the burden of showing that the challenged regulation advances the Government's interest "in a direct and material way." That burden "is not satisfied by mere speculation and conjecture; rather, a governmental body seeking to sustain a restriction on commercial speech must demonstrate that the harms it recites are real and that its restriction will in fact alleviate them to a material degree."

The Government attempts to meet its burden by pointing to current developments in the consumer market. It claims that beer producers are already competing and advertising on the basis of alcohol strength in the "malt liquor" segment of the beer market. The Government attempts to show that this competition threatens to spread to the rest of the market by directing our attention to respondent's motives in bringing this litigation. Respondent allegedly suffers from consumer misperceptions that its beers contain less alcohol than other brands. According to the Government, once respondent gains relief from § 205(e)(2), it will use its labels to overcome this handicap.

Under the Government's theory, § 205(e)(2) suppresses the threat of such competition by preventing consumers from choosing beers on the basis of alcohol content. It is assuredly a matter of "common sense," that a restriction on the advertising of a product characteristic will decrease the extent to which consumers select a product on the basis of that trait. In addition to common sense, the Government urges us to turn to history as a guide. According to the Government, at the time Congress enacted the FAAA, the use of labels displaying alcohol content

(continued)

had helped produce a strength war. Section 205(e)(2) allegedly relieved competitive pressures to market beer on the basis of alcohol content, resulting over the long term in beers with lower alcohol levels.

We conclude that § 205(e)(2) cannot directly and materially advance its asserted interest because of the overall irrationality of the Government's regulatory scheme. While the laws governing labeling prohibit the disclosure of alcohol content unless required by state law, federal regulations apply a contrary policy to beer advertising. The failure to prohibit the disclosure of alcohol content in advertising, which would seem to constitute a more influential weapon in any strength war than labels, makes no rational sense if the government's true aim is to suppress strength wars.

While we are mindful that respondent only appealed the constitutionality of § 205(e)(2), these exemptions and inconsistencies bring into question the purpose of the labeling ban. To be sure, the Government's interest in combating strength wars remains a valid goal. But the irrationality of this unique and puzzling regulatory framework ensures that the labeling ban will fail to achieve that end. There is little chance that § 205(e)(2) can directly and materially advance its aim, while other provisions of the same act directly undermine and counteract its effects.

The Government argues that a sufficient "fit" exists here because the labeling ban applies to only one product characteristic and because the ban does not prohibit all disclosures of alcohol content—it applies only to those involving labeling and advertising. In response, respondent suggests several alternatives, such as directly limiting the alcohol content of beers, prohibiting marketing efforts emphasizing high alcohol strength (which is apparently the policy in some other Western nations), or limiting the labeling ban only to malt liquors, which is the segment of the market that allegedly is threatened with a strength war. We agree that the availability of these options, all of which could advance the Government's asserted interest in a manner less intrusive to respondent's First Amendment rights, indicates that § 205(e)(2) is more extensive than necessary.

We affirm the decision of the court below.

CASE QUESTIONS

1. What inconsistencies exist in BATF's regulatory scheme?

2. To survive a First Amendment challenge, what must a regulation of commercial speech accomplish?

3. What market perception is Coors trying to correct with its labels?

4. In what ways could BATF accomplish its goals of preventing strength wars other than the § 205(e)(2) complete ban?

5. Did the label control prevent strength wars?

6. What are general government trends with respect to disclosure?

Another theory for challenging a regulation in court is ***ultra vires,*** a Latin term meaning "beyond its powers." An *ultra vires* regulation is one that goes beyond the authority given to the agency in its enabling act. Although most agencies stay clearly within their authority, if an agency tries to change the substance and purpose of the enabling act through regulation, the regulations would be *ultra vires*. For example, the intent of the 1933 Securities Act was to provide full disclosure to investors about a securities sale. The SEC could not, on the basis of its authority, pass a rule that eliminated securities registration in favor of an unregulated securities market.

C O N S I D E R . . .

6.2 The National Credit Union Administration (NCUA) is the federal agency responsible for the regulation of credit unions in the United States. Credit unions were authorized and created under a 1934 congressional enactment that limited membership to "groups having a common bond of occupation or association, or to groups with a well-defined neighborhood, community, or rural district," 12 U.S.C. § 1759.

AT&T Family Federal Credit Union has 110,000 members nationwide, only 35 percent of whom are employees of AT&T. Several banks have brought suit, challenging NCUA's approval of AT&T's ongoing credit union when membership exceeds statutory authority. Are the banks correct? Has NCUA exceeded its statutory authority? [*Nat. Credit Union Adm. v. First Nat. Bank & Trust*, 522 U.S. 479 (1998)]

Proactive Business Strategies in Regulation

Some administrative regulations can be eliminated through the use of legislation. In an enabling act called a **sunset law,** Congress creates an agency for a limited period of time during which the agency must establish its benefits and other justification for its continuation. The enabling act may provide for an audit to determine effectiveness after the agency has been in existence for two years. Without renewal by Congress, the sun sets on the agency and it is terminated. Some businesses lobby for the creation of sunset agencies to better control the number of agencies and their effectiveness.

Some agencies' power is controlled through congressional purse strings. With **zero-based budgeting,** the agency does not automatically receive a budget amount but, rather, starts with a zero budget each year and then is required to justify all its needs for funds. This type of control gives Congress some say each year in how the agency is operating. For example, the budget could be renewed only on the condition that the agency not promulgate certain regulations opposed by Congress.

Another tool for curbing regulation that has been used in recent years has been action by the executive branch. For example, former President George Bush imposed a ninety-day moratorium on all new regulations in 1992. During this period, regulators were not permitted to promulgate new regulations. Additionally, the *Negotiated Rulemaking Act of 1990* helps businesses work with regulators and permits agencies to develop new methods for resolving controversies outside of the traditional rulemaking process.

Informal Rulemaking
The process for informal rulemaking is the same as that for formal rulemaking with the exception that no public hearings are held on the rule. The only input from the public comes in the form of comments, using the same procedures discussed earlier.

BUSINESS RIGHTS IN AGENCY ENFORCEMENT ACTION
Administrative agencies not only make the rules; they enforce them. In so doing, the agencies are also responsible for adjudicating disputes over the scope or interpretation of the rules. Exhibit 6.9 is a chart of the steps involved in agency enforcement and adjudication.

Licensing and Inspections

Much of an administrative agency's role enforcement is carried out by requiring the submission of certain types of paperwork. Many agencies issue licenses or permits as a way of enforcing the law. For example, state administrative agencies may require building contractors to be licensed so that their dues can finance a recovery fund for the victims of bankrupt or negligent contractors. The Environmental

EXHIBIT 6.9
Steps for Administrative Agency Enforcement and Adjudication

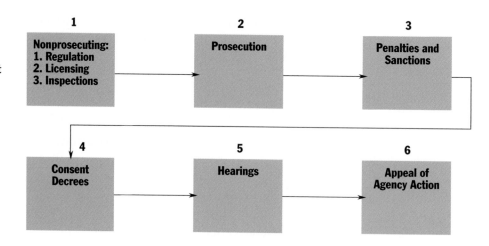

Protection Agency (EPA) carries out its function of protecting the environment in part by requiring licenses or permits for the discharge of foreign substances into the air or water and by requiring advance approval for the construction of projects substantially affecting the environment (see Chapter 12 for more details). The idea behind the licensing and permit method of enforcement is to curtail illegal activity up front and also to have records in case problems arise.

Agencies also have the authority to conduct inspections, such as when an agency responsible for restaurant licenses inspects restaurant facilities to check for health code violations. The Occupational Safety and Health Administration (OSHA) at the federal level has the authority to inspect plants to check for violation of OSHA standards. This power of inspection at unannounced times is an enforcement tool by itself. There is strong incentive to comply with regulations when an inspection could happen at any time. A business can refuse an inspection, but an agency can obtain a warrant and return for a mandatory inspection.

Visit the Occupational Safety and Health Administration:
http://www.osha.gov

Prosecution of Businesses

Administrative agencies are also given the authority to prosecute violators. These agency prosecutions, however, are not traditional criminal prosecutions; the sanctions imposed for agency violations are not jail terms but, rather, are fines, penalties, and injunctions. The penalties required to be paid are not criminal penalties but, rather, civil penalties. For example, in the case of false advertising—a violation of Federal Trade Commission (FTC) rules—the agency could impose restitution as a sanction: The violator would have to reimburse all those individuals who bought the product based on false advertising. In some cases, an agency may merely want a violator to stop certain conduct and promise not to engage in that type of conduct again.

Beginning Enforcement Steps

Regardless of the remedy an agency seeks, all action begins with the agency's issuing a **complaint** against the violating party. The complaint describes when and what the company did and why it is a violation.

Once a complaint is filed, an agency can negotiate with a party for an order or proceed to a hearing to obtain an order from an administrative law judge. The remedies in an order vary according to the type of violation and whether it is ongoing. The FTC could, and typically does, order companies running deceptive ads to stop using the ads and promise not to use them again in the future. These sanctions usually come in the form of an **injunction,** which is a court order that prohibits specifically described conduct. Many statutes are unclear about the extent of authority an agency is given in enforcement proceedings and what types of sanctions an agency can impose for violations. The authority to assess civil penalties, for example, varies from agency to agency.

Consent Decrees

Rather than go through a hearing and the expense of the administrative process, some companies will agree to penalties proposed by an agency. They do so in a document called a **consent decree,** which is comparable to a *nolo contendere* plea in the criminal system. The party does not admit or deny a violation but simply negotiates a settlement with the administrative agency. The negotiated settlement includes the same types of sanctions the agency would have the power to impose if the case went to hearing. The agency may be willing to give up a little in exchange for the violator's willingness to settle and save the agency time and costs of full prosecution. The consent decree is a contract between the charged party and the regulatory agency. Exhibit 6.10 provides an FTC consent decree.

Hearings

If the parties cannot reach an agreement through a consent decree, then the question of violations and penalties will go to an administrative hearing, which is quite different from the litigation procedures described in Chapter 4. Here, there is no jury. The plaintiff or prosecutor is the administrative agency, represented by one of its staff attorneys. The defendant is the person or company accused of violating an administrative regulation. The judge is called an **administrative law judge** (ALJ) at the federal level and in some state-level agencies is called a **hearing examiner** or **hearing officer.** The defendant can be represented by an attorney.

An ALJ has all the powers of a judge. He conducts the hearing, rules on evidentiary and procedural questions, and administers oaths. The ALJ also has certain unique powers, such as the ability to hold settlement conferences between the parties. The ALJ also has the responsibility of making the decision in the case. That decision is cast in the form of a written opinion that consists of findings of facts, conclusions of law, and an order specifying the remedies and sanctions.

The ALJ also has the ethical responsibilities of a trial judge; that is, the judges are prohibited from having *ex parte* **contacts,** which are contacts with one side or one of the parties in the dispute without the knowledge of the others. Staff members of the agency are prohibited from supplying information to the ALJ except when they are witnesses or attorneys in the hearings.

Administrative hearings can have as participants more than just the agency and the party charged with a violation. Other parties with an interest in the case can intervene. These **intervenors** file motions to intervene and are usually permitted to do so at any time before the start of a hearing. Typical intervenors are industry organizations; should the FCC hold hearings on charges against a television station on the content of ads on the station, the National Association of Broadcasters would probably want to intervene in the hearing.

EXHIBIT 6.10 **Excerpts from an FTC Consent Decree**

In the matter of the National Media Group, Inc. et al. Consent Order, etc., in regard to Alleged Violation of The Federal Trade Commission Act

This consent order, among other things, requires a King of Prussia, Pa. firm and a corporate officer, engaged in the advertising and sale of "Acne-Statin," an acne "treatment," to cease disseminating or causing the dissemination of advertisements that represent that Acne-Statin cures acne, eliminates or reduces the bacteria and fatty acids responsible for acne blemishes, and is superior to all other acne preparations and soap for the antibacterial treatment of acne. . . . Additionally, they are required to establish an independent, irrevocable trust account containing sixty thousand dollars ($60,000) to be used to pay half of all requests for restitution by Acne-Statin purchasers; and obligated to conduct and be totally responsible for the administration of the restitution program.

(The original complaint appeared here.)

Order

It is ordered, That respondents, The National Media Group, Inc. a corporation, . . . and the corporate respondent's officers, agents, representatives, and employees . . . do forthwith cease and desist from:

A. Disseminating or causing the dissemination of any advertisement by means of the United States mails or by any means in or affecting commerce, . . . which directly or indirectly:

1. Represents that use of Acne-Statin will cure acne or any skin condition associated with acne.

2. Represents that Acne-Statin will eliminate or reduce the bacteria responsible for pimples, blackheads, whiteheads, or other acne blemishes or any skin condition associated with acne.

3. Represents that Acne-Statin will eliminate or reduce the fatty acids responsible for pimples, blackheads, whiteheads, other acne blemishes or any skin condition associated with acne.

4. Represents that Acne-Statin is superior to prescription or over-the-counter antibacterial acne preparations in the treatment of acne.

5. Represents that Acne-Statin is superior to soap in the antibacterial treatment of acne.

It is further ordered, That:

A. With thirty (30) days of final acceptance of this consent order by the Federal Trade Commission (hereinafter the "Commission"), respondent, The National Media Group, Inc., shall establish an interest-bearing trust account containing the sum of sixty thousand dollars ($60,000), for the purpose of paying restitution to Acne-Statin purchasers. . . .

The rules of evidence and procedure are somewhat relaxed in administrative hearings. Agencies involved in the hearings can issue subpoenas for documents, but the subpoenas can only be enforced by the courts. All of the investigation and adjudication processes of administrative agencies are subject to the constitutional standards of due process, which include the following rights: right to notification of the charges; right to notification of the hearing day; right to present evidence; right to be represented by an attorney; right to an impartial judge; right to a decision based on the law or regulation; and right to cross-examine the witnesses of the agency or intervenors.

Administrative Law of Appeals

Once the ALJ has issued a decision, the decision can be appealed. However, the appellate process in administrative law is slightly different. The first step in an appeal of an ALJ decision is not to a court but to the agency itself. This gives the agency a chance to correct a bad decision before the courts become involved.

The appeal is to the next higher level in the agency. For example, in the FTC, an appeal of an ALJ's decision goes to the commissioners of the FTC for reconsideration. In some agencies, the structure is such that there may be appeals to more than one person in the structure. Those appealing an ALJ decision, however, must go through all the required lines of authority in the agency before they can go to court. This process is known as **exhausting administrative remedies.** If an appeal is made before administrative remedies are exhausted, the court will reject the case on those grounds.

There are some exceptions to the exhaustion rule. A decision by a zoning board to allow construction of a building project could go directly to court because, if the building is started but the decision to allow construction later overruled, the builder is damaged. Alternatively, if the building is not started, other purchasers of the land and the builder are harmed. In other words, fast action is required to maintain all parties' positions.

If an agency has gone beyond its enabling act, a party can also go directly to court. This is more of a challenge to a regulation than it is to the agency's decision, and direct appeal is therefore permitted.

Finally, an agency decision can be appealed directly to court if exhaustion of administrative remedies would be futile, as evidenced by public statements of officials of the agency. When the FTC was trying to develop rules on children's television advertising, for example, a group of interested parties brought a court action to have then FTC chairman Michael Pertschuk removed from the rulemaking process because he had indicated strong feelings in the press about his position. It would have been futile to try administrative remedies because the appeal would have been taken to the party they were trying to remove.

A decision of a federal administrative agency is appealed to one of the U.S. courts of appeals (as indicated in Chapter 2). In most states, appeals from state administrative agencies also go to state courts of appeals. However, some states require a **trial** *de novo,* which means the case is appealed to the state's general trial court, where it is tried. In other words, the hearing is repeated but this time under strict rules of procedure and evidence.

An appellate court can simply affirm an agency action, find that an agency has exceeded its authority, find that an agency has violated the U.S. Constitution, or rule that an agency has acted arbitrarily or that an agency's decision or action is not supported by the evidence. The *State Farm* seat belt case is an example of a court's reversal of administrative agency action in the area of rulemaking.

Exhibit 6.11 provides a summary of the roles of administrative agencies.

ETHICAL ISSUES 6.4

Some businesses take a backdoor approach to getting around administrative regulations. They go over an agency's head to its source of funding, namely Congress. After the Association of National Advertisers succeeded in having Michael Pertschuk removed from the development of regulations for children's television advertising, its attention turned to Congress. As a result of strong lobbying efforts. Congress passed the FTC Improvements Act of 1980. In addition to cutting the FTC budget severely, one of the sections of the act provided that the FTC could not use section 5 (its general power in its enabling act to regulate "deceptive trade practices"; see Chapter 11) to regulate children's television advertising. Shortly after passage, the FTC withdrew all of its rulemaking procedures for children's television advertising.

The organizations and businesses lobbying for the FTC Improvements Act contributed PAC (political action committee) money to members of Congress. Does the ability of businesses to circumvent administrative agencies hinder the agencies' effectiveness? Was the lobbying just an exercise of the businesses' rights? Was the lobbying a way to curtail forever the FTC's power in this area? Is such lobbying an ethical business practice? Does this type of circumvention allow businesses to operate unregulated? *Note:* In 1990, the FTC was able to pass some rules on children's television advertising and Congress held hearings in 1993 to determine whether more regulation of children's television was needed. The industry agreed to self-regulation in the form of clear delineations between programming and commercials.

EXHIBIT 6.11 **The Roles of Administrative Agencies**

ACTIVITY	STEPS	PARTIES	RESULTS
Passing rules	Rule proposed	Agency	New rules
	Comments	Consumers	Modified rules
	Modification, withdrawal, or promulgation	Business Congress Agency	Withdrawn rules
Enforcement	Licensing	Agency Business	
	Inspections	Agency Courts (if warrant is required) Business	Search and inspection
	Complaints	Agency	Fines Penalties Injunctions Consent decrees Hearings

THE RISING STAR WHO FELL

Mike Espy was elected to Congress as a representative from Mississippi in 1988. Bright and young, he was welcomed to the House and given substantial responsibilities. When Bill Clinton was elected president, he tapped Mr. Espy (only 40 at the time) for his cabinet as secretary of agriculture. Mr. Espy was described as a fast-rising political star.

Tyson Foods, Inc., the world's largest producer of fresh and processed poultry product, soon developed a close relationship with Mr. Espy. At the time of Mr. Espy's appointment, Tyson and other regulators were fighting proposed Department of Agriculture guidelines (ultimately not promulgated) that would have imposed a "zero tolerance" on the presence of fecal matter during processing. The proposed regulations would have substantially increased costs for Tyson and other processors.

Tyson offered and Mr. Espy accepted numerous benefits from Tyson, including a ride on a Tyson corporate jet, free lodging at a lakeside cabin owned by Tyson, and seats in Tyson's skybox at a Dallas Cowboys game. Additionally, Mr. Espy's girlfriend received a $1,200 college scholarship from Tyson Foods. Mr. Espy went to the 1994 Super Bowl at government expense, saying he made the trip because Smokey the Bear was being honored in public service announcements at the game.

When information about these corporate gifts and government spending was reported, there was tremendous public outcry. Mr. Espy paid back Tyson Foods for the jet rides and the tickets. However, a special prosecutor was appointed to look into these issues and others, including Quaker Oat's furnishing Mr. Espy a ticket to a Chicago Bulls playoff game after he contacted the company and made the request. In addition, a lobbyist for Sun-Diamond, a raisin and almond firm, sponsored a birthday party for Mr. Espy and 150 Department of Agriculture employees.

By December 1994, Mr. Espy, who had pledged that he would clean up the U.S. poultry business, resigned, saying, "It seemed as if I was just twisting in the wind."

Manley C. Molpus, president of the Grocery Manufacturers Association and a friend of Mr. Espy's, said, "Clearly, there were some lapses of judgment in the administration of his affairs that should have been taken care of with greater sensitivity to the law as well as perception."

A former congressional colleague noted. "It seems as though he behaved as though he was still a member (of Congress). This is not a corrupt or venal guy."

Sun-Diamond was found guilty of making illegal gifts and fined $1.5 million. On appeal, the U.S. Supreme Court reversed the conviction, finding that there was not a sufficient connection between the gifts and alleged influence on various matters pending before Espy and his agency. Tyson Foods entered a guilty plea to making illegal gifts and paid a $6 million fine. Mr. Espy's former aide, Ronald H. Blackley, was tried and convicted of taking money from growers in exchange for the award of subsidies and also lying to federal agents in the subsequent investigation. Mr. Blackley was sentenced to two years in prison despite the federal sentencing guidelines recommending probation, because Judge Lambreth felt lying during an investigation was inexcusable. Richard Douglas, a lobbyist for Sun-Diamond, was also found guilty of making illegal gifts to Mr. Espy but has appealed his case.

In 1996, Mr. Espy's brother Henry was indicted on charges related to campaign finance in his 1993 bid for his brother's vacant congressional seat. Sun-Diamond also pleaded guilty to illegal campaign contributions to Henry's campaign.

In 1997, Mr. Espy was charged, in a thirty-nine–count indictment with accepting and soliciting gifts and favors from Tyson Foods, lying to the FBI, witness tampering, and soliciting NBA tickets from the chairman of Quaker Oats. A judge dismissed six counts, and, after a trial, Mr. Espy was acquitted on all thirty-three remaining counts and said, "I just expected each and every day that I would be found not guilty."

ISSUES

1. Was Mr. Espy's role as an administrator different from his role in Congress?

2. Why wasn't paying back Tyson enough?

3. How did such a web of indictments develop? There were fifteen prosecutions, fifteen convictions, and $11 million in fines resulting from the Espy investigation.

4. Why, for example, were Tyson, Blackley, and Sun-Diamond culpable but Mr. Espy was acquitted?

ETHICAL ISSUES 6.5

Some businesses are able to take advantage of one government's regulations. For example, the Energy Policy Act of 1992 requires that toilets installed after the act took effect (1994) use only 1.6 gallons of water rather than the nearly century-old standard of 3.5 gallons. As of 2000, about one-fourth of the nation's toilets are the 1.6-gallon type.

As homeowners remodel and replace older toilets, they have learned that the 3.5-gallon toilets are no longer sold in the United States. However, just across the U.S./Canadian border near Detroit, Canadian hardware stores are doing a land office business selling 3.5-gallon tanks to U.S. citizens.

Those who are remodeling and even some building new homes generally install a $100 toilet from Home Depot in order to pass inspection. They then purchase a Canadian toilet, in the neighborhood of $500 to $1,000 for a standard fixture because the demand is so high, and install it. Plumbing stores all over Canada report sales are brisk. In a survey conducted in May 2000, the Canadian plumbing store owners said that they sell, on average, one toilet per day to U.S. citizens either via direct sale or shipment.

Do the citizens break any laws by what they do? Is what they do ethical?

THE ROLE OF ADMINISTRATIVE AGENCIES IN THE INTERNATIONAL MARKET

The United States wins the award for the most administrative agencies and regulations. Some businesses have argued that the amount of regulation hinders them in the international marketplace. For example, just the readability level of regulations, as shown in Exhibit 6.12, demands much time and energy as companies attempt to interpret and comply with the laws.

EXHIBIT 6.12 **Various Reading Levels of Documents and Populations**

DOCUMENTS AND POPULATIONS	GRADE LEVEL
1. *Love Story*	7.64
2. Reading Level of U.S. Population over Age 65	9.71
3. *Playboy*	11.46
4. Reading Level of General U.S. Population	11.68
5. *Sports Illustrated*	12.82
6. *Your Medicare Handbook*	14.94
7. *ERISA Summary Plan Description*	15.29
8. *Wall Street Journal*	16.34
9. *Social Security Handbook*	17.51
10. Reading Level of Lawyers	19.00
11. *Albermarle* (U.S. Supreme Court Ruling)	20.30
12. Occupational Safety and Health Act	30.79
13. Employment Retirement Income Safety Act	32.10
14. Section 18 of the Social Security Act	41.04

Sources: Warren S. Blumenfeld et al., "Readability of an ERISA Summary Plan Description vis-à-vis Intended Readership: An Empirical Test of Local Legal Compliance with a Federal Regulation." Paper presented at the Western American Institute for Decision Science Meeting, Reno, Nevada, March 1979. Warren S. Blumenfeld et al., "Readability of the Real Estate Settlement Procedures Act." Paper presented at the Southeastern Regional Business Law Association Meeting, Chapel Hill, North Carolina, October 1980.

Many regulators, legislators, and businesses have advocated elimination and streamlining of existing regulations, as well as careful consideration before new regulations are promulgated.

SUMMARY

What is an administrative agency?

- Administrative agency—statutory creature with the ability to make, interpret, and enforce laws

What laws govern the operation of administrative agencies?

- Administrative Procedure Act—general federal law governing agency process and operations

- Government in the Sunshine Act—federal law requiring public hearings by agencies (with limited exceptions)

- Federal Privacy Act—federal law protecting transfer of information among agencies unless done for enforcement reasons

- Freedom of Information Act—federal law providing individuals with access to information held by administrative agencies (with some exemptions such as for trade secrets)

What do administrative agencies do?

- Rulemaking—process of turning proposed regulations into actual regulations that requires public input

- *Federal Register*—daily publication that updates agency proposals, rules, hearing notices, and so forth

- *Code of Federal Regulations*—federal government publication of all agency rules

- Licensing—role in which an agency screens businesses before permitting operation

- Inspections—administrative agency role of checking businesses and business sites for compliance

How do agencies pass rules?

- Public comment period—period in rulemaking process when any individual or business can provide input on proposed regulations

- Promulgation—approval of proposed rules by heads of agencies

How do agencies enforce the law?

- Consent decree—settlement (*nolo contendere* plea) of charges brought by an administrative agency

- Administrative law judge (ALJ)—overseer of hearing on charges brought by administrative agency

QUESTIONS AND PROBLEMS

1. Residents of New York City who were receiving financial aid under the federally assisted program of Aid to Families with Dependent Children (AFDC) brought a class-action suit alleging that the New York officials responsible for the administration of the program were terminating aid to them without notice of the termination or without a hearing prior to the termination. The residents challenged the actions of the state officials as violative of their constitutional right to due process. The procedures for termination changed after the complaints of these residents, and notices and hearings were provided. What types of procedures would be necessary to protect the residents' due process rights? Must a court afford these procedures? [*Goldberg* v. *Kelly*, 397 U.S. 254 (1970)]

2. In 1979, Congress passed the Chrysler Corporation Loan Guarantee Act. The act was passed to keep the Chrysler Corporation in business and out of bankruptcy. The act established the Chrysler Corporation Loan Guarantee Board, made up of top federal officials, to oversee Chrysler's bailout. The meetings of this board necessarily involved sensitive discussions about Chrysler and its status. Would the meetings be covered under the Sunshine Act and thus open to the public? [*Symons* v. *Chrysler Corp. Loan Guarantee*, 670 F.2d 238 (D.C. 1981)]

3. Because of overcrowded conditions at the nation's airports during the late 1960s, the Federal Aviation Administration (FAA) promulgated a regulation to reduce takeoff and landing delays at airports by limiting the number of landing and takeoff slots at five major airports to sixty slots per hour. The airports were Kennedy, LaGuardia, O'Hare, Newark, and National. At National Airport (Washington), forty of the sixty slots were given to commercial planes, and the commercial carriers allocated the slots among themselves until October 1980. In 1980, New York Air, a new airline, requested some of the forty slots, but the existing airlines refused to give up any. The secretary of transportation, in response and "to avoid chaos in the skies" during the upcoming holidays, proposed a rule to allocate the slots at National. The allocation rule was proposed on October 16, 1980, and appeared in the *Federal Register* on October 20, 1980. The comment period was seven days starting from the October 16, 1980, proposal date. The airlines and others submitted a total of thirty-seven comments to the secretary. However, Northwest Airlines filed suit on grounds that the APA required a minimum of thirty days for a public comment period. The secretary argued that the thirty-day rule was being suspended for good cause (the holiday season was upon them). Who is correct? Should an exception be made, or should the FAA be required to follow the thirty-day rule? [*Northwest Airlines, Inc.* v. *Goldschmidt*, 645 F.2d 1309 (8th Cir. 1981)]

4. Richardson-Vicks, Inc., is the manufacturer and seller of Vick's Pediatric Formula 44 (Pediatric 44), a cough medicine for children. In its ads for Pediatric 44, Vicks claims that the syrup contains active ingredients that enable it to begin working instantly. However, Pediatric 44 is considered to have only inactive ingredients, according to FDA regulations on "active" and "inactive" ingredients. A competitor has alleged that Vicks is "misbranding" its products. Can the FDA take any action? What steps could it take? Will the FDA be required to make an interpretation of the "active"/"inactive" regulation? [*Sandoz Pharmaceuticals* v. *Richardson-Vicks, Inc.*, 902 F.2d 222 (3d Cir. 1990)]

5. Read the following excerpt from the *Wall Street Journal:*

> The smell of the greasepaint and the roar of the crowd, indeed.
>
> The circus of yesteryear, loved by children and fondly remembered by older folk, keeps running smack into the modern world. In 1992, tents must fall within local fire codes. If the clown isn't a U.S. citizen, he had better have a valid work visa along with his makeup kit and big false nose. And the kid who wants to run away from home and join the circus? Forget it. . . .

> Consider Carson & Barnes, the last of the five-ring road shows. The circus is traveling an 18-state route this year, from March 21 to Nov. 15, doing one-night stands. Each morning, about 200 performers and other employees, 150 animals, 80 trucks roll into town. Roustabouts race to erect the "Biggest Big Top On Earth." The circus performs two shows, packs, goes to sleep, rises at dawn and heads for the next stop.

> With scheduling tight, satisfying the local tests is no mean feat. The 237 small towns where the circus is performing this year all usually require about half a dozen permits, with regulations varying from place to place.

> This summer, the circus's soft-drink concession got shut down briefly because of bad water. An Illinois inspector found a high bacteria count and sent word to Wisconsin, so the water flunked inspection in Racine and Jefferson. . . .

> If a sucker isn't born every minute, it is true that people are easily fooled and that can cause the circus trouble. While his circus was crossing Texas this year, someone complained about the stunt Argentine acrobat Sulliana Montes de Oca does with her French poodle. The dog sits on a platform as Ms. Montes de Oca appears to execute a handstand on the poor dog's head.

> It's an illusion, of course, but a local inspector even came out to investigate an abuse complaint, circus officials say. They showed him the steel rod the circus crowd doesn't see that actually supports Ms. Montes de Oca when she does the trick. Dave Brandt, the show's press agent, says, "Who would ever think a nine-pound French poodle can hold up a 90-pound woman?" . . .

> Local officials worry about the welfare of children as well as animals. About half a century ago, the Miller family circus actually did hire some young teenagers. And local kids willing to help set up the show got in free. But child-labor laws and insurance policy problems have put a stop to that. Applicants must be 18.

> Nevertheless, Carson & Barnes has problems even with the only minors it does employ—those who perform in acts with their parents. Last year, California inspectors demanded that 14-year-old Dulce Vital quit holding target balloons for her father's archery act. Though the act is risky and Ms. Vital is young, she knew the routine. When she was replaced in Desert Hot Springs by a 19-year-old stand-in, Isabel Macias, the new girl caught an arrow in the forehead and today has a scar to show for it.

> Then there is the foreign-performer problem. Carson & Barnes employs about 80 Latin Americans a year, and tangles for months with immigration officials to get papers for them. Last year, temporary-visa applications for the Chimals, a Mexican family of acrobats, got lost

in the bureaucracy, say circus officials. The up-shot: For 10 days, the circus performed with an empty ring.

Certain towns make it harder on Carson & Barnes than others. "The fire marshall from hell is here today," reads the general manager's journal entry for Ojai, Calif. The fireman was concerned, among other things, that the inspector's ID number wasn't printed on fire extinguishers.

The hang-up forced the gathering afternoon audience to wait in the hot sun while circus officials jumped through hoops. Finally, at showtime, the fireman was willing to let the show go on if one fire extinguisher could be shown to function properly. One was tested, it worked, and the circus started half-an-hour late. . . .

Source: "Bunting & Red Tape: The Modern Circus Walks a High Wire," *Wall Street Journal*, 31 August 1992, A1, A4. Reprinted by permission of The Wall Street Journal, © 1992 Dow Jones & Company, Inc. All Rights Reserved Worldwide.

Is too much regulation exerted upon the circus? Is all the regulation necessary?

6. Suppose that the SEC has proposed a new rule for the filing of registered companies' annual reports (see Chapter 22). One of the provisions of the rule requires the reports to be filed within three months after the close of the company's financial year. All of the companies commenting on the rule mentioned that the time for filing should be extended at least thirty days because most accounting firms require ninety days to complete their work for an annual report. After the comment period, the SEC changed the rule's time limit to 120 days. Is another public comment period required, or can the rule now be promulgated?

7. Hooked on Phonics is a reading program that departs from the current educational reading philosophy of "whole-language learning." The program emphasizes the more traditional reading process of having children sound out letters and combinations of letters. The Federal Trade Commission (FTC) filed a false advertising complaint against Gateway Educational Products, Inc., the owner of the Hooked on Phonics program. The FTC claimed that Gateway's television claim that those with reading disabilities would be helped "quickly and easily" and that Hooked on Phonics could "teach reading in a home setting without additional assistance" was misleading. Gateway does not feel the claims are false, but it does not want to have bad publicity. What advice can you give Gateway on handling the FTC charges?

8. In March 1992, the Federal Communications Commission (FCC) proposed rules that would increase the maximum number of radio stations a company could own from twelve AM stations and twelve FM stations to thirty of each. The FCC proposed the changes because more than half of the nation's 11,000 radio stations are unprofitable and the larger ownership blocks would allow some economies of scale. Critics were vocal about domination and monopolization. As a result, the FCC changed the ownership maximums to eighteen FM and eighteen AM stations and issued its final rules on August 5, 1992. Describe the process the FCC employed to make these changes. Explain what public outcry accomplished.

9. The Food and Drug Administration (FDA) is concerned about laser eye surgery, noting that the industry concerned with correcting vision is spawning joint ventures, wine-and-cheese seminars to court potential investors, and databases of nearsighted consumers. There are 800 numbers and some dissatisfaction among the 700 patients who've had the surgery, including complaints of farsightedness. The corrective laser surgery costs $2,000 per eye and is not covered by insurance. Further, the only regulation the FDA has in the field covers granting permission to laser manufacturers, which has been given, to sell their machines to opthalmologists. The FDA would like to know more and perhaps control some aspects of patients' care. Describe the steps the FDA must take.

10. The following federal regulation—15 *C.F.R.* § 1511—governs the design and manufacture of pacifiers for babies. Read the regulation and then answer the following questions:
a. What companies would be affected by this type of regulation?
b. How could the companies provide input on the regulations?
c. What types of tests must a pacifier pass under these regulations?
d. What is done after the heat cycle deterioration? Why must a pacifier pass heat deterioration tests?

15 C.F.R. § 1511

(a) A <u>pacifier</u> is an article consisting of a nipple that is intended for a young child to suck upon, but is not designed to facilitate a baby's obtaining fluid, and usually includes a guard or shield and a handle or ring.

(b) <u>Guard</u> or <u>shield</u> means the structure located at the base of the nipple used to prevent the pacifier from being completely drawn into the child's mouth.

(c) <u>Handle</u> or <u>ring</u> means the structure usually located adjacent to the guard or shield used for holding or grasping the pacifier. A hinged handle or ring is one that is free to pivot about an axis parallel to the plane of the guard or shield.

§ 1511.3. Guard or shield requirements.

(a) <u>Performance requirements</u>. Place the pacifier in the opening of the fixture illustrated in Figure 1(a) of this part so that the nipple of the pacifier is centered in the opening and protrudes through the back of the fixture as shown in Figure 1(b). For pacifiers with non-circular guards or shields, align the major axis of the guard or shield with the major axis of the opening in the fixture. Apply a tensile force to the pacifier nipple in the direction shown. The force shall be applied gradually attaining but not exceeding 2.0 pounds (8.9 newtons) within a period of 5 seconds and maintained at 2.0 pounds for an additional 10 seconds. Any pacifier which can be completely drawn through an opening with dimensions no greater than those of Exhibit 1(a) by such a force shall fail the test in this part.

(b) <u>Ventilation holes</u>. The pacifier guard or shield shall contain at least two holes symmetrically located and each being at least 0.20 inches (5 millimeters) in minor dimension. The edge of any hole shall be no closer than 0.20 inches (5 millimeters) to the perimeter of the pacifier guard or shield.

§ 1511.5 Structural integrity tests.

(a) <u>Nipple</u>. Hold the pacifier by the shield or guard, grasp the nipple end of the pacifier and gradually apply a tensile to the pacifier nipple in any possible direction. The force shall be applied gradually, attaining but not exceeding 10.0 pounds (44.5 newtons) within a period of 5 seconds and maintained at 10.0 pounds for an additional 10 seconds.

(b) <u>Handle</u> or <u>ring</u>. Hold the pacifier by the shield or guard or base of the nipple, and push or pull on the handle or ring in any possible direction. The force shall be applied gradually attaining but not exceeding 10.0 pounds (44.5 newtons) within a period of 5 seconds and maintained at 10.0 pounds for an additional 10 seconds.

(c) <u>Heat cycle deterioration</u>. After the testing prescribed in paragraphs (a) and (b) of this section, all pacifiers shall be subject to the following: submerge the pacifier in boiling water for 5 minutes and then remove the pacifier and allow it to cool for 5 minutes in room temperature air, 60° to 80° F. (16° to 27° C). After the cooling period, resubmerge the pacifier in the boiling water for 5 minutes. The process shall be repeated for a total of 6 boiling/cooling cycles. After the sixth cycle, the pacifier shall again be subjected to the structural tests in paragraphs (a) and (b) of this section and section 1511.3.

RESEARCH PROBLEM

Campaign Contributions Decisions Are Pending

11. Read *Sokaogon Chippewa Community* v. *Babbit*, 961 F.Supp. 1276 (W.D. Wis. 1997), and discuss the issues, the role of the agency, and the role of politics.

BUSINESS STRATEGY APPLICATION

The CD-ROM exercise for this chapter takes an in-depth look at the other comments provided on the proposed telemarketing rule in Exhibit 6.5. You have some comments in the book, but a look at more of the businesses and consumers participating in the comment period and their thoughts gives you an idea of what strategic steps businesses must take in rulemaking that affects them.

Chapter Seven

International Law

S hakespeare was ahead of his time when he wrote that "the world is your oyster." Today's global business environment is the dream of economists, who have fostered the notion of free trade since the publication of Adam Smith's *The Wealth of Nations* about two hundred years ago. Trade barriers are down, resources are flowing, and even the smallest of businesses are involved in international trade. Trade across borders still involves additional issues and laws and carries risks that do not exist in transactions within nations. Businesses must understand the legal environment of international trade to enter into contracts and conduct operations in ways that minimize legal risks because, as noted in Chapter 4, litigation across borders can be difficult. This chapter covers the legal environment of international business. What laws affect businesses in international trade? What international agreements affect global businesses? What contract issues exist in international business?

> It's not necessary to use chopsticks. A knife and fork are okay.
>
> MAYOR ZHANG
> *Suzhou, China (in encouraging businesspeople to come to his town)*

> If a foreign country can supply us with a commodity cheaper than we ourselves can make it, better buy it of them with some part of our own industry, employed in a way in which we have some advantage.
>
> ADAM SMITH

> I don't believe you can run a major U.S. company from abroad. George III tried to run the United States from Britain and look what happened to him.
>
> SIR GORDON WHITE
> *Chairman, Hanson Industries, Inc.*

CONSIDER...

In November 1967, Zapata Off-Shore Company, a U.S. corporation based in Houston, contracted with Unterweser, a German corporation, to have Unterweser tow its ocean-going, self-elevating drilling rig (the *Chaparral*) from Louisiana to a point off Ravena, Italy, near the Adriatic Sea, where Zapata had agreed to drill wells.

Unterweser, as the low bidder on the towing service, submitted a contract to Zapata that provided that any dispute arising under the contract would be "treated" before the London Court of Justice.

Unterweser personnel left Venice, Louisiana, on January 5, 1968. On January 9, 1968, Unterweser's towing barge hit a severe storm in the Gulf of Mexico. The elevator legs of the *Chaparral* broke off during the storm, and the rig was severely damaged. Unterweser was instructed to tow the rig to Tampa.

Zapata filed suit for damages against Unterweser in federal district court in Tampa, seeking $3.5 million in damages. Unterweser asked for a dismissal because the case needed to go before the London Court of Justice according to their agreement. Who is correct? Where should the dispute be decided? [*The Bremen* v. *Zapata Off-Shore Co.*, 407 U.S. 1 (1971)]

SOURCES OF INTERNATIONAL LAW

"When in Rome, do as the Romans do" is advice that can be modified for business: When in Rome, follow Roman law. In each country where a business has operations, it must comply with the laws of that nation. Just as each U.S. business must comply with all the tax, employment, safety, and environmental laws of each state in which it operates, each international business must comply with the laws of the countries in which it operates.

Types of International Law Systems

The various systems of laws can be quite different, and businesses are well advised to obtain local legal counsel for advice on the peculiarities of each nation's laws. Generally, a nation's laws are based on one of three types of systems. The United States has a **common law** system. Like England, our laws are built on tradition and precedent (see Chapter 1). Not every possible situation is codified; we rely on our courts to interpret and apply our more general statutes and, in many cases, to develop principles of law as cases are presented (as with the common-law doctrine of negligence; see Chapter 10).

Other countries rely on civil law or code law. This form of law is found in European nations that are not tied to England: France, Germany, Spain, and countries influenced through their colonial activities. Countries with code law systems do not rely on court decisions but rely instead on statutes or codes that are intended to cover all types of circumstances and attempt to spell out the law so there is little need for interpretation.

A final system of law is Islamic law, which is followed in some form in twenty-seven countries. Islamic legal systems are based on religious tenets and govern all aspects of life, from appropriate dress in public to remedies for contract breaches. Many of the Islamic countries have a combination of civil and Islamic systems that result from the influences of both colonization and Islam.

Before its collapse in the former Soviet Union and Eastern Europe, communism was also classified as a legal system. Now the former Communist nations struggle with evolving cultural, market, and governmental systems. In fact, much international work is being completed by U.S. lawyers, accountants, and other professionals, who are assisting in the development of constitutions, legislation, and even such issues as development of tax codes and collection systems.

Nonstatutory Sources of International Law

Customs and values in a culture often have a controlling effect on negotiations, contracts, and performance in international business. The American Bar Association recommends that businesspeople and their lawyers examine seven cultural factors and do background work in these cultural areas before attempting negotiations and business in a particular country. Referred to as the LESCANT factors, the following issues should be researched as if they were legal background for doing business: language, environment and technology, social organization, contexting, authority, nonverbal behavior, and time concept.

Language

Businesspeople should determine which language is preferred in a particular country for conducting business. Mexico and Latin American countries are accus-

Re: English: The Language of Contracts

A new trend is emerging in international contracts. The dominant language for contracts has become English, even for contracts among natives of a country.

The trend is attributed by some to the Internet. Those in non–English speaking countries have become increasingly familiar with English as they have surfed the Net. One French businessman learned English so that he could enjoy the jokes his son sent to him over the Internet. The jokes were in English, and his son was stunned when he visited to find his father so fluent in English following several years of joke exchanges.

Others attribute the trend to, as H. L. Mencken once wrote, the "sheer weight of [the English language's] merit." Businesspeople appreciate the simplicity of grammar as well as the larger vocabulary available in English. English has also incorporated phrases from other languages and continues to evolve while other languages, such as French, prohibit change.

Others attribute the change to the rise of the EU. Because the EU needs one uniting language, most have landed upon English as the choice. Most new contracts being negotiated in Europe are choosing English as their language. The EU released the following information:

47% of Western Europeans speak English.
Only 32% speak German, and only 28% speak French.
77% of all Western European college students speak English.
69% of all Western European business managers speak English.
65% of those between the ages of 15 to 24 speak English.
91% of all school-age children study English.

One Italian CEO says, "The only business language worldwide is English."

Source: Justin Fox, "The Triumph of English," *Fortune*, 18 September 2000, 209–212.

tomed to doing business in English. In Quebec, Canada, there are government regulations on the use of French in conducting business.

Environment and Technology

Communications systems vary in quality and universality in countries around the world. Because U.S. companies are used to rapid communication and verification of offers and acceptances (see Chapter 13 on contract formation), doing business in a country in which communication will be much slower and by different means requires advance knowledge and appropriate adjustments and provisions for negotiations.

For more information on the culture of various countries, visit:

http://www.miti.go.jp/index-e
http://www.chineseculture.about.com. *Click on business.*
http://www.mexicanculture.about.com. *Click on business.*
http://www.jinjapan.org

Social Organization

Businesspeople should know the social order in the country: May women negotiate deals? Is it appropriate to discuss business during a meal? The Manager's Desk feature on tact outlines some of the preparation companies should do in the area of social and cultural research on a country and companies.

Contexting

Low-context cultures are those that rely on the written word as the controlling factor in their relationship. Little weight is given to the context in which that agreement is reached. Low-context cultures include the North American countries, Switzerland, Germany, and Scandinavian countries (not Finland). Midlevel-context cultures are France, England, and Italy; and the high-context cultures are

Re: Tact Can Seal a Global Deal

A Silicon Valley corporate chief and some of his aides recently went to Asia to meet with a number of foreign officials. "We decided to show them the real us and go the way we show up in our offices every day—baseball caps and T-shirts," he said.

Invariably, the boys from Silicon Valley were ushered into offices that looked more like galleries in art museums, where Asian gentlemen in Savile Row attire would rise to greet them.

"Being American, I got right to it," the chief said, recalling his remarks at one luncheon. In his opening statement, he said the host country's President and Cabinet ministers were inept. Upon reflection, he understood that his *modus operandi* caused a loss of face for his Asian hosts. Hardly a basis for a harmonious relationship.

Another painful and destructive scene played out recently at Orly Airport in Paris:

> *An executive—let's call him Jimmy-Joe Real Estate Mogul—and two other Americans arrive on the Concorde as guests of a senior French banker with whom they want to do business. The Frenchman, Pierre Politesse, fetches his guests by limousine and inquires politely about their journey.*
>
> *Slapping his host on the back, Mr. Mogul drawls: "Waal, Pierre, I threw up all the way over. Your French food is jes too rich."*

Is it even necessary to point out what's wrong with this picture? The slap on the back and the use of the host's first name were excessively familiar. And the insult to French cuisine? Mon dieu!

Lorrie Foster, the director of the World Trade Institute of Pace University, estimates that the number of ventures that fail between American and foreign companies could be as high as 60 percent. Executives and entrepreneurs armed with M.B.A.s and dazzling proposals fly overseas full of enthusiasm, only to return deflated. They expect too much too soon.

Building successful, fruitful alliances requires finesse and must be regarded as courtship. Patient, courteous wooing is the key.

One senior vice president at a Fortune 500 company had spent several months gathering figures for a presentation in Tokyo. (Her luggage for the trip also showed that she meant business: a wardrobe of $3,000 suits and an attaché case with an identifiable logo.) At the presentation, she thought she was delivering an offer the Japanese couldn't refuse. But refuse they did.

Clearly, she hadn't considered local traditions. She looked very young and was not aware that her very presence negotiating as a peer with three older male executives had caused them to lose face in their colleagues' eyes. (The businessmen felt that they were being vetted by a low-level employee on behalf of a senior executive—a man, of course—who would arrive later for serious talks.) To compound the problem, she knew nothing about East Asian rituals of respect, including the exchange of business cards.

Of course, Asia is big, and generalizations can be tricky. Women have been heads of state in India, Pakistan, and the Philippines. But in Japan, it is difficult to find a woman executive of senior-level prominence.

Following are some simple guidelines for getting your foot in the door, not in your mouth, when dealing in the global marketplace:

- Spend at least 10 percent of preparation time on interpersonal skills.
- Learn at least key phrases in your host's language. "S'il vous plaît" and "Dankeschön" can go a long way.
- Be conversant in your host country's cultural landmarks, painters, writers, national shrines, and outstanding personalities. It shows that you have respect for cultural heritage.
- Use your own translator, one with established loyalty to you.
- If you're a woman, remember that equality may not be a reality. Adapt to the local customs.

Re: Nonverbal Communication in International Business

In his book **Gestures: The Do's and Taboos of Body Language around the World** *(1991), Roger E. Axtell notes that body language can create problems in international trade negotiations. For example, while a "thumbs up" in the United States translates to "Good going!" such a hand signal in Bangladesh and Australia is the equivalent of a raised middle finger in the United States.*

In many Latin American countries, the A-OK sign formed with the index finger and thumb in a circle is considered an insult. In France, the same gesture means "zero" or "worthless." In Japan, this same symbol is a means of asking for money. The use of the A-OK sign in Japan is particularly dangerous, because businesspeople there are likely to interpret the unintentional request for money as a request for a bribe.

Patting a child's head in India is offensive because the head houses the soul in India. Executives should not touch the heads of children when invited to dinner at the homes of executives in that country.

Rotating your index finger near your ear in the United States is a symbol for "crazy." In Argentina, the same signal means that you have a phone call.

Many U.S. businesspeople have tried to avoid any misinterpretation of their hand signals by consciously placing their hands in their pockets. However, such a gesture is considered impolite in Belgium, Finland, France, Indonesia, Japan, and Sweden.

Latin American countries, Arabic nations, and Asian countries, including Japan. In the high-context cultures, how and in what setting an agreement is reached are as important as the words in the document itself.

Authority

Who has negotiating authority is important in a business meeting, and who is sent to a meeting sends a signal about importance in the high-context cultures. Lawyers are not considered part of the negotiating team in Japan but are considered critical in the United States. Often, in Asian cultures, the negotiators do not have the authority to commit to a deal and must take proposals back to their companies and those who do have authority.

Nonverbal Behavior

In the United States, there is a tendency to interpret nonverbal behavior differently from the way it is perceived in other cultures. For example, silence during negotiations in the United States creates a compulsion for businesspeople to fill the awkward silence or interpret the silence as a rejection. In Asian cultures, such silence is simply a method of contemplating and considering and is not indicative of a rejection.

Time Concept

The United States is a monochronic nation: Time is everything, and the goal of businesspeople is to get the deal done. Other monochronic nations include Great Britain, Germany, Canada, New Zealand, Australia, the Netherlands, Norway, and Sweden. Countries that operate with great flexibility in time and negotiate within the context of building a relationship as opposed to completing a deal are called polychronic nations. The remainder of the world operates within this flexible form of time culture.

Contracts for the International Sale of Goods (CISG)

Visit the UNCITRAL:
http://www.un.or.at/
uncitral
Review the CISG:
http://www.cisg.law.
pace.edu

Sometimes referred to as the Vienna Convention, the United Nations Convention on Contracts for the International Sale of Goods (CISG) began its development in 1964 as an idea that was later discussed and formulated at the 1980 Vienna Convention. The CISG first became effective in 1988 with its adoption in the United States along with a small group of other countries. Today, CISG has been adopted in fifty-three countries, with ratification processes underway in many other countries.

The CISG is designed to provide for international contracts the convenience and uniformity that the Uniform Commercial Code provides for contracts across state lines in the United States. While there are some differences (see Chapters 13 and 14), the CISG is a reflection of the Uniform Commercial Code.

Treaties, Trade Organizations, and Controls on International Trade

In international trade, there are a number of treaties, tariffs, and organizations that govern and guide international contracts.

Whether supported or despised by economists, tariffs and restrictions on trade have existed for as long as trade itself. Duties, quotas, and tariffs have all been used to control the flow of goods over and across national boundaries. For most of history, these limits on trade have been imposed on a nation-by-nation basis. However, new forms of trade agreements are developing, and nations are organizing in larger groups in an attempt to eliminate many of the individually based barriers to trade.

The General Agreement on Tariffs and Trade (GATT)

Review GATT:
http://trading.www.gatt.org

Adopted in 1994, GATT is a multilateral treaty (a treaty among more than two nations), currently subscribed to by 125 nations.

The General Agreement on Tariffs and Trade (GATT) is the most expansive attempt to negotiate free trade and boasts one hundred member countries. The GATT has been able to reduce tariffs nearly 70 percent through meetings of its members, called "rounds." The president of the United States is authorized by Congress to participate in these rounds and agree to reductions in tariffs.

While there was a 1947 GATT, one of the principal differences between that original GATT and the 1994 GATT is the establishment of the World Trade Organization (WTO). WTO is the body charged with the administration and achievement of the GATT objectives. GATT's primary objectives are trade without discrimination and protection through tariffs. Trade without discrimination is achieved through GATT's most-favored-nation clause. Because China has not subscribed to GATT, the issue of its status as a most favored nation continues to be debated, particularly along with the political and social context of human rights issues in that country.

Under the most-favored-nation clause, subscribing countries treat each other equally in terms of import and export duties and charges. Subscribing countries do not give more favorable treatment to one country as opposed to another. Domestic production is protected by tariffs and not through any other commercial measures.

There are some exceptions under GATT for regional trading arrangements undertaken through other treaties, such as the North American Free Trade Agreement (NAFTA) and the European Union (EU).

The WTO has also established a Dispute Settlement Body (DSB), which is an international arbitration body created to bring countries together to resolve trade disputes rather than have those nations resort to trade sanctions. If a WTO panel finds that a country has violated the provisions of GATT, it can impose trade sanctions on that country. The sanctions imposed are generally equal to the amount of economic injury the country caused through its violation of GATT.

European Union (EU)

Visit the European Union:
http://europa.eu.int/
index.htm

The European Economic Community (EEC) was created by the Treaty of Rome and was formerly known as the Common Market; it is often referred to as the European Community (EC) and is now known as the European Union (EU). The EU members are Austria, Belgium, Cyprus, Denmark, Finland, France, Germany, Greece, Ireland, Italy, Luxembourg, the Netherlands, Portugal, Spain, Sweden, and the United Kingdom.

Under the Single European Act, the EU, in an effort to provide for the free flow of goods, services, and human and financial capital, eliminated internal barriers to trade. The Maastricht Treaty (Treaty on the European Union signed in Maastricht, the Netherlands) set the goals of the EU as single monetary and fiscal policies (including a common currency), common foreign policies, and cooperation in the administration of justice.

In addition, the EU has undertaken the ambitious goals of uniformity in laws, with proposals on product liability and litigation for member countries to ensure uniform costs and results. The EU has progressed to the point of having some enforceable international law. For example, the EU has created the European Commission, which has the authority to issue regulations and decisions that are binding on all EU members. The goal of the EU is to build one market of 340 million consumers. In January 1999, the EU introduced a single currency known as the euro.

In addition to the European Commission, the EU has created other institutions to assist it in carrying out its goal of unified European commercial operations. The European Council, which consists of the heads of state of the various members, is the policy-making body and establishes the broad directives for the operation of the EU. The next step below the council is the European Parliament, an advisory legislative body with some veto powers. Finally, the European Court of Justice (ECJ) is the judicial body created to handle disputes and any violations of regulations and the EU treaty itself. The EU has in place 282 directives that govern everything from health and safety standards in the workplace to the sale of mutual funds across national boundaries.

The North American Free Trade Agreement (NAFTA)

Review NAFTA:
http://the-
tech.mit.edu/Bulletins/
nafta.html

The North American Free Trade Agreement (NAFTA) is a treaty among Canada, the United States, and Mexico effective in 1994, which will eliminate all tariffs among the three countries in their trade over a fifteen-year period.

Products covered under NAFTA include only those that originate in these countries. All goods traded across the boundaries of these countries must carry a NAFTA certificate of origin, which verifies the original creation of the goods in that country from which they are being exported. NAFTA has eliminated nearly all of the barriers to trade among these three nations. However, NAFTA is unlike EU in that a common labor market, governing body, and currency were not created.

Prohibitions on Trade: Individual Nation Sanctions

In some countries, international tensions have resulted in trade sanctions being imposed so that commerce with certain nations is prohibited. There are two types of trade sanctions countries can impose. With primary trade sanctions, companies based in the United States are prohibited from doing business with certain countries. For example, the United States has prohibited trade with Iraq since the time of the Gulf War. Primary boycotts can be limited to certain categories of goods. The status of "most favored nation" in trade (MFN) means that the country has no restrictions on the types of goods and services that can be imported and exported. Other category restrictions can include extreme limitations such as trade being limited to food and medical supplies. In some restrictions, the United States prohibits domestic companies from selling certain types of equipment to certain nations. For example, U.S. firms have severe restrictions on selling certain component parts to China. These parts are primarily those that could be used in the development of nuclear weapons and other military capabilities.

The second form of trade prohibition is the secondary boycott, which is a step beyond the primary boycott in that companies from other nations doing business with a sanctioned country will also experience sanctions for such activity. For example, in 1996, the United States passed the Iran and Libya Sanctions Act (ILSA) as a secondary boycott against two nations against which the United States already had imposed trade restrictions. This law was passed as a result of active lobbying by the families of those killed when Pan Am Flight 103 exploded over Lockerbie, Scotland, as a result of bombs planted on the flight by Libyan terrorists. Under the secondary boycott trade prohibition, the United States will not grant licenses to, permit its financial institutions to loan money to, award government contracts to, and will ban imports from any company that finances, supplies, or constructs oil procurement in Iran or Libya. Generally, these types of secondary boycotts do not apply retroactively so that companies already invested need not divest themselves of business in these countries. However, there can be no new business once the act takes effect if the companies wish to continue to do business with the United States.

The International Monetary Fund (IMF) and the World Bank

Created at Bretton Woods, New Hampshire, the International Monetary Fund (IMF) was established following World War II with the goal of expanding international trade through a bank with a lending system designed to bring stability to national currencies. The IMF created the International Bank for Reconstruction and Development (commonly called the World Bank), which allows signing nations to have Special Drawing Rights (SDR) or the ability to draw on a line of credit in order to maintain the stability of their currency.

The idea of IMF was to enhance and encourage international trade through assurances about monetary stability in various countries. Each time a particular nation, such as Japan or Russia, experiences a difficult economic swing, there is significant debate about the use of IMF funds to buoy that nation's currency so that international trade with that country is not destroyed.

Review the Kyoto Treaty:
http://www.unfccc.de

The Kyoto Treaty

The Kyoto Protocol, often called the Kyoto Treaty or the global-warming treaty, is a twenty-four–page document that focuses on the reduction of greenhouse gas emissions. All developed countries would be required to reduce their emissions "by at least 5 percent below 1990 levels," and the United States would be required to reduce its emissions by at least 7 percent below 1990 levels. China, India, and Mexico are excluded from the treaty's coverage. The EU will reduce emissions by 8 percent below 1990 levels, but their fulfillment can be met jointly and need not be on a country-by-country basis. An international body would be created to monitor emissions. For more information on the Kyoto Treaty, see Chapter 12.

Trust, Corruption, Trade, and Economics

Perhaps the greatest activity in multilateral agreements among countries has been in the area of curbing bribes because of their devastating impact on trust and the resulting impact on the investment and economic environments of a country. In his departure speech as secretary of the U.S. Treasury, Paul Rubin cautioned government employees to never accept any sort of gift as part of their duties for, he noted, "Corruption and bribery benefit a few at the expense of many."

The Foreign Corrupt Practices Act

Perhaps the most widely known criminal statute affecting firms that operate internationally is the **Foreign Corrupt Practices Act** (FCPA). The FCPA applies to business concerns that have their principal offices in the United States. It contains antibribery provisions as well as accounting controls for these firms, and it is meant to curb the use of bribery in foreign operations of companies.

The act prohibits making, authorizing, or promising payments or gifts of money or anything of value with the intent to corrupt. The prohibition is against payments designed to influence the official acts of foreign officials, political parties, party officials, candidates for office, any non-governmental organization (NGO), or any person who will transmit the gift or money to one of the other types of persons.

The FCPA is the result of an SEC investigation that uncovered questionable foreign payments by large stock issuers who were based in the United States. Approximately 435 U.S. corporations had made improper or questionable payments in Japan, the Netherlands, and Korea. The most common type of payment was made to foreign government officials. Most of the payments were made in relation to tax valuation or assessments. First passed in 1977, the act was most recently amended in 1998.

For a payment to a foreign official to constitute a violation of the FCPA, payment or something of value must have been given to a foreign official with discretionary authority, a foreign political candidate, or a foreign political party for the purpose of getting the recipient to act or refrain from acting to help business operations or, under the 1998 changes, to "secure any improper advantage" in doing business in that country. Also under the 1998 changes, foreign officials now include public international figures, such as officials with the UN or the IMF.

Payments to any foreign official for "facilitation," often referred to as grease payments, are not prohibited under FCPA so long as these payments are made only to get these officials to do their normal jobs that they might not do or would do slowly without some payment. These grease payments can be made only to

(1) secure a permit or license; (2) obtain paper processing; (3) secure police protection; (4) provide phone, water, or power supply; or (5) secure any other similar actions. Penalties for violations of the FCPA can run up to $100,000 and five years' imprisonment for individuals. Corporate fines are up to $2 million per violation. There are no civil penalties.

The following case deals with a violation of the FCPA.

CASE 7.1

United States v. Liebo
923 F.2d 1308 (8th Cir. 1991)

The Niger Connection: Influence in Exchange for an International Honeymoon

FACTS

Between January 1983 and June 1987, Richard H. Liebo was vice president in charge of the Aerospace Division of NAPCO International, Inc., of Hopkins, Minnesota. NAPCO's primary business consisted of selling military equipment and supplies throughout the world.

In early 1983, the Niger government contracted with a West German company, Dornier Reparaturwerft, to service two Lockheed C-130 cargo planes. After the Niger Ministry of Defense ran into financial troubles, Dornier sought an American parts supplier in order to qualify the Ministry of Defense for financing through the U.S. Foreign Military Sales program. The Foreign Military Sales program is supervised by the Defense Security Assistance Agency of the U.S. Department of Defense. Under the program, loans are provided to foreign governments for the purchase of military equipment and supplies from U.S. contractors.

In June 1983, representatives from Dornier met with officials of NAPCO and agreed that NAPCO would become the prime contractor on the C-130 maintenance contracts. Under this arrangement, NAPCO would supply parts to Niger and Dornier, and Dornier would perform the required maintenance at its facilities in Munich.

Once NAPCO and Dornier agreed to these terms, Mr. Liebo and Axel Kurth, a Dornier sales representative, flew to Niger to get the president of Niger's approval of the contract. In Niger they met with Captain Ali Tiemogo, chief of maintenance for the Niger Air Force. Captain Tiemogo testified that during the trip, Mr. Liebo and Mr. Kurth told him that they would make "some gestures" to him if he helped get the contract approved. When asked whether this promise played a role in deciding to recommend approval of the contract, Captain Tiemogo stated, "I can't say 'no,' I cannot say 'yes,' at that time," but "it encouraged me." Following Captain Tiemogo's recommendation that the contract be approved, the president of Niger signed the contract.

Tahirou Barke, Tiemogo's cousin and close friend, was the first consular for the Niger Embassy in Washington, D.C. Mr. Barke testified that he met Mr. Liebo in Washington sometime in 1983 or 1984. Mr. Barke stated that Mr. Liebo told him he wanted to make a "gesture" to Captain Tiemogo and asked Mr. Barke to set up a bank account in the United States. With Mr. Barke's assistance, Mr. Liebo opened a bank account in Minnesota in the name of "E. Dave," a variation of the name of Mr. Barke's then girlfriend, Shirley Elaine Dave. NAPCO deposited about $30,000 in the account, and Mr. Barke used the money to pay bills and purchase personal items and also gave a portion of the money to Captain Tiemogo.

In August 1985, Mr. Barke returned to Niger to be married. After the wedding, he and his wife honeymooned in Paris, Stockholm, and London. Before leaving for Niger, he informed Mr. Liebo of his honeymoon plans, and Mr. Liebo offered to buy, as a gift, Mr. Barke's airline tickets for both Mr. Barke's return to Niger and his honeymoon trip. Mr. Liebo made the flight arrangements and paid for the tickets, which cost $2,028, by charging them to NAPCO's Diners Club account. Mr. Barke considered the tickets a personal "gift" from Mr. Liebo.

Over a two-and-a-half-year period beginning in May 1984, NAPCO made payments totaling $130,000 to three "commission agents." The practice of using agents and paying them commissions on international contracts was acknowledged as a proper, legal, and accepted business practice in Third World countries. NAPCO issued commission checks to three "agents," identified as Amadou Mailele, Captain Tiemogo's brother-in-law; Fatouma Boube, Captain Tiemogo's sister-in-law; and Miss E. Dave, Mr. Barke's girlfriend. At Captain Tiemogo's request, both Mr. Mailele and Mr. Boube set up bank accounts in Paris. Neither Mr. Mailele, Ms. Boube, nor Miss Dave, however, received the commission checks or acted as NAPCO's agent. These individuals were merely intermediaries through whom NAPCO made payments to Captain Tiemogo and Mr. Barke. NAPCO's corporate president, Henri Jacob, or another superior of Mr. Liebo's approved these "commission payments." No one approved the payment for the honeymoon trip.

Following a three-week trial, the jury acquitted Mr. Liebo on all FCPA charges except for the count concerning NAPCO's purchase of Mr. Barke's honeymoon airline tickets and the related false statement count. Mr. Liebo appealed.

JUDICIAL OPINION

GIBSON, Circuit Judge

Liebo first argues that his conviction on Count VII for violating the bribery provisions of the Foreign Corrupt Practices Act by giving Barke airline tickets for his honeymoon should be reversed because insufficient evidence existed to establish two elements of the offense. First, Liebo contends that there was insufficient evidence to show that the airline tickets were "given to obtain or retain business." Second, he argues that there was no evidence to show that his gift of honeymoon tickets was done "corruptly."

There is sufficient evidence that the airplane tickets were given to obtain or retain business. Tiemogo testified that the President of Niger would not approve the contracts without his recommendation. He also testified that Liebo promised to "make gestures" to him before the first contract was approved, and that Liebo promised to continue to "make gestures" if the second and third contracts were approved. There was testimony that Barke helped Liebo establish a bank account with a fictitious name, that Barke used money from that account, and that

Barke sent some of the money from that account to Tiemogo. Barke testified that he understood Liebo deposited money in the account as "gestures" to Tiemogo for some "of the business that they do have together."

Although much of this evidence is directly related to those counts on which Liebo was acquitted, we believe it appropriate that we consider it in determining the sufficiency of evidence as to the counts on which Liebo was convicted.

Moreover, sufficient independent evidence exists that the tickets were given to obtain or retain business. Evidence established that Tiemogo and Barke were cousins and best friends. The relationship between Barke and Tiemogo could have allowed a reasonable jury to infer that Liebo made the gift to Barke intending to buy Tiemogo's help in getting the contracts approved. Indeed, Tiemogo recommended approval of the third contract and the President of Niger approved that contract just a few weeks after Liebo gave the tickets to Barke. Accordingly, a reasonable jury could conclude that the gift was given to "obtain or retain business."

Liebo also contends that the evidence at trial failed to show that Liebo acted "corruptly" by buying Barke the airline tickets. In support of this argument, Liebo points to Barke's testimony that he considered the tickets a "gift" from Liebo personally. Liebo asserts that "corruptly" means that the offer, payment, or gift "must be intended to induce the recipient to misuse his official position. . . ." Because Barke considered the tickets to be a personal gift from Liebo, Liebo reasons that no evidence showed that the tickets wrongfully influenced Barke's actions.

We are satisfied that sufficient evidence existed from which a reasonable jury could find that the airline tickets were given "corruptly." For example, Liebo gave the airline tickets to Barke shortly before the third contract was approved. In addition, there was undisputed evidence concerning the close relationship between Tiemogo and Barke and Tiemogo's important role in the contract approval process. There was also testimony that Liebo classified the airline tickets for accounting purposes as a "commission payment." This evidence could allow a reasonable jury to infer that Liebo gave the tickets to Barke intending to influence the Niger government's contract approval process. We conclude, therefore, that a reasonable jury could find that Liebo's gift to Barke

(continued)

was given "corruptly." Accordingly, sufficient evidence existed to support Liebo's conviction.
    Remanded on other grounds.

CASE QUESTIONS

1. Describe the relationships of NAPCO; Messrs. Liebo, Jacob, Mailele, and Barke; Ms. Fatouma Boube; Captain Tiemogo; and Ms. Dave.

2. Was there a violation of the FCPA?

3. Were any of the payments bribes?

4. Would these types of payments be permitted to U.S. government officials?

5. If you were Mr. Liebo, would you have objected to the trip and payments?

6. Was NAPCO's conduct ethical?

CONSIDER...

7.1 A Philip Morris subsidiary, C. A. Tabacalera National, and a B.A.T. subsidiary known as C. A. Cigarrera Bigott entered into a contract with La Fundacion del Nino (the Children's Foundation) of Caracas, Venezuela. The agreement was signed on behalf of the foundation by the foundation's president, who also was the wife of the then president of Venezuela. Under the terms of the agreement, these two tobacco firms were to make periodic donations to the Children's Foundation totaling $12.5 million. In exchange, the two firms would receive price controls on Venezuelan tobacco, elimination of controls on retail cigarette prices in Venezuela, tax deductions for donations, and assurances that the existing tax rates applicable to tobacco companies would not be increased.

Is the donation to the charity a violation of the FCPA? [*Lamb* v. *Philip Morris, Inc.*, 915 F.2d 1024 (6th Cir. 1990; *cert. denied*, 498 U.S. 1086 (1995))]

Visit the U.S. Justice Department Web site on the FCPA at http://www.usdojgov/ criminal/fraud/fcpa/ dojdocb

Many businesses have been critical of the FCPA because of the lack of uniformity among various nations concerning the propriety of facilitating (grease) payments and the legality of bribes. A foreign agent can legally receive the payment, but a U.S. corporation cannot make the payment. However, a survey by the U.S. Government Accounting Office of the companies affected by the FCPA found that the ability of companies from other countries to bribe officials did not give them a competitive advantage. The survey found that U.S. trade increased in fifty-one of fifty-six foreign countries after the FCPA went into effect. The increase was attributed to the position adopted by U.S. companies with respect to their competitors—if they could not bribe government officials, they would disclose publicly any information about bribes made by any of the companies from other nations.

The **Organization for Economic Cooperation and Development** (OECD) is now extremely supportive of the already existing U.S. position on bribery and its member countries are enacting legislation for compliance with its international pact against bribery. The OECD passed an anti-bribery provision in December 1997, which, if accepted by the 33 member nations, will result in a form of the FCPA being passed in those individual countries.

When Congress amended the FCPA in order to implement the OECD Convention on Combating Bribery of Foreign Public Officials in International Business Transactions, the amendments expanded the act's jurisdiction to cover all U.S. citizens acting outside the United States and to all non-U.S. citizens acting inside the United States.

BUSINESS STRATEGY

The Costs of Slipping on the FCPA

In companies with 100,000 employees worldwide, supervision of employees with regard to the FCPA can be difficult. Without clear signals from executive management and strong policies, even companies with the best intentions in terms of compliance with the law can fall short. For example, IBM entered into a consent decree with the SEC on charges that it engaged in bribery in violation of the FCPA. The charges filed by the SEC alleged that an IBM subsidiary, IBM Argentina S. A., was awarded a $250 million contract for modernizing the systems of Banco de la Nacion Argentina (BNA), a government-owned commercial bank in Argentina. As part of the arrangement, the IBM subsidiary entered into a $37 million contract to do business with a corporation owned by directors of BNA, with the directors receiving $4.5 million of that $37 million contract as compensation. Those directors then voted to award IBM the contract.

The consent decree requires IBM to pay a $300,000 fine. The fine is minimal because IBM did conduct its own internal investigation to uncover what had happened and fired thirteen employees in its subsidiary when the preceding relationships were uncovered.

BNA revoked the contract after paying IBM $80 million, and IBM has agreed to reimburse BNA

© Reuters NewMedia, Inc./CORBIS

$34 million of that amount. Other Argentine agencies also revoked their contracts with IBM, with the total amount of business lost in the Argentina market estimated to be $500 million.

IBM has announced a new company policy that prohibits company bids for government projects that are not done in an open bidding process with full public access to documents.*

The costs to IBM in this situation, both in terms of its lost contracts and revenues and its reputation, are nearly incalculable. Many companies take the position that they will not even make facilitation payments so that their worldwide staff understand a clear and definitive line. A Procter & Gamble executive explains that, once a government official knows that a company will pay to get things done or get them done quickly, the price keeps rising and that such payments never serve the shareholders well. Long-term growth in a country is limited when even facilitation payments become part of a company's operations there. Strategically, more than ethically and legally, these types of payments are questionable in their benefits and results.

*In the Matter of International Business Machines Corp., Administrative Proceeding File No 3-13097, Rel. No. 34-43761 (Dec. 21, 2000).

The convention basically adopts the standards of the United States under the FCPA and requires nations signing the agreement to: (1) criminalize bribery of foreign public officials; (2) define public official to include officials in all branches of government, whether appointed or elected; any person exercising a public function, including for a public agency or public enterprise; and any official or agent of a public international organization; (3) include as public functions any activity in the public interest; (4) cover business-related bribes to foreign public officials made through political parties and party officials; (5) include as illegal payments made to someone who will become a public official in anticipation of favorable treatment; (6) provide for "effective, proportionate and dissuasive criminal penalties" to those who bribe foreign public officials[1]; (7) authorize the seizure or confiscation of the bribe and bribe proceeds (i.e., net profit), or property of similar value, or impose monetary sanctions of comparable effect; (8) prohibit the establishment of off-the-books accounts and similar practices used to bribe foreign public officials or to hide such bribery; (9) establish jurisdiction over acts that take place in their countries even if there is not extensive physical contact by those paying the bribes; (10) pledge to work together to provide legal assistance relating to

BUSINESS PLANNING TIP

Compliance with the FCPA requires great effort and diligence on the part of companies involved in international operations.

1. Use great caution on any payments to government officials, even for things as simple as getting the phone lines in your office connected. The task may be administrative or bureaucratic, but the understanding of employees about what is and is not illegal is influenced by each choice to pay even so-called legal grease payments.

2. Do background checks on all your foreign employees and agents. Obtain financial information and personal references for them.

3. Publish your complete and unambiguous policy on FCPA payments. Include details and examples for employees, and post the policy in all offices.

4. Establish effective financial controls in all your offices and facilities. Send the outside auditors to your international offices to make surprise visits and spot checks of the records.

5. Voluntarily report any slips or misunderstandings. Come forward with the information and disclose all relevant actions and records to the U.S. government.

investigations and proceedings and to make bribery of foreign public officials an extraditable offense. The United States was the first country to pass implementing procedures in its laws and did so by the end of 1998. Under these amendments to the existing FCPA, all officers, employees, agents, and even foreign nationals working for U.S. companies are covered under the act in order to comply with the OECD requirements.

OECD will continue to monitor its members' compliance with the policies in their laws as well as continue to study the impact of the convention on stopping corruption in international trade.

RESOLUTION OF INTERNATIONAL DISPUTES

As was discussed in Chapters 1, 3, and 4, there really is no way to enforce international laws. The International Court of Justice established by the United Nations is a court of voluntary jurisdiction for disputes between nations; it is not a court for the resolution of business disputes between nations. More and more companies and individuals favor arbitration as a chosen means for resolving disputes. The most popular forum chosen for such arbitrations and quasi-trials is London's Commercial Court (which was chosen in *The Bremen* case contract noted in the chapter opening "Consider")—founded over 100 years ago, on March 1, 1895, when it heard its first case, which involved a dispute over the quality of cloth sold by a Flemish manufacturer to a London agent. The court was perhaps the first to recognize the role of arbitration in deciding international business disputes; such innovation restored the confidence of business in the settlement of disputes by third parties. The London Commercial Court is viewed as a neutral forum with highly experienced judges who are also experienced commercial litigators.

PRINCIPLES OF INTERNATIONAL LAW

The sources of international law simply serve to govern businesses as they operate in a particular country, and the laws may vary from country to country. However, some principles of international law apply to all countries and people in the international marketplace. The principles of international law do affect the decisions and operations of businesses, regardless of the availability of court resolution of rights.

Sovereign Immunity

Visit the International Court of Justice:
http://www.icj-cij.org

The concept of **sovereign immunity** is based on the notion that each country is a sovereign nation. This status means that each country is an equal with other countries; each country has exclusive jurisdiction over its internal operations, laws, and people; and no country is subject to the jurisdiction of another country's court system unless it so consents. Our court system cannot be used to right injustices in other countries or to subject other countries to penalties. For example, in *Schooner Exchange* v. *McFaddon*, 7 Cr. 116 (1812), a group of American citizens attempted to seize the vessel *Exchange* when it came into port at Philadelphia because the citizens believed that the ship had been taken improperly on the high seas by the French emperor Napoleon and that the ship rightfully belonged to them. The U.S. Supreme Court held that the ship could not be seized because sovereign immunity applied, and France could not involuntarily be subjected to the jurisdiction of U.S. courts.

Review the Foreign Sovereign Immunities Act of 1976: http://www.law.cornell.edu/ uscode/28/1602.html

The Foreign Sovereign Immunities Act of 1976 clarified the U.S. government's position on sovereign immunity and incorporated the *Schooner Exchange* doctrine. Not only are countries immune, but the act also adds a clarification to the concept of sovereign immunity of sovereign nations for illegal acts. For example, in *Argentine Republic* v. *Amerada Hess Shipping Co.,* 488 U.S. 428 (1989), the Supreme Court dismissed a suit brought in a U.S. federal court by a Liberian-chartered commercial ship company against the government of Argentina for its unprovoked and illegal attack on a company ship that was in neutral waters when the war between Great Britain and Argentina broke out over the Falkland Islands. The attack by the Argentine navy was unprovoked and in clear violation of international law. However, the U.S. Supreme Court clarified that under the Sovereign Immunities Act and principles of international law, all sovereign nations are immune from suits in other countries, even for those acts—like that of Argentina's—that are clear violations of international law.

A distinction has been made, however, by both the Foreign Sovereign Immunities Act and the courts with respect to the commercial transactions of a sovereign nation. For example, the sale of services and goods; loan transactions; and contracts for marketing, public relations, and employment services entered into by a country are, in essence, voluntary agreements that subject that country's government to civil suits in another nation's courts according to the terms of the agreement or according to the basic tenets of judicial jurisdiction (see Chapter 3).

Expropriation, or the Act of State Doctrine

Under this doctrine, the acts of governments of foreign nations are recognized as valid by U.S. courts, even though under our system of legal rights there may be some question whether the acts were legal or appropriate. This doctrine has been challenged most frequently in cases in which a foreign country has expropriated or nationalized private property in a country by an order of attachment. In effect, the foreign government has seized control of private property. Under our standards of due process, such a taking would be unconstitutional without just compensation (see Chapter 5 for a discussion of eminent domain and just compensation), but the **act of state doctrine** provides that "the courts of one country will not sit in judgment on . . . the acts of another done within its own territory" [*Underhill* v. *Hernandez,* 168 U.S. 250 (1897)].

The effect of the act of state doctrine is to leave foreign affairs in the hands of the legislative and executive branches of government and keep courts out of the loop. There are many cases in which **expropriation** violates principles of international law. In most cases, expropriation or nationalization violates our notions of equity and justice. However, some protection exists for businesses and individuals who invest in foreign nations, because the Sovereign Immunities Act exemption for commercial activity also applies in cases of expropriation. The following case clarifies the distinction between expropriation and commercial activity, one of which enjoys immunity and the other of which does not.

CASE 7.2

Riedel v. *Bancam*
792 F.2d 587 (6th Cir. 1986)

Pesos to Dollars: Exchange Rates Can Kill Investments

FACTS

W. Christian Riedel, a resident of Ohio, had an account with Unibanco, S. A., and asked that it transfer $100,000 to Banca Metropolitana, S. A. (Bamesa) (predecessor to Bancam) for investment in a certificate of deposit (CD). Bamesa merged with another bank to form Bancam, and Riedel's CD was renewed with the newly merged bank.

Shortly after Riedel's renewal, the government of Mexico issued new rules governing accounts from foreigners in Mexican banks. The rules required the banks to pay the CDs in pesos at a rate that was substantially below exchange rates. A month after these rules were put into effect, Bancam was nationalized.

When Riedel's CD came due, the exchange rate was 74.34 pesos to the dollar. He was paid $53,276.23 for his $100,000 investment.

Riedel brought suit in a U.S. federal district court, alleging that Bancam had violated both federal and Ohio securities laws in selling the CDs in the United States without registration. Bancam filed a motion to dismiss the suit on the ground that the Sovereign Immunities Act of 1976 precluded U.S. courts from taking jurisdiction over the matter. Bancam also claimed protection under the act of state doctrine. Finally, Bancam claimed that the CD was not a security for purposes of U.S. securities laws.

The district court dismissed Riedel's suit on the ground that it lacked jurisdiction over the claims under Ohio law and also on grounds of sovereign immunity and the act of state doctrine. Riedel appealed.

JUDICIAL OPINION

KENNEDY, Circuit Judge

In this appeal, Riedel does not challenge the District Court's conclusion that the certificates of deposit that Bancam issued are not "securities" under federal securities law. Instead, Riedel argues that the "act of state doctrine" does not bar his breach of contract and Ohio securities law claims. The District Court, however, did not refer to the "act of state doctrine" in

denying Riedel's motion for a new trial. In addition to holding, as a matter of law, that the certificate of deposit involved in this case was not a "security" under federal securities law, the District Court ruled that it did not have jurisdiction over Riedel's breach of contract and Ohio securities law claims. The District Court concluded that: "Diversity jurisdiction pursuant to 28 U.S.C. Section 1332 does not permit a citizen of this state to sue a foreign government, or agency thereof, in a federal district court."

We agree that the District Court did not have jurisdiction under 28 U.S.C. § 1332 over the breach of contract and Ohio securities law claims. Title 28 U.S.C. § 1332(a)(4) confers original jurisdiction on the district courts over civil actions between a foreign state, as plaintiff, and a citizen of a State. Title 28 U.S.C. § 1332(a)(4), however, does not apply to suits between a citizen of a State and a foreign state, as defendant. A "foreign state," under 28 U.S.C. § 1603(a), "includes a political subdivision of a foreign state or an agency or instrumentality of a foreign state. . . ." Since the Government of Mexico nationalized Bancam on September 1, 1982, Bancam qualifies as an "agency or instrumentality of a foreign state" under 28 U.S.C. § 1603(b)(2). Therefore, this action involves an Ohio citizen and a "foreign state," as a defendant. Consequently, 28 U.S.C. § 1332(a)(4) does not apply. Accordingly, we hold that the District Court properly concluded that it did not have jurisdiction under 28 U.S.C. § 1332 over the breach of contract and Ohio securities law claims.

We conclude, however, that the District Court may have had jurisdiction over the breach of contract and Ohio securities law claims under the [Foreign Sovereign Immunities Act (FSIA) 28 U.S.C. § 1330]. Although the FSIA ordinarily entitles foreign states to immunity from federal jurisdiction, 28 U.S.C. § 1605(a)(2) creates a "commercial activity" exception to this immunity. Title 28 U.S.C. § 1605(a)(2) provides in pertinent part:

A foreign state shall not be immune from the jurisdiction of courts of the United States or of the States in any case . . . in which the action is based upon commercial activity carried on in the United States by the foreign state; or upon an act performed in the United States in connection with a commercial activity of the foreign state elsewhere or upon an act outside the territory of the United States in connection with a commercial activity of the foreign state elsewhere and that act causes a direct effect in the United States.

Accordingly, 28 U.S.C. § 1605(a)(2) applies only when a foreign state's "commercial activity" has the required jurisdictional nexus with the United States.

We hold that the sale of the certificates of deposit in this case was a "commercial activity." . . .

The "act of state doctrine" precludes courts in this country from questioning the validity and effect of a sovereign act of a foreign nation performed in its own territory. . . .

Under the "act of state doctrine," courts exercise jurisdiction but prudentially "decline to decide the merits of the case if in doing so we would need to judge the validity of the public acts of a sovereign state performed within its own territory."

Accordingly, we affirm the portion of the District Court's order denying Riedel's motion for a new trial on the breach of contract claim. The "act of state doctrine," however, does not bar the Ohio securities law claim. Riedel bases that claim on Bancam's failure to register the certificate of deposit with the Ohio Division of Securities and not on Bancam's failure to repay dollars at the certificate's maturity.

Since the District Court may have had the subject matter jurisdiction, we remand the Ohio securities law claim for further proceedings consistent with this opinion. We also note that even if the District Court concludes that it has subject matter jurisdiction, Bancam has also argued that the District Court does not have personal jurisdiction. Assuming that the District Court decides that it has subject matter jurisdiction under the FSIA, the District Court will also have to make findings of fact to determine whether Bancam has sufficient "contacts" with the United States to satisfy due process.

Reversed in part.

CASE QUESTIONS

1. Describe Riedel's investment.

2. What did he get back from his original investment?

3. What are the bases for his suit against Bancam in Ohio?

4. Does the act of state doctrine apply?

5. Does Mexico have sovereign immunity for its expropriation of the bank?

6. What issues will the court be determining when the case is remanded?

C O N S I D E R . . .

7.2   Scott Nelson was employed at the Kingdom of Saudi Arabia, a hospital in Saudi Arabia. He had signed an employment contract to act as a monitoring systems engineer at the hospital. Mr. Nelson responded to an ad run in the United States, was hired, and began work in December 1983.

In the course of his employment, Mr. Nelson discovered numerous safety violations. When, in March 1984, he brought them to the attention of hospital officials, they told him to ignore it.

On September 27, 1994, Mr. Nelson was summoned to the security office, where he was arrested by agents of the Saudi government.

He was transported to a jail cell, where he was shackled, tortured, and beaten. He was kept for four days with no food and confined to an overcrowded cell area infested with rats. When food was eventually provided, he was required to fight other prisoners for it.

> After thirty-nine days and U.S. intervention, Mr. Nelson was released from jail. He refused to return to the hospital and left to return to the United States.
>
> Mr. Nelson and his wife brought a damages suit against his former employer for their failure to warn him about the government. The Saudi government sought to dismiss the suit under the Foreign Sovereign Immunities Act.
>
> Was the activity commercial? Should the Nelsons be permitted to sue? [*Saudi Arabia v. Nelson*, 507 U.S. 349 (1993)]

CONSIDER . . .

7.3 What if a U.S. citizen were sexually harassed in the office of the Brazilian embassy located in Washington, D.C.? Would the Brazilian official be immune from suit for the harassment? What policy implications do you see in the decision in such a matter? [*Zveiter v. Brazilian National Superintendency of Merchant Marine*, 841 F. Supp. 111 (S.D.N.Y. 1993)]

Protections for U.S. Property and Investment Abroad

Review the Hickenlooper amendment:
http://www.law.cornell.edu/
uscode/22/2370.html

The effect of nationalization and expropriation combined with the act of state doctrine and sovereign immunity is to chill U.S. investments in foreign countries. To discourage expropriation, the Foreign Assistance Act of 1962 contained what has been called the Hickenlooper amendment, which requires the president to suspend all forms of assistance to countries that have expropriated the property of U.S. citizens or regulated the property in such a way as to effectively deprive a U.S. citizen of it (through taxation or limits on use).

Many trade treaties that have been negotiated or are being negotiated with other countries contain protections against expropriation. Some treaties provide U.S. companies and investors with the same levels of protection as the citizens of those countries. For example, if a country affords its citizens due process before taking over private property, U.S. citizens and companies must be afforded those same protections prior to expropriation.

Finally, Congress has created a federal insurer for U.S. investments abroad. The Overseas Private Investment Corporation (OPIC) is an insurer for U.S. investment in those countries in which the per capita income is $250 or less. OPIC will pay damages for expropriation, for inability to convert the currency of the country, or for losses from war or revolution.

Consumer protections in other countries are dependent upon those countries' laws. For example, many U.S. citizens have constructed luxury homes along the coast near Ensenada in Baja California. They did so because the land and construction were so much cheaper that they could afford large, luxury homes. However, the land on which many of the homes were located was the subject of fourteen years of litigation and more than sixty court decisions over disputed ownership rights. With the Mexican Supreme Court's decision on land ownership, most of the current U.S. owners have been told that they must vacate their homes and leave everything behind. While there might be due process and property rights in the United States, the homeowners in Ensenada have no hope so long as the Mexican Supreme Court has declared the law for its country and land there.

BIOGRAPHY

The International Cruise Ship

With more people able to afford a cruise, the cruise line industry is booming. In the year 2000, there were nearly 7 million U.S. citizens who took a cruise, an increase of 51 percent from 1995. There were thirty-eight cruise ships scheduled for delivery between 1999 and 2002, including two for the new Disney Cruise Lines. Many of these cruise ships hold in excess of 3,000 passengers each, with the industry estimating continuing increases in numbers of passengers at a rate of about 10 percent per year. Profit margins in the industry are high, with Carnival Cruise's net profits per day averaging about $3 million.*

One interesting issue that has arisen because of the increasing numbers, passengers and business-related issues, and litigation is what law applies to cruise ships? What country has jurisdiction over Royal Caribbean Cruise Lines, Inc., a company incorporated in Liberia with headquarters in Miami and boats registered in Norway? All cruise ships fly foreign country flags because the companies register their ships in other nations to avoid both the substantial U.S. taxes and the tighter labor and environmental regulations imposed on U.S. companies. There are five keys areas of law for cruise ships that have resulted in answers to the questions of which law applies and which countries have jurisdiction.

The first issue relates to the employees on the cruise ships. Workers on many cruise ships work twelve- to fourteen-hour days and are paid $400–$450 per month. The workers are not entitled to U.S. labor and wage protections. While nearly 90 percent of cruise ship passengers are U.S. citizens, the cruise lines are incorporated in countries where they can minimize their tax bills, such as Panama and Liberia. U.S. labor laws do not apply to the ships and their crews. The International Labor Organization of the United Nations suggests a workweek limit of seventy hours. Some of the workers do earn around $2,000 per month in tips. They work four to ten months per year and are not covered by medical insurance when they are not working on the ships. Most cruise ship workers are recruited from the Philippines where average earnings are $1,000 per year.

A second problem is that of dumping. Cruise ships release effluent into the oceans because the cost of waste disposal for boats with 3,000 passengers can run into the hundreds of thousands per day. Questions of jurisdiction arise: what country has authority to take action? Of the 111 complaints of cruise ship dumping (including everything from waifs to waste) brought in countries outside the United States, enforcement action was taken in only two of the cases. The U.S. Environmental Protection Agency (EPA) (see Chapter 12) has brought enforcement action against companies dumping in U.S. waters. For example, Holland America, a division of Carnival Cruises, pleaded guilty in 1998 to discharging waste into Alaska's Inside Passage and agreed to pay a fine of $2 million.

A third problem is criminal activity, such as large numbers of thefts and sexual assaults aboard cruise ships. Litigation in federal district court in Miami resulted in revelations through discovery of a high number of sexual assaults on cruise ships with few of those reported to local law enforcement authorities. The lawsuit, against Carnival, produced records during discovery in which it was revealed that members of Carnival Cruise crews had sexually assaulted passengers and fellow crew members sixty-two times over a five-year period.

When such crimes were committed on the high seas, no country really had jurisdiction and those aboard the ship were not even required to report the crimes. For example, a woman who was assaulted by a crew member she had invited to her cabin was asked not to report the incident by the ship's staff. When the ship docked in Miami, she reported the incident to the FBI. However, when FBI agents boarded the ship to investigate the crime, the ship's captain indicated that the crew member had been escorted to the airport and had boarded a flight for his native Italy.

The reporting stance of the cruise lines has, however, changed because of concerns passengers had about their safety; and prosecution for crimes not being possible, the cruise industry agreed to begin a practice of relaying all crimes reported on board ship to law enforcement agencies. The

(continued)

decision was made by the International Council of Cruise Lines, which is comprised of representatives from sixteen different cruise lines. The Council includes representatives from 90 percent of the industry. The cruise industry had followed a policy of letting passengers decide whether to report these crimes, and the reporting level was low.

A fourth area of concern is that of consumer rights in cruise ship contracts. If there is misrepresentation or the cruise does not fulfill promised destinations, what rights do consumers have? Where can they litigate? Are arbitration clauses in cruise ship contracts valid? The *Carnival Cruise Line* v. *Shute* case answers these questions.

Finally, there is litigation. Passengers who are injured are bringing suit against the companies for their injuries. Several recent examples include a passenger who experienced a back injury in an organized pillow fight, a passenger who was injured while dancing the lindy as part of cruise activities, and a passenger who slipped and fell on a grape left behind from a passenger impersonating Carmen Miranda as part of a skit. Passengers are increasingly using long-arm statutes to require the companies to defend lawsuits in federal district court. Miami seems to be the most common location for such litigation because all major cruise lines have ships and offices there and meet the standards for minimum contacts. (See Chapter 3 for more discussion of long arm statutes.)

Are these ships subject to U.S. laws and courts? Are they floating cities? Sovereign nations?

*Douglas Frantz, "For Cruise Ships' Workers, Much Toil, Little Protection," *New York Times,* 24 December 1999, A1, A16.

Source: Michael D. Goldhaber, "Ticket to Paradise or a Trip From Hell?" *National Law Journal,* 22 March 1999, C1.

BUSINESS PLANNING TIP

Limits on repatriation should be checked before an investment is made in a foreign country. Limits could be set strictly on amounts, or on amounts over certain time periods. Financial planning requires foreknowledge of these types of limits.

Repatriation

Repatriation is the process of bringing back to your own country profits earned on investments in another country. In some nations, there are limits on repatriation; businesses can remove only a certain amount of the profits earned from the operations of a business within a country. Repatriation limits are considered acts of state and are immune from litigation in the United States.

Forum Non Conveniens, or "You Have the Wrong Court"

The doctrine of *forum non conveniens* is a principle of U.S. justice under which cases that are brought to the wrong court are dismissed. The doctrine allows judicial discretion whereby such issues as the location of the evidence, the location of the parties, and the location of the property that will be used to satisfy any judgment that is made are examined. For example, when the Union Carbide disaster occurred at its Bhopal, India, plant, victims and families brought suit against Union Carbide in New York City. A U.S. court of appeals dismissed the case and sent it back to India on the grounds of *forum non conveniens* [*In re Union Carbide Corp. Gas Plant Disaster,* 809 F.2d 195 (2d Cir. 1987)].

Conflicts of Law

No two countries match in terms of the structure of their legal system or in their laws. For example, the law in the United States, codified by the widely adopted Uniform Commercial Code (UCC), is that all contracts and contract relationships are subject to a standard of good faith. In Canada, the good faith exists only if the parties place such a provision in their agreement. Under German law, protections are given not on the basis of good faith but, rather, on the basis of who is the weaker party. Just among three major commercial powers, laws on contracts are significantly different. The rules on conflicts of law in international transactions are as follows: (1) if the parties choose which law applies, that law will apply; (2) if no provision is made, the law of the country where the contract is performed will be used. Agreeing to and understanding the set of laws to be applied in a contract is a critical part of international transactions. The following case is the U.S. Supreme Court's decision on party agreements for resolution of disputes. Look carefully for the answer for the chapter opening "Consider" in the opinion.

CASE 7.3

Carnival Cruise Lines v. *Shute*
499 U.S. 585 (1991)

Cruising for Forums: Contracts Clauses on the High Seas

FACTS

Eulala and Russel Shute (respondents), through an Arlington, Washington, travel agent, purchased passage for a seven-day cruise on petitioner's ship, the *Tropicale*. The Shutes paid the fare to the agent who forwarded the payment to Carnival's (petitioner) headquarters in Miami, Florida. Carnival then prepared the tickets and sent them to the Shutes in Washington. The face of each ticket, at its left-hand lower corner, contained this admonition:
"*SUBJECT TO CONDITIONS OF CONTRACT ON LAST PAGES IMPORTANT! PLEASE READ CONTRACT—ON LAST PAGES 1, 2, 3*" App. 15.

The following appeared on "contract page 1" of each ticket:
"*TERMS AND CONDITIONS OF PASSAGE CONTRACT TICKET . . .*

"*3. (a) The acceptance of this ticket by the person or persons named hereon as passengers shall be deemed to be an acceptance and agreement by each of them of all of the terms and conditions of this Passage Contract Ticket. . . .*"

"*8. It is agreed by and between the passenger and the Carrier that all disputes and matters whatsoever arising under, in connection with or incident to this Contract shall be litigated, if at all, in and before a Court located in the State of Florida, U.S.A., to the exclusion of the Courts of any other state or country.*"

The Shutes boarded the *Tropicale* in Los Angeles, California. The ship sailed to Puerto Vallarta, Mexico, and then returned to Los Angeles. While the ship was in international waters off the Mexican coast, Eulala Shute was injured when she slipped on a deck mat during a guided tour of the ship's galley. The Shutes filed suit against petitioner in the U.S. District Court for the Western District of Washington, claiming that Mrs. Shute's injuries had been caused by the negligence of Carnival Cruise Lines and its employees.

Carnival moved for summary judgment, contending that the forum clause in the tickets required the Shutes to bring their suit in a court in the State of Florida. Carnival also contended that the District Court lacked personal jurisdiction over it because its contacts with the State of Washington were insubstantial. The District Court granted the motion, holding that Carnival's contacts with Washington were constitutionally insufficient to support the exercise of personal jurisdiction.

The Court of Appeals reversed. Reasoning that "but for" Carnival's solicitation of business in Washington, the Shutes would not have taken the cruise and Mrs. Shute would not have been injured, the court concluded that Carnival had sufficient contacts with Washington to justify the District Court's exercise of personal jurisdiction.

JUDICIAL OPINION

BLACKMUN, Justice
Turning to the forum-selection clause, the Court of Appeals acknowledged that a court concerned with

(continued)

the enforceability of such a clause must begin its analysis with *The Bremen v. Zapata Off-Shore Co., 407 U.S. 1, 92 S.Ct. 1907, 32 L.Ed.2d 513 (1972),* where this Court held that forum-selection clauses, although not "historically . . . favored," are "prima facie valid." The appellate court concluded that the forum clause should not be enforced because it "was not freely bargained for." As an "independent justification" for refusing to enforce the clause, the Court of Appeals noted that there was evidence in the record to indicate that "the Shutes are physically and financially incapable of pursuing this litigation in Florida" and that the enforcement of the clause would operate to deprive them of their day in court and thereby contravene this Court's holding in *The Bremen.*

[r]espondents urge that the forum clause should not be enforced because, contrary to this Court's teachings in *The Bremen,* the clause was not the product of negotiation, and enforcement effectively would deprive respondents of their day in court. Additionally, respondents contend that the clause violates the Limitation of Vessel Owner's Liability Act, 46 U.S.C.App. § 183c.

Both petitioner and respondents argue vigorously that the Court's opinion in *The Bremen* governs this case, and each side purports to find ample support for its position in that opinion's broad-ranging language. This seeming paradox derives in large part from key factual differences between this case and *The Bremen,* differences that preclude an automatic and simple application of *The Bremen*'s general principles to the facts here.

In *The Bremen,* this Court addressed the enforceability of a forum-selection clause in a contract between two business corporations. An American corporation, Zapata, made a contract with Unterweser, a German corporation, for the towage of Zapata's oceangoing drilling rig from Louisiana to a point in the Adriatic Sea off the coast of Italy. The agreement provided that any dispute arising under the contract was to be resolved in the London Court of Justice.

After a storm in the Gulf of Mexico seriously damaged the rig, Zapata ordered Unterweser's ship to tow the rig to Tampa, Fla., the nearest point of refuge. Thereafter, Zapata sued Unterweser in admiralty in federal court at Tampa. Citing the forum clause, Unterweser moved to dismiss. The District Court denied Unterweser's motion, and the Court of Appeals for the Fifth Circuit, sitting en banc on rehearing, and by a sharply divided vote, affirmed.

This Court vacated and remanded, stating that, in general, "a freely negotiated private international agreement, unaffected by fraud, undue influence, or overweening bargaining power, such as that involved here, should be given full effect." The Court further generalized that "in the light of present-day commercial realities and expanding international trade we conclude that the forum clause should control absent a strong showing that it should be set aside." The Court did not define precisely the circumstances that would make it unreasonable for a court to enforce a forum clause. Instead, the Court discussed a number of factors that made it reasonable to enforce the clause at issue in *The Bremen* and that, presumably, would be pertinent in any determination whether to enforce a similar clause.

In this respect, the Court noted that there was "strong evidence that the forum clause was a vital part of the agreement, and [that] it would be unrealistic to think that the parties did not conduct their negotiations, including fixing the monetary terms, with the consequences of the forum clause figuring prominently in their calculations." Further, the Court observed that it was not "dealing with an agreement between two Americans to resolve their essentially local disputes in a remote alien forum," and that in such a case, "the serious inconvenience of the contractual forum to one or both of the parties might carry greater weight in determining the reasonableness of the forum clause." The Court stated that even where the forum clause establishes a remote forum for resolution of conflicts, "the party claiming [unfairness] should bear a heavy burden of proof."

[u]nlike the parties in *The Bremen,* respondents are not business persons and did not negotiate the terms of the clause with petitioner. Alternatively, the Court of Appeals ruled that the clause should not be enforced because enforcement effectively would deprive respondents of an opportunity to litigate their claim against petitioner.

The Bremen concerned a "far from routine transaction between companies of two different nations contemplating the tow of an extremely costly piece of equipment from Louisiana across the Gulf of Mexico and the Atlantic Ocean, through the Mediterranean Sea to its final destination in the Adriatic Sea." These facts suggest that, even apart from the evidence of negotiation regarding the forum clause, it was entirely reasonable for the Court in *The Bremen* to have expected Unterweser and Zapata to have negotiated with care in selecting a forum for the resolution of disputes arising from their special towing contract.

In contrast, respondents' passage contract was purely routine and doubtless nearly identical to every commercial passage contract issued by petitioner and most other cruise lines. In this context, it would be entirely unreasonable for us to assume that respondents—or any other cruise passenger—would negotiate with petitioner the terms of a forum-selection clause in an ordinary commercial cruise ticket. Common sense dictates that a ticket of this kind will be a form contract the terms of which are not subject to negotiation, and that an individual purchasing the ticket will not have bargaining parity with the cruise line. But by ignoring the crucial differences in the business contexts in which the respective contracts were executed, the Court of Appeals' analysis seems to us to have distorted somewhat this Court's holding in *The Bremen.*

In evaluating the reasonableness of the forum clause at issue in this case, we must refine the analysis of *The Bremen* to account for the realities of form passage contracts. First, a cruise line has a special interest in limiting the fora in which it potentially could be subject to suit. Because a cruise ship typically carries passengers from many locales, it is not unlikely that a mishap on a cruise could subject the cruise line to litigation in several different fora. Additionally, a clause establishing *ex ante* the forum for dispute resolution has the salutary effect of dispelling any confusion about where suits arising from the contract must be brought and defended, sparing litigants the time and expense of pretrial motions to determine the correct forum and conserving judicial resources that otherwise would be devoted to deciding those motions. Finally, it stands to reason that passengers who purchase tickets containing a forum clause like that at issue in this case benefit in the form of reduced fares reflecting the savings that the cruise line enjoys by limiting the fora in which it may be sued.

Furthermore, the Court of Appeals did not place in proper context this Court's statement in *The Bremen* that "the serious inconvenience of the contractual forum to one or both of the parties might carry greater weight in determining the reasonableness of the forum clause." The Court made this statement in evaluating a hypothetical "agreement between two Americans to resolve their essentially local disputes in a remote alien forum." In the present case, Florida is not a "remote alien forum," nor—given the fact that Mrs. Shute's accident occurred off the coast of Mexico—is this dispute an essentially local one

inherently more suited to resolution in the State of Washington than in Florida. In light of these distinctions, and because respondents do not claim lack of notice of the forum clause, we conclude that they have not satisfied the "heavy burden of proof" required to set aside the clause on grounds of inconvenience.

It bears emphasis that forum-selection clauses contained in form passage contracts are subject to judicial scrutiny for fundamental fairness. In this case, there is no indication that petitioner set Florida as the forum in which disputes were to be resolved as a means of discouraging cruise passengers from pursuing legitimate claims. Any suggestion of such a bad-faith motive is belied by two facts: Petitioner has its principal place of business in Florida, and many of its cruises depart from and return to Florida ports. Similarly, there is no evidence that petitioner obtained respondents' accession to the forum clause by fraud or overreaching. Finally, respondents have conceded that they were given notice of the forum provision and, therefore, presumably retained the option of rejecting the contract with impunity. In the case before us, therefore, we conclude that the Court of Appeals erred in refusing to enforce the forum-selection clause.

Respondents also contend that the forum-selection clause at issue violates 46 U.S.C.App. § 183c. That statute, enacted in 1936, see ch. 521, 49 Stat. 1480, provides:

"It shall be unlawful for the . . . owner of any vessel transporting passengers between ports of the United States or between any such port and a foreign port to insert in any rule, regulation, contract, or agreement any provision or limitation (1) purporting, in the event of loss of life or bodily injury arising from the negligence or fault of such owner or his servants, to relieve such owner . . . from liability, or from liability beyond any stipulated amount, for such loss or injury, or (2) purporting in such event to lessen, weaken, or avoid the right of any claimant to a trial by court of competent jurisdiction on the question of liability for such loss or injury, or the measure of damages therefor. All such provisions or limitations contained in any such rule, regulation, contract, or agreement are hereby declared to be against public policy and shall be null and void and of no effect."

By its plain language, the forum-selection clause before us does not take away respondents' right to "a trial by [a] court of competent jurisdiction" and thereby contravene the explicit proscription of § 183c. Instead, the clause states specifically that

(continued)

actions arising out of the passage contract shall be brought "if at all," in a court "located in the State of Florida," which, plainly, is a "court of competent jurisdiction" within the meaning of the statute.

There was no prohibition of a forum-selection clause. Because the clause before us allows for judicial resolution of claims against petitioner and does not purport to limit petitioner's liability for negligence, it does not violate § 183c.

The judgment of the Court of Appeals is reversed.

DISSENTING OPINION

Justice STEVENS, with whom Justice MARSHALL joins, dissenting.

The Court prefaces its legal analysis with a factual statement that implies that a purchaser of a Carnival Cruise Lines passenger ticket is fully and fairly notified about the existence of the choice of forum clause in the fine print on the back of the ticket. Even if this implication were accurate, I would disagree with the Court's analysis. But, given the Court's preface, I begin my dissent by noting that only the most meticulous passenger is likely to become aware of the forum-selection provision. I have therefore appended to this opinion a facsimile of the relevant text, using the type size that actually appears in the ticket itself. A careful reader will find the forum-selection clause in the 8th of the 25 numbered paragraphs.

Of course, many passengers, like the respondents in this case, will not have an opportunity to read paragraph 8 until they have actually purchased their tickets. By this point, the passengers will already have accepted the condition set forth in paragraph 16(a), which provides that "[t]he Carrier shall not be liable to make any refund to passengers in respect of . . . tickets wholly or partly not used by a passenger." Not knowing whether or not that provision is legally enforceable, I assume that the average passenger would accept the risk of having to file suit in Florida in the event of an injury, rather than canceling—without a refund—a planned vacation at the last minute. The fact that the cruise line can reduce its litigation costs, and therefore its liability insurance premiums, by forcing this choice on its passengers does not, in my opinion, suffice to render the provision reasonable.

Even if passengers received prominent notice of the forum-selection clause before they committed the cost of the cruise, I would remain persuaded that the clause was unenforceable under traditional principles of federal admiralty law and is "null and void" under the terms of Limitation of Vessel Owners Liability Act.

Exculpatory clauses in passenger tickets have been around for a long time. These clauses are typically the product of disparate bargaining power between the carrier and the passenger, and they undermine the strong public interest in deterring negligent conduct. For these reasons, courts long before the turn of the century consistently held such clauses unenforceable under federal admiralty law.

The stipulation in the ticket that Carnival Cruise sold to respondents certainly lessens or weakens their ability to recover for the slip and fall incident that occurred off the west coast of Mexico during the cruise that originated and terminated in Los Angeles, California. It is safe to assume that the witnesses—whether other passengers or members of the crew—can be assembled with less expense and inconvenience at a west coast forum than in a Florida court several thousand miles from the scene of the accident.

CASE QUESTIONS

1. Explain where the parties are located and where the accident occurred.

2. What was the nature of the clause, and where was it located?

3. Does it make any difference to the court that this was a consumer and not a business-to-business contract?

4. Is the clause enforceable?

5. What problems does the dissent see in the majority's decision?

CONSIDER . . .

7.4   International Ambassador Programs, Inc., is a Washington-based nonprofit organization that arranges tours and informational visits in foreign countries, including Russia. Archpexpo, once a Soviet state enterprise and now a Russian limited partnership, facilitates and expedites tours such as those sponsored by Ambassador to Russia and the other former Soviet republics.

Archpexpo and Ambassador entered into several agreements relating to tours. An April 1989 agreement provided that "all disputes and differences without recourse to courts of law shall be referred to the arbitration tribunal with the USSR Trade and Industry Chamber for resolution, such resolution acknowledged as final by the parties."

A dispute arose between the parties when Archpexpo alleged that it had not been paid certain fees due, and Ambassador claimed it was entitled to an offset of $20,000 for refunds it had to give to travelers who were dissatisfied with Archpexpo's service.

Archpexpo filed for arbitration, and Ambassador brought suit in federal district court in the United States. Does the federal district court have jurisdiction? Must Ambassador submit to arbitration in the USSR? What if Ambassador had more than one contract with Archpexpo and some of the contracts contained the arbitration clause and some did not? Would Ambassador be required to submit to arbitration then? [*International Ambassador Programs, Inc.* v. *Archpexpo*, 68 F.3d 337 (9th Cir. 1995)]

PROTECTIONS IN INTERNATIONAL COMPETITION

Although trade barriers are coming down and a global marketplace seems to be a reality, there is still much regulation of international competition. Regulation can be found in the forms of antitrust laws, protections for intellectual property, and trade treaties.

Antitrust Laws in the International Marketplace

All U.S. firms are subject to the antitrust laws of the United States, regardless of where their operations and anticompetitive behavior may occur. Firms from other countries operating in the United States or engaging in trade that has a substantial impact in the United States are also subject to U.S. antitrust laws. These firms are not covered under the act of state doctrine because they are not governmental entities and are engaging in commercial activity. For example, Go Video, a U.S. firm from Arizona, brought a successful antitrust suit against Japanese manufacturers for their alleged refusal to deal with the company in its attempt to develop a dual-deck VCR. U.S. courts and antitrust laws had jurisdiction because of the

> **BUSINESS PLANNING TIP**
>
> Businesses should examine all aspects of a country's development before deciding to do business there. The following issues should be researched and deliberated prior to opening operations in another country:
>
> **1.** What is the economic climate?
>
> **2.** What is the government structure?
>
> **3.** What are cultural attitudes about economic development? Are there any ill feelings by indigenous people toward other nations?
>
> **4.** What is the legal structure of the country? What laws exist? How are they made? Are they changed easily?
>
> **5.** How is the court system? Will it provide an appropriate and fair forum for resolution of disputes?
>
> **6.** What experiences have other businesses had in dealing with this nation?

substantial impact the actions of the Japanese manufacturers would have on the VCR market in the United States.

The converse is also true. Firms outside the United States may enjoy the protections and benefits of our antitrust laws and bring suit for violations if it can be established that the violations they are alleging had a substantial impact on trade in the United States.

Review the Export Trading Company Act of 1982:
http://www.law.cornell.edu/uscode/15/4001.html
Visit the Department of Justice:
http://www.usdoj.gov

The Export Trading Company Act of 1982 carved an exception to the antitrust laws for U.S. firms that combine to do business in international markets. Large U.S. firms that would otherwise be prohibited from merging for anticompetitive reasons are permitted to form export trading companies (ETC) for the purpose of participating in international trade. The Justice Department approves applications for ETCs in advance, provided the applicants can demonstrate that the proposed joint venture will not reduce competition in the United States, increase U.S. prices, or cause unfair competition. Thus, companies like Mobil and Exxon are able to work together to explore Siberian oil fields in a combination that would otherwise be prohibited both under the antitrust laws and for purposes of ongoing operations. These combinations are necessary for effective negotiation of large foreign contracts.

Exhibit 7.1 provides a summary of international law principles and doctrines.

EXHIBIT 7.1 The Treaties, Principles, and Statutes of International Law

NAME	PURPOSE
North Atlantic Treaty North Atlantic Treaty Organization (NATO)	Treaty between U.S. and European nations that establishes a deployment of armed forces and security setup in Europe
Foreign Sovereign Immunities Act of 1976	U.S. statute that clarifies the immunity of foreign countries and officials from prosecution for crimes in the United States
Act of state doctrine (expropriation)	Recognition of foreign government's actions as valid; U.S. courts may not be used to challenge another country's actions, even toward U.S. citizens
Foreign Assistance Act of 1962 (Hickenlooper amendment)	Authorization given to president to cut off aid to countries where U.S. citizens' property has been taken by the government or regulated so as to deprive owner of use
Overseas Private Investment Corporation (OPIC)	Federal insurer for U.S. companies' investments in countries with low per capita income
Repatriation	Bringing back to your own country money earned on investments in other countries
Export Trading Company Act of 1982	Antitrust combination exemption for companies joining to compete in international markets
Maastricht Treaty	Agreement that created European Union
General Agreement on Tariffs and Trade (GATT)	Agreement among 100 countries to increase trade by reducing tariffs
North American Free Trade Agreement (NAFTA)	Agreement among United States, Canada, and Mexico that eliminates 65 percent of the tariffs across borders now, with the goal of tariff elimination by 2010

ETHICAL ISSUES 7.1

"You can't be a global player without a presence in the United States." The advice is from James McDermott, president of Keefe, Bruyette & Woods, a consulting firm, and he was speaking of international banking. Many agreed with Mr. McDermott's assessment, including Daiwa Bank of Japan. Daiwa was established in Japan in 1918, and, as of November 2, 1995, was the tenth largest bank in Japan and the twenty-first largest bank in the world. Its 1994 assets were $183.5 billion, and its earnings for 1994 were booked as $1.3 billion. Daiwa set up its U.S. offices with headquarters in New York under the name of Daiwa Bank Trust Company. There were branches and offices of Daiwa Bank Trust in eleven states in the largest U.S. cities. The U.S. division of the bank employed about 400 people.

Toshihide Iguchi was the executive responsible for running the U.S. bank's trading operations. It would be the trading operations that would result in the bank's downfall. The losses in the bank's trading operations began in 1983 but were not entered on the books. Between 1983 and 1995, more than $1 billion in trading losses were not reported. Indeed, the records of the bank were falsified to conceal the losses. Records were also falsified to conceal another $97 million in losses from 1984 to 1987 in bank operations for the Manhattan offices.

Throughout this period, federal regulators had warned Daiwa officials to separate its trading activities from its record-keeping and custody of funds. The functions were never separated.

In July 1995, Mr. Iguchi confessed his wrongdoing to senior management officials in Japan and urged them to buy back some of the Treasury bonds he had sold illegally to cover up the losses. His letter assured the senior management that there was "zero possibility" that federal regulators would discover what

they were doing. In late July, an officer from Japan met with Iguchi in New York and told him to continue the cover-up until Daiwa issued its six-month financials for the period ending September 30, 1995.

But Daiwa officials reported the problems of the U.S. division and Iguchi's activities to Japanese regulators on August 8, 1995. The same report was made to U.S. regulators in Washington, D.C., on September 15, 1995.

In early November 1995, federal and state regulators "deported" Daiwa operations in the United States, requiring that all U.S. operations be shut down. In addition to deportation, the federal government issued a twenty-four–count indictment charging the bank with deception of federal regulators and cover-ups of losses. Fines for the violations could be $1.3 billion.

Iguchi pleaded guilty to trying to conceal the losses. He converted $377 million in securities held to make up the losses. Masahiro Tsuda, the general manager of the New York office, was also named in the indictments.

Takashi Kaiho, Daiwa's president, complained about the criminal charges and vowed to fight them, contending that "blaming Daiwa Bank for thievery and other unauthorized activities makes no sense."

Do you agree? Is it unfair to hold Daiwa accountable? If Daiwa is not responsible for what happened, who is? The term *rogue trader* has been used frequently in financial debacles. Barings Bank, the 200-year-old international bank that collapsed because of derivative trading, claimed its bankruptcy was the result of one trader. What signals and atmosphere allow a rogue trader to operate?

Protections for Intellectual Property

Protections for intellectual property in the international marketplace are constantly undergoing refinements. Worldwide registration for patents, copyrights, and trademarks are goals that are within reach as the mechanisms for administration are being put into place. Details on international protections are found in Chapter 16.

Criminal Law Protections

All persons and businesses present within a country are subject to that nation's regulatory scheme for business as well as to the constraints of the country's criminal code. Compliance with the law is a universal principle of international business operations. Expulsion, fines, penalties, and imprisonment are all remedies available to governments when foreign businesses break the law in a particular nation.

Often, the complexities of international operations produce layers of business organizations throughout the world. These layers are often necessary for individual countries and proper business structure under the law. However, the layers of organizations may provide opportunities for laundering of money, concealment of transactions, and other complex transactions that can often escape regulatory detection for a time. However, the activities are eventually discovered, and countries are cooperating more to be certain the complexities of international business do not conceal illicit activities.

SUMMARY

What laws affect businesses in international trade?

- Foreign Sovereign Immunities Act of 1976
- Foreign Assistance Act of 1962 (Hickenlooper amendment)
- Overseas Private Investment Corporation (OPIC)
- Export Trading Company Act of 1982
- Contracts for the International Sale of Goods (CISG)

What treaties, agreements, practices, and principles affect international business and trade?

- North Atlantic Treaty
- North Atlantic Treaty Organization (NATO)
- Maastricht Treaty
- General Agreement on Tariffs and Trade (GATT)
- North American Free Trade Agreement (NAFTA)
- International Monetary Fund (IMF)
- Duties, quotas, tariffs—controls on prices and quantities of goods by nations with the goal of balancing imports and exports
- Foreign Corrupt Practices Act—controls on means of accessing governments

What principles of international law affect business?

- Sovereign immunity—freedom of one country from being subject to orders from another country
- Expropriation; act of state doctrine—recognition by U.S. courts of the actions of other governments as valid despite noncompliance with traditional U.S. rights and procedures
- Repatriation—returning profits earned in other countries to one's native land
- Conflict of laws—issue as to which country's law applies in international transactions
- Antitrust issues
- *Forum non conveniens*—doctrine requiring dismissal of cases that should be heard in another country's courts

What protections exist in international competition?

- Antitrust laws
- Protections for intellectual property
- Criminal law protections

QUESTIONS AND PROBLEMS

1. Describe the sources of international law.

2. Suppose that the government of Brazil took possession of the cacao farms of a chocolate factory owned by a U.S. firm. What rights would the U.S. factory have? What limits exist on those rights?

3. LaFair Products is a company based in Mexico that manufactures and sells the bonnet type of hair dryer. The hair dryers are marketed in the United States through several catalog merchants who are based in the United States. One of the hair dryers was defective and severely burned Susan Queenan, a resident of North Carolina. Queenan has filed suit against LaFair in federal district court in North Carolina. Does this court have jurisdiction?

4. Suppose that a foreign country is shipping batteries to the United States and, in violation of our antitrust laws, has refused to sell its batteries to retailers who charge below their minimum price. Would the foreign country be subject to prosecution and civil suit for violation of the antitrust laws?

5. United Arab Shipping Company (UASC) is a corporation formed under the laws of Kuwait. Its capital stock is wholly owned by the governments of Kuwait, Saudi Arabia, the United Arab Emirates, Qatar, Iraq, and Bahrain. No single government owned more than 19.33 percent of UASC's shares, and the corporation was created by a treaty among the owner nations.

Three seamen who were injured while working for UASC brought suit against it in federal district court in the United States. UASC maintains it enjoys sovereign immunity. The seamen claim it is a commercial enterprise and not entitled to immunity. Who is correct? [*Mangattu v. M/V IBN Hayyan*, 35 F.3d 205 (5th Cir. 1994)]

6. Smith & Smith, a U.S. computer firm, contracted to install a computer system for Volkswagen, Germany, in the company's headquarters in Berlin. Smith's contract included the following liability limitation: "We are only liable for loss of data which is due to a deliberate action on our part. We are not responsible for lost profits in any event." The contract had no provisions on choice of law. A crash in the Smith & Smith system caused a loss of ninety-two days' worth of financial data. Volkswagen was required to use its auditors to restructure the database at a substantial cost. Smith &

Smith says it did nothing deliberate and is, therefore, not liable. Volkswagen cites German law that mandates protection by sellers against such losses and permits recovery of lost profits. U.S. law would honor the Smith & Smith clause. Which law applies? Why?

7. In 1995, the French passed a law known as *Loi Toubon* that requires contracts in which performance will occur in France to be written in French. What disadvantages for foreign firms do you see in this policy?

8. The European Union has developed a directive on privacy and e-mail. Nations within the EU are permitted to use e-mail for commercial transactions and can exchange information via e-mail. However, businesses from countries outside the EU will not be permitted access to EU business information and EDI systems for contracting purposes unless they can guarantee that there are adequate privacy protections in place for the data transmitted via e-mail. Most legal experts believe the EU privacy directive applies to all forms of transmissions in business, including commercial contracts and ordering information.

What would happen if a business tapped into an EU business and began entering into transactions without an adequate privacy guarantee? Would there be criminal sanctions? Trade sanctions? How does this directive affect international trade with the EU? The EU has provided that trading privileges can be withdrawn from countries with businesses that violate the privacy standards on e-mail information and data transmission. What happens when trading privileges are withdrawn? Is the EU directive a commercial control of trade?

9. Walid Azab Al-Uneizi was an employee of the Ministry of Defense of Kuwait. Liticia Guzel was an employee of the Willard Inter-Continental Hotel in Washington, D.C. One of her duties was restocking minibars in guest rooms. Al-Uneizi approached Miss Guzel outside Rooms 610 and 612 and conferred with her about restocking Room 612. After Miss Guzel had finished restocking Room 612, Al-Uneizi assaulted and raped her. After the rape, Al-Uneizi gave her a Kuwaiti flag pin. Miss Guzel has brought suit against both Al-Uneizi and the Kuwaiti government, who seek a dismissal under the act of state doctrine. Should the case be dismissed against both? [*Guzel v. State of Kuwait*, 818 F. Supp. 6 (1993)]

10. When the Barings Bank bankruptcy occurred in 1995, Mr. Nick Leeson, the trader responsible for the immense losses the bank experienced after heavy derivative investments, fled to Germany. He was brought back to Hong Kong, the site of his trades, for trial. He is a British citizen who was arrested in Germany. Describe all the principles and issues of international law involved in his arrest, return, and eventual trial in Hong Kong.

RESEARCH PROBLEM

Selling Computer Arms Technology

11. IBM entered a guilty plea to selling sixteen computer work stations and a super computer to a Russian nuclear weapons laboratory. The sales occurred in 1996 and 1997 and were completed without IBM's having obtained the necessary federal licenses required to sell computers for military purposes. IBM agreed to pay an $8.5 million fine, and executives with IBM acknowledge that they knew the computers might be used for the building and testing of nuclear weapons.

U.S. officials requested assistance from Russian officials in conducting the investigation but were rebuffed. U.S. officials have requested the return of the computers, but Russian officials have also refused. Russian officials say the U.S. officials promised them the computer hardware in exchange for the Russians signing the Comprehensive Test Ban Treaty. U.S. officials maintain no such promise was made.

Determine the answers to the following questions:
a. Can U.S. officials demand investigatory cooperation?
b. Can U.S. officials demand return of the computers?
c. Can U.S. officials take any action under the Comprehensive Test Ban Treaty?
d. Can IBM still be paid for the computers?

NOTE

1. Some countries do not provide criminal penalties for corporations under their laws and they are required only to provide for substantial civil penalties.

BUSINESS STRATEGY APPLICATION

In this CD application you will be able to see the FCPA statute as well as a company policy for its employees. You will have the chance to determine what is a violation of the FCPA and then develop some guidelines for your company on compliance.

CHAPTER EIGHT

Cyber Law

In Chapter 7 the issue of whether the parties to a contract can agree where and how their disputes will be resolved. You learned there that the parties to a contract could indeed decide up front on the hows, whens, and wheres of their contract disputes. In this chapter, you will study the same issue with the additional wrinkle of "point and click." That is, we now have the question of whether a contract, formed in cyberspace using not signatures but affirmative responses supplied by computer technology and the Internet, is valid and if its clauses are all part of it.

Today, 80 percent of employees have a computer at work and use it as a part of their jobs. Nearly half of the homes in the United States also have a computer. Computers are an integral part of the way we do business and live. They have become tools of commerce.

Business managers, consumers, business students, and even some lawyers worry when they hear the term *cyber law.* Their concern results from not having had a course called "Cyber Law." This chapter was written to allay those fears. While there are certainly new laws governing aspects of using and operating systems that have come to us in this technological era, most people are surprised to learn that the law, with those qualities of flexibility and stability studied in Chapter 1, is quite capable of handling cyberspace issues without significant departure from the basic principles that have applied to all economic revolutions in the past. While the industrial revolution meant more contracts, the basic principles of formation did not change; and, though the increase in sheer numbers of employees required new laws on safety and unions, the basic principles of fairness and disclosure were the purposes of those laws. The basic principles of law and precedent in the form of judicial decisions that have seen businesses through the many economic revolutions of the past still apply. Cyberspace has simply accelerated the pace at which law works to provide stability while fostering innovation in a flexible environment.

This chapter is called "Cyber Law," but its name is more accurately "The Law in Cyberspace." You will not be learning a whole new body of law. You will be learning how the principles of law apply to new ways of doing things. The law still remains the source of justice, and issues in cyberspace still focus on fundamental principles of fairness, protection of property rights, disclosure, and privacy. For example, you still have a right to privacy in your purchases and buying habits. The fact that an e-business can gather that information about you so easily does not change that right.

The purpose of this chapter is not to explore every possible legal issue in cyber law. Rather, its purpose is to acquaint you with the areas of focus in cyber law and provide a framework for analyzing cyberspace legal issues. This chapter answers two simple questions: what are the issues in and what are the laws affecting business in cyberspace? You will explore both new-to-cyberspace laws and how existing laws apply in cyberspace. Not only will you understand the challenges of legal issues in cyberspace, you will gain a more complete appreciation for a legal system so capable of adjusting and absorbing the changes business brings about.

> **It's enough to send Cardinal Richelieu spinning, if not surfing, in his grave.**
> THE ACADEMIE FRANCAISE ON THE POLLUTION OF THE FRENCH LANGUAGE BY THE INVASION OF THE WORLD WIDE WEB (LE WEB)

> **The Internet presents age-old issues with a new face.**
> PROFESSOR TAMARA MADDOX
> *George Mason University*

> **For all the sophisticated work on firewalls, intrusion-detection systems, encryption, and computer security, e-businesses are at risk from a relatively simply technique that's akin to dialing a telephone repeatedly so that everyone else trying to get through will hear a busy signal.**
> BUSINESS WEEK, FEBRUARY 21, 2000

CONSIDER . . .

Steven Caspi, Ronald Jonas, Arden Cone, and Laurel Barrie were all Microsoft Network (MSN) subscribers. Microsoft rolled over their MSN memberships into more expensive plans without their knowledge or permission, a practice condemned by the attorneys general in twenty-one states. When the four objected, Microsoft offered no relief and the four became representatives in a class action suit brought against Microsoft in New Jersey with approximately 1.5 million class members. Microsoft moved to have the complaint dismissed because of a clause that rolled through the screens of members as they signed up by clicking, "I agree." All four had clicked "I agree" to the following clause:

This agreement is governed by the laws of the State of Washington, U.S.A., and you consent to the exclusive jurisdiction and venue of courts in King County, Washington, in all disputes arising out of or relating to your use of MSN or your MSN membership.

Can Microsoft have the case dismissed in New Jersey? Did the MSN customers make a contract over the Internet? Are these Internet contract forum clauses enforceable?

© Eyewire

Visit a cyber law site:
http://www.cyberlaw.com

AN OVERVIEW OF LAW IN CYBERSPACE

Cyber law is best studied when it is broken down into existing areas of law. The laws affecting business in cyberspace fall into the following six categories: tort issues, contract issues, intellectual property issues, criminal violations, constitutional restraints and protections, and securities law issues. Because of the global nature of the Internet, there are also the international issues that have already begun to arise in contract disputes. Under each of these six categories of law are a number of issues. For example, under contracts, there are the formation issues presented in the chapter opening "Consider": When is a contract formed over the Internet? How is a contract formed over the Internet? What are the terms of a contract formed over the Internet? In the area of torts are the issues of privacy and the use of information e-businesses obtain about you through the use of Web sites or the purchase of goods over the Internet. Just the nature of the Internet as a rapid means of international communication creates critical issues in the tort of libel, particularly with regard to damages because the information is spread so quickly. Chat rooms are technologically sophisticated means of transferring damaging and often false information.

The issues in intellectual property law related to cyberspace are no different in substance. We are still concerned with protecting copyrights and patents; however, now our concerns focus on issues such as copying software programs licensed for your employer onto your personal computer or even downloading music through Napster. Is burning CDs simply peer-to-peer file sharing or is it copyright infringement?

Cyber law is not so new. The breakdown of topics for this chapter into the same groups of law covered on a chapter-by-chapter basis in the book is a good indication that the existing body of law is working quite well in resolving issues that arise in cyberspace. Each of the following sections covers the law in cyberspace as it relates to specific topic areas.

TORT ISSUES IN CYBER LAW

Three main tort issues arise because of the use of cyberspace for doing business: privacy, appropriation, and defamation. Remember, for more background on these torts and related issues, refer to the other chapters in the text.

Privacy Issues in Cyber Law

E-Mail and Worker Privacy

Ninety million American workers send 2.8 billion e-mail messages per day or an average of 190 e-mails per worker per day.[1] E-mail is a means of both commercial and personal communication. A cross between the written letter and the telephone call, e-mail does not have the boundaries of either of those forms of communication. A telephone call is a one-time interaction dependent upon the memories of the parties for its recreation. A letter is tangible, but its one-copy existence means that it can be kept private. E-mail exists not only between the sender and receiver; it is also preserved within the computer hard drive, the system in which it is transmitted, and also via any forwarding of the message to others. What may have been intended as a private exchange actually has several backup copies in a system that others can access. The question becomes, Are we entitled to a right to privacy in our e-mail communications? Can the messages themselves be protected from disclosure on the basis of a right to privacy? Do sender and receiver have the same right to privacy? Is reading the e-mail messages of others the intrusion into private affairs? Is the right to privacy waived when the message is forwarded to someone else?

The answers to these questions depend on the expectation of privacy. Did the sender have an expectation of privacy? Do those using e-mail systems have an expectation of privacy? Do employees have an expectation of privacy while using their employers' e-mail systems? The following case, decided by the U.S. Supreme Court, provides a look at the issue of expectation of privacy (with regard to search warrants) when the search is done in a new and highly sophisticated fashion.

CASE 8.1

Kyllo v. *U.S.*
533 U.S. 27 (2001)

Thermal Marijuana Dynamics

FACTS

In 1991 Agent William Elliott of the United States Department of the Interior came to suspect that marijuana was being grown in the home belonging to Danny Kyllo (petitioner), part of a triplex on Rhododendron Drive in Florence, Oregon. Indoor marijuana growth typically requires high-intensity lamps. In order to determine whether an amount of heat was emanating from petitioner's home consistent with the use of such lamps, at 3:20 A.M. on January 16, 1992, Agent Elliott and Dan Haas used an Agema Thermovision 210 thermal imager to scan the triplex.

Thermal imagers detect infrared radiation, which virtually all objects emit but which is not visible to the naked eye. The imager converts radiation into images based on relative warmth—black is cool, white is hot, shades of gray connote relative differences; in that respect, it operates somewhat like a video camera showing heat images.

The scan of Kyllo's home took only a few minutes and was performed from the passenger seat of Agent Elliott's vehicle across the street from the front of the house and also from the street in back of the house. The scan showed that the roof over the garage and a side wall of Kyllo's home were relatively hot compared to the rest of the home and substantially warmer than neighboring homes in the triplex. Agent Elliott concluded that Kyllo was using halide lights to grow marijuana in his house, which indeed he was. Based on tips from informants, utility bills, and the thermal imaging, a Federal Magistrate Judge issued a warrant authorizing a search of Kyllo's home, and the agents found an indoor growing operation involving more than 100 plants. Kyllo was indicted on one count of manufacturing marijuana. Kyllo unsuccessfully moved to suppress the evidence seized from his home and then entered a conditional guilty plea.

The Court of Appeals for the Ninth Circuit remanded the case for an evidentiary hearing regarding the intrusiveness of thermal imaging. On remand the District Court upheld the validity of the warrant that relied in part upon the thermal imaging, and reaffirmed its denial of the motion to suppress. A divided Court of Appeals initially reversed, but that opinion was withdrawn and the panel affirmed. Kyllo appealed.

JUDICIAL OPINION

SCALIA, Justice

This case presents the question whether the use of a thermal-imaging device aimed at a private home from a public street to detect relative amounts of heat within the home constitutes a "search" within the meaning of the Fourth Amendment.

The Fourth Amendment provides that "[t]he right of the people to be secure in their persons, houses, papers, and effects, against unreasonable searches and seizures, shall not be violated." "At the

(continued)

very core" of the Fourth Amendment "stands the right of a man to retreat into his own home and there be free from unreasonable governmental intrusion." With few exceptions, the question whether a warrantless search of a home is reasonable and hence constitutional must be answered no.

On the other hand, the antecedent question of whether or not a Fourth Amendment "search" has occurred is not so simple under our precedent. The permissibility of ordinary visual surveillance of a home used to be clear because, well into the 20th century, our Fourth Amendment jurisprudence was tied to common-law trespass. Visual surveillance was unquestionably lawful because " 'the eye cannot by the laws of England be guilty of a trespass.' " We have since decoupled violation of a person's Fourth Amendment rights from trespassory violation of his property, but the lawfulness of warrantless visual surveillance of a home has still been preserved. "[T]he Fourth Amendment protection of the home has never been extended to require law enforcement officers to shield their eyes when passing by a home on public thoroughfares."

In assessing when a search is not a search, we have applied somewhat in reverse the principle first enunciated in *Katz* v. *United States,* 389 U.S. 347, 88 S.Ct. 507, 19 L.Ed.2d 576 (1967). *Katz* involved eavesdropping by means of an electronic listening device placed on the outside of a telephone booth—a location not within the catalog ("persons, houses, papers, and effects") that the Fourth Amendment protects against unreasonable searches. We held that the Fourth Amendment nonetheless protected *Katz* from the warrantless eavesdropping because he "justifiably relied" upon the privacy of the telephone booth. As Justice Harlan's oft-quoted concurrence described it, a Fourth Amendment search occurs when the government violates a subjective expectation of privacy that society recognizes as reasonable.

We have applied this test in holding that it is not a search for the police to use a pen register at the phone company to determine what numbers were dialed in a private home, and we have applied the test on two different occasions in holding that aerial surveillance of private homes and surrounding areas does not constitute a search.

The present case involves officers on a public street engaged in more than naked-eye surveillance of a home. We have previously reserved judgment as to how much technological enhancement of ordinary perception from such a vantage point, if any, is too much. While we upheld enhanced aerial photography of an industrial complex in *Dow Chemical* [see Chapter 9], we noted that we found "it important that this is not an area immediately adjacent to a private home, where privacy expectations are most heightened, . . ."

It would be foolish to contend that the degree of privacy secured to citizens by the Fourth Amendment has been entirely unaffected by the advance of technology. For example, as the cases discussed above make clear, the technology enabling human flight has exposed to public view (and hence, we have said, to official observation) uncovered portions of the house and its curtilage that once were private. The question we confront today is what limits there are upon this power of technology to shrink the realm of guaranteed privacy.

While it may be difficult to refine *Katz* when the search of areas such as telephone booths, automobiles, or even the curtilage and uncovered portions of residences are at issue, in the case of the search of the interior of homes—the prototypical and hence most commonly litigated area of protected privacy—there is a ready criterion, with roots deep in the common law, of the minimal expectation of privacy that exists, and that is acknowledged to be reasonable. To withdraw protection of this minimum expectation would be to permit police technology to erode the privacy guaranteed by the Fourth Amendment. We think that obtaining by sense-enhancing technology any information regarding the interior of the home that could not otherwise have been obtained without physical "intrusion into a constitutionally protected area," constitutes a search—at least where (as here) the technology in question is not in general public use. This assures preservation of that degree of privacy against government that existed when the Fourth Amendment was adopted. On the basis of this criterion, the information obtained by the thermal imager in this case was the product of a search. The dissent's comparison of the thermal imaging to various circumstances in which outside observers might be able to perceive, without technology, the heat of the home—for example, by observing snowmelt on the roof, is quite irrelevant. The fact that equivalent information could sometimes be obtained by other means does not make lawful the use of means that violate the Fourth Amendment. The police might, for example, learn how many people are in a particular house by setting up year-round surveillance; but that does not make breaking and entering to find out the same information lawful. In any event, on the night of January 16, 1992, no outside observer could have discerned the relative heat of Kyllo's home without thermal imaging.

The Government maintains, however, that the thermal imaging must be upheld because it detected "only heat radiating from the external surface of the house." The dissent makes this its leading point, contending that there is a fundamental difference between what it calls "off-the-wall" observations and "through-the-wall surveillance." But just as a thermal imager captures only heat emanating from a house, so also a powerful directional microphone picks up only sound emanating from a house—and a satellite capable of scanning from many miles away would pick up only visible light emanating from a house. We rejected such a mechanical interpretation of the Fourth Amendment in *Katz,* where the eavesdropping device picked up only sound waves that reached the exterior of the phone booth. Reversing that approach would leave the homeowner at the mercy of advancing technology—including imaging technology that could discern all human activity in the home. While the technology used in the present case was relatively crude, the rule we adopt must take account of more sophisticated systems that are already in use or in development. The dissent's reliance on the distinction between "off-the-wall" and "through-the-wall" observation is entirely incompatible with the dissent's belief that thermal-imaging observations of the intimate details of a home are impermissible.

The Government also contends that the thermal imaging was constitutional because it did not "detect private activities occurring in private areas." It points out that in *Dow Chemical* we observed that the enhanced aerial photography did not reveal any "intimate details." *Dow Chemical,* however, involved enhanced aerial photography of an industrial complex, which does not share the Fourth Amendment sanctity of the home. The Fourth Amendment's protection of the home has never been tied to measurement of the quality or quantity of information.

Limiting the prohibition of thermal imaging to "intimate details" would not only be wrong in principle; it would be impractical in application, failing to provide "a workable accommodation between the needs of law enforcement and the interests protected by the Fourth Amendment." To begin with, there is no necessary connection between the sophistication of the surveillance equipment and the "intimacy" of the details that it observes—which means that one cannot say (and the police cannot be assured) that use of the relatively crude equipment at issue here will always be lawful. The Agema Thermovision 210 might disclose, for example, at what hour each night the lady of the house takes her daily sauna and bath—a detail that many would consider "intimate";

and a much more sophisticated system might detect nothing more intimate than the fact that someone left a closet light on. We could not, in other words, develop a rule approving only that through-the-wall surveillance which identifies objects no smaller than 36 by 36 inches, but would have to develop a jurisprudence specifying which home activities are "intimate" and which are not. And even when (if ever) that jurisprudence were fully developed, no police officer would be able to know in advance whether his through-the-wall surveillance picks up "intimate" details—and thus would be unable to know in advance whether it is constitutional.

We have said that the Fourth Amendment draws "a firm line at the entrance to the house." That line, we think, must be not only firm but also bright—which requires clear specification of those methods of surveillance that require a warrant. While it is certainly possible to conclude from the videotape of the thermal imaging that occurred in this case that no "significant" compromise of the homeowner's privacy has occurred, we must take the long view, from the original meaning of the Fourth Amendment forward.

Where, as here, the Government uses a device that is not in general public use, to explore details of the home that would previously have been unknowable without physical intrusion, the surveillance is a "search" and is presumptively unreasonable without a warrant.

Since we hold the Thermovision imaging to have been an unlawful search, it will remain for the District Court to determine whether, without the evidence it provided, the search warrant issued in this case was supported by probable cause—and if not, whether there is any other basis for supporting admission of the evidence that the search pursuant to the warrant produced.

Reversed.

CASE QUESTIONS

1. Describe how the federal agents were able to obtain a warrant to search Kyllo's home.

2. What is the general rule on searches of the home?

3. What does the court see as the difference between thermal scanning and observing patches of snow on a roof with some areas showing more melting than others?

4. Was the use of thermal scanning a search? Was it an invasion of privacy?

5. What does the court say about the issue of the method of invasion of privacy?

For more information on technology developing in this field, visit:
http://www.nlectc.org/techproj

CONSIDER...

8.1   Based on the decision in *Kyllo*, do you think that a warrant would be necessary to obtain your e-mails sent over your America Online server from your home? Why, or why not?

As the *Kyllo* case illustrates, the law already exists to handle the question of invasion of privacy. The only issue that courts continue to resolve is whether some new technology for invading privacy somehow can evade the standards for protection of privacy or whether, given technology, there is an expectation of privacy.

The tort of invasion of privacy, or intrusion into private affairs, is as applicable to the issues of privacy in e-mail and Internet account information as it was when telephone service to private homes was first made available. The fact that the phone company could listen in to conversations did not mean it was entitled to do so. Privacy affords protection from both physical and technological invasion. For example, the Federal Trade Commission recently ruled that the use of information about consumers' purchasing history and activity cannot be used without their permission, even when that information was obtained over the Internet. In other words, the source of the information is not the issue; its use and disclosure, a breach of their right to privacy, is.

Whether there has been a tortious invasion of privacy with regard to someone's e-mail depends on the nature of the e-mail system used for the message that is revealed to others. Employers have a right of access to their employees' e-mail. The courts have been consistent in their rulings that employees do not have an expectation of privacy in their employers' e-mail systems. To be certain that employees understand this limitation on privacy at work, most employers provide their employees with notice about the e-mail system and that all e-mail is subject to review. However, most courts have also held that the lack of notice does not mean that the employee has an expectation of privacy. Any messages sent or received on an employer's e-mail system can be retrieved and read by the employer, even those messages of a personal nature. Nearly 70 percent of all mid- to large-size firms do monitor employee's e-mail, and 84 percent of those firms tell their employees they will be monitoring their e-mails.[2] The following case deals with an issue of termination over an employee's e-mails that the boss read.

CASE 8.2

Smyth v. Pillsbury Co.
914 F. Supp. 97 (E.D. Pa. 1996)

Reading My E-Mail? Does My Boss Dare?

FACTS

Michael Smyth (plaintiff) worked at Pillsbury (defendant). Pillsbury's e-mail system was used for both intracompany and intercompany communication among and between employ- ees and suppliers, customers, and others outside the company. Pillsbury repeatedly assured its employees, including Mr. Smyth, that all e-mail communications would remain confidential and privileged. Pillsbury also assured its employees that e-mail communications could not be intercepted and used against employees as grounds for termination or reprimand.

In October 1994, Mr. Smyth received e-mail communications from his supervisor over Pillsbury's e-mail system on his computer at home. Smyth responded and exchanged e-mails with his supervisor. Pillsbury employees did read the e-mail exchange. The e-mails concerned sales management and contained threats to "kill the backstabbing bastards" and referred to the planned Holiday party as the "Jim Jones Koolaid affair."

As a result of what Mr. Smyth said, which Pillsbury executives called "inappropriate and unprofessional," he was terminated. Mr. Smyth sued for invasion of privacy. Pillsbury moved to have Mr. Smyth's complaint dismissed.

JUDICIAL OPINION

WEINER, District Judge

In this diversity action, plaintiff, an at-will employee, claims he was wrongfully discharged from his position as a regional operations manager by the defendant.

A claim may be dismissed under Fed.R.Civ.P. 12(b)(6) only if the plaintiff can prove no set of facts in support of the claim that would entitle him to relief. The reviewing court must consider only those facts alleged in the Complaint and accept all of the allegations as true. Applying this standard, we find that plaintiff has failed to state a claim upon which relief can be granted.

As a general rule, Pennsylvania law does not provide a common law cause of action for the wrongful discharge of an at-will employee such as plaintiff. Pennsylvania is an employment at-will jurisdiction and an employer "may discharge an employee with or without cause, at pleasure, unless restrained by some contract."

However, in the most limited of circumstances, exceptions have been recognized where discharge of an at-will employee threatens or violates a clear mandate of public policy. A "clear mandate" of public policy must be of a type that "strikes at the heart of a citizen's social right, duties and responsibilities." This recognized public policy exception is an especially narrow one. To date, the Pennsylvania Superior Court has only recognized three such exceptions.

First, an employee may not be fired for serving on jury duty. Second, an employer may not deny employment to a person with a prior conviction. And finally, an employee may not be fired for reporting violations of federal regulations to the Nuclear Regulatory Commission. [A] public policy exception must be clearly defined. The sources of public policy can be found in "legislation, administrative rules, regulation, or decision; and judicial decisions. . . . Absent legislation, the judiciary must define the cause of action in case by case determinations."

Plaintiff claims that his termination was in violation of "public policy which precludes an employer from terminating an employee in violation of the employee's right to privacy as embodied in Pennsylvania common law." In support for this proposition, plaintiff directs our attention to a decision by our Court of Appeals in *Borse* v. *Piece Goods Shop, Inc.*, 963 F.2d 611 (3d Cir.1992). In *Borse*, the plaintiff sued her employer alleging wrongful discharge as a result of her refusal to submit to urinalysis screening and personal property searches at her work place pursuant to the employer's drug and alcohol policy. After rejecting plaintiff's argument that the employer's drug and alcohol program violated public policy encompassed in the United States and Pennsylvania Constitutions, our Court of Appeals stated "our review of Pennsylvania law reveals other evidence of a public policy that may, under certain circumstances, give rise to a wrongful discharge action related to urinalysis or to personal property searches. Specifically, we refer to the Pennsylvania common law regarding tortious invasion of privacy."

The Court of Appeals in *Borse* observed that one of the torts which Pennsylvania recognizes as encompassing an action for invasion of privacy is the tort of "intrusion upon seclusion." As noted by the Court of Appeals, the Restatement (Second) of Torts defines the tort as follows:

One who intentionally intrudes, physically or otherwise, upon the solitude or seclusion of another or his private affairs or concerns, is subject to liability to the other for invasion of his privacy, if the intrusion would be highly offensive to a reasonable person. Restatement (Second) of Torts § 652B.

Liability only attaches when the "intrusion is substantial and would be highly offensive to the 'ordinary reasonable person.' " [quotes as in original] Although the Court of Appeals in *Borse* observed that "[t]he Pennsylvania courts have not had occasion to consider whether a discharge related to an employer's tortious invasion of an employee's privacy violates public policy," the Court of Appeals

(continued)

predicted that in any claim where the employee claimed that his discharge related to an invasion of his privacy "the Pennsylvania Supreme Court would examine the facts and circumstances surrounding the alleged invasion of privacy. If the court determined that the discharge was related to a substantial and highly offensive invasion of the employee's privacy, [the Court of Appeals] believe[d] that it would conclude that the discharge violated public policy." In determining whether an alleged invasion of privacy is substantial and highly offensive to a reasonable person, the Court of Appeals predicted that Pennsylvania would adopt a balancing test which balances the employee's privacy interest against the employer's interest in maintaining a drug-free workplace. Because the Court of Appeals in *Borse* could "envision at least two ways in which an employer's drug and alcohol program might violate the public policy protecting individuals from tortious invasion of privacy by private actors," the Court vacated the district court's order dismissing the plaintiff's complaint and remanded the case to the district court with directions to grant *Borse* leave to amend the Complaint to allege how the defendant's drug and alcohol program violates her right to privacy.

Applying the Restatement definition of the tort of intrusion upon seclusion to the facts and circumstances of the case *sub judice,* we find that plaintiff has failed to state a claim upon which relief can be granted. In the first instance, unlike urinalysis and personal property searches, we do not find a reasonable expectation of privacy in e-mail communications voluntarily made by an employee to his supervisor over the company e-mail system notwithstanding any assurances that such communications would not be intercepted by management. Once plaintiff communicated the alleged unprofessional comments to a second person (his supervisor) over an e-mail system which was apparently utilized by the entire company, any reasonable expectation of privacy was lost. Significantly, the defendant did not require plaintiff, as in the case of an [sic] urinalysis or personal property search to disclose any personal information about himself. Rather, plaintiff voluntarily communicated the alleged unprofessional comments over the company e-mail system. We find no privacy interests in such communications.

In the second instance, even if we found that an employee had a reasonable expectation of privacy in the contents of his e-mail communications over the company e-mail system, we do not find that a reasonable person would consider the defendant's interception of these communications to be a substantial and highly offensive invasion of his privacy. Again, we note that by intercepting such communications, the company is not, as in the case of urinalysis or personal property searches, requiring the employee to disclose any personal information about himself or invading the employee's person or personal effects. Moreover, the company's interest in preventing inappropriate and unprofessional comments or even illegal activity over its e-mail system outweighs any privacy interest the employee may have in those comments.

In sum, we find that the defendant's actions did not tortiously invade the plaintiff's privacy and, therefore, did not violate public policy. As a result, the motion to dismiss is granted.

CASE QUESTIONS

1. What was Pillsbury's policy with regard to e-mails?

2. How were the messages with Smyth's supervisor sent?

3. Is there a public policy interest in protecting Smyth's privacy?

4. Did the promises by Pillsbury regarding e-mail make any difference to the court?

5. What should employees learn from this decision?

ETHICAL ISSUES 8.1

What do you think of Pillsbury's promise regarding privacy that it later ignored? Was there a breach of ethics in company officials not complying with the promises made to employees? Would it be better to change the policy? Is it a breach of ethics to monitor employees' e-mails?

Re: How Employees Use Their Computers at Work

The American Society of Chartered Life Underwriters sponsored another survey of ethics and technology. Forty-five percent of all employees say they have engaged in one or more unethical or illegal actions in the past year using technology. The following are the types of unethical acts and the percentage of employees surveyed who say they did it in the last year:

- 4 percent sabotaged the company system or data.
- 5 percent visited pornographic Web sites using office equipment.

- 19 percent created a dangerous driving situation using new technology.
- 11 percent used office equipment to search for another job.
- 13 percent used office equipment for shopping on the Internet.
- 19 percent used office equipment to help a child or spouse with schoolwork.
- 29 percent used the company e-mail for personal reasons.

Which of the preceding do you think are legal? Do you think they are ethical? Why, or why not?

E-Mail Privacy and Statutory Protections

Employers have access to employee e-mail and can monitor; but is there a right to privacy in other e-mail systems that can be "hacked" into and read by others? In this type of activity, there may be some statutory protections. The **Electronic Communications Privacy Act** (ECPA) of 1986 prohibits the interception of "live" communications such as using a listening device to intercept a telephone conversation. The only issue for resolution is whether e-mail is "live" communication or stored information and whether the act is applicable.

A second statutory protection on privacy issues in e-mail is the use of information that businesses and Web sites glean from their users. For example, if you use Amazon.com's Web site to purchase books, Amazon.com knows your reading interests, types of purchases, and amount of purchases. If you buy gardening books on a regular basis, Amazon.com could take your name together with other frequent gardening book purchasers and sell that list to firms selling various items used in gardening. Such a targeted list is a very valuable marketing tool for gardening-type merchants and a potential source of income for Amazon.com. The issue is whether Amazon.com has the right to communicate that information about you—obtained through your use of a Web site for book purchases—to others for their use.

BUSINESS PLANNING TIP

Employers probably do need to monitor employee e-mails in order to protect themselves from liability. For example, both the *New York Times* and the U.S. Navy uncovered sexually suggestive e-mails among and between their employees. The presence of such e-mail can be part of a Title VII sexual harassment via employment atmosphere of harassment (see Chapter 20). Sexually suggestive e-mail circulating on e-mail systems can create an atmosphere of harassment. For example, one case involving e-mail and sexual harassment involved the circulation of a joke entitled: Why Beer Is Better than Women.

Because liability results, employers need to provide warnings to employees and monitor to be certain that e-mails are not creating an atmosphere of harassment.

One of the lessons of cyberspace already discussed in Chapter 4 is that not only is e-mail not private for employees, it is not private for the company and is completely discoverable if the company is a party to litigation. All of the jokes, correspondence, and other information employees put in their e-mail can be reviewed by opponents in litigation.

While cyberspace has presented many legal difficulties for courts and businesses, the technology that created cyberspace has also developed solutions. Many companies are incorporating systems that automatically destroy e-mails after a selected period of time. The idea is to destroy the electronic trail of e-mail messages. Companies offering such technology have their own Web sites:

© Wolfgang Kaehler/CORBIS

> http://www.authentica.com
> http://www.disappearinginc.com

Microsoft has taken the consumer's desire for privacy over the Internet and developed the Platform for Privacy (P3P), a program that lets consumers choose the amount of privacy they want when they use various Internet sites. AOL, Time Warner, and IBM have all agreed to make their sites P3P compatible. The program would save these companies from the additional expense of steps in their programs that are required to allow consumers to choose their privacy protection. Such a program would, however—as competitors have noted to Congress, the Justice Department, and the Federal Trade Commission—give Microsoft a dominant position in the Internet market. Microsoft has used knowledge of technology and the law as it applies to privacy and consumers to develop a product and a potential market edge.

Source: Glenn R. Simpson, "The Battle Over Web Privacy," *Wall Street Journal*, 21 March 2001, B1, B4.

While the Internet makes collection of information easier, this issue of consumer privacy with regard to purchasing habits is not new and is certainly not peculiar to cyberspace commerce. Credit card companies are already restricted in the use and sale of information they can gather through the spending habits of their customers. Credit card customers have the right to restrict the use of information about them, including simply the sales of lists with their names and addresses. Cyberspace companies must follow the same rules and obtain permission from their customers to use information about them or compile their information into marketing lists. While cyberspace companies obtain permission by a "point-and-click" technology, they are still complying with the same laws and following the same protections afforded consumers under existing laws that were written with credit card companies in mind.

The Tort of Appropriation in Cyberspace

Appropriation is the tort of taking of an image, likeness, or name and then using it, without permission, for commercial advantage (see Chapter 10 for more information). Use of a name or image without permission, whether in a newspaper or in cyberspace, is still the tort of appropriation. For example, a screen-saver program that uses a likeness of Richard, the million-dollar winner on CBS television's program *Survivor* is the tort of appropriation. His likeness, in cartoon form for the *Conniver* screen-saver program with the *Survivor* logo, without his permission, constitutes appropriation.

Defamation in Cyberspace

The only difference between **defamation** (see Chapter 10 for more details) in cyberspace and defamation in a newspaper is that the defamation in cyberspace may reach more people more quickly and perhaps increase the level of damages.

The elements of defamation remain the same: that someone wrote or said something false that portrayed you in a bad light and that what was written or said was heard or read by others and understood. Chat rooms do not require any changes in the elements of defamation. Chat rooms only increase the likelihood that someone read and understood the defamatory remarks.

Perhaps one of the most costly cases of defamation occurred in an investor chat room. Mark S. Jakob was a day trader who had lost $100,000 in August 2000 through his poor predictions on how Emulex, Inc., stock options would perform. Desperate to recoup his losses, Mr. Jakob posted a fake press release on the Internet via a chat room that Emulex, Inc.'s earnings were overstated and that its CEO would resign. Various Web sites picked up the press release, and the impact was instantaneous. Emulex shareholders lost $2.5 billion in value before trading was stopped when company officials were able to convince the exchanges that the press release was phony. Mr. Jakob, however, was able to net $240,000 during the trading frenzy following his fake press release.[3] Mr. Jakob's statements about earnings and the resignation of the CEO constituted defamation. Damages for the defamation would be quite easy to establish because of the immediate and radical decline in the company's stock value, directly caused by frenetic trades made immediately following the posting of the press release. For more information on the issues surrounding securities trading and "pump and dump," refer to Chapter 22.

One issue that arises in cases such as the Jakob/Emulex matter is whether outsiders can require servers or companies to disclose the identity of those who are posting information. For example, can companies demand that servers provide information about account holders who have posted damaging information, as Mr. Jakob did, on Web sites and chat rooms? In one situation, a company did ask Yahoo! to reveal the identity of "Aquacool_2000," the screen name for someone who had posted false and misleading information about the company. Yahoo! did reveal the identity of Aquacool, and he then filed a multimillion dollar invasion of privacy suit against Yahoo.[4]

These types of disclosures are disclosures in a civil sense. Remember the earlier discussion on technology and searches by law enforcement agents and the *Kyllo* case. Revealing account holder information pursuant to a private request by a company is an issue of invasion of privacy. However, server companies have no choice when such information is requested pursuant to a valid warrant from a law enforcement agency. However, as noted, the information for the warrant must also be obtained in a legal way that does not violate Fourth Amendment privacy protection. For more information on warrants and the Fourth Amendment, see Chapter 9. For more information on defamation, see Chapter 10.

Trespass in Cyberspace

While the notion of property may be somewhat more complex, the courts have already grappled with the issues of protecting Web sites and servers as a form of property. Those using these "cyberspace facilities" can be held liable for trespass, just as if they had used a company's headquarters without permission for a meeting or soliciting business on the property. The following case is one of the first on the issue of trespass in cyberspace.

CASE 8.3

CompuServe Incorporated v. *Cyber Promotions, Inc.*
962 F.Supp. 1015 (S.D. Ohio 1997)

If You've Got Mail, You Need Our Permission to Send It

FACTS

CompuServe Incorporated ("CompuServe") (plaintiff) is one of the major national commercial online computer services. It operates a computer communication service through a proprietary nationwide computer network. In addition to allowing access to the extensive content available within its own proprietary network, CompuServe also provides its subscribers with a link to the much larger resources of the Internet. This allows its subscribers to send and receive electronic messages, known as "e-mail," by the Internet. Cyber Promotions, Inc., and its president Sanford Wallace (defendants) are in the business of sending unsolicited e-mail advertisements on behalf of themselves and their clients to hundreds of thousands of Internet users, many of whom are CompuServe subscribers. CompuServe has notified Cyber Promotions that it cannot use CompuServe's computer equipment to process and store the unsolicited e-mail and has requested that Cyber Promotions terminate the practice. Instead, Cyber Promotions has sent an increasing volume of e-mail solicitations to CompuServe subscribers. CompuServe has attempted to employ technological means to block the flow of the e-mail transmissions to its computer equipment, but to no avail.

CompuServe moved for a preliminary injunction which would extend the duration of the temporary restraining order issued earlier.

JUDICIAL OPINION

GRAHAM, District Judge
This case presents novel issues regarding the commercial use of the Internet, specifically the right of an online computer service to prevent a commercial enterprise from sending unsolicited electronic mail advertising to its subscribers. For the reasons which follow, this Court holds that where defendants engaged in a course of conduct of transmitting a substantial volume of electronic data in the form of unsolicited e-mail to plaintiff's proprietary computer equipment, where defendants continued such practice after repeated demands to cease and desist, and where defendants deliberately evaded plaintiff's affirmative efforts to protect its computer equipment from such use, plaintiff has a viable claim for trespass to personal property and is entitled to injunctive relief to protect its property.

[T]here is no per-message charge to send electronic messages over the Internet and such messages usually reach their destination within minutes. Thus electronic mail provides an opportunity to reach a wide audience quickly and at almost no cost to the sender. It is not surprising therefore that some companies, like defendant Cyber Promotions, Inc., have begun using the Internet to distribute advertisements by sending the same unsolicited commercial message to hundreds of thousands of Internet users at once. Defendants refer to this as "bulk e-mail," while plaintiff refers to it as "junk e-mail." In the vernacular of the Internet, unsolicited e-mail advertising is sometimes referred to pejoratively as "spam."*

CompuServe subscribers use CompuServe's domain name "CompuServe.com" together with their own unique alpha-numeric identifier to form a distinctive e-mail mailing address. That address may be used by the subscriber to exchange electronic mail with any one of tens of millions of other Internet users who have electronic mail capability. E-mail sent to CompuServe subscribers is processed and stored on CompuServe's proprietary computer equipment. Thereafter, it becomes accessible to CompuServe's subscribers, who can access CompuServe's equipment and electronically retrieve those messages.

Over the past several months, CompuServe has received many complaints from subscribers threatening to discontinue their subscription unless CompuServe prohibits electronic mass mailers from using its equipment to send unsolicited advertisements. CompuServe asserts that the volume of messages generated by such mass mailings places a significant burden on its equipment which has finite processing and storage capacity. CompuServe receives no payment from the mass mailers for processing their unsolicited advertising. However, CompuServe's subscribers pay for their access to CompuServe's services in increments of time and thus the process of accessing, reviewing and discarding unsolicited e-mail costs them money, which is one of the reasons for their complaints. CompuServe has notified defendants that they are prohibited from using its proprietary computer equipment to process and store unsolicited e-mail and has requested them to cease and desist from sending unsolicited e-mail to its subscribers. Nonetheless, defendants have sent an increasing volume of e-mail solicitations to CompuServe subscribers.

In an effort to shield its equipment from defendants' bulk e-mail, CompuServe has implemented software programs designed to screen out the messages and block their receipt. In response, defendants have modified their equipment and the messages they send in such a fashion as to circumvent CompuServe's screening software. Allegedly, defendants have been able to conceal the true origin of their messages by falsifying the point-of-origin information contained in the header of the electronic messages. Defendants have removed the "sender" information in the header of their messages and replaced it with another address. Also, defendants have developed the capability of configuring their computer servers to conceal their true domain name and appear on the Internet as another computer, further concealing the true origin of the messages. By manipulating this data, defendants have been able to continue sending messages to CompuServe's equipment in spite of CompuServe's protests and protective efforts.

*This term is derived from a skit performed on the British television show Monty Python's Flying Circus, in which the word "spam" is repeated to the point of absurdity in a restaurant menu.

Trespass to chattels has evolved from its original common law application, concerning primarily the asportation of another's tangible property, to include the unauthorized use of personal property. Trespass to chattels survives today, in other words, largely as a little brother of conversion. The scope of an action for conversion recognized in Ohio may embrace the facts in the instant case. The Supreme Court of Ohio established the definition of conversion under Ohio law in *Baltimore & O.R. Co.* v. *O'Donnell*, 49 Ohio St. 489, 32 N.E. 476, 478 (1892) by stating that:

[I]n order to constitute a conversion, it was not necessary that there should have been an actual appropriation of the property by the defendant to its own use and benefit. It might arise from the exercise of a dominion over it in exclusion of the rights of the owner, or withholding it from his possession under a claim inconsistent with his rights. If one takes the property of another, for a temporary purpose only, in disregard of the owner's right, it is a conversion. Either a wrongful taking, an assumption of ownership, an illegal use or misuse, or a wrongful detention of chattels will constitute a conversion.

The Restatement § 217(b) states that a trespass to chattel may be committed by intentionally using or intermeddling with the chattel in possession of another. Electronic signals generated and sent by computer have been held to be sufficiently physically tangible to support a trespass cause of action.

Defendants, citing Restatement (Second) of Torts § 221, which defines "dispossession," assert that not every interference with the personal property of another is actionable and that physical dispossession or substantial interference with the chattel is required. Defendants then argue that they did not, in this case, physically dispossess plaintiff of its equipment or substantially interfere with it. An interference resulting in physical dispossession is just one circumstance under which a defendant can be found liable.

An unprivileged use or other intermeddling with a chattel which results in actual impairment of its physical condition, quality or value to the possessor makes the actor liable for the loss thus caused. In the great majority of cases, the actor's intermeddling with the chattel impairs the value of it to the possessor, as distinguished from the mere affront to his dignity as possessor, only by some impairment of the physical condition of the chattel.

In the present case, any value CompuServe realizes from its computer equipment is wholly derived from the extent to which that equipment can serve its subscriber base. Michael Mangino, a software developer for CompuServe who monitors its

(continued)

mail processing computer equipment, states by affidavit that handling the enormous volume of mass mailings that CompuServe receives places a tremendous burden on its equipment. Defendants' more recent practice of evading CompuServe's filters by disguising the origin of their messages commandeers even more computer resources because CompuServe's computers are forced to store undeliverable e-mail messages and labor in vain to return the messages to an address that does not exist. To the extent that defendants' multitudinous electronic mailings demand the disk space and drain the processing power of plaintiff's computer equipment, those resources are not available to serve CompuServe subscribers. Therefore, the value of that equipment to CompuServe is diminished even though it is not physically damaged by defendants' conduct.

Plaintiff asserts that defendants' messages are largely unwanted by its subscribers, who pay incrementally to access their e-mail, read it, and discard it. Also, the receipt of a bundle of unsolicited messages at once can require the subscriber to sift through, at his expense, all of the messages in order to find the ones he wanted or expected to receive. These inconveniences decrease the utility of CompuServe's e-mail service and are the foremost subject in recent complaints from CompuServe subscribers. Patrick Hole, a customer service manager for plaintiff, states by affidavit that in November 1996 CompuServe received approximately 9,970 e-mail complaints from subscribers about junk e-mail, a figure up from approximately two hundred complaints the previous year. Approximately fifty such complaints per day specifically reference defendants. Defendants contend that CompuServe subscribers are provided with a simple procedure to remove themselves from the mailing list. However, the removal procedure must be performed by the e-mail recipient at his expense, and some CompuServe subscribers complain that the procedure is inadequate and ineffectual.

Many subscribers have terminated their accounts specifically because of the unwanted receipt of bulk e-mail messages. Defendants' intrusions into CompuServe's computer systems, insofar as they harm plaintiff's business reputation and goodwill with its customers, are actionable.

[O]ne who intentionally intermeddles with another's chattel is subject to liability only if his intermeddling is harmful to the possessor's materially valuable interest in the physical condition, quality, or value of the chattel, or if the possessor is deprived of the use of the chattel for a substantial time, or some other legally protected interest of the possessor is affected. Sufficient legal protection of the possessor's interest in the mere inviolability of his chattel is afforded by his privilege to use reasonable force to protect his possession against even harmless interference.

Plaintiff CompuServe has attempted to exercise this privilege to protect its computer systems. However, defendants' persistent affirmative efforts to evade plaintiff's security measures have circumvented any protection those self-help measures might have provided. In this case CompuServe has alleged and supported by affidavit that it has suffered several types of injury as a result of defendants' conduct. The foregoing discussion simply underscores that the damage sustained by plaintiff is sufficient to sustain an action for trespass to chattels.

Defendants argue that plaintiff made the business decision to connect to the Internet and that therefore it cannot now successfully maintain an action for trespass to chattels. Their argument is analogous to the argument that because an establishment invites the public to enter its property for business purposes, it cannot later restrict or revoke access to that property, a proposition which is erroneous.

Further, CompuServe expressly limits the consent it grants to Internet users to send e-mail to its proprietary computer systems by denying unauthorized parties the use of CompuServe equipment to send unsolicited electronic mail messages. [Its limited consent follows:]

CompuServe is a private online and communications services company. CompuServe does not permit its facilities to be used by unauthorized parties to process and store unsolicited e-mail. If an unauthorized party attempts to send unsolicited messages to e-mail addresses on a CompuServe service, CompuServe will take appropriate action to attempt to prevent those messages from being processed by CompuServe. Violations of CompuServe's policy prohibiting unsolicited e-mail should be reported to. . . .

Defendants Cyber Promotions, Inc., and its president Sanford Wallace have used plaintiff's equipment in a fashion that exceeds that consent. The use of personal property exceeding consent is a trespass. It is arguable that CompuServe's policy statement, insofar as it may serve as a limitation upon the scope of its consent to the use of its computer equipment, may be insufficiently communicated to potential third-party users when it is merely posted at some location on the network. However, in the present case the record indicates that defendants were actually notified that they were using CompuServe's equipment in an unacceptable manner. To prove that a would-be trespasser acted with the intent required to support liability in tort it is crucial that defendant be placed on notice that he is trespassing.

In response to the trespass claim, defendants argue that they have the right to continue to send unsolicited commercial e-mail to plaintiff's computer systems under the First Amendment to the United States Constitution. The First Amendment states that "Congress shall make no law respecting an establishment of religion, or prohibiting the free exercise thereof; or abridging the freedom of speech, or of the press." The United States Supreme Court has recognized that "the constitutional guarantee of free speech is a guarantee only against abridgement by government, federal or state."

Very recently, in an action filed by Cyber Promotions, Inc., against America Online, Inc., ("AOL") the United States District Court for the Eastern District of Pennsylvania held that AOL, a company selling services that are similar to those of CompuServe, is private actor. *Cyber Promotions, Inc.* v. *American Online, Inc.*, 948 F.Supp. 436, 443–44 (E.D.Pa.1996). That case involved the question of whether Cyber Promotions had the First Amendment right to send unobstructed e-mail to AOL subscribers. The court held that Cyber Promotions had no such right.

This Court agrees with the conclusions reached by the United States District Court for the Eastern District of Pennsylvania. In the present action, CompuServe is a private company. Moreover, the mere judicial enforcement of neutral trespass laws by the private owner of property does not alone render it a state actor.

Defendants in the present action have adequate alternative means of communication available to them. Not only are they free to send e-mail advertisements to those on the Internet who do not use CompuServe accounts, but they can communicate to CompuServe subscribers as well through online bulletin boards, Web page advertisements, or facsimile transmissions, as well as through more conventional means such as the U.S. mail or telemarketing. Defendants' contention, referring to the low cost of the electronic mail medium, that there are no adequate alternative means of communication is unpersuasive.

Defendants' intentional use of plaintiff's proprietary computer equipment exceeds plaintiff's consent and, indeed, continued after repeated demands that defendants cease. Such use is an actionable trespass to plaintiff's chattel. The First Amendment to the United States Constitution provides no defense for such conduct.

Injunction granted.

CASE QUESTIONS

1. What is Cyber Promotions doing to get its advertisements to Internet users?

2. What happens to CompuServe as a result of this use?

3. Is there a trespass? How does the court deal with the fact that there is no actual physical contact?

4. What does the court conclude about Cyber Promotions' arguments on the First Amendment?

5. Is CompuServe entitled to an injunction?

CONSIDER...

8.2 Intel filed suit against Kourosh Hamidi because on six occasions during 1996, 1997, and 1998, Mr. Hamidi sent e-mail messages concerning Intel employment practices to over 30,000 Intel employees at their e-mail addresses on Intel's proprietary computer system. Intel has requested that Hamidi stop sending the messages, but Hamidi has refused and has employed surreptitious means to circumvent Intel's efforts to block entry of his messages into Intel's system.

Intel's e-mail system is part of its general proprietary computer system affording access to the Internet. The e-mail system is dedicated for use in conducting business, including communications between Intel employees and its customers and vendors. Employee e-mail addresses are not published for use outside company business. Hamidi has been using an outdated employee e-mail address list not released for public use.

Reasonable personal use of the e-mail access to the Internet by employees is permitted but is subject to various restrictions, and communications are expressly not private. The company guidelines regarding e-mail Internet and computer use expressly provide that employees have no proprietary interest in any part of the system or its use.

The intrusion by Hamidi into the Intel e-mail system has resulted in the expenditure of company resources to seek to block his "mailings" and to address employee concerns about the mailings. Given Hamidi's evasive techniques to avoid blocking, the self-help remedy available to Intel is ineffective.

Is Intel entitled to an injunction against Hamidi? [*Intel Corp.* v. *Hamidi*, 1999 WL 450944 (Cal.Super.1999)]

CONTRACT LAW IN CYBERSPACE

Formation Issues

Visit Georgetown's cyberspace law center:
http://www.cli.org

Formation of contracts in cyberspace is the culmination of over two decades of effort by businesses to form contracts in an efficient manner. The increasing technology available to businesses for communications has enabled them to move from complicated supply chain distribution systems that involved manufacturers, wholesalers, distributors, and eventually the customers to **business-to-business (B2B) transactions** where there is direct contact between manufacturers and customers. Under business's supply chain twenty years ago, Wal-Mart would have placed an order through a distributor when its supply of Huggies diapers was running low. Now Procter & Gamble and Wal-Mart have linked computers, and Procter & Gamble knows Wal-Mart's inventory and sales and knows exactly when to send Huggies and which stores need them.

This efficient means of orders and deliveries has evolved as technology has. Speed, direct communication, and simplicity have driven the reforms in contract formation. Twenty years ago, businesses negotiated contracts by sending drafts of agreements back and forth through the mails. With the advent of overnight delivery service, businesses were able to speed up the negotiation processes with contract proposals being sent overnight. The fax machine—or telefax, as it was originally known—made for even faster negotiations and exchanges of drafts of contracts. However, the desire for less paper was still there. Paperless contracts actually have existed for some time in B2B transactions because of **electronic digital interchange (EDI)**. EDI has been such an integral part of business that companies using EDI actually have a set of contract formation guidelines that they follow. EDI was the forerunner of today's Internet contracting, and its concept was simple. EDI was the electronic exchange of business forms. Buyers sent purchase orders, and sellers sent receipts by computer.[5] Today, at least one high-tech company specializes in software that lets companies combine their EDI capability with the Internet in order to form contracts.

EDI still had transmission issues and the problems with system capability and interchanges. E-mail and the ability to attach documents have provided greater clarity in document appearance and ease of transmission. In cyberspace, businesses have found both the speed and paperless nirvana they sought for contract formation.

However, the law was not quite ready for the new formation scenario businesses had created. How do we decide when a contract is formed? Do we still require signatures? What constitutes a signature in cyberspace? Businesses were ready to embrace a form of communication for negotiating contracts that the law had not anticipated and for which there were not yet definitive answers.

The same laws that apply when a contract is formed in a business office govern the formation of contracts in cyberspace. Was there an offer and acceptance? When did those two requirements come together? Some issues that arise in contract formation in the new economy are, for example, whether a contract is formed when someone downloads a program from the Internet. He may have paid for the program by credit card and simply downloaded it at his computer. Does the click of the mouse accepting the program mean that he has accepted all the terms of the contract? How does the seller of the program make sure that the buyer is aware of all the terms in the contract that governs the sale of the program? Can the click of the mouse constitute a signature for purposes of contracting? Is "point and click" enough to form a contract? While a more complete discussion of formation is found in Chapter 13, the following case, an answer to the chapter opening "Consider," gives some idea of how we determine acceptance of terms when contracts are formed over the Internet.

For Internet arbitration information, visit:
http://www.ombuds.org *or*
http://www.squaretrade.com *or*
http://www.CyberSettle.com

CASE 8.4

Caspi v. *Microsoft Network, L.L.C.*
732 A.2d 528 (N.J. Sp. 1999)

Point, Click, Accept?

FACTS

Steven Caspi, Ronald Jonas, Arden Cone, and Laurel Barrie (plaintiffs) were all Microsoft Network (MSN) subscribers. Microsoft rolled over their MSN memberships into more expensive plans without their knowledge or permission, a practice condemned by the attorneys general in twenty-one states. When the four objected, Microsoft offered no relief and the four became representatives in a class action suit brought against Microsoft in New Jersey with approximately 1.5 million class members. Microsoft moved to have the complaint dismissed because of the following clause that rolled through the screens of members as they signed up by clicking, "I agree." All four had clicked "I agree" to the following clause:

This agreement is governed by the laws of the State of Washington, USA, and you consent to the exclusive jurisdiction and venue of courts in King County, Washington, in all disputes arising out of or relating to your use of MSN or your MSN membership.

The district court found that a contract had been formed and that the clause was part of it. The plaintiffs appealed.

JUDICIAL OPINION

KESTIN, J.A.D.

We are here called upon to determine the validity and enforceability of a forum selection clause contained in an on-line subscriber agreement of the Microsoft Network (MSN), an on-line computer service.

Before becoming an MSN member, a prospective subscriber is prompted by MSN software to view multiple computer screens of information, including a membership agreement which contains the above clause. MSN's membership agreement appears on the computer screen in a scrollable window next to blocks providing the choices "I Agree" and "I Don't Agree." Prospective members assent to the terms of the agreement by clicking on "I Agree" using a computer mouse. Prospective members have the option

(continued)

to click "I Agree" or "I Don't Agree" at any point while scrolling through the agreement. Registration may proceed only after the potential subscriber has had the opportunity to view and has assented to the membership agreement, including MSN's forum selection clause. No charges are incurred until after the membership agreement review is completed and a subscriber has clicked on "I Agree."

Generally, forum selection clauses are prima facie valid and enforceable in New Jersey. New Jersey courts will decline to enforce a clause only if it fits into one of three exceptions to the general rule: (1) the clause is a result of fraud or "overweening" bargaining power; (2) enforcement would violate the strong public policy of New Jersey; or (3) enforcement would seriously inconvenience trial.

The burden falls on the party objecting to enforcement to show that the clause in question fits within one of these exceptions. Plaintiffs have failed to meet that burden here.

New Jersey follows the logic of the United States Supreme Court decision in *Carnival Cruise Lines* v. *Shute,* 499 U.S. 585, 111 S.Ct. 1522, 113 L.Ed.2d 622 (1991). In *Carnival,* cruise ship passengers were held to a forum selection clause which appeared in their travel contract. The clause enforced in *Carnival* was very similar in nature to the clause in question here, the primary difference being that the *Carnival* clause was placed in small print in a travel contract while the clause in the case *sub judice* was placed on-line on scrolled computer screens.

Plaintiffs' consent to MSN's clause does not appear to be the result of fraud or overweening bargaining power. In New Jersey, fraud consists of (1) material misrepresentation of a past or present fact; (2) knowledge or belief by the declarant of its falsity; (3) an intention that the recipient rely on it; (4) reasonable reliance by the recipient; and (5) resulting damages. Plaintiffs have not shown that MSN's forum selection clause constitutes fraud. The clause is reasonable, clear and contains no material misrepresentation.

Further, plaintiffs were not subjected to overweening bargaining power in dealing with Microsoft and MSN. The Supreme Court has held that a corporate vendor's inclusion of a forum selection clause in a consumer contract does not in itself constitute overweening bargaining power. In order to invalidate a forum selection clause, something more than merely size difference must be shown. A court's focus must be whether such an imbalance in size resulted in an inequality of bargaining power that was unfairly exploited by the more powerful party.

Plaintiffs have shown little more than a size difference here. The on-line computer service industry is not one without competition, and therefore consumers are left with choices as to which service they select for Internet access, e-mail and other information services. Plaintiffs were not forced into a situation where MSN was the only available server. Additionally, plaintiffs and the class which they purport to represent were given ample opportunity to affirmatively assent to the forum selection clause. Like *Carnival,* plaintiffs here "retained the option of rejecting the contract with impunity." In such a case, this court finds it impossible to perceive an overwhelming bargaining situation.

Given the fact that the named plaintiffs reside in several jurisdictions and that, if the class were to be certified, many different domestic and international domiciles would also be involved, "the inconvenience to all parties is no greater in Washington than anywhere else in the country."

If a forum selection clause is clear in its purport and has been presented to the party to be bound in a fair and forthright fashion, no consumer fraud policies or principles have been violated. Moreover, as a matter of policy interest and apart from considerations bearing upon the choice-of-law provision in the forum selection clause, plaintiffs have given us no reason to apprehend that the nature and scope of consumer fraud protections afforded by the State of Washington are materially different or less broad in scope than those available in this State.

The only viable issues that remain bear upon the argument that plaintiffs did not receive adequate notice of the forum selection clause, and therefore that the clause never became part of the membership contract which bound them. A related, alternative argument is that the question of notice is a factual matter that should be submitted to a jury. Defendants respond by arguing that 1) in the absence of fraud, a contracting party is bound by the provisions of a form contract even if he or she never reads them; 2) this clause met all reasonable standards of conspicuousness; and 3) the sign-up process gave plaintiffs ample opportunity to review and reject the agreement. Defendants also contend that notice is a question of law, decidable by a court, not a jury.

The holding in *Carnival Cruise Lines* v. *Shute,* 499 U.S. 585, 111 S.Ct. 1522, 113 L.Ed.2d 622 (1991), does not dispose of the notice question because the plaintiffs there had "essentially . . . conceded that they had notice of the forum-selection provision[,]" by stating that they " '[did] not contest . . . that the forum selection clause was reasonably communicated to [them], as much as three pages of fine print can be communicated.' " The dissenting justices described the format in which the forum selection clause had been presented as "in the fine print on the back of the [cruise] ticket."

The scenario presented here is different because of the medium used, electronic versus printed; but, in any sense that matters, there is no significant distinction. The plaintiffs in *Carnival* could have perused all the fine-print provisions of their travel contract if they wished before accepting the terms by purchasing their cruise ticket. The plaintiffs in this case were free to scroll through the various computer screens that presented the terms of their contracts before clicking their agreement.

Also, it seems clear that there was nothing extraordinary about the size or placement of the forum selection clause text. By every indication we have, the clause was presented in exactly the same format as most other provisions of the contract. It was the first item in the last paragraph of the electronic document. We note that a few paragraphs in the contract were presented in upper case typeface, presumably for emphasis, but most provisions, including the forum selection clause, were presented in lower case typeface. We discern nothing about the style or mode of presentation, or the placement of the provision, that can be taken as a basis for concluding that the forum selection clause was proffered

unfairly, or with a design to conceal or de-emphasize its provisions. To conclude that plaintiffs are not bound by that clause would be equivalent to holding that they were bound by no other clause either, since all provisions were identically presented. Plaintiffs must be taken to have known that they were entering into a contract; and no good purpose, consonant with the dictates of reasonable reliability in commerce, would be served by permitting them to disavow particular provisions or the contracts as a whole.

We agree with the trial court that, in the absence of a better showing than has been made, plaintiffs must be seen to have had adequate notice of the forum selection clause.

Affirmed.

CASE QUESTIONS

1. What are the two issues the court examines in determining the validity of the clause requiring disputes to be resolved in Washington under Washington law?
2. What is different about this case from the *Carnival* case (see Chapter 3)?
3. Was there an acceptance by point and click?
4. Will the plaintiffs have to take their case to Washington?

New Laws on Contract Formation

The ABA digital signature guidelines are at: http://www.abanet.org/ scitech/ec/isc/dsg.html

There are several new laws to govern the formation of contracts (see Chapters 13 and 14 for more information on formation of contracts in cyberspace). The **Electronic Signatures in Global and National Commerce Act (called E-sign)** is a federal law that recognizes digital signatures as authentic for purposes of contract formation. While E-sign recognizes the validity of electronic signatures, states are responsible for passing laws regulating the authenticity and security of signatures. The important aspect of E-sign is that electronic signatures are in parity, or treated equally, with paper signatures.

States have begun to adopt two uniform laws that were drafted to provide the same uniformity in electronic contracts that the Uniform Commercial Code has provided for written contracts. The **Uniform Electronic Transactions Act** (UETA) and the **Uniform Computer Information Transaction Act** (UCITA) have been adopted in eighteen states and two states respectively.[6]

Misrepresentation and Fraud in Cyberspace

Perhaps because there is no face-to-face contact, the Internet has proven to be fertile grounds for many types of frauds, schemes, and misrepresentations. The types of complaints consumers file about their contract experiences on the Web include

FOR THE MANAGER'S DESK

Re: Employee Internet Use

Vault.com conducted a survey of workers and asked how they use the Internet at work for nonwork-related activity and found the following:

News reading	72%
Travel arrangements	45%
Shopping	40%
Job searching	37%
Special interests (hobbies)	37%
Stock-checking	34%
Planning social events	28%
Instant messaging	26%
Music downloads	13%
Games	11%
Chatting	9%
Pornography	4%

Employers have software that enables them to see which Web sites employees have visited, when they visited, and how long they stayed there. Some employers issue reports that indicate which employees are spending large amounts of time. One employer warned an employee about too much online shopping during working hours and then blocked the sites so that the emloyee could no longer access them.

While employees are concerned about privacy, employers are concerned about productivity and the fact that downloading music, for example, can result in the employer's network jamming. Also, employers are concerned that some types of sites being visited, such as pornographic sites, may result in liability for the employer for an atmosphere of harassment.

The same Vault.com survey found that 90 percent of all employees surf the net during work hours for things unrelated to their jobs and 37 percent have used their computers at work to access the Internet to look for another job. About 13 percent say that they spend two or more hours per working day surfing the net for things unrelated to their jobs. Ten percent say that they receive 21 or more personal e-mails per day at work. However, 53 percent say that they limit their non-work Internet access to 30 minutes per working day.

There are also companies that will police employee use for employers. Websense, Inc., serves this function for 12,000 companies, including 239 of the *Fortune 500.* The cost is approximately $15 per employee per year.

Source: Alan Cohen, "Worker Watchers," *Fortune,* Summer 2001 (special issue *Fortune/CNET Technology Review*), p. 70.

BUSINESS PLANNING TIP

To avoid an Internet scam:

1. Know your seller.

2. Check your seller's background.

3. Verify the seller's authenticity with your credit card company.

4. Check the bricks and mortar address given on the Web site. If there is no address, be wary.

5. Check the business status of the seller: use the Better Business Bureau, state attorney general fraud division, and even the secretary of state or other government agency responsible for receiving documents of organization for corporations, limited partnerships, and LLCs (see Chapter 21 for more information on these business organizations).

6. Trust, but verify.

everything from late delivery to lack of delivery to misstatements about the nature of goods being offered for sale.

Once again, misrepresentation, fraud, and nonperformance are not new legal issues. The forum for their occurrence is new and high tech, but the elements remain the same. Even federal regulation of retailers and their sales over the Internet are no different. For example, for the past ten years, the Federal Trade Commission has regulated catalog retailers with rules on performance and disclosure. Catalog retailers are not permitted to charge your credit card for merchandise you order until the merchandise is actually shipped. These retailers must also notify you if there will be a delay in shipping goods to you and also provide you with the opportunity to cancel the order in the event that time for shipment is unacceptable to you.

When retailers who also had catalogs began doing business over the Internet, many of them did not follow the FTC rules on catalogs because they saw this form of sale as being different. However, the FTC saw the Internet as simply an electronic catalog to which the same rules on consumer rights applied. In 2000, the FTC issued a rule making the catalog rules applicable to Internet consumer sales. Using the rule as its enforce-

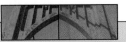

ETHICAL ISSUES 8.3

Concerned about their reputations as search engines, a small group of search engine companies has proposed a code of ethics for search engine firms. Mike Adams, founder and owner of WebSeed.com, has developed a code of ethics called "Search Engine Promotion Code of Ethics." Mr. Adams was concerned about companies that make technologically impossible claims about the number of Web sites and links its service provides. The key provisions of the search engine code of ethics are:

1. Search engine optimization services shall not impose undue bandwidth burdens on search engines.

2. Services shall abide by each search engine's page-submission guidelines and will not attempt to subvert them.

3. No service shall say it can submit pages to more search engines than actually exist.

4. No service shall engage in keyword repetition, page repetition, invisible HyperText Markup language tags, or the use of robot pages.

---

ment tool, the FTC filed a complaint against seven Internet retailers for their failure to deliver Christmas merchandise on time. The retailers, including Macys.com, Toysrus.com and CDNOW, then entered into a consent decree (see Chapter 6 for more details on consent decrees) that requires them to pay fines totaling $1.5 million.

Federal agency activity has stepped up because of fraudulent activity on the Web. The FBI reported that for the year 2000 its number one source of fraud complaints was the Internet. The FBI Internet Fraud Computer Center receives 1,000 complaints per day with 4,000 cases forwarded in 2000 to local authorities for prosecution. The FBI has even created an ethics Web site to provide information on the importance of honesty in business. One of the Internet fraud cases forwarded by the FBI for prosecution was the offer for sale of kidneys for transplantation, which was used to bilk thousands from those awaiting transplants before it could be exposed as a fraud. The average loss per fraud complaint submitted to the FBI is $800.[7]

Another area of misrepresentation comes when search engine companies misrepresent the capabilities of their product or are not fully forthcoming about how they display those who subscribe to have their sites listed as part of the engine or how the search engine lists or provides for links for those using the engine. Companies relying on these search engine firms have the traditional remedies available in all service contracts where the service provider has not performed as promised or has misrepresented the extent or

BUSINESS PLANNING TIP

Privacy and Internet theft of identity have become concerns for consumers who would like to use the Internet for purchases of goods but feel uncomfortable about the level of security. Leading retailers have been developing and perfecting "secure sites," or areas within their Web sites that are secure. These secure sites mean that some form of password is necessary to be able to obtain the information. In effect, the retailers are locking up the information and only giving the returning consumer access. Several of the so-called "big five" accounting firms now offer certification programs under their names for business secure Web sites. The results of such a program is the accounting firm's seal of approval for the security of the Web site for those companies whose sites meet minimum standards for security of customers' identities, records, and financial information. These seals are not seals of approval for products or services. They are only seals on the adequacy of the format and protocol for the company's secure site.

results from the service. Those remedies include the traditional contract remedies of misrepresentation and fraud (see Chapter 14 for more information on these traditional contract defenses). Remedies for such misrepresentation and/or fraud include rescission of the agreement and/or money damages.

One of the biggest areas of fraud that the Internet has facilitated is identity theft. There is, as noted earlier, a tremendous amount of personal and financial information available over the Internet. Hackers are able to collect information on individuals and then piece together sufficient personal information on someone else to obtain credit; make purchases; and even secure government benefits, such as Social Security, using that individual's identity via his Social Security number, credit card numbers, and even bank accounts. In 1999, the Social Security Administration received 30,000 identity theft complaints. That number was nearly tripled from the 11,000 complaints received in 1998 and nearly quadrupled from the 7,868 complaints lodged in 1997. Because the exponential growth parallels the Internet explosion, the Social Security administration attributes the increases to the ease with which information can be obtained.

INTELLECTUAL PROPERTY ISSUES IN CYBERSPACE

The law on intellectual property rights has not changed. The Internet has simply facilitated the copying of everything from trademarks to songs to the cutting and pasting of literary works. For universal access to the Internet, we necessarily opened the door universally to the downloading and copying of both patented and copyrighted software. Even some of the techniques and tools used in accessing and using the Internet have been the subject of intellectual property right legal battles. For example, Jeff Bezos, the founder of amazon.com, patented his one-click system for ordering and was met with great resistance because so many others wished to use such a system in their retail Internet sites.

The *Napster* case from Chapter 1 was also a highly emotional battle over a technological revolution and its effect on copyrights. Rap star Dr. Dre argued that the unauthorized copying of his music via the Napster Web site deprived him of his royalties for his music and his means for making a living. Others called the peer-to-peer file sharing no different from watching a video with a friend. Others saw new opportunities on the Internet because of Napster. Andy Grove, the CEO of Intel, noted, "The whole Internet could be re-architected by Napster-like technology."

Because of the innovation that surrounds the Internet, intellectual property rights require the same or perhaps greater protection so that the incentives for innovation because of resulting ownership are protected. The Internet has presented new challenges for interpretation and application of intellectual property law. For example, Mr. Bezos of Amazon.com has advanced the idea of changing the period for patent protection from twenty years to three to five years because he believes anything longer to be "a silly length of time for software patents."[8] These debates continue both in court and through new legislation written with the Internet in mind.

Copyright Infringement and Technology

The Internet and the nature of cyberspace have made the use, downloading, and copying of copyrighted materials in all forms very easy and very fast. Copyright holders continue to pursue clarifications about the application of federal copyright laws as well as the extent of any protection they have in cyberspace. Some of these issues are being addressed by litigation and others are requiring new legislation or amendments.

The **Digital Millennium Copyright Act (DMCA)**[9] is an amendment to the federal copyright statute that was passed to address some of the new issues of copyright infringement that exist because of digital technology and cyberspace. For example, the statute deals with issues such as the use of copyrighted music in a presentation or program when that music has been downloaded to the computer. Is such a use a fair use or an infringement? Also, the Act addresses an issue that has been the center of much cyberspace litigation, that is, whether linking to a copyrighted site constitutes a copyright infringement.

The DMCA deals with the infringement liability of those who facilitate the infringement of copyrighted materials. For example, in *Sega Enterprises, Ltd.* v. *Maphia*, 857 F. Supp. 679 (N.D. Call. 1994), the court held that the creator of a bulletin board that permitted the free downloading of computer games had committed a violation of federal copyright law because the DMCA applies to those who facilitate infringement as well as those who actually infringe.

Domain Names and Their Protection in Cyberspace

The name of a Web site carries certain appeal and marketability. While a "www.____" may not fit the traditional definition of a trademark or trade name, it is intellectual property with some value. Because there is fierce competition for easy-to-remember as well as clever domain names, there have been many disputes over the use and registration of these names, called **domain registration.** Disputes over who owns what domain name are similar to the disagreements in the early days of the western United States over land ownership through squatter's rights. Numerous questions arise over domain ownership: If someone has registered a domain name for a site and then just sits on that name without using it, do they own the rights to the name? What if someone simply registers the name of a person or company and now that person or company wishes to use the domain name? Who owns it? There is now in place a means for owning a domain name and controlling its use as well as a way to resolve disputes over domain names.

In October 1999 the **Internet Corporation for Assigned Names and Numbers** (ICANN) approved the **Uniform Domain Name Dispute Resolution Policy** (UDRP). Prior to this policy, the Network Solutions, Inc. (NSI) had followed a policy of allowing trademark holders to halt the use of trademarked names for Web sites until the issue of ownership was resolved.

The UDRP provides for arbitration to resolve disputes over domain names. The current user of the disputed name is permitted to continue use of the name until the matter is resolved. The UDRP also does not require a registration as a prerequisite for bringing a complaint against another for name use. The complaint can be based on a Web site's name being deceptively similar to the complainant's Web site name so that users are likely to be confused.

The first UDRP decision was issued in January 2000 and granted the rights to worldwidewrestlingfederation.com to the WWF. Since then, there have been 591 UDRP proceedings commenced with 120 decisions.

Trade Marks and Cyberspace

While there are new ways to protect the new Internet intellectual property, many of the old laws and rights still apply. For example, the **Federal Trademark Dilution Act** permits a company whose name is harmed or diluted through its use by

Explore the Web site with UDRP decisions
http://www.icann.org/udrp/proceedings-list.htm

The registration site is at
http://www.
domainmagistrate.com/
publish/faq.html

another to bring suit for injunctions and damages. Also, the Federal Trade Commission rules on trademark protection are equally applicable on the Internet and are self-enforcing. That is, the parties can bring actions against others for the deception caused by the use of similar domain names.

More detail on intellectual property issues on the Internet is found in Chapter 16.

CRIMINAL LAW ISSUES IN CYBERSPACE

Just as fraud and misrepresentation have exploded on the Internet, so also has crime been committed using the Internet. The FBI calls the levels of cybercrime "epidemic."[10] Over 25 percent of the Fortune 500 corporations have fallen victim to computer crime.[11] Computer viruses cost companies $7.6 billion in lost productivity and repairs through August 1999.[12] In 1999, one man was able to perpetuate a fraud of $45 million by simply making credit card charges to various credit cards from around the world. He had obtained the credit card numbers and information simply by searching Web sites with consumer information.[13]

Most Internet or computer crime is just some form of a conventional crime carried out through the use of a computer. Whether you steal a wallet and use the credit cards in it to purchase goods and services for yourself or use the credit card number for Web transactions, the crime is still credit card fraud, obtaining goods by false pretenses, and other similar existing crimes as designated by each of the states.

There are, however, some crimes that have evolved because of the capabilities of the Internet. If a computer hacker is able to reroute users from the domain they were trying to access to a pornographic Web site, no existing crime is exactly applicable. While such activity may not rise to the level of a common-law crime, it is perhaps a new crime often referred to as the wrongful use of a computer and its systems.[14] Special computer crime statutes have been developed to deal with the use of a computer in an unauthorized manner or to carry out fraud and take unfair advantage.[15] These statutes cover computer crimes committed when the computers are the tools of the crime (identity theft), the targets of crime (hacking into a system of another), or used incidentally to commit a crime (as when they are used for money laundering).

The Internet has been used to transport pornography across state lines and to children; to facilitate contacts with children by pedophiles; to harass employees via e-mail; to stalk victims; to make threats of harm or death; to commit fraud; to facilitate bets and other means of illegal gambling; to commit industrial and economic espionage; to extort money; to sell controlled substances without authorization; to pirate software; to vandalize, trespass, and steal; to shut down companies and services; and even to facilitate terrorism.

In all of these activities, there is either an underlying criminal statute to address the conduct (such as prohibitions on bribery, money laundering, and gambling) or there are computer-specific statutes passed to place criminal sanctions for such computer use. The criminal law statutes particularly applicable to computer crime are covered in Chapter 9 and include the Computer Fraud and Abuse Act[16] and the Economic Espionage Act (EEA).[17] The following case shows that while the computer may be a sophisticated means for committing a crime, the prosecutors in a case are still required to prove the basic elements of a crime: intent and actions.

CASE 8.5

U.S. v. Czubinski
106 F.3d 1069 (1st Cir. 1997)

Surfing for Tax Returns of Friend and Foe: Criminal or Voyeur?

FACTS

Richard Czubinski (defendant-appellant) was an IRS employee in its Boston office. As a member of the IRS's Taxpayer Services Division, Czubinski had full access to taxpayer files. He could retrieve taxpayer information on anyone in the United States who has filed a federal income tax return.

During lunch hours and breaks, Czubinski retrieved the tax returns of the following:

An assistant district attorney in Boston who was prosecuting Czubinski's father
A woman he was dating
David Duke (at the time he was a presidential candidate)

Czubinski was charged with violations of the Computer Fraud and Abuse Act and convicted. He appealed.

JUDICIAL OPINION

TORRUELLA, Chief Judge
Defendant-appellant Richard Czubinski ("Czubinski") appeals his jury conviction on nine counts of wire fraud, 18 U.S.C. §§ 1343, 1346, and four counts of computer fraud, 18 U.S.C. § 1030(a)(4).

Czubinski was employed as a Contact Representative in the Boston office of the Taxpayer Services Division of the Internal Revenue Service ("IRS"). To perform his official duties, which mainly involved answering questions from taxpayers regarding their returns, Czubinski routinely accessed information from one of the IRS's computer systems known as the Integrated Data Retrieval System ("IDRS"). Using a valid password given to Contact Representatives, certain search codes, and taxpayer social security numbers, Czubinski was able to retrieve, to his terminal screen in Boston, income tax return information regarding virtually any taxpayer—information that is permanently stored in the IDRS "master file" located in Martinsburg, West Virginia. In the period of Czubinski's employ, IRS rules plainly stated that employees with passwords and access

codes were not permitted to access files on IDRS outside of the course of their official duties.

In 1992, Czubinski carried out numerous unauthorized searches of IDRS files. He knowingly disregarded IRS rules by looking at confidential information obtained by performing computer searches that were outside of the scope of his duties as a Contact Representative, including, but not limited to, the searches listed in the indictment. Audit trails performed by internal IRS auditors establish that Czubinski frequently made unauthorized accesses on IDRS in 1992. For example, Czubinski accessed information regarding: the tax returns of two individuals involved in the David Duke presidential campaign; the joint tax return of an assistant district attorney (who had been prosecuting Czubinski's father on an unrelated felony offense) and his wife; the tax return of Boston City Counselor Jim Kelly's Campaign Committee (Kelly had defeated Czubinski in the previous election for the Counselor seat for District 2); the tax return of one of his brothers' instructors; the joint tax return of a Boston Housing Authority police officer, who was involved in a community organization with one of Czubinski's brothers, and the officer's wife; and the tax return of a woman Czubinski had dated a few times. Czubinski also accessed the files of various other social acquaintances by performing unauthorized searches.

Nothing in the record indicates that Czubinski did anything more than knowingly disregard IRS rules by observing the confidential information he accessed. No evidence suggests, nor does the government contend, that Czubinski disclosed the confidential information he accessed to any third parties. The government's only evidence demonstrating any intent to use the confidential information for nefarious ends was the trial testimony of William A. Murray, an acquaintance of Czubinski who briefly participated in Czubinski's local Invisible Knights of the Ku Klux Klan ("KKK") chapter and worked with him on the David Duke campaign. Murray testified that Czubinski had once stated at a social gathering in "early 1992" that "he intended to use some of that information to build dossiers on people" involved in "the white supremacist movement." There is, however, no evidence that Czubinski created dossiers, took steps toward making dossiers (such as by printing out or recording the information he browsed), or shared any of the information he accessed in the years following the single comment to Murray. No other witness testified to having any knowledge of Czubinski's alleged intent to create "dossiers" on KKK members.

In this case, the government has charged Mr. Czubinski with devising a scheme or artifice, that is, a plan, to do two things:

(1) to defraud the IRS, the United States Government, and the citizens and taxpayers of the United States by depriving them of their intangible right to his honest services as an IRS employee; and

(2) to defraud the IRS and to obtain its property, that is, confidential taxpayer information, by false pretenses, representations and promises.

The government correctly notes that confidential information may constitute intangible "property" and that its unauthorized dissemination or other use may deprive the owner of its property rights. Thus, a necessary step toward satisfying the "scheme to defraud" element in this context is showing that the defendant intended to "deprive" another of their protected right.

The government, however, provides no case in support of its contention here that merely accessing confidential information, without doing, or clearly intending to do, more, is tantamount to a deprivation of IRS property under the wire fraud statute. We do not think that Czubinski's unauthorized browsing, even if done with the intent to deceive the IRS into thinking he was performing only authorized searches, constitutes a "deprivation" within the meaning of the federal fraud statutes.

Binding precedents, and good sense, support the conclusion that to "deprive" a person of their intangible property interest in confidential information under section 1343, either some articulable harm must befall the holder of the information as a result of the defendant's activities, or some gainful use must be intended by the person accessing the information, whether or not this use is profitable in the economic sense. Here, neither the taking of the IRS's right to "exclusive use" of the confidential information, nor Czubinski's gain from access to the information, can be shown absent evidence of his "use" of the information. Accordingly, without evidence that

Czubinski used or intended to use the taxpayer information (beyond mere browsing), an intent to deprive cannot be proven, and, *a fortiori,* a scheme to defraud is not shown.

Had there been sufficient proof that Czubinski intended either to create dossiers for the sake of advancing personal causes or to disseminate confidential information to third parties, then his actions in searching files could arguably be said to be a step in furtherance of a scheme to deprive the IRS of its property interest in confidential information. The government's case regarding Czubinski's intent to make any use of the information he browsed rests on the testimony of one witness at trial who stated that Czubinski once remarked at a social gathering that he intended to build dossiers on potential KKK informants.

Nevertheless, the fact that during the months following this remark—that is, during the period in which Czubinski made his unauthorized searches—he did not create dossiers (there was no evidence that he created dossiers either during or after the period of his unauthorized searches); given the fact that he did not even take steps toward creating dossiers, such as recording or printing out the information; given the fact that no other person testifying as to Czubinski's involvement in white supremacist organizations had any knowledge of Czubinski's alleged intent to create dossiers or use confidential information; and given the fact that not a single piece of evidence suggests that Czubinski ever shared taxpayer information with others, no rational jury could have found beyond a reasonable doubt that, when Czubinski was browsing taxpayer files, he was doing so in furtherance of a scheme to use the information he browsed for private purposes, be they nefarious or otherwise. In addition, there was no evidence that Czubinski disclosed, or used to his advantage, any information regarding political opponents or regarding the person prosecuting his father.

Mere browsing of the records of people about whom one might have a particular interest, although reprehensible, is not enough to sustain a wire fraud conviction on a "deprivation of intangible property" theory. Curiosity on the part of an IRS officer may lead to dismissal, but curiosity alone will not sustain a finding of participation in a felonious criminal scheme to deprive the IRS of its property.

We add a cautionary note. The broad language of the mail and wire fraud statutes is both their blessing and their curse. They can address new forms of serious crime that fail to fall within more specific legislation. On the other hand, they might be used to prosecute kinds of behavior that, albeit offensive to the morals or aesthetics of federal prosecutors, cannot reasonably be expected by the instigators to form the basis of a federal felony. The case at bar falls within the latter category. Also discomforting is the prosecution's insistence, before trial, on the admission of inflammatory evidence regarding the defendant's membership in white supremacist groups purportedly as a means to prove a scheme to defraud, when, on appeal, it argues that unauthorized access in itself is a sufficient ground for conviction on all counts. Finally, we caution that the wire fraud statute must not serve as a vehicle for prosecuting only those citizens whose views run against the tide, no matter how incorrect or uncivilized such views are.

The defendant's conviction is thus reversed on all counts.

CASE QUESTIONS

1. What was Czubinski doing with his computer at work?
2. Is it computer fraud? Is it wire fraud?
3. Did his conduct violate any statute?
4. Was his conduct ethical?
5. What comment does the court make in conclusion about the use of wire and fraud statutes on computer activities?

Criminal Procedure and Rights in Cyberspace

Browse Web sites for criminal law area:
http://www.fbi.gov/
http://jaring.nmhu.edu/
http://www.cert.org
http://cyber.findlaw.com/
criminal
http://cybercrimes.net

The Fourth Amendment applies not only to searches of offices and homes but also to searches of computers. As noted earlier in the *Kyllo* case, the right to privacy does not change simply because technology permits invasion with ease. At least one court has ordered that the warrant be specific as to whether they are including home and/or office computers and files.[18] For more information on search warrants and the Fourth Amendment, refer to Chapter 9.

CONSTITUTIONAL RESTRAINTS AND PROTECTIONS IN CYBERSPACE

The constitutional issues that arise from cyberspace focus on many aspects of the Constitution. The following sections deal with some of those issues.

First Amendment Rights in Cyberspace

While some speech on the Internet is commercial, other forms of Internet speech are communications relating to voting and ballot initiatives. Speech on the Internet enjoys the same constitutional protections of the First Amendment as other forms of business, personal, and political speech. One of the first speech-related cases to arise related to the Internet was the right of access by businesses to Internet service providers' networks. As noted in the *Cyber Promotions* case earlier in the chapter, and in another case, *Cyber Promotions, Inc.* v. *American Online, Inc.*, 948 F.Supp. 436 (E.D. Pa. 1996), Internet servers are not required under the Constitution to give commercial advertisers unfettered access to their customers for purposes of distribution of e-mail to them. Another speech-related issue that has long been a subject of litigation is the right to publish and access pornographic materials. The Internet has also facilitated the transport of pornography in a forum to which children have easy access. The **Child Pornography Prevention Act**[19] made it a crime to knowingly sell, possess, or distribute child pornography on the Web. However, the U.S. Supreme Court ruled that the statute was both void for vagueness and violative of First Amendment rights.[20]

BIOGRAPHY

Jonathan Lebed: The 15-Year-Old Who Roared Across Wall Street

Jonathan Lebed, a 15-year-old New Jersey middle-school student, shocked the investment world when the Securities Exchange Commission came knocking at his parents' door with a charge of securities fraud. It seems that Jonathan had taken his $8,000 in savings and gifts from family members into nearly $900,000 in gains on stocks traded using a pump-and-dump strategy. Jonathan did so without ever missing a day of school.

Master Jonathan, using over twenty screen names on a computer his parents had given him as a gift, would buy shares of stock and then post positive information about the stock around the Internet in various chat rooms. When the price of his chosen stock would rise, he would then sell it and move on to another stock.

Mrs. Lebed said that Jonathan had always been fascinated with the market and would often sit by the television and watch the stock prices go across the screen on MSNBC and CNN. His mother also indicated he was not a bad stock picker having given some of her friends and family members some good investment advice on stock.

When the SEC stepped in to halt his trading and take his computer, Jonathan became the first minor ever prosecuted by the SEC for securities fraud. His father noted that his son did nothing more than what others in the market do and yet the SEC chose to come after "a kid." The Lebeds entered into a consent decree. They repaid all of the money Jonathan had made except for $273,000, a sum equal to about what is no doubt owed by his parents as taxes on the gains Jonathan made in his trading activity.

Source: Gretchen Morgenson, "S.E.C. Says Teenager Had After-School Hobby: Online Stock Fraud," *New York Times*, 21 September 2000, A1, C10.

The Commerce Clause in Cyberspace

The Commerce Clause has also come into play in the Internet because of the desire of both the states and the federal government to tax the transactions taking place via the Internet. The U.S. Constitution requires that there be some "nexus" between the taxing authority and the business paying the tax (see Chapter 5 for more information on constitutional issues in taxation), and many questions arise about the constitutionality of taxing Internet sales because of the lack of "bricks and mortar" in these businesses. Some Internet retailers are located in one state and have no contact, physically, with any other states. Their only contact is through the computers of their customers who may be located in all fifty states. Is it constitutional for Colorado to tax a New Jersey company operating out of a small office in Trenton? While the nature of business has changed, the constitutional tests remain the same and courts will simply apply the standards of fairness and allocation that they have in other eras as businesses grew in terms of reach even though their physical locations did not change.

Due Process in Cyberspace

Related to the "nexus" doctrine and taxation of Internet sales is the issue of whether an Internet business site with few physical facilities and no real presence in other states can be required to travel to the states where their customers are to litigate cases brought by those customers. The notion of long-arm jurisdiction (see

Re: The Panic That Preceded the NASDAQ Freefall

In the month preceding the drop in the NASDAQ, many insiders at the so-called "dot.com" companies sold their stock and avoided the losses a 17 percent drop in NASDAQ has caused. Insider sales of stocks on the NASDAQ typically average $1 billion to $3 billion per month, but the average jumped to $12 billion per month from November 1999 to February 2000.

Some analysts are noting that the sell-offs by insiders may have prompted the drop in the market. Some examples of the trading include:

- Drugstore.com founder Jed Smith sold 150,000 of his 950,000 shares at a price of $23 per share. The price now is $9.88.

- MicroStrategy CEO Michael Saylor sold $80 million in his company's shares. The price of MicroStrategy shares dropped 62 percent within a few weeks of his sales.
- Beyond.com CEO Mark Breier (now ex-CEO) sold 80,000 shares of his company for $440,000 after he quit as CEO.
- Former Surgeon General C. Everett Koop sold $3 million in shares of his drkoop.com at about $9 per share in February. The spokespersons for drkoop.com indicated the insiders there were "diversifying their portfolios."

Source: Del Jones, "Net Execs Sold Stock before Big Drop," *USA Today*, 6 April 2000, B1.

Chapter 3) becomes even more critical because of the Internet. When does a company have a sufficient presence in a state to require them to defend a lawsuit in that state? The answer is the same as the answer for the presence of a "bricks and mortar" business. Is requiring the Internet retailer to come to a state to defend a lawsuit fair or does it offend notions of justice and fair play? Is reaching out to customers in a state through the Internet sufficient to require the Internet company to come to that state and defend a lawsuit brought by that customer or should the customer be required to travel to the state where the Internet company is located? Refer to the *Bensusan Restaurant Corporation* v. *King* case in Chapter 3 for an answer to that question as well as the *Carnival Cruise Lines* case in that same chapter and the *Caspi* case earlier in this chapter.

SECURITIES LAW ISSUES IN CYBERSPACE

The Internet has provided more information to more investors than at any other time in the capital markets' history. Day traders exist because of computers' ability to track stock prices and trade instantaneously. However, a universally accessible market and full information mean that some of the players may use tactics not entirely consistent with the existing legal framework or that encourage the level playing field necessary to preserve trust in the stock markets.

"Pump and dump," when traders buy a certain stock and then post information on the Web to increase interest in it to drive up the price and hence their gain on that stock, existed long before the Internet and day traders. However, as noted in the section on defamation earlier in the chapter, the rapid exchange of information makes the practice of pump and dump much easier. While the Internet is a new tool for pump and dump, it is still regulated the old-fashioned way with the Securities Exchange Act of 1934 and the regulations on securities fraud (see Chapter 22 for more details on fraud and insider trading). If the trader spreads false information in order to gain from sales of shares based on trading inspired by that information, then the trader has committed fraud.

The SEC has also found that the very nature of new economy companies has created accounting and disclosure dilemmas and questions. When is revenue booked? What is the value of hits to a Web site and how is that reflected? For example, America Online entered into a consent decree with the SEC for its accounting practices that had the company predicting sales on the basis of advertising expenses. The SEC found the model for predicting sales untested and misleading and the reporting of income based on the model, therefore, deceptive. The advertising methods and the company and its technology were all new, but the same securities principles and laws applied: the financial projections must be based on adequate information.[21]

Insider trading issues (see Chapter 22) have been of particular concern in dot.com companies. The companies' sources of revenues and operations are very different, but the rule on insider trading remains the same: insiders cannot trade on nonpublic information.

CYBERSPACE AND INTERNATIONAL LAW

It is only natural that cyberspace would bring to a head international business questions and disputes. With the barriers of distance broken down by the Internet, those in Germany were easily doing business over e-Bay with those in Wisconsin. However, the courts are still left with the issues of which law applies and which courts have jurisdiction. In the following case, A U.S. court grapples with issues of First Amendment protections, international jurisdiction, and the conflicts of law among and between countries.

CASE 8.6

Yahoo! Inc. v. *La Ligue Contre le Racisme et L'Antisemitisme*
145 F.Supp. 2d 1168 (N.D. Cal. 2001)
See also 2001 WL 1381157 (N.D. Cal. 2001)

Pardon My French: Rejecting an Order of a Foreign Court

FACTS

LICRA and UEJF are citizens (defendants) of France. Yahoo! is a corporation (plaintiff) organized under the laws of Delaware with its principal place of business in Santa Clara, California. Yahoo! is an Internet service provider which operates various Internet web sites and services which end users can access at the Uniform Resource Locater ("URL") "http://www.yahoo.com." According to Yahoo!'s complaint, Yahoo! services ending in the suffix, ".com," without an associated country code as a prefix or extension (collectively, "Yahoo!'s U.S. Services"), use the English language and target users who are residents of, utilize servers based in, and operate under the laws of the United States.

Yahoo! subsidiary corporations operate regional Yahoo! sites and services in twenty (20) other countries, including, for example, Yahoo! France, Yahoo! India, and Yahoo! Spain.

Certain services provided by Yahoo! allow end users to post materials on Yahoo! servers which then can be accessed by end users at Yahoo!'s Internet sites. As relevant here, Yahoo! end users are able to post, and have in fact posted, highly offensive matter, including Nazi-related propaganda and memorabilia, the display and sale of which are illegal in France. While Yahoo! avers that its French subsidiary sites do not permit such postings, Yahoo!'s U.S.-based site ending in ".com" does not impose such a restriction because to do so might infringe upon the First Amendment to the United States Constitution. End users in France are able to access Yahoo!'s U.S. services via the web site located at www.yahoo.com.

LICRA sent a "cease and desist" letter to Yahoo!'s headquarters in Santa Clara, California, stating that "unless you cease presenting Nazi objects for sale [on the U.S. Auction Site] within 8 days, we shall size [sic] the competent jurisdiction to force your company to abide by [French] law." Defendants then employed the United States Marshal's Office to serve process on Yahoo! in California and filed civil complaints against Yahoo! in the Tribunal de Grande Instance de Paris (the "French Court") for alleged violation of a French criminal statute barring the public display in France of Nazi-related "uniforms, insignia or emblems" (the "Nazi Symbols Act"). See Le Nouveau Code Penal Art. R.645-2. On May 22, 2000, the French Court issued an order (the "French Order") directing Yahoo! to "take all necessary measures" to "dissuade and render impossible" any access via "yahoo.com" by Internet users in France to the Yahoo! Internet auction service displaying Nazi artifacts. On November 20, 2000, the French Court "reaffirmed" its Order of May 22 for Yahoo to: 1) recognize French Internet Protocol ("IP") addresses and block access to Nazi material by end users assigned such IP addresses; 2) require end users with "ambiguous" IP addresses to provide Yahoo! with a declaration of nationality when they arrive at Yahoo!' s home page or when they initiate any search using the word "Nazi"; and 3) comply with the Order within three (3) months or face a penalty of 100,000 Francs (approximately U.S. $13,300) for each day of non-compliance. The Court denied Defendants' request to enforce its Order or impose any penalties directed at Yahoo! Inc. against Yahoo! France. Thereafter, Defendants again utilized the United States Marshal's Office to serve Yahoo! in Santa Clara with the French Order.

Yahoo challenges both the jurisdiction of the French court and the applicability of French law to its activities.

JUDICIAL OPINION

FOGEL, Judge

This case presents novel legal issues arising from the global nature of the Internet. See *Reno* v. *ACLU*, 521 U.S. 844 (1997) (describing the Internet as a unique and wholly new medium of worldwide human communication). Defendants La Ligue Contre Le Racisme Et L'Antisemitisme ("LICRA") and L'Union Des Etudiants Juifs De France ("UEJF") have obtained a court order in France which requires Plaintiff Yahoo!, Inc. ("Yahoo!") to "render impossible" access by persons in France to certain content on servers based in the United States. Yahoo! now seeks a declaration by this Court that the order of the French court is unenforceable in the United States because it contravenes the Constitution and laws of the United States. Defendants move for dismissal of this action on the ground that this Court lacks personal jurisdiction over them.

Where no applicable federal statute indicates otherwise, a district court has personal jurisdiction over a nonresident defendant to the extent that the law of the forum state constitutionally provides. California law permits courts to exercise jurisdiction to the full extent authorized by the Due Process Clause of the Fourteenth Amendment to the United States Constitution. The Due Process Clause, in turn, has been interpreted to authorize the exercise of personal jurisdiction over a nonresident defendant if that defendant has "minimum contacts" with the forum state such that maintenance of the suit "does not offend 'traditional notions of fair play and substantial justice.' "

Personal jurisdiction over a nonresident of the forum state can be either "general" or "specific." If the nonresident defendant's contacts with the forum state are "substantial" or "continuous and systematic," the defendant is subject to "general jurisdiction" in the forum state even if the cause of action is unrelated to the defendant's activities within the state. See *Helicopteros Nacionales de Colombia, S.A.* v. *Hall*, 466 U.S. 408, 416 (1984). Where the defendant's activities within the forum are not so pervasive as to subject it to general jurisdiction, the defendant still may be subject to specific jurisdiction depending upon the nature and quality of its contacts in relation to the cause of action. The Court of Appeals for the Ninth Circuit applies a three-part test to determine whether a court may exercise specific jurisdiction: 1) the nonresident defendant must do some act or consummate some transaction within the forum or perform some act by which the defendant purposefully avails itself of the privilege of conducting activities in the forum, thereby invoking the benefits and protection of its laws; 2) the claim must be one which arises out of or results from the defendant's forum-related activities; and 3) the exercise of jurisdiction must be reasonable.

The purposeful availment requirement is intended to give notice to a nonresident that it is

(continued)

subject to suit in the forum state, thereby protecting it from being haled into local courts solely as the result of "random, fortuitous or attenuated" contacts over which it had no control. Yahoo! asserts that Defendants' conduct meets this requirement under the "effects test" articulated by the United States Supreme Court in *Calder* v. *Jones,* 465 U.S. 783 (1984). "Under Calder personal jurisdiction can be based upon: '(1) intentional actions (2) expressly aimed at the forum state (3) causing harm, the brunt of which is suffered—and which the defendant knows is likely to be suffered—in the forum state.' "

This Court concludes that Yahoo! has made a sufficient prima facie showing of purposeful availment under the effects test. Yahoo! alleges that Defendants knowingly have engaged in actions intentionally targeted at its Santa Clara headquarters for the express purpose of causing the consequences of such actions to be felt in California, including 1) LICRA's "cease and desist" letter to Yahoo!'s Santa Clara headquarters; 2) Defendants' request of the French Court that Yahoo! be required to perform specific physical acts in Santa Clara (e.g., re-engineering of its Santa Clara–based servers); and 3) Defendants' utilization of United States Marshals to effect service of process on Yahoo! in California. Yahoo! further alleges that the conscious intent of these actions was to compel it to censor "constitutionally protected content on its U.S.-based Internet services."

This Court concludes, however, that the application of the effects test in the present case is fully consistent not only with the rationale of the test but also with traditional principles of personal jurisdiction and international law. While filing a lawsuit in a foreign jurisdiction may be entirely proper under the laws of that jurisdiction, such an act nonetheless may be "wrongful" from the standpoint of a court in the United States if its primary purpose or intended effect is to deprive a United States resident of its constitutional rights. Several of the cases discussing the purposeful availment have focused less on the characterization of the plaintiff's cause of action than on whether the defendant's forum-related acts evidenced intentional, or at the very least knowing, targeting of a forum resident(s).

In the present case, Yahoo! has alleged with particularity that Defendants "purposefully targeted" its Santa Clara headquarters and thus reasonably could have expected to be haled into a California forum in order to defend the Order they obtained from the French Court.

The second element of a specific jurisdiction analysis is a determination as to whether the plaintiff's claims arise out of the defendant's forum-related conduct. As to this element, the Court of Appeals for the Ninth Circuit employs a "but for" test. Accordingly, in the present case Yahoo! must demonstrate that it would have no need for a judicial declaration but for Defendants' forum-related activities. This requirement is easily met. But for Defendants' filing and prosecution of the French lawsuit, which in turn was obtained by Defendants' use of formal process in California, Yahoo! would have no need for a declaration that the French Order is unenforceable in the United States.

The final requirement for specific jurisdiction is that the exercise of jurisdiction be reasonable. For the exercise of jurisdiction to be reasonable it must comport with fair play and substantial justice [which] requires the consideration of several specific factors: (1) the extent of the defendant's purposeful interjection into the forum state; (2) the burden on the defendant in defending in the forum; (3) the extent of the conflict with the sovereignty of the defendant's state; (4) the forum state's interest in adjudicating the dispute; (5) the most efficient judicial resolution of the controversy; (6) the importance of the forum to the plaintiff's interest in convenient and effective relief; and (7) the existence of an alternative forum.

Here, Defendants' acts were aimed at Yahoo! in California. Defendants purposefully accessed Yahoo!'s U.S.-based web site, mailed a demand letter to Yahoo! in Santa Clara, used U.S. Marshals to serve Yahoo! in Santa Clara, and purposefully sought and obtained an order requiring Yahoo! to reconfigure its U.S.-based servers, specifically including servers located in California. The purposeful interjection factor thus weighs in favor of this Court's exercise of personal jurisdiction.

The Court recognizes that the burden on Defendants as non-profit organizations organized in France of litigating in California is not trivial. However, it does not appear that requiring Defendants to litigate this particular case in California is constitutionally unreasonable. Further, it is likely that this case will be resolved largely if not entirely by dispositive motions addressing issues of law which do not require extensive fact discovery in this forum. Defendants have made no factual showing as to the severity of their burden other than making a generalized reference to the financial expense of participating in litigation in a foreign country and noting correctly that the jurisdictional barrier is higher when the defendant is not a resident of the United States.

Generally, as just noted, a plaintiff seeking to hale a foreign defendant into court in the United States must meet a "higher jurisdictional threshold" than is required when a defendant is United States resident. However, since sovereignty concerns inevitably arise whenever a United States court exercises jurisdiction over a foreign national, this factor is "by no means controlling," otherwise "it would always prevent suit against a foreign national in a United States court." The instant action involves only the limited question of whether this Court should recognize and enforce a French Order which requires Yahoo! to censor its U.S.-based services to conform to French penal law. While this Court must and does accord great respect and deference to France's sovereign interest in enforcing the orders and judgments of its courts, this interest must be weighed against the United States' own sovereign interest in protecting the constitutional and statutory rights of its residents.

California has an interest in providing effective legal redress for its residents. This interest appears to be particularly strong in this case in light of Yahoo!'s claim that its fundamental right to free expression has been and will be affected by Defendants' forum-related activities. Many nations, including France, limit freedom of expression on the Internet based upon their respective legal, cultural or political standards. Yet because of the global nature of the Internet, virtually any public web site can be accessed by end-users anywhere in the world, and in theory any provider of Internet content could be subject to legal action in countries which find certain content offensive. Defendants' approach would force the provider to wait indefinitely for a determination of its legal rights, effectively causing many to accept potentially unconstitutional restrictions on their content rather than face prolonged legal uncertainty. California's interest in adjudicating this dispute thus weighs strongly in favor of the exercise of personal jurisdiction.

Yahoo! contends that only a United States court has jurisdiction to adjudicate the question of whether the French Order is enforceable in the United States. Defendants contend that Yahoo! could have challenged the Order's validity, scope and extraterritorial application in France. The Court concludes that even if it were to assume that Yahoo! could challenge the extraterritorial application of the French Order in either jurisdiction or in both, it would hold that this Court is the more efficient and effective forum in which to resolve the narrow legal issue in question: whether the French Order is enforceable in the United States in light of the Constitution and laws of the United States.

While the parties disagree as to whether the French Court offers an alternative forum for determining whether the French Order is enforceable in the United States, the point is moot in light of the superiority of a United States forum for addressing the limited legal question at issue here.

The Court concludes that Defendants have failed to make the "compelling case" necessary to rebut the presumption that jurisdiction is reasonable.

Accordingly, the motion to dismiss is denied.

CASE QUESTIONS

1. What is Yahoo! doing in France that is the subject of a French court order?
2. How have the French sought to enforce the order?
3. Can the U.S. court take jurisdiction over the French parties?
4. What interest does California have in resolving the parties' dispute?

SUMMARY

What is cyber law?

- More accurate to refer to the law in cyberspace
- Cyber law is law as applied to issues that have arisen by doing business in cyberspace

What are the tort issues in cyber law?

- Privacy—e-mail

- Privacy in the disclosure of buying information about consumers using the Internet for purchasing

- The Electronic Communications Privacy Act of 1986 (ECPA)—prohibits the interception of "live" communications such as using a listening device to intercept a telephone conversation and has been raised as a way to prevent e-mail "eavesdropping" if e-mail is considered "live" communications

- Appropriation—use of an image or likeness over the Internet
- Defamation—the issues of identifying those who post information on Web sites and in chat rooms
- Trespass—the use of cyberspace facilities without permission of the owner of those facilities

What are the contract issues in cyber law?

- Trend is business-to-business (B2B) transactions wherein supplier and buyer have direct connections, possibly through customer's supply needs connected directly to manufacturer
- Electronic Digital Interchange (EDI)—precursor to the Internet and B2B transactions that permitted direct ordering and replenishment between manufacturers and their customers
- Point and click—the process of using the Internet and a computer to form a contract; pointing to a box that indicates affirmation and clicking the mouse
- Electronic Signatures in Global and National Commerce Act (called E-sign) is a federal law that recognizes digital signatures as authentic for purposes of contract formation. E-sign puts electronic signatures on equal footing with paper contracts.
- Uniform Electronic Transactions Act (UETA)—uniform law for states that provides the rules for formation of electronic contracts
- Uniform Computer Information Transaction Act (UCITA)—uniform law for states that provides requirements for disclosure in advance of formation
- Misrepresentation and fraud—false and misleading statements made in contract negotiation and formation stages; there are increases in both in Internet transactions because there is no face-to-face contact and such rapid dissemination of information

What are the Intellectual Property Issues in Cyberspace?

- Digital Millennium Copyright Act (DMCA) is a federal statute that amends existing copyright law in order to address some of the new issues of copyright infringement that exist because of digital technology and cyberspace, such as facilitating copyright infringement and whether linking to a copyrighted site can constitute an infringement.

- Domain registration—public filing for ownership of the name for a Website; names can be registered under an international umbrella and disputes are settled by arbitration
- Digital Millennium Copyright Act is a federal statute passed to address some of the new issues of copyright infringement that exist because of digital technology and cyberspace.
- Internet Corporation for Assigned Names and Numbers (ICANN)—organization that registers domain names for purposes of protection of that name as intellectual property
- Uniform Domain Name Dispute Resolution Policy (UDRP)—policy of ICANN that provides the means, timing and rules for resolving disputes over domain names
- Federal Trademark Dilution Act—federal law that permits litigation to halt the use of a trademark that results in the loss of unique appeal for its owner

What are the Criminal Law Issues in Cyberspace?

- Some old statutes such as theft and credit card fraud still apply to Internet crimes
- Some new statutes have been passed to cover those types of activities that do not fit into the traditional common law crimes
- Regardless of whether the crime is under a new statute or old common law standard, the burden of proof on all elements is still with the prosecutor
- Fourth Amendment protections against search and seizure still apply

What Are the Constitutional Law Issues in Cyberspace?

- First Amendment rights exist. No one can be forced to carry information over servers.
- Child Pornography Prevention Act—federal law that prohibited the transmission of child pornography over the Internet; struck down as unconstitutional the infringement of right to free speech
- Commerce Clause—the issue of taxation and the requirement of a nexus or connection to a state for taxation to be imposed on Internet transactions
- Due Process—issues on long arm jurisdiction have already evolved and some courts permit jurisdiction over Web sites sponsors and others do not, depending on the level of contact within the state and the nature of the parties and claim

What are the Securities Law Issues in Cyberspace?

- Pump-and-Dump—practice of buying a stock, touting it to many who then buy it and then selling the stock at an inflated price; not a new practice, but it is easier and faster over the Internet

- Laws on securities fraud and insider trading still apply.

- Accounting policies of dot-coms created new securities fraud issues.

What are the International Law Issues in Cyberspace?

- Long arm jurisdiction over foreign citizens remains an issue.

- Which country's laws apply in case of a conflict between the laws of two nations when both are using the same Internet server with the same content is also an issue.

QUESTIONS AND PROBLEMS

1. In the midst of the litigation surrounding its program for downloading music, Napster, Inc., discovered that a company was using its logo for T-shirts and selling the T-shirts. Can Napster do anything to prevent the use of its logo? Is the use of the logo for T-shirts any different from the use of songs for purposes of downloading for individual listening? Do you see an inconsistency in the defense of downloading music and then taking offense at the copying of the Napster logo?

2. The *New York Times* discovered that twenty-four of its employees in its payroll-processing center were sending "inappropriate and offensive e-mail in violation of corporate policy." Do the employees have any right to privacy with regard to the jokes they send over their e-mail accounts at work? Does the *New York Times* have the right to review the e-mails of the employees to find out about the jokes?

3. California, Nevada, and Washington recently enacted "anti-spam" laws. Anti-spam laws are laws designed to protect Internet users from receiving unsolicited or unwanted junk e-mail. The growth of spam or junk e-mail has been so extensive that systems for companies and organizations are often incapacitated by its inflow.

California's new legislation (Ca. Bus. and Prof. Code Sections 17538.4 and 17538.5 and Penal Code Section 502) prohibits commercial messages from being sent to those with whom the sender does not have an existing business relationship or from whom they have not received express consent. Questions that have already arisen because of the legislation are, What constitutes a business relationship, and Does a one-time transaction qualify for a business relationship?

In addition to controlling to whom the messages may be sent, advertisers must code their message on the subject line with a beginning "ADV." If there is adult material in the ad, the subject line must begin "ADV:ADLT."

Do you think these statutes violate the First Amendment?

Under the new California legislation, servers are permitted to adopt guidelines on the acceptance of ads and may adopt a policy of nonacceptance for unsolicited ads. These companies can then offer protections and screens to their customers and customers can choose options on receipt of junk e-mail. Would this form of statute meet First Amendment standards?

4. Toys " Я " Us has noted that Mohamad Ahmad Akkaoui has created a Web site for the sale of his merchandise which consists of sexual devices and clothing. The name of his Web site is "Adults " Я " Us Lingerienet." Toys " Я " Us worries that the " ' Я ' Us" use might confuse users and buyers at Akkaoui's site about its affiliation with Toys " Я " Us. What rights and protections exist here?

5. A firm that sold Christmas trees over the Internet used the name "Sporty's" in its Web site name. Sporty's has been registered to Sportsman, Inc., for use in its catalogs. The Christmas tree company, Sporty's Farm, explains that it had simply used the name of the owner's dog for the name of the tree Web site and its farm. Who will have the right to use the name on the Web? [*Sporty's Farm* v. *Sportman's Market*, 202 F.3d 489, *cert.* denied, 120 S.Ct. 2719 (2000)]

6. The Melissa virus infected computers around the world and has the record for the fastest moving virus to date. New Jersey law enforcement officials arrested 30-year-old David Smith for the creation of the now famous Melissa virus that has circulated and infected a number of computers. America Online helped the investigators determine the source of the original e-mail sent across the Internet that included the virus.

The virus was part of a message that included an attachment.

Mr. Smith's computer and disks were seized.

Discuss the legal issues in America Online cooperating to reveal the identity and activities of one of its customers. Discuss the seizure of the computer and disks. Discuss what crimes Mr. Smith could be charged with.

What types of criminal charges could be brought against those who develop such viruses? Are there crimes beyond computer crimes that they may have committed?

7. The *Cincinnati Enquirer* ran a story called "Chiquita's Secrets Revealed," in which the reporter documented allegations about the company through the use of e-mail messages that had been obtained by tapping into the company's computer system. Chiquita alleges that Michael Gallagher, a reporter, illegally cracked open the company's voice mail system. Mr. Gallagher was fired by the *Enquirer*.

Gallagher recorded over 2,000 voice mail messages, most of them from Chiquita's legal department. The messages also were delivered anonymously to the Securities and Exchange Commission (SEC). The SEC declined to reveal whether it was conducting an investigation of the company. The company's system logs more than 12,500 messages per week.

Mr. Gallagher submitted questions to the company and then listened to the voice mail of executives as they discussed their answers to his questions. The voice mail conversations were covered under the attorney/client privilege and would not have been discoverable in civil proceedings or usable in any type of criminal or regulatory proceedings.

The *Enquirer* printed an apology to Chiquita on the front page of its paper for three days and also agreed to pay $10 million.

Do you think Mr. Gallagher's conduct was legal? Ethical? What if Chiquita is found to have violated the law? Is his conduct then justified?

8. E-mail messages from a Microsoft executive, revealed as part of the antitrust case brought against it by the Justice Department, indicate that Microsoft engineers were working to program a software bug into an early version of Windows that would detect when a competitor's operating system was being used and then halt that use. One e-mail indicated that if such a program bug could be installed, it would "put competitors on a treadmill" and "crash at some point shortly later." One executive cautioned that the plan should be kept secret: "We need to make sure this

doesn't distract the team for a couple of reasons. One, the pure distraction factor, and two, the less people know about exactly what gets done, the better." Are these e-mails private or can the government have access to them?

9. Two critics of the Mormon Church took portions of the Mormon Church's "church handbook" and placed them on their Web site, which is highly critical of Mormon doctrine and practices. Called *Church Handbook of Instructions,* the materials in the book are copyrighted and constitute the protocol, processes, and procedures for the lay clergy of the Mormon church.

On October 20, 1999, the Mormon Church filed suit in federal district court in Salt Lake City for copyright infringement and requested as a remedy that Jerald and Sandra Tanner be required to remove the excerpted portions of the handbook from their Web site.

Discuss why the suit was filed in federal district court when the Mormon Church is headquartered in Salt Lake City and the Tanners are Utah residents (see also Chapter 3).

If copies of the handbook are made regularly by members and shared with many, are there any problems with enforcing the copyright? Also refer to Chapter 16.

Should it make any difference that the materials are on the Internet as opposed to reprinting? How does the recent court decision that allows authors to prevent their columns from being reprinted on the newspapers' Web sites without their permission help in finding the answer in this case?

10. Douglas Colt was a second-year law student who developed a way to make money from the Internet. He set up a free Web site promising folks hot tips on stocks. However, Mr. Colt bought the stocks himself at low prices before then pumping them up at his Web site. Once the shares were pumped up to a high enough price from the users of his Web site buying the shares, he would then sell all of his shares, that is, dump them. Mr. Colt made over $345,000 using the old tool of "pump and dump" in the new technology, the Internet.

Colt had attracted 9,000 investors to his Web site (Fast-Trades.com). One of his shares, American Education Corporation, climbed 700 percent before he sold his holdings.

Those who participated in the pump-and-dump scam, including Mr. Colt's mother, a councilwoman from Colorado, agreed to a consent decree settlement. None will pay a fine and none will repay their profits.

They have simply agreed not to violate federal securities laws in the future. Georgetown University, Mr. Colt's law school, said there would be no disciplinary action.

Did Colt violate insider trading laws or any federal securities laws?

Was Colt's conduct ethical?

NOTES

1. Julie Cook, "Big Brother Goes to Work," *Office Systems*, August 1999, 43–45.

2. American Management Association Web Site, Research Reports, "More U.S. Firms Checking E-Mail, Computer Files, and Phone Calls, says AMA Survey," April 1999, see http://www.amanet.org/research/ to request a copy

3. Alex Berenson, "Man Charged in Stock Fraud Based on Fake News," *New York Times,* 1 September 2000, C1, C2.

4. *Ibid.*

5. L. J. Kutten, Bernard D. Reams, and Allen E. Strehler, *Electronic Contracting Law* (1991).

6. Virginia and California have adopted UETA and UCITA. Both laws can be found online: http://www.uetaonline.com and http://www.ucitaonline.com

7. Noelle Know, "Online Auctions Top List of Internet Fraud," *USA Today,* 29 August 2000, 1A.

8. Matt Richtel, "Chairman of Amazon Urges Reduction of Patent Terms," *New York Times*, 11 March 2000, B4.

9. 17 USC 1201 *et seq.*

10. See http://Emergency.com/cybrcr98.htm; see also http://www.fbi.gov/nipc/welcome

11. http://jaring.nmhu.edu

12. http://www.computereconomics.com

13. http://www.computerworld.com

14. See http://www.zdnet.com

15. *U.S.* v. *Peterson,* 98 F.3d 502 (9th Cir. 1996).

16. 18 U.S.C. 1030 (1999).

17. 18 U.S.C. 1831 *et seq.* (1999).

18. *U.S.* v. *Hunter,* 13 F. Supp. 2d 574 (D. Vt. 1998).

19. 18 U.S.C. 2252 *et seq.* (1999).

20. *U.S.* v. *Hilton,* 167 F.3d 61 (1st Cir. 1999), cert. denied, 120 S. Ct. 115 (1999); *U.S.* v. *Acheson,* 195 F.3d 645 (11th Cir. 1999) and *Free Speech Coalition* v. *Reno,* 1999 U.S. App. LEXIS 32704 (1999).

21. Floyd Norris, "AOL Pays A Fine to Settle a Charge That It Inflated Profits," *New York Times,* 16 May 2000, C6.

BUSINESS STRATEGY APPLICATION

The Federal Trade Commission now requires those who have Web sites to make disclosures about their policies on the use of information. The users must "point and click" in order to agree to the use of information about them that becomes available because of their use of the Web site. In this exercise you can see the FTC guidelines, view some sample policies and then develop your own privacy policy for your company's Web site.

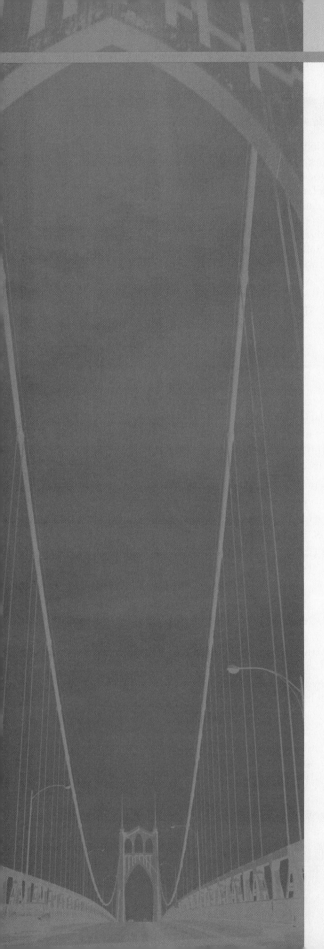

CHAPTER NINE

Business Crime

Business and crime have jointly occupied the headlines of newspapers for much of the past decade. During the year 2000, the Securities Exchange Commission opened over 200 investigations for fraud by corporations. The General Accounting Office estimated in 2000 that more than $100 million of annual health care costs may be attributable to fraud. In the year 2001, the U.S. Justice Department obtained 6,868 white-collar crime convictions, recovered $3.89 billion for victims of white-collar crime, and collected $880 million in criminal penalties from corporations and their managers.

In 1999, credit card fraud through the Internet created more than $400 million in losses.

In its annual strategic plan for the year 2001, the United States Department of Justice concluded that there would be a substantial increase in securities violations, mail fraud, and computer crime because of the Internet and its use for conducting business. Their plan calls for focusing on the "masterminds" who establish the companies that engage in fraud and other forms of business crime.

Every businessperson needs a background in the nature of business crimes. This chapter offers that background for the businessperson by answering the following questions: Why does business crime occur? Who is liable for crimes committed by businesses? What penalties are imposed for business crimes? What are the rights of corporate and individual defendants in the criminal justice system?

Did you ever expect a corporation to have a conscience, when it has no soul to be damned and no body to be kicked?

LORD CHANCELLOR EDWARD THURLOW, 1731–1806

Your crimes show a pattern of skirting the law.

JUDGE KIMBA WOOD,
on sentencing junk-bond king Michael Milken to prison

You don't put Michelangelo or da Vinci in jail. To lose that mind for even a day would be a tragedy.

CHARLES KEATING,
on the sentencing of junk-bond king Michael Milken

I haven't committed a crime. What I did was fail to comply with the law.

DAVID DIMKINS
Former mayor of New York City, on facing charges that he failed to pay taxes

To run him to earth and brand him, as long ago pirate and traitor were branded, is the crying need of our time. . . . Every year that sees him pursue in insolent triumph his nefarious career . . . hurries society toward moral bankruptcy.

EDWARD A. ROSS
on "criminaloids," his term for white-collar criminals in Sin and Society

CONSIDER...

John Park is the president of Acme Markets, a national retail food chain. Acme operated sixteen warehouses that were subject to inspection by the Food and Drug Administration (FDA). During 1970 and 1971, FDA inspectors found rodents in Acme's Philadelphia and Baltimore warehouses. The FDA's chief of compliance wrote to Park and asked that he direct his attention to cleaning up the warehouses. Park directed a subordinate officer to take care of the problems. When the FDA inspected the warehouses again, rodent infesta-

© Robert Holmes/CORBIS

tion was still evident. The FDA charged Acme and Park with criminal violations of the Federal Food, Drug, and Cosmetic Act. Park says he tried to clean up the warehouses but his subordinates failed and that he should not be liable. Is Park correct?

WHAT IS BUSINESS CRIME? THE CRIMES WITHIN A CORPORATION

Many business crimes are committed because the companies apply pressure to managers and employees to produce results. Economic pressure is responsible for much business crime. Upper- and middle-level managers feel the pressure to meet earnings goals or to reach incentive bonus plan figures, and they pass along the pressure they feel to employees. The drive to succeed or present a good earnings record can then lead many employees into crimes on behalf of the corporation. These crimes do not directly line employee pockets. The business benefits, and employees benefit indirectly through profit sharing, salary increases, bonuses, or through just being able to keep their jobs.

For example, in May 2001, the Securities Exchange Commission charged the former CEO of Sunbeam, "Chainsaw" Al Dunlap, with securities fraud for the earnings statements released by Sunbeam while he was its CEO. The SEC complaint alleges that Dunlap and others booked a $5–$6 million sale of inventory as earnings when that sale had not occurred and never did occur. Those who permitted the revenues from a nonexistent sale to be booked indicated that they were simply trying to meet projected earnings statements so that they could preserve shareholder value and share price on the market. In addition to pressure to meet company goals, some individual employees feel personal financial pressure and resort to embezzlement as a means of remedying their bleak personal financial positions. Estimates of losses from internal business thefts range from $4 billion to $44 billion a year. Law enforcement officials claim that 90 percent of all crime occurs inside businesses. They also estimate that the losses attributable to business crimes are forty times greater than losses from crimes committed on the street.

These losses from business crimes do not include the indirect costs businesses now have because of the amount of crime—the costs of security (estimated at $30 billion) and of insurance against internal thefts. A 2001 survey found that 92 percent of employees interviewed admitted taking something from their employers, such as computer time or reimbursement for inflated travel expenses. A survey of businesses and government units found that the average amount each organization loses from check fraud such as forgeries and mail room thefts by employees is $624,000. Medical insurance fraud by employees is estimated at $3 million per company, and false expenses are put at $141,000 per company. These numbers are at least triple what they were in 1994.

The Justice Department estimates that computer hackers steal $2 billion per year over the Internet. The number of forensic accountants has increased from 200 in 1992 to 480 in the FBI today. Indeed, there are now 25,000 members, up from 5,000 in 1994, in the forensic accounting field's professional organization as everyone from internal auditors to special agents tries to ferret out fraud within corporations.

For up-to-date information on crimes, visit the Bureau of Justice statistics:
http://www.ojp.usdoj.gov/
bjs/dtdata.htm
and
http://www.ojp.usdoj.gov/
bjs/welcome.html

Small businesses have higher employee theft costs because they cannot afford the sophisticated monitoring measures larger corporations adopt. Most employee theft is systematic: It goes on over a period of time and is well planned. For example, employees of an aircraft plant filled their pockets with nuts and bolts each day at the end of the shift. Over time, enough hardware was accumulated to fill kegs, which were then sold. Garment workers for apparel manufacturers have gone home with jeans in their purses. Nine out of every ten purchasing agents take kickbacks. All of these acts can be prosecuted under some criminal statute.

These crimes committed for and against a business are business crimes, often referred to as **white-collar crime**. Exhibit 9.1 provides a summary of companies and business executives that have had encounters with laws, regulators, and courts.

EXHIBIT 9.1 **A Roster of Wrongdoing**

NAME/COMPANY	ALLEGATIONS	OUTCOME
Robert Altman, attorney; officer in BCCI subsidiary (1992)	Conspiracy; fraud; commercial bribery; falsifying business records; filing false documents	Acquitted
Archer Daniels, Midland (1996)	Price-fixing	Guilty plea; $100 million fine, $90 million to settle shareholder suits
Bausch & Lomb (1997)	Violations of federal securities laws for overstatement of earnings	Fines paid by officers ($10,000); shareholder lawsuits
BCCI (1992)	RICO violations; fraud; money laundering; larceny; falsification of documents	Guilty plea; $550 million fine
Beverly Enterprises	Fabricated costs; overstated Medicare bills; wire fraud; Medicare fraud	$5 million criminal fine; $170,000 civil fine
Ivan Boesky, arbitrager; worked with Michael Milken (1988)	Securities fraud	Guilty plea; three-year prison with sentence; $100 million in fines and restitution
Brown, Columbia, Cornell, Harvard, Pennsylvania, Princeton, and Yale universities and Dartmouth College (1992)	Monopolization in financial aid awards	Consent decrees agreeing to halt agreements on standard financial aid practices
Clark Clifford, officer in BCCI subsidiary; former secretary of defense (1992)	Conspiracy; fraud; commercial bribery	Too ill to stand trial (now deceased)
Columbia/HCA HealthCare (1998)	Overbilling Medicare	Three executives indicted; two convicted; $745 million fine; 53 percent profit drop; 100 hospitals spun off
Dun & Bradstreet (1992)	Misleading customers into overpurchasing credit services in five suits	Settlement of $18 million
Drexel Burnham Lambert, Inc. (1990)	Securities fraud	Plea bargain; $650 million for criminal charges; $1.6 billion in settlement of investor lawsuits (9,000 investors); agreement to fire Michael Milken
E. F. Hutton (1985)	Check kiting; mail and wire fraud	Guilty plea; $2 million fine
Exxon (1989)	Oil spill; felony pollution charges	$1.3 billion plus $100 million additional damages; cleanup
Ford (1980)	Negligent homicide (Pinto)	Indicted; civil suits nationally
General Electric (1991)	Fraud (defense contract); false billing	$70 million fine; guilty plea
Hertz Rent-A-Car (1988)	Criminal overcharging on repair of damaged rental cars	$13 million refund to consumers
Honda USA (1995)	Bribes; kickbacks	Guilty pleas and convictions of 16 officers

(continued)

EXHIBIT 9.1 *(continued)*

NAME/COMPANY	ALLEGATIONS	OUTCOME
Charles Keating, former CEO of Lincoln S & L (1991)	Securities fraud; federal charges of bankruptcy fraud pending	Convicted; serving 10-year term; partial reversal of case
Kidder Peabody & Co. (1994)	Negligence in supervision of fraudulent bond trader	Firm sold by GE; SEC investigation
Merril Lynch & Co., Inc. (1992)	SEC/congressional investigation into junk bonds	Settled with SEC
Microsoft (1998)	Antitrust monopolization	Settled; $80 million in software donated to schools
Michael Milken, head of bonds for Drexel Burnham (1990)	Securities fraud; income tax evasion; violating ban	Guilty plea; $200 million in fines and penalties; $400 million to settle civil suits; 10-year prison sentence; permanent ban from securities industry; paroled; fined for violating ban—$38 million
MiniScribe (1990)	SEC charges (fraud)	$550 million verdict in civil trial
MIT (1992)	Monopolization in financial aid awards	Barred from future combinations with other schools
Phar-Mor, Inc. (1994)	Fraud; embezzlement	Bankruptcy (Chapter 11—emerged in 1995); CEO sentenced to 35 months
Salomon Brothers (1992)	Cornering bond market; false bids; false records	$290 million fine; two-month suspension
Sears Roebuck (1992)	Consumer fraud in its auto repair shops	Settlement of $8 million (California); 933,000 coupons to repair shop customers ($50 each)
Smith Kline (1997)	False billings to Medicare in 42 states	$325 million fine
Sun-Diamond Foods	Making illegal gifts (Mike Espy)	Guilty plea; $1.5 million fines
U.S. Savings & Loans (1995)	Banking law violations; fraud	$45 million in fines; $2.9 billion in restitution; over 4,000 executives sentenced to prison
U.S. Aviation Underwriters	Fraud in failure to pay airlines' claims	Guilty; $20.5 million fine; CEO sentenced to 5 years
Orange County, California	Mismanagement of investment funds (derivatives)	Robert Citron, treasurer, enters guilty plea (1-year sentence)
Tyson Foods	Making illegal gifts to government officials (Mike Espy)	Guilty plea; $6 million fine
ValuJet	Unlawful transportation of tanks	$11.1 million fine

WHAT IS BUSINESS CRIME? THE CRIMES AGAINST A CORPORATION

Interbusiness crime occurs among competitors and results in one business's gaining a competitive advantage over others. For example, a federal grand jury indicted General Electric for allegedly defrauding the Air Force of more than $800,000 on defense contracts. The Defense Department asked Pratt & Whitney for a $40 million refund on profits made by the firm in supplying jet engine spare parts. Archer Daniels Midland paid a $100 million fine as part of a plea bargain on price-fixing antitrust charges brought against it and several of its officers. Columbia Health Care paid a $745 million fine to settle charges that it had overbilled the government for Medicare and Medicaid patients treated in its facilities. Microsoft was charged with violations of the Sherman Antitrust Act for alleged monopolization through the tying of its Internet browser to its Windows 95 program.

Banks and other financial institutions become involved in interbusiness crime through failure to carefully check their systems operations. Such was the failure of First National Bank of Boston, which facilitated the laundering of proceeds from racketeering and loan sharking by not giving the required notice to the Treasury Department of the conversion of large amounts of cash to cashier's checks. With computer technology so advanced, competitors are tapping into other companies' systems for access to data and other proprietary information.

Once again, it is competitive pressure that results in these types of crimes. Employees within one company engage in illegal behavior in order to achieve what they believe will be a competitive advantage. However, as the remainder of the chapter shows, any competitive advantage is only temporary.

WHO IS LIABLE FOR BUSINESS CRIME?

One of the major differences between nonbusiness and business crimes is that more people can be convicted for business crimes. For nonbusiness crimes, only those actually involved in the planning or execution of the crime or assistance after it is committed can be convicted. In other words, those who were somehow involved in the criminal act or aftermath are criminally responsible. For business crimes, on the other hand, those in the management of firms whose employees actually commit criminal acts can be held liable if they authorized the conduct, knew about the conduct but did nothing, or failed to act reasonably in their supervisory positions. The following landmark case discusses the liability standards for those who are in charge but may not themselves commit a criminal act. It also provides an answer to the chapter's opening "Consider."

CASE 9.1

United States v. *Park*
421 U.S. 658 (1975)

Is Chasing Rats from the Warehouse in My Job Description?

FACTS

Acme Markets, Inc., was a national food retail chain headquartered in Philadelphia, Pennsylvania. At the time of the government action, John R. Park was president of Acme, which employed 36,000 people and operated 16 warehouses.

In 1970, the Food and Drug Administration (FDA) forwarded a letter to Mr. Park describing, in detail, problems with rodent infestation in Acme's Philadelphia warehouse facility. In December 1971, the FDA found the same types of conditions in Acme's Baltimore warehouse facility. In January 1972, the FDA's chief of compliance for its Baltimore office wrote to Mr. Park about

(continued)

the inspection. The letter included the following language:

We note with much concern that the old and new warehouse areas used for food storage were actively and extensively inhabited by live rodents. Of even more concern was the observation that such reprehensible conditions obviously existed for a prolonged period of time without any detection, or were completely ignored.

We trust this letter will serve to direct your attention to the seriousness of the problem and formally advise you of the urgent need to initiate whatever measures are necessary to prevent recurrence and ensure compliance with the law.

After Mr. Park received the letter, he met with the vice president for legal affairs for Acme and was assured that he was "investigating the situation immediately and would be taking corrective action."

When the FDA inspected the Baltimore warehouse in March 1972, there was some improvement in the facility, but there was still rodent infestation. Acme and Park were both charged with violations of the Federal Food, Drug, and Cosmetic Act. Acme pleaded guilty. Mr. Park was convicted and fined $500; he appealed based on error in the judge's instruction, given as follows:

The individual is or could be liable under the statute even if he did not consciously do wrong. However, the fact that the Defendant is president and chief executive officer of the Acme Markets does not require a finding of guilt. Though he need not have personally participated in the situation, he must have had a responsible relationship to the issue. The issue is, in this case, whether the Defendant, John R. Park, by virtue of his position in the company, had a position of authority and responsibility in the situation out of which these charges arose.

The court of appeals reversed Mr. Park's conviction and the government appealed.

JUDICIAL OPINION

BURGER, Chief Justice

Central to the Court's conclusion [in *United States* v. *Dotterweich*], 320 U.S. 277 (1943), that individuals other than proprietors are subject to the criminal provisions of the Act was the reality that "the only way in which a corporation can act is through the individuals who act on its behalf."

At the same time, however, the Court was aware of the concern . . . that literal enforcement "might operate too harshly by sweeping within its condemnation any person however remotely entangled in the proscribed shipment." A limiting principle, in the form of "settled doctrines of criminal law" defining those who "are responsible for the commission of a misdemeanor," was available. In this context, the Court concluded, those doctrines dictated that the offense was committed "by all who have . . . a responsible share in the furtherance of the transaction which the statute outlaws."

The Act does not, as we observed in *Dotterweich*, make criminal liability turn on "awareness of some wrongdoing" or "conscious fraud." The duty imposed by Congress on responsible corporate agents is, we emphasize, one that requires the highest standard of foresight and vigilance, but the Act, in its criminal aspect, does not require that which is objectively impossible. The theory upon which responsible corporate agents are held criminally accountable for "causing" violations of the Act permits a claim that a defendant was "powerless" to prevent or correct the violation to "be raised defensively at a trial on the merits." *U.S.* v. *Wiesenfeld Warehouse Co.*, 376 U.S. 86 (1964). If such a claim is made, the defendant has the burden of coming forward with evidence, but this does not alter the Government's ultimate burden of proving beyond a reasonable doubt the defendant's guilt, including his power, in light of the duty imposed by the Act, to prevent or correct the prohibited condition.

Turning to the jury charge in this case, it is of course arguable that isolated parts can be read as intimating that a finding of guilt could be predicated solely on respondent's corporate position. . . . Viewed as a whole, the charge did not permit the jury to find guilt solely on the basis of respondent's position in the corporation; rather, it fairly advised the jury that to find guilt it must find respondent "had a responsible relation to the situation," and "by virtue of his position . . . had authority and responsibility" to deal with the situation. The situation referred to could only be "food . . . held in unsanitary conditions in a warehouse with the result that it consisted, in part, of filth or . . . may have been contaminated with filth."

Park testified in his defense that he had employed a system in which he relied upon his subordinates, and that he was ultimately responsible for this system. He testified further that he had found these subordinates to be "dependable" and had "great confidence" in them.

[The rebuttal] evidence was not offered to show that respondent had a propensity to commit criminal acts, that the crime charged had been committed; its purpose was to demonstrate that respondent was on notice that he could not rely on his system of delegation to subordinates to prevent or correct unsanitary conditions at Acme's warehouses, and that he must have been aware of the deficiencies of this system before the Baltimore violations were discovered. The evidence was therefore relevant since it served to rebut Park's defense that he had justifiably relied upon subordinates to handle sanitation matters.

Reversed.

CASE QUESTIONS

1. What problems did the FDA find in the Acme warehouses?

2. Over what period of time did the FDA find the problems?

3. Was Mr. Park warned about the problem?

4. What action did Mr. Park take?

5. What standard of liability did the instruction given by the judge impose?

6. Was the instruction correct?

7. Is Mr. Park guilty of a criminal violation?

FOR THE MANAGER'S DESK

Re: The Savings and Loan Statistics

From 1988 to June 30, 1995, the federal government, through the Office of the Special Counsel of the Justice Department, conducted investigations into failed savings and loans "to find and prosecute those who looted our financial institutions." When the Office of Special Counsel concluded its work, the following statistics were released:

Number of defendants charged:
6,405
Types of crimes:
4,297 bank crimes
1,852 S & L crimes
256 credit union crimes
Convictions:
5,506 defendants convicted (96.5 percent conviction rate)
Types of persons convicted:
Officers, directors or CEOs: 29 percent; accountants, attorneys, and consultants: 71 percent

Types of persons charged:
Directors and officers—1,268 (97.5 percent) convicted
Presidents or CEOs—484 (95.1 percent) convicted
Prison time:
Of the 5,506 defendants convicted, 75.5 percent were sentenced to prison.
Fines imposed:
$45,000,000
Restitution ordered:
$2.9 billion

James G. Richmond, who served as special counsel, noted that the 71 percent conviction rate of outsiders proves his point: "If you get an officer who goes bad, he isn't just going to do it with one guy. The most logical accomplice is the lawyer, accountant, or appraiser."

In 1990, Congress enacted what has been called the "white-collar kingpin" law. A response to the 1980s savings and loan scandals, the law imposes minimum mandatory sentences (ten years in most instances) for corporate officers who mastermind financial crimes such as bank and securities fraud.

Browse the Law & Leading Attorneys (L&LA) Web site addressing white-collar crime:
http://www.lawlead.com

Liability for crimes also extends to employees who participate with the company and its management in illegal acts. An employee who works with her employer in establishing fraudulent tax shelters for customers can be held liable along with the company and its officers. The key to liability is personal knowledge of wrongdoing.

Re: Who Really Ends Up Going to Jail for Corporate Crime?

For the most part, those who are sentenced in federal court for white-collar crimes tend to come from the middle classes rather than the upper classes. Criminal violations committed by Fortune 500 corporations over a two-year period showed that executives were convicted in only 1.5 percent of the cases. However, managers were more likely than not to be sentenced in such cases. And employees, particularly in securities fraud cases, were more likely to be sentenced to prison than the executives for whom they worked. Executives charged with securities violations were also less likely to even be prosecuted criminally than employees. However, executives are far more likely than both groups to be given civil sanctions.

White-collar criminals are most likely to have committed their first offense with their business crime charges (72 percent). They are older than most inmates, with 46 percent being over the age of 40.

The breakdown for federal offenders sent to prison is as follows:

Type of Crime	Percentage of Total White-Collar Crime
Fraud	16.5%
Regulatory offenses	2.4%
Extortion, bribery	5.7%

Other types of federal crimes include tax evasion; Medicare and Medicaid overbilling; false reports; and environmental, antitrust, embezzlement, and other securities violations.

The conviction rate for federal prosecutors in the United States is 88 percent. In China, the rate is 99.7 percent.

CONSIDER...

9.1 Virginia T. Morris was the chief executive officer and chairman of the board of directors of Northwest National Bank, a financial institution located in Fayetteville, Arkansas. She was indicted on several counts of bank fraud, money laundering, making false entries in the books of a federally insured financial institution, and making false material statements to a federal bank examiner. Mrs. Morris was convicted and sentenced to prison. She appealed her case on grounds that all the paperwork for the loans, checks, and drafts involved in the case were completed and signed by employees at the bank and not by her. The government has responded by noting that all overdraft approvals were done orally by her. Can Ms. Morris be held criminally responsible for conduct completed on paper exclusively by others? [*United States* v. *Morris,* 18 F.3d 562 (8th Cir. 1994)]

CONSIDER...

9.2 Rudolf G. "Butch" Stanko began the Cattle King Packing Company in Colorado in 1981. He was an officer and a shareholder of the corporation. Mr. Stanko hired Gary Waderich as general sales manager and operations manager.

Stanko, Waderich, and Cattle King were charged with violations of the Federal Meat Inspection Act for selling adulterated meat (meat mixed with inedible scraps to enhance poundage).

Mr. Stanko lived in Scotts Bluff, Nebraska, and claimed he could not be charged because he did not oversee day-to-day operations. He used the "I-was-in-Scotts-Bluff" defense. Will this defense work? [*United States* v. *Cattle King Packing Co., Inc.,* 793 F.2d 232 (10th Cir. 1986)]

THE PENALTIES FOR BUSINESS CRIME

Statutes specify penalties for crimes. Some statutes have both business and individual penalties. Exhibit 9.2 provides a summary of the penalties under the major federal statutes.

Reforming Criminal Penalties

Some regulators and legislators argue that the difficulty with most criminal law penalties is that they were instituted with "natural" persons in mind, as opposed to "artificial" corporate persons. Fines may be significant to individuals, but a $10,000 fine to a corporation with billions in assets and millions in income is simply a cost of doing business.

A recommendation advanced for the reformation of criminal penalties is that the penalties must cost the corporation as much as a bad business decision would cost. For example, if a company develops a bad product line, net earnings could decline 10 to 20 percent. Penalties expressed in terms of net earnings, as opposed to set dollar amounts, are more likely to have a deterrent effect on business criminal behavior.

Another recommendation advanced, and one that has been implemented to a certain extent, requires prison sentences for officers and directors. The human

EXHIBIT 9.2 **Penalties for Business Crime under Federal Law**

ACT	PENALTIES
Internal Revenue Code 26 U.S.C. 7201	$100,000 ($500,000 corporations) and/or 5 years For evasion (plus costs of prosecution) $350,000 and/or three years
Sherman Act (antitrust) 15 U.S.C. 1	$10,000,000 for corporations Injunctions Divestiture
1933 Securities Act 15 U.S.C. 77x	$10,000 and/or 5 years
Securities and Exchange Act of 1934 15 U.S.C. 78ff	$1,000,000 and/or 10 years $2,500,000 for corporations Civil penalties in addition of up to 3 times profit made or $1,000,000, whichever is greater
Clean Air Act 42 U.S.C. 7413	$1,000,000 and/or 5 years
Clean Water Act 33 U.S.C. 1319	$25,000 per day and/or 1 year for negligent violations $50,000 per day and/or 3 years for knowing violations $100,000 per day and/or 6 years for second violations $10,000 per day and/or 2 years for false statements in reports, plans, or records
Occupational Health Safety Act 29 U.S.C. 666	Willful violation causing death $20,000 and/or 1 year Giving advance notice of inspection $1,000 and/or 6 months False statements or representations $10,000 and/or 6 months
Consumer Product Safety Commission 15 U.S.C. 2070	$50,000 and/or 1 year

VALUJET: THE AIRLINE WITH A CRIMINAL RECORD

ValuJet was a discount regional airline that had captured a good share of the market on the Eastern seaboard. On May 11, 1996, a ValuJet plane, Flight 592, 11 minutes into its flight after taking off from Miami, while over the Florida Everglades, crashed, killing all 105 passengers and the 5 crew members who were aboard. Within two months, the Federal Aviation Administration (FAA) had shut down the airline and grounded its planes, citing safety concerns.

The National Transportation Safety Board (NTSB) found that the crash was caused by a fire that resulted from 144 oxygen-generating canisters that SabreTech, Inc., (ValuJet's maintenance firm) employees had placed in the aircraft without proper security, labeling, and packaging. The result was that the canisters exploded and caused a fire in the cabin that resulted in the crash.

Following the NTSB investigation and simultaneous investigations by the FAA, state authorities, and other federal agencies, numerous violations of the law at both the state and federal level were alleged. The violations included not only ValuJet but also other regional airlines. Following the ValuJet crash and the perception that regional airlines were not well supervised, the FAA promised to step up efforts on safety standards. In 1996, the federal government indicted five former employees of Mesa Air Group, Inc., for falsification of records and the use of substandard parts. Mesa Air Group was a maintenance company used by regional airlines for work on their planes. These charges led the FAA to investigate other maintenance firms, which led them to SabreTech, Inc. The FAA charged SabreTech with improperly packaging oxygen generators on the ValuJet flight with a resulting explosion and fire in the cabin that then led to the plane's crash. The indictment alleged that two SabreTech employees, also indicted in the charges, signed work cards stating that they had installed shipping caps on the oxygen generators. Such caps would have prevented their explosion, but the employees only signed the cards; there had been no caps installed. Neither ValuJet nor SabreTech had the caps in their parts inventory. Caps for the 144 canisters would have cost $9.16.

SabreTech was found guilty of only one of the charges: that they had failed to provide training for employees in handling hazardous materials. The company was acquitted on charges of conspiracy and making false statements. The two employees were both acquitted. During the trial, the prosecutor for the federal government said that the two employees were subjected to a "pencil-whipping," meaning that their supervisor demanded that they sign the cards even though the work had not been done.

Following these charges, several cooperating prosecuting attorneys' offices brought the first criminal charges ever brought against an airline. The Miami-Dade County State Attorney's Office filed 110 counts of murder charges against SabreTech for the deaths of 110 passengers in the 1996 crash. The indictment also named three employees of SabreTech. While ValuJet was charged with other crimes, it was not charged with murder.

The charges carry up to five years in prison for each charged employee as well as fines of $250,000 for the company along with $6 million potential fines in charges of mishandling materials for air shipment. A prosecutor for the Miami-Dade County State Attorney's Office said, "This crash was completely preventable. This was not an accident; it was a crime. It was a homicide."

The three employees named are two mechanics as well as SabreTech's vice president for operations. Their lawyer and a lawyer for the company responded that the men were acting on information furnished to them by the company and that the mislabeling and resulting mishandling were the result of a series of mistakes and not reckless or intentional behavior.*

In 1997, ValuJet was merged with another airline that took over operations and the FAA thereby permitted the use of the grounded planes. In 2001, SabreTech settled its regulatory charges with the FAA by paying a $1.75 million fine. SabreTech, now defunct, made no admissions in reaching the civil settlement. The FAA indicated it was uncertain whether any of the fine could be collected.

SabreTech was convicted and ordered to pay a fine of $2,000,000 and restitution of $9,060,400. SabreTech appealed and the conviction on failure to train was upheld but the hazardous material conviction was reversed.*

Both ValuJet and SabreTech and their insurers have paid hundreds of millions of dollars to settle the wrongful death suits brought by the families of the passengers.

*Matthew L. Wald, "Murder Charges Filed by Florida in ValuJet Crash," *New York Times*, 14 July 1999, A1, A14.

element of the corporation—the action element—is then punished for the acts done in the name of the business.

A new type of sentence for corporations has emerged over the past five years. Judges are increasingly assigning monitors to corporations to follow up on corporate activity. For example, as its sentence in an environmental case, ConEd was assigned a Natural Resources Defense Council lawyer as a monitor for its asbestos activity. While their cases were not criminal in nature, both Coca-Cola and Mitsubishi agreed to a panel of monitors as part of their settlement in discrimination cases.

A final recommendation for reforming criminal penalties would require corporations to stand criminally responsible under traditional criminal statutes for corporate wrongs. For example, when Ford Motor Company manufactured the Pinto automobile with a design flaw involving the gas tank location, many civil suits were brought for deaths and injuries caused by the exploding gas tank. However, Ford was indicted for a criminal charge of homicide. In 1999, the state of Florida charged ValuJet, Inc., with murder and manslaughter for carelessly handling deadly materials for shipment with their omissions resulting in a crash of an airplane and the deaths of 110 passengers and the crew. (See Biography.) A traditional common law crime was applied to corporations for the wrongful death of customers. The owner of Imperial Foods Company in North Carolina pled guilty to workplace hazards that resulted in the burn deaths of twenty-five employees at his chicken processing plant and received a nineteen-year prison sentence. While the crimes he was charged with were violations of business laws, the sentence was traditional in the sense that an individual within a company was held personally and criminally responsible for the crimes.

The following case involves a creative sentence imposed by a judge on a corporation.

CASE 9.2

United States v. *Allegheny Bottling Co.*
695 F.Supp. 856 (E.D. Va. 1988) cert. denied, 493 U.S. 817 (1989)

Coke and Pepsi Wars Turn Criminal: Imprisonment for Price-Fixing

FACTS

Mid-Atlantic Coca-Cola Bottling Company and Allegheny Pepsi-Cola Bottling Company were charged with conspiracy to fix prices on Coke and Pepsi in order to avoid the ruinous competition that price wars were causing. Several officers pleaded guilty to the charges, and some were found guilty by a jury.

The trial evidence showed that in the Baltimore market, Coke sold from 6,200,000 to 7,000,000 cases of soft drinks a year. Prior to the price-fixing agreement, the price per case was $6.00 to $6.40. After the price-fixing agreement in 1982, the price was $6.80

per case, and it remained there for a full year. This additional 40 cents per case allowed the companies to earn over $1 million more. In pronouncing sentence on the corporate defendants, the judge used a creative solution (later affirmed by the appellate court).

JUDICIAL OPINION

DOUMAR, District Judge
The Lord Chancellor of England said some two hundred years ago, "Did you ever expect a corporation to have a conscience when it has no soul to be

(continued)

damned, and no body to be kicked?" Two hundred years have passed since the Lord Chancellor espoused this view, and the whole area of what is and is not permitted or what is or is not prohibited, has changed both in design and application. Certainly, this Court does not expect a corporation to have a conscience, but it does expect it to be ethical and abide by the law. This Court will deal with this company no less severely than it will deal with any individual who similarly disregards the law.

. . . Allegheny Bottling Company [parent of Allegheny Pepsi] is sentenced to three (3) years imprisonment and a fine of One Million Dollars ($1,000,000). Execution of the sentence of imprisonment is suspended and all but $950,000 of said fine is suspended, and the defendant is placed on probation for a period of three years.

As special conditions of the probation, in addition to the normal terms of probation, the defendant, Allegheny Bottling Company, shall provide:

(a) An officer or employee of Allegheny of comparable salary and stature to Jerry Polino (former vice president of sales who pled guilty to the conspiracy charges) to perform forty (40) hours of community service per week in the Baltimore, Maryland area for a two (2) year period without compensation to the defendant. [The court required 40 hours of community service from someone of equal stature for each of the four officers of Allegheny who had been convicted or pleaded guilty to the price fixing conspiracy charges.]

Corporate imprisonment requires only that the Court restrain or immobilize the corporation. Such restraint of individuals is accomplished by, for example, placing them in the custody of the United States Marshal. The United States Marshal would restrain the corporation by seizing the corporation's physical assets or part of the assets or restricting its actions or liberties in a particular manner.

Cases in the past have *assumed* that corporations cannot be imprisoned, without any cited authority for that proposition. This Court, however, has been unable to find any case which actually held that corporate imprisonment is illegal, unconstitutional, or impossible. Considerable confusion regarding the ability of courts to order a corporation imprisoned has been caused by courts mistakenly thinking that imprisonment necessarily involves incarceration in jail. But since imprisonment of a corporation does not necessarily involve incarceration, there is no reason to continue the assumption, which has lingered in the legal system unexamined and without support, that a corporation cannot be imprisoned. Since the Marshal can restrain the corporation's liberty and has done so in bankruptcy cases, there is no reason he cannot do so in this case as he himself has so stated prior to the imposition of this sentence.

Corporate imprisonment not only promotes the purposes of the Sherman Act, but also promotes the purposes of sentencing. The purposes of sentencing, according to the United States Sentencing Commission, include incapacitating the offender, deterring crime, rehabilitating the offender, and providing just punishment. The corporate imprisonment imposed today is specifically tailored to meet each of these purposes.

CASE QUESTIONS

1. Is corporate imprisonment illegal?
2. How will the corporation be imprisoned?
3. Is community service a sufficient punishment for the corporation?
4. Can the corporation's assets be imprisoned?

"Shame punishment" has been on the increase in corporate criminal cases. Shame punishment involves public disclosure of an offense. For example, a Delaware federal judge ordered Bachetti Brothers Market to take out an ad for three weeks confessing to its crime of violating federal law by selling meat consisting "in whole or in part of filthy, putrid and contaminated substances."

Corporate Sentencing Guidelines: An Ounce of Prevention Means a Reduced Sentence

Visit the U.S. Sentencing Commission: http://www.ussc.gov

The U.S. Sentencing Commission, established by Congress in 1984, has developed both federal sentencing guidelines and a carrot-and-stick approach to fighting white-collar crime. Under the commission's guidelines, companies that take substantial steps to prevent, investigate, and punish wrongdoing and cooperate with federal investigators can be treated less harshly in sentencing. The goal of the commission was to ensure that companies would establish internal crime prevention programs.

The sentencing guidelines permit judges to place guilty companies on probation for a period of up to five years if their offense or offenses occurred during a time when they had no crime prevention programs in place. The guidelines use a formula that takes into account the seriousness of the offense, the company's history of violations, its cooperation in the investigation, the effectiveness of its compliance program, and the role of senior management in the wrongdoing. The guidelines are a form of mandatory sentencing. If certain factors are present, the judge must order prison times. For example, corporate officers who are proven to have masterminded criminal activity must be sentenced to some prison time.

The federal sentencing guidelines provide for a score or a number that determines the extent of the sentence of the company and individual officers, managers, and employees. A company's "culpability multiplier" can range from 0.05 to 4.00, which is then used to convert a business's culpability score (a number that ranges from 0 to 10 or above). Every company begins with a score of 5, which can be added to or subtracted from depending upon various factors in the guidelines. The larger the organization, the greater the number of points that will be added. Involvement of top officers in criminal conduct also adds to the score. Prior violations increase a company's score, as do attempts to cover up the conduct (obstruction of justice).

A company's score is decreased by the presence of effective compliance programs designed to prevent and detect violations. If a company comes forward and reports the violations voluntarily, the score is decreased. Cooperation with investigators and acceptance of responsibility also serve to reduce the score.

These multipliers are also used in the computation of fines for a business and its employees and officers. Restitution by a company reduces penalties and fines if restitution is made before sentencing. For example, a fine of $1 million to $2 million could be reduced to as low as $50,000 for a company with the following: (1) a code of conduct, (2) an ombudsman, (3) a hot line, and (4) mandatory training for executives. The sentencing guidelines have been referred to as a "quiet revolution" in changing corporate conduct.

The following landmark case deals with the issue of the importance of compliance programs in a corporation and the responsibility of the board of directors for ensuring that the company's compliance program is in place and functioning effectively.

CASE 9.3

In Re Caremark International, Inc.
698 A.2d 959 (Del. Ch. 1996)

The Board's Supervision or Lack Thereof: Kickbacks and Internal Controls

FACTS

Caremark International Inc. is a Delaware corporation with its headquarters in Illinois, which was created in 1992 as a spin-off from Baxter International, Inc. It became a publicly held company, with its stock traded on the New York Exchange. Caremark operates two main health care segments: patient care and managed care services. In these two segments, a substantial portion of Caremark's revenues

(continued)

comes from third-party payments from insurers and Medicare and Medicaid reimbursements.

As part of its operations, Caremark paid physicians fees for monitoring in-home care for patients even though those physicians were not treating the patients. Caremark said the system was created to have outside physicians monitoring home care for quality. However, the federal government, through the Office of Inspector General, in its interpretation of applicable federal regulations, concluded that the fees paid to these physicians constituted referral fees or kickbacks paid with the idea of obtaining patient referrals from these physicians in exchange for their monitoring fees. (Referral payments violate the Anti-Referral Payments Law—ARPL.)

Caremark also had consulting and research payment arrangements with physicians for the promotion of the human growth hormone Protropin, a drug marketed by Caremark (originally the drug was marketed by Baxter).

Caremark did disclose the ongoing federal investigation in 1992 (the investigation had begun before the 1992 spin-off), and, in 1993, Caremark received a clean opinion from Price Waterhouse on internal controls in the company.

In 1994, a federal grand jury in Minnesota issued a 47-page indictment charging Caremark, two of its officers, a physician, and a sales employee with violations of federal law in the forms of research grants, consulting fees, and other payments made by the company in exchange for the promotion of Protropin.

After the indictment became public, five shareholder derivative suits were filed. The shareholders petitioned the Delaware court for approval of a settlement with the company.

JUDICIAL OPINION

ALLEN, Chancellor
In relevant part the terms upon which these claims asserted are proposed to be settled are as follows:

1. That Caremark, undertakes that it and its employees, and agents not pay any form of compensation to a third party in exchange for the referral of a patient to a Caremark facility or service or the prescription of drugs marketed or distributed by Caremark for which reimbursement may be sought from Medicare, Medicaid, or a similar state reimbursement program;

2. That Caremark, undertakes for itself and its employees, and agents not to pay to or split fees with physicians, joint ventures, any business combination in which Caremark maintains a direct financial interest, or other health care providers with whom Caremark has a financial relationship or interest, in exchange for the referral of a patient to a Caremark facility or service or the prescription of drugs marketed or distributed by Caremark for which reimbursement may be sought from Medicare, Medicaid, or a similar state reimbursement program;

3. That the full Board shall discuss all relevant material changes in government health care regulations and their effect on relationships with health care providers on a semiannual basis;

4. That Caremark's officers will remove all personnel from health care facilities or hospitals who have been placed in such facility for the purpose of providing remuneration in exchange for a patient referral for which reimbursement may be sought from Medicare, Medicaid, or a similar state reimbursement program;

5. That every patient will receive written disclosure of any financial relationship between Caremark and the health care professional or provider who made the referral;

6. That the Board will establish a Compliance and Ethics Committee of four directors, two of which will be non-management directors, to meet at least four times a year to effectuate these policies and monitor business segment compliance with the ARPL, and to report to the Board semiannually concerning compliance by each business segment; and

7. That corporate officers responsible for business segments shall serve as compliance officers who must report semiannually to the Compliance and Ethics Committee and, with the assistance of outside counsel, review existing contracts and get advanced approval of any new contract forms.

The complaint charges the director defendants with breach of their duty of attention or care in connection with the ongoing operation of the corporation's business. The claim is that the directors allowed a situation to develop and continue which exposed the corporation to enormous legal liability and that in so doing they violated a duty to be active monitors of corporate performance. The complaint thus does not charge either director self-dealing or the more difficult loyalty-type problems arising from cases of suspect director motivation, such as entrenchment or sale of control contexts. The theory here advanced is possibly the most difficult theory in corporation law upon which a plaintiff might hope to win a judgment.

As the facts of this case graphically demonstrate, ordinary business decisions that are made by officers and employees deeper in the interior of the organization can, however, vitally affect the welfare of the corporation and its ability to achieve its various strategic and financial goals. If this case did not prove the point itself, recent business history would. Recall for example the displacement of senior management and much of the board of Salomon, Inc.; the replacement of senior management of Kidder, Peabody following the discovery of large trading losses resulting from phantom trades by a highly compensated trader; or the extensive financial loss and reputational injury suffered by Prudential Insurance as a result [of] its junior officers' misrepresentations in connection with the distribution of limited partnership interests. Financial and organizational disasters such as these raise the question, what is the board's responsibility with respect to the organization and monitoring of the enterprise to assure that the corporation functions within the law to achieve its purposes?

Modernly this question has been given special importance by an increasing tendency, especially under federal law, to employ the criminal law to assure corporate compliance with external legal requirements, including environmental, financial, employee and product safety as well as assorted other health and safety regulations. In 1991, pursuant to the Sentencing Reform Act of 1984, the United States Sentencing Commission adopted Organizational Sentencing Guidelines which impact importantly on the prospective effect these criminal sanctions might have on business corporations. The Guidelines set forth a uniform sentencing structure for organizations to be sentenced for violation of federal criminal statutes and provide for penalties that equal or often massively exceed those previously imposed on corporations. The Guidelines offer powerful incentives for corporations today to have in place compliance programs to detect violations of law, promptly to report violations to appropriate public officials when discovered, and to take prompt, voluntary remedial efforts.

In 1963, the Delaware Supreme Court in *Graham* v. *Allis-Chalmers Mfg. Co.* addressed the question of potential liability of board members for losses experienced by the corporation as a result of the corporation having violated the anti-trust laws of the United States. There was no claim in that case that the directors knew about the behavior of subordinate employees of the corporation that had resulted in the liability.

Rather, as in this case, the claim asserted was that the directors ought to have known of it and if they had known they would have been under a duty to bring the corporation into compliance with the law and thus save the corporation from the loss. The Delaware Supreme Court concluded that, under the facts as they appeared, there was no basis to find that the directors had breached a duty to be informed of the ongoing operations of the firm. In notably colorful terms, the court stated that "absent cause for suspicion there is no duty upon the directors to install and operate a corporate system of espionage to ferret out wrongdoing which they have no reason to suspect exists." The Court found that there were no grounds for suspicion in that case and, thus, concluded that the directors were blamelessly unaware of the conduct leading to the corporate liability.

How does one generalize this holding today? Can it be said today that, absent some ground giving rise to suspicion of violation of law, that corporate directors have no duty to assure that a corporate information gathering and reporting system exists which represents a good faith attempt to provide senior management and the Board with information respecting material acts, events or conditions within the corporation, including compliance with applicable statutes and regulations? I certainly do not believe so. I doubt that such a broad generalization of the *Graham* holding would have been accepted by the Supreme Court in 1963. The case can be more narrowly interpreted as standing for the proposition that, absent grounds to suspect deception, neither corporate boards nor senior officers can be charged with wrongdoing simply for assuming the integrity of employees and the honesty of their dealings on the company's behalf.

Secondly, I note the elementary fact that relevant and timely information is an essential predicate for satisfaction of the board's supervisory and monitoring role under Section 141 of the Delaware General Corporation Law. Thirdly, I note the potential impact of the federal organizational sentencing guidelines on any business organization. Any rational person attempting in good faith to meet an organizational governance responsibility would be bound to take into account this development and the enhanced penalties and the opportunities for reduced sanctions that it offers.

In light of these developments, it would, in my opinion, be a mistake to conclude that our Supreme Court's statement in *Graham* concerning "espionage" means that corporate boards may satisfy

(continued)

their obligation to be reasonably informed concerning the corporation, without assuring themselves that information and reporting systems exist in the organization that are reasonably designed to provide to senior management and to the board itself timely, accurate information sufficient to allow management and the board, each within its scope, to reach informed judgments concerning both the corporation's compliance with law and its business performance.

Obviously the level of detail that is appropriate for such an information system is a question of business judgment. And obviously too, no rationally designed information and reporting system will remove the possibility that the corporation will violate laws or regulations, or that senior officers or directors may nevertheless sometimes be misled or otherwise fail reasonably to detect acts material to the corporation's compliance with the law. But it is important that the board exercise a good faith judgment that the corporation's information and reporting system is in concept and design adequate to assure the board that appropriate information will come to its attention in a timely manner as a matter of ordinary operations, so that it may satisfy its responsibility.

Thus, I am of the view that a director's obligation includes a duty to attempt in good faith to assure that a corporate information and reporting system, which the board concludes is adequate, exists, and that failure to do so under some circumstances may, in theory at least, render a director liable for losses caused by non-compliance with applicable legal standards.

CASE QUESTIONS

1. Was there any indication that the board was aware of the payment arrangements?

2. What does the court list as the responsibility of the board?

3. Why do you think the company settled the derivative suits? What did it agree to do?

4. What advice would you give to a board member on setting up and monitoring a compliance program?

5. When would directors be liable for criminal conduct by employees in the corporation?

BUSINESS STRATEGY

Businesses should learn the following from the basic principles of the sentencing guidelines:

1. Have a code of ethics in place.
2. Conduct training on the code of ethics.
3. Have a company hot line and ombudsperson for employees to utilize anonymously in reporting violations.
4. Protect employees who report violations.
5. Investigate all allegations regardless of their sources.
6. Report all violations immediately and voluntarily.

© CORBIS

7. Offer restitution to affected parties.
8. Cooperate and negotiate with regulators.
9. Admit your mistakes and shortcomings.
10. Be very public with your code of ethics and discuss ethics with employees via Web site examples or illustrations of good ethical choices in the news among companies and employees.

ELEMENTS OF BUSINESS CRIME

The **elements,** or requirements for proof, of a business crime vary according to type. Crimes are violations of written laws, such as statutes or ordinances. But all crimes' specific elements can be classified into two general elements: *mens rea* or *scienter* and *actus reus.*

ETHICAL ISSUES 9.1

Kevin Weber, a parolee who had committed two felonies, entered Eric's Gazebo, a restaurant in Santa Ana, California, through a rooftop vent on Mother's Day in May 1995. Mr. Weber's intention was to steal cash from the restaurant safe, but he tripped the burglar alarm and fled with four chocolate chip cookies. When he left the restaurant, police were already waiting outside for him.

In 1994, California had passed a "three-strikes" law. The statute requires a minimum sentence of 25 years on the third felony conviction. Mr. Weber was sentenced to 26 years, or 6½ years per cookie. Mr. Weber, 35, must serve at least 26 years before he will be eligible for parole. Is this a fair sentence?

In 2000, a Texas jury sentenced Kenneth Payne, 29, to 16 years in prison for stealing a $1 candy bar. Payne had ten previous convictions for theft, criminal mischief, assault, and possession of a controlled substance. The district attorney's office had recommended the sentence with the prosecuting attorney adding about the candy bar, "It was a king size." Do you think the sentence is fair? What do you think of the prosecuting attorney's comment?

Mens Rea

A **crime** implies some voluntary action, which is to say that a criminal wrong is calculated or intentional; this element of criminal intent is the *mens rea* of a crime. *Mens rea* is the required state of mind for a crime—the intent to commit the act that is a crime. A criminal wrong is not based on an accident unless there was forewarning about the accident or the accident arose from criminal conduct. Thus, driving while intoxicated is a crime, and an accident that happens while a driver is intoxicated is also a criminal wrong. Concealing income is intentional conduct calculated to avoid paying taxes; it is willful and criminal conduct. An oversight in reporting income is not a crime. The following case discusses the issue of intent in an environmental case.

> **BUSINESS PLANNING TIP**
>
> Do not ever try to withhold a violation or restructure paperwork to cover it up. The truth comes out. Concealment is an additional crime.

CASE 9.4

United States v. *Ahmad*
101 F.3d 386 (5th Cir. 1996)

Gasoline, Drains, and Knowledge of the Two Together: A Crime?

FACTS

Ahmad owns a Spin-N-Market located in Conroe, Texas. Shortly after he purchased the combination gas and convenience store in 1992, a leak was discovered in one of the high-octane gasoline tanks at the location. The leak was at the top of the tank and did not present problems with gasoline seeping out. However, the leak did allow water to get into the tank and contaminate the gas. Because water is heavier than gas, the water sank to the bottom of the tank, and because the tank was pumped from the bottom, Ahmad was unable to sell gas from it.

In October 1993, Ahmad hired CTT Environmental Services, a tank-testing company, to examine the tank. CTT determined that the tank contained

(continued)

800 gallons of water and the rest was mostly gasoline. Jewel McCoy, a CTT employee, told Ahmad that the leak could not be repaired until the tank was completely empty, which CTT offered to do for 65 cents per gallon plus $65 per hour of labor. After McCoy gave Ahmad this estimate, he asked whether he could empty the tank himself. McCoy told him that it would be dangerous and illegal for him to do so. Ahmad then responded, "Well, if I don't get caught, what then?"

On January 25, 1994, Ahmad rented a hand-held motorized water pump from a local hardware store, telling a hardware store employee that he was planning to use it to remove water from his backyard. Ahmad hooked the pump up to his tank at the Spin-N-Market and pumped 5,220 gallons of fluid into a manhole near the store and into Lewis Street alongside the store. Of the fluid pumped, 4,690 gallons were gasoline.

The gasoline from Lewis Street made its way to a storm drain and the storm sewer system and eventually into Possum Creek. When city officials discovered the gasoline in Possum Creek, several vacuum trucks were required to decontaminate it.

The gasoline from the manhole made its way to the city sewage treatment center. The gasoline was diverted into a different storage pool in order to avoid shutting down the plant altogether, but the plant had to evacuate all but essential personnel and the firefighters and hazardous materials crews from the city had to be called to restore the plant to a safe condition. While the crews worked, two area schools had to be evacuated for safety reasons.

The gasoline was traced back to Ahmad's Spin-N-Market and Ahmad was indicted for three violations of the Clean Water Act (CWA), of knowingly discharging a pollutant into navigable waters without a permit, knowingly placing others in imminent danger through a pollutant, and knowingly operating a source in violation of pretreatment requirements. Ahmad did not dispute the conduct, he said he did not meet the "knowingly" requirements because he believed he was discharging water.

The jury found Ahmad guilty on two of the three charges and deadlocked on the charge of imminent danger. Ahmad appealed.

JUDICIAL OPINION

SMITH, Circuit Judge
One of the key pieces of evidence Ahmad attempted to introduce in support of this theory was the testimony of Mohammed Abassi and Shahid Latif, who would have told the jury that Ahmad was at the Spin-N-Market only until 7:30 or 8:00 P.M. on January 25, and not the entire evening as the government contended. The gist of this was an attempt to show that Ahmad did not knowingly discharge gasoline himself, but rather only negligently left the pump in the hands of his employees. The district court found Abassi's and Latif's testimony irrelevant and excluded it.

Ahmad contends that the jury should have been instructed that the statutory *mens rea*—knowledge—was required as to each element of the offenses, rather than only with regard to discharge or the operation of a source. Because Ahmad requested such instruction, we review the refusal to give it for abuse of discretion.

The language of the CWA is less than pellucid. Title 33 U.S.C. § 1319(c)(2)(A) says that "any person who knowingly violates" any of a number of other sections of the CWA commits a felony. One of the provisions that § 1319(c)(2)(A) makes it unlawful to violate is § 1311(a), which, when read together with a series of definitions in § 1362, prohibits the addition of any pollutant to navigable waters from a "point source." That was the crime charged in count one. Section 1319(c)(2)(A) also criminalizes violations of § 1317(d), which prohibits the operation of any "source" in a way that contravenes any effluent standard, prohibition, or pretreatment standard. That was the crime charged in count two.

The principal issue is to which elements of the offense the modifier "knowingly" applies. The matter is complicated somewhat by the fact that the phrase "knowingly violates" appears in a different section of the CWA from the language defining the elements of the offenses. Ahmad argues that within this context, "knowingly violates" should be read to require him knowingly to have acted with regard to each element of the offenses. The government, in contrast, contends that "knowingly violates" requires it to prove only that Ahmad knew the nature of his acts and that he performed them intentionally. Particularly at issue is whether "knowingly" applies to the element of the discharge's being a pollutant, for Ahmad's main theory at trial was that he thought he was discharging water, not gasoline.

The Supreme Court has spoken to this issue in broad terms. In *United States v. X-Citement Video, Inc.,* 513 U.S. 65, ___, 115 S.Ct. 464, 467, 130 L.Ed.2d 372 (1994), the Court read "knowingly" to apply to each element of a child pornography offense, notwithstanding its conclusion that under the "most natural grammatical reading" of the statute it should apply only to the element of having transported, shipped, received, distributed, or reproduced the material at issue. The Court also reaffirmed the long-held view that "the presumption in favor of a *scienter* requirement should apply to each of the statutory elements which criminalize otherwise innocent conduct."

Although *X-Citement Video* is the Court's most recent pronouncement on this subject, it is not the first. In *Staples* v. *United States*, 511 U.S. 600, 619–20, 114 S.Ct. 1793, 128 L.Ed.2d 609 (1994), the Court found that the statutes criminalizing knowing possession of a machinegun, 26 U.S.C. §§ 5845(a)(6) and 5861(d), require that defendants know not only that they possess a firearm but that it actually is a machinegun. Thus, an awareness of the features of the gun—specifically, the features that make it an automatic weapon—is a necessary element of the offense. More generally, the Court also made plain that statutory crimes carrying severe penalties are presumed to require that a defendant know the facts that make his conduct illegal.

Indeed, we find it eminently sensible that the phrase "knowingly violates" in § 1319(c)(2)(A), when referring to other provisions that define the elements of the offenses § 1319 creates, should uniformly require knowledge as to each of those elements rather than only one or two. To hold otherwise would require an explanation as to why some elements should be treated differently from others, which neither the parties nor the case law seems able to provide.

In support of its interpretation of the CWA, the government cites cases from other circuits. We find these decisions both inapposite and unpersuasive on the point for which they are cited. In *United States* v. *Hopkins*, 53 F.3d 533, 537–41 (2d Cir.1995), cert. denied, ___ U.S. ___, 116 S.Ct. 773, 133 L.Ed.2d 725 (1996), the court held that the government need not demonstrate that a § 1319(c)(2)(A) defendant knew his acts were illegal. The illegality of the defendant's actions is not an element of the offense, however. In *United States* v. *Weitzenhoff*, 35 F.3d 1275 (9th Cir.1994), cert. denied, ___ U.S. ___, 115 S.Ct. 939, 130 L.Ed.2d 884 (1995), the court similarly was concerned almost exclusively with whether the language of the CWA creates a mistake-of-law defense. Both cases are easily distinguishable, for neither directly addresses mistake of fact or the statutory construction issues raised by Ahmad.

The government also protests that CWA violations fall into the judicially created exception for "public welfare offenses," under which some regulatory crimes have been held not to require a showing of *mens rea*. On its face, the CWA certainly does appear to implicate public welfare.

As recent cases have emphasized, however, the public welfare offense exception is narrow. The *Staples* Court, for example, held that the statute prohibiting the possession of machine guns fell outside the exception, notwithstanding the fact that "[t]ypically, our cases recognizing such offenses involve statutes that regulate potentially harmful or injurious items." *Staples*, 511 U.S. at 607, 114 S.Ct. at 1794.

Though gasoline is a "potentially harmful or injurious item," it is certainly no more so than are machineguns. Rather, *Staples* held, the key to the public welfare offense analysis is whether "dispensing with *mens rea* would require the defendant to have knowledge only of traditionally lawful conduct." The CWA offenses of which Ahmad was convicted have precisely this characteristic, for if knowledge is not required as to the nature of the substance discharged, one who honestly and reasonably believes he is discharging water may find himself guilty of a felony if the substance turns out to be something else.

The fact that violations of § 1319(c)(2)(A) are felonies punishable by years in federal prison confirms our view that they do not fall within the public welfare offense exception. As the *Staples* Court noted, public welfare offenses have virtually always been crimes punishable by relatively light penalties such as fines or short jail sentences, rather than substantial terms of imprisonment. Serious felonies, in contrast, should not fall within the exception "absent a clear statement from Congress that *mens rea* is not required." Following *Staples*, we hold that the offenses charged in counts one and two are not public welfare offenses and that the usual presumption of a *mens rea* requirement applies. With the exception of purely jurisdictional elements, the *mens rea* of knowledge applies to each element of the crimes.

At best, the jury charge made it uncertain to which elements "knowingly" applied. At worst, and considerably more likely, it indicated that only the element of discharge need be knowingly. The instructions listed each element on a separate line, with the word "knowingly" present only in the line corresponding to the element that something was discharged. That the district court included a

(continued)

one-sentence summary of each count in which "knowingly" was present did not cure the error.

The obvious inference for the jury was that knowledge was required only as to the fact that something was discharged, and not as to any other fact. In effect, with regard to the other elements of the crimes, the instructions implied that the requisite *mens rea* was strict liability rather than knowledge.

There was at least a reasonable likelihood that the jury applied the instructions in this way, so we conclude that the instructions misled the jury as to the elements of the offense. Because the charge effectively withdrew from the jury's consideration facts that it should have been permitted to find or not find, this error requires reversal.

Most of Ahmad's defense, after all, was built around the idea that he thought water, rather than gasoline, was being discharged. A rational jury could so have found, and at the same time could have found that he did not actually know that he was pumping gas.

Reversed and remanded.

CASE QUESTIONS

1. What was wrong with Ahmad's tank?
2. Of what significance is Jewel McCoy's testimony?
3. What is the difference between knowledge of the law and knowledge of conduct?
4. What does the court explain is required for the state of mind under the Clean Water Act?
5. Why is Ahmad's testimony that he thought he was discharging water significant?

Some crimes not only require "knowing" or "willful" conduct but also require a refined or specific intent in relation to the crime. Securities fraud, for example, requires proof of not just intentional conduct but of intentional conduct with the idea of defrauding another. An accountant who makes an error in preparing corporate financial statements, unintentionally defrauding stock purchasers, did not intend to defraud them, and her act is probably one of negligence or omission rather than a knowing or willful act. However, a deliberate overstatement of income to comply with a corporate management request would be an act showing intent to defraud.

C O N S I D E R . . .

9.3 Consider the following and discuss whether the appropriate *mens rea* is present.

A 19-year-old was acquitted of charges of vehicular manslaughter brought against him because he collided into the rear of a car on the shoulder of the road while he was driving 80–105 mph and talking on a cell phone.

Believed to be the first criminal case brought for manslaughter with a vehicle owing to cell-phone distraction, the case attracted national attention because Jason Jones killed John and Carole Hall when he struck their car. The accident occurred on Thanksgiving weekend in 1999. Jones is a Naval Academy midshipman and was found guilty of negligent driving. Negligent driving is a misdemeanor and carries a $500 fine.

Testimony by experts for the prosecution indicated that cell-phone use while driving is an enormous distraction. The increased accident rate during cell-phone use while driving is placed at between 34 and 300 percent by various experts.[1]

It is not illegal in Maryland to use a cell phone while driving. Three states do have restrictions on their use; and, since 1995, thirty-seven states have debated proposed legislation on cell-phone use controls for vehicles. Can someone be convicted for conduct that is not illegal?

Nathan Hall, 21, was found guilty of criminally negligent homicide in a Colorado case that resulted from Hall's collision with Alan Cobb on the slopes in Vail, Colorado. Hall, who was 18 at the time of the accident, worked as a lift operator at the Vail Resorts. At the end of his shift, he did a run at what witnesses described as a "much too high" rate of speed. Hall had been a member of his high school's ski racing team.[2]

The Vail Resorts settled a claim with Mr. Cobb's family. It was shortly after the Hall incident that Michael Kennedy and Sonny Bono were killed on ski slopes, the former playing football while skiing and the latter colliding with a tree on a downhill run. Following these accidents, the resorts increased their safety patrols as well as the number of warning signs on the slopes.

Hall said that the conditions caused the accident. The snow was slushy, and the result was moguls, or small hills, on the slopes that caused Hall to lose control.

In 1998–99, there were thirty-four fatalities on ski slopes in the United States. In 1999–2000, there were thirty while the number of skier visits annually rose from 52.1 million in 1998–99 to 52.2 million in 1999–2000.

Could the ski resort be held criminally liable for Mr. Cobb's death?

What was the prosecution required to prove for Hall's conviction of the crime of criminally negligent homicide?

Criminal intent has been a particularly significant issue in business crimes. The intent element is significant because there are actually two intents involved when a corporation is prosecuted for a crime: the intent of the corporation to commit the crime and the intent of those in charge of the corporation, officers, and directors to direct the corporation to commit the wrong.

C O N S I D E R . . .

9.4 The Interstate Commerce Commission (ICC) has the following regulation on the shipping of hazardous materials: "Each shipper offering for transportation any hazardous material subject to the regulations in this chapter, shall describe that article on the shipping paper by the shipping name prescribed in Section 172.5 of this chapter and by the classification prescribed in Section 172.4 of this chapter, and may add a further description not inconsistent therewith. Abbreviations may not be used."

International Minerals & Chemicals shipped sulfuric acid but did not label the shipment "Corrosive Liquid," as required under the regulation on the shipping papers. International was charged with a knowing and criminal violation of the regulation but insisted that the failure to identify was simply an oversight in paperwork for the shipment. Can there be a valid criminal charge? What if International had other slip-ups in its paper work? [*United States* v. *International Minerals & Chemical Corp.*, 402 U.S. 558 (1971)]

ETHICAL ISSUES 9.2

In 2001, Arthur Andersen, one of the largest accounting firms in the world, agreed to pay a $7 million fine to the Securities Exchange Commission (SEC), the largest fine ever assessed against an accounting firm. The SEC had charged Andersen with fraud for its role in the overstatement of earnings throughout the 1990s by Waste Management, Inc. Waste Management eventually had to restate its earnings in 1998, which amounted to a $3.5 billion charge. The company had overstated its earnings by $1.43 billion from 1992–96.

The complaint filed by the SEC against Andersen and three of its audit partners alleged charges of fraud. In settling the case, neither Andersen nor the partners (who paid between $30,000 and $50,000 in fines) admitted or denied the allegations. The partners are also barred from doing audit work for publicly traded companies for periods ranging from one to five years. Andersen has already paid $220 million to settle the shareholder litigation that resulted from the overstatement.

The SEC's complaint in the case alleged that the auditors from Andersen had pleaded with Waste Management executives to make changes. While the executives promised future reforms, they refused each year to reduce the profits. Each year Andersen succumbed to pressure from the Waste Management executives and certified the financial statements. Andersen's internal records reveal that it considered Waste Management a "high risk client" and that it "actively managed reported results." When it was auditing Waste Management's 1993 earnings in early 1994, Andersen auditors discovered $128 million in earnings misstatements that it asked management to change, a change that would have resulted in a reduction in earnings of 12 percent. When Waste Management executives refused to restate earnings, Andersen certified the financial statements anyway concluding that the misstatements were "not material."

The SEC issued the following statement on the announcement of the settlement:

Unless the auditor stands up to management the first time it discovers incorrect accounting, the auditor ultimately will find itself in an untenable position: it either must continue issuing unqualified audit reports on materially misstated financial statements and hope that its conduct will not be discovered or it must force a restatement or qualify its report and thereby subject itself to the liability that will likely result from the exposure of its role in the prior issuance of the materially misstated financial statements.

Arthur Andersen's managing partner for North America released the following statement:

This settlement allows the firm and its partners to end a very difficult chapter and move on. There are important lessons to be learned from this settlement by all involved in the financial reporting process. The pressures on management to meet expectations are greater than ever in a market where information and capital move instantly.

Do you think the auditors at Arthur Andersen had intent to mislead? What were they trying to accomplish? Do you think the overstatement of earnings by 12 percent was ethical? What would have helped Waste Management executives see the issue differently? What would have helped the auditors?

Actus Reus

All crimes include, in addition to the mental intent, a requirement of some specific action or conduct, which is the *actus reus* of the crime. For example, in embezzlement the *actus reus* is the taking of an employer's money. Various types of criminal conduct, or *actus reus* examples, are found in subsequent sections on specific crimes. The following case deals with an issue of the federal crime of money laundering and whether the conduct of an agent at a car dealership constituted money laundering.

CASE 9.5

U.S. v. Nelson
66 F.3d 1036 (9th Cir. 1995)

No Money Down—Just the Full Price in Laundered Cash

FACTS

Kevin Lee Nelson (appellant) appeals his conviction for attempting and conspiring to structure a money laundering transaction. Undercover government agents posing as drug dealers came to the car dealership where Nelson worked, proposing to buy a car with cash. Nelson suggested ways to structure the cash purchase of a car to avoid the dealership's requirement under federal law to report cash transactions over $10,000.

In 1992, the Internal Revenue Service ("IRS") learned Prestige Toyota ("Prestige"), a car dealership in Billings, Montana, had been selling cars to drug dealers using deals structured to avoid the IRS requirement that a retail business file a reporting form whenever it receives more than $10,000 in cash.

The IRS began an undercover investigation. IRS Special Agent Pam White and Raymond Malley, an agent of the Montana Criminal Investigation Bureau, set up an appointment with William Rahlf, a saleman at Prestige, and White wore a transmitter to record their conversations. Rahlf took Agents White and Malley for a test drive in a Toyota 4-Runner, during which Agent White told Rahlf that she was "in the dope business" and Malley was her supplier. She added that she wanted to buy a car with cash, but did not want a "paper trail." Rahlf said "It's not a problem," and volunteered that he had previously sold cars to another drug dealer. Agent White asked him if his superiors would have any problems with the deal, and Rahlf answered "We've done it before, we can do it again." Rahlf added that "[i]t won't be a big deal" to use cash and title the car in another name.

Agent White told Rahlf she would offer $22,000, asked him to use the name "Joyce Brown" and a post office box, and suggested he explain her situation to his superiors. Rahlf took the so-called "four-square" car purchase form in to Randy Replogle, the assistant general sales manager, and appellant Kevin Nelson. Nelson was a sales manager or "closer," who helped salespersons finalize offers. As a closer, Nelson reported to the general sales manager or "desk," who had the final authority to put the deal together.

Replogle was filling in as "desk" that day for Dustin Timmons, Prestige's general sales manager. Rahlf and Replogle discussed the deal, with Nelson present.

Rahlf told Replogle that the customers got their money from the drug business, and that they wanted to buy with cash and leave no paper trail. Replogle said he thought they should not get involved in the deal, and called the owner of Prestige, Ray McLean, at his home. McLean told him not to make the deal, and to get the customers out of the store. Replogle told Nelson to tell the customers to leave.

Rahlf and Nelson returned to Agents White and Malley, and Rahlf introduced Nelson, saying that he was aware of the situation. Nelson told Agents White and Malley that retail sellers must report any cash transaction over $10,000, and that Prestige would have to fill out a form to make such a report. He also told the agents they could use the name "Joyce Brown." Nelson went back in to talk to Replogle, telling the agents that the price was the likely sticking point.

Nelson told Replogle that the customers wanted to use an assumed name, and Replogle called McLean again, who reiterated that he wanted them to ask the customers to leave. Nelson returned to Agents White and Malley, telling them that Prestige would not falsify a name on the reporting form because that would be "fraud to the bank." After discussing whether it would be all right to use a different name if it were a real person, Agent White told Nelson that Joyce Brown was her sister. Nelson then said "The hell with it, let's do it. Let me go grab—grab a paper. Keep that pencil ready on site." Nelson left.

When he returned, Nelson told Agent White that Prestige could not use "Joyce Brown" on the reporting form. He then suggested another way to get around the reporting requirement: if Agent White were to come in with a trade-in to keep the cash price under $10,000, no form would be necessary. He said "I got probably ten good friends in the same situation but when they do it, they always come in and

(continued)

they trade something so they keep it under $10,000 . . . so it doesn't have to be reported." He also suggested that Agent White consider buying two vehicles at Prestige for less than $10,000 each, which the dealership later could take back as trade-ins to keep the cash price of the 4-Runner below the reporting threshold. Nelson explained that he had done this "all the time" so that "we don't have the money trail." Nelson added that he was "more than willing" to do this: "All I want to do is cover my butt and cover yours at the same time." Nelson and Rahlf suggested the agents call Prestige the next day, and the agents left.

Later that evening, Rahlf contacted Jim Sinhold, a friend who worked as a salesperson at a Ford dealership, telling him that he had a female customer with "a purse full of money" who wanted to buy a car. Sinhold testified that Rahlf explained that "the deal didn't happen" at Prestige, and that Rahlf would send Agent White over. Although Rahlf testified that he thought he had told Sinhold that the customer was a dope dealer, Sinhold did not remember that, and thought Rahlf was looking for a referral fee for sending the woman over to the Ford dealership.

Agent White called Rahlf later that same morning. Rahlf told her that he and the agents "blew it" by telling Replogle the whole story, although Nelson was not the problem. Agent White told him the trade-in scheme sounded too complicated. Rahlf then put Prestige's general manager, Dustin Timmons, on the line, and Timmons told Agent White that she would have to get the trade-ins from other dealerships to avoid throwing up a flag. Agent White said the plan was not going to work for her. Rahlf then referred her to Sinhold at the Ford dealership to buy a Ford Explorer. Rahlf also stated "you don't need to tell [Sinhold] anything because I've already told him . . . just do whatever it is you got to do and they'll . . . make the paper work right."

Rahlf and Nelson were found guilty of one count of conspiring to conduct or attempt to conduct financial transactions involving property represented to be the proceeds of unlawful controlled substance trafficking, with the intent to avoid a transaction reporting requirement, and one count of conducting or attempting to conduct such a financial transaction. Nelson was sentenced to a ten-month "split sentence" in the pre-release center in Great Falls, Montana, with five months in the custody component and five months in the pre-release component of the center.

JUDICIAL OPINION

BOOCHEVER, Circuit Judge

To prove a violation of the transaction reporting requirement (money laundering), the Government must prove (1) that the defendant conducted or attempted to conduct a financial transaction, (2) with the intent to avoid a transaction reporting requirement, and (3) that the property involved in the transaction was represented by a law enforcement officer to be the proceeds of specified unlawful activity.

Nelson first claims there was insufficient evidence that the cash involved was "represented by a law enforcement officer to be the proceeds of specified unlawful activity." Nelson argues that the government did not prove that Agents White and Malley specifically told Nelson that the cash was direct earnings from drug sales.

To establish a violation of the statute, the government need not show that the law enforcement officers explicitly stated that the cash in question was the direct product of unlawful activity. We have found sufficient evidence of a representation when the undercover operator "hinted, but never specifically stated, that the funds he needed laundered were proceeds from [drug] trafficking."

In this case, it is clear from Nelson's tape-recorded statements that Nelson believed Agent White was a drug dealer. Further, Nelson was present when Rahlf told Replogle that the customers got their money from the drug business. The evidence was sufficient to show that Agent White represented the cash to be the proceeds of unlawful activity.

Nelson argues that there was insufficient evidence to show that he attempted to conduct a financial transaction, or conspired to conduct such a transaction. Nelson claims that the evidence does not show that he attempted to initiate or to participate in initiating a car sale. Nelson argues that because he was not involved at the time Rahlf completed the four-square form, he took no substantial step toward the completion of the transaction, and all his other acts were mere preparation.

An attempt conviction requires evidence that the defendant intended to violate the statute, and that he took a substantial step toward completing the violation. Nelson advised Agent White that she could use "Joyce Brown," her "sister's" name, on the reporting form and took that idea inside to the "desk" (Replogle) for approval. Replogle told Nelson to ask the customers to leave. Telling the agents that he would do the transaction with a different name "in a heartbeat," but his superiors were unwilling, Nelson then proposed the trade-in scheme using vehicles purchased at Prestige or elsewhere for under $10,000. When the agents said they wanted to think it over and got up to leave, Nelson urged them to call him or Rahlf back.

There is no question that a jury could conclude that Nelson intended to violate the statute when he proposed structuring the car sale to avoid the reporting requirement.

Nelson discussed the assumed name scheme with Replogle, who had the final authority, and Replogle rejected it. He proposed the trade-in scheme to the agents, who said they would think it over. He continued to urge the trade-in idea when Agent White expressed reluctance. Nevertheless, Nelson's expressed eagerness to consummate the deal and his efforts towards doing so are evidence of intent, rather than evidence supporting a finding that Nelson took a step "of such substantiality that, unless frustrated, the crime would have occurred." His actions are also consistent with his job, which was to keep customers on the hook while he helped the salesperson (Rahlf) finalize the offer, which is consistent with mere preparation. Nelson did not break up a cash payment already received, complete paperwork or accept a cash payment, or prepare a detailed plan and receive payment. Nelson's actions were too "tentative and unfocussed" to be an appreciable fragment of the crime of avoiding a reporting requirement. Nor were they a step toward the commission of the crime so substantial that without an intervening act the crime would have occurred. We agree that "[w]hen criminal intent is clear, identifying the point at which the defendants' activities ripen into an attempt is not an analytically satisfying enterprise." We conclude, however, that even viewing the evidence in the light most favorable to the government, the evidence does not show beyond a reasonable doubt that Nelson took a substantial step toward violation of the statute. His actions were mere preparation, and were not sufficient to show an attempt to launder money.

Because the evidence does not support a finding that either Nelson or Rahlf took a substantial step toward violating § 1956 after Nelson joined the conspiracy, we reverse Nelson's conviction for attempt.

Nelson also argues that there was insufficient evidence to sustain his conviction for conspiracy. "The essential elements of a conspiracy are (1) an agreement to engage in criminal activity, (2) one or more overt acts taken to implement the agreement, and (3) the requisite intent to commit the substantive crime." Any rational jury could find from the evidence of Nelson's conversations with Rahlf and the agents that he agreed with Rahlf to engage in the avoidance of the reporting requirement.

In this case, however, Nelson did not join an ongoing conspiracy when he agreed with Rahlf to avoid the reporting requirement. Until that point, Rahlf had entered into an agreement only with the agents, and no conspiracy exists when the only other persons involved are government agents. We therefore consider only Rahlf's actions following the beginning of Nelson's involvement. Nelson twice went to talk with Replogle, the general manager, to discuss the possible use of the false name. Nelson suggested that the agents avoid the reporting requirement by buying and trading in other vehicles, to keep each transaction under $10,000 in cash. Rahlf involved Dustin Timmons, who advised the agents to purchase their trade-ins at other dealers to cover their tracks. Finally, Rahlf referred the agents to the Ford dealership, which would "make the paper work right."

From this evidence, a jury could conclude that at least one overt act took place to implement the agreement to avoid the reporting requirement. There was sufficient evidence to convict Nelson of conspiracy.

We reverse his conviction for attempt and affirm his conviction for conspiracy.

CASE QUESTIONS

1. What does the statute Nelson is accused of violating require?
2. Describe the scenario in which Nelson was involved that led to the charges.
3. Why wasn't there enough of the *actus reus* to commit the crime?
4. How can Nelson be convicted of conspiracy if he did not commit the actual crime?

EXAMPLES OF BUSINESS CRIMES

Theft and Embezzlement

The action of employees who take their employers' property is **theft** or **embezzlement.** For theft, the following elements are necessary: (1) intent to take the property, (2) an actual taking of the property for permanent use, and (3) no authorization to take the property. These three elements are the *actus reus* of the crime. The *mens rea* is the taking of the property with the intent of permanently depriving the owner of use and possession.

For embezzlement, the elements are the same as for theft, with the addition of one more element: The person commits the crime while in the employ or position of trust of the property owner. In other words, embezzlement is theft from a specific type of person—an employer. Although it is usually limited to funds, embezzlement can cover such items as inventory and equipment of a business.

C O N S I D E R . . .

9.5 Darrin James was the manager of Allsup's Store in Clovis, New Mexico. Jay Finnell, his immediate supervisor, found $2,400 in cash below the checkstand, behind some books and papers. Mr. Finnell later discovered irregularities in the records of the store maintained by Mr. James. The sales receipts for the store were greater than the bank deposits. Is there sufficient evidence to convict Mr. James of embezzlement? [*State v. James,* 784 P.2d 1021 (N.M. App. 1989)]

Computer Crime

Review a summary of federal computer crimes:
http://rampages.onramp.net/~dgmccown

The dependence of businesses upon computer technology is great today. Often, such technology evolves more rapidly than the means for developing internal controls on its use. The result is that the ability for the commission of crimes using computers exceeds the ability to control or detect those crimes. Computer crimes fit into four categories:

1. *The unauthorized use of a computer or computer-related equipment.* Even the use of computers for personal projects and the theft of computer hardware and software for nonoffice use have resulted in losses to businesses.

2. *The alteration or destruction of a computer, its files, its programs, or data.* One of the most difficult problems facing businesses is a computer virus, a program that damages computers and/or computer data. Beyond such damage, the costs to businesses in dealing with these viruses include the man-hours and perhaps man-years of work spent in attempting to prevent or detect them. For example, the 52,000 outside researchers hooked up to computers at NASA's Ames Center spent four to eight hours each month trying to determine whether their computers were infected with a virus. Their total time commitment in this task amounted to 142 man-years. The Melissa Virus and the ILUVYOU Virus that spread worldwide in just a day caused an estimated $3 billion damage to businesses.

3. *The entering of fraudulent records or data into a computer system.* The alteration of an academic record or a credit report would fit into this category.

4. *The use of computer facilities to convert ownership of funds, financial instruments, property, services, or data.* The ability to transfer funds electronically has brought about new areas of criminal activity and necessitated the development of statutes to cover the peculiar aspects of crimes facilitated by computers.

Some Computer Crime Terminology

The previous list covers all the types of computer crimes, which may also be referred to by various lay terms. For example, a popular form of financial computer crime is called the "salami technique." In a bank computer system, changes can be made randomly to reduce accounts by a few cents and then transfer that money to one account from which the person who has changed the system can make a legitimate withdrawal. Because the reduction is so small and spread over so many accounts, those affected are unlikely to report any problems. The salami technique has also been used effectively in businesses with programs covering large amounts of inventory of various kinds. Small amounts of inventory are transferred out to warehouses or fictitious firms. The employee making these changes in the system is then able to embezzle these inventory items.

"Scavenging" is the name given to crimes perpetrated by collecting data from discarded materials. For example, ATM receipts, which contain the cardholder's account number and other information, can be recovered from trash bins and that information then used to acquire goods and services.

For those computer systems hooked into communications systems, there is the potential for a more traditional type of crime: wiretapping. There are equipment costs associated with wiretapping, however, and it is not as popular as other forms of computer crime.

State Statutes Covering Computer Crime

All of the states have some form of computer fraud or crime statutes but are still struggling with definitions and the application of existing laws to computer crimes. For example, if a government employee uses part of her computer database to keep personal or small business records, has the employee taken government property through use of the database for nongovernment purposes? Computer crime statutes are examples of laws being developed in response to changing technology. Recently, counterfeit check and document scandals have emerged as a result of the use of desktop publishing capabilities of many home computers. A counterfeit check scheme in Louisiana yielded a home computer operator over $10,000. Prosecution of the case involves the difficult task of showing that the sophisticated check copies were forgeries. Forgeries have become so costly that banks have begun fingerprinting customers as part of new systems designed to catch counterfeit instruments.

Provisions in computer crime statutes that address viruses first appeared in 1989; changes in the statutes involved designating the distribution of a computer virus as a criminal offense. The difficulty in many of the statutes and proposals is catching those who develop the virus.

A number of traditional criminal statutes do not properly apply to computer crime. For example, burglary requires entering a facility unlawfully; and, although a burglary statute would apply to someone entering a building to take computer hardware, it would not apply to someone gaining access to customer lists, formulas, or trade secrets. As the *National Law Journal* notes, cyber criminals thrive because the laws lag behind technology. Also, enforcement is not as fast-paced as the crimes themselves and cases against cyber criminals still take time to build. In fact, these cases may take more time and expertise because of the sophistication of the perpetrators.

States have begun passing laws with both criminal and civil penalties for junk e-mail, often called spam. For example, California's law requires an existing personal or business relationship to avoid prosecution for sending unsolicited e-mail to a person or business. Violation of the law carries a six-month sentence and/or $1,000 fine for each offense, and each e-mail could be considered a separate offense.

Explore the Berne Convention for the Protection of Literary and Artistic Works (Paris text 1971):
http://www.law.cornell.edu/treaties/berne/overview.html

International Conventions on Computer Crime

The Berne (copyright) and Paris Conventions have provisions that permit businesses in member countries to obtain international copyright protection for their software products. Fifty-nine nations are members of one or more of the conventions (see Chapter 16).

Federal Statutes Covering Computer Crimes

Some existing federal statutes cover certain computer crimes. The Copyright Act provides protection for certain computer programs. Once a program is copyrighted, its unauthorized use or reproduction can be prosecuted as a copyright violation.

Review the Copyright Act of 1976, as amended (1994):
http://www4.law.cornell.edu/uscode/17/index.html

The Fair Credit Reporting Act (FCRA) limits access, by computer or otherwise, to individuals' financial and credit histories; unauthorized use or access carries penalties. Equifax and TRW, both credit reporting agencies, settled cases during the 1990s involving charges that they released credit lists to marketing firms, selling the grouped lists on the basis of income and buying histories.

Review the Counterfeit Access Device and Computer Fraud and Abuse Act:
http://www.law.cornell.edu/uscode/18/1001.html

Counterfeit Access Device and Computer Fraud and Abuse Act In 1984, Congress passed the Counterfeit Access Device and Computer Fraud and Abuse Act (CADCFA). This act makes it a federal crime to use or access federal or private computers without authorization in several types of situations. The CADCFA was amended in 1994 to cover additional new technologies, such as scanners, hand-held computers, and laptops.

CADCFA prohibits unauthorized access to U.S. military or foreign policy information, FDIC financial institutions' data, or to any government agency computer. For example, in *Sawyer* v. *Department of the Air Force*, 31 MPSR 193 (1986), a federal employee was terminated from his position for tampering with Air Force invoices and payments. Penalties under CADCFA range from five to twenty-one years' imprisonment.

Federal Computer Fraud and Abuse Act The Federal Computer Fraud and Abuse Act (CFAA) classifies unauthorized access to a government computer as a felony, and trespass into a federal government computer as a misdemeanor. CFAA covers "intentional" and "knowing" acts and includes a section that makes it a felony to cause more than $1,000 damage to a computer or its data through a virus program.

No Electronic Theft Act Passed at the end of 1997, this federal law makes it a criminal offense to willfully infringe copyrighted material worth over $1,000 using the Internet or other electronic devices even when the infringer does not profit from the use of the material. For example, many Internet users clip articles from subscriber services on the Internet and then send them along via e-mail to nonsubscriber friends. There is no transaction for profit, but the transfer of such copyrighted material is considered a violation of this federal law, nonetheless. The act was lobbied for by the software and entertainment industries and was opposed by scientific and academic groups.

CONSIDER...

9.6 David LaMacchia, a twenty-one-year-old student at the Massachusetts Institute of Technology (MIT) and a computer hacker, used MIT's computer network to gain entree to the Internet. Using pseudonyms and an encrypted address, LaMacchia set up an electronic bulletin board, which he named Cynosure. He encouraged his correspondents to upload popular software applications (Excel 5.0 and WordPerfect 6.0) and computer games (Sim City 2000). These he transferred to a second encrypted address (Cynosure II) where they could be downloaded by other users with access to the Cynosure password. The worldwide traffic generated by the offer of free software attracted the notice of university and federal authorities.

On April 7, 1994, a federal grand jury returned a one-count indictment charging LaMacchia with conspiring with "persons unknown" to violate 18 U.S.C. § 1343, the wire fraud statute. According to the indictment, LaMacchia devised a scheme to defraud that had as its object the facilitation "on an international scale" of the "illegal copying and distribution of copyrighted software" without payment of licensing fees and royalties to software manufacturers and vendors. The indictment alleged that LaMacchia's scheme caused losses of more than one million dollars to software copyright holders. The indictment did not allege that LaMacchia sought or derived any personal benefit from the scheme to defraud. [*U.S.* v. *LaMacchia*, 871 F. Supp. 535 (D. Mass. 1994)]

Economic Espionage Act Effective January 1, 1997, the Economic Espionage Act (EEA) makes it a criminal offense to steal trade secrets from an employer. EEA includes fines of up to $250,000 for individuals and $5 million for corporations, as well as up to ten years in prison and possible property forfeitures. The EEA makes it a crime for employees to copy, download, or transmit in any fashion trade secrets of their employer. The EEA is largely the result of the Volkswagen/GM case in which an executive with GM was sued for allegedly taking proprietary information about GM's supply chain management system in its European operations for use in his new position with Volkswagen.

Criminal Fraud

Business crimes against individuals usually result from sales transactions. **Criminal fraud** is an example of this type of crime, the elements of which are the same as those the person defrauded would use to establish a contract defense: There was a false statement; the statement was material—that is, it was the type of information that would affect the buying decision; and there was reliance on the statement. The only differences between contract fraud and criminal fraud is that criminal fraud requires proof of intent that the seller intended to mislead the buyer for the purpose of effecting the transaction and making money. In most of the savings

Re: What Crimes Does a Virus Commit?

David L. Smith was charged with creating the Melissa virus that infiltrated computers worldwide causing millions of dollars in damage in the spring of 1999. New Jersey state prosecutors charged Mr. Smith with interruption of public communication, theft of computer services, and wrongful access to computer systems. While there were federal crimes with which Mr. Smith could be

charged, federal prosecutors deferred to the New Jersey authorites because the crimes carried a possible fine of $480,000 and/or forty years.

Mr. Smith had long been fascinated with hackers and viruses and created the Melissa virus, named after a topless dancer he had met in Florida, as part of an e-mail attachment that, when opened, automatically spread to fifty other e-mail users.

and loans cases in which charges were brought, fraud charges were included, because often documents and appraisals were forged or falsified. Forgery provides proof of the level of intent needed for criminal fraud.

Racketeer Influenced and Corrupt Organization (RICO) Act

The RICO Act (18 U.S.C. Sections 1961–1968), a complex federal statute, was passed with the intent of curbing organized crime activity. The ease of proof and severity of penalties for RICO violations have made it a popular charge in criminal cases in which organized crime may not actually be involved.

For RICO to apply, it must be established that there has been a "pattern of racketeering activity." That pattern is defined as the commission of at least two racketeering acts within a ten-year period. Racketeering acts are defined under the federal statute to include murder; kidnapping; gambling; arson; robbery; bribery; extortion; dealing in pornography or narcotics; counterfeiting; embezzlement of pension, union, or welfare funds; mail fraud; wire fraud; obstruction of justice or criminal investigation; interstate transportation of stolen goods; white slavery; fraud in the sale of securities; and other acts relating to the Currency and Foreign Transactions Reporting Act (an act passed to prevent money laundering).

Explore the Racketeer Influenced and Corrupt Organizations Act:
http://www.law.cornell.edu/uscode/18/1961.html

RICO provides for both criminal penalties and civil remedies. In a RICO civil suit, injured parties can recover treble damages, the cost of their suit, and reasonable attorney fees. According to the *Journal of Accountancy,* 91 percent of all RICO civil actions have been based on the listed pattern crimes of mail fraud, wire fraud, or fraud in the sale of securities. The statute has been used frequently against corporations. For example, Northwestern Bell Telephone Company lobbyists, who took public utility commissioners to dinner and hired two of them as consultants after they left their commission jobs, were sued under RICO. A lawyer representing phone company customers brought a RICO civil suit based on an alleged pattern of bribing the utility regulators [*H. J., Inc.* v. *Northwestern Bell Telephone Co.,* 492 U.S. 229 (1989)].

Another portion of the RICO statute permits prosecutors to freeze defendants' assets to prevent further crimes. When RICO charges are brought against corporations, the seizure of corporate assets can mean the termination of the business. The Justice Department has issued guidelines requiring prosecutors to seek a forfeiture of assets in proportion to the crime rather than seize all of the business assets. A

Re: International Organized Crime

The 1999 Human Development Report of the United Nations concludes that organized crime has greater economic output than all but three of the world's nations. The U.N. report states that organized crime syndicates gross about $1.6 trillion per year. The total gross domestic product for the United Kingdom is $1.28 trillion.

The primary business of crime syndicates is drugs, and that industry is larger than auto manufacturing throughout the world. The report puts the gross revenue for drugs as $400 billion, which represents 8 percent of the world's total trade dollars.

The report points to three factors that have contributed to the growth in organized crime:

1. International trade facilitates greater activity across borders.

2. The lack of currency controls and trade barriers facilitates international monetary exchanges.

3. High-tech equipment and the presence of telecommunications in countries where phone services were a problem for decades make transactions move rapidly but also facilitates forgeries, frauds, and computer theft.

Many of the crime families have also been able to establish legitimate business fronts in other nations such as the Chinese triads with restaurants in London and the Japanese yakuza selling pornography (legalized) in the Netherlands. Even the criminal segments have been exported with the Sicilian Mafia benefiting from its strong heroin presence in New York City.

What do you think regulators can do about the flow of organized crime funds? What can legitimate businesses and individuals, as well as regulators, do to prevent the technological types of crimes via phone, fax, and computer?

Source: Anthony Browne, "Organized Crime Prospers Globally, Tops Output of Most Nations," *London Observer,* as reported in *Washington Times,* 12 July 1999, p. 25

growing number of states have enacted their own versions of the RICO statute for application at the state level. Some state RICO laws are specifically directed at narcotics, but over twenty include securities fraud as one of the covered acts.

RICO violations have become added charges in many criminal cases. For example, if someone is charged with ongoing bribery of a state or local official, RICO charges can be added because of the pattern of corruption. Only one U.S. Supreme Court case has served to restrict RICO's application. In *Reves* v. *Ernst & Young,* 507 U.S. 170 (1993), the accounting firm of Arthur Young (later merged into Ernst & Young) was hired to conduct audits for the Farmer's Cooperative of Arkansas and Oklahoma. An investment by the co-op in a gasohol plant proved to be a financial disaster, and the farmers who held co-op notes that had served as the organization's means of financing over the years lost their investment when the co-op filed for bankruptcy. The investors filed suit against Arthur Young for violations of federal securities laws (see Chapter 22) and RICO. However, the Supreme Court exempted the accounting firm from RICO charges because it found that the firm did not participate in the management of the co-op. The auditor's participation was not that of directing the co-op's affairs, only that of offering its opinions on the financial statements of the firm. The case represents one of the few restrictions on RICO application.

Over the past few years, businesses have been lobbying very heavily for reforms to the broad civil and criminal liabilities created by RICO. It seems unlikely that Congress will change the rights of plaintiffs to bring treble damage suits under the act's protective and deterrent mechanisms.

C O N S I D E R . . .

9.7 Brigido Marmolejo Jr. and Mario Salinas, the former sheriff and chief deputy sheriff of Hidalgo County, Texas, were convicted of various offenses arising from a series of bribes that Marmolejo received and Salinas aided and abetted in exchange for permitting conjugal visits for a federal prisoner, Homero Beltran-Aguirre, housed at the Hidalgo County Jail. The two operated the Hidalgo County Jail for local prisoners as well as under a contract with the U.S. Marshals Service for housing federal prisoners.

The bribes were paid during two different periods of incarceration of Beltran, from June 7, 1991, to April 14, 1992, and from November 6, 1992, to April 26, 1993. The federal prosecutor alleged the series of bribes comprised the pattern of racketeering charged in the indictment against Marmolejo and Salinas for RICO violations. The prosecutor also charged the two with money laundering. Marmolejo and Salinas were convicted, and they appealed challenging the use of only federal crimes to establish a RICO violation. Are other kinds of underlying crimes required for RICO violation or does violation of a federal statute satisfy the underlying crime requirement? Also, Marmolejo and Salinas appealed on the grounds that they were only local law enforcement officials and not involved in interstate commerce and therefore could not be charged with federal crimes. Are they correct? [*U.S. v. Marmolejo*, 89 F.3d 1185 (5th Cir. 1996)]

Federal Crimes

A great many of the statutes on business crimes are found at the federal level. Violations of the Securities Exchange Acts (Chapter 22), the Sherman Act (Chapter 17), the Internal Revenue Act, the Pure Food and Drug Act, the environmental statutes (Chapter 12), the Occupational Safety and Health Act (Chapter 19), and Consumer Product Safety statutes (Chapter 11) carry criminal penalties.

State Crimes

Similar criminal statutes at the state level cover such areas as criminal fraud and securities. In addition, states have particular regulations and laws for certain industries. The sale of liquor in most states is strictly regulated. The result is that there are many incidents of bribes and kickbacks in these highly regulated industries as businesses try to work around the regulatory restrictions.

PROCEDURAL RIGHTS FOR BUSINESS CRIMINALS

Business criminals are treated the same procedurally as other criminals. They have the same rights under the criminal justice system. The U.S. Constitution guarantees protection of certain rights. The **Fourth Amendment** protects the individual's privacy and is the basis for requiring warrants for searches of private property. The **Fifth Amendment** provides the protection against self-incrimination and is also the "due process" amendment, which guarantees that an accused individual will have the right to be heard. The **Sixth Amendment** is meant to ensure a speedy trial; it is the basis for the requirement that criminal proceedings and trials proceed in a timely fashion. These constitutional rights are discussed in the following sections.

Fourth Amendment Rights for Businesses

The Fourth Amendment to the U.S. Constitution provides that "the right of the people to be secure in their persons, houses, papers, and effects, against unreasonable searches and seizures, shall not be violated." This amendment protects individual privacy by preventing unreasonable searches and seizures. Before a government agency can seize the property of individuals or businesses, there must be a valid **search warrant**—or an applicable exception to the warrant requirement—which must be issued by a judge or magistrate and must be based on probable cause. In other words, there must be good reason to believe that instruments or evidence of a crime are present at the business location that is to be searched. The Fourth Amendment applies equally to individuals and corporations. In an unauthorized search, a corporation's property is given the same protection. If an improper search is conducted (without a warrant and without meeting an exception), then any evidence recovered is inadmissible at trial for the purposes of proving the crime.

Exceptions to the warrant requirement are based on emergency grounds. For example, if an office building with relevant records is burning, government agents could enter the property without a warrant to recover the papers. Similarly, if the records are being destroyed, the government need not wait for a warrant. Another exception to the warrant requirement is the "plain view" exception. This exception allows police officers to seize evidence that is within their view. No privacy rights are violated when evidence is exposed to the view of others. The *Kyllo* case in Chapter 8 dealt with the issue of technology affording access where eyes could not ordinarily see. The following case deals with a business issue and the Fourth Amendment exception.

CASE 9.6

Dow Chemical Co. v. *United States*
476 U.S. 1819 (1986)

Low-Flying Federal Agents: Photographic Searches

FACTS

Dow Chemical (petitioner) operates a two-thousand-acre chemical plant at Midland, Michigan. The facility, with numerous buildings, conduits, and pipes, is visible from the air. Dow has maintained ground security at the facility and has investigated fly-overs by other, unauthorized aircraft. However, none of the buildings or manufacturing equipment is concealed.

In 1978, the Environmental Protection Agency (EPA) conducted an inspection of Dow. EPA requested a second inspection, but Dow denied the

request. The EPA then employed a commercial aerial photographer to take photos of the plant from 12,000, 3,000, and 1,200 feet. The EPA had no warrant, but the plane was always within navigable air space when the photos were taken.

When Dow became aware of the EPA photographer, it brought suit in federal district court and challenged the action as a violation of its Fourth Amendment rights. The district court found that the EPA had violated Dow's rights and issued an injunction prohibiting the further use of the aircraft. The court of appeals reversed and Dow appealed.

(continued)

JUDICIAL OPINION

BURGER, Chief Justice

The photographs at issue in this case are essentially like those used in map-making. Any person with an airplane and an aerial camera could readily duplicate them. In common with much else, the technology of photography has changed in this century. These developments have enhanced industrial processes, and indeed all areas of life; they have also enhanced enforcement techniques. Whether they may be employed by competitors to penetrate trade secrets is not a question presented in this case. Governments do not generally seek to appropriate trade secrets of the private sector, and the right to be free of appropriation of trade secrets is protected by law.

That such photography might be barred by state law with regard to competitors, however, is irrelevant to the questions presented here. State tort law governing unfair competition does not define the limits of the Fourth Amendment. The Government is seeking these photographs in order to regulate, not compete with, Dow.

Dow claims first the EPA has no authority to use aerial photography to implement its statutory authority of "site inspection" under the Clean Air Act.

Congress has vested in EPA certain investigatory and enforcement authority, without spelling out precisely how this authority was to be exercised in all the myriad circumstances that might arise in monitoring matters relating to clean air and water standards.

Regulatory or enforcement authority generally carries with it all the modes of inquiry and investigation traditionally employed or useful to execute the authority granted. Environmental standards cannot be enforced only in libraries and laboratories, helpful as those institutions may be.

The EPA, as a regulatory and enforcement agency, needs no explicit statutory provisions to employ methods of observation commonly available to the public at large; we hold that the use of aerial photography is within the EPA's statutory authority.

DISSENTING OPINION

POWELL, MARSHALL, BRENNAN, and BLACKMUN, Justices

The Fourth Amendment protects private citizens from arbitrary surveillance by their Government. Today, in the context of administrative aerial photography of commercial premises, the Court retreats from that standard. It holds that the photography was not a Fourth Amendment "search" because it was not accompanied by a physical trespass and because the equipment used was not the most highly sophisticated form of technology available to the Government. Under this holding the existence of an asserted privacy interest apparently will be decided solely by reference to the manner of surveillance used to intrude on that interest. Such an inquiry will not protect Fourth Amendment rights, but rather will permit their gradual decay as technology advances.

EPA's aerial photography penetrated into a private commercial enclave, an area in which society has recognized that privacy interests may legitimately be claimed. The photographs captured highly confidential information that Dow had taken reasonable and objective steps to preserve as private.

CASE QUESTIONS

1. Of what significance is the fact that Dow's plant could be seen from the air?

2. Did Dow take any steps to protect its privacy?

3. Is the EPA specifically given aerial surveillance authority?

4. Did the EPA need a warrant for taking its aerial photographs?

5. What objections does the dissent raise to the decision?

CONSIDER...

9.8 The IRS attached levies to the property and other assets of G.M. Leasing Corp. for nonpayment of taxes. To satisfy the levy, the IRS seized several automobiles from the street in front of G.M.'s offices. Also, without a warrant, the IRS entered G.M.'s offices and seized business books and records. Has the Fourth Amendment been violated with the seizure of the cars? Of the books and records? [*G.M. Leasing Corp.* v. *United States*, 429 U.S. 338 (1977)]

In many business crimes, the records used to prosecute the defendant are not in the possession of the defendant. The records are, instead, in the hands of a third party, such as an accountant or a bank. Does the Fourth Amendment afford the defendant protection in documents that discuss the defendant or reflect the defendant's finances and transactions when those documents are in the hands of another? In some cases, there is a privilege between the third party and the defendants, and certain documents are protected and need not be turned over. Notes on trial strategy, audit procedures, and other plans and thoughts are not discoverable because such communications are privileged between lawyers and clients. Some states recognize an accountant/client privilege. The priest/parishioner privilege generally exists; however, there are exceptions in which reporting is required, such as in cases of abuse.

Fifth Amendment Rights for Businesses

The Fifth Amendment extends several protections to those facing criminal charges.

C O N S I D E R . . .

9.9   The FBI currently uses an Internet wiretapping system called Carnivore to conduct surveillance of Internet messages and activity. The American Civil Liberties Union says that such a device, even with a warrant, is a violation of the Fourth Amendment because the information and messages of those who are innocent are read by federal agents.

Technology has also facilitated wiretaps, and there were 1,350 authorized wiretaps in 1999, a 2 percent increase over 1998, a steady trend. However, Internet interception need only be authorized by an attorney and does not require a court order. Those seeking the interception need only show that the interception is related to the investigation.

Do you think there is a violation of privacy by Carnivore? Do you think warrants should be required? Why do you think wiretaps are treated differently from Internet interceptions?

Self-Incrimination

The statement "I take the Fifth" is used so often that it has made the Fifth Amendment well known for its protection against self-incrimination. For example, Denise Rich took the Fifth Amendment when asked by both congressional committees and the U.S. Attorney's office in New York to explain her role in securing the presidential pardon for her ex-husband, Marc Rich. No one can be compelled to be a witness against herself. However, this protection applies only to natural persons; corporations are not given this privilege. A corporation cannot prevent the required disclosure of corporate books and records on grounds that they are incriminating.

Corporate officers cannot assert Fifth Amendment protection to prevent compulsory production of corporate records. Nor can corporate officers use the Fifth Amendment to prevent the production of corporate records on grounds that those records incriminate them personally. The rules applicable to corporate officers have been extended to apply to those involved in labor unions, close corporations, and even unincorporated associations. The same rule is applicable to sole shareholders of small corporations as well.

In Chapter 4, the issues of attorney/client privilege and work product are discussed. Often, when a business is investigated for criminal activity, the issues all come together, as in the following landmark case on the rights of corporate employees during a criminal investigation.

CASE 9.7

Upjohn Co. v. United States
449 U.S. 382 (1980)

The Upside and Downside of Internal Investigations

FACTS

Upjohn Company (petitioner) is U.S. manufacturer and international seller of pharmaceuticals. In January 1976, independent auditors for the company notified Gerard Thomas, Upjohn's corporate secretary and general counsel, that they had discovered that an Upjohn subsidiary had made payments to foreign government officials in order to secure business for the company. Mr. Thomas, a member of the Michigan and New York bars, had been Upjohn's general counsel for twenty years.

After consulting with Upjohn's Chairman of the Board, Thomas began an internal investigation to determine whether "questionable payments" had been made. Thomas sent a memo to "All Foreign General and Area Managers" over the Chairman's signature and disclosed the "possibly illegal" payments and management's need for full information on any such payments made by Upjohn. Managers were asked to participate in an investigation to be conducted by "the company's General Counsel," to provide information on such payments, and to treat the information as "highly confidential."

Thomas received and compiled responses and interviewed thirty-three Upjohn officers and employees.

Thomas then submitted a voluntary report to the Securities Exchange Commission (SEC) disclosing certain questionable payments. A copy of the same report was also given to the Internal Revenue Service (IRS). The IRS began an investigation of the tax consequences of the payments and served Upjohn with a summons for

All files relative to the investigation conducted under the supervision of Gerard Thomas to identify payments to employees of foreign governments and any political contributions made by the Upjohn Company or any of its affiliates since January 1, 1971 and to determine whether any

funds of the Upjohn Company had been improperly accounted for on the corporate books during the same period.

The records should include but not be limited to written questionnaires sent to managers of the Upjohn Company's foreign affiliates, and memorandums or notes of the interviews conducted in the United States and abroad with officers and employees of the Upjohn Company and its subsidiaries.

Upjohn declined to turn over the documents requested in the summons on the grounds of attorney/client privilege and claims of work product. The U.S. filed a petition seeking enforcement of the summons. The District Court enforced the summons. The Court of Appeals found the work product claim not applicable and reversed the District Court's conclusion that the attorney-client privilege had been waived. Upjohn appealed.

JUDICIAL OPINION

REHNQUIST, Justice

Federal Rule of Evidence 501 provides that "the privilege of a witness . . . shall be governed by the principles of the common law as they may be interpreted by the courts of the United States in light of reason and experience." The attorney-client privilege is the oldest of the privileges for confidential communications known to the common law. Its purpose is to encourage full and frank communication between attorneys and their clients and thereby promote broader public interests in the observance of law and administration of justice. The privilege recognizes that sound legal advice or advocacy serves public ends and that such advice or advocacy depends upon the lawyer's being fully informed by the client.

The Court of Appeals, however, considered the application of the privilege in the corporate context to present a "different problem," since the client was an inanimate entity and "only the senior management, guiding and integrating the several operations, . . . can be said to possess an identity analogous to the corporation as a whole." The first case to articulate the so-called "control group test" adopted by the court below, *General Electric Co.* v. *Kirkpatrick,* 312 F. 2d 742 (CA3 1962) cert. denied, 372 U.S. 943 (1963), reflected a similar conceptual approach:

Keeping in mind that the question is, Is it the corporation which is seeking the lawyer's advice when the asserted privileged communication is made?, the most satisfactory solution, I think, is that if the employee making the communication, of whatever rank he may be, is in a position to control or even to take a substantial part in a decision about any action which the corporation may take upon the advice of the attorney, . . . then, in effect, he is (or personifies) the corporation when he makes his disclosure to the lawyer and the privilege would apply.

Such a view, we think, overlooks the fact that the privilege exists to protect not only the giving of professional advice to those who can act on it but also the giving of information to the lawyer to enable him to give sound and informed advice.

In the case of the individual client the provider of information and the person who acts on the lawyer's advice are one and the same. In the corporate context, however, it will frequently be employees beyond the control group as defined by the court below—"officers and agents . . . responsible for directing [the company's] actions in response to legal advice"—who will possess the information needed by the corporation's lawyers. Middle-level—and indeed lower-level—employees can, by actions within the scope of their employment, embroil the corporation in serious legal difficulties, and it is only natural that these employees would have the relevant information needed by corporate counsel if he is adequately to advise the client with respect to such actual or potential difficulties.

The control group test adopted by the court below thus frustrates the very purpose of the privilege by discouraging the communication of relevant information by employees of the client to attorneys seeking to render legal advice to the client corporation. The attorney's advice will also frequently be more significant to noncontrol group members than to those who officially sanction the advice, and the control group test makes it more difficult to convey full and frank legal advice to the employees who will put into effect the client corporation's policy.

The narrow scope given the attorney-client privilege by the court below not only makes it difficult for corporate attorneys to formulate sound advice when their client is faced with a specific legal problem but also threatens to limit the valuable efforts of corporate counsel to ensure their client's compliance with the law. In light of the vast and complicated array of regulatory legislation confronting the modern corporation, corporations, unlike most individuals, "constantly go to lawyers to find out how to obey the law.". . .

But if the purpose of the attorney-client privilege is to be served, the attorney and client must be able to predict with some degree of certainty whether particular discussions will be protected. An uncertain privilege, or one which purports to be certain but results in widely varying applications by the courts, is little better than no privilege at all. The very terms of the test adopted by the court below suggest the unpredictability of its application. The test restricts the availability of the privilege to those officers who play a "substantial role" in deciding and directing a corporation's legal response. Disparate decisions in cases applying this test illustrate its unpredictability.

The communications at issue were made by Upjohn employees to counsel for Upjohn acting as such, at the direction of corporate superiors in order to secure legal advice from counsel. As the Magistrate found, "Mr. Thomas consulted with the Chairman of the Board and outside counsel and thereafter conducted a factual investigation to determine the nature and extent of the questionable payments *and to be in a position to give legal advice to the company with respect to the payments.*" Information, not available from upper-echelon management, was needed to supply a basis for legal advice concerning compliance with securities and tax laws, foreign laws, currency regulations, duties to shareholders, and potential litigation in each of these areas. The communications concerned matters within the scope of the employees' corporate duties, and the employees themselves were sufficiently aware that they were being questioned in order that the corporation could obtain legal advice. The questionnaire identified Thomas as "the company's General Counsel" and referred in its opening sentence to the possible illegality of payments such as the ones on which information was sought.

The Court of Appeals declined to extend the attorney-client privilege beyond the limits of the control group test for fear that doing so would entail severe burdens on discovery and create a broad "zone of silence" over corporate affairs. Application of the attorney-client privilege to communications

(continued)

such as those involved here, however, puts the adversary in no worse position than if the communications had never taken place. The privilege only protects disclosure of communications; it does not protect disclosure of the underlying facts by those who communicated with the attorney.

Here the Government was free to question the employees who communicated with Thomas and outside counsel. Upjohn has provided the IRS with a list of such employees, and the IRS has already interviewed some twenty-five of them. While it would probably be more convenient for the Government to secure the results of petitioner's internal investigation by simply subpoenaing the questionnaires and notes taken by petitioner's attorneys, such considerations of convenience do not overcome the policies served by the attorney-client privilege. As Justice Jackson noted in his concurring opinion in *Hickman* v. *Taylor*, 329 U.S., at 516: "Discovery was hardly intended to enable a learned profession to perform its functions . . . on wits borrowed from the adversary."

Our decision that the communications by Upjohn employees to counsel are covered by the attorney-client privilege disposes of the case so far as the responses to the questionnaires and any notes reflecting responses to interview questions are concerned. The summons reaches further, however, and Thomas has testified that his notes and memoranda of interviews go beyond recording responses to his questions. To the extent that the material subject to the summons is not protected by the attorney-client privilege as disclosing communications between an employee and counsel, we must reach the ruling by the Court of Appeals that the work-product doctrine does not apply to summonses.

The Government concedes, wisely, that the Court of Appeals erred and that the work-product doctrine does apply to IRS summonses.

Rule 26 accords special protection to work product revealing the attorney's mental processes. The Rule permits disclosure of documents and tangible things constituting attorney work product upon a showing of substantial need and inability to obtain the equivalent without undue hardship. Rule 26 goes on, however, to state that "[i]n ordering discovery of

such materials when the required showing has been made, the court shall protect against disclosure of the mental impressions, conclusions, opinions or legal theories of an attorney or other representative of a party concerning the litigation." Although this language does not specifically refer to memoranda based on oral statements of witnesses, the *Hickman* court stressed the danger that compelled disclosure of such memoranda would reveal the attorney's mental processes.

While we are not prepared at this juncture to say that such material is always protected by the work-product rule, we think a far stronger showing of necessity and unavailability by other means than was made by the Government or applied by the Magistrate in this case would be necessary to compel disclosure. Since the Court of Appeals thought that the work-product protection was never applicable in an enforcement proceeding such as this, and since the Magistrate whose recommendations the District Court adopted applied too lenient a standard of protection, we think the best procedure with respect to this aspect of the case would be to reverse the judgment of the Court of Appeals for the Sixth Circuit and remand the case to it for such further proceedings in connection with the work-product claim as are consistent with this opinion.

Accordingly, the judgment of the Court of Appeals is reversed, and the case remanded for further proceedings.

CASE QUESTIONS

1. What illegal activity was Upjohn investigating?

2. How did a criminal investigation start?

3. Why wasn't Upjohn charged with violations of the Foreign Corrupt Practices Act?

4. What is the difference between work-product and the attorney-client privilege?

5. What advice would you have for someone conducting an internal company investigation? What advice would you have for the employees involved?

Miranda *Rights*

The famous *Miranda* doctrine resulted from an interpretation of the Fifth Amendment by the U.S. Supreme Court in *Miranda* v. *Arizona*, 384 U.S. 436 (1966). **Miranda** **warnings** must be given to all people who are subjected to custodial interrogation. Custody does not necessarily mean "locked in jail," but it is generally based on an individual's perceptions of a situation. If a person feels she is without freedom to leave a place by choice, the level of custody at which *Miranda* rights must be issued has been reached. The warnings tell those in custody of their Fifth Amendment right to say nothing, as well as their right to an attorney. The failure to give *Miranda* warnings is not fatal to a case so long as the crime can be proved through evidence other than the statement of the defendant; the prosecution can still proceed based on other evidence.

Due Process Rights

The Fifth Amendment also contains due process language. The same language is found in the Fourteenth Amendment and made applicable to the states. **Due process,** as Chapters 5 and 6 discuss, means that no one can be convicted of a crime without the opportunity to be heard, to question witnesses, and to present evidence.

Due process in criminal proceedings guarantees certain procedural protections as a case is investigated, charged, and taken to trial. The Sixth Amendment complements due process rights by requiring that all these procedures be completed in a timely fashion. The following subsections discuss the basic steps in a criminal proceeding as diagrammed in Exhibit 9.3.

Warrant and/or Arrest A criminal proceeding can begin when a crime is witnessed, as when a police officer attempts to apprehend a person who has just robbed a convenience store. When the convenience store is robbed but the robber escapes, and if the police can establish that a certain individual was probably responsible for the robbery, a **warrant** can be issued and the individual then arrested. Whether with or without a warrant, the due process steps begin with the arrest.

Initial Appearance Once an arrest has been made, the defendant must have an opportunity to appear before a judicial figure within a short time period (usually twenty-four hours) to be informed of his charges, rights, and so on. This proceeding is generally referred to as an **initial appearance.** Dates for other proceedings are set at this time and, if the individual can be released, the terms of the release are also established. The individual may

---

BUSINESS PLANNING TIP

What to do when federal agents come to search your business:

1. If the agents have a warrant, it is highly unlikely that the search can be prevented or delayed. The warrant has already been before a judicial figure (magistrate) who has determined that there is probable cause to conduct the search. If you have corporate counsel, have them handle the search. If you have an outside lawyer, call her to see if the lawyer has any specific advice.

2. Check the warrant to be certain the agents have the right location. There have been cases where chaos has been created in the execution of a warrant, only to have all the parties realize they were at the wrong location for the needed records.

3. Read the warrant's parameters. The agents can search only in the areas specified and for the documents and materials specified. Offer directions and instructions on locations of the named documents and items from the warrant.

4. Identify who the leader of the search team is and pledge full cooperation by your business.

5. Request the name of the prosecutor handling the case and ask to see the affidavits used to obtain the warrant.

6. Assign employees to work with the agents so that business data and equipment can be preserved and that permanent damage or loss does not result from retrieval of records.

7. Cooperate and work with the agents to minimize disruption but do not give permission for the agents to search areas not named or documents not delineated in the warrant.

8. Develop a company plan for responding to warrant searches. In these days of computer crime and required databases, the likelihood of a business search is quite high. Include in your plan who will coordinate the search, who is to be contacted, and how records of the search process are to be made.

EXHIBIT 9.3
**Steps in Criminal
Proceedings**

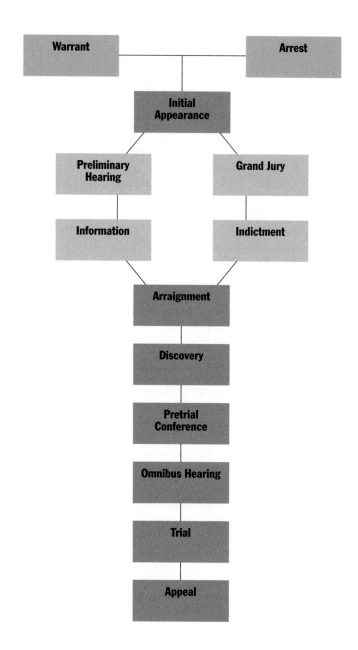

be required to post a bond to be released; others are held without release terms (release terms are generally dependent upon the nature of the crime and the defendant). The terms *released on his own recognizance* and *released OR* mean the defendant is released without having to post a bond.

Preliminary Hearing or Grand Jury Up to this step in the criminal proceedings, the defendant's charges are based on the word of a police officer; there has not yet been any proof brought forth linking the crime and the defendant. The purpose of a preliminary hearing or grand jury proceeding is to require the prosecution to establish that there is some evidence that the defendant committed the crime.

Jim G. Locklear was a purchasing agent. His spectacular career as a buyer began in 1977 with Federated Stores in Dallas, Texas. Federated officers described him as a man with an eye for fashion and a keen ability to negotiate. In 1987, Locklear was offered a position with Jordan Marsh, in the Boston area, with an annual salary of $96,000.

Citing a desire to return to Dallas, Locklear left the Jordan Marsh position after only three months. He returned to Dallas as a buyer for J. C. Penney at an annual salary of $56,000. Mr. Locklear did a phenomenal job as the buyer for the J. C. Penney Home Collection. Penney was the first department store to feature coordinated lines of dinnerware, flatware, and glasses. Under Mr. Locklear's purchasing, annual sales in Penney's tabletop line went from $25 million to $45 million.

Based on an anonymous tip, Penney hired an investigator to look into Mr. Locklear's conduct. The investigator found and reported that Mr. Locklear had personal financial difficulties. He had a $500,000 mortgage on his home and child support payments of $900 a month for four children from four previous marriages. Mr. Locklear also had a country club membership, luxury vehicles, and large securities accounts; and he was known to take vacations at posh resorts. Despite this puzzling lifestyle that was revealed by the investigator, Penney took no action.

ETHICAL ISSUES 9.3

In 1992, Penney received an anonymous letter disclosing a kickback situation between Mr. Locklear and a manufacturer's representative (rep). Penney investigated a second time, referred the case for criminal prosecution, and filed a civil suit against Mr. Locklear.

The investigation conducted by authorities found that Mr. Locklear received payments from vendors through several corporations he had established. During the five-year period from 1987 to 1992, Mr. Locklear had received $1.5 million from vendors, manufacturers' reps, and others.

Mr. Locklear was charged with commercial bribery and entered into a plea agreement that resulted in a five-year prison sentence. Mr. Locklear also served as a witness for the prosecution of those who paid him the bribes. A vendor described his payment of a $25,000 fee to Mr. Locklear as follows: "It was either pay it or go out of business." Mr. Locklear was sentenced to eighteen months in federal prison.

Issues

1. Should Penney have known of the difficulties earlier?

2. Was Mr. Locklear's personal life responsible for his poor value choices at work?

3. Is anyone really harmed by Locklear's activity? Wasn't he a good buyer?

In a **preliminary hearing,** the prosecution presents evidence to a judge to indicate that the accused committed the crime. The prosecution presents witnesses, and the defendant and the defendant's attorney are present for cross-examination of those witnesses. The defense does not present its case at this time but might make an offer of proof to show that the defendant could not have committed the crime. If the judge finds there is sufficient proof, an **information** is issued. The information is to a criminal proceeding what a complaint is to a civil proceeding: It establishes what the defendant did and when and what crimes were committed.

In some crimes, the evidence of the crime is presented to a **grand jury,** which is a panel of citizens who serve for a designated period of time (usually six months) and act as the body responsible for the review of evidence of crimes. If the grand jury finds that there is sufficient evidence that a crime was committed, it issues an **indictment,** which is similar to an information and serves the same function.

Grand jury proceedings are conducted secretly, whereas preliminary hearings are public. Grand juries also have the authority to conduct investigations to determine whether crimes were committed and who did so. Perhaps one of the most famous grand juries was the Washington, D.C., area grand jury that was investigating President Clinton and his wife Hillary for their involvement in a failed savings and loan and its assets. Mrs. Clinton is the only first lady to testify before a grand jury. Despite her public figure status, Mrs. Clinton's testimony remained a secret. In cases that are taken before a grand jury, the criminal process begins with an indictment followed by a warrant to arrest those charged.

The Arraignment An **arraignment** is the proceeding at which the defendant enters a plea of guilty, not guilty, or no contest (*nolo contendere*). If a not guilty plea is entered, a date for trial is set. If the defendant enters a guilty or no contest plea, chances are the plea is the result of a **plea bargain,** which is the term used in criminal proceedings for a settlement. The defendant may plead guilty to a lesser offense in exchange for the prosecution's promise to support a lesser sentence, such as probation or minimum jail time.

Discovery If a case is going to trial, there is a discovery period. Many states have mandatory criminal discovery laws that require each side to turn over certain types of information to the other side, including lists of witnesses they will call and lists of exhibits that will be used at trial. Exhibits include documents, murder weapons, and pictures.

Omnibus Hearing In some cases, the defense attorney wishes to challenge the prosecution evidence on grounds that it was obtained in violation of any of the constitutional protections discussed earlier. Some documents, for example, may have been seized without a warrant. The **omnibus hearing** is the forum wherein all of these challenges can be presented for the judge's ruling as to the admissibility of evidence. It is held before the trial so the jury is not exposed to evidence that should not have been admitted. In the O. J. Simpson double-homicide trial, an omnibus hearing was held on the admissibility of evidence gathered at Mr. Simpson's estate without a warrant.

Trial If no plea agreement is reached before trial, the case then proceeds to trial.

SUMMARY

Who is liable for business crimes?

- Vicarious liability—holding companies accountable for criminal conduct of their officers

- Elements—requirements of proof for crimes

- *Mens rea*—requisite mental state for commission of a crime

- *Actus reus*—physical act of commission of a crime

What penalties exist for business crimes?

- Penalties—punishments for commission of crimes; include fines and imprisonment

- Corporate sentencing guidelines—federal rules used to determine level of penalties for companies and officers; a system that decreases penalties for effort and increases penalties for lack of effort and other problems in company operations

What is the nature of business crime?

- Computer crime—crimes committed while using computer technology; includes such activities as transferring funds (salami technique) and collecting data without authorization (scavenging)

- Counterfeit Access Device and Computer Fraud and Abuse Act—federal law making it a crime to access computers without authorization

- Electronic Espionage Act—makes it a crime to take employer's proprietary information

- Criminal fraud—misrepresentation with the intent to take something from another without her knowledge; to mislead to obtain funds or property

- Foreign Corrupt Practices Act—federal law that regulates financial reports of international firms and prohibits bribes to influence government actions and officials in other countries

- Racketeer Influenced and Corrupt Organizations (RICO) Act—federal law designed to prevent racketeering by making it a crime to engage in certain criminal activities more than once

What are the rights of corporate and individual defendants in the criminal justice system?

- Fourth Amendment—provision in U.S. Constitution that protects against invasions of privacy; the search warrant amendment

- Fifth Amendment—the self-incrimination protection of the U.S. Constitution

- Sixth Amendment—the right-to-trial protection of the U.S. Constitution

- Search warrant—judicially issued right to examine home, business, and papers in any area in which there is an expectation of privacy

- *Miranda* warnings—advice required to be given those taken into custody; details right to remain silent and the right to have counsel

- Due process—right to trial before conviction

- Warrant—public document authorizing detention of an individual for criminal charges; for searches, a judicial authorization

- Initial appearance—defendant's first appearance in court to have charges explained, bail set, lawyer appointed, and future dates set

- Preliminary hearing—presentation of abbreviated case by prosecution to establish sufficient basis to bind defendant over for trial

- Information—document issued after preliminary hearing requiring defendant to stand trial

- Grand jury—secret body that hears evidence to determine whether charges should be brought and whether defendant should be held for trial

- Indictment—document of grand jury issues in requiring defendant to stand trial

- Arraignment—hearing at which trial date is set and plea is entered

- Plea bargain—settlement of criminal charges

- Omnibus hearing—evidentiary hearing outside the presence of the jury

- Trial—presentation of case by each side

QUESTIONS AND PROBLEMS

1. In the summer of 1993, the United States experienced the great, but temporary, Pepsi syringe scare. In several areas throughout the country, "consumers" came forward and claimed they had found medication syringes in cans of Pepsi. The Food and Drug Administration (FDA) and officers of PepsiCo reeled for several days as they attempted to cope with the allegations. Within a short period of time from when the stories on the syringes first appeared, a film taken by a hidden store camera showed one of the "consumers" actually inserting a syringe into a Pepsi drink product prior to purchase.

Assume that a criminal charge of adulteration requires proof of an intentional act. Would the hidden camera film establish the intent element of the crime?

2. Borland International, Inc., and Symantec Corporation are software manufacturers based in Silicon Valley in California. A Borland executive, Eugene Wang, was planning to depart Borland to work for Symantec, considered Borland's archrival. Other Borland executives and its board uncovered evidence, on the evening of Mr. Wang's departure, that Mr. Wang had communicated trade secrets to Gordon Eubanks, Symantec's chief executive. Those secrets included future product specifications, marketing plans through 1993, a confidential proposal for a business transaction, and a memo labeled "attorney/client confidential" summarizing questions asked by the Federal Trade Commission (FTC) in its probe of restraint of trade allegations by Microsoft Corporation.

Mr. Wang had allegedly used his computer to communicate the information to Mr. Eubanks. The local police and Borland executives worked through the night, using Symantec's own software that reconstructs computer files after they have been destroyed.

When Mr. Wang reported for his exit interview, he was detained and questioned by investigators. Searches authorized by warrant of Mr. Eubanks' two homes and his office uncovered evidence that he had received Mr. Wang's information. Borland filed a civil suit against the two men.

Later during the day of the exit interview, Mr. Wang's secretary, who was transferring with him to Symantec, returned to copy from her computer what she called "personal files." A personnel official watched as she copied the files from her computer but became suspicious and notified plainclothes officers in the Borland parking lot. The secretary, Lynn Georganes, was stopped, and the two disks onto which she had copied materials were taken. The disks contained scores of confidential Borland documents, including marketing plans and business forecasts.

Do the actions of Mr. Wang and Mr. Eubanks fit any computer crime statutes? Was there theft involved in their actions? Were Ms. Georganes's actions ethical? Can't a competitor always hire an executive away, and wouldn't Mr. Wang have had most of the information in his head anyway? Can Mr. Eubanks be certain Mr. Wang will not do the same thing to him?

3. Mr. Wittman is a vice president of West Valley Estates, Inc. Under Mr. Wittman's direction, West Valley violated the terms of its dredging permit by dredging and filling land beyond the permit limits. The state of Florida brought criminal charges against West Valley for violation of the permit laws. West Valley said Mr. Wittman did this on his own and that the board never authorized him to go beyond the permit limits, and thus the corporation could not be held liable. Is this a correct analysis? [*West Valley Estates, Inc. v. Florida,* 286 So. 2d 208 (Fla. 1973)]

4. The state of Ohio had a statute that provided criminal penalties for anyone who "with intent to defraud . . . make[s] a check . . . or, with like intent, utter[s] or publish[es] as true and genuine such false . . . matter, knowing it to be false. . . ." Could a violation be established by showing that an individual wrote a check drawn on a bank at which he had no checking account? Is the proper intent established? [*In re Clemons,* 151 N.E.2d 553 (Ohio 1958)]

5. Reuben Sturman was charged with income tax evasion based largely on evidence the Internal Revenue Service and the Justice Department gathered

through records of a Swiss bank in which Mr. Sturman had made substantial deposits over the past five years. The U.S. officials obtained the records from the Swiss bank pursuant to a treaty arrangement the U.S. government has with the Swiss government regarding the exchange of bank and bank record information. Mr. Sturman challenged the charges and the evidence on grounds that he had an expectation of privacy in his Swiss bank account and that U.S. officials were required to have a warrant before obtaining information about specific accounts in the Swiss banking system. Is Mr. Sturman correct? [*United States v. Sturman,* 951 F.2d 1466 (6th Cir. 1991)]

6. Bernard Saul was a salesperson for A. P. Walter Company, a wholesale auto parts business, assigned to the D&S Auto Parts account. Mr. Saul took inventory at D&S each week and phoned in an order to Walter to cover the needed inventory replacements. Between 1976 and 1982, Mr. Saul ordered parts from Walter and invoiced D&S, but actually kept a portion of the parts for himself and sold them to other dealers and pocketed the money himself. Through an audit, D&S discovered that it had paid $155,445.20 for parts that were not received. Can Mr. Saul be charged with any crimes? Can Walter be charged with any crimes? [*D&S Auto Parts, Inc. v. Schwartz,* 838 F.2d 965 (7th Cir. 1988)]

7. Odessa Mae French operated the Pines Motel as a house of prostitution for seven years. During that time, Ms. French avoided any local law enforcement action by allowing the sheriff to have free services at the Pines. Eventually, the federal government brought charges against the operation for tax evasion and RICO violations. Would the services to the sheriff constitute a form of bribe that would support a RICO charge? [*United States v. Tunnell,* 667 F.2d 1182 (5th Cir. 1982)]

8. The New York City Department of Health is responsible for the inspection of Manhattan restaurants to determine whether they comply with the city's health code. Forty-six of the department's inspectors were inducing restaurateurs to pay money to them for permit approval or for a favorable inspection.

Is this activity a basis for a crime? What crime? What would a prosecutor be required to prove? Are the officers and the restaurateurs equally criminally liable? [*U.S. v. Tillem,* 906 F.2d 814 (2d Cir. 1990)]

9. John Blondek and Vernon Tull were employees of Eagle Bus Company, a company based in the United States. Both Mr. Blondek and Mr. Tull were indicted for violations of the FCPA for paying a $50,000 bribe to Donald Castle and Darrell Lowry, officials of the Saskatchewan (Canada) provincial government to ensure that their bid to provide buses to Saskatchewan would be accepted. Messrs. Castle and Lowry were also indicted. Can they, as foreign officials, be prosecuted under the FCPA? [*United States* v. *Blondek,* 741 F. Supp. 116 (N.D. Tex. 1990)]

10. Harlan Nolte and others invested in IFC Leasing Company, a master music recording leasing program. The company was created to acquire and lease master music recordings. Jerry Denby, the executive vice president of IFC, contacted Stephen Weiss, a partner in the law firm of Rosenbaum, Wise, Lerman, Katz & Weiss, to draft the prospectus for investors. Mr. Weiss drafted four documents used in the recruitment of investors for IFC. The complex structure of the investments, according to the documents, would have substantial tax consequences (to their benefit) for the investors.

After Mr. Nolte and others had made their investments, the IRS issued an opinion that the deductions explained in the prospectus and other documents would not be allowed. Criminal fraud actions were brought against IFC and its officers, as well as Stephen Weiss. The Justice Department also indicted both Mr. Weiss's law firm and his partners.

Mr. Weiss's partners and the firm, through its management committee, maintain they cannot be held criminally liable for the actions of one partner. The Justice Department maintains that the firm and the partners were negligent in their supervision of Mr. Weiss and should, therefore, be held criminally liable. Do you agree with the Justice Department's position? Why, or why not? [*Nolte* v. *Pearson,* 994 F.2d 1311 (8th Cir. 1993)]

RESEARCH PROBLEM

Crime, the Internet, and Pornography

11. Read *Reno* v. *American Civil Liberties Union,* 521 U.S. 844 (1997), and determine the following:
a. What criminal statutes were at issue?
b. What provisions of the Constitution were at issue?
c. What is the status of criminal prosecution for transmission of pornography over the Internet?

NOTES

1. Jessie Halladay, "Driver Wins Cell-phone-Crash Verdict," *USA Today,* 7 December 2000, 10A.

2. "Colorado Skier Is Convicted In Fatal Collision on Slopes," *New York Times,* 18 November 2000, A9.

BUSINESS STRATEGY APPLICATION

Refer to the statutes produced on the CD and summarize the areas of a business that are vulnerable to federal criminal charges and what penalties can be imposed. Develop a chart of offenses, area of business, and penalties. You will have the chance to note areas of vulnerability.

CHAPTER TEN

Business Torts

Criminal wrongs require guilty parties to pay a debt to society through a fine, imprisonment, and/or community service. However, criminal wrongs and other types of actions may harm individuals. The harm to an individual or a firm is a civil wrong that entitles those who experience that harm to recover their damages. Torts are civil wrongs that provide a remedy for individuals who are harmed. This chapter answers these questions: What are the types of civil wrongs that create a right of recovery for harm? What are the types and elements of torts? What are the business costs and issues surrounding torts?

The desire for safety stands against every great and noble enterprise.

TACITUS

One does not seriously attack the expertise of a scientist using the undefined phrase "Butt-head."

JUDGE LOURDES G. BAIRD,
*in dismissing the late Carl Sagan's lawsuit against Apple Computer for its code name change
from "Carl Sagan" to "Butt-Head Astronomer."*

CONSIDER...

Dorothy McClung went shopping at the Wal-Mart in the Delta Square Shopping Center in Memphis at around noon. After she had completed her shopping and was returning to her car, she was abducted at gunpoint and forced into her car. She was later found dead in the trunk of her car, after her car was spotted by some hunters in a remote area in Arkansas. Roger McClung, her husband, filed suit against Wal-Mart and the owner of the shopping center, Delta Square. Are these companies liable for the criminal acts of another when those acts occurred in their parking lot?

WHAT IS A TORT?

Tort originates from the Latin term *tortus,* which means "crooked, dubious, twisted." Torts are civil wrongs, actions that are not straight but twisted. A **tort** is an interference with someone's person or with someone's property that results in injury to that person or to that person's property. For example, using someone else's land is an interference with that person's property rights and is the tort of trespass. Damage could result if you held a concert on someone else's land and the concert crowds destroyed the property's vegetation or left litter that had to be removed. The law provides protection for us and our property through the law of torts, which is a way to recover for the damages done to us.

Tort versus Crime

A tort is a private wrong. When a tort is committed, the party who was injured is entitled to collect compensation for damages from the wrongdoer for the private wrong. A crime, on the other hand, is a public wrong and requires the wrongdoer to pay a debt to society through a fine or by going to prison. For example, the crime of assault results in imprisonment, probation, and/or a fine. However, the victim could bring suit against the charged assailant to recover damages, such as medical bills, lost wages, and pain and suffering. The suit would be for the tort of assault.

Types of Torts

There are three types of tort liability: **intentional torts, negligence,** and **strict tort liability.** Intentional torts are the harms that result when parties commit intentional acts. For example, battery, or the striking of another person, is an intentional tort. A person is injured because you chose to hit him. However, suppose that you are stretching your arms in a crowd and you strike a man in the nose and hurt him. You have not committed the tort of battery, but you may have committed the tort of negligence. You did not intentionally strike the man as you would if you were having an argument, but you were carelessly swinging your arms in a crowd of people. These careless actions, or actions done without thinking through the consequences, are torts and constitute negligence. Such accidental harms also impose liabilities on the parties. The key difference between intentional torts and negligence is state of mind. Under the intentional tort standard, the party intended to commit the act. Under negligence, the party may have been careless or may not have thought carefully through his actions but the actions taken were not done with the intent to cause harm. Strict tort liability is generally used in product liability and is discussed extensively in Chapter 11.

Torts are also classified as *property torts* and *personal torts.* The example of trespassing given earlier is a property tort, because the injury is done to someone's property. The tort of defamation is an example of a personal tort, because it involves publishing untrue statements about a person, resulting in harm to that person. The tort of negligence can involve injury to person or property. For example, if someone runs a red light and bumps into your car, he has been careless and the tort of negligence has occurred. If you are injured and your car is damaged, you have experienced both personal and property damage. Regardless of the tort classification, the remedy for the tort is recovery for the damage done to you or your property.

THE INTENTIONAL TORTS

Defamation

Defamation is an untrue statement by one party to another about a third party. It consists of either slander or libel; **slander** is oral or spoken defamation, and **libel** is written (or, in some cases, broadcast) defamation. The elements for defamation are

1. A statement about a person's reputation, honesty, or integrity that is untrue
2. Publication
3. A statement that is directed at a particular person
4. Damages
5. In some cases, proof of malice

Publication

For defamation to occur, the statement must be communicated to a third party. An accountant who addresses a group of lawyers at a luncheon meeting and untruthfully states that another accounting firm has been involved in a securities fraud has met the publication element. So has a supplier who notifies other suppliers that a certain business is insolvent when it is not. Technically, the statement is published if it is communicated to one other person. The more publication, however, the greater the damages.

The Internet has provided a means for instant and international communication of defamatory information. Posting information on the Internet that is false is defamation if it harms another person or company. Internet messages do qualify as publication, and their electronic form qualifies as libel. Also, filing a defamation suit is possible even though the identity of the poster of the defamatory message is not known. The plaintiff can use the power of the courts, through a subpoena, to require servers to reveal the identity of those who have posted such messages.

C O N S I D E R . . .

10.1 Pathologist Dr. Jonathan Oppenheimer anonymously posted a message on a Yahoo Web site accusing Dr. Sam Graham, the chairman of the Department of Urology at the Emory University School of Medicine, of taking kickbacks. The message posted by "fbiinformant" read, "Urocor decided to underbid the Emory Pathology Department for pathology services and give Graham a cut of the money it got from doing pathology. This worked well until the poor SOB got caught with his hand in the cookie jar. Poor guy had to resign his prestigious position."

None of the information in the posting was true. Dr. Graham had left his position to go into private practice. Dr. Graham decided to file suit and filed the suit under the name "John Doe" so that he could then subpoena Yahoo to determine the identity of the person who posted the message. Oppenheimer was not a Yahoo subscriber, but Yahoo was able to provide the Internet service provider (ISP) Oppenheimer used. Dr. Graham's lawyers were able to pursue identity from there.

Is the statement Dr. Oppenheimer made libel? Did the lawyers and AOL act properly in tracking down Oppenheimer's identity? What do you learn about privacy and the Internet from this case? [*Graham v. Oppenheimer*, 2000 WL 33381418 (E.D. Va. 2000)]

Statement about a Particular Person

The general statement "All accountants are frauds" is not sufficiently narrow to be defamatory. The defamatory statement must either be about a particular person or be narrow enough in scope to include only a small group of businesses. For example, the statement "All the accountants in Parkland office complex are dishonest" is specific enough to meet this element.

Damages

The person who is defamed must be able to establish damages, such as lost business, lost profits, lost advertising, lost reputation, or some economic effect resulting from the defamatory statements.

Malice

Malice is not an element of defamation in every case. Malice must be established in those cases in which the defamation is about a public figure. Public figures are those who place themselves voluntarily in the public eye. Elected officials, recording artists, actors, and sports figures voluntarily place themselves in the public eye. Notoriety is often not a function of voluntary conduct. For example, witnesses in a case that has extensive media coverage are not public figures simply because they are in the public eye. However, should they then volunteer for exposure or capitalize on their fame as witnesses, they do become public figures. An example of someone who was a witness and then became a public figure by choice as part of a public relations boost to his career is Kato Kaelin, the once resident at O. J. Simpson's home who became a key witness in Simpson's trial for the murder of his ex-wife Nicole and her friend Ronald Goldman.

Because the First Amendment provides protections for the media, those who are public figures must prove, in addition to the other elements of defamation, that the statements were made or printed with knowledge that they are false or with reckless disregard for whether they are true or false. For example, a newspaper that prints a story on the basis of an unconfirmed source who has been shown to be unreliable in the past would be acting with malice.

The Defenses to Defamation

There are certain times when defamatory statements are made or printed but the tort of defamation is not established because there is a valid defense. A statement may be damaging, but, if it is the truth, it is not defamation. For example, you could publicly disclose that your boss took LSD during the late 1960s when he was in college. The remark might hurt your employer's reputation, but, if it is the truth, it is not the tort of defamation despite the harm it may do to him.

One of the current issues in defamation cases is whether the statements made are protected when they are a columnist's analysis of a situation. That is, courts are trying to determine whether there is some protection for viewpoint in which there is an objection to the conclusions drawn rather than the statements of fact themselves. There is often a fine line between statements of fact and expressions of opinion. In business publications, those opinions can be devastating to companies and their stock performance. In the following case involving an opinion column on litigation in *Forbes,* the court must analyze what is false versus what is true and what is analysis and opinion in order to determine whether a defamation suit can proceed.

CASE 10.1

Wilkow v. Forbes, Inc.
241 F.3d 552 (7th Cir. 2001)

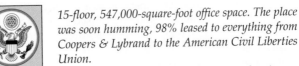

"Pleading Poverty" May Not Be Enough for a Defamation Suit

FACTS

On October 5, 1998, *Forbes* magazine printed the following opinion piece in its biweekly magazine for the business community:

Have the courts gone too far in protecting debtors against creditors? In this case it sure looks like it.

Stiffing the creditor
By Brigid McMenamin

IT HAPPENS EVERY DAY: Business seeks refuge in bankruptcy; owner and creditors make a deal—leaving owner in charge.

Presumably the creditors are satisfied that they got the best possible deal under the circumstances. But what if the owner tries to shaft them by offering only pennies on the dollar? These days, often as not, courts are siding with the bankrupt owners and forcing creditors to accept almost whatever deal the bankrupt party offers them.

In short, many judges, ever more sympathetic to debtors, are allowing unscrupulous business owners to rob creditors.

Unless a creditor is prepared to spend years battling it out in court, he usually caves in. Forget the old rule that in bankruptcy creditors enjoy "absolute priority" over debtors.

The U.S. Supreme Court will soon test the limits of this leniency. It has agreed to review a case in which the Bank of America National Trust & Savings Association claims it was stiffed by a real estate partnership led by Marc Wilkow of M&J Wilkow, Ltd., a Chicago-based manager of strip malls and offices.

The bank is asking the Court to nix a bankruptcy plan under which it might receive as little as $55 million for its $93 million lien against a Chicago office building. Under Wilkow's plan the bank must give up as much as 40% of its claim while Wilkow and his partners get to keep the building.

A lot rides on an eventual Supreme Court decision. That's why eight outsiders have filed friend-of-the-court briefs, including the American Bankers Association, the American Council of Life Insurance, the American College of Real Estate Lawyers, and the Solicitor General.

The whole mess started in 1987 when Bank of America began lending 203 N. LaSalle Street Partnership $93 million to build a sleek building in Chicago with a

15-floor, 547,000-square-foot office space. The place was soon humming, 98% leased to everything from Coopers & Lybrand to the American Civil Liberties Union.

But by the mid-1990s, rents were not keeping up with costs. When the principal came due in January 1995, Wilkow and his partners pleaded poverty. To keep the bank from foreclosing, LaSalle Partnership filed for bankruptcy. Appraisals of the property came in at less than $60 million. In theory the bank was entitled to the entire amount. It suggested selling the property to the highest bidder. Determined to keep the building, LaSalle partners asked the bankruptcy court instead to accept a plan under which the bank would likely receive a fraction of what it was owed while the partners would keep the building. The bank, not the equity holder, would take the hit.

Yet federal judge Paul Plunkett blessed LaSalle's plan. Bank of America will get as little as $55 million plus interest—and even that in monthly payments over seven to ten years.

What happened to the old "absolute priority rule"? To get around that, the partners used a controversial "new value" concept in which the owners agree to kick in fresh capital in return for equity.

To validate the concept, the owners proposed to put in $6.1 million in fresh capital, over five years.

Nice deal—for the debtor. The bank takes an up-to-$38 million haircut, and the owner throws in just $4.1 million in present value.

In September 1997 the federal appeals court that heard the case deferred to the lower court's decision. So the bank petitioned the Supreme Court to step in. On May 4 it agreed.

Bank of America's argument has been boosted by a February ruling from a federal appeals court in New York that found in favor of the creditors in a similar situation. With two such recent conflicting rulings and so much at stake, arguments before the Supreme Court will be heard on Nov. 2.

Realizing the Court could rule against the partnership, Wilkow says he is willing to sweeten his offer. "The time to talk settlement is when there's a cloud of uncertainty over everyone's head," he explains.

The article was accompanied by a photograph of the 203 North LaSalle Street building captioned "Chicago's

(continued)

203 North LaSalle Street, Stiffing the bank with court approval."

The article ran in the magazine seven months prior to the U.S. Supreme Court's decision on the bankruptcy priority rule, a decision that required 8,000 words to explain *(In re 203 North LaSalle Street Limited Partnership,* 526 U.S. 450 (1999)).

Mr. Wilkow filed suit against Forbes alleging that the article was defamatory and had caused him significant harm and damaged his reputation in the business community. The district court dismissed the suit and Mr. Wilkow appealed.

JUDICIAL OPINION

EASTERBROOK, Circuit Judge

The majority opinion in the Supreme Court required about 8,000 words to resolve the case—and without reaching a final decision on the vitality of the new-value exception (though the majority's analysis hog-tied the doctrine).

The majority opinion in this court (on the priority rule prior to its appeal to the U.S. Supreme Court) ran about 9,500 words, with 5,200 more in a dissent. A 670-word article such as the one *Forbes* published could not present either the facts of the case or the subtleties of the law. What the article lacked in analysis, however, it made up for with colorful verbs and adjectives. Taking lenders' side, *Forbes* complained that "many judges, ever more sympathetic to debtors, are allowing unscrupulous business owners to rob creditors." According to the article, a partnership led by Marc Wilkow "stiffed" the bank, paying only $55 million on a $93 million loan while retaining ownership of the building.

Wilkow replied with this libel suit under the diversity jurisdiction, contending that *Forbes* and Brigid McMenamin, the article's author, defamed him by asserting that he was in poverty (or, worse, "pleaded poverty" when he was solvent) and had filched the bank's money. According to Wilkow, *Forbes* should at least have informed its readers that the bank had lent the money without recourse against the partners, so that a downturn in the real estate market, rather than legal machinations, was the principal source of the bank's loss.

The district court dismissed the complaint for failure to state a claim on which relief may be granted. That was a misstep. A complaint is sufficient whenever the plaintiff could prevail under facts consistent with the complaint's allegations, and defamation is a recognized legal claim. The body of this complaint was not self-defeating. Instead the district judge based her decision on the text of the article. But when "matters outside the pleading are presented to and not excluded by the court, the motion shall be treated as one for summary judgment and disposed of as provided in Rule 56, and all parties shall be given reasonable opportunity to present all material made pertinent to such a motion by Rule 56."

In the district court the parties wrangled about choice of law. *Forbes* is based in New York, and Wilkow's business has its headquarters in Chicago. The district judge split the difference, ruling that Illinois law supplies the claim for relief but that New York law supplies an absolute privilege for "the publication of a fair and true report of any judicial proceeding". According to the judge, McMenamin's story is privileged under New York law as a report of proceedings in 203 North LaSalle Street. The judge added, for good measure, that the article is protected by the first amendment because the forceful characterizations to which Wilkow objects are opinions rather than facts. Forbes did not misstate any of the details of the situation, and neither Illinois nor New York requires a reporter to include all facts (such as the nonrecourse nature of the loan) that put the subject in the best light.

We don't think it necessary to consider either constitutional limits on liability for defamation or privileges under New York law, because this article is not defamatory under Illinois law in the first place. In Illinois, a "statement of fact is not shielded from an action for defamation by being prefaced with the words 'in my opinion,' but if it is plain that the speaker is expressing a subjective view, an interpretation, a theory, conjecture, or surmise, rather than claiming to be in possession of objectively verifiable facts, the statement is not actionable."

Characterizations such as "stiffing" and "rob" convey McMenamin's objection to the new-value exception. She expostulates against judicial willingness to allow debtors to retain interests in exchange for new value, not particularly against debtors' seizing whatever opportunities the law allows. Nothing in the article implies that Wilkow did (or even proposed) anything illegal; Forbes informed the reader that the district court and this court approved Wilkow's proposed plan of reorganization. Every detail in the article (other than the quotation in the final paragraph) comes from public documents; the article does not suggest that McMenamin knows extra information implying that Wilkow pulled the wool over judges' eyes or engaged in other misconduct. Colloquialisms such as "pleaded poverty" do not imply that Wilkow was destitute and failing to pay his personal creditors, an allegation that would have been defamatory. Read in context, the phrase conveys the idea that the partnership could not repay the loan out of rents received from the building's tenants. After all, inability to pay one's debts as they come due is an ordinary reason for bankruptcy, and 203 North LaSalle Street Partnership did file a petition in bankruptcy. Filing a bankruptcy petition is one way of "pleading poverty."

Although the article drips with disapproval of Wilkow's (and the judges') conduct, an author's opinion about business ethics isn't defamatory under Illinois law. Informing the reader about the nonrecourse nature of the loan might have made Wilkow look better, but it would not have drawn the article's sting: that the partners got to keep the property even though the bank lost $38 million. The original deal's fundamental structure was that the partnership would repay the loan from rental income, and that if revenue was insufficient the bank could choose to foreclose (cutting its loss and reinvesting at the market rate elsewhere), to renegotiate a new interest rate with the partners, or to forebear in the hope that the market would improve and the full debt could yet be paid. These options collectively would be worth more than the market value of the building on the date of default. Yet the partners refused to honor these promises to the bank. They persuaded judges to eliminate the bank's rights to foreclose, to renegotiate, or to forebear and retain the full security interest. The plan of reorganization stripped down the security interest, prevented the bank from foreclosing, and required it to finance the partnership's operations for the next decade, at a rate of interest below what the bank would have charged in light of the newly revealed riskiness of the loan. If the real estate market fell further during that time, so that the partnership could not repay even the reduced debt, then the bank was going to lose still more money. The present value of the promises made to the bank in the plan of reorganization therefore was less than the appraised value of the building. But the partners stood to make a great deal of money if the market turned up again (as it did), for they had shucked $38 million in secured debt while retaining most appreciation in the property's value. Whether that was a sound use of bankruptcy reorganization, independent of the plan's new-value aspects, is open to question.

A reporter is entitled to state her view that an ethical entrepreneur should have offered the lender a better bargain, such as allowing the bank to foreclose and take its $55 million with certainty, avoiding the additional risk that this plan fastened on the lender. Foreclosure would have had serious consequences for the partners, who would have lost about $20 million in recaptured tax benefits. These potential losses created room for negotiation. Armed with the new-value exception, however, the partners were able to retain the tax benefits, sharing none with the bank in exchange for its approval of a restructuring, while depriving the bank of a security interest that would have been valuable when the market recovered. Although a reader might arch an eyebrow at Wilkow's strategy, an allegation of greed is not defamatory; sedulous pursuit of self-interest is the engine that propels a market economy. Capitalism certainly does not depend on sharp practices, but neither is an allegation of sharp dealing anything more than an uncharitable opinion. Illinois does not attach damages to name-calling. Wilkow's current and potential partners would have read this article as an endorsement of Wilkow's strategy; they want to invest with a general partner who drives the hardest possible bargain with lenders. By observing that Wilkow used every opening the courts allowed, *Forbes* may well have improved his standing with investors looking for real estate tax shelters (though surely it did not help his standing with lenders). No matter the net effect of the article, however, it was not defamatory under Illinois law, so the judgment of the district court is AFFIRMED.

CASE QUESTIONS

1. What type of article did *Forbes* publish, and why is its nature important?

2. Is it defamation to express an opinion about the ethics of a business person?

3. What is the difference between the law and ethics, as this court discusses the question?

4. Does a writer have an obligation to disclose information that makes the subject matter of the piece look better than the writer did?

5. Is a writer expected to explain all the complexities of an issue before expressing an opinion?

Some speech is privileged; that is, there is a strong public interest in protecting the speech regardless of whether it is true. For example, members of Congress enjoy an **absolute privilege** when they are speaking on the floor of the Senate or House because there is a strong public policy to encourage free debate of issues. The same is true of judicial proceedings; in order to encourage people to come forward with the truth, witnesses enjoy an absolute privilege when testifying about the matters at hand. The media enjoy a **qualified privilege,** which is freedom to publish information even though it may be inaccurate, so long as it is not published with malice or with reckless disregard for whether the information published is true or false. Perhaps one of the most famous libel cases addressing the defense of the media privilege involved Carol Burnett and a story about her printed by the *National Enquirer.* The case decision on this incident follows.

CASE 10.2

Burnett v. National Enquirer, Inc.
144 Cal. App. 3d 991 (1983)

Only the *Enquirer* Didn't Know for Sure:
Carol Burnett, Henry Kissinger, and Defamation

FACTS

On March 2, 1976, the *National Enquirer* (appellant) published in its weekly publication a "gossip column" headlined "Carol Burnett and Henry K. in Row" that included the following four-sentence item:

In a Washington restaurant, a boisterous Carol Burnett had a loud argument with another diner, Henry Kissinger. Then she traipsed around the place offering everyone a bite of her dessert. But Carol really raised eyebrows when she accidentally knocked a glass of wine over one diner and started giggling instead of apologizing. The guy wasn't amused and "accidentally" spilled a glass of water over Carol's dress.

Ms. Burnett (respondent) filed suit against the *Enquirer* alleging that the item was entirely false and libelous after the *Enquirer* printed the following retraction:

An item in this column on March 2 erroneously reported that Carol Burnett had an argument with Henry Kissinger at a Washington restaurant and became boisterous, disturbing other guests. We understand these events did not occur and we are sorry for any embarrassment our report may have caused Miss Burnett.

After a jury trial, Ms. Burnett was awarded $300,000 compensatory damages and $1,300,000 punitive damages. The trial court reduced the

amounts to $50,000 compensatory and $750,000 punitive damages. The *Enquirer* appealed.

JUDICIAL OPINION

ROTH, Presiding Justice

Prior to addressing the merits of appellant's contentions and in aid of our disposition, we set out the following further facts pertaining to the publication complained of. . . .

On the occasion giving rise to the gossip column item hereinabove quoted, respondent, her husband and three friends were having dinner at the Rive Gauche restaurant in the Georgetown section of Washington, D.C. The date was January 29, 1976. Respondent was in the area as a result of being invited to be a performing guest at the White House. In the course of the dinner, respondent had two or three glasses of wine. She was not inebriated. She engaged in banter with a young couple seated at a table next to hers, who had just become engaged or were otherwise celebrating. When curiosity was expressed about respondent's dessert, apparently a chocolate souffle, respondent saw to it the couple were provided with small amounts of it on plates they had passed to her table for the purpose. Perhaps from having witnessed the gesture, a family behind respondent then offered to exchange some of their baked alaska for a portion of the souffle, and they, too, were similarly accommodated. As respondent was later leaving the restaurant, she was introduced by a friend to Henry Kissinger, who was dining at another table, and after a brief conversation, respondent left with her party.

There was no "row" with Mr. Kissinger, nor any argument between the two, and what conversation they had was not loud or boisterous. Respondent never "traipsed around the place offering everyone a bite of her dessert," nor was she otherwise boisterous, nor did she spill wine on anyone, nor did anyone spill water on her and there was no factual basis for the comment she ". . . started giggling instead of apologizing."

The impetus for what was printed about the dinner was provided to the writer of the item, Brian Walker, by Couri Hays, a freelance tipster paid by the *National Enquirer* on an ad hoc basis for information supplied by him which was ultimately published by it, who advised Walker he had been informed respondent had taken her Grand Marnier souffle around the restaurant in a boisterous or flamboyant manner and given bites of it to various other people; that he had further but unverified information respondent had been involved in the wine-water spilling incident; but that, according to his sources, respondent was "specifically, emphatically" not drunk. No mention was made by Hays of anything involving respondent and Henry Kissinger.

Having received this report, Walker spoke with Steve Tinney, whose name appears at the top of the *National Enquirer* gossip column, expressing doubts whether Hays could be trusted. Tinney voiced his accord with those doubts. Walker then asked Gregory Lyon, a *National Enquirer* reporter, to verify what Walker had been told by Hays. Lyon's inquiry resulted only in his verifying respondent had shared dessert with other patrons and that she and Kissinger had carried on a good-natured conversation at the restaurant.

In spite of the fact no one had told him respondent and Henry Kissinger had engaged in an argument, that the wine-water spilling story remained as totally unverified hearsay, that the dessert sharing incident was only partially bolstered, and that respondent was not under any view of the question inebriated, Walker composed the quoted item and approved the "row" headline.

The *National Enquirer* is a publication whose masthead claims the "Largest Circulation Of Any Paper in America." It is a member of the American Newspaper Publishers Association. It subscribes to the Reuters News Service. Its staff call themselves newspaper reporters.

By the same token the *National Enquirer* is designated as a magazine or periodical in eight mass media directories and upon the request and written representation of its general manager in 1960 that "In view of the feature content and general appearance [of the publication], which differ markedly from those of a newspaper . . ." its classification as a newspaper was changed to that of magazine by the Audit Bureau of Circulation. It does not subscribe to the Associated Press or United Press International news services. According to a statement by its Senior Editor it is not a newspaper and its content is based on a consistent formula of "how to" stories, celebrity or medical or personal improvement stories, gossip items, and TV column items, together with material from certain other subjects. It provides little or no current coverage of subjects such as politics, sports, or crime, does not attribute content to wire services, and in general does not make reference to time. Normal "lead time" for its subject matter is one to three weeks. Its owner allowed it did not generate stories "day to day as a daily newspaper does."

At appellant's request, the trial court herein made its determination after hearing and based on extensive evidence that the *National Enquirer* was not a newspaper for purposes of the application of Civil Code section 48a.

Seen in this light, the essential question is not then whether any publication is properly denominated a magazine or by some other designation, but simply whether it ought to be characterized as a newspaper or not.

Having so decided, we are also satisfied to conclude without extensive recitation of the evidence that the trial court consistently with the foregoing rationale correctly determined the *National Enquirer* should not be deemed a newspaper for the purposes of the instant litigation.

Nearly twenty years ago, it was announced in *New York Times Co. v. Sullivan*, 376 U.S. 254 (1964) that:

The constitutional guarantees [relating to protected speech] require, we think, a federal rule that prohibits a public official from recovering damages for a defamatory falsehood relating to his official conduct unless he proves that the statement was made with "actual malice"—that

(continued)

is, with knowledge that it was false or with reckless disregard of whether it was false or not.

[W]e are of the opinion the award to respondent of $750,000 in order to punish and deter appellant was not justified.

In so concluding, we are persuaded the evidence fairly showed that while appellant's representatives knew that part of the publication complained of was probably false and that the remainder of it in substance might very well be, appellant was nevertheless determined to present to a vast national audience in printed form statements which in their precise import and clear implication were defamatory, thereby exposing respondent to contempt, ridicule and obloquy, and tending to injure her in her occupation. We are also satisfied that even when it was thought necessary to alleviate the wrong resulting from the false statements it had placed before the public, the retraction proffered was evasive, incomplete and by any standard, legally insufficient. In other words, we have no doubt the conduct of appellant respecting the libel was reprehensible and was undertaken with the kind of improper motive which supports the imposition of punitive damages.

Nevertheless, evidence on the point of appellant's wealth adequately established appellant's net worth to be some $2.6 million and its net income for the period under consideration to be about $1.56 mil-

lion, such that the penalty award, even when substantially reduced by the trial court based on its conclusion the jury's compensatory verdict was "clearly excessive and . . . not supported by substantial evidence," continued to constitute about 35% of the former and nearly half the latter.

The judgment is affirmed except that the punitive damage award herein is vacated and the matter is remanded for a new trial on that issue only, provided that if respondent shall, within 30 days from the date of our remittitur, file with the clerk of this court and serve upon appellant a written consent to a reduction of the punitive damage award to the sum of $150,000, the judgment will be modified to award respondent punitive damages in that amount, and so as modified affirmed in its entirety. . . .

CASE QUESTIONS

1. Was malice established in the case? Why was it necessary to establish malice?

2. Is the *National Enquirer* a newspaper for purposes of the protection of the privilege?

3. Are the damages reduced? To what? Why?

4. Should tabloids like the *National Enquirer* enjoy the protection of the privilege?

CONSIDER . . .

10.2 Benjamin Paul, a personal injury lawyer with the firm of Benjamin Paul & Associates, was running for mayor of Philadelphia and was described by a city council member, Frank Rizzo, as a "slip-and-fall-lawyer running for mayor." *Philadelphia Magazine*, running a story on the candidates in the mayoral race, reprinted the comment about Mr. Paul. Mr. Paul filed suit against *Philadelphia Magazine* for libel. Mr. Paul said the term "slip-and-fall-lawyer" is similar in meaning to "shyster."

Does Mr. Paul have a case? Mr. Paul has handled some slip-and-fall-cases, some on behalf of local members of the Fraternal Order of Police.

CONSIDER . . .

10.3 The *National Enquirer* published an interview with actor Clint Eastwood. The interview had never taken place, and Mr. Eastwood said the publication of such an interview in a sensationalist newspaper made it seem as if he was "washed up as a movie star." Could Mr. Eastwood recover for the publication of the fake interview? What tort has occurred, if any?

BIOGRAPHY

Oprah, Mad Cow Disease, and Veggie Libel Laws

About thirteen states currently have "veggie libel" laws, statutes that permit suit when someone defames a generic product such as eggs, milk, or even broccoli. The laws provide a remedy for generic defamation of a natural food, thus not requiring a business to tie the defamatory remark directly to its particular product. Industry-wide damages can thus be recovered.

The veggie libel laws gained national public attention when Texas cattlemen filed an $11 million suit against talk show host Oprah Winfrey for her remarks during a show on mad cow disease. Following a presentation on the program by an anti-meat campaigner, Howard Lyman, Ms. Winfrey said, "It has just stopped me cold from eating another burger. I'm stopped." Using the Texas False Disparagement of Perishable Food Products Act of 1995, the ranchers and cattlemen alleged that the show presented a one-sided and inaccurate view of the issue of mad cow disease and caused a drop in sales of beef. Cattle futures prices dropped 10 percent on the day following the show, and beef prices went from 62 cents per pound to 55 cents per pound.

Following the judge's dismissal of many counts in the suit, the case proceeded to trial on the basis of a defamation claim, which the jury rejected. Ms. Winfrey emerged from the courthouse and noted, "The First Amendment isn't just alive. It rocks." The constitutionality of the veggie libel laws under the First Amendment has yet to be determined, but a case involving defamation of eggs in Pennsylvania is being taken up on appeal in order to obtain an opinion on that legal issue. In the case, a consumer's group was sued after it reported that an egg producer was washing and repackaging old eggs for sale.

Issues

1. How is vegetable defamation different from defamation of a person?
2. Could Ms. Winfrey have balanced her show?

Contract Interference

The tort of **contract interference** or **tortious interference with contracts** or tortious interference occurs when parties are not allowed the freedom to contract without interference from third parties. The tort developed in England before the twentieth century and still exists today.

While the elements of tortious interference are complex, a basic definition is that the law affords a remedy when someone intentionally persuades another to break a contract already in existence with a third party. Bryan A. Garner, the author of *Tortious Interference*, offers the following examples: "Say you had a contract with Joe Blow, and I for some reason tried to get you to break that contract. Or say that Pepsi has an exclusive contract with a hotel chain to carry Pepsi products, and Coke tries to get the hotel to carry Coke despite that contract. That's tortious interference."

BUSINESS PLANNING TIP

Preventing Shrinkage

• Carson Pirie Scott apprehended 5,000 shoplifters last year at its 57 stores.

• Inventory shrinkage (shoplifting, internal theft, and inventory errors) now constitutes 2.7 percent of sales.

• Nineteen percent of all shoplifting arrests are made during the month of December.

• Suspicious things security guards watch:

1. Baby strollers
2. Cars waiting right outside store exits
3. Shopping bags (when lined with aluminum foil, detector systems fail)
4. Long time periods spent in jewelry area

• Forty-three states now permit store owners to collect civil fines from shoplifters. The fines range from the value of the stolen items up to $5,000 in addition to the value.

Re: A New Twist on the Tort of Interference

Recently, the CBS news show **Sixty Minutes** *pulled from a scheduled airing an interview with a former tobacco executive in a news story about the industry, when threats of both libel and tortious interference with contract suits arose. The former executive of Brown & Williamson, Jeffrey S. Wigand, agreed to have the interview run only if CBS News would indemnify him against the suits. Brown & Williamson lawyers notified CBS News that Wigand had signed a confidentiality agreement and that the company would sue CBS News for interference with that contract if the interview were run.* **Sixty Minutes** *ran a story on tobacco companies without the interview. CBS correspondents Mike Wallace and Morley Safer protested the decision of CBS News executives. However, the* **Wall Street Journal** *ran a story describing CBS News's unusual arrangements with*

Wigand, including the payment of a consulting fee of $12,000 and the promise of full indemnification. Many lawyers commented that the promises CBS made to Wigand could be depicted as inducements for Wigand to breach his contract agreement of confidentiality with Brown & Williamson.

CBS eventually ran the story and interview with Mr. Wigand. The story of Mr. Wigand, CBS, and Brown & Williamson was made into a movie, based on the journalistic expose of the events. The movie, *The Insider,* featured Russell Crowe as Mr. Wigand, and the role earned him an Academy Award nomination. The movie earned protests from many at CBS, particularly Mike Wallace, as an inaccurate depiction of his conduct. Mr. Wallace's producer, Lowell Bergman, left CBS and *Sixty Minutes* after the Wigand story ran. He now teaches journalism at the University of California at Berkeley.

BUSINESS PLANNING TIP

The seven keys to invoking the shopkeeper's privilege are:

1. Stop shoppers discreetly.

2. Don't use physical force unless it is in reponse to the shopper's physical force.

3. Don't question shoppers publicly or make accusations within earshot of others.

4. Call the police quickly to allow them to take over.

5. If you detain shoppers, be certain the physical conditions are appropriate.

6. Don't detain shoppers except for their detention for the police and questioning that resolves the matter.

7. Be especially careful in detaining minors; allow them to call their parents or guardians.

One of the most famous cases involving the question of tortious interference was that of *Texaco, Inc.* v. *Pennzoil Co., 729 S.W.2d 768 (Tex. 1987).* The board of directors of Getty Oil had agreed to sell a substantial portion of its oil to Pennzoil. While Getty and Pennzoil were drafting their agreement, Texaco stepped in and made a competing bid. The Getty board then accepted the Texaco offer. Pennzoil filed suit against Texaco for tortious interference. The trial court awarded Pennzoil $7.53 billion in actual damages and $3 billion in punitive damages. While the appellate court reduced the punitive damages by $2 billion, it did find that Texaco interfered with the Pennzoil contract, because its officers described their conduct as "stop[ping] the train."

False Imprisonment

False imprisonment is often referred to as "the shopkeeper's tort" because it generally occurs as a result of a shoplifting accusation in a store. **False imprisonment** is the detention of a person for any period of time (even a few minutes) against his will. No physical harm need result; the imprisoned party can collect minimal damages simply for being imprisoned without consent. Because shopkeepers need the opportunity to investigate matters when someone is suspected of shoplifting, the tort of false imprisonment does carry the defense of the **shopkeeper's privilege.** This privilege allows a shopkeeper to detain a suspected shoplifter for a reasonable period of time while the matter or incident is investigated. In most states, the shopkeeper must have a reasonable basis for keeping the person; that is, the shopkeeper must have reason to suspect the individual even if it turns out later that the individual has an explanation or did not do what the shopkeeper suspected.

CONSIDER...

10.4 On November 16, 1986, Joseph Canto Jr., then 11 years old, and Samantha Canto, then 16, went shopping at the Ivey department store in Gainesville, Florida. After entering the store, they stopped at a display table to look at metallic chain-link belts. A videotape taken by a security camera shows the children stopping at the display table, handling the items and exchanging conversation while looking around, and Samantha handing something to Joseph, which he placed in his pocket. Jo Ann Williams stopped the children as they were leaving the store and told them she had reason to believe that they had stolen something and to follow her to the security office. The sheriff's report discloses that Ms. Williams called the sheriff's office soon thereafter but that an officer did not arrive for another hour. Another employee, managing agent Kirsten Aalto, arrived at the security office and aided Ms. Williams. The children were released by the officer about two hours after they were initially detained by Ms. Williams. No merchandise was found on the children.

Joseph and Samantha said they were questioned in an intimidating manner, were not allowed to use the bathroom or call their parents, and were called "delinquents" and "shoplifters."

Through their parents, Joseph and Samantha filed suit for damages incurred for their psychological counseling and treatment and for punitive damages. Should they recover? Consider the applicable Florida statutes. Section 812.015(5), Florida Statutes (1989), provides:

> *A merchant, merchant's employee, or farmer who takes a person into custody, as provided in subsection (3) . . . shall not be criminally or civilly liable for false arrest or false imprisonment when the merchant, merchant's employee, or farmer has* probable cause *to believe that the person committed retail theft or farm theft.*

Subsection (3)(a) provides:

> *A law enforcement officer, a merchant, a merchant's employee, or a farmer who has probable cause to believe that retail or farm theft has been committed by a person and that he can recover the property by taking the person into custody may, for the purpose of attempting to effect such recovery or for prosecution, take the person into custody and detain him in a reasonable manner for a reasonable length of time. . . . In the event the merchant, merchant's employee, or farmer takes the person into custody, a law enforcement officer shall be called to the scene immediately after the person has been taken into custody.*

[*Canto v. J. B. Ivey & Co.*, 595 So. 2d 1025 (Fla. 1992)]

Intentional Infliction of Emotional Distress

This tort imposes liability for conduct that goes beyond all bounds of decency and results in emotional distress in the harmed individual. One of the difficulties with this tort is that the only damage the plaintiff is required to prove is that of emotional distress. Although "pain and suffering" damages have been awarded for some time in negligence actions in which the plaintiff recovers damages for physical and property injuries, the awarding of damages for mental distress alone is a relatively new phenomenon. However, the tort of **intentional infliction of emotional distress** has been used quite often by debtors who are harassed by creditors and collection agencies in their attempts to collect funds.

Invasion of Privacy

For information on electronic privacy, see the Electronic Privacy Information Center at:
http://www.epic.org

The intentional tort of *invasion of privacy* is actually three different torts: (1) intrusion into the plaintiff's private affairs; (2) the public disclosure of private facts; and (3) the appropriation of another's name, likeness, or image for commercial advantage. The appropriation tort is discussed subsequently, under competition torts. The two other components of the privacy tort represent rights to be left alone and not to have personal matters publicly disclosed. Intrusion simply requires proof that the defendant was present when the plaintiff was doing something normally considered private.

One of the most famous invasion of privacy cases was *Galella* v. *Onassis*, 353 F. Supp. 196 (S.D.N.Y. 1972). In the case, the late Mrs. Jacqueline Kennedy Onassis brought suit against Ron Galella, a photo journalist, for invasion of her privacy. As a result of the case, Mr. Galella was ordered to remain at least 50 yards from Mrs. Onassis and 100 yards from her children.

COMPETITION TORTS

Appropriation

For information on privacy rights, see the Privacy Rights Clearinghouse:
http://www.privacyrights.org

The appropriation of someone's name, likeness, or voice for commercial advantage without his permission constitutes the tort of **unauthorized appropriation.** For example, if a gas station used your picture in its window to show you as a satisfied customer, you might not be harmed greatly but your privacy is invaded because you have the right to decide when, how, and where your name, face, image, or voice will be used. The fact that you do use the gas station and are a satisfied customer is not the issue in appropriation—it is the use without your permission that constitutes the tort. The following case addresses the unauthorized appropriation of a singer's voice.

CASE 10.3

Midler v. *Ford Motor Co.*
849 F.2d 460 (9th Cir. 1988)

Ford to Bette, "Do You Wanna Dance?"; Bette to Ford, "Not really!"

FACTS

In 1985, Ford Motor Company and its advertising agency, Young & Rubicam, Inc., advertised the Ford Lincoln Mercury with a series of nineteen 30-or-60-second television commer-

cials in what the agency referred to as "The Yuppie Campaign." The aim was to make an emotional connection with Yuppies, bringing back memories of when they were in college. The agency tried to get the "original people," that is, the singers who had popularized the songs, to sing them. When those efforts failed, the agency decided to go with "sound-alikes."

When Young & Rubicam was preparing the Yuppie Campaign it presented the commercial to its client by playing an edited version of Bette Midler (plaintiff/appellant) singing "Do You Want to Dance?" taken from the 1973 Midler album, *The Divine Miss M.*

After Ford accepted the idea and the commercial, Young & Rubicam contacted Midler's manager, Jerry Edelstein. The conversation went as follows: "Hello, I am Craig Hazen from Young & Rubicam. I am calling you to find out if Bette Midler would be interested in doing . . . ?" Mr. Edelstein: "Is it a commercial?" "Yes." "We are not interested."

Undeterred, Young & Rubicam sought out Ula Hedwig, who had been one of the "Harlettes," backup singers for Midler for 10 years. Hedwig was told by Young & Rubicam that "they wanted someone who could sound like Bette Midler's recording of ['Do You Want to Dance?']." She was asked to make a demo tape. She made an a cappella demo and got the job. At the direction of Young & Rubicam, Ms. Hedwig made a record for the commercial. She first had to listen to Miss Midler's recording of it and was then told to "sound as much as possible like the Bette Midler record."

After the commercial aired, Miss Midler was told by a number of people that it sounded exactly like her. Ms. Hedwig was told by friends that they thought it was Miss Midler.

Miss Midler, a nationally known actress and singer, won a Grammy in 1973 as Best New Artist of the Year. She has had both gold and platinum records. She was nominated in 1979 for an Academy Award for Best Female Actress in *The Rose,* in which she portrayed a pop singer. *Newsweek* described her as an "outrageously original singer/comedienne." *Time* hailed her as "a legend" and "the most dynamic and poignant singer-actress of her time."

Miss Midler filed suit against Ford and Young & Rubicam for appropriation. Young & Rubicam had a license from the song's copyright holder to use it. Neither the name nor the picture of Miss Midler was used in the commercial. The district court entered judgment for Ford and Young & Rubicam, and Miss Midler appealed.

JUDICIAL OPINION

NOONAN, Circuit Judge

At issue in this case is only the protection of Midler's voice. The district court described the defendant's

conduct as that "of the average thief." They decided, "If we can't buy it, we'll take it." The court nonetheless believed there was no legal principle preventing imitation of Midler's voice and so gave summary judgment for the defendants.

The First Amendment protects much of what the media do in the reproduction of likenesses or sounds. A primary value is freedom of speech and press. The purpose of the media's use of a person's identity is central. If the purpose is "informative or cultural" the use is immune; "if it serves no such function but merely exploits the individual portrayed, immunity will not be granted." It is in the context of these First Amendment and federal copyright distinctions that we address the present appeal.

Nancy Sinatra once sued Goodyear Tire and Rubber Company on the basis of an advertising campaign by Young & Rubicam featuring "These Boots Are Made for Walkin'," a song closely identified with her; the female singers of the commercial were alleged to have imitated her voice and style and to have dressed and looked like her. The basis of Nancy Sinatra's complaint was unfair competition; she claimed that the song and the arrangement had acquired "a secondary meaning" which, under California law, was protectible. This court noted that the defendants "had paid a very substantial sum to the copyright proprietor to obtain the license for the use of the song and all of its arrangements." To give Sinatra damages for their use of the song would clash with federal copyright law. Summary judgment for the defendants was affirmed. If Midler were claiming a secondary meaning to "Do You Want to Dance" or seeking to prevent the defendants from using that song, she would fail like Sinatra. But that is not this case. Midler does not seek damages for Ford's use of "Do You Want to Dance," and thus her claim is not preempted by federal copyright law. What is put forward as protectible here is more personal than any work of authorship.

Bert Lahr once sued Adell Chemical Co. for selling Lestoil by means of a commercial in which an imitation of Lahr's voice accompanied a cartoon of a duck. Lahr alleged that his style of vocal delivery was distinctive in pitch, accent, inflection, and sounds. The First Circuit held that Lahr had stated a cause of action for unfair competition, that it could be found "that defendant's conduct saturated plaintiff's audience, curtailing his market." That case is more like this one.

A voice is as distinctive and personal as a face. The human voice is one of the most palpable ways identity is manifested. We are all aware that a friend

(continued)

is at once known by a few words on the phone. At a philosophical level it has been observed that with the sound of a voice, "the other stands before me." *A fortiori,* these observations hold true of singing, especially singing by a singer of renown. The singer manifests herself in the song. To impersonate her voice is to pirate her identity.

We need not and do not go so far as to hold that every imitation of a voice to advertise merchandise is actionable. We hold only that when a distinctive voice of a professional singer that is widely known is deliberately imitated in order to sell a product, the sellers have appropriated what is not theirs and have committed a tort in California. Midler has made a showing, sufficient to defeat summary judgment, that the defendants here for their own profit in selling their products did appropriate part of her identity.

CASE QUESTIONS

1. In what context was Miss Midler's voice sought?
2. Did Miss Midler agree to allow her voice to be used?
3. Was there some confusion about who was singing in the commercial?
4. What is the difference between this case and the Nancy Sinatra case?
5. What is the difference between this case and the Bert Lahr case?
6. Was the use of Miss Midler's voice unfair competition?
7. Was the use of Miss Midler's voice appropriation?

Aftermath: Miss Midler's case was tried, and she recovered $400,000 from the defendants in October 1989.

NEGLIGENCE

The tort of **negligence** is one that applies in a variety of circumstances, but it is always used when the conduct of one party did not live up to a certain minimal standard of care we are all expected to use in driving, in our work, and in the care of our property. Negligence imposes liability on us when we are careless. The elements of and defenses to negligence are covered next.

Element One: The Duty

Each of us has the duty to act like an **ordinary and reasonably prudent person** in all circumstances. The standard of the ordinary and reasonably prudent person is not a standard we always live up to; when we do not, we are negligent. The standard of the ordinary and reasonably prudent person is not always what everyone else does or what the law provides. For example, suppose you are driving on a curvy highway late at night and it is raining quite heavily. The posted speed limit is 45 mph. However, the ordinary and reasonably prudent person will not drive 45 mph, because the road and the weather conditions dictate that slower driving is more appropriate. The level of care imposed on us by the ordinary and reasonably prudent person standard is one that requires an examination of all conditions and circumstances surrounding an event that leads to an injury. Many negligence cases struggle with the difficult task of determining whether a duty exists.

Duties, for purposes of negligence actions, can arise because of an underlying statute. Every traffic law carries a criminal penalty (fine and/or imprisonment) for violations of it. However, that law imposes a duty of obedience. A violation of that law is also a breach of duty for purposes of a civil or negligence action. When you run a red light, you have not only committed a crime; you have also breached a duty and are liable for injuries and damages resulting from that breach.

Professionals such as doctors, lawyers, and dentists have the duty of practicing their professions at the level of a reasonable professional. Failure to do so is a breach of duty and a basis for malpractice (negligence by professionals) lawsuits.

Landowners owe duties to people who enter their property. For example, the duty to trespassers, such as thieves, is not to intentionally injure them. Placing man traps would be a breach of this duty.

The following case involves one of the newer issues in whether a duty exists.

CASE 10.4

Randi W. v. *Muroc Joint Unified School District*
929 P.2d 582 (Cal. 1997)

The Glowing Letter of Recommendation That Forgot to Mention Sexual Misconduct with Minors

FACTS

Randi W. (plaintiff) is a 13-year-old minor who attended the Livingston Middle School where Robert Gadams served as vice principal. On February 1, 1992, while Randi was in Gadam's office, Gadams molested and sexually touched Randi.

Gadams had previously been employed at the Mendota Unified School District (from 1985 to 1988). During his time of employment there, Gadams had been investigated and reprimanded for improper conduct with female junior high students, including giving them back massages, making sexual remarks to them, and being involved in "sexual situations" with them.

Gilbert Rossette, an official with Mendota, provided a letter of recommendation for Gadams in May 1990. The letter was part of Gadams's placement file at Fresno Pacific College, where he had received his teaching credentials. The recommendation was extensive and referred to Gadams's "genuine concern" for students, his "outstanding rapport" with everyone, and concluded, "I wouldn't hesitate to recommend Mr. Gadams for any position."

Gadams had also previously been employed at the Tranquility High School District and Golden Plains Unified District (1987–1990). Richard Cole, an administrator at Golden Plains, also provided a letter of recommendation for the Fresno placement file that listed Gadams's "favorable" qualities and concluded that he "would recommend him for almost any administrative position he wishes to pursue." Cole knew, at the time he provided the recommendation, that Gadams had been the subject of various parents' complaints, including that he "led a panty raid, made sexual overtures to students, sexual remarks to students." Cole also knew that Gadams had resigned under pressure because of these sexual misconduct charges.

Gadams's last place of employment (1990–1991) before Livingston was Muroc Unified School District, where disciplinary actions were taken against him for sexual harassment. When allegations of "sexual touching" of female students were made, Gadams was forced to resign from Muroc. Nonetheless, Gary Rice and David Malcolm, officials at Muroc, provided a letter of recommendation for Gadams that described him as "an upbeat, enthusiastic administrator who relates well to the students," and who was responsible "in large part," for making Boron Junior High School (located in Muroc) "a safe, orderly and clean environment for students and staff." The letter concluded that they recommended Gadams "for an assistant principalship or equivalent position without reservation."

All of the letters provided by previous administrators of Gadams were sent in on forms that included a disclosure that the information provided "will be sent to prospective employers."

Through her guardian, Randi W. filed suit against the districts, alleging that her injuries from Gadams's sexual touching were proximately caused by their failure to provide full and accurate information about Gadams to the placement service. The trial

(continued)

court dismissed the case, and the Court of Appeals reversed. The districts appealed.

JUDICIAL OPINION

CHIN, Associate Justice

In finding plaintiff's complaint stated a cause of action against defendants for fraud and negligent misrepresentation, the Court of Appeal majority relied primarily on sections 310 and 311 of the Restatement Second of Torts. Section 310 involves intentional conduct and provides that "[a]n actor who makes a *misrepresentation* is subject to liability to another for *physical harm* which results from an act done by the other *or a third person* in reliance upon the truth of the representation, if the actor (a) intends his statement to induce or should realize that it is likely to induce action by the other, or a third person, which involves an unreasonable risk of physical harm to the other, and (b) knows (i) that the statement is false, or (ii) that he has not the knowledge which he professes." [Italics added.]

Section 311 of the Restatement Second of Torts, involving negligent conduct, provides that: "(1) One who negligently gives *false information* to another is subject to liability for physical harm caused by action taken by the other *in reasonable reliance upon such information,* where such harm results (a) to the other, or (b) *to such third persons as the actor should expect to be put in peril by the action taken.* (2) Such negligence may consist of a failure to exercise reasonable care (a) in ascertaining the accuracy of the information, or (b) in the manner in which it is communicated." [Italics added.]

Although ordinarily a duty of care analysis is unnecessary in determining liability for intentional misrepresentation or fraud, here we consider liability to *a third person* injured as a result of the alleged fraud, an extension of ordinary tort liability based on fraud. Accordingly, in deciding whether to adopt the two Restatement provisions in the circumstances of this case, we consider whether plaintiff has sufficiently pleaded that defendants owed her a *duty of care,* that they breached that duty by making *misrepresentations* or giving *false information,* and that Livingston's *reasonable reliance* on their statements *proximately caused* plaintiff's injury.

Did defendants owe plaintiff a duty of care? In defendants' view, absent some special relationship between the parties, or some specific and known threat of harm to plaintiff, defendants had no duty of care toward her, and no obligation to disclose in their letters any facts regarding the charges against Gadams.

Plaintiff does not argue that a special relationship existed between defendants and her or Gadams. [U]nder section 311 of the Restatement Second of Torts, a parole officer had a duty to exercise reasonable care in giving the victim information regarding the parolee who ultimately killed her. [A]lthough the parole officer had no duty to volunteer information regarding the released criminals he supervised, ". . . the absence of a duty to speak does not entitle one to speak falsely." [T]he parole officer, "having chosen to communicate information about [the parolee] to [the victim], had a duty to use reasonable care in doing so," and that the officer either knew or should have known that the victim's safety might depend on the accuracy of the information imparted.

[N]o California case has yet held that one who intentionally or negligently provides false information to another owes a duty of care *to a third person* who did not receive the information and who has no special relationship with the provider. Accordingly, the issue before us is one of first impression, and we apply the general analytical principles used to determine the existence of duty in particular cases.

In this state, the general rule is that all persons have a duty to use ordinary care to prevent others from being injured as the result of their conduct. *The major [considerations] are* the foreseeability of harm to the plaintiff, *the degree of certainty that the plaintiff suffered injury, the closeness of the connection between the defendant's conduct and the injury suffered, the moral blame attached to the defendant's conduct, the policy of preventing future harm, the extent of the burden to the defendant and consequences to the community of imposing a duty to exercise care with resulting liability for breach, and the availability, cost, and prevalence of insurance for the risk involved.*

The foreseeability of a particular kind of harm plays a very significant role in this calculus, but a court's task—in determining 'duty'—is not to decide whether a particular *plaintiff's injury was reasonably foreseeable in light of a* particular *defendant's conduct, but rather to evaluate more generally whether the category of negligent conduct at issue is sufficiently likely to result in the kind of harm experienced that liability may appropriately be imposed on the negligent party.*

Applying these factors here, we first examine whether plaintiff's injuries were a *foreseeable* result of defendants' representations regarding Gadams's qualifications and character, coupled with their failure to disclose to the Fresno Pacific College placement office information regarding charges or complaints of Gadams's sexual misconduct. Could defendants reasonably have foreseen that the representations and omissions in their reference letters would result in physical injury to someone? Although the chain of causation leading from defendants' statements and omissions to Gadams's alleged assault on plaintiff is somewhat attenuated, we think the assault was reasonably foreseeable. Based on the facts alleged in the complaint, defendants could foresee that Livingston's officers would read and rely on defendants' letters in deciding to hire Gadams. Likewise, defendants could foresee that, had they not unqualifiedly recommended Gadams, Livingston would not have hired him. And, finally, defendants could foresee that Gadams, after being hired by Livingston, might molest or injure a Livingston student such as plaintiff. We must assume, for purposes of demurrer, that plaintiff was indeed *injured* in the manner she alleges, and that a *causal connection exists between defendants' conduct and the injury suffered.* As plaintiff's complaint alleges, her injury was a "direct and proximate result" of defendants' fraud and misrepresentations.

Whether defendants were guilty of any *moral blame* would depend on the proof adduced at trial, although it is certainly arguable that their unreserved recommendations of Gadams, together with their failure to disclose facts reasonably necessary to avoid or minimize the risk of further child molestations or abuse, could be characterized as morally blameworthy.

As for public policy, the law certainly recognizes a *policy of preventing future harm* of the kind alleged here. One of society's highest priorities is to protect children from sexual or physical abuse.

Defendants urge that *competing social or economic policies* may disfavor the imposition of liability for misrepresentation or nondisclosure in employment references. They observe that a rule imposing liability in these situations could greatly inhibit the preparation and distribution of reference letters, to the general detriment of employers and employees alike.

We have recently stated that "[w]hen deciding whether to expand a tort duty of care, courts must consider the potential social and economic consequences." Defendants argue that a rule imposing tort liability on writers of recommendation letters could have one very predictable consequence: employers would seldom write such letters, even in praise of exceptionally qualified employees.

In defendants' view, rather than prepare a recommendation letter stating all "material" facts, posi-

tive and negative, an employer would be better advised to decline to write a reference letter or, at most, merely to confirm the former employee's position, salary, and dates of employment. According to defendants, apart from the former employer's difficulty in deciding how much "negative" information to divulge, an employer who disclosed more than minimal employment data would risk a defamation, breach of privacy, or wrongful interference suit from a rejected job seeker. [C]ases involving only economic loss are subject to a more restrictive rule.

The Court of Appeal thus concluded that it was unnecessary under section 311 of the Restatement Second of Torts for plaintiff to plead her own reliance on defendants' misrepresentations, as long as the recipient of those misrepresentations (ultimately, Livingston) reasonably relied on them in hiring Gadams, as plaintiff alleged here. Citing a comment to section 311, the court observed that "The Restatement, however, makes it clear that the plaintiff need not rely on the misrepresentation and may, indeed, not even know that it was made."

We agree with the Court of Appeal's reliance analysis. Under the Restatement provisions, plaintiff need only allege that her injury resulted from action that *the recipient* of defendants' misrepresentations took in reliance on them. In a case involving false or fraudulent letters of recommendation sent to prospective employers regarding a potentially dangerous employee, it would be unusual for *the person ultimately injured* by the employee actually to "rely" on such letters, much less even be aware of them.

In any event, as the Court of Appeal observed, failure to plead reliance would not be a ground for sustaining a demurrer without leave to amend. We note that questions concerning the reasonableness of Livingston's reliance on letters written well before Livingston allegedly received information regarding Gadams's misconduct are not before us in reviewing the trial court's ruling on demurrer.

As previously discussed, plaintiff's complaint alleges that her injury was a "proximate" result of defendants' fraud and misrepresentations. Defendants do not suggest that the complaint fails to state sufficient facts to establish proximate causation, assuming the remaining elements of duty, misrepresentation and reliance are sufficiently pleaded. Based on the facts alleged in the complaint, plaintiff's injury foreseeably and proximately resulted from Livingston's decision to hire Gadams in reliance on defendants' unqualified recommendation of him.

(continued)

The judgment of the Court of Appeal is affirmed as to counts three and four (negligent misrepresentation and fraud), but reversed as to count five (negligence *per se*).

CASE QUESTIONS

1. Who provided the letters of recommendation for Gadams? What information was missing from the recommendations?

2. What concerns are raised about imposing liability on those who provide letters of recommendation?

3. What was the proximate cause of Randi W.'s injury?

4. Did the former employers owe a duty to anyone with respect to the letters of recommendation?

5. What issues should employers address, in light of this case, in providing letters of reference and recommendation?

Texas State Representative Brian McCall, in debating the Texas legislature's proposed legislation for employer-qualified privilege on references, offered the following:

*Lawyers telling their clients to only give name, rank and serial number are playing a game that puts people in classrooms who shouldn't be there, puts people in operating rooms who shouldn't hold a scalpel and puts people driving trucks who shouldn't have a driver's license.**

Professor Marcia Staff of the University of North Texas has written:

It is time for serious consideration of requiring disclosure of information about violent employees and those who engage in sexual misbehavior in order to provide protection for the public at large, while providing legal protection for the former employer. Without a legal duty to dis-

ETHICAL ISSUES 10.1

close and at least a modicum of legal protection, it appears unlikely that employers, and the attorneys who advise them are going to change their approach to personnel references.[†]

Should employers remain silent about misconduct by former employees? Does the nature of the misconduct matter? Do perfunctory references give a false impression? What about disclosures regarding former employees that were never really established and the employee simply resigned?

*Mary Flood, "References Still Risky, Lawyers Say," *Wall Street Journal*, 22 September 1999, A1.

[†]Marcia Staff, "Personnel References: Legal and Ethical Considerations," Paper presented at the Academy of Legal Studies in Business, August 2001.

Element Two: Breach of Duty

Once the standard of care and the duty are established under element one, there must be a determination that the defendant fell short of that standard or breached that duty for the plaintiff to recover on the basis of negligence. For example, an accountant owes a duty to his client to perform an audit in a competent and professional manner and to conform the audit to the standards and rules established by the American Institute of Certified Public Accounts (AICPA). Failure to comply with these standards would be a breach of duty and would satisfy this second element of negligence.

In many cases, courts try to determine whether the duty was breached to determine whether the defendant's action satisfied the standard of care established in element one.

Re: References, Risk, and Defamation

Paul Calden, a 33-year-old, low-level manager, was fired from his job at Allstate Insurance Company in St. Petersburg, Florida, for carrying a gun to his job. His supervisors at Allstate would later describe him as a "total lunatic."

Mr. Calden applied for a job with Firemen's Fund Insurance in Tampa, Florida. Firemen's Fund contacted the Allstate offices for a reference. Allstate sent a letter signed by a vice president that was neutral in its description of Mr. Calden and did not disclose the true reasons for his termination. Mr. Calden had threatened litigation; there was some fear among the employees about him, and Allstate had agreed to a four-month severance package despite his having worked at Allstate for only nine months. Allstate also agreed to draft and send the neutral letter.

After Mr. Calden was terminated by Firemen's Fund, he shot and killed three executives of the company while they were having lunch at a café. One of the executives' wives filed suit against Firemen's Fund and Allstate. The suit against Allstate was based on its failure to disclose Mr. Calden's bizarre behavior and the risk that he was in the workplace.

Allstate defended its actions on the grounds that the average verdict in a defamation suit by a former employee against his former employer for a job reference is $57,000. In one Florida case, a former employee was awarded $25 million in damages. However, in an unpublished opinion, *Jerner v. Allstate Insurance Co.,* 94-03822 (Fla. App. 1995), the appellate court held that there could be an action against an employer for misrepresentation if the employer gives a neutral reference on an employee who is a danger, as in this case.

Thirty-two states currently (2001) have some form of law that creates a privilege for employers in providing references. The privilege is designed to free managers in their discussions of former employees and their performances. A survey indicates that without such protection, disclosures about violent tendencies will not be made and the risk to employees at a new firm is high. Fifty-four percent of all employers indicate they would not disclose violent behavior when asked for a reference.

In nearly all states, there is a qualified privilege for those who have a moral obligation to speak. These types of privilege statutes provide protection for whistle-blowers (see Chapter 18), in that a controlled (limited) disclosure of information made in good faith will not subject a businessperson to liability for defamation. However, verification of the truth of such statements is critical. Also adding to the complexity of the reference issue is a U.S. Supreme Court decision in which the court held that giving a negative reference on a former employee who has sued the company for discrimination can be considered retaliatory and a violation of Title VII [*Robinson v. Shell Oil Co.,* 519 U.S. 337 (1997)].

BUSINESS STRATEGY

If you are assigned the task of developing a new reference policy for your company, remember the following:

1. Stick with factual disclosures: Use "There was an accusation of embezzlement and he resigned," not "He is an embezzler."
2. Stick with easily defined terms: Use "Angers easily," not "He is a lunatic."
3. Report what happened, not your view: Use "Other staff members complained about her con-duct and work," not "She was a constant pain in the neck."
4. Implement an exit interview in which you disclose the information you have on file that will be given when references are requested.
5. Verify the protections offered under your state law, if any.

The following case focuses on the issues of safety and the liability of businesses and property owners for injuries that result from the acts of third parties. The focus of this case and others similar to it is whether sufficient precautions were taken to prevent the criminal activity. This case provides the answer to the chapter's opening "Consider."

CASE 10.5

McClung v. Delta Square Limited Partnership
937 S.W.2d 891 (Tenn. 1996)

Kidnapped at the Local Wal-Mart: High Noon and No One Was Watching

FACTS

Dorothy McClung, 37, went shopping on December 7, 1990, at the Delta Square Shopping Center Wal-Mart in Memphis at around noon. After she had completed her shopping and was returning to her car, she was abducted at gunpoint by Joseph Harper, a fugitive from Chattanooga, and forced into her car. She was later found dead in the trunk of her car when her car was spotted by some hunters in a remote area in Arkansas. Harper was later caught and confessed to kidnapping, raping and murdering Mrs. McClung. Roger McClung, her husband (plaintiff), filed suit against Wal-Mart and the owner of the shopping center, Delta Square (defendants), for himself as well as on behalf of their three minor children. Mr. McClung alleged that both Wal-Mart and Delta Square were negligent in their failure to provide adequate security. The trial court granted Wal-Mart's and Delta Square's motions for summary judgment. The court of appeals affirmed and Mr. McClung appealed.

JUDICIAL OPINION

WHITE, Justice

To establish negligence, one must prove: (1) a duty of care owed by defendant to plaintiff; (2) conduct falling below the applicable standard of care that amounts to a breach of that duty; (3) an injury or loss; (4) cause in fact; and (5) proximate, or legal, cause.

We have defined duty of care to be the legal obligation owed by defendant to plaintiff to conform to a reasonable person standard of care for protection against unreasonable risks of harm.

The trial court and the Court of Appeals based the award of summary judgment in this case on *Cornpropst v. Sloan*, 528 S.W.2d 188 (Tenn. 1975), in which this Court held that shop owners do not owe to customers a duty to protect them against criminal acts of third parties unless the owner knew or should have known the acts were occurring or about to occur. In that case, decided more than two decades ago, a female shopper, while walking to her car in a shopping center's parking lot, was assaulted and narrowly escaped being kidnapped. She sued the shopping center's owners, operators, and tenants for negligence in failing to provide adequate security measures to protect customers from reasonably foreseeable criminal conduct. She alleged that there were no security guards in the parking lot and that no other protective measures were used or installed. She claimed that, prior to her attack, other acts of violence had occurred either on the premises or in the immediate area of the shopping center.

The Court in *Cornpropst* began its analysis by observing that the common law imposed no duty on anyone, except the government, to protect others from criminal acts of unknown third persons, even though it did impose upon merchants a duty to exercise reasonable care to maintain their premises in a reasonably safe condition. The Court noted, however, that exceptions to the common law rule had developed in circumstances in which a "special relationship," such as a common carrier and passenger or innkeeper and guest, existed between the parties, but refused to base liability on the relationship between the owner or occupier of business property and the customer.

Choosing to follow the then-prevailing rule, the *Cornpropst* Court refused to impose a duty in the case which it characterized as involving "vague allegation[s] that various crimes, assaults and other acts of violence had been committed either on the premises or in the immediate area." The Court deemed it unfair to impose a duty upon the shopping center owner because the attacker "gave no notice by word, act, dress or deed prior to the commission of the attack that would have indicated to anyone an intention of purpose to commit an assault."

The Court's decision was not unanimous. In a dissent, Justice Henry opined that the standard "affords virtually no protection to shopping center invitees . . . and virtually immunizes the owner against liability. . . ." He found the rule to be unduly restrictive and "not in the best interest of the consuming public" given the "modern phenomenon of merchandising and marketing through community shopping centers" that result in "enormous congregations of potential and actual shoppers in relatively compact areas. . . ." Justice Henry advocated (as did the trial judge in this case) the adoption of the rule expressed in the *Restatement (Second) of Torts*, § 344 (1965). That rule provides:

A possessor of land who holds it open to the public for entry for . . . business purposes is subject to liability to members of the public while they are upon the land for such a purpose, for physical harm caused by the accidental, negligent, or intentionally harmful acts of third persons or animals, and by the failure of the possessor to exercise reasonable care to (a) discover that such acts are being done or are likely to be done, or (b) give a warning adequate to enable the visitors to avoid the harm, or otherwise to protect them against it.

The *Cornpropst* Court had little case law to guide its decision. Since *Cornpropst*, however, numerous courts and commentators have considered a business owner's duty to protect its customers from injuries caused by criminal acts of unknown third persons. Not only has the subject received considerable attention in the legal literature, courts, as a result of the prevalence of violent crimes at commercial establishments, have reexamined the law. Parking lots in particular have provided fertile ground for crime because customers usually possess money or recently purchased merchandise. Thus, the criminal "in search of valuables need not take a chance on the unknown assets of some passerby."

In the early cases, courts generally denied recovery to customer victims under the theory that the business had no duty to protect its patrons from criminal attacks. The initial reluctance to impose a duty was attributed to several reasons, including general principles of fairness given the unpredictable nature of criminal conduct.

Notwithstanding the reluctance to impose a duty on business owners, the majority of courts that have considered the issue have been unwilling to hold that a business never has a duty to protect customers from criminal acts. Instead, most have held that, while not insurers of their customers' safety, businesses do have a duty to take reasonable precautions to protect customers from foreseeable criminal acts.

Based on this analysis of the decisions of other jurisdictions, we must disavow the observation made in *Cornpropst* that "conditions in the area [of the defendant business] are irrelevant" in assessing the foreseeability of a criminal act. It makes little sense to ignore the frequency and nature of criminal activity in the immediate vicinity of the business, such as an adjacent parking lot, if the crucial inquiry is the foreseeability of a criminal act occurring on defendant's premises. Conditions in the immediate vicinity of defendant's premises are relevant in making this determination. We also find that foreseeability of harm on which liability may be imposed is not limited to criminal acts of third parties that are known or should be known to pose an imminent probability of harm to customers. Conditions other than those which pose an imminent threat to persons on the premises are relevant to the foreseeability of harm.

We, therefore, join those courts which generally impose a duty upon businesses to take reasonable measures to protect their customers from foreseeable criminal attacks. Because those courts do not universally agree on the meaning of "foreseeability," further consideration is required. In determining foreseeability, some courts have utilized the so-called "prior incidents rule." . . . Courts vary, however, on whether the prior crimes must be of the same general type and nature as the present offense.

After careful consideration of the jurisprudence of other jurisdictions and our own, we adopt the following principles to be used in determining the duty of care owed by the owners and occupiers of business premises to customers to protect them against the criminal acts of third parties: A business ordinarily has no duty to protect customers from the criminal acts of third parties which occur on its premises. The business is not to be regarded as the insurer of the safety of its customers, and it has no absolute duty to implement security measures for the protection of its customers. However, a duty to take

(continued)

reasonable steps to protect customers arises if the business knows, or has reason to know, either from what has been or should have been observed or from past experience, that criminal acts against its customers on its premises are reasonably foreseeable, either generally or at some particular time.

In determining the duty that exists, the foreseeability of harm and the gravity of harm must be balanced against the commensurate burden imposed on the business to protect against that harm. In cases in which there is a high degree of foreseeability of harm and the probable harm is great, the burden imposed upon defendant may be substantial. Alternatively, in cases in which a lesser degree of foreseeability is present or the potential harm is slight, less onerous burdens may be imposed. By way of illustration, using surveillance cameras, posting signs, installing improved lighting or fencing, or removing or trimming shrubbery might, in some instances, be cost effective and yet greatly reduce the risk to customers. In short, "the degree of foreseeability needed to establish a duty decreases in proportion to the magnitude of the foreseeable harm" and the burden upon defendant to engage in alternative conduct.

As a practical matter, the requisite degree of foreseeability essential to establish a duty to protect against criminal acts will almost always require that prior instances of crime have occurred on or in the immediate vicinity of defendant's premises. Courts must consider the location, nature, and extent of previous criminal activities and their similarity, proximity, or other relationship to the crime giving rise to the cause of action. To hold otherwise would impose an undue burden upon merchants.

Having established the appropriate test for determining the duty of care in cases involving business premises liability for the acts of unknown third parties and for the purpose of offering an illustration of the analysis required of courts in these types of cases, we return to the facts of the case at bar. Here, plaintiff's wife was returning to her car in defendants' parking lot when she was accosted. Plaintiff argues that because of past crimes committed on or near defendants' parking lot, a requisite degree of foreseeability to impose a duty to take reasonable precautions was established. To support this contention, plaintiff relies upon records from the Memphis Police Department, which indicate that from May, 1989 through September, 1990, when plaintiff's wife was abducted, approximately 164 criminal incidents had occurred on or near defendants' parking lot. He also relies on the fact that defendants' nearby competitors

provide outdoor security measures and that Wal-Mart uses heightened security measures at other locations.

In response, defendants argue that no duty of reasonable care should be imposed because the attack on plaintiff's wife was neither foreseeable nor preventible. Defendants claim they had no notice that Harper was likely to abduct plaintiff's wife, no reason to have anticipated the attack when it occurred, and no reasonable way to have prevented it. They also assert that providing security is prohibitively expensive, and that security has little impact on preventing crime.

The modern trend, however, does not deem foreseeability as necessarily dependent upon evidence of the same type of prior crimes occurring on or near defendant's premises, but requires "inquiry [into] the location, nature and extent of previous criminal activities and their similarity, proximity or other relationship to the crime in question."

The prior incidents approach to foreseeability has been lauded as preventing businesses from effectively becoming insurers of public safety since "[i]t is difficult, if not impossible, to envision any locale open to the public where the occurrence of violent crime seems improbable."

Several courts have rejected the prior incidents rule in favor of a "totality of the circumstances" approach, in which the foreseeability of criminal conduct may be determined by considering all of the circumstances including the nature or character of the business, its location, and prior incidents of crime, if any.

Nonetheless, the totality of the circumstances approach has been criticized as well, as being too broad a standard, effectively imposing an unqualified duty to protect customers in areas experiencing any significant level of criminal activity.

Having found that because of its severe limitations, the rule advanced in *Cornpropst* is obsolete, and having found further that the prior incidents rule and the totality of the circumstances approach do not provide a suitable balance between the burden of the duty to be imposed and the nature of the rights to be protected, we turn to our own decisions for guidance in determining the appropriate duty of care.

Our recent pronouncements concerning the duty of care in negligence cases reveal a balancing approach consistent with our prevailing principles of fairness and justice.

We reject defendants' argument that it owed plaintiff's wife no duty because the attack was not reasonably foreseeable. In the seventeen months prior to the abduction, the numerous reports of crime to police on or near defendants' premises included a bomb threat, fourteen burglaries, twelve reports of malicious mischief, ten robberies, thirty-six auto thefts, ninety larcenies, and one attempted kidnaping on a parking lot adjacent to defendants' parking lot. All of these crimes occurred on or in the immediate vicinity of defendants' parking lot, took place within a relatively short period of time prior to the abduction of plaintiff's wife, and involved a significant threat of personal harm. The record also establishes that defendants' premises was located in a high crime area, and that other nearby major retail centers utilized security measures to protect customers. The manager of the Wal-Mart store at the time of the abduction testified that he would not hold "sidewalk sales" or place merchandise outside the store, except for "dirt," out of fear it would be stolen.

Considering the number, frequency, and nature of the crimes reported to police, management's acknowledgment of security problems, and other evidence in the record, we conclude that the proof would support a finding that the risk of injury to plaintiff's wife was reasonably foreseeable.

Finally, we must address defendants' argument that random criminal acts of unknown third persons amount to superseding, intervening causes for which defendants cannot be held liable as a matter of law. It is true, as pointed out by defendants, that a superseding, intervening cause can break the chain of causation.

Proximate cause, as well as the existence of a superseding, intervening cause, are jury questions unless the uncontroverted facts and inferences to be drawn from the facts make it so clear that all reasonable persons must agree on the proper outcome.

For the reasons stated above, the judgments of the lower courts are reversed.

CASE QUESTIONS

1. What was the *Cornpropst* case and what is its significance in this case?

2. What was the common law on the duty to protect others from criminal acts?

3. Why is foreseeability an issue in this case and others?

4. What is the "prior incidents" rule?

5. Is the nature of the area of location and the level of crime there a part of foreseeability?

6. Will the merchant and landowner be held liable here? Why, or why not?

7. What public policy issues do you see on both sides of the argument on whether property owners/merchants should be held liable for the injuries to customers and guests caused by the criminal acts of third parties?

Element Three: Causation

After establishing that a duty existed and that there was a breach of duty, the plaintiff in a negligence suit must also establish that the breach of the duty was the cause of his damages. A test that is often used to determine **causation** is the **"but for" test**—"but for the action or lack of action of the defendant, the plaintiff would not have been injured." For example, suppose that a guest is enjoying a scenic view of the ocean from a cliff, near his hotel. At the edge of the cliff, there is a fence that had been installed by the hotel but that the hotel does not keep in good repair. When the guest leans against the fence to take a picture, the fence breaks and the guest falls over the cliff. The hotel breached its duty to keep its premises in reasonably safe condition, and its failure to do so caused the injury to the guest. The "but for" test is limited by the so-called zone of danger rule, which requires that the plaintiff be in the zone of danger when the injury occurs. The zone of danger includes all those people who could foreseeably be injured if a duty is breached. For example, the hotel would also be liable to those injured by the guest as he fell through the weak fence because they are in the zone of danger.

BUSINESS PLANNING TIP

There are several safety tips that all businesses should follow with respect to safety of their customers, especially with respect to criminal acts. The list follows:

1. Good lighting

2. Access to public phones

3. Security patrols

4. Locked gates to parking lots; gate or security access

5. Escorts provided for customers and employees to their vehicles after closing hours

6. Camera security

7. Assigned parking spaces for tenants and employees

8. Warning signs to use caution and be alert

Many hotels change key access codes with each guest and post security personnel near guest elevators at night so that there is no access to the elevators unless you can show your room key. Some hotels have floors for women who are traveling alone, and extra security is provided on those floors.

Element Four: Proximate Cause

Some cutoff line must be drawn between the "but for" causation and events that contribute to the injury of the plaintiff—an element of a negligence case called *proximate cause.* Suppose that you have a tire replaced at a tire store and the technician fails to tighten the wheel sufficiently. As you drive down the street, the tire comes loose, rolls off, and strikes another car. Did the tire store cause the damage to the other car? Yes. Any accidents caused by that car? Yes. Suppose the tire comes off, rolls to the sidewalk, and strikes a pedestrian. Did the tire store cause that injury? Yes. Suppose the pedestrian sees the tire coming and jumps out of the way but, in so doing, injures another pedestrian. Did the tire store cause that injury? Yes. In all of these accidents, the following statement can be made: "But for the failure to tighten the wheel, the accident would not have occurred." Suppose that the tire injures a pedestrian, although not fatally, but a doctor treating the pedestrian, through malpractice, causes the pedestrian's death. Did the tire store cause the death? No; another's negligence intervened.

The Palsgraf case below is a landmark case on the element of proximate cause.

Element Five: Damages

The plaintiff in a negligence case must be able to establish *damages* that resulted from the defendant's negligence. Such damages could include compensation for damages such as medical bills, lost wages, and pain and suffering, as well as any property damages. In many of the cases in this chapter, plaintiffs have also recovered punitive damages. Often referred to as "smart money," punitive damages are similar to civil penalties that are paid to plaintiffs because of the high level of carelessness involved on the defendant's part.

CASE 10.6

Palsgraf v. *Long Island Ry. Co.*
162 N.E. 99 (N.Y. 1928)

Fireworks in the Passenger's Package and Negligence in the Air

FACTS

Helen Palsgraf (plaintiff) had purchased a ticket to travel to Rockaway Beach on the Long Island Railway (defendant). While she was standing on a platform at the defendant's station waiting for the train, another train stopped at the station. Two men ran to catch the train, which began moving as they were running. One of the men made it onto the train without difficulty, but the other man, who was carrying a package, was unsteady as he tried to jump aboard. Employees of the defendant helped pull the man in and push him onto the train car, but in the process the package was dropped. The package contained fireworks, and when it was dropped, it exploded. The vibrations from the explosion caused some scales (located at the end of the platform on which Palsgraf was standing) to fall. As they fell, they hit Palsgraf, who was injured. Palsgraf filed suit against the railroad for negligence.

JUDICIAL OPINION

CARDOZO, Chief Justice

The conduct of the defendant's guard, if a wrong in its relation to the holder of the package, was not a wrong in its relation to the plaintiff, standing far away. Nothing in the situation gave notice that the falling package had in it the potency of peril to persons thus removed. Negligence is not actionable unless it involves the invasion of a legally protected interest, the violation of a right. "Proof of negligence in the air, so to speak, will not do." The plaintiff, as she stood upon the platform of the station, might claim to be protected against intentional invasion of her bodily security. Such invasion is not charged. She might claim to be protected against unintentional invasion by conduct involving in the thought of reasonable men an unreasonable hazard that such invasion would ensue. These, from the point of view of the law, were the bounds of her immunity, with perhaps some rare exceptions, survivals for the most part of ancient forms of liability, where conduct is held to be at the peril of the actor. If no hazard was apparent to the eye of ordinary vigilance, an act innocent and harmless, at least to outward seeming, with reference to her, did not take to itself the quality of a tort because it happened to be a wrong, though apparently not one involving the risk of bodily insecurity, with reference to some one else.

A different conclusion will involve us, and swiftly too, in a maze of contradictions. A guard stumbles over a package which has been left upon a platform. It seems to be a bundle of newspapers. It turns out to be a can of dynamite. To the eye of ordinary vigilance, the bundle is abandoned waste, which may be kicked or trod on with impunity. Is a passenger at the other end of the platform protected by the law against the unsuspected hazard concealed beneath the waste? If not, is the result to be any different, so far as the distant passenger is concerned, when the guard stumbles over a valise which a truckman or a porter has left upon the walk? The passenger far away, if the victim of a wrong at all, has a cause of action, not derivative, but original and primary. His claim to be protected against invasion of his bodily security is neither greater nor less because the act resulting in the invasion is a wrong to another far removed. In this case, the rights that are said to have been violated, the interests said to have been

invaded, are not even of the same order. The man was not injured in his person or even put in danger. The purpose of the act, as well as its effect, was to make his person safe. If there was a wrong to him at all, which may very well be doubted, it was a wrong to a property interest only, the safety of his package. Out of this wrong to property, which threatened injury to nothing else, there has passed, we are told, to the plaintiff by derivation or succession a right of action for the invasion of an interest of another order, the right to bodily security. The diversity of interests emphasizes the futility of the effort to build the plaintiff's right upon the basis of a wrong to some one else. The gain is one of emphasis, for a like result would follow if the interests were the same. Even then, the orbit of the danger as disclosed to the eye of reasonable vigilance would be the orbit of the duty. One who jostles one's neighbor in a crowd does not invade the rights of others standing at the outer fringe when the unintended contact casts a bomb upon the ground. The wrongdoer as to them is the man who carries the bomb, not the one who explodes it without suspicion of the danger. Life will have to be made over, and human nature transformed, before prevision so extravagant can be accepted as the norm of conduct, the customary standard to which behavior must conform.

The risk reasonably to be perceived defines the duty to be obeyed, and risk imports relation; it is risk to another or to others within the range of apprehension. Here, by concession, there was nothing in the situation to suggest to the most cautious mind that the parcel wrapped in newspaper would spread wreckage through the station. If the guard had thrown it down knowingly and willfully, he would not have threatened the plaintiff's safety, so far as appearances could warn him. His conduct would not have involved, even then, an unreasonable probability of invasion of her bodily security. Liability can be no greater where the act is inadvertent.

DISSENTING OPINION

ANDREWS, Justice

Assisting a passenger to board a train, the defendant's servant negligently knocked a package from his arms. It fell between the platform and the cars. Of its contents the servant knew and could know nothing. A violent explosion followed. The concussion broke some scales standing a considerable distance away. In falling, they injured the plaintiff, an intending passenger.

(continued)

Upon these facts, may she recover the damages she has suffered in an action brought against the master? The result we shall reach depends upon our theory as to the nature of negligence. Is it a relative concept—the breach of some duty owing to a particular person or to particular persons?

Or, where there is an act which unreasonably threatens the safety of others, is the doer liable for all its proximate consequences, even where they result in injury to one who would generally be thought to be outside the radius of danger? This is not a mere dispute as to words. We might not believe that to the average mind the dropping of the bundle would seem to involve the probability of harm to the plaintiff standing many feet away whatever might be the case as to the owner or to one so near as to be likely to be struck by its fall. If, however, we adopt the second hypothesis, we have to inquire only as to the relation between cause and effect. We deal in terms of proximate cause, not of negligence.

Negligence may be defined roughly as an act or omission which unreasonably does or may affect the rights of others, or which unreasonably fails to protect one's self from the dangers resulting from such acts.

Where there is the unreasonable act, and some right that may be affected there is negligence whether damage does or does not result. That is immaterial. Should we drive down Broadway at a reckless speed, we are negligent whether we strike an approaching car or miss it by an inch. The act itself is wrongful. It is a wrong not only to those who happen to be within the radius of danger, but to all who might have been there—a wrong to the public at large.

Negligence does involve a relationship between man and his fellows, but not merely a relationship between man and those whom he might reasonably expect his act would injure; rather, a relationship between him and those whom he does in fact injure. If his act has a tendency to harm some one, it harms him a mile away as surely as it does those on the scene.

The proposition is this: Every one owes to the world at large the duty of refraining from those acts that may unreasonably threaten the safety of others. Such an act occurs. Not only is he wronged to whom harm might reasonably be expected to result, but he also who is in fact injured, even if he be outside what would generally be thought the danger zone.

As we have said, we cannot trace the effect of an act to the end, if end there is. Again, however, we may trace it part of the way. An overturned lantern may burn all Chicago. We may follow the fire from the shed to the last building. We rightly say the fire started by the lantern caused its destruction. A cause, but not the proximate cause. What we do mean by the word "proximate" is that, because of convenience, of public policy, of a rough sense of justice, the law arbitrarily declines to trace a series of events beyond a certain point. This is not logic. It is practical politics.

This last suggestion is the factor which must determine the case before us. The act upon which defendant's liability rests is knocking an apparently harmless package onto the platform. The act was negligent. For its proximate consequences the defendant is liable. If its contents were broken, to the owner; if it fell upon and crushed a passenger's foot, then to him; if it exploded and injured one in the immediate vicinity, to him. Mrs. Palsgraf was standing some distance away. How far cannot be told from the record—apparently 25 to 30 feet, perhaps less. Except for the explosion, she would not have been injured. . . . The only intervening cause was that, instead of blowing her to the ground, the concussion smashed the weighing machine which in turn fell upon her. There was no remoteness in time, little in space. And surely, given such an explosion as here, it needed no great foresight to predict that the natural result would be to injure one on the platform at no greater distance from its scene than was the plaintiff. Just how no one might be able to predict. Whether by flying fragments, by broken glass, by wreckage of machines or structures no one could say. But injury in some form was most probable.

Under these circumstances I cannot say as a matter of law that the plaintiff's injuries were not the proximate result of the negligence.

CASE QUESTIONS

1. Who was carrying the package?
2. How far away from the incident was Mrs. Palsgraf?
3. What does Justice Cardozo find?
4. What point does the dissent make?

Defenses to Negligence

Contributory Negligence

In some cases, an accident results from the combined negligence of two or more people. A plaintiff who is also negligent gives the defendant the opportunity to raise the defense of **contributory negligence.** Contributory negligence is simply negligence by the plaintiff that is part of the cause of an accident. For example, suppose that a boat owner is operating his boat late at night on a lake in which the water is choppy and when he is intoxicated. An intoxicated friend is sitting at the bow of the boat trying to put her feet into the water when the owner takes the boat up to high speed. She falls in and is injured. The issue of causation becomes complicated here because there were breaches of duties by both parties. Did he cause the accident by driving at high speed late at night on a choppy lake while intoxicated? Or did she cause the accident by sitting without protection or restraint on the bow of the boat when the boat was being driven like that? The effect of the defense of contributory negligence is a complete bar to both from recovery.

> **BUSINESS PLANNING TIP**
>
> Businesses that have the public on their premises have the duty of taking appropriate precautions for their guests. Shopping malls must provide security for customers in parking lot/garage areas. Adequate lighting is important, as are frequent patrols. Total quality management requires managers to note issues and details and commit resources to solving problems. In the *McClung* case, a few inexpensive changes might have avoided the harm and the liability.

Comparative Negligence

Many states, in order to eliminate the harsh effect of contributory negligence, have adopted a defense of **comparative negligence.** Under this defense, the jury simply determines the level of fault for both the plaintiff and the defendant and, based on this assessment of fault, determines how much each of the parties will be awarded. For example, using our boat example, the jury could find that the boat owner was 75 percent at fault and the passenger was 25 percent at fault. Under comparative negligence, the passenger could recover for her injuries, but the amount recovered would be 25 percent less because of her fault in causing the accident.

The defense of comparative negligence was developed largely because of the perceived unfairness of contributory negligence, which was a complete bar to recovery. The concept of comparative negligence has resulted in more litigation and more verdicts for plaintiffs permitted to use the defense.

Assumption of Risk

The **assumption of risk** defense requires the defendant to prove that the plaintiff knew there was a risk of injury in the conduct he undertook but decided to go forward with it anyway. For example, there are some inherent dangers in activities such as skydiving, skiing, and roller skating. You assume the inherent risks in these activities, but you do not assume the risks caused by the owners of the premises or equipment. For example, when you ski, you assume the natural risks that exist in skiing, but you do not assume the risk of faulty equipment you rent. If the failure of that equipment causes your injuries, the rental company would be responsible for that injury. To assume the risk, you must be completely aware of the risk and you must assume the risk voluntarily. The following case deals with the issue of assumption of risk.

CASE 10.7

Mosca v. *Lichtenwalter*
68 Cal. Rptr. 58 (Cal. App. 1997)

Hooked while Fishing

FACTS

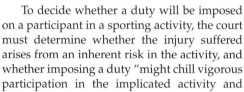

Joseph Mosca and twenty-three others boarded a sportfishing boat for a day of fishing off San Clemente Island. David Lichtenwalter, one of the fishermen, was fishing off the stern near Mosca. Lichtenwalter's line became entangled in kelp and he was unable to get it released. A deck-hand approached Lichtenwalter to help him. Lichtenwalter backed up and handed the pole to the deck-hand just as the line "slingshotted" over the rail toward Mosca, who was struck in the eye with the sinker, which caused a partial vision loss.

Mosca filed suit against Lichtenwalter and others. The trial court, using the defense of assumption of risk, dismissed the case and Mosca appealed.

JUDICIAL OPINION

WALEN, Acting Presiding Justice

The declaration of David Wilhite, a sportfishing expert, was submitted in opposition to the motion for summary judgment. He opined injury from hooks or sinkers when fishing lines slingshot may occur when an improper technique of freeing a stuck line is used. He indicated the danger of injury when extricating a line caught on an underwater object can be minimized by reaching down near the waterline, wrapping the line around a hand, and pulling it at a low angle. Lichtenwalter apparently used that approach when he first tried to release it. When he stepped back for the dockhand to intervene, he allegedly pulled the line in a higher, upward direction.

Mosca contends the trial court erred in granting summary judgment based on assumption of risk.

In *Knight* v. *Jewett* (1992) 3 Cal.4th 296, 11 Cal.Rptr.2d 2, 834 P.2d 696, the Supreme Court discussed the difference between "primary" and "secondary" assumption of risk. Primary assumption of risk is a policy-driven legal concept where the courts declare there is no duty at all.

Primary assumption of risk has often been imposed where the plaintiff and defendant are engaged in a sport. "In the sports setting . . . conditions or conduct that otherwise might be viewed as dangerous often are an integral part of the sport itself."

To decide whether a duty will be imposed on a participant in a sporting activity, the court must determine whether the injury suffered arises from an inherent risk in the activity, and whether imposing a duty "might chill vigorous participation in the implicated activity and thereby alter its fundamental nature."

The trial court, at least implicitly, determined the danger of injury from a hook or sinker flying toward a participant is an inherent risk in sportfishing, and imposing the specter of liability regarding the danger would chill or alter the sport. That determination was reasonable. Hooking and catching fish requires a great deal of knowledge, physical skill, and attention. A participant who worries whether he is hooked on a fish or kelp, and what method should be used to deal with the line in either instance, will not be an effective fisherman, and may be inclined to give up the sport.

Mosca argues that getting hit in the eye by a sinker is not an inherent danger in sportfishing because there was evidence none of the parties, witnesses or the expert had ever heard of this type of injury. The inquiry is not that narrow. The question involved is a broader inquiry: whether injury from flying hooks and sinkers is inherent in the sport.

Relying on expert witness Wilhite's declaration, Mosca also asserts the danger of being hit by a recoiling line which is stuck on an underwater object is not inherent in the sport if care is used to release it, by properly pulling it or even by cutting the line. He begs the question by making this argument. The question whether the sport can be made safer if certain techniques are used bears on the standard of care, and is a question that is reached only if the threshold question of duty is resolved against the defendant. Wilhite admits flying hooks and sinkers are risks in the sport. He merely indicated the danger can be minimized if care is taken and specific techniques to free a line are used.

Courts have recognized these principles in cases dealing with other sports activities. In *Regents of University of California* v. *Superior Court*, 41 Cal.App.4th 1040, 48 Cal.Rptr.2d 922, the court held rock climbers assume the risk climbing anchors may give way, even though it was a standard procedure to double check the anchors to maximize safety. "Falling, whether because of one's own slip, a coclimber's stumble, or an anchor system giving way, is the very risk inherent in the sport of mountain climbing and cannot be completely eliminated without destroying the sport itself." The court found an inherent risk of harm despite the presence of safety measures.

Mosca points out that *Knight* v. *Jewett,* Cal.4th 296, 11 Cal.Rptr.2d 2, 834 P.2d 696, and other cases where primary assumption of risk has been found involved contact sports or other sports where the defendant was an opponent. But there is no such limitation on the doctrine. In *Staten* v. *Superior Court,* 45 Cal.App. 4th at p. 1634, 53 Cal.Rptr.2d 657, the court applied the doctrine to figure skating, a "teamless" sport where one participates in close proximity with others so engaged. Sportfishing is the same type of close-proximity endeavor.

Cases declining to find primary assumption of the risk are distinguishable. In *Yancey* v. *Superior Court* (1994), 28 Cal.App.4th 558, 33 Cal.Rptr.2d 777, the court held a participant throwing a discus owes a duty of due care to check the field before throwing because "[n]othing about the inherent nature of the sport requires that one participant who has completed a throw and is retrieving his or her discus should expect the next participant to throw without looking toward the landing area." (See also *Lowe* v. *California League of Professional Baseball* (1997) 56 Cal.App. 4th 112, 123, 65 Cal.Rptr.2d 105 [antics of team mascot that distracted plaintiff who was struck by foul ball were not integral to the sport].) But Lichtenwalter, in attempting to free his line, was engaged in a typical adjunct of fishing.

In *Morgan* v. *Fuji Country USA, Inc.* (1995) 34 Cal.App.4th 127, 40 Cal.Rptr.2d 249, the court found assumption of the risk was not available to the defendants as grounds for summary judgment because their golf course design could be held by a trier of fact to have affirmatively increased the inherent risk of being struck by errant golf balls. Mosca neither claims, nor did he show, the fishing boat design or anything about the boat owners' fishing policy affirmatively increased the risk of harm. At most he alleges a deckhand was guilty of failing to ensure Lichtenwalter engaged in a preferred line retrieval technique.

Mosca notes that assumption of risk cannot be invoked in hunting accidents, but that is "because of the special danger to others posed by the sport of hunting." Indeed, that concept has been codified by the Legislature. Mosca makes no showing sportfishing has attained a similar status. Although fishing carries with it certain dangers, it does not involve the potentially mortal danger involved in hunting.

The judgment is affirmed.

CASE QUESTIONS

1. What happened on the boat, and how was Mosca injured?
2. Is the risk of being struck by a line inherent in the sport of fishing?
3. Was Mosca's injury typical?
4. What is the difference between assumption of risk in day-to-day activities and assumption of risk in sports?

CONSIDER...

10.5   Benjamin Dayries Wynne, 20, pledged the Sigma Alpha Epsilon fraternity at Louisiana State University in September 1997. To celebrate, Wynne and his fraternity brothers began drinking via "funneling," a process by which a hose from a keg shoots beer into the drinker's mouth.

The fraternity brothers then moved on to a new drinking ritual, "The Three Wise Men," which is a 151-proof mix of rum, Crown Royal, and Jagermeister liqueur. At the end of this ritual, Wynne was staggering and had to be wheeled out of the bar in a shopping cart.

By the next morning, Wynne was found dead of alcohol poisoning. Does the fraternity have liability? Does LSU have liability?

According to a 1994 Harvard study, nearly half of all college students "binge" drink, or drink more than five drinks at one setting. A 1997 Harvard survey found that 52.3 percent of all college students who drink do so with the idea of getting drunk. In 1997, thirty-four students on college campuses died after excessive drinking. Would a complete prohibition on alcohol help? Would a prohibition on fraternity drinking help?

TORT REFORM

As noted in Chapter 3, the United States has a sizable court system equipped with sufficient lawyers for the support of litigation. The United States permits greater recovery for torts while requiring less in terms of proof than other nations. Over the past decade, a number of reforms have been proposed, particularly with respect to tort litigation, to limit recovery or place other limitations on the amount of increasing tort litigation. For example, some reform proposals would limit damages. Those limitations may be general limitations on damage awards or limitations like the Canadian system of $200,000 for pain and suffering. Although nearly all states have adopted some form of limitations in tort recovery, these reforms are a maze of laws differing from state to state, have been subject to judicial challenges (in many cases successful), and have provided little hope for insurers as they try to forecast their risks in insuring businesses and their properties and agents.

Peter W. Huber, a senior fellow at the Manhattan Institute, a conservative New York think tank, maintains that judges should defuse confrontations in tort cases by encouraging the litigants to settle and by establishing rules that would hold defendants liable only in those cases in which they are at fault and a large recovery will deter future accidents that would not otherwise be deterred.

In the following case, the U.S. Supreme Court addressed the issue of large recoveries.

CASE 10.8

BMW of North America, Inc. v. *Gore*
517 U.S. 559 (1996)

The Fussy Doctor, the BMW and Acid Rain

FACTS

Dr. Ira Gore, Jr. (respondent) purchased a new 1990 BMW 535i automobile from German Auto, Inc., a Birmingham, Alabama, dealership. Dr. Gore, a graduate of Harvard and Duke Medical School, signed a "Retail Buyers Order" and "Acknowledgment of Disclosure" in which he acknowledged that the car might have sus-

tained damage, that he had inspected it and agreed to accept it.

Gore drove the car for nine months before taking it to "Slick Finish," an auto detail shop. Gore took the car in to make it "snazzier." The auto detailer told Gore that the car had been partially refinished. Gore later determined that the refinishing had been done because of acid rain damage to the paint on the car during transit from Germany (BMW AG) to the North American vehicle preparation center in Brunswick, Georgia. The preparation center (BMW NA) did not disclose any damage to a dealer or customer if the damage was less than 3 percent of the manufacturer's suggested retail price (MSRP). The refinishing of Gore's auto cost $601.

Upon his discovery that the automobile had been refinished, Gore sued German Auto, BMW AG, and BMW NA, alleging that the failure to disclose the refinishing constituted fraud, suppression of a material fact, and breach of contract. With respect to the BMW defendants, only the suppression claim was submitted to the jury. The jury returned a verdict against all three defendants for $4,000 in compensatory damages, and it assessed $4,000,000 in punitive damages against the BMW defendants jointly, based on a determination that the BMW defendants (BMW) had been guilty of gross, malicious, intentional, and wanton fraud. The trial court entered a judgment on that verdict. BMW defendants appealed. The Alabama Supreme Court reduced the verdict to $2,000,000 and BMW appealed.

JUDICIAL OPINION

STEVENS, Justice

Punitive damages may properly be imposed to further a State's legitimate interests in punishing unlawful conduct and deterring its repetition.

Only when an award can fairly be categorized as "grossly excessive" in relation to these interests does it enter the zone of arbitrariness that violates the Due Process Clause of the Fourteenth Amendment. For that reason, the federal excessiveness inquiry appropriately begins with an identification of the state interests that a punitive award is designed to serve. We therefore focus our attention first on the scope of Alabama's legitimate interests in punishing BMW and deterring it from future misconduct.

No one doubts that a State may protect its citizens by prohibiting deceptive trade practices and by requiring automobile distributors to disclose presale repairs that affect the value of a new car. But the States need not, and in fact do not, provide such protection in a uniform manner. Some States rely on the judicial process to formulate and enforce an appropriate disclosure requirement by applying principles of contract and tort law. Other States have enacted various forms of legislation that define the disclosure obligations of automobile manufacturers, distributors, and dealers. The result is a patchwork of rules representing the diverse policy judgments of lawmakers in 50 states.

Alabama may insist that BMW adhere to a particular disclosure policy in that State. Alabama does not have the power, however, to punish BMW for conduct that was lawful where it occurred and that had no impact on Alabama or its residents. Nor may Alabama impose sanctions on BMW in order to deter conduct that is lawful in other jurisdictions.

In this case, we accept the Alabama Supreme Court's interpretation of the jury verdict as reflecting a computation of the amount of punitive damages "based in large part on conduct that happened in other jurisdictions."

When the scope of the interest in punishment and deterrence that an Alabama court may appropriately consider is properly limited, it is apparent—for reasons that we shall now address—that this award is grossly excessive.

Elementary notions of fairness enshrined in our constitutional jurisprudence dictate that a person receive fair notice not only of the conduct that will subject him to punishment but also of the severity of the penalty that a State may impose. Three guideposts, each of which indicates that BMW did not receive adequate notice of the magnitude of the sanction that Alabama might impose for adhering to the nondisclosure policy adopted in 1983, lead us to the conclusion that the $2 million award against BMW is grossly excessive: the degree of reprehensibility of the nondisclosure; the disparity between the harm or potential harm suffered by Dr. Gore and his punitive damages award; and the difference between this remedy and the civil penalties authorized or imposed in comparable cases. We discuss these considerations in turn.

Perhaps the most important indicium of the reasonableness of a punitive damages award is the degree of reprehensibility of the defendant's conduct. As the Court stated nearly 150 years ago, exemplary damages imposed on a defendant should reflect "the enormity of his offense."

In this case, none of the aggravating factors associated with particularly reprehensible conduct is present. The harm BMW inflicted on Dr. Gore was purely economic in nature. The presale refinishing of the car had no effect on its performance or safety features, or even its appearance for at least nine months after his purchase. BMW's conduct evinced no indifference to or reckless disregard for the health and safety of others. To be sure, infliction of economic injury, especially when done intentionally through

(continued)

affirmative acts of misconduct, or when the target is financially vulnerable, can warrant a substantial penalty. But this observation does not convert all acts that cause economic harm into torts that are sufficiently reprehensible to justify a significant sanction in addition to compensatory damages.

That conduct is sufficiently reprehensible to give rise to tort liability, and even a modest award of exemplary damages, does not establish the high degree of culpability that warrants a substantial punitive damages award. Because this case exhibits none of the circumstances ordinarily associated with egregiously improper conduct, we are persuaded that BMW's conduct was not sufficiently reprehensible to warrant imposition of a $2 million exemplary damages award.

The second and perhaps most commonly cited indicium of an unreasonable or excessive punitive damages award is its ratio to the actual harm inflicted on the plaintiff. The principle that exemplary damages must bear a "reasonable relationship" to compensatory damages has a long pedigree. Scholars have identified a number of early English statutes authorizing the award of multiple damages for particular wrongs. Some 65 different enactments during the period between 1275 and 1753 provided for double, treble, or quadruple damages.

The $2 million in punitive damages awarded to Dr. Gore by the Alabama Supreme Court is 500 times the amount of his actual harm as determined by the jury. Moreover, there is no suggestion that Dr. Gore or any other BMW purchaser was threatened with any additional potential harm by BMW's nondisclosure policy.

Of course, we have consistently rejected the notion that the constitutional line is marked by a simple mathematical formula, even one that compares actual *and potential* damages to the punitive award.

In most cases, the ratio will be within a constitutionally acceptable range, and remittitur will not be justified on this basis. When the ratio is a breathtaking 500 to 1, however, the award must surely "raise a suspicious judicial eyebrow."

Comparing the punitive damages award and the civil or criminal penalties that could be imposed for comparable misconduct provides a third indicium of excessiveness. As Justice O'CONNOR has correctly observed, a reviewing court engaged in determining whether an award of punitive damages is excessive should "accord 'substantial deference' to legislative judgments concerning appropriate sanctions for the conduct at issue."

The maximum civil penalty authorized by the Alabama Legislature for a violation of its Deceptive Trade Practices Act is $2,000; other States authorize more severe sanctions, with the maxima ranging from $5,000 to $10,000.

The sanction imposed in this case cannot be justified on the ground that it was necessary to deter future misconduct without considering whether less drastic remedies could be expected to achieve that goal. The fact that a multimillion dollar penalty prompted a change in policy sheds no light on the question whether a lesser deterrent would have adequately protected the interests of Alabama consumers.

The fact that BMW is a large corporation rather than an impecunious individual does not diminish its entitlement to fair notice of the demands that the several States impose on the conduct of its business. Indeed, its status as an active participant in the national economy implicates the federal interest in preventing individual States from imposing undue burdens on interstate commerce. While each State has ample power to protect its own consumers, none may use the punitive damages deterrent as a means of imposing its regulatory policies on the entire Nation.

Whether the appropriate remedy requires a new trial or merely an independent determination by the Alabama Supreme Court of the award necessary to vindicate the economic interests of Alabama consumers is a matter that should be addressed by the state court in the first instance.

The judgment is reversed, and the case is remanded for further proceedings not inconsistent with this opinion.

Justice SCALIA, with whom Justice THOMAS joins, dissenting.

Today we see the latest manifestation of this Court's recent and increasingly insistent "concern about punitive damages that 'run wild.' " *Pacific Mut. Life Ins. Co.* v. *Haslip*, 499 U.S. 1, 18, 111 S.Ct. 1032, 1043, 113 L.Ed.2d 1 (1991). Since the Constitution does not make that concern any of our business, the Court's activities in this area are an unjustified incursion into the province of state governments.

At the time of adoption of the Fourteenth Amendment, it was well understood that punitive damages represent the assessment by the jury, as the voice of the community, of the measure of punishment the defendant deserved. Today's decision, though dressed up as a legal opinion, is really no more than a disagreement with the community's sense of indignation or outrage expressed in the punitive award of the Alabama jury, as reduced by the State Supreme Court. It reflects not merely, as the concurrence candidly acknowledges, "a judgment about a matter of degree," but a judgment about the appropriate degree of indignation or outrage, which is hardly an analytical determination.

There is no precedential warrant for giving our judgment priority over the judgment of state courts and juries on this matter. The only support for the Court's position is to be found in a handful of errant federal cases, bunched within a few years of one another, which invented the notion that an unfairly severe civil sanction amounts to a violation of constitutional liberties.

One might understand the Court's eagerness to enter this field, rather than leave it with the state legislatures, if it had something useful to say. In fact, however, its opinion provides virtually no guidance to legislatures, and to state and federal courts, as to what a "constitutionally proper" level of punitive damages might be.

In Part III of its opinion, the Court identifies "[t]hree guideposts" that lead it to the conclusion that the award in this case is excessive: degree of reprehensibility, ratio between punitive award and plaintiff's actual harm, and legislative sanctions provided for comparable misconduct.

Of course it will not be easy for the States to comply with the new federal law of damages, no matter how willing they are to do so. In truth, the "guideposts" mark a road to nowhere; they provide no real guidance at all.

As to "degree of reprehensibility" of the defendant's conduct, we learn that "nonviolent crimes are less serious than crimes marked by violence or the threat of violence," and that "trickery and deceit" are "more reprehensible than negligence." As to the ratio of punitive to compensatory damages, we are told that a "general concern of reasonableness . . . enter[s] into the constitutional calculus," though even "a breathtaking 500 to 1" will not necessarily do anything more than "raise a suspicious judicial eyebrow" (an opinion which, when confronted with that "breathtaking" ratio, approved it). And as to legislative sanctions provided for comparable misconduct, they should be accorded " 'substantial deference,' " *ibid*. One expects the Court to conclude: "To thine own self be true."

These criss-crossing platitudes yield no real answers in no real cases. And it must be noted that the Court nowhere says that these three "guideposts" are the *only* guideposts; indeed, it makes very clear that they are not—explaining away the earlier opinions that do not really follow these "guideposts" on the basis of *additional* factors, thereby "reiterat[ing] our rejection of a categorical approach." In other words, even these utter platitudes, if they should ever happen to produce an answer, may be overridden by other unnamed considerations. The Court has constructed a framework that does not genuinely constrain, that does not inform state legislatures and lower courts—that does nothing at all except confer an artificial air of doctrinal analysis upon its essentially ad hoc determination that this particular award of punitive damages was not "fair."

The elevation of "fairness" in punishment to a principle of "substantive due process" means that every punitive award unreasonably imposed is unconstitutional; such an award is by definition excessive, since it attaches a penalty to conduct undeserving of punishment. Indeed, if the Court is correct, it must be that every claim that a state jury's award of *compensatory* damages is "unreasonable" (because not supported by the evidence) amounts to an assertion of constitutional injury. And the same would be true for determinations of liability. By today's logic, *every* dispute as to evidentiary sufficiency in a state civil suit poses a question of constitutional moment, subject to review in this Court. That is a stupefying proposition.

For the foregoing reasons, I respectfully dissent.

CASE QUESTIONS

1. What was wrong with Dr. Gore's car, and how did he discover the problem?

2. What basis did the jury use for awarding $4,000,000 in punitive damages?

3. What arguments does the Court make in requiring that the award be reduced?

4. What constitutional issues are raised?

5. Why do Justices Scalia and Thomas dissent?

6. To whom would the dissent leave the issue of punitive damages?

Re: Wal-Mart's Litigation Strategy

Wal-Mart was sued 4,851 times last year—once every 2 hours every day of the year. Most experts have concluded that Wal-Mart is sued more than any other entity, except the U.S. government. Wal-Mart reports that it currently handles 9,400 open lawsuits.

Wal-Mart is unique in that it has taken the position of fighting many of the suits brought against it. Most corporations take a cost-benefit analysis and settle most lawsuits because it is cheaper for them to do so. Wal-Mart, however, is working to change the nature of litigation against corporations and does fight most suits aggressively. The result of its aggressive stance is that the number of suits has leveled off despite Wal-Mart's increasing size and number of stores.

The types of lawsuits Wal-Mart has pending or has experienced are:

- Slip-and-fall cases where customers have been injured in a Wal-Mart store

- One case brought by the family of a woman shot by her husband who had purchased the rifle at Wal-Mart
- Class action employment suits alleging discrimination
- Wrongful termination of employment cases
- Shoppers injured in a "Furby" stampede when the toy was in demand at Christmas time

Wal-Mart also employs different litigation strategies:

- It hires outside lawyers and pays them a flat fee.
- It has cases moved to federal district court where judges are not elected.
- It settles those cases where the company or employees have done something wrong, but it fights ferociously when there is no fault.

Source: Richard Willing, "Lawsuits Follow Growth Curve of Wal-Mart," *USA Today*, 14 August 2001, A1, A2.

New Verdicts on Tort Reform

Since the time of the *BMW* case, there have been a number of significant decisions on how much is too much in terms of damages awarded to plaintiffs. In *Cooper Industries, Inc.* v. *Leatherman Tool Group*, 532 U.S. 424 (2001), the U.S. Supreme Court held that the Eighth Amendment's prohibition on excessive fines and cruel and unusual punishment requires appellate courts to apply a *de novo* review standard (see Chapter 3) when determining the constitutionality of punitive damages awards made at the trial court level. Several cases have already been decided at the appellate level that have followed the *Leatherman* decision and ordered a reduction of punitive damages. The Alabama Supreme Court reduced one award from $600,000 to $150,000 and another from $300,000 to $180,000. The following is a summary of other examples of punitive damage reductions, even prior to the *Leatherman* decision.

- *Continental Trend Resources, Inc.* v. *Oxy Use, Inc.*, 101 F.3d 634 (10th Cir. 1996), *cert. denied*, 520 U.S. 1241 (1997)—An award of $30 million in punitive damages for the tort of contract interference was ruled as excessive and reduced to $6 million, which was six times the actual damages established by the plaintiff in the case.
- *Neibel* v. *Trans World Assurance Company*, 108 F.3d 1123 (9th Cir. 1997)—An award of $500,000 in punitive damages to plaintiffs who alleged fraud and

conspiracy on the part of an insurance company in its deceptive advertising was ruled as not excessive, in that the amount of $500,000 was approximately six times the plaintiffs' actual damages.

- *Cooper* v. *Casey,* 97 F.3d 914 (7th Cir. 1996)—An award of $22,500 in punitive damages to an inmate who was beaten by prison guards was not excessive even though it was twelve times his actual damages. The case also awarded lawyer's fees for the plaintiffs of $320 per hour, based on the lawyer's evidence that he gave up work for that amount in order to represent the defendants.

- *Benson* v. *Northwest Airlines, Inc.,* 62 F.3d 1108 (8th Cir. 1995), on remand 1997 WL 122897 (D. Minn. 1997)—In a case in which a plaintiff alleged violations of the Americans with Disabilities Act, the damage award included $75,000 in back pay and $2,542,000 in punitive damages. The court reduced the punitive damages to $225,000 because such is the statutory maximum for such cases if the plaintiff can establish malice or reckless indifference on the part of the employer.

- *Scribner* v. *Waffle House, Inc.,* 993 F. Supp. 976 (N.D. Tex. 1998)—In a sexual harassment case, the plaintiff was awarded $6.3 million dollars in punitive damages, which was thirteen times the actual damages Ms. Scribner established at trial. The court held that the lack of management's response and failure to investigate her charges over a period of time warranted "strong medicine." However, the decision was vacated. 62 F.Supp. 2d1186 (N.D. Tex. 1999)

- *Iannone* v. *Frederic R. Harris,* 941 F.Supp. 403 (S.D.N.Y. 1996)—A terminated employee who had alleged sexual harassment was awarded $62,000 in back pay, $5,000 in compensatory damages, and $250,000 in punitive damages. The court reduced the amount to $50,000, stating that the ratio was sufficient recovery in a case that did not involve reprehensible conduct.

- *Florez* v. *Delbovo,* 939 F.Supp. 1341 (N.D. Ill. 1996)—An award of $750,000 as punitive damages in a civil rights case in which there was $55,000 in actual damages was excessive. The punitive damages were reduced to $275,000, for a 5-to-1 ratio.

- *Utah Foam Products Co.* v. *Upjohn Company,* 930 F.Supp. 513 (D. Utah 1996), aff'd 154 F. 3d 1212 (10th Cir. 1998), *cert. denied,* 526 U.S. 1051 (1999)—In a contract action alleging fraud, the plaintiff was awarded $5.5 million in punitive damages, which was 17.5 times the $313,600 in compensatory damages. The court ruled the punitive damage award was excessive and reduced the amount of punitive damages to $617,000, for a 2-to-1 ratio.

- In 1998, the Alabama Supreme Court (Alabama was the state in which the *BMW* case arose) placed restrictions on punitive damages. Now, in Alabama, no punitive damages are awarded without a showing of actual damages.

A study to be published in *Cornell Law Review* raises questions about tort reform and the allegations of runaway juries.[1] The jury may be still out on how extensive the problem of excessive jury verdicts is. The study, conducted by two Cornell professors and the National Center for State Courts, concludes that, particularly with regard to punitive damages, juries are not as generous as once believed. The study looked at 8,724 civil cases in 45 courts around the nation and found the following:

TYPE OF CASE	% OF TIME JURY AWARDED PUNITIVE DAMAGES	% OF TIME JUDGE AWARDED PUNITIVE DAMAGES
All cases	4.0%	4.0%
Individual versus individual	3.5%	5.3%
Individual versus government	2.4%	0.0%
Individual versus corporation	4.7%	6.7%
Individual versus hospital	3.1%	0.0%
Premises liability	1.1%	10.8%
Product liability	7.1%	8.3%
Intentional tort	21.4%	23.8%
Fraud	15.0%	12.6%
Rental/lease	7.3%	0.7%

The study also concludes that there is no difference between the amounts of punitive damages awarded by juries versus those awarded by judges. Others who have studied punitive damages immediately raised questions about the study because it runs contra to existing data.

Source: From a study Ted Eisenberg published in *Cornell Law Review*, March 2002. Used with permission.

SUMMARY

What are the types of civil wrongs that create a right of recovery for harm?

- Tort—a civil wrong; action by another that results in damages that are recoverable

- Intentional tort—civilly wrong conduct that is done deliberately

- Negligence—conduct of omission or neglect that results in damages

- Strict tort liability—imposition of liability because harm results

What are the types and elements of torts?

- Defamation—publication of untrue and damaging statements about an individual or company

- Product disparagement—the tort of defamation for products

- Malice—publication of information knowing it is false or with reckless disregard for whether it is false

- Privilege—a defense to defamation that protects certain statements because of a public interest in having information such as testimony in a trial or media coverage protected from suit

- Interference—the wrong of asking a party to breach a contract with a third party

- False imprisonment—wrongful detention of individual; shopkeepers have a privilege to reasonably detain those they have good cause to believe have taken merchandise

- Shopkeeper's privilege—defense to torts of defamation, invasion of privacy, and false imprisonment for merchants who detain shoppers when shopkeepers have reasonable cause to believe merchandise has been taken without payment

- Intentional infliction of emotional distress—bizarre and outrageous conduct that inflicts mental and possible physical harm on another

- Invasion of privacy—disclosing private information, intruding upon another's affairs or appropriating someone's image or likeness

- Appropriation—the use of another's likeness, image, voice, or trademark for commercial gain and without permission

- Reasonable and prudent person—the standard by which the conduct of others is measured; a hypothetical person who behaves with full knowledge and alertness

- Causation—the "but for" reason for an accident

- Proximate cause—the foreseeability requirement of causation

- Contributory negligence—negligence on the part of a plaintiff that was partially responsible for causing his injuries

- Comparative negligence—newer negligence defense that assigns liability and damages in accidents on a percentage basis and thus reduces a plaintiff's recovery by the amount his negligence contributed to the cause of the accident

- Assumption of risk—plaintiff's voluntary subjection to a risk that caused his injuries

What is the business issue surrounding torts?

- Tort reform—political and legislative process of limiting damages and changing methods of recovery for civil wrongs

QUESTIONS AND PROBLEMS

1. Sylvia Salek is a teacher at Passaic Collegiate School. The yearbook contained a section entitled "The Funny Pages," consisting of pictures of students and faculty accompanied by purportedly humorous captions. One of the pages in this section contained a picture of Ms. Salek sitting next to and facing another teacher, John DeVita, who had his right hand raised to his forehead. The photograph is captioned "Not tonight, Ms. Salek. I have a headache." Another page in the yearbook contains a picture of Mr. DeVita eating, with the caption "What are you really thinking about, Mr. DeVita?"

Ms. Salek brought suit against the school on grounds that the photographs and captions made it seem that Mr. DeVita was refusing to engage in a sexual relationship with her. What tort(s) is Ms. Salek alleging? [*Salek* v. *Passaic Collegiate School,* 605 A.2d 276 (N.J. 1992)]

2. Douglas Margreiter was severely injured in New Orleans on the night of April 6, 1976. He was the chief of the pharmacy section of the Colorado Department of Social Services and was in New Orleans to attend the annual meeting of the American Pharmaceutical Association.

On Tuesday evening, April 6, Mr. Margreiter had dinner at the Royal Sonesta Hotel with two associates from Colorado who were attending the meeting and were staying in rooms adjacent to Mr. Margreiter's in the New Hotel Monteleone. Margreiter returned to his room between 10:30 P.M. and 11:00 P.M.; one of his friends returned to his adjoining room at the same time. Another friend was to come by Mr. Margreiter's room later to discuss what sessions of the meetings each would attend the next day.

About three hours later, Mr. Margreiter was found severely beaten and unconscious in a parking lot three blocks from the Monteleone. The police who found him said they thought he was highly intoxicated, and they took him to Charity Hospital. His friends later had him moved to the Hotel Dieu.

Mr. Margreiter said two men had unlocked his hotel room door and entered his room. He was beaten about the head and shoulders and had only the recollection of being carried to a dark alley. He required a craniotomy and other medical treatment and suffered permanent effects from the incident.

Mr. Margreiter sued the hotel on grounds that the hotel was negligent in not controlling access to elevators and hence to the guests' rooms. The hotel says Mr. Margreiter was intoxicated and met his fate outside the hotel. Is the hotel liable? [*Margreiter* v. *New Hotel Monteleone,* 640 F.2d 508 (5th Cir. 1981)]

3. Carolyn Dolph was shopping at the Dumas, Arkansas, Wal-Mart at 3:00 P.M. on Friday, June 16, 1989. She had just gone through the check-out line and was attempting to leave the store when she was accosted near the exit by the loss-prevention officer for the store, Loretta McNeely. Ms. Dolph testified that Ms. McNeely told her that she knew that Ms. Dolph had been apprehended for shoplifting in the McGehee Wal-Mart the week before, and because of that she was not allowed to shop at any Wal-Mart store. According to Ms. Dolph, Ms. McNeely made the accusation four times. Ms. Dolph countered that Ms. McNeely was mistaken. Ms. McNeely did not believe her; instead, she thought Ms. Dolph was going through typical shoplifter's denial. They were arguing the point, according to Ms. Dolph, where people could overhear, and she felt as if she were on display "right in front of the store."

To resolve the matter, Ms. Dolph and Ms. McNeely moved to a nearby service area, and Ms. McNeely went into a mezzanine office to call the McGehee store. After telephoning McGehee, Ms. McNeely then "hollered down" questions to Ms. Dolph from the office, according to Ms. Dolph. During the time that Ms. McNeely was calling, Ms. Dolph believed that she was being watched by Wal-Mart employees and that she was not free to leave. Ms. McNeely then requested that Ms. Dolph come up to the office, but she refused and asked to see the manager. It turned out that Ms. McNeely was in error and that Ms. Dolph's sister—not Ms. Dolph—had been apprehended in McGehee for shoplifting. Ms. Dolph sued Wal-Mart for slander and was awarded $25,000. Wal-Mart appealed because Ms. Dolph did not produce anyone at the trial who could testify about hearing the "hollered" exchange. Why is this evidence important? Should Wal-Mart win the appeal? [*Wal-Mart Stores, Inc.* v. *Dolph*, 825 S.W.2d 810 (Ark. 1992)]

4. A woman used the women's restroom at a roller-skating rink run by Abate. She discovered that the restroom had see-through panels in the ceiling that allowed observation of those in the restroom. Is this an invasion of privacy? [*Harkey* v. *Abate*, 346 N.W.2d 74 (Mich. 1983)]

5. Two disc jockeys at WPYX-FM radio in Albany, New York have been sued for intentional infliction of emotional distress by Annette Esposito-Hilder, who was identified on the air by the two disc jockeys as the "winner" of the "ugliest bride" contest. The two disc jockeys sponsor an ugliest bride contest based on the wedding pictures in the daily newspaper. Viewers are invited to call in with their guesses as to which bride has been chosen. Generally, the disc jockeys did not reveal last names of the brides. However, in Ms. Esposito-Hilder's case, they broke with past practice and revealed her name.

On appeal of the case from an earlier dismissal, the court held that there was no defamation involved in their statements because they were "pure, subjective opinion." The court did hold, however, that a suit for intentional infliction of emotional distress could go forward. The court held, "Comedic expression does not receive absolute First Amendment protection."

Is opinion protected by the First Amendment? Does it make any difference that Ms. Esposito-Hilder was employed by a competing radio station in the area at the time she "won" the contest? [*Esposito-Hilder* v. *SFX Broadcasting, Inc.*, 665 N.Y.S.2d 697 (1997)]

6. Mae Tom went to Kresge's store on November 15, 1977, slipped, and fell on a clear substance on the floor.

No one ever determined what the substance was, but Kresge's did sell soft drinks in the store, and customers could walk around with their drinks. Mae Tom wishes to recover for her injuries. Can she do so? [*Tom* v. *S. S. Kresge Co., Inc.*, 633 P.2d 439 (Ariz. App. 1981)]

7. Peoples Bank and Trust Company is the conservator of the estate of Nellie Mitchell, a 96-year-old resident of Mountain Home, Arkansas, who has operated a newsstand on the town square since 1963. Before that, she delivered newspapers on a paper route and, according to the evidence, still makes deliveries to certain "downtown" business establishments and select customers.

It appears that Nellie, as she is known to almost everyone in this small Ozark Mountain town, is a town "landmark" or "treasure." She has cared for herself and raised a family as a single parent for all these years on what must have been the meager earnings of a "paper girl."

Her newspaper stand was in a short, dead-end alley between two commercial buildings on the town square. She received permission to put a roof over the alley, and this newsstand was her sole means of support. Her tenacity was evident at trial when she was asked whether she lived with her adult daughter, Betty. She replied, "No, Betty lives with me."

In the October 2, 1990, edition of the *Sun*, published by Globe International, Inc., there was a photograph of Nellie with a story entitled:

Special Delivery
World's oldest newspaper carrier, 101, quits because she's pregnant! I guess walking all those miles kept me young.

The "story" purports to be about a "paper-gal Audrey Wiles" in Stirling, Australia, who had been delivering papers for ninety-four years. Readers are told that Miss Wiles became pregnant by "Will," a "reclusive millionaire" she met on her newspaper route. "I used to put Will's paper in the door when it rained, and one thing just kind of led to another."

In words that could certainly have described Nellie Mitchell, the article, which was in the form and style of a factual newspaper account, in part said:

"[S]he's become like a city landmark because nearly everyone at one time or another has seen her trudging down the road with a large stack of papers under her arm."

The photograph used in the October 2 edition of the *Sun*, of Nellie apparently "trudging down the road with a large stack of papers under her arm," had been used by the defendant in a reasonably factual and accurate article about Nellie published in another of the defendant's publications, the *Examiner*, in 1980.

Peoples Bank, on behalf of Nellie, filed suit against Globe for invasion of privacy and intentional infliction of emotional distress. The jury awarded Nellie $650,000 in compensatory damages and $850,000 in punitive damages. Globe asked the court to reverse the verdict or, in the alternative, reduce the damages. Have any torts been committed? Describe them. Are the damages reasonable? [*Peoples Bank & Trust Co. v. Globe Int'l, Inc.*, 786 F. Supp. 791 (W.D. Ark. 1992)]

8. Benjamin VonBehren, then 2 years old, and his mother paid a visit to their neighbors Edward and Diane Bradley. Mr. and Mrs. Bradley were not home, but Benjamin and his mother were invited into the Bradley home by the Bradleys' 16-year-old daughter, who was at home babysitting her 9-year-old brother, Andy. Andy and Benjamin went to the backyard to play with the Bradleys' dog, a labrador retriever. The Bradleys' dog had a bird in its mouth, which was disturbing to Benjamin. Benjamin hit the dog and pulled its ears and tail to get it to spit out the bird. The dog instead bit Benjamin, who had severe lacerations on his face.

The VonBehrens sued the Bradleys, and the trial court dismissed the case because Benjamin had provoked the dog. The VonBehrens have appealed. What should the appellate court do? Should the Bradleys be held liable? [*VonBehren v. Bradley*, 640 N.E.2d 664 (Ill. 1994)]

9. KSL Recreation Corp. and Boca Partnership signed an agreement on February 23, 1994, to form a joint venture to renovate and expand the 356-acre Boca Raton Hotel & Club resort in Palm Beach County, Florida. The joint venture did not go through because KSL demanded an additional $3.5 million in expenses and fees. Boca then negotiated a loan with Olympus Real Estate Corporation. Boca was about to close on the financing of the renovation with Olympus when KSL faxed a copy of a lawsuit against Boca to Olympus. The lawsuit was not yet filed. Boca had a litigation clause in its agreement with Olympus, and it was required to pay more fees and a higher interest rate. Did KSL interfere with Boca's contract with Olympus?

10. Michael Boone was assaulted in the Palace Bar in Albert Lea, Minnesota, by Aristeo Martinez. Boone suffered a laceration and multiple stab wounds. The fight lasted three minutes and was already ended by the time employees arrived to break up the two warring patrons. Boone sued both Martinez and the Palace Bar. Prior to the fight, Martinez was quite obviously intoxicated, and bar patrons indicated that he was quite loud.

What would Boone have to establish in order to hold the Palace Bar liable for his injuries? [*Boone v. Martinez*, 567 N.W.2d 508 (Minn. 1997)]

RESEARCH PROBLEM

11. Because employers have become dependent on temporary workers and the agencies that provide them, an interesting issue has developed with regard to liability. The question is, Who is responsible for checking the temporary worker's background, especially when the temporary worker is offered a permanent position following a temporary stint?

For example, Robert Half International, Inc., had recruited T'Challa Ross as a bookkeeper and she was placed with Fox Associates, Inc., in Chicago. She did so well at the temporary position that Fox hired her permanently.

However, Robert Half had failed to uncover the fact that Ms. Ross had entered a guilty plea to charges that she embezzled $192,873 from a former employer and had been sentenced to four years' probation and community service. Once hired by Fox, Ms. Ross took blank checks and forged signatures, which resulted in her taking over $70,000 from the company. Her annual salary was $35,000 when she was hired by Fox.

Fox brought suit against Robert Half to recover the $70,000 plus its $6,600 fee, alleging that Robert Half was negligent in that it failed to verify that Ms. Ross, who had checked "No felony convictions" on her application, indeed had no felony convictions. However, two previous employers had given good recommendations and never mentioned any issues of dishonesty or embezzlement.

However, a judge dismissed the case ruling that Robert Half was in the talent business and not the background check or investigation business.

The issue is not limited to staff level. Sunbeam discovered that the executive search firm it used to recruit Al Dunlap did not discover that Dunlap had been dismissed from two previous executive positions. Sunbeam is reeling from losses resulting from Dunlap's tenure as CEO there.

Do you think there is a duty on the part of the temporary agency to check backgrounds? Do you think Fox should have done its own background check? Why do you think the former employers said nothing about her history and gave her good recommendations?

(continued)

RESEARCH PROBLEM

Develop some recommendations and policies for your company on background checks for employees hired through a search firm or temp agency. Be sure to consider what you have learned in this chapter on references, defamation, and negligence. Also, refer to the Web sites of various law firms and others advising clients on this issue: http://www.strassburger.com and http://www.bakerbotts.com

You can also refer to the statutes of various states that have passed laws on privilege with regard to

references: Alaska, Arizona, Arkansas, California, Colorado, Delaware, Florida, Georgia, Idaho, Illinois, Indiana, Kansas, Louisiana, Maine, Maryland, Michigan, Nebraska, New Mexico, North Carolina, North Dakota, Ohio, Oklahoma, Oregon, Rhode Island, South Carolina, South Dakota, Tennessee, Texas, Utah, Wisconsin, and Wyoming. For example, you could go to http://www.capitol.state.tx.us to look for the Texas statute.

NOTE

1. William Glaberson, "A Study's Verdict: Jury Awards Are Not Out of Control," *New York Times*, 6 August 2001, A9.

BUSINESS STRATEGY APPLICATION

The business strategy application for this chapter could be called, "Name That Tort!" You are given a fact pattern and asked to name the possible tort or torts that have been commited. However, you then must take the next step and, based on what you

have seen in the fact pattern and what you know, you must make recommendations for changes in your company's operations that might help to prevent the tort and the liability.

CHAPTER ELEVEN

Product Advertising and Liability

The first jury verdict over $1,000,000 in a product liability suit occurred in 1962. Today there are more than 400 multimillion-dollar verdicts a year. Business payments to claimants are estimated to be $100 billion a year. In 2000, the median award in product liability cases was $520,000.

Product liability cases today are common, the judgments and settlements are large, and insurance coverage costs are now a major expense to businesses. Buyers seem increasingly willing to have matters concerning defective products settled in court.

Product liability is a unique area of law. It has social roots in that it attempts to lessen the burden of losses by requiring a manufacturer or manufacturer's insurer to pay for a defective product. It also has contract roots in that if a product does not do what it is supposed to do, a breach of contract has occurred. Finally, it also has roots in tort law insofar as there is an injury resulting from someone else's carelessness. In these senses, product liability is a combination of contract law, tort law, and social responsibility.

This chapter answers the following questions: How did product liability law develop? What are the contract theories for recovery? What is required for a tort-based recovery on a defective product? How does advertising create liability for a business? What is strict tort liability for products? What reforms are proposed for cutting back liability? Are international product liability standards different?

Caution: This product can burn eyes.

WARNING ON A CURLING IRON

Advertising may be described as the science of arresting human intelligence long enough to get money out of it.

STEPHEN LEACOCK

Advertisements contain the only truths to be relied on in a newspaper.

THOMAS JEFFERSON

Caution: Cape does not enable user to fly.

INSTRUCTIONS ON KENNER PRODUCTS' BATMAN COSTUME

Never iron clothes while they are being worn.

WINNER OF LAWSUIT ABUSE WATCH'S ANNUAL "WACKY LABEL CONTEST" 2000

RUNNERS-UP:

Not for highway use.

ON A WHEELBARROW TIRE

Never use hair dryer while sleeping.

ON A BLOW DRYER

Remove child before folding.

ON A STROLLER

C O N S I D E R . . .

In November 1993, QVC Network advertised, as part of a one-day Thanksgiving promotion, the "T-Fal Jumbo Resistal Roaster." The QVC ad described the roaster as suitable for roasting a 25-pound turkey. At the time that T-Fal and QVC entered into an agreement for the sale of the roasting pan, T-Fal did not have a pan in its line large enough to roast a 25-pound turkey. T-Fal asked its parent company in France to provide a suitable roasting pan as soon as possible. The parent company provided a larger pan to which it added two small handles.

Loyda Castro ordered the roasting pan and used it for roasting her turkey on Thanksgiving Day, 1993. Mrs. Castro was injured when she tried to remove the turkey from the oven. Using two large insulated oven mitts, Mrs. Castro tried to lift the pan from the oven, placing two fingers on each handle on the pan. Two fingers were the maximum grip the small handles on the pan permitted. As the turkey tipped toward her, she lost control of the pan, spilling the hot drippings and fat that had accumulated in the pan during the cooking and basting process. Mrs. Castro suffered second- and third-degree burns to her foot and ankle, which have led to scarring, paresthesia, and swelling. Can she recover from QVC for her injuries? From T-Fal?

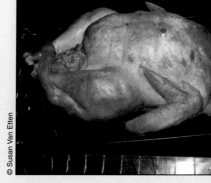

© Susan Van Etten

DEVELOPMENT OF PRODUCT LIABILITY

For some time, courts followed the principle of *caveat emptor,* which means, "Let the buyer beware." This theory meant that sellers were not liable for defects in their products and that it was the buyer's responsibility to be on the alert for defects and take the appropriate precautions.

Following a series of court decisions in which the buyers were allowed recovery and courts questioned the public policy wisdom of *caveat emptor,* the *Restatement Second of Torts* adopted its now famous Section 402A on strict tort liability (discussed later in this chapter). With this adoption, the area of product liability had gone full swing from no liability *(caveat emptor)* to an almost *per se* standard of liability for defective products.

ADVERTISING AS A CONTRACT BASIS FOR PRODUCT LIABILITY

Express Warranties

Learn about advertising law:
http://www.adlaw.com/
adlawindex.html

An **express warranty** as provided in the Uniform Commercial Code (UCC) is an express promise (oral or written) by the seller as to the quality, abilities, or performance of a product (UCC § 2–313). The seller need not use the words *promise* or *guarantee* to make an express warranty. Such a warranty is made when a seller uses a sample or model or provides a description of the goods. Promises of how the goods will perform are also express warranties. Examples of express warranties are: "These goods are 100 percent wool"; "This tire cannot be punctured"; "These jeans will not shrink."

Review UCC § 2-313:
http://www.law.cornell.edu/
ucc/2/2%2d313%2ehtml

Any statements made by the seller to the buyer before the sale is made that are part of the basis of the sale or bargain are express warranties. Opinions, however,

EXHIBIT 11.1   Statements of Fact versus Opinion

STATEMENT	FACT OR OPINION?
This car gets twenty miles per gallon.	Fact
This car gets great gas mileage.	Opinion
These goods are 100 percent wool.	Fact
This is the finest wool around.	Opinion
This truck has never been in an accident.	Fact
This truck is solid.	Opinion
This mace stops assailants in their tracks.	Fact (Promise of Peformance)
This mace is very effective.	Opinion
This makeup is hypoallergenic.	Fact
This makeup is good for your skin.	Opinion
This ink will not stain clothes.	Fact
This ink is safe to use.	Opinion
This computer is IBM-compatible.	Fact
This computer is as good as any IBM.	Opinion
This watch is waterproof.	Fact
This watch is durable.	Opinion

For more on business law and the UCC, go to the ABA's Business Law Web site:
http://www.abanet.org/buslaw/ucc/home.html

are not considered a basis for transactions and are therefore not express warranties. For example, the statement "These jeans are the best on the market" is sales puffing and not an express warranty. Exhibit 11.1 gives some examples of statements of fact versus opinion.

In some cases, such as the following, which provides answers for the chapter opening "Consider," the issue of product liability is one of representations via ad statements.

CASE 11.1

Castro v. QVC Network, Inc.
139 F.3d 114 (2d Cir. 1998)

A Turkey of a Pan: Liability on Thanksgiving Day

FACTS

In November 1993, QVC Network (appellee), an operator of a cable television home-shopping channel, advertised, as part of a one-day Thanksgiving promotion, the "T-Fal Jumbo Resistal Roaster." The roaster was manufactured by U.S.A. T-Fal Corporation. The QVC ad described the roaster as suitable for roasting a 25-pound turkey. At the time that T-Fal and QVC entered into an agreement for the sale of the roasting pan, T-Fal did not have a pan in its line large enough to roast a 25-pound turkey. T-Fal asked its parent company in France to provide a suitable roasting pan as soon as possible. The parent company provided a larger pan to which it added two small handles.

Loyda Castro (appellant) ordered the roasting pan and used it for roasting her turkey on Thanksgiving Day, 1993. Mrs. Castro was injured when she tried to remove the turkey from the oven. Using two large insulated oven mitts, Mrs. Castro tried to lift the pan from the oven placing two fingers on each handle. Two fingers were the maximum grip the small handles on the pan permitted. As the turkey tipped toward her, she lost control of the pan, spilling the hot drippings and fat that had accumulated in the pan during the cooking and basting process. Mrs. Castro suffered second- and third-degree burns to her foot and ankle, which have led to scarring, paresthesia, and swelling.

Mrs. Castro filed suit for strict liability and breach of warranty. The warranty charge was dismissed and the jury returned a verdict for QVC and T-Fal. Mrs. Castro appealed.

JUDICIAL OPINION

CALABRESI, Circuit Judge

Products liability law has long been bedeviled by the search for an appropriate definition of "defective" product design. Over the years, both in the cases and in the literature, two approaches have come to predominate. The first is the risk/utility theory, which focuses on whether the benefits of a product outweigh the dangers of its design. The second is the consumer expectations theory, which focuses on what a buyer/user of a product would properly expect that the product would be suited for.

Not all states accept both of these approaches. Some define design defect only according to the risk/utility approach.

One of the first states to accept both approaches was California, which in *Barker* v. *Lull Engineering Co.*, 20 Cal.3d 413, 143 Cal.Rptr. 225, 573 P.2d 443 (1978), held that "a product may be found defective in design, so as to subject a manufacturer to strict liability for resulting injuries, under either of two alternative tests"—consumer expectations and risk/utility. Several states have followed suit and have adopted both theories.

Prior to the recent case of *Denny* v. *Ford Motor Co.*, 87 N.Y.2d 248, 639 N.Y.S.2d 250, 662 N.E.2d 730 (1995), it was not clear whether New York recognized both tests. In *Denny*, the plaintiff was injured when her Ford Bronco II sports utility vehicle rolled over when she slammed on the brakes to avoid hitting a deer in the vehicle's path. The plaintiff asserted claims for strict products liability and for breach of

(continued)

implied warranty, and the district judge—over the objection of defendant Ford—submitted both causes of action to the jury. The jury ruled in favor of Ford on the strict liability claim, but found for the plaintiff on the implied warranty claim. On appeal, Ford argued that the jury's verdicts on the strict products liability claim and the breach of warranty claim were inconsistent because the causes of action were identical.

This court certified the *Denny* case to the New York Court of Appeals to answer the following questions: (1) "whether, under New York law, the strict products liability and implied warranty claims are identical"; and (2) "whether, if the claims are different, the strict products liability claim is broader than the implied warranty claim and encompasses the latter."

In response to the certified questions, the Court of Appeals held that in a products liability case a cause of action for strict liability is not identical to a claim for breach of warranty.

Moreover, the court held that a strict liability claim is not per se broader than a breach of warranty claim such that the former encompasses the latter. Thus, while claims of strict products liability and breach of warranty are often used interchangeably, under New York law the two causes of action are definitively different. The imposition of strict liability for an alleged design "defect" is determined by a risk-utility standard. The notion of "defect" in a U.C.C.-based breach of warranty claim focuses, instead, on consumer expectations.

Since *Denny*, then, it has been settled that the risk/utility and consumer expectations theories of design defect can, in New York, be the bases of distinct causes of action: one for strict products liability and one for breach of warranty. This fact, however, does not settle the question of when a jury must be charged separately on each cause of action and when, instead, the two causes are, on the facts of the specific case, sufficiently similar to each other so that one charge to the jury is enough.

While eminent jurists have at times been troubled by this issue, the New York Court of Appeals in *Denny* was quite clear on when the two causes of action might meld and when, instead, they are to be treated as separate. It did this by adding its own twist to the distinction—namely, what can aptly be called the "dual purpose" requirement. Thus in *Denny,* the Court of Appeals pointed out that the fact that a product's overall benefits might outweigh its overall risks does not preclude the possibility that

consumers may have been misled into using the product in a context in which it was dangerously unsafe. And this, the New York court emphasized, could be so even though the benefits in other uses might make the product sufficiently reasonable so that it passed the risk/utility test.

In *Denny,* the Ford Bronco II was not designed as a conventional passenger automobile. Instead, it was designed as an off-road, dual purpose vehicle. But in its marketing of the Bronco II, Ford stressed its suitability for commuting and for suburban and city driving. Under the circumstances, the Court of Appeals explained that a rational factfinder could conclude that the Bronco's utility as an off-road vehicle outweighed the risk of injury resulting from rollover accidents (thus passing the risk/utility test), but at the same time find that the vehicle was not safe for the "ordinary purpose" of daily driving for which it was also marketed and sold (thus flunking the consumer expectations test).

That is precisely the situation before us. The jury had before it evidence that the product was designed, marketed, and sold as a multiple-use product. The pan was originally manufactured and sold in France as an all-purpose cooking dish without handles. And at trial, the jury saw a videotape of a QVC representative demonstrating to the television audience that the pan, in addition to serving as a suitable roaster for a twenty-five pound turkey, could also be used to cook casseroles, cutlets, cookies, and other low-volume foods. The court charged the jury that "[a] product is defective if it is not reasonably safe[,] [t]hat is, if the product is so likely to be harmful to persons that a reasonable person who had actual knowledge of its potential for producing injury would conclude that it should not have been marketed in that condition." And, so instructed, the jury presumably found that the pan, because it had many advantages in a variety of uses, did not fail the risk/utility test.

But it was also the case that the pan was advertised as suitable for a particular use—cooking a twenty-five pound turkey. Indeed, T-Fal added handles to the pan in order to fill QVC's request for a roasting pan that it could use in its Thanksgiving promotion. The product was, therefore, sold as appropriately used for roasting a twenty-five pound turkey. And it was in that use that allegedly the product failed and injured the appellant.

In such circumstances, New York law is clear that a general charge on strict products liability based on the risk/utility approach does not suffice. The jury could have found that the roasting pan's overall utility for cooking low-volume foods outweighed the risk of injury when cooking heavier foods, but that the product was nonetheless unsafe for the purpose for which it was marketed and sold—roasting a twenty-five pound turkey—and, as such, was defective under the consumer expectations test. That being so, the appellants were entitled to a separate breach of warranty charge.

In light of the evidence presented by appellants of the multi-purpose nature of the product at issue, the district court, applying New York law, should have granted appellants' request for a separate jury charge on the breach of warranty claim in addition to the charge on the strict liability claim.

Reversed.

CASE QUESTIONS

1. How was the turkey pan purchased?

2. Who designed the turkey pan?

3. Was the pan represented as suitable for roasting a turkey?

4. What is the relationship between tort liability and warranty liability?

5. What is the risk/utility test?

CONSIDER . . .

11.1 John R. Klages was employed as a night auditor at Conley's Motel on Route 8 in Hampton Township. He worked from 11 P.M. until 7 A.M., five days a week. On March 30, 1968, at approximately 1:30 A.M., two individuals entered the motel and announced, "This is a stickup. Open the safe." Mr. Klages indicated that he was unable to open the safe because he did not know the combination. One of the individuals then pointed a gun at his head and pulled the trigger. Fortunately for Mr. Klages, the gun was a starter pistol and he was not seriously injured.

The next day, Mr. Klages and a fellow employee, Bob McVay, decided that they needed something to protect themselves against the possibility of future holdups. After reading an article concerning the effects of mace, Mr. McVay suggested that they consider using mace for their protection and secured from the Mark1 Supply Company four leaflets describing certain mace weapons.

After reading and discussing the literature with their employer, Mr. McVay purchased an MK-II mace weapon from Mark1 Supply Company, which described the mace as follows:

> *Rapidly vaporizes on face of assailant effecting* instantaneous incapacitation. . . . *It will* instantly stop and subdue *entire groups* . . . instantly stops assailants in their tracks. . . . *[A]n attacker is* subdued instantly, *for a period of 15 to 20 minutes.* . . . Time Magazine *stated the Chemical Mace is* "for police the first, if not the final, answer to a nationwide need—a weapon that disables as effectively as a gun and yet does no permanent injury.". . . *The effectiveness is the result of a unique,* incapacitating formulation *(patent pending), projected in a shotgun-like pattern of heavy liquid droplets that, upon contact with the face, cause extreme tearing, and a stunned, winded condition, often accompanied by dizziness and apathy.*

At approximately 1:40 A.M. on September 22, 1968, while Mr. Klages was on duty, two unknown individuals entered the motel office, requested a room, and announced a stickup. One of the intruders took out a gun and directed Mr. Klages to open the safe. Using the cash register as a shield, Mr. Klages squirted the mace, hitting the intruder "right beside the nose." Mr. Klages immediately ducked below the register, but the intruder followed him down and shot him in the head. The intruders immediately departed, and Mr. Klages called the police. The bullet wound caused complete loss of sight in Mr. Klages's right eye. He claims a breach of an express warranty. Is he right? [*Klages* v. *General Ordnance Equipment Corp.*, 19 UCC Rep. Serv. (Callaghan) 22 (Pa. 1976)]

C O N S I D E R . . .

11.2   Lawrence Dorneles purchased a used 1972 Buick GSX from the defendant. Mr. Dorneles had seen an ad that contained a picture of the vehicle and that read as follows: "Buick 1972 GSX, not an original, as close as you can get, all new body parts, 5,000 miles on a new rebuilt 455 Stage 1, car show winner, new exhaust system, mint, tires, never seen rain or snow, garage kept, needs minor interior work, 12 bolt posi rear, hood, tachometer, rear spoiler, all replica details, must sell, $4,500.00. . . ."

Mr. Dorneles answered the ad and spoke with Mr. Carpenito who reiterated the items in the ad and specifically assured that the rebuilt engine had less than 5,000 miles and that the car had been "babied" among other things. Mr. Dorneles neither test drove the vehicle nor had a mechanic inspect the vehicle prior to purchasing it. No written warranty was given by the seller.

Mr. Dorneles paid $4,000.00 for the car and drove it from Port Chester to his home in Pelham. He left the car at home until July 17th when he registered it and was going to drive the car to Valhalla to have a mechanic inspect the car. July 17th was a hot summer day; and on the way to Valhalla, some 15 miles from Pelham, the car began to overheat. The car's engine apparently seized because of the extreme heat and had to be towed back to Pelham. The engine was removed from the Buick at a cost of $450.00, and another new rebuilt engine was installed at a cost of $1,152.00. Additional work has to be done on the car including repairing broken rear suspension springs ($600.00), installing a new transmission ($750.00), and replacing a corroded chain cover ($174.25).

Was an express warranty given that can be the basis of recovery? Do you waive the express warranty when you do not inspect the car? [*Dorneles* v. *Carpenito*, 521 N.Y.S.2d 967 (1987)]

Federal Regulation of Warranties and Advertising

Express warranties are advertisements for goods. Advertising is crucial to both business success and consumers. Because accurate advertising is necessary to ensure full information to support a competitive environment, it is important that advertising be policed for its fairness and accuracy.

Visit the Federal Trade Commission:
http://www.ftc.gov

In 1914, Congress passed the **Federal Trade Commission Act,** which authorized the **Federal Trade Commission** (FTC) to prevent "unfair and deceptive trade practices." Initially, the FTC used its power to regulate all forms of deceptive advertising. However, the Supreme Court, in interpreting the 1914 act, severely restricted the FTC to the regulation of false advertising that adversely affected competition. In reaction to this Court ruling, Congress passed the **Wheeler-Lea Act** of 1938, giving the FTC the power to regulate "unfair and deceptive acts or practices" whenever the public is being deceived regardless of any effects on competition.

Review the Federal Trade Commission Act and the Wheeler-Lea Act:
http://www.law.cornell.edu/
uscode/15/ch2.html#s45

Re: Internet Ads

The number of ads sent to Internet users is staggering. The average Web visitor receives 520 marketing messages each day. Yahoo! sent out 8.8 billion ads in October 2000. Online ads have generated $5.3 billion in revenues so far this year.

Now companies have developed ad-blocking software that consumers can buy or, in some cases, download for free. Examples of such programs include Ad-Killer, Ad Muncher, and Pop-Up Hunter. These programs recognize the domain name of an ad server as it is about to send an ad as a user opens a page. The software blocks the ad and places a blank rectangle where the ads would have appeared. Some users say that their speed in using the Internet increases by three times when using the software.

Software also is being developed with the ability not only to block incoming ads but to substitute its ads in their place. What some experts are predicting is a form of cyber war for advertising with the winners being those who can develop the software that preempts last. These ad blockers and substitutes will make their way to users through free software. But, users are already prepared with their skills on disabling portions of the free software programs.

This issue is a critical one because of the importance of ad revenues on the Internet.

Source: Erika Brown, "Control Geeks," *Forbes*, 27 November 2000, 285–86.

For more information regarding ad-blocking software, go to:
http://www.junkbusters.com
http://www.zeroknowledge.com
http://www.guidescope.com

With the Wheeler-Lea Act, the FTC has expanded its authority over the years. Unsubstantiated or ambiguous advertising claims have been challenged, and deceptive techniques in television ads have also been reviewed by the FTC. The only restriction the FTC has experienced since the Wheeler-Lea Act was passed came after attempts by the agency to regulate the content and number of ads on children's television programming. In that case, the FTC ran into powerful opposition by broadcaster, advertising, and producer groups. These groups brought court actions in an attempt to halt the proceedings and at one point disqualified the FTC chairman from the proceedings. This struggle ended with congressional passage of the **FTC Improvements Act of 1980.** The act actually terminated the FTC's authority in the children's television case and put general restrictions on the FTC. In 1990, some children's television regulations were passed.

Content Control and Accuracy

The FTC has regulated the accuracy of ads in several ways. First, the FTC has challenged certain types of price claims. If an ad announces "50% off," the prices must actually be half the original prices charged for the products or services prior to the sale; that price cannot be inflated to cover the markdown. If an ad quotes a "normal" price, that price must reflect what most sellers in the area are charging.

The FTC has also challenged the accuracy of ads. Claims that goods are "100% wool" are not only the basis for express warranty recovery but also the basis for an FTC challenge. Also, the FTC challenges advertising methods. For example, using "marbles" in soup to make it look thicker as it pours is deceptive. The FTC has used its powers to ensure that ads accurately depict the product as it exists.

BUSINESS PLANNING TIP

Always review the language used in ads for products. Determine whether express warranties are being made. Make sure that warranties, statements of fact, and promises of performance are accurate. Remember that samples are also warranties.

ETHICAL ISSUES 11.1

The Federal Trade Commission (FTC) has been focusing on the concept of "free," particularly as it relates to ads for computers. Many companies have advertised "free computers" or "low-cost computers" with fine print disclosure on requirements such as having to subscribe to CompuServe, Prodigy, or MSN for three-year periods to qualify for the $400 rebates or computer discounts. If the fees for these Internet services are factored in at an average cost of $21.95 per month, then the total cost for those services for three years is $790.20; and there is usually a penalty of $400 if the computer purchaser cancels the Internet service contract before the three-year term expires. Further, some consumers in certain areas must pay long-distance costs to access their Internet service provider that they choose in order to qualify for the rebate or computer price discount.

While most computer retailers do disclose all the terms of the discount or rebate, the FTC notes also that some of the disclosures in the ads are "microscopic." The FTC is considering a rule that would require a conspicuous upfront disclosure of the total cost of purchasing the computer.

Presently, there are no regulations that apply specifically to these discounts and rebates for computer sales other than the generic accuracy in advertising regulations. Refer to Chapter 2 and the discussion of the social, regulatory, and litigation cycle. Is this an issue that has moved into the awareness and activism stage? Is regulation likely? What could the computer retailers do? Do you think they should make more obvious disclosures about the total package cost of these discount computers? Won't they sell more computers with the hook of the $400 rebate and fine-print disclosure?

FTC Control of Performance Claims

Any claims of the ability or efficacy of a product must be supportable. If a sunburn-relief product claims to "anesthetize nerves," the advertiser must be able to prove that claim.

Where an advertising claim cannot be substantiated, the FTC has used **corrective advertising** as a remedy. Corrective advertising requires a seller to correct the unsubstantiated claims made in previous ads. The following landmark case involves an issue of corrective advertising.

CASE 11.2

Warner-Lambert Co. v. *FTC*
562 F.2d 749 (D.C.Cir. 1977)

Does Listerine Prevent Colds?

FACTS

Listerine, a product of the Warner-Lambert Corporation, has been on the market since 1879 and has been represented through advertising to be beneficial for colds, cold symptoms, and sore throats. After a 1972 complaint about Warner-Lambert advertising for Listerine, the FTC held four months of hearings on the ad issues and then ordered Warner-Lambert (petitioner) to do the following:

1. Cease and desist representing that Listerine will cure colds or sore throats, prevent colds or sore throats, or that users of Listerine will have fewer colds than nonusers;

2. Cease and desist representing that Listerine is a treatment for, or will lessen the severity of, colds or sore throats; that it will have any significant beneficial effect on the symptoms of sore throats or any beneficial effect on symptoms of colds; or that the ability of Listerine to kill germs is of medical significance in the treatment of colds or sore throats or their symptoms;

3. Cease and desist disseminating any advertisement for Listerine unless it is clearly and conspicuously disclosed in each advertisement, in the exact language below, that "Contrary to prior advertising, Listerine will not help prevent colds or sore throats or lessen their severity." This requirement extends only to the next 10 million dollars of Listerine advertising.

Warner-Lambert appealed the order.

JUDICIAL OPINION

WRIGHT, Circuit Judge

The first issue on appeal is whether the Commission's conclusion that Listerine is not beneficial for colds or sore throats is supported by the evidence.

First, the Commission found that the ingredients of Listerine are not present in sufficient quantities to have any therapeutic effect.

Second, the Commission found that in the process of gargling it is impossible for Listerine to reach critical areas of the body in medically significant concentration.

Third, the Commission found that even if significant quantities of the active ingredients of Listerine were to reach critical sites where cold viruses enter and infect the body, they could not interfere with the activities of the virus because they could not penetrate the tissue cells.

. . . [T]he Commission found that the ability of Listerine to kill germs by millions on contact is of no medical significance in the treatment of colds or sore throats.

. . . [T]he Commission found that Listerine has no significant beneficial effect on the symptoms of sore throat. The Commission recognized that gargling with Listerine could provide temporary relief from a sore throat by removing accumulated debris irritating the throat. But this type of relief can also be obtained by gargling with salt water or even warm water.

Petitioner contends that even if its advertising claims in the past were false, the portion of the Commission's order requiring "corrective advertising" exceeds the Commission's statutory power. The Commission's position is that the affirmative disclosure that Listerine will not prevent colds or lessen their severity is absolutely necessary to give effect to the prospective cease and desist order; a hundred years of false cold claims have built up a large reservoir of erroneous consumer belief that would persist, unless corrected, long after petitioner ceased making the claims.

If the Commission is to attain the objectives Congress envisioned, it cannot be required to confine its road block to the narrow lane the transgressor has traveled; it must be allowed effectively to close all roads to the prohibited goal, so that its order may not be bypassed with impunity.

We turn next to the specific disclosure required: "Contrary to prior advertising, Listerine will not help prevent colds or sore throats or lessen their severity." Petitioner is ordered to include this statement in every future advertisement for Listerine for a defined period. In printed advertisements it must be displayed in type size at least as large as that in which the principal portion of the text of the advertisement appears and it must be separated from the text so that it can be readily noticed. In television commercials the disclosure must be presented simultaneously in both audio and visual portions. During the audio portion of the disclosure in television and radio advertisements, no other sounds, including music, may occur.

These specifications are well calculated to assure that the disclosure will reach the public. It will necessarily attract the notice of readers, viewers and listeners, and be plainly conveyed. Given these safeguards, we believe the preamble "Contrary to prior advertising" is not necessary. It can serve only two purposes: either to attract attention that a correction follows or to humiliate the advertiser. The Commission claims only the first purpose for it, and this we think is obviated by other terms of the order. The second purpose, if it were intended, might be called for in an egregious case of deliberate deception, but this is not one. While we do not decide whether petitioner proffered its cold claims in good faith or bad, the record compiled could support a finding of good faith. On these facts, the confessional preamble to the disclosure is not warranted.

Accordingly, the order, as modified, is affirmed.

CASE QUESTIONS

1. What claims does the FTC make about Listerine?

2. What proposals for corrective advertising are made in the order?

3. What modifications in the order does the court make?

4. What happens to the preamble, "Contrary to prior advertising"?

5. Is Listerine still required to make disclosures in future ads? For how long?

FTC Control of Celebrity Endorsements

In the past ten years, the FTC has entered a new aspect of ad content control—namely, the use of **celebrity endorsements** for products. At the time the FTC became involved, its director of consumer protection stated:

> *The effectiveness of having a product touted by a well-known movie star or sports figure is apparent from the increasing use of celebrity endorsements in advertising. A sales pitch by a celebrity may be more believable than the same message delivered by an unknown spokesperson. The endorsement can be an important part of sales strategy, and is often quite handsomely rewarded. The endorser may profit from a false advertisement just as much as the manufacturer, and thus it is not unreasonable to obligate him to ascertain the truthfulness of the claims he is being paid to make.*[1]

With a celebrity endorsement, the FTC requires several steps. First, as the quote indicates, the celebrity must ascertain the truth of the ad claims. Second, the celebrity cannot make any claims about product use unless the celebrity has actually used and experienced the product. Finally, if any claims are being made that are not the celebrity's, the source of the information must be disclosed as part of the ad.

FTC Control of Bait and Switch

One of the better-known FTC ad regulations prohibits the use of **bait and switch,** which is a sales tactic in which a cheaper product than the one in stock is advertised to get customers into a store. The seller has no intention of selling the product and in some cases might not even have the product in stock; but the ad is used as "bait" to get the customers in and present them with a "better," more expensive product. Such ad tactics are considered deceptive and subject to FTC remedy.

FTC Control of Product Comparisons

Visit the Better Business Bureau:
http://www.bbb.org

Another aspect of active enforcement by the FTC is in the area of product comparisons. The FTC permits and even welcomes comparisons of products, but such comparisons must be accurate. Results of surveys must be supportable, and product preference tests must be done fairly. In the past few years, the FTC has taken a laissez-faire approach in ad regulation. Other agencies, such as the offices of state attorneys general, the Better Business Bureau, and private companies and individuals, have undertaken public and private enforcement of deceptive ad claims.

The bulk of litigation over comparative ads is now conducted by and against competitors. The FTC generally focuses on deception by companies about their own products. However, federal trademark law permits competitors to recover from companies for ads that include misrepresentations regarding its own products. Companies can be held liable for misrepresentations regarding other products. Litigation over comparative ads is somewhat rewarding because plaintiffs can recover treble damages, the defendant company's profits, and, in some cases, attorney fees. Suits that have been filed for competitor misrepresentations include an action by MCI against AT&T for claims that AT&T is cheaper than MCI and a suit by Gillette against Wilkinson for claims that men preferred Wilkinson's Ultra Glide razor to Gillette's Ultra Plus. The following case is a competitor litigation over misrepresentation.

CASE 11.3

S. C. Johnson & Son, Inc. v. *Clorox Company*
241 F.3d 232 (2d Cir. 2001)

Something Fishy: It's in the Bag It Leaks and It Leaks

FACTS

In August 1999, Clorox (defendant/appellant) introduced a 15-second and a 30-second television commercial ("Goldfish I"), each depicting an S. C. Johnson (plaintiff/appellee) Ziploc Slide-Loc resealable storage bag side-by-side with a Clorox Glad-Lock bag. The bags are identified in the commercials by brand name. Both commercials show an animated, talking goldfish in water inside each of the bags.

In the commercials, the bags are turned upside-down, and the Slide-Loc bag leaks rapidly while the Glad-Lock bag does not leak at all. In both the 15- and 30-second Goldfish I commercials, the Slide-Loc goldfish says, in clear distress, "My Ziploc Slider is dripping. Wait a minute!," while the Slide-Loc bag is shown leaking at a rate of approximately one drop per one to two seconds. In the 30-second Goldfish I commercial only, the Slide-Loc bag is shown leaking while the Slide-Loc goldfish says, "Excuse me, a little help here," and then, "Oh, dripping, dripping." At the end of both commercials, the Slide-Loc goldfish exclaims, "Can I borrow a cup of water!!!"

On November 4, 1999, S. C. Johnson brought an action against Clorox under section 43(a) of the Lanham Act, 15 U.S.C. § 1125(a), for false advertising in the Goldfish I commercials.

Dr. Phillip DeLassus, an outside expert retained by S. C. Johnson, conducted "torture testing," in which Slide-Loc bags were filled with water, rotated for 10 seconds, and held upside-down for an additional 20 seconds. He testified about the results of the tests he performed, emphasizing that 37 percent of all Slide-Loc bags tested did not leak at all. Of the remaining 63 percent that did leak, only a small percentage leaked at the rate depicted in the Goldfish I television commercials. The vast majority leaked at a rate between two and twenty times slower than that depicted in the Goldfish I commercials.

The district court found that the great majority of leaks from the bag are very small and at a very slow rate. On January 7, 2000, the district court held that "the Clorox commercial in question misrepresents the Slide-Loc bag product," and issued an injunction against further runs of the Goldfish I ad.

In February 2000, Clorox released a modified version of the Goldfish I television commercials as well as a related print advertisement ("Goldfish II"). In the 15-second Goldfish II television commercial, a Ziploc Slide-Loc bag and Glad-Lock bag are again shown side-by-side, filled with water and containing an animated, talking goldfish. The bags are then rotated, and a drop of water is shown forming and dropping in about a second from the Slide-Loc bag.

During the approximately additional two seconds that it is shown, the Slide-Loc goldfish says, "My Ziploc slider is dripping. Wait a minute." The two bags are then off-screen for approximately eight seconds before the Slide-Loc bag is again shown, with a drop forming and falling in approximately one second. During this latter depiction of the Slide-Loc bag, the Slide-Loc goldfish says, "Hey, I'm gonna need a little help here." Both bags are identified by brand name, and the Glad-Lock bag does not leak at all. The second-to-last frame shows three puddles on an orange background that includes the phrase "Don't Get Mad."

In the print advertisement, a large drop is shown forming and about to fall from an upside-down Slide-Loc bag in which a goldfish is partially out of the water. Bubbles are shown rising from the point of the leak in the Slide-Loc bag. Next to the Slide-Loc bag is a Glad-Lock bag that is not leaking and contains a goldfish that is completely submerged. Under the Slide-Loc bag appears: "Yikes! My Ziploc© Slide-Loc™ is dripping!" Under the Glad-Lock bag is printed: "My Glad is tight, tight, tight." On a third panel, three puddles and the words "Don't Get Mad" are depicted on a red background. In a fourth panel, the advertisement recites: "Only Glad has the Double-Lock™ green seal. That's why you'll be glad you got Glad. Especially if you're a goldfish."

After these advertisements appeared, S. C. Johnson moved to enlarge the January 7 injunction to

(continued)

enjoin the airing and distribution of the Goldfish II advertisements. On April 6, 2000, after hearing oral argument, the district court entered another order permanently enjoining the distribution of the Goldfish II television commercial and print advertisement. S. C. Johnson appealed.

JUDICIAL OPINION

HALL, District Judge

This case involves a Lanham Act challenge to the truthfulness of a television commercial and print advertisement depicting the plight of an animated goldfish in a Ziploc Slide-Loc bag that is being held upside down and is leaking water. S. C. Johnson & Son manufactures the Ziploc bags targeted by the advertisements.

The district court found that S. C. Johnson had shown by a preponderance of the evidence that the Goldfish I commercials are "literally false in respect to its depiction of the flow of water out of the Slide-Loc bag." The court found that "the commercial impermissibly exaggerates the facts in respect to the flow of water or the leaking of water out of a Slide-Loc bag."

The court entered an injunction, noting that S. C. Johnson had shown irreparable harm sufficient to support an injunction because, as the court found, the Goldfish I commercials are literally false.

[When the Goldfish II ads ran], the court incorporated by reference its prior findings of fact from its January 7, 2000 opinion. The court observed that the Goldfish II commercial "does not literally portray a rate of leakage which was portrayed in the earlier ad and which was the subject of certain of my findings in the earlier decision." Instead, the court noted,

[E]ssentially the same problem that I commented upon in the earlier decision exists with this commercial, ... [T]here is nothing to indicate that this kind of leakage occurs in only some particular percentage of bags, and there is nothing to indicate the degree of risk of such leakage. There is only one image, and that is of a big drop falling out.

The court further found that the Goldfish II commercial "portray[s] . . . a goldfish in danger of suffocating in air because of the outflow of water from the bag."

The court concluded that the Goldfish II television commercial "is decidedly contrary to what was portrayed in the actual evidence about the bags at the first trial, and all in all the television commercial in my view is literally false." The court then addressed the Goldfish II print advertisement, which, it found "is, if anything, worse," because "[i]t has a single image of a Slide-Loc bag with a large drop about to fall away and a goldfish in danger of suffocating because the water is as portrayed disappearing from the bag." The district court concluded that the Goldfish II print advertisement "is literally false." The court also found that the inability of a Ziploc Slide-Loc bag to prevent leakage is portrayed as an inherent quality or characteristic of that product. Accordingly, the court found that the Goldfish II television commercial and print advertisement "portray the leakage as simply an ever-present characteristic of the Slide-Loc bags." The district court found, in the alternative, that the Goldfish II ads were false by necessary implication, a doctrine this court has not yet recognized, because consumers would necessarily believe that more viscous liquids such as soups and sauces would leak as rapidly as water.

The district court found that the Goldfish II television commercial and print advertisement are literally false in violation of section 43(a). That section provides, in pertinent part:

(1) Any person who, on or in connection with any goods or services, or any container for goods, uses in commerce any word, term, name, symbol, or device, or any combination thereof, or any false designation of origin, false or misleading description of fact, or false or misleading representation of fact, which— . . . (B) in commercial advertising or promotion, misrepresents the nature, characteristics, qualities, or geographic origin of his or her or another person's goods, services, or commercial activities, shall be liable in a civil action by any person who believes that he or she is or is likely to be damaged by such act.

To establish a false advertising claim under Section 43(a), the plaintiff must demonstrate that the statement in the challenged advertisement is false. "Falsity may be established by proving that (1) the advertising is literally false as a factual matter, or (2) although the advertisement is literally true, it is likely to deceive or confuse customers. . . ."

It is also well-settled that, "in addition to proving falsity, the plaintiff must also show that the defendants misrepresented an 'inherent quality or characteristic' of the product. This requirement is essentially one of materiality, a term explicitly used in other circuits."

Where the advertising claim is shown to be literally false, the court may enjoin the use of the claim 'without reference to the advertisement's impact on the buying public.' Additionally, a plaintiff must show that it will suffer irreparable harm absent the injunction.

We find no clear error in the district court's findings of fact in support of its conclusion that the Goldfish II television commercial and print advertisement are literally false as a factual matter. We note that the court made its finding of literal falsity after a seven-day bench trial. The evidence presented at trial clearly indicates that, as the court found, only slightly more than one out of ten Slide-Loc bags tested dripped at a rate of one drop per second or faster, while more than one-third of the Slide-Loc bags tested leaked at a rate of less than one drop per five seconds. Over half of the Slide-Loc bags tested either did not leak at all or leaked at a rate no faster than one drop per 20 seconds. Moreover, less than two-thirds, or 63 percent, of Slide-Loc bags tested showed any leakage at all when subjected to the testing on which Clorox based its Goldfish I and II advertisements.

The only Slide-Loc bag depicted in each of the two Goldfish II advertisements, on the other hand, is shown leaking and, when shown, is always leaking.

Moreover, each time the Slide-Loc bag is on-screen, the Goldfish II television commercial shows a drop forming immediately and then falling from the Slide-Loc bag, all over a period of approximately two seconds. Accordingly, the commercial falsely depicts the risk of leakage for the vast majority of Slide-Loc bags tested.

Clorox argues that, because approximately eight seconds pass between the images of the drops forming and falling in the Goldfish II television commercial, the commercial depicts an accurate rate of leakage. However, the commercial does not continuously show the condition of the Slide-Loc bag because the Slide-Loc bag is off-screen for eight seconds. Likewise, the print ad does not depict any rate of leakage at all, other than to indicate that the Slide-Loc bag is "dripping." Clorox's argument that its commercial shows a "continuum" also fails given that in each of the Goldfish II advertisements is a background image containing three puddles of water, when only two drops form and fall in the television commercial and just one drop forms and nearly falls in the print advertisement.

Clorox alleges that the district court erred in finding literal falsity because "no facially false claim or depiction was present in the advertisements at issue in this case." As such, Clorox argues, the district court's finding of literal falsity "was based upon an interpretation of the ads that went beyond their facial or explicit claims." According to Clorox, the district court therefore must have based it[s] injunction on the implied falsity of the ads. Clorox argues that the district court erred as a matter of law because "any alleged message beyond the literal claims in the advertisements [must] be proved by extrinsic evi-

dence," upon which the district court undeniably did not rely in reaching its conclusions.

We disagree. The district court properly concluded that the Goldfish II advertisements are literally false in violation of section 43(a) of the Lanham Act. The court looked at the Goldfish II television commercial and print advertisement in their entirety and determined that the risk of leakage from the Slide-Loc storage bag depicted in the ads is literally false based on the evidence presented at trial of the real risk and rate of leakage from Slide-Loc bags.

Because we affirm the injunction on the basis of literal falsity, we need not reach the issue of whether the district court erred in concluding as an alternative ground that Clorox's Goldfish II television commercial and print advertisement are false "by necessary implication" because consumers would necessarily believe that more viscous liquids than water would also leak rapidly from Ziploc Slide-Loc storage bags.

Clorox argues that the April 6, 2000 Order "does not 'describe in reasonable detail' the conduct it seeks to restrain, and offers Clorox no clear guidance on what it may and may not depict in future Glad-Lock advertising." Clorox further claims that it "has no way of knowing whether it can show water leaking from a Slide-Loc bag and, if so, what rate of leakage it can depict."

Clorox's arguments are unavailing. [T]he district court [need not] "predict exactly what [Clorox] 'will think of next'" or . . . describe all possible, permissible future commercials that Clorox may produce involving Ziploc Slide-Loc storage bags. [T]he district court can do no more to assist Clorox in determining whether a proposed advertisement conveys a message that is literally false with regard to a depiction of Ziploc Slide-Loc bags.

Affirmed.

CASE QUESTIONS

1. Describe how the ads portrayed the two competing brands of plastic storage bags.

2. What did the court find to be "literally false" about the ads?

3. Why were the second series of Goldfish ads enjoined as well?

4. How will consumers be misled by the ads?

5. What does Clorox want from the court that the appellate court says it is not entitled to have for its ad content?

Re: Better Business and Ads

The National Advertising Division of the Council of Better Business Bureaus has undertaken a role of private scrutiny of television ad content. Most particularly, the ad division is focusing on the infomercial, the 30-minute show-type formats for advertising products. There are approximately 600 new infomercials run each year, an amount that has doubled in the last four years. In 1997, the ad division examined 96 different infomercials for misleading claims. About 25 to 30 percent of the complaints on infomercial content come from local Better Business Bureaus, with the remaining 70–75 percent of the claims coming from competitors. Only five of those cases were referred to federal regulators, with the remaining cases resolved by discussions with the product manufacturer or ad sponsor.

The ad division has not taken any action against the psychic reader infomercials, because whether a reading "brings joy" to humans is difficult to define, let alone prove a breach of any type of express promise. Further, the ad division does not become involved in "puffery." An example cited by the division would be the claim by BMW that its cars are "the ultimate driving machine." Such a claim is not actionable.

One product the ad division has investigated is a 30-minute infomercial for the DeLonghi America Caffe Sienna espresso/cappuccino machine. The ad included this statement from the host/announcer:

> *Brew cappuccino just like the pros do right at home. Up until now, the home machines, they just didn't work.*

The ad division approached Jim McCrusker, the president of the U.S. unit of DeLonghi, on the grounds that the ad was misleading. The ad division, reacting to complaints from competitors, wanted McCrusker to add language that indicated it wasn't that other machines didn't work. The machines worked, but their frothing processes were not good.

Mr. McCrusker brought in other machines and consumers to talk with the ad division. The presentation of competitors' machines along with testimonials from consumers about the problems with other machines convinced the ad council that the statement "They didn't work" was indeed accurate for more than just the frothing process.

What lessons are learned from McCrusker's experience? Is documentation for ad claims important? Is it appropriate for competitors to complain to a regulatory body about ad content?

FTC Remedies

The FTC has a wide range of remedies available in the event of deceptive advertising. Corrective ads can be mandated. The FTC can also obtain injunctions to prevent the running of deceptive ads. Companies and endorsers can be required to reimburse purchasers misled by ads. As noted in the *Listerine* case, companies can be required to run corrective advertisements.

BUSINESS STRATEGY

Nestle and the Infant Formula and Product Marketing

Reprinted with permission from Marianne M. Jennings, *Case Studies in Business Ethics*, 4th ed., 2002.

While the merits and problems of breast-feeding versus using infant formula are debated in the United States and other developed countries, the issue is not so balanced in Third World nations. Studies have demonstrated the difficulties and risks of bottle-feeding babies in such places.

First, refrigeration is not generally available, so the formula, once it is mixed or opened (in the case of premixed types), cannot be stored properly. Second, the lack of purified water for mixing with the formula powder results in diarrhea or other diseases in formula-fed infants. Third, inadequate education and income, along with cultural differences, often lead to the dilution of formula and thus greatly reduced nutrition.

Medical studies also suggest that regardless of the mother's nourishment, sanitation, and income level, an infant can be adequately nourished through breast-feeding.

In spite of medical concerns about using their products in these countries, some infant formula manufacturers heavily promoted bottle-feeding.

These promotions, which went largely unchecked through 1970, included billboards, radio jingles, and posters of healthy, happy infants, as well as baby books and formula samples distributed through the health care systems of various countries.

Also, some firms used "milk nurses" as part of their promotions. Dressed in nurse uniforms, "milk nurses" were assigned to maternity wards by their companies and paid commissions to get new mothers to feed their babies formula. Mothers who did so soon discovered that lactation could not be achieved and the commitment to bottle-feeding was irreversible.

In the early 1970s, physicians working in nations where milk nurses were used began vocalizing their concerns. For example, Dr. Derrick Jelliffe, the then director of the Caribbean Food and Nutrition Institute, had the Protein-Calorie Advisory Group of the United Nations place infant formula promotion methods on its agenda for several of its meetings.

Journalist Mike Muller first brought the issue to public awareness with a series of articles in the *New Internationalist* in the 1970s. He also wrote a pamphlet on the promotion of infant formulas called "The Baby Killer," which was published by a British charity, War on Want. The same pamphlet was published in Switzerland, the headquarters of Nestlé, a major formula maker, under the title "Nestlé Kills Babies." Nestlé sued in 1975, which resulted in extensive media coverage.

In response to the bad publicity, manufacturers of infant formula representing about 75 percent of the market formed the International Council of Infant Food Industries to establish standards for infant formula marketing. The new code banned the milk nurse commissions and required the milk nurses to have identification that would eliminate confusion about their "nurse" status.

The code failed to curb advertising of formulas. In fact, distribution of samples increased. By 1977, groups in the United States began a boycott against formula makers over what Jelliffe called "comerciogenic malnutrition."

One U.S. group, Infant Formula Action Coalition (INFACT), worked with the staff of Senator Edward Kennedy of Massachusetts to have hearings on the issue by the Senate Subcommittee on Health and Human Resources, which Kennedy chaired. The hearings produced evidence that 40 percent of the worldwide market for infant formula, which totaled $1.5 billion at the time, was in Third World countries. No regulations resulted, but Congress did tie certain forms of foreign aid to the development by recipient countries of programs to encourage breast-feeding.

Boycotts against Nestlé products began in Switzerland in 1975 and in the United States in 1977. The boycotts and Senator Kennedy's involvement heightened media interest in the issue and led to the World Health Organization (WHO) debating the issue of infant formula marketing in 1979 and agreeing to draft a code to govern it.

After four drafts, and two presidential administrations (Carter and Reagan), the 118 member nations of WHO finally voted on a code for infant formula marketing. The United States was the only nation to vote against it; the Reagan administration opposed the code being mandatory. In the end, WHO made the code a recommendation only, but the United States still refused to support it.

The publicity on the vote fueled the boycott of Nestlé, which continued until the formula maker announced it would meet the WHO standards for infant formula marketing. Nestlé created the Nestlé Infant Formula Audit Commission (NIFAC) to

(continued)

demonstrate its commitment to and ensure its implementation of the WHO code.

In 1988, Nestlé introduced a new infant formula, Good Start, through its subsidiary, Carnation. The industry leader, Abbott Laboratories, which held 54 percent of the market with its Similac brand, revealed Carnation's affiliation: "They are Nestlé," said Robert A. Schoellhorn, Abbott's chairman and CEO. Schoellhorn also disclosed that Nestlé was the owner of Beech-Nut Nutrition Corporation, officers of which had been indicted and convicted (following one reversal) for selling adulterated apple juice for babies.

Carnation advertised Good Start in magazines and on television. The American Academy of Pediatrics (AAP) objected to this direct advertising, and grocers feared boycotts.

The letters "H.A." came after the name"Good Start," indicating the formula was hypoallergenic. Touted as a medical breakthrough by Carnation, the formula was made from whey and advertised as ideal for babies who were colicky or could not tolerate milk-based formulas.

Within four months of Good Start's introduction in November 1988, the FDA was investigating the formula because of six reported cases of vomiting due to the formula. Carnation then agreed not to label the formula hypoallergenic and to include a warning that milk-allergic babies should be given Good Start only with a doctor's approval and supervision.

In 1990, with its infant formula market share at 2.8 percent, Carnation's president, Timm F. Crull, called on the AAP to "examine all marketing practices that might hinder breast-feeding." Crull specifically cited manufacturers' practices of giving hospitals education and research grants, as well as free bottles, in exchange for having exclusive rights to supply the hospital with formula and to give free samples to mothers. He also called for scrutiny of the practice of paying pediatricians' expenses to attend conferences on infant formulas.

The AAP looked into prohibiting direct marketing of formula to mothers and physicians' accepting cash awards from formula manufacturers for research.

The distribution of samples in Third World countries continued during this time. Studies by the United Nations Children's Fund found that a million infants were dying every year because they were not breast-fed adequately. In many cases, the infant starved because the mother used free formula samples and could not buy more, while her own milk dried up. In 1991, the International Association of Infant Food Manufacturers had agreed to stop distributing infant formula samples by the end of 1992.

In the United States in 1980, the surgeon general established a goal that the nation's breast-feeding rate be 75 percent by 1990. The rate remains below 60 percent, however, despite overwhelming evidence that breast milk reduces susceptibility to illness, especially ear infections and gastrointestinal illnesses. The AAP took a strong position that infant formula makers should not advertise to the public, but as a result, new entrants into the market (such as Nestlé with its Carnation Good Start) were disadvantaged because long-time formula makers Abbott and Mead Johnson were well established through physicians. In 1993, Nestlé filed an antitrust suit alleging a conspiracy among AAP, Abbott, and Mead Johnson.

Some 200 U.S. hospitals have voluntarily stopped distributing discharge packs from formula makers to their maternity patients because they felt it "important not to appear to be endorsing any products or acting as commercial agents." A study at Boston City Hospital showed that mothers who receive discharge packs are less likely to continue nursing, if they nurse at all. UNICEF and WHO offer "Baby Friendly" certification to maternity wards that take steps to eliminate discharge packs and formula samples.

Discussion Questions

1. If you had been an executive with Nestlé, would you have changed your marketing approach after the boycotts began? Didn't the first mover approach make sense?

2. Did Nestlé suffer long-term damage because of its Third World marketing techniques?

3. How could a marketing plan address the concerns of the AAP and WHO?

4. Is anyone in the infant formula companies morally responsible for the deaths of infants described in the United Nations study?

5. Is the moratorium on distributing free formula samples voluntary? Would your company comply?

6. If you were a hospital administrator, what policy would you adopt on discharge packs?

7. Should formula makers advertise directly to the public? What if their ads read, "Remember, breast is best"?

Sources

"Breast Milk for the World's Babies." *New York Times*, 12 March 1992, A18.

Burton, Thomas B. "Methods of Marketing Infant Formula Land Abbott in Hot Water." *Wall Street Journal*, 25 May 1993, A1, A6.

Freedman, Alix M. "Nestlé's Bid to Crash Baby-Formula Market in the U.S. Stirs a Row." *Wall Street Journal*, 6 February 1989, A1, A10.

Garland, Susan B. "Are Formula Makers Putting the Squeeze on the States?" *Business Week*, 18 June 1990, 31.

Gerlin, Andrea. "Hospitals Wean from Formula Makers' Freebies." *Wall Street Journal*, 29 December 1994, B1.

Meier, Barry. "Battle over the Market for Baby Formula." *New York Times*, 15 June 1993, C1, C15.

"Nestlé Unit Sues Baby Formula Firms, Alleging Conspiracy with Pediatricians." *Wall Street Journal*, 1 June 1993, B4.

Post, James E. "Assessing the Nestlé Boycott: Corporate Accountability and Human Rights." *California Management Review* 27 (1985): 113–31.

Star, Marlene G. "Breast Is Best." *Vegetarian Times*, June 1991, 25–26.

One of the most frequently used FTC remedies is the consent decree. A **consent decree** is a negotiated settlement between the FTC and the advertiser. It is the equivalent of a no-contest plea. The FTC and the advertiser agree to remedies, and the case is disposed of through the decree without further action.

Ad Regulation by the FDA

Visit the Food and Drug Administration:
http://www.fda.gov

The Food and Drug Administration (FDA) also has authority over some forms of advertising. For example, the FDA has control over direct advertising to the public of prescription medications. Products such as Retin A have had direct ads and news releases subject to FDA regulation. For example, in the case of Retin A, the FDA warned Ortho, its manufacturer, that Retin A had been approved as an anti-acne cream, not as an anti-aging cream, and that it could not be advertised to the public as such.

Professional Ads

Most states have limitations on the types of ads professionals (such as doctors, lawyers, dentists, and accountants) can use in reaching the public. At one time, states had complete bans on ads by professionals. However, the U.S. Supreme Court held such bans to be too restrictive and violative of First Amendment protections on commercial speech. Restrictions may include requirements on fee disclosures or caveats on distinctions in individual cases and needs. The extent and validity of the restrictions continue to be refined through judicial application of First Amendment rights.

CONTRACT PRODUCT LIABILITY THEORIES: IMPLIED WARRANTIES

The UCC's Article II governs contracts for the sale of goods and includes several provisions for implied warranties. The requirements for each of the implied, in addition to coverage of express, warranties are discussed in the following sections.

The Implied Warranty of Merchantability

The **implied warranty of merchantability** (UCC § 2-314) is given in every sale of goods by a merchant seller. This warranty is a promise that the goods are fit for their ordinary purposes. The warranty is not given by all sellers, only by merchant sellers. Briefly defined, merchants are those sellers who are engaged in the business of selling the good(s) that are the subject of the contract. The warranty means the goods are of fair or average quality and are fit for ordinary purposes. Under this warranty, basketballs must bounce, book bindings must hold together, and food items must be free of foreign objects.

For example, in *Metty v. Shurfine Central Corp.*, 736 S.W.2d 527 (Mo. 1987), the court found that a breach of the implied warranty of merchantability occurred because part of a grasshopper in a can of green beans was eaten by a pregnant woman who purchased the beans. Shurfine was liable to the woman for resulting complications in her pregnancy. But what happens if there is something natural, such as a cherry pit in a cherry pie, that harms someone? Is there still a breach of warranty? The following case provides an answer to these questions.

CASE 11.4

Mitchell v. *T.G.I. Friday's*
748 N.E.2d 89 (Ohio App. 2000)

Clamming Up Because of Shell-Shock

FACTS

On April 11, 1996, Sandra Mitchell (appellant) was having dinner at Friday's restaurant (here-inafter "Friday's" or appellee). Ms. Mitchell was eating a fried clam strip when she bit into a hard substance that she believed to be a piece of a clam shell. She experienced immediate pain and later sought dental treatment. Some time later, the crown of a tooth came loose. It was determined that the crown could not be reattached and the remaining root of the tooth was extracted.

Ms. Mitchell filed a product liability action against Friday's, which served the meal, and Pro Source Distributing (hereinafter "Pro Source" or appellee), the supplier of the fried clams. Both Friday's and Pro Source filed motions for summary judgment, which the trial court granted without explanation.

Ms. Mitchell appealed.

JUDICIAL OPINION

WAITE, Judge

Appellant argues that in light of Ohio's product lia-bility legislation, the trial court should have applied the "reasonable-expectation test" to her claim and in doing so the court should not have granted appellees' motions for summary judgment. R.C. 2307.74 provides that "[a] product is defective [if] * * * [i]t deviated in a material way from the design specifications, formula, or performance standards of

the manufacturer * * *." R.C. 2307.75(A)(2) pro-vides that a product is defective in design or formulation if "[i]t is more dangerous than an ordinary consumer would expect when used in an intended or reasonably foreseeable man-ner." According to appellant, by the enactment of these statutes the "reasonable-expectation" test supersedes the traditional "foreign-natural test" applied in cases where injury is caused by substances in food. Appellant asserts that there is a reasonable expectation that clams are completely cleaned of their shells and free of foreign materials.

Before addressing the merits of this argument, we begin by noting that the trial court's journal entries granting summary judgment to appellees failed to delineate any basis for the decisions. Such practice has become common in courts subject to our review. While on review, we must and do conduct a meticulous *de novo* review on appeal, a trial court that gives careful consideration to a motion for sum-mary judgment along with a concise explanation of its decision will benefit the whole of the judicial process. The trial court will not only serve the parties by providing the basis for more expeditious appeals, but may encourage the termination of claims by use of conspicuous and irrefutable logic. The interests of justice are only well served if the parties are informed as to the basis for decisions that affect them.

In the present case, Friday's set forth in its motion for summary judgment appellant's deposition testimony to the effect that while eating a clam strip, she bit down on "a hard, foreign substance." Appellant stated that she assumed it was a piece of a clam shell. Appellant described the size of the object as about a quarter of the size of a small fingernail or about a quarter of an inch or smaller and irregular in shape. Moreover, Friday's attached an affidavit from its manager, Eric Hicks, who immediately responded to appellant's report of the incident. In that affidavit, Hicks confirmed that the object appellant presented to him was indeed a piece of clam shell and that it was approximately one-quarter inch in length and irregularly shaped. In its motion for summary judgment, Pro Source adopted and incorporated the statement of Friday's, appellant's deposition testimony, and the affidavit of Eric Hicks. In her response, appellant set forth no facts to dispute that the object in the clam strip was in fact a piece of clam shell.

Both Friday's and Pro Source presented essentially the same argument, that regardless of whether the foreign-natural test or reasonable-expectation test was applied, appellant has no claim against appellees.

The basis of appellant's argument for application of the reasonable-expectation test is found in R.C. 2307.75, which provides that a product is defective if it is more dangerous than an ordinary consumer would reasonably suspect. However, appellant has not set forth any case law or analysis that would suggest that food products fall under the purview of the statute. We can find no case that has analyzed a food item in that context. Indeed, the weight of product liability cases deal with synthetic products, for example, a cargo door hinge, a glass bottle, or a prosthetic hip joint. Thus, we see no compelling reason to abandon any established test due to the enactment of Ohio's product liability legislation.

However, it does not appear necessary to determine which test applies to the present case. Save for reference to the product liability statute, a similar argument was addressed in *Mathews v. Maysville Seafoods, Inc.* (1991), 76 Ohio App.3d 624, 602 N.E.2d 764. In *Mathews,* the plaintiff suffered a bowel injury when he swallowed a fish bone while eating a fish fillet served by the defendant. The trial court granted the defendant's motion for summary judgment. On appeal, the defendant argued for the adoption of the reasonable-expectation test as opposed to the foreign-natural test.

The *Mathews* court set forth both tests. Under the foreign-natural test:

Bones which are natural to the type of meat served cannot legitimately be called a foreign substance, and a consumer who eats meat dishes ought to anticipate and be on his guard against the presence of such bones.
[Q]uoting *Mix v. Ingersoll Candy Co.* (1936), 6 Cal.2d 674, 682, 59 P.2d 144, 148.

The reasonable-expectation test states:
*The test should be what is "reasonably expected" by the consumer in the food as served, not what might be natural to the ingredients of that food prior to preparation. * * * As applied to the action for common-law negligence, the test is related to the foreseeability of harm on the part of the defendant. The defendant is not an insurer but has the duty of ordinary care to eliminate or remove in the preparation of the food he serves such harmful substances as the consumer of the food, as served, would not ordinarily anticipate and guard against.*
Mathews, 602 N.E.2d at 765.

The *Mathews* court looked to *Allen v. Grafton* (1960), 164 N.E.2d 167, where the plaintiff was injured after swallowing a piece of oyster shell contained in a serving of fried oysters. The Supreme Court held:
The presence in one of a serving of six fried oysters of a piece of oyster shell approximately 3×2 centimeters (about 1 1/5 inches by 4/5 of an inch) in diameter will not justify a legal conclusion either (a) that that serving of fried oysters constituted "food" that was "adulterated" within the meaning of Section 3715.59, Revised Code, or (b) that that serving constituted food not "reasonably fit for" eating.

The *Mathews* court further noted:
*In the instant case, it is not necessary to hold * * * that, because an oyster shell is natural to an oyster and thus not a substance "foreign" to an oyster, no liability can be predicated upon the sale of a fried oyster containing a piece of oyster shell. However, the fact, that something that is served with food and that will cause harm if eaten is natural to that food and so not a "foreign substance," will usually be an important factor in determining whether a consumer can reasonably anticipate and guard against it. * * ***

In our opinion, the possible presence of a piece of oyster shell in or attached to an oyster is so well known to anyone who eats oysters that we can say as a matter of law that one who eats oysters can reasonably anticipate and guard against eating such a piece of shell, especially where it is as big a piece as the one described in plaintiff's petition.

Most courts which have relied on *Allen* conclude that the Ohio Supreme Court has adopted the foreign-natural test. However, other courts have found that *Allen* endorses the reasonable-expectation test.

(continued)

Despite the opposing interpretations of *Allen*, the *Mathews* court stated that " * * * it is not necessary to decide whether the 'reasonable expectation' test or the 'foreign-natural' test holds sway in Ohio * * *." The court stated that it must be reasonably expected that even a fish fillet may contain fish bones. Id., citing *Polite* v. *Carey Hilliards Restaurants, Inc.* (1985). The *Mathews* court noted that in *Polite*, the court applied the foreign-natural test in affirming a summary judgment for the defendant where the plaintiff swallowed an obviously naturally occurring one-inch fish bone concealed in a fish fillet.

*An occasional piece of clam shell in a bowl of clam chowder is so well known to a consumer * * * that we can say the consumer can reasonably anticipate and guard against it.*

Courts cannot and must not ignore the common experience of life and allow rules to develop that would make sellers of food or other consumer goods insurers of the products they sell.

In the present case, it cannot be disputed that the piece of clam shell that caused appellant's injury was natural to the clam strip she consumed. Turning to the question of whether appellant should have reasonably anticipated the presence of the clam shell, we are reminded of the Ohio Supreme Court's holding in *Allen*, supra, that "the possible presence of a piece of oyster shell in or attached to an oyster is so

well known to anyone who eats oysters that we can say as a matter of law that one who eats oysters can reasonably anticipate and guard against eating such a piece of shell * * *." The facts of the present case are virtually indistinguishable from *Allen* except for the type of injury and that, here, appellant was eating fried clams rather than fried oysters. We therefore hold that, as a matter of law, one who eats clams can reasonably anticipate and guard against eating a piece of shell.

As appellant's claim fails under both tests, we overrule her assignment of error and affirm the judgment of the trial court.

Judgment affirmed.

CASE QUESTIONS

1. What did Ms. Mitchell eat, and what were her resulting injuries?

2. What did the lower court do in the case that caused an admonition from the appellate court?

3. What test does Ohio follow—the foreign-natural or the reasonable-expectation test?

4. Does the court feel which test Ohio applies makes a difference in this case?

5. Is the reasonable-expectation test one that makes the food producer or provider an insurer?

CONSIDER...

11.3 Jack A. Clark ordered a chicken enchilada at Mexicali Rose restaurant (defendants). Because of a one-inch-long chicken bone in the enchilada, Mr. Clark choked and received throat injuries. He brought suit for breach of implied warranty, negligence, and strict liability. Should he recover? [*Mexicali Rose* v. *Superior Court*, 822 P.2d 1292 (Cal. 1992)]

CONSIDER...

11.4 On 11 November 1994, Loretta Jones was injured when she bit into a meatball at an Olive Garden Restaurant owned by GMRI, Inc. in Pineville, North Carolina. Ms. Jones attempted to take her first bite of the meatball, she bit down into an unidentified metal object. At that time, she experienced an "incredible stabbing pain in [her] tooth and [her] jaw," caused by a broken tooth. Because she was startled, she "sucked in and immediately sucked down the food" and the object. Ms. Jones said that she cut the meatball into eight pieces prior to taking the bite, and that she did not detect any foreign object in the meatball at that time.

She filed suit against GMRI, Inc., and Rich Products Corporation, which allegedly supplied or manufactured the meatball, asserting claims of negligence, breach of implied warranty, and loss of consortium. GMRI asserted as a defense to the implied warranty claim that it did not have a reasonable opportunity to inspect the meatball in a way that would have discovered the defect.

GMRI said that most of the restaurant's meatballs come into the store frozen and in sealed bags. The restaurant does a visual inspection of the sealed bags of meatballs, and sends back those that do not meet the inspection. The meatballs are put into the freezer at the restaurant until needed, then put into a plastic holding container and placed in a refrigerator. The meatballs, which are slightly larger than a golf ball, are then mixed with a tomato sauce, heated, and served whole. Restaurant personnel indicated that they do not poke or slice the meatballs, other than to check the temperature with a probe.

Is GMRI liable to Ms. Jones? [*Jones* v. *GMRI, Inc.*, 2001 WL 747812 (N.C.App. 2001)]

CONSIDER...

11.5   Ms. Hubbs, 80, suffered from arthritis and osteoporosis. She purchased "The Clapper," a device designed to turn electrical appliances on by responding to sound, namely, the clapping of hands.

Ms. Hubbs did not follow the instructions in the product to adjust its sensitivity. As a result of continual hard clapping, Ms. Hubbs broke her wrists. Ms. Hubbs also did not follow the product instructions to use (buy) a clicker available for the product if clapping is a chore. She has sued the Clapper's manufacturer for breach of the warranty of merchantability. Should she recover? [*Hubbs* v. *Joseph Enterprises*, 604 N.Y.S.2d 292 (1993)]

CONSIDER...

11.6   Wendi James was already eating her taco when she noticed that there was a bloody thumbprint on the flour tortilla shell. She and her brother, who had just obtained their food from a Taco Bell drive-through restaurant, then examined all of their food purchases and discovered that they were spattered with blood. Wendi became ill.

Wendi and her brother, James, then called the Taco Bell restaurant requesting an explanation. A cook there told them that he had cut his finger and had not realized it. He then volunteered that he had recently been tested for the HIV virus and that the test had come back negative. Wendi asked why he had been tested for the virus, and the cook refused to provide an explanation.

Wendi and James have filed suit against Taco Bell. What bases could they allege for liability?

The Implied Warranty of Fitness for a Particular Purpose

The **implied warranty of fitness for a particular purpose** (UCC § 2-315) arises when the seller promises a buyer that the goods will be suitable for a use the buyer has proposed. For example, the owner of a nursery makes an implied warranty for a particular purpose when telling a buyer that a weed killer will work in the buyer's rose garden without harming the roses. An exercise enthusiast is given this warranty when the seller recommends a particular shoe as appropriate for aerobics.

The requirements for this warranty are as follows:

1. The seller has skill or judgment in use of the goods.
2. The buyer is relying on that skill or judgment.
3. The seller knew or had reason to know of the buyer's reliance.
4. The seller makes a recommendation for the buyer's use and purpose.

C O N S I D E R . . .

11.7   Cynthia Rubin went to Marshall Field's department store (one of two defendants) on April 5, 1986. While browsing, she got into a conversation with Julianna Reiner, a sales clerk, and she told Ms. Reiner that she used Vaseline to remove her eye makeup. Ms. Reiner said Vaseline could clog her eye ducts and cause cataracts or other permanent eye damage, and recommended Princess Marcella Borghese Instant Eye Make-Up Remover manufactured by Princess Marcella Borghese, Inc., the other defendant. Ms. Rubin asked if the product was safe. Ms. Reiner showed her the box, which said, "Recommended for all skin types." Ms. Reiner said, "If it wouldn't be safe for you, it wouldn't say this on the box." Relying on Ms. Reiner's representations, Ms. Rubin purchased the product.

That night she used the product to remove her eye makeup. Her eyelids and the skin around her eyes turned red, became taut and rough, and started to sting. She washed her skin repeatedly and kept a cold washrag on her eyes all night. Two days later, when the burning did not subside, she called an ophthalmologist and went to see him the next day. He told her that she had contact dermatitis and prescribed an ointment.

A few weeks later, because the burning and roughness of her eyelids persisted, Ms. Rubin decided to see Dr. Katherine Wier, a dermatologist. Dr. Wier prescribed a similar ointment and told Ms. Rubin that the chemical causing the burning would remain in her system for three or four months. The stinging subsided, but Ms. Rubin could not wear eye makeup again regularly until summer of 1987. When she tried to wear makeup again before that, her eyelids turned bright red and began swelling upon removal of the makeup.

Ms. Rubin filed suit for breach of implied warranty of fitness for a particular purpose. Should she recover? [*Rubin* v. *Marshall Field & Co.* 597 N.E.2d 688 (Ill. 1992)]

Eliminating Warranty Liability by Disclaimers

Warranties can be eliminated by the use of **disclaimers.** The proper method for disclaiming a warranty depends on the type of warranty. Express warranties, however, cannot be given and then taken back. Basically, an express warranty cannot be disclaimed.

The implied warranty of merchantability and the implied warranty of fitness for a particular purpose can be disclaimed by using a phrase such as "WITH ALL FAULTS," or "AS IS." Either warranty alone can be disclaimed by using the name of the warranty: "There is no warranty of merchantability given" or "There is no implied warranty of fitness for a particular purpose."

Even though the UCC is clear on the language to be used for warranty disclaimers and the process seems to be easy, even the warranty disclaimers are subject to the general UCC constraint of good faith. Unconscionable disclaimers of warranties or waiver of warranties when one party has no bargaining power may not be valid. For example, a disclaimer of liability for personal injury resulting from a breach of the warranty of merchantability for a consumer good would be unconscionable. "Consider 11.8" deals with a warranty disclaimer and whether it is valid.

C O N S I D E R . . .

11.8 Nunes Turfgrass, Inc., was the largest independent sod grower in California. Based in Modesto with outlets in seven other California cities, it had been in business since 1962. Vaughan-Jacklin Seed Company was a corporate grower, developer, and commercial retailer of grass seed and was based in Post Falls, Idaho. At the time of the dispute, Vaughan-Jacklin had been in business for fifty years and was one of the largest seed companies in the world.

Nunes sold its sod fields and seed mixes under the Nunes name to landscapers, golf courses, and the general public. In 1980, Nunes began to notice that its customers wanted a hardier, more drought-resistant type of grass (bluegrass-perennial ryegrass blend). Nunes contacted Doyle Jacklin, the sales and marketing manager for Vaughan-Jacklin, and discussed its needs. Mr. Jacklin researched the needs and recommended to Nunes the Jackpot perennial ryegrass. Nunes relied on the recommendation and ordered 8,000 pounds of Jackpot in September 1981.

Before the seed was shipped, Vaughan-Jacklin sent a written confirmation of sale with this warranty and disclaimer:

JACKLIN SEED COMPANY, DIVISION OF VAUGHAN-JACKLIN CORPORATION, warrants that seed it sells conforms to the label description as required by State and Federal Seed Laws. IT MAKES NO OTHER WARRANTIES, EXPRESS OR IMPLIED, OF MERCHANTABILITY, FITNESS FOR PURPOSE, OR OTHERWISE, AND IN ANY EVENT ITS LIABILITY FOR BREACH OF ANY WARRANTY OR CONTRACT WITH RESPECT TO SUCH SEEDS IS LIMITED TO THE PURCHASE PRICE OF SUCH SEEDS. JACKLIN SEED COMPANY FURTHER LIMITS TO SUCH PURCHASE PRICE ITS LIABILITY OF ANY KIND ON ACCOUNT OF ANY NEGLIGENCE WHATSOEVER ON ITS PART WITH RESPECT TO SUCH SEEDS.

The seed bags had the same language, to which was added the following:

LIABILITY for damages for any cause, including breach of contract or breach of warranty, with respect to this sale of seeds IS LIMITED TO A REFUND OF THE PURCHASE PRICE OF THE SEEDS. THIS REMEDY IS EXCLUSIVE. IN NO EVENT SHALL THE LABELER BE LIABLE FOR ANY INCIDENTAL OR CONSEQUENTIAL DAMAGES, INCLUDING LOSS OF PROFIT.

In September and October 1981, Nunes overseeded fifty-six acres with the Jackpot seed. Within weeks of overseeding, large clumps of off-colored ryegrass appeared in the fields, rendering them unfit for sod production. The result was that Nunes could not make sod sales and was forced to liquidate its business in 1984.

Can Nunes recover for breach of warranty? [*Nunes Turfgrass, Inc.* v. *Vaughan-Jacklin Seed Co.*, 246 Cal. Rptr. 823 (1988)]

Privity Standards for UCC Recovery

If you have a contract to buy a car and the seller breaches the contract by refusing to deliver, you can bring suit for breach of contract. There is **privity** between you and the seller. The people in your car pool, however, could not sue the seller for breach if you no longer have a car to use (even though they are affected) because they have no privity of contract with the seller. Traditionally, a recovery for a breach of contract requires privity of contract. A breach of warranty is a breach of contract, and until the time of the UCC, privity was required to be able to recover on a breach of warranty theory.

Section 2-318 of the UCC establishes requirements for breach of warranty recovery. The section has three alternatives that states can adopt, each of which provides warranty protections for *more* than the buyer. For example, Alternative A covers the buyer and members of the buyer's household and guests. Alternative B covers any natural person who is reasonably expected to use the goods and suffers personal injury. Alternative C extends the warranty protection to any person who may be expected to use the goods and is injured. Alternative C also prohibits the disclaimer of liability for personal injury to those covered by the warranty.

Exhibit 11.2 summarizes the UCC warranty protections and disclaimers.

EXHIBIT 11.2   UCC Warranties: Creation, Restrictions, and Disclaimers

TYPE	CREATION	RESTRICTION	DISCLAIMER
Express	Affirmation of fact or promise of performance (samples, model, descriptions)	Must be part of the basis of the bargain	Cannot make a disclaimer inconsistent with an express warranty
Implied warranty of merchantability	Given in every sale of goods by a merchant ("fit for ordinary purposes")	Only given by merchants	(1) Must use "merchantability" or general disclaimer of "as is" or "with all faults" (2) if written must be conspicuous
Implied warranty of fitness for a particular purpose	Seller knows of buyer's reliance for a particular use (buyer is ignorant)	Seller must have knowledge; buyer must rely on that knowledge	Can disclaim with "as is" or "with all faults" or use of specific terms
Title	Given in every sale	Does not apply in circumstances where apparent warranty is not given	
Magnuson-Moss (Federal Consumer Product Warranty Law)	Applies to consumer products of $5 or more	Must label "Full" or "Limited" Applies to consumer products of $10 or more	

STRICT TORT LIABILITY: PRODUCT LIABILITY
UNDER SECTION 402A

Visit the American Law Institute:
http://www.ali.org

The first tort theory for recovery for defective products is **strict liability** in tort. This tort was created and defined by Section 402A of the *Restatement (Second) of Torts*. Restatements of the law are developed by the American Law Institute, an educational group of professors and practicing attorneys. Restatements are not the law, even though they are adopted and recognized in many states as the controlling statement of law in that state. The adoption of a restatement generally comes in the form of judicial acceptance of the doctrines provided.

Restatement § 402A:
-402A. Special Liability of Seller of Product for Physical Harm to User or Consumer

(1) One who sells any product in a defective condition unreasonably dangerous to the user or consumer or to his property is subject to liability for physical harm thereby caused to the ultimate user or consumer, or to his property if
  (a) the seller is engaged in the business of selling such a product, and
  (b) it is expected to and does reach the user or consumer without substantial change in the condition in which it is sold.
(2) The rule stated in Subsection (1) applies although
  (a) the seller has exercised all possible care in the preparation and sale of his product, and
  (b) the user or consumer has not bought the product from or entered into any contractual relations with the seller.

Section 402A has no privity requirements and is not subject to the disclaimers that can eliminate warranty liability. Negligence requires proof of some knowledge of a defect. Section 402A applies if a product is defective, regardless of whether knowledge of a defect existed.

The *Restatement (Third) of Product Liability* has been proposed and would clarify the definition of "defective" with regard to knowledge requirements and recovery.

Unreasonably Dangerous Defective Condition

This part of 402A requires that a product be in a condition of danger such that an ordinary person would not contemplate its use. Eggs are not unreasonably dangerous because of their effects on body cholesterol levels. However, eggs that contain a harmful disease or that were injected with a virus would be unreasonably dangerous.

A product can be unreasonably dangerous because it contains a foreign substance. Most product liability cases relating to food are based on this tenet. Rats in pop bottles, moldy bananas in cereal, parts of a snake in frozen vegetables, and stones in soup are all factual circumstances that have been recognized as 402A defective conditions.

Section 402A applies to defective conditions regardless of the precautions taken by the manufacturer. Manufacturers or food processors who take great precautions in their procedures could overcome a charge of negligence; however, strict liability focuses on the fact that a defect exists, not whether the manufacturer could or could not have prevented the problem. In other words, strict liability does not require a showing of a breach of duty; it only requires a showing of a defective product.

The most common types of product liability cases are based on the following:

1. Design defects
2. Dangers of use that were not warned about or dangers because unclear use instructions were given
3. Errors in manufacturing, handling, or packaging of the product

---

CASE 11.5

Greif v. *Anheuser-Busch Companies, Inc.*
114 F. Supp.2d 100 (D.Conn.2000)

Is Beer Inherently Dangerous?

FACTS

Mrs. Greif was stopped on a bicycle on the edge of Route 4 in Farmington, Connecticut, when a motor vehicle driven by Elmer Michaud crossed over the roadway and struck her, causing serious injuries to her. Michaud had consumed the Anheuser-Busch (defendants) "products" and was under their influence. Michaud was found guilty of assault in the second degree with a motor vehicle and served two years in prison. The Greifs filed a civil suit against him for damages but do not indicate the status of that suit. Mr. Michaud may be judgment proof or close to it.

The "products" in question are beer and beer-type beverages (e.g., light beer, malt liquor, and other alcoholic beverages). Mr. Michaud was driving while intoxicated and was charged with a violation of Connecticut General Statutes § 14-227.

Mr. and Mrs. Greif filed suit under Connecticut's Products Liability Act maintaining that the beer was defective because it contained alcohol which can lead to intoxication and thereby impair the consumer's ability to drive, and that the manufacturers have breached warranties made to consumers. The Greifs also allege that Anheuser-Busch failed to warn about the dangers of drinking their products and has made misrepresentations about them.

JUDICIAL OPINION

GOETTEL, District Judge.
The defendants move to dismiss the plaintiffs' action in Connecticut State Court and removed to the federal court by them on diversity grounds.

Beer has been brewed for tens of thousands of years, although the method of making beer in ancient times varied greatly from place to place. Beer is brewed by fermentation in which microscopic fungi known as yeast consume sugars in the grain, converting them to alcohol and carbon dioxide gas. Typically, a beer contains from two to six percent alcohol. There is now merchandised a nonalcoholic "beer," but whether it can be accurately called "beer" is another matter.

While beer is a relatively mild form of alcoholic beverage, the complaint alleges, and everyone knows, that anyone who consumes enough of any product containing alcohol will become, to some degree, inebriated. Indeed, the complaint alleges that the defendants should have known that some consumers like Mr. Michaud would drink to excess and that intoxication impairs motor skills including driving. According to paragraph 22 of the complaint, the defendants should reduce the intoxicating effects of the products by lowering or removing the alcohol content. In effect, the complaint alleges that the defendants produced a product that can and does have anti-social effects and should be banned or, at the least, the manufacturer should be responsible for all ultimate misuse of the product by consumers. This essentially is a call for the return of Prohibition, the "great experiment" which not only failed seventy years ago but, according to some, actually led to a substantial increase in the drinking of alcoholic beverages.

At first blush, the theories of the complaint are so bizarre that one is tempted not to treat them seriously. However, similar types of suits have been brought in recent years concerning other products with at least some degree of success. For example, suits against gun manufacturers brought by the estates of persons killed by criminals using legally manufactured guns (or brought by those who had supplied medical assistance to those injured in such events) are a recent phenomenon. See, e.g., *Hamilton v. Beretta U.S.A. Corp.*, Nos. 99-7753, 7785, 7787, 2000 WL 1160699 (2d Cir. August 16, 2000) (certifying certain questions to the New York Court of Appeals). Such cases, however, are based upon a claim that the manufacturers had a duty to exercise reasonable care in the marketing and distribution of the hand guns they manufactured. No such claim is made here since there is no claim that the defendants sold their product directly to Michaud, simply that they allegedly manufactured products ultimately consumed by him.

There is of course no way in which a product containing alcohol can be marketed so as to prevent the type of criminal conduct engaged in by Michaud in this case. Moreover, the Connecticut Products Liability Act, on which the plaintiffs rely, requires proof that the product is unreasonably dangerous, i.e., that it must be dangerous to an extent beyond that which would be contemplated by the ordinary consumer who purchases it, with the ordinary knowledge common to the community as to its characteristics.

That comment addresses and rejects the very design defect claim made in this case, stating "Good whiskey is not unreasonably dangerous merely because it will make some people drunk, and is especially dangerous to alcoholics. . . ." A beverage is not unreasonably dangerous because it contains alcohol, providing that its presence is disclosed. The Connecticut courts have consistently held that the potential risks of alcohol intoxication and drunk driving are matters of common knowledge. Consumers expect there to be alcohol in beer and should anticipate that, if they have more than one or two, they will experience a degree of intoxication. The product was not, therefore, defective.

Turning to the plaintiffs' failure to warn claim, it too mimics another new style of case. In recent tobacco litigations, plaintiffs have claimed that, while they were aware of the serious health risks involved in smoking (indeed, they could hardly deny it, since the Surgeon General's warnings have been on cigarette packages for many years), the manufacturers knew of dangerous aspects of their products beyond those commonly understood and therefore were responsible for the smokers' continued addiction. Such cases were not generally suc-

cessful until a recent huge Florida class action verdict which has now been removed to federal court. *Engle v. R. J. Reynolds Tobacco Co.*, No. 00-CV-2641 (removal on July 24, 2000 following July 14, 2000 jury verdict awarding $145 billion punitive damages in state court, No. 94-8273-CA-22 (Fla.Cir.Ct.)). Plaintiffs maintain that while there may have been a common understanding about the risks of consuming alcohol and driving, recent studies have indicated the dangers to be greater than had previously been understood and that therefore the existing case law should be ignored. Plaintiffs cite no new breakthrough in the study of alcoholic beverages which could produce such a change. Plaintiffs rely on *Burton v. R. J. Reynolds Tobacco Co.*, 884 F.Supp. 1515 (D.Kan.1995), but that case rests on the fact that the plaintiff began smoking some sixty years ago, so that, the Court held, the state of knowledge concerning smoking's dangers were not as well known. (Perhaps they were not, but even in the thirties, cigarettes were referred to as "coffin nails.")

Among other things, the plaintiffs claim the defendants failed to warn consumers and the general public that consumption level effects of products differ from person to person, so that an amount which may not cause inebriation in one consumer might do so to another. We doubt that there is any practical way of conveying such a warning in a meaningful way, but there is clearly no claim that any doubts in that regard were the proximate cause of Mr. Michaud's drunkenness.

Those who drink a substantial amount of alcohol within a relatively short period of time are given clear warning that to avoid possible criminal behavior they must refrain from driving. . . . Considering also today's heightened level of public awareness regarding the problem, we cannot believe that any person who drives after drinking would be unaware of the possibility that his blood-alcohol level might equal or exceed the statutory standard. . . .

As if the foregoing were not enough, pursuant to the Alcohol Beverage Labeling Act of 1988, 27 U.S.C. §§ 213 et seq., every bottle or can of beer brewed and sold in the United States contains a federally mandated warning that "consumption of alcohol beverages impairs your ability to drive a car . . . ." 27 U.S.C. § 215(a). That warning was required not because of newly discovered evidence of the effects of alcohol but rather as a "reminder" of such hazards. 27 U.S.C. § 213.

In the final analysis, the plaintiffs cannot prevail against the defendants, because the sole proximate cause of their injuries was the conduct of the

(continued)

drunken driver whose excessive use of alcoholic beverages intoxicated him but who nevertheless drove in a dangerous condition causing injury to the plaintiffs. While the dram shop laws under appropriate circumstances can create liability on the part of those who serve alcoholic beverages, a claim cannot be made against the manufacturer "for the reason that the subsequent injury has been held to have been proximately caused by the intervening act of the immoderate consumer whose voluntary and imprudent consumption of the beverage brings about

intoxication and the subsequent injury." Consequently we GRANT the motion to dismiss.

CASE QUESTIONS

1. What was the accident that led to this litigation?
2. What product is alleged to be defective?
3. Is beer defective because it makes people drunk?
4. Is beer defective because of a lack of warning?
5. Is beer inherently dangerous?

A cell-phone controversy continues on several fronts. There are the vehicle safety issues surrounding the use of cell phones while driving with some states and cities prohibiting their use while operating a vehicle. The other controversy is whether the cell phones cause cancer.

ETHICAL ISSUES 11.2

Some studies conclude that they do not, but the Wireless Technology Research program, a program funded by the cellular-phone industry, has concluded that there are enough questions about their safety that no one should assure users that the phones are absolutely safe.

The FDA's Center for Devices and Radiological Health has concluded that there are no adverse health effects from cell phones and that no additional

warnings are needed. Following a lawsuit filed by a cell-phone user in 1993 in which the allegation was made that the cell phone caused his cancer, the industry placed $27 million into a blind trust for research projects supported by the funding. The Wireless Technology Research program was one of the beneficiaries of the trust.

Review the findings on cell phone safety at http://www.medscape.com

If you were a cell-phone manufacturer, would you take any action? Would you provide warnings? What about those who drive with cell phones and cause accidents? Are cell-phone manufacturers liable to those who are injured by cell-phone-using drivers?

Design Defect

A product with a faulty design exposes its users to unnecessary risks, and products must be designed with all foreseeable uses in mind. Thus, cars must be designed in view of the probability of accidents. A design that creates an otherwise unnecessary explosion upon a rear-end collision is a faulty design.

To make the best possible case in the event of a product liability suit, it is helpful for the manufacturer to have complied with all federal and state regulations on the product. It is also helpful if the manufacturer has used the latest technology and designs available within the industry and has met industry standards in designing its product.

Proper Warnings and Instructions

Manufacturers have a duty to warn buyers when there is a foreseeably dangerous use of a product that buyers are not likely to realize is dangerous. They also have a duty to supplement the warnings. For example, as defects are discovered in autos, the manufacturers send recall notices to buyers. Similarly, manufacturers of airplanes have sent warnings on problems and proper repair procedures to airlines throughout the life of a particular plane design's use.

Manufacturers must also give adequate instructions to buyers on the proper use of the product. Over-the-counter drugs carry instructions about proper dosages and the limitations on dosages.

The quotes in the chapter opening give an indication of the levels of warnings required on products.

Manufacturing, Handling, or Packaging Errors

This breach of duty is the most difficult form of negligence to prove. There are usually so many handlers in the process of manufacturing and packaging a product that it becomes difficult to prove when and how the manufacturer was negligent. One of the issues in drug manufacturing cases is whether the packaging for the materials is sufficient. Does it protect against tampering? Is it childproof? These types of dangers are foreseeable and require special duties with regard to packaging drugs.

C O N S I D E R . . .

11.9   Classify the following as design, manufacture, or warning defects:

- Failure to disclose changes in fuel and operations for a helicopter in hot weather and higher altitudes
- A polio vaccine that produces not immunity, but polio in a child
- Teflon-induced autoimmune system disease caused by Teflon used in the manufacture of an implanted TMJ jaw device
- Diamond represented as a grade V.V.S. that is actually a lower grade
- Infant swing that causes infants to fall out backward if they fall asleep and their weight shifts
- Tobacco that causes lung cancer
- Fondue pot tipping over and burning 2-year-old child
- Bleeding of pizza-box ink onto pizza

Reaching the Buyer in the Same Condition

The requirement that a product reach the buyer without "substantial change" is a protection for the seller. A seller will not be liable for a product that has been modified or changed. The reason for this requirement is that once a product is modified or changed, it becomes unclear whether the original product or the modifications caused the unreasonably dangerous condition. Volkswagen would not be held liable for a dune buggy accident just because the builder and owner of the dune buggy happened to use a Volkswagen engine in building the vehicle. Because Volkswagen's product has been taken apart and modified, its liability has ended. One issue that arises in airplane crash cases is whether the air carrier followed the manufacturer's repair procedures. The failure to follow these procedures could eliminate the manufacturer's liability because the aircraft may have been altered.

The Requirement of a Seller Engaged in a Business

Section 402A requires the seller to be "engaged in the business of selling the product." This requirement sounds like the merchant requirement for the UCC warranty of merchantability. However, the meaning of "selling the product" is slightly broader under 402A than the UCC meaning of merchant. For example, a baseball club is not a merchant of beer, but, if the club sells beer at its games, it is a seller for purposes of 402A. Section 402A covers manufacturers, wholesalers, retailers, food sellers, and even those who sell products out of their homes.

In recent years, some courts have allowed recovery from groups of sellers. For example, in the controversy over diethylstilbestrol (DES, a drug taken by pregnant women), the plaintiffs could show that their harms resulted from DES but could not show exactly who manufactured the drug their mothers took. The courts permitted recovery against the group of manufacturers of DES during that time period [*Sindell* v. *Abbott Lab.*, 607 P.2d 924 (Cal. 1980)].

NEGLIGENCE: A SECOND TORT FOR PRODUCT LIABILITY

A suit for product defects can also be based in negligence. The elements for establishing a negligence case are the same as those for a Section 402A case with one addition: establishing that the product seller or manufacturer either knew of the defect before the product was sold or allowed sales to continue with the knowledge that the product had a defect. Establishing this knowledge is difficult in an evidentiary sense in court, but a plaintiff in a product liability suit who shows that the defendant-seller knew of the problem and sold or continued to sell the product will be able to collect punitive damages in addition to damages for personal injury and property damage. Establishing knowledge in a product liability case usually produces a multimillion-dollar verdict because punitive damages are awarded in addition to compensatory ones.

Examples of cases in which establishing knowledge has been an issue include the Ford Pinto exploding gas tank cases (in which the plaintiffs used internal memos from engineers) and the Dow Corning breast implant suits (in which an engineer, Thomas Talcott, who worked for Dow Corning in 1976, testified for the plaintiffs regarding his feelings during the product's development that leakage was possible).

Comparisons of the various product liability theories are found in Exhibit 11.3 and Exhibit 11.4.

CONSIDER...

11.10   Firestone ATX, ATX II, and Wilderness tires have come under fire in the media because of complaints about the failure of those tires being linked to so many accidents. In May, following a report by a Houston television station on a correlation between the tires and accidents in that area, the National Highway Traffic Safety Administration (NHTSA) received a flurry of complaints about the tires.

The treads on the tires, about 48 million of them, found on many trucks and SUVs and used mostly on Ford Explorers, seem to suddenly separate, although no one yet understands why. One theory is heat and poor tire maintenance. A former Firestone tire engineer, however, theorizes that these particular tires lack nylon caps between their steel belts and the rubber to keep the belts from sawing through the tread. Such caps are common in other tires and cost about $1.00.

EXHIBIT 11.3 **Comparison of Product Liability Theories**

TYPE	PRIVITY REQUIRED?	KNOWLEDGE OF PROBLEM REQUIRED?	WARRANTY PROMISE REQUIRED?
Negligence	No	Yes	No
Section 402A/ strict tort liability	No	No	No
Express warranty	Yes	No	Yes
Implied warranty of merchantability	Yes	No	No
Implied warranty of fitness for a particular purpose	Yes	No	Yes

EXHIBIT 11.4 **Legal Basis for Product Liability**

CONTRACT	TORT
Express warranty	402A—Strict Tort Liability
Implied warranty of merchantability	Elements
Implied warranty of fitness for particular purpose	(1) Defective condition unreasonably dangerous: design; manufacturing defect; or inadequate warning
	(2) Defendant in business of using, selling, or manufacturing product
	(3) Condition of product is the same
	Negligence
	Same; and add (4) Knowledge of defect

Currently, 100 lawsuits are pending around the country that involve accidents resulting from the tires separating. Records for the agency reveal that it has 4 deaths documented as well as 193 accidents from the tires. Reports of tread failure have been documented at speeds of 20 mph, and the vehicle appearing most often in the reported crashes is the Ford Explorer. Many of the tire failures have occurred in vehicles with less than 2,000 odometer miles.

The NHTSA has known of the Firestone tire issues for at least ten years. At least six other nations have issued product recall notices on the tires. Ford has replaced tires in Venezuela, Ecuador, Thailand, Malaysia, Colombia, and Saudi Arabia. Ford referred to the replacements in those nations as a "customer satisfaction issue."

What theories of liability could the plaintiffs in the litigation use? Against whom would they be bringing their suits? Is Firestone liable to the drivers? Does prior knowledge of the tire issue and no action present additional problems for defending against the suits?[2]

Bridgestone/Firestone, Inc., issued a recall of its defective tires for a recall totaling 6.5 million tires, the largest ever in the United States. However, the company simply does not have the inventory to replace the tires at one time and many drivers and car owners will have to wait. The company plans to up production to 500,000 per month, but even that rate will take one year. The company has provided dealers with a list of ten acceptable substitutes for the tires, including tires from other manufacturers for which there will be reimbursement.

Does the company have any liability during the waiting period? What if customers wanted substitute transportation during the time they were waiting for tire replacements?

Most of the tires were on Ford Explorers, and Ford has distanced itself from the recall saying it did not know until the time of the recall of the tire problems and that it wants the recall accelerated. Why is Ford concerned?[3]

PRIVITY ISSUES IN TORT THEORIES OF PRODUCT LIABILITY

Privity is not the standard for recovery in negligence actions. The standard for recovery in negligence actions is whether the injury that resulted was foreseeable and foreseeable to that particular party. For example, a manufacturer of toasters can foresee use by children of the equipment and would have a duty to warn that they should not use it unless supervised by adults. A manufacturer of a weed killer could foresee the presence of dogs, cats, and other pets in a yard sprayed with the killer and should either make the product not harmful to them or warn of the need to keep them away from the sprayed area for a certain period of time. Children and pets certainly have no privity with the manufacturers, but they can recover from the manufacturer (or their parents and owners can) on the basis of the foreseeability of the pets' presence and the foreseeability of the danger causing their injuries.

Likewise, parties other than the product manufacturer may be responsible for defective conditions in the products and can be held liable for their participation. For example, parts manufacturers may be held liable if it can be shown that defects in their parts resulted in a product's defect and the injury to the plaintiff.

C O N S I D E R . . .

11.11   John Evraets underwent eye surgery in September 1983 at a hospital in Long Beach, California. He had a cataract removed and an artificial lens implanted. The lens was manufactured, designed, tested, distributed, and sold by Intermedics Intraocular, Inc., and Pharmacia Opthalmics, Inc.

After the operation, Mr. Evraets suffered pain; irritation; decreased vision; light sensitivity; deterioration of his eye structures, including macular, retinal, and corneal damage; edema; and a detached retina and vitreous humor. He was ultimately obliged to undergo another surgery to replace the lens. In addition to his physical suffering, Mr. Evraets experienced emotional distress, shock, and fright.

In August 1991, Mr. Evraets read a published article in which he learned that defects in Intermedic's and Opthalmic's lenses were the source of his injuries. Could Mr. Evraets recover from these companies? On what basis? [*Evraets v. Intermedics Intraocular, Inc.*, 34 Cal. Rptr. 2d 852 (1994)]

DEFENSES TO PRODUCT LIABILITY TORTS

Three defenses are available to a defendant in a product liability tort:

1. Misuse or abnormal use of a product
2. Contributory negligence
3. Assumption of risk

Misuse or Abnormal Use of a Product

Any use of a product that the manufacturer has specifically warned against in its instructions is a **misuse.** Using a forklift to lift 25,000 pounds when the instructions limit its capacity to 15,000 pounds is a misuse of the product, and any injuries resulting from such misuse will not be the liability of the manufacturer. Product misuse also occurs when a plaintiff has used the product in a manner that the defendant could not anticipate and warn against.

Contributory Negligence

Contributory negligence is traditionally a complete defense to a product liability suit in negligence. For example, although a front loader might have a design failure of no protective netting around the driver, a driver who is injured while using the front loader for recreational purposes is contributorily negligent. Contributory negligence overlaps greatly with product misuse.

Some states, as discussed previously, have adopted a standard of **comparative negligence,** under which the plaintiff's negligence is not a complete defense: The negligence of the plaintiff merely serves to reduce the amount the plaintiff is entitled to recover. For example, a jury might find that the defendant is 60 percent at fault and the plaintiff is 40 percent at fault. The plaintiff recovers, but the amount of that recovery is reduced by 40 percent.

Assumption of Risk

When a plaintiff is aware of a danger in the product but goes ahead and uses it anyway, **assumption of risk** occurs. If a car manufacturer recalled your car for repair and you failed to have the repair done, despite full opportunity to do so, you have assumed the risk of driving with that problem.

The *Binakonsky* case involves issues of assumption of risk in a product liability suit.

PRODUCT LIABILITY REFORM

Visit FMC Corporation:
http://www.fmc.com

"Our product liability system discourages innovation because of unforeseeable potential liability," says Robert Malcott, CEO of FMC Corporation. Mr. Malcott issued this statement as the chair of the Business Roundtable's task force on product liability. This task force and others have proposed several changes, including limiting punitive damages; meeting government standards as a defense; instituting liability shields for drugs, medical devices, and aircraft; and requiring higher standards of proof for recovery of punitive damages.

In each session since 1977, a bill on product liability reform has been introduced in Congress. However, such a bill faces significant opposition from consumer groups and trial lawyers. As trade barriers fall, the ability of the United

CASE 11.6

Binakonsky v. *Ford Motor Co.*
133 F.3d 281 (4th Cir. 1998)

The Sliding Gas Tank Hits a Brick Wall

FACTS

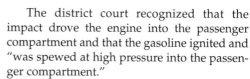

In February 1988, David Binakonsky purchased a 1988 E-150 Ford Econoline van equipped with a 5.8 liter fuel-injected engine. Like most full-size vans, the Ford E-150 contained a shortened engine compartment, which was located between the driver and passenger seats. The engine was encased in an insulated, fiberglass cover, often called a "doghouse."

The fuel system of the van consists of fuel lines and plastic "snap-together" fuel line connectors. The plastic fuel lines carried fuel from two 20-gallon fuel tanks through a high-pressure electronic fuel pump and up to the fuel injection rail at the rear of the engine. The van also had a cut-off switch to stop the flow of fuel to the engine in the event of an accident.

On August 20, 1992, Binakonsky drove his van off the road into a large tree. Upon impact, the engine was pushed into the passenger compartment. Gasoline ignited an intense fire and Binakonsky, unable to escape, was killed. Accident reconstruction experts put the speed of the vehicle at between 40 and 47 mph at the time of the crash (the speed limit was 30 mph in the area). A postmortem examination of Binakonsky revealed a blood-alcohol content of between .14 percent and .16 percent and that he died as a result of the fire (thermal injury to the larynx and fourth degree burns over 100 percent of his body as well as carbon monoxide level of 8 percent). Binakonsky was an alcoholic with a long history of serious traffic violations. At the time of the accident, he did not have a valid license.

Binakonsky's widow, Charlotte, and his four children brought suit against Ford Motor Company on the basis of the crashworthiness doctrine—that the van was defectively designed because it caused or aggravated injuries in an accident. The lower court held that the design of the van was reasonable and granted summary judgment for Ford. Charlotte and the children appealed.

JUDICIAL OPINION

BUTZNER, Senior Circuit Judge
The plaintiffs contend that the fuel delivery system was defectively designed. The defendant contends that the system was safe.

The district court recognized that the impact drove the engine into the passenger compartment and that the gasoline ignited and "was spewed at high pressure into the passenger compartment."

The district court also believed that the fuel cut-off switch "could hardly have been expected to operate properly in a collision of this magnitude."

Though the inertia switch may have operated, the plaintiffs, through the use of Ford documents and by cross-examination of Ford's designated corporate representative, established that gasoline siphoned from the gas tanks into the engine and passenger compartments when the fuel line ruptured.

This is not the first time Ford has addressed the Econoline fuel system. A Ford employee in 1986 commented: "Design should consider getting rid of plastic connectors to improve overall integrity of the system." A Ford 1987 "Concern Analysis Report: Econoline Fuel Line Leaks" addressed problems with the fuel line leaks in the 1985–87 E-series vans. The same plastic fuel system, consisting of plastic fuel lines and plastic connectors, was incorporated into the 1988 E150 van Binakonsky drove.

The plaintiffs' expert testified that the plastic fuel connectors in the Binakonsky van unsnapped during the accident, either by vibration from the accident or by the movement of the various components of the fuel system. He testified that if the fuel lines had been made of braided stainless steel and held together with nut and feral connectors, the fire would not have been fed by fuel and would have been much more manageable. He also testified that in his opinion Ford should not use nylon 11 or 12 within the heat distribution zone of the engine.

The plaintiffs produced sufficient evidence to show a likelihood that the fuel delivery system in the event of an accident was unreasonably dangerous and caused serious injury.

The fact that metal components of the fuel delivery system were relatively undamaged and intact after the collision, while the plastic components succumbed to fire, gives rise to a reasonable inference that steel lines and connectors would have been safer than plastic. Because the evidence disclosed that other 1988 Ford trucks and cars were using steel rather than plastic fuel lines, steel lines and connectors were available as a suitable substitute for the plastic.

Section 402A com. h provides: "A product is not in a defective condition when it is safe for normal handling and consumption." Maryland has relied on comment h to fashion a defense to strict liability known as "misuse" of the product. This defense is explained in *Ellsworth* v. *Sherne Lingerie, Inc.*, 303 Md. 581, 495 A.2d 348 (1985):

We conclude, as have most courts which have considered the issue, that "reasonable foreseeability" is the appropriate test, and thus a seller is required to provide a product that is not unreasonably dangerous when used for a purpose and in a manner that is reasonably foreseeable. If a product is unreasonably dangerous for such use it is "defective" within the meaning of § 402A of the Restatement, and if that defect is a cause of damage the seller will be responsible. On the other hand, if the product is not unreasonably dangerous when used for a purpose and in a manner that is reasonably foreseeable, it simply is not defective, and the seller will not be liable.

Misuse of a product may also bar recovery where the misuse is the sole proximate cause of damage, or where it is the intervening or superseding cause.

Maryland courts have held that whether an accident was so unusual as to be unforeseeable is an issue for the jury. In none of those cases did the court rule that the accident was so bizarre that it was unforeseeable as a matter of law.

We cannot say that a car crashing into a tree at as high as 47 miles per hour is "unquestionably bizarre." The same 40–47 mile per hour single car collision could have been produced by a myriad of other events, such as a car veering off the road to avoid an oncoming collision, or a car losing control on a patch of ice or because of drowsiness.

The fact that Binakonsky was drunk does not make the physical aspects of the crash any more bizarre. In this respect, care must be exercised not to confuse contributory negligence with misuse. On this issue, Maryland law is clear. "The fact that a negligent driver may be the initial cause of an accident does not abrogate the manufacturer's duty to use reasonable care in designing an automobile to reduce the risk of 'secondary impact injuries.' "

Assumption of risk, sometimes called a form of contributory negligence, is a defense to claims based on strict liability. The defense is available against a plaintiff who unreasonably uses a product despite a known risk of danger. Drunk driving is an unreasonable use of a car, and it is common knowledge that a driver who strikes a tree will cause damage. For this reason, a drunk driver, such as Binakonsky, assumes the risk of injury from the initial impact.

It is not generally known, however, that plastic lines and connectors and the lack of an antisiphoning device will cause a vehicle to burst into a devastating postcollision fire. Moreover, Ford gave no warning about the likelihood of such a fire. For these reasons the plaintiffs are entitled to the reasonable inference that Binakonsky did not assume the risk of a lethal fire. To reiterate, Binakonsky assumed the risk of injury from the initial impact. For the purpose of summary judgment, it cannot be inferred that he assumed the risk of an allegedly defective fuel delivery system.

Plaintiffs must prove that a defectively designed fuel system caused the postcollision fire and that the fire was the cause of death.

Dr. Margarita Korella, the assistant medical examiner who performed the autopsy, testified that her examination indicated no nonthermal fractures to the extremities and no evidence of external bleeding. She also testified that there was no "internal evidence of blunt force or penetrating injury to the thoracoabdominal area." Based upon burns found in the larynx, she concluded that the specific thermal injury that caused Binakonsky's death was "the inhalation of super-heated hot air."

We reverse that aspect of the summary judgment pertaining to the van's fuel delivery system and remand the case for trial.

NIEMEYER, Circuit Judge, dissenting
The majority opinion rules, by implication, that an automobile manufacturer has a duty to design its automobiles to withstand risks of injury from a head-on collision with an oak tree at a speed of 40–47 miles per hour. Because I believe that the majority's holding in this case imposes a duty far greater than that imposed by Maryland law, I dissent.

The impact occurred in the center front of the van so that the sides of the van wrapped around the tree, forming a sharp V in the center front bumper area. The tree penetrated the front of the vehicle two to three feet, driving the engine rearward, seriously damaging all of the major components of the vehicle and rupturing the fuel line. The spilling gasoline caught fire, and Binakonsky was dead by the time he was removed from the vehicle. His family contends that the fire caused his death, while Ford contends that he was killed upon impact with the tree.

(continued)

The majority opinion also correctly notes that Maryland recognizes a misuse defense to strict liability.

To rule that this case presents a jury question, the majority states, "We cannot say that a car crashing into a tree at as high as 47 miles per hour is 'unquestionably bizarre.'" This, I respectfully submit, misses the issue. The question is not whether an accident is so bizarre as not to be foreseeable, but whether the risk of injury or death is reasonably foreseeable if a design feature is not adopted. Applied to this case, the question is whether it was foreseeable that a slide valve, which has never been used in any motor vehicle, could reasonably have prevented Binakonsky's death. I submit that as a matter of law we must say that this goes beyond foreseeability and into rank speculation. In order to anticipate that such a valve would reasonably have participated in Binakonsky's death, Ford would have had to assume:

1. That Binakonsky could survive a head-on crash with a tree at 47 miles per hour;

2. That the gas tank would survive such a crash and retain the gasoline in it;

3. That the slide valve would survive sufficiently intact as to contain the gasoline;

9. That the fuel pump would not shut off; and

5. That a fire from some other source or that some other post-collision condition would not have killed Binakonsky.

In speculating about such remote possibilities, and others, we would then have to decide whether such a duty applies if the vehicle were driven into a tree, say, at 65 miles per hour, or 85 miles per hour. There must be a legally established limit to a manufacturer's duty. I believe that that limit should be set at a speed where the risk of death can meaningfully be addressed by the design feature at issue.

I find it difficult to conclude that we must assume, in imposing duties of design, that any human-being will survive the impact of a fall from a seven-story window—the force that Binakonsky was exposed to in this case. If we cannot reasonably foresee that Binakonsky would, except in freakish circumstances, have survived such an impact, we certainly cannot impose a duty on a manufacturer to design a vehicle to prevent post-collision injury from a cause other than the collision itself.

I believe that the holding made by the majority applies a clinical rule in a formulaic way, without considering the common sense factors that must come into play. Rules developed in this manner are antagonistic to the law's role in preserving the manufacturer's duty to produce practicable and desirable safety devices without destroying their ability to continue to develop consumer products. No product can withstand the scrutiny of an absolute safety standard. Yet, that is the direction in which the majority opinion unfortunately is headed.

CASE QUESTIONS

1. How did the accident occur?

2. How did Binakonsky die?

3. What role does Binakonsky's blood-alcohol level play in the case? If Binakonsky would have died regardless of the design, should there be recovery under product liability?

4. How does the majority define the issue in the case? How does the dissent define it?

5. Does this case impose liability regardless of the cause of the crash?

Visit THOMAS, a service of the U.S. Congress, for the status of current congressional bills:
http://thomas.loc.gov

States to compete with nations with limits on product liability will be hindered. The Business Roundtable and other business groups continue to work for reform at the federal and state levels. Further, businesses continue to emphasize total quality management as a tool for minimizing product liability.

The American Law Institute (ALI) has proposed the *Restatement (Third) of Torts*, which would change the current strict liability standard to a negligence standard for defective design and informational defect cases. In other words, plaintiffs who bring product liability cases based on defective design and instruction would have to establish negligence to recover. The strict liability standard would be eliminated under this new proposal. Strict liability would still be the standard for manufacturing defects.

FEDERAL STANDARDS FOR PRODUCT LIABILITY

Consumer Product Safety Commission

Visit the Consumer Product Safety Commission:
http://www.cpsc.gov

The federal level of government generally is not involved in product liability issues. However, the **Consumer Product Safety Commission** (CPSC) is a regulatory agency set up under the Consumer Product Safety Act to regulate safety standards for consumer products. The commission has several responsibilities in carrying out its purposes:

1. *To protect the public against unreasonable risks of injury from consumer products*— To perform this function, the commission has been given the authority to recall products and order their repair or correction. The commission also has the power to ban products completely. This ban can apply only if a product cannot be made less dangerous. The ban on asbestos is an example of the commission's powers. For example, in 1994, the CPSC recalled nearly all types of metal bunk beds.

2. *To develop standards for consumer product safety*—These standards take the form of regulations and minimum requirements for certain products.

3. *To help consumers become more informed about evaluating safety*—Certain regulations require disclosure of the limits of performance and hazards associated with using a particular product.

4. *To fund research in matters of product safety design and in product-caused injuries and illnesses*

The act carries civil penalties of up to a maximum of $500,000. Knowing or willful violations carry a criminal fine of up to $50,000 and/or one year imprisonment, and willful repeat violations carry penalties of up to $500,000 and ten years. In addition, consumers have a right to sue in federal district court for any damages they sustain because of a violation of a regulation or law.

Uniform Product Liability Act

Visit the Department of Commerce:
http://www.doc.gov

In a number of different attempts, the Department of Commerce has tried to issue drafts and recommendations to the states on a set of uniform product liability laws. The proposed act would change the law substantially by establishing several defenses, such as state-of-the-art manufacturing or design. In addition, the proposed law establishes how a product can be defective. In view of the confusion as to standards in product liability, the high awards for damages, and the high insurance premiums paid by businesses, a change seems necessary but has been slow in coming (see "Litigation Thwarts Innovation in the United States," p. 446). Tort reform efforts continue at both federal and state levels.

INTERNATIONAL ISSUES IN PRODUCT LIABILITY

In 1985, the European Community Council of Ministers adopted a directive on product liability. The directive limits liability to "producers"; this is not as inclusive as U.S. law, which holds all sellers liable. There is a ten-year limit on liability, and the "state-of-the-art" defense applies to most member countries: If a product upon its release was as good as any available, there is no product liability.

THE SPACE SHUTTLE, NASA, AND O-RINGS

On January 28, 1986, NASA launched the space shuttle *Challenger* in 30° F weather. Seventy-four seconds into the launch, the low temperature caused the O-ring seals on the *Challenger's* booster rockets to fail. The *Challenger* exploded, killing all seven persons aboard (six astronauts and Christa McAuliffe, a school teacher chosen and trained for the mission).

Morton Thiokol was the NASA subcontractor responsible for the booster rocket assembly. Roger Boisjoly was an engineer at Morton Thiokol who had raised concerns about the O-rings. Boisjoly had given a presentation on the O-ring issue at a conference, but Thiokol took no action. Boisjoly noted the problems in his activity report and finally, in July 1985, wrote a confidential memo to R. K. Lund, Thiokol's vice president for engineering. Excerpts follow:

This letter is written to insure that management is fully aware of the seriousness of the current O-ring erosion problem. . . . The mistakenly accepted position on the joint problem was to fly without fear of failure. . . . [This position] is now drastically changed as a result of the SRM [shuttle recovery mission] 16A nozzle joint erosion which eroded a secondary O-ring with the primary O-ring never sealing. If the same scenario should occur in a field joint (and it could), then it is a jump ball as to the success or failure of the joint. . . . The result would be a catastrophe of the highest order— loss of human life. . . .

It is my honest and real fear that if we do not take immediate action to dedicate a team to solve the problem, with the field joint having the number one priority, then we stand in jeopardy of losing a flight along with all the launch pad facilities.

In October 1985, Boisjoly presented the O-ring issue at a conference of the Society of Automotive Engineers and requested suggestions for resolution. On January 27, 1986, the day before the launch, Boisjoly attempted to halt the launch. However, four Thiokol managers, including Lund, voted unanimously to recommend the launch. One manager urged Lund to "take off his engineering hat and put on his management hat." The managers then developed the following revised

recommendations. Engineers were excluded from the development of these findings and the final launch decision.

- Calculations show that SRM-25 [the designation for the *Challenger's* January 28 flight] O-rings will be 20° colder than SRM-15 O-rings.
- Temperature data not conclusive on predicting primary O-ring blow-by
- Engineering assessment is that
  —Colder O-rings will have increased effective durometer [that is, they will be harder].
  —"Harder" O-rings will take longer to seat. More gas may pass primary [SRM-25] O-ring before the primary seal seats (relative to SRM-15).
  —If the primary seal does not seat, the secondary seal will seat.
  Pressure will get to secondary seal before the metal parts rotate.
  O-ring pressure leak check places secondary seal in outboard position, which minimizes sealing time.
  —MTI recommends STS-51L launch proceed on 28 January 1986.
  SRM-25 will not be significantly different from SRM-15.

After the decision was made, Boisjoly returned to his office and wrote in his journal:

I sincerely hope this launch does not result in a catastrophe. I personally do not agree with some of the statements made in Joe Kilminster's [Kilminster was one of the four Thiokol managers who voted to recommend the launch] written summary stating that SRM-25 is okay to fly.

The subsequent investigation by the presidential commission placed the blame for the faulty O-rings squarely with Thiokol. Charles S. Locke, Thiokol's CEO, maintained, "I take the position that we never agreed to the launch at the temperature at the time of the launch. The *Challenger* incident resulted more from human error than mechanical error. The decision to launch should have been referred to headquarters. If we'd been consulted here, we'd never have given clearance, because the temperature was not within the contracted specs."

Boisjoly testified before the presidential panel regarding his opposition to the launch and the decision of his managers (who were also engineers) to override his recommendation. Boisjoly, who took medical leave for post-traumatic stress disorder, has left Thiokol, but he does receive disability pay from the company. Currently, Mr. Boisjoly operates a consulting firm in Mesa, Arizona. He speaks frequently on business ethics to professional organizations and companies.

In May 1986, then CEO Locke stated, in an interview with the *Wall Street Journal,* "This shuttle thing will cost us this year 10¢ a share." Locke later protested that his statement was taken out of context.

Roger Boisjoly offers the following advice on whistle-blowing:

a. You owe your organization an opportunity to respond. Speak to them first VERBALLY. Memos are not appropriate for the first step.

b. Gather collegial support for your position. If you cannot get the support, then make sure you are correct.

c. Then spell out the problem in a letter.

ISSUES

1. Do you think Mr. Boisjoly feels some responsibility for the *Challenger* accident?

2. Would you have done anything differently?

3. What can companies do to be certain they listen to a Roger Boisjoly?

Source: From *Case Studies in Business Ethics,* 4th edition, by Marianne M. Jennings. © 2002. Reprinted with permission of South-Western College Publishing, a division of International Thomson Publishing. Fax 800 730-2215.

ETHICAL ISSUES 11.3

In some cases, products outlawed in the United States are sold outside the United States. Referred to as dumping, the products are sold without mention of the U.S. litigation pending. What can be done about firms that sell defective products in Third World countries? For example, IUDs and non–flame-retardant pajamas were dumped after problems developed in the United States. Discuss the ethical issues.

Visit the International Organization for Standardization:
http://www.iso.ch

In addition to the council's guidelines are the International Standards Organization's 9000 Guidelines for Quality Assurance and Quality Management. These directives require products to carry a stamp of compliance with standards and procedures as a means of limiting product defects.

Under the CISG (see Chapter 7 for more details), there are similar provisions to the UCC warranty protections for goods sold in international transactions. However, disclaimers are made more easily under the CISG and the notions of consequential damages are limited because the United States' level of damages in product liability cases far exceeds the levels for any other country in the world. Further, the notion of strict liability for products is unique to the United States, and under EU guidelines the notion of knowledge is used as a standard for imposing liability.

Re: Litigation Thwarts Innovation in the United States

American innovation is in trouble in the courts. Burt Rutan, the pioneering designer of the **Voyager,** *used to sell construction plans for novel airplanes to do-it-yourselfers. In 1985, concerned about the lawsuits that would follow if a home-built plane crashed, he took the plans off the market.*

The Monsanto Company decided in 1987 not to market a promising new filler and insulator made of calcium sodium metaphosphate. The material is almost certainly safer than asbestos, which it could help to replace in brakes and gaskets. But safer is not good enough in today's climate of infectious litigation.

Liability fears have caused the withdrawal of exotic drugs that the Food and Drug Administration consider safe and effective, including some for which no close substitute is known.

In the past fifteen years most companies have halted U.S. research on contraceptives and drugs to combat infertility and morning sickness. "Who in his right mind," the president of one pharmaceutical company asked in 1986, "would work on a product today that would be used by pregnant women?"

Liability is supposed to fall on "defective," unduly dangerous products and services. What has gone wrong?

The old rules of negligence, which lasted until the 1960s in most states, looked closely at the human actors on the scene. Were they careful? Had they been well trained? Thus tested, engineers, surgeons, chemists and pharmacologists at the leading edge of their professions fared well.

The new rules of "strict liability," invented by U.S. courts in the 1960s and 1970s, place technology itself in the dock. After an accident, jurors are given a few days to evaluate the design of a mass-vaccination program, a power plant, or an advanced military aircraft. Sympathy for the victims clouds the analysis, and if finding a design defect is what it takes to help out the unfortunate claimant, then that is what many juries find.

Moreover, human nature is predisposed to accept the old and familiar risk while rejecting the novel and the exotic. [C]onsulting engineers favor older design options in their specifications, fearing that

new ones will carry greater risk—not physical risk but legal.

The various elements of liability in the courts today all join to thwart innovation. Take the duty to warn of hazards, great and small, common and bizarre, in staggering detail. It is a game that sellers master only by playing for a long time. The warnings on birth-control pills have been honed for 30 years and now run on for several pages of dense detail. No equivalent warning can be offered for a next-generation mode of contraception, even if on balance it is safer.

Modern law also demands that risky products come, in effect, with their own insurance contract attached, underwritten by some producer's liability insurer. Insurance, by design, spreads costs broadly and somewhat indiscriminately; when one product comes under intense liability attack, an entire industry may lose its coverage. For the prudent business, no insurance usually means no product.

The most regressive effects are felt precisely where fruitful innovation is most urgently needed. Liability today is highly—and often indiscriminately—contagious. Progress is undercut the most in the markets already battered by a hurricane of litigation: contraceptives, vaccines, obstetrical services, and light aircraft, for example.

More often than not, the best anticipatory defense in the modern legal environment is to sit still. Age, familiarity, and ubiquity provide the surest legal protection. When it encourages improvement at all, today's liability system promotes the trivial and marginal change. The drug manufacturer endlessly fine-tunes the warning or microscopically adjusts the dosage in the capsule. The doctor orders more tests and x-rays in order to pile up a protective paper trail. Companies hire squadrons of risk managers, industrial hygienists, and consumer psychologists. Liability-driven safety management becomes a mirror image of the legal process itself—fussy, cumulative, bureaucratic, and preoccupied with paper.

Meanwhile, the threat of liability impedes or prevents the sharp break with technological tradition, the profound change in method or material, design or manufacture. Over the long term, however, the bold leap forward is all-important in the quest for safety, and it is precisely in the riskiest areas of life, where the litigation climate is worst, that such change is most urgently needed.

Today's U.S. liability system, unique in the world in its reach and impact, is all too adept at condemning services and technologies deemed unacceptable for one reason or another. What it lacks is a reliable way to say yes.

What is the solution? When we deal with essentially private risks (in transportation or personal consumption, for example), fair warning and conscious choice by the consumer must be made to count for much more than they do today—not because individual choices will always be wise (they surely will not be) but because such a system at least allows positive choice and the acceptance of change.

Informed consent by the individual is not, however, going to take care of such complex or far-reaching safety issues as chemical-waste disposal, mass vaccination, or central power generation. Those are, and obviously must continue to be, delegated to expert agencies acting for the collective good. But if

they are to be useful at all, agents must be able to buy as well as sell. For safety agencies, this means not only rejecting bad safety choices but also embracing good ones. Yet the long-standing rule, vigorously applied by our courts, is that even the most complete conformity to applicable regulations is no shield against liability.

The courts should be strongly encouraged, instead, to respect the risk and safety choices made by expert agencies. It may be politically unrealistic to propose that liability should be entirely foreclosed even in cases where activities are conducted with the express approval of qualified regulatory agencies, but surely it could be firmly curtailed in such circumstances. At the very least, full compliance with a comprehensive licensing order should provide liability protection against punitive, if not compensatory, damages. It has always been true that ignorance of the law is no excuse. Today, knowledge of the law is no excuse either. It should be.

Source: Peter Huber, *Scientific American*, March 1989. Mr. Huber is a fellow at the Manhattan Institute. Reprinted courtesy of *Scientific American*, March 1989.

SUMMARY

How does advertising create liability for a business?

- Express warranty—contractual promise about nature or potential of product that gives right of recovery if product falls short of a promise that was a basis of the bargain

- Bait and switch—using cheaper, unavailable product to lure customers to store with a more expensive one then substituted or offered instead

- Federal Trade Commission (FTC)—federal agency responsible for regulating deceptive ads

- Wheeler-Lea Act—federal law that allows FTC to regulate "unfair and deceptive acts or practices"

- Celebrity endorsements—FTC area of regulation wherein products are touted by easily recognized public figures

- Consent decree—voluntary settlement of FTC complaint

What are the contract theories of product liability?

- Implied warranty of merchantability—warranty of average quality, purity, and adequate packaging given in every sale by a merchant

- Implied warranty of fitness for a particular purpose—warranty given in circumstances in which the buyer relies on the seller's expertise and acts to purchase according to that advice

- Disclaimer—act of negating warranty coverage

- Privity—direct contractual relationship between parties

What is required for tort-based recovery on a defective product? What is strict tort liability for products?

- Strict liability—standard of liability that requires compensation for an injury regardless of fault or prior knowledge

- Restatement § 402A—American Law Institute's standards for imposing strict liability for defective products

- Negligence—standard of liability that requires compensation for an injury only if the party responsible knew or should have known of its potential to cause such injury

- Punitive damages—damages beyond compensation for knowledge that conduct was wrongful

What defenses exist in product liability?

- Misuse—product liability defense for plaintiff using a product incorrectly

- Contributory negligence—conduct by plaintiff that contributed to her injury; serves as a bar to recovery

- Comparative negligence—negligent conduct by plaintiff serves as a partial defense by reducing liability by percentage of fault

- Assumption of risk—defense to negligence available when plaintiff is told of product risk and voluntarily uses it

What reforms have occurred and are proposed in product liability?

- Consumer Product Safety Commission—federal agency that regulates product safety and has recall power

- Uniform Product Liability Act—proposed federal statute that would limit product liability suits and recovery

---

QUESTIONS AND PROBLEMS

1. Roger Gonzales purchased a Volvo station wagon for himself and his family. While the Volvo was pulling a U-Haul trailer and Mrs. Gonzalez was driving, there was an accident in which the Volvo rolled over. Mrs. Gonzalez was killed, and the Gonzalez daughter was severely injured. The trailer hitch used on the Volvo was unsuitable for the Volvo's bumper. Mr. Gonzalez brought suit against Volvo for its failure to warn him not to use certain trailer hitches on the bumper that could cause accidents. Is Volvo liable? What is U-Haul's liability? [*Gonzalez v. Volvo of America Corp.*, 752 F.2d 295 (7th Cir. 1985)]

2. Joyce Payne got a permanent wave from a beautician, Ms. Thrower. Ms. Thrower used a permanent wave product called Soft Sheen, and she carefully read and followed all instructions on the wave kit. While Ms. Thrower applied one step ("rearranger") in the process, Ms. Payne complained of a burning sensation in her back. The wave was completed, but two days later Ms. Payne was diagnosed in a hospital emergency room as having second degree burns on her back. She brought suit against the manufacturer of the wave and Ms. Thrower. Ms. Thrower says there were no warnings about the rearranger possibly burning skin. Who is liable? [*Payne v. Soft Sheen Products, Inc.*, 486 A.2d 712 (D.C. 1985)]

3. Seven-Up Co. began distributing its soft drinks, including its lemon-lime 7UP, in the 1920s, and by the time Coca-Cola introduced its lemon-lime soft drink, Sprite, in 1961, 7UP dominated the market.

Coca-Cola had been trying for years to break 7UP's hold on the market. In 1991, it launched a sales

presentation known as "The Future Belongs to Sprite." The sales presentation consisted of charts, graphs, and overhead displays comparing the relative sales performance of Sprite and 7UP during the 1980s. After the sales presentation had been made to eleven bottlers, five of them decided to switch their lemon-lime soft drink from 7UP to Sprite.

7UP filed suit, alleging that Coca-Cola had skewed the data in its presentations and misrepresented what was happening with 7UP's market share. Is the presentation a form of advertising for which 7UP has a remedy? Is there damage from a competitor through misleading ads? [*Seven-Up Co. v. Coca-Cola Co.*, 86 F.3d 1379 (5th Cir. 1996)]

4. Wade Lederman, 31, was at a Fourth of July pool party at a relative's house in 1991. At about 10:30 P.M., Lederman, his brother, and two others decided to go swimming. They jumped from the sides of the pool into the water and also dove from the pool's diving board. At about midnight, Mr. Lederman dove into the pool from the side and struck his head on the bottom, sustaining permanent physical and neurological injuries.

The pool in which Lederman was injured is a residential swimming pool that is in-ground and oval-shaped, with a shallow end and a deep end. The pool has three steps at the shallow end by which swimmers can enter the pool. There is a white line one foot wide painted on the bottom of the pool between the shallow end and the deep end. At the start of that line, the depth increases to 7 feet and then slowly descends to a depth of 10 feet at the diving-board end of the pool.

Mr. Lederman filed suit against Pacific Industries, Inc., the pool manufacturer, for its failure to display water depths in and around the pool; failure to warn as to which areas were not appropriate for diving; failure to warn that at night, with pool lights on, the depth of the pool was deceptive; and failure to warn that the white line was just the start of the deep end and not a line for diving versus nondiving areas of the pool.

Should Mr. Lederman recover from Pacific? [*Lederman* v. *Pacific Industries Inc.*, 119 F.3d 551 (7th Cir. 1997)]

5. On September 6, 1986, Floyd Simeon, 63, and his son, Edward Simeon, 38, went to the Sweet Pepper Grill, a restaurant at the River Walk in New Orleans. They ordered a dozen and a half raw oysters. Floyd ate six oysters, and Edward ate nine or ten. The men had eaten raw oysters before, and these looked and smelled "good."

Two days later, Mr. Simeon began running a fever and complained of pain in his ankle. Several physicians were consulted, and it was determined that Mr. Simeon was suffering from vibrio vulnificus septicemia, an infection resulting from eating raw oysters with vibrio vulnificus bacteria. As the disease progressed, Mr. Simeon developed severe blisters on his legs and began to lose subcutaneous tissue. Plastic surgeons and other physicians tried to stop the spread of the disease, but they were unsuccessful and Mr. Simeon died on September 23, 1986.

Mrs. Simeon brought a suit against Sweet Pepper Grill for breach of the warranty of merchantability. Should the restaurant be held liable? [*Simeon* v. *Doe*, 618 So. 2d 848 (La. 1993)]

6. In 1994, a group of Chrysler engineers met to review proposals and recommendations for improving their Chrysler Minivan lines in order to make them more competitive. Paul Sheridan, one of the engineers on Chrysler's Minivan Safety Team, raised the No. 1 issue on the lists of proposals and recommendations: The latches on the minivan rear doors appeared to be popping open even in low-speed crashes. The Chrysler Minivan latches did not appear to have the strength of either the Ford Windstar minivan or the Chevy minivan rear-door latches. Sheridan proposed that Chrysler make the latches stronger and use that strength as a marketing tool.

After Sheridan made his proposal, and according to testimony in a subsequent product liability suit, a top production engineer told Sheridan, "That ship has sailed. We told you that last time. Next subject."

In *Jimenez* v. *Chrysler Corporation,* the parents of Sergio Jimenez brought suit against Chrysler for their son's wrongful death when he was thrown from the back of their 1985 Dodge Caravan. The Jimenezes alleged that the latch on the rear door popped open and Sergio was thrown from the minivan and killed.

The Jimenezes introduced the proposal and response by the production engineer. The engineer

maintains that he was misunderstood in his statement; his attitude did not go unnoticed by the jury in the case. The jury deliberated only 2.5 hours before returning a verdict for the Jiminezes of $262.5 million, $250 million of which was punitive damages. The jury disregarded Chrysler's allegations during the case that Mrs. Jimenez had run a red light, that Sergio was not wearing a seat belt at the time of the accident, and that Sergio was more likely thrown from a side window of the van.

Chrysler has agreed with the National Highway Traffic Safety Administration (NHTSA) to replace the latches on 4.3 million minivans manufactured since 1984. Chrysler has spent $115 million for that replacement program on everything from notification to installation and estimates that about 61 percent of the van latches have now been replaced.

The number of deaths from ejection through the rear minivan doors is 37, which is 11 more than the fatalities from the Ford Pinto exploding gas tank defect but well short of GM's 168 fatalities in side-saddle gas tank collisions in their pickups. Chrysler has forty lawsuits pending around the country that involve rear-door ejection deaths and injuries.

The damage award in the Jimenez case is likely to be reduced on appeal (see the *Gore* v. *BMW* case in Chapter 10). However, damaging evidence brought out in the *Jimenez* case tends to be the focus of jury interest and awards:

- Chrysler initially used a latch in its vans that the rest of the industry had abandoned.
- When it switched to a better latch, still not meeting federal standards for passenger vehicles, it did not notify the owners of existing vans of the change and safety issues.
- Chrysler destroyed documentation on minivan crash tests, including films and computer records. (The company says that such destruction was part of its routine document destruction program; however, a juror noted, following the trial, that only the documentation on the collisions in which the rear door was affected was destroyed. Chrysler still had the documentation on the vans' front-end collision tests.)
- Engineers proposed adding a latch strengthener for about $0.25 per vehicle in 1990, but the plan was vetoed by Chrysler executives because it was believed such an addition would be tantamount to an admission to regulators that the latches were not safe and Chrysler had been taking the position that the latches were indeed safe.
- Chrysler used political clout to prevent a 1994 recall by NHTSA of the vehicles for latch replacement; a letter from Chrysler Vice Chairman Tom Denomme to Chairman Robert Eaton and President Robert Lutz read, "If we want to use political pressure to try to quash a recall letter, we need to go now."

Chrysler officials helped staff members for Representative John Dingell of Michigan (the ranking Democrat on the House Commerce Committee, which supervises the NHTSA) draft a letter objecting to the recall. NHTSA postponed the recall. When the recall was made in 1995, there was no acknowledgment that the latches were defective or that there was any safety issue.

Following the verdict, one juror said the evidence painted a picture of corporate indifference and added, "We want people to understand why we made the decision we did. We knew what we were doing. When you speak to a company as big as Chrysler, you've got to speak on terms they understand." Another juror said that the political interference with the recall was an "8" on a scale of 10 for damage to the company. Still another juror noted that executives answered, "I don't know. I don't remember. I can't recall," too often to have much credibility.

Chrysler had been the first mover in the minivan market. Its product filled a niche in the family auto market, and it occupied a unique position in terms of federal regulation in that there were no applicable federal standards for the lifting rear door on the van. Chrysler used latch designs and parts that had been banned in passenger vehicles for years precisely because of the risk of ejection and associated high fatality rates. However, the lack of federal regulations on the minivan meant that Chrysler violated no law in using the outmoded systems and parts.

When Chrysler began to receive notice of accidents and began holding design and marketing meetings in 1993, lawyers ordered that no notes be taken at meetings, and minutes of meetings were collected and destroyed.
a. Why were punitive damages appropriate in this case? Are they too high? What message do the punitive damages send to businesses?
b. What should Chrysler do internally to be certain such a series of events does not happen again?
c. Why are the running of a red light and the lack of a seat belt not issues in the *Jimenez* case?

7. Roy E. Farrar Produce Co. (Farrar) ordered a shipment of boxes from International Paper Company (International) that were to be suitable for the packing and storage of tomatoes. The dimensions of the two sizes of boxes were to be such that either 20 or 30 pounds of tomatoes could be packed without the necessity of weighing each box. Mr. Farrar requested that boxes be the same type as those supplied to Florida packers for shipping tomatoes. Mr. Farrar told Mr. Wilson, an agent for International, to obtain the correct specifications for the Florida-type box.

International shipped Mr. Farrar 21,500 unassembled boxes at a unit price of 64 cents per box. The boxes were not tomato boxes, were not Florida boxes, did not have adequate stacking strength, and would not hold up during shipping. Mr. Farrar had to repack 3,624 boxes (at a cost of $1.92 per box). Substitute boxes were purchased for 10 cents above the International price. The replacement boxes were Florida boxes and did not collapse. Mr. Farrar was also forced to pay growers $6 a box for tomatoes damaged during shipping. He could not use 6,100 boxes, and his sales dropped off, resulting in financial deficiencies in his operation. Can Mr. Farrar recover for his damages? Why, or why not? [*International Paper Co.* v. *Farrar*, 700 P.2d 642 (N.M. 1985)]

8. Cindi Cott, her husband Charles Price, and her father John Cott joined friends for an evening at the Peppermint Twist bar nightclub in Topeka, Kansas, on September 23, 1989. That evening, Peppermint Twist advertised watermelon shots for one dollar by posting it on a portable sign in the nightclub's parking lot. A watermelon shot contains Southern Comfort, Creme de Noyaux, and orange juice. Mary Cottrell was the Peppermint Twist waitress assigned to the table where Cindi, Charles, John, and their friends were sitting. Three shots were ordered. Mary poured the watermelon shots from a pour-and-serve container on her tray.

Unbeknownst to Mary, the bar staff had confused a pour-and-serve container with Eco-Klene—a heavy-duty commercial dishwasher detergent with lye. Eco-Klene is red in color like the watermelon shots, and the bartenders had been using Eco-Klene near their sinks because they had run out of the normal dishwashing liquid they used. Eco-Klene contains sodium hydroxide, a cause of severe chemical burns that can be fatal.

Cindi took a drink of the Eco-Klene, became very ill, and went to the restroom. John, curious, then tasted his Eco-Klene. Both were rushed to the hospital, experienced permanent physical damage, lost work time, and endured extensive rehabilitation. Cindi and John have sued Peppermint Twist. Can they recover? Are the manufacturers of Eco-Klene liable? [*Cott* v. *Peppermint Twist Management Co., Inc.*, 856 P.2d 906 (Kan. 1993)]

9. On February 14, 1999, Garry O. Hickman opened a pack of Big Red gum, which is manufactured by Wrigley. The gum was purchased by Hickman at a grocery store on the evening of February 13, 1999. Hickman unwrapped the package, which was still sealed, and put two pieces of the gum into his mouth. Hickman provided the following description of the events that occurred after he began to chew the gum:

> [A]fter I started chewing the gum I bit down on it, uh, when I bit down on it the tooth exploded in my mouth. I begin to get all of this stuff out of my mouth, tooth fragments all over my mouth and everything. The screw turned up and stuck up in the top of my gum. I had to pull it out which caused me a lot of pain and all and everything and it was very uncomfortable there for a while.

Hickman's gums stayed sore for several weeks and he sought treatment from Dr. Conly on February 18, 1999. One of Hickman's bottom teeth was fragmented. Those fragments chipped his top front teeth. Dr. Conly recommended that Hickman have surgery, which would total approximately $905.00, to remove the fractured tooth. However, Hickman had been unable to do so because he was unable to afford the surgery.

Hickman filed suit against Wrigley. Can he recover? What theories might he try? [*Hickman* v. *Wm. Wrigley, Jr. Co., Inc.*, 768 So.2d 812) (La. App. 2000)]

10. On August 11, 1995, David Lyall was adding chlorine to his swimming pool in the backyard of his home. The chlorine was in tablet form and was called "Leslie's Chlorinator Tablets 1." The tablets were contained in a 5.5-gallon bucket-like container with a childproof lid. Plastican, Inc., was the designer of the container.

When Lyall attempted to open the container, the lid blew off, allegedly due to the buildup of the gas, nitrogen trichloride. The lid, chlorine, and chlorine gas blew into his face causing him to lose his right eye and suffer several chemical burns and cuts to his face, which resulted in scarring and permanent disfigurement. Lyall's right eye has been replaced with a prosthetic device.

Lyall filed suit for the defective container and the failure to warn about the effects of gas buildup. Lyall filed suit against both Leslie's and Plastican. What theories of liability do you think Lyall used and why? [*Lyall* v. *Leslie's Poolmart*, 984 F.Supp. 587 (E.D. Mich. 1997)]

RESEARCH PROBLEM

11. Review the following hypotheticals as well as the cited case and develop a policy for a restaurant that you own or a chain in which you are a manager on coffee temperatures, serving coffee, types of cups, and any related issues. Write a memo discussing your new policies and explain why you are implementing them.

Stella Liebeck, 81, suffered third-degree burns when coffee spilled on her lap inside her car after she went through a McDonald's drive-through in Albuquerque, New Mexico. The temperature of the coffee, according to corporate guidelines, is 180 to 190 degrees Fahrenheit. Ms. Liebeck has sued McDonald's to recover for her injuries resulting from the coffee spill.

Should Ms. Liebeck be allowed to recover? What theories could she use to recover?

George Morgan, 58, purchased coffee at a Burger King drive-through. He suffered third-degree burns when the bottom of his coffee cup collapsed, spilling hot coffee over his legs and groin. What is different about Mr. Morgan's accident from Ms. Liebeck's accident? Are there different liability issues?

For some insight, read *Austin* v. *W. H. Braum, Inc.*, 249 F.3d 805 (8th cir. 2001)

NOTES

1. *FTC News Summary,* 19 May 1978, 1–2.

2. For more information, see James R. Healey and Sara Nathan, "More Deaths Linked to Tires," *USA Today,* 2 August 2000, 1A; and Healey and Nathan, "Officials Have Known SUV Tire Suspicions for Decade," *USA Today,* 2 August 2000, 1B.

3. For more information, see Norihiko Shirouzu and Timothy Aeppel, "Firestone Says It Acted to Improve Problem Tires," *Wall Street Journal,* 18 August 2000, A3; and David Kiley, "Ford Chief Wants to Speed Tire Recall," *USA Today,* 17 August 2000, 1A.

BUSINESS STRATEGY APPLICATION

The CD-ROM exercise for Chapter 11 provides you with the opportunity to manage the production and distribution chain for your company so that you minimize product liability. You'll learn to check the legal implications of everything from ad copy to warranties.

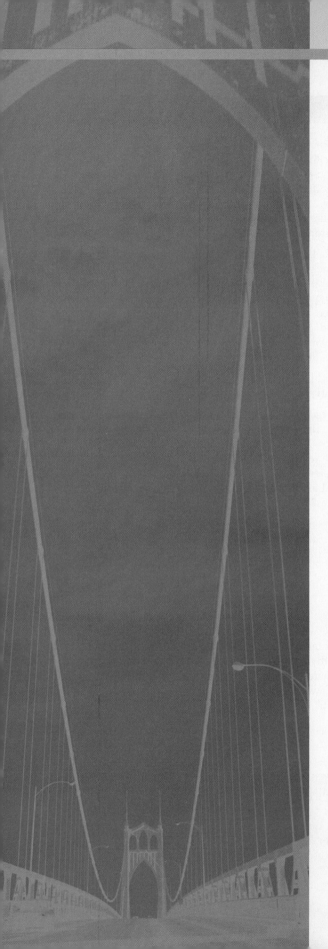

CHAPTER TWELVE

Environmental Regulation

When producing its products or providing its services, a firm has an obligation to do so in a manner that does not illegally affect the environment. Apart from the damage claims and penalties that can result from the unlawful pollution of the environment, social responsibility is a major issue. Keeping a clean environment is a long-range goal not only for society but also for the businesses that hope to continue operating in that society. This chapter answers the following questions: What are the public and private environmental laws? What protections and requirements are there in environmental laws? Who enforces environmental laws? What are the penalties for violations?

By the shores of Gitche Gumee,

By the shining Big-Sea-Water, . . .

How they built their nests in summer,

Where they hid themselves in winter,

How the beavers built their lodges,

Where the squirrels hid their acorns,

How the reindeer ran so swiftly,

Why the rabbit was so timid . . .

HENRY WADSWORTH LONGFELLOW
"Hiawatha's Childhood"

The landscape and the language are the same

For we ourselves are landscape and land.

CONRAD AIKEN
A Letter from Li Po and Other Poems (1955)

© EyeWire

CONSIDER...

In 1990, the U.S. Fish and Wildlife Service listed the northern spotted owl as an endangered species. Further, the service concluded that logging in the Northwest threatened the owl's continued existence. Lumber companies and trade associations protested, "Is it owls or is it jobs?" As the economies of the Northwest states suffered, the lumberjacks and lumber companies took their issue to Congress. A temporary measure allows continued harvesting through legislation overriding the U.S. Fish and Wildlife order. The battle continues in the pages of newspapers and over the airways. How much environmental regulation do we need? When can development be curtailed through regulation?

Visit an environmental educational site:
http://www.lib.lsu.edu/gov/fedgov.html

COMMON-LAW REMEDIES AND THE ENVIRONMENT

From earliest times, landowners have enjoyed the protections of the courts and various doctrines to prevent bad smells, noises, and emissions. Common law affords relief to adjoining landowners and communities when activities rise to the level of a **nuisance.** A nuisance exists when the activities of one landowner interfere with the use and enjoyment of their properties by other landowners or by members of the community in which the nuisance occurs. Bad smells, ongoing damage to paint on buildings, excessive noise, polluted air, and the operation of facilities that present health problems can all be enjoined as nuisances. In the following case, the New Jersey Supreme Court was faced with an issue of contamination of property and the liability of the transferors and transferees for the hazard that was created. In many environmental problems, concerned parties do not want money for damages as much as they want the harmful activity halted. The courts have the power to issue injunctions against those who are harming land, individuals, or the environment. Injunctions are granted in those cases in which the party (or parties) requesting the injunctive relief is able to establish ongoing harm as a result of the defendant's activities.

CASE 12.1

T & E Industries, Inc. v. *Safety Light Corp.*
587 A.2d 1249 (N.J. 1991)

Toxic Waste Radiates: You Can't Bury the Past

FACTS

United States Radium Corporation (USRC) owned an industrial site on Alden Street in Orange, New Jersey, where it processed radium from 1917 until 1926. USRC sold the radium for medical purposes and also used it to manufacture luminous paint for instrument dials, watches, and other products. Radium processing permitted recovery of only 80 percent of the radium from the carnotite ore transported to the plant from Colorado and Utah. The unextracted radium was contained in "tailings" that USRC discarded onto unimproved portions of the Alden Street site.

Through a complex series of chemical processes, the discarded radium emits radon, which can cause lung cancer when inhaled. Epidemiological studies had not been done at the time the tailings were discarded, and the federal government did not regulate the disposal of the tailings until 1978. However, many people had suspicions about handling radium, and as early as 1917 USRC employees measured the radioactivity of radium. One story told of how Dr. Van Sochocky, the president of USRC, "hacked" off his fingertip when radium lodged beneath his fingernail because he feared the effects of radium.

Radium processing ceased at the Alden site in 1926, and the site was leased to various commercial tenants until it was sold in 1943 to Arpin, a plastics manufacturer. The tailings were not removed from the site in spite of continually developing evidence about the danger. In fact, Arpin constructed a new portion of plant that rested on the discarded tailings. The property changed hands several times. T&E (plaintiff), a manufacturer of electronic components, leased the premises in 1969 and purchased it in 1974.

The Uranium Mill Tailings Radiation Control Act (1978) calls for the evaluation of inactive mill-tailing sites. New Jersey's Department of Environmental Protection (DEP) inspected the plaintiff's site and found radon levels exceeding state and federal standards. In spite of soil removal and other actions, the site could not be brought into compliance; T&E was forced to move its operations. The site could not be sold until cleanup of the tailings was complete.

to which its value to the community is out-
_d by its dangerous attributes.

_t does not dispute that liability can be
_nterprisers who engage in abnormally
_ities that harm others; but it contends
_ty is contingent on proof that the
_ or should have known of the
_erous character of the activity."
_dant, absent such knowledge,
_ no position to make the cost-
_t will enable him to spread the
_ optimal level of activity."
_bsent such an opportunity,
_ing strict liability on those
_lly dangerous activities,
_g, cannot be realized.

_not, however, determine whether
_ge is a requirement in the context of a strict-
_oility claim predicated on an abnormally danger-
ous activity. Even if the law imposes such a requirement, we are convinced, for the reasons set forth more
fully below, that defendant should have known about
the risks of its activity, and that its constructive
knowledge would fully satisfy any such requirement.

Radium has always been and continues to be an
extraordinarily dangerous substance. Although
radium processing has never been a common activity, the injudicious handling, processing, and disposal of radium has for decades caused concern; it
has long been suspected of posing a serious threat to
the health of those who are exposed to it.

Furthermore, although the risks involved in the
processing and disposal of radium might be curtailed, one cannot safely dispose of radium by dumping it onto the vacant portions of an urban lot.
Because of the extraordinarily hazardous nature of
radium, the processing and disposal of that substance is particularly inappropriate in an urban setting. We conclude that despite the usefulness of
radium, defendant's processing, handling, and disposal of that substance under the facts of this case
constituted an abnormally dangerous activity, plaintiff's property is befouled with radium because
of defendant's abnormally dangerous activity. Radiation levels at the site exceed those permitted under
governmental health regulations. Moreover, the
property has been earmarked as a Superfund site.
Because plaintiff vacated the premises in response
to the health concern posed by the radium-
contaminated site and because the danger to health is
"the kind of harm, the possibility of which [made

_,ities can be so
_ly infrequent occur-
_,ustifiably allocated as a cost
_ enterpriser who engages in such
conduct. Although the law will tolerate the hazardous activity, the enterprise must pay its way.

Because the former owner of the property whose
activities caused the hazard might have been in the
best position to bear or spread the loss, liability for the
harm caused by abnormally dangerous activities does
not necessarily cease with the transfer of property.

A real-estate contract that does not disclose the
abnormally dangerous condition or activity does not
shield from liability the seller who created that condition or engaged in that activity.

The *Restatement* sets forth six factors that a court
should consider in determining whether an activity
is "abnormally dangerous."

(a) existence of a high degree of risk of some harm to
the person, land, or chattels of others;

(b) likelihood that the harm that results from it will
be great;

(c) inability to eliminate the risk by the exercise of
reasonable care;

(d) extent to which the activity is not a matter of
common usage;

(e) inappropriateness of the activity to place where it
is carried on; and

(continued)

defendant's] activity abnormally dangerous," defendant is strictly liable for the resulting harm.

Here defendant knew that it was processing radium, a substance concededly fraught with hazardous potential. It knew that its employees who handled radium should wear protective clothing; it knew that some employees who had digested radium had developed cancer, and prior to the sale of the property, it knew that the inhalation of radon could cause lung cancer. Despite that wealth of knowledge concerning the harmful effects of radium exposure, defendant contends that it could not have known that disposal of the radium-saturated by-products behind the plant would produce a hazard. That contention appears to rest on the idea that somehow the radium's potential for harm miraculously disappeared once the material had been deposited in a vacant corner of an urban lot, or at the least that one might reasonably reach that conclusion—a proposition that we do not accept.

Surely someone engaged in a business as riddled with hazards as defendant's demonstrably was should realize the potential for harm in every aspect of that dangerous business. If knowledge be a requirement, defendant knew enough about the abnormally dangerous character of radium processing to be charged with knowledge of the dangers of disposal.

Final[...] argument, [...] uncertainty [...] business comm[...] We have already [...] ing in that it exten[...] that meets the crite[...] activity. Second, we [...] tion any conveyance [...] would be made not in a [...] tion of regulatory require[...] embrace a condition such a[...] Street property.

Affirmed.

CASE QUESTIONS

1. Who originally owned the property
2. How was the property originally used
3. How did the original owners feel about radium?
4. What was disposed of on the site?
5. What made the disposal an abnormally dangerous activity?
6. What does the court say about the "parade of horribles" argument?

C O N S I D E R . . .

12.1 Spur Industries has operated a feedlot in an area about 20 miles from the city of Phoenix since 1956. Del E. Webb began the development of Sun City, a retirement community, in 1959. Spur expanded its operations in 1960 from 35 acres to 115 acres. Spur was feeding between 20,000 and 30,000 head of cattle. Each head produced 35 to 40 pounds of wet manure each day. Residents of Sun City are complaining about the odors and flies. Webb has been unable to sell 1,300 lots located next to the feedlot. Could the residents win a nuisance suit against Spur? Does it matter that Spur was there first? [*Spur Industries, Inc.* v. *Del E. Webb Dev. Co.,* 494 P.2d 700 (Ariz. 1972)]

e-commerce Because any electrical current sets up a magnetic field, computers and wire transmissions to and from computers set up magnetic fields that might affect electrical equipment in buildings on neighboring land. The stronger the current, the greater the magnetic field. Also, if there is a loose or broken circuit that sparks, the interference with neighbors is increased. If that interference rises to an unreasonable level, it may be stopped as a nuisance and damages recovered for the harm.

For example, the Meridian Data Processing Center was an independent contractor that performed all the data processing for a large number of banks and stockbrokers within the state. Because of the large number of computers and direct wire lines to its customers, the center's operation set up a substantial magnetic field that interfered with some of the electronic display equipment in several neighboring stores. The stores sued the data processing center to obtain an injunction against it for nuisance.

Because of the social utility of the activity, it is unlikely a court would enjoin this form of activity. It might, however, impose some limitations on hours of operation or require investment in technology to find a means around the problem.[1]

STATUTORY ENVIRONMENTAL LAWS

At the federal level, most environmental laws can be placed in one of three categories: those regulating air pollution, those regulating water pollution, and those regulating solid waste disposal on land. In addition, the federal regulatory scheme has several laws affecting property rights that do not fit into these categories but are discussed in this subsection nonetheless.

Air Pollution Regulation

Early Legislation

The first legislation dealing with the problem of air pollution passed in 1955 and was the **Air Pollution Control Act.** However, the 1955 act did very little to control or even to take steps to control the problem of air pollution.

Little action was taken to encourage greater involvement in the air pollution issue until Congress passed the **Air Quality Act** in 1967. Under this act, the Department of Health, Education and Welfare (HEW) was authorized to oversee the states' adoption of air quality standards and the implementation of those plans. Again, this legislation proved ineffective, for by 1970 no state had adopted a comprehensive plan.

1970 Amendments to the Clean Air Act: New Standards

Review the Clean Air Act and Amendments:
http://www.law.cornell.edu/
uscode/42/
ch85.html#s7401

Visit the Environmental Protection Agency:
http://www.epa.gov

Because the states did not take action concerning air pollution, Congress passed the 1970 amendments to the original but ineffective 1963 **Clean Air Act** (42 U.S.C. § 7401); these amendments constituted the first federal legislation with any real authority for enforcement. Under the act, the **Environmental Protection Agency** (EPA) was authorized to establish air quality standards; and, once those standards were developed, states were required to adopt implementation plans to achieve the federally developed standards. These **state implementation plans** (SIPs) had to be approved by the EPA, and adoption and enforcement of the plans were no longer discretionary but mandatory. To obtain EPA approval, the implementation plans had to meet deadlines for compliance with the EPA air quality standards, and thus the Clean Air Act established time periods for achieving air quality.

The air quality standards set by the EPA specify how much of a particular substance in the air is permissible. It was up to each state to devise methods for meeting those standards. The first step taken by the states was to measure existing air content of substances such as sulfur dioxide, carbon monoxide, and hydrocarbons. Based on the results, the states then took appropriate steps to reduce the amounts of any substances that exceeded federal standards. The EPA required those state standards to mandate the development of air pollution devices. The lack of technology could not be used as a defense to air pollution.

1977 Amendments

With the 1977 amendments came authority for the EPA to regulate business growth in an attempt to achieve air quality standards. With this authority, the EPA classified two types of areas in which business growth could be contained. **Nonattainment areas** included those areas with existing, significant air quality problems, the so-called dirty areas. Clean areas were called **prevention of significant deterioration (PSD) areas.**

EPA Economic Controls for Nonattainment Areas

For information on development of solar technology, see
http://www.ncsc.ncsu.edu

For nonattainment areas, the EPA developed its **emissions offset policy,** which requires three elements before a new facility can begin operation in a nonattainment area: (1) The new plant must have the greatest possible emissions controls; (2) the proposed plant operator must have all other operations in compliance with standards; and (3) the new plant's emissions must be offset by reductions from other facilities in the area.

In applying these elements, the EPA follows the **bubble concept,** which examines all the air pollutants in the area as if they came from a single source. If it can be shown that a new plant will have no net effect on the air in the area (after offsets from other plants), then the new facility will not be subject to a veto.

Although the EPA did not regulate initially the construction of plants in areas already meeting air quality standards, environmentalists' protests and suits brought about the application of EPA regulations to PSD areas. Basically, the purpose of PSD regulations is to permit the EPA to have the right to review proposed plant constructions prior to their construction. In their submissions for EPA review, the plant operators are required to establish that there will be no significant effect on air quality and that emissions will be controlled with appropriate devices.

New Forms of Control: The 1990 Amendments to the Clean Air Act

The Clean Air Act was revised substantially with the **Clean Air Act Amendments of 1990.** These amendments focus on issues such as acid rain, urban smog, airborne toxins, ozone-depleting chemicals, and the various regional economic concerns and political problems attendant to these issues.

As of 1990, ninety-six cities were already three years late in achieving the attainment levels mandated by their SIPs in 1977, and forty-one cities had carbon monoxide levels exceeding the goals in their SIPs. Under the 1990 amendments, the EPA was authorized to establish a **federal implementation plan** (FIP) within two years of a state's failure to submit to the EPA an adequate SIP. New deadlines were established for polluted areas according to current levels of pollution. Except for Los Angeles, compliance deadlines were set for the year 2000, with annual pollution-reduction goals for cities set at 3 to 4 percent a year.

The 1990 amendments have had a substantial impact on smaller businesses, such as dry cleaners, paint shops, and bakeries, because the definition of a major source of pollution was changed from those businesses emitting 100 tons or more a year to those emitting 50 tons or more per year.

To meet the new EPA standards and deadlines that have resulted from the 1990 Act, cities and counties are imposing even residential regulations such as "no-burn" days for fireplaces and restrictions on charcoal barbeques.

One of the effects of the Clean Air Act of 1990 has been the buying and selling of EPA sulfur dioxide emissions permits. If, for example, a utility has an EPA permit to discharge one ton of sulfur dioxide per year, but its equipment permits it to run "cleaner," the utility can sell the permit to another utility. In fact, the Chicago Board of Trade conducts a national auction for the sale of such permits. The price for a permit for one ton of sulfur dioxide ranges from $122 to $450. The first day of trading these permits—March 30, 1993—produced sales of 150,000 permits worth $21.4 million. One percent of the bids were from environmental groups seeking to prevent use of the permits.

The nine worst nonattainment areas were required to use reformulated gasolines to reduce emissions by 25 percent by 2000. Tighter tailpipe standards for autos were phased in to require emissions reductions ranging from 30 to 60 percent for various pollutants. Plants that are major sources of toxic emissions must use **maximum achievable control technology** (MACT), or the best available methods for limiting emissions, regardless of cost.

Penalties under the act allow field citations and civil penalties of up to $5,000 a day in addition to the $25,000 a day in general fines. The $5,000-per-day penalty applies to even minor violations, including record keeping. The EPA is also authorized under the amendments to pay $10,000 rewards to people who provide information leading to criminal convictions or civil penalties. Stiffer criminal penalties were added, with a possibility of up to two years imprisonment for false statements or failures to report violations. Willful violations carry penalties of up to fifteen years and/or $1,000,000 in fines. The act specifically holds as criminally liable any responsible corporate officers.

C O N S I D E R . . .

12.2 Union Electric Company is an electric utility serving St. Louis and large portions of Illinois and Iowa. It operates three coal-fired generating plants in metropolitan St. Louis that are subject to sulfur dioxide restrictions under Missouri's SIP. Union Electric did not seek review of the implementation plan but applied for and obtained variances from the emissions limitations. When an extension for the variances was denied, Union Electric challenged the implementation plan on the grounds that it was technologically and economically infeasible and should therefore be amended. Will Union Electric succeed in having the plan amended? Consider the question in light of the 1990 Clean Air Act Amendments. [*Union Electric Co. v. EPA*, 427 U.S. 246 (1976)]

Water Pollution Regulation

Early Legislation

In 1965, the first federal legislation on water quality standards was passed—the **Water Quality Act.** The act established a separate enforcement agency—the **Federal Water Pollution Control Administration** (FWPCA)—and required states to establish quality levels for the waters within their boundaries. Because the act contained few expeditious enforcement procedures, only about half of the states had developed their zones and standards by 1970, and none of the states were engaged in active enforcement of those standards with their implementation plans.

The **Rivers and Harbors Act of 1899,** which prohibits the discharge into navigable rivers and harbors of refuse that causes interference with navigation, was used for a time to enforce water standards since state action was minimal. Specifically, the act prohibited the release of "any refuse matter of any kind or

Clean Air and the Popular SUV

In 1990, the SUV/light truck market consisted of approximately 4,000,000 units sold out of 14,000,000 of total vehicle sales in the United States. By 1999, the percentage of the total market had increased and total sales were higher. SUVs/light truck sales were 8,200,000 of 16,400,000 units sold. 47.6 percent of Ford Motor Company's sales are of SUVs, primarily its Ford Explorer and larger Expedition, but also of its even larger Excursion.

In 1997, most auto manufacturers entered the luxury SUV market. These SUVs, with prices around $50,000, featured in-vehicle televisions and VCRs, leather interiors, and all the amenities of luxury cars.

Market data on SUV buyers indicate that the primary reason for their purchase of an SUV is safety (44 percent) followed by need (due to family size—33 percent) followed by a desire to go off-roading (10 percent) and finally by "wanted to be with the latest trend" (10 percent).

The SUV has proven to be a lightning rod in public discussion in areas as diverse as environmentalism and safety. Focusing on safety concerns and the use of fuel and resulting emissions, there has been intense media coverage of SUVs.

In 1997, the *New York Times* ran a report entitled "License to Pollute: Light Trucks, Darlings of Drivers, Are Favored by Law, Too." The article concluded that, because of a loophole, these vehicles, including SUVs, had emissions 20 to 100 percent higher than cars. The article noted that if Americans had continued buying just cars instead of light trucks and SUVs, then CO_2 emissions would have been "down by 9.3 percent."

Later in 1997, California air quality officials revealed a proposal to require trucks, minivans, and most SUVs to meet the same emissions standards as passenger cars by the year 2004. That proposal is now law.

Following the Kyoto treaty of December 12, 1997, in which the United States agreed (subject to ratification by the Senate) to reduce its emissions to its 1990 levels by the year 2012, Ford and Chrysler announced on January 5, 1998, that they would cut the emissions of their SUVs and minivans. At a cost of $100 per vehicle or $100 million per year, Ford announced that its Windstar vans would immediately meet the same emissions standards as its passenger vehicles. The

ETHICAL ISSUES 12.1

New York Times reported on the Ford decision as follows:

. . . Jacques Nasser [Ford's president of worldwide automotive operations] made clear in an interview that Ford wanted to maintain the acceptability of sports utility vehicles as alternatives to cars, while gaining an advantage over rival automakers in catering to environmentally aware families. 'Anybody who has concerns about the environment can set them aside,' Nasser said adding that Ford was also influenced by recent articles in the New York Times *on the environmental problems of light trucks.*

USA Today ran a series of articles during 1999 on the following topics: the disadvantages of driving a small car in an SUV-dominated market and road; the high center of gravity in small SUVs and the danger of rollovers; and the car makers detours around CAFÉ rules. CAFÉ (Corporate Average Fuel Economy) rules are the mileage standards the federal government requires each automaker to attain when the fuel economies of all the vehicles they sell in a model year are averaged together. The standard for cars is 27.5 miles per gallon in combined city and highway driving, and the standard for trucks and SUVs is 20.7 miles per gallon. The fine for failing to meet CAFÉ is $5.50 for each 0.1 mpg short of the CAFÉ standard. If an automaker sells 1 million cars that average 27 mpg instead of 27.5 mpg, then the fine is $27.5 million. Foreign automakers generally ignore the CAFÉ standards and simply pay the fines as they say "as a cost of doing business." U.S. automakers are in compliance because criminal sanctions include prison time for officers and managers. *USA Today* concluded, however, that U.S. automaker compliance was meaningless because the automakers are permitted to carry credits forward when they exceed CAFÉ and juggling model years, by mid-year introduction of vehicles, can result in exclusion of large chunks of sales of larger vehicles that would decrease the mpg.

Following the series in the *New York Times* and *USA Today,* Ford announced that it would escalate its emissions standards for its trucks and SUVs. Jacques Nasser announced on May 17, 1999, that Ford's trucks, including its Explorer and Expedition, would meet EPA (Environmental Protection Agency) emissions standards for 2004 by the year 2000. Nasser said he wants customers to have the choice of a full range of Ford products and not have to choose "between the one that is environmentally friendly and the one that isn't."

In early 2000, Ford released its social responsibility report, called "Corporate Citizenship Report," and its chairman announced it to the shareholders at Ford's annual meeting in May 2000. William Clay Ford Jr. read the Sierra Club's description of the Ford Excursion at the meeting as "a gas-guzzling rolling monument to environmental destruction." Mr. Ford promised that his company would do better. Sales of the Excursion in 1999 were 15,838 units, in excess of the 15,000 produced. There is a waiting list for buyers. The following day, the *Detroit Free Press* carried the story of the Ford announcement with the following headline in its business section, "Ford admits its trucks hurt the earth." The Associated Press headline was, "Ford admits dilemma: SUVs vs. environment." Environmental groups said that they would use the report for lobbying in Washington for more stringent regulations. Debbie Zemke, director of

Ford's corporate governance said Ford still stood by its decision to be forthright, "We just said: 'For heaven's sake, everybody else is talking about it, so why shouldn't we?'"

GM and DaimlerChrysler announced that while they would not be accelerating their emissions reductions programs, they were working on alternative fuel vehicles. "We have different objectives on how we get to lower emissions," was the DaimlerChrylser response. GM noted, "It is taking its own path to lower vehicle emissions in the U.S. and around the world."

Do you think Ford is correct? Would you admit your best-selling products were dangerous for the environment?

Source: Adapted from Marianne M. Jennings, *Case Studies and Readings in Business Ethics*, 4th edition, West 2002.

description" into navigable waters in the United States without a permit from the Army Corps of Engineers. For a time, the act was used to prosecute those industrial polluters that were discharging without permit.

Present Legislation

Review the Clean Water Act:
http://www.law.cornell.edu/
uscode/33/ch26.html

It was not until 1972 that meaningful and enforceable federal legislation was enacted with the passage of the **Federal Water Pollution Control Act of 1972** (33 U.S.C. § 1401). Under this act, two goals were set: (1) swimmable and fishable waters by 1983 and (2) zero discharge of pollutants by 1985. The act was amended in 1977 to allow extensions and flexibility in meeting the goals and was renamed the **Clean Water Act.** One of the major changes brought about by the act was the move of water pollution regulation from local to federal control. Federal standards for water discharges were established on an industry-wide basis, and all industries, regardless of state location, are required to comply.

Under the act, all direct industrial dischargers are placed into twenty-seven groups, and the Environmental Protection Agency (EPA)—now responsible for water pollution control since the FWPCA was merged into it—establishes ranges of discharge allowed for each industrial group. The ranges for pulp mills, for example, differ from those for textile manufacturers, but all plants in the same industry must comply with the same ranges.

The ranges of discharges permitted per industrial group are referred to as **effluent guidelines.** In addition, the EPA has established within each industrial group a specific amount of discharge for each plant, which is the effluent limitation. Finally, for a plant to be able to discharge wastes into waterways, it must obtain from the EPA a **National Pollution Discharge Elimination System** (NPDES) permit. This type of permit is required only for direct dischargers, or **point sources,** and is not required of plants that discharge into sewer systems (although these secondary dischargers may still be required to pretreat their discharges). Obtaining a permit is a complicated process that requires not only EPA approval but also state approval, public hearings, and an opportunity for the proposed plant owners to obtain judicial review of a permit decision.

In issuing permits, the EPA may still prescribe standards for release. Generally, the standards that are set depend upon the type of substance the discharger proposes to release. For setting standards, the EPA has developed three categories of pollutants: **conventional, nonconventional,** and **toxic pollutants.** If a discharger is going to release a conventional pollutant, the EPA can require it to pretreat the substance with the **best conventional treatment** (BCT). If the pollutant to be discharged is either toxic or nonconventional, then the EPA can require the **best available treatment** (BAT), which is the highest standard imposed. In issuing permits and requiring these various levels of treatment, the EPA need only consider environmental effects, and not the economic effects, on the applicant discharger.

For information on wetlands, visit http://www.bergen.org/ AAST/Projects/ES/WL

C O N S I D E R . . .

12.3 Inland Steel Company applied for a permit from the EPA under the Federal Water Pollution Control Act of 1972. Although Inland was granted the permit, the EPA made the permit modifiable, as new standards for toxic releases and treatment were being developed. Inland claimed the modification restriction on the permit was invalid because the EPA did not have such authority and also because Inland would be subject to every technological change or discovery made during the course of the permit. Inland filed suit. Was the restriction invalid? [*Inland Steel Co. v. EPA*, 547 F.2d 367 (7th Cir. 1978)]

Review the Safe Water Drinking Act: http:// www.law.cornell.edu/ uscode/42/300g-1.html

In 1986, Congress passed the **Safe Drinking Water Act** (42 U.S.C. Section 300f), which provides for the EPA to establish national standards for contaminant levels in drinking water. The states are primarily responsible for enforcement and can have higher standards than the federal standards, but they must at least enforce the federal standards for their drinking water systems.

In 1990, Congress passed the **Oil Pollution Act** (OPA) (33 U.S.C. Section 1251). The act was passed in response to large oil tanker spills, such as the one resulting from the grounding of the *Exxon Valdez* in Prince William Sound, Alaska, that resulted in a spill of 11 million gallons of crude oil that coated 1,000 miles of Alaskan coastline. Another example was the 1990 explosion aboard the *Mega Borg* in Galveston Bay that resulted in a 4-million-gallon spill and a fire that burned for more than a week.

Review the Oil Pollution Act: http://www.law.cornell.edu/ uscode/33/ch40.html

The OPA applies to all navigable waters up to 200 miles offshore and places the federal government in charge of all oil spills. Once full liability for cleanup is imposed on the company responsible for the spill, the federal government may step in and clean up a spill and then demand compensation for the costs incurred. The Oil Spill Liability Trust Fund, established by a five-cent-per-barrel tax, covers cleanup costs when the party responsible is financially unable to do the cleanup.

Those responsible for spills are liable for penalties of $25,000 a day or $1,000 a barrel spilled. If the spill is the result of negligence or willful misconduct, the penalties are $3,000 per barrel spilled. Failure to report a spill can bring a $250,000 fine for an individual (sole proprietor or officer, according to agency and criminal liability principles) and up to five years imprisonment or $500,000 for a corporation. Civil penalties run higher and include the full cost of cleanup (up to $50 million) should those responsible not clean up the oil spill.

Re: The Exxon Valdez

On March 24, 1989, the oil tanker Exxon Valdez ran aground on Bligh Reef, south of Valdez, Alaska, and spilled approximately 10.8 million gallons of oil into Prince William Sound. The captain of the tanker was Joseph Hazelwood.

Captain Hazelwood had a history of drinking problems and had lost his New York driver's license after two drunk-driving convictions. In 1985, with the knowledge of Exxon officials, Captain Hazelwood joined a twenty-eight–day alcohol rehabilitation program. Almost a week after the Prince William Sound accident, Exxon revealed that Captain Hazelwood's blood-alcohol reading was 0.061 in a test taken 10 1/2 hours after the spill occurred. When announcing the test results, Exxon also announced Captain Hazelwood's termination.

Then U.S. Interior Secretary Manual Lujan called the spill the oil industry's "Three Mile Island." After ten days, the spill covered 1,000 square miles and leaked out of Prince William Sound onto beaches along the Gulf of Alaska and Cook Inlet. A cleanup army of 12,000 was sent in with hot water and oil-eating microbes. The workers found more than 1,000 dead otters among a local otter population of 15,000 to 22,000. Approximately 34,400 sea birds died, as did 151 bald eagles that ate the oil-infested remains of the sea birds.

Joseph Hazelwood was indicted by the state of Alaska on several charges, including criminal mischief, operating a watercraft while intoxicated, reckless endangerment, and negligent discharge of oil. He was found innocent of all charges except the negligent discharge of oil, was fined $50,000, and was required to spend 1,000 hours helping in the cleanup of the Alaskan beaches.

Following the spill, critics of Exxon maintained that the company's huge personnel cutbacks during the 1980s affected the safety and maintenance levels aboard the tankers. Subsequent hearings revealed that the crew of the *Valdez* was overburdened with demands of speed and efficiency. The crew was working ten- to twelve-hour days and often had interrupted sleep. Lookouts were often improperly posted, and junior officers were permitted control on the bridge without the required supervision. Robert LeResche, oil-spill coordinator for the state of Alaska, said, "It wasn't Captain Ahab on the bridge. It was Larry and Curly in the Exxon boardroom." In response to Exxon's critics, then CEO Lawrence Rawl stated, "And we say, `We're sorry, and we're doing all we can.' There were 30 million birds that went through the sound last summer, and only 30,000 carcasses have been recovered. Just look at how many ducks were killed in the Mississippi Delta in one hunting day in December! People have come up to me and said, `This is worse than Bhopal.' I say, 'Hell, Bhopal killed more than 3,000 people and injured 200,000 others!' Then they say, 'Well, if you leave the people out, it was worse than Bhopal.' "

Late in February 1990, Exxon was indicted by a grand jury in Anchorage on federal felony charges of violations of maritime safety and antipollution laws. The charges were brought after negotiations between Exxon and the Justice Department had been terminated. Both the state of Alaska and the Justice Department also brought civil suits against Exxon for the costs associated with cleaning up the spill.

By May 1990, Exxon had resumed its cleanup efforts using 110 employees at targeted sites. In 1991, Exxon reached plea agreements with the federal government and the state of Alaska on the criminal charges. In the agreements, Exxon consented to plead guilty to three misdemeanors and pay a $1.15 billion fine.

At the end of 1991, an Alaska jury awarded sixteen fishermen more than $2.5 million in damages and established a payout formula for similar plaintiffs in future litigation against Exxon. The jury awarded $5 billion in punitive damages, the largest verdict in history, but the Ninth Circuit called the award excessive in 2001 and remanded the case for a redetermination of the damages. Eight hundred other civil cases remained pending at the time of the verdict.

What was Exxon's "attitude" with regard to the spill? What was the company's purpose in cutting back on staff and maintenance expenditures? Was Captain Hazelwood morally responsible for the spill? Was Exxon management morally responsible for the spill?

As part of amendments to the Oil Pollution Act of 1990, Congress banned the *Valdez* from ever sailing into Prince William Sound again. The *Valdez* is not named in the act specifically, but the language of the statute is as follows:

> Notwithstanding any other law, tank vessels that have spilled more than 1,000,000 gallons of oil into the marine environment after March 22, 1989, are prohibited from operating on the navigable waters of Prince William Sound, Alaska.

33 U.S.C.A. § 2737

Solid Waste Disposal Regulation

Early Regulation

During the 1970s, there were two major toxic waste debacles that resulted in a new federal regulatory scheme of toxic waste disposal. In 1978, "Love Canal," as it came to be called, made national news as 80,000 tons of hazardous waste were found in the ground in an area that was primarily residential and included an elementary school. Epidemiological studies of cancer and illness rates in the area led to the discovery and eventual cleanup. Also, in Sheppardsville, Kentucky, an area that came to be called "Valley of the Drums," 17,000 drums of hazardous waste leaked tons of chemicals into the ground and water supply before their removal.

The emotional reaction to these two problem areas and the public outcry resulted in the passage of legislation that provided the federal government with some enforcement power for improper solid waste disposal. The **Toxic Substances Control Act** (TOSCA) (15 U.S.C. § 601) was passed in 1976 and authorized the EPA to control the manufacture, use, and disposal of toxic substances. Under the act, the EPA is authorized to prevent the manufacture of dangerous substances and stop the manufacture of substances subsequently found to be dangerous.

Also passed by Congress in reaction to dangerous dumping practices was the **Resource Conservation and Recovery Act of 1976** (RCRA) (42 U.S.C. § 6901). The two goals of the act are to control the disposal of potentially harmful substances and to encourage resource conservation and recovery. A critical part of the act's control is a manifest or permit system that requires manufacturers to obtain a permit for the storage or transfer of hazardous wastes so that the location of such wastes can be traced through an examination of the permits issued.

The Superfund

In 1980, Congress passed the **Comprehensive Environmental Response, Compensation, and Liability Act** (CERCLA) (42 U.S.C. § 9601), which authorized the president to issue funds for the cleanup of areas that were once disposal sites for hazardous wastes. Under the act, a **Hazardous Substance Response Trust Fund** was set up to provide funding for cleanup. If funds are expended in such a cleanup, then, under the provisions of the act, the company responsible for the disposal of the hazardous wastes can be sued by the federal government and required to repay the amounts expended from the trust fund. Often called the **Superfund,** the funds are available for governmental use but cannot be obtained through suit by private citizens affected by the hazardous disposals.

In 1986, CERCLA was amended by the **Superfund Amendment and Reauthorization Act.** Under the amendments in that act, liability provisions were included, and the EPA is now permitted to recover cleanup funds from those responsible for the release of hazardous substances. Approximately 700 hazardous substances are now covered. (They are listed at 40 C.F.R. § 302.) Since the passage of the 1986 amendments, there has been judicial expansion of the concept of "responsibility." Clearly, those who release the substances are liable, but that liability has been expanded to include those who purchase the property and did not perform adequate checks on the property's history.

CERCLA Lender Liability One of the more intriguing issues that resulted from CERCLA liability was whether a lender has the responsibility of cleanup because it was back in possession of the property due to a foreclosure sale or a deed in lieu

Review the Toxic Substances Control Act:
http://www.law.cornell.edu/uscode/15/ch53.html

Review the Resource Conservation and Recovery Act of 1976:
http://www.law.cornell.edu/uscode/42/ch82.html

Review the Comprehensive Environmental Response, Compensation, and Liability Act and Amendments:
http://www.law.cornell.edu/uscode/42/ch103.html

See CERCLA documents at:
http://www.citation.com/hpages/cercla.html

For Superfund information, try:
http://www.monitor.net/monitor/free/luftcleanup.html
or
http://www.epa.gov/superfund/index.htm
or
http://www.house.gov/democrats/ht_environ.html

of foreclosure. In *U.S.* v. *Fleet Factors Corp.*, 901 F.2d 1550 (11th Cir. 1990), the court held that a lender could be held responsible and liable for the cleanup of real property it finds itself holding due to a loan default. The finding of the court appeared to create great liability for lenders when they did not have control over the conduct of the mortgagor prior to their repossession or foreclosure. The result was that the EPA promulgated rules on lender liability in 1992. However, the rules did not provide lenders with sufficient guidelines for managing property obtained through default or foreclosure. To clarify liability issues, Congress passed the **Asset Conservation, Lender Liability, and Deposit Insurance Protection Act of 1996.** This statute provides a specific exclusion for lenders in that the definition of "owner/operator" does not include someone who "holds indicia of ownership primarily to protect his security interest." This new provision has been labeled the "secured lender exemption" from CERCLA liability. However, the new act does provide that a lender can lose its status if it "actually participate[s] in the management or operational affairs of a vessel or facility." But, the "capacity" to assert control does not result in lender liability as the *Fleet Factors* case held. A lender can do the following and still not be subject to environmental liability:

- Monitor or enforce terms of the security agreement.
- Monitor or inspect the premises or facility.
- Mandate that the debtor take action on hazardous materials.
- Provide financial advice or counseling.
- Restructure or renegotiate the loan terms.
- Exercise any remedies available at law.
- Foreclose on the property.
- Sell the property.
- Lease the property.

CERCLA—Four Classes of Liability Rules There are four classes of parties that can be held liable under CERCLA. "Owners and operators" of a contaminated piece of property comprise one group. While "owner" is self-explanatory, "operator" would include those who lease property and then contaminate it, such as those who lease factories, operate storage facilities, and so forth. A second group would be owners and operators at the time the property was contaminated. This group brings under CERCLA jurisdiction those who were responsible for the property contamination, as opposed to present owners who had the problem deeded to them. For example, many gas stations have been converted to other businesses. Suppose that one of the underground gas tanks once used by the gas station has been leaking hazardous materials into the surrounding soil. Not only would the present owners be liable; so also would be all those who owned the gasoline station previously.

The final two groups consist of those who transport hazardous materials and those who arrange for the transportation of hazardous materials. There are virtually no liability exemptions for those who fit into these four groups. Further, it is important to understand that the liability exists under CERCLA for both corporations and corporate officers. For example, the EPA has been successful in criminal prosecutions against officers of corporations who have been ordered to conduct a cleanup but who failed to do so.

CERCLA and Corporate Liability CERCLA liability has also extended to corporate board members and corporate successors and officers in cases in which a company is purchased by another firm. Those who merge or buy corporations also buy into CERCLA liability—liability under CERCLA cannot be avoided by a transfer of ownership. The U.S. Supreme Court ruled in *U.S. v. Bestfoods,* 525 U.S. 51 (1998) (see Chapter 21) that a parent corporation is not automatically liable under CERCLA for a subsidiary corporation's conduct but may be responsible if the subsidiary is simply a shell. In other words, CERCLA liability of parent corporations for the actions of their subsidiaries is governed by corporate law on piercing the corporate veil (see Chapter 21). Under the *Best Foods* case, liability of the parent corporation for actions of a subsidiary results if:

1. the parent corporation operates the facility, is a joint venturer in the operation of the facility, or works side-by-side with the subsidiary in operations;

2. the parent and subsidiary corporations share officers and directors such that it becomes impossible to separate out the decision-making processes; or

3. an officer of the parent corporation (or other designated or authorized employee) operates the facility of the subsidiary.[2]

The best safeguard for lenders against CERCLA liability is screening the property carefully before accepting it as collateral. The lender's sale to another is not covered, and the lender is in the position of trying to sell property with a CERCLA problem. The value of the collateral is reduced substantially. The lender and any purchaser of a piece of property should conduct a *due diligence review* of the property. There are three phases in a due diligence review. Phase 1 consists of a search to determine whether there is evidence of past or current environmental problems on the property. Evidence reviewed in a Phase 1 search would be private and public records, aerial photographs, and a site inspection. If Phase 1 reveals some concerns, then the parties proceed to Phase 2, which consists of chemical analysis of soil, structures, and water from the property. If Phase 2 finds the presence of contaminants, the report for Phase 2 estimates the cost of cleanup. Phase 3 is the actual cleanup plan.

C O N S I D E R . . .

12.4 Grand Auto Parts Stores receives used automotive batteries from customers as trade-ins. Grand Auto drives a screwdriver through spent batteries and then sells them to Morris Kirk & Sons, a battery-cracking plant that extracts and smelts lead. Tons of crushed battery casings were found on Kirk's land. The EPA sought to hold Grand Auto liable for cleanup. Can Grand Auto be held liable? [*Catellus Dev. Corp. v. United States,* 34 F.3d 748 (9th Cir. 1994)]

New Developments under CERCLA

Judicial Developments One issue that courts continue to face with respect to CERCLA cleanup efforts is whether insurance policies for comprehensive general liability apply to a company's cost of cleanup. The wording of individual policies and intent of the parties are controlling in these cases.

Other issues within CERCLA are developing in various types of CERCLA cases. One federal district court declared CERCLA unconstitutional for its retroactive effect (*U.S. v. Olin Corp.*, 927 F.Supp. 1502), but it was reversed [*U.S. v. Olin Corp.*, 107 F.3d 1506 (11th Cir. 1997)]. Other courts have begun to examine the issue of causation between the contaminants present on a piece of property and its relation to any injury as a means of a cost/benefit analysis. For example, in *Licciardi* v. *Murphy Oil U.S.A.*, 111 F.3d 396 (5th Cir. 1997), one federal circuit court held that there must be some causation established between the cleanup and what the owner or operator is alleged to have dumped at the site. However, not all the federal circuit courts have followed that line of reasoning in their decisions [*Johnson* v. *James Langley Operation Co., Inc.*, 226 F.3d 957 (8th Cir. 2000)].

Another basis for CERCLA challenges has been one grounded in the basic administrative law principle of an arbitrary and capricious challenge to an EPA demand for cleanup of a site when the demand for cleanup is not linked to any danger. The EPA cleanup was upheld in *U.S. v. Broderick Investment Co.*, 200 F.3d 679 (10th Cir. 1999), despite the cleanup being very costly because the EPA ordered a cleanup to the point that the cancer rate in the area would be reduced to one in 100,000, a rate higher than in non-Superfund sites. However, because a day-care center was planned for the land, the court held that the cleanup level was not arbitrary or capricious.

The Self-Audit Companies have been responding to CERCLA liability with voluntary disclosures through the EPA's self-audit procedures. The EPA encourages companies to self-identify problem lands and areas in exchange for reduced fines. Companies have hired executive-level managers such as vice presidents for environment or vice presidents for health, safety, and environment to manage a staff

> **BUSINESS PLANNING TIP**
>
> Due diligence is necessary not only when buying property but also when buying companies with land holdings. Liability under CERCLA is transferred via land ownership or corporate ownership.

of in-house professionals who do everything from supervising a company's current activities to investigating past activities to determine environmental problems. These problems are then reported to the EPA, and the company and agency work together to solve the problem and be certain cleanup is done where warranted. These self-audits and disclosures also help the companies be more accurate in their disclosures in materials to shareholders and analysts. The "Manager's Desk" "The In-House Investigation and the EPA" gives background on the requirements for self-audits.

Environmental Quality Regulation

Review the National Environmental Policy Act: http://www.law.cornell.edu/ uscode/42/ch55.html

Environmental controls of air, water, and waste are directed at private parties in the use of their land. However, as part of the environmental control scheme, Congress also passed an act that regulates what governmental entities can do in the use of their properties. The **National Environmental Policy Act** (NEPA) of 1969 (42 U.S.C. § 4321) was passed to require federal agencies to take into account the environmental impact of their proposed actions and to prepare an **environmental impact statement** (EIS) before taking any proposed action.

An EIS must be prepared and filed with the EPA whenever an agency sends a proposed law to Congress and whenever an agency will take major federal action significantly affecting the quality of the environment. The information required in an EIS is as follows:

1. The proposed action's environmental impact
2. Adverse environmental effects (if any)

FOR THE MANAGER'S DESK

Re: The In-House Investigation and the EPA

In 1997, the EPA initiated 562 criminal investigations and referred 256 cases to the U.S. Justice Department for criminal prosecution. Both environmental investigations and referrals for prosecutions under federal law have been increasing each year. The criminal investigation staff for the EPA has grown from 150 in 1996 to 200 in 1997.

The definition of "criminal intent" or *"mens rea"* (see Chapter 9) required for prosecution of environmental crimes is quite broad, and even the barest degree of knowledge can result in the imposition of liability for corporate officers. Those who should have known and could have prevented environmental violations are held accountable, even though they may not have had complete knowledge about a problem.

This potential level of liability has created an atmosphere of self-investigation and self-reporting among corporations, in-house legal counsel, and officers designated as environmental officers. Concerns developed about privilege issues and self-incrimination as the companies, employees, and officers tried to determine whether there have been any violations within the company.

To encourage self-reporting and self-investigation, the EPA has developed a policy on recommending *against* criminal prosecutions. Companies complying with the steps provided in the policy enjoy some guarantee that the officers and companies will not be prosecuted criminally. These steps include:

1. The company must fully cooperate with the EPA, including turning over to EPA officials all information and materials from the investigation, audit, or due diligence studies that led to the discovery of the criminal violation.

2. The reported violation must have come from the company's own self-discovery processes, and it must not be reported because of another's discovery or threat of disclosure.

3. The voluntary disclosure must be made before the EPA has launched a criminal investigation.

4. The voluntary disclosure must be made before the EPA—while not having yet opened an investigation—is talking with citizens, whistle-blowers, or others about potential violations.

5. The voluntary disclosure must be made in a timely fashion (generally ten days from the time of discovery).

6. The company making the voluntary disclosure must remedy the problem within 60 days and provide verification of such closure or, if additional time is needed, make a request with accompanying justification for extended time.

7. The company must agree to take whatever steps are necessary to prevent a recurrence.

8. The reported violation must not be a repeat of previous conduct.

Decisions on criminal prosecution under environmental statutes will be made by a Voluntary Disclosure Board comprised of employees from both the EPA and the Department of Justice.

Source: Adapted from an in-house memo from Earl Devaney, director of the EPA's Office of Criminal Enforcement, Forensics, and Training.

3. Alternative methods

4. Short-term effects versus long-term maintenance, enhancement, and productivity

5. Irreversible and irretrievable resource uses

Examples of federal agency actions that have faced the issue of preparation of EISs include the Alaska oil pipeline, the extermination of wild horses on federal lands, the construction of government buildings, the NAFTA treaty, and highway construction.

The following case involves the question of whether an EIS was needed.

CASE 12.2

Sierra Club v. *United States Dep't of Transportation*
753 F.2d 120 (D.C. 1985)

Skiing and Landing at Jackson Hole

FACTS

In 1983, the Federal Aviation Administration (FAA) issued two orders amending the operations specifications for Frontier Airlines, Inc., and Western Airlines, Inc. These amendments gave the airlines permanent authorizations to operate Boeing 737 jet airplanes (B-737s) out of Jackson Hole Airport, which is located within the Grand Teton National Park in Wyoming. These two airlines are the only major commercial carriers that schedule flights to and from Jackson Hole.

Private jets have flown into the airport since 1960; and Western Airlines has been flying into Jackson Hole since 1941. The airport is the only one in the country located in a national park, and Congress has continually funded expansions and improvements of the once single dirt-runway airport.

In 1978, Frontier applied for permission to fly B-737s into the Jackson Hole Airport. The FAA released its EIS on the application in 1980, which found that B-737s were comparable with C-580 propeller aircraft (the type then being used by Western and Frontier) for noise intrusion but were substantially quieter than the private jets using the airport. The study also showed that fewer flights would be necessary because the B-737 could carry more passengers and that different flight paths could reduce noise. Based on this EIS, Frontier was given the right to use B-737s for two years. When Frontier applied for permanent approval, the FAA used the 1980 EIS statement and found that with flight time restrictions, the impact would not harm the environment.

The Sierra Club (Petitioner), a national conservation organization, brought suit for the FAA's failure to file an EIS for the 1983 amendments and for the use of national park facilities for commercial air traffic without considering alternatives.

JUDICIAL OPINION

BORK, Circuit Judge

We do not think the FAA violated NEPA by failing to prepare an additional EIS. Under NEPA, an EIS must be prepared before approval of any major federal action that will "significantly affect the quality of the human environment." The purpose of the Act is to require agencies to consider environmental issues before taking any major action.

Under the statute, agencies have the initial and primary responsibility to determine the extent of the impact and whether it is significant enough to warrant preparation of an EIS. This is accomplished by preparing an Environmental Assessment (EA). An EA allows the agency to consider environmental concerns, while reserving agency resources to prepare full EIS's for appropriate cases. If a finding of no significant impact is made after analyzing the EA, then preparation of an EIS is unnecessary. An agency has broad discretion in making this determination, and the decision is reviewable only if it was arbitrary, capricious or an abuse of discretion.

This court has established four criteria for reviewing an agency's decision to forego preparation of an EIS. First, the agency must have accurately identified the relevant environmental concern. Second, once the agency has identified the problem, it must take a "hard look" at the problem in preparing the EA. Third, if a finding of no significant impact is made, the agency must be able to make a convincing case for its finding. Last, if the agency does find an impact of true significance, preparation of an EIS can be avoided only if the agency finds that changes or safeguards in the project sufficiently reduce the impact to a minimum.

The first test is not at issue here. Both the FAA and Sierra Club have identified the relevant environmental concern as noise by jet aircraft within Grand Teton National Park. The real issues raised by Sierra Club are whether the FAA took a "hard look" at the problem, and whether the methodology used by the agency in its alleged hard look was proper.

We find that the FAA did take a hard look at the problem. The FAA properly prepared an EA to examine the additional impact on the environment of the plan. The EA went forward from the 1980 EIS. The 1980 EIS, which was based on extensive research by Dr. Hakes of the University of Wyoming, noise testing by the FAA, and data derived from manufacturer

(continued)

information, showed that noise intrusions of B-737 jets over the level caused by C-580 propeller aircraft amounted to only 1 dbl near the Airport and decreased in proportion to the distance from the Airport. The agency, exercising its expertise, has found that an increase this minute is not significant for any environment. In addition, the EIS and Hakes studies were based on a worst case scenario, and it was determined that if certain precautions were taken the actual noise levels could be diminished greatly.

Petitioner argues that because Jackson Hole Airport is located within national parkland a different standard—i.e., individual event noise level analysis—is mandated. Both individual event and cumulative data were amassed in preparing the 1980 EIS on which the EAs were based. The fact that the agency in exercising its expertise relied on the cumulative impact levels as being more indicative of the actual environmental disturbance is well within the area of discretion given to the agency. We agree with petitioner that although noise is a problem in any set-ting, "airplane noise is fundamentally inconsistent with the type of recreational experience Park visitors are seeking" and should be minimized. Here the FAA found that a cumulative noise increase of 1 dbl or less is not significant—even for the pristine environment in which Jackson Hole Airport is located.

Given all of these facts, we think the FAA was not required to prepare yet another EIS before granting permanent authorizations for the use of B-737s.

The orders of the FAA are hereby affirmed.

CASE QUESTIONS

1. What airport noise is at issue?
2. Who is involved in the case?
3. Was an EIS prepared?
4. What is the basis for the appeal?
5. What has the FAA allowed? Will the authorizations stand?

Other Federal Environmental Regulations

In addition to the previously discussed major environmental laws, many other specific federal statutes protect the environment.

Surface Mining

The **Surface Mining and Reclamation Act of 1977** (42 U.S.C. § 6907) requires those mining coal to restore land surfaces to their original conditions and prohibits surface coal mining without a permit.

Noise Control

Under the **Noise Control Act of 1972** (42 U.S.C. § 4901), the EPA, along with the Federal Aviation Administration (FAA), can control the amount of noise emissions from low-flying aircraft for the protection of landowners in flight paths.

Pesticide Control

Review an environmental group's pesticide Web site:
http://www.beyondpesticides.org

Under the **Federal Environmental Pesticide Control Act,** the use of pesticides is controlled. All pesticides must be registered with the EPA before they can be sold, shipped, distributed, or received. Also under the act, the EPA administrator is given the authority to classify pesticides according to their effects and dangers.

OSHA

Review the Environmental Pesticide Control Act:
http://www.law.cornell.edu/uscode/7/ch6.html

The **Occupational Safety and Health Administration** (OSHA) is responsible for workers' environments. OSHA controls the levels of exposure to toxic substances and requires safety precautions for exposure to such dangerous substances as asbestos, benzene, and chloride.

*Review the Asbestos Hazard
Emergency Response Act:*
http://www.law.cornell.edu/
uscode/15/2641.html

Asbestos

Buildings that contain asbestos materials remain a problem for buyers, sellers, and occupants. The **Asbestos Hazard Emergency Response Act** (AHERA), passed in 1986, required all public and private schools to arrange for the inspection of their facilities to determine whether their buildings had asbestos-containing materials (ACMs). Schools are required to develop plans for containment, but other buildings are not regulated. The Clean Air Act does, however, define airborne asbestos as a toxic pollutant, and liability may result from the release of fibers from this known carcinogen. Further, an amendment to the Superfund Act classified asbestos as a **community-right-to-know substance,** which means that there is probably a duty to disclose the presence of asbestos to buyers, tenants, and employees. Numerous ethical questions arise with respect to the presence of asbestos and the obligations of landowners to replace the asbestos given that the phaseout of its use did not end until 1997. Questions such as the impact of the release of asbestos from the walls when tenants, employees, and others hang photos and other objects by nailing them onto the walls remain. The issues of the degree of harm and the cost of replacement continue to be debated among property owners.

*Review the Endangered
Species Act:*
http://www.law.cornell.edu/
uscode/22/2151q.html

*For information on forests,
see*
http://forests.org

Endangered Species

In 1973, Congress passed the **Endangered Species Act,** a law that has been a powerful tool for environmentalists in protecting certain species through their advocacy of restrictions on commercial use and development when the habitats of certain species are interfered with. Under the act, the secretary of the interior is responsible for identifying endangered terrestrial species, and the secretary of commerce identifies endangered marine species. In addition, these cabinet members must designate habitats considered crucial for these species if they are to thrive. In many instances, there is litigation concerning what species should or should not be on the list. Once a species is on the list, its critical habitat cannot be disturbed by development, noise, or destruction. The following case, which provides an answer to the chapter opening "Consider," has given federal agencies broad authority in protecting endangered species.

CASE 12.3

Babbitt v. Sweet Home Chapter of Communities for a Great Oregon
515 U.S. 687 (1995)

Owls versus Jobs: Lumber versus Endangered Species

FACTS

Two U.S. agencies halted logging in the Pacific Northwest because it endangered the habitat of the northern spotted owl and the red-cockaded woodpecker, both endangered species. Sweet Home Chapter (respondents) is a group of landowners, logging companies, and fami-

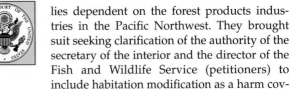

lies dependent on the forest products industries in the Pacific Northwest. They brought suit seeking clarification of the authority of the secretary of the interior and the director of the Fish and Wildlife Service (petitioners) to include habitation modification as a harm covered by the Endangered Species Act (ESA).

(continued)

The federal district court found for the secretary and director and held that they had the authority to protect the northern spotted owl through a halt to logging. The court of appeals reversed. Babbitt, the secretary of the interior, appealed.

JUDICIAL OPINION

STEVENS, Justice

Section 9(a)(1) of the Endangered Species Act provides the following protection for endangered species:

Except as provided in sections 1535(g)(2) and 1539 of this title, with respect to any endangered species of fish or wildlife listed pursuant to section 1533 of this title it is unlawful for any person subject to the jurisdiction of the United States to—(B) take any such species within the United States or the territorial sea of the United States[.] 16 U.S.C. § 1538(a)(1).

Section 3(19) of the Act defines the statutory term "take":

The term 'take' means to harass, harm, pursue, hunt, shoot, wound, kill, trap, capture, or collect, or to attempt to engage in any such conduct. 16 U.S.C. § 1532(19).

The Act does not further define the terms it uses to define "take." The Interior Department regulations that implement the statute, however, define the statutory term "harm":

Harm *in the definition of 'take' in the Act means an act which actually kills or injures wildlife. Such act may include significant habitat modification or degradation where it actually kills or injures wildlife by significantly impairing essential behavioral patterns, including breeding, feeding, or sheltering.*
50 CFR § 17.3 (1994).

We assume respondents have no desire to harm either the red-cockaded woodpecker or the spotted owl; they merely wish to continue logging activities that would be entirely proper if not prohibited by the ESA. On the other hand, we must assume *arguendo* that those activities will have the effect, even though unintended, of detrimentally changing the natural habitat of both listed species and that, as a consequence, members of those species will be killed or injured. Under respondents' view of the law, the Secretary's only means of forestalling that grave result— even when the actor knows it is certain to occur—is to use his § 5 authority to purchase the lands on which the survival of the species depends. The Secretary, on the other hand, submits that the § 9 prohibition on takings, which Congress defined to include "harm," places on respondents a duty to avoid harm

that habitat alteration will cause the birds unless respondents first obtain a permit pursuant to § 10.

The text of the Act provides three reasons for concluding that the Secretary's interpretation is reasonable. First, an ordinary understanding of the word "harm" supports it. The dictionary definition of the verb form of "harm" is "to cause hurt or damage to: injure." Webster's Third New International Dictionary 1034 (1966). In the context of the ESA, that definition naturally encompasses habitat modification that results in actual injury or death to members of an endangered or threatened species.

Respondents argue that the Secretary should have limited the purview of "harm" to direct applications of force against protected species, but the dictionary definition does not include the word "directly" or suggest in any way that only direct or willful action that leads to injury constitutes "harm." Moreover, unless the statutory term "harm" encompasses indirect as well as direct injuries, the word has no meaning that does not duplicate the meaning of other words that § 3 uses to define "take." A reluctance to treat statutory terms as surplusage supports the reasonableness of the Secretary's interpretation.

Second, the broad purpose of the ESA supports the Secretary's decision to extend protection against activities that cause the precise harms Congress enacted the statute to avoid. As stated in § 2 of the Act, among its central purposes is "to provide a means whereby the ecosystems upon which endangered species and threatened species depend may be conserved."

Third, the fact that Congress in 1982 authorized the Secretary to issue permits for takings that § 9(a)(1)(B) would otherwise prohibit, "if such taking is incidental to, and not the purpose of, the carrying out of an otherwise lawful activity," 16 U.S.C. § 1539(a)(1)(B), strongly suggests that Congress understood § 9(a)(1)(B) to prohibit indirect as well as deliberate takings. The permit process requires the applicant to prepare a "conservation plan" that specifies how he intends to "minimize and mitigate" the "impact" of his activity on endangered and threatened species, 16 U.S.C. § 1539(a)(2)(A), making clear that Congress had in mind foreseeable rather than merely accidental effects on listed species.

The Court of Appeals made three errors in asserting that "harm" must refer to a direct application of force because the words around it do. First, the court's premise was flawed. Several of the words that accompany "harm" in the § 3 definition of "take," especially "harass," "pursue," "wound," and "kill," refer to actions or effects that do not require direct applications of force. Second, to the extent the court read a requirement of intent or purpose into the words used to define "take," it ignored § 9's express provision that a "knowing" action is enough to violate the Act. Third, the court employed *noscitur a sociis* to give "harm" essentially the same function as other words in the definition, thereby denying it independent meaning. The canon, to the contrary, counsels that a word "gathers meaning from the words around it." The statutory context of "harm" suggests that Congress meant that term to serve a particular function in the ESA, consistent with but distinct from the functions of the other verbs used to define "take." The Secretary's interpretation of "harm" to include indirectly injuring endangered animals through habitat modification permissibly interprets "harm" to have "a character of its own not to be submerged by its association."

When it enacted the ESA, Congress delegated broad administrative and interpretive power to the Secretary. See 16 U.S.C. §§ 1533, 1540(f). The task of defining and listing endangered and threatened species requires an expertise and attention to detail that exceeds the normal province of Congress. Fashioning appropriate standards for issuing permits under § 10 for takings that would otherwise violate § 9 necessarily requires the exercise of broad discretion. The proper interpretation of a term such as "harm" involves a complex policy choice. When Congress has entrusted the Secretary with broad discretion, we are especially reluctant to substitute our views of wise policy for his. In this case, that reluc-

tance accords with our conclusion, based on the text, structure, and legislative history of the ESA, that the Secretary reasonably construed the intent of Congress when he defined "harm" to include "significant habitat modification or degradation that actually kills or injures wildlife."

In the elaboration and enforcement of the ESA, the Secretary and all persons who must comply with the law will confront difficult questions of proximity and degree; for, as all recognize, the Act encompasses a vast range of economic and social enterprises and endeavors. These questions must be addressed in the usual course of the law, through case-by-case resolution and adjudication.

The judgment of the Court of Appeals is reversed.

CASE QUESTIONS

1. Is habitat modification harming endangered species?

2. Does the Court's interpretation mean no intent is required to violate ESA?

3. Did Congress intend to give the secretary authority to shut down an industry?

4. Is logging prevented now?

5. What ethical issues arise from this case?

Aftermath: In August 1995, Congress passed, as a rider to a budget-reduction bill, a provision that suspended environmental laws in some national forest areas in Washington and Oregon through 1996.

Since the time of these head-on confrontations, the logging and paper industries have adopted a "Sustainable Forestry Initiative." The Initiative, adopted by 200 members of the American Forest and Paper Association, supports ecofriendly logging. The Nature Conservancy supports the Initiative, which has had the effect of negotiated solutions to the issue of logging versus environmental protection. No further legislation has been needed at the federal level because of the cooperation between and among these groups.

In the following case, the U.S. Supreme Court interpreted the Endangered Species Act as also permitting lawsuits by landowners who are affected by the statute's application.

CASE 12.4

Bennett v. *Spear*
520 U.S. 154 (1997)

Falling for the Lost River Sucker: Ranchers, ESA, and Water Levels

FACTS

The Fish and Wildlife Services issued an opinion on the operation of the Klamath Irrigation Project and the project's impact on two varieties of endangered fish. The Klamath Project is one of the oldest of the federal reclamation projects and is a series of lakes, rivers, dams, and irrigation canals in northern California and southern Oregon. The opinion concluded that the operation of the project might impact on the Lost River Sucker (*Deltistes luxatus*) and Shortnose Sucker (*Chasmistes brevirostris*) species of fish that were listed as endangered in 1988. The opinion further provided for alternative means of operation for the project that included the maintenance of minimum water levels in certain portions of the project.

Brad Bennett and other ranchers (petitioners) operate their ranches within the areas designated to receive less water pursuant to the biological opinion issued. Bennett filed suit alleging that the opinion was incorrect in its conclusions on the impact of the project on the two species of fish and that the opinion failed to take into account the resulting economic impact of lessening the water levels. Bennett's complaint alleged that the Endangered Species Act (ESA) and the Administrative Procedure Act (APA) required the federal government to take his interests into account in making the determination as to what to do about the project. The federal district court dismissed the complaint and the court of appeals affirmed the dismissal. Mr. Bennett appealed.

JUDICIAL OPINION

SCALIA, Justice
We first turn to the question the Court of Appeals found dispositive: whether petitioners lack standing by virtue of the zone-of-interests test. Although petitioners contend that their claims lie both under the ESA and the APA, we look first at the ESA because it may permit petitioners to recover their litigation costs, and because the APA by its terms independently authorizes review only when "there is no other adequate remedy in a court," 5 U.S.C. § 704.

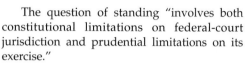

The question of standing "involves both constitutional limitations on federal-court jurisdiction and prudential limitations on its exercise."

Numbered among these prudential requirements is the doctrine of particular concern in this case: that a plaintiff's grievance must arguably fall within the zone of interests protected or regulated by the statutory provision or constitutional guarantee invoked in the suit.

We have made clear, however, that the breadth of the zone of interests varies according to the provisions of law at issue, so that what comes within the zone of interests of a statute for purposes of obtaining judicial review of administrative action under the "generous review provisions" of the APA may not do so for other purposes.

The first question in the present case is whether the ESA's citizen-suit provision negates the zone-of-interests test (or, perhaps more accurately, expands the zone of interests). We think it does. The first operative portion of the provision says that "any person may commence a civil suit"—an authorization of remarkable breadth when compared with the language Congress ordinarily uses. Even in some other environmental statutes, Congress has used more restrictive formulations, such as "[any person] having an interest which is or may be adversely affected," or "any person having a valid legal interest which is or may be adversely affected . . . whenever such action constitutes a case or controversy." And in contexts other than the environment, Congress has often been even more restrictive. In statutes concerning unfair trade practices and other commercial matters, for example, it has authorized suit only by "[a]ny person injured in his business or property."

Our readiness to take the term "any person" at face value is greatly augmented by two interrelated considerations: that the overall subject matter of this legislation is the environment (a matter in which it is common to think all persons have an interest) and that the obvious purpose of the particular provision in question is to encourage enforcement by so-called "private attorneys general"—evidenced by its elimination of the usual amount-in-controversy and diversity-of-citizenship requirements, its provision for recovery of the costs of litigation (including even expert witness fees), and its reservation to the Government of a right for first refusal to pursue the action initially and a right to intervene later. Given these factors, we think the conclusion of expanded standing follows.

It is true that the plaintiffs here are seeking to prevent application of environmental restrictions rather than to implement them. But the "any person" formulation applies to all the causes of action authorized by § 1540(g)—not only to actions against private violators of environmental restrictions, and not only to actions against the Secretary asserting underenforcement under § 1533, but also to actions against the Secretary asserting overenforcement under § 1533. As we shall discuss below, the citizen-suit provision does favor environmentalists in that it covers all private violations of the Act but not all failures of the Secretary to meet his administrative responsibilities; but there is no textual basis for saying that its expansion of standing requirements applies to environmentalists alone. The Court of Appeals therefore erred in concluding that petitioners lacked standing under the zone-of-interests test to bring their claims under the ESA's citizen-suit provision.

By the Government's own account, while the Service's Biological Opinion theoretically serves an "advisory function," 51 Fed.Reg. 19928 (1986), in reality it has a powerful coercive effect on the action agency:

The statutory scheme . . . presupposes that the biological opinion will play a central role in the action agency's decision-making process, and that it will typically be based on an administrative record that is fully adequate for the action agency's decision insofar as ESA issues are concerned. . . . [A] federal agency that chooses to deviate from the recommendations contained in a biological opinion bears the burden of "articulat[ing] in its administrative record its reason for disagreeing with the conclusions of a biological opinion."

51 Fed.Reg. 19, 956 (1986).

What this concession omits to say, moreover, is that the action agency must not only articulate its reasons for disagreement (which ordinarily requires species and habitat investigations that are not within the action agency's expertise), but that it runs a substantial risk if its (inexpert) reasons turn out to be wrong. A Biological Opinion of the sort rendered here alters the legal regime to which the action

agency is subject. When it "offers reasonable and prudent alternatives" to the proposed action, a Biological Opinion must include a so-called "Incidental Take Statement"—a written statement specifying, among other things, those "measures that the [Service] considers necessary or appropriate to minimize [the action's impact on the affected species]" and the "terms and conditions . . . that must be complied with by the Federal agency . . . to implement [such] measures."

The Service itself is, to put it mildly, keenly aware of the virtually determinative effect of its biological opinions. The Incidental Take Statement at issue in the present case begins by instructing the reader that any taking of a listed species is prohibited unless "such taking is in compliance with this incidental take statement," and warning that "[t]he measures described below are nondiscretionary, and must be taken by [the Bureau]." Given all of this, and given petitioners' allegations that the Bureau had, until issuance of the Biological Opinion, operated the Klamath Project in the same manner throughout the twentieth century, it is not difficult to conclude that petitioners have met their burden—which is relatively modest at this state of the litigation—of alleging that their injury is "fairly traceable" to the Service's Biological Opinion and that it will "likely" be redressed—i.e., the Bureau will not impose such water level restrictions—if the Biological Opinion is set aside.

Whether a plaintiff's interest is "arguably . . . protected . . . by the statute" within the meaning of the zone-of-interests test is to be determined not by reference to the overall purpose of the Act in question (here, species preservation), but by reference to the particular provision of law upon which the plaintiff relies. It is difficult to understand how the Ninth Circuit could have failed to see this from our cases. As we said with the utmost clarity in *National Wildlife Federal*, "the plaintiff must establish that the injury he complains of . . . falls within the 'zone of interests' sought to be protected by the statutory provision whose violation forms the legal basis for his complaint."

The Court of Appeals erred in affirming the District Court's dismissal of petitioners' claims for lack of jurisdiction. Petitioners' complaint alleges facts sufficient to meet the requirements of Article III standing, and none of their ESA claims is precluded by the zone-of-interests test. Petitioners' § 1533 claim is reviewable under ESA's citizen-suit provision, and

(continued)

petitioners' remaining claims are reviewable under the APA.

The judgment of the Court of Appeals is reversed.

CASE QUESTIONS

1. Who has brought the suit, and why?

2. Can those affected by the protection of an endangered species bring suit under the ESA?

3. How does the court deal with the issue raised by the government that the opinion is only an opinion and not government action?

4. Do the ranchers have standing to challenge the endangered species protection under the ESA?

5. The court's opinion was unanimous. Do you agree that both sides in an environmental case, those representing the interests of the species and those representing economic interests, should have the right to challenge a finding by the federal government?

STATE ENVIRONMENTAL LAWS

In addition to federal enactments, all the states have enacted some form of environmental law and have established their own environmental policies and agencies. Some states may require new industrial businesses to obtain a state permit along with the required federal permits for the operation of their plants. Some states regulate the types of fuels that can be used in vehicles and offer incentives for carpooling.

ENFORCEMENT OF ENVIRONMENTAL LAWS

Federal environmental laws can be enforced through criminal sanctions, penalties, injunctions, and suits by private citizens. In addition to federal enforcement rights, certain common-law remedies, such as nuisance or trespass, exist for the protection of property rights. This portion of the chapter discusses the various remedies available for environmental violations.

Parties Responsible for Enforcement

Although many federal agencies are involved with environmental issues, the Environmental Protection Agency (EPA), established in 1970, is the agency responsible for the major environmental problems of air and water pollution, solid waste disposal, toxic substance management, and noise pollution. The EPA is responsible for the promulgation of specific standards and the enforcement of those standards with the use of the remedies discussed in the following subsections. The federal EPA may work in conjunction with state EPAs in the development and enforcement of state programs.

The **Council on Environmental Quality** (CEQ) was established in 1966 under the National Environment Act and is part of the executive branch of government. Its role in the environment regulatory scheme is that of policymaker. The CEQ is responsible for formulating national policies on the quality of the environment and then making recommendations to lawmakers regarding its policy statements.

In addition to these major environmental agencies, other federal agencies are involved in enforcement of environmental issues, such as the Atomic Energy Commission, the Federal Power Commission, the Department of Housing and Urban Development, the Department of the Interior, the Forest Service, the Bureau of Land Management, and the Department of Commerce. Basically, all federal

EXHIBIT 12.1 **Penalties for Violation of Federal Environmental Laws**

ACT	PENALTIES	PRIVATE SUIT
Clean Air Act	$25,000 per day, up to one year imprisonment; fifteen years for willful or repeat violations; $10,000 rewards	Citizen suits; authorized EPA suit for injunctive relief
Clean Water Act	$25,000 per day, up to one year imprisonment, or both; $50,000/three years for violations with knowledge; $100,000/six years for subsequent violations	Citizen suits; authorized EPA suit for injunctive relief
Resource Conservation and Recovery Act (Solid Waste Disposal Act)	$250,000 and/or fifteen years for intentional; $1,000,000 for corps; $50,000 and/or five years for others	Citizen and negligence suits after EPA refuses to handle
Oil Pollution Act	$25,000 per day, or $1,000 per barrel; $3,000 per barrel if willful or negligent; $250,000 and/or five years for failure to report	Hazardous Substance/Response Trust Fund for cleanup; EPA suit for injunctive relief and reimbursement of trust funds; Private actions in negligence

agencies that deal with the use of land, water, and air are involved in compliance with and enforcement of environmental laws.

Criminal Sanctions for Violations

Most of the federal statutes previously discussed carry criminal sanctions for violations. Exhibit 12.1 summarizes the various penalties provided under each of the discussed acts. In exercising its enforcement power, the EPA may require businesses to maintain records or to install equipment necessary for monitoring the amounts of pollutants being released into the air or water.

The following case deals with the issue of criminal liability for environmental law violations.

CASE 12.5

United States v. *Johnson & Towers, Inc.*
741 F.2d 662 (3d Cir. 1984)

Changing Your Oil: It Can Be Criminal

FACTS

Johnson & Towers (Johnson) repairs and overhauls large motor vehicles. In its operations, Johnson uses degreasers and other industrial chemicals that contain methylene chloride and trichlorethylene, classified as "hazardous wastes" under the Resource Conservation and Recovery Act (RCRA) and as pollutants under the Clean Water Act.

(continued)

The waste chemicals from Johnson's cleaning operations were drained into a holding tank and, when the tank was full, pumped into a trench. The trench flowed from the plant's property into Parker's Creek, a tributary of the Delaware River. Under RCRA, generators of such wastes must obtain a permit from the EPA, but Johnson had not received or even applied for such a permit.

Jack Hopkins, a foreman, and Peter Angel, the service manager for Johnson, were charged with criminal violations of the RCRA and the Clean Water Act. Johnson was also charged and pled guilty. Messrs. Hopkins and Angel pled not guilty on grounds that they were not "owners" or "operators" as required for RCRA violations. The trial court agreed and dismissed all charges against Messrs. Hopkins and Angel except for the criminal conspiracy charges.

The government appealed the dismissal.

JUDICIAL OPINION

SLOVITER, Circuit Judge

The single issue in this appeal is whether the individual defendants are subject to prosecution under RCRA's criminal provision, which applies to:

any person who— . . . (2) knowingly treats, stores, or disposes of any hazardous waste identified or listed under this subchapter either—(A) without having obtained a permit under Section 6925 of this title . . . or (B) in knowing violation of any material condition or requirement of such permit.

If we view the statutory language in its totality, the congressional plan becomes . . . apparent. First, "person" is defined in the statute as "an individual, trust, firm, joint stock company, corporation (including a government corporation), partnership, associa-tion, State, municipality, commission, political subdivision of a State, or any interstate body." Had Congress meant to take aim more narrowly, it could have used more narrow language. Second, under the plain language of the statute, the only explicit basis for exoneration is the existence of a permit covering the action. Nothing in the language of the statute suggests that we should infer another provision exonerating persons who knowingly treat, store or dispose of hazardous waste but are not owners or operators.

Finally, though the result may appear harsh, it is well established that criminal penalties attached to regulatory statutes intended to protect public health, in contrast to statutes based on common law crimes, are to be construed to effectuate the regulatory purpose.

In summary, we conclude that the individual defendants are "persons" within the RCRA, that all elements of that offense must be shown to have been knowing, but that such knowledge, including that of the permit requirement, may be inferred by the jury as to those individuals who hold the requisite responsible positions with the corporate defendant. For the foregoing reasons, we will reverse the district court's dismissal and we will remand for further proceedings consistent with this opinion.

CASE QUESTIONS

1. Who is charged with criminal violations?
2. What violations are charged?
3. What violations did the lower court dismiss?
4. Did Congress intend to prosecute corporate employees?
5. Does the appellate court reinstate the charges?
6. What proof is required to show violations by the "persons" involved?

Group Suits: The Effect of Environmentalists

In many circumstances, private suits have had the most effect either in terms of obtaining compliance with environmental regulations or in terms of abating existing nuisances affecting environmental quality. The reason for the success of these suits may be the ultimate outcome of the litigation—possible business shutdowns and, at the least, the payment of tremendous amounts of damages and costs.

Private suits have been brought by environmental groups that have both the organizational structure and sufficient funding for the initiation and completion of such suits. In some cases, the environmental groups are formed to protest one specific action, as is the case of Citizens Against the Squaw Peak Parkway; other

Visit the Sierra Club:
http://www.sierraclub.org

groups are national organizations that take on environmental issues and litigation in all parts of the country. Examples of these national groups include the Sierra Club, the Environmental Defense Fund, Inc., the National Resources Defense Council, and the League of Conservation Voters. Some environmental groups represent business interests in environmental issues, as does the Mountain States Legal Foundation, which becomes involved in presenting business issues when private organizations and individuals bring environmental suits.

These environmental groups have been successful not only in bringing private damage and injunctive relief suits but also in forcing agencies to promulgate regulations and to enjoin projects when EISs should have been filed but were not.

INTERNATIONAL ENVIRONMENTAL ISSUES

The EU and Environmentalism

Visit the European Environment Agency:
http://www.eea.eu.int

By the end of 1992, the European Union (EU) had passed more than 200 environmental directives that focus on noise restrictions; protection of endangered species; energy efficiency; recycling; and air, land, and water quality. The view of the EU is that environmental planning is to be conducted by member states as part of their economic development plans and processes. In 1990, the EU created the European Environment Agency to serve as a clearinghouse for environmental information; eventually the agency will operate for members in a manner similar to the EPA.

Many EU directives are designed to eliminate the need for regulation by encouraging different business choices and educating consumers. One directive required manufacturers to make 90 percent of all packaging materials recyclable by the year 2000. Another directive awards companies the use of an "eco-audit" sticker on their labels and stationeries if they comply with an annual environmental audit of their manufacturing, waste management, materials use, and energy choices. The audits can be done in-house or conducted by registered eco-auditors, but results must be released to the public. An innovative directive of the EU has created an EU-wide "eco-label" to be placed on all consumer goods to provide information about the environmental impact of a product's production, distribution, life, and disposal. Germany has had such a label, called the "Blue Angel," for a number of years, and the EU has adopted the concept for its continental marketplace.

Visit the International Organization for Standardization:
http://www.iso.ch

ISO 14000

Information about ISO 14000 is available at
http://www.iso.ch

The International Organization for Standardization (ISO) has developed its ISO 14000 series of international environmental standards. Some environmental scholars have predicted that the ISO standards will become the model for regulators and prosecutors in their enforcement and sentencing activities for environmental violations.

Visit the CERES organization and review its principles:
http://www.ceres.org

Under ISO 14000, companies can become ISO certified, which will permit them to place special insignias on their materials, correspondence, and products to indicate their ISO standing. ISO standards emphasize not only compliance but also self-audits and self-correction. Genuine dedication to improvement is a key standard for this environmental certification.

ETHICAL ISSUES 12.2

The following chart is a summary of environmental issues in various industries, the solutions companies developed, and the resulting benefits from the changes made pursuant to environmental regulation.

What stakeholders benefit from these types of environmentally motivated production changes? Were benefits to the environment the same as benefits to the shareholders? Should companies consider innovation in environmental modifications beyond just what the law requires? Why, or why not?

Environmental Regulation Has Competitive Implications

SECTOR/ INDUSTRY	ENVIRONMENTAL ISSUES	INNOVATIVE SOLUTIONS	INNOVATION OFFSETS
Pulp and paper	Dioxin released by bleaching with chlorine	Improved cooking and washing processes Elimination of chlorine by using oxygen, ozone, or peroxide for bleaching Closed-loop processes (still problematic)	Lower operating costs through greater use of by-product energy sources 25% initial price premium for chlorine-free paper
Paint and coatings	Volatile organic compounds (VOCs) in solvents	New paint formulations (low-solvent-content paints, water-borne paints) Improved application techniques Powder or radiation-cured coatings	Price premium for solvent-free paints Improved coatings quality in some segments Worker safety benefits Higher coatings-transfer efficiency Reduced coating costs through materials savings
Electronics manufacturing	Volatile organic compounds (VOCs) in cleaning agents	Semiaqueous, terpene-based cleaning agents Closed-loop systems No-clean soldering where possible	Increase in cleaning quality and thus in product quality 30% to 80% reduction in cleaning costs, often for one-year payback periods Elimination of an unnecessary production step
Refrigerators	Chlorofluorocarbons (CFCs) used as refrigerants Energy usage Disposal	Alternative refrigerants (propane-isobutane mix) Thicker insulation Better gaskets Improved compressors	10% better energy efficiency at same cost 5% to 10% initial price premium for "green" refrigerator
Dry cell batteries	Cadmium, mercury, lead, nickel, cobalt, lithium, and zinc released in landfills or to the air (after incineration)	Rechargeable batteries of nickel-hydride (for some applications) Rechargeable lithium batteries (now being developed)	Nearly twice as efficient at same cost Higher energy efficiency Expected to be price competitive in the near future
Printing inks	VOCs in petroleum inks	Water-based inks and soy inks	Higher efficiency, brighter colors, and better printability (depending on application)

BIOGRAPHY

THE EPA ADMINISTRATORS

1971–1973: WILLIAM D. RUCKELSHAUS

Served as the first EPA administrator, appointed by Richard Nixon. Mr. Ruckelshaus continued to serve under Gerald Ford and was responsible for the implementation of both the Clean Water Act and the Clean Air Act. By the time of his departure, the EPA had 9,077 employees.

1973–1977: RUSSELL E. TRAIN

Established close congressional relationships. Agency size ranged from 9,200 to 10,200 employees during his tenure.

1977–1981: DOUGLAS M. COSTLE

The first EPA administrator under a Democratic president; appointed by Jimmy Carter. Saw the role of the EPA as that of a health agency. Often credited for the beginning of environmental activism. Responsible for the Superfund Amendments being passed in Congress. Agency grew to 11,000 employees. Budget of EPA went from $1 billion in 1971 to $5.4 billion in 1981.

1981–1983: ANNE BURFORD GORSUCH

Appointed by Ronald Reagan. Questions arose about how effective the EPA had been in Superfund cleanup. Constitutional confrontation with Congress on executive privilege regarding documents relating to Superfund cleanups. Agency was reduced from 13,000 employees to 12,000.

1983–1985: WILLIAM D. RUCKELSHAUS

Appointed by Ronald Reagan. His seasoned experience was required in order to restore the EPA's reputation following the Burford years. Pursued an asbestos-removal program in schools. Began global environmental relations and meetings. Agency grew to 13,000 employees.

1989–1993: WILLIAM K. REILLY

Key figure in getting the Clean Air Act of 1990 through Congress. Issues with contractors and subcontractors in Superfund cleanups plagued his administration. Pushed the 1992 Earth Summit in Rio de Janiero. Agency grew to 17,000 employees during his tenure.

1993–2001: CAROL M. BROWNER

Formerly head of Florida's environmental agency. Pushes "environmental justice." Implemented strictest air quality standards to date. Agency budget was increased to $7.5 billion and employees to 18,375 during her tenure.

2001–PRESENT: CHRISTINE TODD WHITMAN

Formerly the governor of New Jersey, Mrs. Whitman was appointed by President George W. Bush in early 2001. Mrs. Whitman's first budget is for $7.2 Million. EPA Employees at the end of 2001 were 18,050.

The Kyoto Protocol

Visit the Business Roundtable site for their Kyoto Treaty report:
http://www.brtable.org

The United Nations Framework Convention for Climate Change (UNFCCC) is a group of government officials and nonprofit leaders who have been meeting regularly over the past eight years about the issues of global warming, air pollution, acid rain, and other environmental concerns. Citing automobile production as the world's leading industry and oil production the second, the UNFCCC, in its Kyoto meeting, adopted the Kyoto Treaty, which proposes the reduction of six greenhouse gases (mostly carbon dioxide) in the United States and other industrialized nations. The year 1990 was the baseline for omissions under the treaty. The Kyoto Treaty has not yet been adopted in the United States, and the Bush Administration has taken a strong position against the treaty.

Can U.S. Businesses Do Well under Kyoto?

When some businesses consider the UN global-warming treaty, known as the Kyoto Protocol, and what it would mean for them if adopted by the United States, they see red. The treaty would require dramatic cuts in the use of fossil fuels. Conventional estimates place the costs of implementing the treaty at over $100 billion per year in the United States alone. A new study by the Energy Information Administration estimates that it could increase retail electricity prices anywhere from 20 to 80 percent.

© PhotoDisc, Inc.

But still other companies—in a development that may bode ill for treaty opponents—see green, green as in profits. Joseph Romm, an energy consultant who once oversaw alternative-energy programs at the Energy Department, had glad tidings for members of the Energy Efficient Building Association at a recent Washington, D.C., conference. "It's going be great business for everyone at this conference," Romm said of the treaty. "By 2010, climate change will be driving every major energy-related investment." And that, he explained, creates great economic opportunities for EEBA members and other companies producing "green" products.

Romm is not alone in predicting tremendous profits from the Kyoto Protocol. In recent months, several Fortune 500 firms have come out in favor of immediate action to curb greenhouse gas emissions, despite lingering scientific uncertainty about the threat of global warming and clear indications that emissions controls will entail substantial costs to consumers. British Petroleum, one of the world's largest petroleum companies, resigned from the anti-Protocol Global Climate Coalition and called upon industry to play a "positive and responsible part in identifying solutions." Honeywell CEO Michael Bonsignore likewise proclaimed that industry "can't sit back and wait for the perfect, obvious solutions to present itself" and must instead begin to act.

Earlier this year, the Pew Charitable Trusts launched the Center for Climate Change to bolster support for greenhouse gas controls. Recognizing the political value of getting business leaders to support new regulatory measures, the Center, in one of its first actions, created the Business Environmental Leadership Council. In addition to Honeywell and BP, Council members include Enron, United Technologies, International Paper, 3M, and DuPont.

The Council hails the Kyoto Protocol as a "first step in the international process" and is already receiving wide media attention. . . .

Companies such as Enron and BP are revered as role models of the new corporation citizen who places the demands of ecological sustainability ahead of revenues, profits—and shareholders. . . .

Yet the companies are hardly acting out of enlightened concern for the earth. As Clemson economist Bruce Yandle notes, "Actions that might be seen as attempts by industries to restrict output and raise rivals' costs are encouraged rather than frowned upon in the name of global environmental protection. . . ." For years, many corporations have sought to turn government intervention in the economy to their benefit. All the better when, as in the climate-change debate, they can pretend to be on the side of the angels in the bargain.

Yet not all corporate leaders pretend they are jumping on the greenhouse bandwagon for altruistic reasons. "We're a beneficiary of environmental regulations because we have for a long time invested in providing energy-efficient services," Enron's John Palmisano told *Investor's Business Daily.* "Our main product, natural gas, is relatively clean. This market is emerging for technologies not just because of Kyoto but also because of domestic regulations and regulations worldwide. . . .

Companies that do not stand to profit from the Kyoto Protocol are still hedging their bets to ensure a "place at the table," if and when the United States begins to issue new emissions-control regulations. A General Motors official pledged that the company would "constructively address the global-climate issue" while still opposing the Kyoto Protocol and higher fuel-economy standards. Similarly, many companies that are lukewarm about the treaty are endorsing a proposal by the International Climate Change Partnership (ICCP)—a business group devoted to finding a middle ground with environmentalists before the treaty is in place.

If you were in charge of your company's environmental program, what position would you take on Kyoto? Would it matter what the nature of your company's business is? Where should political activity be focused?

Source: Reprinted with permission © 1998 by National Review Inc., 215 Lexington Ave., New York, NY 10016, "Greenbacks" by Jonathan H. Adler.

Environmental concerns have prompted voluntary actions on the part of the U.S. business community. Consider the programs initiated by the following companies.

None of the programs initiated by these companies is mandated by law. Why are the companies taking

ETHICAL ISSUES 12.3

such steps? Discuss the benefits each company derives from its programs. Do some of the benefits meet Milton Friedman's test for social responsibility?

COMPANY	PROGRAM
Amana	Initiated companywide recycling program for newspapers, plastic jugs, and motor oil; proceeds donated to nonprofit environmental groups
Arco Chemical	Promotes the antifreeze agent propylene glycol over the more toxic ethylene glycol
AT&T	Publishes annual environmental report
Chevron	Publishes annual environmental report
Conoco	Ordered two double-hulled tankers and plans to add more to fleet
Du Pont	Will reduce air emissions on an ongoing basis and explore new technologies for doing so; publishes annual environmental report
General Mills	Requires use of recycled paper in all cereal boxes; banned use of metals in heavy printing ink
H. J. Heinz	Developed easy recycling ketchup bottles; will not buy tuna caught with dolphins in nets
Johnson & Johnson	Eliminated use of Styrofoam cups in the workplace; started companywide recycling program at employee desks
Kodak	Established camera recycling program
McDonald's	Shortened straws; uses recycled paper for napkins and trays
Polaroid	Publishes annual environmental report
Procter & Gamble	Is developing recycling of disposable diapers
Scott Paper	Sponsors tree-planting programs
Union Carbide	Will spend $310 million over four years on environmental and recycling programs; publishes annual environmental report
Herman Miller	Stopped using rain forest mahogany in Eames signature chair; gave employees mugs and stopped using Styrofoam cups

The Precautionary Principle

The **precautionary principle** has become a dominant force in environmental regulation in Canada, Australia, and Europe. The precautionary principle requires those who propose change to demonstrate that their proposed actions will not cause serious or irreversible harm to the environment. The standard is used, for example, in Australia as the burden of proof for anyone who seeks to obtain a permit to dump hazardous waste. The government will not issue the permit unless and until the applicant demonstrates that the action will not cause serious or irreversible harm. It has been used in applications for logging permits and building construction.

Advocates of the precautionary principle urge that it be used to initiate legislation. That is, if new regulations and/or legislation are not passed, there will be serious or irreversible harm to the environment. Many also see its potential in application to particular products that may harm the environment and as a means to force the development of more environmentally friendly products if the burden of proof for the precautionary principle were not met.[3]

SUMMARY

What are the public and private environmental laws? What protections and requirements are there in environmental laws?

- Nuisance—bad smells, noises, or dirt from one property that interferes with another's use and enjoyment of their property

- Nonattainment areas—areas with significant air pollution problems

- Emissions offset policy—new plants not built until new emissions are offset by reductions elsewhere

- Bubble concept—EPA policy of maximum air emissions in one area

- Clean Air Act—federal law that controls air emissions

- Maximum Achievable Control Technology (MACT)—best means for controlling emissions

- Clean Water Act—federal law that regulates emissions in various water sources

- Effluent guidelines—EPA maximum allowances for discharges into water

- Safe Drinking Water Act—federal law establishing standards for contaminants

- Oil Pollution Act—federal law imposing civil and criminal liability for oil spills

- Resource Conservation and Recovery Act—federal law controlling disposal of hazardous waste through a permit system

- Superfund—funds available for government to use to clean up toxic waste sites

- Comprehensive Environmental Response, Compensation, and Liability Act (CERCLA)—federal law providing funds and authority for hazardous waste site cleanups

- Endangered Species Act—powerful federal law that can curb economic activity if it presents harm to endangered species or their habitat

Who enforces environmental laws?

- Environmental Protection Agency (EPA)—federal agency responsible

- Coalition for Environmentally Responsible Economies (CERES)—international environmental organization

- National Environmental Policy Act (NEPA)—federal law that requires federal agencies to assess environmental issues before taking actions

- Environmental Impact Statement (EIS)—report by federal agency on study of proposed action's effect on the environment

What are the penalties for violations?

- Injunction—judicial order halting an activity

- Fines and criminal penalties

QUESTIONS AND PROBLEMS

1. Philip Carey Company owned a tract of land in Plymouth Township, Pennsylvania, on which it deposited a large pile of manufacturing waste containing asbestos. Carey sold the land to Celotex, and Celotex sold the land to Smith Land & Improvement Corporation. The EPA notified Smith in July 1984 that unless Smith took steps to eliminate the asbestos hazard, the EPA would do the work and pursue reimbursement. Smith proceeded with the cleanup to the EPA's satisfaction at a total cost of $218,945.44. Smith then turned to Celotex and Carey, as previous owners of the property, for reimbursement.

These firms say they have no liability under CERCLA. Which firms are liable? [*Smith Land & Improvement Corp.* v. *Celotex*, 851 F.2d 86 (3rd Cir. 1988)]

2. A group of landowners situated near the Sanders Lead Company brought suit to recover for damages to their agricultural property from accumulations of lead particulates and sulfur oxide deposits released in Sanders' production process. The landowners' property had increased in value because of its commercial potential in being close to the plant. Sanders employs most of the town's residents in its operations. What common-law and statutory rights do the landowners have, and what relief can be obtained? [*Borland* v. *Sanders Lead Co., Inc.*, 369 So. 2d 523 (Ala. 1979)]

3. In 1985, Manufacturers National Bank of Detroit issued a letter of credit for Z&Z Leasing, Inc., an industrial firm, in order to enable Z&Z to obtain bond financing from Canton Township, Michigan.

   After six years of operation, Z&Z was not doing well and had defaulted on its bond obligations. A consultant for the bank found underground storage tanks on Z&Z's site. The tanks contained a yellowish liquid that was found to be a solvent and a hazardous substance. The bank paid off the Canton township bond obligation and foreclosed on the Z&Z property. By 1993, Z&Z had still not sold the property, and the EPA sought to hold the bank liable as an operator for the costs of cleaning up the tanks.

   Can the bank be held liable? [*Z&Z Leasing, Inc.* v. *Graying Reel, Inc.*, 873 F. Supp. 51 (E.D. Mich. 1995)]

4. Reynolds Metal has been held to the same technological standards in its pollution control for can-manufacturing plants as those applied to aluminum manufacturers. Reynolds claims the processes are different and that the technology is not yet available for can manufacturing. Does Reynolds have a point? [*Reynolds Metals Co.* v. *EPA*, 760 F.2d 549 (D.C. 1985)]

5. The Mitchells lived in a residential section of Beverly Hills, Michigan, and sought to enjoin the operation of a nearby piggery. The pigs were fed in an open field, and any garbage not eaten by the pigs was plowed under by tractors. The odors from the operation, particularly in the spring and summer, were such that the use and enjoyment of the Mitchells' property was impaired. Could the Mitchells file a suit? On what basis? Could they win? Are any federal statutory violations involved? [*Mitchell* v. *Hines*, 9 N.W. 2d 547 (Mich. 1943)]

6. Peabody Mine No. 47 was located one-fourth mile from Walter Patterson's land. Mr. Patterson used his land for farming and operated on a low-maintenance schedule. His house had never been painted.

Mr. Patterson said that gas, smoke, fumes, and dust traveled to his property, and he complained his clothes turned black, his bedclothes were dusty, his food was covered in coal dust, and his throat and nostrils were affected. Mr. Patterson said he was forced to sleep with the windows closed, even in the summer, to avoid blowing coal dust. The coal mine facilities operated twenty-four hours a day, six days each week. Does Mr. Patterson have any remedy? [*Patterson* v. *Peabody Coal Co.*, 122 N.E.2d 48 (Ill. 1954)]

7. Brad Bennett and Mario Giordano operate ranches in Oregon. Each has a reservoir used for water sources for their cattle. The U.S. Fish and Wildlife Service has issued an opinion that the water level in the reservoirs must be maintained at a specific level in order to preserve the habitat of two species of fish, the shortnose sucker and the Lost River sucker. Bennett and Giordano protest, saying that in dry spells if their cattle cannot drink, they will lose their herds. Can the government order the maintenance of a water level? [*Bennett* v. *Plenert*, 63 F. 3d 915 (9th Cir. 1995)]

8. The Nuclear Regulatory Commission (NRC) was responsible for the decision to allow the once-crippled Three Mile Island Unit I nuclear plant to resume operation. Pursuant to the NEPA, the NRC considered the impact on the surrounding community and determined that there would be no adverse impact. A group, People Against Nuclear Energy (PANE), intervened in the action by the NRC and asked that the court require the NRC to consider whether the risk of a nuclear accident (as had been experienced with the original shutdown of the plant) might harm the community in a psychological sense. The NRC says the risk of an accident is not an effect on the environment. Is psychological health a factor in EIS evaluations? [*Metropolitan Edison Co.* v. *People Against Nuclear Energy*, 460 U.S. 766 (1983)]

9. The Tennessee Valley Authority (TVA) proposed the construction of Tellico Dam. If the dam is constructed, the known population of snail darters will be eradicated. A snail darter is a 3-inch-long fish that is protected by the Endangered Species Act, which requires all federal agencies (like the TVA) not to fund, authorize, or carry out projects that would jeopardize the continued existence of an endangered species. At the time an environmental group brought the issue to light, the TVA had already expended $100 million in the construction of the dam, which would bring great economic benefits to the area. What factors are important in resolving such a dispute? Is it a matter of the significance of the species? Should an EIS have discussed this problem? [*Tennessee Valley Authority* v. *Hill*, 437 U.S. 153 (1978)]

10. Albert J. Hubenthal operated a fifty-five–acre worm-farming operation in Winona County, Minnesota. Mr. Hubenthal maintained that large amounts of scrap materials, such as tires, wood, metal, leather, and solid waste were necessary for a successful worm operation. The fifty-five acres were "messy, smelly, and germy," as described by the neighbors. The county attorney called the farm a nuisance and warned Mr. Hubenthal that he had thirty days to clean up the farm. He refused, and the county removed all materials from the worm farm. Could the county do this? Was the farm a nuisance? [*Hubenthal* v. *County of Winona*, 751 F.2d 243 (8th Cir. 1984)]

RESEARCH PROBLEM

11. PETA has been a powerful force in demanding changes in corporate behavior. Its latest target has been Burger King for its treatment of chickens—to stop removing the beaks of laying hens and also to enlarge the animals' cages. Also, PETA would like Burger King to ensure that its animals are stunned before they are slaughtered. PETA has developed a new logo and name for the company, MURDER KING. Burger King is suffering from flat sales and does not welcome the negative publicity. How would you respond to PETA's concerns? Visit the Web sites of both PETA and Burger King for more information on these issues: http://www.burgerking.com and http://www.peta.org

---

NOTES

1. E-commerce selection reprinted with permission from *Anderson's Business Law and the Legal Environment* (2002) by David Twomey, Marianne Jennings, and Ivan Fox, p. 1011.

2. The work of Professors Cindy A. Schipani and Lynda J. Oswald is an excellent resource for discussions on parent liability for CERCLA violations as well as a history of the development and scope of CERCLA. *See e.g.,* Lynda J. Oswald & Cindy A. Schipani, "CERCLA and the `Erosion' of Traditional Corporate Law Doctrine," 86 *Northwestern Law Review* 259 (1990). Their work was referred to in the *Best Foods* case.

3. For more information on the precautionary principle, see Charmian Barton, "The Status of the Precautionary Principle in Australia: Its Emergence in Legislation as a Common Law Doctrine," 22 *Harvard Environmental Law Review* 509 (1998).

BUSINESS STRATEGY APPLICATION

The CD-ROM exercise gives you the chance to study the environmental, health, and safety (EHS) policies of several companies and then develop such a policy for your company.

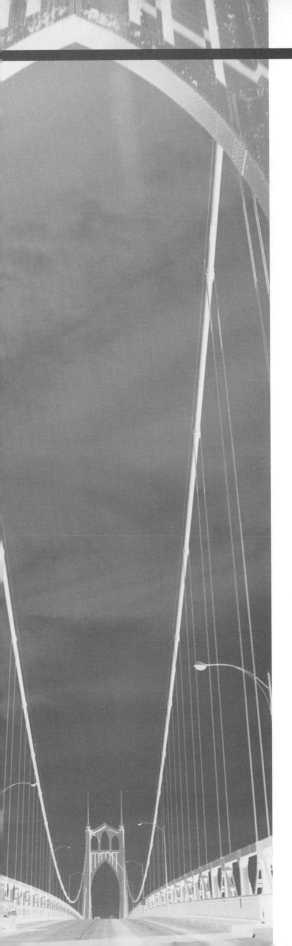

PART THREE

Business Competition and Sales

This section of the book covers the laws and regulations that apply to what a business sells, how it sells its product, and how the sales transaction for the product is set up and financed. Do you have the right to sell a product?—or have you appropriated someone else's idea? What can you say and write in your advertising? What is fair and legal in competition? When do you have a contract, and what kinds of terms do you need to have in it? In this era of electronic commerce, what exactly is a contract and when is it formed? What constitutes performance on a contract, and what is a breach? Can you be compensated if the other side fails to perform? How can transactions be financed, and what forms do you need? What are your rights as a seller for collecting payments under a contract?

This portion of the text covers all the preliminary aspects of contracts, as well as the performance and collection issues in contract relations. The materials walk through the heart of business operations: sales, competition, property rights, advertising, contract formation and performance, and receivable collection.

CHAPTER THIRTEEN

Contracts and Sales: Introduction and Formation

Contracts have been necessary in business since business began. They allow businesses to count on money, supplies, and services. Contracts are the private law of business; the parties develop their own private set of laws through their contracts. These private laws have the benefit of judicial enforcement in all states. This chapter covers contract basics: What is a contract? What laws govern contracts? What are the types of contracts? How are contracts formed? What contracts must be in writing?

> **A verbal contract isn't worth the paper it's written on.**
> SAMUEL GOLDWYN

> **The number of people shopping online increased 65 percent in the year 2000.**
> *USA TODAY*, "WHO'S DRIVING E-COMMERCE?" JANUARY 9, 2001 1B.

CONSIDER...

In the summer of 1996, PepsiCo, Inc., ran a marketing campaign involving Pepsi Points. The Pepsi Points, obtained by drinking Pepsi, could be redeemed for prizes. In one television ad promoting Pepsi Points, a Harrier jet is pictured outside a school yard with the campaign's slogan beneath it: DRINK PEPSI GET STUFF. The jet pictured in the ad was generated by computer. The ad said the jet could be yours for 7 million Pepsi Points. PepsiCo maintains the ad was a spoof. John Leonard, then a 21-year-old business student, saw the ad and delivered to Pepsi fifteen original Pepsi Points plus a check for $700,008.50—sufficient for the cost of a Harrier jet, plus shipping and handling.

Pepsi refused to deliver the jet. Pentagon spokesman Kenneth Bacon (famous now for the release of Linda Tripp's personnel records from the Pentagon) indicated that no Harrier jets were available at that time because before a member of the public can buy one the jets must be demilitarized.

© John H. Clark/CORBIS

Pepsi also said the ad was a joke and not an offer. Leonard said that the ad induced conduct on his part, as would all Pepsi Points ads, and that Pepsi was required to deliver to him a Harrier jet. Who was correct? Was the ad an offer?

WHAT IS A CONTRACT?

Businesses cannot expand and grow without being able to rely on commitments; resources are wasted if promises are not fulfilled. For example, suppose that Wonder Bread Company constructs a new wing and buys new equipment to expand production, but, when the wing is ready to operate, the wheat supplier backs out of the supply contract with Wonder Bread. Wonder Bread has wasted resources and will lose the opportunity and motivation to expand because of the problems created by unenforceable agreements. These strong economic considerations brought about the involvement of the courts in enforcing contractual promises.

"A **contract** is a promise or set of promises for breach of which the law gives a remedy, or the performance of which the law in some way recognizes as a duty." This definition comes from the *Restatement (Second) of Contracts,* a statement of contract law by the American Law Institute (ALI), which recognizes a contract as a set of voluntary promises that the law will enforce for private parties. The remainder of this chapter focuses on the creation, performance, and enforcement of those promises.

SOURCES OF CONTRACT LAW

There are three general sources of contract law: common law, the Uniform Commercial Code, and the new sources of law evolving in response to e-commerce—the Uniform Electronic Transactions Act, the Uniform Computer Information Transactions Act, and the Electronic Signatures in Global and National Commerce Act of 2000 (E-sign).

Common Law

Common law was the first law of contracts. As discussed in Chapter 1, common law consists today of those traditional notions of law and that body of law developed by judicial decisions dealing with contract issues. Although it is not statutory law, the traditional English common law of contracts has been modified by statute in some states. Thus, certain types of contracts have unique and specific content requirements—for example, listing agreements for real estate agents, insurance policies, and consumer credit contracts (see Chapter 15 for a more complete discussion of the statutory requirements in consumer credit contracts); but, however much specific language and statutory requirements these contracts have, their formation and enforcement are still governed by common law. Common law applies to contracts that have land or services as their subject matter. A rental agreement for an apartment may be covered by common law or specific landlord-tenant statutes, but a contract for the construction of a home or an employment contract is governed by common law.

A general treatment of the common law for contracts can be found in the *Restatement (Second) of Contracts.* A group of legal scholars wrote the *Restatement,* and changes have been made to reflect the changes in contract law over the years.

The Uniform Commercial Code

One of the problems with common law is its lack of uniformity. The states do not follow the same case decisions on contract law, and some states do not follow the *Restatement;* the result is that different rules apply to contracts in different states.

Consequently, businesses once had great difficulty and expense when they contracted across state lines because of differences in state contract common law. To address the need for uniformity, the National Conference of Commissioners on Uniform State Laws and the American Law Institute worked to draft a set of commercial laws appropriate for businesspeople, lawyers, and lawmakers. The result of their efforts was the **Uniform Commercial Code** (UCC). The final draft of the UCC first appeared in the 1940s. With several revisions and much time and effort, the Code was adopted, at least in part, in all the states.

Article 2 of the UCC governs contracts for the sale of goods and has been adopted in all states except Louisiana. Although sections of Article 2 may have various forms throughout the states, the basic requirements for contracts remain consistent; businesses now have uniform requirements that have expedited interstate contracts. Article 2 is more liberal than common law, and contracts are more easily formed and performed and remedies are easier to determine under Article 2. Specific differences are covered in the remaining sections of the chapter. Excerpts of Article 2 are reproduced in Appendix G. Determining which contracts are UCC contracts and which are common law contracts is often difficult. The following case addresses this issue.

Review Article 2 of the UCC:
http://www.law.cornell.edu/ucc/2/overview.html

Examine drafts of proposed changes to the UCC, published by the National Conference of Commissioners on Uniform State Laws:
http://www.law.upenn.edu/library/ulc/ulc.htm

CASE 13.1

Cook v. *Downing*
891 P.2d 611 (Ok. Ct. App. 1995)

The Dentures Sold Were a "Bill of Goods," but Were They UCC Goods?

FACTS

Dr. Cook (appellant) is a licensed dentist who has a practice with less than 50 percent in the work of fitting and making dentures. Mrs. Downing (appellee) is a patient of Dr. Cook who was fitted for dentures. Mrs. Downing filed suit against Dr. Cook after she took delivery of her dentures because she said they were ill-fitting and produced sore spots in her mouth. Dr. Cook's expert witness testified that Mrs. Downing's problems were probably due to candidas, an autoimmune reaction, or an allergy to the dental material. No expert testified that her problems were due to ill-fitting dentures.

The trial court awarded damages to Mrs. Downing on the basis of a breach of UCC Article 2 implied warranty of fitness for a particular purpose. Dr. Cook appealed, maintaining that the dentures were not a sale of goods.

JUDICIAL OPINION

HUNTER, Judge

Section 2-105(1) defines *goods* as meaning "all things (including specially manufactured goods) which are movable at the time of identification to the contract for sale other than the money in which the price is to be paid, investment securities (Article 8) and things in action. 'Goods' also includes the unborn young of animals and growing crops and other identified things attached to realty. . . ." The law of implied warranty in the commercial code is found in § 2-315 which states:

Where the seller at the time of contracting has reason to know any particular purpose for which the goods are required and that the buyer is relying on the seller's skill or judgment to select or furnish suitable goods, there is unless excluded or modified under the next section an implied warranty that the goods shall be fit for such purpose.

(continued)

We agree with Appellant's position that any claim Appellee might have sounds in tort. In Oklahoma, dentists, professionals who are regulated by the state, furnish dentures. In general, dentists must use ordinary skill in treating their patients. A patient does not establish the elements of legal detriment by only showing nonsuccess or unsatisfactory results.

A dentist is not a merchant and the Uniform Commercial Code is not the law to apply to these facts. Finding no Oklahoma law on point, we align ourselves with the reasoning stated by the Court of Appeals of North Carolina in *Preston v. Thompson*, 53 N.C.App. 290, 280 S.E.2d 780 [31 UCC Rep Serv 1592] (1981). In the *Preston* case, the patient determined through her research in the yellow pages that the dentist was a specialist in dentures. The patient claimed the doctor made oral assurances that the dentures would fit satisfactorily. The dentures did not fit well and subsequent attempts at correcting the problem were not successful. The patient sued the dentist on an implied warranty theory pursuant to the Uniform Commercial Code. The court held that the transaction was not of "goods" and that a dentist was not a "merchant" under the UCC. We adopt the rule as enunciated by the North Carolina court, that "those who, for a fee, furnish their professional medical services for the guidance and assistance of others are not liable in the absence of negligence or intentional misconduct." (citation omitted). The court further held that "the fact that defendant holds himself out as specializing in the preparing and fitting of dentures does not remove him from the practice of dentistry and transform him into a merchant." We hold that under the laws of Oklahoma, a dentist is not a merchant and dentures, furnished by a dentist, are not goods under the UCC.

A dentist could be sued for breach of contract, if such contract were alleged to exist, but that is not the fact as revealed in the record in our case. Appellee presented evidence of an advertisement guaranteeing dentures to fit, but testified that she did not see this ad until after she had begun her treatment with appellant. The evidence does not support any breach of contract action.

As a matter of law, appellee erroneously based her cause of action on the Uniform Commercial Code rather than negligence. The court erred in entering judgment in favor of appellee based on this law. For this reason, we reverse the judgment of the trial court and remand the matter with directions to enter judgment in favor of appellant.

Reversed and remanded with directions.

JONES, Judge dissenting

As is typical of small claims cases, there were no pleadings here to define the issues. At trial, however, issues were raised as to dental malpractice and breach of implied warranties under the UCC. Although the trial court based its decision on a finding of a breach of the implied warranty of fitness for a particular purpose, the trial court's decision must be affirmed if sustainable on any ground.

The decision cannot be affirmed on the basis of professional negligence as the necessary evidence of such negligence was lacking. But neither can the trial court's decision's [sic] be affirmed on the basis of implied warranty of fitness for a particular purpose. There was no particular or special purpose involved as is required by § 2-315. The use appellee was to make of the dentures was their ordinary use, and that they may not have been suitable for the ordinary purpose for which they were to be used is the concept of "merchantability."

The implied warranty of merchantability is codified at 12A O.S. 1991 § 2-314 and deserves a closer look.

(1) . . . a warranty that the goods shall be merchantable is implied in a contract for their sale if the seller is a merchant with respect to goods of that kind. . . .
(2) Goods to be merchantable must be at least such as . . . (c) are fit for the ordinary purposes for which such goods are used; . . .

A "merchant" is defined as:
. . . a person who deals in goods of the kind or otherwise by his occupation holds himself out as having knowledge or skill peculiar to the practices or goods involved in the transaction or to whom such knowledge or skill may be attributed by his employment of an agent or broker or other intermediary who by his occupation holds himself out as having such knowledge or skill.

"Goods" means "all things (including specially manufactured goods) which are movable at the time of identification to the contract for sale other than the money in which the price is to be paid, investment securities . . . and things in action. . . ."

"Dentists" and "dentures" appear to be included in the definitions of merchants and goods.

The transaction of a patient being fitted for and purchasing dentures from a dentist is actually a hybrid. It is not purely a sale of goods by a merchant, nor is it purely the providing of a service by a health care professional. Whether implied warranties under

Article 2 of the U.C.C. apply to such a transaction should depend on whether the predominant element of the transaction is the sale of goods or the rendering of services. If the sale of goods predominates, it would be within the scope of Article 2 and the implied warranties contained therein. However, if the service aspect predominates, there would be no implied warranties.

Although the record contains no specific findings of fact, the record does contain evidence from which it could be concluded that this transaction was principally a sale of goods and that the implied warranty of merchantability applies thereto. The evidence was also sufficient that the trier of fact could have concluded that the dentures were not fit for their ordinary purpose as required to establish a prima facie case for breach of the implied warranty of merchantability. We must affirm a law action tried to the court if there is any competent evidence to support the judgment.

In contemporary society the old distinctions separating health care professionals from other businessmen are blurring in many respects. This court's holding that a dentist is *not* a merchant, and den-

tures, furnished by a dentist, are *not* goods ignores the fact that nothing excludes them from the statutory definitions of merchant and goods. It also ignores the fact that health care professionals in some instances *are* selling goods to their "patients," with the providing of professional services being secondary to the sale. To such transactions there is no reason Article 2 of the UCC should not apply.

I respectfully dissent.

CASE QUESTIONS

1. Did the fitting for dentures constitute a sale of goods?

2. Does classifying the dentures as something other than the sale of goods deprive Mrs. Downing of a remedy?

3. Do you think eyeglasses and contact lenses should be classified as sales of goods? Why, or why not?

4. What public policy issues does the dissenting judge raise?

CONSIDER . . .

13.1   In September of 1988, Jane Pittsley contracted with Hilton Contract Carpet Co. for the installation of carpet in her home. The total contract price was $4,402. Hilton paid the installers $700 to put the carpet in Pittsley's home. Following installation, Pittsley complained to Hilton that some seams were visible, that gaps appeared, that the carpet did not lie flat in all areas, and that it failed to reach the wall in certain locations. Although Hilton made various attempts to fix the installation by attempting to stretch the carpet and other methods, Pittsley was not satisfied with the work. Eventually, Pittsley refused any further efforts to fix the carpet. Pittsley initially paid Hilton $3,500 on the contract but refused to pay the remaining balance of $902.

Pittsley filed suit, seeking rescission of the contract, return of the $3,500, and incidental damages. Hilton answered and counterclaimed for the balance remaining on the contract. Hilton also defended on the grounds that the only issue was the installation and that the damages were minimal. Pittsley argued that the contract was under the UCC and that she was entitled to remedies because the carpet was defective. Hilton disagreed on the application of the UCC. Who is correct? Does the UCC apply to the contract for the carpet sale and installation? Is Pittsley entitled to the warranty protection of the UCC? [*Pittsley* v. *Houser*, 875 P.2d 232 (Idaho 1994)]

The UCC has added a new section called "Article 2 Leases," which applies to leases of goods. Over the past ten years, many new forms of goods transactions have developed, such as the long-term auto lease, which appears to be more of a sale than a lease. Because of the nature of these agreements, leases did not fit well under common law or traditional Article 2. Article 2 Leases, drafted for these types of contracts, covers such issues as the statute of frauds (leases in which payments exceed $1,000, for example, must be in writing), contract formation, and warranties associated with a lease. This new section of the UCC has been adopted in most states.

Evolving E-Commerce Contract Laws

Uniform Electronic Transactions Act (UETA)

Visit the UETA online for updates on legislation: http://www.uetaonline.com

The **Uniform Electronic Transactions Act** (UETA) is a uniform law drafted in 1999, adopted in twenty-eight states, and proposed as legislation in sixteen others. The UETA was promulgated in response to contracts being formed over the Internet and includes provisions on issues such as electronic signatures. However, there is not near the uniformity of the UETA in state adoptions as under the UCC and the issues of what constitutes a valid signature and the effect of electronic verification continue to evolve.

Electronic Signatures in Global and National Commerce Act of 2000

The UETA is state recognition of the **Electronic Signatures in Global and National Commerce Act of 2000 (E-sign),** 15 U.S.C. Section 7001, the federal law that mandates the recognition of electronic signatures for the formation of contracts (see p. 522 for more information). While states may vary in their specifics under the UETA, it is clear from E-sign that all states cannot deny legal effect to contracts that are entered into electronically and that bear electronic signatures.

Uniform Computer Information Transaction Act (UCITA)

Visit the UCITA online for updates on legislation: http://www.ucita.org

The **Uniform Computer Information Transaction Act** (UCITA) was promulgated in 1999 and has been adopted in two states and proposed in eight others (as of December 2001). The UCITA would govern all contracts involving the sale, licensing, maintenance, and support of computer software. Those contracts not involving software that are contracts for the sale of other goods would still be governed by the UCC along with the UETA, if adopted in the state.

TYPES OF CONTRACTS

Contracts exist in many different forms, and these forms can control many of the parties' rights and remedies with respect to the relationship. The following sections cover the various types of contracts and offer an introduction to contract terminology.

Bilateral versus Unilateral Contracts

A contract can result from two parties exchanging promises to perform or from one party exchanging a promise for the other party's actions. A **bilateral contract** is one in which both parties promise to perform certain things. For example, if you sign a contract to buy a used pink Cadillac for $2,000, you have entered into a bilateral contract with the seller. The seller has promised not to sell the car to anyone else and will give you the title to the car when you pay the $2,000. You have promised to buy that pink Cadillac and will turn over the $2,000 to the seller in exchange for the title. The contract consists of two promises: your promise to buy and the seller's promise to sell.

Some contracts have one party issuing a promise and the other party simply performing. This type of contract is called a **unilateral contract.** For example, suppose that your uncle said, "I will pay you $500 if you will drive my new Mercedes to San Francisco for me within the next five days." Your uncle has promised to pay, but you have not promised to do anything. Nonetheless, you can hold your uncle to his promise if you drive his car to San Francisco. Your agreement is a promise in exchange for performance. If you drive the car to San Francisco, your uncle's promise will be enforceable as a unilateral contract.

Express versus Implied Contracts (Quasi Contracts)

Some contracts are written, signed (even notarized), and very formal in appearance. Others are simply verbal agreements between the parties (see page 519 for a discussion of the types of contracts that can be oral). A contract that is written or orally agreed to is an **express contract.** In still other situations, the parties do not discuss the terms of the contract but nonetheless understand that they have some form of contractual relationship. A contract that arises from circumstances and not from the express agreement of the parties is called an **implied contract,** as when you go to a doctor for treatment of an illness. You and the doctor do not sit down and negotiate the terms of treatment or the manner in which the doctor will conduct the examination or how much you will pay. You understand that the doctor will do whatever examinations are appropriate to determine the cause of your illness and that there is a fee associated with the doctor's work. The payment and treatment terms are implied from general professional customs. You have an **implied-in-fact contract.**

A second type of implied or enforceable agreement is called an **implied-in-law contract** or a **quasi contract.** The term *quasi* means "as if" and describes the action of a court when it treats parties who do not have a contract "as if" they did. The courts enforce a quasi contract right if one party has conferred a benefit on another, both are aware of the benefit, and the retention of the benefit would be an enrichment of one party at the unjust expense of the other.

It is important to understand that the theory of quasi contract does not apply to what has been referred to as "the officious meddler." The officious meddler is someone who performs unrequested work or services and then, based on a quasi contract theory, seeks recovery. For example, you could not be required to compensate a painting contractor who came by and painted your house without your permission because the contractor acted both without your knowledge and without your consent. However, if you are aware the painting is going on and you do nothing to stop it, you would be held liable in quasi contract.

Void and Voidable Contracts

A **void contract** is an agreement to do something that is illegal or against public policy or it may lack legal elements (see Chapter 14). For example, a contract to sell weapons to a country on which a weapons ban exists is a void contract. Neither side can enforce the contract, even if the weapons have already been delivered, because allowing the seller to collect payment would encourage further violations of the law banning the weapons sales.

A contract may be partially void; that is, only a portion of the contract violates a statute or public policy and is therefore unenforceable. For example, in many states, it is illegal to charge excessive rates of interest (known as usury; see Chapter 15 for more discussion). In a usurious loan contract, the loan repayment would be enforceable but the interest terms would not be. As another example, suppose that an owner has sold her business and in the contract has agreed never to start another such business. Although the buyer deserves some protection for the payment of goodwill, the complete elimination of the seller's right to start a business is an excessive restraint of trade that is against public policy and would not be enforced, even though the actual sale of the business would be enforced.

A **voidable contract** is a contract that can be unenforceable at the election of one of the parties. For example, if there has been misrepresentation, the party who is the victim can elect to void the contract. Likewise, a minor who signs a contract can choose to be bound by the agreement or can choose to disaffirm the contract. These types of contracts are voidable at the option of one of the parties.

Unenforceable Contracts

An **unenforceable contract** is a contract that cannot be enforced because of some procedural problem. A contract that should be in writing to comply with the statute of frauds but is not is unenforceable. When suit to enforce a contract is not brought within the statute of limitations, the contract becomes unenforceable.

Executed versus Executory Contracts

Contracts are **executed contracts** when the parties have performed according to their promises or required actions (under unilateral agreements). Contracts are **executory contracts** when the promise to perform is made but the actual performance has not been done. A contract could be wholly executed, wholly executory, or partially executed. For example, referring to the offer your uncle made about the Mercedes trip to California, the contract is wholly executory at the time your uncle makes the offer. If you drive the car to San Francisco, your performance is complete but your uncle's is not; hence, the contract is partially executed. When your uncle pays you, the contract is wholly executed because both of you have performed your responsibilities under this unilateral contract. Courts often distinguish between executed and executory contracts in determining both the rights of the parties (particularly with respect to issues of public policy and capacity) and the remedies available to the parties.

FORMATION OF CONTRACTS

A contract is formed when two parties with the correct mental intent, under the correct circumstances, within the boundaries of the law, and with some detriment to each of them agree to do certain acts in exchange for the other's acts. This formation requires the presence of all of these elements; the lack of one element or the presence of a problem, such as illegality, can result in the invalidity of the contract. The elements necessary for the formation of a valid contract are outlined in Exhibit 13.1.

EXHIBIT 13.1
Overview
of Contracts

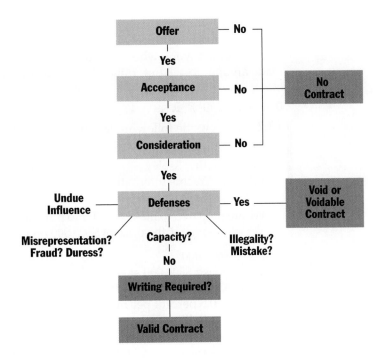

Offer

The **offer** is the first part of a contract. The person who makes the offer is called the **offeror,** and the person to whom the offer is made is called the **offeree.** The requirements for a valid offer are covered in the following sections.

Intent to Contract versus Negotiation

The offeror must intend to contract at the time the offer language is used. This requirement distinguishes offers from negotiations. For example, a letter from a business person may contain the following: "I am interested in investing in a franchise. I have heard about your opportunities. Please send me all necessary information." The letter expresses an interest in possibly contracting in the future, but there is no present intention to enter into a contract expressed in the language. But suppose the above letter of inquiry was followed by another letter with the following language: "I have decided to invest in one of your franchises. Enclosed are the necessary documents, signatures, and a deposit check." Here the parties have passed the negotiation stage and entered into part one of the contract—there is an offer.

Courts use an objective standard in determining the intent of the parties, which means that courts look at how a reasonable person would perceive the language, the surrounding circumstances, and the actions of the parties in determining whether a contract was formed. For example, a businessperson who is exasperated with the poor financial performance of her firm may say jokingly to someone over lunch, "I'd sell this company to anyone willing to take it." If that statement is made in the context of a series of complaints about the firm and the workload, it would not be an offer. That same language used in a luncheon meeting with a prospective buyer would create a different result.

For a look at how auction sales look on the Internet, see:
http://www.ebay.com
http://www.haggle.com
http://www.priceline.com

In many situations, one party has simply requested bids or is inviting offers. The frustrated business owner could say, "I am interested in selling my firm. If you run into anyone who is interested, have them call me." The owner has not made an offer to sell but, rather, has made an invitation for an offer.

CONSIDER...

13.2 Review the following language and determine whether an offer has been made.

TO: Brit Ripley
FROM: Yachts International
RE: Sailing Vessel *Infinity*

We are prepared to make an offer to purchase the U.S. Coast Guard Documented Vessel *Infinity* for the price of $600,000 on the following terms and conditions:

Price: $600,000
Terms: Cash $300,000 at close of escrow
Note: $300,000 (unsecured) due in one year
Interest: 0.5 percent per month on unpaid balance versus 100,000 shares of stock of a public company
Will guarantee $3.00 per share in one year. Buyer reserves the right to repurchase shares at $3.00 in one year if guarantee given.
Escrow: ASAP
Conditions:
1. All insurance to remain in effect until close.
2. Seller to deliver to Port of San Francisco in seaworthy and sailable condition.

/s./J. P. Morgan
YACHTS INTERNATIONAL

Ads are simply invitations for offers. The following case provides the answer for the chapter opening problem.

CASE 13.2

Leonard v. *Pepsico*
210 F.3d 88 (2d Cir. 2000)

Does "Pepsi Stuff" Include a Harrier Jet?

FACTS

Pepsico (defendant/appellee), the producer and distributor of the soft drinks Pepsi and Diet Pepsi, ran a promotion, entitled "Pepsi Stuff," which encouraged consumers to collect "Pepsi Points" from specially marked packages of Pepsi or Diet Pepsi and redeem these points for merchandise featuring the Pepsi logo. John Leonard (plaintiff/appellant) is a resident of Seattle, Washington, who saw the Pepsi Stuff commercial that he contends constituted an offer for obtaining a Harrier Jet as part of the Pepsi Stuff.

The commercial opens upon an idyllic, suburban morning, where the chirping of birds in sun-dappled trees welcomes a paperboy on his morning route. As the newspaper hits the stoop of a conventional two-story house, the tattoo of a military drum introduces the subtitle, "MONDAY 7:58 AM." The stirring strains of a martial air mark the appearance of a well-coiffed teenager preparing to leave for school, dressed in a shirt emblazoned with the Pepsi logo, a red-white-and-blue ball. While the teenager confidently preens, the military drumroll again sounds as the subtitle "T-SHIRT 75 PEPSI POINTS" scrolls across the screen. Bursting from his room, the teenager strides down the hallway wearing a leather jacket. The drumroll sounds again, as the subtitle "LEATHER JACKET 1450 PEPSI POINTS" appears. The teenager opens the door of his house and, unfazed by the glare of the early morning sunshine, puts on a pair of sunglasses. The drumroll then accompanies the subtitle "SHADES 175 PEPSI POINTS." A voiceover then intones, "Introducing the new Pepsi Stuff catalog," as the camera focuses on the cover of the catalog. At this point, the following message appears at the bottom of the screen: "Offer not available in all areas. See details on specially marked packages."

The scene then shifts to three young boys sitting in front of a high school building. The boy in the middle is intent on his Pepsi Stuff Catalog, while the boys on either side are each drinking Pepsi. The three boys gaze in awe at an object rushing overhead, as the military march builds to a crescendo. The Harrier Jet is not yet visible, but the observer senses the presence of a mighty plane as the extreme winds generated by its flight create a paper maelstrom in a classroom devoted to an otherwise dull physics lesson. Finally, the Harrier Jet swings into view and lands by the side of the school building, next to a bicycle rack. Several students run for cover, and the velocity of the wind strips one hapless faculty member down to his underwear. While the faculty member is being deprived of his dignity, the voiceover announces: "Now the more Pepsi you drink, the more great stuff you're gonna get."

The teenager opens the cockpit of the fighter and can be seen, helmetless, holding a Pepsi. "[L]ooking very pleased with himself," the teenager exclaims, "Sure beats the bus," and chortles. The military drumroll sounds a final time, as the following words appear: "HARRIER FIGHTER 7,000,000 PEPSI POINTS." A few seconds later, the following appears in more stylized script: "Drink Pepsi—Get Stuff."

With that message, the music and the commercial end with a triumphant flourish.

Inspired by this commercial, Leonard set out to obtain a Harrier Jet. The Catalog specifies the number of Pepsi Points required to obtain promotional merchandise. The Catalog includes an Order Form which lists, on one side, fifty-three items of Pepsi Stuff merchandise redeemable for Pepsi Points. Conspicuously absent from the Order Form is any entry or description of a Harrier Jet. The amount of Pepsi Points required to obtain the listed merchandise ranges from 15 (for a "Jacket Tattoo" ("Sew 'em on your jacket, not your arm.")) to 3300 (for a "Fila Mountain Bike" ("Rugged. All-terrain. Exclusively for Pepsi.")).

The rear foldout pages of the Catalog contain directions for redeeming Pepsi Points for merchandise. These directions note that merchandise may be ordered "only" with the original Order Form. The Catalog notes that in the event that a consumer lacks enough Pepsi Points to obtain a desired item, additional Pepsi Points may be purchased for ten cents each; however, at least fifteen original Pepsi Points must accompany each order.

Although Leonard initially set out to collect 7,000,000 Pepsi Points by consuming Pepsi products, it soon became clear to him that he "would not be able to buy (let alone drink) enough Pepsi to collect the necessary Pepsi Points fast enough." Reevaluating his strategy, Leonard realized that buying Pepsi Points would be a more promising option. Through acquaintances, Leonard ultimately raised about $700,000.

On March 27, 1996, Leonard submitted an Order Form, fifteen original Pepsi Points, and a check for $700,008.50. At the bottom of the Order Form, Leonard wrote in "1 Harrier Jet" in the "Item" column and "7,000,000" in the "Total Points" column. In a letter accompanying his submission, Leonard stated that the check was to purchase additional Pepsi Points "expressly for obtaining a new Harrier jet as advertised in your Pepsi Stuff commercial."

On May 7, 1996, Pepsico rejected Leonard's submission and returned the check, explaining that:
The item that you have requested is not part of the Pepsi Stuff collection. It is not included in the catalogue or on the order form, and only catalogue merchandise can be redeemed under this program.

The Harrier jet in the Pepsi commercial is fanciful and is simply included to create a humorous and entertaining ad. We apologize for any misunderstanding or confusion that you may have experienced and are enclosing some free product coupons for your use.

(continued)

Leonard then responded:

Your letter of May 7, 1996 is totally unacceptable. We have reviewed the video tape of the Pepsi Stuff commercial . . . and it clearly offers the new Harrier jet for 7,000,000 Pepsi Points. Our client followed your rules explicitly. . . .

This is a formal demand that you honor your commitment and make immediate arrangements to transfer the new Harrier jet to our client. If we do not receive transfer instructions within ten (10) business days of the date of this letter you will leave us no choice but to file an appropriate action against Pepsi. . . .

After some complex manuevers related to diversity jurisdiction, Leonard filed suit and Pepsico moved for summary judgment. The court granted summary judgment and Leonard appealed.

JUDICIAL OPINION
PER CURIAM

Plaintiff-appellant John D. R. Leonard alleges that the ad was an offer, that he accepted the offer by tendering the equivalent of 7 million points, and that Pepsico has breached its contract to deliver the Harrier jet. Pepsico characterizes the use of the Harrier jet in the ad as a hyperbolic joke ("zany humor"), cites the ad's reference to offering details contained in the promotional catalog (which contains no Harrier fighter plane), and argues that no objective person would construe the ad as an offer for the Harrier jet.

The United States District Court for the Southern District of New York (Wood, J.) agreed with Pepsico and granted its motion for summary judgment on the grounds (1) that the commercial did not amount to an offer of goods; (2) that no objective person could reasonably have concluded that the commercial actually offered consumers a Harrier Jet; and (3) that the alleged contract could not satisfy the New York statute of frauds.

We affirm for substantially the reasons stated in Judge Wood's opinion. See 88 F.Supp.2d 116 (S.D.N.Y.1999). [To help understand the issues in the case, portions of Judge Wood's opinion follow.]

WOOD, District Judge

The general rule is that an advertisement does not constitute an offer. The Restatement (Second) of Contracts explains that

Advertisements of goods by display, sign, handbill, newspaper, radio or television are not ordinarily intended or understood as offers to sell. The same is true of catalogues, price lists and circulars, even though the terms of suggested bargains may be stated in some detail.

It is of course possible to make an offer by an advertisement directed to the general public, but there must ordinarily be some language of commitment or some invitation to take action without further communication.

Restatement (Second) of Contracts § 26 cmt. b (1979). Similarly, a leading treatise notes that:

It is quite possible to make a definite and operative offer to buy or sell goods by advertisement, in a newspaper, by a handbill, a catalog or circular or on a placard in a store window. It is not customary to do this, however; and the presumption is the other way. . . . Such advertisements are understood to be mere requests to consider and examine and negotiate; and no one can reasonably regard them as otherwise unless the circumstances are exceptional and the words used are very plain and clear.

An advertisement is not transformed into an enforceable offer merely by a potential offeree's expression of willingness to accept the offer through, among other means, completion of an order form.

Under these principles, plaintiff's letter of March 27, 1996, with the Order Form and the appropriate number of Pepsi Points, constituted the offer. There would be no enforceable contract until defendant accepted the Order Form and cashed the check.

The exception to the rule that advertisements do not create any power of acceptance in potential offerees is where the advertisement is "clear, definite, and explicit, and leaves nothing open for negotiation," in that circumstance, "it constitutes an offer, acceptance of which will complete the contract." *Lefkowitz* v. *Great Minneapolis Surplus Store,* 251 Minn. 188, 86 N.W.2d 689, 691 (1957). In *Lefkowitz,* defendant had published a newspaper announcement stating: "Saturday 9 AM Sharp, 3 Brand New Fur Coats, Worth to $100.00, First Come First Served $1 Each." Mr. Morris Lefkowitz arrived at the store, dollar in hand, but was informed that under defendant's "house rules," the offer was open to ladies, but not gentlemen. The court ruled that because plaintiff had fulfilled all of the terms of the advertisement and the advertisement was specific and left nothing open for negotiation, a contract had been formed.

The present case is distinguishable from *Lefkowitz.* First, the commercial cannot be regarded in itself as sufficiently definite, because it specifically reserved the details of the offer to a separate writing, the Catalog. The commercial itself made no mention of the steps a potential offeree would be required to take to accept the alleged offer of a Harrier Jet. The advertisement in *Lefkowitz,* in contrast, "identified the person who could accept." Second, even if the Catalog had included a Harrier Jet among the items that could be obtained by redemption of Pepsi Points, the advertisement of a Harrier Jet by both television commercial and catalog would still not constitute an offer. As the *Mesaros* court explained, the absence of any words of limitation such as "first come, first served," renders the alleged offer sufficiently indefinite that no contract could be formed.

The Court finds, in sum, that the Harrier Jet commercial was merely an advertisement. The Court now turns to the line of cases upon which plaintiff rests much of his argument.

2. Rewards as Offers

In opposing the present motion, plaintiff largely relies on a different species of unilateral offer, involving public offers of a reward for performance of a specified act. Because these cases generally involve public declarations regarding the efficacy or trustworthiness of specific products, one court has aptly characterized these authorities as "prove me wrong" cases. The most venerable of these precedents is the case of *Carlill v. Carbolic Smoke Ball Co.*, 1 Q.B. 256 (Court of Appeal, 1892), a quote from which heads plaintiff's memorandum of law: "[I]f a person chooses to make extravagant promises . . . he probably does so because it pays him to make them, and, if he has made them, the extravagance of the promises is no reason in law why he should not be bound by them."

The case arose during the London influenza epidemic of the 1890s. Among other advertisements of the time, for Clarke's World Famous Blood Mixture, Towle's Pennyroyal and Steel Pills for Females, Sequah's Prairie Flower, and Epp's Glycerine Jube-Jubes, appeared solicitations for the Carbolic Smoke Ball. The specific advertisement that Mrs. Carlill saw, and relied upon, read as follows:

£100 reward will be paid by the Carbolic Smoke Ball Company to any person who contracts the increasing epidemic influenza, colds, or any diseases caused by taking cold, after having used the ball three times daily for two weeks according to the printed directions supplied with each ball. £1000 is deposited with the Alliance Bank, Regent Street, shewing our sincerity in the matter.

During the last epidemic of influenza many thousand carbolic smoke balls were sold as preventives against this disease, and in no ascertained case was the disease contracted by those using the carbolic smoke ball.

Mrs. Carlill purchased the smoke ball and used it as directed, but contracted influenza nevertheless. The advertisement was construed as offering a reward because it sought to induce performance, unlike an invitation to negotiate, which seeks a reciprocal promise. As Lord Justice Lindley explained, "advertisements offering rewards . . . are offers to anybody who performs the conditions named in the advertisement, and anybody who does perform the condition accepts the offer." Because Mrs. Carlill had complied with the terms of the offer, yet contracted influenza, she was entitled to £100.

Other "reward" cases underscore the distinction between typical advertisements, in which the alleged offer is merely an invitation to negotiate for purchase of commercial goods, and promises of reward, in which the alleged offer is intended to induce a potential offeree to perform a specific action, often for noncommercial reasons.

In the present case, the Harrier Jet commercial did not direct that anyone who appeared at Pepsi headquarters with 7,000,000 Pepsi Points on the Fourth of July would receive a Harrier Jet. Instead, the commercial urged consumers to accumulate Pepsi Points and to refer to the Catalog to determine how they could redeem their Pepsi Points. The commercial sought a reciprocal promise, expressed through acceptance of, and compliance with, the terms of the Order Form. As noted previously, the Catalog contains no mention of the Harrier Jet. Plaintiff states that he "noted that the Harrier Jet was not among the items described in the catalog, but this did not affect [his] understanding of the offer."

In evaluating the commercial, the Court must not consider defendant's subjective intent in making the commercial, or plaintiff's subjective view of what the commercial offered, but what an objective, reasonable person would have understood the commercial to convey.

If it is clear that an offer was not serious, then no offer has been made. . . .

An obvious joke, of course, would not give rise to a contract. On the other hand, if there is no indication that the offer is "evidently in jest," and that an objective, reasonable person would find that the offer was serious, then there may be a valid offer.

Plaintiff's insistence that the commercial appears to be a serious offer requires the Court to explain why the commercial is funny. Explaining why a joke is funny is a daunting task; as the essayist E. B. White has remarked, "Humor can be dissected, as a frog can, but the thing dies in the process. . . ." The commercial is the embodiment of what defendant appropriately characterizes as "zany humor."

First, the commercial suggests, as commercials often do, that use of the advertised product will

(continued)

transform what, for most youth, can be a fairly routine and ordinary experience. The commercial in this case thus makes the exaggerated claims similar to those of many television advertisements: that by consuming the featured clothing, car, beer, or potato chips, one will become attractive, stylish, desirable, and admired by all. A reasonable viewer would understand such advertisements as mere puffery, not as statements of fact. Second, the callow youth featured in the commercial is a highly improbable pilot, one who could barely be trusted with the keys to his parents' car, much less the prize aircraft of the United States Marine Corps. Rather than checking the fuel gauges on his aircraft, the teenager spends his precious preflight minutes preening. The youth's concern for his coiffure appears to extend to his flying without a helmet. Finally, the teenager's comment that flying a Harrier Jet to school "sure beats the bus" evinces an improbably insouciant attitude toward the relative difficulty and danger of piloting a fighter plane in a residential area, as opposed to taking public transportation.

Third, the notion of traveling to school in a Harrier Jet is an exaggerated adolescent fantasy. In this commercial, the fantasy is underscored by how the teenager's schoolmates gape in admiration, ignoring their physics lesson. The force of the wind generated by the Harrier Jet blows off one teacher's clothes, literally defrocking an authority figure. As if to emphasize the fantastic quality of having a Harrier Jet arrive at school, the Jet lands next to a plebeian bike rack. This fantasy is, of course, extremely unrealistic. No school would provide landing space for a student's fighter jet, or condone the disruption the jet's use would cause.

Fourth, the primary mission of a Harrier Jet, according to the United States Marine Corps, is to "attack and destroy surface targets under day and night visual conditions." United States Marine Corps, Factfile: AV-8B Harrier II (last modified Dec. 5, 1995) <http://www.hqmc.usmc.mil/factfile.nsf>. Manufactured by McDonnell Douglas, the Harrier Jet played a significant role in the air offensive of Operation Desert Storm in 1991. The jet is designed to carry a considerable armament load, including Sidewinder and Maverick missiles. . . . [D]epiction of such a jet as a way to get to school in the morning is clearly not serious even if, as plaintiff contends, the jet is capable of being acquired "in a form that eliminates [its] potential for military use."

Fifth, the number of Pepsi Points the commercial mentions as required to "purchase" the jet is 7,000,000. To amass that number of points, one would have to drink 7,000,000 Pepsis (or roughly 190 Pepsis a day for the next hundred years—an unlikely possibility), or one would have to purchase approximately $700,000 worth of Pepsi Points. The cost of a Harrier Jet is roughly $23 million dollars, a fact of which plaintiff was aware when he set out to gather the amount he believed necessary to accept the alleged offer.

In light of the obvious absurdity of the commercial, the Court rejects plaintiff's argument that the commercial was not clearly in jest.

The absence of any writing setting forth the alleged contract in this case provides an entirely separate reason for granting summary judgment. Under the New York Statute of Frauds, a contract for the sale of goods for the price of $500 or more is not enforceable by way of action or defense unless there is some writing sufficient to indicate that a contract for sale has been made between the parties and signed by the party against whom enforcement is sought or by his authorized agent or broker.

There is simply no writing between the parties that evidences any transaction. Plaintiff argues that the commercial, plaintiff's completed Order Form, and perhaps other agreements signed by defendant which plaintiff has not yet seen, should suffice for Statute of Frauds purposes, either singly or taken together.

The commercial is not a writing; plaintiff's completed order form does not bear the signature of defendant, or an agent thereof.

In sum, there are three reasons why plaintiff's demand cannot prevail as a matter of law. First, the commercial was merely an advertisement, not a unilateral offer. Second, the tongue-in-cheek attitude of the commercial would not cause a reasonable person to conclude that a soft drink company would be giving away fighter planes as part of a promotion. Third, there is no writing between the parties sufficient to satisfy the Statute of Frauds.

For the reasons stated above, the Court grants defendant's motion for summary judgment. Summary judgment granted and affirmed.

CASE QUESTIONS

1. What offer does Leonard allege was made?

2. When does the court think an offer was made?

3. Why is whether the ad is funny an important issue?

4. Does the commercial satisfy the statute of frauds?

5. Will Leonard get his Harrier jet? Why, or why not?

Re: Checklist for Contract Preliminaries

1. Do your contract homework.
   a. Do background checks—check references, complaints at state and private agencies, court dockets.
   b. Learn the nature of the business and industry custom—learn to use the language.
2. Negotiate details.
   a. Agree on terms that help you accomplish your purpose (apple powder for bakery equipment, not just apple powder).
   b. Make sure your written agreement is complete.

Re: Checklist for Drafting Contracts

1. Identify both parties clearly. Be certain corporate names are correct. Make sure the parties have the proper authority to enter into the transaction. (Are copies of board resolutions approving the contract available?)
2. Define the terms used in the contract, including industry terms.
3. List all terms: price, subject matter, quantity, delivery, payment terms.
4. Answer "what if" questions. (What if payment is not made? What if deliveries are late?)

Certain and Definite Terms

One of the ways to determine whether there is intent to contract is also the second requirement for a valid offer. The offer must contain certain and definite language and cover all the terms necessary for a valid contract, which include the following:

- Parties
- Subject matter of the contract
- Price
- Payment terms
- Delivery terms
- Performance times

Under the UCC, the requirements for an offer are not as stringent as the requirements under common law. So long as the offer identifies the parties and the subject matter, the Code sections can cover the details of price, payment, delivery, and performance (see § 2-204 in Appendix G).

Also under the UCC, courts give great weight to industry custom and the previous dealings of the parties in determining whether the terms are certain and definite enough to constitute an offer (see § 2-208 in Appendix G). For example, the parties may have done business with each other for ten years and their agreement simply contains a quantity and a price. Whatever payment and delivery terms have been used in their relationship in the past (their **course of dealing**) will be the terms for their ongoing relationship.

Communication of the Offer

An offer must be communicated to the offeree before it is valid. A letter in which an offer is made is not an offer until the letter reaches the offeree. For example, suppose Office Max had prepared an offer letter that included a substantial price

BUSINESS STRATEGY

The Art and Law of Negotiations: Rocky, Bullwinkle, and Binding Contracts

Jay Ward Productions owns the copyrights and trademarks in the cartoon characters Rocky the Flying Squirrel, Bullwinkle the Moose, Boris, Natasha, and Dudley Do-Right (the Ward characters). I.R.V. (plaintiff) licenses characters, copyrights, and trademarks for a variety of businesses.

On March 27, 1991, Mrs. Ramona Ward and Ms. Tiffany Ward, the principals of Jay Ward Productions, met with Mr. Irving Handelsman, I.R.V.'s president, to discuss I.R.V. serving as the licensing agent for the Ward characters. I.R.V. had previously been the licensing agent for several of the Ward characters from 1969 through 1991.

Before the March 27th meeting, I.R.V. had held telephone discussions with Ramona and Tiffany Ward, outlining its proposal for obtaining the licensing work for the Ward characters. Handelsman claims that he was assured by Ramona that I.R.V. would continue to represent the Ward characters.

At the meeting, the Wards emphasized that they wished to maximize their licensing income and that Handelsman should proceed quickly in order to obtain licensing agreements. At the meeting, Tiffany Ward typed a memo on Jay Ward Productions letterhead, which provided as follows:

March 27, 1991

Dear Irv:

This is to signify our intention to do business with I.R.V. Merchandising on an exclusive merchandising basis with the exception of three companies listed below. When we receive our lawyers go ahead per a contract to be signed and official written release from Peter Piech regarding merchandising rights we are prepared to pay at 25% com-

© AFP/CORBIS

mission on the first $500,000.00; 30% on the next million; 35% on the next $500,000.00 and 40% on everything over $2,000,000.00.

Details of payments, accounting details, etc. to be included in the contract. This contract is to be effective March 27, 1991, for two years.

This intention to do business pertains only to Bullwinkle, Rocky, Boris, Natasha, Mr. Peabody, Sherman, Dudley Do-Right, Aesop, Fractured Fairy Tales. [Hoppity Hooper]

Sincerely,

/s/ Ramona C. Ward

EXCLUSIONS TO CONTRACT; KRAFT FOODS [pasta], RALSTON PURINA [10%], KENTUCKY FRIED CHICKEN

[Note: grammatical errors unchanged]

The Wards told Handelsman to proceed and that their attorney would be in touch in a few days with the final agreement. Handelsman negotiated several licensing agreements over the next few days. He notified Ramona Ward of such agreements and indicated that she expressed pleasure.

On April 4, 1991, I.R.V. received a letter from Jay Ward Productions indicating that it had reconsidered its "preliminary feeling" and decided against entering into an agreement with I.R.V. Jay Ward Productions eventually granted the licensing rights to MCA, and MCA subsequently signed up those clients Handelsman had obtained between the time of the March 27th meeting and the April 4 letter of withdrawal. Ward did not pay Handelsman license fees on any of these arrangements.

Do you think Handelsman is entitled to the license fees? List the errors you think the parties made in trying to establish a contractual relationship. Refer to the language, the timing, and the assumptions.

discount for computers that was about to be mailed to Renco Rental Equipment so that Renco might buy the computers at the substantial discount. Before the letter is mailed, the machines offered in the letter are in high demand and Office Max decides that, rather than make its discount offer, it will just sell the machines easily in the retail market. The letter to Renco and other Office Max customers is never mailed. Renco, realizing the value of the computers and learning of the unmailed letter, cannot accept the discount computer offer because it was never communicated to them.

ETHICAL ISSUES 13.1

David Pelzman owns a restaurant called "David's on the Main" in Columbus, Ohio. It is a trendy and popular restaurant that is always fully booked for New Year's Eve. Jeff Burrey of Columbus called and made a reservation for New Year's Eve at David's, but did not go to David's as he had planned.

Mr. Pelzman sued Mr. Burrey for breach of contract. Mr. Pelzman says he paid for food and scheduled staff based on the number of reservations he had received. In his suit, Mr. Pelzman asked for $440 in damages or the price of the two-person package for New Year's Eve that parties who wish to participate pay.

Mr. Burrey, upon being served with the suit for his failure to arrive, said, "Never in a million years did I think it was a contract. If they can sue a customer for not showing up for a reservation, then a customer can sue the restaurant for having to wait 15 minutes to be seated when they have a reservation."

Do you think that Mr. Burrey and David's had a contract? Was it fair of Mr. Burrey to make a reservation and then not show up? Was it ethical for Mr. Burrey to do so? Is it a proper use of the courts to have Mr. Pelzman filing this type of suit?

Some forms of communication are not treated as offers. For example, as the *Leonard* v. *Pepsico* case indicates, television ads are generally not offers. Mass communications of information about deals and prices are generally treated as invitations for offers.

Termination of an Offer by Revocation

Because an offer is one-sided, it can be revoked anytime before acceptance by the offeree. **Revocation** occurs when the offeror notifies the offeree that the offer is no longer good.

There are some limitations on revocation. One such limitation has already been mentioned: Acceptance by the offeree cuts off the right to revoke. Also, under common law, **options** cannot be revoked. An option is a contract in which the offeree pays the offeror for the time needed to consider the offer. For example, suppose that Yolanda's Yogurt is contemplating opening a new restaurant, and Yolanda has a property location in mind but is uncertain about the market potential. Yolanda does not want the property to be sold to someone else until she can complete a market study. Yolanda could pay the seller (offeror) a sum of money to hold the offer open for thirty days. During that thirty-day period, the offeror can neither revoke the offer nor sell to anyone else.

Under the UCC, there is a form of an option that, without the offeree's payment, makes an offer irrevocable. Under a **merchant's firm offer** (see § 2-205 in Appendix G), the offer must be made by a merchant, put in writing, and signed by the merchant; moreover, the merchant must hold the offer open for a definite time period (but no longer than three months). A merchant is someone who is in the business of selling the goods that are the subject matter of the contract or who holds particular skills or expertise in dealing with the goods. A rain check for sale merchandise from a store is an example of this type of offer. The firm offer cannot be revoked if the requirements are met, and money or consideration is not one of those requirements.

Termination of an Offer by Rejection

An offer carries no legally binding obligation for the offeree, who is free to accept or reject the offer. Once the offeree rejects the offer, the offer is ended and cannot later be accepted unless the offeror renews the offer.

Rejection by Counteroffer under Common Law An offer also ends when the offeree does not fully reject the offer but rejects some portion of the offer or modifies it before acceptance. These changes and rejections are called **counteroffers.** The effect of a counteroffer is that the original offer is no longer valid, and the offeree now becomes the offeror as the counteroffer becomes the new offer. Consider the following dialogue as an example:

> Alice: I will pay you $50 to paint the trim on my house.
> Brad: I will do it for $75.

Alice made the first offer. Brad's language is a counteroffer and a rejection at the same time. Alice is now free to accept or reject the $75 offer. If Alice declines the $75 counteroffer, Brad cannot then force Alice to contract for the original $50 because the offer ended. The following "Consider" deals with an issue of offers and counteroffers.

CONSIDER...

13.3 December 30, 1977: John Hancock Insurance Company sends a commitment letter to Houston Dairy offering to loan Houston $800,000 at 9.25 percent interest; acceptance must be in writing within seven days and must be accompanied by a $16,000 letter of credit or cashier's check.

January 17, 1978: President of Houston Dairy sends letter of acceptance to Hancock along with cashier's check.

January 23, 1978: Hancock cashes the check (check went through standard company processing).

Hancock claims there is no contract because the acceptance occurred after the offer had expired. Houston Dairy maintains that its letter of acceptance was a new offer that was accepted by Hancock with the cashing of the check. Who is correct? Is there a contract?

Rejection by Counteroffer under the UCC Under the UCC, modification by offerees was seen as a necessary part of doing business, and Section 2-207 (see Appendix G) allows flexibility for such modifications. Section 2-207 has two separate rules for modifications; one governs merchants, and the other governs nonmerchant transactions. Exhibit 13.2 provides a visual overview of the UCC's rules for additional terms in acceptance.

For nonmerchants, the addition of terms in the counteroffer does not result in a rejection; there will still be a contract if there is a clear intent to contract, but the additional terms will not be a part of the contract. For example, consider the following dialogue:

> Joe: I will sell you my pinball machine for $250.
> Jan: I'll take it. Include $10 in dimes.

Joe and Jan have a contract, but the $10 in dimes is not a part of the contract. If Jan wanted the dimes, she should have negotiated before formally accepting the offer.

EXHIBIT 13.2
UCC Rules for Additional Terms in Acceptance

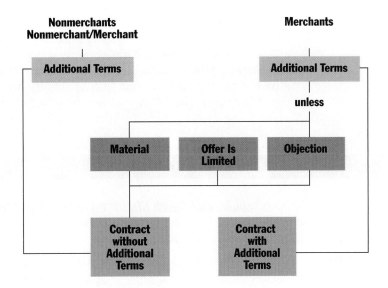

For merchants (both parties must be merchants), Section 2-207 has more complicated rules and details on additional terms in acceptance. Sometimes called the **battle of the forms,** Section 2-207 covers situations in which offerors and offerees send purchase orders and invoices back and forth with the understanding that they have a contract. Under Section 2-207, if the parties reach a basic agreement but the offeree has added terms, there will be an enforceable contract; the added terms are not a rejection under Section 2-207. Whether the added terms will become a part of the contract depends on the following questions:

1. Are the terms material?
2. Was the offer limited?
3. Does one side object?

If the terms the offeree adds to the original offer terms are *material,* they do not become a part of the contract. For example, suppose that Alfie sent a purchase order to Bob for twelve dozen red four-inch balloons at 4 cents each. Bob sends back an invoice that reflects the quantity and price, but Bob's invoice also has a section that states, "There are no warranties express or implied on these goods." Do Alfie and Bob have a contract with or without warranties? The waiver of warranties is a material change in what Alfie gets: now a contract without warranties. Because it is material, Section 2-207 protects Alfie and the warranty waiver is not part of the contract.

Terms that can be added but are not considered material are such payment terms as "30 days same as cash." Shipment terms are generally immaterial unless the method of shipment is unusually costly.

An offeror can avoid the problems of form battles and Section 2-207 by simply *limiting* the offer to the terms stated. Language that could be used would be: "This offer is limited to these terms." If the offeree attempts to add terms in the acceptance, there will be a contract, but the added terms will not be part of the contract. For example, suppose Alfie's offer on the balloons was limited and Bob accepted but added that the payment terms were "30 days same as cash." They would still have a contract but without the additional payment term.

A final portion of Section 2-207 allows the parties to take action to eliminate additional terms. They can do so by *objecting* to any added terms within a reasonable time. For example, if Alfie's offer was not limited and Bob accepted the payment terms, Alfie could object to the payment terms and they would then not be a part of the contract. Exhibit 13.2, as already noted, summarizes the UCC's Section 2-207 rules. The following case deals with 2-207 issues.

CASE 13.3

Schulze and Burch Biscuit Co. v. Tree Top, Inc.
831 F.2d 709 (7th Cir. 1987)

Chunky Apple Powder, Clogged Machines, and Purchase Orders

FACTS

Schulze and Burch Biscuit Company (Schulze) purchased low-moisture 16-mesh dehydrated apple powder from Tree Top, Inc. (Tree Top) to use in making strawberry and blueberry "Toastettes," which it sells to Nabisco, Inc.

On April 27, 1984, E. Edward Park, Schulze's director of procurement, telephoned Rudolph Brady, a broker for Tree Top, and ordered 40,000 pounds of Tree Top's apple powder. Mr. Park told Mr. Brady that the purchase was subject to a Schulze purchase order and gave Mr. Brady the number of the purchase order, but Mr. Park did not send the purchase order or a copy of it to Mr. Brady or to Tree Top. On the front of the purchase order was the following clause:

Important: *The fulfillment of this order or any part of it obligates the Seller to abide by the terms, conditions and instructions on both sides of this order. Additional or substitute terms will not become part of this contract unless expressly accepted by Buyer; Seller's acceptance is limited to the terms of this order, and no contract will be formed except on these terms.*

Shortly after the telephone conversation, Mr. Brady sent Schulze a form entitled simply "Confirmation" that listed Mr. Brady as broker, Schulze as buyer, and Tree Top as seller as well as the quantity, price, shipping arrangements, and payment terms. It also showed the purchase order number that Mr. Park had given to Mr. Brady. Several preprinted provisions, including an arbitration clause, stood on the lower portion of the form:

Seller guarantees goods to conform to the national pure food laws. All disputes under this transaction shall be arbitrated in the usual manner. This confirmation shall

be subordinate to more formal contract, when and if such contract is executed. In the absence of such contract, this confirmation represents the contract of the parties. If incorrect, please advise immediately.

Mr. Brady had sent a similar confirmation form to Schulze in each of at least ten previous transactions between Tree Top and Schulze. Schulze had never objected to any of the preprinted provisions. Schulze had sent Mr. Brady a purchase order in two of those transactions; in each of the other transactions, as in the present case, Schulze simply informed Mr. Brady of the number of the appropriate purchase order.

Subsequently, Schulze brought suit seeking damages for breach of contract, alleging that the dehydrated apple powder had been so full of apple stems and wood splinters that it clogged the machinery of Schulze's Toastette assembly line, causing the line to shut down, with various financial losses. Schulze alleged that the powder thus failed to meet Schulze's specifications, which had governed the previous sales of apple powder. Tree Top alleged that the dispute was subject to arbitration because of the arbitration clause in the confirmation sent by Mr. Brady to Schulze.

The trial court ordered Schulze to submit to arbitration. Schulze appealed.

JUDICIAL OPINION

ESCHBACH, Senior Circuit Judge
The resolution of this case depends upon UCC § 2-207.

In this case, Brady, acting as Tree Top's agent, sent a confirmation that contained terms additional to those discussed by Brady and Schulze. Schulze did not object to the additional terms. Whether the contract was formed orally by the telephone call or by the confirmation acting as an acceptance, the arbitration clause was a term "additional to or different from those offered or agreed upon." The parties have proceeded on the assumption that they are both "merchants" for the purposes of § 2-207. The principal issue is thus whether the addition of the arbitration term would "materially alter" the contract. If so . . . it would not become part of the contract.

Illinois courts, in deciding whether particular clauses are material alterations, have looked to the [UCC] Comment's formulation that a material alteration is one that would "result in surprise or hardship if incorporated without express awareness by the other party." Under Illinois law, the test for whether an additional term would be a material alteration in the contract is "whether the addition constitutes an unreasonable surprise to one of the bargaining parties." No Illinois court has addressed the question whether addition of a clause providing for arbitration of disputes between the contracting parties is a material alteration. Some courts in other jurisdictions have held that to be a question that depends on the circumstances of each case. Other courts have followed the "New York rule" that addition of an arbitration clause is a material alteration.

But even in New York, courts have held that addition of an arbitration clause is not a material alteration if the party had reason to know that such a clause would be included in a confirmation.

In the present case, Tree Top did not offer proof of a trade usage of using arbitration to resolve disputes. But Tree Top did offer evidence of a prior course of dealing between the parties that would give notice to Schulze that an arbitration clause would likely be included in the confirmation.

In the present case, Tree Top's agent Brady had sent a confirmation form containing the same arbitration provision to Schulze in each of the previous nine transactions he brokered between the two parties. Schulze had ample notice that the tenth confirmation would be likely to include an arbitration clause. To prevent the clause from becoming part of the contract, Schulze needed only to give notice of objection within a reasonable time. As a matter of law, inclusion of such a clause in the tenth confirmation was not "unfair surprise." Therefore the addition of the arbitration clause was not a material addition to the contract, under the test used in Illinois law.

The next issue is whether Schulze's offer was one that "expressly limits acceptance to the terms of the offer" under § 2-207(2)(a). If so, under § 2-207(2)(a), additional terms in the acceptance do not become part of the contract. During the telephone conversation in which Park placed the order for the apple powder, he informed Brady that the transaction was "subject to" Schulze purchase order 11621. Schulze never sent the purchase order to Brady or to Tree Top. . . . In two of the previous ten transactions between Schulze and Tree Top that Brady had brokered, Schulze had sent the purchase order to Brady.

Even assuming that the purchase order became part of the parties' contract, we hold that it was not, for the purposes of UCC § 2-207, an offer that *"expressly* limits acceptance to the terms of the offer" [emphasis added]. In this case, neither Brady nor Tree Top could have seen the purchasing offer with the limiting language. Although Schulze had sent a purchase order in two of the previous nine transactions, that is insufficient to give notice that mere reference to the number of a purchase order is intended "expressly" to make the order acceptable only on the terms in a purchase order that remains unseen. That indirect incorporation falls short of an "express" limitation.

Because the offer did not expressly limit acceptance to its terms and because, as discussed above, the addition of the arbitration clause was not a material addition to the contract, the arbitration clause became part of the contract under § 2-207(2). For the reasons stated, the judgment of the district court is affirmed.

CASE QUESTIONS

1. What was the problem with the powder?
2. In which document did the arbitration clause appear?
3. Is arbitration a material change?
4. Was the offer limited to the terms of the offer?
5. Did Tree Top have an ethical obligation to furnish apple powder that did not clog the machinery of Schulze and Burch? Does industry custom require that the apple powder be free of non-powder items? Did Tree Top know of Schulze and Burch's planned use? Does that make a difference in your view of the ethics in the case?

Aftermath: Schulze and Burch still manufactures "Toastettes," and its name can be found on the box.

C O N S I D E R . . .

13.4   In the following three dialogues, determine whether there would be a contract if two nonmerchants were having the dialogue and then whether there would be a contract if two merchants were having the dialogue. If there is a contract, determine for both merchants and nonmerchants whether the additional terms mentioned during the dialogue would be part of their contract.

  1. A: "I'll sell you my Peugot bicycle for $100."

  B: "I'll take it. Include your tire pump."

  Result:

  Nonmerchants _____

  Merchants _____

  2. A: "I'll sell you my white 1974 Ford Torino for $358. This offer is limited to these terms."

  B: "I'll take it. Furnish a history of repairs."

  Result:

  Nonmerchants _____

  Merchants _____

  3. A: "I'll sell you my antique Coca-Cola sign."

  B: "I'll take it if you will deliver it."

  Result:

  Nonmerchants _____

  Merchants _____

Termination by Offer Expiration

An offer can end by expiring and, once expired, can no longer be accepted by the offeree. For example, if an offer states that it will remain open until November 1, it automatically terminates on November 1 and no one has the power to accept the offer after that time. The death of the offeror also ends the offer, unless the offeree holds an option. Even offers without time limits expire after a reasonable time has passed. For example, an offer to buy a home is probably only good for one or two weeks because the offeror needs to know whether to try for another house. The offeror's offer terminates naturally if the offeree fails to accept within that time frame.

Acceptance: The Offeree's Response

An **acceptance** is the offeree's positive response to the offeror's proposed contract, and only persons to whom the offer is made have the power of acceptance. That acceptance must be communicated to the offeror using the proper method of communication, which can be controlled by the offeror or left to the offeree. In either case, the method of communication controls the effective time of the acceptance.

Acceptance by Stipulated Means

Some offerors give a required means of acceptance that is called a specified or **stipulated means.** If the offeree uses the stipulated means of acceptance, the

EXHIBIT 13.3 **Timing Rules for Acceptance**

TYPE OF OFFER	METHOD OF ACCEPTANCE	ACCEPTANCE EFFECTIVE?
No means given	Same or reasonable method of communication	When properly mailed, dispatched (mailbox rule)
No means given	Slower or unreasonable method of communication	When received, if offer still open
Means specified (specified or stipulated means)	Stipulated means used	Mailbox rule
Means stipulated (specified or stipulated means)	Stipulated means not used	Counteroffer and rejection

acceptance is effective sooner than the offeror's receipt; the acceptance is effective when it is properly sent. For example, if the offeror has required the acceptance to be mailed and the offeree properly mails the letter of acceptance, the acceptance is effective when it is sent. This timing rule for acceptance is called the **mailbox rule,** and it applies in stipulated means offers so long as the offeree uses the stipulated means to communicate acceptance.

Acceptance with No Stipulated Means

If the offeror does not stipulate a means of acceptance, the offeree is free to use any method for communication of the acceptance. If the offeree uses the same method of communication or a reasonable means, the mailbox rule also applies. If the offeree uses a slower method of acceptance, the acceptance is not effective until it is received. Exhibit 13.3 summarizes the timing of acceptance rules, and the following case deals with an issue of timing on offer and acceptance.

CASE 13.4

Cantu v. *Central Education Agency*
884 S.W.2d 565 (Tex. App. 1994)

The Teacher's Lesson on Acceptance

FACTS

Cantu had a teaching contract with the San Benito Consolidated Independent School District. She hand-delivered to her supervisor a written offer to resign. Three days later the superintendent of schools mailed her a letter accepting the offer of resignation. Cantu then changed her mind and the next day hand-delivered a letter withdrawing her resignation. The superintendent refused to recognize the attempted rescission of the resigna-

tion. Cantu appealed to the state district court. It decided against her and she again appealed.

JUDICIAL OPINION

SMITH, J.

. . . Cantu was hired as a special-education teacher by the San Benito Consolidated Independent School District under a one-year contract for the 1990–91 school year. On Saturday, August 18, 1990, shortly

(continued)

before the start of the school year, Cantu hand-delivered to her supervisor a letter of resignation, effective August 17, 1990. In this letter, Cantu requested that her final paycheck be forwarded to an address in McAllen, Texas, some fifty miles from the San Benito office where she tendered the resignation. The San Benito superintendent of schools, the only official authorized to accept resignations on behalf of the school district, received Cantu's resignation on Monday, August 20. The superintendent wrote a letter accepting Cantu's resignation the same day and deposited the letter, properly stamped and addressed, in the mail at approximately 5:15 P.M. that afternoon. At about 8:00 A.M. the next morning, August 21, Cantu hand-delivered to the superintendent's office a letter withdrawing her resignation. This letter contained a San Benito return address. In response, the superintendent hand-delivered that same day a copy of his letter mailed the previous day to inform Cantu that her resignation had been accepted and could not be withdrawn.

The State Commissioner of Education concluded that, because the school district's acceptance of Cantu's resignation was effective when mailed, an agreement to rescind Cantu's employment contract was in force when she attempted to withdraw her offer of resignation and the school district's refusal to honor her contract was not unlawful.

The sole legal question presented for our review is the proper scope of the "mail-box rule"* under Texas law and whether the rule was correctly applied. . . . Cantu contends . . . that the trial court erred in ruling that the agreement to rescind her contract of employment became effective when the superintendent deposited his letter accepting Cantu's resignation in the mail. Cantu argues that, under Texas law, an acceptance binds the parties in contract on mailing only if the offeror has sent the offer by mail or has expressly authorized acceptance by mail. There was no express authorization for the school district to accept Cantu's offer by mail. The question presented is whether authorization to accept by mail may be implied only when the offer is delivered by mail or also when the existing circumstances make it reasonable for the offeree to so accept.

The aphorism "the offeror is the master of his offer" reflects the power of the offeror to impose conditions on acceptance of an offer, specify the manner of acceptance, or withdraw the offer before the offeree has effectively exercised the power of acceptance. However, more often than not, an offeror does not expressly authorize a particular mode, medium, or manner of acceptance. Consequently, particularly with parties communicating at a distance, a rule of law is needed to establish the point of contract formation and allocate the risk of loss and inconvenience that inevitably falls to one of the parties between the time that the offeree exercises, and the offeror receives, the acceptance. See 1 Arthur L. Corbin, *Contracts* § 78 (1963).

As Professor Corbin notes, courts could adopt a rule that no acceptance is effective until received, absent express authorization by the offeror; however, the mailbox rule, which makes acceptance effective on dispatch, closes the deal and enables performance more promptly, and places the risk of inconvenience on the party who originally has power to control the manner of acceptance. . . . "Even though the offer was not made by mail and there was no [express] authorization, the existing circumstances may be such as to make it reasonable for the offeree to accept by mail and to give the offeror reason to know that the acceptance will be so made." . . . In short, acceptance by mail is impliedly authorized if reasonable under the circumstances.

The *Restatement* approves and adopts this approach: an acceptance by any medium reasonable under the circumstances is effective on dispatch, absent a contrary indication in the offer. *Restatement (Second) of Contracts* §§ 30(2), 63(a), 65, 66 (1979). In addition, the *Restatement* specifically recognizes that acceptance by mail is ordinarily reasonable if the parties are negotiating at a distance or *even if a written offer is delivered in person to an offeree in the same city.* . . . The same standard, *viz.,* whether the manner of acceptance is reasonable under the circumstances, governs offer and acceptance in commercial transactions under the Texas Business and Commerce Code. (Uniform Commercial Code § 2-206.)

Cantu relies primarily on a 1903 opinion of the Texas Supreme Court to support her contention that an offeree is impliedly authorized to accept by mail only if the offer is submitted through the mail. *Scottish-American Mortgage Co.* v. *Davis,* 96 Tex. 504, 74 S.W. 17 (1903).

A more recent opinion of the supreme court, *McKinney* v. *Croan,* 144 Tex. 9, 188 S.W.2d 144 (1945), suggests that circumstances indicating the reasonableness of an acceptance be considered in determining whether an acceptance by mail is impliedly authorized and effective on mailing. In holding that a reply to a request for admissions was effective when mailed, the *McKinney* court specifically noted that the "parties resided about 350 miles apart," in addition to noting that the request was sent by mail. . . . The court also cited to 17 C.J.S. *Contracts* § 52, which reads: The request or authorization to communicate the acceptance by mail is implied in two cases, namely: (1) Where the post is used to make the offer . . . (2) *Where the circumstances are such that it must have been within the contemplation of the parties that according to the ordinary usages of mankind the post might be used as a means of communicating the acceptance.* . . .

The *McKinney* court's express mention of the distance between the parties as a circumstance making acceptance by mail reasonable and its affirmation of an authority following the modern trend that *either* mail delivery of the offer *or* reasonable circumstances might impliedly authorize communication by mail convince us that Texas law is not frozen into the rigid 1903 position urged by appellant. As we noted earlier, Texas courts are directed by statute to consider whether acceptance by mail is reasonable under the circumstances in commercial transactions. . . . § 2.206 . . . We hold that it is proper to consider whether acceptance by mail is reasonably implied under the circumstances, whether or not the offer was delivered by mail.

. . . It was reasonable for the superintendent to accept Cantu's offer of resignation by mail. Cantu tendered her resignation shortly before the start of the school year—at a time when both parties could not fail to appreciate the need for immediate action by the district to locate a replacement. In fact, she delivered the letter on a Saturday, when the Superintendent could neither receive nor respond to her offer, further delaying matters by two days. Finally, Cantu's request that her final paycheck be forwarded to an address some fifty miles away indicated that she could no longer be reached in San Benito and that she did not intend to return to the school premises or school-district offices. The Commissioner of Education and district court properly considered that it was reasonable for the school district to accept Cantu's offer by mail. . . .

Judgment affirmed.

CASE QUESTIONS

1. Who was the offeror? Does the UCC apply in this case?

2. Why did the court refer to the fact that Cantu's forwarding address was fifty miles away from the place where she delivered her offer to resign?

3. What is the distinction between the *Davis* case and the *McKinney* case?

*The mailbox rule provides that the properly addressed acceptance of an offer is effective when deposited in the mail, unless otherwise agreed or provided by law. *Black's Law Dictionary,* 952 (6th ed., 1990).

E-Commerce and Contract Formation

The Internet has provided a means for contracting online. However, the courts have been left to deal with the issue of whether and when a contract has been formed. The new rules that have emerged in cyberspace contract focus on whether the parties knew the terms and whether they voluntarily accepted those terms once aware of them. In other words, the rules on contract formation in cyberspace require that the parties prove that a click was something more than an accidental one and that the click was made after there has been full disclosure of the terms.

Sellers generally accomplish these two goals by establishing on their Web sites "clickon," "clickthrough," or "clickwrap" agreements. The company or offeror simply lists all the terms of the agreement that the visitor/offeree is about to enter into. The visitor/offeree must click on "I agree" or "I agree to these terms," or she cannot proceed to the completion of the contract segments of the site. The terms include cost, payment, warranties, arbitration provisions, and so on, and all applicable terms must be spelled out in advance of the "I agree" click point.

Because this form of contract formation is so new, case law is rare, but the following case is one example of a "Clickwrap" dispute.

CASE 13.5

M.A. Mortenson Co., Inc. v. Timberline Software Corp.
998 P.2d 305 (Wash. 2000)

Wrapping up the Acceptance on Shrinking Liability

FACTS

M.A. Mortenson Company, Inc. (Mortenson) (Petitioner), a general construction contractor, purchased licensed computer software from Timberline Software Corporation (Timberline) (Respondent) through Softworks Data Systems, Inc. (Softworks) (Respondent), Timberline's local authorized dealer.

Since at least 1990, Mortenson has used Timberline's Bid Analysis software to assist with its preparation of bids. Mortenson had used Medallion, an earlier version of Bid Analysis, at its Minnesota headquarters and its regional offices. In early 1993, Mortenson installed a new computer network operating system at its Bellevue office and contacted Mark Reich (Reich), president of Softworks, to reinstall Medallion. Reich discovered, however, that the Medallion software was incompatible with Mortenson's new operating system. Reich informed Mortenson that Precision, a newer version of Bid Analysis, was compatible with its new operating system.

After Reich provided Mortenson with a price quote Mortenson issued a purchase order dated July 12, 1993, confirming the agreed upon purchase price, set up fee, delivery charges, and sales tax for eight copies of the software. The purchase order indicated that Softworks, on behalf of Timberline would "[f]urnish current versions of Timberline Precision Bid Analysis Program Software and Keys" and "[p]rovide assistance in installation and system configuration for Mortenson's Bellevue Office." The purchase order also contained the following notations:

Provide software support in converting Mortenson's existing Bid Day Master Files to a format accepted by the newly purchased Bid Day software. This work shall be accomplished on a time and material basis of $85.00 per hour. Format information of conversion of existing D-Base Files to be shared to assist Mortenson Mid-West programmers in file conversion.

-System software support and upgrades to be available from Timberline for newly purchased versions of Bid Day Multi-User.

-At some future date should Timberline upgrade "Bid Day" to a windows version, M.A. Mortenson would be able to upgrade to this system with Timberline crediting existing software purchase toward that upgrade on a pro-rated basis to be determined later.

Below the signature line the following was stated: "ADVISE PURCHASING PROMPTLY IF UNABLE TO SHIP AS REQUIRED. EACH SHIPMENT MUST INCLUDE A PACKING LIST. SUBSTITUTIONS OF GOODS OR CHANGES IN COSTS REQUIRE OUR PRIOR APPROVAL." The purchase order did not contain an integration clause.

Reich signed the purchase order and ordered the requested software from Timberline. When Reich received the software, he opened the three large shipping boxes and checked the contents against the packing invoice. Contained inside the shipping boxes were several smaller boxes, containing program diskettes in plastic pouches, installation instructions, and user manuals. One of the larger boxes also contained the sealed protection devices for the software.

All Timberline software is distributed to its users under license. Both Medallion and Precision Bid Analysis are licensed Timberline products. In the case of the Mortenson shipment, the full text of Timberline's license agreement was set forth on the outside of each diskette pouch and the inside cover of the instruction manuals. The first screen that appears each time the program is used also references the license and states, "[t]his software is licensed for exclusive use by: Timberline Use Only." Further, a license to use the protection device was wrapped around each of the devices shipped to Mortenson. The following warning preceded the terms of the license agreement:

CAREFULLY READ THE FOLLOWING TERMS AND CONDITIONS BEFORE USING THE PROGRAMS. USE OF THE PROGRAMS INDICATES YOUR ACKNOWLEDGEMENT THAT YOU HAVE READ THIS LICENSE, UNDERSTAND IT, AND AGREE TO BE BOUND BY ITS TERMS AND CON-

DITIONS. IF YOU DO NOT AGREE TO THESE TERMS AND CONDITIONS, PROMPTLY RETURN THE PROGRAMS AND USER MANUALS TO THE PLACE OF PURCHASE AND YOUR PURCHASE PRICE WILL BE REFUNDED. YOU AGREE THAT YOUR USE OF THE PROGRAM ACKNOWLEDGES THAT YOU HAVE READ THIS LICENSE, UNDERSTAND IT, AND AGREE TO BE BOUND BY ITS TERMS AND CONDITIONS.

Under a separate subheading, the license agreement limited Mortenson's remedies and provided:

LIMITATION OF REMEDIES AND LIABILITY NEITHER TIMBERLINE NOR ANYONE ELSE WHO HAS BEEN INVOLVED IN THE CREATION, PRODUCTION OR DELIVERY OF THE PROGRAMS OR USER MANUALS SHALL BE LIABLE TO YOU FOR ANY DAMAGES OF ANY TYPE, INCLUDING BUT NOT LIMITED TO, ANY LOST PROFITS, LOST SAVINGS, LOSS OF ANTICIPATED BENEFITS, OR OTHER INCIDENTAL, OR CONSEQUENTIAL DAMAGES ARISING OUT OF THE USE OR INABILITY TO USE SUCH PROGRAMS, WHETHER ARISING OUT OF CONTRACT, NEGLIGENCE, STRICT TORT, OR UNDER ANY WARRANTY, OR OTHERWISE, EVEN IF TIMBERLINE HAS BEEN ADVISED OF THE POSSIBILITY OF SUCH DAMAGES OR FOR ANY OTHER CLAIM BY ANY OTHER PARTY. TIMBERLINE'S LIABILITY FOR DAMAGES IN NO EVENT SHALL EXCEED THE LICENSE FEE PAID FOR THE RIGHT TO USE THE PROGRAMS.

In December 1993, Mortenson utilized the Precision Bid Analysis software to prepare a bid for a project at Harborview Medical Center in Seattle. On the day of the bid, the software allegedly malfunctioned multiple times and gave the following message: "Abort: Cannot find alternate." Mortenson received this message 19 times that day. Nevertheless, Mortenson submitted a bid generated by the software. After Mortenson was awarded the Harborview Medical Center project, it learned its bid was approximately $1.95 million lower than intended.

Mortenson filed an action in King County Superior Court against Timberline and Softworks alleging breach of express and implied warranties. After the suit was filed, a Timberline internal memorandum surfaced, dated May 26, 1993. The memorandum stated, "[a] bug has been found [in the Precision software] . . . that results in two rather obscure problems," and explained, "[t]hese problems only happen if the following [four] conditions are met." The memorandum concluded, "[g]iven the unusual criteria for

this problem, it does not appear to be a major problem." Apparently, other Timberline customers had encountered the same problem and a newer version of the software was sent to some of these customers. After an extensive investigation, Timberline's lead programmer for Precision Bid Analysis acknowledged if the four steps identified in the memo were "reproduced as accurately as possible," Mortenson's error message could be replicated.

Timberline moved for summary judgment of dismissal in July 1997, arguing the limitation on consequential damages in the licensing agreement barred Mortenson's recovery. Mortenson countered that its entire contract with Timberline consisted of the purchase order and it never saw or agreed to the provisions in the licensing agreement. The trial court granted Timberline's motion for summary judgment. The trial judge stated, "if this case had arisen in 1985 rather than 1997, I might have a different ruling" but "the facts in this case are such that even construing them against the moving party, the Court finds as a matter of law that the licensing agreements and limitations pertaining thereto were conspicuous and controlling and, accordingly, the remedies that are available to the plaintiff in this case are the remedies that were set forth in the licensing agreement. . . ."

Mortenson appealed the summary judgment order to the Court of Appeals. The Court of Appeals affirmed the trial court and held (1) the purchase order was not an integrated contract; (2) the license terms were part of the contract; and (3) the limitation of remedies clause was not unconscionable and, therefore, enforceable. Mortenson appealed.

The Court of Appeals affirmed and Mortenson appealed.

JUDICIAL OPINION

JOHNSON, J.

This case presents the issue of whether a limitation on consequential damages enclosed in a "shrink-wrap license" accompanying computer software is enforceable against the purchaser of the licensed software.

Mortenson contends because the purchase order fulfilled the basic requirements of contracting under the U.C.C., it constituted a fully integrated contract. As a result, Mortenson argues the terms of the license, including the limitation of remedies clause, were not part of the contract and, thus, are not enforceable. Timberline counters that the parties did not intend the purchase order to be an exclusive

(continued)

recitation of the contract terms, and points to the absence from the purchase order of several key details of the agreement. Timberline argues, and the trial court and Court of Appeals agreed, that the purchase order did not prevent the terms of the license from becoming part of the contract or render the limitation of remedies clause unenforceable.

Whether the parties intend a written document to be a final expression of the terms of the agreement is a question of fact. Whether the purchase order qualifies as a contract at all does not resolve the issue of whether it is an integrated contract. Even if we assume the purchase order could, standing alone, constitute a complete contract under the U.C.C., such was not the case here. The language of the purchase order makes this clear. For example, the purchase order sets an hourly rate for Timberline's provision of "software support," but does not specify how many hours of support Timberline would provide. The purchase order also states: "[a]t some future date should Timberline upgrade 'Bid Day' to a windows version, M.A. Mortenson would be able to upgrade to this system with Timberline crediting existing software purchase toward that upgrade on a pro-rated basis to be determined later." Finally, the purchase order does not contain an integration clause. The presence of an integration clause "strongly supports a conclusion that the parties' agreement was fully integrated. . . ." Here, the absence of such a clause further supports the conclusion that the purchase order was not the complete agreement between the parties. The trial court and the Court of Appeals correctly determined the purchase order did not constitute an integrated contract.

Mortenson next argues even if the purchase order was not an integrated contract, Timberline's delivery of the license terms merely constituted a request to add additional or different terms, which were never agreed upon by the parties. Mortenson claims the additional terms did not become part of the contract because they were material alterations. Timberline responds that the terms of the license were not a request to add additional terms, but part of the contract between the parties. Timberline further argues that so-called "shrinkwrap" software licenses have been found enforceable by other courts, and that both trade usage and course of dealing support enforcement in the present case.

For its section 2-207 analysis, Mortenson relies on *Step-Saver Data Sys., Inc.* v. *Wyse Tech.*, 939 F.2d 91 (3d Cir.1991). There, Step-Saver, a value added retailer, placed telephone orders for software and confirmed with purchase orders. The manufacturer then forwarded an invoice back to Step-Saver. The software later arrived with a license agreement printed on the packaging. Finding the license "should have been treated as a written confirmation containing additional terms," the Third Circuit applied U.C.C. section 2-207 and held the warranty disclaimer and limitation of remedies terms were not part of the parties' agreement because they were material alterations. Mortenson claims *Step-Saver* is controlling, as "virtually every element of the transaction in the present case is mirrored in *Step-Saver.*" We disagree.

First, *Step-Saver* did not involve the enforceability of a standard license agreement against an end user of the software, but instead involved its applicability to a value added retailer who simply included the software in an integrated system sold to the end user. In fact, in *Step-Saver* the party contesting applicability of the licensing agreement had been assured the license did not apply to it at all. Such is not the case here, as Mortenson was the end user of the Bid analysis software and was never told the license agreement did not apply.

Further, in *Step-Saver* the seller of the program twice asked the buyer to sign an agreement comparable to their disputed license agreement. Both times the buyer refused, but the seller continued to make the software available. In contrast, Mortenson and Timberline had utilized a license agreement throughout Mortenson's use of the Medallion and Precision Bid Analysis software. Given these distinctions, we find *Step-Saver* to be inapplicable to the present case. We conclude this is a case about contract formation, not contract alteration.

[t]he Seventh Circuit held software shrinkwrap license agreements are a valid form of contracting under Wisconsin's version of U.C.C. section 2-204, and such agreements are enforceable unless objectionable under general contract law such as the law of unconscionability. The court stated, "[n]otice on the outside, terms on the inside, and a right to return the software for a refund if the terms are unacceptable (a right that the license expressly extends), may be a means of doing business valuable to buyers and sellers alike."

The UCITA embraces the theory of "layered contracting," which acknowledges while "some contracts are formed and their terms fully defined at a single point in time, many transactions involve a rolling or layered process. An agreement exists, but terms are clarified or created over time." UCITA § 208 cmt. 3 (Approved Official Draft).

We, therefore, hold under RCW 62A.2-204 the terms of the license were part of the contract between Mortenson and Timberline, and Mortenson's use of the software constituted its assent to the agreement, including the license terms.

The terms of Timberline's license were either set forth explicitly or referenced in numerous locations. The terms were included within the shrinkwrap packaging of each copy of Precision Bid Analysis; they were present in the manuals accompanying the software; they were included with the protection devices for the software, without which the software could not be used. The fact the software was licensed was also noted on the introductory screen each time the software was used. Even accepting Mortenson's contention it never saw the terms of the license, as we must do on summary judgment, it was not necessary for Mortenson to actually read the agreement in order to be bound by it.

Furthermore, the U.C.C. defines an "agreement" as "the bargain of the parties in fact as found in their language or by implication from other circumstances including course of dealing or usage of trade or course of performance. . . ." Mortenson and Timberline had a course of dealing; Mortenson had purchased licensed software from Timberline for years prior to its upgrade to Precision Bid Analysis. All Timberline software, including the prior version of Bid Analysis used by Mortenson since at least 1990, is distributed under license. Moreover, extensive testimony and exhibits before the trial court demonstrate an unquestioned use of such license agreements throughout the software industry. Although Mortenson questioned the relevance of this evidence, there is no evidence in the record to contradict it. While trade usage is a question of fact, undisputed evidence of trade usage may be considered on summary judgment.

Mortenson contends even if the limitation of remedies clause is part of its contract with Timberline, the clause is unconscionable and, therefore, unenforceable.

Limitations on consequential damages are generally valid under the U.C.C. unless they are unconscionable. Whether a limitation on consequential damages is unconscionable is a question of law.

Mortenson asserts Timberline's failure to inform it of the "defect" in the software prior to its purchase renders the licensing agreement substantively unconscionable.

Comment 3 to [U.C.C.] § 2-719 generally approves consequential damage exclusions as "merely an allo-

cation of unknown or undeterminable risks." Thus, the presence of latent defects in the goods cannot render these clauses unconscionable. The need for certainty in risk-allocation is especially compelling where, as here, the goods are experimental and their performance by nature less predictable.

Mortenson also contends the licensing agreement is procedurally unconscionable because "the license terms were never presented to Mortenson in a contractually-meaningful way."

Procedural unconscionability has been described as the lack of a meaningful choice, considering all the circumstances surrounding the transaction including " '[t]he manner in which the contract was entered,' whether each party had 'a reasonable opportunity to understand the terms of the contract,' and whether 'the important terms [were] hidden in a maze of fine print. . . .' "

Examining the contracting process between the parties based on the above factors, we hold the clause to be procedurally conscionable. The clause was not hidden in a maze of fine print. The license was set forth in capital letters on each diskette pouch and on the inside cover of the instruction manuals. A license to use the protection device was wrapped around each such device. The license was also referenced in the opening screen of the software program. This gave Mortenson more than ample opportunity to read and understand the terms of the license. Mortenson is also not an inexperienced retail consumer, but a nationwide construction contractor that has purchased licensed software from Timberline in the past.

We find Mortenson's unconscionability claim unpersuasive and, therefore, find the limitation of remedies clause to be enforceable.

Affirmed.

CASE QUESTIONS

1. When did Mortenson agree to the limitation on damages?

2. Where does the liability limitation clause fit in the 2-207 scenario?

3. What choices do software buyers have when they read a screen that limits the software company's liability?

4. Is the damage limitation clause unconscionable?

Consideration

Consideration is what distinguishes gifts from contracts and is what each party—offeror and offeree—gives up under the contract; it is sometimes called **bargained-for exchange.** If you sign a contract to buy a 1980 Mercedes for $17,000, your consideration is the $17,000 and is given in exchange for the car. The seller's consideration is giving up the car and is given in exchange for your $17,000. On the other hand, if your grandmother tells you that she will give you her Mercedes, there is no consideration, and your grandmother's promise (unfortunately) is not a contract and is not enforceable.

The courts are not concerned with the amount or nature of consideration so long as it is actually passed from one party to the other. A contract is not unenforceable because a court feels you paid too little under the contract terms. The amount of consideration is left to the discretion of the parties, but one party cannot demand greater consideration once the contract is finalized.

C O N S I D E R . . .

13.5   In 1977, George Lucas granted Kenner Toys the exclusive right to produce *Star Wars* toys—the action figures and other replicas from the movie—in perpetuity for $100,000 per year. At the time the contract was negotiated, no one understood how valuable the contract rights were.

In 1991, Hasbro Toys purchased Kenner. By this time, the sales of Princess Leia dolls and R2D2 replicas were nonexistent. Because there was no market for the toys, the toys were no longer produced, and an accountant with Kenner decided to save $100,000 and not send the check to Mr. Lucas.

In 1992, a Lucas employee saw a line of Galoob toys at a trade show and asked if Galoob was interested in making the *Star Wars* toy line. Galoob jumped at the chance and did quite well marketing the toys. Some executives believe that the popularity of the toys motivated Lucas to rerelease the movies, which turned out to be a money-maker for Lucas as well as for the Galoob toy line.

In 1996, Lucas did grant some rights to Hasbro, but it has lost market share and footing to Galoob. Was the failure to make the payment a failure of consideration? Has Hasbro lost its rights?

Unique Consideration Issues

The concept of consideration and its requirement for contract formation has presented courts with some unique problems. Often an element of fairness and reliance exists in circumstances in which there is an offer and acceptance but no consideration. For example, many nonprofit organizations raise funds through pledges. Such pledges are not supported by consideration, but the nonprofit organizations rely on those pledges. Called **charitable subscriptions,** these agreements are enforced by courts despite the lack of consideration.

The doctrine of **promissory estoppel** is also used as a substitute for consideration in those cases in which someone acts in reliance on a promise that is not supported by consideration. For example, suppose an employer said, "Move to Denver and I'll hire you." There is no detriment on your part until you begin work. The employer has no detriment either. However, if you sold your home in Phoenix and incurred the expense of moving to Denver, it would be unfair to allow the employer to claim the contract did not exist because of no consideration. You have acted in reliance on a promise, and that reliance serves as a consideration substitute.

CONSIDER. . .

13.6   Alan Fulkins, who owns a construction company that specializes in single-family residences, is constructing a small subdivision with twenty-three homes. Tretorn Plumbing, owned by Jason Tretorn, was awarded the contract for the plumbing work on the homes at a price of $4,300 per home.

Plumbing contractors complete their residential projects in three phases. Phase 1 consists of digging the lines for the plumbing and installing the pipes that are placed in the foundation of the house. Phase 2 consists of the pipes within the walls of the home, and phase 3 is the surface plumbing, such as sinks and tubs. However, industry practice dictates that the plumbing contractor receive one-half of the contract amount after completion of phase one.

Tretorn completed the digs of phase one for Fulkins and received payment of $2,150. Tretorn then went to Fulkins and demanded an additional $600 per house for completion of the work. Fulkins said, "But you already have a contract for $4,300!" Tretorn responded, "I know, but the costs are killing me. I need the additional $600."

Fulkins explained the hardship of the demand, "Look, I've already paid you half. If I hire someone else, I'll have to pay them two-thirds for the work not done. It'll cost me $5,000 per house." Tretorn responded, "Exactly. I'm a bargain because the additional $600 I want only puts you at $4,900. If you don't pay it, I'll just lien the houses and then you'll be stuck without a way to close the sales. I've got the contract all drawn up. Just sign it and everything goes smoothly."

Should Fulkins sign the agreement? Does Tretorn have the right to the additional $600? Was it ethical for Tretorn to demand the $600? Is there any legal advice you can offer Fulkins?

Contract Form: When Writing Is Required

For a look at electronic signatures and contracts, visit:
http://www.unisys.com/home/e-signatures

Some contracts can exist just on the basis of an oral promise. Others, however, are required to be in writing to be enforceable, and these contracts are covered under each state's **statute of frauds.**

Common Law Statute of Frauds

The term *statute of frauds* originated in 1677 when England passed the first rule dealing with written contracts: the Statute for the Prevention of Frauds and Perjuries. The purpose of the first statute and the descendant statutes today is to have written agreements for the types of contracts that might encourage conflicting claims and possible perjury if oral agreements were allowed. The following is a partial list of the types of contracts required to be in writing under most state laws:

1. Contracts for the sale of real property. This requirement includes sales, certain leases, liens, mortgages, and easements.

2. Contracts that cannot be performed within one year. These contracts run for long periods and require the benefit of written terms.

3. Contracts to pay the debt of another. Cosigners' agreements to pay if a debtor defaults must be in writing. A corporate officer's personal guarantee of a corporate note must be in writing to be enforceable.

UCC Statute of Frauds

Under the UCC, there is a separate statute of frauds for contracts covering the sale of goods. Contracts for the sale of goods costing $500 or more are required to be in writing to be enforceable.

C O N S I D E R . . .

13.7   Which of the following contracts must be in writing to be enforceable?

1. A contract for the sale of an acre of land for $400

2. A contract for management consulting for six months for $353,000

3. A contract for the sale of a car for $358

4. A contract for a loan cosigned by a corporation's vice president

5. A contract for the sale of a mobile home for $12,000

Exceptions to the Statute of Frauds

For a summary of electronic signature legislation, visit: http://www.mbc.com

There are some exceptions to the UCC and common law statute of frauds provisions that were created for situations in which the parties have partially or fully performed their unwritten contract. Under both the UCC and common law, if the parties go ahead and perform the oral contract, courts will enforce the contract for what has already been done. For example, if Alan agreed to sell land to Bertha under an oral contract and Bertha has paid, has the deed, and has moved in, Alan cannot use the statute of frauds to remove Bertha and get the land back.

E X H I B I T   13.4   Common-Law versus UCC Rules on Formation

AREA	UCC	COMMON LAW
Application	Sales of goods	Services, real estate, employment contracts
Offers	Need subject matter (quantity); code gives details	Need subject matter, price, terms, full details agreed upon
Options	Merchant's firm offer—no consideration needed	Need consideration
Acceptance	Can have additional terms	Mirror image rule followed
	Mailbox rule works for reasonable means of acceptance	Must use same method to get mailbox rule*
Consideration	Required for contracts but not for modification or firm offers	Always required
Writing requirement	Sale of goods for $500 or more	Real estate, contracts not to be performed in one year; paying the debt of another
Defenses[†]	Must be free of all defenses for valid contract	Must be free of all defenses for valid contract

*Some courts have adopted the UCC rule for common law contracts.
[†]See Chapter 14.

For a summary of proposed electronic signature legislation, visit: http://www.ilpf.org

What Form of Writing Is Required?

The form of writing required under the statute of frauds is not formal. Evidence of a written agreement can be pieced together from memos and letters. Under the UCC, merchants can meet the statute of frauds by sending confirmation memos (see § 2-201 in Appendix G). These **merchants' confirmation memoranda** summarize the oral agreement and are signed by only one party, but they can be used to satisfy the statute of frauds so long as the memo has been sent to the nonsigning party for review and there is no objection upon that party's receipt. Exhibit 13.4 provides a summary of UCC and common law-formation provisions.

In the following case, the sufficiency of the contract writing is discussed.

CASE 13.6

Rosenfeld v. Basquiat
78 F.3d 184 (2d Cir. 1996)

The Artist, the Crayon, and the Contract

FACTS

Michelle Rosenfeld, an art dealer, alleges she contracted with artist Jean-Michael Basquiat to buy three of his paintings. The works that she claims she contracted to buy were entitled *Separation of the K, Atlas,* and *Untitled Head.* Rosenfeld testified that she went to Basquiat's apartment on October 25, 1982; while she was there, he agreed to sell her three paintings for $4,000 each, and she picked out three. Basquiat asked for a cash deposit of 10 percent; she left his loft and later returned with $1,000 in cash, which she paid him. When she asked for a receipt, he insisted on drawing up a contract and got down on the floor and wrote it out in crayon on a large piece of paper, remarking that some day this contract would be worth money. The handwritten document listed the three paintings, bore Rosenfeld's signature and Basquiat's signature, and stated: "$12,000—$1,000 DEPOSIT—Oct 25 82." Rosenfeld later returned to Basquiat's loft to discuss delivery, but Basquiat convinced her to wait for at least two years so that he could show the paintings at exhibitions. After Basquiat's death, the estate argued that there was no contract because the statute of frauds made the agreement unenforceable. The estate contended that a written contract for the sale of goods must include the date of delivery. From a judgment in favor of the estate, the plaintiff appealed.

JUDICIAL OPINION

CARDAMONE, J.

. . . Because this case involves an alleged contract for the sale of three paintings, any question regarding the Statute of Frauds is governed by the U.C.C. (applicability to "transactions in goods") (contract for $500 or more is unenforceable "unless there is some writing sufficient to indicate that a contract for sale has been made between the parties and signed by the party [charged]"). Under the U.C.C., the only term that *must* appear in the writing is the quantity. See N.Y.U.C.C. § 2-201.

Beyond that, "[a]ll that is required is that the writing afford a basis for believing that the offered oral evidence rests on a real transaction." The writing supplied by the plaintiff indicated the price, the date, the specific paintings involved, and that Rosenfeld paid a deposit. It also bore the signatures of the buyer and seller. Therefore, the writing satisfied the requirements of § 2-201.

Citing *Berman Stores Co.* v. *Hirsh*, 240 N.Y. 209 (1925), the estate claims that a specific delivery date, if agreed upon, must be in the writing. *Berman Stores* was decided before the enactment of the U.C.C. and was based on the principle that "the note or memorandum . . . should completely evidence the contract which the parties made." 240 N.Y. at 214 (quoting *Poel* v. *Brunswick-Balke-Collender Co.*, 216 N.Y. 310,

(continued)

314 [1915]). The rule that a specific delivery date is "an essential part of the contract and must be embodied in the memorandum," *Berman Stores*, 240 N.Y. at 215, was rejected by the legislature—at least for sale-of-goods cases—when it enacted the U.C.C. That rule and the statute upon which it was based were repealed to make way for the U.C.C.

. . . Because the writing, allegedly scrawled in crayon by Jean-Michel Basquiat on a large piece of paper, easily satisfied the requirements of § 2-201 of the U.C.C., the estate is not entitled to judgment as a matter of law. It is of no real significance that the jury found Rosenfeld and Basquiat settled on a particular time for delivery and did not commit it to writing. . . . As a consequence, . . . the alleged contract is not invalid on Statute of Frauds grounds. . . .

Judgment reversed.

CASE QUESTIONS

1. Why was the contract required to be in writing?
2. Did the contract comply with the statute of frauds?
3. Does a writing that does not comply with the statute of frauds make the alleged contract void?

BUSINESS PLANNING TIP

Many businesses are relying on fax machines for offers and acceptances. These machines offer the benefit of quick, written documents. However, clarity is often sacrificed, and fax paper can fade. Further, in several recent cases signatures had been taped onto faxed copies. There was no authentic signature, and the taped signature could not be detected on the fax. Always follow up your faxes with actual documents for signature.

BUSINESS PLANNING TIP

Electronic Contracts

The fax, the phone, and electronic data interchange (EDI) allow businesses to do business rapidly. Often, transactions are completed electronically, with little or no paperwork. Managers should follow these tips in using these technological methods of communication:

1. Follow up and verify to be certain someone with authority entered the transaction or sent the transmission.

2. Keep a hard copy for your records—"delete" *often* works too well.

3. Meet once each year to update your understanding of terms and your relationship.

4. Have your computer network checked for access and possible espionage.

The Writing Requirement in the Electronic Contract

As noted earlier in the chapter, the UETA is the proposed uniform law on making contracts via electronic means. However, whatever form of law the states adopt individually for signature requirements for electronic contacts, those laws cannot violate the federal E-sign provisions. Under E-sign, states must provide parity for electronic and paper signatures. That is, electronic contracts and signatures must be held to meet the statute of frauds requirements in the same way that paper contracts and signatures do. Some documents are, however, exempt from this equal treatment and include wills, trusts, checks, letters of credit, court documents, and cancellation of health and life insurance policies. States may require paper documentation for protection of legal rights in these transactions.

E-sign does not deal with the issues of digital signatures and security. Those are issues each of the states must grapple with in adopting their legislation giving e-contracts parity in terms of the writing requirement. Some companies are not comfortable without some form of **digital signature.** The digital signature can be accomplished in different ways. Encryption is used for the encoding of messages so that they cannot be read without the code. This process allows a form of electronic or digital signature that can have the same authenticity and verification of source as a notarized document once had. A digital signature is defined as a "transformation of a message using an asymmetric cryptosystem such that a person having the initial message and the signer's public key can accurately determine whether (a) the transformation was created using the private key that corresponds to the signer's public key; and (b) the message has been altered since the transformation was made." In other words, using a public/private electronic code system, the authenticity of transmissions codes can be determined.

Problems faced by businesses and those working to draft effective legislation and uniform laws on encryption commerce include the concerns of law enforcement officials with the use of encryption devices. Law enforcement officials want the capacity to decode mes-

For a look at Article 2B, go to:
http://www.law.upenn.edu/bll/ulc.htm

sages because of the national security issues that arise when communications include illegal activities and information. The FBI has asked for some controls on encryption.

The Effect of the Written Contract: Parol Evidence

Once a contract is reduced to its final written form and is complete and unambiguous, the parties to the contract are not permitted to contradict the contract terms with evidence of their negotiations or verbal agreements at the time the contract was executed. This prohibition on extrinsic evidence for fully integrated contracts is called the **parol evidence** rule and is a means for stopping ongoing contradictions to contracts that have been entered into and finalized. It is a protection for the application of the document to the parties' rights as well as a reminder of the need to put the true nature of the agreement into the contract.

There are some exceptions to the parol evidence rule. If a contract is incomplete or the terms are ambiguous, extrinsic evidence can be used to clarify or complete the contract, as in the case of UCC contracts in which price, delivery, and payment terms can be added (see § 2-202 in Appendix G). Also, if one of the parties to the contract is alleging a defense to the contract's formation, then evidence of the circumstances creating that defense can be used as evidence. Evidence of lack of capacity or fraud does not violate the parol evidence rule.

ISSUES IN FORMATION OF INTERNATIONAL CONTRACTS

International business contracts are very similar to domestic contracts. However, the unique aspect of international contracts is that additional risks and questions arise over the choice of currency, the impact of culture on contract interpretation and performance, and the stability of the governments of the parties involved in the contract. In other words, international contracts carry certain risks that are not part of contracts between businesses in the same country. Over the past few years, the increased number of international transactions has resulted in recognition of the need for a more uniform law on international contract formation and performance. The United Nations has developed such a set of laws, called the **United Nations Convention on Contracts for the International Sale of Goods** (CISG) (see Chapter 7).

BUSINESS PLANNING TIP

Avoiding Legal Pitfalls in International Transactions

1. Use short, simple contracts. The tendency to place all possibilities in a contract is a U.S. tradition. In Germany, for example, the parties have a one-page agreement that references and incorporates terms and conditions of one of the parties.

2. Watch unconscionability protections. While the United States focuses its unfairness protections on consumers, other countries afford these same protections to commercial transactions.

3. Some disclaimers are void in other countries. For example, the clause, "We are only liable for loss of data which is due to a deliberate act on our part. We are not responsible for lost profits in any event," would be valid in the United States but void in Germany. In Germany, sellers of software must assume liability for at least gross negligence.

4. One party's attempt to limit liability would be void in Germany. Any liability limitation must be specifically addressed and negotiated for such a clause to be valid.

5. Unusually long periods for performance are typical in the United States but void in Germany.

6. Price increase limitations are typical in non-U.S. contracts.

7. In other countries, parties can refuse to pay on a current contract if performance on an earlier contract was less than satisfactory and damages are owed.

Visit the Institute of International Commercial Law, sponsored by the Pace University School of Law, to review the CISG:

http://cisgw3.law.pace.edu/ cisg/text/database.html

The CISG, which applies to those contracts in which buyer and seller have their businesses in different countries (unless the parties agree otherwise), has four parts: Part I: Application; Part II: Formation; Part III: Sale of Goods; and Part IV: Final Provisions. Part II includes provisions for the requirements for offers and acceptance, including a merchant's firm offer provision. Acceptance is effective only upon receipt; and, whenever forms do not match, there is no contract unless the nonmatching terms are immaterial.

Party autonomy continues to remain a priority. The parties can always choose the applicable law, the nation for the location of courts for resolving disputes, and remedies. Details on global contracts are found in Chapter 7.

There are several significant differences between the UCC and the CISG. For example, the CISG follows the common law mirror image rule and not the more liberal UCC "battle of the forms" modification exception. The CISG also requires the presence of a price for an offer to be definite enough to be valid. Merchants' firm offers exist under the CISG, but there are no time limitations on their validity, as with the UCC three-month limit. Parties in international trade need to be familiar with the hybrid nature of the CISG in order to protect their contract rights.

Those firms and countries not relying on the CISG should be familiar with the nuances of commercial law in the countries in which they are doing business. The tendency of many U.S. businesses is to draft a form contract using the home country legal concepts and carry them over to other countries. As the earlier planning tips indicate, such a practice and reliance on form contracts can be dangerous.

For the United Nations' model law on electronic commerce, visit:

http://www.un.or.at/ uncitral/english/texts/ electcom/index.htm

One of the content and interpretation issues in international contracts focuses on the method of payment. Currently, many contracts specify that payment is to be made in deutsche marks or pounds. On January 1, 1999, the EU began the use of one currency. Payment under various contracts will become more of an issue for parties to negotiate in international transactions. Some parties are negotiating now to put substitutes into their contracts, and all parties working on new agreements are covering the issue in their negotiations. In *Intershoe* v. *Bankers Trust*, confusion on payment issues proved expensive for one party.

In negotiating an international contract, parties should determine which country's laws will govern the transaction. Courts will not interfere with this decision so long as the law chosen has some relation to the transaction. The parties should also agree to submit to the jurisdiction of a particular court so that litigation does not begin with the issue of whether there is or is not jurisdiction in a particular court. If the parties wish to submit to arbitration prior to litigation, the terms and nature of arbitration should be delineated in the contract.

For information on law, contracts, and contract forms in international transactions, visit the Web site for the National Law Center for Inter-American Free Trade:

http://www.natlaw.com

International contracts carry peculiar and additional risks. One of the lessons of the 1991 war in the Persian Gulf, for example, is that international contracts should have provisions for war, interruption of shipping lines, and other political acts. Often referred to as *force majeure* clauses, these provisions in international contracts allow the parties to agree what will happen in the event of sudden changes in government or in the global political climate rather than rely on a court to determine after the fact what rights, if any, the parties had. (See Chapter 14 for more details on contract issues.)

CASE 13.7

Intershoe, Inc. v. Bankers Trust
569 N.Y.S.2d 33 (1991)

Lira, Shoes, and Exchange Rates

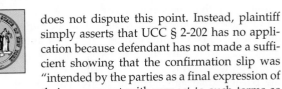

FACTS

Intershoe, Inc. (plaintiff), is a shoe importer that uses various foreign currencies, including Italian lira, in its business.

On March 3, 1985, Intershoe phoned Bankers Trust (defendant) and entered into several foreign currency transactions, one being a futures transaction involving lira. On March 13, Bankers Trust sent Intershoe a confirmation slip with the following terms: "WE [Bankers] HAVE BOUGHT FROM YOU [Intershoe] ITL 537,750,000" and "WE HAVE SOLD TO YOU USD 250,000.00."

The confirmation slip specified a rate of 2,151 lira per dollar and called for delivery of the lira approximately seven and a half months later, between October 1 and October 31, 1985. Intershoe's treasurer signed the slip and returned it to Bankers Trust on March 18, 1985.

By letter dated October 11, 1985, Bankers Trust notified Intershoe that it was awaiting instructions as to Intershoe's delivery of the lira. Intershoe responded in a letter dated October 25, 1985, that the transaction was a mistake and that it would not go through with it. To cover commitments in other currency transactions, Bankers Trust was forced to purchase lira on the open market at a higher price than that on March 13, 1985, resulting in a loss of $55,014.85. Intershoe filed suit claiming that it had purchased, not sold, lira and that it had sustained damages of $59,336.40. Bankers Trust counterclaimed for its damages.

The trial court held that there were issues of fact. Bankers Trust maintained that the case should be decided in its favor by summary judgment because of the parol evidence rule and appealed.

JUDICIAL OPINION

HANCOCK, Jr., Justice

We turn to defendant's argument that UCC § 2-202 bars the parol evidence submitted in opposition to its motion.

There seems to be no question that the UCC applies to foreign currency transactions. Plaintiff does not dispute this point. Instead, plaintiff simply asserts that UCC § 2-202 has no application because defendant has not made a sufficient showing that the confirmation slip was "intended by the parties as a final expression of their agreement with respect to such terms as are included therein." Something more is required, plaintiff says, either language in the confirmation slip indicating that it was intended to be the final expression of the parties' agreement or uncontroverted evidence that the writing was so intended. Otherwise, according to plaintiff, there are factual issues as to the effect the parties intended the confirmation slip to have and summary judgment must be denied. We disagree.

Here, the essential terms of the transaction are plainly set forth in the confirmation slip: that plaintiff had sold lira to defendant, the amount of the lira it sold, the exchange rate, the amount of dollars to be paid by defendant for the lira, and the maturity date of the transaction. The signature of plaintiff's agent who signed and returned the confirmation slip five days later on March 18, 1985, signifies plaintiff's acceptance of these terms. Nothing in the confirmation slip suggests that it was to be a memorandum of some preliminary or tentative understanding with respect to these terms. On the contrary, it is difficult to imagine words which could more clearly demonstrate the final expression of the parties' agreement than "WE HAVE BOUGHT FROM YOU ITL 537,750,000" and "WE HAVE SOLD TO YOU USD 250,000.00."

The confirmation is not of some bargain to be made in the future but expresses the parties' meeting of the minds as to a completed bargain's essential terms—a sale of 537,750 lira at a rate of 2151 for 250,000 dollars—made in a telephone conversation on March 13, 1985. The only evidence plaintiff has tendered does no more than contradict the stated terms of the confirmation slip—the very evidence which UCC § 2-202 precludes. It does not address the critical question of whether the terms in the confirmation slip were intended to represent the parties' final agreement on those matters. We conclude that

(continued)

where, as here, the form and content of the confirmation slip suggest nothing other than that it was intended to be the final expression of the parties' agreement as to the terms set forth and where there is no evidence indicating that this was not so, UCC § 2-202 bars parol evidence of contradictory terms.

We reject plaintiff's contentions that UCC § 2-202 requires that there be some express indication in the writing itself or some other evidence that the parties intended it to be the final expression of their agreement. . . . To require that the record include specific extraneous evidence that the writing constitutes the parties' final agreement as to its stated terms would in many instances impose a virtually insurmountable obstacle for parties seeking to invoke UCC § 2-202, particularly in cases involving large commercial banks and other financial institutions, which typically close hundreds of transactions over the telephone during a business day. As a practical matter, a confirmation slip or similar writing is usually the only reliable evidence of such transactions, given the unlikely prospect that one who makes scores of similar deals each day will remember the details of any one particular agreement. Indeed, this case is illustrative inasmuch as neither of the participants had a specific recollection of the March 13, 1985, telephone conversation.

Plaintiff also argues that UCC § 2-202 does not bar the parol evidence submitted in opposition to defendant's motion because it is offered to show that there was never a contract between the parties. This argument is unavailing. Plaintiff does not dispute that it entered into a foreign currency transaction with defendant; its only contention is that the transaction called for it to purchase and not sell lira. Hence, the parol evidence is being used to contradict a term of the contract, not to show that there was no contract, and UCC § 2-202 applies.

Reversed.

CASE QUESTIONS

1. Describe the transaction.
2. Who sold, according to the memo?
3. Who sold, according to Intershoe?
4. Is the memo a final writing?
5. What dangers would the court introduce if orders such as this were contradicted by oral testimony?
6. Did someone fail to read a document carefully before signing? Does the parol evidence rule allow "failure to read" as a defense?

CONSIDER...

13.8 Terrorist acts, such as the September 11, 2001, destruction of the World Trade Center towers in New York City, have become more frequent over the past few years. What happens when there is a substantial interruption in a business's operations because a bombing destroys or damages its leased facilities? Would you add provisions and protections to your lease? What terms would you want if you were the landlord?

In addition to the risks of political changes, international contracts have the risks of changing currency exchange rates, long distances in transportation, and difficulties with collection of payments. Most international contracts have built-in performance guarantees. For example, a seller ships goods with a **bill of lading** (a document of title that the carrier will have). To be able to pick up the goods from the carrier, the buyer must have a copy of the bill of lading. The seller can have a bank release the bill of lading to the buyer when the buyer has paid or when the buyer's bank issues a letter of credit (which is the bank's commitment to pay) to the seller for the amount due for the goods. The effect of these two documents is that the seller or carrier does not release the goods until the payment is made or assured. The flow of goods is controlled across borders through documents that travel with the goods and through banks that will issue the payment. At the same time, the buyer is assured that the goods are there before payment is made or authorized.

BIOGRAPHY

THE STORY OF TELEVISION CONTRACTS

In 1996, the six stars of the cast of the NBC-TV situation comedy *Friends* (Jennifer Aniston, Courtney Cox, Lisa Kudrow, Matt LeBlanc, Matthew Perry, and David Schwimmer) each demanded a salary increase from $40,000 per episode to $100,000 per episode, which was more than double their contract salaries. Further, the six stars threatened to walk out on the beginning of the fall season if their salary demands were not met. *Friends* was one of a handful of highly successful programs on NBC, indeed on any network. The six actors had examined the ad revenues for their show and concluded that with their short-lived careers and fame, they needed to negotiate as much salary as possible. The six stars were successful in renegotiating their contracts, but they also created a new phenomenon in the television industry whereby stars are able to command high salaries when nervous executives feel their departure is imminent.

Some sample salaries are as follows:

Tim Allen	*Home Improvement*	$1.25 million per episode
Paul Reiser	*Mad about You*	$1.00 million per episode
Helen Hunt	*Mad about You*	$1.00 million per episode

(Note: Both Mr. Reiser and Ms. Hunt received an increase from $750,000 to $1,000,000 per episode following the end of the *Seinfeld* series, which was the heart of NBC's successful Thursday night lineup. Mr. Seinfeld had been the first and only television actor to receive $1 million per episode—Mr. Allen's contract was negotiated at about the same time as Reiser's and Hunt's, and Mr. Allen's show is with ABC Television.)

Julia Louis-Dreyfuss	*Seinfeld*	$600,000 per episode
Jason Alexander	*Seinfeld*	$600,000 per episode
Michael Richards	*Seinfeld*	$600,000 per episode
Kelsey Grammer	*Frasier*	$250,000 per episode
John Lithgow	*Third Rock from the Sun*	$150,000 per episode
Tom Selleck	*The Closer*	$150,000 per episode
David Duchovny	*The X-Files*	$110,000 per episode
Gillian Anderson	*The X-Files*	$100,000 per episode
Roma Downey	*Touched by an Angel*	$75,000 per episode
Drew Carey	*Drew Carey Show*	$60,000 per episode
Della Reese	*Touched by an Angel*	$55,000 per episode
Calista Flockhart	*Ally McBeal*	$40,000 per episode
Jenna Elfman	*Dharma & Greg*	$40,000 per episode
Sarah Michelle Geller	*Buffy the Vampire Slayer*	$30,000 per episode

Just recently, the actors who work two days each week to do the voices of the characters for *The Simpsons* received an increase from their $15,000 to $25,000 per episode to $50,000 per episode. These voice actors work only two days each week, whereas actors in television series work five days per week. Julie Kavner, the voice of Marge Simpson, has a separate deal and did not participate in the threatened walkout by the voice talents for the show.

(continued)

ISSUES

Are the actors justified in threatening to walk out if they do not receive pay increases? Is there a legal basis for their walkouts? Some of the actors point to the earnings for the shows as justification for the walkouts. The net profits for the eight-year run of *The Simpsons* have been $500 million. Reruns for the

Drew Carey Show recently sold for $2 million each. Are unanticipated earnings and success a reason for increased payments under existing contracts?

When Mr. Jay Leno was asked about the tactics of the *Friends* stars, he responded, "You have to get what you can while you can in this business." Is Mr. Leno right? Is such an attitude ethical?

FOR THE MANAGER'S DESK

Re: Service, Interpretation of Terms, and the Art of Communication in Contract Relations

A contract relationship is only as good as the communication between the parties. The following is a series of communications between a hotel guest and various hotel employees.

Dear Maid,

Please do not leave any more of those little bars of soap in my bathroom since I have brought my own bath-sized Dial. Please remove the six unopened little bars from the shelf under the medicine chest and another three in the shower soap dish. They are in my way. Thank you,

S. Berman

Dear Room 238,

I am not your regular maid. She will be back tomorrow, Thursday, from her day off. I took the 3 hotel soaps out of the shower soap dish as you requested. The 6 bars on your shelf I took out of your way and put on top of your Kleenex dispenser in case you should change your mind. This leaves only the 3 bars I left today which my instructions from the management is to leave 3 soaps daily. I hope this is satisfactory.

Kathy, Relief Maid

Dear Maid—I hope you are my regular maid.

Apparently Kathy did not tell you about my note to her concerning the little bars of soap. When I got back to my room this evening I found you had added 3 little Camays to the shelf under my medicine cabinet. I am going to be here in the hotel for two weeks and have brought my own bath-size Dial so I don't need those 6 little Camays which are on the shelf. They are in my way when shaving, brushing teeth, etc.

Please remove them.

S. Berman

Dear Mr. Berman,

My day off was last Wed. so the relief maid left 3 hotel soaps which we are instructed by the management. I took the 6 soaps which were in your way on the shelf and put them in the soap dish where your Dial was. I put the Dial in the medicine cabinet for your convenience. I didn't remove the 3 complimentary soaps which are always placed inside the medicine cabinet for all new check-ins and which you did not object to when you checked in last Monday. Please let me know if I can be of further assistance.

Your regular maid,

Dotty

Dear Mr. Berman,

The assistant manager, Mr. Kensedder, informed me this A.M. that you called him last evening and said you were unhappy with your maid service. I have assigned a new girl to your room. I hope you will accept my apologies for any past inconvenience. If you have any future complaints please contact me so I can give it my personal attention. Call extension 1108 between 8 A.M. and 5 P.M. Thank you.

Elaine Carmen

Housekeeper

Dear Miss Carmen,

It is impossible to contact you by phone since I leave the hotel for business at 7:45 A.M. and don't get back before 5:30 or 6 P.M. That's the reason I called Mr. Kensedder last night. You were already off duty. I only asked Mr. Kensedder if he could do anything about those little bars of soap. The new maid you assigned me must have thought I was a new check-in today, since she left another 3 bars of hotel soap in my medicine cabinet along with her regular delivery of 3 bars on the bath-room shelf. In just 5 days here I have accumulated 24 little bars of soap. Why are you doing this to me?

S. Berman

Dear Mr. Berman,

Your maid, Kathy, has been instructed to stop delivering soap to your room and remove the extra soaps. If I can be of further assistance, please call extension 1108 between 8 A.M. and 5 P.M. Thank you,

Elaine Carmen,
Housekeeper

Dear Mr. Kensedder,

My bath-size Dial is missing. Every bar of soap was taken from my room including my own bath-size Dial. I came in late last night and had to call the bellhop to bring me 4 little Cashmere Bouquets.

S. Berman

Dear Mr. Berman,

I have informed our housekeeper, Elaine Carmen, of your soap problem. I cannot understand why there was no soap in your room since our maids are instructed to leave 3 bars of soap each time they service a room. The situation will be rectified immediately. Please accept my apologies for the inconvenience.

Martin L. Kensedder
Assistant Manager

Dear Mrs. Carmen,

Who the hell left 54 little bars of Camay in my room? I came in last night and found 54 little bars of soap. I don't want 54 little bars of Camay. I want my one damn bar of bath-size Dial. Do you realize I have 54 bars of soap in here. All I want is my bath-size Dial. Please give me back my bath-size Dial.

S. Berman

Dear Mr. Berman,

You complained of too much soap in your room so I had them removed. Then you complained to Mr. Kensedder

that all your soap was missing so I personally returned them. The 24 Camays which had been taken and the 3 Camays you are supposed to receive daly (sic). I don't know anything about the 4 Cashmere Bouquets. Obviously your maid, Kathy, did not know I had returned your soaps so she also brought 24 Camays plus the 3 daily Camays. I don't know where you got the idea this hotel issues bath-size Dial. I was able to locate some bath-size Ivory which I left in your room.

Elaine Carmen
Housekeeper

Dear Mrs. Carmen,

Just a short note to bring you up-to-date on my latest soap inventory.

As of today I possess:

—On shelf under medicine cabinet—18 Camay in 4 stacks of 4 and 1 stack of 2.

—On Kleenex dispenser—11 Camay in 2 stacks of 4 and 1 stack of 3.

—On bedroom dresser—1 stack of 3 Cashmere Bouquet, 1 stack of 4 hotel-size Ivory, and 8 Camay in 2 stacks of 4.

—Inside medicine cabinet—14 Camay in 3 stacks of 4 and 1 stack of 2.

—In shower soap dish—6 Camay, very moist.

—On northeast corner of tub—1 Cashmere Bouquet, slightly used.

—On northwest corner of tub—6 Camays in 2 stacks of 3.

Please ask Kathy when she services my room to make sure the stacks are neatly piled and dusted. Also, please advise her that stacks of more than 4 have a tendency to tip. May I suggest that my bedroom window sill is not in use and will make an excellent spot for future soap deliveries. One more item, I have purchased another bar of bath-sized Dial which I am keeping in the hotel vault in order to avoid further misunderstandings.

S. Berman

SUMMARY

What are contracts?

- Contract—promise or set of promises for breach of which the law gives a remedy, or the performance of which the law in some way recognizes as a duty

What laws govern contracts?

- Common law—traditional notions of law and the body of law developed in judicial decisions

- *Restatement (Second) of Contracts*—general summary of the common law of contracts

- Uniform Commercial Code (UCC)—set of uniform laws (forty-nine states) governing commercial transactions

What are the types of contracts?

- Bilateral contract—contract of two promises; one from each party

- Unilateral contract—contract made up of a promise for performance

- Express contract—written or verbally agreed-to contract

- Implied contract—contract that arises from parties' voluntary conduct

- Quasi contract—theory for enforcing a contract even though there is no formal contract because the parties behaved as if there were a contract

- Implied-in-fact contract—contract that arises from factual circumstances, professional circumstances, or custom

- Implied-in-law contract—legally implied contract to prevent unjust enrichment

- Void contract—contract with illegal subject matter or against public policy

- Voidable contract—contract that can be avoided legally by one side

- Unenforceable contract—agreement for which the law affords no remedy

- Executed contract—contract that has been performed

- Executory contract—contract not yet performed

How are contracts formed?

- Offer—preliminary to contract; first step in formation

- Offeror—person making the offer

- Offeree—recipient of offer

- Course of dealing—UCC provision that examines the way parties have behaved in the past to determine present performance standards

- Revocation—offeror canceling offer

- Options—offers with considerations; promises to keep offer open

- Merchant's firm offer—written offer signed by a merchant that states it will be kept open

- Counteroffer—counterproposal to offer

- Battle of the forms—UCC description of merchants' tendency to exchange purchase orders, invoices, confirmations, and so on

- Acceptance—offeree's positive response to offer

- Mailbox rule—timing rule for acceptance

- Consideration—something of value exchanged by the parties that distinguishes gifts from contracts

- Charitable subscriptions—enforceable promises to make gifts

- Promissory estoppel—reliance element used to enforce otherwise unenforceable contracts

When must contracts be in writing?

- Statute of frauds—state statutes governing the types of contracts that must be in writing to be enforceable

- Merchants' confirmation memorandum—UCC provision that allows one merchant to bind another based on an oral agreement with one signature

- Parol evidence—extrinsic evidence that is not admissible to dispute an integrated unambiguous contract

What issues for contracting exist in international business?

- CISG—Contracts for the International Sale of Goods; a proposed uniform law for international commercial transactions

QUESTIONS AND PROBLEMS

1. L. A. Becker Co., Inc., sent D. A. Clardy a $100 down payment along with a merchandise order. Clardy deposited the check, as was its usual daily practice for payments. After examining the offer, Clardy sent a rejection letter along with a check for $100 to Becker, who claims Clardy accepted by cashing the check. Is Becker correct? [*L. A. Becker Co.* v. *Clardy*, 51 So. 211 (Miss. 1910)]

2. Consider the following proposal description: Attached are an original and two (2) carbon copies of our Proposal No. 620-M-86R covering the subject as agreed upon in your office last Friday, June 20, 1986. Please sign the original and one (1) copy on the lower left corner of page 9 and return to us for our execution. We will return one (1) executed copy for your files.

Again we thank you for selecting us for this project. We assure you it is receiving our best attention. Our Engineering Department is proceeding with the designs, fabrication drawings, and material orders.

We look forward to your receiving the necessary permits.

The "proposal" consists of five pages of typewritten terms, setting forth specifications for the manufacture, assembly, and erection of a television tower and related items, and four pages of preprinted "Terms and Conditions of Sale." The printed portion includes the following relevant terms:

Acceptance of Proposal

This proposal is for immediate acceptance and prior to such acceptance is subject to modification or withdrawal without notice.

Acceptance of this proposal will evidence Buyer's intent that the sale be governed solely by the terms and conditions of this proposal.

Any modifying, inconsistent or additional terms and conditions of Buyer's acceptance shall not become a part of any contract resulting from this proposal unless agreed to in writing by Kline.

Any order or offer by Buyer as a result of this proposal shall not be binding upon Kline until accepted by Kline in writing by an officer of Kline. If accepted by Kline, this proposal shall constitute the agreement between the Buyer and Kline.

At the bottom of the final page are the following signature spaces:

KLINE IRON & STEEL CO., INC.

By _____

Its   (Seller)

GRAY COMMUNICATIONS, INC.

By _____

Its   (Buyer)

Is there an offer? When would the earliest acceptance be? [*Kline Iron & Steel Co., Inc.* v. *Gray Communications Consultants, Inc.*, 715 F. Supp. 135 (D.S.C. 1989)]

3. Would an arbitration clause added to the reverse side of a buyer's purchase order be a material change for purposes of the merchant's battle of the forms under Section 2-207 of the UCC? [*Berquist Co.* v. *Sunroc Corp.*, 777 F. Supp. 1236 (E.D. Pa. 1991)]

4. Mace Industries, Inc., sent a quotation to Paddock Pools for water treatment equipment. Paddock responded with a purchase order that had the following written on its reverse side:

"THE SELLER AGREES TO ALL OF THE FOLLOWING TERMS AND CONDITIONS"

The clause was then followed by language stating that acceptance was expressly conditional upon Mace's acceptance of the terms.

Problems between the parties developed. Paddock says there is no contract because of its conditional acceptance. Mace maintains that Section 2-207 applies and that there was a contract, with the only issues being the additional terms Paddock wrote on its purchase order and whether they are part of the contract. Who is correct? [*Mace Industries, Inc.* v. *Paddock Pool Equipment Co., Inc.*, 339 S.E.2d 527 (S.C. 1986)]

5. Consider the following sequences of offers and acceptances and determine whether in each case there would be a contract.

a. September 1, 2001:   A mails an offer to B.
   September 2, 2001:   B receives the offer.
   September 3, 2001:   A mails a revocation.
   September 4, 2001:   B mails an acceptance.
   September 5, 2001:   B receives the revocation.
   September 6, 2001:   A receives the acceptance.
   RESULT: _____

b. September 1, 2001:   A mails an offer to B.
   September 2, 2001:   B receives the offer.
   September 3, 2001:   B wires an acceptance.
   September 4, 2001:   B wires a rejection.
   September 4, 2001 (later): A receives the acceptance.
   September 5, 2001:   A receives the rejection.
   RESULT: _____

c. September 1, 2001: A mails an offer to B.
   September 2, 2001: B receives the offer.
   September 3, 2001: A wires a revocation.
   September 3, 2001: B wires an acceptance.
   September 4, 2001: B receives the revocation.
   September 5, 2001: A receives the acceptance.
   RESULT: _____

Would your answers be different under the UCC from those under common law?

6. Corinthian Pharmaceuticals Systems, Inc., placed a telephone order with Lederle Laboratories for 1,000 vials of vaccine. Corinthian then followed the telephonic/computer order with two written confirmations. Neither the phone order nor the confirmations mentioned a price. Is there a valid offer? [*Corinthian Pharmaceuticals Systems, Inc. v. Lederle Lab.,* 724 F. Supp. 605 (S.D. Ind. 1989)]

7. Hillcrest Country Club contacted N. D. Judds Company about replacement of the roof on its clubhouse. Rick Langill served as Judds's representative in negotiating the contract. Hillcrest managers were in possession of a brochure that described the RS-18 roofing manufactured by Roof Systems made of galvanized steel laminated with acrylic film called Korad.

Judds maintains Hillcrest received the brochure by calling Roof Systems. Hillcrest managers maintain Langill gave them the brochures. Mr. Langill generally stamps brochures and attaches a cover letter before mailing them out, but Hillcrest's brochure was not stamped although it was used as a basis for Hillcrest's specification sheet. The brochure touted a twenty-year warranty and promised no chalking, fading, chipping, peeling, or other forms of coating deterioration.

Judds submitted a bid with language that waived all warranties once final payment was made. Hillcrest accepted Judds's bid; and the roof was installed in July 1982.

By September 1984, the roof panels on the Hillcrest clubhouse were flaking and required replacement. Judds cited the warranty waiver. Hillcrest replaced the roof at a cost of $80,000 and filed suit against Judds and Roof Systems.

Did Roof Systems's warranty extend to Hillcrest? Was there privity of contract? Is this a UCC Section 2-207 problem? Was a contract formed? Does Hillcrest have a warranty? [*Hillcrest Country Club v. N. D. Judds Co.,* 12 U.C.C.2d Rep. Serv. (Callaghan) 990, 236 Neb. 233 (1990)]

8. Ben Diskin, a clothing manufacturer, placed an order with J. P. Stevens for 290 pieces of all-wool flannel material. Mr. Diskin issued a check to Stevens for $151,380. On the reverse side of the check, Mr. Diskin wrote:

In full payment for 290 pcs. of flannel as per contract, less anti. to be figured upon billing. Final total subject to adjustment.

Stevens sent to Mr. Diskin its standard sales contract that was initialed as approved by the sales and credit departments, but there were no signatures. Do the parties have a contract? [*Diskin v. J. P. Stevens & Co.,* 652 F. Supp. 553 (D. Mass. 1987)]

9. Thomas Koenen signed a car-purchase order form to buy a limited edition Buick Regal. GM would manufacture only 500 of these Regals. The order form was also signed by the car dealer's salesman and sales manager. Mr. Koenen gave Royal Buick Company (the dealer) a check for $500. No price is mentioned on the order form. Is there a contract? [*Koenen v. Royal Buick Co.,* 783 P.2d 822 (Ariz. 1989)]

10. Nation Enterprises, Inc., purchased a large (36 by 3 feet) gas-fired convection oven from Enersyst, Inc., to make its pizza crusts. There were problems with the oven that the parties were working to resolve, but Nation needed a second oven. It was going to purchase one from someone else, but Enersyst orally promised to fix the first oven if Nation bought the second oven from it. (Oven 1 was beyond its sixty-day warranty.) Nation bought the second oven, but Enersyst did not fix the first one. Nation sued, but Enersyst claims its promise on the first oven is inadmissible under the parol evidence rule. Is this correct? [*Nation Enterprises, Inc. v. Enersyst, Inc.,* 749 F. Supp. 1506 (N.D. Ill. 1990)]

RESEARCH PROBLEM

A Draft of a Beer Contract

11. On March 23, 1994, Northern Distributing Company made two offers to purchase two brands of beer carried by Keis Distributors, Inc.: 683,136 cases of Genesee beer at $1.75 per case and 95,632 cases of LaBatt's/Rolling Rock beer at $2 per case. The offer contained a termination date of April 11, 1994, and directed Keis to "accept this offer by signing below." Keis countersigned as requested and sent the offer back to Northern with a cover letter that stated both sides should retain counsel to work out "the wording of the final details."

A proposed "closing and consulting agreement" was drafted but never signed, and Keis then withdrew from these distribution areas. Northern did purchase some of Keis's inventory after the distributorship termination, and a dispute arose as to the price due on that inventory. Northern claimed the contract price, and Keis said they had no contract so the price was higher. Who is correct?

Read the case and decide. [*Keis Distributors, Inc.* v. *Northern Distributing Co.,* 641 N.Y.S. 2d 417 (App. Div. 1996)]

BUSINESS STRATEGY APPLICATION

In the CD-ROM exercise for this chapter, you will learn to recognize when you have a contract—that is, when formation occurs. You will see items that are unclear and some inconsistencies. You will make a list of items that would concern you if it were your contract negotiations.

CHAPTER FOURTEEN

Contracts and Sales: Performance and Remedies

Once the parties have reached the point of form-ing a contract with an offer, acceptance, and consideration (as discussed in Chapter 13), it would seem that their troubles are over and that all they need to do is carry through with performance. How-ever, their agreement may be subject to challenge because new information arises; or perhaps what is considered sufficient performance to one party may not be sufficient to another. This chapter focuses on contract problems and answers the following ques-tions: What if the assumptions made in formation turn out to be untrue? Must the parties go through with the contract? If one party does not perform, is the other excused? When is performance required, and when is it sufficient? What remedies exist? Do third parties have rights in a contract?

For want of a nail the shoe was lost;
For want of a shoe the horse was lost;
And for want of a horse the rider was lost;
For the want of a rider the battle was lost;
For the want of the battle the kingdom was lost
And all for the want of a horseshoe-nail.

POOR RICHARD'S ALMANAC (1758)

CONSIDER...

Dorris Reed purchased a home from Robert King for $76,000. After Mrs. Reed moved in, she learned that the house had been the site of the murders of a mother and her four children. King and the real estate agents were aware of these events but did not disclose them to Mrs. Reed prior to the sale. The neighbors told Mrs. Reed of the murders after she moved into her home. Is Mrs. Reed stuck with the house? Is there any way she can get out of the contract?

EXHIBIT 14.1 Defenses in Contract Formation

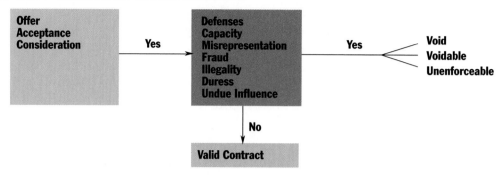

DEFENSES IN CONTRACT FORMATION

Even though a contract may have been formed with the three elements of offer, acceptance, and consideration, one of the elements may be flawed. The result is a contract that may be void, voidable, or unenforceable. When one of the required elements of formation is flawed, the contract is subject to a defense. A **contract defense** is a situation, term, or event that makes an otherwise valid contract invalid. These defenses ensure that the parties enter into contracts voluntarily and on the basis of accurate information. The defenses are displayed in Exhibit 14.1 and are discussed in the following sections.

Capacity

Both parties to a valid contract must have **capacity,** which includes both age and mental capacity.

Age Capacity

Age capacity means the parties must have reached the age of majority. In most states, that age is 18, but in some states the age of contractual capacity is 21. Before the time a party reaches the age of capacity, his or her contracts are voidable: A **voidable contract** of a minor allows the party lacking the necessary age (**minor** or **infant**) to choose not to honor the contract, in which case the other party to the contract will have no remedy. But there are some exceptions to the minors' contracts rules. Some statutes make such contracts enforceable; for example, student loan agreements are enforceable against minors. Minors' contracts for such necessities as food and clothing are still voidable, but courts do hold minors liable for the reasonable value of those necessities.

C O N S I D E R . . .

14.1 Because of a domestic relations problem, on May 9, 1983, John D. Gilbert canceled, on the advice of counsel, a Visa card held jointly with his wife. Mr. Gilbert made a new application, and a new credit card was issued to him.

The card was mailed to Mr. Gilbert at his business address. After a month, he received a Visa bill for $1,341.54 in purchases. Mr. Gilbert acknowledges that his married daughter Christine charged $85.44 and that he charged $89.88. The remaining $1,166.22 was charged by Ann Gilbert, Mr. Gilbert's minor daughter.

Mr. Gilbert refused to pay Ann's share of the bill, and Visa brought suit. Can Visa recover from Ann? Can Visa recover from Mr. Gilbert? [*Fifth Third Bank/Visa* v. *Gilbert,* 478 N.E. 2d 1324 (Ohio 1981)]

ETHICAL ISSUES 14.1

LeAnn Rimes, a country western singer, signed a contract at age 12 with Curb Records. Curb Records is owned by Mike Curb, a longstanding presence in the music industry who began his career with a group known as "The Mike Curb Congregation." Under the terms of the contract, Ms. Rimes will be 35 before she has delivered the twenty-one albums required under the terms of the agreement. "At 12, I didn't understand everything in my contract. All I know is that I really wanted to sing." Ms. Rimes testified at a hearing of the California Senate Select Committee on the Entertainment Industry looking into the labor issues surrounding the long-term/album requirements contracts.

Other artists testified about their lack of health insurance benefits under these contracts. Singer Courtney Love testified, in reference to her minimal insurance coverage, "I can maybe get six days in rehab."

Don Henley, a solo artist formerly with The Eagles, testified, "The deck is stacked and has been stacked for sixty years in the recording companies' favor."

Record industry executives testified that the long-term contracts are necessary because of the time, money, and effort required to build young artists. One executive said, "There is one thing that all labels have in common and that's risk."

The Dixie Chicks are in litigation with their label, Sony, and Ms. Love is in litigation with her label, Vivendi Universal, for what they say are questionable accounting practices in arriving at the artists' share of the profits. Both companies have responded with countersuits alleging that the artists have not produced the albums required under their contracts.

Does Ms. Rimes have a possible defense? Are the recording contracts binding or are they unconscionable? Are the long-term contracts and their requirements ethical?

Mental Capacity

Contracting parties must also have *mental capacity*, which is the ability to understand that contracts are enforceable, that legal documents have significance, and that contracts involve costs and obligations. Contracts of those lacking mental capacity are also voidable. Moreover, if a party to a contract has been declared legally incompetent, that person's contracts are void. A **void contract** is one the courts will not honor, and neither party is obligated to perform under that agreement.

Misrepresentation

When one party to a contract is not given full or accurate information by the other party about the contract subject matter, **misrepresentation** occurs. Misrepresentation allows a **rescission** of the contract, which means the contract is rescinded or set aside. Misrepresentation occurs when a seller makes inaccurate statements about its product or fails to disclose pertinent information about its product that should be disclosed. For example, failing to disclose that a deluxe model car has a standard car engine is misrepresentation. The elements required for innocent misrepresentation are as follows:

1. Misstatement of a material fact (or the failure to disclose a material fact)
2. Reliance by the buyer on that material misstatement or omission
3. Resulting damages to the buyer

To be a basis for rescission, the misrepresentation must have been one regarding a **material fact.** A material fact is the type of information that would affect someone's decision to enter into the contract. For example, if a buyer for your stock in XYZ Corporation failed to disclose that a takeover was pending, there would be misrepresentation of a material fact. A takeover affects the price of stock, and the price of stock in the future affects your decision to buy and sell presently.

Misrepresentation cannot be based on sales **puffing,** which is opinion about the subject matter of a contract. For example, suppose that a real estate agent told you a house you were considering buying was located in the "best area in town." Such a statement is an opinion and cannot be a basis for misrepresentation.

C O N S I D E R . . .

14.2 Analyze the following statements. Are they opinion, or could they be the basis for misrepresentation?

This lightbulb will last 200 hours.
These suits are 100 percent wool.
This fabric is the finest money can buy.
This sweater is 50 percent cashmere.
This toothpaste reduces cavities by 20 percent.
This car gets 22 miles to the gallon.
This stock has never decreased in value.
This house has no easements running through the backyard.
This car has not been in an accident.
These bicycle locks are theft-proof.
This carpet-cleaning machine will remove every type of spot on your rugs.

The buyer must have reliance on (that is, attach some importance to) the statement that was made. For a buyer of stock to claim financial misrepresentation, the buyer must have actually examined the false financial statements of the company selling the stock and based the buying decision on the company's financial condition. A buyer who is buying cars only to take them apart for their used parts does not rely on a misrepresentation that the car has not been in an accident. Whatever information is given must be part of the reason the buyer has agreed to enter into the contract.

Fraud

Although misrepresentation can result simply because of inaccurate information, **fraud** is the knowing and intentional disclosure of false information or the knowing failure to disclose relevant information. Fraud has the same elements of proof as misrepresentation, with the added element of *scienter,* or knowledge that the information given is false. An example of the distinction could be in a situation in which the seller of a home obtains an exterminator's report that says the house is clear of termites and passes it along to the buyer. Because the house actually has termites, there has been misrepresentation, but not fraud, because the seller was simply passing along the information without the knowledge of its accuracy. If, however, that same seller received a report from an exterminator that indicated there were termites and then found another exterminator to report there were no termites and passed that report along to the buyer, there would be fraud because there was knowledge of the false report and the intent to defraud the buyer. The following case includes a discussion of the elements of misrepresentation and provides the answer for the chapter's opening "Consider."

CASE 14.1

Reed v. King
193 Cal. Rptr. 130 (1983)

Buying Property from the Addams Family: How Scary Must It Be?

FACTS

Dorris Reed purchased a home from Robert King for $76,000. Mr. King and his real estate agents did not disclose to Mrs. Reed that 10 years before, the house had been the site of the murders of a mother and her four children. After Mrs. Reed moved into the home, neighbors disclosed to her the story of the murders and the fact that the house carried a stigma. Because of its history, appraisers evaluated the true worth of the house to be $65,000. Mrs. Reed filed suit on the basis of misrepresentation and sought rescission and damages. Her complaint was dismissed by the trial court, and she appealed.

JUDICIAL OPINION

BLEASE, Associate Justice

In the sale of a house, must the seller disclose it was the site of a multiple murder?

Does Reed's pleading state a cause of action? Concealed within this question is the nettlesome problem of the duty of disclosure of blemishes on real property which are not physical defects or legal impairments to use.

Reed seeks to state a cause of action sounding in contract, i.e., rescission, or in tort, i.e., deceit. In either event her allegations must reveal a fraud. "The elements of actual fraud, whether as the basis of the remedy in contract or tort, may be stated as follows: There must be (1) a *false representation* or concealment of a material fact (or, in some cases, an opinion) susceptible of knowledge, (2) made with *knowledge* of its falsity or without sufficient knowledge on the subject to warrant a representation, (3) with the *intent* to induce the person to whom it is made to act upon it; and such person must (4) act in *reliance* upon the representation (5) to his *damage*."

The trial court perceived the defect in Reed's complaint to be a failure to allege concealment of a material fact. "Concealment" and "material" are legal conclusions concerning the effect of the issuable facts pled. As appears, the analytic pathways to these conclusions are intertwined.

Reed's complaint reveals only nondisclosure despite the allegation King asked a neighbor to hold his peace. There is no allegation the attempt at suppression was a cause in fact of Reed's ignorance. Accordingly, the critical question is: does the seller have duty to disclose here? Resolution of this question depends on the materiality of the fact of the murders.

In general, a seller of real property has a duty to disclose: "where the seller knows of facts *materially* affecting the value or desirability of the property which are known or accessible only to him and also knows that such facts are not known to, or within the reach of the diligent attention and observation of the buyer, the seller is under a duty to disclose them to the buyer."

Whether information "is of sufficient materiality to affect the value or desirability of the property . . . depends on the facts of the particular case." Materiality "is a question of law, and is part of the concept of right to rely or justifiable reliance." Accordingly, the term is essentially a label affixed to a normative conclusion. Three considerations bear on this legal conclusion: the gravity of the harm inflicted by nondisclosure; the fairness of imposing a duty of discovery on the buyer as an alternative to compelling disclosure, and its impact on the stability of contracts if rescission is permitted.

Numerous cases have found nondisclosure of physical defects and legal impediments to use of real property are material. However, to our knowledge, no prior real estate sale case has faced an issue of nondisclosure of the kind presented here. Should this variety of ill-repute be required to be disclosed? Is this a circumstance where "nondisclosure of the fact amounts to a failure to act in good faith and in accordance with reasonable standards of fair dealing"[?]

The paramount argument against an affirmative conclusion is it permits the camel's nose of unrestrained irrationality admission to the tent. If such an "irrational" consideration is permitted as a basis of rescission the stability of all conveyances will be seriously undermined. Any fact that might disquiet the enjoyment of some segment of the buying public

(continued)

may be seized upon by a disgruntled purchaser to void a bargain. In our view, keeping this genie in the bottle is not as difficult a task as these arguments assume. We do not view a decision allowing Reed to survive a demurrer in these unusual circumstances as endorsing the materiality of facts predicating peripheral, insubstantial, or fancied harms.

The murder of innocents is highly unusual in its potential for so disturbing buyers they may be unable to reside in a home where it has occurred. This fact may foreseeably deprive a buyer of the intended use of the purchase. Murder is not such a common occurrence that *buyers* should be charged with anticipating and discovering this disquieting possibility. Accordingly, the fact is not one for which a duty of inquiry and discovery can sensibly be imposed upon the buyer.

Reed alleges the fact of the murders has a quantifiable effect on the market value of the premises. We cannot say this allegation is inherently wrong and, in the pleading posture of the case, we assume it to be true.

Reputation and history can have a significant effect on the value of realty. "George Washington slept here" is worth something, however physically inconsequential that consideration may be. Ill-repute or "bad will" conversely may depress the value of property. Failure to disclose such a negative fact where it will have a foreseeably depressing effect on income expected to be generated by a business is tortious. Some cases have held that *unreasonable* fears of the potential buying public that a gas or oil pipeline may rupture may depress the market value of land and entitle the owner to incremental compensation in eminent domain.

Whether Reed will be able to prove her allegation, the decade-old multiple murder has a significant effect on market value we cannot determine. If she is able to do so by competent evidence she is entitled to a favorable ruling on the issues of materiality and duty to disclose. Her demonstration of objective tangible harm would still the concern that permitting her to go forward will open the floodgates to rescission on subjective and idiosyncratic grounds.

CASE QUESTIONS

1. What information about the house was not disclosed to Mrs. Reed before she purchased it?
2. How did she discover the information and when?
3. Is the information material?
4. What does Mrs. Reed need to establish to be entitled to rescission and damages?
5. Is Mrs. Reed's case dismissed, or will she be permitted to go forward with the suit?
6. Would the information about the house make a difference to you in making a buying decision?
7. Should Mr. King and the real estate agents have disclosed the information to Mrs. Reed? Was there an ethical obligation to do so?

BUSINESS PLANNING TIP

When employees and agents are working for commissions as well as salary (or are on commission alone), there is great temptation to engage in misrepresentation. For example, in the Sears Roebuck & Company controversy over the allegations that its auto repair centers overcharged customers, Sears CEO Edward Brennan issued a statement indicating that the presence of incentives for selling parts and services may have contributed to poor decisions by employees in handling customers. Incentive-based pay systems must also have ethical guidelines.

The failure to disclose material information about the subject matter of a contract can also constitute fraud. For example, a car dealership that fails to disclose to a customer that the car he is buying was in an accident is misrepresentation. If the car dealership performed the body work on the car in its own body shop, the failure to disclose the accident and repairs would be fraud.

With respect to real estate transactions, most states have passed some form of disclosure statutes. In some states, the history of criminal activity on a property must be disclosed. In other states, there are prohibitions on disclosure. Some of these states prohibit disclosure of information such as whether an occupant of the property died of AIDS. However, even in these states, the truth must be revealed if the buyer asks specifically about the occupants and their health.

Re: The Insurer Who Felt Overdrawn

American Insurance Group, Inc., has a reputation for taking on any client the company believes has filed an unjust claim.

Now, AIG and several other insurers are taking on Mary Poppins. More to the point, they appear to be questioning her truthfulness.

The central issue: Did Julie Andrews—renowned as the beloved Miss Poppins, the heroic Maria Von Trapp, and the gender-bending Victoria Grant—fib when she filled out medical forms needed for an insurance policy for the musical "Victor/Victoria"? According to a suit filed in a New York state court in Manhattan by the producers of the play, the insurers have rescinded a policy they wrote on "Victor/Victoria." The insurers claim Ms. Andrews falsely answered questions about her medical past, the suit says.

The policy was purchased in March 1995 from a group of insurers led by Lexington Insurance Co., an AIG subsidiary, for a premium of $157,985. For that, the producers say, they thought they were getting coverage that would pay as much as $2 million for missed appearances by Ms. Andrews and $8.5 million if Ms. Andrews was forced to abandon the show altogether. The policy carried a two-show deductible—standard procedure in show business—that meant the insurers wouldn't have to pay until two consecutive performances were missed. AIG shared much of the liability with eight other insurance companies but remained the lead underwriter, according to the lawsuit.

Broadway shows with superstars generally offer ticketholders the option of leaving the theatre and taking a refund if the star can't make it. Seldom is a show, other than a one-person performance, canceled. Well-trained understudies are usually waiting in the wings for such a chance to strut their stuff—as was the case in "Victor/Victoria."

"Most people have adjusted to the fact that if the star is out they'll still watch a darn good show," says Carol Bressi-Cilona, who brokered the insurance policy for the play through her employer, the DeWitt Stern Group.

That wasn't entirely the case for this musical, heavily dependent on Ms. Andrews's star power. In fact, most of the times it was announced that Ms. Andrews wouldn't appear, dozens of patrons headed for the exits—with a stop at the refund window.

Ms. Andrews had a spate of rough spells during the show's run. The musical opened in October 1995, but the following January, she came down with a sore throat and a hacking cough. At her doctors' request, the suit says, she missed 10 performances, resulting in losses of $442,435.

Several weeks later, according to the suit, she had a gallbladder operation and missed 21 shows: Cost: $980,850.

A few months down the road, she missed several more performances because of a bad larynx. Those losses amounted to about $183,000, according to the suit, which says that insurers refused to pay any of these claims.

Indisputably, Ms. Andrews worked hard. And to the tens of thousands of theatergoers who watched her sing and dance her way through the strenuous routines as a cross-dressing cabaret star, she is a hero. To take on that role at her age—she is 61 years old—was no mean feat.

"It's a very demanding part. There are only two scenes Julie is not in," says Ms. Bressi-Cilona. "One costume is so heavily beaded they have to lift it onto her. First she's running around with practically no clothes, and then she has lots of clothes and she's sweating."

To date, Ms. Andrews has performed in nearly 600 performances of the musical, which shows eight times a week, Tuesday through Saturday, with matinees three days a week. Her husband, Blake Edwards, directs the show and, according to an interview Ms. Andrews gave to Newsday, he put up $2 million of the family's money to fund the show.

According to the lawsuit, the insurers rescinded the policy on the grounds that Ms. Andrews had allegedly falsely answered two questions in an affidavit submitted when the producers applied for the policy.

One question asked if she ever had suffered from tuberculosis, asthma, emphysema, persistent cough or any other disease or abnormality of the lungs or respiratory system, according to the suit. Her answer was "no," the suit says. The second question asked if she had had "any disease, disorder or

(continued)

injury of the bones, joints, muscles, back, spine, or neck." Again, the suit says, the answer was "no."

It isn't clear what the insurers think was incorrect about those responses—and New York-based AIG wouldn't comment yesterday. About the only thing the producers say in the suit about Ms. Andrews's health is that she "occasionally experiences mild bronchial symptoms solely in response to specific external factors such as infection, smog or other environmental factors, and occasionally has mild osteoarthritic symptoms in her hands."

As for Ms. Andrews, she couldn't comment yesterday afternoon. Peter Cromarty, publicist for "Victor/Victoria," says she was in "vocal rest." "When you sing seven or eight times a week for two hours," he says, "the only way you can humanly do that is not talking between shows."

Source: Leslie Scism, "Maybe Julie Andrews Could Offer Insurers a Spoonful of Sugar," *Wall Street Journal*, April 4, 1997, A1. Reprinted by permission of *The Wall Street Journal*, © 1997 Dow Jones & Company, Inc. All Rights Reserved Worldwide.

Duress

Duress occurs when a party is physically forced into a contract or deprived of a meaningful choice when deciding whether to enter into a contract. Requiring employees to sell company stock holdings in order to keep their jobs is an example of duress because of a lack of choice. If there has been duress, the contract is voidable. The party who experienced the duress has the right to rescind the agreement, but rescission is a choice; the law does not make the contract illegal or unenforceable because duress was present. The choice of enforcement or rescission is left to the party who experienced the duress.

Undue Influence

Undue influence occurs when one party uses a close personal relationship with another party to gain contractual benefits. Before undue influence can be established, a **confidential relationship** of trust and reliance must exist between the parties. Attorneys and clients have a confidential relationship. Elderly parents who rely on a child or children for their care have a confidential relationship with those children. To establish undue influence, there must be an abuse of this confidential relationship. For example, conditioning an elderly parent's care upon the signing over of his land to a child is an abuse of the relationship. An attorney who offers advice on property disposition to his benefit is abusing the confidential relationship. Again, contracts subject to undue influence defenses are voidable. They can be honored if the party who experienced the influence desires to honor the contract.

Illegality and Public Policy

A contract that violates a statute or the general standards of public policy is void and cannot be enforced by either party. To enforce contracts that violate statutes or public conscience would encourage the commission of these illegal acts, and so contract law is controlled by the statutory prohibitions and public policy concerns of other areas of law.

Contracts in Violation of Criminal Statutes

Contracts that are agreements to commit criminal wrongs are void. For example, the old saying that "there is a contract out on his life" may be descriptive, but it is

ETHICAL ISSUES 14.2

Beech-Nut Nutrition Corporation was a division of Squibb Corporation. Its chewing gum segment was profitable but was sold in 1973. The baby food division of Beech-Nut, which had 15 percent of the baby food market, had never been profitable, and by 1978 creditors were increasingly anxious.

Beech-Nut had entered into a contract in 1977 with Interjuice Trading Corporation for Interjuice to furnish apple juice concentrate to Beech-Nut at a price that was 20 percent below market prices. This contract was a huge break for Beech-Nut since it used apple concentrate in 30 percent of its baby food products. The Interjuice contract attracted enough attention that Nestlé purchased Beech-Nut in 1979.

Jerome J. LiCari was the director of research and development for Beech-Nut. Mr. LiCari and the chemists in his department were concerned about the Interjuice contract for two reasons: (1) rumors of adulteration (substituted product or inferior product) in the apple juice concentrate market were rampant, and (2) the price was simply too good to be true.

At that time there were no tests to determine adulteration, but Mr. LiCari sent two of his employees to the Interjuice plant in Queens, New York. Interjuice officials refused to allow them to see processing operations but did provide them access to the plant storage tanks.

Mr. LiCari then tried, in 1981, to develop a test for adulteration. He could not, but he took his circumstantial evidence and concerns for Beech-Nut's reputation to John F. Lavery, Beech-Nut's head of operations. Mr. LiCari suggested Beech-Nut adopt Gerber's policy requiring suppliers to establish authenticity or lose their contracts. Mr. Lavery called Mr. LiCari "Chicken Little" and told him he had no proof.

In late 1981, Mr. LiCari, feeling that his tests showed the Interjuice concentrate had no apple juice, wrote a memo to Mr. Lavery suggesting Beech-Nut switch suppliers. Mr. Lavery did not respond.

Mr. LiCari then took his cost and chemical analysis to Neils Hoyvald, the president and CEO of Beech-Nut, who told LiCari, "I'll look into it." He did nothing and told Mr. LiCari he had great technical ability but that his judgment was "colored by naivete and impractical ideals."

Mr. LiCari resigned from Beech-Nut and wrote a letter to the FDA disclosing the Interjuice adulteration and signing it, "Johnny Appleseed."

Mr. LiCari's letter started an FDA inquiry and the eventual discovery that Interjuice concentrate was a chemical concoction with no apple juice at all. After what the FDA called a cat-and-mouse game of shipping juice lots to avoid regulatory testing, the FDA found and tested a lot with no juice.

Messrs. Hoyvald and Lavery were indicted.* Mr. LiCari, located as a witness through company files, testified at both trials, "I thought apple juice should be made from apples."

Beech-Nut still struggles with market share and consumer loyalty.

Issues

1. Was there misrepresentation in the sale of Beech-Nut baby food?

2. Was there fraud?

3. Was Mr. LiCari harmed by his discovery and disclosure?

4. Was Beech-Nut's conduct with respect to the Interjuice contract ethical?

5. Was Beech-Nut's conduct with respect to Mr. LiCari ethical?

*Following two trials and appeals, Hoyvald entered a guilty plea.

not accurate in the legal sense. There could never be a valid contract to kill someone because the agreement is one to commit a criminal wrong and is therefore void. No one is permitted to benefit from contracts to commit illegal acts. For example, a beneficiary for a life insurance policy will not collect the proceeds from the insured's policy if the beneficiary arranged for the death of the insured (contract for murder). The following "Consider" deals with the issue of benefits from an illegal contract.

C O N S I D E R . . .

14.3   Robert Hackett was made a substitute fireman for the city of New Britain, Connecticut, in 1949. In 1950, he was made a full-time fireman and in 1968 became a lieutenant. After earning the highest mark on the captain's examination, he was promoted to captain in 1974. He then scored the highest score on the deputy chief exam and was promoted to that rank in 1977.

Mr. Hackett had paid an employee in the city department responsible for administering the exams to ensure that he earned the highest grades (which he did). He had, in effect, purchased his last two promotions. When these acts were discovered (after Mr. Hackett had retired), criminal charges were brought against him and the city employee. Both were convicted of felonies.

The pension board of New Britain then met and voted to reduce Mr. Hackett's pension by $5,483.97 a year because that reduction placed his pension at the level it would have been without the last two promotions. The board said the reduction was necessary because the last two promotions were obtained through illegal conduct. Mr. Hackett filed suit. Is illegality a defense to the pension? [*Hackett* v. *City of New Britain*, 477 A.2d 148 (Conn. 1984)]

Contracts in Violation of Licensing Statutes

In some cases, contracts are not contracts to commit illegal acts but are simply contracts for a legal act to be done by one not authorized to perform such services. Every state requires some professionals or technicians to be licensed before they can perform work for the public. For example, a lawyer must be admitted to the bar before representing clients. A lawyer who contracts to represent a client before having been admitted to the practice of law has entered into a void contract. Even if the lawyer successfully represents the client, no fee could be collected because the agreement violated the licensing statute and to allow the lawyer to collect the fee, even in *quasi* contract, would encourage others to violate the licensing requirements. In some cases, licensing requirements are in place not for competency reasons but, rather, to raise revenues. For example, an architect may be required to pass a competency screening to be initially licensed in a state and after that the license may be renewed simply by paying an annual fee. Suppose that the architect forgot to pay the annual renewal fee and, after the license had lapsed, entered into a $300,000 contract with a developer. The developer discovers the renewal problems after the work is completed and wants to get out of paying the architect. In this case, the issue is not one of competency screening but of financial oversight and the architect would be permitted to collect the fee.

Contracts in Violation of Usury Laws

These contracts are credit or loan contracts that charge interest in excess of the state's limits for interest or finance charges. These statutes are discussed in detail in Chapter 15.

Contracts in Violation of Public Policy

Some contracts do not violate any criminal laws or statutory provisions but do violate certain standards of fairness or encourage conduct in violation of public policy. For example, many firms will include **exculpatory clauses** in their contracts that purport to hold the firms completely blameless for any accidents occurring on their premises. Most courts consider a firm's trying to hold itself com-

MORAL ROLE MODELS IN ADS

Michael Irvin, a football star with the Dallas Cowboys, signed an endorsement contract with the North Texas Toyota Dealers Association in exchange for a fee as well as a $50,000 Toyota Landcruiser auto.

Shortly after the endorsement agreement was signed, Mr. Irvin was arrested for cocaine possession. Mr. Irvin was arrested in a motel room with a teammate and two topless dancers. The police found marijuana, cocaine, and drug paraphernalia in the room as well. In the middle of his trial, following the testimony of one of the dancers, Mr. Irvin entered a no-contest plea to the charges and was fined $10,000 and ordered to perform 800 hours of community service. The sentence for cocaine possession (10.3 grams) can be twenty years in Texas.

The Toyota Dealers brought suit against Mr. Irvin, seeking to rescind the agreement as well as recover the cost of the ad campaign with Mr. Irvin's image and lost sales estimated at $1.2 million. The Toyota Dealers claim there was a morals clause in the contract, or an underlying assumption that Mr. Irvin's character and personal life were sufficiently clean that he was an appropriate role model for car sales.

Mr. Irvin did return his Landcruiser to the dealers.

ISSUES

1. Is there an implied morals clause in endorsement contracts?

2. Should there be?

3. Is private life subject to scrutiny in endorsement contracts?

---

pletely blameless for all accidents, regardless of the degree of care or level of fault against public policy, and will not, therefore, enforce such clauses.

Also grouped into the public policy prohibition are contracts that restrict trade or employment. For example, when a business is sold, part of the purchase price is paid for the business's goodwill. The benefit of that payment is lost if the seller moves down the street and starts another similar business. Hence, the courts have permitted **covenants not to compete** to be included in these contracts so long as they are reasonable in time and geographic scope. These covenants and their legality are discussed in detail in Chapter 17.

Some contracts are not actually contracts for criminal or illegal activities, but the terms of the contract are grossly unfair to one party. A contract that gives all the benefits to one side and all the burdens to the other is an **unconscionable** contract. The standards for determining whether a contract is unconscionable are the public policy standards for fairness that cover all types of contract provisions and negotiations. Many consumer rental contracts have been declared unconscionable because the consumers were paying more in rent than it would cost to buy the rented appliance outright.

The standards for unconscionability are set on a case-by-case basis. The courts have not given a firm definition of unconscionability. Even the UCC does not specifically define unconscionability, although one section (2-302) prohibits the enforcement of unconscionable contracts.

The *Water* v. *Min Ltd.* case deals with a contract that involves several different defenses.

CASE 14.2

Water v. *Min Ltd.*
587 N.E.2d 231 (Mass. 1992)

Young, Drugged, and Wealthy: Capable of Contracting?

FACTS

Gail A. Waters (plaintiff) was injured in an accident when she was 12 years old. At age 18 she settled a negligence claim with Commercial Union Insurance Company and purchased an annuity contract, the income from which was her support.

At age 21, Gail became romantically involved with Thomas Beauchemin (defendant), an ex-convict who introduced her to drugs and to Min Ltd., a partnership consisting of David and Robert DeVito and Michael D. Steamer (defendants), and suggested that she sell her annuity contract to them.

Gail signed a contract to sell her policy, with a cash value of $189,000, to the defendants for $50,000. The contract was signed on the hood of a car in the parking lot of a restaurant. The guaranteed return to the owner of the policy over its 25-year life was $694,000.

Gail filed suit to rescind the contract. The trial court found, among other things, that the contract was unconscionable. The DeVitos, Mr. Steamer, and Mr. Beauchemin appealed.

JUDICIAL OPINION

LYNCH, Justice

The defendants contend that the judge erred by (1) finding the contract unconscionable (and by concluding the defendants assumed no risks and therefore finding the contract oppressive); (2) refusing them specific performance; and (3) failing to require the plaintiff to return all the funds received from them.

Unconscionability. The defendants argue that the evidence does not support the finding that the contract was unconscionable or that they assumed no risks and therefore that the contract was oppressive.

The doctrine of unconscionability has long been recognized by common law courts in this country and in England. "Historically, a [contract] was considered unconscionable if it was 'such as no man in his senses and not under delusion would make on the one hand, and as no honest and fair man would

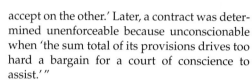

accept on the other.' Later, a contract was determined unenforceable because unconscionable when 'the sum total of its provisions drives too hard a bargain for a court of conscience to assist.'"

The doctrine of unconscionability has also been codified in the Uniform Commercial Code (code), G.L.C. 106, § 2-302 (1990 ed.), and, by analogy, it has been applied in situations outside the ambit of the code.

Unconscionability must be determined on a case-by-case basis, with particular attention to whether the challenged provision could result in oppression and unfair surprise to the disadvantaged party and not to allocation of risk because of "superior bargaining power." Courts have identified other elements of the unconscionable contract. For example, gross disparity in the consideration alone "may be sufficient to sustain [a finding that the contract is unconscionable]," since the disparity "itself leads inevitably to the felt conclusion that knowing advantage was taken of [one party]." High pressure sales tactics and misrepresentation have been recognized as factors rendering a contract unconscionable. If the sum total of the provisions of a contract drive too hard a bargain, a court of conscience will not assist its enforcement.

The judge found that Beauchemin introduced the plaintiff to drugs, exhausted her credit card accounts to the sum of $6,000, unduly influenced her, suggested that the plaintiff sell her annuity contract, initiated the contract negotiations, was the agent of the defendants, and benefited from the contract between the plaintiff and the defendants. The defendants were represented by legal counsel; the plaintiff was not. The cash value of the annuity policy at the time the contract was executed was approximately four times greater than the price to be paid by the defendants. For payment of not more than $50,000 the defendants were to receive an asset that could be immediately exchanged for $189,000, or they could elect to hold it for its guaranteed term and receive $694,000. In these circumstances the judge could correctly conclude the contract was unconscionable.

The defendants assumed no risk and the plaintiff gained no advantage. Gross disparity in the values exchanged is an important factor to be considered in determining whether a contract is unconscionable. "[C]ourts [may] avoid enforcement of a bargain that is shown to be unconscionable by reason of gross inadequacy of consideration accompanied by other relevant factors."

We are satisfied that the disparity of interests in this contract is "so gross that the court cannot resist the inference that it was improperly obtained and is unconscionable."

Amount of repayment order. The defendants also argue that the judge erred in failing to require the plaintiff to return the full amount paid by them for the annuity.

The defendants paid $18,000 cash after deducting $7,000 for a debt which was owed to them by Beau-

chemin. The remaining $25,000 due on the contract was never paid.

The judge's order was consistent with his findings that Beauchemin was the agent of the defendants, and that the plaintiff only received $18,000 for her interest in the annuity.

Judgment affirmed.

CASE QUESTIONS

1. List the possible defenses to this contract.

2. What made the contract unconscionable?

3. What protections for Gail could have been built into the annuity contract?

4. Is there any criminal conduct here?

CONTRACT PERFORMANCE

Once parties have contracted, they have the obligation of performance. The following subsections cover when performance is due, what constitutes performance, and when performance is excused.

When Performance Is Due

Performance is due according to the times provided in the contract. In some contracts, however, prescribed events must occur before there is an obligation of performance. These events are called **conditions. Conditions precedent** are events that give rise to performance. Suppose that Zelda has agreed to buy Scott's house and their contract provides that Zelda does not have to pay until she is able to obtain a reasonable loan to finance the purchase. This financing clause is a condition precedent to contract performance. If Zelda is denied financing, she is not required to perform under the contract. Another example of a condition precedent is in a contract for construction of jackets out of a material to be furnished by the seller. Unless the seller gives the manufacturer the fabric to work with, the manufacturer has no obligation to perform. **Conditions concurrent,** or **conditions contemporaneous,** exist in every contract; there is an exchange of benefits at the same time. One is willing to perform because the other side does.

Standards for Performance

The contract details what the parties are required to do for complete performance. In some contracts, performance is easily determined. If there is a contract between an employment agency and a potential employee to find work for the employee, performance is complete once the work is found.

But in some contracts, performance is complicated, and there may be errors in its execution. For example, construction contracts are long-term, complicated agreements. During the construction of a building, it is possible that some mistakes might be made. Is an owner allowed to not pay a contractor because there is a mistake or two? The doctrine of **substantial performance** applies in construction contracts, and it means that the constructed building is for practical purposes just as good as the one contracted for. For example, a builder might have substituted a type of pipe when the brand name specified in the contract was not available. The substitution is a technical breach of contract, but it is a substitute that is just as good. The builder will be paid for the construction, but the owner will be entitled to damages.

E-Commerce: Payments Have Changed

One aspect of contract performance is payment. With the Internet and online transactions, methods of payment have changed substantially. The following methods have been developed to provide means for payment. Parties choose these methods largely on the basis of their perceptions about the security in the method of payment:

1. *Digital cash.* Retailers create their own currency on the Internet, and customers with the right software can purchase the currency and then pay for items with their currency account. It is a virtual phone card and is good for those who do not have credit cards or would prefer not to use those credit cards on the Web.

2. *Digital wallets.* The one-stop payment location authorized by a buyer. Retailers can be paid from the wallet when given access by the buyer. Some digital wallet programs also include shipping information so that buyers can shop faster because they need not fill out all the seller's forms and information.

3. *Virtual points.* This is an Internet frequent flyer program. Web users accumulate points and then can make purchases using those points. These systems must have a sufficient number of retailers to make them work well and entice consumers.

4. *Person-to-person payment.* Most commonly called PayPal, this is a system in which the buyer authorizes payment and the seller then drops by a site to give information needed in order to authorize the payment. The amount is taken from the buyer's bank account.

5. *Virtual escrow.* A third party handles the Internet transaction and makes sure that the seller has performed according to the contract before releasing payment to the buyer.

6. *Virtual credit card.* A system for those who doubt security of the Internet. This system creates a new credit card number for each transaction that cannot be reused.

When Performance Is Excused

There are times when all conditions of a valid contract are met but performance of the contract is excused. Under common law, the parties are excused from performance if performance has become impossible. **Impossibility** means that the contract cannot be performed by the parties or anyone else. For example, performance under a contract for the purchase and sale of land that has been washed away into a lake is impossible. Completing a year of dance lessons is impossible for someone who has had a paralyzing accident.

Under the UCC (and under the *Restatement*), performance can be excused if there is commercial impracticability. **Commercial impracticability** (see § 2-615 in Appendix G) excuses performance if the basic assumptions the parties made when they entered into the contract have changed. Although this definition makes it seem that the UCC excuses performance when wars, embargoes, and unusually high price increases occur, courts have been reluctant to apply the excuse of commercial impracticability. The standard of commercial impracticability has been interpreted to mean nothing more or less than the common law standard of impossibility.

Parties can protect themselves from unusual events by putting in their contracts *force majeure* clauses, which excuse the parties from performance in the event of such problems as wars, depression, or embargoes. Following the attack on the World Trade Center in New York City, there were many contracts that were excused for impossibility. For example, because air traffic was halted, all overnight shipping contract performances were excused.

CONSIDER . . .

14.4 Trans World Airlines (TWA) had a sales/leaseback arrangement on ten aircraft with Connecticut National Bank. TWA was experiencing difficulty making payments, attributing the difficulties to the Gulf War, which resulted in decreased air travel because of terrorism and decreased oil flow. Is this an example of commercial impracticability? [*Connecticut Nat'l. Bank* v. *Trans World Airlines, Inc.,* 762 F. Supp. 76 (S.D.N.Y. 1991)]

CONSIDER . . .

14.5 In December 1983, the Department of Energy agreed that it would take possession of 100,000 metric tons of spent radioactive fuel rods from nuclear power plants around the country beginning February 1, 1998. In order to be able to take possession of the nuclear waste from the plants, the Department of Energy agreed to construct a nuclear waste repository. The utilities with nuclear plants agreed to pay in funds for the construction of such a site. Over the years, seventy-two utilities in thirty-four states paid in $13.5 billion for construction of such a site with the funds for the storage plan collected in rates from customers. The site was to be the Yucca Mountain facility, located near Yucca Mountain in Nevada. However, presently Yucca Mountain has a five-mile-long tunnel and there are no storage bays or concrete walls. It is estimated that it will take another fifteen years before the site is ready to accept the spent nuclear fuel.

The utilities are reaching a point of maximization for storage at their plant sites, and the fuel rods remain radioactive for 20,000 years. Has the federal government breached its contract? What damages would the utilities have?

In the following case, there are issues of performance and termination of a contract in a case that some experts have labeled a landmark one in terms of imposing a duty of a good faith in performance.

CASE 14.3

Sons of Thunder, Inc. v. Borden, Inc.
690 A.2d 575 (N.J. 1997)

Ships and Liability Passing in the Night?

FACTS

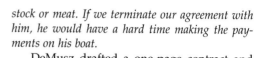

Borden, Inc., owned Snow Food Products Division, a leading producer of clam products, including Snow's Clam Chowder. Borden had used its own four-vessel fleet as well as independent boats in order to obtain clams for processing. Boats delivered the clams to Borden's Cape May plant, where the shell stock was processed into clam meat. From there the meat was shipped to Pine Point, Maine, where final products were made and canned.

In 1978, Borden hired Donald DeMusz to be the captain of the *Arlene Snow,* one of Borden's four boats. Eventually, DeMusz was hired as an independent contractor to manage Borden's boats, and DeMusz formed Sea Labor, Inc., as the company responsible for the management of those boats. Sea Labor received five cents per bushel of clams harvested by the four boats. DeMusz still also received his compensation as captain of the *Arlene Snow.*

At about the same time as DeMusz was hired, Borden began its "Shuck-at-Sea" program, which enabled the fishermen to shuck the clams on the boat, thus allowing the boats to bring back larger amounts of clams, thereby reducing costs and eliminating the need for more plant and facilities. However, the existing boats were not large enough for the shucking equipment.

Wayne Booker, a manager for Borden and Snow's, discussed with DeMusz the possibility that DeMusz might buy a larger boat and undertake the Shuck-at-Sea program. DeMusz submitted a proposal which Booker and other executives approved. Along with two partners, DeMusz formed Sea Works, Inc., and for $750,000 purchased the *Jessica Lori,* a clam-fishing boat with shucking equipment. DeMusz financed the purchase through a bank loan.

An internal company memo from Booker included the following paragraph along with a description of how Musz's purchase of a boat would save money:

[W]e still have a significant mutual interest with DeMuse [sic]. His principal business will still be in chartering the Snow fleet and in captaining Arlene. He needs a dependable customer for the clams that he catches, either shell

stock or meat. If we terminate our agreement with him, he would have a hard time making the payments on his boat.

DeMusz drafted a one-page contract and Booker approved it with one small change.

DeMusz then formed Sons of Thunder, Inc., with Bill Gifford and Bob Dempsey in order to purchase the second boat. The final contract was entered into on January 15, 1985, and included the following provision:

IT IS understood and Agreed to by the parties hereto that Snow Food Products shall purchase shell stock from Sons of Thunder Corp. for a period of one (1) year, at the market rate that is standardized throughout the industry. The term of this contract shall be for a period of one (1) year, after which this contract shall automatically be renewed for a period up to five years. Either party may cancel this contract by giving prior notice of said cancellation in writing Ninety (90) days prior to the effective cancellation date.

Sons of Thunder Corp. will offer for sale all shell stock that is landed to Snow Food.

In March 1985, Sons of Thunder bought a boat, which it named *Sons of Thunder.* The cost to rig and purchase the boat was $588,420.26. Sons of Thunder sought financing from First Jersey National Bank, but was unable to obtain a loan until Booker intervened in the negotiations. Booker told the representative of the bank that DeMusz had a solid relationship with Borden and that although the contract could be terminated within one year, Borden expected the contract to run for five years. Moreover, Booker explained to the representative that the five-year term of the contract would be sufficient to pay back the loan. Ultimately, DeMusz obtained a $515,000 loan, which he, Gifford, Dempsey, and their spouses personally guaranteed. DeMusz used a personal note to cover the remaining balance.

Meanwhile, in August 1984, Booker and DeMusz had begun negotiations about DeMusz purchasing a second boat that would provide clams to Borden. If the Shuck-at-Sea project was successful, Borden would want a second vessel shucking at sea. Moreover, a second large boat would give Borden the advantage of receiving clam meat in bad weather because small boats generally cannot go out to sea in bad weather.

The boat, *Sons of Thunder,* was not ready to fish until February 1986. After some preliminary testing the *Sons of Thunder* started to operate and to fulfill its contract with Borden. For most weeks, the records show that Borden did not buy the minimum amount specified in the contract.

Problems continued with the Shuck-at-Sea program, and the original boat, the *Jessica Lori,* had to be rerigged with resulting delays. At the same time problems with the program were being worked through, there were changes in Borden's management. DeMusz explained to new managers that Borden was not purchasing the amounts it had promised but received no assurances that the contract would be honored. Also at this time, Borden was experiencing difficulties with plant managers in terms of conflicts and kickbacks with resulting terminations.

The relationship between DeMusz and his companies and Borden began to deteriorate and when Borden discovered that a $500,000 accounting error had actually overstated the benefits of the Shuck-at-Sea program, Borden elected to exercise its termination rights under the contracts and sent DeMusz (through the various companies) notice of termination. DeMusz and his companies experienced substantial losses as a result of the termination of contracts. DeMusz filed suit. Borden moved for summary judgment on the grounds that it had properly exercised its termination rights. The jury found for DeMusz, the court of appeals affirmed, and Borden appealed.

JUDICIAL OPINION

GARIBALDI, Justice
The question whether Borden performed its obligations in good faith appears before the Court. . . .

The obligation to perform in good faith exists in every contract, including those contracts that contain express and unambiguous provisions permitting either party to terminate the contract without cause. See *United Roasters, Inc.* v. *Colgate-Palmolive Co.,* 649 F2d 985 (4th Cir.), cert. denied, 454 U.S. 1054, 102 S.Ct. 599, 70 L. Ed.2d 590 (1981). In *United Roasters,* United Roasters gave Colgate the right to manufacture and distribute Bambeanos, its roasted soybean snack. The contract governing the relationship allowed Colgate to terminate its performance at any time during the test-marketing period so long as it

gave United Roasters thirty days notice. After two years of testing Bambeanos, Colgate announced plans to merge with Riviana Foods, Inc., and in the next five months, it ceased producing Bambeanos, stopped advertising them, sold its entire inventory of raw soybeans and Bambeanos, and transferred its product manager to another project. Eventually, Colgate terminated the contract.

Interpreting North Carolina law in the diversity action, the Fourth Circuit concluded that North Carolina had not decided whether there was a good faith limitation on an unconditional right to terminate a contract. The Fourth Circuit did, however, evaluate United Roaster's claim that Colgate violated the covenant of good faith and fair dealing. The panel stated

What is wrong with Colgate's conduct in this case is not its failure to communicate a decision to terminate. . . , but its cessation of performance. Clearly it had an obligation of good faith performance up until its right of termination was actually effective. The contract expressly obliged it to use its best efforts in the promotion of Bambeanos. Instead of doing that, it simply ceased performance. . . . Quite simply, it broke its contract when it terminated its performance, which was United Roasters' contractual due.

In *Bak-A-Lum Corp.,* supra, 69 N.J. 123 (1976), this Court reached a similar conclusion even though the contract was oral and the parties had not discussed how the contract could be terminated. In that case, Bak-A-Lum and Alcoa made an oral agreement, which gave Bak-A-Lum an exclusive distributorship of aluminum siding and related products manufactured by Alcoa. Alcoa eventually terminated the exclusive part of the agreement by appointing four additional distributors. Even though Alcoa planned on terminating the distributorship, it encouraged Bak-A-Lum to expand its warehouse facilities, which substantially increased its operating costs.

Despite acknowledging Alcoa's unconditional right to terminate the contract, the Court upheld the verdict for Bak-A-Lum because it found that Alcoa had breached the implied covenant of good faith and fair dealing by withholding its plans to terminate the contract while encouraging the plaintiff to expand its facilities. As the Court explained: "While the contractual relation of manufacturer and exclusive territorial distributor continued between the parties an obligation of reciprocal good-faith dealing persisted between them." The Court found that the implied covenant of good faith and fair dealing required the defendant to give the plaintiff reasonable notice of its

(continued)

termination. Ultimately, the Court concluded that "a reasonable period of notice of termination of the distributorship . . . would have been twenty months."

The case most heavily relied on by Borden and the majority at the Appellate Division, *Karl's Sales & Service, Inc.* v. *Gimbel Brothers Inc.*, 249 N.J.Super. 487 (App. Div.), cert. den., 127 N.J. 548 (1991), is distinguishable from this matter. In that case, the Appellate Division stated that where the contractual right to terminate is express and unambiguous, the motive of the terminating party is irrelevant. As stated previously, we agree with that view of the law. However, in *Karl's Sales*, unlike this case and *Bak-A-Lum*, there were no allegations of bad faith or dishonesty on the part of the terminating party. Accordingly, *Karl's Sales* did not address the issue we are concerned with here.

Borden knew that Sons of Thunder depended on the income from its contract with Borden to pay back the loan. Yet, Borden continuously breached that contract by never buying the required amount of clams from the Sons of Thunder. Furthermore, after Gallant took Booker's place, he told DeMusz that he would not honor the contract with Sons of Thunder. Nicholson also told DeMusz that he did not plan to honor that contract. Borden's failure to honor the contract left Sons of Thunder with insufficient revenue to support its financing for the Sons of Thunder.

Borden was also aware that Sons of Thunder was guaranteeing every loan that Sea Work had taken to finance the rerigging and purchasing costs for the [boat]. Thus, Borden knew that the corporations were dependent on each other, and that if one company failed, the other would most likely fail. Borden, however, fulfilled its obligations to Sea Work only for a short time before it began to breach that agreement. Eventually, Borden terminated its contract with Sea Work even though it knew that terminating the contract would leave Sea Work with no market to fish the *Jessica Lori*.

The final issue is whether the jury's assessment of $412,000, approximately one year's worth of additional profits, for the breach of the implied covenant of good faith and fair dealing was a reasonable verdict. Specifically, can a plaintiff recover lost profits for a breach of the implied covenant of good faith and fair dealing? We agree with Judge Humphreys that the jury's award of one year's additional profits "is a reasonable and fair estimate of 'expectation damages.'" Moreover, we agree with the trial court that lost profits are an appropriate remedy when a buyer breaches the implied covenant of good faith and fair dealing.

In order to recover for lost profits under [section 2-708(2)], the plaintiffs must prove the amount of damages with a reasonable degree of certainty, that the wrongful acts of the defendant caused the loss of profit, and that the profits were reasonably within the contemplation of the parties at the time the contract was entered into.

The jury's award of $412,000, approximately one year's profit, for the breach of the implied covenant of good faith and fair dealing is reasonable and fair.

CASE QUESTIONS

1. Explain the nature of the relationships between DeMusz and Borden.

2. Were all the DeMusz corporations completely dependent upon Borden?

3. What is the effect of following a termination clause in a contract?

4. What impact does "good faith" have on termination of a contract?

5. What are the damages when there is a lack of good faith in the termination of a contract?

6. What provisions would you suggest be added to a contract such as this in which the relationship is one of contract but also one of dependence?

To look at form contracts, go to
http://www.legaldocs.com
or
http://www.lectlaw.com/forma.htm

Often the obligation to perform is discharged by agreement of the parties. In some cases, the parties agree to substitute someone else for the obligation in an agreement called a **novation.** For example, suppose that before forming a corporation, a business owner had signed a lease for store premises and then incorporates the business. The landlord agrees to substitute the new corporation as the tenant. All three parties (landlord, owner, and corporation) sign a novation. The owner is excused from individual liability and performance, and the corporation is substituted. Note that the landlord must agree; the owner cannot discharge his performance obligations by unilaterally substituting the corporation.

BUSINESS STRATEGY

Dealing with High-Powered Talent

Paula Zahn was under contract with the Fox News Channel as the anchor of a nightly news show called, "The Edge." She was hired by Fox News in 1999 after her stint as a co-host of the CBS Morning Show ended. Her contract with Fox News ran through February 2002. Her 10 P.M. talk show earned the lowest ratings of any of Fox News' evening talk shows.

CNN has been in a tight competitive battle with Fox News because Fox has ousted CNN from the number one position in terms of news networks.

© Mitchell Gerber/CORBIS

Through Ms. Zahn's agent, Richard Liebner, who also represents Diane Sawyer of ABC and Dan Rather of CBS, CNN approached Ms. Zahn about jumping to CNN. Mr. Liebner than asked Fox News if it could begin contract negotiations early for Ms. Zahn. Fox News refused, and Mr. Liebner disclosed the third-party offer from CNN.

Ms. Zahn's contract with Fox News includes a provision that prohibits her from talking with other news networks and programs while her contract with Fox News is still in effect.

When Fox News learned of the negotiations and discussions with CNN, Roger Ailes, the chairman of Fox News, fired Ms. Zahn calling the discussions and negotiations a breach of contract. Mr. Ailes also alleges that CNN induced the breach.

Shortly after her termination at Fox, Ms. Zahn was hired by CNN. Walter S. Isaacson, chairman of CNN, said, "We're totally jazzed that Paula is out of her contract and is now available."

Ms. Zahn had been making $600,000 per year with Fox News and was hired by CNN for $2.1 million.

Did negotiating with CNN constitute a breach? Is such a prohibition on negotiations legal? Did CNN commit the tort of interference with contract relations? Is there any way for networks to protect themselves against such anchor-hopping? Could you develop a strategy for them?

Ms. Zahn is not the only example of difficulties with talent. George Michael, an English recording artist, rocketed to international fame in the 1980s as the lead singer with the pop group Wham! Mr. Michael was signed in 1988 by Sony Music Entertainment for a fifteen-year exclusive recording con-

tract. His first solo album with Sony was "Faith," which sold 14 million copies worldwide. Mr. Michael conducted a year-long world tour to promote the "Faith" album. After the tour, he became dissatisfied with his lack of privacy. Sony wanted him to do more tours, but he felt the tours would only create more privacy problems for him.

Mr. Michael also became dissatisfied with the image Sony had created for him. Mr. Michael said that Sony had created a "sex-saturated" image of him and that his music and the quality of his songs were lost in the promotion of him as a sex symbol.

Mr. Michael brought suit alleging Sony had breached its contract with him through its insistence on the cultivated image. At the trial of the case in London, Sony barristers introduced evidence that Mr. Michael's agent had sought more money from Sony between 1988 and 1990. Sony barristers also established that Mr. Michael did not complain to Sony about his marketing during the 1988 "Faith" tour, nor did Mr. Michael's agents express any concerns.

Was Mr. Michael's suit about artistic freedom? Was there any breach of contract by Sony? Did Mr. Michael want more money than the original contract provided? Why can't he just be paid more? Didn't Sony make Mr. Michael a star? Is it ethical for him to leave Sony after its investment in his debut album?

Note: Mr. Michael lost his suit. But Dreamworks SKG and Virgin Records purchased his record contract from Sony for $40 million. [*Panayiotou v. Sony Music Entertainment (UK) Ltd.*, 8711 (1993)]

Some artists try a different route from contract litigation. The music group TLC (T-Boz, Left-Eye, and Chili), a three-woman group based in Atlanta, rose to the top of the music charts in 1993 and has since had two multiplatinum albums along with six top singles.

At the end of 1995, all three women filed for bankruptcy. If the bankruptcy judge grants their petition, the three women will be excused from the record contracts they signed five years ago with independent producers. When groups are unknown, as TLC was five years ago, the major record producers will not sign them. These groups rely on independent producers. The contracts negotiated with "new kids" are extremely lopsided in the producer's

(continued)

favor. For example, a producer has the right to drop an artist at any time, but the artist has no right to leave the contract relationship. However, when groups' music takes off and they begin selling records, the stars want renegotiated contracts or contracts with other producers. They want more than the customary industry figure of 12 percent royalties for new artists.

From 1995 to 1996, three other groups filed for bankruptcy after achieving success in the pop music charts. Section 365 of the Federal Bankruptcy Code permits the bankruptcy court to release a debtor from contracts that are burdensome or onerous or that impair the ability of the debtor to make a fresh start.

The lawyer for TLC maintains that the women have debts and meet the test for bankruptcy. The lawyer for their producer says the women face only a cash-flow problem and that $2.2 million in royalties is in the system for them. He also adds, "I think they

wanted to be bankrupt because they think they can get out of their contract on the basis of bankruptcy."

Is it ethical to run up debts in order to declare bankruptcy to get out of a contract? Is it ethical to declare bankruptcy to obtain a higher royalty percentage on your sales through another contract? Could you develop a strategy for the record companies to use in their contracts to avoid these bankruptcy evasions by stars?

Do you think highly visible contracts and employees must be handled differently from regular employee contracts? Do you think the high visibility affords less rights under the contract? Refer back to Ethical Issues 14.1. Do the issues of the fairness of contracts and public visibility make contract enforcement more difficult? What do you learn about celebrity contracts from these examples and those given in Ethical Issues 14.1?

ETHICAL ISSUES 14.3

Jan and Jeff Bennett were married on January 21, 1996. Their honeymoon was a ten-day cruise. They flew from Seattle to Puerto Rico where they were to begin their cruise, but their luggage did not arrive in Puerto Rico. They were assured by American Airlines that it was on its way. As each day passed, they were notified that their luggage would be waiting for them at the next port, but their luggage never arrived and they spent their ten-day cruise and honeymoon in the same clothes. They had no clothes for swimming, tennis, exercise, or other activities that were part of the cruise.

The Bennetts, who still do not have their luggage, returned home and filed suit against American Airlines for $500,000. They based the damages on their ruined honeymoon and their inability to take time from work for another year to take a similar cruise.

Is their demand for damages reasonable? What about the airlines' liability limitations for loss of passenger luggage? Is it fair to allow the Bennetts to recover so much for their lost luggage?

In other situations, the parties reach an agreement for payment in full on a contract; such an agreement is called an **accord and satisfaction.** The amount they agree to pay may be less than the original contract amount, but disputes over warranties, repairs, and other issues change the value of the contract. The accord and satisfaction serves to discharge the performance of both parties.

CONTRACT REMEDIES

If performance is not excused and there is a valid contract, the nonbreaching party can recover for damages from the nonperforming party. The purpose of such **compensatory damages** is to put the nonbreaching party in the same position he would have been in had there not been a breach. The law has formulas to calculate the amount of compensatory damages for breach of every type of contract. For example, if a seller has agreed to sell a buyer a car for $5,000 and the seller

Re: Killer Performance Requirements in Retail

It's called "the Squeeze." The Squeeze refers to the increasingly onerous logistical demands retailers place on clothing suppliers. The logistical demands add tremendous costs to suppliers, they are rigid, they are complex (some retailers' rules run fifty pages), and they carry penalties. Noncompliance with logistical requirements allows the retailer to take a "chargeback," or a deduction from its payment.

Here are some sample logistical requirements:

Shipping and Packing Guidelines from Retailers to Vendors

Packing Hanging Garments

You must have written authorization from Federated to ship GOH. All ready-to-wear merchandise should be shipped in conveyable cartons in order to maximize the use of UCC-128 shipping container label. . . .

Lazarus, unit of Federated Department Stores

Routing Instructions

Determine your RPS Zone number on the Zone Chart. . . . Determine your LTL [less than truckload] Zone number from the Zone Chart and follow the LTL Routing for that zone.

Kaufmann's, unit of May Department Stores

Paperwork Documentation

Provide a separate packing list for each store and for each purchase order, detailed as to purchase order #, department #, store # and two letter code, style #, color (when ordered by color), size (when ordered by size), number of cartons, and total units shipped.

Hecht's, unit of May Department Stores

Charges include $300 for incorrect labels, $500 for incorrect packing materials, and a 5 percent penalty if a shipment arrives late.

Schwab Co., the manufacturer of "Little Me" infants clothes, was charged $400 for late delivery of a $500 shipment.

A buyer for Federated Department Stores says, ". . . [I]t's not our responsibility to keep vendors afloat. We have a separate philanthropy program." Small vendors complain they must hire extra people to handle special boxing and that retailers' chargebacks are reversed if they offer proof of compliance.

Smaller vendors are taking their products to specialty stores and boutiques. Large retailers say, "This is all still negotiable." Some vendors say that retailers are wrong on their charges about 25 to 50 percent of the time, but "They throw it up to see what will stick." Vendors note that their cash flow is affected and that until the disputes are resolved, it often takes a year for them to be paid on their invoices.

Discussion Questions

1. Is there a problem with unconscionability?
2. Would you deal with large retailers?
3. Is this kind of behavior anticompetitive?
4. Do you feel the guidelines and chargeback fees are truly negotiable?

breaches, the buyer could collect the extra $1,000 it would cost to buy a substitute car priced at $6,000.

In addition to compensatory damages, nonbreaching parties are entitled to collect the extra damages or **incidental damages** involved because of the breach. If a seller must run an ad in a newspaper to sell a car a buyer has refused to buy, the costs of the ad are incidental damages.

Some parties agree in their contracts on the amounts they will pay in the case of nonperformance. Damages agreed upon in advance are **liquidated damages,** and the contractual clauses containing them are enforceable so long as they are not excessive and compensatory damages are not awarded in addition to the liquidated damages.

Re: The Apology Bonus

With the burst of the economic bubble and the fall of so many dot-coms during 2001, many business school graduates who thought that they had employment contracts ended up with letters from their future employers telling them there would be no job. However, the letters also offered an "apology bonus" or a "reverse hiring bonus." For example, Cisco Systems offered its new hires ninety days' pay plus outplacement and resume services. Intel agreed to pay its new hires their promised hiring bonuses plus two months' pay. Nortel

Networks agreed to pay all bonuses in excess of $1,000. Dell Computer offered one month's pay plus reimbursement for any expenses incurred in preparation for moving and beginning work with Dell. Dell also offered the same package to those who lost their internships with Dell.

Why would the companies agree to pay these bonuses? What is the nature of these obligations to the graduating students? What are the ethical issues?

In some cases, the nonbreaching party may be able to collect **consequential damages.** Consequential damages are damages that result because of the breach and generally involve such damages as lost business, lost profit, or late penalties. For example, if a contractor must pay a penalty of $200 per day for each day a building is late after the completion date stipulated in the contract and the contractor is late because the steel supplier did not meet its deadline, the $200-per-day penalty would be a consequential damage that the steel supplier would be required to pay. Whether a party will be able to collect consequential damages depends on whether the breaching party knew or should have known what the consequences of the breach would be.

C O N S I D E R . . .

14.6 Boeing Company was scheduled to deliver several of its 747-400 jumbo jetliners to Northwest Airlines by December 31, 1988. Northwest set that deadline because it needed the $16 million in investment tax credits the planes would bring. Boeing missed the December 31 deadline, and Northwest wants to recover compensation from Boeing for the lost tax credits. Could Northwest recover for these lost credits?

C O N S I D E R . . .

14.7 Dan O'Connor paid $125 to have Notre Dame University's leprechaun mascot tattooed on his upper arm with the words "Fighting Irish" inscribed above the little gnome. The tattoo parlor inscribed the chosen leprechaun and "Fighing Irish."

Mr. O'Connor's girlfriend pointed out the spelling error, and Mr. O'Connor filed suit against the Tattoo Shoppe in Carlstadt, New Jersey, seeking unspecified damages.

Mr. O'Connor noted, "I was irate, and for a minute or two after I cooled down I kind of giggled. But I can't just live with this. You're not talking about a dented car where you can get another one . . . you're talking about flesh."

What damages should Mr. O'Connor receive? Would a refund of $125 be enough? What if the Tattoo Shoppe had a clause in its contract limiting damages to a refund? Would it be valid?

THIRD-PARTY RIGHTS IN CONTRACTS

Generally, a contract is a relationship between or among the contracting parties and is not enforceable by others who happen to benefit. For example, suppose a landowner and a commercial developer enter into an agreement for the construction of a shopping mall. Such a project means jobs for the area and additional business for restaurants, hotels, and transportation companies, but these businesses would not have the right to enforce the contract or collect damages for breach if the developer pulled out of the project. However, certain groups of people do have rights in contracts even though they may not have been parties to the contracts. A good example would be a beneficiary of a life insurance policy. The beneficiary does not contract with the insurance company and does not pay the premiums, but the beneficiary has contract rights because the purchaser of the policy directed so.

In other types of third-party contract rights, the third parties are not part of the original contract, as is the life insurance beneficiary, but are brought in after the fact. For example, suppose that a plumbing contractor is owed $5,000 by a homebuilder for work done on homes in the builder's subdivision. In the sales contracts for the homes, the homebuilder is the seller, and the buyer's purchase monies will go to the homebuilder. However, the homebuilder could assign payment rights to the plumber as a means of satisfying the debt. This process, called **assignment,** gives the plumber the right to collect the contract amount from the buyer. The plumber takes the place of the homebuilder in terms of contract rights.

In some cases, the duty or obligation to perform under a contract is transferred to another party. The transfer of contractual duties and obligation is called a **delegation.** Generally, a delegation of duties carries with it an assignment of benefits. For example, suppose that Neptune Fisheries, Inc., has a contract with Tom Tuna, Inc., to sell thirty fresh lobsters each day. Neptune is stopping its lobster line and delegates its duties under the Tom Tuna contract to Louie's Lobsters, Inc. Louie's takes over Neptune's obligation to furnish the thirty lobsters and is assigned the right to benefits (payment for the lobsters) under the contract. Both Louie's and Neptune are liable to Tom Tuna for performance. A delegation, unlike a novation, does not release the original contracting party.

INTERNATIONAL ISSUES IN CONTRACT PERFORMANCE

Assuring Payment

Review bills of lading:
http://www.showtrans.com/
bl.htm

International contract transactions for goods necessarily involve shipment. To control access to the goods and, hence, payment for the goods, many sellers use a **bill of lading** for transacting business. The bill of lading is a receipt for shipment issued by the carrier to the seller. It is also a contract for the shipment of the goods and evidence of who has title to the goods listed on the bill of lading. If a bill of lading is used, the buyer will not gain access to the goods unless and until the seller provides the necessary documents for release of the goods. Once the seller has the bill of lading, the seller can choose to transfer title to the goods by transferring the bill of lading. The seller could also pledge the bill of lading as security for the payment of a debt. A bill of lading can be made directly to the buyer, or it can be a negotiable bill of lading that can be transferred to anyone.

The bill of lading is often used in conjunction with a line of credit in international transactions because the two together offer the seller assurance of payment and the buyer assurance of arrival of the goods. In international transactions, in which resolution of disputes over great distances can be difficult, this means of controlling access to goods and payment is very helpful.

In this type of transaction, the seller delivers goods to a carrier for transportation and receives a bill of lading. The seller then sends the bill of lading through his bank to the buyer's bank to give the buyer's bank title to the goods, which will be turned over to the buyer once the funds are deducted from the line of credit established by the bank for the buyer.

The buyer may also arrange for a **letter of credit** to be used in conjunction with the bill of lading. The letter of credit is issued by the buyer's bank and is sent to a corresponding bank where the seller is located. The letter of credit lists the terms and conditions under which the seller can draw on the letter of credit or be paid. For example, turning the bill of lading over to the corresponding bank may be the condition of drawing on the letter of credit; the bill of lading is then used by the corresponding bank and the buyer's bank to allow the buyer to take possession of the goods. Because banks are involved in these transactions through credit assurances, the seller enjoys more of an assurance of payment prior to shipment because a letter of credit is actually a confirmation of payment.

Assuring Performance: International Peculiarities

International contracts have a particular need for a *force majeure* clause. Wars, revolutions, and coups are often included in international contracts as justification for noncompletion of the contract. The *force majeure* clauses are summaries of potential international events that could hamper production or trade.

One other risk of international contracts is the stability of various currencies and their possible devaluation. The method and means of payment should be specified in the contract, and a clause covering devaluation may also be included so that full payment is ensured.

The following case illustrates what can happen between the negotiation of an international contract and the time for contract payment.

CASE 14.4

Lakeway Co. v. Bravo
576 S.W.2d 926 (Tex. 1979)

Falling Pesos: Negotiating an Exchange Rate

FACTS

Lakeway and Bravos (in a contract drawn and executed in both English and Spanish) agreed that Bravos would buy a certain Lakeway lot in Travis County, Texas. The purchase price was $25,820, with payment by Bravos to be in pesos. The agreement was executed July 31, 1976.

By the time the check was presented for final payment, it was August 30, 1976. The Mexican government devalued the peso on August 31, 1976, and the result was that Lakeway received $8,188.45 less than it would have had the transaction not been subject to an interim devaluation. Lakeway brought suit. Summary judgment was granted for Bravos, and Lakeway appealed.

JUDICIAL OPINION

SUMMERS, Chief Justice

Appellant (Lakeway) contends that the intention of the parties, as set forth in the contract, was for a total purchase price of $25,820.00; that how it was paid, whether in dollars or in pesos, was immaterial so long as the result to the seller was the required number of dollars; and that the peso figure in parenthesis was simply for the convenience of the buyer to let him know how many pesos would be required to buy the property. It urges that this intention is supported by the fact that the contract provides that "Seller agrees to notify Buyers in writing of the total amount due in Mexican pesos if a change in the official exchange rate occurs prior to such payment." We agree with these contentions.

However, in the instant case a check payable in the correct amount of pesos for final payment under

the contract was delivered to Lakeway by the Bravos on August 18, 1976; such check was received by Lakeway without objection; said check was honored and cleared appellees' bank account on August 30, 1976, prior to the devaluation of the peso, which occurred on August 31, 1976; and when honored and paid in due course, the payment became absolute and related back to the date of delivery of the check on August 18, 1976; and as of said date of delivery it produced the specified value in dollars and satisfied the terms of the contract.

The judgment of the trial court is affirmed.

CASE QUESTIONS

1. What was the land purchase price?
2. How much did Lakeway lose once there was devaluation?
3. Will Lakeway get more money?
4. How did the contract address the issue of devaluation?

SUMMARY

What if the assumptions made and the information given turn out to be untrue? Must the parties still go forward with the contract?

- Contract defense—situation, term, or event that excuses performance

- Capacity—mental and age threshold for valid contracts

- Voidable contract—one party can choose not to honor the contract

- Puffing—statements of opinion

- Material fact—basis of the bargain

- Void contract—contract that courts will not honor

- Misrepresentation—incomplete or inaccurate information prior to contract execution

- Rescission—setting aside of contract as a remedy

- Fraud—intentional misrepresentation

- *Scienter*—knowledge that information given is false

- Duress—physical or mental force that deprives party of a meaningful choice with respect to a proposed contract

- Undue influence—exerting control over another party for purposes of gain

- Confidential relationship—trust, confidence, reliance in a relationship

- Public policy—standards of decency

- Exculpatory clauses—attempt to hold oneself harmless for one's own conduct

- Unconscionable contract—contract that is grossly unfair

If one party does not perform, is the other side excused? When is performance required and when is it excused?

- Conditions precedent—advance events that must occur before performance is due, for example, obtaining financing

- Substantial performance—performance that, for practical purposes, is just as good as full performance

- Commercial impracticability—defense to performance of sales contract based on objective impracticability

- Novation—agreement to change contract among all affected, for example, agreement to substitute parties

- Accord and satisfaction—agreement entered into as settlement of a disputed debt

- The obligation of good faith—must perform in a reasonable fashion; performance must meet commercial standards

What remedies exist?

- Compensatory damages—amount required to place party in as good a position as before breach

- Incidental damages—costs of collecting compensatory damages

- Liquidated damages—agreement clause in contract that preestablishes and limits damages

- Consequential damages—damages owed to third parties from a breach

Do third parties have rights in a contract?

- Incidental beneficiary—an indirect beneficiary

- Donee beneficiary—a beneficiary designated in the contract; third party intended to benefit from the contract, for example, life insurance

- Creditor beneficiary—a beneficiary designated in one contract who will compensate him for services given pursuant to a separate contract, for example, health insurance

What are the contract performance issues in international business?

- Bill of lading—title document used to control transfer of goods

- Letter of credit—pledge by bank of availability of funds for a transaction

- Exchange rate and risk issues in contracts

QUESTIONS AND PROBLEMS

1. Robert G. Rawlinson was employed by Germantown Manufacturing in Marple Township as its assistant controller. He embezzled $372,113.21 from the company, which discovered the theft, though not the exact amount, on May 21, 1982. Mr. Rawlinson admitted his wrongdoing and was fired. He did not tell his wife, and it was not until she eavesdropped on a telephone conversation between her husband and Peter Kulaski that she discovered something was amiss. Mr. Rawlinson told her (after his phone conversation) that he had taken $20,000 from the company and was fired. Mrs. Rawlinson testified that her "whole world fell apart" upon hearing the news. She was already depressed and tired because of a miscarriage she had suffered in late April.

The following day, Mr. Kulaski came to the Rawlinson home and asked them to sign two judgment notes. The first note was for $160,000, the amount Mr. Rawlinson admitted taking from the company. The second note was for any amounts above and beyond the $160,000 that would be established by the company president as having been taken by Mr. Rawlinson. Mrs. Rawlinson's name was on the documents, and she asked if they should not have an attorney. Mr. Kulaski told them they did not need an attorney because the company was acting in good faith and that no criminal charges would be brought if the Rawlinsons would cooperate. Mrs. Rawlinson felt

that if she signed the notes, her husband would not go to jail.

Mrs. Rawlinson had never before seen a judgment note and cried while trying to read these. She thought she was signing only for $160,000 and, because her husband had a check for $150,000 ready to turn over, that they could easily come up with the remaining $10,000.

In August 1982, the president of the company verified that the total amount taken was $212,113.21 more than the $160,000 already paid. When demand for payment was made, Mrs. Rawlinson requested that the confession of judgment be opened and disallowed on the basis of misrepresentation. The lower court found for Mrs. Rawlinson, and Germantown Manufacturing appealed. Give a list of defenses Mrs. Rawlinson could use. [*Germantown Mfg. Co.* v. *Rawlinson,* 491 A.2d 138 (Pa. 1985)]

2. Tony Curtis, a respected actor, entered into a contract to write a novel for Doubleday & Company, publishers. Because of complex divorce proceedings and other personal factors, Mr. Curtis was unable to submit a satisfactory manuscript. Doubleday demanded a return of the $50,000 advance Mr. Curtis had received. Are they entitled to it? [*Doubleday & Co.* v. *Curtis,* 763 F.2d 495 (2d Cir. 1985)]

3. Bernina Sewing Machines imports sewing machines and parts for U.S. distribution. Its contract prices are in francs. Because of the devaluation of the U.S. dollar, Bernina wants to be excused from its contracts. Can it be excused under any contract doctrine? [*Bernina Distributors, Inc.* v. *Bernina Sewing Machines*, 646 F.2d 434 (10th Cir. 1981)]

4. Would failure to disclose a delinquency on your mortgage on a loan application be a misrepresentation? [*Barrer* v. *Women's National Bank*, 761 F.2d 752 (D.C. 1985)]

5. Orkin investigated Helen M. Clarkson's home for termites and found none, but continued routine inspections. After one monthly inspection, Ms. Clarkson hired another firm to inspect for termites. The firm found termite tunnels and damage. Ms. Clarkson had to spend approximately $1,200 for repairs. Could she recover that amount from Orkin? [*Clarkson* v. *Orkin Exterminating Co., Inc.*, 761 F.2d 189 (4th Cir. 1985)]

6. Northland Ford Dealers sponsored a hole-in-one contest at the Moccasin Creek Country Club in South Dakota. The contest winner would receive a new Ford Explorer. Jennifer Harms registered for the contest. She stood at the women's marker for teeing off and hit a hole-in-one. She was denied her car because the dealers' insurance policy for the event indicated the following, "ALL AMATEUR MEN AND WOMEN SHALL UTILIZE THE SAME TEE." That tee was established in the policy as 170 yards. However, the men and women participating in the contest were not told of this rule or restriction. Must the dealers give Jennifer her Ford Explorer or will she remain "tee'd off"? *Harms* v. *Northland Ford Dealers*, 602 N.W. 2d 58 (S.D. 1999).

7. Amy was a 78-year-old widow who lived alone. She drove an hour each day to take care of her disabled sister, Mary. When Mary died, Amy drove to take care of Mary's husband, Bill. Bill left Amy a fourth of his estate when he died. Was there undue influence? [*Totman* v. *Vernon*, 494 A.2d 97 (R.I. 1985)]

8. On February 21, 1990, Robert Barto and his wife signed an agreement with Estate Motors, Ltd., of Birmingham, Michigan, to purchase a Mercedes Benz 500 SL automobile. They signed the agreement that follows.

Retail Buyers Order

ESTATE MOTORS LTD.
464 S. Woodward Telephone 644-8400
BIRMINGHAM, MICHIGAN 48011

Purchasers
Name ___Robert Barto___   Date __Feb. 21, 1990__
— NEW — CAR

PLEASE ENTER MY ORDER FOR ONE __Mercedes Benz__   —   USED —
TRUCK
AS FOLLOWS

Year	Make	Model or Series	Body Type	Color	Trim
1991	Mercedes Benz	500SL	2 Door	199 Black Pearl	Gray Leather

MVI or Serial No.   Stock No.   To Be Delivered
                                        On or About   19

CASH PRICE OF VEHICLE _____

199	BLACK PEARL—
	Gray Leather—
740	Black Soft Top

                                        TOTAL
                                        TAX
              TOTAL CASH DELIVERED PRICE
CASH DEPOSIT SUBMITTED WITH ORDER   500—
SALESMAN /s/ (Doug MacFarlane)   SIGNED /s/ (Robert Barto)
                                        PURCHASER
                              PURCHASER'S
                              NAME ___Robert Barto___
                              STREET
THIS ORDER IS NOT VALID UN-   ADDRESS 1 Winward Place
LESS SIGNED BY DEALER OR   CITY &
HIS AUTHORIZED REPRESEN-   STATE Gross Pointe Farms   ZIP 48236
TATIVE.
APPROVED _____   BUS. PHONE _____
         Dealer or Authorized RES. PHONE 886-2277
         Representative

      THIS ORDER IS NOT A BINDING CONTRACT
      CASH OR CASHIER'S CHECK UPON DELIVERY

Doug MacFarlane, their salesman, told the Bartos that because of high demand, their car might not be delivered for eighteen months.

In mid-August 1991, Mr. MacFarlane telephoned Mr. Barto and informed him that his Mercedes would be at the dealership and ready for pickup on August 30. Mr. MacFarlane also informed Mr. Barto in that telephone conversation for the first time that he would have to pay a luxury tax on his new car (in addition to the purchase price, state sales tax, and license/title fees) when he came to pick it up.

Mr. Barto was angry about having to pay the luxury tax because he believed that his car fell within the scope of the preexisting binding contract exception, as his order for the car had been placed before September 30, 1990. During the ensuing weeks before his car arrived at Estate Motors, Mr. Barto telephoned the Mercedes-Benz district sales representatives and legal counsel and was informed that Mercedes-Benz was advising their dealers that the new luxury tax was not to be assessed on cars ordered before September 30, 1990. Mr. Barto also learned that of the 114 Mercedes-Benz dealers within the midwest region, only Estate Motors was assessing the tax on cars ordered before September 30, 1990.

Mr. Barto attempted to negotiate a manner of payment of the tax with Estate Motors. He first proposed that he bring with him two checks when he picked up his car—one check payable to Estate Motors for everything but the amount of the luxury tax, and one check for the luxury tax payable to the IRS. The dealer refused this arrangement. Mr. Barto then suggested that he pay the luxury tax into an escrow account. Again the dealer refused. Because Mr. Barto wanted his new car, he ultimately agreed to pay Estate Motors the full purchase price, including the luxury tax assessment.

On August 30, 1991, when Mr. Barto went to Estate Motors to pick up his Mercedes-Benz, he tendered to the dealer his check for $111,446 to cover the $99,950 purchase price of the car, the sales tax/license/title fees of $4,501, and the 10 percent luxury tax amounting to $6,995. Mr. Barto and the dealer also executed on August 30 Estate Motors' "Statement of Vehicle Sale," which reflected the breakdown of his $111,946 total purchase price, license/title transfer and proof of insurance information, and the odometer disclosure.

Mr. Barto continued to protest having to pay the $6,995 luxury tax on his new Mercedes after picking the car up. The dealer provided Mr. Barto with a blank IRS 843 form for a tax refund. When the IRS denied Mr. Barto's claim for refund, he filed suit against Estate.

Mr. Barto wished to rescind the agreement. He wanted his $500 back. Is Mr. Barto entitled to it? Is there a contract at all? [*Barto v. United States*, 823 F. Supp. 1369 (E.D. Mich. 1993)]

9. Betty Lobianco had a burglar alarm system installed in her home by Property Protection, Inc. The contract for installing the system provided:

Alarm system equipment installed by Property Protection, Inc. is guaranteed against improper function due to manufacturing defects or workmanship for a period of 12 months. The installation of the above equipment carries a 90-day warranty. The liability of Property Protection, Inc., is limited to repair or replacement of security alarm equipment and does not include loss or damage to possessions, persons, or property.

On November 22, 1975, Ms. Lobianco's home was burglarized and $35,815 in jewelry was taken. The alarm system, which had been installed less than ninety days earlier, included a standby source of power in case the regular source of power failed. On the day of the fateful burglary, the alarm did not go off because the batteries installed in the system had no power.

Ms. Lobianco brought suit to recover the $35,815. She claimed that the liability limitation was unconscionable and unenforceable under the UCC. Property Protection claimed that the UCC did not apply to the installation of a burglar alarm system. Who is correct? [*Lobianco v. Property Protection, Inc.*, 437 A.2d 417 (Pa. 1981)]

10. Northrup King Company produces and sells seeds to farmers and others throughout the United States. Northrup placed the following disclaimer on its product:

NOTICE: Northrup King Co. warrants that seeds sold have been labeled as required under State and Federal Seed Laws and that they conform to the label description. No liability hereunder shall be asserted unless the buyer or user reports to the warrantor within a reasonable period after discovery (not to exceed 30 days), any condition that might lead to a complaint. <u>Our liability on this warranty is limited in amount to the purchase price of the seeds. This warranty is in lieu of all other warranties, express or implied, including warranties of merchantability and fitness for a particular purpose. There are no warranties which extend beyond the face hereof.</u>

The underlined language was in red print on containers. Northrup sold pepper seeds to Floyd Ammons, whose pepper crop developed bacterial rust-spotting disease. Mr. Ammons brought suit for damages (loss of his crop), saying the disclaimer is unconscionable and void. Is he right? [*Northrup King Co. v. Ammons*, 9 U.C.C.2d Rep. Serv. (Callaghan) 836 (4th Cir. 1989)]

RESEARCH PROBLEM

11. Visit the following Websites and determine how the companies have computer users enter into contracts. Determine how the computer user knows that a contract has been formed and what the terms of that contract are. Also, watch for liability limitation clauses (when they are disclosed) and what types of liability limitations companies use.

www.fedex.com

www.hertz.com

www.dell.com

www.ups.com

BUSINESS STRATEGY APPLICATION

In the CD-ROM application for this chapter, you'll have the chance to write a memo on what types of *force majeure* clauses you would include in your company's contracts based on what you learn from background research and examples.

CHAPTER FIFTEEN

Financing of Sales and Leases: Credit and Disclosure Requirements

The English refer to credit sales as "buying on the never never" because you never really pay for everything; there is always some outstanding credit. Credit sales are a way of life in the United States. Nearly all sellers advertise not only their products but also the availability of credit terms for buyers. Credit is used so often that both Congress and state legislatures have enacted statutes regulating credit contracts. This chapter covers those regulations and credit contracts. How is a credit contract set up? What are the requirements? What statutes affect the credit contract? How are credit contracts enforced?

> Neither a borrower nor a lender be,
> For a loan oft loses both itself and friend
> And borrowing dulls the edge of husbandry.
>
> HAMLET
> *Act 1, Scene 3*

Consumer Credit Outstanding (per American Bankers Association)

1993	$850 million
1995	$1.100 billion
1997	$1.250 billion
1998	$1.500 billion
1999	$1.390 billion
2000	$1.550 billion
2001	$1.590 billion

Delinquency Rate of Consumer Loans

Year	Percent of Loans Outstanding
1990	2%
1991	1.65%
1992	2.74%
1993	2.6%
1994	2.66%

CONSIDER...

In February 1995, A.B.&S., an auto repair shop owned by Bonner, an African-American male, applied for a $230,000 business loan from the South Shore Bank. Bonner submitted the required Small Business Administration Loan Form 912 on December 27, 1994. In response to the question about arrests and convictions, Bonner noted the following:

1. Domestic matter between 1982 and 1984

2. Conviction for aggravated battery and assault in 1983 (claims self-defense)

3. Possession of a controlled substance in 1985

4. Disorderly conduct between 1985 and 1990

5. Possession of a controlled substance in 1990

6. Possession of a stolen car in September 1994

The bank denied the loan.

Bonner filed suit under the Equal Credit Opportunity Act, alleging that the bank's practice of considering criminal records has an unlawful disparate impact on African-American men. Can the bank consider Bonner's criminal record in making a loan decision?

© Susan Van Etten

ESTABLISHING A CREDIT CONTRACT

Gather consumer credit protection information:
www.federalreserve.gov.
Click on Consumer Information

A credit contract not only needs the usual elements of a contract (as covered in Chapter 13), including offer, acceptance, and consideration, but it requires additional information for the credit agreement to be valid. The following list covers the extra details needed in a credit contract:

1. How much the buyer/debtor is actually carrying on credit or financing
2. The rate of interest the buyer/debtor will pay
3. How many payments will be made, when they will be made, and for how long
4. Penalties and actions for late payments
5. Whether the creditor will have collateral
6. The necessary statutory disclosures on credit transactions

STATUTORY REQUIREMENTS FOR CREDIT CONTRACTS

The following statutes affect and, in some cases, control the terms in a credit contract. A summary of the federal statutes appears in Exhibit 15.1.

EXHIBIT 15.1 **Summary of Federal Laws on Consumer Credit**

CREDIT STATUTE (FEDERAL)	PURPOSE AND SCOPE
Equal Credit Opportunity Act 15 U.S.C. § 1691 (1974)	Prohibits discrimination on the basis of sex, race, age, or national origin in credit extension decision
Consumer Credit Protection Act (CCPA) 15 U.S.C. § 1601 (1968)	Umbrella statute passed to deal with fairness of consumer credit transactions
Truth-in-Lending Act 15 U.S.C. § 1601 (1968)	Part of CCPA that governs disclosure of credit terms
Amendments (1995) 15 U.S.C. § 1605	Closes loopholes for avoiding loan repayments based on clerical errors in loan documents
Fair Credit and Charge Card Disclosure Act 15 U.S.C. § 1646 (1988)	Provides for disclosure requirements in the solicitation of credit cards
Regulation Z 12 C.F.R. § 226 (1981)	Federal Reserve Board regulations providing details for all disclosure statutes
Home Equity Loan Consumer Protection Act 15 U.S.C. § 1647 (1988)	Disclosure requirements for home equity loans and a rescission period
Home Ownership and Equity Protection Act 15 U.S.C. § 1637 (1994)	Disclosure requirements on payment amounts for home equity loans and cancellation rights
Fair Credit Billing Act 15 U.S.C. § 1637 (1974)	Rights of debtors on open-end credit billing disputes
Fair Credit Reporting Act 15 U.S.C. § 1681 (1970)	Right of debtors with respect to reports of their credit histories
Consumer Leasing Act 15 U.S.C. § 1667 (1976)	Disclosure requirements for leases of goods by consumers
Fair Debt Collections Practices Act 15 U.S.C. § 1692 (1977)	Regulation of conduct of third-party bill collectors and attorneys

Re: ATM Fees and Other Creative Bank Charges

In California, there is a heated battle between banks and consumers over ATM fees. Consumers have been upset recently with ATM usage charges that can be as much as $3.50 for the withdrawal of $20. For example, a bank can charge $2.00 when a customer uses an ATM from a different bank. The bank the customer uses can also charge money, generally $1.50, for the foreign customer using its system. The result is a total charge for the consumer of $3.50.

When ATMs were first gaining popularity, banks waived such fees in order to encourage usage of the electronic forms of banking as opposed to the labor-intensive and costly physical tellers. In fact, the two major ATM systems had joined together to fight charging fees. However, legislatures in fifteen states passed statutes permitted the ATM surcharges.

Now states are swinging the other way, with Connecticut and Iowa being two examples of states that do not permit the surcharges. The litigation in the San Francisco area involves the issue of whether states can regulate banking surcharges. The issue of preemption has been raised with respect to state statutes on ATM fees.

Credit card holders have discovered new and creative fees being assessed to them by their credit card companies. The following is a list of the latest new forms of charges on credit card bills:

- Foreign transaction fees—foreign transaction fees have increased from 1 percent to 3 percent.
- Cash advance fees have increased from 1 percent to between 3 percent and 5 percent, and the minimum fee has increased from $1 to between $5 and $10.
- Balance transfer fees for transferring the balance from one credit card to another with lower interest is typically 3 percent of the balance, with minimum transfer fees ranging from $5 to $50.
- On some of the credit cards, cancellation of the card can lead to an accelerated interest rate such as the 26.99 percent charged by Fleet Financial.

The fees are in response to a new consumer trend to pay off their credit card balances. In 1991, 29 percent of consumers paid off their monthly credit card bills. In 1999, the figure had risen to 44 percent. With so little interest income from the cards, the cards are generating revenue in other ways, such as by the aforementioned new fees and charges.

The Federal Reserve Bank is proposing rules with greater disclosure requirements. Those rules can be seen at http://www.regs.comments@federalreserve.gov

State Usury Laws

Usury is charging an interest rate higher than the maximum permitted by law. If the maximum rate of interest permitted by statute is 21 percent, a creditor charging 24 percent has violated a statute and created a void contract.

The usury rate varies from state to state, and many states have different usury rates for the various types of transactions. For example, the usury rate for real estate loans may be lower than the usury rate for credit cards or installment credit transactions. Some states' usury rates are just a percentage figure, whereas other states include loan origination charges, finders' fees, service charges, and other fees paid by the debtor in determining the actual rate of interest charged.

Penalties for charging a usurious rate also vary. Some states treat the usurious agreement as completely void, and the penalty for the creditor is forfeiture of interest and principal. Other states allow the creditor to recoup the principal but deny any interest. Some states simply require the creditor to forfeit any interest above the maximum; others also impose a penalty on the creditor by allowing the debtor to collect two or three times the amount of excess interest charged as damages.

CONSIDER...

15.1   The mail-order business is a large part of the retail industry. This segment of retail sales has grown so significantly that state attorneys general have litigated to be able to charge some sales taxes within their state despite a mail-order company's out-of-state location and a minimal catalog mailing to in-state residents. With more companies, more catalogs, and more customers, consumer protection issues are increasing.

Currently, the Federal Trade Commission (FTC) regulates catalog forms and disclosures about merchandise availability and costs. As with the evolving credit laws, however, some areas are not regulated and do present costly problems for consumers. For example, a Talbots catalog used the shipment cost for a pair of $12.00 ragg trouser socks as $5.50 or 45.8 percent of the purchase price. If a shopper wanted to send those socks to a daughter at college and thus at a different address than the catalog shopper's, there is an additional $3.00 for a "shipped to" address. Then the customer would pay shipping costs of 70.8 percent of the purchase price. Further, shipping and handling costs are not related to item weights or sizes; they are related to total ordered amount; and the shipping and handling costs decrease as a percentage of total price the more one buys. The following chart is from a Talbots catalog:

Shipping and handling

Total merchandise (exclude tax)	Add	Shipping and Handling (%)
$20.00 and under	$5.50	27.5%
$20.01 to $30.00	$6.50	22–32.5%
$30.01 to $50.00	$7.50	15–25%
$50.01 to $100.00	$8.50	8.5–17%
$100.01 to $150.00	$9.50	6.3–9.5%
$150.01 to $200.00	$10.50	5.25–7%
$200.01 and over	$11.50	5.7% and less

Please add $3.00 for each additional shipping address.

Some companies, such as LL Bean, base their shipping and handling charges on actual weight, and each item in the catalog carries the weight of the item beside the price. What do you think the basis for catalog shipping and handling charges is? Is it to encourage customers to order more? Do you think companies have determined the most common price range for orders and charged the most in those ranges? Could this be considered usury? Why, or why not? Do you think this area will be a new focus for consumer protection?

The Equal Credit Opportunity Act

Review the Equal Credit Opportunity Act:
http://www.law.cornell.edu/uscode/15/1691.html

The **Equal Credit Opportunity Act** (ECOA) was passed to ensure that credit was denied or awarded on the applicant's merits—the ability to pay—and not on such extraneous factors as sex, race, color, religion, national origin, or age. (See Exhibit 15.1 on p. 566.) Questions regarding these matters can be asked of applicants for record-keeping purposes, but the decision to extend or deny credit must be based on factors other than these. The following types of information also cannot be considered in making the credit decision:

1. Marital status of the applicant
2. Applicant's receipt of public assistance income
3. Applicant's receipt of alimony or child support payments
4. Applicant's plans for having children

The ECOA also provides married persons the right to have individual credit applications, lines, and ratings. Credit applications must specify that a spouse's income need not be disclosed unless the applicant is relying on that income to qualify for credit. Further, even on joint accounts, debtors can require creditors to report credit ratings individually for the spouses.

Visit the Federal Trade Commission:
http://www.ftc.gov

Violations of the ECOA carry statutory penalties. The ECOA is enforceable by the Federal Trade Commission (FTC), by the U.S. attorney general, and by private actions by debtors. Debtors can sue for their actual damages for embarrassment and emotional distress and also for punitive damages of up to $10,000. If a group of debtors brings a class action against a creditor, they can collect punitive damages of up to the lesser of $500,000 or 1 percent of the creditor's net worth. Punitive damages are recoverable even when there are no actual damages. The *A.B.&S. Auto Service* case involves an issue of an ECOA violation and also provides the answer to the chapter opening "Consider."

CASE 15.1

A.B.&S. Auto Service, Inc. v. South Shore Bank of Chicago
962 F.Supp. 1056 (N.D.Ill. 1997)

Do the Crime, Forget the Loan

FACTS

A.B.&S. Auto Service, Inc. (AB&S) is an automobile repair shop located in Chicago, Illinois. Jerry L. Bonner is AB&S's president, and he is an African-American. South Shore is a commercial bank that maintains three branches on Chicago's South Side and a loan office in the Austin neighborhood of Chicago's West Side. South Shore participates in the Small Business Administration's (SBA) loan guarantee program.

The SBA requires all applicants for the loan guarantee program to fill out an SBA Form 912 Statement of Personal History. SBA Form 912 asks applicants if they have ever been charged with or arrested or convicted for any criminal offense other than a minor motor vehicle violation and if so, asks the applicant to provide details. Form 912 also provides:
The fact that you have an arrest or conviction record will not necessarily disqualify you.

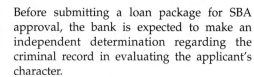

Before submitting a loan package for SBA approval, the bank is expected to make an independent determination regarding the criminal record in evaluating the applicant's character.

In February 1995, AB&S applied for a $230,000 business loan from the bank after having a similar SBA request denied by La Salle Bank Lakeview. Bonner submitted a Form 912 on December 27, 1994. In response to the question about arrests and convictions, Bonner noted the following:

1. Domestic matters between 1982 and 1984
2. Conviction for aggravated battery and assault (1983) (claims self-defense)
3. Possession of a controlled substance in 1985
4. Disorderly conduct between 1985 and 1990
5. Possession of a controlled substance in 1990
6. Possession of a stolen car in September 1994

(continued)

Leslie Davis, an African-American Vice President at South Shore Bank, recommended approval of Bonner's application. However, the loan committee agreed that because of Bonner's criminal record the application should be denied. The bank then decided to deny the loan.

During the last 15 years, the South Shore Bank has made at least three business loans to applicants with criminal records. One of these three applicants was an African-American. South Shore evaluates each application on an individual basis and examines criminal record and other information for purposes of determining character.

Bonner and his company (plaintiffs) filed suit under the ECOA alleging that the bank's practice of considering criminal record has an unlawful disparate impact on African-American men. South Shore Bank (defendants) moved for summary judgment because Bonner did not establish a case of discrimination. Bonner also moved for summary judgment on the grounds that consideration of criminal record without tying it to creditworthiness violated the ECOA.

JUDICIAL OPINION

WILLIAMS, Anne Claire, District Judge
The court must determine whether South Shore Bank's policy of inquiring about a credit applicant's criminal record, in compliance with SBA's requirements, violates the ECOA. The ECOA provides, in relevant part, that:

it shall be unlawful for any creditor to discriminate against an applicant, with respect to any aspect of a credit transaction—

(1) on the basis of race, color, religion, national origin, sex or marital status, or age (provided the applicant has the capacity to contract)

15 U.S.C. § 1691(a)(1). A credit applicant can prove discrimination under the ECOA by using any one of the following three different approaches used in the employment discrimination context: 1) direct evidence of discrimination; 2) disparate impact analysis, also called the "effects" test; or 3) disparate treatment analysis.

In order to prove discrimination under the disparate impact analysis or "effects" test, an applicant must show how "a policy, procedure, or practice specifically identified by the [applicant] has a significantly greater discriminatory impact on members of a protected class." Plaintiffs traditionally establish this prima facie case by making "a statistical comparison of the representation of the protected class in the applicant pool with representation in the group actually accepted from the pool. "If the statistical disparity is significant, then plaintiff is deemed to have made out a prima facie case." However, courts have found that "proof of disparate impact need not be shown by statistics in every case nor need it be shown by proof of actual disproportionate exclusion from the applicant pool."

Once the plaintiff has made the prima facie case, the defendant-lender must demonstrate that any policy, procedure, or practice has a manifest relationship to the creditworthiness of the applicant. In other words, the onus is on the defendant to show that the particular practice makes defendant's credit evaluation system more predictive than it would be otherwise.

Courts have held that the use of general population statistics is insufficient to make out a prima facie case under the ECOA.

In *Saldana v. Citibank*, 1996 WL 332451 (N.D.Ill. 1996), the plaintiff, loan-applicant, sued Citibank claiming it denied her loan based on its policy of redlining. Saldana tried to make her case under the disparate impact theory. Specifically, she claimed that Citibank had an unwritten policy that set the minimum amount for a rehab loan at $100,000. This policy, she claims, disproportionately impacted the African-American community because few African-Americans could meet this financial test based on their income and net worth. Saldana offered statistical evidence regarding 1) the bank's loan approval rate for loans over $100,000 in the Austin area; 2) the bank's loan rejection rate for white and African-American applicants in comparison with their representation in the greater Chicago community; and 3) the bank's average refinancing approval and average rejection rate in Austin in comparison to the City of Chicago's average approval and rejection rates. While the court found that this last set of statistics successfully presented some statistical evidence comparing the Austin community to the greater Chicago community, the court still found that "these statistics are of a very general nature and do not relate specifically to the policy identified as having a discriminatory impact. Thus, Saldana has failed to establish her claim under a disparate impact analysis."

Similarly, in *Cherry v. Amoco Oil Co.*, 490 F.Supp. 1026 (N.D.Ga. 1980), the credit-card applicant sued Amoco Oil Company, alleging that Amoco's use of zip code ratings in Atlanta, which assigned low-ratings to those zip code areas where Amoco had unfavorable delinquency experience, adversely effected [sic] black applicants disproportionately.

Plaintiffs claim that South Shore Bank's practice of considering an applicant's criminal record in making commercial lending decisions has a disparate impact on African-Americans. To make the prima facie case plaintiffs offer the testimony of Dr. Jaslin U. Salmon. Dr. Salmon testified that any decision that is based on arrest records would militate against people of color. He suggests that, based on his research, there are many cases in which the black applicant is qualified, credit worthy, but was not given the loan for other reasons and among those reasons, arrest records had been taken into consideration. However, the bank disputes this point because Dr. Salmon was unable to identify a single study showing that consideration of arrest records has a disproportionate impact on African-American applicants for any type of credit, much less any study addressing the impact on business loan applicants.

In addition to Dr. Salmon's testimony, plaintiffs offer the general population statistics of arrest by race in 1990. Considering these general population statistics, the court finds that these statistics are insufficient to make out a prima facie case under the ECOA. The court recognizes that the ECOA prohibits creditors from inquiring into the race, sex, or marital status of an applicant. This in turn places plaintiffs in a difficult position of trying to prove disproportionate impact without any access to a creditor's statistical lending profile. Plaintiffs can refer to the general population as long as plaintiffs clearly demonstrate that the applicant pool would possess approximately the same characteristics. Considering the statistical proof and the testimony of Dr. Salmon, the court finds that plaintiffs have not made this showing that the applicant pool possesses approximately the same characteristics as the general population.

Both the statistics and Dr. Salmon's supporting testimony do not answer the following questions: 1) how many African-Americans with convictions or arrests are otherwise qualified for the loan: and 2) how many African-Americans are deterred from applying because of the bank's practice. Plaintiffs' evidence is further undermined, as it was in *Hill,* by the fact that the bank's practice of considering an applicant's criminal record was not consistently applied to disqualify applicants with criminal records. Rather, the bank has made at least three business loans to applicants with criminal records.

One of these three applicants with criminal records is African-American.

South Shore Bank's practice of inquiring into a credit applicant's criminal history is legitimately related to its extension of credit for two reasons. First, the regulations require the SBA, in evaluating a loan guarantee application, to consider "the character, reputation, and credit history of the applicant, its associates, and guarantors." 13 C.F.R. § 120.150. As a participant in the SBA loan guarantee program, South Shore Bank is obligated to consider an applicant's criminal record provided on SBA Form 912 in its evaluation of a loan applicant's character.

Secondly, the bank's inquiry into an applicant's criminal record provides relevant information about an applicant's creditworthiness, particularly his judgment and character. Plaintiff Bonner admits that several of the incidents described in his completed SBA Form 912: possession of a controlled substance, domestic abuse, and disorderly conduct, reflected negatively on his judgment and character. Specifically, Bonner admits that these incidents involved an exercise of bad judgment. Therefore, because an applicant's judgment and character may legitimately be considered in making commercial lending decisions, South Shore Bank's practice of considering criminal history as it relates to character and judgment bears a legitimate and manifest relationship to the extension of credit. Therefore, the court finds that the bank has successfully demonstrated that its practice of inquiring into a credit applicant's criminal record is legitimately related to the extension of credit.

For the foregoing reasons, the court grants defendant South Shore Bank's motion for summary judgment and denies plaintiff Bonner and AB&S's motion for summary judgment.

CASE QUESTIONS

1. Who asked for the information about the loan applicant's criminal record?

2. What, according to Bonner's expert, is the impact of considering criminal records of applicants?

3. Is the use of the criminal record in making a decision to extend credit a violation of the ECOA?

4. Do you think a criminal record is an indication of character?

C O N S I D E R . . .

15.2   Medmark, Inc., a small corporation, requested a loan from Merchant's Bank. Merchant's Bank agreed to make the loan if Bruce Shalberg, a director of the company, obtained his wife's signature on the loan guaranty he had agreed to make. Merchant's Bank had made an independent investigation of Mr. Shalberg and found him to be creditworthy.

When Merchant's Bank failed, the Federal Deposit Insurance Corporation (FDIC) took over all accounts and filed against Medmark as well as Mr. and Mrs. Shalberg on their guaranty of the note. Mrs. Shalberg filed a motion for summary judgment on the grounds that she had been required, in violation of the ECOA, to sign as a guarantor for an obligation for which her husband qualified independently. Why did Merchant's Bank require Mrs. Shalberg to sign? Had the bank violated the ECOA? [*Federal Deposit Insurance Corporation* v. *Medmark, Inc.,* 897 F.Supp. 511 (Kan. 1995)]

Business Planning Tip

The following questions of credit applicants are prohibited under ECOA:

1. Are you receiving public assistance income?
Comment: Applicant may voluntarily disclose income if relying on it to obtain credit but need not disclose it.

2. Are you planning on starting a family?
Comment: Questions about family and marital status are prohibited.

3. Are you pregnant?
Comment: Questions about family and marital status are prohibited.

4. Are you married?
Comment: Applicant can voluntarily disclose marriage if she is relying on spouse's income.

5. Please circle: Miss, Ms., Mrs., Mr.
Comment: Would reveal marital status.

6. Will your spouse serve as a guarantor?
Comment: Would reveal marital status.

7. Do you have alimony or child support income?
Comment: Cannot require disclosure; applicant could reveal if relying on income to qualify.

The Truth-in-Lending Act

The **Truth-in-Lending Act** (TILA) is actually part of the **Consumer Credit Protection Act** passed in 1968 by Congress (15 U.S.C. § 1601), which was the first federal statute to deal with credit issues. Its purpose was to make sure debtors were treated fairly through adequate disclosure of credit terms. The Federal Reserve Board was delegated the responsibility for enforcement of the TILA and has promulgated various regulations to carry out the details of the act. One of them, **Regulation Z**, is perhaps better known than the statute that gave rise to it (12 C.F.R. § 226).

TILA Applications

The TILA does not apply to all credit transactions; it is limited to consumer credit transactions, which are contracts for goods or services for personal or home use. Thus, a computer purchased for a law office is not covered by TILA, but a computer purchased for the home is.

Wherever consumer credit is extended, the TILA applies regardless of the type of credit transaction. **Open-end credit transactions,** like the use of a credit card, are covered under the TILA. **Closed-end transactions,** also covered under the TILA, are those in which the debtor is buying a certain amount and repaying it. A loan to buy a car that will be paid back over a fixed time, such as four years, is a closed-end transaction.

Open-End Disclosure Requirements

In charge card credit arrangements, the creditor has several responsibilities at different stages in the transaction. When a debtor is first sent the credit card, the creditor must include the following information: what the interest (finance) charges and annual percentage rate are for charges on the credit card; when bills will be sent; what to do about questions on the bills; and when payments are due.

The monthly bill that the creditor is required to send must contain the balance from the last statement, payments and credits made during the billing period, new charges made during the billing period, and computation of finance charges.

↓ DETACH HERE AND KEEP LOWER PART FOR YOUR RECORDS ↓

DATE	STORE	REFERENCE #	DEPT. #	MERCHANDISE AND TRANSACTION DESCRIPTION	PURCHASES	PAYMENTS/CREDITS
AUG 2	RE	0810014	21	MISSES SUITS	217.19	
AUG 2	RE	0840051	146	GIRLS ACCESS./LINGERIE &		
AUG 2	RE	0840051	61	TODDLERS CLOTHING	121.16	
AUG 2	RE	0930042	404	LANCOME	23.32	
AUG 2	RE	1580015	110	CLUBHOUSE	96.99	

CLOSING DATE	PREVIOUS BALANCE	PLUS: FINANCE CHARGE	PLUS: TOTAL PURCHASES	LESS: TOTAL PAYMENTS AND CREDITS	NEW BALANCE	ACCOUNT NUMBER	
AUG 22 89	0.00	0.00	458.66	0.00	458.66	PAYMENT FOR CURRENT BILLING CYCLE	45.00
						PLUS PAST DUE AMOUNT	0.00
						EQUALS TOTAL MINIMUM PAYMENT DUE	45.00
						DUE DATE	SEP 17

Periodic Rate	Applied to following portion of Previous Balance	ANNUAL PERCENTAGE RATE
1.65	0.00	19.8

PLANNING A MAJOR PURCHASE? ASK ABOUT OUR TIME OPTION PLAN (TOP) ACCOUNT. SUBJECT TO APPROVAL, THIS PLAN OFFERS LOWER MONTHLY PAY-MENTS ON PURCHASES EXCEEDING $300 IN SELECTED DEPARTMENTS.

NOTICE: See Reverse Side for Important Information. Purchases or credits not shown will appear on your next statement.

To avoid FINANCE CHARGE on next statement, full payment of New Balance must be received by due date shown above. macy's CALIFORNIA NC

EXHIBIT 15.2 Sample Billing Statement

Other required information on credit card bills includes the following: the dates of the billing period, the free-ride period or the time the debtor has to pay the balance to avoid any finance charges, and where to inquire about billing errors. Any changes in credit terms, billing, or charges must be sent to the debtor at least one month in advance of the change. Exhibit 15.2 is a sample billing statement.

In 1988, the Board of Governors of the Federal Reserve promulgated new rules pursuant to the **Fair Credit and Charge Card Disclosure Act of 1988** for the solicitation of credit card customers. The rules require the disclosure up front of certain information to these potential customers, such as the fees for issuing the card, the annual percentage rate for the card, any finance or transaction charges, and whether a grace period for payment exists. In addition, potential customers must be told how the average daily balance is computed, when payments are due, whether there is a late payment fee, and whether there are charges for going over the credit limit.

The federal law focuses on the need for disclosure of all possible charges that can occur if a customer accepts the card, charges that may entail much more than the finance charges on the balance. Model forms are available for these disclosures and must be given in writing to a customer at the time of application or solicitation.

Credit Cards and Privacy

The FTC found through an investigation that credit card companies were selling lists of their credit card holders, including their purchasing patterns, to marketing firms so that they could engage in targeted marketing. As a result, all credit card companies were required in 2001 to send out a disclosure and election form to all customers. The disclosures explained how the company might use information about the credit card holder and purchasing patterns. The election form permits credit card holders options on disclosure ranging from full disclosure to anyone to complete removal of the customer's name from all mailing lists used for promotional materials.

In its annual report for 1999, Yahoo, Inc., included a disclosure that it was cooperating with the Federal Trade Commission (FTC) in its inquiry into how Internet sites gather personal information about users. Yahoo also filed a Form 8 disclosure with the SEC indicating its cooperation. Yahoo said that it made the disclosure in its financial reports because it is "extremely conservative in legal documents" and downplayed the significance of the FTC inquiry.

The FTC inquiry resulted in new rules for gathering information via the Internet and for curtailing the current activities of many Internet companies. The change has had an impact on the important aspect of mining the Internet for information. With restrictions on use of consumer information obtained through the Internet, the marketing lists are far less target-directed. Advertisers are willing to pay 7 to 10 times as much for ad space that goes to prescreened audiences. Internet providers are able to mine users and provide just such access. If denied that ability, ad revenues would drop.

The FTC also investigated DoubleClick, Inc., for its data-gathering processes. One industry analyst said, "DoubleClick is not doing anything that anyone else isn't doing."

Evaluate the ethical implications of that last statement. Evaluate the strategic choices of Yahoo and others in waiting for the FTC to take action as opposed to taking voluntary action themselves.

Closed-End Disclosure Requirements

In a closed-end contract, in which the amount to be paid is definite from the beginning, the creditor must include in the credit contract the following terms:

1. The amount the debtor is financing
2. The **finance charges,** that is, the rate of interest charged for repayment
3. The **annual percentage rate** (APR), which is the finance charge reflected in a percentage figure
4. The number and amount of payments and when they are due
5. The total cost of financing (this figure is a total of the actual price of the goods or services along with all interest charges that will be paid over the scheduled repayment time)
6. Whether there are any additional penalties such as prepayment penalties or late payment penalties
7. Any security interest (lien or collateral) the creditor has in the goods sold by credit
8. The cost of credit insurance if the debtor is paying for credit insurance

Exhibit 15.3 is an example of a closed-end credit contract.

Errors on the form or disclosure are viewed in light of their seriousness as well as the overall picture presented to the consumer. Recent amendments to the TILA eliminated the once petty and highly technical violations so costly to creditors for an inconsequential omission.

Big Wheel Auto   Alice Green

ANNUAL PERCENTAGE RATE	FINANCE CHARGE	Amount Financed	Total of Payments	Total Sales Price
The cost of your credit as a yearly rate.	The dollar amount the credit will cost you.	The amount of credit provided to you or on your behalf.	The amount you will have paid after you made all payments as requested.	The total cost of your purchase on credit including your down payment of $ *1500—*
14.84%	$ *1496.80*	$ *6107.50*	$ *7604.30*	$ *9129.30*

You have the right to receive at this time an itemization of the Amount Financed.
☐ I want an itemization. ☒ I do not want an itemization.

Your payment schedule will be:

Number of Payments	Amount of Payments	When Payments are Due
36	$ *211.23*	*Monthly beginning 6-1-95*

Insurance
Credit life insurance and credit disability insurance are not required to obtain credit, and will not be provided unless you sign and agree to pay the additional cost.

Type	Premium*	Signature
Credit Life	$ *120—*	I want credit life insurance. *Alice Green* ___ Signature
Credit Disability		I want credit disability insurance. ___ Signature
Credit Life and Credit Disability		I want credit life and disability insurance. ___ Signature

Security: You are giving a security interest in: ☒ the goods being purchased.
☐ _____.

Filing fee $ *12.50*   **Non-filing Insurance** $_____
Late charge: If a payment is late you will be charged $10.00

Prepayment: If you pay early, you
☐ may   ☐ will not   have to pay a penalty.
☒ may   ☐ will not   be entitled to a refund of part of the finance charge.

See your contract documents for any additional information about nonpayment, default, any required repayment in full before the scheduled date, and prepayment refunds and penalties.

I have received a copy of this document.

Alice Green _____   *5-1-99*
Signature   Date

*Means an estimate

EXHIBIT 15.3 Sample Closed-End Credit Contract

In addition to ensuring adequate disclosures in credit contracts, Regulation Z covers advertising that includes credit terms. If any part of the credit arrangement is mentioned in an advertisement, all terms must be disclosed. For example, if a creditor advertises payments "as low as $15 per month," the ad must also disclose the APR, the down payment required, and the number of payments.

The following case deals with credit advertising.

CASE 15.2

State v. Terry Buick, Inc.
520 N.Y.S.2d 497 (1987)

$99 per Month plus Fine Print

FACTS

Terry Buick, Inc., is an automobile retailer that displayed across the street-side face of its building large yellow signs in block letters that read:

NO MONEY DOWN INSTANT CREDIT! $99/MO.

Terry Buick was located on Route 9, a very busy public highway in Poughkeepsie, New York. The actual credit terms of the sales were printed on 2¼″ × 3⅜″ stickers, which could be read only by close inspection and were attached to the windshields of cars that were for sale. These small stickers showed the price of the car, the down payment, the term in months, and the average interest rate applied to installment payments. Suit was brought by the state of New York for violation of the credit advertisement regulations of TILA.

JUDICIAL OPINION

BENSON, Justice

This action for an injunction under 15 U.S.C. § 1664 (Truth in Lending Act), General Business Law Article 22-A and CPLR § 6301 enjoining Terry Buick, Inc. from continuing to advertise the terms for credit on vehicles it is selling in an illegal, false and deceptive manner is determined as follows:

The Court viewed the defendant's place of business with the attorneys and examined a number of the windshield stickers. They were legible only upon inspection from a distance of a few feet and set forth the financial details of each offer. Examination of the stickers showed that almost every offering required a down payment to obtain $99 per month financing. Other used cars had only "99/MO" painted on their windshields. According to the testimony of one witness, the salesman did not know the price of several of such cars. He testified that no cars were offered for sale for $2,000 down and $99 per month.

The plaintiff relied heavily upon the testimony of an undercover agent, a woman in the employ of the Attorney General who went to the defendant's place of business in the guise of a prospective purchaser and engaged a salesman in conversation about the

cars. She recorded the conversation secretly and offered the tape, which the Court admitted into evidence. The plaintiff emphasized in argument a statement which the salesman made to the plaintiff's agent in which he admitted that the purpose of the advertising was to capture people's attention as they drove by and get them into the dealership.

The Truth in Lending statutes which govern the defendant's conduct are 15 U.S.C. § 1664(d) and New York General Business Laws §§ 350 and 350-a. The Federal statute is amplified by Regulation Z, 12 C.F.R. § 226.24. State courts have concurrent jurisdiction to enforce the Federal statute.

§ 1664(d) reads as follows:

If any advertisement . . . states the amount of the down-payment, if any, the amount of any installment payment, the dollar amount of any finance charge, or the number of installments or the period of repayment, then the advertisement shall state all of the following items . . .

1. the downpayment, if any;

2. the terms of repayment;

3. the rate of the finance charge expressed as an annual percentage rate.

The regulation adopted pursuant to the statute requires that "The creditor shall make the disclosures required by this subpart clearly and conspicuously."

The Court's inspection of the defendant's place of business and its advertising material showed beyond question that the announcement signs were a "come on" designed to lure the eager seeker of a good deal. It also showed that "what you see is not what you get." We have not given the testimony of the undercover agent much weight. It was a contrived tactic practiced upon a relatively guileless salesman by a young woman who pretended to be a purchaser. Her testimony is not necessary, however, to convince the Court that defendant's public announcement of its deals fell far short of the candid display which the law requires. The law requires full disclosure described in the plain language of the statute. A look at the defendant's advertising scheme leads directly to the conclusion that it was designed to attract customers by half truths or falsity. No customer could buy a car on the terms boldly announced on the face of the building. The defendant's intentions did not have to be explained by testimony. No undercover agent was needed to obtain admissions. The message spoke for itself and could not be misread. It was "misleading in a material respect."

Truth in lending laws were not adopted for the canny shopper. They were made for the gullible and those easily led. . . . "In weighing a statement's capacity, tendency or effect in deceiving or misleading customers, we do not look to the average customer but to the vast multitude which the statutes were enacted to safeguard, including the ignorant, the unthinking and the credulous who, in making purchases, do not stop to analyze but are governed by appearances and general impressions." The plaintiff was not required to show that anyone had been deceived or that the advertising had injured anyone. It met its burden by showing its misleading effect.

The defendant's violation of Federal and New York State truth in lending laws has been demonstrated.

The motion for an order granting a preliminary injunction enjoining the defendant Terry Buick, Inc. from continuing to advertise the terms for credit on vehicles it is selling in an illegal, false and deceptive manner is granted.

CASE QUESTIONS

1. Describe the location of the large credit terms.
2. Where were the details of the credit transaction explained?
3. Did the court need the testimony concerning the salesman's words?
4. Did it matter that no one was deceived by the ads?
5. What will the court order Terry to do?

Credit Card Liabilities

Regulation Z provides protection for credit card holders in addition to the required open-end disclosures. These additional protections are designed to limit the liability of a debtor for unauthorized use of a credit card.

First, a creditor cannot send an unsolicited credit card to a debtor. The debtor must have applied for the card or consented to have one sent. This protection is necessary so that debtors will be aware of what cards are coming and will know when to report losses or thefts.

Second, even if a credit card is stolen, Regulation Z provides dollar limitations for debtor liability. The maximum amount of liability a debtor can have for the misuse of a credit card is $50. This liability limitation applies only if the debtor takes the appropriate steps for notifying the creditor of the theft or loss. The procedures for notification are given when the credit card is first sent to the debtor.

C O N S I D E R . . .

15.3 Suppose an employee of a firm forged a credit application for his company and then used the card for personal purchases. Would the credit card issuer be liable? Should the issuer verify the request and check references? [*Transamerica Ins. Co. v. Standard Oil Co.*, 325 N.W.2d 210 (N.D. 1981)]

Canceling Credit Contracts: Regulation Z Protections

In addition to all the usual disclosures for a closed-end contract, certain types of credit contracts must include a **three-day cooling-off period** for the debtor, which is a buyer's protection for "cold feet." The buyer has the right to rescind certain types of credit contracts anytime during the seventy-two hours immediately following execution of a credit contract.

The types of credit contracts covered by the cooling-off period are those in which the creditor takes a security interest in the debtor's home. For example, if Alfie is installing a solar hot water system in his home, has purchased it on credit, and is giving the solar company a lien on his house, the three-day period applies; Alfie has three days to change his mind after he signs the contract. The three-day period also applies to **home solicitation sales,** which are those in which the buyer is first approached in her home by the seller/creditor. The protection here allows the buyer to recoup from any sales pressure that might have been used.

Where the three-day rescission period applies, the creditor must include both a description of the rights in the contract and a full explanation of the procedures the debtor should follow to rescind the contract during the three-day period.

Under the **Home Equity Loan Consumer Protection Act of 1988,** additional disclosures are required for those transactions in which consumers use their homes as security for the credit. These additional disclosures must explain that in the event the consumer does not pay the debt, she could lose the dwelling because it could be sold to pay the debt. The three-day rescission period also applies to home equity credit lines. If notice of this three-day rescission right is not given to the homeowner/debtor, the right of rescission will continue for three years. Variable rate loans require specific disclosures on maximum increases in interest rates and the impact on payments.

Exhibit 15.4 is an example of a three-day cancellation provision.

TILA Penalties

The TILA provides specific penalties for violations of disclosure provisions. A creditor is liable to an individual for twice the amount of finance charges and for attorney fees of the debtor. The minimum recovery for an individual is $100 and the maximum, $1,000. A group of debtors bringing a class action against a creditor can collect the lesser of $500,000 or 1 percent of the creditor's net worth as damages.

Fair Credit Billing Act

The **Fair Credit Billing Act** affords debtors the opportunity to challenge the figures on an open-end transaction monthly statement. Errors on credit card accounts are covered by this act and, to a lesser degree, by Regulation Z. Creditors are required to supply on the monthly statement an address or phone number to write or call in the event a debtor has questions or challenges regarding the bill. The language must read: "IN CASE OF ERRORS, CALL OR WRITE . . ."

Under the act, debtors can collect damages if they comply with all the act's procedural requirements. First, a debtor must notify the creditor of any errors within sixty days of the receipt of the statement. The notification must be in writing for the damage sections to apply. If a creditor supplies a phone number for inquiries, the notice must explain that oral protests do not preserve all Regulation Z rights. The written protest of the debtor must include the debtor's name, the account number, and a brief explanation of the claimed error.

Once the creditor has received the written protest, thirty days are allotted for the creditor to acknowledge to the debtor receipt of the protest. The creditor has ninety days from receipt of the protest to take final action, either giving the debtor's account a credit or reaffirming that the charges are valid.

H-9 Rescission Model Form (Refinancing)

NOTICE OF RIGHT TO CANCEL

Your Right to Cancel
You are entering into a new transaction to increase the amount of credit provided to you. We acquired a [mortgage/lien/security interest] [on/in] your home under the original transaction and will retain that [mortgage/lien/security interest] in the new transaction. You have a legal right under federal law to cancel the new transaction, without cost, within three business days from whichever of the following events occurs last:

(1) the date of the new transaction, which is _____; or
(2) the date you received your new Truth-in-Lending disclosures; or
(3) the date you received this notice of your right of cancel.

If you cancel the new transaction, your cancellation will apply only to the increase in the amount of credit. It will not affect the amount that you presently owe or the [mortgage/ lien/security interest] we already have [on/in] your home. If you cancel, the [mortgage/lien/security interest] as it applies to the increased amount is also cancelled. Within 20 calendar days after we receive your notice of cancellation of the new transaction, we must take the steps necessary to reflect the fact that our [mortgage/lien/security interest] [on/in] your home no longer applies to the increase of credit. We must also return any money you have given to us or anyone else in connection with the new transaction.

You may keep any money we have given you in the new transaction until we have done the things mentioned above, but you must then offer to return the money at the address below. If we do not take possession of the money within 20 calendar days of your offer, you may keep it without further obligation.

How to Cancel
If you decide to cancel the new transaction, you may do so by notifying us in writing, at
_____ (creditor's name and business address).

You may use any written statement that is signed and dated by you and states your intention to cancel, or you may use this notice by dating and signing below. Keep one copy of this notice because it contains important information about your rights.

If you cancel by mail or telegram, you must send the notice no later than midnight of _____ (date) _____ (or midnight of the third business day following the latest of the three events listed above). If you send or deliver your written notice to cancel some other way, it must be delivered to the above address no later than that time.

I WISH TO CANCEL

_____   _____
Consumer's Signature   Date

EXHIBIT 15.4 Three-Day Cancellation Notice

For information on debtor's rights and credit issues, visit the National Foundation for Credit Counseling:
http://www.nfcc.org

During the time the creditor is considering the debtor's protest, the debtor is not required to pay the questioned amount or any finance charges on that amount. If the charges are in fact accurate, the debtor will be charged for the finance charges during this time period. If the creditor fails to comply with any of the requirements or deadlines on bill protests, the debtor can be excused from payment even if the charges disputed were actually accurate.

Fair Credit Reporting Act

Review the Fair Credit Reporting Act:
http://www4.law.cornell.edu/uscode/

The **Fair Credit Reporting Act** (FCRA) is designed to provide debtors some rights and protections regarding the credit information held by third parties about them. Before the passage of the FCRA, many debtors were denied the right to see their credit reports and were often victims of inaccurate reports. The FCRA brought credit reports out in the open.

When the FCRA Applies

The FCRA applies to consumer reporting agencies, which are third parties (not creditors or debtors) that compile, evaluate, and sell credit information about **consumer debt** and debtors. Commercial credit reporting agencies and commercial debtors are not subject to FCRA standards.

Limitations on FCRA Disclosures

Under the FCRA, consumer reporting agencies can disclose information only to the following:

1. A debtor who asks for his own report
2. A creditor who has the debtor's signed application for credit
3. A potential employer
4. A court pursuant to a subpoena

When a debtor files for credit, she has the right to know where a credit report came from. However, the creditor cannot show the report to the debtor, who must get the report through a credit reporting agency.

Consumer agencies are limited not only as to whom disclosures can be made but also as to what can be disclosed. The following are the general limitations on debtor disclosures:

1. No disclosure of bankruptcies that occurred more than ten years ago
2. No disclosure of lawsuits finalized more than seven years ago
3. No disclosure of criminal convictions and arrests that have been disposed of more than seven years ago

When a debtor applies for a loan of more than $50,000 or a job that pays more than $20,000, these limitations on disclosures do not apply.

Visit two sites for companies that handle credit reports:
http://www.equifax.com
http://www.transunion.com

Under the FCRA, debtors have not only the right to see reports but also the right to make corrections of inaccurate information included in those reports. A debtor simply notifies the reporting agency of the alleged error. If the agency acknowledges the error, the debtor's report must be corrected and anyone who has received a report on that debtor during the previous two years must be notified.

If the agency still stands by the information challenged by the debtor, the debtor has the right to have included in the credit report a 100-word statement explaining her position on the matter. This statement is then included with the actual credit report in all future reports sent to third parties.

The following case deals with a problem of an inaccurate credit report.

CASE 15.3

Stevenson v. *TRW, Inc.*
987 F.2d 288 (5th Cir. 1993)

The Father with the Prodigal Son's Credit Rating

FACTS

TRW, Inc., is one of the nation's largest credit reporting agencies. Subscribing companies report to TRW both the credit information they obtain when they grant credit to a consumer and the payment history of the consumer. TRW then compiles a credit report on that consumer to distribute to other subscribers from whom the consumer has requested credit.

John M. Stevenson is a 78-year-old real estate and securities investor. In late 1988 or early 1989, Mr. Stevenson began receiving numerous phone calls from bill collectors regarding arrearages in accounts that were not his. Stevenson first spoke with TRW's predecessor, Chilton's, to try to correct the problem. When TRW purchased Chilton's, Mr. Stevenson began calling TRW's office in Irving, Texas. In August 1989, he wrote TRW and obtained a copy of his credit report dated September 6, 1989. He discovered many errors in the report. Some accounts belonged to another John Stevenson living in Arlington, Texas, and some appeared to belong to his estranged son, John Stevenson, Jr. In all, Mr. Stevenson disputed approximately 16 accounts, seven inquiries, and much of the identifying information.

The reverse side of the credit report contained a printed notice describing how consumers could send a written dispute of the accuracy of their credit reports to the local TRW office. Mr. Stevenson, however, called TRW to register his complaint and then wrote TRW's president and CEO on October 6, 1989, requesting that his credit report be corrected. His letter worked its way to TRW's consumer relations department by October 20, 1989, and on November 1, 1989, that office began its reinvestigation by sending consumer dispute verification forms (CDVs) to subscribers that had reported the disputed accounts. The CDVs ask subscribers to check whether the information they have about a consumer matches the information in TRW's credit report. Subscribers who receive CDVs typically have 20 to 25 working days to respond. If a subscriber fails to respond or indicates that TRW's account information is incorrect, TRW deletes the disputed information. Mr. Stevenson understood from TRW that the entire process should take from three to six weeks.

As a result of its initial investigation, TRW removed several of the disputed accounts from Mr. Stevenson's report by November 30, 1989.

TRW retained one of the remaining accounts on the report because the subscriber insisted that the account was Mr. Stevenson's. The others were still either pending or contained what TRW called "positive information." It also began to appear that Mr. Stevenson's estranged son had fraudulently obtained some of the disputed accounts by using his father's Social Security number. This information led TRW to add a warning statement in December 1989, advising subscribers that Mr. Stevenson's identifying information had been used without his consent to obtain credit. Meanwhile, Mr. Stevenson paid TRW a fee and joined its Credentials Service, which allowed him to monitor his credit report as each entry was made. TRW finally completed its investigation on February 9, 1990. By then, TRW claimed that all disputed accounts containing "negative" credit information had been removed. Inaccurate information, however, either continued to appear on Stevenson's reports or was reentered after TRW had deleted it.

Mr. Stevenson filed suit in Texas state court alleging both common law libel and violations of the Fair Credit Reporting Act (FCRA). TRW removed the case to federal court, and on October 2, 1991, the case was tried before a federal court without a jury. The district court granted judgment for Mr. Stevenson on both the libel and FCRA claims, and TRW appealed.

JUDICIAL OPINION

WILLIAMS, Circuit Judge

Congress enacted FCRA "to require that consumer reporting agencies adopt reasonable procedures for meeting the needs of commerce for consumer credit, personnel, insurance, and other information in a manner which is fair and equitable to the consumer, with regard to the confidentiality, accuracy, relevancy, and proper utilization of such information. . . ." To guard against the use of inaccurate or

(continued)

arbitrary information in evaluating an individual for credit, insurance, or employment, Congress further required that consumer reporting agencies "follow reasonable procedures to assure maximum possible accuracy of the information concerning the individual about whom" a credit report relates.

Consumers have the right to see their credit information and to dispute the accuracy or completeness of their credit reports. When it receives a complaint, a consumer reporting agency must reinvestigate the disputed information "within a reasonable period of time" and "promptly delete" credit information that has been found to be inaccurate or unverifiable. (15 U.S.C. § 1681i(a).) The parties here stipulated that TRW began its reinvestigation within a reasonable period of time after receiving Stevenson's written dispute. Nevertheless, the court found that TRW had negligently and willfully violated § 1681i(a) by not deleting inaccurate and unverifiable information promptly and by allowing deleted information to reappear.

The record, however, contains evidence from which the district court could find that TRW did not delete unverifiable or inaccurate information promptly. First, TRW did not complete its reinvestigation until February 9, 1990, although TRW's subscribers were supposed to return the CDVs by December 4, 1989. Second, § 1681i(a) requires prompt deletion if the disputed information is inaccurate or unverifiable. If a subscriber did not return a CDV, TRW claims that it deleted the disputed information as unverifiable. Yet, some disputed accounts continued to appear on Stevenson's credit report for several weeks. One subscriber failed to return the CDV, but its account appeared on the report issued on February 9, 1990. Another subscriber returned its CDV by December 4, 1989, indicating that TRW's information was inaccurate, yet the information was not deleted until after February 9, 1990.

Allowing inaccurate information back onto a credit report after deleting it because it is inaccurate is negligent. Additionally, in spite of the complexity of Stevenson's dispute, TRW contacted the subscribers only through the CDVs. Although testimony at trial revealed that TRW sometimes calls subscribers to verify information, it made no calls in Stevenson's case. TRW relied solely on the CDVs despite the number of disputed accounts and the allegations of fraud. TRW also relied on the subscribers to tell TRW whether to delete information from Stevenson's report. In a reinvestigation of the

accuracy of credit reports, a credit bureau must bear some responsibility for evaluating the accuracy of information obtained from subscribers.

The bureau had exhibited no ill will toward the plaintiff and had acted to fix the problem. Likewise, TRW provided Stevenson's credit report on request, did not conceal information about his report, investigated the disputed accounts, and attempted to resolve the complaints. TRW moved slowly in completing its investigation and was negligent in its compliance with the prompt deletion requirement. The record does not reveal, however, any intention to thwart consciously Stevenson's right to have inaccurate information removed promptly from his report.

TRW maintains that most of Stevenson's distress was the result of the many calls he received from creditors of the fraudulently obtained accounts. TRW correctly questions the relevance of these creditors' calls to violations of FCRA. Nearly all of these calls occurred before Stevenson filed his written dispute and TRW began its reinvestigation. Only after that did the FCRA violations occur. Stevenson's distress because of creditors' calls arose before TRW's FCRA violations.

The record reveals evidence, however, that Stevenson suffered mental anguish over his lengthy dealings with TRW after he disputed his credit report. First, Stevenson testified that it was a "terrific shock" to him to discover his bad credit rating after maintaining a good credit reputation since 1932. Second, Stevenson was denied credit three times during TRW's reinvestigation: by Bloomingdale's, by Bank One, and by Gabbert's Furniture Company. Stevenson testified that he had to go "hat in hand" to the president of Bank One, who was a business associate and friend, to explain his problems with TRW. As a result, he obtained credit at Bank One. Third, Stevenson had to explain his credit woes to the president of the First City Bank Colleyville when he opened an account there. With a new president at First City Bank, Stevenson had to explain his situation again. Despite the fact that he was ultimately able to obtain credit, Stevenson testified to experiencing "considerable embarrassment" from having to detail to business associates and creditors his problems with TRW. Finally, Stevenson spent a considerable amount of time since he first disputed his credit report trying to resolve his problems with TRW.

The district court properly found that Stevenson had suffered humiliation and embarrassment from TRW's violations of FCRA. We affirm the award of

$30,000 in actual damages based upon the finding of mental anguish. We also affirm the award of $20,700 in attorney's fees.

CASE QUESTIONS

1. What caused Mr. Stevenson's anguish? Was it the correction process?

2. What suggestions could you offer to TRW to prevent the problems with Mr. Stevenson's credit report?

3. What would you do differently if you were trying to correct your report?

4. Are the damages reasonable?

CONSIDER...

15.4   Jennifer Cushman has a permanent residence in Pennsylvania but attended college in Vermont. In the summer of 1993, an unknown person, possibly a member of her household in Philadelphia, applied under Cushman's name for credit cards from three credit grantors: American Express ("Amex"), Citibank Visa ("Citibank"), and Chase Manhattan Bank ("Chase"). The person provided the credit grantors with Cushman's social security number, address, and other identifying information. Credit cards were issued to that person in Cushman's name, and that person accumulated balances totaling approximately $2,400 on the cards between June of 1993 and April of 1994. All this occurred without Cushman's knowledge.

In August of 1994, an unidentified bill collector informed Cushman that TUC was publishing a consumer credit report indicating that she was delinquent on payments to these three credit grantors. Cushman notified TUC that she had not applied for or used the three credit cards in question, and suggested that a third party had fraudulently applied for and obtained the cards. In response, a TUC clerk called Amex and Chase to inquire whether the verifying information (such as Cushman's name, social security number, and address) in Amex's and Chase's records matched the information in the TUC report. The TUC clerk also asked if Cushman had opened a fraud investigation with the credit grantors. Because the information matched, and because Cushman had not opened a fraud investigation, the information remained in the TUC report. TUC was unable to contact Citibank, so TUC deleted the Citibank entry from the report. TUC's investigations are performed by clerks paid $7.50 per hour and who are expected to perform ten investigations per hour.

There is no evidence that TUC took the necessary steps to obtain access to pertinent documents from the credit grantors that would enable TUC to perform a handwriting comparison. Cushman was denied credit because of the report. She filed suit under the FCRA. Did TUC violate the law? [*Cushman* v. *Trans Union Corp.*, 115 F.3d 220 (3d Cir. 1997)]

Identity Theft

e–commerce

With the increasing use and popularity of the Internet, identity theft has been increasing. In 1997, the Social Security Administration received 7,868 identity theft complaints. By 1999, that number had grown to 30,000. Retailers provide secure sites in order to minimize these thefts through outsiders obtaining access to credit card information, social security numbers, and other background information from sites consumers use to make purchases.

Consumer Leasing Act

Get information on issues in auto leasing:
www.leasetips.com

The **Consumer Leasing Act** is an amendment to TILA that provides disclosure protection for consumers who lease goods. Under this act, the lessor must disclose how much will be paid over the life of the lease, whether any money will be owed at the end of the lease, and whether the lease can be terminated.

In 1998, the Federal Trade Commission (FTC) and the Federal Reserve Board developed a new disclosure form for consumer leases. The new form requires disclosure of the following:

1. The amount due at the lease signing (must be itemized, too)
2. Total of payments
3. Monthly payments and other charges
4. Capitalized cost (shows the actual price of the goods—was previously missing from most lease agreements so as to discourage consumer shopping, especially for cars)
5. Residual value (value at the end of the lease, which helps determine the monthly payments)
6. Rent charge (really is the interest rate)
7. Trade-ins, rebates, and other credits given at signing
8. Early termination conditions and terms
9. Excessive wear, use, and mileage provisions

Examine Article 2A of the UCC:
http://www.law.cornell.edu/ucc/2A/overview.html

Consumer leasing has become an important part of our economy. Recently, Article 2A was added to the Uniform Commercial Code. In this article, which immediately follows the sales article, all aspects of consumer leases are covered. The topics in Article 2A include information about lease contracts, warranties, and remedies.

ENFORCEMENT OF CREDIT TRANSACTIONS

Although a debtor has the benefit of paying over time, a creditor has the worry of trying to ensure payment. A creditor may be able to increase sales by extending credit, but risks of nonpayment also increase with each extension of credit. Fortunately, the law affords creditors some additional protections that can be used to guarantee repayment.

The Use of Collateral: The Security Interest

One way a creditor can have additional assurances of repayment is to obtain a pledge of collateral from the debtor. For goods, this collateral pledge is called a **security interest.** The creation of security interests is governed by Article IX of the Uniform Commercial Code.

A security interest is created by a written agreement called a *security agreement.* Once a security interest is created, the creditor is given the right to repossess the pledged goods in the event the debtor defaults on repayment. When a debtor purchases a car on credit, there is nearly always a security interest in that car that allows the lender the right to repossess the car and sell it to satisfy the loan in the event the debtor defaults. This right to sell gives the creditor some additional assurances that the debt will be repaid. For more information on security interests, see Chapter 16.

Collection Rights of the Creditor

Review the Fair Debt Collection Practices Act:
http://www4.law.cornell.edu/uscode/15/1692.html

If a debtor falls behind on payments, the creditor has the right to proceed with collection tactics. Many creditors refer or sell their delinquent credit accounts to collection agencies. There was a time when some of these agencies engaged in questionable conduct in the collection of debts, including harassing debtors with phone calls and embarrassing them by contacting their friends and relatives. To control abuses in the collection process, Congress passed the **Fair Debt Collections Practices Act** (FDCPA) in 1977. The FDCPA became effective in 1978 and controls a great deal of debt collection. About two-thirds of the states have adopted some form of debt collection statutes. If state law, relative to the federal act, provides the same or greater protection for debtors in the collection process, the state law governs. In states without a collection law, the FDCPA applies.

When the FDCPA Applies
The FDCPA applies to consumer debts and debt collectors. Consumer debts are defined here as they are under the TILA: debts for personal, home, or family purposes. Debt collectors are third-party collectors. The FDCPA does not apply to original creditors collecting their own debts; for example, Sears collecting Sears debts is not governed by the FDCPA. However, if Sears referred its collection accounts to Central Credit Collection Agency, Central Credit would be under the FDCPA. If Sears created its own collection agency with a name other than Sears, the FDCPA would apply to that agency as well.

The FDCPA does not apply to the collection of commercial accounts or to banks and the Internal Revenue Service. In a rule revision, attorneys collecting debts for clients were made subject to coverage of the FDCPA.

C O N S I D E R . . .

15.5 Telecredit Service Corporation's business is the collection of dishonored checks. Telecredit purchases these checks and then contacts the drawers to collect the funds. Stanley Holmes wrote a $315 check to Union Park Pontiac that was dishonored. Union Park sold the check to Telecredit, and Telecredit sent letters and made contacts to collect the check. Some contacts would be violations of FDCPA, but Telecredit says it is not covered by FDCPA because it is not collecting the debts of another. Is this correct? [*Holmes* v. *Telecredit Service Corp.*, 736 F. Supp. 1289 (D. Del. 1990)]

Collector Requirements under the FDCPA
One of the requirements for collectors under the FDCPA is written verification of debt. A collector must provide such verification if a debtor asks. The collector must also automatically provide written verification within five days after contacting the debtor. Written verifications must include the following information:

1. The amount of the debt
2. The name of the creditor
3. The debtor's right to dispute the debt and the procedures for doing so. If a debtor disputes a debt, the collector has thirty days to verify the debt and its amount before any collection contact can continue.

Collector Restrictions under the FDCPA

In addition to affirmative disclosure requirements, collectors are subject to certain prohibitions under the FDCPA. The following subsections cover the prohibitions.

Debtor Contact One of the most frequent abuses of collectors prior to the FDCPA was constant debtor contact and harassment. The FDCPA curbs the amount of contact: Debtors cannot be contacted before 8:00 A.M. or after 9:00 P.M., and debtors who work night shifts cannot be disturbed during their sleeping hours in the daytime.

The place of contact is also controlled by the FDCPA: Collectors must avoid contact at inconvenient places. Home contact is permitted, but contact in club, church, or school meetings is prohibited. Collectors can approach debtors at their places of employment unless employers object or have a policy against such contact.

To prevent harassment, the FDCPA gives debtors a chance to "call off" a collector. If a debtor tells the collector that she wants no more contact, the collector must stop and take other steps, such as legal action, to collect the debt. If the debtor is represented by an attorney and gives the name of the attorney to the collector, the collector can contact only the attorney from that point.

Third-Party Contact The FDCPA also prohibits notifying other parties of the debtor's debts and collection problems. However, the debtor's spouse and parents can be contacted regarding the debt. Other parties can be contacted for information, but the collector cannot disclose the reason for the contact. Further, the only information that can be obtained from these third parties is the address, phone number, and place of employment of the debtor.

These third parties cannot be told about the debt, the amount, delinquencies, or any other information about the debtor. The collector must even be careful to use appropriate stationery when writing for information so that the letterhead does not disclose the nature of the collector's business. Postcard contact with the debtor or third parties is prohibited because of the likelihood that others will see the information about the debtor.

Prohibited Acts Collectors have certain other restrictions on their conduct under the FDCPA. The general prohibition in the FDCPA is that collectors cannot "harass, oppress, or abuse" the debtor. Using abusive language or physical force is prohibited. Misrepresenting the authority of a collector is also prohibited, as is posing as a law enforcement official or producing false legal documents. Debtors cannot be threatened with prison or other actions not authorized by law.

The *Trull* case involves an issue of FDCPA violations.

BUSINESS PLANNING TIP

Generating form collection letters by computer must be carefully monitored. The FDCPA imposes notice and content requirements that must flow in sequence. Threatened actions must be taken, or the threat is a violation.

Penalties for FDCPA Violations

The Federal Trade Commission (FTC) is responsible for enforcement of the FDCPA. The FTC can use its cease and desist orders to stop collectors from violating the FDCPA and can also assess penalties for violations. However, the greatest power of enforcement under the FDCPA lies with individual debtors. Debtors who can prove collector violations can collect for actual injuries and mental distress. Debtors can also collect up to $1,000 in addition to actual damages for actions by collectors that are extreme, outrageous, malicious, or repeated. Attorney fees incurred by debtors in bringing their suits are also recoverable.

CASE 15.4

Trull v. *GC Services Ltd. Partnership*
961 F. Supp. 1199 (N.D. Ill. 1997)

Debts, Threats, and FDCPA

FACTS

Lisa Trull owed $68.05 to BMG Music Service. BMG Music Service referred the account to GC Services Limited Partnership for collection. BMG sent the following pieces of correspondence to Trull.

LETTER #1

FOR   : L A TRULL
DATE   : MAY 23, 1995
SUBJECT: BMG MUSIC SERVICE'S CLAIM
            AGAINST L A TRULL

Your account has now been referred to GC Services and we intend to obtain payment from you.

In the process of writing this memorandum to you, this firm has accessed the computer information on you provided by BMG MUSIC SERVICE, which is now contained in our National Database. Please be advised that this information will be used by GC Services, including my office, to proceed with our formal collection procedures to settle your account with BMG MUSIC SERVICE.

If you do not think this debt is a just one, you may want to obtain advice on this question. Otherwise, we will expect payment promptly to remedy this claim. When remitting your payment, detach and return the upper portion of this notice. A return envelope is enclosed for your convenience.

LETTER #2

YOU OWE   : BMG MUSIC SERVICE
ACCOUNT#   : 3683915395
BALANCE DUE : $68.05
June 13, 1995

The debt listed above has been placed with us for collection. (Since you ignored our previous notice, we assume this debt is correct.) We intend to take all appropriate steps to see that you pay it.

Your failure to pay has been listed by BMG MUSIC SERVICE with a National Credit Reporting Bureau as an outstanding delinquency. This delinquent credit report will be maintained and available as part of your personal file by the National Credit Reporting Bureau. This may be used by interested consumer product and service companies, or other creditors in case you should attempt to obtain goods or credit from them.

Pay what you owe and further collection activities on your account will stop. Failure to resolve this delinquent account will result in continued collection activity.

LETTER #3

July 5, 1995
WARNING!

Don't even think about ignoring this notice as you've ignored others in the past requesting you to pay what you owe BMG MUSIC SERVICE.

Buying on credit can be highly convenient. Why run the risk of losing that privilege? You need to take action immediately in order to avoid being labeled as a bad credit risk by BMG MUSIC SERVICE.

Pay your bill and wipe your record clean today!
IMPORTANT NOTICE

YOUR ACCOUNT HAS BEEN TRANSFERRED FROM BMG MUSIC SERVICE TO GC SERVICES' AGENCY MASTER DEBTOR FILE. YOUR PAYMENT MUST BE RECEIVED BY GC SERVICES AT THE ADDRESS INDICATED ABOVE IN ORDER TO ENSURE PROPER CREDIT OR ADJUSTMENT TO YOUR ACCOUNT.

LETTER #4

August 15, 1995

This is the last effort I will be making to settle your account with BMG MUSIC SERVICE.

Your lack of response to date indicates to us that you do not intend to pay for the merchandise you received from BMG MUSIC SERVICE. Your name will be retained as part of our records along with others who, despite their good name and reputation, have shirked their payment responsibility.

Is it not about time you settled this matter, especially in view of the consequences? We are anxious to clear your record as well as ours. Send your payment!
IMPORTANT NOTICE

YOUR ACCOUNT HAS BEEN TRANSFERRED FROM BMG MUSIC SERVICE TO GC SERVICES' AGENCY MASTER DEBTOR FILE. YOUR PAYMENT MUST BE RECEIVED BY GC SERVICES AT

(continued)

THE ADDRESS INDICATED ABOVE IN ORDER TO ENSURE PROPER CREDIT OR ADJUSTMENT TO YOUR ACCOUNT.

Further, each letter concludes with the following sentence: "NOTICE: see reverse side for important consumer information." The reverse side then provides the following in all capital letters:

"This is an attempt to collect a debt and any information obtained will be used for that purpose. Consumer information:

"Unless you, within thirty (30) days after your receipt of GC Services' initial written notice to you concerning this debt, dispute the validity of the debt, or any portion hereof, the debt will be assumed to be valid by GC Services. If you notify GC Services in writing within the above described thirty (30) day period that the debt, or any portion thereof, is disputed, GC Services will obtain verification of the debt or a copy of a judgment against you and a copy of such verification or judgment will be mailed to you by GC Services upon your written request within the above described thirty (30) day period, GC Services will provide you with the name and address of the original creditor, if different from the current creditor.

"The demands for payment in this letter do not reduce your rights to dispute this debt, or any portion thereof, and/or to request verification within the thirty (30) day period as set forth above."

Trull brought suit against GC alleging violations of the FDCPA. GC filed a motion to dismiss Trull's claim.

JUDICIAL OPINION

NORDBERG, District Judge

Plaintiff complains that the correspondence from Defendant violates [the FDCPA].

The Seventh Circuit has identified the "unsophisticated consumer" as "the hypothetical consumer whose reasonable perceptions will be used to determine if collection messages are deceptive or misleading." This standard is designed to protect consumers who are of below-average sophistication or intelligence, uninformed, naive, or trusting, while incorporating an objective element of reasonableness that "shields complying debt collectors from liability for unrealistic or peculiar interpretations of collection letters."

Applying the standard to this case, the Court concludes that an unsophisticated consumer, who has been informed that "This is the last effort I will be making to settle your account with BMG MUSIC SER-

VICE," reasonably could interpret the statement, "Your name will be retained as part of our records along with others who, despite their good name and reputation, have shirked their payment responsibility," followed by a reference to (1) the need to "settle[ ] this matter, especially in view of the consequences," (2) the statement that "[w]e are anxious to clear your record as well as ours," and (3) the "***IMPORTANT NOTICE***" that "YOUR ACCOUNT HAS BEEN TRANSFERRED TO GC SERVICES' AGENCY MASTER DEBTOR FILE," to imply that GC operates a consumer reporting agency that assembles consumer credit information for the purpose of furnishing consumer reports to third parties.

[In] the present case, GC Services has implied that, despite the letter being its last effort to settle the debt, Plaintiff's inclusion in GC Services' "master debtor file" will have "consequences." The reasonable unsophisticated consumer could construe the furnishing of this master debtor file to third parties to be among those vague consequences and, therefore, the purpose behind the "master debtor file." Thus, Trull has sufficiently stated a claim upon which relief may be granted.

Plaintiff further claims in Count II that Exhibit C (Letter #3) simulates a telegram, thus deceptively overstating and misrepresenting the urgency of the communication, in violation of the Act.

Plaintiff's Complaint merely alleges that the letter simulates a telegram, without specifying in what manner. Nevertheless, as the letter is attached to the Complaint, the Court may consider the letter in determining whether Plaintiff states a claim upon which relief may be granted. Plaintiff argues in her responsive brief that the letter of June 13, 1995 simulates a telegram because it is on yellow paper and headed "STAR High Priority Communication" and because of the layout and type face.

The Staff Commentary on the Fair Debt Collection Practices Act advises that "A debt collector may not communicate by a format or envelope that misrepresents the nature, purpose, or urgency of the message. It is a violation to send any communication that conveys to the consumer a false sense of urgency." The only case cited by Plaintiff that held a simulated telegram violates Section 1692e(10) is distinguishable, as the letter was headed "Tell-A-Gram." Nevertheless, assuming, without purporting to decide, that simulating a telegram violates the Act, the Court finds that Plaintiff cannot state such a claim, as even an unsophisticated consumer could not reasonably construe the letter at issue to be a telegram. First, unlike a telegram, the letter was sent through the mail. One who lacks the information to appreciate the distinction would be similarly unaware of the expense that attaches to a telegram and, thus, would not interpret the letter with the same urgency as one who believed it was hand delivered. Further, no derivation of the word telegram appears on the letter; rather, a sentence appears below the heading, stating in all capital letters that "This star high priority letter is being sent to you by GC Services," clearly identifying it as a letter. This is a situation where the standard's objective element of reasonableness "shields complying debt collectors from liability for unrealistic or peculiar interpretations of collection letters." Accordingly, that claim is dismissed, with prejudice.

Plaintiff claims that the correspondence violated Section 1692g in two ways: (1) each letter contained a validation notice, diluting the meaning of the warning and confusing the consumer, and (2) the second letter was sent within 30 days of the initial communication, overshadowing and effectively invalidating the validation notice.

Drawing all reasonable inferences in favor of Plaintiff, the Court finds that it appears beyond doubt that she can prove no set of facts in support of the claim arising from repeated validation notices that would entitle her to relief. The validation notice defines the validation period as being "within thirty (30) days after your receipt of GC Services' *initial* written notice to you concerning this debt." It is unreasonable for even the consumer of below-average sophistication or intelligence, who is uninformed, naive, or trusting, to ignore the word "initial," and, the standard protects the compliant debt collector from a peculiar interpretation.

In contrast, Plaintiff states a claim arising from the letter of June 13, 1996, because it states "Since you ignored our previous notice, we assume this debt is correct," contradicting notice of the thirty-day period before which the debt will be assumed to be valid. The Court finds that an unsophisticated consumer reasonably could be misled reading that statement within the validation period.

CASE QUESTIONS

1. How much money did Trull owe?
2. What was the nature of the four pieces of correspondence?
3. What violations of FDCPA does the court find?
4. Will Trull be permitted to go forward with her suit?

Suits for Enforcement of Debts

Occasionally, collection is ineffective and there is no collateral to repossess. The creditor has few options left but to bring suit to enforce collection of the debt. In bringing a successful suit, the creditor will obtain a **judgment,** which is the court's official document stating that the debtor owes the money and the collector is entitled to that money. However, in debt cases, the judgment is only the beginning. Once the creditor has the judgment, it must be executed to obtain funds.

A judgment is executed by having it attach to various forms of the debtor's property. For example, a judgment can attach to real property. A judgment can also attach to funds by **garnishment,** which is the attachment of a judgment to an account, paycheck, or receivables. Once there is attachment, the creditor is entitled to those funds. The third party holding the funds must comply with the terms of the garnishment and release the appropriate amount of funds to the creditor.

Employees are given some protection under the Consumer Credit Protection Act with respect to garnishments. One such protection is the limitation on the employer's ability to fire employees who have their wages garnisheed by a single creditor.

Re: The Collection Process

Businesses generally try to collect a debt for six months after the first missed payment before they turn the account over to a collection agency. Approximately 3 percent of all consumer debt remains uncollected after six months. That amount is approximately $150 billion.

Of that uncollected amount, almost 60 percent is turned over to collection agencies. The creditor will pass the account from agency to agency in an attempt to collect the money due. It is not unusual for uncollected consumer debts to cycle through three different collection agencies. Of the amount referred to collection agencies by creditors, only 7.5 cents on every dollar is collected and the collection agencies receive 20 to 25 percent of that amount.

Businesses usually refer only those debts over $2,000 to lawyers for litigation. However, all nonpaying debtors are listed in monthly reports to the credit bureaus. In 1996, the fastest-growing type of small business was credit collection and reporting. With all of the increases in credit availability and resulting defaults, the collection and reporting companies have continued to expand in numbers and size.

CONSIDER...

15.6   Clarence J. Ellis was employed by Glover & Gardner as a laborer and carpenter from August 1979 until June 18, 1980. On June 18, 1980, Charles Gardner, the president and owner of Glover & Gardner, received a notice of garnishment of Mr. Ellis's wages and fired Mr. Ellis that day. It was Mr. Ellis's first garnishment. Gardner said he fired Mr. Ellis because of alcoholism, poor job performance, insubordination, and dishonesty. However, Mr. Ellis's separation notice, which was sent to the Tennessee Department of Employment Security, gave as the reason for termination the garnishment. Did Mr. Gardner violate the law? [*Ellis* v. *Glover & Gardner Construction Co.*, 562 F. Supp. 1054 (M.D. Tenn. 1983)]

Under the Consumer Credit Protection Act, the amount that consumer creditors can garnishee on debtor wages is limited to 25 percent of the net wages. Garnishment for past-due child support is limited to 50 percent of net wages.

The End of the Line on Enforcement of Debts: Bankruptcy

Visit the American Bankruptcy Institute for more about bankruptcy: http://www.abiworld.org/home.html

Federal laws afford debtors shelter when their obligations cannot be paid. *Bankruptcy* is the legal process of having a debtor—individual, partnership, corporation, LLC (see Chapter 21)—turn over all nonexempt assets in exchange for a release from debts following the distribution of those assets to creditors. There are three forms of bankruptcy. *Chapter 7* bankruptcy is the liquidation form in which the entity is dissolved or the individuals debts are discharged. *Chapter 11* is the reorganization form in which a business enjoys protection from collection and creditors until a new plan for satisfying the business obligations is approved. *Chapter 13* is the consumer debt adjustment plan under which consumers can be given a new repayment plan for their debts.

Once an individual or business voluntarily declares bankruptcy, all collection efforts must stop. A voluntary petition in bankruptcy provides the debtor with immediate relief from creditors. A debtor can be involuntarily petitioned into bankruptcy

BUSINESS STRATEGY

How to Evaluate Credit Risk

Lawrence B. Lindsey, 41, who earns $123,100 a year, applied for a Toys "Я" Us credit card through the Delaware division of the Bank of New York. He pays his mortgage on time each month and has a clean credit record and job security. Mr. Lindsey's application was rejected; the letter from the bank explained as follows: "We have received your new account application. We regret that we are not able to approve it at this time."

The bank used a computerized scoring system to evaluate credit applications, and Mr. Lindsey's was rejected, according to his letter, because "Multiple companies requested your credit report in the past six months."

Mr. Lindsey was, at the time, a member of the Federal Reserve Board (presently, he is an economic advisor in the Bush Administration), the federal agency that sets interest rates and regulates banks. He has expressed concerns about computerized

© AP/Wide World Photos

credit scoring and has said: "I would expect credit-scoring type procedures to be overwhelmingly dominant by the end of the decade. We will obtain the fairness of the machine but lose the judgments, talents, and sense of justice that only humans can bring to decision making."

Discussion Questions

1. How is computer scoring more fair in credit applications?
2. What are the advantages of credit scoring?
3. Are lenders using computer screening to ensure compliance with the ECOA?
4. Are people unfairly affected by that use?
5. What problems does it create?
6. Do you foresee a time when computer scoring is regulated?
7. Would you use computer scoring for credit extension in your business?

---

by creditors. In an involuntary petition case, the debtor has the opportunity for a hearing. The standard for declaring voluntary bankruptcy is that the individual or business has debts. The standard for creditors petitioning a debtor into involuntary bankruptcy is that the debtor is unable to pay debts as they become due.

Not all debts are discharged in bankruptcy. Alimony, child support, student loans, and taxes are examples of debts that survive bankruptcy.

Bankruptcy reform has been passed in the House and Senate and awaits joint conference committee approval as well as the president's signature. The reforms under the new law include limitations on the exemptions debtors can claim, more stringent requirements for declaring bankruptcy and more types of debts surviving bankruptcy. Also, the reforms would require consumers to first go through the Chapter 13 process before going to Chapter 7 liquidation.

For an update on the status of the bankruptcy bill, visit: http://www.clla.org

BUSINESS PLANNING TIP

When there is any question as to whether a consumer credit transaction is involved or whether a protective statute applies, the question is resolved in favor of the credit applicant. Many businesses treat all credit applications as consumer credit applications and apply the statutes (even though they are not required to do so) so that they can avoid any issues and questions on consumer credit.

INTERNATIONAL CREDIT ISSUES

With the problems in the world economy, bankruptcies are increasing substantially. However, there are significant differences between declaration of bankruptcy in the United States and other countries. In Japan, for example:

- Debtors can keep only kitchen utensils and $1,500 in cash.

ETHICAL ISSUES 15.1

Lindsey Appliances follows a policy of reporting any and all late payments to a credit reporting agency. Lindsey includes a disclosure in its contracts that "late payments, even those late by one day, are reported to credit monitoring agencies." Is Lindsey's policy a fair one?

BIOGRAPHY

JOEL KRISOLOFSKY: HAVE SKILLS, WILL COLLECT

Joel Krisolofsky dials the phone about 300 times a day. Nobody he calls wants to hear from him.

"I want to give you some information that you might not have been aware of," Mr. Krisolofsky tells a Minnesota woman who answers the phone. He cites a figure—$3,271—the charges she and her husband ran up on a credit card and never repaid.

"We're dealing with unemployment," the woman says, as a baby cries in the background. "That's why its hard to meet that."

After 15 minutes of cajoling, Mr. Krisolofsky persuades her to accept a payment schedule in which $75 a month will be deducted automatically from the family's checking account. Hanging up the phone, he notes the easy time he had. "This is like taking candy from a baby," he says.

Mr. Krisolofsky loves collecting debt, and why not? The more than $1 million a year of repayments he reels in makes him the star performer at Abacus Financial Management Services LP, a collection agency here. "He's a very driven individual—no doubt about it," says Bradford J. Gustin, the executive vice president.

And he earns good money. Abacus pays collectors $24,000 plus commission. "This year I will make 95 grand and next year $120,000," says Mr. Krisolofsky, who is 31. "Where else can you make this kind of money without a college degree?"

As more Americans fail to repay debt, collecting has become lucrative work. Bad debt placed with collection agencies soared 39 percent to $117 billion in 1995 from $84 billion in 1994, according to the latest estimates by the American Collectors Association in Minneapolis. During that period, debt collected by agencies rose 40 percent to

$31 billion, says M. Kaulkin & Associates, Inc., a Bethesda, Md., firm that advises on mergers and acquisitions in the industry.

With the field growing so rapidly, the nation's 6,000 collection agencies need more and more collectors. Between 1994 and 2005, agency employment will rise 37 percent, according to a study by the Bureau of Labor Statistics, more than double the 14 percent average growth the bureau projected for all other industries.

Some agencies are growing even faster. Anderson Financial Network, Inc., of Bloomington, Ill., expects to quadruple its collection force by the end of next year to about 2,400. In Phoenix, the workforce at Associated Creditors Exchange, Inc., has increased to 350 from 150 in 18 months and soon will grow by another 75.

Driving this growth is the rising delinquency rate on credit cards. In the second quarter, bank credit card losses climbed to 5.2 percent of total credit card debt outstanding, the highest annualized level in the 14 years that the Federal Deposit Insurance Corp. has tabulated the numbers. Among retailers feeling the pinch, Sears, Roebuck & Co. has said rising credit card charge-offs will hurt fourth-quarter earnings.

MANY KINDS OF DEBT

Besides credit card debt, collection agencies are pursuing the receivables of utilities, wireless-phone companies, and government agencies for such matters as parking tickets, court judgments, child support, and state and municipal taxes. An especially fast-growing category: medical facilities stiffed by uninsured patients.

The industry isn't popular. "If I had a dime for everyone who says they are going to blow us up, I would have a million dollars," says Bruce Passen, president of Abacus Financial.

Debt collectors have been around as long as debt. Many of them resort to intimidation, though the 1977 Fair Debt Collection Practices Act put some limits on it. It restricted collection calls to the hours of 8 A.M. to 9 P.M. and prohibited harassing language and idle threats, such as litigation.

"There are still agencies out there twisting people's arms and making false representations," says Gary Klein, a staff attorney at the National Consumer Law Center, a consumer-advocacy group in Boston. "But there is a sophisticated end of the business that has cleaned up its act quite a bit."

The industry also has an economic incentive to mind its manners: competition. Most debtors have multiple creditors and receive calls from a number of collectors, each wanting the money due it to get top priority. And pleasantry usually works better than intimidation.

The industry is nearly invisible because its clients, the creditors, demand confidentiality, and the law protects the identity of debtors. But several days at Abacus Financial offer some insight into the growth potential and operating procedures of the collection industry.

Abacus collects debt for some major credit card companies, retailers, and medical organizations. Its 150 collectors work in tiny cubicles with two main tools: a telephone, with headset, and a computer screen that pulls up debtor names, phone numbers, credit records, and even neighbors' phone numbers.

The room gets noisy as the collectors talk to debtors, joke with each other and, on rare occasions, lose their temper with someone on the other end of the line. "Why do you have to use that kind of language with me?" one collector bellows into his headset. "Did your dog die, or has your wife been on your back?"

Mr. Krisolofsky scoffs at the collector: "I'll show you someone who is butting heads during a call. I'll show you somebody who does not make a commission."

Unlike many collectors, who often go to the vending room to guzzle beverages, Mr. Krisolofsky rarely leaves his desk. He sometimes goes three hours between breaks, making call after call. "You got to get into a zone," he says. He doesn't mind the grind. "It beats manual labor," he says. "You get to use your brains and communicate with customers."

A Buddha paperweight sits on his desk, beside pinned-up slogans such as "Values: Integrity, Love, Friendship, Money."

Mr. Krisolofsky, a muscular 235-pounder with the loudest and most animated voice in the office, nonetheless says the most important part of the job is to listen and offer counsel, even when debtors are swearing. "Even angry people tell you their problems," he says. "You have to read between the lines."

He favors positive reinforcement.

"It's that you want to pay, but you just can't pay now," he says to a woman who owes $5,440 in credit card debt.

"I had perfect credit until this year," she confides. "I am a single parent. I'm the one I have to depend on. I got divorced."

He suggests paying $100 a month on the debt, on which the creditor, after writing it off, is no longer charging interest. "At least there is no interest, and all this will go toward your balance," he says. After she agrees to the plan, he ends the call with, "Best of luck to you, ma'am."

Not that he can't get tough. "If we can't work out something temporarily, I am going to have to recommend further action," he says to a South Carolina woman who owes $5,893 in credit card debt. (Although he doesn't expressly threaten litigation, because Abacus doesn't sue debtors, a debtor could infer that that might be the next step—and the creditor could eventually decide to file suit.)

Even here, though, Mr. Krisolofsky is quick to soften his tone and add: "I just want to know where you stand and put our heads together to create a win-win situation." After he describes the benefits of cleaning up her credit record, the woman agrees to make four $150 payments over four months via Western Union.

Collectors try to get the full balance first. They also sometimes offer settlements at 85 cents on the dollar. But if they see no hope of getting even that, they negotiate monthly payments because some money is better than nothing. In October, Mr. Krisolofsky brought in $66,251 in such payments, either through Western Union, postdated checks, or direct drafts from checking accounts—payments he calls "my annuities."

Mr. Krisolofsky, a collector since age 22, mainly seeks payments for one major credit card company and for issuers of student loans. Last year, he collected $1,180,000 and expects to hit $1.5 million this year. The son of a debt collector, he says the business is in his blood.

(continued)

Most of his calls get an answering machine. "This is Mr. Kay from Abacus Financial," Mr. Krisolofsky usually says. "It's important that you return my call." He uses the alias "Mr. Kay" because it is easier to pronounce and remember than his real name and to protect himself from vindictive debtors.

A recent call on a delinquent student loan is answered by the debtor's mother in Illinois. The debtor isn't home. His mother asks why Mr. Krisolofsky is calling, but the law allows collectors to say that only to the debtor. She says she is suffering from cancer and asks him not to call back.

"Ma'am, I'm sorry, but I am going to have to keep calling," he says. She screams hysterically into the phone and hangs up.

That prompts calls of complaint first from the woman's husband and then from the debtor himself, who swears loudly into the phone. "If you are going to talk to me like that, you better start with Mister," says Mr. Krisolofsky, grinning. "Sometimes you have to fight a nasty attitude with a sense of humor," he says later. Mr. Krisolofsky is confident that he will collect the debt because the man has a good credit record and probably won't want an unpaid student loan to spoil it.

Abacus's second-highest-performing collector, Jerome Bridges, is empathetic with debtors. Seven years ago, he and his wife had a premature baby that saddled the family with $70,000 in medical debt. His credit card bills soared because his wife stopped working to care for the baby.

"I got a lot of calls from bill collectors," recalls Mr. Bridges, now 39. He himself was a collector at the time. "It humbles you. It makes you want to treat people like you want to be treated."

Compared with Mr. Krisolofsky, Mr. Bridges uses a low-key approach. "I call it seasoning," he says. He gives a demonstration after tracking down a debtor at the bookstore where the man works. Mr. Bridges tells the debtor, "It sounds like you are a person who wants to take care of their responsibility but is a little stressed because you have some bills that are behind." He adds that his bad credit will hurt him in applying for jobs.

The man concedes that much, saying he couldn't get a better-paying job because employers did credit checks on him. He earns $18,000 a year, has $18,000 in bad debt on seven credit cards and $19,000 in student loans outstanding.

Mr. Bridges asks the man what he can pay per month. The man begrudgingly says $75. Mr. Bridges raises it to $100 and sets up a $100 direct draft from the man's bank account. Hanging up, Mr. Bridges excitedly pumps one arm in the air.

On another call, Mr. Bridges learns that the debtor has scheduled a meeting with a bankruptcy attorney. This news is discouraging because collection activity must stop once a debtor files for bankruptcy-court protection, as record numbers of people are doing these days.

But most debtors don't, and Mr. Bridges says that assures him, and many others, of a job. By next March, Abacus plans to more than double its number of collectors to nearly 400. And just wait until a recession hits, says Mr. Passen, its president. "There are not going to be enough of us to go around."

Source: Robert Berner, "Dun Deals: As Many People Sink into Debt, One Group of Workers Prospers," *Wall Street Journal,* November 20, 1997, A1, A15. Reprinted by permission of *The Wall Street Journal,* © 1997 Dow Jones & Company, Inc. All Rights Reserved Worldwide.

- A meeting, called *dogeza,* is held wherein the company owner sits on the floor among creditors and begs for forgiveness while the creditors are permitted to yell abusive epithets at the debtor.

Other aspects of Japanese law make a company's failure and the impact on individual business people very different. Japanese creditors routinely require guarantors, even on business debts, and most business people rely on family for such guarantors. As a result, many in-laws find themselves responsible for debt when the business of their son-in-law fails. The divorce rate for executives of bankrupt Japanese business people is twice that of the national average.

The suicide rate for failed Japanese business people is 50 percent greater than in the general population. Under Japanese law, insurance companies do pay benefits even when death results from suicide so long as the policy has been in effect for at least one year. And the suicide rate for people with insurance policies is 50 percent higher than in the general population.

SUMMARY

What are the statutes that affect credit contracts?

- Usury—charging interest in excess of the statutory maximum

- Equal Credit Opportunity Act—federal law prohibiting denial of credit on the basis of sex, race, color, religion, national origin, age, marital status, public assistance income, alimony, or child support income and plans for additional family

- Truth-in-Lending Act—federal law governing disclosures in credit contracts

- Consumer Credit Protection Act—first federal statute on credit disclosure requirements

- Open-end transactions—credit card transactions

- Closed-end transactions—preestablished-amount finance contract, as in the financing of a television purchase

- Fair Credit and Charge Card Disclosure Act of 1988—federal law governing solicitation of credit card customers

- Regulation Z—federal regulation governing credit disclosures

- Three-day cooling-off period—right of rescission on credit contracts initiated in the home

- Home Equity Loan Consumer Protection Act of 1988—federal law requiring disclosures for home equity consumer loans

- Fair Credit Billing Act—federal law governing rights of debtors to dispute credit card charge

- Fair Credit Reporting Act—federal law regulating disclosure of credit information to and by third parties

- Consumer Leasing Act—federal law governing consumer lease transactions

How are credit contracts enforced?

- Security interest—pledge of collateral for credit

- Fair Debt Collections Practices Act—federal law regulating collection of consumer debt by third parties

- Judgment—court order authorizing collection of money from party

- Garnishment—attachment of account, paycheck, or receivables to collect judgment

- Bankruptcy—federal process of collecting assets to pay creditors and discharge debts.

- Chapter 7—liquidation bankruptcy

- Chapter 11—reorganization bankruptcy

- Chapter 13—consumer debt adjustment plan

QUESTIONS AND PROBLEMS

1. In May 1976, TRW (a credit reporting agency) issued a consumer report on Bennie E. Bryant in connection with his application for a federally insured home loan under the Veterans Administration. The consumer report had several inaccuracies, and Mr. Bryant went to TRW to point out the matters needing correction. For unrelated reasons, the mortgage did not close.

In August 1976, Mr. Bryant applied for another mortgage. On September 28, TRW called the mortgage company to let them know his credit report would be unfavorable. When the mortgage company notified Mr. Bryant, he again went to TRW offices and explained that the September report contained new inaccuracies in addition to those that were part of the May report. After this meeting, a memo about possible inaccuracies was placed in Mr. Bryant's file. However,

the credit report without corrections was issued to the mortgage company on September 30. No follow-through had been done on the file memo.

Mr. Bryant's August mortgage application was originally denied. After personal efforts on his part, however, the credit report was corrected and the mortgage was eventually given.

Does Mr. Bryant have any rights and protections? [*Bryant v. TRW, Inc.*, 689 F.2d 72 (6th Cir. 1982)]

2. Michael S. Lamar had held a First USA Bank credit card for five years. He paid the entire balance each month. In July 1998, he missed the July 26th due date for his payment. He was assessed a $29 late fee on charges of $21.66. Upon complaint, First USA rescinded the charge but warned that it does so only once each year. Are these charges legal?

3. Maurice Miller obtained an American Express credit card in 1966, and his wife, Virginia, was given a supplementary card. Her card had a different number, was issued in her name, and had a separate annual fee. When Mr. Miller died in 1979, American Express canceled both credit cards. Mrs. Miller sued for violation of the ECOA. Has there been a violation? [*Miller* v. *American Express Co.,* 688 F.2d 1235 (9th Cir. 1982)]

4. In community property states, signatures of both spouses are required on real property transactions. Would a mortgagee that requires both spouses' signatures on a mortgage application be violating the ECOA? [*McKenzie* v. *U.S. Home Corp.,* 704 F.2d 778 (5th Cir. 1983)]

5. Would the collection of a dishonored check for $23.15 written by a consumer to a Circle-K Store by a collection agency be covered under the FDCPA? [*Wade* v. *Regional Credit Association,* 87 F.3d 1098 (9th Cir. 1996)]

6. James A. Swanson received a letter from a collection agency, the Southern Oregon Credit Service, indicating that if payment in full or definite arrangements for payment of his account were not made within forty-eight hours, the agency would begin a complete investigation into his employment and assets. Is the agency's threat a violation of the FDCPA? [*Swanson* v. *Southern Oregon Credit Service, Inc.,* 869 F.2d 1222 (9th Cir. 1988)]

7. A loan agreement provided for total number of payments as "one × $128.00 and 24 × $128.00." Is this sufficient disclosure of the total number of payments? Is it too confusing to be disclosure? Would it make any difference if the agreement showed how much would be paid in total? [*Sunamerica Finance Corp.* v. *Williams,* 442 N.E.2d 83 (Ohio 1982)]

8. American Future Systems, Inc. (AFS), sells china, cookware, crystal, and tableware, and extends credit to its customers for such purchases. Sales on a credit basis amount to over 95 percent of AFS sales. First National Acceptance Corporation (FNAC) is AFS's credit company and is wholly owned by AFS. AFS affords young people and minorities a chance to obtain credit in spite of their lack of prior credit histories.

Its general standards for credit are (1) a telephone in the residence, (2) positive credit experience of at least $100, and (3) employment with regular income. AFS has three specific marketing programs: a summer program; a winter program for single white females; and a winter program for minorities, married persons, and males.

Under the summer program, target customers are single white females living at home with a parent who could cosign for the credit. AFS does not always require the parent's signatures and might ship goods to this group without checking credit histories. This market is reached by salespeople who are sent only to white neighborhoods and instructed to avoid neighborhoods where there might be a racial mix.

If salespeople encounter a minority customer in their presentations, AFS will sell the goods and extend credit to them, but a credit check is done on both the applicant and cosigner before goods are shipped. About 20 percent of the applications of minority applicants are denied.

The winter program has two parts. The preferred part of the winter program consists of sales to single white women who are sophomores, juniors, or seniors in four-year colleges or nursing schools. The other part of the program focuses on minorities, males, and married persons attending college or vocational schools. Shipment to preferred customers is immediate, with automatic credit approval. Shipment to the nonpreferred winter group is deferred until the applicant makes three timely monthly payments.

AFS presented evidence that minority customers are, as a group, less creditworthy than their white counterparts. However, the statistics presented did not account for AFS's failure to solicit in minority neighborhoods.

The U.S. government brought suit for violation of the ECOA. Is the AFS program a violation of ECOA? [*United States* v. *American Future Systems, Inc.,* 743, F2d 169 (3d Cir. 1984)]

9. In 1984, Jean Mayes purchased Albert L. Silva, d/b/a Rainbow Motors, a Nantucket car dealership. In May 1985, Jean Mayes entered into financing arrangements with Chrysler Credit Corporation to finance his car inventory. The borrower was Rainbow Motors, Jean Mayes as president and sole shareholder.

Chrysler demanded that Mr. Mayes and his wife, Michele Mayes, sign a "continuing guaranty" before it would extend credit. Mrs. Mayes, a well-compensated corporate attorney, was listed as a director and officer of Rainbow, but she did not participate in managing it. Rainbow defaulted, and Chrysler brought suit against Michele Mayes, seeking $750,126.41. Mrs. Mayes said Chrysler was estopped from collecting the debt because of the ECOA. Is she correct? [*Mayes* v. *Chrysler Credit Corp.,* 37 F.3d 9 (1st Cir. 1994)]

10. William Daniel Thompson Jr. opened a credit account with Gordon's Jewelers and then failed to pay off a $77.25 balance. The failure to pay was recorded with the computerized credit reporting agency of the

San Antonio Retail Merchants Association (SARMA). When William Douglas Thompson III applied for credit, it was denied because of the unfavorable report from Gordon's. Mr. Thompson III notified SARMA of the error but was still denied credit. Is SARMA liable if Mr. Thompson III files suit? [*Thompson v. San Antonio Retail Merchants Ass'n*, 682 F.2d 509 (5th Cir. 1982)]

RESEARCH PROBLEM

Burgeoning Credit, Burgeoning Debt, Burgeoning Bankruptcies

11. Consumers' available credit limits on their credit cards have jumped significantly. Between 1996 and 1998, credit limits on consumer credit cards increased by 50.3 percent to a total of $1.78 trillion dollars of available credit lines for consumers. This increase means that consumers could be in total debt up to 4.2 times their current outstanding debt balance—a figure that increased from 3.4 times current outstanding debt in March 1996.

The most common credit card line is now $3,500, as opposed to the typical $2,000 limit just two years ago. The average account balance has also increased from $1,479 to $1,987. On gold card credit cards, the increase in account balances is not as significant: from $2,334 to $2,497.

Meanwhile, consumer bankruptcies also continue at an all-time high, largely fueled by excessive credit card debt, according to the Consumer Federation of America. The proposed Bankruptcy Act reforms would make declaration of bankruptcy more difficult. The Consumer Federation of America has also issued a report on what it calls the "irresponsible" promotion of credit cards and credit card debt and points to the increase in limits as an example of banks' willingness to lure consumers into an often dangerous path of credit dependency.

Are banks acting in a responsible fashion with their solicitations of consumers for credit cards and increases in credit card lines? What responsibility do consumers have with regard to credit card debt? What disclosure rules apply in banks' solicitation of credit card customers? What should the banks do to influence legislation?

For More Information

Robert D. Hershey Jr., "The Sky Is Becoming the Only Limit for Credit Card Users," *New York Times*, 9 August 1998, Money & Business, 11.

Refer to the National Bankruptcy Review Commission Report: http://www.abiworld.org/legis/bulletins/97nov4.html

Also see the Chamber of Commerce News: http://www.uschamber.org

For House debate on this issue: http://thomas.loc.gov

For a look at the American Bankruptcy Institute: http://www.abiworld.org/stats/4thqtr97pr.html

---

BUSINESS STRATEGY APPLICATION

Using materials on the CD-ROM, you have the chance to develop the credit policies for a company from its application to its collection procedures.

After walking through one company's policies and issues, you will be able to develop your own credit system.

CHAPTER SIXTEEN

Business Property

The Vatican Library. The House of Windsor. Spuds McKenzie. The common thread? They all have lucrative arrangements for the licensing of their images and symbols. The law affords protection for these images and symbols even though the property right is a bundle of images and feelings about a person, business, or logo. According to a 2000 survey by the *National Law Journal*, intellectual property has been and remains the fastest-growing legal specialty.

This chapter covers the rights of businesses and their property. Property comes in different forms: personal, intellectual, and real; and the rights and protections differ for each type. What does a business own? What are the types of business property? What are the rights and issues in personal property owned by a business? What statutory protections exist for intellectual property? What issues of property protection exist in international business operations? What are real property interests, and what rights are included? Protecting the goodwill that symbols, names, and motifs provide for a business is an important part of the ongoing success of a business.

Possession is nine points of the law. No, it's not. Paperwork is.

HARVARD BUSINESS REVIEW
September/October 1995

We must take care to guard against two extremes equally prejudicial: the one, that men of ability, who have employed their time for the service of the community, may not be deprived of their just merits, and the reward for the ingenuity and labour; the other, that the world may not be deprived of improvements, nor the progress of the arts retarded.

SAYRE V. MOORE, 102 ENG. REP. 138, 140 (1785)

CONSIDER . . .

2 Live Crew, a popular rap musical group, recorded and performed a rap music version of Roy Orbison's famed 1964 "Oh, Pretty Woman" rock ballad. The song was written by Mr. Orbison and William Dees, and the rights to the song were assigned to Acuff-Rose Music, Inc. The rap version was called "Pretty Woman." Rap music is a "style of black American popular music consisting of improvised rhymes performed to rhythmic accompaniment." 2 Live Crew's manager had written to Acuff-Rose requesting permission to do the parody and offering to pay for rights to do so. Acuff-Rose responded by saying, "I am aware of the success enjoyed by the '2 Live Crew,' but I must inform you that we cannot permit the use of a parody of 'Oh, Pretty Woman.' "

2 Live Crew recorded the parody anyway. Acuff-Rose maintains the 2 Live Crew parody is infringement. Is it?

© Neal Preston/CORBIS

WHAT CAN A BUSINESS OWN? PERSONAL PROPERTY: THE TANGIBLE KIND

When we see a Dreyer's Ice Cream truck driving along beside us, we understand that Dreyer's Ice Cream owns that truck; it is a part of the Dreyer's fleet and is carried as business equipment on the books of the Dreyer's corporation. If someone took that truck, it would be theft and Dreyer's would be entitled to compensation if the truck were damaged or destroyed by the theft. Dreyer's would also be entitled to compensation if someone hit the truck in an accident and damaged it. Because the truck is Dreyer's property, Dreyer's enjoys certain rights of ownership in it. The delivery truck is **tangible property.** Tangible property is the type of property we can see and touch. Delivery trucks, desks, computers, inventory, and the building and land in which a business is located are all forms of tangible property. We have specific laws governing real and personal property rights for tangible property. We have laws to protect us against theft of our property and laws that provide remedies if someone harms or destroys that property.

Types of Personal Property

The Dreyer's truck would be an example of one form of personal property that businesses own—equipment. Everything from the laser printer in the office to the Thermos brand water coolers that construction crews have attached to their company trucks is included as a form of business equipment. Businesses also have personal property interests in the form of inventory or the goods that they hold for sale to customers.

Transfer of Personal Property

Business property that is equipment or inventory may or may not have **documents of title** associated with them. Vehicles in a company's fleet have the standard title documents for motor vehicles. Other types of tangible personal property that would have title documents include airplanes, helicopters, and even pure-bred animals. Title to these forms of personal property is transferred by the transfer of the document of title.

Many other forms of business property do not have any formal documents of title. Computers, desks, and file cabinets are typical forms of business property that do not have any title documents. These forms of personal property are transferred by a **bill of sale.** A bill of sale is simply a contract that reflects the sale of personal property and provides all the proof necessary to establish ownership.

Leases and Bailments of Personal Property

Many businesses choose to lease their equipment. A **lease** is a right of use and possession of property for a fixed or open-end period of time. The key difference between a lease of personal property and ownership is that in a lease the possession of the property transfers, but ownership does not. Upon termination of the lease, possession reverts back to the lessor.

In some circumstances, personal property is rented for a short period of time. A temporary transfer of possession of personal property is called a **bailment.** If you rent an extra bed for company, you are the **bailee** in the bailment relationship. The rental store is the **bailor.** If you check your coat at the coatroom in a Broadway theater, a bailment is created. The coat-check person as an agent for the theater is the bailee, and you are the bailor. If you leave your watch at a jeweler's for repair, you are the bailor and the jeweler is the bailee.

The bailment relationship is created with very simple requirements: The bailor turns possession over to the bailee with the understanding that the personal property will be returned, and both parties intend to create a bailment relationship. The intention to create a bailment distinguishes the bailment relationship from a **license.** For example, if you park your car yourself in a parking lot and pay for parking upon entry or departure, you have been given a license, the right to park on a lot that is owned by another. If you drive to a lot and a valet takes your keys and car and parks it for you, a bailment is created because possession of your car has been turned over to another. In those circumstances, you are the bailor and the parking lot owner is the bailee.

The bailment relationship carries duties and responsibilities. The bailee has the duty to return the bailment at the end of the agreed-upon period of possession. The bailee also has the duty of using reasonable care to protect the bailor's property while it is in his possession. In a parking valet situation, the bailee has a duty to take reasonable care to protect your car. A bailee cannot eliminate its liability for damage to the bailor's property. Often, parking stubs issued by valets read: "RESTAURANT ASSUMES NO LIABILITY FOR DAMAGE TO PROPERTY." Such a disclaimer of liability is called an **exculpatory clause,** but it is generally not valid because it is against public policy to allow someone to hold himself completely harmless for his negligent acts. It is, however, valid for the restaurant to limit its liability. For a parking stub from a valet that reads, "RESTAURANT NOT LIABLE FOR ITEMS VALUED AT OVER $50 LEFT IN VEHICLE," the bailee is not disclaiming all liability but, rather, is letting the bailor know in advance not to leave valuable items in the car. Many parking valet stubs now disclaim liability for theft of cellular phones and stereo systems. Such disclaimers are valid because they limit, but do not eliminate, liability.

In rental bailments, the bailor has the duty of checking the rented equipment to be certain it is in working order and has no defects that could injure the bailee. For example, if you leased a snowblower from a rental equipment franchise and a loose belt on the snowblower caused it to injure you, the franchise would have liability for your injuries because of its failure to maintain the equipment. The franchise that rents equipment, however, is not responsible for injuries that you experience because an activity for which

> ### BUSINESS PLANNING TIP
>
> Businesses that rent equipment should follow a regular maintenance schedule for their equipment. Also, their rental forms should include disclosures about the nature of activities for which their equipment is used. For example, businesses that rent ski equipment have disclosures on their rental forms about the risks that are inherent in skiing.

you use their equipment is dangerous. If you rent in-line skates from a rental franchise, the franchise is not responsible for any injuries you experience because of the inherent dangers in in-line skating. They would, however, be responsible if a defective buckle caused your skate to come loose and you fell and were injured as a result.

Creditors' Rights and Personal Property

Often, a business may not have the cash available for the purchase of equipment or inventory. Many businesses rely on the extension of credit to purchase both these forms of business personal property. Creditors, on the other hand, are concerned about the ability of a business to pay for property, particularly in those situations where the business is new and the capitalization is small. To provide more security for a creditor, a business can provide a **lien** or **security interest** to the creditor in the property that is purchased. Sometimes called a **chattel mortgage,** this form of security is created under Article 9 of the **Uniform Commercial Code** (UCC). The UCC is a near-universal uniform law in the United States that governs commercial transactions, including contracts (see Chapters 13 and 14) and financial transactions such as notes, checks, and drafts.

Review Article 9 of the UCC:
http://www.law.cornell.edu/ucc/9/overview.html

Article 9 of the UCC, revised in 2000, allows creditors to take a security interest in debtors' personal property. That security interest is created when a debtor authenticates a **security agreement** in exchange for the extension of credit or as security for an underlying debt. Once the creditor has a security interest in the personal property, that creditor has priority above other unsecured creditors in the event of the debtor's bankruptcy as well as the right of repossession of the secured property, often referred to as the **collateral,** if the debtor fails to make the necessary payments. Repossession under Article 9 can take place without court action. The creditor is permitted to take back the property from the debtor without first going to court to obtain a foreclosure. The only restrictions on creditors' repossession of debtors' property when there has been a **default,** or nonpayment of the debt, is that the creditor cannot "breach the peace." A breach of the peace is a violation of the law. A creditor cannot trespass or use physical force to repossess the property. Perhaps the most common example of repossession is taking back cars for which payment has not been made. Those responsible for the actual repossession may take the car from a public place, but they cannot enter the debtor's private property to repossess the car because that would be a trespass, a violation of the law, and thus a breach of the peace.

One additional protection that an Article 9 creditor can obtain is through perfection, generally accomplished by the filing of a **financing statement.** A financing statement is filed with a public agency (generally either the secretary of state or county recorder or clerk) to provide public notice that the creditor has an interest in the debtor's property. Under the 2000 version of Article 9, these financing statements generally are filed in a central location; and the move is toward an electronic system that permits easy access to information. The process of perfection is important because it often gives the creditor priority over subsequent creditors who might take a security interest in the same equipment or inventory.

WHAT CAN A BUSINESS OWN? PERSONAL PROPERTY:
THE INTANGIBLE OR INTELLECTUAL KIND

In addition to the Dreyer's truck itself, referred to earlier, you also see painted on the truck the signature brown and white stripes that are part of the ice cream's packing. You see the distinctive writing, "Dreyer's Grand Ice Cream." You recognize the truck from its distinctive paint and writing probably before you even read the name "Dreyer's." That distinctive color scheme, name, and writing are also business property that belongs to Dreyer's. The recognition and goodwill that come from those brown stripes and the name are forms of **intangible property** that also enjoys statutory protections, which include Dreyer's right to prevent others from using its distinctive name and colors and taking from it the goodwill those items have come to symbolize. The symbols represent a bundle of very valuable rights for the business.

Forms of intangible property include patents, copyrights, trademarks, trade names, and trade dress. Protections include federal rights, international protections, and common law rights of action for the damage to or taking of these forms of intangible property.

Protection for Business Intellectual Property

Federal law provides competitive protection for ideas, formulas, and trademarks. This section of the chapter covers these statutory protections of competition.

Patents

Visit the U.S. Patent and Trademark Office (PTO): http://www.uspto.gov

Patents are a type of legal monopoly obtained with the filing of certain information and forms with the U.S. Patent Office. So fundamental is the protection of new products and processes that the protection for inventors is found in Article 1, Section 8, of the U.S. Constitution.

While there are several types of patents, the most common are utility or functional patents and design patents. Utility or function patents are those that cover machines, processes, and improvements to existing devices. For example, a computerized method for tracking a dry cleaner's inventory of clothing is protected by a patent. Prior to 1995, a patent was valid for seventeen years. However, in order to bring the U.S. laws into compliance with GATT provisions, the protection was extended to twenty years in 1995. Design patents are those that protect the features of a product. The lace configuration on Eve of Milady bridal gowns and Procter & Gamble's method for elasticized legs on their disposable diapers are examples of product designs protected by patent. Design patents are granted for fourteen years.

During these exclusive rights periods of fourteen and twenty years, the patent holder has the sole rights for profits on sales. Because protection is so extensive, an idea is patentable only if it is nonobvious, novel, and useful; and the idea must be reduced to some tangible form. For example, a discovery of a reproductive hormone in the male body is not patentable, but a product to stop production of that hormone for birth control purposes can be patented.

Anyone who sells or uses a patented product or process without the consent of the patent holder has committed patent **infringement.** Infringement entitles the patent holder to a statutory action for damages. The patent holder (the plaintiff) in such a case need only show that a patent was held and that the defendant infringed that patent. A Patent Office registration for a product or process, however, is not a guarantee of recovery. A court must still agree with the Patent Office determination that the product or process is nonobvious, useful, and novel.

> ### BUSINESS PLANNING TIP
>
> To be certain federal protection for your intangible property rights is maximized, put either the "®" by the trade name or trademark or on the packaging or product, or place the words "Registered in U.S. Patent and Trademark Office" or "Reg. U.S. Pat. & TM. Off." Once you are registered with the U.S. Patent and Trademark Office, obtaining registrations in other countries becomes much easier. Also, a registered product enjoys protection at the borders of the United States. Customs officials can exclude products that are being imported if they infringe a registered property right.

Amazon.com has had an ongoing battle with Barnes and Noble.com over the "One Click" shopping method. Amazon.com obtained a patent for its buyers' shopping method that permits shoppers to place items in a virtual shopping cart and then click just one button when they are ready to purchase. The buyers need not go through the time of filling in shipping, billing, and credit information for each purchase.

Barnes and Noble created a similar "One Click" shopping experience for its online customers, and Amazon.com sued for patent infringement. On appeal, a court held that Barnes & Noble could continue to use the "one click" method while the parties proceeded to trial on the issue of whether the "one click" patent was a valid one or simply an obvious convenience for online shoppers. While the outcome of the case is unknown, Barnes & Noble at least introduced enough evidence to prevent the court from issuing an injunction against it pending the trial [*Amazon.com, Inc.* v. *Barnes & Noble.com,* 239 F.3d 1343 (Fed. Cir. 2001)].

CONSIDER...

16.1 Procter & Gamble (P&G) was issued patent #4,455,333 on June 19, 1984, for an invention entitled "Doughs and Cookies Providing Storage-Stable Texture Variety." The patent covers a method of manufacturing ready-to-serve cookies that remain crispy on the outside and chewy on the inside for an extended shelf life. P&G markets these cookies under the Duncan Hines label.

P&G brought a patent infringement action against Nabisco Brands, Inc., which markets its own line of dual-textured cookies called "Almost Home" and "Chewy Chips Ahoy." P&G also sued Keebler Company for its dual-textured cookie called "Soft Batch" and Frito-Lay, Inc., for its "Grandma's Rich and Chewy." Each of the defendants denies infringement. They have moved for dismissal of the case on grounds that the patent is invalid because baking cookies is not patentable. Do you agree? Would you protect P&G's process? [*Procter & Gamble Co.* v. *Nabisco Brands, Inc.,* 604 F. Supp. 1485 (D.C. Del. 1985)]

Copyrights

Visit the issue of fair use at the Copyright and Fair Use site:
http://www.fairuse.com

Patents protect inventors. Copyrights protect authors of books, magazine articles, plays, movies, songs, dances, recordings, and so on, as well as the creators of photographs. A copyright protects the expression of ideas. A copyright gives the holder of the copyright the exclusive right to sell, control, or license the copyrighted work. A copyright exists automatically for works created after 1989. While the placement of the traditional C or copyright symbol is not required, it is recommended. Further, the existence of a copyright in the United States is recognized in all nations that have signed the Berne Convention. Under the terms of the Berne Convention and U.S. law, copyright registration is not required, but it is also recommended. Registration is a means of preventing someone violating the copyright from claiming a lack of knowledge about the work's protection. In order to register a copyright, the creator need only file two copies of the work with the Copyright Office in Washington, D.C. Without copyright registration, the owner cannot bring a suit for copyright infringement.

A copyright runs for the life of the creator plus seventy years. If the work produced was done in the employ of a business, the business then registers the copyright. These types of copyrights run for 120 years from the time of creation or

95 years from publication of the work, whichever is shorter. These time limits for protection have been expanding over the years with the most recent extension, from fifty to seventy years, passed with the **Sonny Bono Copyright Term Extension Act** (CTEA). The late Representative Bono was concerned because the copyright on the cartoon character Mickey Mouse was about to expire. While the Constitution prohibits granting copyrights in perpetuity, there has been a clear trend in congressional actions to keep extending out that protection period.

A copyright holder has control over the use of the created work. That control includes control over reproduction, distribution, public performances, derivative works, and public displays. Some copyright holders assign or license these rights to others in exchange for royalties. For example, most songwriters assign their rights for public performances of their songs to the American Society of Composers, Authors, and Publishers (ASCAP) and Broadcast Music, Inc. (BMI), who then pay the writers each time their song is used, according to a previously determined schedule of fees. There is an international fee schedule for payment for tapes, CDs, and records; it could be a flat fee, a per-minute fee, a per-record fee, or a per-song fee.

Damages for copyright infringement include the profits made by the infringer, actual costs, attorney fees, and any other expenses associated with the infringement action. All illegal copies can be obtained through court injunction and any distribution of the illegal copies halted by the same court order.

In addition to the civil suits that can be brought for infringement and resulting damages to a business owner, there are federal criminal penalties for copyright infringement. Criminal penalties are available when infringement is willful and for "commercial advantage or private financial gain."

Visit "The Copyright Web Site" for more information on copyrights: http://www.benedict.com *For a copyright quiz, visit:* http://www.cyberbee.com

e-commerce

Technology has created new issues in copyright infringement, particularly in the areas of copyrighted software and music, with the availability of digital technology. For example, an MIT student uploaded and downloaded copyrighted software programs and then gave fellow students passwords for access. The result was that students at MIT enjoyed free access to the Internet at a cost of $1 million to the system's owners. However, the student did not charge for the access and thus realized no personal financial gain from the project. Technically, there was no violation of the copyright laws.

As a result of this case, music producers and software developers added protection technology to their copyrighted products and lobbied for a change in copyright law, which came with the **Digital Millennium Copyright Act** in 1998. This act criminalizes the circumvention of protection technology in order to make copies of copyrighted materials as well as assisting others, providing expertise, or manufacturing products to circumvent protection technology. This act is at the root of the *Napster* case (see Chapter 1), in which music was downloaded without

> **BUSINESS PLANNING TIP**
>
> Be certain your employees understand the copyrighted nature of computer software and the protections afforded the owners of those programs. Be sure they understand that both criminal and civil penalties exist for infringement of the software programs.

> **BUSINESS PLANNING TIP**
>
> Most employers acquire site licenses for computer software programs so that they enjoy a type of discount by not being required to purchase a full program for each employee. Have appropriate controls in place for the master disks and access to the programs so that the site license is not violated. Be certain employees understand the content of and reasons for the site license agreements.

In the summer of 1996, the dance song "Macarena" hit the pop music scene and charts in the United States. The line-type dance inspired by the song is called the Macarena. At camps around the country, the song was played and children were taught the dance.

The American Society of Composers, Authors, and Publishers (ASCAP) is the organization that serves as a clearinghouse for fee payments for use of copyrighted materials belonging to its members. ASCAP sent a letter to the directors of camps and nonprofit organizations sponsoring camps (Girl Scouts, Boy Scouts, Camp Fire Girls, American Cancer Association, and so forth) that warned them that licensed songs should not be used without paying ASCAP the licensing fees and that violators would be pursued. ASCAP's prices for songs are, for example,

$591 for the camp season for "Edelweiss" (from *The Sound of Music*) or "This Land Is Your Land."

Some of the nonprofit-sponsored camps charge only $44 per week per camper. The directors could not afford the fees, and the camps eliminated their oldies dances and dance classes. ASCAP declined to offer discounted licensing fees for the camps.

Why did ASCAP work so diligently to protect its rights? What ethical and social responsibility issues do you see with respect to the nonprofit camps? Some of these camps are summer retreats for children who suffer from cancer, AIDS, and other terminal illnesses. Does this information change your feelings about ASCAP's fees? What would you do if you were an ASCAP member and owned the rights to a song a camp wished to use?

charge via peer-to-peer file sharing. Shawn Fanning, Napster's founder, argued that his technology did not violate copyright laws because his service was a nonprofit enterprise. However, the acts of circumvention and facilitating circumvention are now violations of copyright laws.

Under the **Computer Software Copyright Act of 1980,** all software can be copyrighted, whether it is written in ordinary language (source code) or machine language (object code). While software copyrights do not cover methods of operation (such as menus), they do cover the underlying programs themselves.

Fair Use and Copyrights

Review the Copyright Act of 1976, as Amended (1994):
http://www.law.cornell.edu/topics/copyright.html

When the copyright laws were amended in 1976, one change permitted "fair use" of copyrighted materials. **Fair use** is occasional and spontaneous use of copyrighted materials for limited purposes—for example, a short quote from a copyrighted work. Fair use also allows instructors to reproduce a page or chart from a copyrighted work to use in the classroom; and copies of book pages can be made for research purposes. One interesting question that has arisen is the relationship between the notion of fair use and the prohibitions under the Digital Millennium Copyright Act. Can a professor circumvent protection technology for fair use in the classroom? Some feel the professor can do so if he has purchased the work. In other words, the professor can use an excerpt from the Beatles' *White Album* if the professor owns that album.

Another issue in fair use involves questions about such use and the First Amendment. For example, satirical works use the lyrics and speech of others as a form of social commentary such as those found in *Mad Magazine* and *Saturday Night Live.* The First Amendment protects social commentary, and the copyright laws protect original work. The following case involves an issue of a parody of copyrighted material being used for commercial gain. The case provides the answer for the chapter's opening "Consider."

CASE 16.1

Campbell v. Acuff-Rose Music, Inc.
510 U.S. 569 (1994)

Justice Souter Does the Pretty Woman Rap

FACTS

2 Live Crew, a popular rap musical group, recorded and performed a rap music version called "Pretty Woman" of Roy Orbison's famed 1964 "Oh, Pretty Woman" rock ballad. The song was written by Mr. Orbison and William Dees, and the rights to the song were assigned to Acuff-Rose Music, Inc. (respondent). Rap music is a style of black American popular music that consists of often-improvised rhymes performed to rhythmic accompaniment. 2 Live Crew's manager had written to Acuff-Rose to request permission to do the parody and offered to pay for rights to do so. Acuff-Rose's response: "I am aware of the success enjoyed by the '2 Live Crew,' but I must inform you that we cannot permit the use of a parody of 'Oh, Pretty Woman.'"

2 Live Crew recorded the parody anyway and named Messrs. Orbison and Dees as the songwriters and Acuff-Rose as the publisher on the CD cover. After over 250,000 copies of the CD had been sold and over one year later, Acuff-Rose Music, Inc., filed suit against Luther Campbell (also known as Luke Skywalker), Christopher Wongwon, Mark Ross, and David Hobbs, members of the 2 Live Crew group, for infringement. 2 Live Crew maintained that its song was a parody and thus protected under the fair use exceptions of the copyright laws. The district court granted summary judgment for 2 Live Crew. The court of appeals held that the commercial nature of the parody rendered it presumptively unfair. 2 Live Crew (petitioners) appealed.

JUDICIAL OPINION

SOUTER, Justice

We are called upon to decide whether 2 Live Crew's commercial parody of Roy Orbison's song, "Oh, Pretty Woman," may be a fair use within the meaning of the Copyright Act of 1976, 17 U.S.C. § 107 (1988 ed. and Supp. IV).

It is uncontested here that 2 Live Crew's song would be an infringement of Acuff-Rose's rights in "Oh, Pretty Woman," under the Copyright Act of 1976, 17 U.S.C. § 106 (1988 ed. and Supp. IV), but for a finding of fair use through parody.

The first factor in a fair use enquiry is "the purpose and character of the use, including whether such use is of a commercial nature or is for nonprofit educational purposes." The central purpose of this investigation is to see whether the new work merely "supersede[s] the objects" of the original creation, or instead adds something new, with a further purpose or different character, altering the first with new expression, meaning, or message; it asks, in other words, whether and to what extent the new work is "transformative." Although such transformative use is not absolutely necessary for a finding of fair use, *Sony Corp. of America* v. *Universal City Studios, Inc.,* 464 U.S. 417 (1984), the goal of copyright, to promote science and the arts, is generally furthered by the creation of transformative works. Such works thus lie at the heart of the fair use doctrine's guarantee of breathing space within the confines of copyright and the more transformative the new work, the less will be the significance of other factors, like commercialism, that may weigh against a finding of fair use.

Suffice it to say now that parody has an obvious claim to transformative value, as Acuff-Rose itself does not deny. Like less ostensibly humorous forms of criticism, it can provide social benefit, by shedding light on an earlier work, and, in the process, creating a new one. We thus line up with the courts that have held that parody, like other comment or criticism, may claim fair use under § 107.

Parody needs to mimic an original to make its point, and so has some claim to use the creation of its victim's (or collective victims') imagination, whereas satire can stand on its own two feet and so requires justification for the very act of borrowing.

The fact that parody can claim legitimacy for some appropriation does not, of course, tell either parodist or judge much about where to draw the line. Like a book review quoting the copyrighted material criticized, parody may or may not be fair use, and petitioner's suggestion that any periodic use is

(continued)

presumptively fair has no more justification in law or fact than the equally hopeful claim that any use for news reporting should be presumed fair.

As the District Court remarked, the words of 2 Live Crew's song copy the original's first line, but then "quickly degenerate[e] into a play on words, substituting predictable lyrics with shocking ones . . . [that] derisively demonstrate[e] how bland and banal the Orbison song seems to them." Judge Nelson, dissenting below, came to the same conclusion, that the 2 Live Crew song "was clearly intended to ridicule the white-bread original" and "reminds us that sexual congress with nameless streetwalkers is not necessarily the stuff of romance and is not necessarily without its consequences. The singers (there are several) have the same thing on their minds as did the lonely man with the nasal voice, but here there is no hint of wine and roses." Although the majority below had difficulty discerning any criticism of the original in 2 Live Crew's song, it assumed for purposes of its opinion that there was some.

We have less difficulty in finding that critical element in 2 Live Crew's song than the Court of Appeals did, although having found it we will not take the further step of evaluating its quality. The threshold question when fair use is raised in defense of parody is whether a periodic character may reasonably be perceived. Whether, going beyond that, parody is in good taste or bad does not and should not matter to fair use. As Justice Holmes explained, "[i]t would be a dangerous undertaking for persons trained only to the law to constitute themselves final judges of the worth of [a work], outside of the narrowest and most obvious limits. At the one extreme some works of genius would be sure to miss appreciation. Their very novelty would make them repulsive until the public had learned the new language in which their author spoke."

While we might not assign a high rank to the periodic element here, we think it fair to say that 2 Live Crew's song reasonably could be perceived as commenting on the original or criticizing it, to some degree. 2 Live Crew juxtaposes the romantic musings of a man whose fantasy comes true, with degrading taunts, a bawdy demand for sex, and a sigh of relief from paternal responsibility. The later words can be taken as a comment on the naivete of the original of an earlier day, as a rejection of its sentiment that ignores the ugliness of street life and the debasement that it signifies. It is this joinder of reference and ridicule that marks off the author's choice of parody from the other types of comment and criticism that traditionally have had a claim to fair use protection as transformative works.

The use, for example, of a copyrighted work to advertise a product, even in a parody, will be entitled to less indulgence under the first factor of the fair use enquiry, than the sale of a parody for its own sake, let alone one performed a single time by students in school.

We agree with both the District Court and the Court of Appeals that the Orbison original's creative expression for public dissemination falls within the core of the copyright's protective purposes. This fact, however, is not much help in this case, or ever likely to help much in separating the fair use sheep from the infringing goats in a parody case, since parodies almost invariably copy publicly known, expressive works.

We think the Court of Appeals was insufficiently appreciative of parody's need for the recognizable sight or sound when it ruled 2 Live Crew's use unreasonable as a matter of law. It is true, of course, that 2 Live Crew copied the characteristic opening bass riff (or musical phrase) of the original, and true that the words of the first line copy the Orbison lyrics. But if quotation of the opening riff and the first line may be said to go to the "heart" of the original, the heart is also what most readily conjures up the song for parody, and it is the heart at which parody takes aim. Copying does not become excessive in relation to parodic purpose merely because the portion taken was the original's heart. If 2 Live Crew had copied a significantly less memorable part of the original, it is difficult to see how its parodic character would have come through.

This is not, of course, to say that anyone who calls himself a parodist can skim the cream and get away scot free. In parody, as in news reporting, context is everything, and the question of fairness asks what else the parodist did besides go to the heart of the original. It is significant that 2 Live Crew not only copied the first line of the original, but thereafter departed markedly from the Orbison lyrics for its own ends. 2 Live Crew not only copied the bass riff and repeated it, but also produced otherwise distinctive sounds, interposing "scraper" noise, overlaying the music with solos in different keys, and altering the drum beat. This is not a case, then, where "a substantial portion" of the parody itself is composed of a "verbatim" copying of the original. It is not, that is, a case where the parody is so insubstantial, as compared to the copying, that the third factor must be resolved as a matter of law against the parodists.

It was error for the Court of Appeals to conclude that the commercial nature of 2 Live Crew's parody of "Oh, Pretty Woman" rendered it presumptively unfair. No such evidentiary presumption is available to address either the first factor, the character and purpose of the use, or the fourth, market harm, in determining whether a transformative use, such as parody, is a fair one. The court also erred in holding that 2 Live Crew had necessarily copied excessively from the Orbison original, considering the parodic purpose of the use. We therefore reverse the judgment of the Court of Appeals.

The case was remanded for trial.

APPENDIX A

"Oh, Pretty Woman," by Roy Orbison and William Dees
Pretty Woman, walking down the street,
Pretty Woman, the kind I like to meet,
Pretty Woman, I don't believe you,
you're not the truth,
No one could look as good as you
Mercy
Pretty Woman, won't you pardon me,
Pretty Woman, I couldn't help but see,
Pretty Woman, that you look lovely as can be
Are you lonely just like me?
Pretty Woman, stop a while,
Pretty Woman, talk a while,
Pretty Woman give your smile to me
Pretty Woman, yeah, yeah, yeah
Pretty Woman, look my way,
Pretty Woman, say you'll stay with me
'Cause I need you, I'll treat you right
Come to me baby, Be mine tonight
Pretty Woman, don't walk on by,
Pretty Woman, don't make me cry,
Pretty Woman, don't walk away,
Hey, O.K.
If that's the way it must be, O.K.
I guess I'll go on home, it's late
There'll be tomorrow night, but wait!
What do I see
Is she walking back to me!
Oh, Pretty Woman.

APPENDIX B

"Pretty Woman," as recorded by 2 Live Crew
Pretty woman walkin' down the street
Pretty woman girl you look so sweet
Pretty woman you bring me down to that knee
Pretty woman you make me wanna beg please
Oh, pretty woman
Big hairy woman you need to shave that stuff

Big hairy woman you know I bet it's tough
Big hairy woman all that hair it ain't legit
'Cause you look like 'Cousin It'
Big hairy woman
Bald headed woman girl your hair won't grow
Bald headed woman you got a teeny weeny afro
Bald headed woman you know your hair could look nice
Bald headed woman first you got to roll it with rice
Bald headed woman here, let me get this hunk of biz for ya
Ya know what I'm saying you look better than rice a roni
Oh bald headed woman
Big hairy woman come on in
And don't forget your bald headed friend
Hey pretty woman let the boys
Jump in
Two timin' woman girl you know you ain't right
Two timin' woman you's out with my boy last night
Two timin' woman that takes a load off my mind
Two timin' woman now I know the baby ain't mine
Oh, two timin' woman
Oh pretty woman

CASE QUESTIONS

1. What constitutes fair use?
2. What is the significance of 2 Live Crew's commercial gain from the parody?
3. Why is the *Sony* case cited?
4. Why did 2 Live Crew's manager seek permission first?
5. Do you agree with the court's decision? Was it a fair use? Should the owner of the rights be allowed to decide how a song will be parodied for commercial gain?
6. Does the court comment on bad taste and parody quality? Why?

Aftermath: The 2 Live Crew case began a trend in the music parody industry, based on what has become known as "Footnote 10." In Footnote 10 in the Supreme Court opinion, the Court noted its concern for the use of injunctions in parody cases. The footnote indicates that automatic injunctive relief when the parody goes beyond fair use is wrong because there may be a strong public interest in the publication of the secondary work, as in the 2 Live Crew parody, in which social commentary is present.

CONSIDER...

16.2   The San Diego Chicken, a mascot at professional baseball games, has a portion of his act in which he grabs a purple dinosaur and stomps it, stamps it, pounds it, and pummels it. Lyons Partnership, L.P., the producer of the *Barney the Dinosaur* (a purple dinosaur) television show and the holder of all its product licenses, filed suit against Ted Giannoulas (the man beneath the San Diego Chicken costume) for copyright infringement.

A Texas court classified the portion of Mr. Giannoulas's act that involved a purple dinosaur as a form of parody or satire that was thereby protected by the First Amendment. Kenneth Fitzgerald, the lawyer for Mr. Giannoulas, said Mr. Giannoulas will seek to recover his attorney's fees in the case.

Mr. Fitzgerald noted during the case that Barney has been spoofed by Jay Leno as well as on the television show *Saturday Night Live,* but Lyons chose only to pursue Giannoulas.

What is wrong with selective enforcement of one's copyright protections? Is Barney the Dinosaur something that can be copyrighted?

CONSIDER...

16.3   Jesse "The Body" Ventura, the former professional wrestler who is now governor of Minnesota, was concerned when Garrison Keillor announced that he was so inspired by Mr. Ventura's election that he had written a comic novel. The novel, with a lead character of Jimmy "Big Boy" Valente, is also the story of a professional wrestler's life and rise to a governorship. Governor Ventura accused Mr. Keillor of "cheating" because he was "making money off of me." Governor Ventura was writing a book about himself, but Mr. Keillor's book was to appear long before the Ventura autobiography.

Does Governor Ventura have any grounds for stopping Mr. Keillor's efforts? Does he have the right to protect his life story? Does he have exclusive rights on that story? Is it protectable under any intellectual property provisions? What effect does his being elected governor have on his rights?

Trademarks

Review the Lanham Act:
http://www.law.cornell.edu/
topics/trademark.html

Trademarks are words, pictures, designs, or symbols that businesses place on goods to identify those goods as their product. "Xerox," the Mercedes-Benz triangle, and "M and M's" are all examples of trademarks. The **Lanham Act** of 1946 is a federal law passed to afford businesses protection of their trademarks. This law is really a protection of a company's goodwill. A trademark becomes associated with that company and is used as a means of identifying that company's goods or services. The Lanham Act assures the right to retain that unique identification.

To obtain protection, goods must move in interstate commerce. When this requirement is met, a trademark is registered on the *Principal Register.* The trademark must be unique and nongeneric. For example, "cola" is a generic term; "Coca-Cola" is a trademark. Before recent changes in the law, a trademark must have been in use before registration; but a recent amendment to the Lanham Act allows preregistration, a practice followed in Europe for many years.[1] Once a trademark is registered, its registration can be challenged for five years. If no challenge is brought, the trademark becomes incontestable and is protected as long as its owner enforces it.

Once a trademark is registered, the holder has the obligation of maintaining the unique nature of that trademark. To do so, there must be a generic term that can be associated with the trademark so the public does not turn the trademark itself into a generic term. For example, there are "Band-Aid brand adhesive strips" instead of "Band-Aids." There is "Jell-O brand gelatin dessert" instead of "Jell-O." There are "Formica brand kitchen countertops" instead of "Formica" and "Rollerblade in-line skates" instead of "Rollerblades." Parker Brothers recently lost its "Monopoly" trademark because there is no generic term for the type of board game it was. Other examples are "aspirin" and "cellophane."

CASE 16.2

Harley-Davidson, Inc. v. *Grottanelli*
164 F.3d 806 (2d Cir. 1999)
cert. denied *531 U.S. 1103 (2001)*

When Is a Hog Generic?

FACTS

Harley-Davidson (Harley-Davidson, Harley, or the company), a corporation based in Milwaukee, Wisconsin, manufactures and sells motorcycles, motorcycle parts and accessories, apparel, and other motorcycle-related merchandise. It brought suit against The Hog Farm, owned by Ronald Grottanelli (Grottanelli), for its use of the word "hog" in its business name and in reference to other products. Harley maintains that "hog" is a trademark associated with its motorcycles.

The lower court enjoined Mr. Grottanelli from using the term "hog" in his store except as to his store's name, which he could keep so long as confined to a narrow geographic area. Mr. Grottanelli appealed as well as Harley-Davidson to request a more narrow geographic scope for use of "The Hog Farm" name by Mr. Grottanelli.

JUDICIAL OPINION

NEWMAN, Circuit Judge

This appeal primarily involves trademark issues as to whether the mark "HOG" as applied to large motorcycles is generic. [We] conclude that the word "hog" had become generic as applied to large motorcycles before Harley-Davidson began to make trademark use of "HOG" and that Harley-Davidson's attempt to withdraw this use of the word from the public domain cannot succeed.

In the late 1960s and early 1970s, the word "hog" was used by motorcycle enthusiasts to refer to motorcycles generally and to large motorcycles in particular. The word was used that way in the press at least as early as 1965, and frequently thereafter, prior to the 1980s when Harley first attempted to make trademark use of the term. Several dictionaries include a definition of "hog" as a motorcycle, especially a large one. The October 1975 issue of *Street Chopper* contained an article entitled "Honda Hog," indicating that the word "hog" was generic as to motorcycles and needed a trade name adjective.

See *The Oxford Dictionary of Modern Slang* (1992) ("hog noun U.S. A large, often old, car or motorcycle.1967 -."); *American Heritage Dictionary* (3d ed. 1992) ("hog . . . 4. Slang. A big, heavy motorcycle"); Eric Partridge, *A Dictionary of Slang and Unconventional English* (8th ed. 1984) ("hog n . . . 8. a homebuilt motorcycle . . ."); see also Glossary of Sportscycle Terms, *Bike and Rider*, Aug. 1992, at 84 ("HOG Old fashioned, heavyweight sportscycle").

A likely etymology of "hog" to mean a motorcycle is suggested in the entry for "road-hog" in Eric Partridge, *A Dictionary of Slang and Unconventional English* (6th ed. 1996), which reports that in the United States as early as 1891 "road-hog" was applied to an "inconsiderate" cyclist and somewhat later to motorists.

(continued)

Beginning around the early 1970s and into the early 1980s, motorcyclists increasingly came to use the word "hog" when referring to Harley-Davidson motorcycles. However, for several years, as Harley-Davidson's Manager of Trademark Enforcement acknowledged, the company attempted to disassociate itself from the word "hog." The Magistrate Judge drew the reasonable inference that the company wished to distance itself from the connection between "hog" as applied to motorcycles and unsavory elements of the population, such as Hell's Angels, who were among those applying the term to Harley-Davidson motorcycles.

In 1981, Harley-Davidson's new owners recognized that the term "hog" had financial value and began using the term in connection with its merchandise, accessories, advertising, and promotions. In 1983, it formed the Harley Owners' Group, pointedly using the acronym "H.O.G." In 1987, it registered the acronym in conjunction with various logos. It subsequently registered the mark "HOG" for motorcycles. That registration lists Harley-Davidson's first use as occurring in 1990.

Grottanelli opened a motorcycle repair shop under the name "The Hog Farm" in 1969. Since that time his shop has been located at various sites in western New York. At some point after 1981, Grottanelli also began using the word "hog" in connection with events and merchandise. He has sponsored an event alternatively known as "Hog Holidays" and "Hog Farm Holidays," and sold products such as "Hog Wash" engine degreaser and a "Hog Trivia" board game.

Though the Magistrate Judge made no ultimate finding as to whether "hog" was generic as applied to large motorcycles prior to Harley-Davidson's trademark use of the word, his subsidiary findings point irresistibly toward that conclusion. He found that there was "substantial evidence which would indicate that in those years the term referred to motorcycles (or motorcyclists) generally." He cited the various press and dictionary usages of the word that we have set forth above. Though not conclusive, dictionary definitions of a word to denote a category of products are significant evidence of genericness because they usually reflect the public's perception of a word's meaning and its contemporary usage. In this case, one dictionary cites a generic use of "hog" to mean a large motorcycle as early as 1967, long before Harley's first trademark use of the word, and the recent dictionary editions continuing to define the word to mean a large motorcycle indicate that the

word has not lost its generic meaning. We have observed that newspaper and magazine use of a word in a generic sense is "a strong indication of the general public's perception" that the word is generic.

However, rather than recognize that the word "hog," originally generic as applied to motorcycles, cannot subsequently be appropriated for trademark use, the Magistrate Judge upheld Harley-Davidson's anti-dilution claim on the ground that its "HOG" mark has become a strong trademark. This was error. Even the presumption of validity arising from federal registration, . . . cannot protect a mark that is shown on strong evidence to be generic as to the relevant category of products prior to the proprietor's trademark use and registration.

Supporting the generic nature of "hog" as applied to motorcycles is Harley-Davidson's aversion to linking the word with its products until the early 1980s, long after the word was generic. Harley's Manager of Trademark Enforcement acknowledged that in the past Harley had attempted to disassociate itself from the term "hog." As the Magistrate Judge noted, Harley's own history of the company, "The Big Book of Harley-Davidson," makes no reference to "hog" as relating to its products before the early 1980s. Though Harley-Davidson was not shown to have used the word "hog" in a generic sense, its deliberate resistance to linking the word to its products is nonetheless probative.

Harley-Davidson cites the rulings in *Harley-Davidson Motor Co.* v. *Pierce Foods Corp.,* 231 U.S.P.Q. 857 (T.T.A.B.1986), and *Harley-Davidson, Inc.* v. *Seghieri,* 29 U.S.P.Q.2d 1956 (N.D.Cal.1993), but we are not bound by those decisions, and, more significantly, there is no indication that the bodies making those rulings had the extensive record of early generic usage that we have. In *Pierce Foods,* the litigation did not even raise the issue of the genericness of "hog." Seghieri apparently had scant evidence of genericness; the Court relied on articles from Harley's own newsletter, which indicated that "hog" meant Harley-Davidson motorcycles.

Professor McCarthy contends that, in some contexts, there might be a doctrine whereby trademark use can be reacquired in a generic term, and he cites the "SINGER" and "GOODYEAR" marks as examples. But Professor McCarthy recognizes that his examples are words that were originally proper names of the manufacturer and that the cases he enlists, *Singer Mfg. Co.* v. *Briley,* 207 F.2d 519 (5th Cir.1953), and *Goodyear Tire & Rubber Co.* v. *H. Rosenthal Co.,* 246 F.Supp. 724 (D.Minn.1965), "do not stand for the proposition that a commonly used name of an article like 'computer,' 'typewriter' or 'flashlight' can be appropriated by one seller as a trademark." Moreover, if a generic word could ever be infused with trademark significance, the word must have ceased to have current generic meaning. The recent editions of the dictionaries cited by the District Court demonstrate that generic usage of "hog," applied to motorcycles, still exists.

Nor does Professor McCarthy's discussion of so-called "dual usage" terms provide any help to Harley-Davidson. "Dual usage" in trademark law refers to a mark that starts out as proprietary and gradually become [sic] generic as to some segments of the public. If such a mark "retains" trademark significance, injunctive relief must be carefully tailored to protect only the limited trademark use and not to bar the generic use. Our case, however, concerns a mark that starts out generic and is sought to be given trademark significance by a manufacturer.

Harley-Davidson suggests, albeit in a footnote, that it is entitled to trademark use of "HOG" as applied to motorcycles because a substantial segment of the relevant consumers began to use the term specifically to refer to Harley-Davidson motorcycles before the company made trademark use of the term. Some decisions have invoked this principle to accord a company priority as to its subsequent trademark use of a term. Whether or not we would agree with these decisions, they present a significantly different situation. Neither "ACE" nor "BUG" was a generic term in the language as applied, respectively, to a category of film editors or a category of automobiles prior to the public's use of the terms to refer to the American Cinema Editors and Volkswagen cars. By contrast, "hog" was a generic term in the language as applied to large motorcycles before the public (or at least some segments of it) began using the word to refer to Harley-Davidson motorcycles. The public has no more right than a manufacturer to withdraw from the language a generic term, already applicable to the relevant category of products, and accord it trademark significance, at least as long as the term retains some generic meaning.

The public may also take a trademark and give it a generic meaning that is new. See *Lucasfilm, Ltd.* v. *High Frontier*, 622 F. Supp. 931 (D.D.C.1985) ("Strategic Defense Initiative" referred to as "Star Wars Program" without infringing movie trademark STAR WARS).

For all of these reasons, Harley-Davidson may not prohibit Grottanelli from using "hog" to identify his motorcycle products and services. Like any other manufacturer with a product identified by a word that is generic, Harley-Davidson will have to rely on all or a portion of its tradename (or other protectable marks) to identify its brand of motorcycles, e.g., "Harley Hogs."

Reversed.

CASE QUESTIONS

1. Who used the term "hog" first among the two parties?

2. When did the term "hog," as applied to motorcycles, appear in the dictionary?

3. Did Harley-Davidson reclaim the term "hog" from its generic standing?

4. Is the term "hog" generic now?

Not all commonly used terms, however, are generic. In *San Francisco Arts & Athletics, Inc.* v. *United States Olympic Committee*, 483 U.S. 522 (1987), the Supreme Court held that the term *Olympic* belongs to the U.S. Olympic Committee and could not be used by San Francisco Arts & Athletics, Inc. (SFAA), in promoting its "Gay Olympic Games."

The SFAA did not have permission to use the term *Olympic*. Use of a **trade name** without the registered owner's permission is infringement. Suit can be brought for injunctive relief to stop the use of the trademark. The plaintiff owner can also recover all damages and attorneys' fees. If the plaintiff can show a willful infringement, the Lanham Act allows the plaintiff to recover treble damages. Relief is also available for using a trademark without authorization in advertising.

Recent changes in the law allow a competitor to seek treble damages when its product is used deceptively in a comparative ad.

A more recent and critical aspect of the Lanham Act is the concept of **trade dress.** Trade dress consists of the colors, designs, and shapes associated with a product. If someone copies the color schemes and shapes, they are likely to benefit from the goodwill of the owner and developer of the trade dress. The subtle copying of trade dress dilutes the value of the company's goodwill and reputation. The following case is a landmark one on the extent of federal protection for trade dress.

CASE 16.3

Two Pesos, Inc. v. *Taco Cabana, Inc.*
505 U.S. 763 (1992)

Two Pesos, Two Cabanas, and Infringement

FACTS

Taco Cabana, Inc. (respondent), operates a chain of fast-food restaurants in Texas that serve Mexican food. The first Taco Cabana restaurant opened in 1978 in San Antonio, and five more opened by 1985. Taco Cabana's theme or trade dress is self-described as follows:

A festive eating atmosphere having interior dining and patio areas decorated with artifacts, bright colors, paintings and murals. The patio includes interior and exterior areas with the interior patio capable of being sealed off from the outside patio by overhead garage doors. The stepped exterior of the building is a festive and vivid color scheme using top border paint and neon stripes. Bright awnings and umbrellas continue the theme.

In December 1985, Two Pesos (petitioner) opened its first restaurant in Houston. Its motif was very similar to Taco Cabana's self-described motif above. Two Pesos expanded rapidly in Houston but did not enter the San Antonio market. Taco Cabana entered the Houston and Austin markets in 1986 and expanded into Dallas and El Paso, where Two Pesos was doing business.

In 1987, Taco Cabana sued Two Pesos in federal district court for trade dress infringement under the Lanham Act. The jury found that Taco Cabana has a trade dress; taken as a whole, the trade dress is non-functional; the trade dress is inherently distinctive; the trade dress has not acquired a secondary meaning (which means that people associate the colors, configurations, and designs of the trade dress with Taco Cabana) in the Texas market; and the alleged

infringement creates a likelihood of confusion on the part of ordinary customers about the source or association of the restaurant's goods or services. The trial court held that Two Pesos had infringed Taco Cabana's trade dress.

The court of appeals affirmed and Two Pesos appealed maintaining that, without a finding of secondary meaning, there was no infringement.

JUDICIAL OPINION

WHITE, Justice

The Lanham Act was intended to make "actionable the deceptive and misleading use of marks" and "to protect persons engaged in . . . commerce against unfair competition."

A trademark is defined in 15 U.S.C. § 1127 as including "any word, name, symbol, or device or any combination thereof" used by any person "to identify and distinguish his or her goods, including a unique product, from those manufactured or sold by others and to indicate the source of the goods, even if that source is unknown." In order to be registered, a mark must be capable of distinguishing the applicant's goods from those of others. Marks are often classified in categories of generally increasing distinctiveness; following the classic formulation set out by Judge Friendly, they may be (1) generic; (2) descriptive; (3) suggestive; (4) arbitrary; or (5) fanciful. The latter three categories of marks, because their intrinsic nature serves to identify a particular source of a product, are deemed inherently distinctive and are entitled to protection. In contrast, generic marks—those that "refe[r] to the genus of which the particular product is a species"—are not registrable as trademarks.

The general rule regarding distinctiveness is clear: An identifying mark is distinctive and capable of being protected if it *either* (1) is inherently distinctive *or* (2) has acquired distinctiveness through secondary meaning.

Petitioner argues that the jury's finding that the trade dress has not acquired a secondary meaning shows conclusively that the trade dress is not inherently distinctive.

Engrafting onto § 43(a) a requirement of secondary meaning for inherently distinctive trade dress also would undermine the purposes of the Lanham Act. Protection of trade dress, no less than of trademarks, serves the Act's purpose to "secure to the owner of the mark the goodwill of his business and to protect the ability of consumers to distinguish among competing producers. National protection of trademarks is desirable, Congress concluded, because trademarks foster competition and the maintenance of quality by securing to the producer the benefits of good reputation."

[A]dding a secondary meaning requirement could have anticompetitive effects, creating particular burdens on the start-up of small companies. It would present special difficulties for a business, such as respondent, that seeks to start a new product in a limited area and then expand into new markets. Denying protection for inherently distinctive nonfunctional trade dress until after secondary meaning has been established would allow a competitor, which has not adopted a distinctive trade dress of his own, to appropriate the originator's dress in other markets and to deter the originator from expanding into and competing in these areas.

We agree with the Court of Appeals that proof of secondary meaning is not required to prevail on a claim under § 43(a) of the Lanham Act where the trade dress at issue is inherently distinctive, and accordingly the judgment of that court is affirmed.

CASE QUESTIONS

1. Does the court make a distinction between trade name and trade dress? Why, or why not?

2. Does the Lanham Act require a showing of secondary meaning to acquire protection for trade dress?

3. What would happen to a new business if the secondary meaning requirement were imposed?

4. How could this suit have been resolved alternatively?

5. Evaluate the ethics of Two Pesos.

In *Wal-Mart* v. *Samara*, 529 U.S. 205 (2000), the U.S. Supreme Court limited its ruling in *Two Pesos* to product packaging and held that there is no trade dress protection for product design absent some form of registration under federal law such as trademark or patent or the product design having achieved some level of distinctiveness. In the case, Samara designed, produced, and sold a line of seersucker children's clothes with bold appliques and large collars. Wal-Mart had introduced its own line of clothing that was similar. Product design trade dress enjoys no inherent protection. Product packaging, which the court noted was involved in *Two Pesos*, does enjoy protection as in the shape of a Coca-Cola bottle. However, absent some other statutory protection, product design requires legislative change for protection.

e-commerce

The Semiconductor Chip Protection Act of 1984 (17 U.S.C. Sections 901 *et seq.*) provides intellectual property protection for a new form of property in the computer age: the semiconductor chip. The act permits civil recovery and penalties of up to $250,000 for chip piracy, which includes infringing the design of another's chip during the ten-year period in which the chip design and manufacturing stencils enjoy exclusive protection under federal law. Reverse engineering of chips themselves is not prohibited so long as any new products developed as a result are not simply a product of that process of examining a competitor's work. Any design based on reverse engineering must build on the examined design and offer some new innovation or capability.

C O N S I D E R . . .

16.4 They can be spotted from a distance. The classic Ferrari design with its lined side panels and hidden headlights is unique. Although the Ferrari name is a registered trademark, the design of the Ferrari is not. Roberts Motor Company designed a car with a look similar to the Ferrari, but the Roberts car would sell for a much lower price. Ferrari brought suit against Roberts alleging infringement. Is Ferrari correct? Can a nonpatented, noncopyrighted design belong exclusively to Ferrari? [*Ferrari* v. *Roberts Motor Co.*, 944 F.2d 1235 (6th Cir. 1991), *cert. denied*, 505 U.S. 1219 (1992)]

C O N S I D E R . . .

16.5 Mr. Orenthal James Simpson has applied for trademark registration for his widely used nicknames of O.J. and Juice. Joseph J. Gleason, vice president and general counsel of Florida Citrus Mutual, a trade group, responded, "I'd question if he could copyright something that generic."

Are the nicknames entitled to trademark and trade name protection? The trade names and trademarks will be used for the merchandising of Simpson products. Mr. Simpson was acquitted of the double homicide charges against him for the killing of his ex-wife, Nicole Brown, and her friend Ronald Goldman, but was later held liable monetarily in a civil suit for wrongful death. His name and nicknames are household words because of the notoriety of the trial. Evaluate the likelihood of Mr. Simpson obtaining the trademarks.

In 1996, the Federal Trademark Dilution Act took effect. Its purpose is to prevent "the lessening of the capacity of a famous mark to identify and distinguish goods or services." The act covers the problem of blurring or creating confusion among consumers about the source of a product and tarnishment or the portrayal of a product in an unsavory manner.

Consumer surveys have become a critical part of infringement trials. Where the issue is whether the public has been misled by a trademark infringement, the responses of a representative sample are critical evidence in a case. One such case involved a survey of consumers in twenty-four shopping malls nationwide. The Baltimore Colts had become the Indianapolis Colts, and the Canadian Football League proposed calling one of its teams the Baltimore CFL Colts. The survey showed consumers were confused, and the data carried the case for the former Baltimore Colts's owners.

C O N S I D E R . . .

16.6 Jim Henson Productions created a new character, Spa'am, a high priest of the wild boars, which is a group of boars that worship Miss Piggy, another Henson creation and a pig puppet. The movie *Muppet Treasure Island* introduced Spa'am as a character and also as a stuffed animal toy for children to purchase. Spa'am acts childish.

Hormel Foods Corporation brought suit against Henson Productions, alleging that the new character will cause the public to spurn Spam, Hormel's popular luncheon meat. Hormel's suit asked for an injunction against Henson Productions to prohibit it from releasing the movie until the character's name was changed. Hormel spokesman Alan Krejci notes, "Henson Productions is seeking to use our trademark . . . for monetary gain." Should the injunction be granted? Are the puppet and its name infringements of the Spam trademark?

EXHIBIT 16.1   **Summary of Intellectual Property Rights**

TYPE OF INTELLECTUAL PROPERTY	TRADEMARKS	COPYRIGHTS	PATENTS	TRADE SECRETS
Protection	Words, names, symbols, or devices used to identify a product or service	Original creative works of authorship, such as writings, movies, records, and computer software	Utility, design, and plant patents	Advantageous formulas, devices, or compilation of information
Applicable standard	Identifies and distinguishes a product or service	Original creative works in writing or in another format	New and nonobvious advances in the art	Not readily ascertainable, not disclosed to the public
Where to apply	Patent and Trademark Office	Register of Copyrights	Patent and Trademark Office	No public registration necessary
Duration	Indefinite so long as it continues to be used	Life of author plus 70 years, or 95 years from publication for "works for hire"	Utility and plant patents, 20 years from date of application; design patents, 14 years	Indefinite so long as secret is not disclosed to public

Adapted from Anderson's Business Law, © 2001 by David Twaney, Marianne Jennings and Ivan Fox.

Exhibit 16.1 provides a summary of intellectual property rights and protections.

BUSINESS PROPERTY PROTECTION IN INTERNATIONAL BUSINESS

Patent Protection

A patent in the United States affords protection for inventors only in the United States. To ensure international protection, the inventor needs to register the patent in each country where he will be selling the product or idea.

The period for patent protection varies from country to country. The United States does not permit patent protection for products until the patent is granted, whereas other countries afford protection from the time application is made. Procedures for obtaining patents also vary significantly from country to country. For example, many countries hold **opposition proceedings** as part of the patent process. Much like the federal regulatory promulgation steps (see Chapter 6), the description of the patent is published, and the public is invited to study the description and possibly oppose the granting of a patent.

Some countries impose **working requirements** on the patent holder, which means that the idea or product must be produced commercially within a certain period of time or the patent protection is revoked.

Re: Pokemon

The Pokemon phenomenon has swept the United States with the trading cards of the video game, cartoon, and movie characters carrying unusually high values. For example, a Charizard card sells for around $45. Because of the high value of the trading cards, a large counterfeit industry has begun. Knock-offs from just the trading card portion of the Pokemon fad are estimated to have cost Nintendo $725 million in 1998.

Nintendo has hired private investigators around the globe to stop the distribution of knock-off cards and Pokemon video games. The investigators spot the fake cards by holding them up to the light. One cannot see through a real Pokemon card but can see through a knock-off. The private investigators then tear up the fake cards they find. In a recent raid in New York City, a team of Nintendo private investigators recovered 8,000 pirated Pokemon goods in 29 retail stores.

With the retail distribution halted there, Nintendo has been able to trace the items to importers in Los Angeles and obtained a court order halting their distribution of products to retailers. From there Nintendo plans to find the manufacturers of the knock-off goods that they believe are located in Taiwan.

What intellectual property rights does Nintendo hold in its Pokemon game software and its trading cards? Are injunctions a remedy available under federal law? Can Nintendo destroy the knock-off goods?

For more information: Dean Takahashi, "In Pursuit of Pokemon Pirates," *Wall Street Journal*, 8 November 1999, B1, B4.

Trademark Protection

In the United States, trademarks are registered to afford protection. However, like patents, the U.S. registration is effective only in the United States. For protection in other countries, a trademark must be registered (if the country affords the protection of registration). In some countries, known as common law countries, trademark protection is established through use in that country and through the recognition by others of the use and distinction provided by the trademark. In a recent change in the United States, protection for trademarks is afforded without actually introducing the product on the market. Beginning on November 16, 1989, companies could register trademarks without first marketing the product. This change has been perceived as one that will help the United States in its efforts to compete in the international market, because European protection is afforded from the time of application, which can be before the product is used or marketed.

Visit the World Intellectual Property Organization:
http://www.wipo.org

Several international registries attempt to offer international protection. For example, the 1891 **Madrid Agreement Concerning the International Registration of Trademarks** provides a central form of registration through the International Bureau, which is part of the World Intellectual Property Organization (WIPO) in Geneva, Switzerland. Registrations with the bureau are effective for five years in all member countries unless one of the members objects to the trademark registration, in which case the registration is not effective in that country. In addition, the United States is a party to the 1929 **Pan American Convention,** which includes a provision affording trademark protection in all member countries.

In 1989, a diplomatic convention in Madrid resulted in the adoption of the Madrid Protocol Concerning the International Registration of Marks, which created WIPO. WIPO would serve, for those countries participating in the Madrid Protocol System established in 1891, as a central clearinghouse for all trademarks. National or local application would also result in WIPO application for participating nations. The system is designed to simplify, streamline, and reduce the costs of international trademark protection.

Visit BUFETE AF, a Spanish intellectual property law firm, to learn more about the Community Trademark:
http://www.bufeteaf.es

In 1996, the European Union began its one-stop trademark registration known as Community Trademark (CTM). Under the provisions of this program, U.S. companies register their trademarks once and enjoy protection in all countries that are part of the European Union. The trademark and backup materials are filed with the Office of Harmonization of the Internal Market (OHIM). The OHIM will then notify the trademark offices in each of the member states of the European Union.

Many countries have permitted the unauthorized use of trademarks in an effort to develop local economies. These countries permit the production of **knock-off goods,** which are goods that carry the trademark or trade name of a firm's product but are not actually produced by that firm. A costly problem for trademark holders is the **gray market.** Manufacturers in foreign countries are authorized to produce a certain amount of goods, but many foreign manufacturers exceed their licensed quota and dump the goods into the market at a much lower price and thereby reduce the trademark owner's market. Such excessive use is an infringement.

CONSIDER...

16.7 Congoleum Corporation holds the American patents for the manufacture of chemically embossed vinyl floor covering and owns corresponding patents in twenty-six foreign countries. Mannington is also involved in the manufacture of vinyl flooring and is authorized to use Congoleum patents in the United States. However, Mannington has just expanded its operations to other countries and is using its license rights in them. Congoleum claims that the patent license for the other countries must be obtained in those countries as well as in the United States. Is Congoleum correct? [*Mannington Mills, Inc. v. Congoleum Corp.,* 595 F.2d 1287 (3d Cir. 1979)]

CONSIDER...

16.8   Illia Lekach and Simon Falic are brothers-in-law who founded Perfumania, Inc. Perfumania is a chain of no-frills stores that sells 170 brands of upscale perfumes, such as Estée Lauder, Calvin Klein, and Chanel, at prices 20 to 70 percent below department store prices. Lekach referred to the company as the Toys R Us of perfume sales.

Manufacturers of the expensive perfumes like to sell only to their full-price department store customers. Perfumania must get its supplies from the gray market—unauthorized and authorized distributors in other countries where manufacturers charge less than in the United States.

Givenchy, Boucheron, and Cosmair have sued Perfumania for copyright infringement and patent violations. The manufacturers maintain that they must pay the promotion fees on the perfumes and Perfumania enjoys the benefits of the expensive promotions without paying costs. One manufacturer notes, "I don't want to sell to the gray market. It's not a strategy. You kill your name."

Evaluate the legalities and ethics of Perfumania's gray market purchases and discount sales.

Copyrights in International Business

Review the Berne Convention for the Protection of Literary and Artistic Works (Paris Text 1971):
http://www.law.cornell.edu:80/treaties/berne/overview.html

The United States was a party to the 1986 Berne Convention agreement and made it a part of U.S. copyright law through the **Berne Convention Implementation Act of 1988.** Under the convention and the act, a collective work can bear its own notice of copyright and still afford protection for the individual contributions within the work. Under prior copyright law, each contribution had to carry its own notice to be afforded full protection. These new provisions apply to books, magazines, and records. The purpose of the Berne Convention, called the Convention for the Protection of Literary and Artistic Works, was to establish international uniformity in copyright protection. The convention was signed on September 9, 1986, and became effective in the United States on March 1, 1989. Twenty-four countries are members of Berne, which is administered by WIPO. However, the Berne Convention gives backdoor copyright protection to works originating in non-Berne member countries if the work is simultaneously published in a Berne member country. Presently, some copyright holders are governed under previous U.S. copyright laws, which required separate and collective copyrights for full protection.

Differing International Standards

The protection of intellectual property in other countries is a difficult task, particularly when the standards of those countries do not recognize computer software as a property right.

China has led the world with software piracy. In 1994, the U.S. Trade Representative placed China on its Special 301 Priority Watch List. By February 1995, the United States threatened to impose more than $1 billion in trade sanctions if China did not take action to curb software pirating. In August 1995, the United States and China reached an agreement to prevent the sanctions. China agreed to take immediate action against known software pirates and to confiscate software packages without seals that U.S. companies would place on their software packages and materials. China remains on the trade watch list as the cultural change for appreciation of ownership rights with respect to computer programs takes place.

ENFORCING BUSINESS PROPERTY RIGHTS

Product Disparagement

When an untrue statement is made about a business product or service, the defamation is referred to as **disparagement** and is either **trade libel** (written) or **slander of title** (oral). These business torts occur when one business makes untrue statements about another business, its product, or its abilities. The elements for disparagement follow:

1. False statement about a business product or about its reputation, honesty, or integrity
2. Publication
3. Statement that is directed at a business (in many cases, businesses are considered public figures, and the statement must be made with malice and the intent to injure that business)
4. Damages

These elements are the same as those discussed in Chapter 10 for the personal tort of defamation (see pgs. 365–373). The *Bose* case deals with the tort of disparagement.

CASE 16.4

Bose Corporation v. Consumers Union of United States, Inc.
466 U.S. (1984)

Woofers, Tweeters, and Disparagement

FACTS

Bose Corporation is the manufacturer of the Bose 901, a stereo loudspeaker. In May 1970, the Consumers Union publication, *Consumer Reports,* analyzed and evaluated loudspeaker systems. The middle-range price group was analyzed, and the Bose 901 was included. It was described in a two-page boxed-off section as "unique and unconventional," but the description also pointed out that a listener could "pinpoint the location of various instruments much more easily with a standard speaker than with the Bose system." The following is an excerpt from the boxed description:

Worse, individual instruments heard through the Bose system seemed to grow to gigantic proportions and tended to wander about the room. For instance, a violin appeared to be ten feet wide and a piano stretched from wall to wall. With orchestral music, such effects seemed inconsequential. But we think they might become annoying when listening to soloists. . . .

We think the Bose system is so unusual that a prospective buyer must listen to it and judge it for himself. We would suggest delaying so big an investment until you were sure the system would please you after the novelty value had worn off.

(continued)

The article was not written by the same people who made the observation of the speakers. The observers described the sound as moving around the room and the article described the sounds as wandering back and forth.

Bose Corporation took exception to many of the statements made and asked *Consumer Reports* to publish a retraction. *Consumer Reports* would not retract the statements, and Bose sued for disparagement. The district court found that Bose was a public figure and, as such, was required to prove that the statements were made with knowledge they were false (malice). However, the court did find that some of the remarks constituted disparagement and held for Bose (petitioner). The court of appeals reversed on the grounds that the statements were not made with malice, that the article did not accurately reflect what evaluators heard but was written for a mass audience and not with reckless disregard for the truth. Bose appealed.

JUDICIAL OPINION

STEVENS, Justice
Respondent (Consumers Union) correctly reminds us that in cases raising First Amendment issues we have repeatedly held that an appellate court has an obligation to "make an independent examination of the whole record" in order to make sure "that the judgment does not constitute a forbidden intrusion on the field of free expression."

. . . There are categories of communication and certain special utterances to which the majestic protection of the First Amendment does not extend because they "are no essential part of any exposition of ideas, and are of such slight social value as a step to truth that any benefit that may be derived from them is clearly outweighed by the social interest in order and morality." Libelous speech has been held to constitute one such category. . . .

We agree with the Court of Appeals that the difference between hearing violin sounds move around the room and hearing them wander back and forth fits easily within the breathing space that gives life to the First Amendment. We may accept all of the purely factual findings of the District Court and nevertheless hold as a matter of law that the record does not contain clear and convincing evidence that [Consumers Union] prepared the loudspeaker article with knowledge that it contained a false statement, or with reckless disregard for the truth.

The judgment of the Court of Appeals is affirmed.

CASE QUESTIONS

1. Who prepared the *Consumer Reports* article?
2. Why is malice an important part of the case?
3. What classes of speech are exceptions to First Amendment protection?
4. Is disparagement a difficult tort to prove?

Palming Off

Palming off, one of the oldest unfair methods of competition, occurs when one company sells its product by leading buyers to believe it is really another company's product. For example, there were many cases of palming off during the early 1980s, when Cabbage Patch dolls were popular, in demand, and scarce. Many replicas were made and called "Cabbage Patch dolls" even though they were not manufactured by Coleco, the original creator.

Establishing palming off requires proof that there is likely to be confusion because of the appearance or name of the competing product. For example, labeling a diamond DeBiers instead of DeBeers is likely to cause confusion. Competitors' packaging with the same colors and design as an original product creates confusion. Potential buyers are likely to be confused as to who actually made the product and who has what market and quality reputation.

BUSINESS STRATEGY

When Is Your Product Too Close for Competition?

Bristol-Myers develops, produces, and markets over-the-counter ("OTC") medicines, including Excedrin PM. Excedrin PM is an analgesic/sleep aid that is the largest seller in the United States.

© Susan Van Etten

Extensive advertising and promotional campaigns by Bristol-Myers have resulted in Excedrin PM's excellent reputation and public acceptance.

McNeil markets the leading line of analgesics in the United States under the Tylenol trademark. In 1991, McNeil filed for trademark protection for a new analgesic/sleep aid, Tylenol PM.

Both Excedrin PM and Tylenol PM contain essentially the same ingredients—namely, 500 mg of acetaminophen. The outer cartons of both Tylenol PM caplets and Excedrin PM caplets are predominantly dark blue. The trademarks "Tylenol" and "Excedrin" appear in white capital letters immediately followed by the yellow letters "PM." Below the products' name line appears the phrase "For pain with sleeplessness" for Tylenol and "For pain with accompanying sleeplessness" for Excedrin. At the lower right portion of the carton, McNeil has depicted the two light blue caplets imprinted with the Tylenol PM product name. Bristol-Myers has depicted two light blue tablets imprinted with the letters "PM."

Bristol-Myers claims product confusion, misappropriation, and infringement. McNeil's says its Tylenol PM name is generic and will not cause confusion.

Donald Casey, the product manager for McNeil, revealed the following in a deposition in the litigation Bristol-Myers brought for trade name and trade dress infringement:

Q: After you get by the mark could you pick out the package from exhibits 6, 7, 8 and 9 which look the most like this one? This one being Excedrin PM. . . .
A: 8B.
Q: 8B. Okay. Let me now ask you the question in kind of reverse. Looking at the Tylenol PM package, blue package, would you agree that it has some similarity to the Excedrin PM package?
A: Yes. . . .
Q: Is there any package you see on here which has a greater similarity to Excedrin PM than the Tylenol PM package you marketed. . . .
A: Not really.
Q: So if I'm understanding you then you spent about four hundred thousand dollars to have Gerstman & Meyers create about 60 or 70 of these package markups, right?
A: Yes.
Q: And in the end what you brought to market was the one package markup that looked—that had the greatest similarity to Excedrin PM, right?
A: As we phrased it, yes.
Bristol-Myers Squibb Co. v. McNeil PCC, Inc., 786 F. Supp. 1982 (E.D.N.Y. 1992); affirmed in part and reversed in part, 973 F.2d 1033 (2d Cir. 1992)

Was Tylenol PM getting a free ride on Excedrin PM's success? Was this litigation a good strategy for pushing the envelope on the similarities in the products' names and appearances?

Could you, as a product manager, have made the same decision to pick the product package that most looked like Excedrin PM? Is it ethical to copy a product to create confusion?

Misappropriation

Some businesses have a **trade secret**—chemical formula, procedure, customer list, data, or device that only that business has. Generally, these types of secrets should be given patent or copyright protection. However, those that do not qualify for these federal statutory protections (discussed earlier in this chapter) have only the tort of **misappropriation** as protection. Misappropriation occurs when a competitor figures out the formula for a product or takes a customer list or other data and puts the product or information to use competitively. Misappropriation is conversion of a trade secret, and proof of misappropriation requires that there be some theft, industrial espionage, or bribery as the means used for obtaining the trade secret. These tort actions are in addition to the criminal issues discussed earlier.

BIOGRAPHY

CALVIN KLEIN AND LINDA WACHNER: A BATTLE OF JEANS AT PRICE CLUB

One of the most dramatic intellectual property suits of this era involved Calvin Klein and Linda Wachner, head of the Warnaco Group. Warnaco Group was the licensed manufacturer for Calvin Klein jeans but was sued by Mr. Klein because he said that Warnaco exceeded its licensing authority for the trademark jeans by selling them to warehouse clubs where they were sold at discount prices. Mr. Klein said the sales diminished the value of the Calvin Klein trademark and called Ms. Linda Wachner "a cancer on the value and integrity of my business." He also referred to Ms. Wachner as "vulgar and unprofessional."

Ms. Wachner says that Mr. Klein was simply disturbed by the public revelation that most designers do not manufacture their own clothing but, rather, have mass-market manufacturers handle the production and distribution.

At the time the suit was filed in 2000, Warnaco's stock had declined 83 percent since 1998 and the company was carrying debt of $1.2 billion.

Mr. Klein hired David Boies' (of the Microsoft litigation and *Bush* v. *Gore*) firm to represent him in his suit to have the license for his jeans returned to him.

Warnaco responded to the suit by alleging that Klein only took action after he failed to sell his company and that his financial problems could not be solved by "throwing stones at Warnaco." Klein responded that he could not sell the company because of its affiliation with Warnaco.

By March 2001, the two settled their litigation. The terms of the settlement, announced as the parties left the courtroom just prior to selecting a jury in the case, were sealed but the parties did disclose that Warnaco agreed to substantially curb its sales of the jeans to warehouse clubs.

However, Warnaco's stock continued to tumble and its troubles mounted as its auditors rebelled on disclosures and its canceled calls with analysts. Its losses mounted and banks were attempting to unload their Warnaco debt for as little as 35 cents on the dollar. By the summer of 2001, Warnaco was in bankruptcy in what many industry insiders called "poetic justice" for Wachner, Warnaco's CEO since 1986.

Why would Mr. Klein worry about the sales to warehouse clubs? Does a trademark owner have the right to restrict the number of sales and the types of buyers? What business lessons should both sides learn from the dispute and litigation?

For more information: Leslie Kaufman, "Calvin Klein Suit against Warnaco Is Settled," *New York Times*, 23 January 2001, C1, C7.

WHAT CAN A BUSINESS OWN? REAL PROPERTY

The Nature of Real Property

Land

Real property consists of more than just land itself; it is a bundle of rights. An old saying in property law is, "The owner of the soil owns also to the sky and to the depths." When you own real property, you own the surface that we actually see and upon which buildings are placed, but you also own **air rights** and **mineral rights.**

Air Rights

Air rights in real property consist of the right to use the air above the surface land that is described as your real property interest. Your land interest can actually be separated into two interests so that you can keep the surface rights and transfer the air rights. The ownership of air rights is important in large cities because building up is the only way to expand available space in cities limited in expansion on the ground. For example, in New York City, the Met Life building is built in the air rights above Grand Central Station. This fifty-nine–story building occupies the air rights above the station. The foundation of the building rests on the surface of the land through an **easement,** or a right to use the land of another for a limited purpose.

The sale of the air space above one's surface land can be profitable. In cities in which horizontal growth is limited, the only means of expansion for businesses is to build vertically. Excessive demand coupled with a finite supply make air space rights extremely valuable. In Los Angeles, the air space above the owned surface rights has its own value for which property taxes are assessed. Some businesses purchase air rights for possible future expansion and simply hold the rights until their expansion occurs.

There are limitations on air rights. All property owners take their air rights subject to the right of flight. Airplanes may use the air lots over your property in travel without committing trespass and without being required to pay compensation.

Mineral Rights

Mineral rights are rights to what rests below the surface of land. Examples of valuable commodities that a landowner can own beneath a property's surface include oil, gas, coal, geothermal energy pockets, and water. Just as with air rights, these subsurface rights can be transferred separately. The right to drill for oil and gas can be conveyed to another (possibly in exchange for royalty payments) and the surface rights retained. Those who purchase the mineral rights are again given an easement for access to the property for drilling.

Fixtures

There is yet another form of real property rights that crosses personal property with real property. **Fixtures** are a part of the property that were once personal property but have become a part of the land or a structure on the land. For example, a microwave oven is personal property when it is purchased from a store. But if that oven is installed in a home in a place built especially for it and it is bolted to the walls or cabinets in the kitchen, it becomes a part of the real property. Fixtures often create confusion in the transfer of real property, as the parties disagree over whether the personal property was intended to become a part of the real property. Questions that are important in determining whether an item is a fixture and part of the real property or personal property are as follows:

1. What did the parties intend? If the parties have agreed that an item is a fixture, it will be treated as such. For example, draperies in a home are a frequent source of disagreement among buyers and sellers over whether they stay with the home or go with the seller. If their contract includes draperies, then they are treated as fixtures and will transfer with the home to the buyer.

2. How is the item attached to the real property? The greater the degree of attachment and the more the item has become a part of the real property, the greater the likelihood that it will be classified as a fixture. One exception to this general rule is the classification of **trade fixtures.** Many forms of personal property that a business uses will be attached to the real property,

but they are a part of the business and are not intended to remain a part of the real property. Retail stores have counters bolted to the floor. These counters are an integral part of the store, but they are trade fixtures and would be classified as personal property and not a part of the real property.

3. What is the relationship between the attacher and the property? Who attached the fixture to the real property, and is the attacher a tenant or a landowner? Shelves attached by a tenant are probably not intended to remain as part of the real property. Those same shelves attached by a homeowner would probably be classified as a fixture. A commercial tenant is different from a residential tenant because of the rules about trade fixtures being personal property.

4. Who wants to know? Courts vary in their classifications of fixtures according to who is asking whether an item is a fixture. If an insurer is seeking classification of an item as personal property so that an insurance claim for damage to the real property is less, the courts will probably find in favor of the insured and classify the item as a fixture. For assessments of value for property tax purposes, the courts label items as fixtures more frequently because of the increased value of the property they bring.

CONSIDER...

16.9   Consider the following items and determine whether the items would be fixtures or personal property. Assume that the parties have not reached an agreement on the nature of the fixtures.

1. A pipe organ installed in a building owned and operated by Organ Stop Pizza. Organ Stop Pizza features an organist each night who works with the patrons to play appropriate music and offer entertainment to children. What additional information would help you in determining whether the organ would be a fixture and real property or simply just personal property?

2. Refrigerators, washers, and dryers found in the apartments of a twenty-unit complex a buyer has just purchased.

3. The garage door opener and keys to a house just purchased.

4. A neon sign purchased by a tattoo parlor and installed above the door of its leased premises in a strip mall.

5. The color-coordinated bedspreads and curtains in a hotel just sold.

Interests in Real Property

There are various forms of ownership interests in real property. The highest degree of land ownership is called a **fee simple** interest. If a company or individual has a fee simple interest in property, it owns full rights to the property and has the freedom to mortgage the property, sell the property, and, in the case of individuals, transfer the property by will.

A lesser degree of real property ownership is the **life estate.** In this form of real property interest, one person is given the right to use and occupy the property for life. When that person, the **life tenant,** dies, the property either goes back to the grantor (the person who originally transferred it) or, in most cases, to another person—called the **remainderman.** Generally, the remainderman receives a fee simple interest. The life estate is used often in estate planning. A surviving spouse is given a life estate in the family residence with the couple's children (remaindermen) receiving the fee simple interest when the spouse passes away.

Another real property interest is the **easement,** which is a right to use another's property. There are access easements that permit the owner of the easement to use a path or road on another's property in order to gain access to his own real property. There are negative easements, where the easement holder is promised by another property holder that the latter will not, for example, plant trees that will block sunlight from the solar panels on the easement holder's property. There are easements in gross that run through most properties that are given to utility companies for the right to run wires and pipes through segments of property so individual property owners and the surrounding community can enjoy utility service.

A final form of real property interest is the **lease,** which is temporary possession of real property. A lease can be a fixed lease in which there is a beginning and ending date, or the lease can be a **periodic tenancy** in which the landlord and tenant go from period to period renewing the lease. For example, a month-to-month tenancy is a form of a periodic tenancy in which a tenant pays rent on a given day each month and thereby renews the lease. To end a periodic tenancy, the other party must be given a full period's notice of termination. If the rent in a periodic tenancy is paid on the first day of each month and the tenant wishes to end the lease, notice must be given on the first of the month. If, for example, a tenant notified the landlord on October 15 that the tenant wished to terminate the lease, the tenant's obligation to pay rent continues through November, because the tenant will not have given a full period's notice until the end of November.

A lease for a fixed period has the benefit of fixed rent that cannot be changed until the lease is over. A periodic tenant's rent can be raised at any time once a full period's notice is given.

Most states have full statutory provisions on residential leases, and many have requirements on commercial leases. These statutory provisions cover such issues as the condition of the property when the lease begins, maintenance, security deposits, and when lease agreements must be in writing to be enforceable.

Transferring Real Property

The transfer of real property is more complex than the transfer of personal property. Real property is transferred through a document called a **deed.** A deed must be in writing, it must be signed by the owner (grantor) of the property, and it must contain a full legal description of the property in order to transfer title to real property.

There are several different types of deeds. The type of deed determines the degree of title protection the transferee is given by the transferor or grantor. A **warranty deed** or **general warranty deed** provides the highest degree of title protection from the grantor. When the grantor gives the grantee a warranty deed, he promises that he has good title, that he has the authority to transfer title, and that there are no liens or title problems other than anything noted on the deed. A deed may include a qualification, "subject to public utility easements," which means that the grantee takes the title subject to the utility easements through the property.

A **special warranty deed** or **bargain and sale deed** is one in which the grantor makes the same promises as under a warranty deed but does so only for the time during which he held title to the property. In this form of deed, the grantor is simply saying that he did nothing during his ownership of the property to cloud the title. Most buyers elect to purchase **title insurance,** which is a policy that affords reimbursement to the buyer in the event a title defect arises after the purchase. Title insurance is protection in addition to the grantor's promises, but it covers only defects in title that are of record, such as tax liens and easements.

A **quitclaim deed** is a deed that carries no warranties about the title to the land. In effect, the grantor in a quitclaim deed is saying, "I hereby transfer whatever interest I have in this real property, but there is no guarantee that I hold any interest in this property." The quitclaim deed is often used in situations where someone is trying to clear title to property and obtains quitclaim deeds from many individuals who might or might not have a claim on title.

While the delivery of a complete and signed deed is all that is necessary to transfer title to real property, the process of **recording** is done in nearly all property transfers. Recording is the filing of the deed with a government agency, usually a county recorder or county clerk, so that public notice is given of the transfer and ownership. The risk of not recording a deed is that the grantor could make a subsequent transfer of the land, and, depending upon particular state statutes, the original grantee could lose title to the land to that subsequent transferee.

BUSINESS PLANNING TIP

Before purchasing property, check the area for noise and other activity. Determine flight paths and plans for construction of airports, runways, and possible expansion of airport capacity and facilities.

Title to real property can be transferred in other ways. Real property can be transferred by will, and heirs obtain title through the probate of the estate (still by use of a deed). Title to land can also be transferred through **adverse possession.** Adverse possession is use of another's land for a statutory period of time (generally ranging from ten to twenty years) in an open manner. In effect, what begins as a trespass can ripen into title if the owner of the land takes no action to remove a trespasser from the land. Often called *squatter's rights,* adverse possession can occur in situations as simple as placing a fence incorrectly along a property's border. If the fence encroaches on a neighbor's land by six inches, and the fence remains there for twenty years, the fence builder acquires title to those extra six inches by adverse possession. Parties who succeed each other in land interests, such as a daughter inheriting from a father or a buyer purchasing from a seller, can add together their years of adverse possession to qualify for ownership. This is called *tacking.* A buyer who buys land from a seller who has owned it for ten years and used adjoining property adversely needs only ten more years to claim ownership in a twenty-year jurisdiction.

Financing Real Property Purchases

The purchase of real property is a major transaction for individuals and businesses. Most property buyers are unable to pay cash for their property. Financing arrangements that allow the creditor to take a lien on the purchased property have existed since English common law. The most common form of property security for a creditor is the **mortgage.** In this form of security, a borrower pledges property to the lender as security for the debt that arises because the lender advances the money for purchase of the property. In the event the buyer/borrower does not make the necessary payments to the lender, the lender can **foreclose** on the mortgage. **Foreclosure** is a judicial process in which the lender takes possession and title of mortgaged property and then sells it to satisfy the unpaid debt.

Another form of creditor security for real property purchases is the **deed of trust.** Popular in the western states, this form of security places title to property in

Re: Solar Easements

One form of an easement that is negotiated in more and more sales contracts today is the solar easement. Under common law, there is no "right to light"; someone can build a building next to your property that blocks all of your light and not be liable for any damages. In the case of **Fontainebleau Hotel Corp.** *v.* **Forty-Five Twenty-Five, Inc., 114 So.2d 357 (Fla. 1959),** *a Miami hotel could not obtain relief from a court when the neighboring property owner constructed a fourteen-story addition to its existing hotel that blocked the afternoon sun from the plaintiff hotel's swimming pool and sunbathing areas. The court held that absent an agreement, there were no restrictions on the blockage of light.*

However, with a properly negotiated contract, the right to light can be obtained and protected. The contract can specify that the seller gives a solar easement or right of light to the buyer, or neighbors can agree to a solar easement among themselves. Even residential property owners can benefit from solar easement clauses, particularly when they have a solar heating system that requires the panels of the system to be near direct sunlight to maximize efficiency.

Some cities have passed ordinances that prevent solar panel obstruction. Often a part of zoning laws, these ordinances give the solar system owner a statutory right of light. In these cities, title insurance companies physically inspect neighboring properties for solar systems so that they can exclude solar easements from their policy or offer additional insurance for increased "solar premium."

the hands of a trustee, who holds title until a debtor repays the creditor the full amount of the debt. If the debtor defaults on payments, the trustee may then proceed to sell the property to satisfy the debt. The deed of trust financing arrangement is beneficial to lenders because judicial foreclosure is not required in order to hold a property sale.

Because of the importance of these interests and the need to have priority over subsequent real property creditors, mortgages and deeds of trust are also recorded in the public offices where deeds and other land interests are recorded.

SUMMARY

What does a business own? What are the types of business property?

- Tangible property—physical: real and personal property

- Intangible property—bundles of rights with respect to goodwill, trade names, copyrights, patents, trade dress, and trade secrets

- Real property—bundles of rights with respect to land, attachments, air space, and subsurface materials

What are the rights and issues in personal property owned by a business?

- Documents of title—formal legal document that serves to prove and transfer title to tangible personal property

- Bill of sale—informal document or contract that serves to prove and transfer title to tangible personal property

- Lease—right of use and possession of property for fixed or open-end period

- Bailment—temporary transfer of possession of personal property

- Bailor—party who owns property and surrenders possession

- Bailee—party who has temporary possession of the property of another

- License—right granted of access; generally oral; personal right that is nontransferrable

- Exculpatory clause—clause that attempts to hold a party harmless in the event of damage or injury to another or another's property

- Lien—creditor's right in property to secure debt

- Security interest—UCC lien on personal property

- Chattel mortgage—term for lien on personal property

- Uniform Commercial Code—uniform statute governing commercial transactions adopted in forty-nine states

- Security agreement—contract that creates a security interest

- Collateral—property subject to lien, security interest, or chattel mortgage

- Financing statement—publicly-filed document reflecting security interest

What statutory protections exist for intellectual property?

- Patents—statutory protection for products and processes

- Copyrights—statutory protection for words, thoughts, ideas, music

- Trademarks—statutory protection for product symbols

- Trade names—statutory protection for unique product labels and names

- Trade dress—statutory protection for product colors and motifs

- Trade secrets—criminal sanctions for unauthorized transfer or use

What issues of intellectual property protection exist in international operations?

- OPTH—European Community trademark registration

- WIPO—World Intellectual Property Organization

What private remedies exist for property protections?

- Product disparagement—false and damaging statements

- Misappropriation—use of another's ideas or trade secrets

- Palming off—causing deception about the maker or source of a product

What are real property interests, and what rights are included?

- Air rights—rights of surface owner to air above land surface

- Mineral rights—rights of surface owner to materials beneath the land surface

- Easement—right or privilege in the land of another

- Fixtures—property that was once personal in nature that is affixed to real property and becomes a part of it

- Trade fixtures—personal property used in a trade or business that is attached to real property but is considered personal property

- Fee simple—highest degree of land ownership; full rights of mortgage and transferability

- Life estate—right to use and occupy property for life

- Remainderman—interest in third party following a life estate

- Lease—temporary possession and use of real property

- Periodic tenancy—lease that runs from period to period such as month to month

- Warranty deed—highest level of title protection in real property transfer

- Special warranty deed—promises of title protection only for grantor's period of ownership

- Bargain and sale deed—a special warranty deed

- Title insurance—insurance purchased for buyer's benefit of land title

- Quitclaim deed—transfer of title with no warranties

- Recording—public filing of land documents

- Adverse possession—acquisition of land title through use for statutory period

- Mortgage—lien on real property

- Foreclosure—process of creditor's acquiring mortgaged land for resale

- Deed of trust—alternative form of creditor security in land purchase

QUESTIONS AND PROBLEMS

1. Lotus 1-2-3 is a spreadsheet program that enables users to perform accounting functions electronically on a computer. Users manipulate and control the program with a series of menu commands such as "Copy," "Print," and "Quit." Lotus 1-2-3 has 469 commands arranged into more than 50 menus and submenus and includes what is known as a "macro" feature. Users can write a series of command choices that can then be executed with a single keystroke.

Borland introduced its Quattro spreadsheet program in 1987, after three years of development work by its engineers. Borland's objective was to build a superior spreadsheet program and take over the market, but its product contains an identical copy of the entire Lotus 1-2-3 menu tree. Borland does not dispute its inclusion; it simply notes that the Quattro system builds on the Lotus commands.

Lotus filed suit against Borland for infringement. Borland removed the interface part of its program, but Lotus contends the commands in the Quattro program are virtually the same as the Lotus program—just the first letters are different. Borland maintains the menus are not protected by copyright. Should they be protected? [*Lotus Dev. Corp.* v. *Borland Int'l., Inc.,* 49 F.3d 807 (1st Cir. 1995); *cert.* granted, 515 U.S. 1191 (1995). The Supreme Court deadlocked on the merits, resulting in an affirmance by an equally divided court (516 U.S. 233 [1996]).]

2. Storck Candy manufactures Werther's Original Butter Toffee Candy. The toffee is sold in an eight-ounce bag with a brown background, a picture of a mound of unwrapped candy, an Alpine village, and an old-fashioned container pouring white liquid.

Farley Candy Company introduced its butter toffee candy in a bag the same size and shape as Werther's, with a pair of containers pouring liquid.

Storck says that Farley is using its trade dress in trying to sell its candy. Has Farley done anything that is a tort? Do federal laws offer protection? [*Storck USA, L.P.* v. *Farley Candy Co., Inc.,* 785 F. Supp. 730 (N.D. Ill. 1992)]

3. Moe's Pizza, a restaurant located on Watts Street in New York City, leased its premises from Manhattan Mansions. Water from the bathroom of the residential apartment located above Moe's has been leaking into the kitchen at Moe's. On many occasions, the water leaked directly onto the grill and Moe's was forced to close in order to clean up the water. Additionally, many customers would leave when they saw the water dripping from the ceiling into the cooking area. Moe's withheld its rent of $3,418.76 for the month of February after repeated requests for repairs of the floor and leak were made. Manhattan Mansions has filed suit for nonpayment of rent and eviction. Moe's claims a breach of the implied warranty of habitability. Does the warranty apply here? [*Manhattan Mansions* v. *Moe's Pizza,* 561 N.Y.S. 2d 331 (1990)]

4. Robert Conroy invented and holds the patent for "inflatable bladders used in athletic footgear." The patent is called "Athletic Armor and Inflatable Bag Assembly." The "Bladders" can be inflated with air to cushion and protect the feet of the athletic shoe wearer.

Reebok International, Ltd., manufactures a basketball shoe with inflatable bladders that it sells under the name of the PUMP. Conroy brought suit, claiming Reebok infringed his patent. Reebok says the design and method of inflation are different from Mr. Conroy's patented system. Mr. Conroy says the idea of an inflatable shoe is his and he is entitled to royalties from Reebok. Is Mr. Conroy correct? [*Conroy* v. *Reebok International, Ltd.,* 29 U.S. P. Q.2d 1373 (Mass. 1994)]

5. Roger Burten submitted his "Triumph" electronic game to Milton Bradley for possible mass production, but it was rejected twice after review. One year later, however, Milton Bradley began marketing a new electronic board game under the name of "Dark Tower." There were structural and design similarities between "Triumph" and "Dark Tower." Mr. Burten brought suit for fraud, breach of contract, and trade secret misappropriation. Can Burten recover under any of these theories? [*Burten* v. *Milton Bradley Co.,* 763 F.2d 461 (1st Cir. 1985)]

6. Vanna White is the hostess of *Wheel of Fortune*, one of the most popular game shows in television history. An estimated 40 million people watch the program daily. Capitalizing on the fame that her participation in the show has bestowed on her, Miss White markets her identity to various advertisers.

Samsung Electronics ran a series of ads in at least half-a-dozen publications with widespread, and in some cases national, circulation. Each of the advertisements in the series followed the same theme: Each depicted a current item from popular culture and a Samsung electronic product. Each was set in the twenty-first century and conveyed the message that the Samsung product would still be in use at that time. By hypothesizing outrageous future outcomes for the cultural items, the ads created humorous effects. For example, one lampooned current popular notions of an unhealthy diet by depicting a raw steak with the caption: "Revealed to be health food. 2010 A.D." Another depicted irreverent "news" show host Morton Downey Jr. in front of an American flag with the caption: "Presidential candidate. 2008 A.D."

The advertisement that prompted a Vanna White dispute was for Samsung video cassette recorders (VCR). The ad depicted a robot dressed in a wig, gown, and jewelry that was consciously selected to resemble Vanna White's hair and dresses. The robot was posed next to a game board instantly recognizable as the *Wheel of Fortune* game show set in a stance for which Miss White is famous. The caption of the ad read: "Longest-running game show. 2012 A.D." Defendants referred to the ad as the "Vanna White ad." Unlike the other celebrities used in the campaign, Miss White neither consented to the ads nor was paid. Have Vanna White's rights been violated? Did Samsung violate federal law? [*White* v. *Samsung Elect. Am., Inc.*, 971 F.2d 1395 (9th Cir. 1992)]

7. Spuds MacKenzie is a ring-eyed dog known as the mascot/trademark for Bud Light beer. Beneath Spuds's picture, the following line appears: "The original Party Animal." Another company has begun using the slogan. Anheuser-Busch claims the slogan is a trademark for Bud. Is Anheuser-Busch correct? [*In Re Anheuser-Busch,* No. 17,939, slip op. (May 16, 1990)]

8. Freddie Fuddruckers, Inc., uses glass-enclosed bakeries and butcher areas exposed to the public to emphasize its freshness as a decor theme in all its Fuddruckers restaurants. Fuddruckers floors are checkered, walls tiled, and lighting bright to communicate cleanliness and quality. Ridgeline opened its restaurants with nearly identical decor. Does Fuddruckers have any rights? [*Freddie Fuddruckers, Inc.* v. *Ridgeline, Inc.,* 589 F. Supp. 72 (1984)]

9. Do the following slogans constitute protectable business properties?
a. MetLife: "Get Met, It Pays"
b. General Electric: "GE Brings Good Things to Life"
c. Nike: "Just Do It"
d. Toys "Я" Us: "Я Us"

10. At your hair salon, you notice collections of Gucci, Louis Vuitton, and Fendi handbags, wallets, and briefcases in several glass display cases. As you examine them, you find that no article is priced over $68. You know that no item in any of the genuine collections is priced at or below $68 (key chains and small change purses excluded). Would you buy any of the items for yourself? For gifts? Would you report the salon to anyone? Is it fair to those foreign manufacturers to have these sales of knock-off goods?

RESEARCH PROBLEM

It's a Wonderful Life, but Whose Is It? Using Property Rights to Preserve Earnings

11. In 1946, director Frank Capra produced *It's a Wonderful Life,* a movie based on a short story by Philip Van Doren Stern called "The Greatest Gift." The movie, starring Jimmy Stewart, did not perform well at the box office, and, although it received five Academy Award nominations, it won no awards. The movie's copyright was allowed to lapse. Television stations showed the classic without paying fees since the copyright had lapsed.

However, the U.S. Supreme Court decision in *Stewart* v. *Abend,* 495 U.S. 207 (1990), offering an extension of the copyright protection of the underlying story to the movie, affected Jimmy Stewart's life once again. The original story owner, Mr. Stern, had the rights to the story since the movie rights had lapsed. With his story copyright in place, royalties for its use in the movie had to be paid once again. The owners of *It's a Wonderful Life* began charging fees to cover their fees to Mr. Stern, and the result was costly access. *It's a Wonderful Life* was seen on television day and night during the holiday season when the copyright on the movie had lapsed. Now, with the copyright clarification, the movie rights have been reprotected. The story's continuing protection and the high royalty fees make *It's a Wonderful Life* a singular holiday event.

What is the relationship between movie copyrights and the rights to the underlying story? Who owns what between story authors and movie producers? What should businesses negotiating movie rights and royalties be certain about before signing an agreement?

NOTE

1. Some states do have provisions for registration of trade names for businesses, such as when a company is named Carla's Hair Salon, DBA (doing business as) "The Mane Place."

BUSINESS STRATEGY APPLICATION

In this CD-ROM exercise, you have the chance to follow a company through its ongoing property issues. You then have the opportunity to develop intellectual property policies and systems for your company.

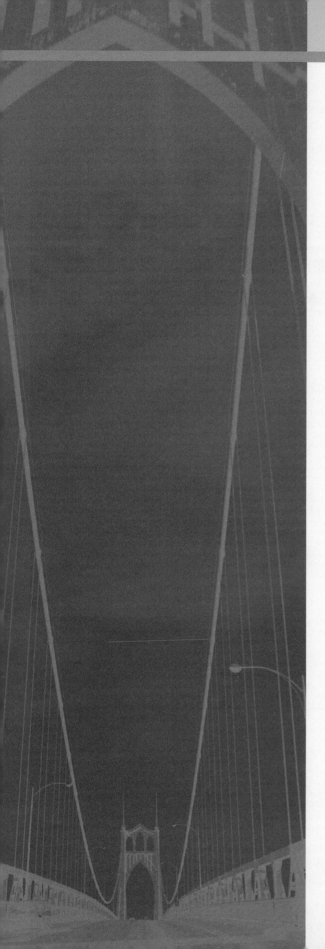

CHAPTER SEVENTEEN

Trade Practices: Antitrust

Economic power is an inevitable result of the free enterprise system. Building a better mousetrap should result in attracting more customers and developing economic power. But gaining economic power through other means destroys the free enterprise system and often precludes purchasers from buying the better mousetrap. They are stuck with a mousetrap that may be mediocre but is built by a firm with perhaps ill-gained economic power and resulting market control.

Antitrust law exists to regulate the growth of economic or market power; it does so in part by ensuring that competition remains a part of the free enterprise system. This chapter answers the following questions: What restraints of trade are permissible? What antitrust laws exist? What penalties can be imposed for violations? What are the forms of horizontal trade restraints and defenses? What are the forms of vertical trade restraints and defenses?

People of the same trade seldom meet together, even for merriment and diversion, but the conversation ends in some contrivance to raise prices. It is impossible indeed to prevent such meetings, by any law which would be consistent with liberty and justice. But though the law cannot hinder people of the same trade from sometimes assembling together, it ought to do nothing to facilitate such assemblies.

ADAM SMITH
The Wealth of Nations

While the law of competition may be sometimes hard for the individual, it is best for the race, because it ensures the survival of the fittest in every department.

ANDREW CARNEGIE

CONSIDER...

Microsoft Corporation virtually controls the software market for personal computers. Over 90 percent of the operating systems used in personal computers have Microsoft software. Rival Novell CEO Robert J. Frankenberg says, "There is no doubt Microsoft is out to kill us. This is not paranoia. They really are out to get us."

Bill Gates, CEO of Microsoft, has responded, "This is a fiercely competitive business."

Microsoft requires its customers who manufacture computers to pay a fee for each computer they ship, even if the computer contains another software maker's operating system. These manufacturers thus have an incentive to use Microsoft because they must pay double royalties if they do not.

The Justice Department and Microsoft entered into a consent decree under which Microsoft halted the payment requirements, but Microsoft then refused to sell Windows to manufacturers using other Net browser systems. Can Microsoft do this?

COMMON LAW PROTECTIONS AGAINST RESTRAINT OF TRADE

Early Common Law of Trade Restraints

In the sixteenth century, the earliest trade restraint cases held that it was void *per se* for parties to agree that one party would not engage in a lawful trade or profession. Oddly enough, the void *per se* rule was not followed with the intent of encouraging competition; rather, it was followed out of fear that those not able to practice their trade would become a burden to society.

In the seventeenth and eighteenth centuries, the courts began to recognize that certain circumstances required some form of trade restraint. The first permissible type of restraint was allowed in the sale of a business: In the sale provisions, the seller agreed not to open a competing business. This trade restraint, called a **covenant not to compete,** was valid so long as it was reasonable in its length and scope. For example, in *Mitchell* v. *Reynolds,* 24 Eng. Rep. 347 (1711), a baker who sold his bakery agreed not to compete in the immediate area for five years, and a court held the covenant valid because it was limited in time and geographic scope.

Modern Common Law of Trade Restraints

Under common law, contracts and covenants that restrain trade are not illegal *per se.* Such contracts are enforceable so long as they are not unreasonable—that is, they go no further than necessary for protection. Exceeding reasonable time and geographic limits would be examples of unreasonable trade restraints. For example, a covenant in a contract for the sale of a dry cleaning business that prohibits the seller from opening another dry cleaning business anywhere in the state is unreasonably broad, but a similar covenant limited to the town where the business is located is probably reasonable. The reasonable restraint is related to the sale of a business and preservation of its goodwill.

Restraints in leases are also related to a business transaction and are valid. For example, a restriction in a shopping center lease that prohibits a lessee from operating a business that competes with other tenants is appropriate so long as the purpose of the restriction is to obtain a proper mix in the shopping center with the idea of attracting more business. Partners' and employees' restrictions that prevent them from competing for a certain time period after they leave a partnership or corporation are also reasonable so long as they are not excessive.

In the following case, the court addresses the issue of a shopping center lease covenant and its reasonableness under common law standards.

BUSINESS PLANNING TIP

When negotiating valid covenants not to compete:

1. Be certain the covenant is necessary.

2. Be certain the covenant is reasonable.

a. Covers only the geographic scope necessary (a five-mile radius for the sale of a dry cleaning business is reasonable; a worldwide prohibition is not)

b. Covers only the time necessary (five years is reasonable; a lifetime prohibition is not)

3. Make the covenant part of the agreement of sale, lease, or employment. Separate agreements not to compete arouse suspicions.

4. Be certain the noncompete clause or paragraph is initialed by both parties.

5. Legal representation helps ensure validity by assumed understanding.

CASE 17.1

Child World, Inc. v. South Towne Center, Ltd.
634 F. Supp. 1121 (S.D. Ohio 1986)

Toys "Я" Us Only

FACTS

Child World, Inc. (plaintiff), operates large retail toy stores throughout Ohio and other states called Children's Palace. South Towne Centre, Ltd. (defendant), is a limited partnership in Ohio that leases space in its South Towne Centre shopping complex to a Children's Palace store. Section 43(A) of the lease, executed in February 1976, provided as follows:

Except insofar as the following shall be unlawful, the parties mutually agree as follows:

A. Landlord shall not use or permit or suffer any other person, firm, corporation or other entity to use any portion of the Shopping Center or any other property located within six (6) miles from the Shopping Center and owned, leased, or otherwise controlled by the landlord (meaning thereby the real property or parties in interest and not a "straw" person or entity) or any person or entity having a substantial identity of interest, for the operation of a toys and games store principally for the sale at retail of toys and games, juvenile furniture and sporting goods such as is exemplified by the Child World and Children's Palace stores operated by Tenant's parent company, Child World, Inc. at the demised premises and elsewhere.

The lease was for 20 years and was signed by Barbara Beerman Weprin, the sole general partner of South Towne. Mad River Ltd. is another limited partnership in which Ms. Weprin is the sole general partner. Mad River owns another parcel of land approximately one-half mile from the South Towne Centre. On December 24, 1985, Mad River entered into an agreement to sell the parcel of land to Toys "Я" Us, Inc. Toys "Я" Us intends to construct a retail facility similar to the description in the above-noted lease clause. When Children's Palace was informed of the sale, they brought suit seeking to enforce the covenant not to lease or sell to a competitor of Children's Palace.

JUDICIAL OPINION

RICE, Circuit Judge

The consensus of the federal courts which have considered covenants in shopping center leases is one

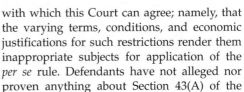

with which this Court can agree; namely, that the varying terms, conditions, and economic justifications for such restrictions render them inappropriate subjects for application of the *per se* rule. Defendants have not alleged nor proven anything about Section 43(A) of the lease which would indicate that it has only anticompetitive consequences. Indeed, in Finding of Fact #9, Defendants agree that Section 43(A) was negotiated as an inducement for Plaintiff to erect a Children's Palace store on Defendants' premises and to enter into a 20-year lease. This economic justification for exclusivity clauses is among the primary reasons that clauses such as Section 43(A) have not been found to be *per se* illegal, but rather have been found consistent with the public interest in economic development. Such laws can induce tenants to establish stores and to enter into a particular marketplace, often then encouraging the entry of other, often smaller, merchants.

A number of factors have been considered by the courts which have excluded restrictive covenants in shopping center leases: (1) the relevant product and geographic markets, together with the showing of unreasonable impact upon competition in these markets, due to the restrictive covenant; (2) the availability of alternate sites for the entity excluded by the operation of such a covenant; (3) the significance of the competition eliminated by the exclusivity clause, and whether present or future competitors were the parties excluded; (4) the scope of the restrictive covenant and whether it varied depending on particular circumstances; and (5) the economic justifications for the inclusion of the restrictive covenant in the lease.

Due to the particular facts of this case, however, the Court needs not, and specifically does not, reach the validity of the six-mile limitation contained in Section 43(A). Regardless of possible overbreadth, a restrictive covenant challenged as unreasonable . . . will be upheld to the extent that a breach of the covenant has occurred or is threatened to occur within a reasonable geographic area and time period. The parties have agreed, in Finding of Fact #12, that

(continued)

the parcel which Defendants seek to convey to Toys "Я" Us is approximately one-half mile from the Children's Palace store covered by the Lease. The Court finds that Section 43(A) is lawful and enforceable to the extent of one-half mile, as required by the facts of this case.

Turning to the impact which enforcement of Section 43(A), as applied in this case, would have upon the Defendants, the burdens of enforcement are not unduly great. As noted *supra*, Section 43(A) does not appear to preclude rental or sale, even within a one-half mile radius, to any number of stores which can compete with a Children's Palace toy and game store but which are not "copycat" stores. On the financial level, there is testimony from a representative of Defendants in the record to the effect that the value of the parcel in question increases almost daily. Moreover, Defendants believe that they will have no difficulty in finding another purchaser, should Section 43(A) preclude their sale of the parcel to Toys "Я" Us.

Enforcement of Section 43(A) to the extent of one-half mile would also not appear to foreclose the entry of Toys "Я" Us into competition with Plaintiff's store in the environs of the South Towne Centre shopping center. In his deposition, J. Tim Logan indicated that,

even were Section 43(A) upheld, presumably in its entirety, Toys "Я" Us would still establish a store in the vicinity of Plaintiff's store.

Other courts have believed that restrictive covenants of a scope of one-half mile or more, albeit less than six miles, are legitimate lures by landlords in order for shopping center tenants to enter particular marketplaces and to thereby enhance the economic development of the community. The public has surely benefitted from the development of South Towne Centre. As a restriction of six miles appeared reasonable to Defendants' predecessors at the time of bargaining, enforcement of Section 43(A) of the Lease to the extent of one-half mile is consistent with that original calculation of value, and certainly reasonable.

CASE QUESTIONS

1. Who leased what from whom?

2. What restrictions were there in the lease agreement?

3. How did Toys "Я" Us become involved?

4. Is the sale a violation of the anticompetition clause?

5. Is the same shopping center involved?

CONSIDER...

17.1 In April 1965, Berkeley Heights Shopping Center leased 11,514 square feet of space to A&P Supermarkets. Under the terms of the lease, Berkeley agreed not to lease any other shopping center space to another grocery store. On April 16, 1977, A&P informed Berkeley that it was ceasing operations and subleasing the premises to Drug Fair, a modern drug store chain that sells food stuffs. In 1985, Berkeley sought to lease other space in the center to another grocery store and Drug Fair objected on the grounds of the covenant not to compete. Berkeley maintains the covenant only applies when the premises Drug Fair occupies are used as a grocery store operation. Who is correct? [*Berkeley Dev. Co.* v. *Great Atlantic & Pacific Tea Co.*, 518 A.2d 790 (N.J. 1986)]

FEDERAL STATUTORY SCHEME ON RESTRAINT OF TRADE

During the last half of the nineteenth century, the United States experienced a tremendous change in its economy. A primarily agricultural economy changed to an industrial economy. Law on business combinations was largely undeveloped and unsuitable for the types of predatory business practices this new industrial age brought. Furthermore, because common law was the only source of law for dealing with these business problems, those laws that did exist were nonuniform. In reaction to the lack of laws and the public outcry over business abuses, Con-

BUSINESS STRATEGY

Keeping Employees in Place When You're Selling the Subsidiary

In July 1995, AT&T decided to sell one of its affiliates, Paradyne Corp., a manufacturer of network access products for the telecommunications industry. AT&T wanted to ensure that Paradyne remained a viable entity because AT&T and its other affiliates, including Lucent Technologies, purchased many of the network access products Paradyne manufactured. To make Paradyne more attractive to buyers as an ongoing business, AT&T adopted a human resource plan that placed restrictions on Paradyne employees' ability to transfer to other divisions of AT&T. Specifically, the Preliminary Net (the initial restriction agreement) precluded an employee who voluntarily left Paradyne from being hired by any other division of AT&T. AT&T believed that one of Paradyne's most marketable assets was its skilled employees. The retention of Paradyne's employees, therefore, was considered essential for the sale of Paradyne.

On July 31, 1996, Lucent sold Paradyne to Texas Pacific Group. Before closing, Lucent agreed, on behalf of itself and the other former AT&T affiliates,

PARADYNE
Courtesy Paradyne

that it would not hire, rehire, retain, or solicit the services of any Paradyne employee or consultant whose annual income exceeded $50,000. This "Pre Closing Net" (another version of the restriction agreement) was consistent with the understanding that Texas Pacific Group's interest in purchasing Paradyne was based on its desire to acquire the technical skills of Paradyne's employees for a sufficient period of time to ensure a successful transition of ownership.

Once the deal was closed, Lucent and Texas Pacific Group entered a post-closing agreement in which Lucent warranted on behalf of itself and the other AT&T affiliates that for 245 days (8 months) following the sale and the expiration of the Pre Closing Net, it would not seek to hire, solicit or rehire any Paradyne employee or consultant whose compensation exceeded $50,000. The employees filed suit contending that the effect of the covenant in the agreements was to reduce competition as well as their ability to work for other companies. Is the covenant enforceable? [*Eichorn* v. *AT & T Corp.*, 248 F.3d 131 (3d Cir. 2001)]

gress became involved, passing federal statutes on antitrust issues in the late nineteenth and early twentieth centuries. With some amendments and changes, this scheme still exists and applies today. Exhibit 17.1 summarizes the general federal statutory antitrust statutes covered in detail in the following topic sections.

Jurisdiction of Federal Antitrust Laws

Federal laws cannot apply to business conduct unless interstate commerce is involved (see Chapter 5 for a complete discussion of interstate commerce). All federal antitrust statutes define interstate commerce for purposes of applying the statutes to businesses and are discussed in the following subsections.

Sherman Act Jurisdiction

The standards for Sherman Act jurisdiction are the same as the standards established under the Commerce Clause (see Chapter 5). Even if an activity is purely intrastate, it is subject to Sherman Act jurisdiction if the activity has a substantial economic effect on interstate commerce. Even if the activity of a business is purely local in nature, its economic impact and resources are examined to determine whether interstate commerce has been affected. There are very few times when interstate commerce is not found under the Sherman Act standard.

In *McClain* v. *Real Estate Board of New Orleans*, 441 U.S. 942 (1980), for example, an antitrust action against real estate brokers who worked only in the New

EXHIBIT 17.1 **Federal Antitrust Statutes**

STATUTE	ORIGINAL DATE	JURISDICTION	COVERAGE	PENALTIES
Sherman Act 15 U.S.C. § 1	1890	Commerce Clause	Monopolies; attempts to monopolize; boycotts; refusals to deal; price fixing; resale price maintenance; division of markets	Criminal; $350,000 for individuals; $10 million for corps.; private suits
Clayton Act 1914 15 U.S.C. § 12	1914	Persons engaged in commerce	Tying; treble damages; mergers; interlocking directorates	Private suits
Federal Trade Commission Act 15 U.S.C. § 41	1914	Commerce Clause	Unfair methods of FTC competition	
Robinson-Patman Act 15 U.S.C. § 13	1936	Persons engaged in commerce and selling goods across state lines	Price discrimination	Private suits and criminal for international acts
Celler-Kefauver (part of Clayton Act) 15 U.S.C. § 18	1950		Asset acquisitions	
Hart-Scott-Rodino Antitrust Improvements Act 15 U.S.C. § 1311	1976 amended 1980, 1994	Gives greater authority to Justice Department for prosecution; requires premerger notification to Justice Department		

Orleans area was permitted under the Sherman Act because the U.S. Supreme Court found that the brokers facilitated the loans and insurance for the properties they sold. The loans and insurance were provided by national firms, and funding came from outside the state. This involvement of interstate commerce, even in an indirect fashion, is sufficient for Sherman Act jurisdiction.

Clayton Act Jurisdiction

The jurisdictional standard for the Clayton Act is different from the broad Sherman Act jurisdiction of any interstate commerce. The Clayton Act can be applied *only* to transactions and persons *engaged* in interstate commerce, not just businesses *affecting* interstate commerce.

Robinson-Patman Act Jurisdiction

The Robinson-Patman Act has the most stringent jurisdictional requirements. The seller accused of price discrimination must be engaged in interstate commerce, and at least one of two claimed discrimination sales must be across state lines. A firm that sells only to in-state customers is not subject to Robinson-Patman jurisdiction.

EXHIBIT 17.2 Antitrust Remedies

	SHERMAN ACT	CLAYTON ACT	ROBINSON-PATMAN ACT	FTC ACT
Criminal	$350,000 and/or three years in prison for individuals; $10 million for corporations; directors and officers also liable as to intent and knowledge	None	Section 4 for intentional price discrimination	None
Civil	Treble damages plus costs and attorney fees	Same	Same	None
Equitable	Injunctions, divestitures, asset distributions, sales	Same	Same	Same
Enforcers	Justice Department; U.S. attorney; state attorneys general; private persons	Same	Same	FTC

Antitrust Penalties and Remedies

The federal antitrust laws have powerful incentives for compliance that include substantial penalties and remedies. The following subsections discuss these provisions, and a summary appears in Exhibit 17.2.

Criminal Penalties

The Sherman Act carries felony criminal penalties. For individuals, the penalties are fines of up to $350,000 and/or up to three years in prison. For corporations, there are fines of up to $10 million. These criminal penalties require proof that the violator intended the anticompetitive conduct and realized the consequences of the action taken.

The FTC and Clayton Acts do not carry criminal penalties. However, certain forms of intentional price discrimination are made criminal under Section 4 of the Robinson-Patman Act. It is important to note that officers and directors of violating corporations can also be held criminally liable for antitrust violations. The Antitrust Division of the Department of Justice or the local U.S. attorney's office is responsible for bringing criminal action under the antitrust laws.

Equitable Remedies

Equitable remedies can be obtained by either the government or private parties. Equitable relief is an order from a court that restrains or prevents anticompetitive conduct. An injunction is a frequent form of antitrust relief; it is a court order prohibiting a violating party from engaging in anticompetitive conduct.

Equitable remedies are also affirmative in nature. They can require parties to take appropriate steps to eliminate the results of anticompetitive behavior. A firm can be ordered to divest itself of an acquired firm, for example; or in an unlawful asset acquisition, a court order can require that the assets be divided with a competing firm. Contracts whose terms violate the antitrust laws can be canceled by court order.

Equitable remedies give the courts discretion to fashion remedies that will eliminate the results of anticompetitive behavior.

Private Actions for Damages

Section 4 of the Clayton Act allows any person whose business or property is injured as a result of an antitrust violation to recover "threefold the damages by him sustained"—commonly referred to as **treble damages**—along with the costs of the suit and reasonable attorney fees. This section, with its substantial recovery provisions, is strong incentive for private enforcement of antitrust laws. Consumers, businesses, and state attorneys general can all bring private damage actions under Section 4.

Visit the Corporate Counsel Web site for information on current antitrust issues:
http://www.ljx.com/ corpcounselor/index.html

The types of damages that can be recovered include lost profits, increased costs, and decreased value in property. These damage suits have a four-year statute of limitations; that is, suit must be brought within four years of the alleged violation. Those who bring private damage suits enjoy a proof benefit: If the government has brought suit and a violation is found, that judgment can be used in a private suit as *prima facie* evidence against the violating defendant. A *prima facie* case allows a plaintiff to survive a directed verdict and entitles the plaintiff to a judgment if the defendant offers no contradictory evidence (see Chapter 4 for more discussion).

Exhibit 17.1 provides a summary of the federal antitrust laws, the jurisdictional requirements for their application, the types of activities covered under each statute, and the applicable penalties. Exhibit 17.2 provides a summary of penalties and remedies under the federal antitrust laws.

HORIZONTAL RESTRAINTS OF TRADE

Horizontal restraints of trade are designed to lessen competition among a firm's competitors. For example, Ford's and GM's fixing prices to drive Chrysler out of business would be a horizontal restraint. The Sherman Act covers the horizontal restraints of **price fixing,** market division, **group boycotts** and refusals to deal, **joint ventures,** and monopolization. The Clayton Act also covers the problem of anticompetitive horizontal mergers or mergers with competitors.

Sherman Act Restraints

Monopolization

Section 2 of the Sherman Act prohibits the act of **monopolizing.** Notice that the Sherman Act does not prohibit monopolies; there are certain types of monopolies recognized as exceptions to Section 2. For example, in a small town there is usually only enough economic base to support one newspaper; such an operation is not a Section 2 violation. Some businesses simply produce a product that is superior or unique; this type of monopoly is not a violation. When a business has obtained a large market share by **superior skill, foresight, and industry,** it has simply put its product in the market in a superior way and is entitled to its market share.

Acquiring a large market share through methods other than legitimate competition is prohibited under Section 2. To prove such monopolization, the following elements must be established:

1. The possession of **monopoly power** in the **relevant market**
2. The willful acquisition or maintenance of that power

Monopoly Power Judicial decisions have defined monopoly power under Section 2 as the power to control prices or exclude competition in a relevant market. To determine whether a firm has this ability, or monopoly power, the courts have examined the firm's **market power,** which is an economic term that means the firm has a relatively inelastic demand curve. An elastic demand curve means that the firm's products have competition from other firms or from firms with substitute products. For example, cosmetic firms have an elastic demand; buyers can switch to other products when there are price increases in one line or can even give up the use of cosmetics. On the other hand, the demand curve for gasoline is less elastic. Although there are substitute means of transportation, most drivers need to use their cars and hence need gasoline.

At some point, ever-increasing market power will turn into monopoly power. High profits and the lack of substitute goods are indications that market power has made this transition. Some courts examine the firm's market share to determine whether it has monopoly power. There is, however, no set percentage figure used to make this determination. Most of the cases dealing with the percentage-of-market approach have involved firms with market shares greater than 50 percent.

Relevant Market In determining market share, a court must first determine a firm's market. The context in which market share is measured is called the **relevant market;** and each product has a relevant **geographic market.** For example, a beer producer may have 50 percent of all nationwide beer sales, but, in a suit involving a local competitor, the producer's share might be only 20 percent because of the local beer's popularity. This local or **submarket** could be used as the relevant geographic market. A product may have an international market but may have only 10 percent market share in a particular area.

Each firm also has its own relevant **product market,** which is determined by consumers' preferences and their willingness to substitute other products for the product at issue. For example, a market could be defined as plastic wrapping materials, or it could be defined as food storage materials and include such wraps as wax paper, aluminum foil, and plastic storage bags. The product market is determined by the **cross elasticity** of demand. Cross-elastic demand means consumers are willing to substitute other products in the event of unavailability or price changes.

The definition of relevant market is one of the key elements in monopolization cases. There will always be contradictory testimony from expert economists. As a result, the decisions on relevant market vary widely.

Purposeful Act Requirement Proving that a firm has monopoly power is only half of an antitrust monopolization case. The second element requires a showing that the firm acquired or is maintaining monopoly power by some purposeful or deliberate act that is not "superior skill, foresight, and industry" (which in short is the ability to build a better mousetrap). Some examples of prohibited purposeful conduct are **predatory pricing** and **exclusionary conduct.** Predatory pricing is pricing below actual cost for a temporary period to drive a potential competitor out of business. Exclusionary conduct is conduct that prevents a potential competitor from entering the market. For example, interfering with the purchase of a factory by a competitor would be improper exclusionary conduct. The following landmark case, both judicially and economically, deals with nearly all legal issues under the Sherman Act and other federal antitrust laws.

CASE 17.2

U.S. v. Microsoft
253 F.3d 34 (C.A. D.C. 2001)

You Have Performed an Illegal Operation

FACTS

Microsoft Corporation, a company based in Washington and doing business in all 50 states and around the world is the leading supplier of operating systems for personal computers (PCs). Although Microsoft licenses its software programs directly to consumers, the largest part of its sales consists of licensing the products to manufacturers of personal computers.

Microsoft was concerned about its strategic position with respect to the Internet, a global electronic network consisting of smaller interconnected networks, which allows millions of computers to exchange information over telephone wires, dedicated data cables, and wireless links.

The United States Justice Department had an ongoing inquiry into the market shares and practices of Microsoft and 23 state attorneys general were also looking into the company's practices. The concerns of the Justice Department and attorneys general include:

1. Microsoft's position in the market as a monopolist (90 percent market share for operating systems).

2. Microsoft's barriers to entry for operating systems and Web browsers. Microsoft has refused to sell its software operating system to computer companies that installed Microsoft's competitive browser, Netscape, which was gaining popularity as Microsoft's Explorer (IE) struggled.

3. Microsoft worked to inhibit the efforts of Netscape with its browser by first trying to acquire Netscape and then working to "cut off [its] air supply" by retarding Sun Corporation's development and implementation of the Java program. When Microsoft altered the portions of Sun's Java program that allowed it to work without Windows, Sun notified Microsoft that such was a violation of its licensing agreement. Microsoft's response was, "Sue us." Sun sued Microsoft one week before the Justice Department brought its suit against Microsoft. Sun's suit then ran parallel with the Justice Department's.

In issuing a three-part opinion, Judge Thomas Penfield Jackson of the district court found that Microsoft had violated the antitrust laws and ordered a remedy of breaking up the company. Microsoft appealed the decision.

JUDICIAL OPINION

PER CURIAM

What is somewhat problematic . . . is that just over six years have passed since Microsoft engaged in the first conduct plaintiffs allege to be anticompetitive. As the record in this case indicates, six years seems like an eternity in the computer industry. By the time a court can assess liability, firms, products, and the marketplace are likely to have changed dramatically. This, in turn, threatens enormous practical difficulties for courts considering the appropriate measure of relief in equitable enforcement actions, both in crafting injunctive remedies in the first instance and reviewing those remedies in the second. Conduct remedies may be unavailing in such cases, because innovation to a large degree has already rendered the anticompetitive conduct obsolete (although by no means harmless). And broader structural remedies present their own set of problems, including how a court goes about restoring competition to a dramatically changed, and constantly changing, marketplace. That is just one reason why we find the District Court's refusal in the present case to hold an evidentiary hearing on remedies—to update and flesh out the available information before seriously entertaining the possibility of dramatic structural relief—so problematic.

We do not mean to say that enforcement actions will no longer play an important role in curbing infringements of the antitrust laws in technologically dynamic markets, nor do we assume this in assessing the merits of this case. Even in those cases where forward-looking remedies appear limited, the Government will continue to have an interest in defining the contours of the antitrust laws so that law-abiding firms will have a clear sense of what is permissible and what is not. And the threat of private damage actions will remain to deter those firms inclined to test the limits of the law.

The second matter of note is more theoretical in nature. We decide this case against a backdrop of significant debate amongst academics and practitioners over the extent to which "old economy" § 2 monopolization doctrines should apply to firms competing in dynamic technological markets characterized by network effects. In markets characterized by network effects, one product or standard tends towards dominance, because "the utility that a user derives from consumption of the good increases with the number of other agents consuming the good." Once a product or standard achieves wide acceptance, it becomes more or less entrenched. Competition in such industries is "for the field" rather than "within the field."

In technologically dynamic markets, however, such entrenchment may be temporary, because innovation may alter the field altogether. Rapid technological change leads to markets in which "firms compete through innovation for temporary market dominance, from which they may be displaced by the next wave of product advancements." Microsoft argues that the operating system market is just such a market.

Whether or not Microsoft's characterization of the operating system market is correct does not appreciably alter our mission in assessing the alleged antitrust violations in the present case.

Moreover, it should be clear that Microsoft makes no claim that anticompetitive conduct should be assessed differently in technologically dynamic markets. It claims only that the measure of monopoly power should be different. For reasons fully discussed below, we reject Microsoft's monopoly power argument.

II. Monopolization

Section 2 of the Sherman Act makes it unlawful for a firm to "monopolize." The District Court found that Microsoft possesses monopoly power in the market for Intel-compatible PC operating systems. Focusing primarily on Microsoft's efforts to suppress Netscape Navigator's threat to its operating system monopoly, the court also found that Microsoft maintained its power not through competition on the merits, but through unlawful means.

A. Monopoly Power

While merely possessing monopoly power is not itself an antitrust violation, it is a necessary element of a monopolization charge. Because direct proof is only rarely available, courts more typically examine market structure in search of circumstantial evidence of monopoly power.

The District Court considered these structural factors and concluded that Microsoft possesses monopoly power in a relevant market. Defining the market as Intel-compatible PC operating systems, the District Court found that Microsoft has a greater than 95% share. It also found the company's market position protected by a substantial entry barrier.

Microsoft argues that the District Court incorrectly defined the relevant market. It also claims that there is no barrier to entry in that market. Alternatively, Microsoft argues that because the software industry is uniquely dynamic, direct proof, rather than circumstantial evidence, more appropriately indicates whether it possesses monopoly power. Rejecting each argument, we uphold the District Court's finding of monopoly power in its entirety.

1. Market Structure
   a. Market definition
In this case, the District Court defined the market as "the licensing of all Intel-compatible PC operating systems worldwide," finding that there are "currently no products—and . . . there are not likely to be any in the near future—that a significant percentage of computer users worldwide could substitute for [these operating systems] without incurring substantial costs." Calling this market definition "far too narrow," Microsoft argues that the District Court improperly excluded three types of products: non-Intel compatible operating systems (primarily Apple's Macintosh operating system, Mac OS), operating systems for non-PC devices (such as handheld computers and portal websites), and "middleware" products, which are not operating systems at all.

The District Court found that consumers would not switch from Windows to Mac OS in response to a substantial price increase because of the costs of acquiring the new hardware needed to run Mac OS (an Apple computer and peripherals) and compatible software applications, as well as because of the effort involved in learning the new system and transferring files to its format. The court also found the Apple system less appealing to consumers because it costs considerably more and supports fewer applications.

Microsoft's challenge to the District Court's exclusion of non-PC based competitors, such as information appliances (handheld devices, etc.) and portal websites that host serverbased software applications, suffers from the same defect: the company fails to challenge the District Court's key

(continued)

factual findings. In particular, the District Court found that because information appliances fall far short of performing all of the functions of a PC, most consumers will buy them only as a supplement to their PCs.

This brings us to Microsoft's main challenge to the District Court's market definition: the exclusion of middleware. Because of the importance of middleware to this case, we pause to explain what it is and how it relates to the issue before us. Operating systems perform many functions, including allocating computer memory and controlling peripherals such as printers and keyboards.

Operating systems also function as platforms for software applications. They do this by "exposing"— i.e., making available to software developers— routines or protocols that perform certain widely-used functions. These are known as Application Programming Interfaces, or "APIs."

Every operating system has different APIs. Accordingly, a developer who writes an application for one operating system and wishes to sell the application to users of another must modify, or "port," the application to the second operating system. This process is both timeconsuming and expensive.

"Middleware" refers to software products that expose their own APIs. Because of this, a middleware product written for Windows could take over some or all of Windows's valuable platform functions— that is, developers might begin to rely upon APIs exposed by the middleware for basic routines rather than relying upon the API set included in Windows. If middleware were written for multiple operating systems, its impact could be even greater. The more developers could rely upon APIs exposed by such middleware, the less expensive porting to different operating systems would be. Ultimately, if developers could write applications relying exclusively on APIs exposed by middleware, their applications would run on any operating system on which the middleware was also present. Netscape Navigator and Java—both at issue in this case—are middleware products written for multiple operating systems.

Microsoft argues that, because middleware could usurp the operating system's platform function and might eventually take over other operating system functions (for instance, by controlling peripherals), the District Court erred in excluding Navigator and Java from the relevant market. The District Court found, however, that neither Navigator, Java, nor any other middleware product could now, or would soon, expose enough APIs to serve as a platform for popular applications, much less take over all operating system functions. Again, Microsoft fails to challenge these findings, instead simply asserting middleware's "potential" as a competitor.

Microsoft claims that even a predominant market share does not by itself indicate monopoly power. Although the "existence of [monopoly] power ordinarily may be inferred from the predominant share of the market," we agree with Microsoft that because of the possibility of competition from new entrants, looking to current market share alone can be "misleading." In this case, however, the District Court was not misled. Considering the possibility of new rivals, the court focused not only on Microsoft's present market share, but also on the structural barrier that protects the company's future position. That barrier—the "applications barrier to entry"—stems from two characteristics of the software market: (1) most consumers prefer operating systems for which a large number of applications have already been written; and (2) most developers prefer to write for operating systems that already have a substantial consumer base. This "chicken-and-egg" situation ensures that applications will continue to be written for the already dominant Windows, which in turn ensures that consumers will continue to prefer it over other operating systems.

The consumer wants an operating system that runs not only types of applications that he knows he will want to use, but also those types in which he might develop an interest later. Also, the consumer knows that if he chooses an operating system with enough demand to support multiple applications in each product category, he will be less likely to find himself straitened later by having to use an application whose features disappoint him. Finally, the average user knows that, generally speaking, applications improve through successive versions. He thus wants an operating system for which successive generations of his favorite applications will be released—promptly at that. The fact that a vastly larger number of applications are written for Windows than for other PC operating systems attracts consumers to Windows, because it reassures them that their interests will be met as long as they use Microsoft's product.

2. Direct Proof

Having sustained the District Court's conclusion that circumstantial evidence proves that Microsoft possesses monopoly power, we turn to Microsoft's alternative argument that it does not behave like a monopolist. Claiming that software competition is uniquely "dynamic," the company suggests a new rule: that monopoly power in the software industry should be proven directly, that is, by examining a company's actual behavior to determine if it reveals the existence of monopoly power. According to Microsoft, not only does no such proof of its power exist, but record evidence demonstrates the absence of monopoly power. The company claims that it invests heavily in research and development.

Microsoft's argument fails because, even assuming that the software market is uniquely dynamic in the long term, the District Court correctly applied the structural approach to determine if the company faces competition in the short term.

Even if we were to require direct proof, moreover, Microsoft's behavior may well be sufficient to show the existence of monopoly power. Certainly, none of the conduct Microsoft points to—its investment in R&D and the relatively low price of Windows—is inconsistent with the possession of such power. The R&D expenditures Microsoft points to are not simply for Windows, but for its entire company, which most likely does not possess a monopoly for all of its products. Moreover, because innovation can increase an already dominant market share and further delay the emergence of competition, even monopolists have reason to invest in R&D. Microsoft's pricing behavior is similarly equivocal. The company claims only that it never charged the short-term profit-maximizing price for Windows. Faced with conflicting expert testimony, the District Court found that it could not accurately determine what this price would be. In any event, the court found, a price lower than the short-term profit-maximizing price is not inconsistent with possession or improper use of monopoly power. Microsoft does argue that the price of Windows is a fraction of the price of an Intel-compatible PC system and lower than that of rival operating systems, but these facts are not inconsistent with the District Court's finding that Microsoft has monopoly power.

More telling, the District Court found that some aspects of Microsoft's behavior are difficult to explain unless Windows is a monopoly product. For instance, according to the District Court, the company set the price of Windows without considering rivals' prices, something a firm without a monopoly would have been unable to do. The District Court also found that Microsoft's pattern of exclusionary conduct could only be rational "if the firm knew that it possessed monopoly power." It is to that conduct that we now turn.

B. Anticompetitive Conduct

In this case, after concluding that Microsoft had monopoly power, the District Court held that Microsoft had violated § 2 by engaging in a variety of exclusionary acts (not including predatory pricing), to maintain its monopoly by preventing the effective distribution and use of products that might threaten that monopoly.

Whether any particular act of a monopolist is exclusionary, rather than merely a form of vigorous competition, can be difficult to discern: the means of illicit exclusion, like the means of legitimate competition, are myriad. The challenge for an antitrust court lies in stating a general rule for distinguishing between exclusionary acts, which reduce social welfare, and competitive acts, which increase it.

With these principles in mind, we now consider Microsoft's objections to the District Court's holding that Microsoft violated § 2 of the Sherman Act in a variety of ways.

1. Licenses Issued to Original Equipment Manufacturers

The District Court condemned a number of provisions in Microsoft's agreements licensing Windows to OEMs, because it found that Microsoft's imposition of those provisions (like many of Microsoft's other actions at issue in this case) serves to reduce usage share of Netscape's browser and, hence, protect Microsoft's operating system monopoly.

Therefore, Microsoft's efforts to gain market share in one market (browsers) served to meet the threat to Microsoft's monopoly in another market (operating systems) by keeping rival browsers from gaining the critical mass of users necessary to attract developer attention away from Windows as the platform for software development.

[T]he District Court condemned the license provisions prohibiting the OEMs from: (1) removing any desktop icons, folders, or "Start" menu entries; (2) altering the initial boot sequence; and (3) otherwise altering the appearance of the Windows desktop.

The District Court concluded that the first license restriction—the prohibition upon the removal of desktop icons, folders, and Start menu entries—thwarts the distribution of a rival browser by preventing OEMs from removing visible means of user access to IE. The OEMs cannot practically install a second browser in addition to IE, the court found, in part because "[p]re-installing more than one product in a given category . . . can significantly increase an

(continued)

OEM's support costs, for the redundancy can lead to confusion among novice users."

The second license provision at issue prohibits OEMs from modifying the initial boot sequence—the process that occurs the first time a consumer turns on the computer. Prior to the imposition of that restriction, "among the programs that many OEMs inserted into the boot sequence were Internet sign-up procedures that encouraged users to choose from a list of IAPs assembled by the OEM." Microsoft's prohibition on any alteration of the boot sequence thus prevents OEMs from using that process to promote the services of IAPs, many of which—at least at the time Microsoft imposed the restriction—used Navigator rather than IE in their internet access software. Upon learning of OEM practices including boot sequence modification, Microsoft's Chairman, Bill Gates, wrote: "Apparently a lot of OEMs are bundling non-Microsoft browsers and coming up with offerings together with [IAPs] that get displayed on their machines in a FAR more prominent way than MSN or our Internet browser." Microsoft does not deny that the prohibition on modifying the boot sequence has the effect of decreasing competition against IE by preventing OEMs from promoting rivals' browsers. Because this prohibition has a substantial effect in protecting Microsoft's market power, and does so through a means other than competition on the merits, it is anticompetitive.

b. Microsoft's justifications for the license restrictions

Microsoft argues that the license restrictions are legally justified because, in imposing them, Microsoft is simply "exercising its rights as the holder of valid copyrights." Microsoft's primary copyright argument borders upon the frivolous. The company claims an absolute and unfettered right to use its intellectual property as it wishes: "[I]f intellectual property rights have been lawfully acquired," it says, then "their subsequent exercise cannot give rise to antitrust liability." That is no more correct than the proposition that use of one's personal property, such as a baseball bat, cannot give rise to tort liability. As the Federal Circuit succinctly stated: "Intellectual property rights do not confer a privilege to violate the antitrust laws."

* * *

Microsoft denies, as a factual matter, that it commingled browsing and non-browsing code, and it maintains the District Court's findings to the contrary are clearly erroneous. According to Microsoft,

its expert "testified without contradiction that '[t]he very same code in Windows 98 that provides Web browsing functionality' also performs essential operating system functions—not code in the same files, but the very same software code."

Microsoft's expert did not testify to that effect "without contradiction," however. A Government expert, Glenn Weadock, testified that Microsoft "design[ed] [IE] so that some of the code that it uses co-resides in the same library files as other code needed for Windows." Another Government expert likewise testified that one library file, SHDOCVW.DLL, "is really a bundle of separate functions. It contains some functions that have to do specifically with Web browsing, and it contains some general user interface functions as well." One of Microsoft's own documents suggests as much.

In view of the contradictory testimony in the record, some of which supports the District Court's finding that Microsoft commingled browsing and non-browsing code, we cannot conclude that the finding was clearly erroneous.

3. Agreements with Internet Access Providers

The District Court also condemned as exclusionary Microsoft's agreements with various IAPs. The IAPs include both Internet Service Providers, which offer consumers internet access, and Online Services ("OLSs") such as America Online ("AOL"), which offer proprietary content in addition to internet access and other services. The District Court deemed Microsoft's agreements with the IAPs unlawful because: Microsoft licensed [IE] and the [IE] Access Kit to hundreds of IAPs for no charge. Then, Microsoft extended valuable promotional treatment to the ten most important IAPs in exchange for their commitment to promote and distribute [IE] and to exile Navigator from the desktop. Finally, in exchange for efforts to upgrade existing subscribers to client software that came bundled with [IE] instead of Navigator, Microsoft granted rebates—and in some cases made outright payments—to those same IAPs.

Although offering a customer an attractive deal is the hallmark of competition, the Supreme Court has indicated that in very rare circumstances a price may be unlawfully low, or "predatory." The rare case of price predation aside, the antitrust laws do not condemn even a monopolist for offering its product at an attractive price, and we therefore have no warrant to condemn Microsoft for offering either IE or the IEAK free of charge or even at a negative price. Likewise, as we said above, a monopolist does not violate the Sherman Act simply by developing an attractive product.

4. Dealings with Internet Content Providers, Independent Software Vendors, and Apple Computer

The District Court held that Microsoft engages in exclusionary conduct in its dealings with ICPs, which develop websites; ISVs, which develop software; and Apple, which is both an OEM and a software developer.

With respect to the deals with ICPs, the District Court's findings do not support liability. After reviewing the ICP agreements, the District Court specifically stated that "there is not sufficient evidence to support a finding that Microsoft's promotional restrictions actually had a substantial, deleterious impact on Navigator's usage share." Because plaintiffs failed to demonstrate that Microsoft's deals with the ICPs have a substantial effect upon competition, they have not proved the violation of the Sherman Act.

As for Microsoft's ISV agreements, however, the District Court did not enter a similar finding of no substantial effect. The District Court described Microsoft's deals with ISVs as follows:

In dozens of "First Wave" agreements signed between the fall of 1997 and the spring of 1998, Microsoft has promised to give preferential support, in the form of early Windows 98 and Windows NT betas, other technical information, and the right to use certain Microsoft seals of approval, to important ISVs that agree to certain conditions. One of these conditions is that the ISVs use Internet Explorer as the default browsing software for any software they develop with a hypertext-based user interface.

Another condition is that the ISVs use Microsoft's "HTML Help," which is accessible only with Internet Explorer, to implement their applications' help systems.

[T]he effect of these deals is to "ensure [ ] that many of the most popular Web-centric applications will rely on browsing technologies found only in Windows," and that Microsoft's deals with ISVs therefore "increase [ ] the likelihood that the millions of consumers using [applications designed by ISVs that entered into agreements with Microsoft] will use Internet Explorer rather than Navigator."

When Microsoft entered into the First Wave agreements, there were 40 million new users of the internet. Because, by keeping rival browsers from gaining widespread distribution (and potentially attracting the attention of developers away from the

APIs in Windows), the deals have a substantial effect in preserving Microsoft's monopoly, we hold that plaintiffs have made a *prima facie* showing that the deals have an anticompetitive effect.

Of course, that Microsoft's exclusive deals have the anticompetitive effect of preserving Microsoft's monopoly does not, in itself, make them unlawful. A monopolist, like a competitive firm, may have a perfectly legitimate reason for wanting an exclusive arrangement with its distributors. Accordingly, Microsoft had an opportunity to, but did not, present the District Court with evidence demonstrating that the exclusivity provisions have some such procompetitive justification.

5. Java

Java, a set of technologies developed by Sun Microsystems, is another type of middleware posing a potential threat to Windows' position as the ubiquitous platform for software development. Programs calling upon the Java APIs will run on any machine with a "Java runtime environment," that is, Java class libraries and a JVM.

In May 1995 Netscape agreed with Sun to distribute a copy of the Java runtime environment with every copy of Navigator, and "Navigator quickly became the principal vehicle by which Sun placed copies of its Java runtime environment on the PC systems of Windows users." Microsoft, too, agreed to promote the Java technologies—or so it seemed. For at the same time, Microsoft took steps "to maximize the difficulty with which applications written in Java could be ported from Windows to other platforms, and vice versa." Specifically, the District Court found that Microsoft took four steps to exclude Java from developing as a viable cross-platform threat: (a) designing a JVM incompatible with the one developed by Sun; (b) entering into contracts, the so-called "First Wave Agreements," requiring major ISVs to promote Microsoft's JVM exclusively; (c) deceiving Java developers about the Windows-specific nature of the tools it distributed to them; and (d) coercing Intel to stop aiding Sun in improving the Java technologies.

When specifically accused by a *PC Week* reporter of fragmenting Java standards so as to prevent crossplatform uses, Microsoft denied the accusation and indicated it was only "adding rich platform support" to what remained a crossplatform implementation. An e-mail message internal to Microsoft, written shortly after the conversation with the reporter, shows otherwise:

[O]k, i just did a followup call. . . . [The reporter] liked that i kept pointing customers to w3c standards

(continued)

[(commonly observed internet protocols)]. . . . [but] he accused us of being schizo with this vs. our java approach, i said he misunderstood [—] that [with Java] we are merely trying to add rich platform support to an interop layer. . . . this plays well. . . . at this point its [sic] not good to create MORE noise around our win32 java classes. instead we should just quietly grow j++ [(Microsoft's development tools)] share and assume that people will take more advantage of our classes without ever realizing they are building win32-only java apps.

Finally, other Microsoft documents confirm that Microsoft intended to deceive Java developers, and predicted that the effect of its actions would be to generate Windows-dependent Java applications that their developers believed would be cross-platform; these documents also indicate that Microsoft's ultimate objective was to thwart Java's threat to Microsoft's monopoly in the market for operating systems. One Microsoft document, for example, states as a strategic goal: "Kill cross-platform Java by grow[ing] the polluted Java market."

Microsoft's conduct related to its Java developer tools served to protect its monopoly of the operating system in a manner not attributable either to the superiority of the operating system or to the acumen of its makers, and therefore was anticompetitive. Unsurprisingly, Microsoft offers no procompetitive explanation for its campaign to deceive developers. Accordingly, we conclude this conduct is exclusionary, in violation of § 2 of the Sherman Act.

d. The threat to Intel
In 1995 Intel was in the process of developing a high-performance, Windows-compatible JVM. Microsoft wanted Intel to abandon that effort because a fast, cross-platform JVM would threaten Microsoft's monopoly in the operating system market. At an August 1995 meeting, Microsoft's Gates told Intel that its "cooperation with Sun and Netscape to develop a Java runtime environment . . . was one of the issues threatening to undermine cooperation between Intel and Microsoft." Three months later, "Microsoft's Paul Maritz told a senior Intel executive that Intel's [adaptation of its multimedia software to comply with] Sun's Java standards was as inimical to Microsoft as Microsoft's support for non-Intel microprocessors would be to Intel."

Intel nonetheless continued to undertake initiatives related to Java. By 1996 "Intel had developed a JVM designed to run well . . . while complying with Sun's cross-platform standards." In April of that year, Microsoft again urged Intel not to help Sun by distributing Intel's fast, Sun-compliant JVM. And

Microsoft threatened Intel that if it did not stop aiding Sun on the multimedia front, then Microsoft would refuse to distribute Intel technologies bundled with Windows.

Intel finally capitulated in 1997.

Microsoft's internal documents and deposition testimony confirm both the anticompetitive effect and intent of its actions. Microsoft does not deny the facts found by the District Court, nor does it offer any procompetitive justification for pressuring Intel not to support cross-platform Java. Microsoft lamely characterizes its threat to Intel as "advice." The District Court, however, found that Microsoft's "advice" to Intel to stop aiding cross-platform Java was backed by the threat of retaliation, and this conclusion is supported by the evidence cited above. Therefore we affirm the conclusion that Microsoft's threats to Intel were exclusionary, in violation of § 2 of the Sherman Act.

REMEDIES

The District Court's remedies-phase proceedings are a different matter. It is a cardinal principle of our system of justice that factual disputes must be heard in open court and resolved through trial-like evidentiary proceedings. Any other course would be contrary "to the spirit which imbues our judicial tribunals prohibiting decision without hearing."

This rule is no less applicable in antitrust cases. Despite plaintiffs' protestations, there can be no serious doubt that the parties disputed a number of facts during the remedies phase. In two separate offers of proof, Microsoft identified 23 witnesses who, had they been permitted to testify, would have challenged a wide range of plaintiffs' factual representations, including the feasibility of dividing Microsoft, the likely impact on consumers, and the effect of divestiture on shareholders.

The reason the court declined to conduct an evidentiary hearing was not because of the absence of disputed facts, but because it believed that those disputes could be resolved only through "actual experience," not further proceedings. But a prediction about future events is not, as a prediction, any less a factual issue. Indeed, the Supreme Court has acknowledged that drafting an antitrust decree by necessity "involves predictions and assumptions concerning future economic and business events." Trial courts are not excused from their obligation to resolve such matters through evidentiary hearings simply because they consider the bedrock procedures of our justice system to be "of little use."

In sum, we vacate the District Court's remedies decree for three reasons. First, the District Court failed to hold an evidentiary hearing despite the presence of remedies-specific factual disputes. Second, the court did not provide adequate reasons for its decreed remedies. Finally, we have drastically altered the scope of Microsoft's liability, and it is for the District Court in the first instance to determine the propriety of a specific remedy for the limited ground of liability which we have upheld.

The judgment of the District Court is affirmed in part, reversed in part, remanded in part. We vacate in full the Final Judgment embodying the remedial order, and remand the case to the District Court for reassignment to a different trial judge for further proceedings consistent with this opinion.

CASE QUESTIONS

1. Make a list of the conduct Microsoft engaged in that the court finds indicated it was a monopoly.

2. What is the relevant market? What does Microsoft say the relevant market is?

3. What intellectual property argument does Microsoft make as a defense to the antitrust charges?

4. What error did the trial judge make with respect to the remedies?

5. Did Microsoft violate the Sherman Act?

6. Why is the case remanded?

Aftermath: The Justice Department reached a settlement of the case with Microsoft near the end of 2001. There would be no breakup of Microsoft as part of the remedies for the antitrust violation. Microsoft agreed to pay penalties, the majority of which ($180 million) would be in software donations to schools. Several states had not yet agreed to the settlement.

ETHICAL ISSUES 17.1

The Running Fox is a small running-shoe manufacturer well known among professional runners for its high-quality, highly protective shoe. Athletic Feet is a manufacturer of a full line of running shoes, from track to long-distance running. Athletic Feet also publishes *Runner's Monthly*, a top magazine in the field of running with an almost exclusively runner circulation. For the past three years, *Runner's Monthly* has published its "annual shoe survey" in which all the running shoes on the market are rated. Athletic Feet's shoes have been ranked as the top three in every category. Running Fox did not perform well in the ratings and has brought a monopolization suit against Athletic Feet. Athletic Feet says the relevant market is athletic shoewear because it not only manufactures running shoes but also tennis, basketball, baseball, and other types of sport shoes. In the athletic shoe market, Athletic Feet holds a 20 percent share of the market; but in the running-shoe market, it holds an 80 percent share. Obviously, Running Fox wants to argue that running shoes are the relevant market. Who is correct? What is the relevant market? Does *Runner's Monthly* have a conflict of interest?

Attempts to Monopolize

Section 2 of the Sherman Act can be violated even though actual monopolization might not be the result. In other words, attempts at monopolization are also part of Section 2. There need not be an actual successful effort so long as it can be shown that the conduct created a "dangerous probability" of monopolization.

CONSIDER...

17.2 Amanda Reiss had completed her residency in ophthalmology in Portland, Oregon, and was moving to Phoenix, Arizona, to start her practice. She began looking for office space and met with a leasing agent who showed her several complexes of medical suites. Dr. Reiss was ready to sign for one of them when the leasing agent turned to her and said, "Oh, by the way, you're not one of those advertising doctors, are you? Because they don't want that kind in any of my complexes." Has there been a violation of the antitrust laws?

For an update on the Intel antitrust litigation, visit: http://www.zdnet.com/ zdnn/special/intelftc.html

Price Fixing

Any agreement or collaboration among competitors "for the purpose and with the effect of raising, depressing, fixing, pegging, or stabilizing the price of a commodity" is the Supreme Court's definition of price fixing. Under Section 1 of the Sherman Act, price fixing is a *per se* violation, which means that the conduct is illegal and unreasonable as a matter of law. The effect of a *per se* violation of the antitrust laws is to shorten trials substantially because a *per se* violator has no defenses to present in the case. Some antitrust scholars feel the Supreme Court is moving away from its *per se* standard for price fixing. Price fixing can result from several different activities, covered in the following subsections.

Minimum Prices A minimum fee or price schedule discourages competition, puts an artificial restriction on the market, and provides a shield from market forces. There is no defense to this type of agreement. Even proof that the minimum price is a reasonable price is irrelevant once there is proof of an agreement.

Maximum Prices Although maximum prices sound like an excellent benefit for consumers, the effect is to stabilize prices, which translates into a restriction on free-market forces.

List Prices An agreement among competitors to use list prices as a guideline in sale prices is also a *per se* violation. There is still a violation even though the agreement was not mandatory and even though the list price was just a starting point in price negotiations. Just the exchange of price information has an effect on the market and interferes with the ability to price in relation to demand, supply, and competition.

Production Limitations An agreement to limit production is an agreement to fix prices because the parties are controlling the supply, which in turn controls the right to demand the resulting price.

Limitations on Competitive Bidding Some competitors have tried to avoid "ruinous competition" by eliminating bidding. In *National Soc'y of Professional Engineers* v. *United States*, 435 U.S. 679 (1978), a professional society agreed that there should not be bidding on engineering projects because the bidding process encouraged cost cutting and posed possible safety risks in the construction of the projects bid. Although its motives were well intentioned, it was still found to have committed a violation because the agreement was price fixing and a *per se* violation of the Sherman Act.

Why do Companies Succumb to Price Fixing?

Down through the centuries social analysts have frequently charged, "Laws are like spiderwebs, which may catch small flies but let wasps and hornets break through." As more and more corporations have been caught in the web of price fixing laws, however, this charge has lost its punch. Senior business managers in industries that have never before known these problems, as well as previous offenders, are probably more concerned now about their corporate exposure to being indicted and convicted of price fixing than they were in any other recent period.

The costs of violating price fixing laws are very high: lawyers' fees, government fines, poor morale, damaged public image, civil suits, and now prison terms. Justice Department statistics indicate that 60 percent of antitrust felons are sentenced to prison terms. Thus, for very pragmatic reasons as well as for personal convictions, America's top executives are searching for fail-safe ways of meeting legal requirements.

One CEO well expressed the frustration common to executives in convicted companies:

> We've tried hard to stress that collusion is illegal. We point out that anticompetitive practices hurt the company's ethical standards, public image, internal morale, and earnings. Yet we wind up in trouble continually. When we try to find out why employees got involved, they have the gall to say that they "were only looking out for the best interests of the company." They seem to think that the company message is for everyone else but them. You begin to wonder about the intelligence of these people. Either they don't listen or they're just plain stupid.

General Management Signals

Some executives talked very explicitly about the problem of changing the culture of a problem division. Having been burned in the past, the financial vice president of a convicted company has adopted an inventive approach. He has communicated new acquisition criteria to his investment brokers. He is now at least as interested in information about a company's ethical practices as in its financial performance. One chief executive officer said that he and his top managers learned the hard way from troubles soon after making an acquisition. He felt that retraining management is helpful.

Some managers have been reviewing their practices and making tighter definitions of who can legitimately take part in pricing decisions. It takes careful analysis of the multiple sources of relevant information concerning prices as well as an explicit commitment procedure to make such rules both workable and prudent.

Attempts to move beyond top-level role modeling have led some executives to prepare codes of ethics on company business practices. In some companies this document circulates only at top levels and, again, the word seems to have trouble getting down the line. Even those documents that were sent to all employees seemed to have been broadly written, toothless versions of the golden rule. One company tried to get more commitment by requiring employees to sign and return a pledge.

For codes to really work, substantial specificity is important. One executive said his company's method was successful because the code was tied in with an employee's daily routine:

> There is a code of business conduct here. To really make it meaningful, you have to get past the stage of endorsing motherhood and deal with the specific problems of policy in the different functional areas. We wrote up 20 pages on just purchasing issues.

Auditing for Compliance

Once these more specific codes of business conduct are distributed, top managers may want more than a signed statement in return. Individuals can be held responsible if they have been informed on how to act in certain gray areas. The company can show its commitment to the code by checking to see that it is respected and then disciplining violators.

Several companies are developing ways to implement internal policing. Some executives think that audits could hold people responsible for unusual pricing successes as well as for failures. Market conditions, product specifications, and factory scheduling could be coded, put on tables, and compared to prices. High variations could be investigated. One division vice president also plans to audit expense accounts to see that competitor contact is minimized.

Source: Reprinted by permission of *Harvard Business Review.* "Why Do Companies Succumb to Price Fixing?" by Jeffrey A. Sonnenfeld and Paul R. Lawrence, July–August 1978. Copyright © 2002 by the Harvard Business School Publishing Corporation; all rights reserved.

Credit Arrangement Agreements The cost of credit is part of the price of goods and services. Any agreement among creditor-competitors to limit credit terms or to charge a universal credit fee is an agreement relating to price and a *per se* violation.

C O N S I D E R . . .

17.3 Visx of Santa Clara, California, and Summit Technology of Waltham, Massachusetts, have formed a joint venture (to be called Pillar Point Partners), pooling their resources for a new surgical technique called refractive keratectomy, which corrects vision by removing corneal tissue with lasers. The process is an advancement over popular radial keratotomy, which requires a scalpel.

Pillar Point Partners was created to resolve patent disputes and FDA-approval issues. Visx holds patents for the lasers but does not have regulatory approval. Summit has FDA approval for the sale of its laser. Pillar Point will license laser users and require licensees to pay a $250 royalty per procedure.

Dr. Frank O'Donnell, chairman of a competitor, Laser Sight of St. Louis, notes, "I've always thought this sounds like price fixing." Is the fixed royalty fee price fixing?

Division of Markets

Any agreement between competitors to divide up an available market is a *per se* violation under the Sherman Act. The result of such an agreement is to give the participants monopolies in their particular area. Such a market division introduces an unnatural force into the competitive market. For example, office product supply companies agreeing to operate only in certain cities throughout a state would be a division of markets and a *per se* violation.

C O N S I D E R . . .

17.4 BRG of Georgia, Inc. (BRG), and Harcourt Brace Jovanovich Legal and Professional Publications (HJB) are the nation's two largest providers of bar review materials and lectures. HJB began offering a Georgia bar review course on a limited basis in 1976 and was in direct, and often intense, competition with BRG from 1977 to 1979. BRG and HJB were the two main providers of bar review courses in Georgia during this period. In early 1980, they entered into an agreement that gave BRG an exclusive license to market HJB's materials in Georgia and to use its trade name "Bar/Bri." The parties agreed that HJB would not compete with BRG in Georgia and that BRG would not compete with HJB outside of Georgia.

Under the agreement, HJB received $100 per student enrolled by BRG and 40 percent of all revenues over $350. Immediately after the 1980 agreement, the price of BRG's course was increased from $150 to over $400.

Is this an illegal division of markets? [*Palmer v. BRG of Georgia, Inc.*, 498 U.S. 46 (1990)]

Group Boycotts and Refusals to Deal

A group of competitors that agrees not to deal with buyers unless those buyers agree to standard credit or arbitration clauses has committed a *per se* violation.

BIOGRAPHY

CHRISTIE'S AND SOTHEBY'S: ARTISTIC PRICE FIXING

Christie's International and Sotheby's are international auction houses for art and estate items known for their handling of the estates and property of the rich and famous such as: the estate of Jaqueline Kennedy Onassis; the gowns of Diana, Princess of Wales; and the effects of Marilyn Monroe. Together, the two firms controlled 95 percent of the international auction market. They became the subject of a price fixing investigation by the Federal Trade Commission and Justice Department in 1997.

The allegations of price fixing against the auction houses involve "conscious parallelism." That is, the two federal agencies were investigating why the two auction houses raised their commissions in lock step over the years with virtually no price competition in auction commissions.

The drama and media coverage surrounding the Christie's and Sotheby's antitrust investigation continued, but the case seemed to have no substance until the end of 1999.

In December 1999, Christopher M. Davidge, the CEO of Christie's, was terminated. Upset about what he called his "paltry" severance package and others say was his concern that he might have been set up to take the blame for any antitrust charges, Davidge demanded all of his business records from Christie's. He took everything from his files, including handwritten notes he had sent to Christie's CEO, Diana (Dede) Brooks. Also implicated in his files was then chairman of Sotheby's, A. Alfred Taubman.

Mr. Davidge had initially denied, when questioned by the Justice Department, that he had any inappropriate communications with Sotheby's and Ms. Brooks. However, Mr. Davidge's former assistant, Irmgrad Pickering, told the Justice Department that she believed Mr. Davidge and Ms. Brooks had held meetings.

He turned the records over to his lawyer who, in turn, turned them over to the Justice Department. The records have been described as establishing "classic cartel behavior—price fixing pure and simple" between Christie's and Sotheby's. The correspondence in his files was between him and Diana Brooks, CEO of Sotheby's. The correspondence reflects a pattern of the two auction

houses matching their commission rates. For example, in March 1995, Christie's announced it was increasing its sellers' fees from a flat rate to a sliding scale ranging from 2 percent to 20 percent. Sotheby's made an announcement of the same change in sellers' rates one month later.

Soon after Christie's became aware of the documents and correspondence in the hands of the Justice Department, it announced its cooperation with the federal government and was given amnesty. At the same time, Christie's announced that it was raising its buyer's commission from 17.5 percent to 18 percent (for buyers spending up to $80,000 and 10 percent for buyers above that amount) and charging its sellers less taking its commission for sales down 1 percent to 5 percent and as low as 1.25 percent for amounts greater than $1,000.

Both changes placed Sotheby's, Christie's prime competitor, in the position of charging higher commissions. The disparity in commission was the first time there was any difference in the competitors' prices in over a decade.

Mr. Taubman denied any involvement in the price fixing and offered a lie detector test conducted by a former FBI agent to establish that he did not know of the arrangements and communications between Ms. Brooks and Mr. Davidge. The two key questions in the polygraph exam, which Mr. Taubman passed, were:

Did you tell Dede Brooks to try and reach an agreement with Davidge regarding amounts to be charged to buyers or sellers?

Did Dede Brooks ever tell you that she had reached an agreement with Davidge about amounts to be charged to buyers and sellers?

Mr. Taubman's answers of "no" to each of these questions were found to be truthful by the examiner for the polygraph. The test was conducted without any law enforcement agents present.

At nearly the same time, Christie's agreed to pay $256 million, one-half of a $512 million civil suit brought against the company, and settled a shareholder lawsuit for $30 million. Sotheby's also agreed to pay its $256 million of the suit amount to settle civil claims. Mr. Taubman agreed to be responsible for paying $156 million of that

(continued)

corporate obligation. Representing the plaintiffs in the antitrust suit against the two auction houses was David Boies, the lawyer who represented Al Gore in the 2000 presidential election litigation, Shawn Fanning and Napster in their copyright litigation, and the federal government in the Microsoft antitrust case.

Davidge got immunity in exchange for his cooperation. Ms. Brooks entered a guilty plea on October 5, 2000, and declined all of her stock options. Her friends say she refused the options so as to put all of the case behind her. Others say she declined them so that she will not be held responsible for any of the costs the company has incurred related to the antitrust activities. In exchange for favorable sentencing, Ms. Brooks, Mr. Taubman's one-time protégé, turned state's evidence and cooperated with the Justice Department in its investigation.

In May 2001, four years after the investigation began, the Justice Department announced the indictment of Mr. Taubman as well as his counterpart at Christie's, Sir Anthony Tennant. The indictment charged price fixing over a 6-year period involving over 13,000 customers. The criminal case proceeded to trial near the end of 2001. Ms. Brooks testified against Mr. Taubman. Mr. Taubman was found guilty of price fixing and related charges.

Both Christie's and Davidge are immune from prosecution for antitrust violations because of their cooperation.

Following the settlements, Sotheby's, a 256-year-old company, hired Michael I. Sovern, the former president of Columbia University, as chairman of the board. Sotheby's stock suffered during the time of the daily disclosures about the investigations, the evidence, and the resulting litigation. At the beginning of the investigation, Sotheby's stock was trading in March 1999 at $42 per share. By March 2000, it was down to $15 per share.

Why do we worry that two auction houses were agreeing on increases in their commission rates? What do you think of Mr. Davidge's ethics? Did his intent to sue Christie's for terminating him turn out to provide Christie's with a break in the antitrust case? What do you think of Ms. Brooks providing evidence on her former mentor?

Sources

Alexandria Peers and Ann Davis, "Christie's Overhauls Commissions," *Wall Street Journal*, 8 February 2000, A3, A10.

Douglas Frantz, with Carol Vogel and Ralph Blumenthal, "Files of Ex-Christie's Chief Fuel Inquiry into Art Auction," *New York Times*, 8 October 2000, A1, A28.

Visit the American Medical Association:
http://www.ama-assn.org

Some group boycotts appear to have the best intentions. Many garment manufacturers once agreed not to sell to buyers who sold discount or pirated designer clothing. Certainly their intentions were good, but the result still has the anticompetitive effect of controlling the marketplace. Competitors cannot enforce the law through boycotts; other avenues of relief are available. The American Medical Association's rules that prohibited salaried medical practices and prepaid medical plans are illegal boycotts in spite of the protection motivations behind the restrictions.

The following case involves an issue of a well-intentioned but still illegal boycott.

CASE 17.3

FTC v. Superior Court Trial Lawyers Ass'n
493 U.S. 411 (1990)

A Legal Boycott: Legal Aid, Legal Fees

FACTS

The U.S. Constitution requires that legal counsel be provided to indigent defendants. The District of Columbia, like other local governments, fulfills this responsibility through a program that hires private lawyers at a rate of $30 per hour. In 1982 these lawyers handled 25,000 indigent defendant cases at a cost of $4,579,572 to the District. Over 1,200 lawyers were registered for the indigent defendant program, with 100 lawyers classified as "regulars." Three of these 100 lawyers derived all of their income from indigent representation cases.

The Superior Court Trial Lawyers Association (SCTLA) had been concerned about the low fees paid in the program and had met with the mayor to encourage higher fees to ensure quality representation. The mayor was sympathetic but indicated that no funds were available for an increase.

In 1983 SCTLA formed a strike committee that recommended, as the only way to increase fees, encouraging members to stop signing indigent representation agreements until a rate schedule of $45 for out-of-court time and $55 for in-court time was achieved. About 100 lawyers signed a petition to this effect and agreed not to accept new cases. The result was that 90 percent of the regulars refused to accept new cases.

Within 10 days of the September 6, 1983, petition, the criminal justice system in the District of Columbia was in chaos; the mayor met with the SCTLA strike committee and, declaring a crisis, increased the fees to the $45–$55 per hour rates. The agreement was approved by the city council on September 21, 1983.

The Federal Trade Commission (FTC) filed a complaint against SCTLA alleging that SCTLA's conduct was a conspiracy to fix prices and conduct a boycott, and it violated Section 5 of the FTC Act as an unfair method of competition. The administrative law judge (AJL) found for the FTC, the FTC found that a boycott had occurred that caused harm, and the court of appeals remanded the case for a determination of whether SCTLA (respondents) had market power. The FTC appealed.

JUDICIAL OPINION

STEVENS, Justice

Respondents' boycott may well have served a cause that was worthwhile and unpopular. We may assume that the preboycott rates were unreasonably low, and that the increase has produced better legal representation for indigent defendants. Moreover, given that neither indigent criminal defendants nor the lawyers who represent them command any special appeal with the electorate, we may also assume that without the boycott there would have been no increase in District fees at least until Congress [acted]. These assumptions do not control the case, for it is not our task to pass upon the social utility or political wisdom of price fixing agreements.

It is of course true that the city purchases respondents' services because it has a constitutional duty to provide representation to indigent defendants. It is likewise true that the quality of representation may improve when rates are increased. Yet neither of these facts is an acceptable justification for an otherwise unlawful restraint of trade. As we have remarked before, the "Sherman Act reflects a legislative judgment that ultimately competition will produce not only lower prices, but also better goods and services." *National Society of Professional Engineers* v. *United States*, 435 U.S. 679 (1978). This judgment recognizes that all elements of a bargain—quality, service, safety, and durability—and not just the immediate cost, are favorably affected by the free opportunity to select among alternative offers. That is equally so when the quality of legal advocacy, rather than engineering design, is at issue.

The social justifications proffered for respondents' restraint of trade thus do not make it any less unlawful. The statutory policy underlying the Sherman Act "precludes inquiry into the question whether competition is good or bad." Respondents' argument, like that made by petitioners in *Professional Engineers*, ultimately asks us to find that their boycott is permissible because the price it seeks to set is reasonable. But it was settled shortly after the Sherman Act was passed that it "is no excuse that the

(continued)

prices fixed are themselves reasonable." Respondents' agreement is not outside the coverage of the Sherman Act simply because its objective was enactment of favorable legislation.

The lawyers' association argues that if its conduct would otherwise be prohibited by the Sherman Act and the Federal Trade Act, it is nonetheless protected by the First Amendment rights.

The activity the FTC order prohibits is a concerted refusal by [the] lawyers to accept any further assignments until they receive an increase in their compensation; the undenied objective of their boycott was an economic advantage for those who agreed to participate. No matter how altruistic the motives of respondents may have been, it is undisputed that their immediate objective was to increase the price that they would be paid for their services.

Respondents' concerted action in refusing to accept further assignments until their fees were increased was thus a plain violation of the antitrust laws.

Affirmed as to the finding of a violation. Reversed for further proceedings on the issue of market power.

CASE QUESTIONS

1. Explain the District of Columbia system for providing legal representation for indigent defendants.
2. What was the rate of compensation for lawyers in the program?
3. What fees did the lawyers want?
4. What was the effect of the refusal to take new cases?
5. How long did the boycott last?
6. Did the lawyers get the fees they desired?
7. Of what relevance is the motivation of the lawyers in staging the boycott?
8. Was the boycott a violation of antitrust laws?
9. Was the violation *per se?*

CONSIDER...

17.5 The Federal Trade Commission is conducting an investigation into the informal agreements reached between Toys "Я" Us and toy manufacturers. Toys "Я" Us holds a 19.4 percent share of the U.S. toy market and has informal agreements with Mattel and Hasbro with respect to the sale of their toys to discount warehouse clubs such as Costco and Sam's Club. The clubs are sold toys only in more expensive packaging arrangements. For example, Hollywood Hair Barbie can be purchased at Toys "Я" Us for $10.95, but can only be purchased in a package with a dress at the warehouse clubs for $15.95. Some of the most popular toy items are never sold to the warehouse clubs. For example, Hasbro has not sold its Hall of Fame GI Joe action figures to warehouse clubs and Mattel will not sell its Fisher Price pool table to the clubs.

The FTC commissioners voted 5 to 3 to begin the investigation because toy manufacturers are put into a situation of choosing between selling to Toys "Я" Us and other retailers. Toys "Я" Us maintains that the warehouse clubs do not have the overhead of advertising the toys and simply choose those items that sell the best at very low margins. The low margins can be maintained because, for example, Costco took in more in membership fees over the last ten years than its total net profit.

Is there illegal restraint of trade? Is there price fixing? Have the antitrust laws been violated?

Joint Ventures

A **joint venture** is an undertaking by two or more businesses for a limited purpose. An oil corporation working with an engineering firm for the development of a new drill would be a joint venture; they would be business partners for that limited purpose and project.

Competitors who become involved in joint ventures are a natural concern. These combinations are subject, not to a *per se* violation standard, but to the **rule-of-reason** violation standard, which allows a court to consider the various benefits and detriments involved in a joint venture. For example, in one case all coal producers formed a joint venture sales agency during a time of a depressed coal market to increase sales and save selling costs. This joint venture was held reasonable under the Sherman Act [*United States v. Appalachian Coal*, 228 U.S. 334 (1933)].

In another case, a joint venture between movie producers and movie theaters was held unreasonable because it gave the theaters exclusive showing rights to the producers' movies [*United States v. Paramount Pictures*, 334 U.S. 131 (1948)].

Exceptions to Sherman Act Violations

Some activities by competitors are protected even though the competitors are acting as a group and even though the effect may be to reduce competition. One such exception is the *Noerr-Pennington* **doctrine,** under which competitors are permitted to work together for the purpose of governmental lobbying and other political action.[1] Their conduct cannot be restrained under the Sherman Act because their activity enjoys the protection of the First Amendment. Competitors who work together to influence legislators and administrative agencies are protected even though they may be working for anticompetitive benefits. For example, competitors can make appearances at new licensee hearings and oppose the granting of a license. The resulting reduction in competition is done within the confines of the First Amendment and is not subject to Sherman Act jurisdiction.

The *Noerr-Pennington* doctrine strikes a delicate balance between anticompetitive behavior and First Amendment rights. That balance often fluctuates as new issues in regulation, lobbying, and licensing arise. In some instances, market domination is at issue in regulatory proceedings. In *City of Columbia v. Omni Outdoor Advertising*, 499 U.S. 365 (1991), a company that was controlling the outdoor advertising market in one city attempted to use its lobbying First Amendment rights to protect its market control. An objection and suit by a competitor still resulted in the protection of *Noerr-Pennington* and First Amendment rights. Courts are hesitant to intervene in a business's right to lobby and petition government agencies even if the purpose is preservation of market superiority.

CONSIDER...

17.6 In Arizona, fees for title insurance searches and policies were established by rating bureaus established by the title companies. The bureaus recommended rates to the state, and the state adopted those rates unless some specific objection was made. The result was that title search and insurance fees were the same for all companies within the state. The FTC filed a complaint against the title companies, alleging that they were engaged in price fixing. The companies responded that government regulation of prices is not price fixing. Do you agree? [*FTC v. Ticor Title Ins. Co.*, 504 U.S. 621 (1992)]

Review the Local Government Antitrust Act of 1984:
http://www.law.cornell.edu/uscode/15/34.html

There are additional exceptions to the antitrust laws. The Local Government Antitrust Act of 1984 was passed to eliminate the effects of several Supreme Court decisions that would not allow state and local governments to be exempted from the application of federal antitrust laws unless there was a state policy that specifically exempted such activities. The Local Government Antitrust Act has provided an exemption for these localities, which were facing over 300 antitrust lawsuits at the time the act was passed.

In order to compete effectively in the international market, U.S. businesses have been permitted to form selling cooperatives or joint ventures with prior approval from the Justice Department. The Joint Venture Trading Act of 1983 allows joint ventures of competitors for the purpose of competing with foreign competitors (with Justice Department approval). The Shipping Act of 1984 allows carriers to enter into joint venture shipping arrangements so shippers can more effectively compete in the international market, where rates are set and routes and shipments are divided among competitors.

Clayton Act Restraints

Interlocking Directorates

The first Clayton Act horizontal restraint concerns the use of directors on the boards of competitive firms to lessen the effects of competition—**interlocking directorates.** Section 8 prohibits a director of a firm with $10 million or more in capital from being a director of a competing company. The intent of this prohibition is to lessen the likelihood of the exchange of anticompetitive information about price, markets, and other competitors.

Horizontal Mergers

Horizontal mergers are mergers between competitors. To determine when they have taken place, courts have applied a test of "presumptive illegality": Any merger that produces an undue percentage share of the market or significantly increases market concentration is a violation. In these cases, the courts examine market share and the relevant markets to determine whether there is undue concentration.

There are some defenses that justify a horizontal merger. One is the **failing-company doctrine,** which allows the acquisition of a competitor that is clearly failing if it is an asset or inventory acquisition. Another defense is the **small-company doctrine,** which applies when two small companies merge with the hope of being better able to compete with the larger businesses in that market.

In *United States* v. *Von's Grocery Co.,* 384 U.S. 270 (1966), the Supreme Court held that a merger between Von's Grocery Company and Shopping Bag Food Stores, which would have given the two companies together a 7.5 percent share of the retail grocery market in Los Angeles, was violative of the Clayton Act because its effect would be to substantially lessen competition. In 1988, the Justice Department approved the merger of Von's and Safeway in southern California. The merger made the new Von's the largest competitor in terms of market percentage as well as in the number of stores. Justice Department attitudes and guidelines on mergers have changed largely because geographic markets have changed. Geographic markets are now defined in light of international trade. Some domestic combinations that would have been illegal in 1966 are now permissible because of size requirements for companies in international competition.

The Federal Trade Commission (FTC) has charged AOL Time Warner, Inc., and its subsidiaries, Warner Music Group and Vivendi Universal SA, with price fixing in connection with the sales of the Three Tenors' audio and video CDs and tapes. (The three tenors are Luciano Pavarotti, Placido Domingo, and Jose Carreras).

The Three Tenors make a record of their live performances together—done once every four years. The first two CDs and videos in the series sold millions, with both becoming two of the highest volume opera recordings in history. However, by the third performance and CD and video, the public demand was not as great and the FTC charges that Warner felt the first two releases would cannibalize the sales for the third. As a result, all parties involved in the sales of these CDs and tapes had to agree not to discount the first two performance tapes so that the third would have an opportunity to sell. The FTC also

ETHICAL ISSUES 17.2

alleges that there were agreements on when advertisements could run for the third series sales and availability.

The FTC stumbled across a memo on the marketing plan and advertising constraints as it was reviewing documents in connection with the Warner/EMI Music merger proposal, a merger that fell through after European officials balked at the idea. The FTC pursued the case, and Warner settled the charges by agreeing not to restrain competition or set prices in the future.

Is it permissible for an agency investigating one issue to use evidence it comes across related to another issue? What lessons does this situation offer on the percolating nature of the truth? Is establishing a minimum price a violation of the Sherman Act? Is restricting advertising a violation of the Sherman Act?

VERTICAL TRADE RESTRAINTS

Various steps are involved in getting a product from its creation to its ultimate consumer. For example, producing packaged sandwich meats requires the manufacturer to obtain bulk-butchered meat (originally from a ranch) through a distributor and turn it into packaged sandwich meat that is sold to another distributor. This distributor sells to a grocery wholesaler, who sells to grocery stores, where consumers buy the packaged meat. This entire process has different levels of production and distribution, but there is one vertical chain from start to finish.

The types of vertical restraints, which are discussed in the following subsections, are:

- Resale price maintenance
- Sole outlets and exclusive distributorships
- Customer and territorial restrictions
- Tying arrangements
- Exclusive dealing or requirements contracts
- Price discrimination

Resale Price Maintenance

Resale price maintenance is an attempt by a manufacturer to control the price that retailers charge for the manufacturer's product. Resale price maintenance is a rule-of-reason violation (see *Khan* case) of Section 1 of the Sherman Act. Resale price maintenance includes either minimum or maximum prices, or both. A minimum price encourages a retailer to carry a certain product because its profit margin will be higher. One explanation offered to justify minimum prices is that, without them, dealers who advertise and offer service may be used by consumers for information only, after which these consumers actually buy at discount houses.

A manufacturer who attempts to set a maximum price is trying to prevent retailers with market power from charging a price higher than that set for the manufacturer's goods, thereby reducing the number of sales. The economic theory is that fewer goods would be sold under such circumstances than if there were open competition.

Resale price maintenance can also occur in ways other than actual price controls—for example, through the use of consignments. If the packaged-sandwich-meat manufacturer required all grocery stores to act as agents for the sale of its meats and paid a commission on each sale, there would be a consignment. The manufacturer could control the price through such an arrangement, but such price-controlled consignments are violations of Section 1 of the Sherman Act.

Manufacturers can offer a "suggested retail price" without violating Section 1, although any attempt to enforce that suggested price would be a violation. For example, a manufacturer who refuses to sell to a retailer who does not use the suggested price is engaging in resale price maintenance.

At one time, states were permitted to allow resale price maintenance by statute. That power was taken away in 1975, and states cannot, by statute, allow minimum price schedules or require dealers to adhere to **fair trade contracts,** which are agreements on maximum or minimum prices.

The following case deals with the issue of resale price maintenance and the change from its *per se* violation to a rule-of-reason standard.

CASE 17.4

State Oil v. *Khan*
522 U.S. 3 (1997)

Fill It Up, but Only at My Price

FACTS

Barkat U. Khan and his corporation (respondents) entered into an agreement with State Oil (petitioner) to lease and operate a gas station and convenience store owned by State Oil. The agreement provided that Khan would obtain the gasoline supply for the station from State Oil at a price equal to a suggested retail price set by State Oil, less a margin of 3.25 cents per gallon. Khan could charge any price he wanted, but if he charged more than State Oil's suggested retail price, the excess was rebated to State Oil. Khan could sell the gasoline for less than State Oil's suggested retail price, but the difference came out of his allowed margin.

After a year, Khan fell behind on his lease payments and State Oil gave notice of and began proceedings for eviction. The court had Khan removed and appointed a receiver for operation of the station. The receiver operated the gas station without the price constraints and received an overall profit margin above the 3.25 cents imposed on Khan.

Khan filed suit alleging that the State Oil agreement was a violation of Section 1 of the Sherman Act because State Oil was controlling price. The district court held that there was no *per se* violation and that Khan had failed to demonstrate antitrust injury. The Court of Appeals reversed and State Oil appealed.

JUDICIAL OPINION

O'CONNOR, Justice

Under § 1 of the Sherman Act, 26 Stat. 209, as amended, 15 U.S.C. § 1, "[e]very contract, combination . . . , or conspiracy, in restraint of trade" is illegal. In *Albrecht v. Herald Co.,* 390 U.S. 145, 88 S.Ct. 869, 19 L.Ed.2d 998 (1968), this Court held that vertical maximum price fixing is a per se violation of that statute. In this case, we are asked to reconsider that decision in light of subsequent decisions of this Court. We conclude that *Albrecht* should be overruled.

Although the Sherman Act, by its terms, prohibits every agreement "in restraint of trade," this Court has long recognized that Congress intended to outlaw only unreasonable restraints.

As a consequence, most antitrust claims are analyzed under a "rule of reason," according to which the finder of fact must decide whether the questioned practice imposes an unreasonable restraint on competition, taking into account a variety of factors, including specific information about the relevant business, its condition before and after the restraint was imposed, and the restraint's history, nature, and effect.

Some types of restraints, however, have such predictable and pernicious anticompetitive effect, and such limited potential for procompetitive benefit, that they are deemed unlawful per se.

Thus, we have expressed reluctance to adopt per se rules with regard to "restraints imposed in the context of business relationships where the economic impact of certain practices is not immediately obvious."

In *White Motor Co. v. United States,* 372 U.S. 253, 83 S.Ct. 696, 9 L.Ed.2d 738 (1963), the Court considered the validity of a manufacturer's assignment of exclusive territories to its distributors and dealers. The Court determined that too little was known about the competitive impact of such vertical limitations to warrant treating them as per se unlawful.

Four years later, in *United States v. Arnold, Schwinn & Co.,* 388 U.S. 365, 87 S.Ct. 1856, 18 L.Ed. 2d 1249 (1967), the Court reconsidered the status of exclusive dealer territories and held that, upon the transfer of title to goods to a distributor, a supplier's imposition of territorial restrictions on the distributor was "so obviously destructive of competition" as to constitute a per se violation of the Sherman Act. In *Schwinn,* the Court acknowledged that some vertical restrictions, such as the conferral of territorial rights or franchises, could have procompetitive benefits by allowing smaller enterprises to compete, and that such restrictions might avert vertical integration in the distribution process. The Court drew the line, however, at permitting manufacturers to control product marketing once dominion over the goods had passed to dealers.

Albrecht, decided the following Term, involved a newspaper publisher who had granted exclusive territories to independent carriers subject to their adherence to a maximum price on resale of the newspapers to the public. Influenced by its decisions in *Socony-Vacuum, Kiefer-Stewart,* and *Schwinn,* the Court concluded that it was per se unlawful for the publisher to fix the maximum resale price of its newspapers. The Court acknowledged that "[m]aximum and minimum price fixing may have different consequences in many situations," but nonetheless condemned maximum price fixing for "substituting the perhaps erroneous judgment of a seller for the forces of the competitive market."

Albrecht was animated in part by the fear that vertical maximum price fixing could allow suppliers to discriminate against certain dealers, restrict the services that dealers could afford to offer customers, or disguise minimum price fixing schemes. The Court rejected the notion (both on the record of that case and in the abstract) that, because the newspaper publisher "granted exclusive territories, a price ceiling was necessary to protect the public from price gouging by dealers who had monopoly power in their own territories."

In a vigorous dissent, Justice Harlan asserted that the majority had erred in equating the effects of maximum and minimum price fixing.

Nine years later, in *Continental T.V., Inc. v. GTE Sylvania, Inc.,* 433 U.S. 36, 97 S.Ct. 2549, 53 L.Ed.2d 568 (1977), the Court overruled *Schwinn,* thereby rejecting application of a per se rule in the context of vertical nonprice restrictions. The Court acknowledged the principle of *stare decisis,* but explained that the need for clarification in the law justified reconsideration of *Schwinn:*

Since its announcement, Schwinn *has been the subject of continuing controversy and confusion, both in the scholarly journals and in the federal courts. The great weight of scholarly opinion has been critical of the decision, and a number of the federal courts confronted with analogous vertical restrictions have sought to limit its reach.*

Thus, our reconsideration of *Albrecht's* continuing validity is informed by several of our decisions, as well as a considerable body of scholarship discussing the effects of vertical restraints. Our analysis is also guided by our general view that the primary

(continued)

purpose of the antitrust laws is to protect interbrand competition. See, e.g., *Business Electronics Corp. v. Sharp Electronics Corp.,* 485 U.S. 717, 726, 108 S.Ct. 1515, 1520–1521, 99 L.Ed.2d 808 (1988). "Low prices," we have explained, "benefit consumers regardless of how those prices are set, and so long as they are above predatory levels, they do not threaten competition." Our interpretation of the Sherman Act also incorporates the notion that condemnation of practices resulting in lower prices to consumers is "especially costly" because "cutting prices in order to increase business often is the very essence of competition." *Matsushita Elec. Industrial Co. v. Zenith Radio Corp.,* 475 U.S. 574, 594, 106 S.Ct. 1348, 1360, 89 L.Ed.2d 538 (1986).

So informed, we find it difficult to maintain that vertically-imposed maximum prices could harm consumers or competition to the extent necessary to justify their per se invalidation. As Chief Judge Posner wrote for the Court of Appeals in this case:

As for maximum resale price fixing, unless the supplier is a monopsonist he cannot squeeze his dealers' margins below a competitive level; the attempt to do so would just drive the dealers into the arms of a competing supplier. A supplier might, however, fix a maximum resale price in order to prevent his dealers from exploiting a monopoly position. . . . [S]uppose that State Oil, perhaps to encourage . . . dealer services . . . has spaced its dealers sufficiently far apart to limit competition among them (or even given each of them an exclusive territory); and suppose further that Union 76 is a sufficiently distinctive and popular brand to give the dealers in it at least a modicum of monopoly power. Then State Oil might want to place a ceiling on the dealers' resale prices in order to prevent them from exploiting that monopoly power fully. It would do this not out of disinterested malice, but in its commercial self-interest. The higher the price at which gasoline is resold, the smaller the volume sold, and so the lower the profit to the supplier if the higher profit per gallon at the higher price is being snared by the dealer.

93 F.3d, at 1362.

See also R. Bork, The Antitrust Paradox 281–282 (1978) ("There could of course, be no anticonsumer effect from [the type of price fixing considered in *Albrecht*], and one suspects that the paper has a legitimate interest in keeping subscriber prices down in order to increase circulation and maximize revenues from advertising").

Further, although vertical maximum price fixing might limit the viability of inefficient dealers, that consequence is not necessarily harmful to competition and consumers.

After reconsidering *Albrecht*'s rationale and the substantial criticism the decision has received, however, we conclude that there is insufficient economic justification for per se invalidation of vertical maximum price fixing. That is so not only because it is difficult to accept the assumptions underlying *Albrecht*, but also because *Albrecht* has little or no relevance to ongoing enforcement of the Sherman Act.

Despite what Chief Judge Posner aptly described as *Albrecht*'s infirmities, [and] its increasingly wobbly, moth-eaten foundations," there remains the question whether *Albrecht* deserves continuing respect under the doctrine of *stare decisis.* The Court of Appeals was correct in applying that principle despite disagreement with *Albrecht,* for it is this Court's prerogative alone to overrule one of its precedents.

We approach the reconsideration of decisions of this Court with the utmost caution. *Stare decisis* reflects "a policy judgment that 'in most matters it is more important that the applicable rule of law be settled than that it be settled right.' "

But "[s]*tare decisis* is not an inexorable command." Ibid. In the area of antitrust law, there is a competing interest, well-represented in this Court's decisions, in recognizing and adapting to changed circumstances and the lessons of accumulated experience. Thus, the general presumption that legislative changes should be left to Congress has less force with respect to the Sherman Act in light of the accepted view that Congress "expected the courts to give shape to the statute's broad mandate by drawing on common-law tradition." *National Soc. of Professional Engineers* v. *United States,* 435 U.S. 679, 688, 98, S.Ct. 1355, 1363, 55 L.Ed.2d 637 (1978). As we have explained, the term "restraint of trade," as used in § 1, also "invokes the common law itself, and not merely the static content that the common law had assigned to the term in 1890." Accordingly, this Court has reconsidered its decisions construing the Sherman Act when the theoretical underpinnings of those decisions are called into serious question.

In overruling *Albrecht,* we of course do not hold that all vertical maximum price fixing is per se lawful. Instead, vertical maximum price fixing, like the majority of commercial arrangements subject to the antitrust laws, should be evaluated under the rule of reason. In our view, rule-of-reason analysis will effectively identify those situations in which vertical maximum price fixing amounts to anticompetitive conduct.

There remains the question whether respondents are entitled to recover damages based on State Oil's conduct. Although the Court of Appeals noted that "the district judge was right to conclude that if the rule of reason is applicable, Khan loses," its consideration of this case was necessarily premised on *Albrecht*'s per se rule. Under the circumstances, the matter should be reviewed by the Court of Appeals in the first instance. We therefore vacate the judgment of the Court of Appeals and remand the case for further proceedings consistent with this opinion.

Remanded.

CASE QUESTIONS

1. What were the terms of Khan's lease?
2. Could Khan charge a different price?
3. What happened when a receiver operated the station without the State Oil lease constraints?
4. Is vertical price fixing a *per se* violation?
5. What does the court say about inefficient retailers and vertical price controls?
6. What does the court say about a long-standing precedent and *stare decisis*?

Sole Outlets and Exclusive Distributorships

A **sole outlet** or **exclusive distributorship** agreement is one in which a manufacturer appoints a distributor or retailer as the sole or exclusive outlet for the manufacturer's product. This type of arrangement can be a violation of Section 1 but is subject to a rule of reason analysis. When the rule of reason is applied to alleged antitrust violators, the alleged violators have an opportunity to present justifications for their conduct.

In a rule of reason analysis of sole outlets or exclusive distributorships, courts examine several factors. One factor is a manufacturer's freedom to pick and choose certain buyers to deal with. However, the extent of the manufacturer's freedom is limited by the amount of **interbrand competition,** which is the competition available for the manufacturer's product. For example, in the case of the sandwich-meat manufacturer, so long as there are other manufacturers selling their products in the area, the manufacturer could agree to sell to only one chain of grocery stores. But if there is little interbrand competition, the antitrust laws require that **intrabrand competition** be more available. Thus, if the manufacturer were the only one distributing sandwich meats in the area, dealing with only one grocery chain might not be reasonable and could not survive an antitrust challenge.

The rule of reason also allows a court to consider other factors involved in a manufacturer's arrangements. For example, if the manufacturer agrees to limit outlets merely to benefit one of the outlets, there may be a violation.

CONSIDER...

17.7 Department 56 is a company that manufactures and sells collectible Christmas village houses and other replica items to allow collectors to create the whimsical "Snow Village" town or "Dickens Christmas." Department 56 has only authorized dealers. Sam's Club, a division of Wal-Mart Stores, Inc., began selling Department 56 pieces from The Heritage Village Collection.

Susan Engel, president and CEO of Department 56, attempted to contact Wal-Mart because it is not an authorized Department 56 dealer. Wal-Mart did not respond, and Ms. Engel sent by Federal Express to National Collector clubs a letter that contained the following language:

> *Sam's Club should not have any Department 56 merchandise. In a marketing environment where most companies are fighting to get their merchandise into the Wal-Marts of the world, we are fighting to get our merchandise out. While we recognize there is surely a place for mass market and warehouse stores, Department 56 Villages enjoy a strong heritage of dealer sales and service support. Our products simply do not fit the warehouse-style selling environment of Sam's Club.*
>
> *Of strong importance to us—and we hope to you too—is the tradition of selling our villages through an exclusive dealer network made up almost entirely of independent retailers. Wal-Mart Stores, Inc., and its subsidiaries are predators on these hard working individuals. Sales of our products mean virtually nothing to the bottom line of a company the size of Wal-Mart. But to many of our loyal dealers, healthy Department 56 product sales mean survival.*
>
> *Do you really need to shop at Sam's Club or Wal-Mart? Let's refuse to purchase villages or any other products from local Wal-Mart owned stores.*

The letter asked collector club members to write Wal-Mart executives and local store managers. Names, mailing addresses, and telephone and fax numbers were offered.

Has Ms. Engel violated any laws? How do you think Sam's Club obtained the Department 56 products?

Evaluate the conduct of Ms. Engel in sending out the letter. Were her state- **ETHICAL ISSUES 17.3** ments about Wal-Mart and calls to action fair? Should Wal-Mart respond? How?

Customer and Territorial Restrictions

Sole outlets allow manufacturers to decide (within limitations) to whom they will sell goods. However, manufacturers are not given the right to control what the buyer does with goods and how those goods are sold. Under Section 1 of the Sherman Act, restricting to whom and where a buyer of a manufacturer's goods can sell is a rule-of-reason violation. The restrictions are subject to the rule of reason because interbrand competition may be increased even though intrabrand competition is reduced.

In applying the rule of reason to **customer and territorial restrictions,** there are several issues to be considered. The first is whether there is an increase in interbrand competition because of decreased intrabrand competition. A second consideration is whether the manufacturer imposing the restriction has market power. The more market power the manufacturer has, the fewer substitute goods consumers have, resulting in less interbrand competition.

Vertical restrictions are likely to be judged reasonable when the manufacturer is new to the market or is having financial or sales difficulties. If the restrictions will help the manufacturer get started or keep going, the objective of interbrand competition is met by the restrictions on intrabrand competition.

Tying Arrangements

Tying sales are those that require buyers to take an additional product in order to buy a needed product. For example, requiring the buyer of a copier machine to buy the seller's paper when there are other brands of paper suitable for use in the machine is a tying arrangement. The copier machine is the tying product or the desired product, and the paper is the tied product or the required product.

Tying is usually an illegal *per se* violation of Section 3 of the Clayton Act (for goods contracts) and Section 1 of the Sherman Act (for services, real property, and intangibles). Both acts prohibit tying but cover different subject matters. Whether there is a violation depends on whether market power results from the tying arrangement and whether there are any defenses.

Market power is established if the tying product is unique. For example, requiring the purchase of inferior movie films in order to buy copyrighted quality films is an example of the presence of market power. Because the seller is the only one with the copyrighted films, there is market power that is being used to sell another unnecessary, low-demand product.

Two defenses have been recognized in tying cases. The first is the *new-industry defense*. Under this defense, the manufacturer of the tying product is permitted to have a tied product to protect initially the quality control in the start-up of a business. For example, a cable television antenna manufacturer required purchasers to take a service contract also. The tying was upheld during the outset of the business so that the system could begin functioning properly and this new cable television industry could catch hold.

A second defense is *quality control for the protection of goodwill*. This defense is rarely supportable. The only time it would apply is if the specifications for the tied goods were so detailed that they could not possibly be supplied by anyone other than the manufacturer of the tying product.

The following case involves an issue of whether a tying arrangement was valid.

CASE 17.5

Jefferson Parish Hosp. Dist. No. 2 v. *Hyde*
466 U.S. 2 (1984)

B.Y.O. Anesthesiologist: Tying Hospital Arrangements

FACTS

Dr. Edwin G. Hyde, a board-certified anesthesiologist, applied for permission to practice at East Jefferson Hospital (petitioners) in Louisiana. An approval was recommended for his hiring, but the hospital's board denied him employment on grounds that the hospital had a contract with Roux & Associates for Roux to provide all anesthesiological services required by the hospital's patients. Dr. Hyde filed suit, which the district court dismissed. The court of appeals reversed that decision and held that the contract for the services with Roux was illegal *per se*. The hospital appealed.

(continued)

JUDICIAL OPINION

STEVENS, Justice

The exclusive contract had an impact on two different segments of the economy: consumers of medical services, and providers of anesthesiological services. Any consumer of medical services who elects to have an operation performed at East Jefferson Hospital may not employ any anesthesiologist not associated with Roux. No anesthesiologists except those employed by Roux may practice at East Jefferson.

There are at least twenty hospitals in the New Orleans metropolitan area and about 70 percent of the patients living in Jefferson Parish go to hospitals other than East Jefferson. Because it regarded the entire New Orleans metropolitan area as the relevant geographic market in which hospitals compete, this evidence convinced the District Court that East Jefferson does not possess any significant "market power"; therefore it concluded that petitioners could not use the Roux contract to anticompetitive ends. The same evidence led the Court of Appeals to draw a different conclusion. Noting that 30 percent of the residents of the Parish go to East Jefferson Hospital, and that, in fact, "patients tend to choose hospitals by location rather than price or quality," the Court of Appeals concluded that the relevant market was the East Bank of Jefferson Parish. The conclusion that East Jefferson Hospital possessed market power in that area was buttressed by the facts that the prevalence of health insurance eliminates a patient's incentive to compare costs, that the patient is not sufficiently informed to compare quality, and that family convenience tends to magnify the importance of location.

The Court of Appeals held that the case involves a "tying arrangement" because the "users of the hospital's operating rooms (the tying product) are also compelled to purchase the hospital's chosen anesthesia service (the tied product)."

It is clear, however, that every refusal to sell two products separately cannot be said to restrain competition. For example, we have written that "if one of a dozen food stores in a community were to refuse to sell flour unless the buyer also took sugar it would hardly tend to restrain competition if its competitors were ready and able to sell flour by itself." Buyers often find package sales attractive; a seller's decision to offer such packages can merely be an attempt to compete effectively—conduct that is entirely consistent with the Sherman Act.

Accordingly, we have condemned tying arrangements when the seller has some special ability—usually called "market power"—to force a purchaser to do something that he would not do in a competitive market. When "forcing" occurs, our cases have found the tying arrangement to be unlawful.

The hospital has provided its patients with a package that includes a range of facilities and services required for a variety of surgical operations. At East Jefferson Hospital the package includes the services of the anesthesiologist. Petitioners argue that the package does not involve a tying arrangement at all—that they are merely providing a functionally integrated package of services.

Unquestionably, the anesthesiological component of the package offered by the hospital could be provided separately and could be selected either by the individual patient or by one of the patient's doctors if the hospital did not insist on including anesthesiological services in the package it offers to its customers. As a matter of actual practice, anesthesiological services are billed separately from the hospital services petitioners provide. There was ample and uncontroverted testimony that patients or surgeons often request specific anesthesiologists to come to a hospital and provide anesthesia, and that the choice of a hospital is particularly frequent in respondent's specialty, obstetric anesthesiology.

Thus, the hospital's requirement that its patients obtain necessary anesthesiological services from Roux combined the purchase of two distinguishable services in a single transaction. As noted above, there is nothing inherently anticompetitive about packaged sales. Only if patients are forced to purchase Roux's services as a result of the hospital's market power would the arrangement have anticompetitive consequences.

It is safe to assume that every patient undergoing a surgical operation needs the services of an anesthesiologist; at least this record contains no evidence that the hospital "forced" any such services on unwilling patients. The record therefore does not provide a basis for applying the *per se* rule against tying to this arrangement.

In order to prevail in the absence of *per se* liability, respondent has the burden of proving that the Roux contract violated the Sherman Act because it unreasonably restrained competition.

All the record establishes is that the choice of anesthesiologists at East Jefferson has been limited to one of the four doctors who are associated with Roux and therefore have staff privileges. Even if Roux did not have an exclusive contract, the range of alternatives open to the patient would be severely limited by the nature of the transaction and the hospital's unquestioned right to exercise some control over the identity and number of doctors to whom it accords staff privileges.

Petitioner's closed policy may raise questions of medical ethics, and may have inconvenienced some patients who would prefer to have their anesthesia administered by someone other than a member of Roux & Associates, but it does not have the obviously unreasonable impact on purchasers that has characterized the tying arrangements that this Court has branded unlawful.

Reversed.

CASE QUESTIONS

1. What is East Jefferson's share of the medical care market?

2. Do patients ever indicate any choice or knowledge regarding anesthesiologists?

3. Is the arrangement illegal *per se?*

4. Is the arrangement unreasonable?

5. Why was the issue of "force" important?

CONSIDER...

17.8 David Ungar holds a Dunkin' Donuts franchise. The terms of his franchise agreement require him to use only those ingredients furnished by Dunkin' Donuts. He is also required to buy their napkins, cups, and so on with the Dunkin' Donuts trademark on them. Is this an illegal tying arrangement? What if Dunkin' Donuts maintains that it needs these requirements to maintain its quality levels on a nationwide basis? [*Ungar v. Dunkin' Donuts of Am., Inc.,* 531 F.2d 1211 (3d Cir. 1976)]

Exclusive Dealing or Requirements Contracts

Under **exclusive dealing** or **requirements contracts,** a buyer agrees to handle only one manufacturer's goods and not to carry any competitors' brands. These contracts also exist when a buyer agrees to purchase all of its requirements from one seller, such as when the sandwich-meat manufacturer agrees to buy meat from only one slaughterhouse.

These types of agreements are treated as tying arrangements because the buyer has, in effect, agreed not to use another's products; but they are treated more leniently. The contracts must cover a substantial dollar amount of the market, and a substantial share of the market must be foreclosed by the agreement. For example, if the sandwich-meat manufacturer is a national manufacturer, the agreement to buy from one slaughterhouse is substantial. However, if the manufacturer is a local one with limited distribution, the agreement will probably not foreclose much of the market from other slaughterhouses.

Price Discrimination

The Robinson-Patman Act prohibits **price discrimination,** which is selling goods at prices that have different ratios to the marginal cost of producing them. If two goods have the same marginal cost and are sold to different people at different prices, there is price discrimination. Four elements are required in a price discrimination case:

1. A seller engaged in commerce

2. Discrimination in price among purchasers

3. Commodities sold that are of like grade or quality

4. A substantial lessening of competition in any line of commerce or a tendency to create a monopoly; or competition is injured, destroyed, or prevented

If all the elements are established, both the buyer and the seller have violated the Robinson-Patman Act.

Price Discrimination among Purchasers

For price discrimination to occur, there must actually be a purchase; Robinson-Patman does not cover leases and consignments. Also, the purchases must be made at about the same time. The discrimination can come in the form of the actual price charged but can also come from indirect charges. For example, offering different credit terms to equally qualified buyers can constitute price discrimination.

Commodities of Like Grade or Quality

For the Robinson-Patman Act to apply, the products sold must be of **like grade or quality,** which means that there are no physical differences in the product. Label differences do not make the products different. For example, the sandwich-meat manufacturer who makes a private label meat cannot discriminate in price for the sale of that meat if the contents are the same as the manufacturer's advertised label meat and only the label is different. However, if the private-label meat has lesser quality meat in it, there can be a price difference because the products are not the same.

Lessening or Injuring Competition

Generally, injury to competition can be demonstrated by showing that there is a substantial price cut in a certain area by a large manufacturer with the effect of injuring or destroying a smaller competitor. Price discrimination is an example of the use of vertical restraints to lessen horizontal competition. Predatory pricing or pricing below cost is an example of conduct that will injure or destroy competition.

The following case involves an issue of competition injury through price discrimination.

CASE 17.6

Utah Pie Co. v. Continental Baking Co.
386 U.S. 685 (1967)

Pie in the Sky: Free Market Competition and Pricing

FACTS

Utah Pie Company (petitioner) is a Utah corporation that for 30 years has been baking pies in its plant in Salt Lake City and selling them in Utah and surrounding states. It entered the frozen pie business in 1957 and was immediately successful with its new line of frozen dessert pies—apple, cherry, boysenberry, peach, pumpkin, and mince.

Continental Baking Company, Pet Milk, and Carnation (respondents), based in California, sell pies in Utah primarily on a delivered-price basis.

The major competitive weapon in the Utah pie market was price. Between 1958 and 1961, there was a deteriorating price structure for pies in the Utah market. Utah Pie was selling pies for $4.15 per dozen at the beginning of the period; at the time it filed suit for price discrimination, it was selling the same pies for $2.75 per dozen. Continental's price went from $5.00 per dozen in 1958 to $2.85 at the time suit was filed. Pet's prices went from $4.92 per dozen to $3.46, and Carnation's from $4.82 per dozen to $3.30.

Utah Pie filed suit charging price discrimination by respondents based on allegations outlined in the opinion that follows. The district court found for Utah Pie. The court of appeals reversed, and Utah Pie appealed.

JUDICIAL OPINION

WHITE, Justice

We deal first with petitioner's case against the Pet Milk Company. . . . Pet's initial emphasis was on quality, but in the face of competition from regional and local companies and in an expanding market where price proved to be a crucial factor, Pet was forced to take steps to reduce the price of its pies to the ultimate consumer. These developments had consequences in the Salt Lake City market which are the substance of petitioner's case against Pet.

First, Pet successfully concluded an arrangement with Safeway, which is one of the three largest customers for frozen pies in the Salt Lake market, whereby it would sell frozen pies to Safeway under the latter's own "Bel-air" label at a price significantly lower than it was selling its comparable "Pet-Ritz" brand in the same Salt Lake market and elsewhere. . . .

Second, it introduced a 20-ounce economy pie under the "Swiss Miss" label and began selling the new pie in the Salt Lake market in August 1960 at prices ranging from $3.25 to $3.30 for the remainder of the period. This pie was at times sold at a lower price in the Salt Lake City market than it was sold in other markets.

Third, Pet became more competitive with respect to the prices for its "Pet-Ritz" proprietary label. . . . According to the Court of Appeals, in seven of the 44 months Pet's prices in Salt Lake were lower than prices charged in the California markets. This was true although selling in Salt Lake involved a 30- to 35-cent freight cost.

The burden of proving cost justification was on Pet and, in our view, reasonable men could have found that Pet's lower priced "Bel-air" sales to Safeway were not cost justified in their entirety. Pet introduced cost data for 1961 indicating a cost saving on the Safeway business greater than the price advantage extended to that customer. These statistics were not particularized for the Salt Lake market, but assuming that they were adequate to justify the 1961 sales, they related to only 24 percent of the Safeway sales over the relevant period. The evidence concerning the remaining 76 percent was at best incomplete and inferential. It was insufficient to take the defense of cost justification from the jury, which reasonably could have found a greater incidence of unjustified price discrimination than that allowed by the Court of Appeals' view of the evidence.

The Court of Appeals almost entirely ignored other evidence which provides material support of the jury's conclusion that Pet's behavior satisfied the statutory test regarding competitive injury. This evidence bore on the issue of Pet's predatory intent to injure Utah Pie. As an initial matter, the jury could have concluded that Pet's discriminatory pricing was aimed at Utah Pie; Pet's own management, as early as 1959, identified Utah Pie as an "unfavorable factor," one which "d[u]g holes in our operation" and posed a constant "check" on Pet's performance in the Salt Lake City market. Moreover, Pet candidly admitted that during the period when it was establishing its relationship with Safeway, it sent into Utah Pie's plant an industrial spy to seek information that would be of use to Pet in convincing Safeway that Utah Pie was not worthy of its customers. . . . Finally, Pet does not deny that the evidence showed it suffered substantial losses on its frozen pie sales during the greater part of time involved in this suit, and there was evidence from which the jury could have concluded that the losses Pet sustained in Salt Lake City were greater than those incurred elsewhere. It would not have been an irrational step if the jury concluded that there was a relationship between the price and the losses.

It seems clear to us that the jury heard adequate evidence from which it could have concluded that Pet had engaged in predatory tactics in waging competitive warfare in the Salt Lake City market. Coupled with the incidence of price discrimination attributable to Pet, the evidence as a whole established, rather than negated, the reasonable possibility that Pet's behavior produced a lessening of competition proscribed by the Act.

Petitioner's case against Continental is not complicated. Continental was a substantial factor in the

(continued)

market in 1957. But its sales of frozen 22-ounce dessert pies, sold under the "Morton" brand, amounted to only 1.3 percent of the market in 1958, 2.9 percent in 1959, and 1.8 percent in 1960. Its problems were primarily that of cost and in turn that of price, the controlling factor in the market. In late 1960 it worked out a co-packing arrangement in California by which fruit would be processed directly from the trees into the finished pies without large intermediate packing, storing, and shipping expenses. Having improved its position, it attempted to increase its share of the Salt Lake City market by utilizing a local broker and offering short-term price concessions in varying amounts. Its efforts for seven months were not spectacularly successful. Then in June 1961, it took the steps which are the heart of petitioner's complaint against it. Effective for the last two weeks of June it offered its 22-ounce frozen apple pies in the Utah area at $2.85 per dozen. It was then selling the same pies at substantially higher prices in other markets. The Salt Lake City price was less than its direct cost plus an allocation for overhead. . . . Utah's response was immediate. It reduced its price on all of its apple pies to $2.75 per dozen. . . . Continental's total sales of frozen pies increased from 3,350 dozen in 1960 to 18,800 dozen in 1961. Its market share increased from 1.8 percent in 1960 to 8.3 percent in 1961. The Court of Appeals concluded that Continental's conduct had had only minimal effect, that it had not injured or weakened Utah Pies as a competitor, that it had not substantially lessened competition and that there was no reasonable possibility that it would do so in the future.

We again differ with the Court of Appeals. Its opinion that Utah was not damaged as a competitive force apparently rested on the fact that Utah's sales volume continued to climb in 1961 and on the court's own factual conclusion that Utah was not deprived of any pie business which it otherwise might have had. But this retrospective assessment fails to note that Continental's discriminatory below-cost price caused Utah Pie to reduce its price to $2.75.

Even if the impact on Utah Pie as a competitor was negligible, there remain the consequences to others in the market who had to compete not only with Continental's 22-ounce pie at $2.85 but with Utah's even lower price of $2.75 per dozen for both its pro-

prietary and controlled labels. . . . The evidence was that there were nine other sellers in 1960 who sold 23,473 dozen pies, 12.7 percent of the total market. In 1961 there were eight other sellers who sold less than the year before—18,565 dozen or 8.2 percent of the total—although the total market had expanded from 184,569 dozen to 226,908 dozen. We think there was sufficient evidence from which the jury could find a violation of § 2(a) by Continental.

Section 2(a) does not forbid price competition which will probably injure or lessen competition by eliminating competitors, discouraging entry into the market or enhancing the market shares of the dominant sellers. But Congress has established some ground rules for the game. Sellers may not sell like goods to different purchasers at different prices if the result may be to injure competition to either the sellers' or the buyers' market unless such discriminations are justified as permitted by the Act. In this case there was some evidence of predatory intent with respect to each of these respondents. There was also other evidence upon which the jury could rationally find the requisite injury to competition. The frozen pie market in Salt Lake City was highly competitive. At times Utah Pie was a leader in moving the general level of prices down, and at other times each of the respondents also bore responsibility for the downward pressure on the price structure. We believe that the Act reaches price discrimination that erodes competition as much as it does price discrimination that is intended to have immediate destructive impact. In this case, the evidence shows a drastically declining price structure which the jury could rationally attribute to continued or sporadic price discrimination.

Reversed.

CASE QUESTIONS

1. Describe the competitors in the Utah Pie frozen pie market.

2. Is it significant that the national competitors were selling their pies at different prices in Utah?

3. Does it matter that the size of the pie market (i.e., number of pies sold) increased during the period examined?

CONSIDER...

17.9   A&P Grocery Stores decided to sell its own brand of canned milk (referred to as "private label" milk). A&P asked its longtime supplier, Borden, to submit an offer to produce the private label milk. Bowman Dairy also submitted a bid, which was lower than Borden's. A&P's Chicago buyer then contacted Borden and said, "I have a bid in my pocket. You people are so far out of line it is not even funny. You are not even in the ballpark." The Borden representative asked for more details but was told only that a $50,000 improvement in Borden's bid "would not be a drop in the bucket."

A&P was one of Borden's largest customers in the Chicago area. Furthermore, Borden had just invested more than $5 million in a new dairy facility in Illinois. The loss of the A&P account would result in underutilization of the plant. Borden lowered its bid by more than $400,000. The Federal Trade Commission has charged Borden with price discrimination, but Borden maintains it was simply meeting the competition. Has Borden violated the Robinson-Patman Act? Does it matter that the milk was a private label milk and not its normal trade name Borden milk? Are the ethics of the A&P representative troublesome? [*Great Atlantic & Pacific Tea Co., Inc.* v. *FTC*, 440 U.S. 69 (1979)]

Defenses to Price Discrimination

If there are legitimate cost differences in the manufacture or handling of a product, there cannot be price discrimination. Additional costs of delivery or of adding specifications to a product can increase the price without violating the Robinson-Patman Act. For example, if a sandwich-meat manufacturer produces a special low-fat bologna, the price for that product can be different. If the manufacturer uses different shipping companies for its customers, there again may be a price differential.

Quantity discounts are permitted so long as the seller can show that there are actual cost savings in the sale of increased quantities and not just an assumption that larger sales are more economical. Limiting the number of buyers who qualify for quantity discounts is some proof that the actual cost savings are not present.

Prices for products also can change according to market, inflation, material costs, and other variable factors. The seller must simply establish that a price change was initiated in response to one of these factors.

Another defense to a charge of price discrimination is **meeting the competition.** This defense must establish that a price change was made in a certain market to meet the competition there. Also, the seller must charge the same as its competitors and not a lower price. Finally, the price differences must be limited to an area or individuals. For example, a national firm may have a different price in one state because of more competition within that particular state.

Visit "Antitrust Policy" for more about mergers, price fixing, and vertical restraints:
http://www.antitrust.org

Vertical Mergers

Vertical mergers are between firms that have a buyer-seller relationship. For example, if a sandwich-meat manufacturer merged with its meat supplier, there would be a vertical merger. In determining whether a vertical merger violates the Clayton Act, the courts determine the relevant geographic and product markets and then determine whether the effect of the merger will be to foreclose or lessen competition.

Re: E-Commerce, E-Mail, and Technology

E-mail is redefining the way cases are tried. In the U.S. Justice Department's case against Microsoft, a lawyer commented, "The Government does not need to put Mr. Gates on the stand because we have his e-mail and memoranda." The lawyer's comment reflects the tendency of e-mail to speak for itself. Witnesses can shrug and assert they cannot remember, but an e-mail from them is always available for recollection purposes as well as admission as evidence. At Microsoft, e-mail supplanted the telephone as the primary means of communication and the Government was able to tap into the entire e-mail system. There are 30 million pages of e-mail used as evidence in the Microsoft trial.

E-mail provides what is known as a contemporaneous record of events and has the added bonus that, for whatever psychological reason, those communicating with e-mail tend to be more frank and informal than they would be in a memo. E-mail can also contradict a witness's testimony and serve to undermine credibility. For example, when asked whether he recalled discussions with a subordinate about whether Microsoft should offer to invest in Netscape, Mr. Gates responded in his deposition, "I didn't see that as something that made sense." But Mr. Gates's e-mail included an urging to his subordinates to consider a Netscape alliance, "We could even pay them money as part of the deal, buying a piece of them or something."

E-mail is discoverable, it is admissible as evidence, and it is definitely not private. Employees should follow the admonition of one executive whose e-mail was used to fuel a million-dollar settlement by his company with a former employee, "If you wouldn't want anyone to read it, don't send it in e-mail." The impact of e-mail in the Microsoft antitrust case on companies and their e-mail policies was widespread. For example, amazon.com launched a company-wide program called "Sweep and Keep," under which employees are instructed to purge e-mail messages no longer needed for conducting business. Amazon.com is offering employees who purge immediately free lattes in the company cafeteria.

The company had a two-part program. The first portion included instructions on document retention and deletion. The second part of the program was on document creation and included the following warning for employees: "Quite simply put, there are some communications that should not be expressed in written form. Sorry, no lattes this time."

The American Management Association reports that there was a 5 percent increase in the number of companies monitoring their employees' e-mail, from 15 percent to 20 percent during 1998.

Employees around the country report that they are now holding back on their e-mail communications and being careful about their choices of words.

Sources: Steve Lohr, "Antitrust Case is Highlighting Role of E-Mail," *N.Y. Times,* Nov. 2, 1998, C1, C4. John R. Wilke, "Old E-Mail Dogs Microsoft in Fighting Antitrust Suits," *Wall Street Journal,* August 27, 1998, B1.

ANTITRUST ISSUES IN INTERNATIONAL COMPETITION

As the level of international trade has increased, so also has the number of competitors. For example, three domestic manufacturers produce cars in the United States. However, the availability of international trade markets has resulted in the importing of cars from Japan, Great Britain, Germany, Sweden, and Yugoslavia; and international competition changes the market perspective, because the relevant market is not the United States, but the world.

As a result of increased levels of international competition, more joint ventures of competitors and large companies that once would have seemed unthinkable under antitrust protections will be permitted. For example, American Telephone and Telegraph (AT&T) has entered into a joint venture agreement with the Economic Ministry of Taiwan to improve that nation's telecommunications systems. General Mills, Inc., was permitted to acquire RJR Nabisco's cold-cereal business in both the United Kingdom and the United States so that it could compete more effectively in the large North American and European markets.

The EU has developed its own antitrust guidelines and has even questioned the merger of two of the largest U.S. accounting firms in their European operations. There is an increasing concern internationally about antitrust issues, because there has been significant merger activity as U.S. companies merge in order to compete effectively in international markets. The Justice Department is very liberal in permitting both joint ventures and mergers in international markets because of the need for U.S. companies to compete on a global basis. As these large mergers are proposed, the EU and other countries are taking a closer look at their anticompetitive effects. In 2001, General Electric was handed one of the few management setbacks legendary CEO Jack Welch has ever experienced. The proposed acquisition of Honeywell International by GE was opposed by EU antitrust enforcers. The EU's Merger Task Force recommended that the $41 billion proposed merger not be permitted to go through in its present form.

The U.S. Supreme Court has held that companies from other countries that engage in commerce in the United States will be subject to U.S. antitrust laws. Foreign corporations doing business here are subject to the same rules of competition required of U.S. corporations.

SUMMARY

What restraints of trade are permissible?

- Covenant not to compete—clause in employment or business sale contracts that restricts competition by one of the parties; must be reasonable in scope and time

What antitrust laws exist?

- Sherman Act—first federal antitrust law; prohibits monopolization and horizontal trade restraints such as price fixing, boycotts, and refusals to deal

- Clayton Act—federal antitrust statute that prohibits tying and interlocking directorates; controls mergers

- Federal Trade Commission Act—federal law that allows the FTC to regulate unfair competition

- Robinson-Patman Act—anti–price discrimination federal statute

- Celler-Kefauver Act—regulates asset acquisitions

- Hart-Scott-Rodino Antitrust Improvements Act—antitrust law that broadened Justice Department authority and provided new merger guidelines

What penalties can be imposed for restraints of trade?

- Equitable remedies—nonmonetary remedies such as injunctions

- Treble damages—three times actual damages available in antitrust cases

What are the forms of horizontal trade restraint and defenses?

- Horizontal restraints of trade—anticompetitive behavior among a firm's competitors

- Price fixing—controlling price of goods through agreement, limiting supply, controlling credit

- Group boycotts—agreement among competitors to exclude competition

- Joint ventures—temporary combinations that may restrain trade

- *Per se* violation—violation of antitrust laws that has no defense or justification

- Monopolization—possession of monopoly power in the relevant market by willful acquisition

- Market power—power to control prices or exclude competition

- Relevant market—geographic and product market used to determine market power

- Predatory pricing—pricing below actual cost to monopolize

- *Noerr-Pennington* doctrine—protection of First Amendment activities from antitrust laws

- Exclusive distributorship—limited dealership rights; not an antitrust violation so long as horizontal competition exists

- Tying—requiring buyers to take an additional product in order to purchase the product they wish

- Price discrimination—selling goods across state lines at prices that have different ratios to marginal costs

What are the forms of vertical trade restraints and defenses?

- Resale price maintenance—requiring prices be set in vertical distribution

---

QUESTIONS AND PROBLEMS

1. Harold Vogel, an experienced gem appraiser, is a member of the American Society of Appraisers. Vogel's fee for his work is based on a percentage of the value of the appraised item. The society expelled him under the authority of a bylaw that provides: "It is unprofessional and unethical for the appraiser to do work for a fixed percentage of the amount of value." Mr. Vogel brought suit under Section 1 of the Sherman Act alleging that his expulsion was a boycott and that he no longer had referrals from the society. Mr. Vogel also claims the bylaw is a means of fixing prices. Is he right? [*Harold Vogel* v. *American Society of Appraisers*, 744 F.2d 598 (7th Cir. 1984)]

2. Denny's is a full-service marine dealer located near Peru, Indiana, that sells fishing boats, motors, trailers, and marine accessories in the central Indiana market. Renfro Productions and others are marine dealers in the same market area who compete with Denny's to sell boats to Indiana consumers. CIMDA is a trade association of marine dealers in that area. Renfro and others are producers of two boat shows held annually at the Indiana State Fairgrounds (the "Fairgrounds Shows"). The February Fairgounds Show (the "Spring Show") originated over thirty years ago. It is one of the top three boat shows in the United States, attracting between 160,000 and 191,000 consumers annually. The October show (the "Fall Show") is smaller and began in 1987.

Denny's participated in the Fall Show in 1988, 1989, and 1990; it participated in the Spring Show in 1989 and 1990. At all of these shows Denny's was very successful, apparently because it encouraged its customers to shop the other dealers and then come to Denny's for a lower price. During and after the 1989

Spring Show, some of the other dealers began to complain about Denny's sales methods. After the 1990 Spring Show, these dealers apparently spent a good part of one CIMDA meeting "vent[ing] their . . . frustration" about Denny's. The complaints escalated. As a result, Renfro informed Denny's that after the 1990 Fall Show (in which Denny's was contractually entitled to participate) it could no longer participate in the Fairgrounds Shows. Is this an antitrust violation? [*Denny's Marina, Inc.* v. *Renfro Productions, Inc.*, 8 F.3d 1217 (7th Cir. 1993)]

3. Professional Real Estate Investors, Inc. (PRE), operated LaMancha Private Club and Villas, a resort in Palm Springs, California. PRE installed videodisk players in the resort's hotel rooms and assembled a library of more than 200 motion pictures for guests to rent for in-room viewing. PRE was working to develop a market for the sale of similar systems to other hotels.

Columbia Pictures Industries, Inc., and seven other motion picture studios held copyrights on the films PRE was renting. Columbia also licensed transmission of copyrighted motion pictures to hotel rooms through a wired cable system called Spectradyne.

Columbia sued PRE for copyright infringement. PRE countersued, claiming Columbia's suit was a sham that cloaked underlying acts of monopolization and restraint of trade and that Columbia was simply tying up PRE in litigation while it expanded its Spectradyne service in hotels.

Under the law, PRE could sell or lease lawfully purchased videodisks under the "first sale" doctrine of the Copyright Act. The only issue that remained was whether in-room viewing was a performance that required PRE to pay royalties.

Is Columbia's activity subject to antitrust regulation or is it protected under the *Noerr-Pennington* doctrine? [*Professional Real Estate Investors, Inc.* v. *Columbia Pictures, Inc.*, 508 U.S. 49 (1993)]

4. Budget Rent-a-Car and Aloha Airlines have developed a "fly-drive" program. Under their agreement, customers of Aloha receive a $7 first-day rental rate for car rentals (the usual rate is $14). Robert's Waikiki U-Drive has brought suit challenging the agreement as a tying arrangement and unlawful. Is Robert's correct? [*Robert's Waikiki U-Drive* v. *Budget Rent-a-Car*, 732 F.2d 1403 (9th Cir. 1984)]

5. Eastman Kodak Company introduced its new "pocket 110 cameras" to the market in 1972. The cameras used special film that only Kodak manufactured. Also, only Kodak labs had the technology for developing the 110 film. Foremost Color Lab, a film processor, has brought suit on the basis that the 110 system creates a monopoly and is unlawful tying. Is Foremost correct? [*Foremost Pro Color* v. *Eastman Kodak Co.*, 703 F.2d 534 (9th Cir. 1984)]

6. Gardner-Denver, the largest manufacturer of ratchet wrenches and their replacement parts in the United States, has a dual pricing system for wrench parts and components. Its blue list had parts that, if purchased in quantities of five or more, were available for substantially less than its white list prices. Has Gardner-Denver engaged in price discrimination with its two price lists? [*D. E. Rogers Assoc., Inc.* v. *Gardner-Denver Co.*, 718 F.2d 1431 (6th Cir. 1983)]

7. Russell Stover is a candy manufacturer that ships its products to 18,000 retailers nationwide. Stover designates resale prices for its dealers but does not request assurances from them that they are honoring the prices. It has, however, refused to sell to those retailers it believes will sell below the prices suggested. Is there an antitrust violation in this conduct? [*Russell Stover Candies, Inc.* v. *FTC*, 718 F.2d 256 (8th Cir. 1982)]

8. William Inglis & Sons is a family-owned wholesale bakery with production facilities in Stockton, California, that manufactured and distributed bread and rolls in northern California. ITT Continental is one of the nation's largest wholesale bakeries and was a competitor of Inglis in the northern California market.

Both Inglis and Continental sold their bread under a private label and an advertised label. Continental's advertised bread was "Wonder" bread, whereas Inglis's advertised bread was "Sunbeam." The private label bread is sold at a lower price than the advertised brand, but the principal difference between the two is the profit. Inglis filed a complaint stating that Continental was selling its private label bread at below-cost prices in a predatory price scheme designed to drive Inglis out of the market. Inglis also says the lower price on private bread earned Continental more grocery-shelf space for its "Wonder" bread. Is such conduct illegal under the Sherman Act? Is predatory pricing a *per se* violation? [*William Inglis* v. *ITT Continental Baking Co.*, 668 F.2d 1014 (9th Cir. 1980)]

9. On August 1, 1957, Procter & Gamble, the nation's leading manufacturer of soaps, detergents, and other high-turnover household products, acquired Clorox Chemical Company, the nation's leading producer of liquid bleach. Purex Corporation, the second leading producer of liquid bleach, brought suit challenging the acquisition as violative of the Clayton Act. At the time of the acquisition, Clorox held 48.8 percent of sales and Purex held 15.7 percent of sales. Purex says the enormous financial strength, advertising budget, and marketing skills of P&G would make it nearly impossible for any bleach manufacturer to compete. What factors are important in determining whether the merger is a valid one? [*Purex Corp.* v. *Procter & Gamble Co.*, 596 F.2d 881 (9th Cir. 1979)]

10. MacDonald Group, Ltd., owned and operated the Fresno Fashion Fair Mall and leased space to Edmond's, a California retail jeweler. The lease contained a covenant that limited MacDonald to one additional jewelry store as a tenant in the mall. The lease was entered into in 1969. In 1978, MacDonald was involved in the construction of an expansion to the mall and began negotiations to include a retail jeweler in the new space. Edmond's objected and brought suit. The covenant provides that only two jewelry stores would be tenants in the Fresno Fashion Fair Mall. The expansion would still be part of the Fresno Fashion Fair Mall and would not have a separate name. Would the covenant apply to the new addition to the mall? [*Edmond's of Fresno* v. *MacDonald Group, Ltd.*, 217 Cal. Rptr. 375 (1985)]

Old, Onerous, and Still on the Books: Are Dusty Consent Decrees Hobbling Corporate America? Strategies for Coping with Regulatory Constraints

11. As anniversaries go, October 12 was an odd one for General Electric Co. It was on that day eighty-three years ago that GE signed an agreement with the government designed to weaken the company's dominance of the lighting industry. Among other measures, the consent decree banned GE from manufacturing private label or generic lighting products and required the company to disclose its ownership of several lighting businesses that had been thought to be independent.

Today, GE and a growing number of other companies constrained by decades-old consent decrees say it's time to remove the shackles. GE is negotiating with the Justice Department's Antitrust Division to lift the order, arguing that its provisions are hindering the company's ability to compete in a global economy. "By lifting this order, we would be able to do exactly what our competitors are doing," says company spokesman John J. Betchkal.

What has suddenly spurred these challenges, after years of little or no activity? Part of the answer, say experts, is that global competition has greatly intensified over the past decade. IBM, for instance, has been hit particularly hard and has been frustrated watching competitors flourish under practices it is barred from using.

Slacking Off

Another factor has been a change in the government's attitude. It used to be almost impossible to persuade regulators and courts to abandon or modify consent decrees. But in July, the Federal Trade Commission announced that its antitrust decrees would lapse after twenty years. The agency also invited companies to seek reviews of old decrees. The average life span of the Justice Department's antitrust orders is now ten years. Experts say regulators finally realize that some decrees can impede competition if left unchecked too long. "The problem with these decrees is that they don't learn with society," says Daniel M. Wall, an antitrust lawyer in San Francisco.

GE, for example, wants to begin offering private label lightbulbs to retailers—a business segment that global competitors such as Philips Lighting and Osram Sylvania, Inc., already have. In addition, the company wants to sell generic products to compete in the lower-priced end of the lighting market. The company won't say how much these endeavors would be worth but is concerned that rivals are profiting from its predicament. The government is weighing GE's request.

Experts estimate that more than 100 of these decades-old decrees are still controlling some corporate behavior. Most antitrust agreements entered into today are not open-ended. For example, the settlement reached recently between the government and Microsoft Corp. is due to expire in just 6½ years.

Release?

Yet, for all the sentiment that has been expressed in favor of updating outmoded enforcement measures, companies are encountering stiff opposition. Critics say it is because even with the passage of time and a more global marketplace, many companies still retain too much control over their industries to be freed from certain restraints. IBM is butting heads with a number of its competitors over a 1956 consent decree that, among other things, forced it to offer computer services separately from its manufacturing and sales business. It also required IBM, which had previously only leased its equipment, to sell outright its computers and equipment to competitors.

Such provisions created what are now multibillion-dollar aftermarkets composed of independent leasing and service businesses and dealers of used IBM computer equipment. The 265 independent lessors alone earn more than $15 billion. These companies argue that such revenues would plummet without the decree. "If you don't regulate IBM, it will put handcuffs on companies like ours to compete effectively. And that will cause consumers to suffer," argues Philip A. Hewes, a senior vice president at ComDisco, Inc., the largest independent computer-leasing company.

Independent service organizations (ISOs) agree, arguing that the court should draw a distinction between IBM's diminished strength in manufacturing and its continued dominance of the computer-service business. "There is a superficial appeal to IBM's argument that we need to reassess things after 40 years," says Ronald S. Katz, a San Francisco lawyer who represents the ISOs. "But IBM could hobble or get rid of its competition" if the decree were to be lifted. IBM, which has said it must be free to match such competitors as Electronic Data Systems, Inc., declines to comment.

Ironic

Thus far, the Justice Department has remained silent on the IBM case, which is pending in federal court. Not so with respect to Kodak, which in May persuaded a court to overturn two consent decrees. Kodak successfully argued that it no longer possessed enough power to control prices or hinder competition. Consequently, Kodak claimed it should be allowed to sell private label film and to bundle its film and photo finishing businesses. Robert B. Bell, Kodak's antitrust counsel in Washington, says his client would have come out with a number of innovative products if it were not for the decrees from 1920 and 1954.

The government has appealed the Kodak case, arguing that the company still wields too much market control. The appeal, which is expected to be heard in January, is deemed so important that Assistant Attorney General Anne K. Bingaman is expected to make a rare court appearance to argue the case herself. That Bingaman would be battling the case so hard strikes some critics as ironic. "It's really baffling to companies to have the government fight decrees that are 80 years old when current policy allows them to expire in 10 years," says Bell.

Baffling, maybe. But the Kodak decision could affect dozens of other decrees on the books by creating a new legal standard for overturning them. That is a feat in antitrust law that has not been accomplished since 1932—the time of prohibition and the kidnapping of Charles Lindbergh Jr.

Source: Linda Himelstein, "Old, Onerous, and Still on the Books," *Business Week*, November 7, 1994, 58–59. Reprinted from the November 7, 1994 issue of *Business Week* by special permission, copyright © 1994 by The McGraw-Hill Companies, Inc.

Issues
a. Why are the older decrees still in effect?
b. Why do the companies feel the decrees should be lifted?
c. What updates can you find on the companies and their decrees?

NOTE

1. The doctrine is named after the two U.S. Supreme Court cases in which it was developed: *Eastern R.R. President's Conference* v. *Noerr Motor Freight, Inc.*, 365 U.S. 127 (1961), and *United Mine Workers* v. *Pennington*, 381 U.S. 657 (1965).

BUSINESS STRATEGY APPLICATION

In this CD-ROM application, you have the chance to correct the activities and memos of employees for the antitrust violations you find in them. You have the chance to stop the violations before they occur.

PART FOUR

Business and Its Employees

This portion of the book covers the rights and duties of employers and employees as they work together to operate a business. What are the regulations and restrictions relating to the hiring and firing of employees? How much authority do employees have to make decisions and take actions with respect to their work? How are safety regulations enforced in the workplace? What legal limits exist with respect to work hours? What role do unions play in employee and employer relations? What do federal and state antidiscrimination statutes provide? What are their effects on hiring, firing, promoting, and rewarding?

CHAPTER EIGHTEEN

Management of Employee Conduct: Agency

All businesses have a common thread: employees. They need them, rely on them, pay them, and give them authority to perform certain business tasks. This delegation of authority is the focus of this chapter. When is an employee acting on behalf of an employer? How much authority does an employee have? What duties and obligations do employees owe employers? When is a business liable for an employee's acts? These questions are a preview of the topics covered in this chapter.

How to Fire Someone without Being Sued

1. Do not fire anyone.

2. Fire everyone.

3. Fire everyone in the same division.

4. Fire only those employees with well-documented and written performance problems.

5. Fire only those employees for whom managers can articulate a legitimate business justification.

6. Do not violate any internal company procedures when selecting employees for termination.

7. Offer terminated employees a severance package in exchange for signing a release not to sue the company.

8. Do not threaten the employee.

9. Give the employee a brief but specific reason for the termination.

10. Be kind.

FROM CAMERON STRACHER, "HOW TO FIRE SOMEONE WITHOUT BEING SUED"
New York Times Magazine, 8 April 2001, 54.

CONSIDER...

Jerome Lange was the manager of a small grocery store that carried Nabisco products. Ronnell Lynch had been hired by Nabisco as a cookie salesman-trainee in October 1968. On March 1, 1969, Mr. Lynch was assigned his own territory, which included Lange's store.

On May 1, 1969, Mr. Lynch came to Mr. Lange's store to place previously delivered merchandise on the shelves. An argument developed between the two over Mr. Lynch's service to the store. Mr. Lynch became very angry and started swearing. Mr. Lange told him to either stop swearing or leave the store because children were present. Mr. Lynch then became uncontrollably angry and

said, "I ought to break your neck." He then went behind the counter and dared Mr. Lange to fight. When Mr. Lange refused, Mr. Lynch viciously assaulted him, after which he threw merchandise around the store and left.

Is Nabisco liable for Mr. Lynch's actions?

NAMES AND ROLES: AGENCY TERMINOLOGY

A principal-agent relationship is one in which one party acts on behalf of another. A clerk who helps you to the dressing room and takes your payment in a department store is an agent. Barry Bonds has an agent who negotiates his contracts for him. A power of attorney is a form of agency relationship in which authority is given another to enter into transactions. A special power of attorney is one limited in time or scope, as when a landowner gives another the authority to close a particular land transaction. A general power of attorney is one in which an individual gives another the rights to manage his financial affairs in everything from handling checking accounts to entering into contracts. The common thread in all of these relationships is that one party acts on behalf of another.

Although some terms are used interchangeably, there are exact labels and definitions for the parties in an agency relationship. This section outlines and defines the terminology used to cover that relationship.

Agency

In an agency relationship, one party agrees to act on behalf of another party according to directions. It is a relationship that exists by common consent—both sides agree to it—and a relationship that is fiduciary in nature—there are duties and responsibilities on both sides. The general term *agency* can be used to refer to many different types of relationships. A real estate agent who is hired to help market your house is an agent of yours; a sales clerk in a department store is an agent for that store; talent agents are agents for many actors at the same time.

Principals

In the employer-employee relationship, the employers are referred to as the **principals.** The term *principal* is used because some agents are not truly employees. A literary agent, for example, represents many authors who are the agent's principals, but the principals are not "employers," in the usual sense, of the agent.

Agents

Agents are people hired by a principal to do a task on behalf of the principal. The agent represents the principal in such a way that if the agent negotiates a contract, the principal, but not the agent, is bound by and a party to the contract. A president of a corporation is an agent of the corporation. When the president negotiates a contract, the corporation, not the president, is bound to perform that contract.

All employees are agents of the principal employer, but not all agents are employees. A corporation might hire an architect to design a new office building and obtain bids for the construction of the building. The architect would be an agent for very limited purposes but not an employee of the company.

Employers-Employees: Master-Servant Relationships

A **master-servant relationship** is one in which the principal (master) exercises a great deal of control over the agent (servant). An employer-employee relationship for a production line worker is an example of a master-servant relationship. Among the various factors considered are whether an employee works regular hours, is paid a regular wage, and is subject to complete supervision and control by the employer during work hours. The factors used to determine whether a master-servant relationship exists are as follows:

- Level of supervision of agent
- Level of control of agent
- Nature of agent's work
- Regularity of hours and pay
- Length of employment

Independent Contractors

An **independent contractor** is a person who is hired by another to perform a task but who is not controlled directly by the hiring party. For example, a corporation's attorney is an agent of the corporation only for purposes of legal representation and court appearances. However, the attorney is not a corporate employee and the corporation would have no control over the attorney's office operations. The attorney is an independent contractor. A subcontractor hired for performing partial work on a construction site is also an example of an independent contractor.

Principals have less responsibility for independent contractors than for servants, because they have little control over a contractor's conduct. The distinction between master-servant relationships and independent contractor relationships is important because a principal's liability for an agent's actions varies depending upon the agent's status as servant or contractor.

Agency Law

Agency law is not statutory; rather, its source is common law. The reflection of common law regarding agency is found in the *Restatement of Agency*, which is a summary of the majority view of agency law in the United States that is followed by many courts in handling agency cases.

Studying agency law actually involves examining three different components. The first component is the creation of the agency relationship. The second component involves the examination of the relationship between principals and agents. The third component examines the relationship of the agent and principal to third parties. In this third component, the areas of contracts *and* torts are covered because principals have both contractual and tort liability for certain acts of their agents.

CREATION OF THE AGENCY RELATIONSHIP

In most cases, determining whether an agency relationship exists is a simple task: A business hires an employee, and that employee is an agent of the business. Agency relationships, however, are created in other ways, and the requirements vary.

Express Authority

An employee who is hired by agreement (oral or written) is an agent and has been given **express authority** to act on behalf of the business. That authority, however, may be limited. A driver employee, for example, may only have the authority to

Re: Powers of Attorney

Powers of attorney generally authorize one person (the agent or attorney in fact) to act on behalf of another person (the principal); but these grants can vary in scope and have different purposes. A glossary follows:

SCOPE	PURPOSES
Nondurable or Durable	**Child Care**
A nondurable, or conventional, power of attorney expires upon the incapacitation of the principal. A durable power of attorney either takes effect or remains in effect upon incapacitation.	Often used in cases of prolonged parental absence or incapacity, for decisions on emergency medical care or school-related matters.
Limited or Special	**Financial**
This variety limits the agent's authority to specific areas or transactions, like a real estate closing.	A very common power of attorney. If durable, it can help avoid costly and protracted judicial conservatorship proceedings when a person becomes incompetent.
Springing	**Health Care**
A springing power of attorney does not become effective until a certain event occurs—the incapacity of the principal, for example.	Allows an agent to make medical decisions for an incapacitated principal. The agent may also enforce the principal's living will, which states his treatment preferences in the event of terminal illness or other conditions.

Source: Laura Pedersen-Pietersen, "When a Friend Needs a Legal Stand-In," *New York Times,* March 15, 1998, BU4. Copyright © 1998 by The New York Times. Reprinted by permission.

deliver packages; a sales employee may have the authority to represent the company but is required to obtain another employee's signature to finalize sales contracts. An express contract specifies the limitations of an employee/agent's authority.

The Writing

An agency relationship is created by agreement, which need not be in writing, although it is best for both employer and employee if it is. A written contract specifying the agent's authority is required only if the agent will enter into contracts required to be in writing or if a state statute requires an agent's authority to be in writing. For example, many states require that real estate agents' commission contracts be in writing. An agent who will be negotiating contracts for a principal for longer than a year should have a written agreement.

Capacity

Because agents will enter into contracts for their principals, the principals must have the **capacity** to contract. Capacity here means capacity in the traditional contract sense: age and mental capacity (as covered in Chapter 14).

The contractual capacity of the agent is not an issue in the agency relationship for purposes of the agent's authority to enter into contracts. However, the capacity of the agent to drive, operate equipment, or work with the public is an issue that affects the employer's liability to third parties. Because of this liability, many employers conduct polygraph and psychological tests and drug screening as a precondition to hiring employees. Many firms also have ongoing drug-testing programs to ensure that employees are not reporting for work—or working—under the influence of drugs or alcohol.

One of the most controversial issues in agency law concerns the **unincorporated association,** which is a group that acts as an entity but has no legal existence. Some charitable organizations—churches, for example— have an ongoing existence and have probably built buildings, had fund-raising drives, and entered into many contracts. However, because these organizations are not incorporated and do not have any legal existence, those who sign these contracts are not agents. Moreover, they are liable under contract terms because the organizations are not principals with capacity. For example, suppose that a Little League coach signs a credit contract for the purchase of Little League equipment. The Little League organization is nonprofit and is not incorporated. In the event the league does not raise enough money to pay for the sporting equipment, the signing coach is liable because the league is not a principal with capacity.

The National Conference of Commissioners on Uniform State Laws proposed the *Uniform Unincorporated Nonprofit Association Act* (UUNAA) in 1996, and it has been adopted in ten states. Under the UUNAA, the contract and tort liability of individual members of a nonprofit association would be eliminated if they were acting on behalf of their nonprofit unincorporated association. The UUNAA also gives unincorporated nonprofits the right to bring suits and be sued in their names and to own property in similar fashion.

> **BUSINESS PLANNING TIP**
>
> Before you sign on behalf of an organization, be sure you understand your liability. For example, if you sign a contract with a hotel for a group's meeting, you will have personal liability if your group is not incorporated and if the hotel is not paid. If your group is incorporated, be sure to sign so that the corporation, not you, is personally liable. You can use the following format:
>
> (Your Group Name)
>
> By: (Your Name)
>
> (Your Title)
>
> An example:
>
> Pacific Southwest Academy of Legal Studies in Business, a nonprofit corporation
>
> By: Marianne M. Jennings
>
> Executive Secretary

Implied Authority

An agent under contract not only has the authority given expressly but also has certain **implied authority.** Implied authority is the extension of express authority by custom. For example, a person who is hired as president of a corporation probably does not have his exact duties specified in the contract. However, this president will likely have the same type of authority customarily held by corporate presidents: to sign contracts, to authorize personnel changes, to conduct salary reviews and changes, and to institute operational changes. The law gives the president customary authority unless the president's contract specifies otherwise. This implied authority can be limited by agreement between the parties if they do not want custom and practice to control their relationship.

Apparent Authority

In many cases an agency relationship arises not by express or implied contracts but because of the way a principal presents himself to third parties. This theory of agency law, called **apparent authority** or **agency by estoppel,** holds a principal liable if the principal makes someone else think he has an agent.

Apparent authority exists by appearance. A third party is led to believe that an agent, although not actually holding express and accompanying implied authority, had the proper authority to deal with the third party. The third party is led to believe that certain promises will be fulfilled. For example, a mobile home dealer who has brochures, note pads, and other materials from a mobile home manufacturer has the appearance of having the authority to sell those homes even if there is no actual authority. The following case deals with issues of apparent authority.

CASE 18.1

Streetman v. Benchmark Bank
890 S.W.2d 212 (Tex. App. 1995)

Morphing through Being Overdrawn:
The Nintendo Franchise and the Bouncing Checks

FACTS

Michael Streetman and his wife, Laura (appellants), operated a video rental store. As part of their business, they decided to expand into Nintendo game cartridges for rental. Nintendo, at the time of their decision to expand into this area, was the only game system available and its Super Mario Brothers game had swept the country with children and adults alike entranced by the game. At one point, the games were so popular that Mr. Streetman was selling them out of the back of his truck.

The Streetmans decided to expand their video rental business to include game cartridges for rental. In order to purchase the number of game cartridges that they needed for the rental business, the Streetmans met with Donald Gene Watts, a senior credit officer for Benchmark Bank. They asked for a loan and assurance that their "overdraft" checks would be honored. They opened a checking account for their business, M & L Distributing, in December of 1988.

Over the next several months, the Streetmans wrote approximately 500 overdraft checks. The Bank collected service charges on a majority of these checks. At one point in time, their checking account was over-

drawn $204,863.10. On June 8, 1989, the Streetmans bought a Nintendo distributorship.

The Bank returned five checks with the notation "insufficient funds" on July 18, 1989, but Loan Officer Watts said this was an error and notified the payees that the Bank had erred in returning those checks. All other overdrafts were honored until August 28, 1989, when the Bank suddenly stopped honoring their overdraft checks. Because of their lack of cash, the Streetmans were unable to purchase the Nintendo cartridges as soon as they became available, and they lost the valuable Nintendo distributorship which they had acquired. Their business failed.

Benchmark Bank sued the Streetmans for the balance due on delinquent promissory notes. The Streetmans filed a counterclaim for breach of contract, for breach of warranty, and for deceptive trade practices. The trial court entered a partial summary judgment for the Bank for $440,770.47 (the amount due on the promissory notes). The Streetmans' counterclaims were tried by a jury which found for the Streetmans on some of their claims and which assessed damages at $2,000,000.00. The trial court entered judgment notwithstanding the verdict that the Streetmans take nothing, and the Streetmans appealed.

JUDICIAL OPINION

DICKENSON, Justice

The issue that controls this case is whether there is any evidence to support the jury's finding that Watts had the authority to bind the Bank by promising to pay "all" of the Streetmans' overdrafts. There is evidence that Watts said that the Bank would never return a check unpaid. However, in order to show that the Bank is liable for Watts' promise, there must be some evidence that Watts had the actual or apparent authority to make this agreement for the Bank. [T]here is no competent evidence of Watts' actual or apparent authority to pay "all overdrafts."

In order to show that Watts had actual authority, there must be some evidence that the Bank intentionally conferred the authority upon him; intentionally allowed him to believe that he possessed the authority; or, by want of care, allowed him to believe that he possessed the authority. Actual authority may be express or implied. There is no evidence that the Bank gave Watts the authority or that the Bank allowed Watts to believe that he had the authority to promise to pay all overdrafts drawn on the Streetmans' account. Watts testified that he did not have such authority. Further, the evidence conclusively establishes that banks have federally mandated lending limits and that both Watts and the Bank were aware that the Bank could not exceed this limit. Although the evidence is undisputed that Watts, as the senior credit officer of the Bank, had the authority to loan money and to approve the payment of overdrafts up to the Bank's lending limit, there is no evidence that Watts had the actual authority to promise to pay "all overdrafts" drawn on the account.

There is also no competent evidence that Watts had the apparent authority to make such a promise.

Apparent authority is based upon the doctrine of estoppel and is created when the principal's conduct would lead a reasonably prudent person to believe that the agent has the authority he purports to exercise. Apparent authority is not available where the other party has notice of the limitations of the agent's power. The undisputed evidence clearly shows that the Streetmans knew from dealing with their previous bank that banks have lending limits; consequently, they knew that Watts' authority was limited and that he could not agree to pay "all overdrafts" drawn on their account.

Moreover, a reasonably prudent person would not believe that Watts was acting within the scope of his authority by promising to pay "all overdrafts" drawn on the account. We hold that there is no evidence that Watts was acting within the scope of his authority by promising to pay "all overdrafts" or that the Bank engaged in any false, misleading, or deceptive acts in its course of dealings with the Streetmans. The trial court properly disregarded the jury findings.

The judgment of the trial court is affirmed.

CASE QUESTIONS

1. What did the Streetmans do, and why did they need additional funds?
2. What did the Streetmans say that Watts promised them?
3. Would Watts have the authority to make that promise?
4. What knowledge does the court say the Streetmans had about bank operations that precluded the application of the protection of apparent authority?

CONSIDER...

18.1 On September 20, 1973, a Beech Model 18 Aircraft carrying singer Jim Croce and his entourage (the group) crashed shortly after takeoff from Natchitoches, Louisiana. All were killed.

At the time of the crash, the plane was being flown by Robert N. Elliott, an employee of Roberts Airways. Roberts had been asked by Mustang Aviation to fly the entourage according to a prepared itinerary. Mustang originally had entered into a contract with Lloyd St. Martin of Variety Artists International, a booking agent for popular singers, to fly the group itself. The agreement was entered into on September 18, 1973. Later that same day, Mustang learned that its aircraft was disabled, and it was then that Mustang's director of operations called Roberts and asked it to substitute.

Relatives of Mr. Croce and the others killed in the crash brought suit against Mustang for the crash. What, if any, agency relationships existed in this case? How did they arise? Is Mustang liable for the crash? [*Croce* v. *Bromely Corp.,* 623 F.2d 1084 (5th Cir. 1980)]

Ratification

There are times when an agent without proper authority enters into a contract that the principal later ratifies. **Ratification** occurs when the principal reviews a contract and voluntarily decides that, even though the agent did not have proper authority, the contract will be honored as if the agent had full authority. Once a contract is ratified, it is effective from the time the agent entered into it even though the agent had no authority until after the fact. Ratification is a way for a principal to give an agent authority retroactively.

For example, suppose that an apartment manager does not have the authority to contract for any type of construction work except routine maintenance. Because the fence around the apartment complex is deteriorated, the manager contracts for the construction of a completely new fence at a cost that exceeds by six times any maintenance work he has had done in the past. The contractor begins work on the fence, and the apartment owner drives by and sees the work and says nothing. By his inaction in allowing the contractor to continue building the fence, the apartment complex owner ratifies the contract.

C O N S I D E R . . .

18.2   Benjamin Chavez served as executive director of the National Association for the Advancement of Colored People (NAACP). Mary Stansee, former employee of the NAACP executive offices, charged Mr. Chavez with sexual harassment, and he settled the claim for $332,400. The NAACP was financially troubled at the time of the settlement, with a deficit of $2.7 million in 1993, and Mr. Chavez did not disclose the settlement to the board until after it was completed. Did Mr. Chavez have implied authority to make the settlement? Did he have apparent authority?

THE PRINCIPAL-AGENT RELATIONSHIP

To this point, the focus has been on the relationship between the agent and principal on the one hand and third parties on the other. However, it is important to realize that a contractual relationship exists between the agent and principal, so that each has certain obligations and rights. This section of the chapter covers that relationship.

The Agent's Responsibilities

Principals and agents have a **fiduciary** relationship, which is characterized by loyalty, trust, care, and obedience. An agent in the role of fiduciary must act in the principal's best interests.

Duty of Loyalty: General

An agent is required to act only for the benefit of the principal, and an agent cannot represent both parties in a transaction unless each knows about and consents to the agent's representation of the other. Further, an agent cannot use the information gained or the offers available to or by the principal to profit personally. For example, an agent who is hired to find a buyer for a new invention cannot interfere with the principal's possible sale by demonstrating his own product. Neither can an agent hired to find a piece of property buy the property and then sell it (secretly, of course) back to the principal. The following case involves an issue of an agent's fiduciary duty in a sale transaction.

CASE 18.2

Silva v. Bisbee
628 P.2d 214 (Hawaii 1981)

Did I Forget to Tell You I'm the Buyer as Well as Your Agent?

FACTS

Bernice Bisbee (defendant/appellant) is a real estate broker employed by Midkiff Realty, Inc. In September 1972, she obtained from Richard and Marian Silva (plaintiffs/appellees) an exclusive listing agreement for the sale of their property in Kaleheo, Kauai. The land, which fronted on the Kaumualii highway, consisted of 34,392 square feet and one two-bedroom house and one four-bedroom house. The Silvas told Ms. Bisbee that they wanted $100,000 for the property.

Some time later, Ms. Bisbee obtained an offer for the property from David Larsen. The down payment was set at $35,000, with payments of $2,000 a month at 8 percent a year, but Mr. Larsen backed out before closing. After that, a joint venture of six members formed the Pacific Equity Associates to buy the property. Ms. Bisbee was to manage the joint venture and would receive 10 percent of the profits for her services. One of the joint venture members, Toshio Morikawa, appeared as the buyer at the July 1973 closing of the property sale. Ms. Bisbee did not tell the Silvas of the venture nor of her pecuniary interest in it.

In August 1973, Ms. Bisbee prepared for the venture a financial statement that listed the market value of the Silva property at $149,424. Several times the venture was late making payments, which Ms. Bisbee covered. Mr. Silva and his wife were emotionally distressed about the late payments and told Ms. Bisbee. Eventually, because of defaults on the payments, the Silvas brought suit to cancel the contract and for damages for fraud by Ms. Bisbee, naming Midkiff Realty in the suit as well.

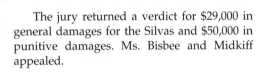

The jury returned a verdict for $29,000 in general damages for the Silvas and $50,000 in punitive damages. Ms. Bisbee and Midkiff appealed.

JUDICIAL OPINION

PADGETT, Judge

Bisbee and Midkiff concede that as brokers under a listing contract, they stood in a fiduciary relationship to the Silvas. It is axiomatic that a fiduciary cannot have a pecuniary interest in the purchase of property from the *cestui que* [beneficiary of the] trust without full disclosure. No such disclosure was made here. Bisbee's conduct in causing the purchase of the property by a joint venture in which she had a pecuniary interest constituted constructive fraud as a matter of law.

As to the issue of emotional distress, the appellants' motion for a directed verdict below was expressly based on the decision of the Supreme Court of Hawaii in *Rodrigues v. State*. Appellants here argue, however, that the emotional distress grew out of the failure to make the payments on time, not out of the fiduciary relationship, and that, therefore, the case is one sounding in contract.

It is well-settled that a party cannot complain on appeal that the motion for a directed verdict should have been granted on a ground not specified.

We read *Rodrigues* to say that given some evidence of emotional distress in the record, the question of whether such distress amounted to serious mental distress which a reasonable man normally constituted could not adequately cope with is one for the jury. Since there was testimony that Bisbee was

(continued)

informed of the fact of emotional upset arising out of the late payments, the test of foreseeability was met.

What we have said disposes of the contention that Midkiff's motion for a new trial was improperly denied. Bisbee was Midkiff's agent and Midkiff is equally liable with her for the damages arising out of her breach of fiduciary duty as well as the damages arising out of the claimed emotional distress.

The last points raised are that the evidence was insufficient to justify the award of punitive damages and that those damages are excessive. There was ample evidence from which the jury could have concluded that what Bisbee did was done willfully, wantonly or maliciously or characterized by some aggravating circumstances. Certainly the jury could have concluded that Bisbee's failure to advise the Silvas that their property was worth more than $100,000 was willful and that Bisbee's failure to advise them of

her pecuniary interest in the purchaser was also willful. We cannot say in the circumstances of this case that the award of $50,000 punitive damages shocks the conscience of the court.

Affirmed.

CASE QUESTIONS

1. What did agent Bisbee fail to disclose?

2. Was Ms. Bisbee representing both sides in a transaction?

3. Can the Silvas recover for their emotional distress?

4. Do you think the jury awarded the difference between the listed value of the property and the actual value as punitive damages?

5. Why is Midkiff also liable?

Duty of Loyalty: Post-Employment Many companies have their employees sign contracts that include covenants not to compete or covenants not to disclose information about their former employers should they leave their jobs or be terminated from their employment.

The laws on noncompete agreements vary from state to state, with California's being the most protective of employees. California's statute in essence prohibits employers from enforcing agreements that prohibit employees from working in their chosen fields. However, across all states, courts are clear in their positions that there must be an underlying reason for the noncompete agreement such as an employee having had access to the company's proprietary information.

Employees' signatures on these agreements are often questioned, particularly when there is some form of compensation attached to surrender of rights. California has provided protection for employees who refuse to sign noncompete agreements, punishing employers with punitive damages in wrongful termination cases brought by employees terminated following their refusals to sign. The *Coady* v. *Harpo* case deals with an interesting type of covenant in an employment contract that covers post-employment activities of departed employees.

The downsizings in the dot-coms have brought back the issue of the noncompete and confidentiality agreements. When employees were recruited by these upstart firms and lured with stock options, it was difficult for them to imagine a time when the company would no longer exist or need to downsize. As a result, most of them signed fairly restrictive covenants not to compete.

For example, one dot-com agreed to give its employees stock options if they would sign a noncompete agreement. Amazon.com offered downsized employees an additional ten weeks' pay plus $500 in addition to the normal severance package if they would sign a three-page "separation agreement and general release" in which they promised not to sue Amazon over the lay-off or disparage it in any way. Amazon did have all employees sign a confidentiality agreement at the beginning of their employment that it has indicated it will enforce and that is likely to be valid because it is not a restraint on employment and is tied to legitimate business protection interests.

e-commerce

CASE 18.3

Coady v. Harpo, Inc.
719 N.E.2d 244 (Ill. App. 1999)

O! Oprah! Do Tell!

FACTS

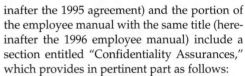

Elizabeth Coady (plaintiff) was employed by Harpo, Inc., (defendant) a company owned by Oprah Winfrey, as a senior associate producer for "The Oprah Winfrey Show" from November 1993 until March 1998. Ms. Coady alleged that for some time prior to March 26, 1998, those working at Harpo engaged in conduct so intolerable as to amount to constructive termination. On March 26, 1998, Ms. Coady notified Harpo by letter from her attorney that she resigned effectively immediately.

Ms. Coady, a trained journalist, indicated her intent to write or otherwise report about her experiences as an employee of Harpo. She asserted that she would write about her experiences as an exercise of her rights of free speech and free press and was not prohibited from doing so by a confidentiality policy, which was entitled "Business Ethics, Objectivity, and Confidentiality Policy," contained in Harpo's September 1996 employee manual.

In a letter dated April 24, 1998, Harpo "reminded" Ms. Coady that she had signed a document entitled "Business Ethics, Objectivity, and Confidentiality Policy" on March 12, 1995, and provided her a copy of the agreement in the letter. The letter further stated that in the March 12, 1995, agreement, Ms. Coady "agreed (among other things) to keep confidential, during her employment and thereafter, all information about the Company, Ms. Winfrey, her private life, and Harpo's business activities which she acquired during or by virtue of her employment with Harpo." Harpo representatives indicated in the letter their intentions to enforce and ensure compliance with the confidentiality agreement.

Ms. Coady filed suit seeking, among other things, a declaration that the covenant is unenforceable. The trial court dismissed the claim and Ms. Coady appealed.

JUDICIAL OPINION

GREIMAN, Justice

Both the independent document entitled "Business Ethics, Objectivity, and Confidentiality Policy" (here-

inafter the 1995 agreement) and the portion of the employee manual with the same title (hereinafter the 1996 employee manual) include a section entitled "Confidentiality Assurances," which provides in pertinent part as follows:

1. During your employment or business relationship with Harpo, and thereafter, to the fullest extent permitted by law, you are obligated to keep confidential and never disclose, use, misappropriate, or confirm or deny the veracity of, any statement or comment concerning Oprah Winfrey, Harpo (which, as used herein, included all entities related to Harpo, Inc., including Harpo Productions, Inc., Harpo Films, Inc.) or any of her/its Confidential Information. The phrase 'Confidential Information' as used in this policy, includes but is not limited to, any and all information which is not generally known to the public, related to or concerning: (a) Ms. Winfrey and/or her business or private life; (b) the business activities, dealings or interests of Harpo and/or its officers, directors, affiliates, employees or contractors; and/or (c) Harpo's employment practices or policies applicable to its employees and/or contractors.

2. During your employment or business relationship with Harpo, and thereafter, you are obligated to refrain from giving or participating in any interview(s) regarding or related to Ms. Winfrey, Harpo, your employment or business relationship with Harpo and/or amy [sic] matter which concerns, relates to or involves any Confidential Information.

The relevant documents also provide that commitment to the stated policies is required as a condition of employment: "Your commitment to the guidelines set forth in this policy is a condition of your employment or business relationship with Harpo."

In addition, defendant's motion to dismiss attached a copy of plaintiff's acknowledgment of the employee manual, which she signed upon the commencement of her employment at defendant in 1993. The acknowledgment signed by plaintiff states in relevant part:

I acknowledge and understand that I may not use any confidential or proprietary information of HARPO for my own purposes either during or after my employment with

(continued)

HARPO, and I understand that I am prohibited from removing, disclosing or otherwise misappropriating any of HARPO's confidential or proprietary information for any reason.

[P]laintiff asserts that the confidentiality policy is not enforceable, primarily arguing that it is overly broad and not reasonably necessary to protect defendant's legitimate business interests. Defendant, however, contends that the confidentiality agreement is enforceable because it does not violate any public policy, was supported by adequate consideration, was not an adhesion contract and properly protected defendant's legitimate business interests.

Until the filing of her appellate reply brief, plaintiff relied on the 1996 employee manual to support her cause of action, contending that the confidentiality policy contained therein was not enforceable because the 1996 employee manual included a contract disclaimer, i.e., "[t]his manual is not a contract." Plaintiff relied on case law that addressed whether an employee handbook creates contractual rights. E.g., *Duldulao* v. *Saint Mary of Nazareth Hospital Center*, 115 Ill.2d 482, 106 Ill.Dec. 8, 505 N.E.2d 314 (1987).

In light of the facts in the present case, the employee-handbook analysis is unnecessary because defendant attached the 1995 agreement to its motion to dismiss as the affirmative matter refuting plaintiff's crucial conclusions of law based on the 1996 employee manual and the language in both documents is identical. As acknowledged by plaintiff in her appellate reply brief, "[t]he covenant in the manual contains precisely the same language and terms as the confidentiality agreement which plaintiff signed on March 12, 1995." Plaintiff further stated that her arguments as to the enforceability of the restrictive covenant remain the same regardless of which version is considered. Accordingly, we will not unnecessarily elongate this opinion by conducting a pointless exercise to determine whether the 1996 employee manual created a contract. Instead, we consider the identical language contained in the 1995 agreement to determine its validity.

"A postemployment restrictive covenant will be enforced if its terms are reasonable." To determine the reasonableness of a restrictive covenant, "it is necessary to consider whether enforcement of the covenant will injure the public, whether enforcement will cause undue hardship to the promisor and whether the restraint imposed by the covenant is greater than is necessary to protect the interests of the employer."

The reasonableness of some types of restrictive covenants, such as nonsolicitation agreements, also is evaluated by the time limitation and geographical scope stated in the covenant. However, a confidentiality agreement will not be deemed unenforceable for lack of durational or geographic limitations where trade secrets and confidential information are involved.

Postemployment restrictive covenants typically involve agreements by a past employee not to compete with the business of her former employer, not to solicit clients or customers of her former employer, and not to disseminate trade secrets of her former employer. The covenants in these typical cases are carefully scrutinized because Illinois courts abhor restraints on trade.

Although restraint of trade is a significant concern, "[a]n equally important public policy in Illinois is the freedom to contract." Furthermore, postemployment restrictive covenants "have a social utility in that they protect an employer from the unwarranted erosion of confidential information."

Unlike the traditional line of restrictive covenant cases, the confidentiality agreement at issue in the instant case does not impose any of the typical restrictions commonly adjudicated in restrictive covenant cases. Defendant does not seek to restrain plaintiff's future career. Plaintiff is free to choose her future occupation, the locale in which she may choose to work, and the time when she can commence her new career. Defendant does not object to plaintiff becoming a journalist, competing with defendant in the same venue and in any locale, including Chicago, and in beginning her new venture immediately. The confidentiality agreement does not restrict commerce and does not restrict plaintiff's ability to work in any chosen career field, at any time. Instead, the 1995 confidentiality agreement restricts plaintiff's ability to disseminate confidential information that she obtained or learned while in defendant's employ. Most certainly, plaintiff had no problem with keeping confidences as long as she was a senior associate producer and continued her work with defendant.

Moreover, we find unpersuasive plaintiff's argument that the confidentiality agreement is too broad because it remains effective for all time and with no geographical boundaries. Whether for better or for worse, interest in a celebrity figure and his or her attendant business and personal ventures somehow seems to continue endlessly, even long after death, and often, as in the present case, extends over an international domain.

Under the facts of this case and the terms of the restrictive covenant at issue, we find that the 1995 confidentiality agreement is reasonable and enforceable. Accordingly, we affirm the trial court's order dismissing plaintiff's cause of action as stated in count I of her complaint. Affirmed.

CASE QUESTIONS

1. What did Ms. Coady agree to when she became a Harpo employee?

2. Does it matter whether it was part of the employee manual or part of a contract?

3. Is there a difference between a confidentiality agreement and a covenant not to compete?

4. Does this restrictive covenant prevent Ms. Coady from working as a journalist?

5. Is the Oprah covenant enforceable?

FOR THE MANAGER'S DESK

Re: Severance Packages and Covenants Not to Compete

When there are layoffs by a company, departing employees may be given generous severance packages, but those packages carry consideration on both sides. The departing employee may be given months of compensation, assistance with placement, retirement buy-outs and even educational loans or grants. However, the employer/company has its right to benefits on its side of the contract. The employer may ask for the following:

- Covenant not to compete
- Promise not to litigate the layoff
- Promise not to share the terms of the agreement with others
- Promise not to work for a competitor

These types of promises extracted by an employer may or may not be enforceable. There are several factors for the employer and employee to consider as they enter into these agreements.

The first factor is voluntariness. Was the agreement voluntary? The burden here is on the employer because, after all, this is someone who is about to be without a job and his or her compensation for the next few weeks or months is tied to signing this agreement.

Whether an agreement is voluntary could be determined by:

- Whether the employee was subject to time constraint in the decision to sign the agreement
- Whether the employee was permitted to have independent advice

- Whether the employee was already subject to noncompete agreements as part of his or her original employment agreement
- Whether the employee was permitted to consult a lawyer
- Whether the employee had the agreement proposed and was then given the opportunity to take it from the workplace for consideration or review

The second factor is whether the state recognizes noncompete agreements. The geographic tendencies are that noncompete agreements tend to be honored more in states east of the Mississippi. These noncompete agreements are more difficult to enforce in the West. Even in those states that have recognized the clauses as enforceable, there is a burden on the employer to show that the enforcement of the clause does not present an unreasonable hardship for the departing employee. And the concept of "unreasonable hardship" is a nebulous one.

Employers should understand these principles as well as the laws of their state of operation prior to proposing such departure agreements. Having the contract subject to the laws of their state is another important clause to put in the agreement, particularly when your state of operation recognizes the validity of noncompete clauses.

Source: Janet Novack, "Just a piece of paper?" *Forbes,* May 5, 1997, p. 156.

ETHICAL ISSUES 18.1

FAO Schwarz has filed suit against its former chairman and CEO, John Eyler, because Mr. Eyler left his position at FAO Schwarz and joined Toys "Я" Us in January 2000. The suit is one for breach of contract that alleges specifically that Mr. Eyler violated a clause in his employment agreement that required him to give one year's notice of his departure and also prevents him from working for a competitor for two years after his departure.

Mr. Eyler was hired at FAO Schwarz in 1992 and last year was paid a $2.4 million bonus that the suit describes as a payment made to keep him at the company.

The suit asks for a hearing to determine whether there should be a preliminary injunction against Mr. Eyler to prevent him from going to work for Toys "Я" Us until the merits of the case are decided.

Toys "Я" Us, also named as a defendant in the suit, issued a response denying any wrongdoing and explaining that it would "vigorously defend" against the lawsuit. Toys "Я" Us and FAO Schwarz had been in merger discussions last year and Toys "Я" Us had signed an agreement that it would not recruit FAO Schwarz employees for two years following the merger discussions if those discussions failed (they did not, in fact, result in a merger).

The suit also alleges that Mr. Eyler took with him trade secrets and that FAO is entitled to protection against their use by Mr. Eyler.

What kinds of trade secrets do you think Eyler might have? What kinds of covenants not to compete are enforceable? Do you think this covenant should be enforced against Mr. Eyler? Evaluate the ethics of Toys "Я" Us and Mr. Eyler.

Source: Dana Canedy, "Schwarz Sues Chief for Move to Toys "Я" Us," *New York Times*, Feb. 18, 2000, C1, C20.

Duty of Obedience

An agent has the duty to obey reasonable instructions from the principal. The agent is not required to do anything criminally wrong or commit torts, of course; but he is required to operate according to the principal's standards and instructions. Failure to do so could mean the agent has gone beyond the authority given and is then personally liable for the conduct.

Duty of Care

For a look at the 100 best companies to work for, visit:
http://www.fortune.com

Agents have a duty to use as much care and to act as prudently as they would if managing their own affairs. Agents must take the time and effort to perform their principals' assigned tasks. For example, officers of corporations must base their decisions on information, not guesses, and must ensure that their decisions are carried out by employees.

An agent who does not use reasonable care is liable to the principal for any damages resulting from a lack of care. When an agent does not make adequate travel arrangements for a speaker, the agent is liable to the speaker for damages that result from the speaker's nonappearance at an engagement.

The Principal's Rights and Responsibilities

A principal has the right to expect that an agent will perform within the standards just described. In exchange, the principal has certain obligations. The first obligation is that of compensation, which can take various forms. Some agents work for a fee on a contingency basis. A real estate agent, for example, may have an arrangement in which he receives compensation only if a buyer for the property is found.

BIOGRAPHY

THE LEAPING EXECUTIVES IN THE AUTO WORLD

Following is a summary of the changes in the executive teams at the world's largest auto manufacturers from 1999–2000.

EXECUTIVE TITLE	ORIGINAL COMPANY	NEW COMPANY/TITLE
James Schroer VP Global Marketing	Ford	Daimler/Chrysler Exec. VP Global Sales/Marketing
John Devine CFO	Ford	General Motors CFO
Bryan Nesbitt Design staff	Daimler/Chrysler	GM Chevrolet Design chief
Dave Smith Design staff	Daimler/Chrysler	GM Saturn Design chief
Sue Cischke VP Regulatory Affairs & Passenger Car Operations	Daimler/Chrysler	Ford VP Environmental & Safety Engineering
Steve Harris VP of Communications	Daimler/Chrysler	GM VP of Communications
Karen Francis General Manager	GM Oldsmobile	Ford Director—Consumer Connect
Mark LeNeve CEO	Volvo (Ford)	GM Cadillac VP/General Manager
Joe Chao Exec. Director Quality & Reliability	GM	Daimler/Chrysler VP Advance Mfring & Engineering
Jeffrey Bell Director—Retail Marketing & E-business	Ford	Daimler/Chrysler Marketing Communications Director
Tony Cervone Communications Director	Daimler/Chrysler	GM Communications Director
Tony Cervone Communications Director	GM	Daimler/Chrysler VP—Communications
Tony Cervone VP—Communications	Daimler/Chrysler	GM Communications Director

Source: "Big Three Auto Execs Jump from Ship to Ship" by David Kiley, May 15, 2001, 3B. Copyright 2001, USA Today. Reprinted with permission.

ISSUES

The companies say that they instruct new employees from other auto companies not to share new product information with them. Do you think that is all the valuable information they might bring with them? Is it ethical to share systems, plans, and management tools with a new company from your former employer, a competitor?

The Dilemma of Team Doctors: Agents of Players or Agents of Management?

ETHICAL ISSUES 18.2

In a 1989 baseball game against the Toronto Blue Jays, Marty Barrett, a second baseman for the Boston Red Sox, "popped" his right knee while running to first base. Mr. Barrett had ruptured his anterior cruciate ligament (ACL). Two days after the game, Dr. Arthur Pappas, the Red Sox team doctor and chair of the University of Massachusetts Medical Center's orthopedic department, performed surgery and removed most of Mr. Barrett's ACL. Dr. Pappas is also a part owner of the Red Sox and at a press conference described the injury as "torn cartilage" and "a stretched ligament."

Sports Illustrated asks the following questions about team doctors:

Team doctors face torturous ethical dilemmas. Are they supposed to be getting players ready to play, or are they supposed to be seeing to it that they heal completely? Should the doctors be more concerned with the immediate needs of the team or with the long-term health of players whose careers will be over while they are still young men? How does a doctor keep from feeling like a member of the team, which, as former Los Angeles Raider team internist Robert Huizenga says, "invariably has a subtle effect on a doctor's decision-making process"? What does a doctor do when a coach or an owner is pressuring a player to get back in the lineup—and the player says he's not ready? More to the point, what does a doctor do in this situation when he knows that the player is not ready?

Is there a conflict of interest? Is there a greater conflict if the physician is a part owner?

There can be a **gratuitous agency,** in which the agent has authority to act for the principal but will not be compensated. For example, some charitable organizations have agents act in fund-raising capacities, but these agents do not expect compensation. Principals also have an obligation to indemnify agents for expenses the agents incur in carrying out the principal's orders. Corporate officers, for example, are entitled to travel compensation; sales agents are entitled to compensation for ads to sell goods, realty, or services.

LIABILITY OF PRINCIPALS FOR AGENTS' CONDUCT: THE RELATIONSHIP WITH THIRD PARTIES

Contract Liability

Although the types of authority an agent has and the terms of the agency agreement define the authority of the agent, the contract liability of a principal is not determined by either what he intended or by the limitations agreed to privately by the agent and the principal. In other words, third parties have certain contract enforcement rights depending on the nature of the agent's work and the authority given by the principal. The liability of the principal for contracts made by an agent is controlled by the perceptions created for and observed by the third party to the contract. Those perceptions vary, and so the liability of the principal varies depending on the way in which the agent does business. For example, an officer of a corporation has the authority to bind the corporation, but what if the officer does not disclose that there is a principal? This section deals with those issues.

The Disclosed Principal
In a situation in which a third party is aware there is a principal involved and also knows who the principal is, the principal is liable to the third party but the agent

is not. This is true whether the agent has express, implied, or apparent authority. If the agent has no authority, however, then the agent, not the principal, is liable. For example, suppose that Paula Abbaduhla is the vice president of Video Television, Inc., and she signs for a line of credit for the corporation at First Bank. So long as she signed the documents "Video Television, Inc., by Paula Abbaduhla, VP," Video would be solely responsible for the line of credit. If, however, she signed that same way but had no authority, she would be liable to Video if it had to honor the agreement. As another example, most title insurers and escrow companies require corporations selling or buying real property to have board authorization in the form of a resolution. If Paula signed to buy land and did not have a resolution, she would have no express authority, and without implied or apparent authority, she would be liable for the land contract. (See Chapter 21 for a more thorough discussion of board resolutions and officers' authority.)

The Partially Disclosed Principal

In this situation, the third party knows that the agent is acting for someone else, but the identity of the principal is not disclosed. For example, an agent might be used to purchase land for development purposes when the developer does not want to be disclosed because disclosure of a major developer's involvement might drive up land prices. In this situation, the third-party seller of the land can hold either the principal or the agent liable on the contract. The agent assumes some risk of personal liability by not disclosing the identity of the principal.

The Undisclosed Principal

In this situation, an agent acts without disclosing either the existence of a principal or the principal's identity. Again, such an arrangement might be undertaken to avoid speculation, or it could be undertaken simply to protect someone's privacy, such as when a famous person purchases a home and does not want any advance disclosure of the purchase or its location. Here, the agent stands alone for liability to the third party. If the third party discovers the identity of the principal, the third party could hold either principal or agent liable. Exhibits 18.1 and 18.2 provide summaries of the liability of agents and principals under the three forms of disclosure of the relationship.

Liability of Principals for Agents' Torts

As for the liability of principals for torts committed by agents, two types of agents must be considered: servants and independent contractors. The amount of liability a principal has for an agent's torts depends first upon the status of the agent.

Master-Servant Relationship

As discussed earlier in the chapter, there is a distinction between the liability of a principal for the acts of a servant and for those of an independent contractor. The principal is liable for the torts of the servant—an agent whose work, assignments, and time are controlled by the principal.

Scope of Employment

Employers (principals) are liable for the conduct of employees (agents/servants) while those employees are acting in the **scope of employment.** Scope of employment means that an employee is doing work for an employer at the time a tort

EXHIBIT 18.1
Contract Liability of
Disclosed Principal

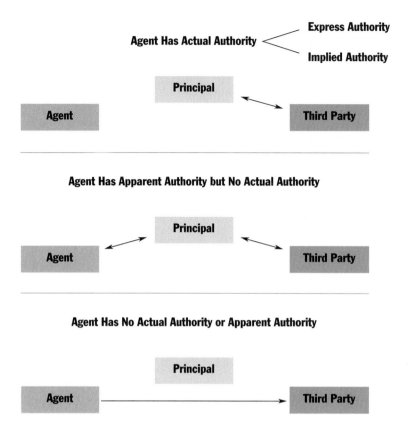

EXHIBIT 18.2
Contract Liability
of Undisclosed or
Partially Disclosed
Principal

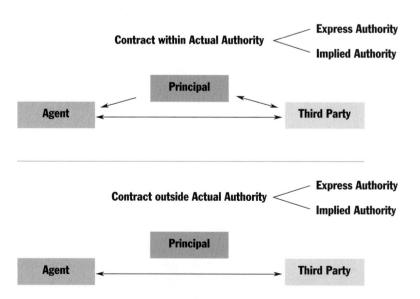

occurs. Suppose a florist delivery driver, while delivering flowers, has an auto accident that is the delivery driver's fault. In addition to the driver's responsibility for the negligence in the accident, the florist is also liable to injured parties under the doctrine of *respondeat superior.*

Scope of employment has been defined broadly by the courts. Negligent torts committed while an employee is driving to a sales call or delivery are clearly within the scope of employment.

An employee who takes the afternoon off is not within the scope of employment, and the principal is not liable if an accident occurs during that time. An employee who uses the lunch hour to shop is not within the scope of employment. When an employee is acting on personal business, the scope of employment ends. The following case deals with an issue of when the scope of employment ends, in a timing sense.

CASE 18.4

Faverty v. *McDonald's Restaurants of Oregon, Inc.*
892 P.2d 703 (Ct. App. Or. 1995)

Triple Shift Overtime: Who Is Liable for the Drive Home Afterward?

FACTS

Matt Theurer was an 18-year-old high school senior who participated in many extracurricular activities and was also a member of the National Guard. Theurer was employed by a McDonald's restaurant in Portland (defendant) on a part-time basis. Theurer was called an enthusiastic worker but his friends and family had expressed concern that he was doing too much and getting too little sleep.

McDonald's employed many high school students on a part-time basis and their restaurants closed at 11:00 PM with clean-up and other procedures taking up an hour until midnight. McDonald's had an informal policy of not permitting high school students to work more than one midnight shift per week. McDonald's also had an informal policy against split shifts which forced the high school students to work in the morning and then evening because the commuting time prevented "people from getting their rest." Despite these policies, the high school employees frequently complained about being tired and at least two of McDonald's employees had accidents while driving home after working the closing shift until midnight.

A few times each year, McDonald's scheduled special clean-up projects at the restaurant that required employees to work after the midnight closing. Student workers were to be used for clean-up shifts only on weekends or during spring break. However, for one scheduled clean-up project, a regular employee was terminated untimely and the manager asked for volunteers for a midnight to 5 AM clean-up shift. Theurer volunteered and the manager knew that Theurer had to drive about 20 minutes to and from work.

During the week of the scheduled clean-up Theurer had worked five nights. One night he worked until midnight, another until 11:30 PM, two until 9 PM, and another until 11 PM. On Monday, April 4, 1988, Theurer worked his regular shift from 3:30 until 7:30 PM, followed by a clean-up shift beginning at midnight until 5 AM on April 5, and then worked another shift from 5 AM until 8:21 AM. During that shift Theurer told his manager that he was tired and asked to be excused from his next regular shift. The manager excused him and Theurer began his drive home.

Theurer was driving 45 miles per hour on a two-lane road when he became drowsy or fell asleep, crossed the dividing line into oncoming traffic, crashed into Frederic Faverty's (plaintiff) van and was killed. Faverty was seriously injured. Faverty

(continued)

settled his claims with Theurer's estate and then filed suit against McDonald's. The jury found for Faverty and McDonald's appealed.

JUDICIAL OPINION

LANDAU, Judge

Defendant argues that it was Theurer's employer and, because of that relationship, it was subject to a limited duty to both Theurer and plaintiff, as a matter of law.

According to defendant, there is no evidence that it knew or should have known that Theurer was so exhausted or fatigued that it should have foreseen that working him three shifts in one 24-hour period would create a foreseeable risk of harm to motorists such as plaintiff. Plaintiff argues that defendant failed to preserve that argument and that, in any event, the evidence is sufficient to support the trial court's ruling.

There is evidence that defendant controlled all work assignments. Therefore, defendant knew or had reason to know of the number of hours Theurer had been working. There also is evidence that defendant ordinarily did not use high school students to work after midnight, and when it did, it tried to limit that late shift to once a week. Defendant also had a policy of not working its employees two shifts in one day. According to at least one of the defendant's managers, those policies were adopted and enforced out of concern that employees not become overly tired on the job. In fact, defendant was aware that at least two of its employees had recently had automobile accidents as a result of falling asleep while driving home after working late shifts. There is evidence that, during and after his late-night shift, Theurer was visibly fatigued, and that defendant's managers were on site and saw Theurer throughout that shift. It is undisputed that defendant knew that Theurer was a high school student, and that most of the high school students who worked there drove to work in their own cars. On the basis of that evidence, a reasonable jury could conclude that defendant knew or should have known that working Theurer so many hours would impair his ability to drive home safely.

Defendant and the dissent insist that, because Theurer "volunteered" to work so many hours, the evidence simply is insufficient to establish defendant's negligence, as a matter of law. First of all, in so characterizing the facts, defendant and the dissent put a "spin" on the evidence to which they are not entitled. The evidence, taken in the light most favorable to plaintiff, shows that Theurer did not, out of the blue, volunteer to take three shifts in one 24-hour

period. Defendant affirmatively asked him to work those hours. Moreover, the evidence shows that defendant—not its employees—generally controlled all work assignments and that defendant penalized its employees for not working as assigned.

Second, even indulging the assumption that Theurer volunteered for his all-night shift, the evidence still is sufficient to support the jury's verdict. Defendant's managers knew that Theurer already had been scheduled to work more than its own policies permitted. Moreover, they saw him in a visibly fatigued state and continued to work him as scheduled. In that regard, defendant was much like a bartender who served alcoholic beverages to a visibly intoxicated person who then caused an automobile accident that harmed another. No one required the intoxicated person to have the extra drink. He or she asked for the drink and "volunteered" to pay for it. Nevertheless, the courts have held that, because the bartender saw the driver in a visibly intoxicated state, and it is reasonably foreseeable that the customer will drive when he or she leaves, the bartender is liable for the consequences of the automobile accident.

Finally, defendant itself conceded at trial that, if it had allowed Theurer to "volunteer" to work around the clock three full days, the "court can almost say as a matter of law, allowing someone to work that long without any rest or sleep might very well constitute affirmative misconduct by an employer, but [it] may be a matter of degrees. . . ."

Thus, whether Theurer volunteered or not simply is not the point. The point is whether, as plaintiff alleged in his complaint, defendant "was negligent in working Theurer more hours than was reasonable." That is, as defendant said at trial, "a matter of degrees." In other words, it is a matter for the jury to decide, not for the court to resolve as a matter of law.

Defendant, the dissent and the *amici curiae* the National Council of Chain Restaurants and the Defense Research Institute, Inc., implore us to reverse the trial court's judgment on the public policy ground that the result is "patently unreasonable," "shocking," "farfetched" and "goes beyond the common-sense application of tort law." However, that argument was not made to the trial court, and we will not consider it for the first time on appeal.

DISSENTING OPINION

EDMUNDS, Judge

The majority holds that a restaurant can be held liable for common law negligence because its adult employee fell asleep while driving home from work, crossed the center line into the oncoming lane of traffic and collided with plaintiff's vehicle. The reason for the restaurant's liability: It accepted the employee's offer to work overtime, and, according to the majority, thereby became responsible for the risk of injury caused by the employee's state of fatigue. That holding is without precedent in the State of Oregon. It makes all employers potentially liable for their employees' off-premises negligence when an employee becomes tired as a result of working. That has never been the law in Oregon nor should it be now.

The majority need have gone no further than defendant's motion for a directed verdict in deciding this case. Defendant is entitled to a directed verdict as a matter of law because of certain uncontroverted facts. First, Theurer was not a minor, but an adult at the time of the accident. He was 18 years old and serving in the National Guard. Defendant did not owe any special responsibility to him because he also attended high school. The fact that he was a student working part time and had over-extended himself physically is of no import to defendant's liability. No rule of negligence requires an employer to inquire into the private lives of its adult employees to determine if, on a given occasion, the employee is not getting enough sleep.

Second, Theurer volunteered to work the cleanup shift. He was not sought out by defendant and "required" to work on April 5, 1988.

Third, Theurer never asked to be relieved from working the shift either before the shift started or during it; nor is there any evidence that defendant refused such a request.

Fourth, Theurer was not on defendant's business premises and was on his own time when he drove home from work that morning. Theurer was not acting on defendant's behalf, nor did defendant have actual control of or the right to control Theurer's driving conduct or where he went after he got off work. Moreover, no omission or affirmative act by defendant prevented Theurer from choosing to have someone pick him up after work, or to take a nap in his car before driving home, or some other preventive measure.

The majority's analysis is wrong because the facts relied on by it are not controlling unless defendant's conduct created an "unreasonable" risk of harm to

plaintiff. In the context of this case, the question is whether defendant created an unreasonable risk of harm to every person on the highway that morning when it scheduled Theurer to work. That question must be answered in the light of the uncontroverted facts that Theurer was an adult employee, that defendant did not require him to work the shift, that Theurer assured defendant's manager that he would rest between shifts and that he would be able to handle the shift physically, that Theurer never asked to be relieved from the shift, and that the harm to plaintiff occurred off defendant's work premises as a result of an activity over which defendant had no right of control. By holding defendant responsible for the safety of all persons on the roadway, the majority makes "general foreseeability" the test for determining whether defendant's conduct is deemed "negligent."

In effect, the opinion says to Oregon employers, "Do not schedule your employees in a manner that will cause fatigue, because if you do, you risk liability for negligence in the event that your employee acts in a negligent manner off-premises and after work." That is not the law of this state and it cannot be unreasonable conduct for an employer to accept an offer from an adult employee, made days in advance of the shift, to work overtime, insofar as the safety of motorists is concerned after the employee gets off work. Because the majority opinion extends the duty of care owed to the general public by employers in the scheduling of their employees' work shifts to beyond any reasonable boundary, I dissent.

CASE QUESTIONS

1. Of what significance is the fact that Theurer volunteered for the all-night shift?

2. Why would a restaurant association have an interest in the outcome of the case?

3. Did McDonald's violate any Oregon statute?

4. Was Theurer acting within the scope of employment?

5. Is McDonald's liable to Faverty?

6. What counterpoints does the dissenting judge make?

A new issue evolving in the area of scope of employment is whether the employer can be held liable for the intentional acts of the employee. Generally, those intentional acts not authorized by employers do not result in liability. However, as the following case discusses, employers may have concerns and potential liability for inaction once they are on notice of problems. The following case also provides the answer for the chapter opening "Consider."

CASE 18.5

Lange v. *National Biscuit Co.*
211 N.W.2d 783 (Minn. 1973)

Shelf Space Is My Life: Flipping Out over Oreos

FACTS

Jerome Lange (plaintiff) was the manager of a small grocery store in Minnesota that carried Nabisco (defendant) products. Ronnell Lynch had been hired by Nabisco as a cookie salesman-trainee in October 1968. On March 1, 1969, Mr. Lynch was assigned his own territory, which included Mr. Lange's store.

Between March 1 and May 1, 1969, Nabisco received numerous complaints from grocers about Mr. Lynch's being overly aggressive and taking shelf space in the stores reserved for competing cookie companies.

On May 1, 1969, Mr. Lynch came to Mr. Lange's store to place previously delivered merchandise on the shelves. An argument developed between the two over Mr. Lynch's service to the store. Mr. Lynch became very angry and started swearing. Mr. Lange told him to either stop swearing or leave the store because children were present. Mr. Lynch then became uncontrollably angry and said, "I ought to break your neck." He then went behind the counter and dared Mr. Lange to fight. When Mr. Lange refused, Mr. Lynch viciously assaulted him after which he threw merchandise around the store and left.

Mr. Lange filed suit against Nabisco and was awarded damages based on the jury's finding that although the acts of Mr. Lynch were outside the scope of employment, Nabisco was negligent in hiring and retaining him. The judge granted Nabisco's motion for judgment notwithstanding the verdict, and Mr. Lange appealed.

JUDICIAL OPINION

TODD, Justice

There is no dispute with the general principle that in order to impose liability on the employer under the doctrine of respondeat superior it is necessary to show that the employee was acting within the scope of his employment. Unfortunately, there is a wide disparity in the case law in the application of the "scope of employment" test to those factual situations involving intentional torts. The majority rule as set out in Annotation, 34 A.L.R.2d 372, 402, includes a twofold test: (a) Whether the assault was motivated by business or personal considerations; or (b) whether the assault was contemplated by the employer or incident to the employment.

Under the present Minnesota rule, liability is imposed where it is shown that the employee's acts were motivated by a desire to further the employer's business. Therefore, a master could only be held liable for an employee's assault in those rare instances where the master actually requested the servant to so perform, or the servant's duties were such that that motivation was implied in law.

The fallacy of this reasoning was that it made a certain mental condition of the servant the test by which to determine whether he was acting about his master's business or not. Moreover, with respect of all intentional acts done by a servant in the supposed furtherance of his master's business, it clothed the master with immunity if the act was right, because it was right, and, if it was wrong, it clothed him with a like immunity, because it was wrong. He thus got the benefit of all his servant's acts done for him, whether right or wrong, and escaped the burden of all intentional acts done for him which were wrong. Under the operation of such a rule, it would always be more safe and profitable for a man to conduct his business vicariously than in his own person. He would escape liability for the consequences of many acts connected with his business springing from the imperfection of human nature, because done by another, for which he would be responsible if done by himself. Meanwhile, the public, obliged to deal or come in contact with his agents, for intentional injuries done by them, might be left wholly without redress. . . . A doctrine so fruitful of mischief could not long stand unshaken in an enlightened system of jurisprudence.

In developing a test for the application of respondeat superior when an employee assaults a third person, we believe that the focus should be on the basis of the assault rather than the motivation of the employee. We reject as the basis for imposing liability the arbitrary determination of when, and at what point, the argument and assault leave the sphere of the employer's business and become motivated by personal animosity. Rather, we believe the better approach is to view both the argument and assault as an indistinguishable event for purposes of vicarious liability.

We hold that an employer is liable for an assault by his employee when the source of the attack is related to the duties of the employee and the assault occurs within work-related limits of time and place. The assault in this case obviously occurred within work-related limits of time and place, since it took place on authorized premises during working hours.

The precipitating cause of the initial argument concerned the employee's conduct of his work. In addition, the employee originally was motivated to become argumentative in furtherance of his employer's business. Consequently, under the facts of this case we hold as a matter of law that the employee was acting within the scope of employment at the time of the aggression and that plaintiff's posttrial motion for judgment notwithstanding the verdict on that ground should have been granted under the rule we herein adopt. To the extent that our former decisions are inconsistent with the rule now adopted, they are overruled.

Plaintiff may recover damages under either the theory of *respondeat superior* or negligence. Having disposed of the matter on the former issue, we need not undertake the questions raised by defendant's asserted negligence in the hiring or retention of the employee.

Reversed and remanded.

CASE QUESTIONS

1. What previous indications did Nabisco have that Lynch might cause some problems?

2. Was the attack of Lange within the scope of employment?

3. What test does the court give for determining scope of employment?

4. What is the "motivation test"?

5. Does this court adopt or reject the "motivation test"?

C O N S I D E R . . .

18.3 Oklahoma Nursing Homes, Ltd., employed numerous health care professionals at its various nursing homes, including nurse's aides, who assisted occupants of the homes with daily activities such as eating, bathing, and dressing.

Glen Rodebush, a victim of Alzheimer's disease, was a resident of one of the company's homes. His condition caused him to be combative sometimes. Rodebush's wife, Zelda, arrived one day for a visit and discovered large welts and red marks on his face. Mrs. Rodebush called her husband's doctor, who found that the marks were caused by slaps of the human hand and were six to twelve hours old. Earlier in the day, Mr. Rodebush had been bathed by a male nurse's aide and, during the course of the bath, Mr. Rodebush had become unruly. Following the bath, a supervisor noted that the aide smelled of liquor and noted from his time card that he had arrived thirty minutes late. He confessed that he had "partied all night." The nurse's aide had been hired without a background check. Following the incident and Mrs. Rodebush's complaint about the marks, the company discovered that the aide had a felony conviction for violent assault and battery with intent to kill, escape, and carrying a weapon following conviction of a felony.

The aide had never been given training by the company, and the company had been cited by the State Department of Human Services for violations of reporting requirements as well as the failure to take proper steps against employees who report to work while intoxicated.

Mrs. Rodebush has filed suit against the nursing home on behalf of her husband. The nursing home claims it cannot be held liable for the intentional and unauthorized acts of its employees. Who is correct? Should there be recovery? [*Rodebush v. Oklahoma Nursing Homes, Ltd.,* 867 P.2d 1241 (Okl.1993)]

The liability of principals for the torts of agents has become a costly part of doing business. Many firms are undertaking various forms of testing to prevent employees who could cause injuries from driving, operating machinery, or otherwise working in situations in which human safety is an issue.

In *Skinner v. Railway Labor Executives Association,* 489 U.S. 602 (1989), the U.S. Supreme Court dealt with the issue of the validity of drug testing in the railroad industry. Under the Federal Railroad Safety Act of 1979, railroads were authorized to administer breath and urine tests to employees who had violated certain safety rules. A union brought suit against the secretary of transportation, alleging that railroad employees' rights to privacy under the Fourth Amendment (see Chapter 9) were intruded upon by the law and the testing. However, the Supreme Court held that the need for safety and the government's responsibility for ensuring railroad safety permitted the testing. Although the court ruled that the tests did violate individual privacy, they were also held to be necessary for the greater interest of public safety, at least in this case, of a governmental employer.

C O N S I D E R . . .

18.4   The FAA announced required drug testing by all airlines for the following employees: flight crew members, flight attendants, flight or ground instructors, flight testing personnel, aircraft dispatchers, maintenance personnel, aviation security or screening personnel, and air traffic controllers. The tests required included screening for marijuana, cocaine, opiates, phencyclidine (PCP), and amphetamines.

Is this testing appropriate? Is it an unnecessary invasion of privacy? Should all employees be tested? [*Bluestein v. Skinner,* 908 F.2d 451 (9th Cir. 1990)]

Independent Contractors

Principals are not generally liable for the torts of independent contractors, but there are three exceptions to this general no-liability rule. The first exception covers **inherently dangerous activities,** which are those that cannot be made safe. For example, using dynamite to demolish old buildings is an inherently dangerous activity. Without this liability exception, a principal could hire an independent contractor to perform the task and then assume no responsibility for the damages or injuries that might result.

The second exception to the no-liability rule occurs when a principal negligently hires an independent contractor. A landlord who hires a security guard, therefore, must check that guard's background, because if a tenant's property is stolen by a guard with a criminal record, the landlord is responsible. Similarly, if a principal hires independent contractors knowing of their past employment history, the principal is liable for the conduct of those independent contractors. Thus, a business that hires a collection agency to collect past due accounts, knowing that agency's reputation for violence, is liable for the agency's torts even though they are independent contractors.

The third exception is the situation in which the principal has provided the specifications for the independent contractor's procedures or process.

TERMINATION OF THE AGENCY RELATIONSHIP

An agency relationship can end in several different ways. First, the parties can have a definite duration for the agency relationship. A listing agreement for the sale of real property usually ends after ninety days. An agency can also end because the agent quits or the principal fires the agent. When the principal dies or is incapacitated, an agency ends automatically because the agent no longer has anyone to contract on behalf of.

Although the agency ends easily when an agent is fired or quits, the authority of the agent does not end so abruptly or easily. An agent can still have **lingering apparent authority** that exists beyond the termination of the agency in relation to third parties who are unaware of the agency termination. For example, if the purchasing agent for a corporation retires after twenty-five years, the agency between the agent and corporation has ended. However, many customers are used to dealing with the agent and may not be aware of the end of the agency. That purchasing agent could still bind the principal corporation even though actual authority has ended. The principal corporation can end lingering apparent authority by giving public or **constructive notice** and private or **actual notice.** Public notice is publication of the resignation. In many trade magazines and business newspapers, there are announcements and personal columns about business associate changes and other personnel news. These are public notices; and, even though not everyone dealing with the agent may see the notice, they are deemed to have been given constructive notice. However, the principal must also give private notice to those firms that have dealt with the agent or have been creditors in the past. This notice is accomplished by a letter sent to each firm or individual who has dealt with the agent. Without this notice, the agent's apparent authority lingers with respect to those third parties who have not received notice.

TERMINATION OF AGENTS UNDER EMPLOYMENT AT WILL

Most employees do not have written contracts that specify the start and duration of their employment. Rather, most employees work at the discretion of their employers, which is to say that they have **employment at will.** Recent cases have placed some restrictions on this employer freedom to hire and fire at will, as courts have been giving employees/agents the benefit of their reliance. Employees have based their protection rights on several theories, including implied contract and public policy. Exhibit 18.3 summarizes the "dos" and "don'ts" of terminating employees.

EXHIBIT 18.3 **The Dos and Don'ts of Laying People Off**

DO	DON'T
Conduct regular reviews of employees, using objective, uniform measures of performance.	Don't make oral promises of job security to employees who might later be laid off. **Danger: breach-of-contract suit.**
Give clear, business-related reasons for any dismissal, backed by written documentation when possible.	Don't put pressure on an employee to resign in order to avoid getting fired. **Danger: coercion suit.**
Seek legal waivers from older workers who agree to leave under an early-retirement plan, and make sure they understand the waiver terms in advance.	Don't make derogatory remarks about any dismissed worker, even if asked for a reference by a prospective employer. **Danger: defamation suit.**
Follow any written company guidelines for termination, or be prepared to show in court why they're not binding in any particular instance.	Don't offer a fired employee a face-saving reason for the dismissal that's unrelated to poor performance. **Danger: wrongful-discharge suit.**

Source: Arthur S. Hayes, "Layoffs Take Careful Planning to Avoid Losing the Suits that Are Apt to Follow," *Wall Street Journal,* November 2, 1990, 131. Reprinted by permission of *The Wall Street Journal,* © 1990 Dow Jones & Company, Inc. All Rights Reserved Worldwide.

The Implied Contract

Many courts have implied the existence of a contract because of the presence of promises, procedures, and policies in an employee personnel manual. Personnel manuals have been held to constitute, both expressly and impliedly, employee contracts or to become part of the employee contracts when they are given to employees at the outset. One of the factors that determines whether a personnel manual and its terms constitute a contract is the reliance of an employee on its procedures and terms.

Visit the ACLU Web site for employment issues: http://www.aclu.org/issues/worker/campaign.html

Because the employee manual represents a potential contract for the employer, its nature and content should be considered carefully. There are two approaches to employee manuals. One approach is the detailed approach in which all rules, rights, and expectations are carefully established. Another approach is the simple one, in which overall general policies and rights are established with details to be filled in as individual issues arise. The following case deals with the issue of implied contract and appears to create a restriction in using it as a means of limiting employment at will.

CASE 18.6

Guz v. *Bechtel*
8 P.3d 1089 (Cal. 2000)

The Will to Challenge at Will

FACTS

John Guz, 49, had worked for Bechtel Corporation for 22 years, in BNI, a division specializing in engineering, construction, and environ-

mental remediation that focuses on federal government programs, principally for the Departments of Energy and Defense (BNI-MI). Between 1986 and 1991, BNI-MI's size was further reduced from 13 to six persons, and its costs were reduced from $748,000 in 1986 to $400,000 in 1991.

Guz had worked for BNI-MI since 1986. He had worked his way up through the company from administrative assistant, beginning at a salary of $750 per month, to financial reports supervisor, earning $70,000 per year. During his time with Bechtel, Mr. Guz had been given generally favorable performance evaluations, steady pay increases and a continuing series of promotions.

During this time, Bechtel maintained Personnel Policy 1101, dated June 1991, on the subject of termination of employment (Policy 1101). Policy 1101 stated that "Bechtel employees have no employment agreements guaranteeing continuous service and may resign at their option or be terminated at the option of Bechtel."

Bechtel began a series of restructuring changes and eliminated Mr. Guz's division. Mr. Guz was discharged as were all the employees in the division. Mr. Guz brought suit against Bechtel alleging that he had an "implied-in-fact contract" with Bechtel that prevented the company from terminating him so long as the company was performing well financially.

The trial court granted Bechtel's motion for summary judgment and dismissed the action. In a split decision, the Court of Appeal reversed. Bechtel appealed.

JUDICIAL OPINION

BAXTER, Justice

This case presents questions about the law governing claims of wrongful discharge from employment as it applies to an employer's motion for summary judgment.

First, the Court of Appeal used erroneous grounds to reverse summary judgment on Guz's implied contract cause of action. The Court of Appeal found triable evidence (1) that Guz had an actual agreement, implied in fact, to be discharged only for good cause, and (2) that the elimination of Guz's work unit lacked good cause because Bechtel's stated reason—a "downturn in . . . workload"—was not justified by the facts, and was, in truth, a pretext to discharge the unit's workers for poor performance without following the company's "progressive discipline" policy. We acknowledge a triable issue that Guz, like other Bechtel workers, had implied contractual rights under specific provisions of Bechtel's written personnel policies. But neither the policies, nor other evidence, suggests any contractual restric-

tion on Bechtel's right to eliminate a work unit as it saw fit, even where dissatisfaction with unit performance was a factor in the decision. The Court of Appeal's ruling on Guz's implied contract claim must therefore be reversed.

Second, the Court of Appeal erred in restoring Guz's separate cause of action for breach of the implied covenant of good faith and fair dealing. Here Guz claims that even if his employment included no express or implied-in-fact agreement limiting Bechtel's right to discharge him, and was thus "at will" (Lab. Code, § 2922), the covenant of good faith and fair dealing, implied by law in every contract, precluded Bechtel from terminating him arbitrarily, as by failing to follow its own policies, or in bad faith. But while the implied covenant requires mutual fairness in applying a contract's actual terms, it cannot substantively alter those terms. If an employment is at will, and thus allows either party to terminate for any or no reason, the implied covenant cannot decree otherwise.

While the statutory presumption of at-will employment is strong, it is subject to several limitations. For instance, as we have observed, "the employment relationship is fundamentally contractual." Thus, though Labor Code section 2922 prevails where the employer and employee have reached no other understanding, it does not overcome their "fundamental . . . freedom of contract" to depart from at-will employment. The statute does not prevent the parties from *agreeing* to any limitation, otherwise lawful, on the employer's termination rights. One example of a contractual departure from at-will status is an agreement that the employee will be terminated only for "good cause" in the sense of "'"a fair and honest cause or reason, regulated by good faith . . ."' [Citations]," as opposed to one that is 'trivial, capricious, unrelated to business needs or goals, or pretextual. . . .'" But the parties are free to define their relationship, including the terms on which it can be ended, as they wish. The parties may reach any contrary understanding, otherwise lawful, "concerning either the term of employment or the grounds or manner of termination."

Thus, the employer and employee may enter "an agreement . . . that . . . the employment relationship will continue indefinitely, pending the occurrence of some event such as the employer's dissatisfaction with the employee's services or the existence of some 'cause' for termination." Among the many available options, the parties may agree that the employer's termination rights will vary with the

(continued)

particular circumstances. The parties may define for themselves what cause or causes will permit an employee's termination and may specify the procedures under which termination shall occur. The agreement may restrict the employer's termination rights to a greater degree in some situations, while leaving the employer freer to act as it sees fit in others.

The contractual understanding need not be express, but may be implied in fact, arising from the parties' conduct evidencing their actual mutual intent to create such enforceable limitations. [w]e [have] identified several factors, apart from express terms, that may bear upon "the existence and content of an . . . [implied-in-fact] agreement" placing limits on the employer's right to discharge an employee. These factors might include "the personnel policies or practices of the employer, the employee's longevity of service, actions or communications by the employer reflecting assurances of continued employment, and the practices of the industry in which the employee is engaged."

Whether that understanding arises from express mutual words of agreement, or from the parties' conduct evidencing a similar meeting of minds, the exact terms to which the parties have assented deserve equally precise scrutiny. Every case thus turns on its own facts.

Guz alleges he had an agreement with Bechtel that he would be employed so long as he was performing satisfactorily and would be discharged only for good cause. Guz claims no express understanding to this effect. However, he asserts that such an agreement can be inferred by combining evidence of several factors, including (1) his long service; (2) assurances of continued employment in the form of raises, promotions, and good performance reviews; (3) Bechtel's written personnel policies, which suggested that termination for poor performance would be preceded by progressive discipline, that layoffs during a work force reduction would be based on objective criteria, including formal ranking, and that persons laid off would receive placement and reassignment assistance; and (4) testimony by a Bechtel executive that company practice was to terminate employees for a good reason and to reassign, if possible, a laid-off employee who was performing satisfactorily.

Guz further urges there is evidence his termination was without good cause in two respects. First, he insists, the evidence suggests Bechtel had no good cause to eliminate BNI-MI, because the cost reduction and workload downturn reasons Bechtel gave for that decision (1) were not justified by the facts, and (2) were a pretext to terminate him and other individual BNI-MI employees for poor performance without following the company's progressive discipline rules. Second, Guz asserts, even if there was good cause to eliminate his work unit, his termination nonetheless lacked good cause because Bechtel failed to accord him fair layoff rights set forth in its written personnel rules, including (1) use of objective force ranking to determine which unit members deserved retention, and (2) fair consideration for other available positions while he was in holding status.

We see no triable evidence of an implied agreement between Guz and Bechtel on additional, different, or broader terms of employment security. As Bechtel suggests, the personnel documents themselves did not restrict Bechtel's freedom to reorganize, reduce, and consolidate its work force for whatever reasons it wished. Thus, contrary to the Court of Appeal's holding, Bechtel had the absolute right to eliminate Guz's work unit and to transfer the unit's responsibilities to another company entity, even if the decision was influenced by dissatisfaction with the eliminated unit's performance, and even if the personnel documents entitled an individual employee to progressive discipline procedures before being fired for poor performance.

We agree that disclaimer language in an employee handbook or policy manual does not necessarily mean an employee is employed at will. But even if a handbook disclaimer is not controlling in every case, neither can such a provision be ignored in determining whether the parties' conduct was intended, and reasonably understood, to create binding limits on an employer's statutory right to terminate the relationship at will. Like any direct expression of employer intent, communicated to employees and intended to apply to them, such language must be taken into account, along with all other pertinent evidence, in ascertaining the terms on which a worker was employed.

At the outset, it is undisputed that Guz received no individual promises or representations that Bechtel would retain him except for good cause, or upon other specified circumstances. Nor does Guz seriously claim that the practice in Bechtel's industry was to provide secure employment. Indeed, the undisputed evidence suggested that because Bechtel, like other members of its industry, operated by competitive bidding from project to project, its work force fluctuated widely and, in terms of raw numbers, was in general decline.

However, Guz insists his own undisputed long and successful service at Bechtel constitutes strong evidence of an implied contract for permanent employment except upon good cause. Bechtel responds that an individual employee's mere long and praiseworthy service has little or no tendency to show an implied agreement between the parties that the employee is no longer terminable at will.

We agree that an employee's mere passage of time in the employer's service, even where marked with tangible indicia that the employer approves the employee's work, cannot alone form an implied-in-fact contract that the employee is no longer at will. Absent other evidence of the employer's intent, longevity, raises and promotions are their own rewards for the employee's continuing valued service; they do not, in and of themselves, additionally constitute a contractual guarantee of future employment security. A rule granting such contract rights on the basis of successful longevity alone would discourage the retention and promotion of employees.

On the other hand, long and successful service is not necessarily irrelevant to the existence of such a contract. Over the period of an employee's tenure, the employer can certainly communicate, by its written and unwritten policies and practices, or by informal assurances, that seniority and longevity do create rights against termination at will. The issue is whether the employer's words or conduct, on which an employee reasonably relied, gave rise to that specific understanding.

We therefore decline to interpret that long, successful service, standing alone, can demonstrate an implied-in-fact contract right not to be terminated at will.

Bechtel's written personnel documents—which, as we have seen, are the sole source of any contractual limits on Bechtel's rights to terminate Guz—imposed no restrictions upon the company's prerogatives to eliminate jobs or work units, for any or no reason, even if this would lead to the release of existing employees such as Guz.

Accordingly, we conclude the Court of Appeal erred in finding, on the grounds it stated, that Guz's implied contract claim was triable. Insofar as the Court of Appeal used these incorrect grounds to overturn the trial court's contrary determination, and thus to reinstate Guz's contractual cause of action, the Court of Appeal's decision must be reversed.

CASE QUESTIONS

1. How long had Guz worked at Bechtel? Describe his work performance over the years.

2. Is Guz correct that a legitimate business reason is overridden by implied contract rights of employees?

3. What does Guz say is the relationship between good performance and the right of the employer to terminate employees at will?

4. Is Bechtel going to have to pay damages to Guz?

5. What lessons should employers learn from the Guz case?

C O N S I D E R . . .

18.5   Joan Leikvold was hired by Valley View Community Hospital in 1972 as its operating room supervisor. In 1978, she became director of nursing. In 1979, she asked to return to her supervisor position. Carl Nusbaum, the director of Valley View, indicated that it was inadvisable for her to go from a managerial position to a subordinate position. In November 1979, Leikvold was fired.

Valley View's personnel manual provided as follows:

Every effort is made to help an employee to adjust himself to his work. If the employee's work, however, should be considered unsatisfactory during the first three months of employment, the hospital reserves the right to discontinue his services without notice. If an employee is discharged for unsatisfactory service after the three-month probationary period is completed, two weeks notice of such discharge will be given. Gross violations of conduct and hospital rules are grounds for immediate dismissal and will cause an employee to forfeit the usual two weeks notice. On such

BUSINESS STRATEGY

The Employee Handbook as a Source of Litigation: Taking Precautionary Steps

The employee handbook continues to be a source of litigation. Every appellate court that has heard a case on the issue of employee handbooks has ruled that there is an implied contract that results from the terms in the employee handbook.

© Deanna Ettinger/Thomson Learning

This focus on employee handbooks has been combined with the majority of courts finding the right of an employee to recover for wrongful discharge. Only Florida, Georgia, North Carolina, and Rhode Island do not recognize wrongful employment action rights. Indiana, Louisiana, and Texas have not ruled on the issue of wrongful discharge.

The law on employee handbooks is as follows:

1. The offer of employment is made to the employee by the employer, and included in the terms of the offer are the terms in the employee handbook.
2. Those handbooks include grounds for termination as well as the process that must be followed in order for termination to occur.
3. The employee accepts these terms by beginning employment.

Some advice from lawyers on employee handbooks:

1. Avoid using general phrases such as "employees may only be terminated for cause."
2. Avoid phrases such as employment continues so long as the employee "does a satisfactory job."
3. Say what you mean and mean what you say.
4. State that the employee relationship is an at-will relationship and can be ended at any time.
5. Make sure supervisors know the terms and procedures in the handbook and follow them.
6. Don't make reference to long-term employment, uninterrupted employment, continuing employment.
7. Don't make promises to employees in the handbook.
8. Update handbooks and review them periodically.
9. Make sure employees receive copies of changes and modified handbooks.
10. Have employees acknowledge receipt of the handbook.

For more information:

Mark W. Bennett, *Employment Relationship: Law & Practice* (2000).
Pleva v. Norquist, 195 F.3d 905 (7th Cir. 1999).
Knight v. Vernon, 214 F.3d 544 (4th Cir. 2000).
Demasse v. ITT Corp., 984 P.2d 1138 (Ariz. 1999).

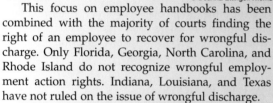

occasion, the employee will be paid in full only to the time of discharge. No notice or terminal pay is given for the following:

1. *Frequent tardiness*
2. *Sleeping on the job*
3. *Insubordination*
4. *Intoxication*
5. *Malicious gossip*
6. *Excessive garnishments*
7. *Conviction of a felony*
8. *Gambling on hospital premises*
9. *Unexcused absences*
10. *Soliciting tips or other serious misconduct*

The discharged employee who feels himself aggrieved by the terms of the discharge may appeal to Administration and will be granted a hearing.

Leikvold claims this section limits Valley View's right to discharge a nonprobationary employee to those cases in which the employee's work has been unsatisfactory or in which the employee has committed a gross violation of conduct or hospital rules. Is she correct? [*Leikvold* v. *Valley View Community Hosp.*, 688 P.2d 170 (Ariz. 1984)]

The Public Policy Exception

Learn more about whistle-blowing:
http://www.whistleblowers.org

In a second group of employment-at-will cases, the courts have afforded protection to those employees, called *whistle-blowers*, who report illegal conduct and to those who refuse to participate in conduct that is illegal or that is violative of public policy. For example, an employee was found to be wrongfully discharged when fired after supplying information to police who were investigating alleged criminal violations by a co-employee [*Palmateer v. International Harvester Co.*, 421 N.E.2d 876 (Ill. 1981)]. Other cases in which courts have found a wrongful discharge involve a refusal by an employee to commit perjury, a refusal by an employee to participate in price fixing, and an employee-reported violation of the Food, Drug, and Cosmetic Act.

In the following case, a court deals with the issue of an employer firing an employee who has taken action in an area not directly related to his employment.

CASE 18.7

Gardner v. Loomis Armored, Inc.
913 P.2d 377 (Wash. 1996)

Termination for Helping during a Knife Attack

FACTS

Kevin Gardner is a driver with Loomis Armored, Inc., which is a company supplying armored truck delivery services to banks, businesses and others requiring secure transport of funds and other valuables. Because of the safety and liability issues surrounding armored truck deliveries, Loomis has adopted a policy for all drivers that their trucks cannot be left unattended. The policy is provided in the employee handbook and the penalty for violation of the rule is as follows:

Violations of this rule will be grounds for termination.

While Gardner was making a scheduled stop at a bank for a pick-up of funds, he noticed a woman was being threatened with a knife by an obviously agitated man. Gardner left his truck unattended as he went to the aid of the woman. The woman was saved, her assailant apprehended, and Gardner was then fired by Loomis for violating the company policy of not leaving the truck unattended. Gardner filed suit for wrongful termination in violation of public policy.

JUDICIAL OPINION

DOLLIVER, Justice

The narrow public policy encouraging citizens to rescue persons from life threatening situations clearly evinces [demonstrates] a fundamental societal interest. . . . The value attached to such acts of heroism is plainly demonstrated by the fact that society has waived most criminal and tort penalties stemming from conduct necessarily committed in the course of saving a life. If our society has placed the rescue of a life above constitutional rights and above the criminal code, then such conduct clearly rises above a company's work rule. Loomis' work rule does not provide an overriding justification for firing Gardner when his conduct directly served the public policy encouraging citizens to save persons from serious bodily injury or death.

We find that Gardner's discharge for leaving the truck and saving a woman from an imminent life threatening situation violates the public policy encouraging such heroic conduct. This holding does not create an affirmative legal duty requiring citizens

(continued)

to intervene in dangerous life threatening situations. We simply observe that society values and encourages voluntary rescuers when a life is in danger. Additionally, our adherence to this public policy does nothing to invalidate Loomis' work rule regarding drivers' leaving the trucks. . . . Our holding merely forbids Loomis from firing Gardner when he broke the rule because he saw a woman who faced imminent life threatening harm, and he reasonably believed his intervention was necessary to save her life. Finally, by focusing on the narrow public policy encouraging citizens to save human lives from life threatening situations, we continue to protect employers from frivolous lawsuits.

CASE QUESTIONS

1. Why is this case different from one in which an employee "rescues" a member of the public from fraud in bids or injury from defective products?

2. Did Gardner do the right thing in leaving his truck unattended? What were his ethical obligations under the circumstances? What would you have done?

3. Does this case create any affirmative legal duty for helping those in danger?

4. Can an employee in Washington be fired for assisting a citizen who is a crime victim?

For information on downsizing, visit the American Psychological Association Web site: http://www.apa.org/books/homepage.html

Review the False Claims Act: http://www.taf.org

There has been a tremendous increase in suits brought by employees for improper discharge. Many companies, in the interest of maintaining fairness and saving expenses, have adopted a *peer review* policy. Peer review is a formal grievance procedure for nonunion employees. Employees who feel that they cannot get an adequate response from their supervisors or by following the lines of authority have the opportunity to present their cases to a panel of fellow employees and managers (three employees, two managers is the general configuration). Panel members listen to the presentation, can ask for more information, vote on the issue, and issue a written opinion with an explanation.

Many companies (including Coors and GTE) are avoiding lawsuits through what seems to be a mutually satisfactory resolution of wrongful termination and other grievance cases. Some employers say this process encourages both managers and employees to make better decisions. The peer review process should be in the employee handbook, should be required prior to court action, and should be widely publicized.

The Antiretaliation Statutes: Protections for Whistle-Blowers

Rather than having employees rely on a case-by-case determination of when they are protected in taking action in the course of employment and when they are not, many states as well as the federal government have passed whistle-blower protections statutes, which prevent employers from firing employees who report violations, note safety concerns, or in some way take action that benefits the public but does not help or reflect well on their employers.

There are two generic federal statutes that afford protection for federal employees: the Civil Service Reform Act of 1978 and the Whistleblower Protection Act of 1989. The statutes protect federal employees who report wrongdoing and permit them to recover both back pay and their attorney's fees in the event they litigate or protest a termination for their disclosure of possible violations of the law. There are also specific provisions in some federal statutes for certain categories of federal employees. For example, a portion of the Energy Reorganization Act provides protection for employees of nuclear facilities who report violations of federal laws and regulations at nuclear plants. The False Claims Act permits employees of government contractors whose tips and disclosures to federal investigators and agencies result in fines and penalties to collect 25 percent of those fines and penalties. Whistle-blowers who have obtained recovery under the False Claims Act include former GE employees who disclosed time-card fraud on defense contracts, and many employees of the health care providers involved in Medicare/Medicaid fraud cases (an employee in one case recovered $17.5 million after a $70 million fine was paid).

All fifty states plus the District of Columbia have antiretaliation whistle-blower protection statutes of some type. About half of the states protect all employees, while the other half provides protection only for government employees. Three states offer monetary rewards for employees who report wrongdoing that results in the collection of fines from a company, as the federal government does. Thirty-two states provide protection for employees who report civil rights violations, and nineteen states provide protections for reporting minimum wage violations. Other areas in which the states provide whistle-blower protection include reporting violations of environmental laws, child welfare laws, and child-care facility health and safety standards.

AGENCY RELATIONSHIPS IN INTERNATIONAL LAW

One of the complexities that has developed in law because of complex global organizations is the liability of various subsidiaries, officers,

> ### BUSINESS PLANNING TIP
>
> Encourage internal whistle-blowing. Publicize your hot line for disclosing illegal activity, and encourage employees to come forward. Eliminate employee fears by directing the investigation of complaints to someone outside a reporting employee's chain of command. Be certain that all complaints are investigated and that investigations are done promptly. Whenever possible, publicize the investigation and its outcome to encourage other employees to come forward.
>
> For the employee, the following suggestions should be followed:
>
> **1.** Consult family and close friends for perspective and support.
>
> **2.** Work within your system and through its chain of command before going public. Go through the various layers of management, even to the board of directors.
>
> **3.** Voice/write your concerns; don't make accusations.
>
> **4.** Maintain records of your internal contacts and their objections.
>
> **5.** Find other employees who also know about this potentially volatile situation.
>
> **6.** Keep a record of your information and carefully document your complaints. Eliminate speculation, personal opinion, and anger. Be objective.
>
> **7.** Maintain copies of records.
>
> **8.** Find support groups in your community (and nationwide, if necessary).

and owners of multinational organizations when the interrelationships and operations may not be clear or even known to them. Perhaps the best example of the pitfalls of complex, global structure is the multinational bank BCCI, a bank that proved elusive as authorities from several countries investigated it for criminal activity. BCCI was a complex, multinational organization with banks in seventy countries, including the United States (First American Bankshares, headed by Clark Clifford and Robert Altman). The banks and businesses in the different countries were staffed by residents of those countries, and the full global network of BCCI was not disclosed to these subsidiaries and the individuals operating them. Regulations of operations were limited to the entities located in each of the various nations. Jurisdiction over other operations was limited. The layers of the organization made it difficult for anyone, even those in the subsidiaries, to be certain of the roles and activities of the full organization or of other subsidiaries.

Source: Patrick McDonnell, *Forbes*, November 28, 1988, 117. Reprinted with permission of Patrick McDonnell © 1988.

BCCI collapsed and surrendered its U.S. assets to U.S. regulators in settlement of various charges. The late Clark Clifford and Robert Altman were indicted for activities involving BCCI, although they were affiliated with U.S. operations only. Mr. Altman was acquitted of the charges, but Mr. Clifford was determined to be too ill to stand trial.

Following this complex case and the structure of principals and agents to evade the laws of any country, England, the United States, and other countries have been working together to determine who was responsible for the bank's collapse and how such tangled and evasive structures can be avoided in the future. One of the proposals considered is to require filing and full disclosure of all principal-agent and parent-subsidiary relationships in all countries in which a bank conducts business.

BIOGRAPHY

JOHN E. SWANSON: AN ETHICS OFFICER AND A WHISTLE-BLOWER

John Swanson was hired by Dow Corning in 1966 at age 30 as an advertising supervisor. He was promoted to manager of industrial marketing a short time later, and in that position he began to write speeches for the then chairman and CEO of the company, William C. Goggin. When Goggin retired, his successor, Jack S. Ludington, continued to rely on Swanson for advice as well as speeches.

Just three years prior to Swanson's arrival at Dow Corning, the company had introduced its silicone breast implants to the market. From the time the product was released to market, there were complaints about ruptures.

Ludington and Swanson, along with three managers, formed a Business Conduct Committee in 1976 and began to draft guidelines for ethical conduct, develop processes for monitoring compliance, and create methods for correction of questionable conduct within the company. Swanson slowly took on the full task of ethics within Dow Corning and developed the company's code of ethics, called *A Matter of Integrity*. One provision in the code explained a standard for employees to use in deciding whether their conduct is appropriate: "We will act with the idea that everything we do will eventually see the light of day."

By 1990, Swanson's job was primarily the updating of the code, making of presentations to employees, and performing conduct reviews.

While Swanson climbed the corporate ladder, his wife, Colleen, became interested in the company's silicone implants. She had implants put in in 1974, and her physician had warned that the long-term implications could not be known because they were so new and also indicated that there were side effects in a small number of cases. Colleen had the implants put in and almost immediately began to experience headaches. Other symptoms followed with no medical explanation obtained despite ongoing doctor visits, tests, and evaluations. Fifteen years later, in 1990, Colleen's daughter called and explained the story of a California woman who had implants and was experiencing similar difficulties. Colleen passed the information along to John.

Swanson took the information about his wife to officers in the company and then recused himself from any further work on the issue. The first lawsuits on the implants had been won in 1984, and Dow Corning continued to battle class action litigation on a national basis. The medical connection has still not been completely established. However, Colleen had her implants removed in 1991 and sued Dow Corning in 1992. John was not a party to the litigation.

When Dow Corning's CEO, Keith McKennon, learned of Colleen's suit, he confronted John, "Look, what does Colleen want out of this? Does she want a zillion dollars? This could be messy. Can't we just talk this out and see if we can get it resolved?" No resolution was reached.

Colleen settled her lawsuit in May 1993, and John retired three months later, in August 1993, on the date he was eligible for retirement. Following a $4.23 billion global settlement on the class action lawsuits, Dow Corning filed for bankruptcy in May 1995.

Colleen and John have since cooperated for a book by *Business Week* reporter John Byrne called *Informed Consent*. John will receive half of the royalties from the book but had no editorial control.

ISSUES

1. Did Swanson do the right thing?
2. How was his timing?

SUMMARY

When is an employee acting on behalf of an employer?

- Principal—employer; responsible party

- Agent—party hired to act on another's behalf

- *Restatement of Agency*—common law view of agent-principal relationship

- Unincorporated association—nonlegal entity; no legal existence as natural or fictitious person

How much authority does an employee hold?

- Express authority—written or stated authority

- Implied authority—authority by custom

- Apparent authority—authority by perceptions of third parties

- Lingering apparent authority—authority left with terminated agent because others are not told of termination

- Actual notice—receipt of notice of termination

- Constructive notice—publication of notice of termination

- Ratification—after-the-fact recognition of agent's authority by principal

- Disclosed principal—existence and identity of principal are known

- Partially disclosed principal—existence but not identity of principal is known

- Undisclosed principal—neither existence nor identity of principal is known

- Gratuitous agency—agent works without compensation

When is a business liable for an employee's acts?

- Master-servant relationship—principal-agent relationship in which principal exercises great degree of control

- Independent contractor—principal-agent relationship in which principal exercises little day-to-day control over agent

- Scope of employment—time when agent is doing work for the principal

- Inherently dangerous activities—activities for which, even if performed by independent contractor, principal is liable

What duties and obligations do employees owe employers?

- Fiduciary—one who has utmost duty of trust, care, loyalty, and obedience to another

How is an agency relationship terminated?

- Employment at will—right of employer to terminate noncontract employees at any time

- Protections for employees through express contract (manuals), implied contracts, and public policy

- Whistle-blowers are protected by antiretaliation statutes

QUESTIONS AND PROBLEMS

1. Dr. Warren Lesch had a leak in his car's gas tank that had been repaired by Malcolm Weeks, an employee of Walker's Chevron, Inc., in Bel Air, Maryland. The tank was not repaired properly, and Dr. Lesch's home and garage were destroyed when the gas tank exploded. Dr. Lesch and his wife were severely burned as a result.

Walker's Chevron is a "branded" station: It displays only Chevron signs and colors and sells only Chevron gas and oil. The Lesches have sued Mr. Weeks, Walker's Chevron, and Chevron USA. Who is liable for the explosion? [*Chevron USA, Inc.* v. *Lesch,* 570 A.2d 840 (Md. 1990)]

2. On September 29, 1984, Wilton Whitlow was taken to Good Samaritan Hospital's emergency room in Montgomery County, Ohio, because he had suffered a seizure and a blackout. He was examined by Dr. Dennis Aumentado, who prescribed the anti-epileptic medication Dilantin. Mr. Whitlow experienced no further seizures and was monitored as an outpatient at Good Samaritan over the next few weeks.

Mr. Whitlow complained to Dr. Aumentado of warm and dry eyes, and his Dilantin dose was reduced. On October 20, 1984, he was again admitted to the emergency room with symptoms that were eventually determined to be from Stevens-Johnson syndrome, a condition believed to be caused by a variety of medications. Mr. Whitlow sued Dr. Aumentado and Good Samaritan for malpractice and Parke-Davis, the manufacturer of Dilantin, for breach of warranty.

The hospital maintains it is not liable because Dr. Aumentado was an independent contractor. Is the hospital correct? [*Whitlow* v. *Good Samaritan Hosp.,* 536 N.E.2d 659 (Ohio 1987)]

3. On March 29, 1983, Barry Mapp was observed in the J. C. Penney department store in Upper Darby, Pennsylvania, by security personnel, who suspected that he might be a shoplifter. Michael DiDomenico, a security guard employed by J. C. Penney, followed Mr. Mapp when he left the store and proceeded to Gimbels department store. There, Mr. DiDomenico notified Rosemary Federchok, a Gimbels security guard, about his suspicions. Even though his assistance was not requested, Mr. DiDomenico decided to remain to assist in case Ms. Federchok, a short woman of slight build, required help in dealing with Mr. Mapp if he committed an offense in Gimbels. It came as no surprise when Mr. Mapp was observed taking items from the men's department of the store; and, when he attempted to escape, he was pursued. Although Ms. Federchok was unable to keep up, Mr. DiDomenico continued to pursue Mr. Mapp and ultimately apprehended him in the lower level of the Gimbels parking lot. When Ms. Federchok arrived with Upper Darby police, merchandise that had been taken from Gimbels was recovered. Mr. Mapp, who had been injured when he jumped from one level of the parking lot to another, was taken to the Delaware County Memorial Hospital, where he was treated for a broken ankle.

Mr. Mapp filed suit against Gimbels for injuries sustained while being chased and apprehended by Mr. DiDomenico. He alleged in his complaint that Mr. DiDomenico, while acting as an agent of Gimbels, had chased him, had struck him with a nightstick, and had beaten him with his fists. Gimbels says it is not liable because Mr. DiDomenico was not its agent. Is Gimbels correct? [*Mapp* v. *Gimbels Dep't Store,* 540 A.2d 941 (Pa. 1988)]

4. Nineteen-year-old Lee J. Norris was employed by Burger Chef Systems as an assistant manager of one of its restaurants. On a day when he was in charge and change was needed, Mr. Norris left to get change but also decided to get Kentucky Fried Chicken at a nearby store for his lunch to take back to Burger Chef. The bank where Mr. Norris usually got change is 1.6 miles from Burger Chef, and the Kentucky Fried Chicken outlet is 2.5 miles from Burger Chef. After Mr. Norris

left the bank and was on his way to the Kentucky Fried Chicken restaurant, he negligently injured Lee J. Govro in an accident. Is Burger Chef liable for the accident? [*Burger Chef Systems* v. *Govro,* 407 F.2d 921 (8th Cir. 1969)]

5. Dewey Nabors operates a real estate brokerage under the trade name Nabors & Company, which shares an office, telephone, and secretary with Midtown, a real estate management corporation that had hired Robert Keaton to oversee the completion of a shopping center. Mr. Nabors asked Mr. Keaton to order siding, pipes, and flooring for his personal residence and directed him to order these materials in the name of Nabors & Company. Mr. Keaton contracted with Richardson, Inc., for the flooring. Richardson understood that Mr. Keaton was working for Midtown and billed Midtown for Mr. Nabors's materials. Mr. Nabors refused to pay for the materials because he was dissatisfied. Is Midtown liable? What theory is Richardson using? [*Midtown Properties, Inc.* v. *Richardson, Inc.,* 228 S.E.2d 303 (Ga. 1976)]

6. Reverend John Fisher is the pastor of St. James Episcopal Church in Ohio. Catherine Davis served there as parish secretary from 1978 until six months after Father Fisher arrived at St. James in January 1988. She was fired by Father Fisher after she went to the bishop of the diocese to complain about sexual harassment by Father Fisher. The bishop promised an investigation, which was not conducted because Father Fisher denied the allegations. Ms. Davis then brought suit against the Episcopal Diocese. The diocese denied liability, claiming it was not in control of Father Fisher's actions because he was an independent contractor. Do you agree? [*Davis* v. *Black,* 591 N.E.2d 11 (Ohio 1991)]

7. Lennen & Newell, Inc., (L&N) is an advertising agency hired by Stokely-Van Camp to do its advertising. L&N contracted for the purchase of ad time from CBS, but no Stokely representative's signature is on the contract. If L&N does not pay for the ad time, is Stokely liable? [*CBS, Inc.* v. *Stokely-Van Camp, Inc.,* 456 F. Supp. 539 (E.D.N.Y. 1977)]

8. Although James A. Schoenberger was promised a raise by his immediate supervisor, company policy was that the personnel department made all decisions on raises. The supervisor was in charge of a full department. Did the supervisor have the authority to give the raise? [*Schoenberger* v. *Chicago Transit Auth.,* 405 N.E.2d 1076 (Ill. 1980)]

9. Richard Woolley was hired by Hoffman-LaRoche (HL, defendant) in October 1969 as an Engineering Section Head in HL's Central Engineering Department at Nutley, New Jersey. There was no written employment contract. Mr. Woolley began work in 1969 and had his first promotion in 1976 and a second promotion to Group Leader for Civil Engineering in 1977. In 1978, he was asked to write a report for his supervisors about piping problems in a building at Nutley.

Mr. Woolley submitted the report a month later, and one month after that he was told that the general manager had lost confidence in him. Mr. Woolley's immediate supervisors asked him to resign, but he refused. A formal letter asking for his resignation followed, and he again refused. He was fired two months after he was asked for his resignation.

Mr. Woolley filed suit based on the express and implied promises in the employment manual, which he had first read in 1969. He maintained that he could not be fired at will and could only be terminated for cause according to the terms of the manual. Is Mr. Woolley correct? [*Woolley v. Hoffman-LaRoche, Inc.,* 491 A.2d 1257 (N.J. 1985)]

10. The physician for the Philadelphia Eagles football team examined Don Chuy, a player, and determined that because of a medical condition, Mr. Chuy should not play football. The team's general manager then reported to a sports columnist that Mr. Chuy had a fatal blood disease. A report of the illness appeared in print and was picked up by other sources. Mr. Chuy's personal physician never diagnosed the disease. Mr. Chuy sued the football club for defamation. Is the club liable for the remarks made by the general manager? [*Chuy v. Philadelphia Eagles Football Club,* 595 F.2d 1265 (3d Cir. 1979)]

RESEARCH PROBLEM

Public Relations Issues, Strategy, and the Problem Employee

11. Former Indiana University basketball coach, Bobby Knight, had a long history of violent temper eruptions both on and off the court. Nonetheless, he had been a successful coach for the teams, often taking Indiana to the NCAA final four competition. The flamboyant coach had been know to confront officials during games, throw chairs during games, and use colorful language continually. A video tape captured the coach lunging for the throat of an Indiana University student and player during a practice session.

Coach Knight initially denied that it happened, and then the video tape was produced. The trustees of Indiana University placed the coach on probation and wrote in a letter to the coach that any violation of the terms of the probation—including no striking of students, no temper eruptions, no foul language—was grounds for termination.

Many fans and alumni were outraged at the agreement and defended keeping the coach in good standing because he never had any NCAA violations (i.e., he ran a "clean" program) and he saw to it that most of his players also graduated from college in addition to playing basketball or being recruited by professional teams.

Write a memo explaining why the trustees took the action that they did. Be sure to include discussion of the principles of agency law, potential liability, and the rights of Coach Knight with regard to his employment contract.

BUSINESS STRATEGY APPLICATION

In the CD-ROM Business Strategy Application for this chapter you will be given several scenarios in which an employer was held liable for the conduct of an employee. You will then learn the steps the employer could have taken to eliminate or minimize the resulting liability. When you have completed these scenarios, you will be able to list the components of an effective risk management program for minimizing employer liability with regard to the conduct of employees.

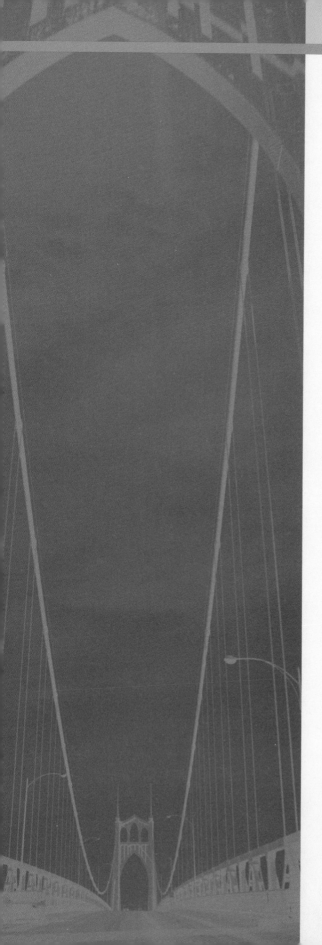

CHAPTER NINETEEN

Management of Employee Welfare

The employer-employee relationship has evolved from one of a paternal nature in the 1600s and 1700s to one of a contractual nature. In the earlier period, employers often assumed responsibility for the well-being of their employees, a personal relationship made possible because of the less-complex nature of business at the time. With the industrial revolution, however, more employees were needed and the personal relationship factor was lost. The employer-employee relationship became thoroughly contractual.

The result of this contractual relationship was that each party became interested in maximizing her own economic benefit. Employers wanted the most work for the least amount of money. Employees wanted maximum pay, safe working conditions, and some type of insurance for retirement, unemployment, and disability. Because employers had the upper hand—they controlled the jobs—their bargaining positions were better than those of employees. As a result, workers organized to give themselves more bargaining power, and the federal government passed legislation to assure workers that some of their needs would be met.

This chapter discusses the work and safety standards covered in federal legislation. The questions answered by the materials in this chapter are: What wage and work hour protections exist for employees? Are there restrictions on children's work? What protections exist for safety in the workplace? What happens when an employee is injured in the workplace? Are workers entitled to pensions, and are they regulated? What is the social security system, and what benefits does it provide? What rights do unemployed workers have? How are labor unions formed, and what is their relationship with employees?

Tendinitis, DeQuervain's tendinitis, carpal tunnel syndrome, and tennis elbow: The four most common workplace injuries following the dot-com bubble

5.7 million: Number of work-related injuries and illnesses in 1999

5,915: Number of fatal occupational injuries in 2000

The fastest-growing category of workplace violence is the kind directed against employers or former employers.

—NATIONAL SAFE WORKPLACE INSTITUTE

CONSIDER...

Dr. Craig Young, an ophthalmologist, founded the Aroostook County Regional Ophthalmology Center, which employs several physicians as well as a significant nursing and clerical staff. The ACROC employee manual provides as follows, "No office business is a matter for discussion with spouses, family or friends. All grievances are to be discussed in private with the office manager or physicians. It is totally unacceptable for an employee to discuss any grievances within earshot of patients." Dr. Young changed the work schedules of an ophthalmic technician and three nurses in order to accommodate an emergency surgery. The four employees were overheard by patients as they complained in the front office. Dr. Young fired the employees. The employees said they were just exercising their right to organize as employees. Is that right protected?

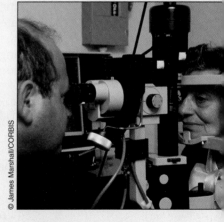

© James Marshall/CORBIS

EXHIBIT 19.1 **Statutory Scheme for Employee Welfare**

STATUTE	DATE	PROVISIONS
Worker's Compensation	1900	Absolute liability of employers for employee injury; no common law tort suits by employees against employers
Social Security Act 42 U.S.C. § 301	1935	FICA contributions; unemployment compensation; retirement benefits
Fair Labor Standards Act 29 U.S.C. § 201	1938	Minimum wages; child labor restrictions; overtime pay
Equal Pay Act 29 U.S.C. § 206	1963	Amendment to FLSA; Equal pay for equal work
Occupational Safety and Health Act 29 U.S.C. § 651	1970	Safety in the workplace; employee rights; employer reporting; inspections
Employment Retirement Income Security Act 29 U.S.C. § 441	1974	Disclosure of contributions, investments, loans; employee vesting; employee statements
Family and Medical Leave Act 29 U.S.C. § 2601	1993	Protection of job after family leave (for pregnancy, child care, adult illness, elderly care)

WAGES AND HOURS PROTECTION

The series of laws affecting employee rights over the past fifty years is summarized in Exhibit 19.1.

The Fair Labor Standards Act

Review the Fair Labor Standards Act:
http://www.law.cornell.edu/ uscode/29/ch8.html

The **Fair Labor Standards Act** (FLSA) is commonly called by workers the "minimum wage law" or the wage and hour law. This act does establish a minimum wage, but it also includes provisions regulating child labor, overtime pay requirements, and equal pay provisions. The FLSA was originally introduced in the Senate by Hugo L. Black when he was a senator from Alabama. His 1937 appointment to the U.S. Supreme Court may have helped it pass the high Court's scrutiny. Having been amended several times, the FLSA is an enabling statute that sets up various administrative agencies to handle the regulations and necessary enforcement.

Coverage of FLSA

The FLSA applies to all businesses that affect interstate commerce. As discussed in Chapter 5, "affecting" interstate commerce is a very broad standard, and even small businesses using mail and phone services are involved in interstate commerce.

FLSA Minimum Wage and Overtime Regulations

Under FLSA, all covered employees must be paid a "minimum wage." The minimum wage is established by Congress and is increased through legislation. The FLSA also includes an hours protection for covered employees in the form of time-and-one-half pay for hours worked above forty hours per week. Regardless of the pay period for covered employees (monthly, weekly, or biweekly), overtime is computed on the basis of forty hours per week. For example, if a covered employee worked thirty-eight, forty-two, thirty-five, and forty-seven hours in four consecutive weeks, and is paid on a monthly basis, that employee is entitled to nine hours of overtime pay.

The definition of "covered employees" is provided in the FLSA. Some categories of employees are "covered" for purposes of minimum wage protections but not for overtime pay. For example, professionals, executives, and others who exercise discretion and judgment in their positions may be covered for purposes of minimum wage protections but not covered for purposes of overtime protections. The reason for this exemption is that these employees, often referred to as "white-collar" workers, possess sufficient training, knowledge, and experience to counter employer unfairness. Certain types of jobs are exempt from overtime protections, such as those of taxicab drivers and railroad employees and those in commercial service and domestic service.

One coverage issue that has received extensive attention during the last decade because of the impact of downsizing has been whether employees can be required to work overtime hours. The FLSA simply provides the right to time-and-one-half pay for overtime worked; it does not include limitations on hours (except in child labor regulation for children under the age of 18). There is no statutory right to refuse to work overtime. Union collective bargaining agreements can impose restraints, and many employers seek volunteers for overtime. However, employers should exercise caution with overly tired employees because, as the *McDonald's* case in Chapter 18 held, employers may be liable for accidents of such employees even when they are on their way home.

FLSA and Child Labor Provisions

The child labor provisions of the FLSA were created to keep children in school for at least a minimum number of years. The provisions of the act govern particular ages and restrict the types of employment those age groups can hold:

1. *18 years old and older.* This group is not covered, as this age is the cutoff for the child labor provisions. Anyone 18 or older can work in any type of job for unlimited hours.

2. *16–17 years old.* This age group can work in any "nonhazardous" job for unlimited hours. Hazardous jobs include mining, logging, roofing, and excavation.

3. *14–15 years old.* This group can work only in nonhazardous, nonmanufacturing, and nonmining jobs, and only during nonschool hours. Work hours are limited to three per day on school days and eighteen per week during school weeks. On nonschool days, this group can work eight hours and during nonschool weeks a maximum of forty hours. Even the hours of the day they may work are restricted: not before 7:00 A.M. or after 7:00 P.M. (except during the summer months, when they can work until 9:00 P.M.).

There are exemptions to the laws; young actors and actresses, for example, are exempt. But even in this field, many states require approval of their contracts and also require that some of the earnings be put in trust for use by the child when the child becomes an adult. Other exemptions apply to work-study programs and farm work. (For information on child labor in international business, see pp. 763–766.)

Enforcement of FLSA

Enforcement of the FLSA requirements may begin in several different ways. Employees can initiate the process by filing a complaint with the U.S. Department of Labor. Upon receipt of the complaint, the department begins an investigation that could lead to a finding of no violation, a violation and a settlement with the employer, or a violation and litigation by the employees for collection of back wages.

In some cases, employers make the laws self-enforcing by requesting interpretations from the Labor Department that are then published in the *Code of Federal Regulations.*

In a final type of case, the Labor Department initiates its own investigation of a firm for possible violations. The department has broad investigatory authority, including the right to ask for records and target particular industries and portions of the law for enforcement. For example, in 1999, the Labor Department focused on the car dealership programs that had high-school-age vocational students working in service departments. While the mechanical work was permissible, using the under-18 students as car jockeys to bring the customers' cars around to them following service was a violation of the age restrictions in the labor laws on certain types of work.

FLSA and Record-Keeping Requirements

Employers subject to the FLSA are required to keep records of hours and wages of their employees. There are no particular formats for these records, but failure to keep them can result in a fine.

Penalties for FLSA Violation

Visit the Department of Labor's Wage and Hour Division:
http://www.dol.gov/dol/esa/public/whd_org.htm

The FLSA carries both civil and criminal penalties. Employees have the right to sue civilly to recover from an employer any wages that were not paid or any overtime compensation that was denied, plus reasonable attorney fees required to bring the action to recover. In addition to the employees' rights, the U.S. Department of Labor's Wage and Hour Division has enforcement power for violations. A willful violation of FLSA carries a maximum $10,000 fine and possible imprisonment of up to six months.

To help employees pursue their rights, the FLSA makes it a violation for any employer to fire an employee for filing an FLSA complaint or for participating in any FLSA proceeding.

Liability for FLSA Violation

Employers, of course, are liable for FLSA violations; but, because most employers are corporations, the question arises as to who in the corporation is liable. The answer is that anyone who actively participates in the running of the business is liable under the FLSA. Officers of the corporation can be held individually liable for the corporation's violations. The FLSA imposes fines on both corporations and officers involved in managing employees.

The Equal Pay Act of 1963

The **Equal Pay Act of 1963** is an amendment to the FLSA that makes it illegal to pay different wages based on gender to men and women who are doing substan-

Review the Equal Pay Act:
http://www.law.cornell.edu/
uscode/29/206.html

tially the same work. If the jobs involve equal responsibility, training, or skill, men and women must have equal pay. Merit systems and seniority systems instituted in good faith do not violate the Equal Pay Act even though they may result in different pay rates for the same jobs. So long as the disparate pay is based on length of employment or a merit-raise system, the disparity is within the act.

It is important to understand that the Equal Pay Act is not an act that requires the application of the doctrine of comparable worth. This doctrine extends the concept of the Equal Pay Act a step further and says men and women should be paid on the same scale, not just for the same jobs but when they are doing different jobs that require equal skill, effort, and responsibility. This issue came to light in 1983 when Louise Peterson, a licensed practical nurse at Western State Hospital in Tacoma, Washington, brought suit when she discovered that her salary of $1,462 per month for her supervision of the daily care of sixty men convicted of sex crimes was $192 less per month than that of the hospital groundskeeper and $700 less per month than men doing similar jobs at Washington's state prisons. Although a trial judge found the pay scales to be discriminatory and ordered the state to reimburse its female employees $838 million in back pay, the ruling was later reversed. Nonetheless, there are strong advocates for the comparable worth system, and it is seen by many women as a means for leveling the wage disparities that have developed over the years as women have come and gone from the workforce in their traditionally female job positions. Others are strongly opposed because of the costs of both evaluation under the doctrine and its implementation. Presently, federal standards do not require comparable worth pay scales.

WORKPLACE SAFETY

The Occupational Safety and Health Act

*Review the Occupational
Safety and Health Act:*
http://www.law.cornell.edu/
uscode/29/651.html

Visit OSHA:
http://www.osha.gov

One of the worker welfare concerns of Congress has been safety in the workplace. In the past, the economic concerns of employers often overshadowed their concern for proper safety precautions. To ensure worker safety, Congress passed the **Occupational Safety and Health Act** of 1970. Its application was broad, protecting virtually every employee in the country. It was an enabling statute that created three agencies responsible for worker safety standards: the **Occupational Safety and Health Administration** (OSHA), the Occupational Safety and Health Review Commission (OSHRC), and the National Institute for Occupational Health and Safety (NIOSH). OSHA is the agency responsible for the promulgation and enforcement of workplace safety standards. OSHA's enforcement powers include investigations, record-keeping requirements, and research. The stated purpose of the act is to "assure so far as possible every working man and woman in the nation safe and healthful working conditions and to preserve our human resources."

The Occupational Safety and Health Act gives the secretary of labor responsibility for administration. OSHA is within the Department of Labor, and its function is to develop safety standards and enforce them through inspections, citations, and court actions. OSHA has created the Occupational Safety and Health Review Commission (OSHRC), whose role is to review OSHA citations and which is the administrative court of appeal for OSHA violators. It consists of three members, who are appointed by the president for staggered six-year terms.

Visit the National Institute for Occupational Safety and Health:
http://www.cdc.gov/niosh/homepage.html

The National Institute for Occupational Safety and Health (NIOSH) often undertakes studies of workplace safety issues. Issues that have been a focus of NIOSH study have included long-term exposure hazards. While OSHA and OSHRC have focused on the traditional issues of equipment use and protective gear, NIOSH has studied the effects of long-term exposure to chemicals and particles.

OSHA Coverage and Duties

OSHA coverage is broad: Every employer with one or more employees who is in a business affecting commerce is covered by OSHA. Several other federal acts regulate safety for particular industries, including the Coal Mine and Safety Act and the Railway Safety Act.

The basic responsibilities of employers are to know and follow OSHA's rules, inspect for hazards and correct them, inform employees of their rights, keep statutorily mandated records, and post citations given by OSHA.

OSHA Responsibilities

Promulgating Rules and Safety Standards

Search for proposed OSHA rules:
http://www.osholine.com

OSHA is responsible for promulgating rules and regulations for safety standards and procedures. The rules are adopted by the standard administrative process of notice in the *Federal Register,* public input, and final decision (see Chapter 6).

Awarding Variances

Once a safety standard is set, employers can still apply for a temporary or permanent variance, which exempts them from compliance with an OSHA regulation. Temporary variances are granted when an employer needs time to comply—for example, to obtain safety equipment or to change the structure or rearrange the workplace. Permanent variances are granted when an employer is able to demonstrate that even with the variance, the workplace is just as safe.

Inspections

OSHA inspections are the administration's enforcement tool. Inspectors can enter the workplace "without delay and at a reasonable time" to inspect. They can check the workplace and the records and can question employees. OSHA's inspection power is limited by numbers, however. Because of OSHA's limited staff, the regulations provide for an order of priority on inspections:

1. Hazards or conditions that could cause death
2. Investigations of fatal accident sites
3. Employee complaints
4. Particularly hazardous industries
5. Random inspections incorporating an emphasis on certain types of industries (roofing, lumbering, meat packing, transportation [car, truck] manufacturing, and longshoring)

The inspections themselves are regulated as to the procedures that must be followed. An OSHA inspector appears at a workplace and upon showing identification asks permission for an inspection. If the employer allows it, the employer or an agent of the employer can accompany the OSHA inspector. After the inspection, the inspector and employer meet to discuss violations, and the problems are often worked out on the spot and the violations remedied immediately.

Employee Rights, Inspections, and OSHA If an inspection is the result of an employee complaint, the employer cannot take any retaliatory action against that employee. Because of OSHA's limited staff, there is reliance on those in the workplace to bring violations to its attention. If workers fear retaliation, the violations will remain unreported. An employee who is fired, demoted, or discriminated against for registering an OSHA complaint can file a complaint, and the Department of Labor can pursue the employee's rights in federal district court. The following is a landmark case on the issue of employer retaliatory conduct.

CASE 19.1

Whirlpool Corporation v. Marshall
445 U.S. 1 (1980)

You Can't Make Me Do It: Employee Defiance and Danger

FACTS

Whirlpool is a manufacturer of household appliances. In its plant in Marion, Ohio, Whirlpool uses a system of overhead conveyor belts to send a constant stream of parts to employees on the line throughout the plant. Beneath the conveyor belt is mesh screen to catch any parts or other objects that might fall from the conveyor belt.

Some items did fall to the mesh screen, located some 20 feet above the plant floor. Maintenance employees had the responsibility for removing the parts and other debris from the screen. They usually stood on the iron frames of the mesh screen, but occasionally they found it necessary to go onto the screen itself. While one maintenance employee was standing on the mesh, it broke and he fell the 20 feet to his death on the floor below. After this fatal accident, maintenance employees were prohibited from standing on the mesh screen or the iron frames. A mobile platform and long hooks were used to remove objects.

Two maintenance employees, Virgil Deemer and Thomas Cornwell, complained about the screen and its safety problems. When the plant foreman refused to make corrections, Mr. Deemer and Mr. Cornwell asked for the name of an OSHA inspector, and Mr. Deemer contacted an OSHA official on July 7, 1974.

On July 8, 1974, Mr. Deemer and Mr. Cornwell reported for work and were told to do their mainte-

nance work on the screen in the usual manner. Both refused on safety grounds, so the plant foreman sent them to the personnel office. They were then forced to punch out and were not paid for the six hours left on their shift.

On behalf of Mr. Deemer and Mr. Cornwell, the secretary of labor brought suit against Whirlpool for the lost six hours of pay and to have the written reprimands for the incident removed from the files of the employees. The trial court found for Whirlpool, and the secretary appealed. The court of appeals found for the secretary, and Whirlpool appealed.

JUDICIAL OPINION

STEWART, Justice

. . . The Secretary is obviously correct when he acknowledges in his regulation that, "as a general matter, there is no right afforded by the Act which would entitle employees to walk off the job because of potential unsafe conditions at the workplace." By providing for prompt notice to the employer of an inspector's intention to seek an injunction against an imminently dangerous condition, the legislation obviously contemplates that the employer will normally respond by voluntarily and speedily eliminating the danger. And in the few instances where this does not occur, the legislative provisions authorizing prompt judicial action are designed to give

(continued)

employees full protection in most situations from the risk of injury or death resulting from an imminently dangerous condition at the worksite.

As this case illustrates, however, circumstances may sometimes exist in which the employee justifiably believes that the express statutory arrangement does not sufficiently protect him from death or serious injury. Such circumstances will probably not often occur, but such a situation may arise when (1) the employee is ordered by his employer to work under conditions that the employee reasonably believes pose an imminent risk of death or serious bodily injury, and (2) the employee has reason to believe that there is not sufficient time or opportunity either to seek effective redress from his employer or to apprise OSHA of the danger.

Nothing in the Act suggests that those few employees who have to face this dilemma must rely exclusively on the remedies expressly set forth in the Act at the risk of their own safety. But nothing in the Act explicitly provides otherwise. Against this background of legislative silence, the Secretary has exercised his rulemaking power and has determined that, when an employee in good faith finds himself in such a predicament, he may refuse to expose himself to the dangerous condition, without being subjected to "subsequent discrimination" by the employer.

The question before us is whether this interpretative regulation constitutes a permissible gloss on the Act by the Secretary.

The regulation clearly conforms to the fundamental objective of the Act—to prevent occupational deaths and serious injuries. The Act, in its preamble, declares that its purpose and policy is "to assure so far as possible every working man and woman in the Nation safe and healthful working conditions and to preserve our human resources. . . ."

To accomplish this basic purpose, the legislation's remedial orientation is prophylactic in nature. The Act does not wait for an employee to die or become injured. It authorizes the promulgation of health and safety standards and the issuance of citations in the hope that these will act to prevent deaths or injuries from ever occurring. It would seem anomalous to construe an Act so directed and constructed as prohibiting an employee, with no other reasonable alternative, the freedom to withdraw from a workplace environment that he reasonably believes is highly dangerous.

Moreover, the Secretary's regulation can be viewed as an appropriate aid to the full effectuation of the Act's "general duty" clause. That clause provides that "[e]ach employer shall furnish to each of his employees employment and a place of employment which are free from recognized hazards that are causing or are likely to cause death or serious physical harm to his employees." Since OSHA inspectors cannot be present around the clock in every workplace, the Secretary's regulation ensures that employees will in all circumstances enjoy the rights afforded them by the "general duty" clause.

The regulation thus on its face appears to further the overriding purpose of the Act, and rationally to complement its remedial scheme.

[T]he Secretary's regulation must, therefore, be upheld, particularly when it is remembered that safety legislation is to be liberally construed to effectuate the congressional purpose.

CASE QUESTIONS

1. What workplace hazard was at issue?
2. What type of remedy does the secretary of labor (acting on behalf of OSHA) want?
3. Is this remedy provided by statute?
4. Is this remedy provided by regulation?
5. Does the decision allow employees to walk off the job when there is a workplace hazard?

OSHA Search Warrant Requirements

Although most businesses voluntarily permit OSHA inspections, on some occasions employers have refused access. In *Marshall* v. *Barlows, Inc.*, 436 U.S. 307 (1978), the U.S. Supreme Court ruled that OSHA inspectors must obtain warrants if employers refused access.

OSHA Penalties

There are five types of OSHA violations, each of which carries a different range of penalties. Exhibit 19.2 is a summary of OSHA penalties.

EXHIBIT 19.2 OSHA Penalties

TYPE OF OFFENSE	DESCRIPTION	PENALTY
Willful	Employer aware of danger or a repeat violator	Up to $70,000 (not less than $5,000) and/or six months imprisonment
Serious	Violation is a threat to life or could cause serious injury	$7,000
Nonserious	No threat of serious injury	Up to $7,000
De minimis	Failure to post rights	Up to $7,000 per violation
Failure to correct	Citation not followed	$7,000 per day

FOR THE MANAGER'S DESK

Re: The Unseen Safety Issues

Often referred to as the sick-building syndrome, there are numerous indoor-air pollutants that affect office employees, causing the following: headaches; eye, nose, and throat irritation; and dry, tight facial skin.

The EPA lists the following indoor pollutants:

    Computer terminals—Electromagnetic fields
    Volatile organic compounds (VOCs)
    Fax machines—VOCs
    Copy machines—Hydrocarbons
    Particulates (toner)
    Ink/bubble jet printers—Hydrocarbons
    Laser printers—Hydrocarbons

To improve conditions and decrease these pollutants: Improve air circulation.

    Inexpensive: Open the windows
    Expensive: Air filtration systems

Check building design for circulation.

Check placement of equipment.

West Bend Mutual Insurance Company of West Bend, Wisconsin, installed an air flow and air filter system for $150,000. Absenteeism is down and productivity is up 8–16 percent.

Most businesses are unaware of its availability, but OSHA funds a program administered by the states that offers free consulting services to small businesses in order to assist them in complying with OSHA rules. The program has forty-two full-time consultants. If a consultant finds a problem in a business, no citation is issued, but the business is given thirty days to bring its plant into compliance.

After an inspection, OSHA can issue a citation, which begins the penalty process. Although some employers enter into a consent decree and settle the matter with OSHA, any citation can be challenged by an employer, who must give notice of challenge within fifteen days of receiving the citation. A hearing is then conducted by an administrative law judge (ALJ). The ALJ makes a recommendation to the OSHRC, which decides what action to take. Once the OSHRC decision is made, the employer has sixty days to seek review of the decision by a U.S. court of appeals.

Re: Fatal Occupational Injuries

*For the year 2000, OSHA reports the following
information on fatal workplace injuries:*

Type of Injury	Number	Percent (Rounded)
Total	5,915	100%
Transportation incidents	2,571	43%
Highway	1,363	23%
Nonhighway	399	7%
Aircraft	280	5%
Worker struck	370	6%
Water vehicle	84	1%
Rail	71	1%
Assaults and violent acts	929	16%
Homicides	677	11%
Self-inflicted	220	4%
Contact with objects/equipment	1,005	17%
Falls	734	12%
Exposure to harmful substances	480	8%
Fires and explosion	177	3%
Other events	19	—

State OSHA Programs

Most federal regulatory laws preempt state laws, but state laws addressing occupational safety are not generally preempted, and the states share responsibility for workplace safety with the federal government. Also, state criminal laws may be used to prosecute officers and companies already sanctioned by OSHA.

For a state to assume responsibility for an OSHA program, it must submit a plan for approval by the secretary of labor. The plan must include an enforcement agency, appropriate safety standards, and the authority of the state agency to inspect randomly, as OSHA does. The secretary must be assured that the state plan will be as effective as federal OSHA would be. Also, OSHA is in charge of the Complaints against State Program Administration, which permits those affected and interested in safety to file complaints with OSHA regarding state performance. OSHA can then investigate and, if necessary, eliminate state approval.

Employee Impairment and Testing Issues

One safety problem in the workplace is the presence of impaired co-workers. An employee operating equipment, whether a drill press or a delivery van, while under the influence of drugs or alcohol presents a substantial safety concern for any business. Current estimates are that between 14 and 20 percent of the U.S. workforce is impaired on the job. Employees who use drugs are almost four times more likely to be involved in workplace accidents. Further, the cost in reduced productivity attributable to impaired workers is $100 billion. In 1989, the U.S. Supreme Court issued two decisions—*Skinner* v. *Railway Labor Executives' Association*, 489 U.S. 602 (1989), and *National Treasury Employees Union* v. *Von Raab*,

489 U.S. 656 (1984)—that upheld the right of government employers to conduct drug screening of federal employees without a warrant and without probable cause if those employees were in "safety sensitive" positions. These two particular cases involved railway employees and customs officers.

In the area of drug and alcohol screening, the interests of employee privacy collide with safety and business issues. Courts at the state and federal level have adopted a near uniform position of holding safety concerns above employees' right of privacy. Their decisions have upheld the right of employer testing even in the private sector, especially in work situations where safety is a concern.

Visit Web sites on workplace and other privacy issues:
http://www.epic.org
and
http://www.privacyrights.org

EMPLOYEE PENSIONS, RETIREMENT, AND SOCIAL SECURITY

One of the concerns of workers is what happens to them when they retire: Will they have an income? Other concerns are whether they will have a source of income in the event of disability, or whether their survivors will have income in the event of their death. Finally, what if no work is available? What income will they have until they find another job? These issues are the social issues of employment law—providing for those who, because of age, disability, or unemployment, are unable to provide for themselves.

> **BUSINESS PLANNING TIP**
>
> When implementing drug testing:
> 1. Disclose in advance the company's policy.
> 2. Provide justification:
>   Safety
>   Productivity
>   Insurance costs
>   Personal well-being of employees
> 3. Ensure fairness of your program:
>   Reliability of lab
>   Randomness of selection
>   Offer of two-lab testing
>   Offer of independent choice
> 4. Protect privacy and dignity of employees:
>   Privacy of giving sample
>   Privacy of results
> 5. Offer rehabilitation where appropriate—counseling, retesting.
> 6. Adhere to disciplinary measures. Termination is the only option in many cases

Social Security

Review the Social Security Act of 1935:
http://www.ssa.gov/history/35act.html

The **Social Security Act of 1935** was a key component of the massive reforms in federal government during Franklin Roosevelt's presidency.

The idea of the Social Security system was to have those who could work shoulder the social burden of providing for those who could not. Every employer and employee is required to contribute to the Social Security programs under the Federal Insurance Contributions Act (FICA). The amount employees contribute is based upon their annual wage, but there is a maximum wage amount for contributions. FICA contributions are paid one-half by employers and one-half by employees. Independent contractors pay their own FICA contributions. There are death benefits for spouses and children, and disability and retirement benefits.

The benefits paid to the retired and disabled are based on formulas. The amount depends on how long an individual worked and her salary range. Surviving spouse and children's benefits are likewise tied to work and salary history.

Private Retirement Plans

Review the Employee Retirement Income Security Act of 1974:
http://www.law.cornell.edu/uscode/29/1001.html

For many, Social Security retirement benefits do not provide enough security, and at present there is no assurance that those employed today will be able to collect their Social Security benefits upon retirement. For these reasons, many employees have invested in their own private retirement plans.

ETHICAL ISSUES 19.1

The pension benefits due to employees under ERISA are substantial expenses for companies. When companies are enduring difficult times, they often employ creative measures to eliminate the pension obligations. For example, the story of Massey-Ferguson and its employees and pension plans is one that took resolution at the U.S. Supreme Court.

Charles Howe and his co-workers were employed by Massey-Ferguson, a wholly owned subsidiary of the parent corporation, Varity Corporation. Massey-Ferguson was not performing well and Varity developed a plan to place Massey-Ferguson and all other weak subsidiaries into a new subsidiary called Massey Combines. Because of the weakness of the companies to be combined in Massey Combines, the officers and board of Varity understood that Massey Combines might fail. However, their goal was to eliminate the debts of these poorly performing subsidiaries. One of the debts they hoped to eliminate through this restructuring was the medical and pension benefits due to Massey-Ferguson employees, including Howe.

Varity held employee information sessions when employees became concerned about their futures and the status of their retirement plans. During these meetings, Varity officers offered their assurances that their benefits would be secure if they transferred to Massey Combines. Known as the Project Sunshine campaign, the meetings offered assurances along with a letter saying: "When you accept employment with Massey Combines Corp. . . . benefit programs will remain unchanged." "We are all very optimistic that our new company has a bright future."

The employees were persuaded to become employees of Massey Combines, but Massey Combines was insolvent from the day of its formation. It was placed into receivership, and the employees of Massey Combines, formerly of Massey-Ferguson, lost all of their pension benefits. Varity Corporation cut off health benefits for retirees, pointing to language in its official health plan: "The company hereby reserves the right, by action of the board, to amend or terminate the plan or trust at any time." Howe and others filed suit under ERISA, and the U.S. Supreme Court held, in *Varity Corp.* v. *Howe*, 516 U.S. 489 (1996), that Howe and the others had the right to bring a private suit against Varity for its breach of its fiduciary duties under ERISA.

Refer to Chapter 2 and list the categories of ethical breaches Varity committed. Was Varity honest with the employees? Did it take unfair advantage of them? Did Varity give a false impression? What ethical test could the officers and board of Varity have employed in avoiding the resulting litigation and eventual liability of Varity to the employees for their pensions?

Many retirement and pension plans are set up by employers, who enjoy tax benefits from some plans. However, when there were indications that employees' funds in plans were being misused, not invested wisely, and in some cases embezzled, Congress enacted the **Employee Retirement Income Security Act of 1974** (ERISA).

Coverage of ERISA

ERISA applies to any employer engaged in or affecting interstate commerce and to any organization (such as a union) representing employees in interstate commerce. ERISA covers any medical, retirement, or deferral-of-income plan.

Requirements of ERISA Plans

For more information on pensions and ERISA, visit: http://www.pbgc.gov

Covered employers and organizations must give participants an annual report on the insurance or retirement fund that must include a financial statement and an actuarial statement. The annual report must also list any loans made from the fund, including amounts and to whom they were made. The cost of reporting and fiduciary duties under ERISA have caused many employers to drop pension plans. ERISA does not require employer pension plans—it only regulates those who have them.

ERISA Employee Rights

ERISA employees are entitled to receive an annual statement showing both their total benefits in any of the covered plans and the amount that is vested or that is nonforfeitable should they leave the job. In addition, ERISA provides minimum vesting requirements or sets standards for when employees will have rights in their retirement, pension, or annuity plans.

FASB 106, Retirees, and Pensions

In 1995, a new rule of the Financial Accounting Standards Board (FASB) took effect that required companies to reflect as a current expense the costs of benefits for retired employees. This accounting rule will continue to affect earnings as the population ages and benefit costs increase.

Unemployment Compensation

Benefits Provided

State laws provide for the amount of **unemployment compensation** that will be paid. The amount is tied to the average amount earned by an individual during the months preceding employment termination. The benefits are usually paid on a weekly or biweekly basis. Most states also have a minimum and maximum amount that can be collected regardless of average earnings during the base period. Further, benefit payments in most states are limited to twenty-six weeks.

Qualifying for Benefits

Each state has its own standards for payment of benefits. Generally, eligibility requirements demand that an individual be (1) involuntarily terminated from her job, (2) able and available for work, and (3) involved in seeking employment.

The payment of unemployment benefits raises many social issues regarding its effects. For example, many opponents of such benefits maintain that awarding them encourages unemployment. In addition, unemployment compensation has created some conflicts in federal labor legislation. In the following case, the U.S. Supreme Court dealt with the conflicting federal rights for labor, management, and unemployment compensation.

For more information on what happens to your pension if your company goes bankrupt, go to:
http://www.dol.gov/dol/pwba

Visit the Financial Accounting Standards Board:
http://www.rutgers.edu/Accounting/raw/fasb

CASE 19.2

Wimberly v. Labor and Indus. Relations Comm'n of Missouri
479 U.S. 511 (1987)

Post-Partum Employment

FACTS

After the birth of her child on November 5, 1980, Linda Wimberly (petitioner) was on pregnancy leave from her job at J. C. Penney. Under Penney policy, she could return to work

only if a position was available. A position was not available when Mrs. Wimberly tried to return and she then filed a claim for unemployment benefits with the Missouri Division of Employment Security. She was denied the claim because she had left "work voluntarily

(continued)

without good cause attributable to [her] work or [her] employer," a provision of a Missouri statute.

Mrs. Wimberly filed suit, and the trial court held that the Missouri statute was inconsistent with the Federal Unemployment Tax Act that prohibits denying compensation "solely on the basis of pregnancy or termination of pregnancy." The court of appeals affirmed, but the Missouri Supreme Court reversed. Mrs. Wimberly appealed to the U.S. Supreme Court.

JUDICIAL OPINION

O'CONNOR, Justice

The Federal Unemployment Tax Act (Act), 26 U.S.C. §§ 3301 *et seq.*, enacted originally as Title IX of the Social Security Act in 1935, 49 Stat. 639, envisions a cooperative federal-state program of benefits to unemployed workers. The standard at issue in this case, § 3304(a)(12), mandates that "no person shall be denied compensation under such State law solely on the basis of pregnancy or termination of pregnancy."

Apart from the minimum standards reflected in § 3304(a), the Act leaves to state discretion the rules governing the administration of unemployment compensation programs.

The treatment of pregnancy-related terminations is a matter of considerable disparity among the States. Most States regard leave on account of pregnancy as a voluntary termination for good cause. Some of these States have specific statutory provisions enumerating pregnancy motivated termination as good cause for leaving a job, while others, by judicial or administrative decision, treat pregnancy as encompassed within larger categories of good cause such as illness or compelling personal reasons. A few states, however, like Missouri, have chosen to define "leaving for good cause" narrowly. In these states, all persons who leave their jobs are disqualified from receiving benefits unless they leave for reasons directly attributable to the work or to the employer.

Petitioner does not dispute that the Missouri scheme treats pregnant women the same as all other persons who leave for reasons not causally connected to their work or their employer, including those suffering from other types of temporary disabilities. She contends, however, that § 3304(a)(12) is not simply an antidiscrimination statute, but rather that it mandates preferential treatment for women who leave work because of pregnancy. According to petitioner, § 3304(a)(12) affirmatively requires states to provide unemployment benefits to women who leave work because of pregnancy when they are next available and able to work, regardless of the state's treatment of other similarly situated claimants.

Contrary to petitioner's assertions, the plain import of the language of § 3304(a)(12) is that Congress intended to prohibit states from singling out pregnancy for unfavorable treatment. The text of the statute provides that compensation shall not be denied under state law "solely on the basis of pregnancy." The focus of this language is on the basis of the state's decision, not the claimant's reason for leaving her job. Thus, a state could not decide to deny benefits to pregnant women while at the same time allowing benefits to persons who are in other respects similarly situated: The "sole basis" for such a decision would be on account of pregnancy. On the other hand, if a state adopts a neutral rule that incidentally disqualifies pregnant or formerly pregnant claimants as part of a larger group, the neutral application of that rule cannot readily be characterized as a decision made "solely on the basis of pregnancy."

Even petitioner concedes that § 3304(a)(12) does not prohibit states from denying benefits to pregnant or formerly pregnant women who fail to satisfy neutral eligibility requirements such as ability to work and availability for work. Missouri does not have a "policy" specifically relating to pregnancy: It neutrally disqualifies workers who leave their jobs for reasons unrelated to their employment.

In *Turner* v. *Department of Employment Security*, this Court struck down on due process grounds a Utah statute providing that a woman was disqualified for 12 weeks before the expected date of childbirth and for 6 weeks after childbirth, even if she left work for reasons unrelated to pregnancy. The Senate Report used the provision at issue in *Turner* as representative of the kind of rule that § 3304(a)(12) was intended to prohibit.

In a number of states, an individual whose unemployment is related to pregnancy is barred from receiving any unemployment benefits. In 1975 the Supreme Court found a provision of this type in the Utah unemployment compensation statute to be unconstitutional. . . . A number of other states have similar provisions although most appear to involve somewhat shorter periods of disqualification.

S. Rep. No. 94-1265, at 19, 21, U.S. Code Cong. & Admin. News 1976, pp. 6031, 6015.

In short, petitioner can point to nothing in the Committee Reports, or elsewhere in the statute's legislative history, that evidences congressional intent to mandate preferential treatment for women on account of pregnancy. There is no hint that Congress disapproved of, much less intended to prohibit, a neutral rule such as Missouri's. Indeed, the legislative history shows that Congress was focused only on the issue addressed by the plain language of § 3304(a)(12): prohibiting rules that single out pregnant women or formerly pregnant women for disadvantageous treatment.

Because § 3304(a)(12) does not require states to afford preferential treatment to women on account of pregnancy, the judgment of the Missouri Supreme Court is affirmed.

CASE QUESTIONS

1. Why was Mrs. Wimberly denied unemployment compensation?
2. Was the pregnancy given as a reason?
3. What is the difference between the Utah statute mentioned in the Court's opinion and the Missouri statute?
4. Is the Missouri statute valid?
5. What implications does the decision carry for maternity leaves?

C O N S I D E R . . .

19.1   Alfred Smith and Galen Black were fired by a private drug rehabilitation center because they ingested peyote for sacramental purposes at a ceremony of the Native American Church, of which both are members. When Messrs. Smith and Black applied for unemployment compensation from the state of Oregon, their requests were denied because they were fired for "misconduct." They challenged the decision as a violation of their religious freedom. Are Messrs. Smith and Black correct? [*Employment Div., Dep't of Human Resources of Oregon* v. *Smith*, 496 U.S. 913 (1990)]

Who Pays for Unemployment Benefits?

Although the idea and mandate for unemployment compensation came from the federal government, the states actually administer their own programs. Employers in each state are taxed based on the number of workers they employ and their wages. Those taxes are collected by the states on a quarterly basis. These funds are deposited with the federal government, which maintains an unemployment insurance program with the funds. Each state has an account in the federal fund on which it can draw. Employers effectively pay the costs of the unemployment compensation system.

WORKERS' COMPENSATION LAWS

For an example of a state workers' compensation law, review the Texas Worker's Compensation Act:
http://www.twcc.state.tx.us/act/toc.html

The purpose of **workers' compensation** laws is to provide wage benefits and medical care to victims of work-related injuries. Although each state has its own system of workers' compensation, several general principles remain consistent throughout the states:

1. An employee who is injured in the scope of employment is automatically entitled to certain benefits (a discussion of work-related injuries and the scope of employment follows).
2. Fault is immaterial. An employee's contributory negligence does not lessen her right to compensation. Employers' care and precaution do not lessen their responsibility.
3. Coverage is limited to employees and does not extend to independent contractors.

4. Benefits include partial wages, hospital and medical expenses, and death benefits.

5. In exchange for these benefits, employees, their families, and dependents give up their common-law right to sue an employer for damages.

6. If third parties (equipment manufacturers, for example) are responsible for an accident, recovery from the third party goes first to the employer for reimbursement.

7. Each state has some administrative agency responsible for administration of workers' compensation.

8. Every employer who is subject to workers' compensation regulation is required to provide some security for liability (such as insurance).

Employee Injuries

As they originated, workers' compensation systems were created to provide benefits for accidental workplace injuries. Over the years, however, the term *accident* has been interpreted broadly. Most injuries are those that result suddenly, such as broken arms, injured backs caused by falls, burns, and lacerations. But workers' compensation has been extended to cover injuries that develop over time. For example, workers involved in lifting heavy objects might eventually develop back problems. Even such medical problems as high blood pressure, heart attacks, and nervous breakdowns have in some cases been classified as work related and compensable.

The standard for recovery under the workers' compensation system is that the injury originate in the workplace, be caused by the workplace, or develop over time in the workplace. Even stress, when shown to be caused or originated by employment, is a compensable injury.

Workers' compensation issues have become more complex, and many of the hearings involve the issue of determining whether a disability originated on the job or would have existed independently of the job. The following case deals with this type of issue.

CASE 19.3

Gacioch v. Stroh Brewery Co.
396 N.W.2d 1 (Mich. 1990)

The Free-Beer Lunches, Alcoholism, and Workers' Comp

FACTS

Casimer Gacioch (plaintiff) began working for Stroh Brewery on February 24, 1947. When he began his work for Stroh, he was predisposed to alcoholism, but he had not yet become an uncontrolled alcoholic.

Beer was provided free at the brewery and was available to all employees on the job at "designated

relief areas." This availability had been negotiated through a collective bargaining agreement. Employees could drink beer during their breaks and at lunch with no limit on the amount.

Mr. Gacioch did not drink at home during the week but drank 3 or 4 bottles of beer on the weekend. At work he drank 12 bottles a day. He was not a test taster; he ran a machine that fed cases of beer to a soaker.

In 1973, Stroh Brewery noticed Mr. Gacioch's drinking problem and required him to sign an agreement stating that he could no longer drink on the job. He continued to drink, and seven months after the first agreement he signed a second agreement not to drink on the job. He again continued to drink, was intoxicated on the job, and could not perform his work. He was fired on August 30, 1974.

From April 1976 until September 1978, Mr. Gacioch worked part-time as a church custodian. He pursued a workers' compensation claim against Stroh, alleging he was disabled because of alcoholism. He was denied recovery and appealed to the Workers' Compensation Appeal Board (WCAB), which found that alcoholism is a disease, that the free-beer policy accelerated the problem, and that Stroh should pay compensation. Stroh appealed.

JUDICIAL OPINION

ARCHER, Justice

This case involves a claim for workers' compensation benefits for the chronic alcoholism suffered by plaintiff. We must determine whether, under the circumstances extant in this case, chronic alcoholism suffered by plaintiff who, during breaks drank beer provided free by Stroh Brewery pursuant to a collectively bargained contract provision negotiated by the union is compensable under the Workers' Disability Compensation Act as a personal injury which arose out of and in the course of plaintiff's employment.

The statute in effect on the last day of plaintiff's employment at Stroh Brewery read:

An employee, who receives a personal injury arising out of and in the course of his employment by an employer who is subject to the provisions of this act, at the time of such injury, shall be paid compensation in the manner and to the extent provided in this act, or in case of his death resulting from such injuries the compensation shall be paid to his dependents as defined in this act. Time of injury or date of injury as used in this act in the case of a disease or in the case of an injury not attributable to a single event shall be the last day of work in the employment in which the employee was last subjected to the conditions resulting in disability or death.

"Personal injury" shall include a disease or disability which is due to causes and conditions which are characteristic of and peculiar to the business of the employer and which arises out of and in the course of the employment. Ordinary diseases of life to which the public is generally exposed outside of the employment shall not be compensable.

Defendants contend that alcoholism is not a disease, but, rather, a "social aberration." All three experts testifying in this case, Drs. Smith and Tanay, plaintiff's experts, and Dr. Rauch, defendants' expert, referred to alcoholism as a disease. Dr. Smith described alcoholism as a "lifelong metabolic disease, much like diabetes." Dr. Tanay testified that alcoholism is associated with particular personality disorders which begin during a person's childhood. The WCAB treated plaintiff's chronic alcoholism as a disease. Our review of the professional literature on the subject indicates that various organizations representing health care professionals have officially pronounced alcoholism as a disease. Hence, plaintiff's chronic alcoholism is a disease for purposes of the above statute.

Plaintiff asserts that his chronic alcoholism was an occupational disease. We disagree. A review of the record indicates that the WCAB also did not conclude that plaintiff's alcoholic condition was an occupational disease. The board treated plaintiff's alcoholism as an ordinary disease of life. The proper inquiry in this case, therefore, is whether plaintiff's chronic alcoholism was a disease or disability which was due to causes and conditions which are characteristic of and peculiar to the business of Stroh and which arose out of and in the course of employment. In reaching the question concerning whether chronic alcoholism is a disease which is due to causes and conditions which are characteristic of and peculiar to the business of Stroh and which arose out of and in the course of plaintiff's employment, we must be careful not to equate "circumstance" of employment with "out of and in the course" of employment. If chronic alcoholism can be categorized as an ordinary disease of life to which the public is generally exposed outside of the employment, plaintiff is not entitled to a workers' compensation award. The pertinent question then is whether the board made specific findings as to whether brewery workers are more prone to develop chronic alcoholism than is the general public.

We are unable to discern from the opinion of the board whether it found as fact that brewery workers are more prone to suffer from chronic alcoholism (an ordinary disease of life) than is the general public. We note that none of the experts testifying in this case stated that plaintiff's alcoholism was due to the inherent characteristics and peculiarities of his employment in the brewery industry as a production worker responsible for running a machine. Dr. Smith, for example, testified that "Mr. Gacioch would have most likely become an alcoholic anyway and his drinking outside of work eventually [was] far greater than during work."

(continued)

Dr. Rauch opined that individuals who are predisposed to alcoholism, like plaintiff herein, are likely to become an alcoholic no matter where they work.

We are unable to determine from the opinion of the WCAB whether it understood the applicable legal standard and what facts it specifically relied upon in reaching its conclusion that plaintiff's alcoholism was compensable under the Workers' Disability Compensation Act.

We therefore remand this case to the WCAB for its statement of the law and the specific facts relied upon to support its conclusion.

CASE QUESTIONS

1. What was Stroh's free-beer policy?
2. Who negotiated the policy?
3. Was Mr. Gacioch predisposed to alcoholism?
4. Is alcoholism a disease?
5. Is alcoholism a disease that originated in the workplace in this case?
6. What additional factual information is needed to resolve the case?
7. How do you feel about the free-beer policy? Can you foresee other issues of liability for Stroh beyond workers' compensation?

C O N S I D E R . . .

19.2   Walt Disney Company hired Victor Salva in 1994 to direct the movie *Powder*. He had been convicted in 1988 of molesting a 12-year-old boy and served fifteen months of a three-year sentence, completing his parole in 1992. The criminal acts occurred while Mr. Salva was directing a short horror film, *Clownhouse*. *Powder* was a film about high-school children, but Disney indicates it did not know of Mr. Salva's background. What liability did Disney have had Mr. Salva molested an actor?

Fault Is Immaterial

The fact that an injury occurs in the workplace is enough for recovery. Employee negligence, employer precautions, contributory negligence, and assumption of risk are generally not issues in workers' compensation cases.

Employees versus Independent Contractors

Workers' compensation applies to employees but not to independent contractors. Employees are those who are present at the workplace on a regular basis, paid a wage, and supervised. **Independent contractors** are those who work on a job basis, work irregular hours, and are not supervised by the employer. A backhoe operator working daily from 5 A.M. to 1 P.M. for a plumbing company and paid a weekly wage is an employee. A backhoe operator hired and paid on a per-job basis is an independent contractor. A more complete discussion of employee status can be found in Chapter 18 and on p. 742.

Re: Curbing Workplace Violence

Over the past few years, the following workplace shootings have made international news:

- Alfred Eugene Miller—August 5, 1999—killed three of his co-workers with an automatic weapon in Billingly, Alabama
- Bryan Uyesugi—Xerox repairman—November 2, 1999—shoots and kills seven of his co-workers during a team meeting

Most employers believe that workers' compensation systems apply to such incidents. However, there are an increasing number of decisions that impose liability on employers to the relatives of deceased employees for their failure to provide adequate security. For example, in a 1994 Texas case, a court imposed liability on an employer who was aware that a man had made threats and took no extra precautions. In *Vaughn* v. *Granite City Steel,* 576 N.E.2d 874 (Ill. App. 1991), an employee's family was awarded $415,000 following the employee's shooting death in the employer's parking lot when the jury determined that security was "grossly inadequate." A North Carolina jury awarded $7.9 million to the families of two employees killed by another employee who the employer knew had a history of violence.

The *National Law Journal* offers the following checklist for employers in reducing workplace violence:

1. Issue a policy statement that the company intends to prevent workplace violence.

2. Implement a zero tolerance policy for threats and violent acts.

3. Encourage employees to report threats and violent acts.

4. Take remedial action, including discharge, against those employees who make threats or show violence in the workplace.

5. Protect employees who report acts and threats of violence.

6. Have procedures in place for taking action if customers become violent.

7. Refer employees for assistance and counseling if they exhibit signs of strain or violent tendencies.

8. Do more comprehensive background checks on potential employees.

9. Provide training on recognizing violent tendencies—offer to all employees.

10. Implement some type of survey or anonymous reporting system.

11. Create a team to assess issues of security and violence.

Source: Donald F. Burke, "When Employees Are Vulnerable, Employers Are, Too. Bosses Can Be Liable for Workplace Violence When They Fail to Prevent a Known Threat." This article is reprinted from January 17, 2000 edition of the New York Law Journal. © 2000 NLP IP Company. All rights reserved. Further duplication without permission is prohibited.

Benefits

Workers' benefits can be grouped into three different categories: medical, disability, and death. Medical benefits include typical insurance-covered costs such as hospital costs, physician and nursing fees, therapy fees, and rental costs for equipment needed for recovery.

Disability benefits are payments made to compensate employees for wages lost because of a disability injury. The amount of benefits is based on state statutory figures. Most states base disability benefits on an employee's average monthly wage, and they also specify a maximum amount. State statutes also generally have a list of **scheduled injuries,** which will carry a percentage disability figure. For example, loss of a body part is a typical injury. In Arizona, the disability amount for a lost thumb is 55 percent of the average monthly wage for fifteen months (Ariz. Rev. Stat. § 23-1044). For a lost foot, the amount is 55 percent of the average monthly wage for fifty months. Total disability is also defined by statute. Workers who have total disability are generally entitled to two-thirds of their

Re: Who Is an Employee and Who Is an Independent Contractor?

For purposes of social security taxes, unemployment compensation, worker's compensation, and, of course, principal liability, the definition of an employee versus that of independent contractor is critical. Many businesses apply a label of "independent contractor" to agents doing work for them, but the activities of those independent contractors may, in fact, make them employees. Employers should check the status of those who are doing work so that they are paying wage taxes properly and have adequate coverage for liability.

In a 1987 revenue ruling, the Internal Revenue Service (IRS) listed the twenty factors for determining whether an employer has sufficient control to label an agent an employee (servant) as opposed to an independent contractor. Those twenty factors are:

1. Instructions on worker's performance of duties versus independent work

2. Training by co-workers versus no training required

3. Integration of worker's services into the business

4. Services benefit the business personally as opposed to a group of employers

5. Worker hires, supervises, and pays his own assistants (more likely to be independent contractor)

6. Continuing relationship as opposed to one-time projects

7. Set hours of work as opposed to flexibility

8. Full time required as opposed to working for others

9. Doing work on the employer's premises as opposed to own facilities

10. Order of tasks established by employer

11. Oral or written reports as opposed to independence

12. Payment by hour, week, or month as opposed to payment by project or task

13. Payment of business or travel expenses as opposed to personal payment as part of fee

14. Furnishing tools and materials versus furnishing own supplies

15. Use of and payment for outside facilities

16. Realization of profit or loss by worker

17. Working for more than one firm at a time

18. Making services available to the general public

19. Employer's right to discharge versus employee processes and procedures

20. Worker's right to terminate without consequences such as breach of contract

These twenty complex and burdensome factors were consolidated by the ninth circuit in *Donovan* v. *Sureway Cleaners*, 656 F.2d 1368 (9th Cir. 1981) into six factors:

1. Degree of control over workers

2. Whether the worker has the risk of profit or loss

3. Whether the worker makes an investment

4. Level of skills and training for the work

5. Permanency of worker

6. Integration into economics of the business

One consistent factor not present in any of the evaluation lists is what the employer labels the worker—the label is irrelevant, and courts are consistent in their unwillingness to accept employers' labels of workers.

A new proposal for determining independent contractor status will require a focus on the degree of control as the key factor. The Internal Revenue Service has a new training manual for examiners who determine whether workers are independent contractors or employees. The twenty-point test is simply background information for the ultimate determination under the guidelines, which are designed to look at the overall relationship of the business with the worker.

average monthly salary for the period of the disability. Total disability usually includes the loss of both eyes or both hands or complete paralysis.

Some injuries suffered by workers are not listed in statutes. Those not specifically described in statutes are called **unscheduled injuries.** The amount allowed for unscheduled injuries is discretionary and an area of frequent litigation.

Death benefits are paid to the family of a deceased employee and generally include burial expenses. In addition, survivors who were economically dependent on an employee are also paid benefits. The amount of death benefits is generally some percentage of the average monthly salary; for example, a surviving spouse might be entitled to a 35 percent benefit.

Forfeiture of the Right of Suit

The majority of states require employees to forfeit all other lawsuit rights in exchange for workers' compensation benefits. Employees receive automatic benefits but lose the right to sue their employers for covered incidents. Some states even prohibit employees from suing their co-workers, but these states allow suits against negligent co-workers for damages. In addition, some states allow family members to sue employers for direct injury to themselves. In those states, a spouse could bring a lawsuit against an employer for loss of consortium (marital companionship).

Third-Party Suits

If an employee is injured by a machine malfunction while on the job, the employee is covered by workers' compensation. However, there is an issue of product liability in the accident. If suit is brought against the machine's manufacturer for product liability, any recovery goes first to the employer to compensate for the cost of the employee's benefits. In other words, third-party recovery is first used to reimburse the employer.

Administrative Agency

Every state has some administrative agency responsible for the administration of claims, hearings, and benefits. In most states, this agency holds hearings for claims, and its decision is appealable in the same manner as any other agency decision.

The procedure for compensation requires employees to file claims with the agency along with medical documentation for the claim. Most claims are paid without contest; but, when there is a challenge to a decision, a hearing with evidence and testimony is held.

Insurance

All states with workers' compensation systems require employers to be financially responsible for benefits under their systems. Employers can show financial responsibility by (1) maintaining an insurance policy, (2) obtaining a policy through the state agency, or (3) offering evidence of sufficient assets and resources to cover potential claims and benefits.

Problems in Workers' Compensation Systems

Increasingly, states and employers are experimenting with reforms to workers' compensation systems. Concerns focus on fraud that stems from incentives in the system. For example, medical benefits in workers' compensation are better than most medical plans. Because nearly all disability payments are tax-free, employees may be living on close to 90 percent of what they lived on (after taxes) before their disability.

Some doubts exist about the legitimacy of many complaints. A janitor moonlighting for HGO, Inc., hurt his little finger while on the job. He collected $16,800 in disability payments over the next three years, even though he was able to continue his regular day job as a police officer.

Suggested reforms have included the elimination of certain claims, as in California, where attempts are being made to eliminate "mental stress" from workers' compensation coverage. Georgia no longer makes lifetime disability payments but instead limits their duration to eight years. Other states have hired more investigators to detect fraud. Companies are also attempting to cut costs by using staff doctors or by returning employees to other jobs that can be done despite an injury.

The nature of work in the United States has changed and continues to change rapidly. The workers' compensation systems were established during the Industrial Revolution, when the injuries sustained were primarily the types of factory and machinery accidents we traditionally associate with workers' compensation claims. However, the majority of jobs in the United States are now in service industries, and the nature of work-related injuries has changed from sudden-accident types to ongoing, progressive problems that are more expensive to treat and correct. For example, the repetitive hand and arm motions of computer keyboard operators cause an injury, often called carpal tunnel syndrome, to word processors, journalists, reservationists, and cashiers. This injury requires expensive surgery and results in many lost work days, if not new job assignments. Such injuries, often called repetitive stress injuries (RSIs), are the basis of pending lawsuits by workers against keyboard and equipment manufacturers.

The office environment itself is presenting new and difficult-to-control health-related problems for workers. As the chapter opening data indicates, ergonomics is a rapidly growing field that examines the design of work areas and office equipment to minimize such worker injuries as repetitive motion syndromes and back problems. Architects and engineers are working together to design buildings that eliminate the so-called sick-building syndrome, in which poor air quality or the lack of fresh air circulation increases the incidence of illness and causes other symptoms in office workers.

Explore the Americans with Disabilities Act:
http://janweb.icdi.wvu.edu/kinder

A final issue in workers' compensation is the relationship between the state systems and the Americans with Disabilities Act (see Chapter 20), which prohibits discrimination against employees with disabilities and requires accommodation of employer facilities to permit disabled persons to work. Traditionally, when an accident caused disability, an employee collected payment in lieu of being rehired. An issue that arises as the systems of laws interact is whether an employer is required to rehire a disabled employee.

LABOR UNIONS

History and Development of Labor Legislation

When workers first began organized efforts to improve their employment situations, the courts were particularly harsh. In early eighteenth-century England, participants in organized labor were prosecuted for criminal conspiracy, which is the crime of organizing with others for the commission of another crime. The first case in the United States (*Commonwealth* v. *Pullis* [1806]) also charged organized laborers with criminal conspiracy that resulted in a criminal conviction for laborers participating in a strike.

Many employers tried to stifle the labor union movement by requiring their employees to sign **yellow-dog contracts,** which prohibited employees from joining unions. With these attempts came the beginning of protective labor legislation.

The Railway Labor Act of 1926

Review the Railway Labor Act:
http://www.law.cornell.edu/uscode/45/151.html

The **Railway Labor Act** was the first federal legislation to address union issues specifically, but its application was limited to labor relations in the railroad industry. However, the act did establish some basic rights for railway employees that would later carry over to general labor statutes. Railway employees were given the right to form and join unions without employer interference. The employees were also given the right to bargain collectively with their employers. The underlying purpose of the act was to promote peaceful labor-management relations. This act is still effective today and was expanded to cover airline employees in 1936.

The Norris-LaGuardia Act of 1932

Review the Norris-LaGuardia Act:
http://www.law.cornell.edu/uscode/29/101.html

In addressing the problem of courts issuing injunctions to stop union strikes, the **Norris-LaGuardia Act** prohibited the injunction as a remedy in labor disputes and eliminated the common law application of the use of government to control employer-employee relations. Under the act, the government (including the courts) became a neutral force in labor-management disputes.

There were some exceptions to the anti-injunction rule. Violent strikes could be enjoined, provided that it was clear there would be or had been violence and that public officers could not control the violence and any resulting damage. Even in these cases, a hearing allowing all parties to attend was required before a violent strike could be enjoined.

The Wagner Act

Review the National Labor Relations Act:
http://www.law.cornell.edu/uscode/29/151.html

The **Wagner Act,** also known as the **National Labor Relations Act** (NLRA) of 1935, gave employees the right to organize and choose representatives to bargain collectively with their employers. Further, it established the **National Labor Relations Board** (NLRB), which had two functions: to conduct union elections and to investigate and remedy unfair labor practices.

The Taft-Hartley Act: The Labor-Management Relations Act of 1947

Visit the NLRB:
http://www.nlrb.gov

Over President Truman's veto, Congress passed the **Taft-Hartley Act,** which was a response to the public's concern about too many strikes, secondary boycotts, and the unrestrained power of union officials. The act amended the Wagner Act by applying the principle of unfair labor practices to unions as well as employers. Strikes to force employers to discharge nonunion employees, secondary boycotts, and strikes over work assignments were prohibited as unfair labor practices. Employees were also given the right to remove a union they no longer wanted as their representative. The act also contains provisions that allow the president to invoke a **cooling-off period** of bargaining before a strike that threatens to imperil the public health and safety can begin. This power has been used by presidents in transportation and coal strikes.

Review the Taft-Hartley Act:
http://www.law.cornell.edu/uscode/29/141.html

The Landrum-Griffin Act: The Labor-Management Reporting and Disclosure Act of 1959

Review the Landrum-Griffin Act:
http://www.law.cornell.edu/uscode/29/ch11.html

Visit the AFL-CIO:
http://www.aflcio.org

As unions grew, evidence of corruption and undemocratic procedures within them came to light. The **Landrum-Griffin Act** was passed to ensure employee protection within union organizations. The act gave union members a bill of rights, required certain procedures for election of officers, prescribed financial reporting requirements for union funds, and established criminal and civil penalties for union misconduct.

Today there are nearly 450 active unions in the United States, from the Screen Actors Guild to the Airline Pilots Association. However, over 75 percent of these unions are affiliated with the AFL-CIO (the American Federation of Labor and Congress of Industrial Organizations), the giant that resulted from the merger of the two original labor unions in 1955. These unions, however, make up only 13.9 percent of today's workforce (a steady figure since 1998), compared to the 35 percent in 1955.

Union Organizing Efforts

Employees make the decisions of whether a union will represent them and, if so, which will serve as their representative. This process is called selecting a bargaining representative, and the NLRB has strict procedures for such selection. The NLRB carefully chooses how employees will be grouped together so that they share common interests.

The Collective Bargaining Unit

The first step in union organization is the establishment of a collective bargaining unit. The **collective bargaining unit** is a group of employees recognized by the NLRB as appropriate for exclusive representation of all employees in that group. Collective bargaining units are determined by a commonality of interest. Because all employees will be represented by a union voted in by the majority, the NLRB requires the unit to consist of homogeneous employees. A union petitioning for representation must carefully define its bargaining unit because a petition will be dismissed if the NLRB determines that the bargaining unit is inappropriate. For example, some bargaining units consist of entire plants of workers, whereas others are specialized units within a plant, such as the maintenance staff or the line workers in an assembly plant. For some national companies, the bargaining unit is all employees, whereas for other national firms the bargaining unit is one particular plant or store. Obviously, defining the bargaining unit is crucial, for it can control whether the union will gain enough votes. A union might not have enough votes in a particular plant, but it could have enough votes if the unit were company-wide; in such cases, the union will want the larger bargaining unit.

In determining the appropriateness of a collective bargaining unit, the NLRB considers the following factors:

1. The type of union and its history of bargaining—types of employees and types of industries
2. The duties, wages, and skills of the employees
3. How the bargaining unit fits in an employer's structure
4. The wishes of the employees

CONSIDER...

19.3   Trump Taj Mahal Associates (Trump), a limited partnership, operates the Trump Taj Mahal Casino Resort in Atlantic City, New Jersey. The entertainment department at the Taj includes stage technicians, convention lounge technicians, and entertainment event technicians.

Trump maintains a list of approximately forty on-call or "casual" employees who perform technical functions and who are called upon on an intermittent basis to perform the same functions as regular technical employees when there are not enough regular employees to perform the work. Trump maintains this casual list because the casino industry is regulated by the New Jersey Casino Control Commission, which requires employees to be "badged" or licensed. The lists and pre-qualifications enable Trump to draw from a pool of technicians who have already met certain procedural and technical requirements in order to satisfy short-term labor needs.

During the first eleven months of operation at the Taj Mahal Casino, Trump operated its entertainment department with three full-time stage technicians and five full-time convention lounge technicians, and did not employ any part-time technicians. About March 1, 1991, Trump increased its staff to twenty-eight full-time technicians and ten regular part-time technicians by hiring from the casual list. Trump selected those employees from the casual list who had worked the most hours at the Taj and had the necessary skills for the particular job. A number of casuals who had worked a considerable number of hours in the past remained on the casual list.

The 1990 list of casual employees entitled "entertainment technicians" shows that those employees worked from 30 to 952 hours during that year. The regional director found that during 1990 the casuals worked an average of 379 hours during the year, or approximately 7 hours a week, and during early 1991 the casuals worked an average of 119 hours, or approximately 17 hours a week.

The employees sought to have their collective bargaining unit expanded to include both the full-time technicians and the on-call (i.e., casual) employees.

Is this a proper bargaining unit? [*Trump Taj Mahal Associates Ltd.* v. *International Alliance of Theatrical Stage Employees*, 306 N.L.R.B. No. 57 (1992)]

The Petition, Cards, and Vote

Once the collective bargaining unit is set, the union, employees, or employers can file a petition for exclusive representation of employees within a unit. The petition is filed with the NLRB and must be supported by at least 30 percent of the members of the bargaining unit. The 30 percent support is shown by signed and dated **authorization cards** filled out by employees. These authorization cards must be signed willingly, and the employee must understand the effect of the cards.

Once the cards are filed, an employer has two choices. First, the employer can voluntarily recognize the union. If the union has obtained authorization cards from a majority of the employees, such recognition is wise unless the employer knows of some illegal conduct used to obtain the cards. If there was illegal conduct, the employer can always file a charge with the NLRB, which will conduct an investigation.

If the authorization cards do not amount to a majority of employees in the bargaining unit, the employer can insist on a formal election. In an election, the employees vote for or against the union that petitions for representation and has the right to campaign and distribute literature before an upcoming election. However, employers can prohibit oral campaigning during work hours and can restrict literature distribution both during and, to a degree, before and after work hours. Employer restrictions cannot be made with the intent of eliminating the possibility of the union. The restrictions must be reasonable and serve some purpose, such as controlling litter and requiring employees to do their work during their work hours.

The election is conducted by secret ballot by the NLRB. A simple majority of the employees must vote in favor of the union for certification to occur.

CONSIDER...

19.4   The Republic Aviation Plant in Suffolk County, New York, was holding a union certification election. The plant had adopted, well before any union activity, a rule against soliciting that provided: "Soliciting of any type cannot be permitted in the factory or offices."

An employee who had been reminded of the rule persisted in passing out cards to fellow employees during his lunch hour. Three other employees wore UAW-CIO union buttons to work and were asked to remove them, but they refused. All four employees were discharged. The four filed a complaint with the NLRB on grounds they had been denied the right to distribute information about the union. Did the plant rule violate the employees' right to distribute information? [*Republic v. NLRB,* 324 U.S. 793 (1945)]

Certification

Once **certification** of a union has taken place, either because of the employer's consent or a valid election, that union has the exclusive right to represent the employees in all contract negotiations. An employer who refuses to deal with the certified union can be forced to by an injunction obtained by the NLRB.

After a union has been certified, an election for a new union cannot be held for twelve months from the time of certification. If the union signs a collective bargaining agreement, no union certification election can be held until the collective bargaining agreement expires. These limitations on elections and certifications prevent chaos in the workplace that would result from constant changeovers in union representation. Exhibit 19.3 summarizes the steps in the union certification process.

EXHIBIT 19.3
Union Certification

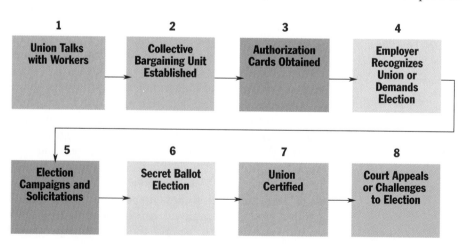

1	2	3	4
Union Talks with Workers	Collective Bargaining Unit Established	Authorization Cards Obtained	Employer Recognizes Union or Demands Election

5	6	7	8
Election Campaigns and Solicitations	Secret Ballot Election	Union Certified	Court Appeals or Challenges to Election

Nonunion Members in the Certified Workplace Although the NLRA gave unions the right to exist, it also gave workers the right to a choice. Workers are not required to join unions and cannot be coerced into supporting union action. Attempts by a union to force its members to participate in strikes and other union activities are considered unfair labor practices. The following case is an interpretation of whether a union coerced employees into participating in a strike.

CASE 19.4

Pattern Makers' League of North America, AFL-CIO v. *NLRB*
473 U.S. 95 (1985)

You Can't Make Me Strike If I Want to Work

FACTS

The Pattern Makers' League of North America, AFL-CIO, provides in its constitution that union members may not resign during a strike or when a strike is imminent. The league fined ten of its members who, in violation of this provision, resigned during a strike and returned to work. The NLRB held that the union rule violated section 8(b) of the NLRA, which provides: "It shall be an unfair labor practice for a labor organization or its agents—(1) to restrain or coerce (A) employees in the exercise of rights guaranteed herein. . . ."

The union rule (League Law 13) provides: "No resignation or withdrawal from an Association or from the League shall be accepted during a strike or lockout, or at a time when a strike or lockout appears imminent."

The U.S. court of appeals for the Seventh Circuit enforced the board's order. The league appealed.

JUDICIAL OPINION

POWELL, Justice

Section 7 of (the NLRA) grants employees the right to "refrain from any or all (concerted) activities." The general right is implemented by § 8(b)(a)(A). The latter section provides that a union commits an unfair labor practice if it "restrains or coerces employees in the exercise" of their § 7 rights. When employee members of a union refuse to support a strike (whether or not a rule prohibits returning to work during a strike), they are refraining from "concerted activity." Therefore, imposing fines on these employees for returning to work "restrains" the exercise of their § 7 rights. Indeed, if the terms "refrain" and

"restrain or coerce" are interpreted literally, fining employees to enforce compliance with any union rule or policy would violate the Act.

Language and reasoning from other opinions of this Court confirm that the Board's construction of § 8(b)(1)(A) is reasonable. In *Scofield* v. *NLRB,* 394 U.S. 423 (1969), the Court upheld a union rule setting a ceiling on the daily wages that members working on an incentive basis could earn. The union members' freedom to resign was critical to the Court's decision that the union rule did not "restrain or coerce" the employees within the meaning of § 8(b)(1)(A).

The decision in *NLRB* v. *Textile Workers,* 409 U.S. 213 (1972) also supports the Board's view that Section 8 prohibits unions from punishing members not free to resign. There, thirty-one employees resigned their union membership and resumed working during a strike. We held that fining these former members "restrained or coerced" them. In reaching this conclusion, we said "the vitality of Section 7 requires that the member be free to refrain in November from the actions he endorsed in May."

League Law 13 curtails (the) freedom to resign from full union membership. Nevertheless, the petitioners (League) contend that League Law 13 does not contravene the policy of voluntary unionism imbedded in the Act. They assert that this provision does not interfere with workers' employment rights because offending members are not discharged, but only fined. We find this argument unpersuasive, for a union has not left a "worker's employment rights inviolate when it exacts (his entire) paycheck in satisfaction of a fine imposed for working." Congress in 1947 (with the Taft-Hartley Act) sought to eliminate

(continued)

completely any requirement that the employee maintain full union membership. Therefore, the Board was justified in concluding that by restricting the right of employees to resign, League Law 13 impairs the policy of voluntary unionism.

Petitioners . . . argue that the proviso to § 8(b)(1)(A) expressly allows unions to place restrictions on the right to resign.

Neither the Board nor this Court has ever interpreted the proviso as allowing unions to make rules restricting the right to resign. Rather, the Court has assumed that "rules with respect to the . . . retention of membership" are those that provide for expulsion of employees from the union. Accordingly, we find no basis for refusing to defer to the Board's conclusion that League Law 13 is not a "rule with respect to the retention of membership" within the meaning of the proviso.

The petitioners next argue that the legislative history of the Taft-Hartley Act shows that Congress made a considered decision not to protect union members' right to resign.

The legislative history does not support this contention. The "right to resign" apparently was included in the original House bill to protect workers unable to resign because of "closed shop" agreements. Union constitutions limiting the right to resign were uncommon in 1947.

The Board has the primary responsibility for applying "the general provisions of the Act to the complexities of industrial life." Where the Board's construction of the Act is reasonable, it should not be rejected. . . . [T]he Board has consistently construed § 8(b)(1)(A) as prohibiting the imposition of fines on employees who have tendered resignations invalid under a union constitution. Therefore we conclude that the Board's decision here is entitled to our deference.

Affirmed.

CASE QUESTIONS

1. What union rule is at issue?
2. Does the rule affect union membership?
3. Can the union enforce the rule?
4. What is the purpose of § 8(b)(1)(A)?
5. Does the legislative history support a prohibition of the union rule?

Union Contract Negotiations

Once a union is certified as the employees' representative, one of its major roles is to obtain a contract or **collective bargaining agreement** between employer and employees. This section discusses the roles of the parties in obtaining that agreement.

Good-Faith Bargaining

Visit the U.S. Department of Labor:
http://www.dol.gov

Section 8(d) of the NLRA defines **good-faith bargaining** as a mutual obligation of employer and union to meet at reasonable times, confer in good faith on employment issues, and execute a written agreement reflecting their oral agreement. Both parties must bargain with an open mind and the sincere intent of reaching an agreement.

Whether there has been good-faith bargaining on the part of the parties depends on each situation and on various factors, such as the reasonableness of the position taken, repeated failures to show up at bargaining sessions or to be available for them, and holding steadfast to a predetermined position during the course of bargaining. Most of the cases dealing with the problem of failure to bargain in good faith are the result of employer conduct.

Subject Matter of Good-Faith Bargaining

Two types of subject matters can be discussed during bargaining: (1) mandatory or compulsory subject matter and (2) permissive subject matter. As to the former, the NLRA describes **mandatory bargaining terms** as those dealing with "wages,

EXHIBIT 19.4 **Usual Topics for a Collective Bargaining Agreement**

COLLECTIVE BARGAINING TOPICS

Recognition of the union	Employee grievances
Wages	Length of agreement/expiration date
Work hours	Incentive plans
Vacations	Union announcements (bulletin board rights)
Sick leave	Definition of terms
Seniority	Leaves of absence
Insurance	Drug testing
Pension/retirement plans	

hours, and other terms and conditions of employment." Obviously, the amount to be paid as wages is included but so also are related issues, such as merit pay, vacations, overtime, work hours, leaves, and pay days. Exhibit 19.4 lists the usual topics covered in a collective bargaining agreement.

One of the issues that has been a subject of good-faith bargaining is the two-tier wage structure. In the past, unions have agreed to two-tier wage structures in order to help financially struggling firms survive. Now, however, many corporations are raising the issue in bargaining in order to control wage increases. For example, in the airline industry, pilots with the greatest seniority work under a wage structure that affords them very high pay levels. But more pilots are available now than before, and some new pilots are willing to enter employment under a different wage and age scale. Although there are many management and labor concerns about a two-tier structure, it appears to be a good-faith bargaining topic that will remain an issue for both groups.

Permissive subject matters, in contrast to compulsory subject matters, would be those the parties are required to negotiate but on which they need not reach an agreement. A strike vote of employees before a strike starts is an example of a permissive subject. Any topic that does not directly concern employer-employee relations is a permissive subject. A refusal to bargain on a permissive subject is not, however, an unfair labor practice; a refusal to bargain on mandatory subject matter *is* an unfair labor practice.

Some subjects are "unbargainable." Employers and employees cannot bargain to give away statutory rights—for example, the procedures for certifying a union. Nor can they bargain about having a **closed shop,** which requires employees to be union members before they can be hired. Such shops are illegal under the Taft-Hartley Act.

C O N S I D E R . . .

19.5 Determine whether the following subjects are mandatory, permissive, or nonbargainable:

- Insurance plans
- Maternity leaves
- Plant rules
- Subcontracting procedures

- Strikes
- Layoffs
- Union bookkeeping procedures
- Meal periods

Failure to Bargain in Good Faith

Failure to bargain on mandatory subject matter is an **unfair labor practice,** which is conduct prohibited by statute or NLRB decision. If there is a failure to bargain on a mandatory topic, a charge can be brought and the NLRB can proceed with a complaint.

C O N S I D E R . . .

19.6   E. I. Du Pont de Nemours & Company is renegotiating its contract with the International Brotherhood of Du Pont Workers. Two issues have arisen during the course of bargaining. The union has asked Du Pont to release a map that was developed as a result of a Du Pont study on its toxic waste locations. The second issue was Du Pont's implementation of its business ethics policy and its application to union members without its being a subject of bargaining. Must the map be released? Is this a mandatory subject? Must the application of the ethics policy be negotiated? [*Du Pont* v. *International Bhd. of Du Pont Workers,* 301 N.L.R.B. No. 14 (1991)]

Protected Concerted Activities

The following forms of union activities are protected under the NRLA as being necessary for union members to give each other "mutual aid and protection," as it is expressed in the statute.

Public Advertisements

Ads and handbills that explain the union's issues and position are permitted and can be an effective tool for obtaining boycotts, yet another protected activity in which employees encourage customers not to deal with their employer until the strike is settled.

Unions and Organizing via E-Mail[1]

A battle over the use of company e-mail systems in unionization efforts has emerged in a case involving Pratt & Whitney, a division of United Technologies, and the Florida Professional Association (FPA). The FPA used the company's e-mail system to contact the company's 2,000 engineers. When Pratt & Whitney blocked usage of the company e-mail system, FPA filed an unfair labor practice with the NLRB. While the charge has been withdrawn, the issue remains unresolved.

Companies consider the use of their system a trespass that opens up the company system to sabotage and spamming. Union organizers call the resistance a block to convenient communication by union organizers. One California court has sided with employers and called the use of company e-mail systems for unionization efforts a trespass.

ETHICAL ISSUES 19.2

There is a new trend among employers to rank employees as part of their annual performance evaluations. For example, Ford Motor Company has 18,000 managers who are grouped into sets of 30 to 50. Of each group, 10 percent must be assigned an "A" grade, 80 percent must be assigned a "B" grade, and 10 percent must be given a "C" grade. Those with the bottom grades are then eased out of the company. Those with a "C" grade cannot be given a pay raise, and those with a "C" grade for two years in a row are demoted or terminated. There are no exceptions made for any of the groups, but Ford did cut back on the "C" requirement to 5 percent for 2001.

Other companies with grading systems include Sun Microsystems. Employees given a "C" there are given ninety days to improve. If they do not improve, they are given one chance to resign and take a severance package or risk termination.

Cisco Systems has established a goal of getting rid of one of every twenty employees with the focus being on employees given substandard performance evaluations.

GE has a 20-70-10 plan for ranking employees. GE follows a carrot approach in that it rewards the top 20 percent so well that few ever leave the company. GE uses the 10 percent group to terminate employees, and it terminates about 8,000 management and professional employees each year. Jack Welch has noted that these in the 10 percent would end up leaving the company anyway because they are unhappy in not performing and GE just makes the inevitable decision for them early.

Workers' rights groups call the systems inhumane. Some say that instead of motivating employees to do better, the result is that they are demoralized and do worse or leave the company.

Do these systems violate any laws? Are they a mandatory collective bargaining issue? Are you comfortable with them from the perspective of business ethics?

Source: Del Jones, "More Firms Cut Workers Ranked at the Bottom to Make Way for Talent," *USA Today*, 30 May 2001, 1B, 2B.

Other employer issues include the fact that e-mail by union organizers must be read during breaks and not on the job, a distinction impossible to monitor. Just as union organizers cannot come into a factory or workplace to talk union during work hours, the use of e-mail is an invasion of the working hours and time of the employer.

In *Timekeeping Systems, Inc.*, 323 N.L.R.B. No. 30 (1997), the NLRB ruled that sending an e-mail message to fellow employees was a protected "concerted activity" and thus applied the same rules of other forms of worker interaction and communication to electronic commerce. However, companies have been resisting such application because of the problems with security as well as the need to monitor employee e-mails for offensive and harassing content.

Picketing

A union currently recognized as a certified collective bargaining agent can **picket** an employer, but picketing for recognition of a union is not permitted.

Nonunion Activities

Employees who, for example, are not unionized but stage a walkout are engaged in protected concerted activities as well. There is a right of employees to discuss employer issues among themselves. A prohibition on such discussions would cut off the possibility of unionization. The following case illustrates the protection of nonunion employees and their concerted activity and provides an answer for the chapter opening "Consider."

CASE 19.5

Aroostook County Regional Ophthalmology Center v. *NLRB*
81 F.3d 209 (D.C. 1996)

Gossip as a Protected Concerted Activity

FACTS

Dr. Craig Young, an ophthalmologist, founded the Aroostook County Regional Ophthalmology Center (ACROC or Company) which employs several physicians as well as a a significant nursing and clerical staff. The ACROC employee manual provides as follows, "No office business is a matter for discussion with spouses, family or friends. All grievances are to be discussed in private with the office manager or physicians. It is totally unacceptable for an employee to discuss any grievances within earshot of patients."

Dr. Young changed the work schedules of an ophthalmic technician and three nurses in order to accommodate an emergency surgery. The four employees were not pleased with their new schedules and were overheard by patients as they complained in the front office. Dr. Young fired the employees. The employees said they were just exercising their right to organize as employees.

Dr. Young then met with the employees and offered to reinstate them if they agreed to bring all complaints directly to him and stopped gossiping as they worked. Two of the employees agreed to the conditions and were rehired. The two who refused to agree to the conditions filed charges with the NLRB alleging that ACROC committed an unfair labor practice under Section 8 of the NLRA in disallowing discussion and curbing their right to organize.

The administrative law judge (ALJ) found that the employees were not engaged in protected concerted activity when they were fired and that their termination did not violate the NLRA, but the NLRB (the Board) reversed and found that it was protected concerted activity. Both the ALJ and the NLRB also found that the conditions placed on rehiring violated employees' right to talk among themselves about dissatisfaction with their employment conditions and did violate the NLRA. ACROC appealed.

JUDICIAL OPINION

EDWARDS, Chief Judge

The board adopted the ALJ's determination that ACROC's rule prohibiting employees from discussing "office business" with "spouses, families or friends" was a prima facie violation of section 8(a)(1) of the NLRA because "employees have the right to seek the assistance of, among others, 'spouses, families or friends' on matters pertaining to their terms of employment." There can be no quarrel with the claim that, under the NLRA, employees are generally free to discuss the terms and conditions of their employment with family members and friends. But to concede this point lends nothing to the analysis in this case, because the rule in question in no way precludes employees from conferring with or seeking support from family and friends with respect to matters directly pertaining to the employees' terms and conditions of employment. Rather, ACROC argues that the rule—when read in context—is designed only to prevent employees from discussing patient medical information with persons outside of the office. This construction of the rule is supported by the rule's placement in the Office Policy Manual as the last sentence of a long discussion regarding patient confidentiality in which the term "office business" is used to refer to confidential patient medical information, and there is nothing to suggest the contrary.

The board does not question ACROC's right to require employees to protect patient privacy; so if the rule means what the company says, it follows that its promulgation and enforcement were not unfair labor practices. In the absence of any evidence that ACROC is imposing an unreasonably broad interpretation of the rule upon employees, the Board's determination to the contrary is unjustified. If an occasion arises where ACROC is attempting to use the rule as the basis for imposing questionable restrictions upon employees' communications, the employees may seek review of the Company's actions at that time. However, the rule on its face is not unlawful.

According to the Board, ACROC's rule requiring grievances to be discussed in private with Company managers or physicians "is an overly broad restriction of the employees' statutory right to engage in protected concerted activity." The Board does not doubt that ACROC may prohibit employees from disturbing patients by discussing grievances in their presence; rather, the Board faults ACROC for failing to draft the rule more artfully to make it clear that the ban relates only to staff discussions that occur in "immediate patient care areas." Once again, the Board has imagined horrible hypothetical situations (which, if true, might violate the Act) that have nothing much to do with the rule as written and enforced by the Company. Even worse, in assessing ACROC's rules, the Board has failed to properly take account of the employment context in which this case arises.

The Supreme Court has noted that, "in the context of the health-care facilities, the importance of the employer's interest in protecting patients from disturbance cannot be gain-said." ACROC does not operate large facilities where the distinction between patient and nonpatient areas can easily be discerned. In a small medical practice, such as ACROC's, the employer has unique concerns about employees acting in a way that might disturb patients; in this situation, a rule prohibiting employees from voicing complaints in front of patients is neither surprising nor unlawful. Although the Board suggested that ACROC's rule might discourage "employees from any discussion of grievances for fear that a patient may overhear the discussion," this speculation is fanciful at best, and it has nothing to do with the case at hand. The opportunities for the employees to discuss grievances (both in or near the workplace out of the earshot of patients, and after working hours) are obvious and numerous. There is nothing in the record suggesting that employees have been barred from using these opportunities to discuss their mutual concerns. If and when ACROC's employees find that the rule is being unreasonably enforced so as to infringe on protected activities, they may seek appropriate redress.

As to the rule's other element, that employees' discussions of grievances be conducted in private conversations with management level staff, we find that such a requirement seems designed merely to provide a reasonable and fair procedure for resolution of employment disputes. This requirement is entirely reasonable when read in context with the accompanying provision that employees should not discuss grievances within earshot of patients, implying that the rule's purpose is to ensure that employee complaints are presented to management in an appropriate manner without the disruption to ACROC's clients. Moreover, the Board has again presented no evidence indicating that the rule has actu-

ally been applied to restrict employees from discussing grievances among themselves or from otherwise engaging in lawful protected concerted activity. In fact, ACROC affirmatively encouraged discussions among employees that did not include physicians or management, for example, through the implementation of "teams" of nurses and technicians. Accordingly, the Board's findings to the contrary on these points must be overturned.

In assessing ACROC's actions in firing the four employees, both the ALJ and the Board focused on whether the employees' actions to which Dr. Young objected constituted protected concerted activity. The ALJ found no evidence to suggest that the employees "engaged in any of the behavior at issue 'with the object of initiating group action,'" and, thus, found that the employees' behavior was not protected by the NLRA. The Board reversed the ALJ's determination, noting that, because the employees were discussing vital elements of their employment, such communications are protected by the NLRA because they could "spawn collective action."

We neither understand nor endorse the Board's "spawning" theory, which, on its face, appears limitless and nonsensical. Certainly, discussion of employment conditions, such as scheduling, could be protected concerted activity; however, adoption of a per se rule that any discussion of work conditions is automatically protected as concerted activity finds no good support in the law.

In this case, an argument could be made that the employees' complaints were concerted activity because the topic of schedule changes is potentially relevant to a labor dispute, particularly because schedule changes had been the subject of ongoing discussions between ACROC employees and management. However, we need not resolve this issue, because, even assuming, arguendo, that the fired employees were engaged in a form of concerted activity when they lamented their schedules in the presence of patients, their conduct was not protected concerted activity.

In the setting of a small medical office, it is inherently bad conduct for medical staff personnel to complain about their jobs while they are tending patients. Indeed, it cannot be doubted that such misconduct is extremely serious, because it has the great potential to unsettle patients. It is hardly reassuring for a patient, concerned over his or her personal well-being, to be confronted by a medical attendant who seems distracted because of displeasure over the work environment. Such grousing in the presence of

(continued)

patients is plainly inconsistent with the reasonable demands of caretaking, and, therefore, it cannot constitute protected activity. Therefore, ACROC's firing of the employees who engaged in such behavior did not violate the NLRA, and the Board's finding is unjustified.

Although the Company committed no unfair labor practice when it fired the employees, substantial evidence supported the Board's determination that the conditions imposed by the Company for rehire were unlawful. Dr. Young conditioned the rehiring of the fired employees upon their agreement that they would bring all of their complaints to Dr. Young, that they would avoid any discussions with particular employees, and that they would cease all "gossiping and complaining" amongst themselves. The effect that these conditions likely would have had on the employees' ability to engage in behavior that is protected under the NLRA is so obvious that ACROC has not seriously attempted to defend the legitimacy of the conditions as imposed. Instead, ACROC claims that the employees should have understood that Dr. Young did not really mean what he said; rather, they should have understood

that his harsh terms were intended to impose the more reasonable demand that employees discuss their grievances outside the presence of patients. Neither the ALJ nor the Board were convinced by this argument, and neither are we. Thus, the finding of the Board that ACROC violated the NLRA by placing improper conditions on the rehiring of fired employees must stand.

Reversed in part. Affirmed in part.

CASE QUESTIONS

1. What is the difference between discussing patient matters outside of work with family and friends and employment matters discussed with the same groups?

2. Are the employees engaged in concerted activity as they discuss their schedule issues in the medical office?

3. Were the conditions for rehiring valid?

4. Is employee discussion of grievances within earshot of patients a protected activity?

The Strike

The **strike** is the best known and most widely used economic weapon of unions. A strike is a work stoppage because employees no longer report to work. As a result of replacement threats and downsizing, strikes in 1995 were at a level one-half of that in 1985. In 1995, there were only 32 strikes involving 1,000 or more workers. Insecurity and fear about their jobs and companies' ability to continue operation during a strike have curbed the use of this economic weapon by union members.

The Shareholders

In recent years, unions have developed a new economic tool—contacting institutional shareholders and board members to put public pressure on corporate officers to work with unions. These public-attention tactics have been effective.

C O N S I D E R . . .

19.7 Local 760 of the Teamsters Union called a strike against fruit packers and warehouses doing business in Yakima, Washington. The firms sold their apples to the Safeway chain of retail grocery stores. Local 760 began a consumer boycott against the firms, with union members picketing outside the forty-six Safeway stores in Seattle. The pickets wore placards that read: "To the Consumer: Non-Union Washington State apples are being sold at this store. Please do not purchase such apples. Thank you. Teamsters Local 760, Yakima, Washington."

The pickets distributed handbills outside the stores and to the public generally. A typical handbill read:

DON'T BUY WASHINGTON STATE APPLES

The 1960 Crop of Washington State Apples is being Packed by Non-Union Firms. Included in this non-union operation are twenty-six firms in the Yakima Valley with which there is a labor dispute. These firms are charged with being

UNFAIR

by their employees who, with their union, are on strike and have been *replaced by non-union strikebreaking workers* employed under substandard wage scales and working conditions.

In justice to these striking union workers who are attempting to protect their living standards and their right to engage in good-faith collective bargaining, we request that you

DON'T BUY WASHINGTON STATE APPLES

Teamsters Union Local 760
Yakima, Washington

This is not a strike against any store or market.

Is the action taken by Local 760 an unfair labor practice, or is it a proper secondary boycott? [*NLRB* v. *Fruit Packers*, 377 U.S. 58 (1964)]

Unfair Employee Practices

While employees have certain rights protected under Section 8 of the NLRA, they are also prohibited from engaging in activities that are classified as unfair labor practices.

Hot Cargo Agreements

A clause in a collective bargaining agreement in which an employer agrees not to use, handle, or sell certain products, or use the services of an unfair employer is a **hot cargo agreement.** In some cases, the agreement prohibits an employer from handling the products of a nonunion company. Because these types of agreements are rarely voluntary, they have been prohibited, with some exceptions for the clothing and construction industries.

The Slowdown

A **slowdown** is an economic tool that interrupts the employer's business but falls short of a stoppage or strike. Slowdowns usually occur when employees refuse to perform work or use certain equipment that is in violation of their collective bargaining agreement with the employer. For example, in early 1999, American Airlines pilots staged a slowdown by calling in sick, known as a sickout. After more than 1,000 flights per day were canceled, a federal court ordered the pilots to halt their slowdown.

Featherbedding

Featherbedding is payment for work not actually performed. It is an unfair labor practice for a union to negotiate an agreement that requires an employer to pay for work that was not actually performed. For example, some bricklayers' unions

BUSINESS STRATEGY

In 1982, Gilmore Steel, located in Oregon, was a company suffering losses. Management tried to get concessions from the union for pay reductions, and a year-long strike resulted. Gilmore hired replacement workers and then developed a plan for a management-led buyout. The Employee Share Ownership Plan offered the newly hired employees 100 percent ownership in what would become Oregon Steel. Top management in the firm would own less than 5 percent, and employees as shareholders would receive 20 percent of the company's pretax earnings in profit sharing. Management perks and time clocks were eliminated, and shop-floor workers were placed on the same compensation system as the top executives.

© Danny Lehman/CORBIS

The initial years were tough; it looked as if the buyout was a failure. By 1988 the company had gone public. The employees' shares that were once worth only pennies climbed to $38 a share. Oregon Steel's profits per ton are now the best in the industry. It has no debt, and productivity is double the steel industry average. Average pay for workers is $50,000, which is 25 percent above the industry average, and many of the employees are millionaires.

Did the union do the right thing with the strike? Are employees better off without union representation? What if the gamble the employees took had not worked?

at one time required payment for a minimum number of bricks even though the work might not have actually involved that many bricks. Other examples include paying workers for tasks completed by someone else. An agreement requiring payment for the task of pressing in a clothing manufacturing firm would be unfair if the clothing was sometimes shipped unpressed.

Secondary Boycotts

If the **primary boycott** is a protected economic weapon of unions, the concept of a **secondary boycott** is a complex and difficult one. Nonetheless, asking a third party not to handle an employer's goods appears to be unfair only if there is coercion involved. Further, the request cannot be one to stop work—it must be simply a request that the third party cease doing business with the employer.

Employer Rights

Freedom of Speech

Employers have the right to give information to employees about unions and the results of union organization. The speech of employers cannot be controlled by the NLRB unless the speech is accompanied by some unlawful conduct, such as a threat of physical force or a promise of benefit. For example, an employer who threatens the loss of jobs if employees join the union is not protected by the free speech rule. An employer who tells employees that it will not negotiate with a union is also not protected by the free speech rule. These types of statements are considered unfair labor practices, as is the promise of temporary benefits.

Right-to-Work Laws

Section 14(b) of the Taft-Hartley Act is in some ways a protection for employers as well as for employees. This section outlaws the closed shop, which, as discussed earlier, is a business that requires union membership before an employee can be

EXHIBIT 19.5 Management Dos and Don'ts in the Unionization Process

DO	DON'T
1. Tell employees about current wages and benefits and how they compare to other firms.	1. Promise employees pay increases or promotions if they vote against the union.
2. Tell employees you will use all legal means to oppose unionization.	2. Threaten employees with termination or discriminate when disciplining employees.
3. Tell employees the disadvantages of having a union (especially cost of dues, assessments, and requirements of membership).	3. Threaten to close down or move the company if a union is voted in.
4. Show employees articles about unions and negative experiences others have had elsewhere.	4. Spy or have someone spy on union meetings.
5. Explain the unionization process to your employees accurately.	5. Make a speech to employees or groups at work within twenty-four hours of the election (before that, it is allowed).
6. Forbid distribution of union literature during work hours in work areas.	6. Ask employees how they plan to vote or if they have signed authorization cards.
7. Enforce in a consistent and fair manner disciplinary policies and rules.	7. Urge local employees to persuade others to vote against the union (such a vote must be initiated solely by the employee).

Source: R. L. Mathis and J. H. Jackson *Human Resource Management*, 8th ed, p. 533. © 1997. Reprinted with permission of South-Western College Publishing, a division of International Thomson Publishing. Fax 800 730-2215.

hired. Based on this section of Taft-Hartley, states can pass **right-to-work laws** that give people the right to work without having to join a union. About half the states have right-to-work statutes.

Exhibit 19.5 is a summary of management dos and don'ts when faced with an upcoming union election.

Right to an Enforceable Collective Bargaining Agreement

Once a union is certified and agrees to the terms of a collective bargaining agreement, an employer has the right to expect that the terms of that agreement will be honored. So long as the employer abides by its terms, the union and other employees cannot stage a strike during the period of its effectiveness. Neither can the agreement be abandoned by employees during this period.

Economic Weapons of Employers

Employers have economic weapons that can be used in response to employee economic weapons.

Plant and Business Closings

In response to union certifications and strikes, some employers have opted to close the affected plants. In some cases, employers have abandoned the business altogether. It is clear that these shutdowns and closures are strong economic weapons, and their legality under the federal labor law scheme has some restrictions. In *Textile Workers Union* v. *Darlington Manufacturing Co.*, 380 U.S. 263 (1965), the Supreme Court ruled that an employer has the right to terminate his or her entire business for any reason. Even if the reason for the closing is vindictiveness toward the union, neither the NLRB nor the courts can require an employer to stay in business. However, the closing of part of a business (such as a particular plant or one store) is subject to review as a possible unfair labor practice.

Employers cannot use a temporary closing with a promise of reopening after a union is defeated in an election. Further, employers cannot stage a **runaway shop,** which is when work is transferred to another plant or a new plant is opened to carry the workload of the old plant.

The concern of the NLRB in the closing of one plant is that employees in other plants, fearful that their plant will be closed, will fail to exercise their rights to unionize. For a plant closure to be an unfair labor practice, the evidence must show that the closure was done with the intent of curbing unionization in that and other plants owned by the employer. The "purpose and effect" of the closing must have been foreclosure of union activity.

Although the NLRB and courts have recognized the legitimate right of a business to close a particular store or plant, there are many concerns about plant closings. Plant-closing legislation has been proposed since the early 1970s, and Congress, some states, and even some cities have enacted such legislation. The purpose of plant-closing legislation is to take the sting out of an employer's closing of a plant by a variety of mechanisms, such as requiring that employees and community and state officials be given thirty days' notice of the closing, requiring employee severance packages to provide for employees during the time they need to find other employment, or requiring the employer to be partially responsible for the workers' unemployment compensation.

Review the Worker Adjustment and Retraining Notification Act:
http://www.law.cornell.edu/uscode/29/2101.html

Federal plant-closing legislation is called the **Worker Adjustment and Retraining Notification Act of 1988** (WARN). Under this act, employers with 100 or more workers are required to give workers sixty days' advance notice of plant shutdowns that would affect at least fifty workers and of layoffs that would last more than six months and affect one-third of the workers at the site. There are some exceptions to the sixty-day notice requirement, such as unforeseeable circumstances and seasonal, agricultural, and construction businesses. Penalties for violations include back pay and benefits for employees for each day of violation and up to $500 per day for each day notice was not given.

Some businesses voluntarily provide for the workers at a closed plant by giving them hiring priority at their other plant locations, but unions often argue that the ability to close a plant gives employers too much power at the bargaining table and that employers can coerce communities into giving them special tax treatment or additional services by threatening to close a facility. On the other hand, employers often argue that plant-closing laws unfairly restrict their ability to manage their resources and can force a business to continue operating an unprofitable unit rather than face the costs of closing.

Plant Flight

One result of the increased globalization of business is the increasing availability of lower-cost labor pools outside the United States. When union demands increase business costs beyond what management feels will allow a firm to remain competitive, plants are closed and work is transferred to plants outside the United States. The global marketplace provides management with a bargaining tool that becomes difficult for unions to address. Demands for wage increases, more benefits, and better working conditions are often met with a plant closing in the United States and a plant opening in another country where the labor pool is large and the wages low.

The Lockout

A **lockout** is an employer's economic weapon in which the employer refuses to allow employees to work. Lockouts have been recognized by the U.S. Supreme

Bleeding from losses of $4.45 billion for 1991, General Motors Corporation (GM) announced on February 24, 1992, that it would close 21 plants over the next few years and named 12 plants it would close in 1992, affecting over 16,300 workers. GM is the nation's largest manufacturer, and the $4.45 billion loss was the largest ever in U.S. corporate history. Robert C. Stempel, GM's then chairman, said the United States was in an unusually deep automotive slump: "The rate of change during the past year was unprecedented. And no one was immune to the extraordinary events which affected our lives and the way in which we do business."*

More than 3,400 workers at GM's North Tarrytown, New York, plant were laid off by 1995. The Tarrytown plant manufactured GM's minivans: the Chevrolet Lumina, the Pontiac Trans Sport, and the Oldsmobile Silhouette. The minivan, originally designed in the United States, was executed by GM with a wide stance and a sloping, futuristic nose. Projections were that 150,000–200,000 of the vans would be sold annually. Instead, sales reached only 100,000 per year, which represented one-half of the Tarrytown plant's capacity. Dealers maintained that the shape of the van was too avant-garde for significant

ETHICAL ISSUES 19.3

sales. "It looks like a Dustbuster," noted a GM manager anonymously.† GM executives acknowledged that building one model per plant was a sloppy and expensive way to do business.

Tarrytown United Auto Workers had negotiated with GM in 1987 to get the minivan plant. The union members voted for innovative and cooperative work rules to replace expensive union practices. Also, state and local governments contributed job training funds, gave tax breaks, and began reconstruction of railroad bridges to win the minivan production plant.

When unions (workers) and governments make payments in exchange for promises from a manufacturer to locate a plant in a particular area, should the plant owner have an obligation to continue operations? Did GM just make a business decision to stop losses? Should workers and governments absorb business risks such as a poor-selling minivan?

*Doran P. Levin, "GM Picks 12 Plants to Be Shut as It Reports a Record U.S. Loss," *New York Times,* 25 February 1992, A1.

†Doran P. Levin, "Vehicle's Design Doomed Van Plant," *New York Times,* 26 February 1992, C4.

Court as a legitimate measure to help an employer avoid a strike at an economically damaging time. The reason for an employer's lockout must be economic. A lockout to discourage union membership, therefore, is an unfair labor practice.

Conferring Benefits

Employers can use benefits as economic weapons; the only restriction is the timing of those benefits. Offering them too close to an election can be an unfair labor practice. Conferring benefits on a temporary basis to gain an advantage (precluding the union) is also an unfair labor practice.

Bankruptcy

Bankruptcy has become a solution for many business problems, labor problems among them. When strikes extend for long periods of time, the financial well-being of the firms affected can deteriorate, often to the degree that some firms declare bankruptcy. The type of bankruptcy proceedings that are initiated will determine the fate of labor contracts. In a reorganization, the contracts remain in force. In a straight bankruptcy, the workers stand in line (although with some priority) to collect any wages due and any contributions made to the firm's retirement plan. Bankruptcy can be an escape for a firm, but the bankruptcy laws themselves limit the availability of this economic weapon. The firm must still meet the tests for declaring bankruptcy, so the weapon is not entirely optional.

Exhibit 19.6 provides a summary of labor weapons, rights, and unfair practices.

EXHIBIT 19.6   **Union Disputes: Economic Weapons and Rights of Employers and Employees**

ECONOMIC WEAPONS	RIGHTS	UNFAIR LABOR PRACTICES
Employer 1. Business closing Plant closings 2. Lockouts 3. Right to confer benefits (timing)	1. Freedom of speech 2. Demand election (30%)	1. Refusal to bargain in good faith 2. Refusal to bargain on a mandatory issue 3. Yellow-dog contracts 4. Violation of collective bargaining agreement 5. Interference with joining union 6. Timing of benefits 7. Observation of union activities 8. Domination of labor union 9. Discrimination in promotion of union members 10. Blacklisting
Employee 1. Strike 2. Ads 3. Picketing 4. Boycotts 5. Shareholders	1. Freedom of speech 2. Right to union representation upon investigation 3. Right to join union 4. Right of members to adequate representation 5. Right to union office	1. Violation of collective bargaining agreement 2. Secondary boycotts 3. Payment for union cards 4. Coercion or discrimination in union membership 5. Causing an employer to pay excessive wages—featherbedding 6. Hot cargo agreements

INTERNATIONAL ISSUES IN LABOR

Today's labor market is considerably different from the market that existed at the time of the enactment of federal labor legislation. Both operations within the United States and operations in other countries are affected by a new international labor force. Domestic operations must be certain that all employees from other countries are documented workers. International operations present numerous ethical and public policy issues in the conditions and operations of plants in other countries with different labor standards.

Immigration Laws

The **Immigration and Naturalization Act** (INA), the **Immigration Reform and Control Act of 1986** (IRCA) and the **Immigration Act of 1990** (8 U.S.C. Section 11101 *et seq.*) are the federal laws that apply to immigrants in the United States and impose requirements on employers in the United States that employ immigrants.

Before hiring a new employee, employers must verify that the employee is either a U.S. citizen or is permitted to work in the United States. All non-U.S. citizens must have an I-9 form on file with the employer. Form I-9 provides complete information about noncitizens and requires the employer to verify the information provided through an Alien Registration Card, commonly called a "green card." Verification of U.S. Citizenship can be provided by a driver's license from a state in the United States, a Social Security card, or a U.S. passport. If someone with a foreign accent can provide evidence of U.S. citizenship, the employer is not permitted to question further or require additional documentation, for such would be an act of discrimination under the immigration laws.

Because of lobbying from the high-tech industries, Congress passed the **American Competitive and Workforce Investment Act of 1998** in order to increase the number of "highly skilled" workers who could enter the United States and stay for purposes of employment. The number of such highly skilled workers was increased on a sliding scale through the year 2000, and then Congress passed the **American Competitiveness in the Twenty-First Century Act of 2000** to increase the number of such workers through 2004. Also, under this statute, employers cannot lay off American employees within the ninety days following their submission of an application for entrance and employment of one of these highly skilled workers. Referred to as *H-1B professionals,* their pay scale is also controlled by the act so that their pay is equivalent to what an equally skilled U.S. worker would earn in the same position. This constraint on wages eliminates the incentive for companies to hire all foreign H-1B professionals at much lower salaries.

Working Conditions and International Labor Law

With the passage of GATT and NAFTA, a worldwide market has been emerging. Today's management is also different from the management in power at the time the labor laws were passed. From true adversaries always looking for a way to "win," labor and management have grown to realize the importance of a working relationship that seeks to avoid confrontation and the use of economic weapons. In 1978, Congress passed the **Labor Management Cooperation Act** (29 U.S.C. § 171), which was designed to use the Federal Mediation and Conciliation Service (set up in 1947) to encourage alternative solutions to labor disputes. The act allocated funds for the study of ways to increase communication and encourage the use of collective bargaining as a means for resolving disputes.

Review the Labor Management Cooperation Act:
http://www.law.cornell.edu/uscode/29/171.html

Companies today are using more conciliatory methods to balance the economic interests of management and labor. Labor law is moving from the strike to arbitration in advance of disputes.

Solutions to labor issues have been occurring outside the statutory protections and rights given in the massive union legislation of earlier decades. Employees have turned to an individual posture and have sought the protection of individual rights, such as employment at will (see Chapter 18 for a discussion of these individual rights).

Many employers have reorganized their companies around teams of employees to empower them and use their knowledge and ideas. Motorola and Ford are among team companies that let workers make key decisions. A concern raised by unions is that the mixing of labor and management violates the Wagner Act. For example, teams of workers at Electromation, Inc., in Elkhart, Indiana, determined that a wage hike should be skipped because of heavy losses and instead developed programs for absenteeism.

Foreign competition has made it difficult for unions to organize and for laborers to command more than minimum wage. Mexican laborers earn 70 cents an

Review the International Covenant on Economic, Social, and Cultural Rights:
http://www.umn.edu/humanrts/instree/b2esc.htm

Visit the International Labour Organization (ILO):
http://www.ilo.org

hour, and Chinese workers 8 cents. During the 1980s, 500,000 of the 1.2 million U.S. manufacturing jobs that were sent abroad were apparel and textile jobs.

The United Nations Commission on Human Rights has developed the International Covenant on Economic, Social, and Cultural Rights. This covenant includes the right to work; join trade unions; enjoy leisure; earn a decent living; and receive education, medical care, and social security. Although this international covenant would carry with it the protections outlined in this chapter for U.S. workers, there is no enforcement of the covenant. Its real strength comes through documentation and disclosure of its violation.

One of the most successful organs of the United Nations is the International Labour Organization (ILO). This commission, founded in 1920, continues to work to develop such principles as the right to work, to join trade unions, and to have a safe work environment. Member nations submit reports on their nation's status and compliance with the standards of the ILO agreement.

Some nations have individual legislation for their workers. For example, Germany has its own OSHA-like agency for the administration of worker safety issues. Germany's agency has existed longer than OSHA and tends to experience more self-reporting by employers.

The National Labor Committee (NLC), an activist group, periodically releases information on conditions in foreign factories and the companies utilizing those factories. In 1998, the NLC issued a report that Liz Claiborne, Wal-Mart, Ann Taylor, Esprit, Ralph Lauren, J. C. Penney, and K-Mart were using subcontractors in China that use Chinese women (between the ages of 17 and 25) to work 60–90 hours per week for as little as 13–23 cents per hour. The Chinese subcontractors do not pay overtime, house the workers in crowded dormitories, feed them a poor diet, and operate unsafe factories.

Levi Strauss & Co. pulled its manufacturing and sales operations out of China in 1993 because of human rights violations but announced in 1998 that it would expand its manufacturing there and begin selling clothing there. Peter Jacobi, the president of Levi Strauss & Co., indicated that it had the assurance of local contractors that they would adhere to the company's guides on labor conditions. Jacobi stated, "Levi Strauss is not in the human rights business. But to the degree that human rights affect our business, we care about it."

The Mariana Islands are currently a site of investigation by the Department of Interior for alleged indentured servitude of children as young as 14 in factories there. Wendy Doromal, a human rights activist, issued a report that workers there have tuberculosis and oozing sores. Approximately $820 million worth of clothing items are manufactured each year on the islands, which are a U.S. territory. Labels manufactured there include The Gap, Liz Claiborne, Banana Republic, J. C. Penney, Ralph Lauren, and Brooks Brothers.

U.S. companies' investments in foreign manufacturing in major developing nations like China, Indonesia, and Mexico have tripled in fifteen years to $56 billion, a figure that does not include the subcontracting work. In Hong Kong, Singapore, South Korea, and Taiwan, where plants make apparel, toys, shoes, and wigs, national incomes have risen from 10 percent to 40 percent of American incomes over the past ten years. In Indonesia, since the introduction of U.S. plants and subcontractors, the portion of malnourished children in the country has gone from one-half to one-third.

In a practice that is widely accepted in other countries, children, ages 10 to 14, labor in factories for fifty or more hours per week. Their wages enable their families to survive. School is a luxury, and a child attends only until she is able to work in a factory. The Gap, Levi Strauss & Co., Esprit, and Leslie Fay have all been listed in social responsibility literature as exploiting their workers.

In the United States, the issue of sweatshops came to the public's attention when it was revealed that talk-show host Kathie Lee Gifford's line of clothing at Wal-Mart had been manufactured in sweatshops in Guatemala and CBS ran a report on conditions in Nike subcontractor factories in Vietnam and Indonesia. The reports on Nike's factories issued by Vietnam Labor Watch included the following: women required to run laps around the factory for wearing nonregulation shoes to work; payment of subminimum wages; physical beatings, including with shoes, by factory supervisors; and most employees are women between the ages of 15 and 28. Philip Knight, CEO of Nike, included the following in a letter to shareholders:

> *Q: Why on earth did Nike pick such a terrible place as Indonesia to have shoes made? A: Effectively the U.S. State Department asked us to. In 1976, when zero percent of Nike's production was in Taiwan and Korea, Secretary of State Cyrus Vance asked Charles Robinson . . . to start the U.S.-ASIAN Business Council to fill the vacuum left by the withdrawal of the American military from that part of the world. . . . Chuck Robinson accepted the challenge, put together the council and served as Chairman of the U.S. side for three years. Mr. Robinson was a Nike Board member at that time as he is today. . . . "Nike's presence in that part of the world," according to a senior state department official at that time, "is American foreign policy in action."*

Nike sent former U.N. Ambassador Andrew Young to its overseas factories in order to issue a report to Knight, the board, and the shareholders. Young did tour factories but only with Nike staff and only for a few hours. Young issued the following findings:

- Factories that produce Nike goods are "clean, organized, adequately ventilated, and well-lit."
- No evidence of a "pattern of widespread or systematic abuse or mistreatment of workers."
- Workers don't know enough about their rights or about Nike's own code of conduct.
- Few factory managers speak the local language, which inhibits workers from lodging complaints or grievances.
- Independent monitoring is needed because factories are controlled by absentee owners and Nike has too few supervisors on site.

On October 18, 1997, there were international protests against Nike in thirteen countries and seventy cities. On October 13, 1997, 6,000 Nike workers went on strike in Indonesia followed by a strike of 1,300 in Vietnam.

On November 8, 1997, an Ernst & Young audit about unsafe conditions in a Nike factory in Vietnam was leaked to the *New York Times* and made front-page news.

Michael Jordan, NBA and Nike's superstar endorser, agreed to tour Nike's factories in July 1998, stating, "the best thing I can do is go to Asia and see for myself. The last thing I want to do is pursue a business with a negative over my head that

I don't have an understanding of. If there are issues . . . if it's an issue of slavery or sweatshops, [Nike executives] have to revise the situation."

From June 1997 to January 1998, Nike distributed 100,000 plastic "code of conduct" cards to plant workers. The cards list workers' rights. Nike's performance dropped. Its stock price has dropped from a 1996 high of $75.75 per share to a March 1998 low of $43 per share. Retailers canceled orders so that sales decreased 3 percent for 1997. Nike reduced its labor force by 10 to 15 percent or 2,100 to 3,100 positions.

Press for Change and Global Exchange, an activist group, made the following demands of Nike in 1998:

1. *Accept independent monitoring by local human rights groups to ensure that Nike's Code of Conduct is respected by its subcontractors.* The GAP has already accepted independent monitoring for its factories in El Salvador, setting an important precedent in the garment industry. If Nike were to accept such monitoring in Indonesia, it would set a similar positive precedent in the shoe industry, making Nike a true leader in its field.

2. *Settle disputes with workers who have been unfairly dismissed for seeking decent wages and work conditions.* There are dozens of Indonesian workers who have been fired for their organizing efforts and thousands who have been cheated out of legally promised wages. Nike must take responsibility for the practices of its subcontractors and should offer to reinstate fired workers and repay unpaid wages.

3. *Improve the wages paid to Indonesian workers.* The minimum wage in Indonesia is $2.26 a day. Subsistence needs are estimated to cost at least $4 a day. While Nike claims to pay double the minimum wage, this claim includes endless hours of overtime. We call on Nike to pay a minimum of $4 a day for an eight-hour day and to end all forced overtime.

The American Apparel Manufacturers Association (AAMA), which counts 70 percent of all U.S. garment makers in its membership as well, has a database for its members to check labor compliance by contractors. The National Retail Federation has established the following statement of Principles on Supplier Legal Compliance (now signed by 250 retailers):

1. *We are committed to legal compliance and ethical business practices in all of our operations.*
2. *We choose suppliers that we believe share that commitment.*
3. *In our purchase contracts, we require our suppliers to comply with all applicable laws and regulations.*
4. *If it is found that a factory used by a supplier for the production of our merchandise has committed legal violations, we will take appropriate action, which may include canceling the affected purchase contracts, terminating our relationship with the supplier, commencing legal actions against the supplier, or other actions as warranted.*
5. *We support law enforcement and cooperate with law enforcement authorities in the proper execution of their responsibilities.*
6. *We support educational efforts designed to enhance legal compliance on the part of the U.S. apparel manufacturing industry.*

BIOGRAPHY

AARON FEUERSTEIN: AN ODD CEO

Methuen, Massachusetts, is a small city not unlike the Bedford Falls of *It's a Wonderful Life*. Over the years, the working-class town on the border of New Hampshire and Massachusetts has come to rely on the good heart of one man. While Aaron Feuerstein may not look much like Jimmy Stewart, he is the protagonist of a Christmas story every bit as warming as the Frank Capra movie—or the Polartec fabric made at his Malden Mills.

On the night of December 11, just as Feuerstein was being thrown a surprise 70th birthday party, a boiler at Malden Mills exploded setting off a fire that injured 27 people and destroyed three of the factory's century-old buildings. Because Malden Mills employs 2,400 people in an economically depressed area, the news was as devastating as the fire. According to Paul Coorey, the president of Local 311 of the Union of Needletrades, Industrial and Textile Employees, "I was standing there seeing the mill burn with my son, who also works there, and he looked at me and said, 'Dad, we just lost our jobs.' Years of our lives seemed gone."

When Feuerstein arrived to assess the damage to a business his grandfather had started 90 years ago, he kept himself from crying by thinking back to the passage from *King Lear* in which Lear promises not to weep even though his heart would "break into a thousand flaws." "I was telling myself I have to be creative," Feuerstein later told the *New York Times*. "Maybe there's some way to get out of it." Feuerstein, who reads from both his beloved Shakespeare and the Talmud almost every night, has never been one to run away. When many other textile manufacturers in New England fled to the South and to foreign countries, Malden Mills stayed put. When a reliance on fake fur bankrupted the company for a brief period in the early '80s, Feuerstein sought out alternatives.

What brought Malden Mills out of bankruptcy was its research-and-development team, which came up with a revolutionary fabric that was extremely warm, extremely light, quick to dry, and easy to dye. Polartec is also ecologically correct because it is made from recycled plastic bottles. Clothing made with Polartec or a fraternal brand name, Synchilla, is sold by such major outdoor

clothiers as L. L. Bean, Patagonia, Eastern Mountain Sports, and Eddie Bauer, and it accounts for half of Malden's $400 million-plus in 1995 sales.

Even though the stock of a rival textile manufacturer in Tennessee, the Dyersburg Corp., rose sharply the day after the fire, L. L. Bean and many of Malden's other customers pledged their support. Another apparel company, Dakotah, sent Feuerstein a $30,000 check. The Bank of Boston sent $50,000, the union $100,000, the Chamber of Commerce in the surrounding Merrimack Valley $150,000. "The money is not for Malden Mills," says Feuerstein. "It is for the Malden Mills employees. It makes me feel wonderful. I have hundreds of letters at home from ordinary people, beautiful letters with dollar bills, $10 bills."

The money was nothing to the workers compared to what Feuerstein gave them three days later. On the night of December 14, more than 1,000 employees gathered at the gym of Central Catholic High School to learn the fate of their jobs. Feuerstein entered the gym from the back, and as he shook the snow off his coat, the murmurs turned to cheers. The factory owner, who had already given out $275 Christmas bonuses and pledged to rebuild, walked to the podium. "I will get right to my announcement," he said. "For the next 30 days— and it might be more—all our employees will be paid their full salaries." What followed, after a moment of awe, was a scene of hugging and cheering that would have trumped the cinematic celebration for *Wonderful Life's* George Bailey.

True to his word, Feuerstein has continued to pay his employees in full, at a cost of some $1.5 million a week and at an average of $12.50 an hour—already one of the highest textile wages in the world. "I really haven't done anything," says Feuerstein. "I don't deserve credit. Corporate America has made it so that when you behave the way I did, it's abnormal."

Update and Aftermath: On January 29, 1996, Mr. Feuerstein extended the pay guarantee for another 30 days as he continued the process of rebuilding the plant. He continued the employees' medical benefits for 90 days. Mr. Feuerstein would continue the pay guarantee through June 1996, when nearly all employees were back to full-time

(continued)

status. Those employees who were not fully employed were those displaced by the rebuilt factory's new technology. Mr. Feurstein developed on-site retraining and retooling for these employees, and Malden Mills has a near 100 percent outplacement record for these former employees. The grand reopening of the fully rebuilt plant was in September 1997. Polartec and the company continue to perform well. However, Mr. Feuerstein did enjoy his first litigation by employees in 1998 over employment practices. He admitted to being stunned by the suit. Near the end of 2001, Malden Mills was teetering near bankruptcy. The union, about to negotiate a new agreement, indicated it would agree to whatever Mr. Feuerstein wanted in order to save the company.

ISSUES

1. Why did Mr. Feuerstein choose to continue paying his employees?

2. How has his company survived when his wages are the highest in the world?

Source: Steve Wulf, "The Glow from a Fire," *Time,* January 8, 1996, p. 49. © Time Inc. Reprinted with permission. Further reproduction prohibited.

The U.S. Department of Labor has recommended the following to improve the current situation:

1. *All sectors of the apparel industry, including manufacturers, retailers, buying agents and merchandisers, should consider the adoption of a code of conduct.*
2. *All parties should consider whether there would be any additional benefits to adopting more standardized codes of conduct [to eliminate confusion resulting from a proliferation of different codes with varying definitions of child labor].*
3. *U.S. apparel importers should do more to monitor subcontractors and homeworkers [the areas where child labor violations occur].*
4. *U.S. garment importers—particularly retailers—should consider taking a more active and direct role in the monitoring and implementation of their codes of conduct.*
5. *All parties, particularly workers, should be adequately informed about codes of conduct so that the codes can fully serve their purpose.*

By 2000, Nike, still experiencing campus protests for its overseas plant conditions, began to experience economic impact as the students protested their colleges and universities signing licensing agreements with Nike. For example, Nike ended negotiations with the University of Michigan for a six-year multi-million dollar licensing agreement because Michigan joined the consortium. Phil Knight withdrew a pledge to make a $30 million donation to the University of Oregon because the university also joined the consortium. Nike continues to support the Fair Labor Association, an organization backed by the White House with about 135 colleges and universities as members, but its membership there has not halted the consortium's activities.[2]

SUMMARY

What wage and hour protections exist for employees?

- Fair Labor Standards Act—federal law that regulates minimum wage and overtime pay

- Minimum wage—federal minimum hourly rate of pay

- Overtime pay—rate of 1½ times the hourly rate for hours over 40-per-week worked

- Equal Pay Act—equal wages for equal work regardless of gender

- Child labor standards—restrictions on hours and types of work for children under the age of 18

What protections exist for safety in the workplace?

- Occupational Safety and Health Act—federal law setting and enforcing workplace safety standards

- Occupational Safety and Health Administration—federal agency responsible for safety in the workplace

- Drug testing—screening of employees for impairment

What happens when a worker is injured in the workplace?

- Workers' compensation—state-by-state system of employer strict liability for injuries of workers on the job; the few exceptions to recovery include self-inflicted injuries

What is the Social Security system, and what benefits does it provide?

- Social Security Act—federal law establishing disability, beneficiary, and retirement benefits

- Federal Insurance Contributions Act (FICA)—statute establishing system for withholding contributions for social security benefits

Are workers entitled to pensions, and are they regulated?

- Employment Retirement Income Security Act (ERISA)—federal law regulating employer-sponsored pension plans

- FASB 106—accounting disclosure for a company's employee retirement obligations

What rights do unemployed workers have?

- Unemployment compensation—federal program handled by states to provide temporary support for displaced workers

- Workers' compensation—system of no-fault liability for employees injured on the job

How are labor unions formed, and what is their relationship with employees?

- Railway Labor Act—first federal law providing union protections

- Norris-LaGuardia Act—federal law prohibiting injunctions to halt strikes

- National Labor Relations Act (Wagner Act)—federal law authorizing employee unionization

- Labor Management Relations Act (Taft-Hartley Act)—federal law limiting union economic weapons

- Labor-Management Reporting and Disclosure Act (Landrum-Griffin Act)—federal law regulating union membership and organizations

- NLRB—National Labor Relations Board, federal agency responsible for enforcing labor laws

- Collective bargaining unit—group of employees recognized as appropriate to have an exclusive bargaining agent

- Authorization cards—employee-signed support for election

- Certification—recognition of union as exclusive bargaining agent

- Collective bargaining agreement—exclusive rights agreement between employer and employee in a collective bargaining unit

- Good-faith bargaining—requirement that parties negotiate terms in earnest

- Unfair labor practice—conduct by labor or management prohibited by statute

- Concerted activities—union-sponsored activities

- Picketing—public appearance of striking union members

- Boycotts—refusal to work for or to buy from or handle products of an employer

- Slowdown—workers report to job but do not operate at full speed

- Right-to-work laws—right to work at a company without being required to join a union

- Worker Adjustment and Retraining Notification Act (WARN)—federal law requiring employers to give sixty days' notice of plant shutdowns

- Lockout—employer closes plant or business so workers cannot work

- Runaway shop—employer transfers work to nonunion plants

QUESTIONS AND PROBLEMS

1. Ruth Saludes is a Harvard University graduate with a master's degree in linguistics and education. She had worked for several years in various counseling and teaching positions. Feeling "burned out," Ms. Saludes decided she wanted to be a carpenter and left her position at the Free Clinic of Tucson, although she had no skill or experience in construction or carpentry. She filed for unemployment compensation but refused to take counseling jobs and insisted on a carpentry job. Her unemployment was cut off when she refused to take a counseling job. Ms. Saludes brought suit. Is she entitled to compensation? [*Saludes* v. *Department of Employment Security,* 628 P.2d 63 (Ariz. 1981)]

2. H. M. Wilson hired H. J. High as the general contractor for the construction of one of its stores in a shopping center in Tampa, Florida. The shopping center was owned and operated by Edward J. DeBartelo Corporation and had eighty-five tenants. The tenants paid a minimum rent plus a percentage of gross sales for maintenance of the common areas in the shopping center.

H. J. High's workers went on strike, posted themselves at the four entrances to the shopping center, and distributed handbills to customers. The handbills asked customers not to shop at any of the eighty-five stores until their dispute with High was settled. Is this an unlawful secondary boycott? [*Edward J. DeBartelo Corp.* v. *NLRB,* 463 U.S. 147 (1983)]

3. Joe Ortiz was discharged from Magma Copper Co. for absenteeism. He missed the last shift of work before he was fired because he was temporarily in custody following an arrest for a criminal offense. He filed for unemployment but was denied. Mr. Ortiz said he notified Magma that he was missing because of being detained in jail. The unemployment compensation agency says Mr. Ortiz is disqualified for benefits because he was fired for misconduct. Who is right? [*Magma Copper* v. *Department of Employment Security,* 625 P.2d 935 (Ariz. 1981)]

4. Donald Thompson worked as a machine operator for Hughes Aircraft for thirteen years. During that time, his skin (hands) was exposed to Wynn's 331, a coolant oil. In 1978, while working with machines and using Wynn's 331 oil, Mr. Thompson developed an active scaly eruption. He required medical attention but continued to work. The scaly eruption stopped only when Mr. Thompson was off work for medical treatment. He was certified to return to work but only if he avoided contact with Wynn's 331 oil. Hughes refused to rehire him, and Mr. Thompson filed for a permanent unscheduled disability. Does he qualify? [*Hughes Aircraft* v. *Industrial Comm'n,* 606 P.2d 819 (Ariz. 1981)]

5. Janice W. Craig was employed by Drenberg and Associates, an insurance agency. She had approximately fifteen years' experience when she started to work at Drenberg in August 1974 and was initially assigned underwriting duties in the personal and commercial lines of insurance. About the time she started to work, Drenberg began a year of explosive growth. Under normal conditions, an agency with 400,000 accounts could expect to acquire approximately 40,000 new accounts in the period of a year. Drenberg grew from 400,000 to 1,200,000 in just over one year. To keep pace with this growth, the agency's employees worked many overtime hours. Yet, in spite of their best efforts, the agency remained thirty days behind in its accounts.

Mrs. Craig was a conscientious employee and a perfectionist. In addition to her duties for personal and commercial lines, she took over a part of what is described as the commercial desk, handling correspondence, renewals, and changes. Her working conditions created an atmosphere in which she was under constant pressure.

On or about April 1, 1975, Drenberg purchased an agency from Earl Woodland, thereby acquiring 500 new accounts and an additional employee. Mrs. Craig was given responsibility for both supervising the new employee and for merging the books of the two agencies. The additional responsibility and mounting pressure began to affect her. She began to feel frustrated and ineffective. She experienced difficulty relating to her co-workers and on occasions had heated exchanges with customers. On September 25, 1975, she engaged in a particularly emotional telephone conversation with one of the agency's customers, after which she eventually left the office in tears. That night she took a slight overdose of sleeping pills. The following day she sought help at the Tri-City Mental Hospital and was subsequently admitted to Camelback Hospital, where her condition was diagnosed as neurotic depression, or a mental breakdown.

Mrs. Craig filed a claim with the Industrial Commission wherein she related facts establishing that she was suffering from a disabling mental condition brought on by the gradual buildup of the stress and strain of her employment.

In addition to Mrs. Craig's difficulties at the office, she was experiencing domestic disharmony. She and her husband argued frequently concerning his drinking habits. She encountered difficulties in relating to her daughters, and her mother's death caused additional internal pressures. It was on the evening of September 25, 1975, that the Craigs again argued, following which she took the overdose of medication. Should Mrs. Craig receive workers' compensation? [*Fireman's Fund Ins. Co.* v. *Industrial Comm'n,* 579 P.2d 555 (Ariz. 1979)]

6. Harry Connelly was an embalmer's helper. When he cut his hand during the preparation of a corpse, germs from the gangrenous corpse got into his cut and caused blood poisoning, and he eventually died. Would Mr. Connelly's survivors be entitled to workers' compensation? [*Connelly* v. *Hunt Furniture,* 147 N.E. 366 (N.Y. 1925)]

7. Beth Israel Hospital had a rule prohibiting solicitation and distribution of literature in all areas of the hospital except the employee locker rooms. The union challenged the rule as unfair because employees could not be approached in the hospital cafeteria or coffee shop. Can an employer restrict literature distribution? Is this rule too restrictive? [*Beth Israel Hosp.* v. *NLRB,* 437 U.S. 483 (1978)]

8. OSHA requires vehicles with an obstructed rear view to be equipped with a reverse signal alarm. Knight, an independent contractor working for Clarkson Construction, operated a Clarkson dump truck that had no warning signal but had an obstructed rear view. If an injury resulted to a pedestrian when Mr. Knight backed onto the highway, what liability would there be? What could OSHA do? What could the pedestrian do? What effect does Mr. Knight's being an independent contractor have? If Mr. Knight were also injured, could he recover? [*Clarkson Constr. Co.* v. *OSHA,* 531 F.2d 451 (10th Cir. 1980)]

9. Earl Webster was a 39-year-old construction worker in good health. While shoveling sand into a wheelbarrow on a Texas road crew in 97-degree heat, he complained to fellow workers that he was sick. He stopped to have a drink of water, pushed two more wheelbarrows, lost consciousness, and was taken unconscious in the car to the company offices. He died a short time later of heat prostration. Is his spouse entitled to death benefits under workers' compensation? Would it make a difference if the water given to him to drink was bad? [*American General Ins.* v. *Webster,* 118 S.W. 2d 1082 (Tex. 1938)]

10. Suppose an employer decided to spin off a particular plant or part of its business to avoid either unionization or the recognition of a collective bargaining agreement. Would the spin-off work, or is this an unfair labor practice? [*International Union, UAW* v. *NLRB,* 470 F.2d 422 (D.C. 1972)]

RESEARCH PROBLEM

Wages, Hours, and Colorful Jobs

11. Analyze the following questions and research the cited cases to discover the complex issues involved in the minimum wage, overtime, and covered employees under the FLSA.

Would the following count as part of hours worked?
- Mandatory training time [*Martin* v. *Parker Fire Protection Dist.*, 988 F.2d 1064 (10th Cir. 1993)]
- Firefighters' sleep time while on 24-hour duty [*Alldread* v. *Granada*, 988 F.2d 1425 (5th Cir. 1993)]
- Being on call in case of emergency [*Berry* v. *County of Sonoma*, 30 F.3d 1174 (9th Cir. 1994)]
- Time spent by employees at meat slaughter/processing plant waiting in line at knife room to get their knives sharpened [*Reich* v. *IBP, Inc.*, 820 F. Supp. 1315 (D.C. Kan. 1993)]

Would the following employees be covered by the minimum wage and overtime protections of FLSA?
- Inmates who are required to work as part of their sentences and perform labor within a state-run correctional facility [*McMaster* v. *Minnesota*, 819 F. Supp. 1429 (D.C. Minn. 1993)]

- Manager of Chick-Fil-A mall restaurant who has a capital investment in the restaurant but must follow corporate standards of operation [*Howell* v. *Chick-Fil-A*, 7 FLW Fed.D. 641 (N.D. Fla. 1993)]
- Migrant farm workers who harvested pickling cucumbers and are paid regardless of employer's profit on sale [*Cavazos* v. *Foster*, 822 F. Supp. 438 (W.D. Mich. 1993)]
- Dancers at an upscale topless nightclub in Dallas who furnish their own costumes but are told when to appear [*Martin* v. *Priba Corp.*, 123 CCH LC 35737 (N.D. Tex. 1992)]
- Formerly homeless alcoholic who is working for the Salvation Army under its rehabilitation program and is residing at the Salvation Army facility [*Williams* v. *Strickland*, 837 F. Supp. 1049 (N.D. Cal. 1994)]

NOTES

1. This section is from Noam S. Cohen, "Corporations Battling to Bar Use of E-Mail for Unions," *New York Times*, 23 August 1999, C1, C6.

2. Steven Greenhouse, "Anti-Sweatshop Group Invites Input by Apparel Makers," *New York Times*, 29 April 2000, A9.

BUSINESS STRATEGY APPLICATION

The CD-ROM exercise for this chapter is a proactive application that takes the basic rights discussion of employees in U.S.-based businesses and shows how companies deal with these issues in their international operations. A look at several companies' philosophies and approaches, as well as the Sullivan principles, give future managers some insight into why these international labor issues are important and how a company should go about developing its international labor and employee policies.

CHAPTER TWENTY

Employment
Discrimination

Employment discrimination has been one of the fastest-growing legal issues of the past decade. There has been a dramatic increase in the number of suits for discrimination and reverse discrimination and of cases in matters of unequal pay, sexual harassment, seniority, and maternity leave. Few employers have remained unaffected by the impact of antidiscrimination laws and cases.

In this chapter the following questions are answered: What laws governing employment discrimination exist? What types of discrimination exist? Are there any defenses to discrimination? What penalties or damages can be imposed for violations?

Nature of Complaint	Number of Complaints
Race	28,819
Sex	23,907
Disabilities	17,007
Age	14,141
National origin	7,108
Religion	1,811
Equal pay	1,071

EEOC 1999 DATA ON EMPLOYMENT DISCRIMINATION CASES

I have a dream that one day this nation will rise up and live out the true meaning of its creed: "We hold these truths to be self-evident; that all men are created equal." I have a dream. . . . I have a dream that my four little children will one day live in a nation where they will not be judged by the color of their skin but by the content of their character. I have a dream. . . .

DR. MARTIN LUTHER KING JR.

© EyeWire

CONSIDER...

Kimberly Ellerth's supervisor, Ted Slowik, was interviewing her for a promotion. He reached over and touched her knee and added that she was not "loose enough." In a conversation between them in which Slowik told Ellerth she got the job, he commented that the men in factories she would be working with "certainly like women with pretty legs." Kimberly complained to no one but then quit and filed suit for sexual harassment. Can she recover?

HISTORY OF EMPLOYMENT DISCRIMINATION LAW

Protections against employment discrimination are strictly statutory. Common law afforded employees no protection against discrimination. Indeed, common law viewed the entire employment relationship as a private contractual matter in which there should be no judicial interference.

Review the Civil Rights Acts of 1866 and 1870:
http://www.law.cornell.edu/uscode/42/1981.html

Notwithstanding the **Civil Rights Acts of 1866 and 1870,** the first effective antidiscrimination employment statute was a long time in coming. The first federal legislation to deal directly with the issue of discrimination was the **Equal Pay Act of 1963** (see Chapter 19 for more details). The statutory right to equality was expanded beyond the issue of pay less than a year later by **Title VII** of the **Civil Rights Act of 1964.** Title VII is the basis for discrimination law and judicial decisions in such matters. Although it has been amended many times, its basic purpose is to prohibit discrimination in employment on the basis of race, color, religion, sex, or national origin.

Explore the Equal Pay Act:
http://www.law.cornell.edu/uscode/29/206.html

Title VII was first amended by the **Equal Employment Opportunity Act of 1972.** This amendment gave the act's enforcer, the **Equal Employment Opportunity Commission** (EEOC), greater powers—for example, the right to file suits in federal district court. In 1975, Title VII was again amended, with the **Pregnancy Discrimination Act,** which defined "sex" discrimination to include discrimination on the basis of pregnancy and childbirth.

Laws have also been enacted to protect against discrimination because of age or handicap. Discrimination on the basis of age was prohibited by the **Age Discrimination in Employment Act of 1967** (discussed later in this chapter). Under the **Rehabilitation Act of 1973,** federal contractors are prohibited from discriminating against certain employees in performing their contracts. With the **Americans with Disabilities Act,** passed in 1990, employers of twenty-five or more employees (progressed to include employers of fifteen or more employees in 1994) are prohibited from discriminating against employees with disabilities and are required to make reasonable accommodations for qualified employees with disabilities. Although the substance of the existing antidiscrimination laws remains, the Civil Rights Act of 1991 made significant changes in procedural aspects of Title VII litigation. Exhibit 20.1 provides a summary of federal antidiscrimination legislation to date.

Review Title VII of the Civil Rights Act of 1964:
http://www.aristotle.net/~hantley/hiedlegl/statutes/title7/title7.htm

In 1993, Congress passed the **Family and Medical Leave Act.** This new federal law provides employees with the right to take twelve weeks of leave for childbirth, adoption, or family illness (see also Chapter 19).

In addition to this legislation, several executive orders that apply to administrative agencies (see Chapter 6) have been issued. These orders require federal government contractors to institute, among other things, affirmative action programs in their labor forces.

EMPLOYMENT DISCRIMINATION: TITLE VII OF THE CIVIL RIGHTS ACT

As mentioned earlier, Title VII of the Civil Rights Act of 1964—also known as the **Fair Employment Practices Act**—as amended in 1991, prohibits discrimination in all areas of employment on the basis of race, color, religion, national origin, and sex (including pregnancy, childbirth, or abortion). Other acts prohibit discrimination based on physical disability or age.

EXHIBIT 20.1 **Employment Discrimination Statutory Scheme**

STATUTE	DATE	PROVISIONS
Civil Rights Acts of 1866 and 1870 42 U.S.C. § 1981	1866 1870	Prohibited intentional discrimination based on race, color, national origin, or ethnicity; permit lawsuits
Equal Pay Act 29 U.S.C. § 206	1963	Prohibits paying workers of one sex different wages from the other when the jobs involve substantially similar skill, effort, and responsibility; Wage and Hour Division of Department of Labor enforces; private lawsuits permitted; double damage recovery for up to three years' wages plus attorney fees
Civil Rights Act of 1964 42 U.S.C. § 1981	1964	Outlaws all employment discrimination on the basis of race, color, religion, sex, or national origin; applies to hiring, pay, work conditions, promotions, discipline, and discharge; EEOC enforces; private law suits permitted; costs and attorney fees recoverable
Age Discrimination in Employment Act 42 U.S.C. § 6101	1967	Prohibits employment discrimination because of age against employees over 40 and mandatory retirement restrictions; EEOC enforces; private lawsuits permitted; attorney fees and costs recoverable
Equal Employment Opportunity Act 42 U.S.C. § 2000	1972	Expanded enforcement power of EEOC
Rehabilitation Act 29 U.S.C. § 701	1973	Prohibits employment discrimination on the basis of handicaps
Pregnancy Discrimination Act 42 U.S.C. § 2000e	1975	Prohibits discrimination on the basis of pregnancy and childbirth
Americans with Disabilities Act 42 U.S.C. § 12101	1990	Prohibits discrimination against the handicapped
Civil Rights Act of 1991 42 U.S.C. § 1981	1991	Clarifies disparate impact suit requirements; clarifies the meaning of "business necessity" and "job related"; changes some Supreme Court decisions (*Wards Cove*); punitive damage recovery
Glass Ceiling Act 42 U.S.C. § 2000e	1991	Creates commission to study barriers to women entering management and decision-making positions
Family and Medical Leave Act 29 U.S.C. § 2601	1993	Establishes 12 weeks of unpaid leave for medical or family reasons

Application of Title VII

Groups Covered

Title VII does not apply to all employers but is limited to the following groups:

1. Employers with at least fifteen workers during each working day in each of twenty or more calendar weeks in the current or preceding year

2. Labor unions that have fifteen members or more or operate a hiring hall that refers workers to covered employers

3. Employment agencies that procure workers for an employer who is covered by the law

4. Any labor union or employment agency, provided it has fifteen or more employees

5. State and local agencies

Noncovered Employers

Certain employers and employment situations that are *not* subject to Title VII follow:

1. Employment of aliens outside the United States is exempt.

2. Religious corporations, associations, educational institutions, or societies are exempt when the employment of individuals of a particular religion is connected with the activities of such corporations, associations, educational institutions, or societies.

3. Congress is exempt from the Civil Rights Act of 1964 (including Title VII).

4. The federal government and corporations owned by the federal government are exempt from Title VII, but the same prohibitions against discrimination appear in other statutes from which they are not exempt.

5. Indian tribes and departments or agencies in the District of Columbia subject to the procedures of the civil service are exempt.

Employment Procedures Covered

Every step in the employment process is covered by Title VII. Hiring, compensation, training programs, promotion, demotion, transfer, fringe benefits, employer rules, working conditions, and dismissals are all covered. In the case of an employment agency, the system for the agency's job referrals is also covered.

THEORIES OF DISCRIMINATION UNDER TITLE VII

There are three basic, but not mutually exclusive, theories of discrimination under Title VII: **disparate treatment, disparate impact,** and **pattern or practice of discrimination.**

Disparate Treatment

The most common form of discrimination at the time Title VII was passed was treating employees of one race or sex differently from employees of another race or sex. This different, or disparate, treatment results in unlawful discrimination when an individual is treated less favorably than other employees because of race, color, religion, national origin, or sex. The U.S. Supreme Court established the elements required to be shown to establish disparate treatment under Title VII in *McDonnell Douglas Corp.* v. *Green,* 411 U.S. 792 (1973). The case involved the rights of a black mechanic who had been laid off during a general workforce reduction and then not rehired. McDonnell claimed Mr. Green was not rehired because of his participation in a lock-in at the plant to protest racial inequality. Mr. Green brought suit for a Title VII violation, and the Supreme Court established the following elements as a *prima facie* case for discrimination:

1. Plaintiff belongs to a racial minority.

2. Plaintiff applied for and was qualified for a job with the employee.

3. Plaintiff, despite job qualifications, was rejected.

4. After plaintiff's rejection, the job remained open and the employer continued to seek applicants.

It is the employer's burden of proof to show that there was a nondiscriminatory reason for the employment decision. That burden arises when the employee-plaintiff establishes the four elements established in *Green*. The following case deals with the issue of how much proof the defendant-employer must offer as to the reason for the employment decision.

CASE 20.1

Chescheir v. Liberty Mutual Ins. Co.
713 F.2d 1142 (5th Cir. 1983)

How Come He Can Go to Law School but I Can't?:
The Case of the Law Student Claims Adjuster

FACTS

Liberty Mutual Insurance Company has a rule prohibiting its adjustors and first-year supervisors from attending law school. This "law school rule" was proposed and implemented on a national basis by Edmund Carr, a vice president and general claims manager, in November 1972.

Joan Chescheir (plaintiff) was hired by Liberty Mutual's Dallas office in March 1973 as a claims adjustor. In January 1975, she voluntarily resigned but in June of that year was hired in Liberty's Houston office as a claims adjustor.

In August 1976, Wyatt Trainer, the claims manager at the Houston office, received an anonymous letter informing him that Ms. Chescheir was attending law school. After consulting with his assistants and superior, Mr. Trainer fired her after she admitted she was attending law school.

Charity O'Connell also worked in the Houston office as a claims adjustor during the same period Ms. Chescheir did. During a coffee break with a new employee, Timothy Schwirtz (also an adjustor), Ms. O'Connell relayed the story of Ms. Chescheir's firing. Mr. Schwirtz then said, "Oh, that's strange, because when I was hired, when Wells (Southwest Division claims manager) interviewed me, he told me that I could go to law school and in fact if I came down to the Houston office, there were law schools in Houston." Ms. O'Connell then went to her supervisor and told him she also was attending law school. She refused to quit law school and was fired.

William McCarthy, Liberty's house counsel in its Houston office, attended law school while working as an adjustor and was retained as house counsel upon his graduation. The trial court found that Mr. McCarthy's supervisors were aware of his contemporaneous law school career. Alvin Dwayne White was employed as an adjustor in Liberty's Fort Worth office and asked for a transfer to Houston so he could attend law school. He was given the transfer and attended law school in Houston. James Ballard worked as an adjustor in Houston, attended law school, and was promoted to supervisor while in law school. Supervisors and employees were aware of his law school attendance, but the law school rule was not enforced against him. In short, none of the male employees known to have been attending law school was fired.

Ms. Chescheir and Ms. O'Connell both filed complaints with the EEOC, were given right of suit letters, and filed suit in federal district court. After a lengthy trial, the court found that Liberty Mutual had violated Title VII. Both women were given back pay.

JUDICIAL OPINION

GOLDBERG, Circuit Judge

Title VII applies . . . not only to the more blatant forms of discrimination, but also to subtler forms, such as discriminatory enforcement of work rules.

The four part test for demonstrating a *prima facie* case for discriminatory discharge due to unequal imposition of discipline [is]:

1. That plaintiff was a member of a protected group;

2. That there was a company policy or practice concerning the activity for which he or she was discharged;

(continued)

3. That nonminority employees either were given the benefit of a lenient company practice or were not held to compliance with a strict company policy; and

4. That the minority employee was disciplined either without the application of a lenient policy, or in conformity with the strict one.

Of course, if an employer is unaware that a non-minority employee is in violation of company policy, the absence of discipline does not demonstrate a more lenient policy. It follows from this that if an employer applies a rule differently to people it believes are differently situated, no discriminatory intent has been shown.

The district court made multitudinous findings of subsidiary facts and concluded in a finding of ultimate fact: "The defendant applied its law school rule differently to male and female employees." The subsidiary facts detail a plethora of individual instances that each tend to suggest discrimination.

It is clear that the plaintiffs are members of a protected group and that there was a company policy or practice concerning the activity for which the plaintiffs were discharged; thus the first two elements of the test are met. It is also clear that minority employees were disciplined without the application of a lenient policy, and in conformity with a strict policy. All women known to violate the law school rule were immediately discharged. Furthermore, even potential violations of the rule by women were investigated promptly. An anonymous letter was sufficient to trigger an investigation of Chescheir, and the fact that Chescheir was attending law school moved the company to interrogate another woman.

The only remaining element of the *prima facie* case is a finding that male employees either were given the benefit of a lenient company practice or were not held to compliance with a strict company policy. This is the element upon which Liberty Mutual focuses its attack. Recasting Liberty Mutual's argument slightly, it claims that other males were strictly disciplined in accord with the law school rule, and that Liberty Mutual never knew that McCarthy, White, and Ballard were attending law school. Thus, claims Liberty Mutual, the third element was not met.

We are not persuaded. First, our review of the record does not disclose any males in the Southwest Division who were discharged because of the law school rule. Second, even were we to accept Liberty Mutual's contention that it did not actually know McCarthy, White, and Ballard were attending law school, we would still affirm the judgment. The operative question is merely whether Liberty Mutual applied a more liberal standard to male employees. The district court found that there were widespread rumors that McCarthy and Ballard were attending law school. Also, the EEOC notified Liberty Mutual that a male adjustor was attending law school (Ballard) and requested an explanation. Key managerial employees, at a minimum, suspected McCarthy was attending law school but preferred not to ask and confirm their suspicions. One male adjustor was told when he was hired that he could attend law school. In contrast to Liberty Mutual's energetic investigation of women it believed might be attending law school, Liberty Mutual never investigated any of these allegations, suspicions, or rumors about male adjustors. The case of Mr. White is even more dramatic. After he expressed a desire to transfer to Houston in order to attend law school, that transfer was granted and he was never told he could not attend law school.

The preceding facts are more than enough to support the third leg [of the test]. Males at Liberty Mutual were subject to lenient enforcement of the law school rule. The district court's ultimate finding of fact that Liberty Mutual applied its law school rule discriminatorily finds firm support in the record; all four elements of the *prima facie* case are present.

Once Chescheir and O'Connell established a *prima facie* case of discrimination, the burden shifted to Liberty Mutual to present a justification. The district court found that Liberty Mutual offered no justification. Accordingly, the judgment of the district court is affirmed.

CASE QUESTIONS

1. What employer rule is at issue?

2. How were the plaintiffs fired using the rule?

3. Had any male employees ever been fired under the rule?

4. Were there examples of disparate use of the rule?

5. Is there a *prima facie* case?

6. What damages were awarded?

Disparate Impact

Many employment hiring, promoting, and firing practices are not intentionally discriminatory. In fact, the basis for such decisions may be quite rational. Even so, the effect or impact of many employment standards is to discriminate against particular races or on the basis of sex.

In one case, the Alabama prison system had a minimum height requirement of 5′2″ and a minimum weight requirement of 120 pounds for all of its "correctional counselors" (prison guards). The impact of the rule was to exclude many females and very few males [*Dothard* v. *Rawlinson*, 433 U.S. 321 (1977)]. Although the rule had a purpose other than one of discrimination, namely, making sure guards were large enough to perform their jobs, the effect of the rule was to exclude women from the job position.

Disparate impact cases do not require the four steps of proof outlined in the *Green* case. Rather, the proof required in disparate impact cases is a statistical showing of the impact of an employment practice.

In the landmark case of *Wards Cove Packing, Inc.* v. *Atonio*, 490 U.S. 642 (1989), the Supreme Court established standards for employer liability in cases in which there was no intentionally discriminating act or policy (as in the *Liberty Mutual* case). The Court held that the plaintiff always had the burden of showing the impact. The plaintiff was required to show which employment practice had a disparate or disproportionate impact and then demonstrate that the employment practice was actually responsible for the disparate impact. The Court also allowed businesses to demonstrate a business justification; the plaintiff then had to disprove that justification or show a way of accomplishing the business goals through some other means.

Review the 1991 amendments to the Civil Rights Act:
http://www.law.cornell.edu/
uscode/42/1981.html

The 1991 amendments to the Civil Rights Act changed the *Wards Cove* ruling. All a plaintiff need establish is that a practice or practices have a disparate impact on a protected class. The burden then shifts to the employer to show "business necessity" for the practice. The employer must show that the practice is "job related for the position in question and consistent with business necessity." Many viewed this as the law prior to the *Wards Cove* decision.

The ruling in *Wards Cove* that statistical comparisons must be made between qualified minorities in the labor market and the persons holding the jobs in question is appropriate and still stands. The 1991 Act did not change that ruling in the case. Disparate impact cases thus cannot be based on an analysis of only the demographics of the labor market; the proper comparison is between the skilled labor force (as defined by the position in question) and those actually holding the position.

Also, the 1991 amendments require the plaintiff to show causation between the practice of the employer and the disparate impact. For example, in one case that immediately preceded the 1991 amendments, the Seventh Circuit found that a company's low percentage of African-Americans in its workforce was due to its location in a Hispanic neighborhood and not because of its practice of hiring by word of mouth [*EEOC* v. *Chicago Miniature Lamp Works*, 947 F. 2d 292 (7th Cir. 1991)].

Pattern or Practice of Discrimination

The "pattern or practice" theory involves discrimination not against one person but, rather, against a group or class of persons (for example, women or African-Americans). Generally, a party bringing suit seeks to show that a particular minority group is underrepresented in an employer's workforce as compared with that group's representation in the population base. Circumstantial evidence and statistics are used to establish a pattern or practice of discrimination. For example, percentages are often compared. An employer's workforce may consist of 6 percent African-Americans, whereas the city's population consists of 30 percent African-Americans.

The standards for establishing a pattern or practice of discrimination are affected by the 1991 amendments to the Civil Rights Act; the burdens of proof are those discussed under disparate impact, with a "reasonable justification" defense for employers. In pattern or practice cases, the initial burden of proof of discrimination is upon the plaintiff or the EEOC.

C O N S I D E R . . .

20.1 Home Depot has 100,000 employees nationwide, with 504 warehouse-style stores. Approximately 70 percent of the stores' sales forces (those who sell lumber, electrical supplies, hardware, etc.) are male. Approximately 70 percent of Home Depot's operations personnel (cashiers, accountants, and clerical employees in back offices who do billing) are women.

A class-action lawsuit has been filed against Home Depot for gender disparity because its statistics on its workforce reinforce "gender stereotypes." The plaintiffs in the case claim Home Depot managers hire assuming that only men possess masculine traits needed for sales. Is there a case of disparate impact here?

SPECIFIC APPLICATIONS OF TITLE VII

The various theories of Title VII discrimination apply to specific types of discrimination. The following sections cover these types of discrimination and Title VII's application to them.

Sex Discrimination

Review the Glass Ceiling Act:
http://www.law.cornell.edu/
uscode/42/2000e.html

Although Title VII included sex discrimination in its prohibitions, its presence and effects were not as obviously in existence as the more blatant racial discrimination. Many of the initial discrimination suits were brought in response to "protective legislation," which consisted of state statutes that prohibited women from working in certain fields and occupations for safety reasons. The reasons for such prohibitions were that the jobs were too strenuous, too dangerous, or too stressful. Because the effect of the statutes was to keep women from certain higher-paying occupations and men from certain female-dominated jobs, the EEOC issued guidelines providing that employers guilty of discrimination could not use these statutory cloaks. As a result, in *Dothard v. Rawlinson*, 433 U.S. 321 (1977), the Supreme Court held that an Alabama Board of Corrections administrative regulation establishing minimum height and weight requirements was violative of Title VII.

A *prima facie* case of sex discrimination by an employer requires proof of the same elements established in the *Green* case. The only difference is that the issue of rejection, firing, or demotion is based on sex rather than race.

Other more subtle hints of discrimination have slowly been eliminated from every area of employment. Even job listings in classified ads cannot carry any sexual preference. For example, an employer cannot advertise for just a "waitress";

the ad must be for a "waiter/waitress." Further, state laws and company policies that prohibit women from working during certain hours if they have school-age children are violations of Title VII.

Sexual Harassment

Sexual harassment has been a very public topic since the Senate confirmation hearings for Justice Clarence Thomas, at which Professor Anita Hill raised allegations of sexual harassment, which is a violation of Title VII of the Civil Rights Act. Company policies on this issue should attempt to make it clear that an environment of harassment is not appropriate for any employee. Companies should also enforce policies uniformly.

In a series of decisions from state and federal courts, the judicial response to sexual harassment has evolved. Employers have been held liable for allowing sexual harassment to occur; firing employees for their failure to accept sexual advances has allowed fired employees to collect damages for wrongful termination.

Sexual harassment cases take two forms. There are the *quid pro quo* cases, in which an employee is required to submit to sexual advances in order to remain employed, secure a promotion, or obtain a raise. There are also the *atmosphere of harassment* cases, in which the invitations, language, pictures or suggestions become so pervasive as to create a hostile work environment.

Employers are held liable for the conduct of employees that amounts to sexual harassment, as the following case, which appears in the chapter opening "Consider," illustrates.

CASE 20.2

Burlington Industries, Inc. v. *Ellerth*
524 U.S. 742 (1998)

The Boorish Supervisor Meets Vicarious Liability

FACTS

Kimberly Ellerth (respondent) worked as a salesperson in one of Burlington's divisions from March 1993–May 1994. During her employment, she reported to a mid-level manager, Ted Slowik. Ellerth worked in a two-person office in Chicago and was one of Burlington's 22,000 employees. Slowik was based in New York, but was responsible for Ellerth's office. The following incidents of boorish and offensive behavior occurred during Ellerth's employment:

Summer 1993 | While on a business trip, Ellerth accepted Slowik's invitation to the hotel lounge. Slowik made remarks about Ellerth's breasts, told her to "loosen up" and said, "You know, Kim, I could make your life very hard or very easy at Burlington."

March 1994 | Ellerth was being considered for a promotion and Slowik expressed concern during the interview that she was not "loose enough." Slowik then reached out and rubbed her knee.

March 1994 | Slowik called Ellerth to give her the promotion and said, "You're gonna be out there with men who work in factories, and they certainly like women with pretty butts/legs."

May 1994 | Ellerth called Slowik for permission to insert a logo into a fabric sample. Slowik said, "I don't have time for you right now, Kim—unless you want to tell me what you're wearing." Ellerth ended the call.

(continued)

May 1994   Ellerth called again for permission and Slowik said, "Are you wearing shorter skirts yet, Kim, because it would make your job a whole heck of a lot easier."

In May 1994, the supervisor in the Chicago office cautioned Ellerth about returning phone calls. Ellerth quit and faxed a letter giving reasons for her decision unrelated to the alleged sexual harassment. Three weeks later, however, she sent another letter complaining of Slowik's behavior.

During her employment at Burlington, Ellerth did not tell anyone about Slowik's behavior. She chose not to tell her supervisor in the Chicago office because, "It would be his duty as my supervisor to report any incidents of sexual harassment."

Ellerth filed suit against Burlington for violation of Title VII in that the sexual harassment forced her constructive discharge.

The District Court found Slowik's behavior created a hostile work environment but found that Burlington neither knew nor should have known about the conduct. The Court of Appeals reversed, with eight separate opinions imposing vicarious liability on Burlington. Burlington appealed.

JUDICIAL OPINION

KENNEDY, Justice

At the outset, we assume an important proposition yet to be established before a trier of fact. It is a premise assumed as well, in explicit or implicit terms, in the various opinions by the judges of the Court of Appeals. The premise is: a trier of fact could find in Slowik's remarks numerous threats to retaliate against Ellerth if she denied some sexual liberties. The threats, however, were not carried out or fulfilled. Cases based on threats which are carried out are referred to often as quid pro quo cases, as distinct from bothersome attentions or sexual remarks that are sufficiently severe or pervasive to create a hostile work environment. The terms quid pro quo and hostile work environment are helpful, perhaps, in making a rough demarcation between cases in which threats are carried out and those where they are not or are absent altogether, but beyond this are of limited utility.

"Quid pro quo" and "hostile work environment" do not appear in the statutory text. The terms appeared first in the academic literature, see C. MacKinnon, *Sexual Harassment of Working Women* (1979); found their way into decisions of the Courts of Appeals, see, e.g., *Henson* v. *Dundee,* 682 F.2d 897, 909 (CA11 1982); and were mentioned in this Court's decision in *Meritor Savings Bank, FSB* v. *Vinson,* 477 U.S. 57 (1986).

Nevertheless, as use of the terms grew in the wake of *Meritor,* they acquired their own significance. The standard of employer responsibility turned on which type of harassment occurred. If the plaintiff established a quid pro quo claim, the Courts of Appeals held, the employer was subject to vicarious liability.

We do not suggest the terms quid pro quo and hostile work environment are irrelevant to Title VII litigation. To the extent they illustrate the distinction between cases involving a threat which is carried out and offensive conduct in general, the terms are relevant when there is a threshold question whether a plaintiff can prove discrimination in violation of Title VII. When a plaintiff proves that a tangible employment action resulted from a refusal to submit to a supervisor's sexual demands, he or she establishes that the employment decision itself constitutes a change in the terms and conditions of employment that is actionable under Title VII. For any sexual harassment preceding the employment decision to be actionable, however, the conduct must be severe or pervasive. Because Ellerth's claim involves only unfulfilled threats, it should be categorized as a hostile work environment claim which requires a showing of severe or pervasive conduct.

We must decide, then, whether an employer has vicarious liability when a supervisor creates a hostile work environment by making explicit threats to alter a subordinate's terms or conditions of employment, based on sex, but does not fulfill the threat. We turn to principles of agency law, for the term "employer" is defined under Title VII to include "agents." In express terms, Congress has directed federal courts to interpret Title VII based on agency principles. Given such an explicit instruction, we conclude a uniform and predictable standard must be established as a matter of federal law. We rely "on the general common law of agency, rather than on the law of any particular State, to give meaning to these terms."

Section 219(1) of the Restatement sets out a central principle of agency law:
A master is subject to liability for the torts of his servants committed while acting in the scope of their employment.

An employer may be liable for both negligent and intentional torts committed by an employee within the scope of his or her employment. Sexual harassment under Title VII presupposes intentional conduct. While early decisions absolved employers of liability for the intentional torts of their employees, the law now imposes liability where the employee's "purpose, however misguided, is wholly or in part to further the master's business."

As Courts of Appeals have recognized, a supervisor acting out of gender-based animus or a desire to fulfill sexual urges may not be actuated by a purpose to serve the employer.

The concept of scope of employment has not always been construed to require a motive to serve the employer.

The general rule is that sexual harassment by a supervisor is not conduct within the scope of employment.

Scope of employment does not define the only basis for employer liability under agency principles. In limited circumstances, agency principles impose liability on employers even where employees commit torts outside the scope of employment.

In a sense, most workplace tortfeasors are aided in accomplishing their tortious objective by the existence of the agency relation: Proximity and regular contact may afford a captive pool of potential victims.

Tangible employment actions are the means by which the supervisor brings the official power of the enterprise to bear on subordinates. A tangible employment decision requires an official act of the enterprise, a company act. The decision in most cases is documented in official company records, and may be subject to review by higher level supervisors.

For these reasons, a tangible employment action taken by the supervisor becomes for Title VII purposes the act of the employer. Whatever the exact contours of the aided in the agency relation standard, its requirements will always be met when a supervisor takes a tangible employment action against a subordinate. In that instance, it would be implausible to interpret agency principles to allow an employer to escape liability, as *Meritor* itself appeared to acknowledge.

Whether the agency relation aids in commission of supervisor harassment which does not culminate in a tangible employment action is less obvious. On the one hand, a supervisor's power and authority invests his or her harassing conduct with a particular threatening character, and in this sense, a supervisor always is aided by the agency relation. On the other hand, there are acts of harassment a supervisor might commit which might be the same acts a co-employee would commit, and there may be some circumstances where the supervisor's status makes little difference.

It is this tension which, we think, has caused so much confusion among the Courts of Appeals which have sought to apply the aided in the agency relation standard to Title VII cases.

An employer is subject to vicarious liability to a victimized employee for an actionable hostile environment created by a supervisor with immediate (or successively higher) authority over the employee. When no tangible employment action is taken, a defending employer may raise an affirmative defense to liability or damages, subject to proof by a preponderance of the evidence. The defense comprises two necessary elements: (a) that the employer exercised reasonable care to prevent and correct promptly any sexually harassing behavior, and (b) that the plaintiff employee unreasonably failed to take advantage of any preventive or corrective opportunities provided by the employer or to avoid harm otherwise. While proof that an employer had promulgated an anti-harassment policy with complaint procedure is not necessary in every instance as a matter of law, the need for a stated policy suitable to the employment circumstances may appropriately be addressed in any case when litigating the first element of the defense. And while proof that an employee failed to fulfill the corresponding obligation of reasonable care to avoid harm is not limited to showing any unreasonable failure to use any complaint procedure provided by the employer, a demonstration of such failure will normally suffice to satisfy the employer's burden under the second element of the defense. No affirmative defense is available, however, when the supervisor's harassment culminates in a tangible employment action, such as discharge, demotion, or undesirable reassignment.

Affirmed.

DISSENTING OPINION

Justice THOMAS, with whom Justice SCALIA joins, dissenting

The Court today manufactures a rule that employers are vicariously liable if supervisors create a sexually hostile work environment, subject to an affirmative defense that the Court barely attempts to define. This rule applies even if the employer has a policy against sexual harassment, the employee knows about that policy, and the employee never informs anyone in a position of authority about the supervisor's conduct. As a result, employer liability under Title VII is judged by different standards depending upon whether a sexually or racially hostile work

(continued)

environment is alleged. The standard of employer liability should be the same in both instances: An employer should be liable if, and only if, the plaintiff proves that the employer was negligent in permitting the supervisor's conduct to occur.

Sexual harassment is simply not something that employers can wholly prevent without taking extraordinary measures—constant video and audio surveillance, for example—that would revolutionize the workplace in a manner incompatible with a free society. Indeed, such measures could not even detect incidents of harassment such as the comments Slowick allegedly made to respondent in a hotel bar. The most that employers can be charged with, therefore, is a duty to act reasonably under the circumstances. As one court recognized in addressing an early racial harassment claim:

The Court's holding does guarantee one result: There will be more and more litigation to clarify applicable legal rules in an area in which both practitioners and the courts have long been begging for guidance. It thus truly boggles the mind that the Court can claim that its holding will effect "Congress' intention to promote conciliation rather than litigation in the Title VII context." All in all, today's decision is an ironic result for a case that generated eight separate opinions in the Court of Appeals on a fundamental question, and in which we granted certiorari "to assist in defining the relevant standards of employer liability."

Popular misconceptions notwithstanding, sexual harassment is not a freestanding federal tort, but a form of employment discrimination. As such, it should be treated no differently (and certainly no better) than the other forms of harassment that are illegal under Title VII. I would restore parallel treatment of employer liability for racial and sexual harassment and hold an employer liable for a hostile work environment only if the employer is truly at fault. I therefore respectfully dissent.

CASE QUESTIONS

1. What is vicarious liability?

2. When will an employer be held liable for sexual harassment despite a lack of actual knowledge?

3. What is the liability of a company for harassment of an employee by an immediate supervisor?

4. What defenses exist to vicarious liability?

5. What impact does a tangible employment action have on vicarious liability?

6. What major issues does the dissenting opinion raise?

CONSIDER...

20.2   Between 1985 and 1990, while attending college, Beth Ann Faragher worked part time and during the summers as an ocean lifeguard for the Parks and Recreation Department of the City of Boca Raton (City).

Faragher worked for three immediate supervisors during this period: Bill Terry, David Silverman, and Robert Gordon. Faragher resigned in June 1990 and brought a Title VII sexual harassment suit against the city in 1992. She alleged a sexually hostile atmosphere because of "uninvited and offensive touching," lewd remarks, and Silverman's comment "Date me or clean the toilets for a year."

Faragher had not complained to higher management, and the lifeguards had no significant contact with higher city officials. Two months before Faragher's resignation, a former lifeguard, Nancy E. Wanchew, wrote to the City's personnel director complaining about Terry and Silverman's harassment of female lifeguards.

Should the City be held liable? Does it matter that Faragher asked only for nominal damages, attorney's fees, and costs? [*Faragher v. City of Boca Raton*, 524 U.S. 775 (1998)]

BUSINESS STRATEGY

Sexual harassment law demands that executives not only avoid inappropriate words and actions, but also take seriously complaints of harassment by their colleagues, even their superiors. A case in point: Earlier this month CNA Financial Corp. announced the resignation of its top life-insurance executive, Jack Kettler, and his deputy, Robert Teske. Mr. Kettler was accused of making "offensive comments" to two female employees; Mr. Teske, of failing to act on the women's complaints.

© Amy Etra/PhotoEdit

complaint against the unit's chief executive, he reportedly called her and asked if she felt her job was "in jeopardy" and if she "felt pressured." Later, the CEO reportedly summoned a female employee to his hotel room, told her he was going to fire another complainant, then directed her to sign an affidavit stating that he had not harassed her. Such overtures are clearly inappropriate, but even routine contact should be minimized or prevented until the situation is resolved. If it's practical, remove both accuser and accused from the workplace, making clear to their colleagues that the separation does not imply any prejudgment but is simply a way to minimize pressure on everyone concerned.

Equal Employment Opportunity Commission guidelines require employers to investigate complaints of sexual harassment "promptly and thoroughly." Based on a review of relevant court cases and on my investigative work for corporate counsel over the past two decades, here are some practical suggestions for minimizing the legal, internal, and public-relations fallout from sexual harassment charges:

Move quickly to begin an investigation. It's tempting to wait until the dust settles, but companies can help protect themselves from liability by starting an investigation immediately—preferably within 24 hours of a complaint. In the case of *Nash* v. *Electrospace System Inc.,* a federal district judge praised the accused company for wrapping up its investigation quickly. "The investigation and transfer were accomplished within one week of [the plaintiff's] first complaints," the court noted. "Surely this [promptness] reflected a prudent response to an unpleasant situation." An appeals court, upholding the district court's ruling in favor of Electrospace, called the company's response "prompt and sensitive."

Interview potential witnesses, as well as people who may be aware of a pattern of harassment. Such testimony is critical, especially when the alleged harasser denies the charge. And co-workers can provide important corroborating or exculpatory details, such as each individual's demeanor at the time of the alleged act, whether the harasser had the opportunity to commit it and whether there existed a broader pattern of behavior. If the accuser is a young female secretary, for example, an investigator should consider interviewing her young female predecessors.

Carefully regulate the alleged harasser's contact with accusers and potential witnesses. Soon after a female employee of Astra USA filed a sexual harassment

Choose the sequence of interviews carefully. The first investigative step is interviewing the accuser to learn about specific alleged acts, dates, and other details. If the alleged harasser is likely to cooperate with the investigation or admit the harassment, interviewing him next could lead to a quick, informal resolution of the situation. But if the alleged harasser is considered hostile and the accuser says there is a pattern of behavior, it's probably best to interview other witnesses first.

Conduct interviews far from prying eyes. While an investigation is in progress, employee interest in who is under suspicion, who is assisting the investigation, and what they're saying is always intense. Even an interview's duration may be fodder for office gossip. To limit speculation and preserve confidentiality, conduct all interviews in a private area, preferably off site. Ask all employees, whether interviewed or not, to refrain from rumor and speculation, which can only hurt morale, productivity, and the company's public image.

Ask for documents and other hard evidence. In one case I worked on, a series of inappropriate messages in birthday cards from a boss to an employee were an important break in the investigation. Ask the complainant, alleged harasser and witnesses for any documents—notes, hotel receipts, and the like—that might corroborate or refute an accuser's claims. Voice and e-mail messages can also provide concrete evidence that harassment has occurred.

Reveal details about the allegation to interview subjects only when absolutely necessary. A company risks a defamation charge if "raw," unconfirmed information obtained during a sexual harassment investigation leaks.

(continued)

Investigate thoroughly, but don't let investigations drag on. A major law firm, Baker & McKenzie, challenged the veracity of a secretary who complained about a partner's alleged groping—only to find later that a number of similar complaints had been made against the same partner. In 1994 a jury ordered the firm to pay its former employee several million dollars. In press interviews after the verdict, one juror cited the firm's failure to follow up on the prior complaints. Yet an overlong, overzealous investigation can do as much damage as a perfunctory one. If victims believe that a company's internal resolution process has failed because the investigation drags on, they may go outside the organization to seek satisfaction. That can escalate the seriousness of the situation that could have been resolved had the investigation been completed in a timely manner.

A badly managed sexual harassment investigation can seriously damage an organization—internally, in the courts, and in the public eye. But a prompt, thorough, professional investigation can help preserve, even enhance, the credibility of its leadership, the morale of its workers, and the value of its stock.

Source: James B. Mintz, "Harassment 101: How to Handle Complaints," *Wall Street Journal,* March 31, 1997, A14. Reprinted with permission of *The Wall Street Journal* © 1997 Dow Jones & Company, Inc. All rights reserved.

CONSIDER...

20.3 Joseph Oncale worked for Sundowner Offshore Services on a Chevron U.S.A. Inc. oil platform in the Gulf of Mexico. He was employed as part of an eight-man crew. Oncale complained in his pink slip when he quit that he "left voluntarily due to sexual harassment and verbal abuse." Oncale said that he was called names suggesting homosexuality and threatened with rape.

Oncale filed suit under Title VII for sexual harassment. Is recovery for same-sex sexual harassment possible under Title VII? [*Oncale* v. *Sundowner Offshore Services, Inc.* 523 U.S. 75 (1998)]

CONSIDER...

20.4 Determine whether the following would constitute sexual harassment (either *quid pro quo* or atmosphere of harassment) under Title VII.

1. A manager who referred to female customers as "bitchy" or "dumb"; flirted with an employee's female relatives; and told of spending a weekend at a nudist camp [*Gleason* v. *Mesirow Financial, Inc.,* 118 F. 3d 1134 (7th Cir. 1997)]

2. A manager who told a single, pregnant female employee that he disapproved of premarital sex [*Brill* v. *Lante,* 119 F. 3d 1266 (7th Cir. 1997)]

3. Calendar photographs of women in swimwear posted in a coemployee's work station [*Guidry* v. *Zale Corp.,* 969 F. Supp. 988 (M.D.La. 1997)]

4. A supervisor who called his wife "ignorant" and women in his department "dumb" and used the term "gals" for all his female employees [*Penry* v. *Federal Home Loan Bank of Topeka,* 970 F.Supp. 833 (D. Kan. 1997)]

5. A supervisor who referred to the architecture of a shopping mall as looking like "two hooters" and a "bra bazaar," while having dinner with an employee on a business trip [*Penry* v. *Federal Home Loan Bank of Topeka,* 970 F. Supp. 833 (D. Kan. 1997)]

6. Two uninvited hugs by a supervisor and notes to employees signed, "Love, Steph" [*Drew* v. *First Sav. of New Hampshire,* 968 F. Supp. 762 (D. N. H. 1997)]

BIOGRAPHY

HEATHER SUE MERCER: A REAL KICKER

Heather Sue Mercer was awarded $2 million by a jury following a trial on her complaint that alleged Duke University violated her rights and discriminated against her by refusing to allow her a position on the football team as a place kicker.

In 1995, Ms. Mercer tried out for the football team and made the squad. She kicked a 28-yard field goal in a 1995 spring intrasquad game. However, Coach Fred Goldsmith indicated she did not have the leg strength to compete at the Division I level. Also, team mates testified that she was not accurate.

Ms. Mercer was listed in the 1995 media guide but was not permitted to suit up for the game, something third and fourth string players are permitted to do. Assistant coach Fred Chatham explained the reason, "We don't need . . . magazines running up and down the sidelines taking pictures of Heather Sue." The following season she became the first athlete ever cut from the squad.

The jury deliberated for two hours before reaching the verdict, which included punitive damages, finding that Duke had acted with malice and reckless indifference. Ms. Mercer says that she will establish a scholarship fund for women who wish to become place kickers.

What laws and rights would Ms. Mercer have used as a basis for her suit?

Source: Alex Tresniowski, et al., "Kicking Up a Storm," *People*, 30 October 2000, pp. 69–70.

---

e-commerce

Derogatory, suggestive, and offensive e-mails and electronic bulletin boards on servers sponsored by an employer can be the basis for a hostile environment sexual harassment suit. Employers not only have the responsibility to prohibit employees from posting such materials; they also have a responsibility to supervise such bulletin boards and e-mails to be certain that there is not an atmosphere of harassment that results.

Further, in litigation over such materials, plaintiffs may rely on printed copies of the materials and messages to use in establishing their cases even though the materials may have already been deleted from the company system.

Sex Discrimination and Pensions

Another area of sex discrimination in employment involves the statistical fact that women live longer than men. It costs more for a female employee to have a pension than a male employee because she will live longer after retirement. In *City of Los Angeles Department of Water v. Manhart*, 435 U.S. 702 (1978), the Supreme Court held that employers could not require female employees to contribute more to their pension plans than males. The additional contributions for the female employees were required by the employer because the pension planner had statistical evidence that longevity of female employees exceeded that of male employees. If the Supreme Court had

Visit the Women's Legal History Biography Project: **http://www.stanford.edu/ group/WLHP**

BUSINESS PLANNING TIP

Office Romances

New York lawyer Sidney Siller, who defends sexual harassment suits, offers this advice for office etiquette to avoid litigation:

1. Leave your office door open during meetings.

2. Don't go out to lunch with opposite sex co-workers.

3. Don't offer rides home (even in inclement weather).

4. Avoid physical contact in the office.

Some companies have adopted a policy of no fraternization among employees.

sanctioned the disparity in pension plan payments, the higher cost of having female employees could have been cited by employers as the reason for their hiring practices. Insurers and employers are required to treat employees as a group and not to break them down by their age, sex, or other characteristics.

Sex Discrimination and Pregnancy Issues

Review the Pregnancy Discrimination Act:
http://www.law.cornell.edu/uscode/29/621.html

The Pregnancy Discrimination Act was added to Title VII in 1974. Prior to this act, women were forced to take maternity leaves at certain times and for certain lengths of time solely because of their pregnancies. Many women who returned to work after their pregnancies discovered that their pay had been cut or that they had been demoted. Even employees' insurance coverage treated pregnancy differently from other medical ailments, and pregnancy was not treated as an illness by most employers in terms of sick leave.

This act revolutionized maternity issues in the employment world. The specific acts prohibited under this statute are as follows:

1. Forcing a resignation
2. Demoting or limiting an employee's job upon her return to work
3. Refusing to allow a mother to return to work after pregnancy
4. Providing different sick leave rules for pregnancy and other medical ailments
5. Providing different medical insurance benefits or disability leave for pregnancy and other ailments
6. Refusing to hire or promote on the basis of pregnancy or family plans

The following landmark case focuses on new issues in sex discrimination.

CASE 20.3

International Union v. Johnson Controls, Inc.
499 U.S. 187 (1991)

The Acid Test for Women: The Right to Choose High-Risk Jobs

FACTS

Johnson Controls, Inc. (respondent), manufactures batteries. In the manufacturing process, the element lead is a primary ingredient. Occupational exposure to lead entails health risks, including the risk of harm to any fetus carried by a female employee.

Before the Civil Rights Act of 1964 became law, Johnson Controls did not employ any woman in a battery-manufacturing job. In June 1977, however, it announced its first official policy concerning its employment of women in jobs with lead exposure risk: *[P]rotection of the health of the unborn child is the immediate and direct responsibility of the prospective parents.*

While the medical profession and the company can support them in the exercise of this responsibility, it cannot assume it for them without simultaneously infringing their rights as persons. . . .

Since not all women who can become mothers wish to become mothers (or will become mothers), it would appear to be illegal discrimination to treat all who are capable of pregnancy as though they will become pregnant.

Consistent with that view, Johnson Controls "stopped short of excluding women capable of bearing children from lead exposure" but emphasized that a woman who expected to have a child should not choose a job in which she would have such exposure. The company also required a woman who wished to be considered for employment to sign a statement indicating that she had been advised of the risk of having a child while she was exposed to lead. The statement informed the woman that although there was evidence "that women exposed to lead have a higher rate of abortion," this evidence was "not as clear . . . as the relationship between cigarette smoking and cancer," but that it was, "medically speaking, just good sense not to run that risk if you want children and do not want to expose the unborn child to risk, however small. . . ."

In 1982, Johnson Controls shifted from a policy of warning to a policy of exclusion. Between 1979 and 1983, eight employees became pregnant while maintaining lead levels in excess of 30 micrograms per decaliter of blood. The company responded by announcing a broad exclusion of women from jobs that exposed them to lead:

[I]t is [Johnson Controls'] policy that women who are pregnant or who are capable of bearing children will not be placed into jobs involving lead exposure or which could expose them to lead through the exercise of job bidding, bumping, transfer or promotion rights.

(App. 85–86).

The policy defined "women . . . capable of bearing children" as "[a]ll women except those whose inability to bear children is medically documented."

Several employees (petitioners) and their unions filed suit alleging that Johnson Controls's fetal protection policy violated Title VII of the Civil Rights Act. Included in the group were:

Mary Craig	sterilized to avoid losing her job
Elsie Nason	50-year-old divorcee who lost compensation when transferred out of lead exposure job
Donald Penney	denied request for leave of absence to lower his lead level before becoming a father

The district court entered summary judgment for Johnson Controls. The court of appeals affirmed, and the employees appealed.

JUDICIAL OPINION

BLACKMUN, Justice

The bias in Johnson Controls' policy is obvious. Fertile men, but not fertile women, are given a choice as to whether they wish to risk their reproductive health for a particular job. Section 703(a) of the Civil Rights Act of 1964, 78 Stat. 255, as amended, 42 U.S.C. § 2000e-2(a), prohibits sex-based classifications in terms and conditions of employment, in hiring and discharging decisions, and in other employment decisions that adversely affect an employee's status. Respondent's fetal-protection policy explicitly discriminates against women on the basis of their sex. The policy excludes women with childbearing capacity from lead-exposed jobs and so creates a facial classification based on gender. Respondent assumes as much in its brief before this Court.

Nevertheless, the Court of Appeals assumed, as did the two appellate courts who already had confronted this issue, that sex specific fetal-protection policies do not involve facial discrimination. These courts analyzed the policies as though they were facially neutral, and had only a discriminatory effect upon the employment opportunities of women. Consequently, the courts looked to see if each employer in question had established that its policy was justified as a business necessity. The business necessity standard is more lenient for the employer than the statutory BFOQ [Bona Fide Occupational Qualification] defense. The court assumed that because the asserted reason for the sex-based exclusion (protecting women's unconceived offspring) was ostensibly benign, the policy was not sex-based discrimination. That assumption, however, was incorrect.

First, Johnson Controls' policy classifies on the basis of gender and childbearing capacity, rather than fertility alone. Respondent does not seek to protect the unconceived children of all its employees. Despite evidence in the record about the debilitating effect of lead exposure on the male reproductive system, Johnson Controls is concerned only with the harms that may befall the unborn offspring of its female employees.

Our conclusion is bolstered by the Pregnancy Discrimination Act of 1978, 42 U.S.C. § 2000e(k), in which Congress explicitly provided that, for purposes of Title VII, discrimination "on the basis of sex" includes discrimination "because of or on the basis of pregnancy, childbirth, or related medical conditions." "The Pregnancy Discrimination Act has now made clear that, for all Title VII purposes, discrimination based on a woman's pregnancy is, on its face, discrimination because of her sex." In its use of the words "capable of bearing children" in the 1982 policy statement as the criterion for exclusion, Johnson Controls explicitly classifies on the basis of potential for pregnancy. Under the PDA, such a classification must be regarded, for Title VII purposes, in the same light as explicit sex discrimination. Respondent has chosen to treat all its female employees as potentially pregnant; that choice evinces discrimination on the basis of sex.

(continued)

We concluded above that Johnson Controls' policy is not neutral because it does not apply to the reproductive capacity of the company's male employees in the same way as it applies to that of the females. Moreover, the absence of a malevolent motive does not convert a facially discriminatory policy into a neutral policy with a discriminatory effect. Whether an employment practice involves disparate treatment through explicit facial discrimination does not depend on why the employer discriminates but rather on the explicit terms of the discrimination.

In sum, Johnson Controls' policy "does not pass the simple test of whether the evidence shows 'treatment of a person in a manner which but for that person's sex would be different.'"

We therefore turn to the question whether Johnson Controls' fetal-protection policy is one of those "certain instances" that come within the BFOQ exception.

Johnson Controls argues that its fetal-protection policy falls within the so-called safety exception to the BFOQ. Our cases have stressed that discrimination on the basis of sex because of safety concerns is allowed only in narrow circumstances. In *Dothard* v. *Rawlinson*, 433 U.S. 321 (1977), this Court indicated that the danger to a woman herself does not justify discrimination. We there allowed the employer to hire only male guards in contact areas of maximum-security male penitentiaries only because more was at stake than the "individual woman's decision to weigh and accept the risks of employment." We found sex to be a BFOQ inasmuch as the employment of a female guard would create real risks of safety to others if violence broke out because the guard was a woman. Sex discrimination was tolerated because sex was related to the guard's ability to do the job—maintaining prison security. We also required in *Dothard* a high correlation between sex and ability to perform job functions and refused to allow employers to use sex as a proxy for strength although it might be a fairly accurate one.

Similarly, some courts have approved airlines' layoffs of pregnant flight attendants at different points during the first five months of pregnancy on the ground that the employer's policy was necessary to ensure the safety of passengers.

The unconceived fetuses of Johnson Controls' female employees, however, are neither customers nor third parties whose safety is essential to the business of battery manufacturing. No one can disregard the possibility of injury to future children; the BFOQ, however, is not so broad that it transforms this deep social concern into an essential aspect of battery making.

Our case law makes clear that the safety exception is limited to instances in which sex or pregnancy actually interferes with the employee's ability to perform the job. This approach is consistent with the language of the BFOQ provision itself, for it suggests that permissible distinctions based on sex must relate to ability to perform the duties of the job. Johnson Controls suggests, however, that we expand the exception to allow fetal-protection policies that mandate particular standards for pregnant or fertile women. We decline to do so. Such an expansion contradicts not only the language of the BFOQ and the narrowness of its exception but the plain language and history of the Pregnancy Discrimination Act.

A word about tort liability and the increased cost of fertile women in the workplace is perhaps necessary. One of the dissenting judges in this case expressed concern about an employer's tort liability and concluded that liability for a potential injury to a fetus is a social cost that Title VII does not require a company to ignore. It is correct to say that Title VII does not prevent the employer from having a conscience. The statute, however, does prevent sex-specific fetal-protection policies. These two aspects of Title VII do not conflict.

More than 40 States currently recognize a right to recover for a prenatal injury based either on negligence or on wrongful death. According to Johnson Controls, however, the company complies with the lead standard developed by OSHA and warns its female employees about the damaging effects of lead. It is worth noting that OSHA gave the problem of lead lengthy consideration and concluded that "there is no basis whatsoever for the claim that women of childbearing age should be excluded from the workplace in order to protect the fetus or the course of pregnancy." Instead, OSHA established a series of mandatory protections which, taken together, "should effectively minimize any risk to the fetus and newborn child." Without negligence, it would be difficult for a court to find liability on the part of the employer. If, under general tort principles, Title VII bans sex-specific fetal-protection policies, the employer fully informs the woman of the risk, and the employer has not acted negligently, the basis for holding an employer liable seems remote at best.

Although the issue is not before us, the concurrence observes that "it is far from clear that compliance with Title VII will preempt state tort liability."

Our holding today that Title VII, as so amended, forbids sex-specific fetal-protection policies is neither remarkable nor unprecedented. Concern for a woman's existing or potential offspring historically has been the excuse for denying women equal employment opportunities.

It is no more appropriate for the courts than it is for individual employers to decide whether a woman's reproductive role is more important to herself and her family than her economic role. Congress has left this choice to the woman as hers to make.

The judgment of the Court of Appeals is reversed and the case is remanded for further proceedings consistent with this opinion.

CASE QUESTIONS

1. Describe Johnson Controls's evolving policy on lead exposure.
2. Describe the plaintiffs who brought suit in the case.
3. Are circumstances given when sex is a BFOQ?
4. What problem is presented by the exclusion of men?
5. What is the court's position on tort liability of the company with respect to the fetus?

CONSIDER...

20.5 Lora Ilhardt began working for Sara Lee in April 1988. She was the first female attorney to be hired in Sara Lee's Chicago office. She was given several raises and promoted to director, which gave her the opportunity to participate in the company's bonus plan.

In October 1989, Ilhardt gave birth to her first child and took a three-month maternity leave. She asked to return, working part time at three days per week. Her request was granted and her salary was adjusted, but she was still given full bonus participation.

Her part-time status caused some inconvenience, but both clients and co-workers gave her high performance reviews.

In July 1991, Ilhardt began her second maternity leave and Sara Lee was undergoing a corporate reduction in force. Gordon Newman, Sara Lee's general counsel, decided, if necessary, to eliminate Ilhardt's position since she was part time. Newman told her that if she worked full time, he could better protect her job.

Ilhardt did not take a full-time job and by April 1993 was in the midst of her third pregnancy. The RIF came at the end of April. Newman offered her an eight-month maternity leave but could not guarantee a job after it was over. Ilhardt refused and was terminated. Ilhardt took her maternity leave and then asked to return. Sara Lee had no openings. Ilhardt filed a Title VII discrimination claim. Should she recover? [*Ilhardt v. Sara Lee Corp.*, 118 F. 3d 1151 (7th Cir. 1997)]

Religious Discrimination

Employers are required to make reasonable efforts to accommodate an employee's religious practices, holidays, and observances. Not all religious or church activities, however, are protected; for example, the observance of a religion's Sabbath is a protected activity, but taking time to prepare for a church bake sale or pageant is an unprotected activity. The 1972 amendments to Title VII defined religion to include "all aspects of religious observance and practice, as well as belief." The accommodation of religion thus defined is required unless an employer is able to establish that allowing the employee such an accommodation would result in "undue hardship on the conduct of the employer's business."

In *Trans World Airlines, Inc. v. Hardison*, 432 U.S. 63 (1977), the Supreme Court confirmed the clear language of the 1972 act that requires an employer to demonstrate inability to accommodate an employee's religious needs. As a member of a church that worshiped on Saturdays, Larry G. Hardison expressed a desire not to work that day. TWA worked through several alternatives to afford Mr. Hardison the opportunity for Saturdays off, including asking the union to waive a seniority rule that limited substitutes for him and looking for an alternative job that would not require Saturday work. The union would not waive its rule, and no managers were available to take the shift. When Mr. Hardison refused to work on Saturdays, he was dismissed and filed suit, but the Court found for TWA because of its extensive efforts and the constraints that prevented shifting of workers without substantial interference in TWA's operations.

Title VII requires only reasonable accommodation. Employees are not necessarily entitled to the accommodation they desire. For example, in *American Postal Workers Union v. Postmaster General*, 781 F.2d 772 (9th Cir. 1986), several postal employees refused to work at a window in the post office where draft registration forms were handled. They asked to be able to direct draft registrants to the windows of employees who did not have religious objections to the draft. The Postal Service transferred the employees to nonwindow jobs, which was supported by the court as a reasonable accommodation.

Further, employees are expected to cooperate with their employers in making an accommodation, such as finding a fellow employee to take a shift. In *TWA v. Hardison*, the Court noted, "The statute is not to be construed to require an employer to discriminate against some employees in order for others to observe their Sabbath."

Racial Discrimination

When Title VII was first enacted, its clear intent was to prevent discrimination against the minority workforce. After Title VII had been in effect for several years, an unanticipated problem arose: Does Title VII's protection extend to all races? Are white employees entitled to the same protection Title VII affords other races?

In 1976, the Supreme Court provided the answer in *McDonald v. Santa Fe Trail Transportation Co.*, 427 U.S. 273 (1976). Here, some black employees had been reinstated after committing the same offense as a group of white employees who were not reinstated. The Court held that Title VII prohibited such racial discrimination.

In *Patterson v. McClean Credit Union*, 491 U.S. 164 (1989), the U.S. Supreme Court was faced with reprehensible conduct by an employer in the consideration of a black female for promotion. The Court held that there was no violation of the Civil Rights Act because a promotion was not part of a contract as required to establish race discrimination under Section 1981, a nineteenth-century antidiscrimination statute. The effect of the case was changed by the 1991 Civil Rights Act, which permits victims of racial or ethnic discrimination to recover unrestricted compensatory and punitive damages without regard to the technical issue of whether the terms of employment fit within the Court's narrow construction of a contract.

ANTIDISCRIMINATION LAWS AND AFFIRMATIVE ACTION

Some employers, either voluntarily or through the EEOC, have instituted **affirmative action** programs. Nothing prohibits such programs under Title VII, and the Supreme Court has sanctioned them as methods for remedying all the past years of discrimination. Although Title VII does not mandate such programs, employers may legally institute them.

Affirmative action has been described by some as the tool necessary to put all races and the sexes on an equal footing after years of discrimination. Others, however, have described it as an unfair system that discriminates against whites and males and often serves to reduce the self-esteem of those who benefit from it because of their feelings about being hired or promoted solely because of their race or sex. Others have argued that affirmative action encourages inefficiency because it prevents the most qualified or the most deserving from earning a promotion or being hired in the first instance.

What Is Affirmative Action?

Although Title VII prohibits discrimination against any group, there is well-established judicial and legislative support for the establishment of affirmative action programs. Affirmative action is a remedial step taken to ensure that those who have been victims of discrimination in the past are given the opportunity to work in positions they would have attained had there not been discrimination.

Affirmative action programs are used to improve job opportunities for African-Americans, Hispanics, Native Americans, Asians, women, persons with disabilities, and Vietnam veterans.

Who Is Required to Have Affirmative Action Programs?

Some federal funding laws, such as those for education and state and local governments, mandate affirmative action programs.

Some employers have an obligation to take steps to equalize the representation of minorities and women in their labor forces. This equalization of representation in the labor force is the process of affirmative action. Those employers who are obligated to undertake affirmative action programs are:

1. Employers who, pursuant to consent decree or court order, must implement plans to compensate for past wrongs
2. State and local agencies and colleges and universities that receive federal funds
3. Government contractors
4. Businesses that work on federal projects (10 percent of their subcontract work must employ minority businesses)

Affirmative action plans cannot simply be **quotas;** a quota program is an unlawful infringement of the rights of a majority group of employees. Rather, affirmative action programs set goals—for example, a certain number of minorities employed by a certain date. If the goal is not met, a business has not violated the law so long as it has made a good-faith effort to recruit and hire minorities. That good-faith effort can be established by a showing of internal and external advertising, monitoring of the program's progress, and changes and improvements in the program's development.

Preparing an Affirmative Action Program

An employer should begin with an equal employment opportunity statement, which says simply that decisions on recruiting, hiring, training, and promotion will be made without regard to race, color, religion, sex, national origin, veteran status, or disability. The statement should be displayed at the place of business, made evident in all recruiting materials, and reaffirmed each year to reestablish commitment to it. The firm should also appoint an affirmative action or equal employment opportunity officer. The role of this employee is to identify problems and propose solutions.

A business should then conduct an initial audit and maintain good records regarding its hiring, promotion, and recruiting of employees. In such an audit, the employer examines job titles and determines key areas in which women and minorities are underrepresented. If the audit finds that these groups are underrepresented with respect to their availability in the workforce, then a system of goals and timetables should be established for each underrepresented job title. The employer then monitors the data to see whether the goals are met. If goals are not met, further steps should be taken, such as more aggressive recruiting.

Affirmative Action Backlash: The Theory of Reverse Discrimination

Currently there are legislative movements and grass roots referenda that mandate the elimination of affirmative action programs. The University of California system eliminated affirmative action programs in 1995, but the programs were reinstated by a court after the elimination was challenged. The issues of fairness, extent, and need of affirmative action continue to be debated.

In *Adarand Constructors, Inc.* v. *Pena,* 515 U.S. 200 (1995), the U.S. Supreme Court was faced with the issue of affirmative action programs in a case brought by a contractor that challenged the federal government's program granting socially and economically disadvantaged contractors and subcontractors preferences in the awarding of government contracts. The case was remanded for trial after a ruling by the Court that such programs were subject to a standard of review known as "strict scrutiny." The Court held that the government's set-aside program offering preferences to minority-owned businesses was a racial classification. To survive the strict scrutiny test, which is derived from the Equal Protection Clause of the U.S. Constitution (see Chapter 5), the federal government must be able to show, when a case goes to trial, that the contractor preferences serve a compelling government interest. *Adarand II,* heard by the U.S. Supreme Court in 2001, was upheld without opinion.[1]

In *Taxman* v. *Board of Education of Piscataway,* 91 F.3d 1547 (3d Cir. 1996), *cert.* granted, 521 U.S. 1117 (1997); *cert.* dismissed, 522 U.S. 1010 (1997), a school district, when facing the need to reduce the size of its teaching staff, decided to retain an African-American school teacher, Debra Williams. Sharon Taxman, a white school teacher, challenged the decision as discriminatory, and the school board defended on the grounds of its affirmative action program. On appeal, the circuit court held that the decision was unconstitutional because the school board's program was adopted to promote diversity and not to remedy any past wrongs the school district had committed. The U.S. Supreme Court granted *certiorari* to review the case, but the school board agreed to a settlement, paying Ms. Taxman $433,500, of which $308,500 was paid by national civil rights organizations. The civil rights organizations indicated that they agreed to pay the bulk of the settlement because they were fearful that the court might outlaw affirmative action programs.

THE DEFENSES TO A TITLE VII CHARGE

Title VII is not a strict liability statute. Some defenses are provided in the act that employers can use to defend against a charge of discrimination.

Bona Fide Occupational Qualification

A **bona fide occupational qualification** (BFOQ) is a job qualification based on sex, religion, or national origin that is necessary for the operation of business. A particular religious belief is a BFOQ for a pastor of a church. Similarly, an actor, to qualify for a role, may need to be a certain sex for purposes of realism and thus sex is a BFOQ for such employment.

The BFOQ exception has been applied narrowly, however. For a discriminatory qualification for employment to fall within the BFOQ exception, the employer must be able to establish that the job qualification is carefully formulated to respond to public safety, privacy, or other public needs; and the formulation of the policy must not be broader than is reasonably necessary to preserve the safety or privacy of individuals involved. For example, a restriction on hiring male employees for work in a nursing home occupied by women is excessive if male employees can work in jobs not involved with the personal care of the residents. Nor is personal preference a justification for a BFOQ; for example, many airlines have argued that there is a customer preference for female as opposed to male flight attendants. But customer preference is not a basis for a BFOQ; it is not a business necessity.

Seniority or Merit Systems

The goals and objectives of Title VII are often inconsistent with labor union rules of operation. Although matters of discrimination and union supervision are both covered by federal law, there are some conflicts between the two statutory schemes. Which controls the other: the remedial effect of Title VII or the long-standing history of seniority and other union rules? Although the exception for seniority and merit systems has always been a part of Title VII, early decisions made Title VII goals superior and invalidated many of the seniority and merit systems.

The criteria to be used in determining whether a seniority or merit system is valid are as follows:

1. The system must apply to all employees.
2. Whatever divisions or units are used for the system must follow the industry custom or pattern; that is, the divisions cannot be set up so as to discriminate against particular races or groups.
3. The origins of the system cannot lie in racial discrimination.
4. The system must be maintained for seniority and merit purposes and not to perpetuate racial discrimination.

Aptitude and Other Tests

Any employer charged with Title VII discrimination because of employee aptitude testing must be able to show that the tests used are valid. Validity means that the tests are related to successful job performance and that a test does not have the effect of eliminating certain races from the employment market.

An employer can validate a test in any of several different ways. Test scores of applicants can later be compared with the applicants' eventual job performance to validate the test. An employer can also give the test to current employees and use the correlation between their scores and job performance as a means for validating the test. Some tests can be validated by their content. For example, requiring potential police officers to complete a driving course, a physical fitness test, and a marksmanship test is valid because the tests are based on the things police officers actually do.

Misconduct

For many years, an absolute defense to discrimination was employee misconduct. If an employee violated company rules, there was no discrimination case. The defense was so broad that even evidence the employer acquired *after* the termination and charge of discrimination could be used as a defense. In the following case, the Supreme Court limited this defense.

CASE 20.4

McKennon v. Nashville Banner Publishing Co.
524 U.S. 742 (1995)

Lying Is Not a Defense for Discrimination

FACTS

For 30 years, Christine McKennon (petitioner) worked for Nashville Banner Publishing Company (respondent), but was terminated as part of a work reduction plan. She was 62 years old at the time of her termination.

Ms. McKennon filed suit alleging her termination was a violation of the Age Discrimination in Employment Act (ADEA).

In preparation of the case, Banner took McKennon's deposition. She testified that during her final year of employment, she had copied several confidential documents bearing upon the company's financial condition. She had access to these records as secretary to Banner's comptroller. Ms. McKennon took the copies home and showed them to her hus-

band. Her motivation, she averred, was apprehension that she was about to be fired because of her age. When she became concerned about her job, she removed and copied the documents for "insurance" and "protection." A few days after these deposition disclosures, Banner sent Ms. McKennon a letter declaring that removal and copying of the records was in violation of her job responsibilities and advising her (again) that she was terminated. Banner's letter also recited that had it known of Ms. McKennon's misconduct, it would have discharged her at once for that reason.

Nashville Banner conceded its discrimination in district court, which granted summary judgment for Banner on grounds that Ms. McKennon's misconduct was a defense. The court of appeals affirmed and Ms. McKennon appealed.

JUDICIAL OPINION

KENNEDY, Justice

We shall assume that the sole reason for McKennon's initial discharge was her age, a discharge violative of the ADEA. Our further premise is that the misconduct revealed by the deposition was so grave that McKennon's immediate discharge would have followed its disclosure in any event. We do question the legal conclusion reached by those courts that after-acquired evidence of wrongdoing which would have resulted in discharge bars employees from any relief under the ADEA. That ruling is incorrect.

The ADEA, enacted in 1967 as part of an ongoing congressional effort to eradicate discrimination in the workplace, reflects a societal condemnation of invidious bias in employment decisions. The ADEA is but part of a wider statutory scheme to protect employees in the workplace nationwide.

The ADEA and Title VII share common substantive features and also a common purpose: "the elimination of discrimination in the workplace." Congress designed the remedial measures in these statutes to serve as a "spur or catalyst" to cause employers "to self-examine and to self-evaluate their employment practices and to endeavor to eliminate, so far as possible, the last vestiges" of discrimination. The ADEA, in keeping with these purposes, contains a vital element found in both Title VII and the Fair Labor Standards Act: it grants an injured employee a right of action to obtain the authorized relief.

The objectives of the ADEA are furthered when even a single employee establishes that an employer has discriminated against him or her. The disclosure through litigation of incidents or practices which violate national policies respecting nondiscrimination in the work force is itself important, for the occurrence of violations may disclose patterns of noncompliance resulting from a misappreciation of the Act's operation or entrenched resistance to its commands, either of which can be of industry-wide significance. The efficacy of its enforcement mechanisms becomes one measure of the success of the Act.

As we have said, the case comes to us on the express assumption that an unlawful motive was the sole basis for the firing. McKennon's misconduct was not discovered until after she had been fired. The employer could not have been motivated by knowledge it did not have and it cannot now claim that the employee was fired for the nondiscriminatory reason. Mixed motive cases are inapposite here, except to the important extent they underscore the necessity of determining the employer's motives in ordering the discharge, an essential element in determining whether the employer violated the federal antidiscrimination law. As we have observed, "proving that the same decision would have been justified . . . is not the same as proving that the same decision would have been made."

The ADEA, like Title VII, is not a general regulation of the workplace but a law which prohibits discrimination. The statute does not constrain employers from exercising significant other prerogatives and discretions in the course of the hiring, promoting, and discharging of their employees. In determining appropriate remedial action, the employee's wrongdoing becomes relevant not to punish the employee, or out of concern "for the relative moral worth of the parties," but to take due account of the lawful prerogatives of the employer in the usual course of its business and the corresponding equities that it has arising from the employee's wrongdoing.

The proper boundaries of remedial relief in the general class of cases where, after termination, it is discovered that the employee has engaged in wrongdoing must be addressed by the judicial system in the ordinary course of further decisions, for the factual permutations and the equitable considerations they raise will vary from case to case. We do conclude that here, and as a general rule in cases of this type, neither reinstatement nor front pay is an appropriate remedy. It would be both inequitable and pointless to order the reinstatement of someone the employer would have terminated, and will terminate, in any event and upon lawful grounds.

The object of compensation is to restore the employee to the position he or she would have been in absent the discrimination, but that principle is difficult to apply with precision where there is after-acquired evidence of wrongdoing that would have led to termination on legitimate grounds had the employer known about it.

Where an employer seeks to rely upon after-acquired evidence of wrongdoing, it must first establish that the wrongdoing was of such severity that the employee in fact would have been terminated on those grounds alone if the employer had known of it at the time of the discharge. The concern that employers might as a routine matter undertake extensive discovery into an employee's background or performance on the job to resist claims under the Act is not an insubstantial one, but we think the authority of the courts to award attorney's fees, mandated under the statute, 29 U.S.C. §§ 216(b), 626(b),

(continued)

and in appropriate cases to invoke the provisions of Rule 11 of the Federal Rules of Civil Procedure will deter most abuses.

The judgment is reversed.

CASE QUESTIONS

1. Why is the timing of the misconduct disclosure important?

2. Does Banner deny discriminatory intent?

3. Why are "mixed motive" cases not relevant in this analysis?

4. Is reinstatement a remedy?

ENFORCEMENT OF TITLE VII

Visit the EEOC at:
http://www.eeoc.gov

Title VII is an enabling act that created the Equal Employment Opportunity Commission for the purpose of administration and enforcement. The EEOC is a five-member commission whose members are appointed by the president with the approval of the Senate. As with all other federal commissions, no more than three members can belong to the same political party.

The EEOC was given very broad powers under Title VII. In addition to its rule-making and charging powers, the EEOC has very broad investigatory authority, including the authority to subpoena documents and testimony.

Steps in an EEOC Case

The Complaint

An EEOC complaint can be filed by an employee or by the EEOC. An employee has 180 days (in some cases, up to 300 days) from the time of the alleged violation to file a complaint. The EEOC does not have such a statute of limitations.

The complaint is filed with either the EEOC or the state administrative agency set up for employment discrimination issues. For the state agency to continue handling the complaint, it must be an EEOC-approved program. If it is not, the EEOC handles the complaint. The EEOC has special forms that can be filled out by any employee wishing to file such a complaint.

Notification to the Employer

Once a complaint has been filed, the EEOC has ten days to notify the employer of the charges. Employers are prohibited from the time of notification from taking any retaliatory action against the charging employee.

EEOC Action

After the complaint is filed, the EEOC has 180 days from that time to take action in the case before the complaining party can file suit on the matter. During this time, the EEOC can use its investigatory powers to explore the merits of the charges. In the case of *University of Pennsylvania* v. *EEOC*, 493 U.S. 182 (1990), the Supreme Court ruled that the EEOC could have access to all information in an employee's file—even evaluation letters in which evaluators were promised confidentiality. This is also a conciliation period during which the EEOC may try to work out a settlement between the employer and the employee.

ETHICAL ISSUES 20.1

Consider the following circumstances and decide whether there has been a violation of Title VII. Consider the ethical implications of the conduct along with the legal.

1. An employee must be dismissed. There are two women, one white and the other black, who have been with a company for the same amount of time and who have the same rate of absenteeism. Their performance evaluations are about the same. Can the black employee be dismissed without violating Title VII?

2. Company B has had a significant problem with absenteeism, tardiness, and failure to follow through on job assignments among the employees who are of a certain race. The personnel director is concerned about company productivity, the costs of training, and the costs of constant turnover. The personnel director is also aware of the constraints of Title VII. The director instructs those staffing the front office to tell members of that particular race who apply for a job that the company is not accepting applications. The director's theory is that his applicant pool will be prescreened and he will not have to make discriminatory hiring decisions. Is the director correct?

The Right-to-Sue Letter

If the EEOC has not settled its complaint within 180 days from the time of its filing, the employee has the right to demand a **right-to-sue letter** from the EEOC, which is a certification that the employee has exhausted his administrative remedies. If a state agency is involved, the time for its settlement of the matter must also expire before the employee can take the matter to court.

The employee has the right to this letter regardless of the EEOC's findings. Even if the EEOC has investigated and determined that there are no merits to the charges, the employee can still pursue the case in court.

Remedies Available under Title VII

Remedies available under Title VII include injunctions, back pay, punitive damages, and attorneys' fees. If a court finds a violation, it may order that corrective or affirmative action be taken to compensate for past wrongs. An injunction usually requires the employer to stop the illegal discrimination and then institute a plan to hire or promote minorities. Back-pay awards are limited to two years under Title VII. Section 706(b) of the act permits successful parties to recover "reasonable attorneys' fees."

An employer cannot take retaliatory action against employees who file charges or who are successful in a suit; Title VII makes such action unlawful.

Title VII originally allowed damages for back pay for all forms of discrimination. Punitive and compensatory damages are now permitted in racial and ethnic discrimination cases. The 1991 amendments extend the recovery of punitive and compensatory damages to cases involving sex, religion, or disability.

OTHER ANTIDISCRIMINATION LAWS

Age Discrimination in Employment Act of 1967

Title VII does not cover the very real problem of age discrimination, which generally involves companies' hiring preference for younger people. To correct this loophole, the Age Discrimination in Employment Act (ADEA) was passed in 1967,

Review the Age Discrimination in Employment Act:
http://www.law.cornell.edu/uscode/29/621.html

and the EEOC was given responsibility for its enforcement. The act covers all employers with twenty or more employees and prohibits age discrimination in the hiring, firing, and compensation of employees. All employment agencies are covered. Those protected under the act are workforce members above age 40.

The elements in an age discrimination case are similar to those in other discrimination cases—simply substitute that the terminated employee was replaced with a younger employee. The replacement need not be below the age of 40 [*O'Connor* v. *Consolidated Coin Caterers Corp.*, 517 U.S. 308 (1996)].

C O N S I D E R . . .

20.6   The superiors for a 58-year-old terminated employee commented that the employee had a "1970s management style." Is such a statement evidence of age discrimination? [*Rifakes* v. *Citizen Utilities Co.*, 968 F. Supp. 315 (N.D. Tex. 1997)]

C O N S I D E R . . .

20.7   On October 29, 1982, Preview Subscription Television, Inc., a subsidiary of Time, Inc., hired Thomas Taggart as a print production manager for Preview's magazine guide. Taggart was 58 years old at the time and had over 30 years experience in the printing industry. In May 1983, Time notified Mr. Taggart that Preview would be dissolved and that Preview employees would receive special consideration for all Time positions.

Mr. Taggart applied for thirty-two positions in various divisions at Time and its subsidiaries, including *Sports Illustrated, People, Life, Money, HBO,* and *Cinemax Guide.* He was interviewed but never hired. The reason given was that he was "overqualified." Mr. Taggart filed suit alleging age discrimination. Time responded by saying he performed poorly at interviews, his letters and résumés for jobs contained numerous typographical errors, and he was argumentative with management and counselors.

Time hired less-qualified younger applicants for all the jobs. Has there been age discrimination? [*Taggart* v. *Time, Inc.*, 924 F. 2d 43 (2nd Cir. 1991)]

Equal Pay Act of 1963

Review the Equal Pay Act:
http://www.law.cornell.edu/uscode/29/206.html

The Equal Pay Act of 1963 is an amendment to the Fair Labor Standards Act. (The details of its coverage are outlined in Chapter 19.) The basic purpose of the act is to ensure that equal pay is given for jobs with equal content regardless of sex. Its application is limited to sex-based discrimination. Most of these kinds of cases deal with the issue of whether two jobs are "equal" in their content and whether the employees are thus entitled to equal pay.

Communicable Diseases in the Workplace

Whether employees can be fired because they may carry a communicable disease has recently become a crucial issue. Court decisions on the treatment of infected employees have varied, but the Supreme Court decision, *School Board of Nassau County* v. *Arline,* 480 U.S. 273 (1987), has been touted as a protectionist measure as a result of its finding that a school board could not discriminate against a teacher because she had tuberculosis (a contagious disease). The Americans with Disabilities Act will provide new issues and remedies with regard to communicable diseases (see below).

Rehabilitation Act of 1973

Review the Rehabilitation Act:
http://www.law.cornell.edu/uscode/29/701.html

Congress enacted the Rehabilitation Act to prohibit discrimination in employment against handicapped persons by persons and organizations that receive federal contracts or assistance. The Labor Department is responsible for enforcement of the act. The Rehabilitation Act laid the ground work for the Americans with Disabilities Act. It is limited to employers who have federal contracts and requires the same reasonable accommodation standards now required under ADA.

Americans with Disabilities Act

Review the Americans with Disabilities Act:
http://www.usdoj.gov/crt/ada/adahoml.htm

The intent of the Americans with Disabilities Act (ADA) was to eliminate discrimination against individuals with disabilities. The ADA has been called the "Emancipation Proclamation" for disabled U.S. citizens.

The ADA is divided into five sections. Title I governs employment issues; Titles II, III, and IV ensure that those with disabilities still have access to public streets, walkways, buildings, and transportation.

The ADA was signed on July 26, 1990. It became effective on July 26, 1992, for employers with twenty-five or more employees and went into effect on July 26, 1994, for employers with fifteen or more employees. The employment provisions (Title I) apply to private businesses and to state and local government agencies but not to the federal government.

Under the ADA, employers cannot discriminate in hiring, promotion, and selection criteria against a "qualified individual with a disability." "Qualified" means that the individual, with reasonable accommodation, can perform all "essential functions" of the job. Impairments such as gambling, kleptomania, pyromania, illegal drugs, and sexual disorders are excluded from protection.

A disability is defined by the ADA as a physical or mental impairment that substantially limits one or more major life activities such as seeing, hearing, speaking, walking, breathing, learning, or self-care. The ADA also includes as a disability having a record of impairment or having something others regard as a disability. Pursuant to a recent U.S. Supreme Court case [*Bragdon v. Abbott*, 524 U.S. 624 (1998)], human immunodeficiency virus (HIV) is considered a physical impairment for purposes of the ADA. In that case, a dentist's refusal to treat an HIV-positive patient who needed a cavity filled violated the ADA public accommodation provisions.

Employers must make "reasonable accommodations" for disabled individuals to enable them to perform essential functions. Included in reasonable accommodations are providing employee facilities that are readily accessible to and usable by disabled individuals, job restructuring, allowing part-time or modified work schedules, reassigning disabled individuals to vacant positions, acquiring or modifying equipment, and providing qualified readers or interpreters. Perhaps the accommodation best known to the public was the right golfer Casey Martin won to use a cart in PGA tournaments because of his circulatory ailment. That case follows.

CASE 20.5

PGA Tour, Inc. v. Martin
531 U.S. 1049 (2001)

A Stroke of Genius for an ADA in Full Swing

FACTS

Casey Martin (respondent) is a talented golfer. As an amateur, he won 17 Oregon Golf Association junior events before he was 15, and won the state championship as a high school senior. He played on the Stanford University golf team that won the 1994 National Collegiate Athletic Association (NCAA) championship. As a professional, Martin qualified for the NIKE TOUR in 1998 and 1999, and based on his 1999 performance, qualified for the PGA TOUR in 2000. In the 1999 season, he entered 24 events, made the cut 13 times, and had 6 top-10 finishes, coming in second twice and third once.

Martin is also an individual with a disability as defined in the Americans with Disabilities Act of 1990 (ADA or Act). Since birth he has been afflicted with Klippel-Trenaunay-Weber Syndrome, a degenerative circulatory disorder that obstructs the flow of blood from his right leg back to his heart. The disease is progressive; it causes severe pain and has atrophied his right leg. During the latter part of his college career, because of the progress of the disease, Martin could no longer walk an 18–hole golf course. Walking not only caused him pain, fatigue, and anxiety, but also created a significant risk of hemorrhaging, developing blood clots, and fracturing his tibia so badly that an amputation might be required. For these reasons, Stanford made written requests to the Pacific 10 Conference and the NCAA to waive for Martin their rules requiring players to walk and carry their own clubs. The requests were granted.

The PGA TOUR, Inc., (Petitioner) a nonprofit entity formed in 1968, sponsors and cosponsors professional golf tournaments conducted on three annual tours. About 200 golfers participate in the PGA TOUR; about 170 in the NIKE TOUR; and about 100 in the SENIOR PGA TOUR. PGA TOUR and NIKE TOUR tournaments typically are 4-day events, played on courses leased and operated by the PGA. The entire field usually competes in two 18-hole rounds played on Thursday and Friday; those who survive the "cut" play on Saturday and Sunday and receive prize money in amounts determined by their aggregate scores for all four rounds. The revenues generated by television, admissions, concessions, and contributions from cosponsors amount to about $300 million a year, much of which is distributed in prize money.

The basic Rules of Golf, the hard cards, and the weekly notices apply equally to all players in tour competitions. As one of petitioner's witnesses explained with reference to "the Masters Tournament, which is golf at its very highest level . . . the key is to have everyone tee off on the first hole under exactly the same conditions and all of them be tested over that 72-hole event under the conditions that exist during those four days of the event."

The lower court and court of appeals found that the rule on no carts violated the Americans with Disabilities Act and required the PGA to permit Martin to use a cart pursuant to the act's rules on reasonable accommodation. The PGA appealed.

JUDICIAL OPINION

STEVENS, Justice

This case raises two questions concerning the application of the Americans with Disabilities Act of 1990, to a gifted athlete: first, whether the Act protects access to professional golf tournaments by a qualified entrant with a disability; and second, whether a disabled contestant may be denied the use of a golf cart because it would "fundamentally alter the nature" of the tournaments, § 12182(b)(2)(A)(ii), to allow him to ride when all other contestants must walk.

The term 'disability' means, with respect to an individual—

(A) a physical or mental impairment that substantially limits one or more of the major life activities of such individual. . . .

On the merits, because there was no serious dispute about the fact that permitting Martin to use a golf cart was both a reasonable and a necessary solution to the problem of providing him access to the tournaments, the Court of Appeals regarded the central dispute as whether such permission would "fundamentally alter" the nature of the PGA TOUR or NIKE TOUR.

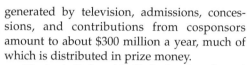

Title III of the ADA prescribes, as a "[g]eneral rule":

No individual shall be discriminated against on the basis of disability in the full and equal enjoyment of the goods, services, facilities, privileges, advantages, or accommodations of any place of public accommodation by any person who owns, leases (or leases to), or operates a place of public accommodation."

42 U.S.C. § 12182(a).

The phrase "public accommodation" is defined in terms of 12 extensive categories, which the legislative history indicates "should be construed liberally" to afford people with disabilities "equal access" to the wide variety of establishments available to the nondisabled.

It seems apparent, from both the general rule and the comprehensive definition of "public accommodation," that petitioner's golf tours and their qualifying rounds fit comfortably within the coverage of Title III, and Martin within its protection. The events occur on "golf course[s]," a type of place specifically identified by the Act as a public accommodation. In addition, at all relevant times, petitioner "leases" and "operates" golf courses to conduct its Q-School and tours.

According to petitioner, Title III [of the ADA] is concerned with discrimination against "clients and customers" seeking to obtain "goods and services" at places of public accommodation, whereas it is Title I that protects persons who work at such places. As the argument goes, petitioner operates not a "golf course" during its tournaments but a "place of exhibition or entertainment," and a professional golfer such as Martin, like an actor in a theater production, is a provider rather than a consumer of the entertainment that petitioner sells to the public. Martin therefore cannot bring a claim under Title III because he is not one of the " 'clients or customers of the covered public accommodation.' " Rather, Martin's claim of discrimination is "job-related" and could only be brought under Title I—but that Title does not apply because he is an independent contractor (as the District Court found) rather than an employee.

We need not decide whether petitioner's construction of the statute is correct, because petitioner's argument falters even on its own terms. If Title III's protected class were limited to "clients or customers," it would be entirely appropriate to classify the golfers who pay petitioner $3,000 for the chance to compete in the Q-School and, if successful, in the subsequent tour events, as petitioner's clients or customers. In our view, petitioner's tournaments (whether situated at a "golf course" or at a "place of exhibition or entertainment") simultaneously offer at least two "privileges" to the public—that of watching the golf competition and that of competing in it. Although the latter is more difficult and more expensive to obtain than the former, it is nonetheless a privilege that petitioner makes available to members of the general public. In consideration of the entry fee, any golfer with the requisite letters of recommendation acquires the opportunity to qualify for and compete in petitioner's tours. Additionally, any golfer who succeeds in the open qualifying rounds for a tournament may play in the event. That petitioner identifies one set of clients or customers that it serves (spectators at tournaments) does not preclude it from having another set (players in tournaments) against whom it may not discriminate.

Petitioner does not contest that a golf cart is a reasonable modification that is necessary if Martin is to play in its tournaments. Martin's claim thus differs from one that might be asserted by players with less serious afflictions that make walking the course uncomfortable or difficult, but not beyond their capacity. In such cases, an accommodation might be reasonable but not necessary. In this case, however, the narrow dispute is whether allowing Martin to use a golf cart, despite the walking requirement that applies to the PGA TOUR, the NIKE TOUR, and the third stage of the Q-School, is a modification that would "fundamentally alter the nature" of those events.

We are not persuaded that a waiver of the walking rule for Martin would work a fundamental alteration in either sense.

As an initial matter, we observe that the use of carts is not itself inconsistent with the fundamental character of the game of golf. From early on, the essence of the game has been shot-making—using clubs to cause a ball to progress from the teeing ground to a hole some distance away with as few strokes as possible. That essential aspect of the game is still reflected in the very first of the Rules of Golf, which declares: "The Game of Golf consists in playing a ball from the teeing ground into the hole by a stroke or successive strokes in accordance with the rules." Rule 1-1, Rules of Golf, App. 104. Over the years, there have been many changes in the players' equipment, in golf course design, in the Rules of Golf, and in the method of transporting clubs from hole to hole. Originally, so few clubs were used that each player could carry them without a bag. Then came golf bags, caddies, carts that were pulled by

(continued)

hand, and eventually motorized carts that carried players as well as clubs. "Golf carts started appearing with increasing regularity on American golf courses in the 1950's. Today they are everywhere. And they are encouraged. For one thing, they often speed up play, and for another, they are great revenue producers." There is nothing in the Rules of Golf that either forbids the use of carts, or penalizes a player for using a cart. That set of rules, as we have observed, is widely accepted in both the amateur and professional golf world as the rules of the game. The walking rule that is contained in petitioner's hard cards, based on an optional condition buried in an appendix to the Rules of Golf, is not an essential attribute of the game itself.

Even if we accept the factual predicate for petitioner's argument—that the walking rule is "outcome affecting" because fatigue may adversely affect performance—its legal position is fatally flawed. Petitioner's refusal to consider Martin's personal circumstances in deciding whether to accommodate his disability runs counter to the clear language and purpose of the ADA. As previously stated, the ADA was enacted to eliminate discrimination against "individuals" with disabilities, and to that end Title III of the Act requires without exception that any "policies, practices, or procedures" of a public accommodation be reasonably modified for disabled "individuals" as necessary to afford access unless doing so would fundamentally alter what is offered. To comply with this command, an individualized inquiry must be made to determine whether a specific modification for a particular person's disability would be reasonable under the circumstances as well as necessary for that person, and yet at the same time not work a fundamental alteration.

To be sure, the waiver of an essential rule of competition for anyone would fundamentally alter the nature of petitioner's tournaments. As we have demonstrated, however, the walking rule is at best peripheral to the nature of petitioner's athletic events, and thus it might be waived in individual cases without working a fundamental alteration.

The judgment of the Court of Appeals is affirmed.

DISSENTING OPINION

Justices SCALIA and THOMAS

In my view today's opinion exercises a benevolent compassion that the law does not place it within our power to impose. The judgment distorts the text of Title III, the structure of the ADA, and common sense. I respectfully dissent.

The Court holds that a professional sport is a place of public accommodation and that respondent is a "custome[r]" of "competition" when he practices his profession. It finds, that this strange conclusion is compelled by the "literal text" of Title III of the Americans with Disabilities Act of 1990(ADA), 42 U.S.C. § 12101 et seq., by the "expansive purpose" of the ADA, and by the fact that Title II of the Civil Rights Act of 1964, 42 U.S.C. § 2000a(a), has been applied to an amusement park and public golf courses. I disagree.

The ADA has three separate titles: Title I covers employment discrimination, Title II covers discrimination by government entities, and Title III covers discrimination by places of public accommodation. Title II is irrelevant to this case. Title I protects only "employees" of employers who have 15 or more employees, §§ 12112(a), 12111(5)(A). It does not protect independent contractors. Respondent claimed employment discrimination under Title I, but the District Court found him to be an independent contractor rather than an employee.

Respondent also claimed protection under § 12182 of Title III. That section applies only to particular places and persons. The place must be a "place of public accommodation," and the person must be an "individual" seeking "enjoyment of the goods, services, facilities, privileges, advantages, or accommodations" of the covered place.

The provision of Title III at issue here (§ 12182, its principal provision) is a public-accommodation law, and it is the traditional understanding of public-accommodation laws that they provide rights for customers.

The one place where Title III specifically addresses discrimination by places of public accommodation through "contractual" arrangements, it makes clear that discrimination against the other party to the contract is not covered, but only discrimination against "clients or customers of the covered public accommodation that enters into the contractual, licensing or other arrangement." And finally, the regulations promulgated by the Department of Justice reinforce the conclusion that Title III's protections extend only to customers. "The purpose of the ADA's public accommodations requirements," they say, "is to ensure accessibility to the goods offered by a public accommodation." Surely this has nothing to do with employees and independent contractors.

The Court, for its part, pronounces respondent to be a "customer" of the PGA TOUR or of the golf courses on which it is played. That seems to me quite incredible. The PGA TOUR is a professional sporting event, staged for the entertainment of a live and TV audience, the receipts from whom (the TV audience's admission price is paid by advertisers) pay the expenses of the tour, including the cash prizes for the winning golfers. The professional golfers on the tour are no more "enjoying" (the statutory term) the entertainment that the tour provides, or the facilities of the golf courses on which it is held, than professional baseball players "enjoy" the baseball games in which they play or the facilities of Yankee Stadium. To be sure, professional ballplayers participate in the games, and use the ballfields, but no one in his right mind would think that they are customers of the American League or of Yankee Stadium. They are themselves the entertainment that the customers pay to watch. And professional golfers are no different. It makes not a bit of difference, insofar as their "customer" status is concerned, that the remuneration for their performance (unlike most of the remuneration for ballplayers) is not fixed but contingent—viz., the purses for the winners in the various events, and the compensation from product endorsements that consistent winners are assured. The compensation of many independent contractors is contingent upon their success—real estate brokers, for example, or insurance salesmen.

Respondent did not seek to "exercise" or "recreate" at the PGA TOUR events; he sought to make money (which is why he is called a professional golfer). He was not a customer buying recreation or entertainment; he was a professional athlete selling it.

The regulations state that Title III "does not require a public accommodation to alter its inventory to include accessible or special goods with accessibility features that are designed for, or facilitate use by, individuals with disabilities."

It is as irrelevant to the PGA TOUR's compliance with the statute whether walking is essential to the game of golf as it is to the shoe store's compliance whether "pairness" is essential to the nature of shoes. If a shoe store wishes to sell shoes only in pairs it may; and if a golf tour (or a golf course) wishes to provide only walk-around golf, it may. The PGA TOUR cannot deny respondent access to that game because of his disability, but it need not provide him a game different (whether in its essentials or in its details) from that offered to everyone else.

Nowhere is it writ that PGA TOUR golf must be classic "essential" golf. Why cannot the PGA TOUR, if it wishes, promote a new game, with distinctive rules (much as the American League promotes a game of baseball in which the pitcher's turn at the plate can be taken by a "designated hitter")? If members of the public do not like the new rules—if they feel that these rules do not truly test the individual's skill at "real golf" (or the team's skill at "real baseball") they can withdraw their patronage. But the rules are the rules. They are (as in all games) entirely arbitrary, and there is no basis on which anyone—not even the Supreme Court of the United States—can pronounce one or another of them to be "nonessential" if the rulemaker (here the PGA TOUR) deems it to be essential.

If one assumes, however, that the PGA TOUR has some legal obligation to play classic, Platonic golf—and if one assumes the correctness of all the other wrong turns the Court has made to get to this point—then we Justices must confront what is indeed an awesome responsibility. It has been rendered the solemn duty of the Supreme Court of the United States, laid upon it by Congress in pursuance of the Federal Government's power "[t]o regulate Commerce with foreign Nations, and among the several States," U.S. Const., Art. I, § 8, cl. 3, to decide What Is Golf. I am sure that the Framers of the Constitution, aware of the 1457 edict of King James II of Scotland prohibiting golf because it interfered with the practice of archery, fully expected that sooner or later the paths of golf and government, the law and the links, would once again cross, and that the judges of this august Court would some day have to wrestle with that age-old jurisprudential question, for which their years of study in the law have so well prepared them: Is someone riding around a golf course from shot to shot really a golfer? The answer, we learn, is yes. The Court ultimately concludes, and it will henceforth be the Law of the Land, that walking is not a "fundamental" aspect of golf.

Either out of humility or out of self-respect (one or the other) the Court should decline to answer this incredibly difficult and incredibly silly question.

CASE QUESTIONS

1. Why does Martin wish an accommodation?
2. Does use of a cart fundamentally alter the game of golf?
3. Is Martin seeking a public accommodation or an employee accommodation?
4. Does the dissent believe that the court must define the essential elements of the game of golf?

EXHIBIT 20.2 Compliance Tips for ADA

MINIMIZING AN EMPLOYER'S ADA RISKS

1. Post notices describing the provisions of the ADA in your workplace.

2. Review job requirements to ensure that they bear a direct relationship to the ability to perform the essential functions of the job in question.

3. Identify, in writing, the "essential functions" of a job before advertising for or interviewing potential candidates.

4. Before rejecting an otherwise qualified applicant or terminating an employee on the basis of a disability, first determine that (a) the individual cannot perform the essential duties of the position, or (b) the individual cannot perform the essential duties of the position without imminent and substantial risk of injury to self or others, and (c) the employer cannot reasonably accommodate the disability.

5. Articulate factors, other than an individual's disability, that are the basis of an adverse employment decision. Document your findings and the tangible evidence on which a decision to reject or terminate was based; make notes of accommodations considered.

6. Ask the disabled individual for advice on accommodations. This shows the employer's good faith and a willingness to consider such proposals.

7. Institute programs of benefits and consultation to assist disabled employees in effectively managing health, leave, and other benefits.

8. Check with insurance carrier regarding coverage of disabled employees and attempt (within economic reason) to maintain provided coverage or arrange for separate coverage.

9. Keep disabled individuals in mind when making structural alterations or purchasing office furniture and equipment.

10. Document all adverse employment actions, including reasons for the employment action with respect to disabled employees; focus on the employee's inability to do the job effectively rather than any relation to the employee's disability.

Source: EEOC Enforcement Guidance
www.eeoc.gov

Employers are not required to make accommodations that would result in "undue hardship," as determined by examining four factors:

1. The nature and cost of the accommodation
2. The size, workforce, and resources of the specific facility involved
3. The size, workforce, and resources of the covered entity
4. The nature of the covered entity's entire operation

Preemployment medical examinations are prohibited under the ADA, as are specific questions about a protected individual's disabilities. However, an employer may inquire about the ability of the applicant to perform job-related functions. "Can you carry fifty pounds of mail?" is an appropriate question; "Do you have the use of both arms?" is not.

Employers can refuse employment if an ADA-protected individual cannot perform necessary job functions. Also, employers can refuse to hire individuals who pose a direct threat to the health and safety of others in the workplace (assuming the risk cannot be minimized through accommodation).

The ADA is enforced through the EEOC and carries the same rights and remedies provided under Title VII. Exhibit 20.2 provides a list of items to help employers comply with ADA. Exhibit 20.3 examines proper and improper questions for job interviews under ADA.

EXHIBIT 20.3 Legal and Illegal Versions of Similar Job Interview Questions

LEGAL	ILLEGAL
1. Do you have 20/20 corrected vision?	What is your corrected vision?
2. How well can you handle stress?	Does stress ever affect your ability to be productive?
3. Can you perform this function with or without reasonable accommodation?	Would you need reasonable accommodation in this job?
4. How many days were you absent from work last year?	How many days were you sick last year?
5. Are you currently illegally using drugs?	What medications are you currently taking?
6. Do you regularly eat three meals per day?	Do you need to eat a number of small snacks at regular intervals throughout the day in order to maintain your energy level?
7. Do you drink alcohol?	How much alcohol do you drink per week?

Source: EEOC's "Enforcement Guidance on Pre-Employment Disability-Related Inquiries," May 12, 1994.

CONSIDER...

20.8 Margaret Christian was fired by St. Anthony's Medical Center after she disclosed to them that she had hyper-cholesterolemia (her cholesterol count is 319 milligrams), which would require blood draining, which would require an extra day or two off per month. After Christian was fired, she filed suit, alleging a violation of ADA. St. Anthony's says she was not currently disabled and ADA does not protect all medically afflicted persons. Christian says the treatment itself is disabling. Who is right? [*Christian* v. *St. Anthony Medical Center, Inc.*, 117 F.3d 1051 (7th Cir. 1997)]

The Family and Medical Leave Act

Visit the family and work Web site: http://www.connectforkids.org

Passed in 1993, the **Family and Medical Leave Act** (FMLA) requires companies with fifty or more employees to provide twelve weeks' leave each year for medical or family reasons, including the birth or adoption of a child or the serious health condition or illness of a spouse, parent, or child. Although pay is not required during the leave, medical benefits of the employee must continue, and the same or equivalent job must be available for the employee upon his return.

Review the Family and Medical Leave Act: http://www.law.cornell.edu/uscode/29/2601.html

THE GLOBAL WORKFORCE

Currently two thousand U.S. companies have 21,000 subsidiary operations in 21 countries throughout the world. With the free trade agreements (see Chapter 7), those numbers will increase, as will the sizes of the global operations. One of the many employment issues that arise with respect to employees in the subsidiary operations is whether the protections of Title VII apply to workers in these foreign operations. In *EEOC* v. *Arabian American Oil Co.*, 499 U.S. 244 (1991), the U.S. Supreme Court was faced with the issue of whether U.S. companies could engage in employment discrimination against U.S. citizens when they are working in countries outside the United States. The Court held that the companies are governed by the employment laws of the country of operations and not the provisions of U.S. legislation.

Re: The FMLA: No Free Vacation

Abusing the FMLA

The abuse of the FMLA centers mostly on the way employees and/or their healthcare providers interpret their own or a family member's serious illness. According to the law's regulations, a serious health condition can include an illness that incapacitates the person for more than three days, requires at least one visit to a healthcare professional, and leads to ongoing treatment. Examples of serious health conditions include heart attack, stroke, most types of cancer, back conditions requiring extensive therapy or surgery, pneumonia, emphysema, asthma, severe arthritis, Alzheimer's disease, diabetes, epilepsy, migraines and appendicitis. Examples of nonserious health conditions that are not given FMLA protections, unless complications develop, include: the common cold, flu, earaches, stomachaches, minor ulcers, headaches other than migraines, and routine dental problems. Workers can take leave in as little as one-hour increments and their managers usually lack discretion to deny leave.

In the following examples, the employees attempted to use FMLA protections but were denied by their employers and the legal system.

"Mommy, It Hurts" and Other Ailments

A 4-year-old child's ear infection kept him home from daycare and his mother home from work for four days. The mother took her child to the doctor once and administered antibiotics herself for 10 days. The mother requested four days of job-protected absence but did not receive it. Was she entitled to FMLA protections? No.

The court in *Seidle* v. *Provident Mutual Life Insurance Co.* found that the child was not incapacitated for more than three days. On the fourth day the child had a runny nose. The only reason the child did not return to daycare on the fourth day was that the daycare center has a policy which prohibits attendance by children with runny noses. There was also no evidence of continuing treatment by a healthcare provider as set forth by the act. In this case, the mother administered the medication herself. She never scheduled a follow-up visit with the doctor and did not telephone the doctor to communicate her child's condition.

In another case, an employee was fired for poor work performance, but she claimed that the firing was due to her need to take time off to attend to her ill daughter, who had to stay in bed due to an asthma attack. Is the woman entitled to FMLA protections? No. The court in *Sakelarion* v. *Judge & Dolph, Ltd.*, found that the employee's assertion that her daughter needed to be in bed due to asthma, without any evidence that she was incapable of self-care, was insufficient for FMLA protections.

An employee claimed to have a case of food poisoning with no evidence of inpatient care and no continued treatment by a healthcare provider. Was he entitled to FMLA protections? No. The court claimed in *Oswalt* v. *Sara Lee Corp.* that because the employee's food poisoning did not require inpatient care or continuing medical treatment, it could not be considered a serious health condition.

The Good Word?

The courts have also proved that FMLA requires more than the patient's word. In *Bauer* v. *Dayton-Walther Corp.*, the company had a "no fault" attendance policy whereby employees who missed work time accumulated points of absenteeism. Upon the accumulation of six absenteeism points in six months, the employee could be automatically terminated. In this case, an employee was terminated, but he tried to be reinstated, claiming to have rectal bleeding. He also claimed that he was afraid his condition could eventually become cancerous. The court did not reinstate him because he was never incapacitated for more than three days, he sought medical attention only once, and treatment was never administered. It also claimed that a condition must be looked at for what it is, not what it can or may become.

Employees in other cases have attempted to misapply the FMLA provisions. In one such case, a Chicago bus driver took leave under the FMLA for constipation, while in another case an employee remained out of work for seven weeks because of the removal and subsequent infection of an ingrown toenail.

To avoid abuse of the FMLA at your company, human resources professionals should consider what I call the EEI strategy; establish and/or update the company's FMLA policy, educate and train supervisors about the FMLA, and inform employees about their rights under the FMLA. These are briefly explained below.

Update company-leave policies. Companies must have an FMLA policy that is clear and consistent in delineating and explaining:

- The right of employees to take leave under the FMLA.
- The steps that employees need to take when requesting leave.
- Whether medical certification, including second and third opinions, are required.
- If applicable, the substitution of paid leave for unpaid family and medical leave.
- Whether an employee who fails to return to work after a leave will be required to reimburse the employer for health-insurance premiums covering the leave period.
- Whether an employee on leave is entitled to earn employment benefits.

It is important to remember that a company's policy must give the same or more protections as the federal law.

Educate and train supervisors. Supervisors must be familiar with the company FMLA policy. They also must understand that there are certain practices prohibited under the act, such as interfering with an employee's right to take leave, discharging or discriminating in any way against people who are exercising their rights under the FMLA, or interfering with proceedings concerning the law.

Inform employees. Employees must be informed of their rights and obligations under the FMLA in the company handbook, manual, and/or fact sheets that outline FMLA protections.

Source: Teresa Brady, "The FMLA: No Free Vacation," *Management Review,* June 1997, 43. Reprinted from *Management Review,* June 1997. Copyright (c) 1997 American Management Association International. Reprinted by permission of American Management Association International, New York, NY. All rights reserved. http://www.amanet.org

FOR THE MANAGER'S DESK

Re: The Respect of Rank

Charlene Barshefsky is the United States trade representative. She is both an ambassador and a cabinet officer. With the recent vote to open trade with China, Ms. Barshefsky saw the culmination of years of negotiations with the Chinese.

When interviewed by the *New York Times* about her experience as a woman serving as the United States' chief negotiator, she explained that in China and other countries, gender is not as important as rank:

> *Because my rank is high, my foreign counterparts treat me with the deference one might expect. Rank is much more important than gender, and rank can tend to overcome any potential gender bias. To the*

extent women are thought to be, in general, more perceptive about people, more aware of their surroundings, more sensitive to body language, it is a decided advantage to be a woman in a negotiation, particularly in watching. The body always speaks well before the mouth ever opens.

Are other nations ahead of the United States in treating women as equals? Should rank matter more than gender? What other examples can you point to outside the United States where women have achieved high ranks?

Source: Eric Schmitt, "The Negotiator," *New York Times Magazine,* 1 October 2000, p. 21.

BIOGRAPHY

TEXACO: THE JELLY BEAN DIVERSITY FIASCO

In November 1996, Texaco, Inc., was rocked by the disclosure of tape-recorded conversations among three executives about a racial discrimination suit pending against the company. The suit, seeking $71 million, had been brought by 6 employees, on behalf of 1,500 other employees, who alleged the following forms of discrimination:

I have had KKK printed on my car. I have had my tires slashed and racial slurs written about me on bathroom walls. One co-worker blatantly called me a racial epithet to my face. Throughout my employment, three supervisors in my department openly discussed their view that African Americans are ignorant and incompetent, and, specifically, that Thurgood Marshall was the most incompetent person they had ever seen.

Sheryl Joseph, formerly a Texaco secretary in Harvey, Louisiana, was given a cake for her birthday, which occurred shortly after she announced that she was pregnant. The cake depicted a black pregnant woman and read, "Happy Birthday, Sheryl. It must have been those watermelon seeds."

The suit also included data on Texaco's workforce:

| 1989 | Minorities as a percentage of Texaco's workforce | 15.2% |
| 1994 | Minorities as a percentage of Texaco's workforce | 19.4% |

Number of Years to Promotion, by Job Classification

Minority Employees	Job	Other Employees
6.1	Accountant	4.6
6.4	Senior Accountant	5.4
12.5	Analyst	6.3
14.2	Financial Analyst	13.9
15.0	Assistant Accounting Supervisor	9.8

Senior Managers

	White	Black
1991	1,887	19
1992	2,001	21
1993	2,000	23
1994	2,029	23

Racial Composition (% of Blacks) by Pay Range

Salary	Texaco	Other Oil Companies
$51,000	5.9%	7.2%
$56,900	4.7%	6.5%
$63,000	4.1%	4.7%
$69,900	2.3%	5.1%
$77,600	1.8%	3.2%
$88,100	1.9%	2.3%
$95,600	1.4%	2.6%
$106,100	1.2%	2.3%
$117,600	0.8%	2.3%
$128,800	0.4%	1.8%

(African-Americans make up 12% of the U.S. population)

The acting head of the EEOC wrote in 1995, "Deficiencies in the affirmative-action programs suggest that Texaco is not committed to insuring comprehensive, facility by facility, compliance with the company's affirmative-action responsibilities."

Faced with the lawsuit, Texaco's former treasurer, Robert Ulrich, senior assistant treasurer, J. David Keough, and senior coordinator for personnel services, Richard A. Lundwall, met and discussed the suit. A tape transcript follows: [They look through evidence, deciding what to turn over to the plaintiffs.]

Lundwall Here, look at this chart. You know, I'm not really quite sure what it means. This chart is not mentioned in the agency, so it's not important that we even have it in there. . . . They would never know it was here.

Keough They'll find it when they look through it.

Lundwall Not if I take it out they won't.

[The executives decide to leave out certain pages of a document; they worry that another version will turn up.]

Ulrich We're gonna purge the [expletive deleted] out of these books, though. We're not going to have any damn thing that we don't need to be in them—

Lundwall As a matter of fact, I just want to be reminded of what we discussed. You take your data and . . .

Keough You look and make sure it's consistent to what we've given them already for minutes. Two versions with the restricted and that's marked clearly on top—

Ulrich But I don't want to be caught up in a cover-up. I don't want to be my own Watergate.

Lundwall We've been doing pretty much two versions, too. This one here, this is strictly my book, your book . . .

Ulrich Boy, I'll tell you, that one, you would put that and you would have the only copy. Nobody else ought to have copies of that.

Lundwall O.K.?

Ulrich You have that someplace and it doesn't exist.

Lundwall Yeah, O.K.

Ulrich I just don't want anybody to have a copy of that.

Lundwall Good. No problem.

Ulrich You know, there is no point in even keeping the restricted version anymore. All it could do is get us in trouble. That's the way I feel. I would not keep anything.

Lundwall Let me shred this thing and any other restricted version like it.

Ulrich Why do we have to keep the minutes of the meeting anymore?

Lundwall You don't, you don't.

Ulrich We don't?

Lundwall Because we don't, no, we don't because it comes back to haunt us like right now—

Ulrich I mean, the pendulum is swinging the other way, guys.

[The executives discuss the minority employees who brought the suit.]

Lundwall They are perpetuating an us/them atmosphere. Last week or last Friday I told . . .

Ulrich [Inaudible.]

Lundwall Yeah, that's what I said to you, you want to frag grenade? You know, duck, I'm going to throw one. Well, that's what I was alluding to. But the point is not, that's not bad in itself but it does perpetuate us/them. And if you're trying to get away and get to the we . . . you can't do that kind of stuff.

Ulrich [Inaudible.] I agree. This diversity thing. You know how black jelly beans agree. . . .

Lundwall That's funny. All the black jelly beans seem to be glued to the bottom of the bag.

Ulrich You can't have just we and them. You can't just have black jelly beans and other jelly beans. It doesn't work.

Lundwall Yeah. But they're perpetuating the black jelly beans.

Ulrich I'm still having trouble with Hanukkah. Now, we have Kwanza (laughter).

The release of the tape prompted the Reverend Jesse Jackson to call for a nationwide boycott of Texaco. Sales fell 8%, Texaco's stock fell 2%, and several institutional investors were preparing to sell their stock.

Texaco did have a minority recruiting effort in place and the "jelly bean" remark was tied to a diversity trainer the company had hired. The following are excerpts from Texaco's statement of vision and values.

RESPECT FOR THE INDIVIDUAL

Our employees are our most important resource. Each person deserves to be treated with respect and dignity in appropriate work environments, without regard to race, religion, sex, age, national origin, disability or position in the company. Each employee has the responsibility to demonstrate respect for others.

The company believes that a work environment that reflects a diverse workforce, values diversity, and is free of all forms of discrimination, intimidation, and harassment is essential for a productive and efficient workforce. Accordingly, conduct directed toward any employee that is unwelcome, hostile, offensive, degrading, or abusive is unacceptable and will not be tolerated.

A federal grand jury began an investigation of Texaco to determine whether there had been obstruction of justice in the withholding of documents.

Within days of the release of the tape, Texaco settled its bias suit for $176.1 million, the largest sum ever allowed in a discrimination case. The money will allow an 11% pay raise for blacks and other minorities who joined in the law suit. Texaco's chairman and CEO, Peter I. Bijur, issued the following statement after agreeing to a settlement. *Texaco is facing a difficult but vital challenge. It's broader than any specific words and larger than any lawsuit. It is one we must and are attacking head-on.*

We are a company of 27,000 people worldwide. In any organization of that size, unfortunately, there are bound to be people with unacceptable, biased attitudes toward race, gender and religion.

Our goal, and our responsibility, is to eradicate this kind of thinking wherever and however it is found in our company. And our challenge is to make Texaco a company of limitless opportunity for all men and women.

(continued)

> *We are committed to begin meeting this challenge immediately through programs with concrete goals and measurable timetables.*
>
> *I've already announced certain specific steps, including a redoubling of efforts within Texaco to focus on the paramount value of respect for the individual and a comprehensive review of our diversity programs at every level of our company.*
>
> *It is essential to this urgent mission that Texaco and African Americans and other minority community leaders work together to help solve the problems we face as a company—which, after all, echo the problems faced in society as a whole.*
>
> *Discrimination will be extinguished only if we tackle it together, only if we join in a unified, common effort.*

> *Working together, I believe we can take Texaco into the 21st century as a model of diversity. We can make Texaco a company of limitless opportunity. We can make Texaco a leader in according respect to every man and woman.*
>
> Even after the announcement, Texaco stock was down $3 per share, a loss of $800 million total, and the boycott was continued. Texaco's proposed merger with Shell Oil began to unravel as Shell's CEO expressed concern about Texaco's integrity.

Source: Marianne M. Jennings, "Texaco: The Jelly Bean Diversity Fiasco," in *Business Ethics: Case Studies and Selected Readings,* 4th ed., by Marianne M. Jennings, 102–110. © 2002. Reprinted with permission of South-Western College Publishing, a division of International Thomson Publishing. Fax 800 730-2215.

Congress responded to the Supreme Court's ruling in *Arabian American Oil* by adding a section to the Civil Rights Act of 1991 addressing the issue of foreign operations. The statutory provision on foreign operations and civil rights protections is neither universal nor automatic. The amendment provides basically that if there is a conflict between U.S. employment discrimination laws and those of a host country, a company should follow the laws of the host country. An example would be a law in the host country that prohibits the employment of women in management. The company would be required to follow that prohibition for operations located in the host country. If the host country has no laws on employment discrimination, the company is then required to follow all U.S. antidiscrimination laws.

Review the Universal Declaration of Human Rights:
http://www.un.org/Overview/rights.html

Several multilateral treaties govern the rights of workers. In 1948, the United Nations adopted its Universal Declaration of Human Rights. The declaration supports, among other things, equality of pay and nondiscriminatory employment policies. Also, the Helsinki Final Act of 1973 supports nondiscriminatory employment policies. In 1977, the International Labor Office issued its Tripartite Declaration of Principles Concerning Multinational Enterprises, which supports equal pay and nondiscriminatory payment policies. The EU has adopted all of these treaties and policies for their implementation.

SUMMARY

What laws governing employment discrimination exist?

- Civil Rights Act 1866, 1964—federal statutes prohibiting discrimination in various aspects of life (employment, voting)
- Equal Pay Act—equal pay for the same work regardless of gender
- Equal Employment Opportunity Act—antidiscrimination employment amendment to Civil Rights Act

- Pregnancy Discrimination Act—prohibits refusing to hire or promote or firing because of pregnancy
- Age Discrimination Act—prohibits hiring, firing, promotion, benefits, raises based on age
- Rehabilitation Act of 1973—federal statute prohibiting discrimination on basis of disability by federal agencies and contractors
- Americans with Disabilities Act—federal law prohibiting discrimination on basis of disability by certain employees

- Family and Medical Leave Act—federal law providing for twelve weeks of leave for childbirth, adoption, or family illness

- Sexual harassment—form of discrimination that involves a *quid pro quo* related to sexual favors or an atmosphere of harassment

What types of discrimination exist?

- Disparate treatment—form of discrimination in which members of different races/sexes are treated differently

- Disparate impact—test or screening device that affects one group more than another

- Pattern or practice of discrimination—theory for establishing discrimination that compares population percentages with workplace percentages

Are there any defenses to discrimination?

- BFOQ—job qualification based on sex, religion, or national origin that is necessary for the operation of a business, such as religious affiliation for the pastor of a church

- Affirmative action—programs created to remedy past wrongs that permit choices on the basis of race, sex, or national origin

QUESTIONS AND PROBLEMS

1. Patricia Lorance is an hourly wage employee at the Montgomery Works AT&T electronics products plant. She had been employed there since the early 1970s and under union rules accrued seniority through her years of service at the plant. In 1979, the union entered into a new collective bargaining agreement providing that seniority would be determined by department and not on a plant-wide basis. The effect of the change was to put Ms. Lorance at the bottom of the seniority ladder in the testing areas despite her longevity in the plant. When layoffs became necessary, she and the other female testers were laid off because of the new seniority rule. Without the new rule, Ms. Lorance and the other women would not have been victims of the cutbacks. Does the seniority system violate Title VII? [*Lorance* v. *AT&T Technologies, Inc.*, 490 U.S. 900 (1989)]

2. Calvin Rhodes began as a salesman with Dresser Industries in 1955. In 1986, the oil industry experienced a severe economic downturn and Rhodes was laid off. His severance report said he was discharged as part of a reduction in force (RIF). Within two months, Dresser had hired a 42-year-old replacement. Rhodes sued for violation of ADEA. Will he win? [*Rhodes* v. *Guiberson Oil Tools* (subsidiary of Dresser), 75 F.3d 989 (5th Cir. 1996)]

3. Vivian Martyszenko was working as a cashier at a Safeway grocery store in Ogallala, Nebraska, when she received a call from the police informing her that her two children might have been molested. Martyszenko's supervisor gave her two weeks' vacation leave to care for her children.

The psychiatrist's exam of the children was inconclusive, and Martyszenko was told it would take time for their recovery. She asked for leave under the FMLA, which Safeway denied. She then filed suit, alleging Safeway had violated FMLA. Was the boys' condition a serious health condition covered under FMLA? [*Martyszenko* v. *Safeway, Inc.*, 120 F.3d 120 (8th Cir. 1997)]

4. On August 11, 1980, Shelby Memorial Hospital hired Sylvia Hayes, a certified x-ray technician, to work the 3–11 P.M. shift in the hospital's radiology department. Two months later, she was fired after she informed her supervisor that she was pregnant. The supervisor fired Ms. Hayes because Dr. Cecil Eiland, the hospital's radiology director and director of radiation safety, recommended that Ms. Hayes be removed from all areas using ionizing radiation and the hospital could not find alternative work for her. After her dismissal, Ms. Hayes filed suit for violation of the Pregnancy Discrimination Act and Title VII. Should she recover? [*Hayes* v. *Shelby Memorial Hosp.*, 726 F.2d 1543 (11th Cir. 1984)]

5. The Masonic nursing home has mostly female, but some male, occupants and hires fewer male attendants than female ones. The administration of the home maintains that the female occupants (for privacy reasons) would not consent to intimate personal care by males and would, in fact, leave the home. A substantial portion of the women at the home are "total care" patients who require assistance in performing virtually all activities, including bathing, dressing, and using toilets, catheters, and bedpans. In a suit brought by a male nurse's aide who was denied employment, who would win? [*Fessel* v. *Masonic Home*, 17 FEP Cases 330 (Del. 1978)]

6. Woolworth Victor Davis applied for a position as a firefighter with the city of Philadelphia in 1977. When he reported for his physical exam, the physician noticed a scar; and Mr. Davis explained that he had used amphetamines in 1972 but had not engaged in drug use since then. He was told he could not be hired because the city would not employ anyone with a drug history. Mr. Davis filed suit under the Rehabilitation Act of 1973. What will be the outcome? Would the ADA have protected him? [*Davis* v. *Butcher,* 451 F. Supp. 791 (E.D. Pa. 1978)]

7. Audra Sommers (aka Timothy Cornesh) a self-claimed "female with the anatomical body of a male," was hired by Budget Marketing on April 22, 1980. She was fired on April 24, 1980, because the female workers at Budget refused to allow her in the women's restroom and threatened to quit if she/he were allowed in. Ms. Sommers brought suit for a violation of Title VII alleging discrimination on the basis that she was a transsexual. Does Title VII apply? [*Sommers* v. *Budget Marketing, Inc.,* 667 F.2d 748 (8th Cir. 1982)]

8. Would the following constitute sexual harassment? Yes, or No?

a. Sexual comments or innuendoes; telling sexual jokes or stories
b. Asking personal questions about social or sexual life
c. Telling lies or spreading rumors about a person's personal sex life
d. Making sexual comments about a person's body
e. Turning work discussions to sexual topics
f. Looking a person up and down

g. Staring repeatedly at someone
h. Blocking a person's path or hindering the other person's movements
i. Giving unwanted gifts and/or materials of a sexual nature
j. Invading a person's body space by standing closer than appropriate
k. Standing close or brushing up against another person
l. Sexual gestures or kissing sounds or massages
m. Posters, cartoons, or handouts that depict men, women, or members of minority groups in a less than businesslike manner

9. American Airlines passed a grooming rule that prohibited a "corn row" hairstyle on all employees. Renee Rogers, a black woman, brought a Title VII suit alleging that the denial of her right to wear the hairstyle intruded upon her rights and discriminated against her. What will be the result? [*Rogers* v. *American Airlines, Inc.,* 527 F. Supp. 229 (S.D.N.Y. 1981)]

10. American Airlines has a policy of not hiring flight officers over the age of 40. The reason for their policy is that it takes ten to fifteen years for a flight officer to become a co-pilot and then another ten to fifteen years for a co-pilot to become a captain. Because the FAA requires retirement at age 60, service would be limited. Edward L. Murnane, age 43, was denied employment on the basis of age and filed an age discrimination suit. Is age a BFOQ for the job? [*Murnane* v. *American Airlines, Inc.,* 667 F.2d 98 (D.C. 1981)]

RESEARCH PROBLEM

Kafka Wasn't Kidding

11. Develop a solution for employers to the problems/conflicts raised in the following report: You know the sad story: In the early hours of the morning of Mar. 24, 1989 the tanker *Exxon Valdez* hit a reef in Price William Sound, Alaska, spilling 11 million gallons of crude oil. Exxon paid billions in fines and cleanup costs. Many people still curse Exxon as a despoiler of the environment.

It is widely believed that the captain of the tanker was drunk. To minimize the chances of another such disaster, Exxon implemented a new policy: While offering employees help in getting treatment for alcohol or drug dependency, the company declared some jobs, where safety is critical—tanker captains, for example—off-limits to anyone who has a history of abuse of alcohol or some other substance.

Now Exxon is in court again.

This time the bureaucrats in the U.S. Equal Employment Opportunity Commission are suing the company to protect ships' captains and the like who have had drinking or drug problems.

No, we are not kidding.

The feds say Exxon's policy, aimed at minimizing accidents, violates the 1990 Americans with Disabilities Act. The EEOC says that Exxon is illegally discriminating against some 50 employees who have had alcohol or drug problems but have since been rehabilitated.

Chrys Meador, an EEOC trial attorney on the case, defends her agency's kafkaesque action. "Exxon believes they cannot get a guarantee that somebody who's had a substance abuse problem will never relapse," she says. "Well, we can't give them that guarantee. But the experts we have consulted have said that there are very positive employee assistance programs that actively monitor individuals, and there are telltale signs so that you can detect these things before they become a problem."

In other words, it's the company's responsibility to know when an ex-drunk is about to slip off the wagon or when a schizophrenic has stopped taking his pills. Only it had better be careful how it monitors these things.

Meador says the agency is just following what Congress said in the 1990 Disabilities Act. Scary thing is, she's right.

Big companies like Exxon can afford to pay these fines and put up with the expensive red tape and legal costs. Owners of small businesses cannot. Talk about discrimination.

Source: David A. Price, "Kafka Wasn't Kidding," *Forbes,* June 2, 1997. Reprinted by Permission of Forbes Magazine © Forbes Inc., 2004.

NOTE

1. Upon remand from the U.S. Supreme Court in 1995, the case was tried and decided at 965 F. Supp. 1556 (D. Colo. 1997). The court decided that the program was not drawn narrowly enough and the affirmative action program violated the equal protection clause. It was reversed at 228 F.3d 1147 (10th Cir. 2000) and *certiorari* was granted at 121 S. Ct. 1598 (2001).

BUSINESS STRATEGY APPLICATION

In this application you have the chance to review the diversity policies of the following companies:
1. ChevronTexaco
2. Denny's
3. Levi Strauss & Co.
4. Unocal
5. Coca-Cola
Some of these companies, as you know from your readings, have had legal issues in terms of their compliance with Title VII. However, they have emerged with new programs on diversity and their corrections and actions provide insight into how to makes changes and improvements in compliance and achieving diversity.

Studying these companies' programs will give you an idea of the components of effective management for diversity so that you would be able to develop an effective diversity program for your company.

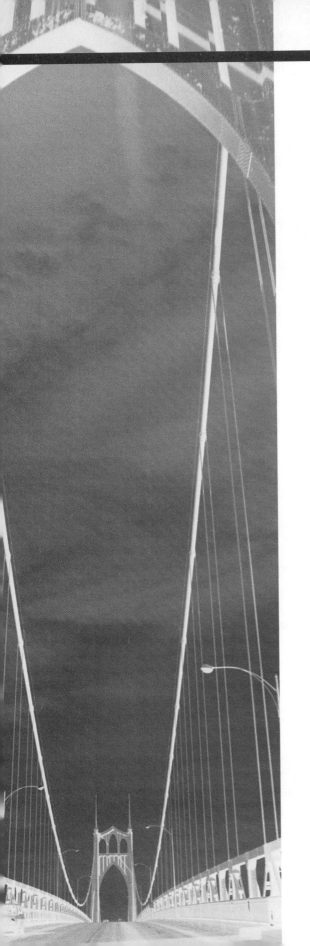

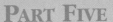

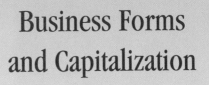

PART FIVE

Business Forms and Capitalization

This portion of the book covers legal issues in forming and financing a business. The structure of a business determines its owners' rights and liabilities. Different business forms afford varying levels of flexibility for operations. In addition, the type of business structure creates opportunities for both initial financing of the business and its expansion.

Some forms of business financing require compliance with state and federal laws for sales of such business interests as securities and bonds. These laws include disclosure requirements for sales and provide remedies for investors and impose liabilities on businesses when disclosures made about the nature of the interest and the business are incomplete or inaccurate.

Some businesses combine or merge in order to compete better in the evolving global economy. State and federal laws afford disclosure and protections for merging businesses and their owners and investors.

CHAPTER TWENTY-ONE

Forms of Doing Business

It is very often the case that businesses are not formed by one person alone. The sole proprietorship is a popular form of doing business, but the greatest amount of income derives from businesses formed by more than one person. Partnerships, limited partnerships, limited liability companies, and corporations are all multi-individual forms of doing business. This chapter answers the following questions: How are various business entities formed? What are the advantages and disadvantages of various entities? What are the rights, responsibilities, and liabilities of the individuals involved?

Each of the forms of doing business is examined by reviewing its formation, sources of funding, the personal liability of owners, tax consequences, management and control, and the ease of transferring interest. Overviews of business forms are found in Exhibits 21.1 and 21.2.

Please accept my resignation. I don't want to belong to any organization that will accept me as a member.

GROUCHO MARX

Although our form is corporate, our attitude is partnership. We do not view the company itself as the ultimate owner of our business assets but instead view the company as a conduit through which our shareholders own the assets.

WARREN BUFFETT
Chairman, Berkshire Hathaway

© Jacques M. Chenet/CORBIS

CONSIDER...

In 1984, General Motors bought 100 percent of Electronic Data Systems' stock, a company founded and chaired by H. Ross Perot, who was also EDS's largest shareholder. Perot was given a 0.8 percent interest in GM voting stock and was elected to the GM Board. Perot became a thorn in the side of GM's board, saying publicly, "Until you nuke the old GM system, you'll never tap the full potential of your people." GM's board voted to reacquire Perot's interest for $745 million. GM shareholders were outraged. Can the board do this? What rights do shareholders have?

EXHIBIT 21.1 **Comparison of Forms of Conducting Business**

FORM	FORMATION	FUNDING	MANAGEMENT
Sole proprietorship	No formal requirements	Individual provides funds	Individual
Partnership	Articles of partnership	Capital contributions of partners	All partners or delegated to one
Limited partnership	Filing of articles of partnership	Capital contributions of general and limited partners	General partner
Corporation	Formal filing of articles of incorporation	Debt (bonds)/equity (shareholders)	Board of directors, officers and/or executive committee
S corporation* or Subchapter S	Same as above (special IRS filings to create special tax [flow-through] status)	Same as above	Same as above
C corporation†	Created as normal corporation	Same as corporation	Same as above
Limited liability company (LLC)	Formal filing—articles of organization	Capital contributions of members	All members manage or delegate to one member
Limited liability partnership	Filing of articles of limited liability partnership	Capital contributions of partners	All partners or delegated to one

*S corporations are formed under state incorporation laws but structured to obtain flow-through or pass-through status for income and losses under IRS regulations.

†C corporation is again a label for tax purpose.

THE SOLE PROPRIETORSHIP

Formation

A **sole proprietorship** is not a true business entity because it consists of only an individual operating a business. Often, a sole proprietorship is evidenced by the following language: "Homer Lane d/b/a Green Grower's Grocery"; "d/b/a" is an acronym for "doing business as." Because a sole proprietorship comprises but one individual and no separate organization exists, there are no formal requirements for formation. The individual simply begins doing business. In some states, "d/b/a" businesspeople are required to publish and file the fictitious names under which they will be doing business.

Sources of Funding

Visit the Small Business Association:
http://www.sbaonline.sba.gov

Most sole proprietorships are small businesses, and initially their business capital needs are small. Their financing usually comes from loans, either direct loans from banks or loans through such government agencies as the Small Business Administration (SBA).

EXHIBIT 21.2 Comparison of Forms of Conducting Business

FORM	TRANSFER CONTROL	TAXES	DISSOLUTION	LIABILITY
Sole proprietorship	No transfer	Individual pays on individual return	Death; voluntary	Individual
Partnership	Transfer interest but not partner status	Partner takes profits and losses on individual return (flow-through)	Dissolution upon death; withdrawal of partner	Partners are personally liable
Limited partnership	More easily transferred	Same as partnership (flow-through)	Death of general partner	General partner is personally liable; limited partners liable to extent of contribution
Corporation	Shares (with reasonable restrictions) are easily transferred	Corporation pays taxes; shareholders pay taxes on dividends	Dissolved only if limited in duration or shareholders vote to dissolve	No shareholder personal liability unless (1) watered or (2) corporate veil
S corporation or Subchapter S	Restrictions on transfer to comply with S corporation	Shareholders pay taxes on profits; take losses	Same as above	Same as above
C corporation	No restrictions	Election of pass-through	Same as above	Same as above
Limited liability company (LLC)	No admission without consent of majority	Flow-through treatment	Dissolved upon death, bankruptcy	Same as above (except professional negligence)
Limited liability partnership	No admission without consent of majority	Flow-through treatment	Dissolved upon death, bankruptcy	Varies by state but liability for acts of partners is limited in some way

Some sole proprietorships are started with financial backing from other people, usually in the form of a personal loan. In such cases, the sole proprietor may have the skills or clients for a successful business but not the funds necessary to begin.

Liability

Because financing for a sole proprietorship is based on the sole proprietor's credit rating and assets, the proprietor is personally liable for the business loan, and her assets are subject to attachment should there be a default. To get financing, a sole proprietor takes personal financial risk.

Tax Consequences

The positive side of unlimited personal liability of a sole proprietor is the right to claim all tax losses associated with the business. The income of the business is the income of the sole proprietor and is reported on the sole proprietor's income tax return. There is no separate filing requirement for the business itself. Moreover, although sole proprietors owe all the taxes, they also get the benefit of all business deductions.

Management and Control

The proprietor is the management of the business. In many businesses, the sole proprietor is both management and employee. The proprietor makes all decisions. This form of business operation is truly centralized management.

Transferability of Interest

Because the business in many ways is the owner, the business can be transferred only if the owner allows it. When a sole proprietor's business is transferred, the transfer consists of the property, inventory, and goodwill of the business. The sole proprietor is generally required to sign a noncompetition agreement so that the goodwill that is paid for is preserved (see Chapters 17 and 18 for more details). In addition, upon the owner's death the heirs or devisees of the owner would inherit the property involved in the business. They could choose to operate the business, but the business usually ends upon the death of the sole proprietor.

THE PARTNERSHIP

Review Arizona's Uniform Partnership Act: www.azleg.state.az.us/ars/ 29/title29

Partnerships are governed by some version of the **Uniform Partnership Act** (UPA), which has been adopted in forty-nine states. The UPA and similar uniform acts are the work of the National Conference of Commissioners on Uniform State Laws, which is a group of lawyers, judges, and professors who develop model laws in the interest of uniformity among the states. In 1994, a new final version of the UPA was adopted by the commissioners. Most states have adopted the **Revised Uniform Partnership Act** (RUPA), but some did not repeal the UPA. The UPA defines a partnership as an "association of two or more persons to carry on as co-owners, a business for profit." "Persons" can include corporations, known as "artificial" persons, and natural persons.

Formation

A partnership can be formed voluntarily by direct action of the parties, or its formation can be implied by the ongoing conduct of the parties.

Voluntary Formation
The most desirable way to form a partnership (at least in terms of protecting partners' rights and liabilities) is to have the partners execute a partnership agreement, or draw up **articles of partnership.** The articles should include certain information, which is summarized in Exhibit 21.3.

Involuntary Formation: Partnerships by Implication
A partnership can arise even though there is no express agreement and the parties do not call themselves partners. In certain circumstances, courts infer that a partnership exists even if the persons involved say they are not partners.

Simply owning property together does not result in a **partnership by implication.** But courts examine a number of factors in determining whether a partner-

EXHIBIT 21.3 **Information Included in Articles of Partnership**

MINIMUM REQUIREMENTS	SUGGESTED PROVISIONS
1. Names of the partners	1. Disability issues
2. Name of the partnership	2. Insurance coverage
3. Nature of the partnership's business	3. Sale of interest
4. The time frame of operation	4. Divorce of one of the partners
5. Amount of each partner's capital contribution	5. Indemnity agreements
6. Managerial powers of partners	6. Noncompetition agreements
7. Rights and duties of partners	7. Leaves of absence
8. Accounting procedures for partnership books and records	
9. Methods for sharing profits and losses	
10. Salaries (if any) of the partners	
11. Causes and methods of dissolution	
12. Distribution of property if the partnership is terminated	

ship exists by implication. Section 7 of the UPA provides that if two or more parties share the profits of a business, it is *prima facie* evidence that a partnership exists. (*Prima facie* evidence means there is a presumption that a partnership exists.) However, the presumption of partnership by profit-sharing can be overcome if someone received profits for any of the following reasons:

1. Profits paid to repay debts
2. Profits paid as wages or rent
3. Profits paid to a widow or estate representative
4. Profits paid for the sale of business goodwill

Many shopping center leases, for example, provide for the payment of both a fixed amount of rent and a percentage of net profits. The owners of the shopping center thus profit as the stores do, but they profit as landlords, not as partners with the shopping center businesses.

The following case addresses the question of whether a partnership exists.

CASE 21.1

Shaw v. Delta Airlines, Inc.
798 F. Supp. 1453 (D. Nev. 1992)

Delta Force: Liability in the Sky

FACTS

Delta Airlines, Inc. (defendant), operates under a contractual arrangement with Sky-West Airlines, Inc., to serve as its ticketing and marketing agent. Delta is a large airline serving large cities, and SkyWest is a commuter airline shuttling passengers from large cities to outlying small towns.

(continued)

Samuel Shaw took a Delta flight to Salt Lake City and then took a flight on SkyWest from Salt Lake City to Elko, Nevada. The SkyWest flight crashed just miles from the Elko airport and Shaw suffered serious personal injuries as a result. He and his wife, Lola (plaintiffs), brought suit against Delta as a partner of SkyWest seeking damages for his injuries. Delta moved for summary judgment on grounds that SkyWest was solely liable.

JUDICIAL OPINION

REED, Senior District Judge

Plaintiffs concede that SkyWest is not a subsidiary or division of Delta. However, Plaintiffs argue that certain facts sustain the conclusion that SkyWest was Delta's agent for the purposes of carrying passengers on less-traveled "commuter" routes that Delta does not itself fly. They present evidence that indicates that SkyWest uses Delta trademarks and insignia, the two companies are often mentioned together by Delta in national print advertisements and airline industry schedules, and that Delta has control over SkyWest routes and timetables. Thus, Plaintiffs claim that Delta presents the image to the public that SkyWest is part of Delta, or at the least Delta's agent. As such, Plaintiffs argue, a jury could hold Delta liable on an apparent authority theory.

Since Delta and SkyWest were parties to a contract under which both would presumably make a profit from their combined efforts, one might argue that these two parties were engaged in a partnership. The position of the vast majority of states is that if two or more parties intend for their relationship to result in a partnership, the law will treat the relationship as a partnership, regardless of whether the parties themselves call the relationship a partnership or intend the legal consequences that flow from that label.

However, the authorities also clearly indicate that there is no specific test to determine the existence of a partnership. An express written agreement to form a partnership is not required. The trier of fact must look to the conduct of the parties and all the circumstances surrounding their relationship and transactions. The key factor is not the subjective intent of the parties to form a partnership, but instead the intent of the parties to do the things that the law will consider a partnership. It is immaterial that the parties do not call their relationship, or believe it to be, a partnership, especially where the rights of third parties are concerned.

The law provides a laundry list of factors to look at in deciding whether or not parties intended to form a partnership. Nevada has adopted the Uniform Partnership Act ("UPA") "Rules for determining existence of partnership." According to this section, "receipt by a person of a share of profits of a business is prima facie evidence that he is a partner in the business. . . ."

On its face, this section might seem to imply that any contractual agreement under which both parties receive profits is a partnership. However, most jurisdictions find that mere participation in profits does not create a partnership unless the partners also share losses. Also, most authorities require that each partner have some degree and right of control over the business. "Although the sharing of profits and losses is prima facie evidence of a partnership, the issue of control is the more important criterion in determining the existence of a partnership."

In the instant case, the agreement between Delta and SkyWest does not indicate any desire to engage in a business as risk-sharing partners with joint-control over the enterprise. It is true that both parties expected to make a profit from the enterprise; however, a person "who has no proprietary interest in a business except to share profits as compensation for services is not a partner or joint venturer." Even where one party exercises some degree of control over the other, and their joint fortunes depend upon the same business factors, a partnership does not necessarily exist.

In this case, SkyWest certainly did not have joint control over the operations of Delta. Nor did SkyWest directly participate in the profits or losses of the Delta corporation. The "Delta Connection" agreement might be characterized as simply a business referral arrangement whereby Delta benefits through its ability to issue tickets to connecting passengers and SkyWest benefits through the payments it receives on the tickets of passengers that Delta has sent to it. The court concludes that, under the above legal standards, no reasonable jury could conclude that Delta and SkyWest were general partners.

The label "joint venture" clearly does not apply in this case. Delta and SkyWest did not agree to a short-term business deal in which they proposed to jointly share in profits or losses. Nor did either party invest capital in a joint business deal. The court's reasoning from its partnership analysis applies equally as well here: Delta and SkyWest are contract parties to a business referral agreement. There is no joint venture under Nevada law.

Plaintiffs' major argument is that SkyWest was the agent of Delta for purposes of carrying passengers like Mr. Shaw. Delta argues that although it may be SkyWest's agent for ticketing, marketing, and scheduling, SkyWest is not *its* agent for any purpose. Since there is no explicit agency agreement, Plaintiffs argue instead that the law may deem SkyWest the agent of Delta on an apparent authority theory. They claim that Delta has used advertising and marketing strategies aimed at creating the impression in the minds of the traveling public that SkyWest is somehow a part of Delta.

Delta makes much of the fact that the Delta Connection agreement expressly states that no employee, independent contractor, or agent of either company shall be deemed to be an employee, independent contractor, or agent of the other. However, it is clear that a clause negating agency in a written contract is not controlling.

A principal is bound by the acts of its agent while acting in the course of his or her employment, and a principal is liable for those acts within the scope of the agent's authority. An agent's authority may be express, implied, or apparent. In Nevada, "apparent authority" is that authority which a principal holds its agent out as possessing, or permits the agent to exercise or to represent him- or herself as possessing, under such circumstances as to estop the principal from denying its existence. The existence or non-existence of an agency relationship is a question of fact for the jury.

If the jury were to find as a matter of fact that Delta fostered the impression in travelers' minds that SkyWest was its agent (or subsidiary or partner) then that would be enough to support the conclusion that there was a principal-agent relationship between the two airlines, whether or not Delta intended an actual legal agency. Under such an analysis, the first question collapses into the second and the only remaining relevant inquiry focuses on the apparent authority issue.

Once an agency is found to exist, the important question is actually one of scope. For example, a principal-agent relationship exists between a home seller and his or her real estate agent. However, if the agent took the initiative of selling the home owner's car, the agent would likely be exceeding the scope of the agent's authority, be it express, implied, or apparent. In this case, the jury could easily find that SkyWest was Delta's agent for *something*, for example, a ticketing agent, a booking agent, etc. Almost all contractual relationships will create agencies of one kind or another between the parties, no matter how small or limited in scope. Once the trier of fact has made that determination, the true issue in any agency case becomes the scope of the agent's authority.

Plaintiffs present uncontroverted evidence that Delta has some measure of control over its relationship with SkyWest. Delta possesses the right to control the printing and distribution of SkyWest timetables as SkyWest's marketing agent. Delta decides where and how this information gets published and may print SkyWest flight information as Delta connecting flights in appropriate airline guides. Delta also has the power to assign the flight numbers to SkyWest flights.

Plaintiffs also present evidence that tends to show that Delta's actions have effectively managed to equate SkyWest with Delta in the minds of the traveling public. Delta publishes SkyWest flight information in Delta timetables and refers to SkyWest's service as the "Delta Connection." The two names (Delta and SkyWest) appear together in national advertising materials along with the same trademark the "Delta Connection." The agreement between Delta and SkyWest provides for the use of Delta slogans and insignia "reflect the Delta Connection and the relationship between SkyWest and Delta." Advertising materials depict the Delta trademark (a red, white, and blue triangle) close by the SkyWest name and Delta includes SkyWest destination cities in its own list of destinations. Delta issues SkyWest tickets on Delta ticket stock and provides its ticket stock to SkyWest for some of its ticketing needs.

The jury must decide if SkyWest was the agent of Delta with the apparent authority to carry passengers for Delta.

Defendant Delta's motion for summary judgment is denied.

CASE QUESTIONS

1. Why is the sharing of profits not enough to create a partnership between SkyWest and Delta?

2. Is the use of Delta's logo by SkyWest important to the case?

3. What two questions must be decided by the jury?

4. Do you believe Delta created the impression that SkyWest and Delta were one and the same?

5. Why do you think Mr. Shaw wishes to have Delta held liable?

C O N S I D E R . . .

21.1   Richard Chaiken entered into agreements with both Mr. Strazella and Mr. Spitzer to operate a barber shop. Mr. Chaiken was to provide barber chairs, supplies, and licenses. Messrs. Strazella and Spitzer were to bring their tools, and the agreements included work hours and holidays for them. The Delaware Employment Security Commission determined that Messrs. Strazella and Spitzer were employees, not partners, and sought to collect unemployment compensation for the two barbers. Mr. Chaiken maintains that they are partners and not employees. Who is correct? [*Chaiken* v. *Employment Security Comm'n*, 274 A.2d 707 (Del. 1971)]

Involuntary Formation: Partnership by Estoppel

There are times when someone can be held to be a partner because she acted like a partner. Some court decisions have held that anyone who helps a new business obtain a loan is holding herself out as a partner. Section 16 of the UPA provides as follows:

> *When a person by words spoken or written or by conduct, represents himself, or consents to another representing him to anyone as a partner in an existing partnership or with one or more persons not actual partners, he is liable to any party to whom such representation has been made.*

In other words, if the conduct of two or more parties leads others to believe a partnership exists, that partnership may be found to exist legally under the notion of **partnership by estoppel.** Partnerships by estoppel arise when others are led to believe there is a partnership. The *Shaw* case also involved this issue.

C O N S I D E R . . .

21.2   Triangle Chemical Company supplied $671.10 worth of fertilizer and chemicals to France Mathis to produce a cabbage crop. When Mr. Mathis first asked for credit, he was denied. He then told Triangle that he had a new partner, Emory Pope. The company president called Mr. Pope, who said he was backing Mr. Mathis. Mr. Pope had loaned Mr. Mathis money to produce the crop, and Mr. Mathis said Mr. Pope would pay the bills. Mr. Pope said, "We're growing the crop together and I am more or less handling the money." When Mr. Mathis could not pay, Triangle wanted to hold Mr. Pope personally liable. Mr. Pope said his promise to pay another's debt would have to have been in writing. Triangle claimed Mr. Pope was a partner and personally liable. Is he? [*Pope* v. *Triangle Chemical Co.*, 277 S.E.2d 758 (Ga. 1981)]

Sources of Funding

Visit the American Bar Association's business law section:
http://www.abanet.org/buslaw/efss/home.html

Funding for a partnership comes from the partners who initially contribute property, cash, or services to the partnership accounts. These contributions are the capital of the partnership. Not only are these contributions put at the risk of the business, but so also are each of the partners' personal assets: Partners are personally liable for the full amount of partnership obligations.

Partner Liability

Each partner is both a principal and an agent to the other partners and is liable both for the acts of others and to the others for individual acts. If one partner enters into a contract for partnership business supplies, all the partners are liable. Similarly, if one partner has a motor vehicle accident while on a partnership delivery, the individual partner is liable for her own negligence, but because she was in the scope of partnership business, the partners and the partnership are also liable. Under the RUPA, partners are jointly and severally liable for all obligations.

If partnership assets are exhausted, each partner is individually liable. Creditors can satisfy their claims by looking to the assets of the individual partners after the partnership assets are exhausted.

The following case deals with an issue of partnership liability.

CASE 21.2

Vrabel v. Acri
103 N.E.2d 564 (Ohio 1952)

Shot Down in a Ma & Pa Cafe: Is Ma Liable When Pa Goes to Jail?

FACTS

On February 17, 1947, Stephen Vrabel and a companion went into the Acri Cafe in Youngstown, Ohio, to buy alcoholic drinks. While Mr. Vrabel and his companion were sitting at the bar drinking, Michael Acri, without provocation, drew a .38-caliber gun, shot and killed Mr. Vrabel's companion, and shot and seriously injured Mr. Vrabel. Michael Acri was convicted of murder and sentenced to a life term in the state prison.

Florence and Michael Acri, as partners, had owned and operated the Acri Cafe since 1933. From the time of his marriage to Florence Acri in 1931 until 1946, Michael Acri had been in and out of hospitals, clinics, and sanitariums for the treatment of mental disorders and nervousness. Although he beat Mrs. Acri when they had marital difficulties, he had not attacked, abused, or mistreated anyone else. The Acris separated in September 1946, and Mrs. Acri sued her husband for divorce soon afterward. Before their separation, Mrs. Acri had operated and managed the cafe primarily only when Mr. Acri was ill. Following the marital separation and until the time he shot Mr. Vrabel, Mr. Acri was in exclusive control of the management of the cafe.

Mr. Vrabel brought suit against Florence Acri to recover damages for his injuries on the grounds that,

as Mr. Acri's partner, she was liable for his tort. The trial court ordered her to pay Mr. Vrabel damages of $7,500. Mrs. Acri appealed.

JUDICIAL OPINION

ZIMMERMAN, Judge

The authorities are in agreement that whether a tort is committed by a partner or a joint adventurer, the principles of law governing the situation are the same. So, where a partnership or a joint enterprise is shown to exist, each member of such project acts both as principal and agent of the others as to those things done within the apparent scope of the business of the project and for its benefit.

Section 13 of the Uniform Partnership Act provides: "Where, by any wrongful act or omission of any partner acting in the ordinary course of business of the partnership or with the authority of his copartners, loss or injury is caused to any person, not being a partner in the partnership, or any penalty is incurred, the partnership is liable therefor to the same extent as the partner so acting or omitting to act."

However, it is equally true that where one member of a partnership or joint enterprise commits a wrongful and malicious tort not within the actual or apparent scope of the agency, or the common business of the particular venture, to which the other

(continued)

members have not assented, and which has not been concurred in or ratified by them, they are not liable for the harm thereby caused.

Because at the time of Vrabel's injuries and for a long time prior thereto Florence had been excluded from the Acri Cafe and had no voice or control in its management, and because Florence did not know or have good reason to know that Michael was a dangerous individual prone to assault cafe patrons, the theory of negligence urged by Vrabel is hardly tenable.

We cannot escape the conclusion, therefore, that the above rules, relating to the nonliability of a partner or joint adventurer for wrongful and malicious torts committed by an associate outside the purposes and scope of the business, must be applied in the instant case. The willful and malicious attack by Michael Acri upon Vrabel in the Acri Cafe cannot reasonably be said to have come within the scope of the business of operating the cafe, so as to have rendered the absent Florence accountable.

Since the liability of a partner for the acts of his associates is founded upon the principles of agency, the statement is in point that an intentional and willful attack committed by an agent or employee, to vent his own spleen or malevolence against the injured person, is a clear departure from his employment and his principal or employer is not responsible therefor.

Judgment reversed.

CASE QUESTIONS

1. What was the nature of the business?
2. What type of injury occurred, and who caused it?
3. Why was Mr. Acri not a defendant?
4. Is Mrs. Acri liable for the injuries?

Tax Consequences in Partnerships

A partnership does not pay taxes. It simply files an informational return. Each partner, however, must report her share of partnership income (or losses) and deductions and must pay taxes on the reported share.

Management and Control

Partnership Authority

Unless agreed otherwise, each partner has a duty to contribute time to manage the partnership. Each partner has an equal management say, and each has a right to use partnership property for partnership purposes. No one partner controls the property, funds, or management of the firm (unless the partners so agree).

The partners may agree to delegate day-to-day management responsibilities to one or more of the partners. However, the agency rules of express, implied, and apparent authority (see Chapter 18) apply to partnerships. Each partner is an agent of the other partners, and each has express authority given by the UPA and any partnership agreement, the implied authority relating to those powers, and apparent authority as is customary in their business. Some management matters are simply a matter of a vote; a majority of the partners makes the decision. The unanimous consent of the partners is required for some decisions, however, such as confessing a judgment (settling a lawsuit), transferring all the partnership's assets, or selling its goodwill. Basically, unusual transactions in which no apparent authority could be claimed require all the partners' approval.

C O N S I D E R . . .

21.3   Silvio Giannetti, his daughter, Anne Marie, and her husband, Jerry Prozinsky, were partners in the Giannetti Investment Company (GIC). GIC owned and operated the Brougham Manor Apartments. Jerry signed a contract with Omnicon to give it the right to install the equipment for and promote cable television in the apartment complex. Silvio was most disturbed when he learned that Jerry had signed the agreement. He refused to allow Omnicon further access to the complex. The result was that cable service was interrupted, lines could not be repaired, and Omnicon was forced to discontinue all its cable customers in the apartment complex. Omnicon filed suit against GIC for breach of contract. Silvio maintains that GIC is not liable because Jerry did not have the authority to sign such a contract. Is Silvio correct? [*Omnicon v. Giannetti Investment Company*, 561 N.W.2d 138 (Mich. App. 1997)]

The partners are not entitled to compensation for their management of the partnership's business, unless so specified in the partnership agreement. Under the UPA, a partner who winds up a dissolved partnership's business can be compensated.

Partner Fiduciary Duties

Because each partner is an agent for the partnership and the other partners as well, she owes the partnership and the other partners the same fiduciary duties an agent owes a principal. Partners' obligations as fiduciaries are the same as agents' duties to principals.

Partnership Property

Partnership property is defined as property contributed to the firm as a capital contribution or property purchased with partnership funds. Partners are co-owners of partnership property in a form of ownership called *tenancy in partnership*. Tenants in partnership have equal rights in the use and possession of the property for partnership purposes. On the death of one of the partners, rights in the property are transferred to the surviving partner or partners. The partnership interest in the property remains, and the property or a share of the property is not transferred to the estate of the deceased partner. The estate of the deceased partner simply receives the value of the partner's interest, not the property.

Partner Interests

Partners' interests in the partnership are different from partnership property. A partner's interest is a personal property interest that belongs to the partner. It can be sold (transferred) or pledged as collateral to a creditor. Creditors (personal) can attach a partner's interests to collect a debt.

There are several effects on the partnership of a transfer of a partner's interest. The transfer does not result in the transferee becoming a new partner because no person can become a partner without the consent of all the existing partners. Further, the transfer does not relieve the transferring partner of personal liability. A transfer of interest will not eliminate individual liability to existing creditors.

Some partnership agreements place restrictions on transfer. For example, there may be a provision that allows the partnership the right to buy out a partner before the partner has the authority to transfer her interest.

Transferability of Interests

A partner cannot transfer her partnership status without the unanimous consent of the other partners. However, if that transfer is approved, the departing or outgoing partner and the incoming partner should be aware of their liability. Absent an agreement from creditors, the outgoing partner remains personally liable for all partnership debts up to the time of departure. If the departing partner gives public notice of her disassociation, no further personal liability results from contracts and obligations entered into after departure. The incoming partner is liable for all contracts after the date she comes into the firm. Incoming partners are liable for existing debts only to the extent of their capital contribution.

The following case deals with an issue of departing partners and liability.

CASE 21.3

Beane v. *Paulsen*
21 Cal.App.4th 89 (Cal.App.3d Dist. 1993)

Liability Doesn't Stop Here: Departing Partners and Debt

FACTS

Madeline Tucker, a retired schoolteacher, and her son, Bernard Ferris, were co-owners of a duplex in Fair Oaks, California. Tucker, 79, and her son had executed loan documents of a note for $105,000 and a deed of trust on the property and given the loan proceeds to Ferris and his partners, Bill and Clay Biscoe, so that they could purchase a bar.

The bar failed, and in order to prevent the bankruptcy trustee from foreclosing on her home, Mrs. Tucker retained William Dunbar in 1987 to represent her in order to have the note and deed of trust set aside on the grounds of undue influence.

Mr. Dunbar was a partner in the firm of Paulsen, Vodonick, and Davis (PVD). Mr. Paulsen, Mr. Vodonick and Mr. Davis had all dealt with Mrs. Tucker's case and claim. The firm was formed as a professional corporation in 1985, and the lawyers severed their relationship in 1988, with Mr. Paulsen and Mr. Davis departing. Mr. Vodonick and Mr. Dunbar formed a practice.

Mr. Vodonick failed to assert Mrs. Tucker's claim in a timely manner and it was dismissed. Mrs. Tucker filed suit for malpractice in April 1991 against Davis, Paulsen, Vodonick, and Dunbar. Davis and Paulsen maintained that their liability ended when they left the firm. Davis and Paulsen were granted summary judgment, and Mrs. Tucker's executor (Beane) appealed.

JUDICIAL OPINION

DAVIS, Judge

Mrs. Tucker was not represented by a partnership but by a professional corporation, PVD. This distinction seems to have escaped the litigants throughout these proceedings. It is not a distinction, however, that affects our analysis of the question of liability of defendants Paulsen and Davis for PVD's negligent provision of professional services.

In California, the Legislature has authorized the formation of professional corporations for the purpose of practicing law if they are registered with the State Bar. The Legislature has also mandated that the State Bar, as a condition of the registration process, require the corporation to "maintain security by insurance or otherwise for claims against it by its clients" for malpractice. Accordingly, the State Bar requires "For law corporations that apply to the State Bar for a Certification of Registration on or after October 27, 1971, security for claims against it by its clients for [malpractice] shall consist of an executed copy of [a written agreement . . . by each of the shareholders, jointly and severally guaranteeing payment by the corporation of all claims established against it by its clients for [malpractice] arising out of the practice of law by the corporation. . . . This written guarantee has certain financial limits per claim and is to be offset by any available malpractice insurance."

[D]efendants Paulsen and Davis have joint and several liability to the former client of their corporation as guarantors of PVD's financial responsibility for malpractice. Considering it appears to be undisputed that PVD is insolvent, this would not be any different than their joint and several liability had they simply been in a partnership at the time the alleged malpractice was committed against Mrs. Tucker.

We now proceed with our analysis of their claim that they severed their liability for an alleged malpractice regarding Mrs. Tucker when they left the corporation (adhering to the less-cumbersome terminology of partnership and the applicable tenets of vicarious partnership liability).

We first briefly dispatch the defendants' alternative ground for affirming the trial court. They claim they effectively severed their relationship with Mr. Vodonick and PVD by August 1988, when Mrs. Tucker was given notice of the break-up of the firm, and consequently cannot be held liable for their former partner's failure in 1987 to prosecute the bankruptcy proceeding. They cite *Redman* v. *Walters* (1979) 88 Cal.App. 3d 448. The principle on which they rely is inapposite.

In *Redman*, the plaintiff engaged the services of a partnership in 1969. In 1970, defendant Walters left the firm, never having met the plaintiff or participated in his lawsuit. There was no communication with the plaintiff about the defendant's separation from the partnership, other than a change in the letterheads in correspondence sent to him or the headings of pleadings. In 1974, the plaintiff's action was dismissed for failure to prosecute, at which point he brought suit against the partnership and defendant Walters. In reinstating the plaintiff's action as to defendant Walters, the *Redman* court first noted the principle of partnership law that in dissolution, the partnership "continues" as to contractual obligations until they are satisfied. Thus, having been a member of a partnership that contracted with the plaintiff, the defendant continued to be a partner for purposes of that contract until it was discharged, and as a partner he would have vicarious liability for the negligent acts of his partners in performing the contract. The only way in which the defendant could have been discharged from future vicarious liability as a member of this "continuing" partnership was if the plaintiff had given express or implied consent to nonrepresentation, "or perhaps by estoppel." The court found that the mere fact the plaintiff had received documents indicating the change in membership of the partnership was insufficient on summary judgment to establish the "existence or absence of estoppel, or waiver" because that was "ordinarily a question of fact" except where the evidence is undisputed and is susceptible of only one reasonable inference.

As characterized in a malpractice treatise, "The court rested its decision upon principles of general partnership law, and cautioned law firms that a partner can only terminate prospective liability if the client knows of the partner's withdrawal and consents to terminating that individual's obligations." We emphasize that key word, because it is one thing to say that a client by conduct can accede to nonrepresentation by a departing partner, absolving that partner of subsequent negligent acts with which he has no connection, and it is quite another matter to assert, as do the defendants before us, that the client also releases the departing partners from liability for negligent acts already committed, without any showing that the client was consciously relinquishing the right to sue. We believe this is the point the trial court sought to make in its minute order, albeit cryptically, when it referenced the fact "[m]ovants represented plaintiff when the injury occurred" and did not refer to this ground for the motion any further. Thus, regardless of whether or not the facts adduced in the trial court are sufficient to infer a release by Mrs. Tucker of any future representation by the defendants, they certainly cannot be read as releasing the defendants from liability for the past tortious acts of their partnership unknown to Mrs. Tucker until 1989.

The undisputed facts adduced by the defendants are insufficient as a matter of law to establish either defense posited by them. The judgment is reversed and remanded with directions to enter a new order denying the motion by defendants Paulsen and Davis for summary judgment.

CASE QUESTIONS

1. What does Mrs. Tucker use as her basis for a malpractice claim?

2. What is the liability of lawyers in a professional corporation?

3. What happens when a partner leaves a firm?

4. Why is there joint and several liability in professional corporations?

5. What should Paulsen and Davis have done when they left their firm?

Dissolution and Termination of the Partnership

Dissolution is not necessarily termination. The UPA defines dissolution as one partner's ceasing to be associated with carrying on the business. The RUPA refers to "dissociation" of partners which may or may not lead to dissolution. When a partner leaves, retires, or dies, the partnership is dissolved, though not terminated. Dissolution is basically a change in the structure of the partnership. Dissolution may have no effect on the business: The partnership will be reorganized and will continue business without the partner who is leaving.

Dissolution *can* lead, however, to termination of the partnership. Termination means all business stops, the assets of the firm are liquidated, and the proceeds are distributed to creditors and partners to repay capital contributions and to distribute profits (if any). There are several grounds for dissolution.

Dissolution by Agreement

The partnership agreement itself may limit the partnership's time of existence. Once that time expires, the partnership is dissolved. If the agreement does not specify the time or there is no partnership agreement, the partners can (by unanimous consent) agree to dissolve the partnership.

Dissolution by Operation of Law

Another way a partnership is dissolved is by operation of law. This means that certain events require the dissolution of the partnership. When one partner dies, the partnership is automatically dissolved. The business could go on, but the partnership as it once existed ends and the deceased partner's estate must be paid for her interest. Also, if the partnership or an individual partner becomes bankrupt, the partnership is dissolved by law.

Dissolution by Court Order

The third method for dissolution of a partnership is by court order. Sometimes partners just cannot work together any longer. In such circumstances, they can petition a court for dissolution in the interest of preserving their investments.

LIMITED PARTNERSHIPS

A **limited partnership** is a partnership with a slight variation in the liability of those involved. There are two types of partners in a limited partnership: at least one **general partner** and one **limited partner.** General partners have the same obligations as partners in general partnerships—full liability and full responsibility for the management of the business. Limited partners have liability limited to the amount of their contribution to the partnership, and they cannot be involved in the management of the firm. General partners run the limited partnership, and the limited partners are the investors.

The Uniform Limited Partnership Act (ULPA) was drafted in 1916. At that time there were very few limited partnerships, and most of them were quite small. The limited partnership, however, has become a significant part of business structure, particularly over the past twenty years. It has been the predominant form of business organization for oil exploration and real estate development because of the significant tax advantages available through limited partnerships. The attractiveness of limited liability combined with tax advantages has resulted in an increase in the numbers and sizes of limited partnerships.

Because of this increased use, the ULPA proved to be inadequate for governing the creation, structure, and ongoing operations of limited partnerships. In 1976, the National Conference of Commissioners on Uniform State Laws developed the **Revised Uniform Limited Partnership Act** (RULPA). The act was designed to update limited partnership law to address the ways limited partnerships were doing business. The RULPA was revised in 1985 and has been adopted in nearly every state.

Formation

As discussed earlier, a valid general partnership can be created through the conduct of the parties and without a formal partnership agreement. A limited partnership, however, is a statutory creature and requires compliance with certain procedures in order to exist. If these procedures are not followed, it is possible that the limited partners could lose their limited liability protection.

The RULPA requires the following information for filing at the appropriate government agency:

1. Name of the limited partnership (It cannot be deceptively similar to another corporation's or partnership's name and must contain the words "limited partnership"; no abbreviations are permitted.)
2. Address of its principal office
3. Name and address of statutory agent
4. Business address of the general partner
5. Latest date for dissolution of the partnership

Under the RULPA, the limited partners need not be named in the certificate, nor are they all required to sign the certificate. These changes resulted from recognition of the size of limited partnerships and the tremendous paperwork burden created by the RULPA. If an error is made in formation, the partnership could be deemed a general partnership and the limited partners could lose the protection of their limited liability. However, under RULPA, limited partners are permitted to file an amendment correcting the problem or withdrawing from the business altogether. A limited partner would still be liable to any third parties for liabilities incurred by the general partnership prior to the time the correction is made.

The certificate of limited partnership is simply public disclosure of the formation and existence of the limited partnership; it does not deal with the many more rights and obligations that the partners may agree on among themselves. Those issues are generally addressed in a much longer document called a **limited partnership agreement** or the **articles of limited partnership.**

Sources of Funding

Capital contributions supply the initial funding for a limited partnership. Both the general and limited partners make contributions upon entering the partnership. Under the RULPA, the contribution can be in the form of cash, property, services already performed, or a promissory note or other obligation to pay money or property. The RULPA requires that limited partners' promises to contribute must be in writing to be enforceable. The limited partners are always personally liable for the difference between what has actually been contributed and the amount promised to be contributed.

Some partners make **advances** or loans to the partnership. The partnership can also borrow money from third parties. However, only the general partner has any personal liability for repayment of the loan to the third party.

Liability

The principal advantage of a limited partnership is the limited personal liability. To ensure personal limited liability, several requirements must be met. First, as already discussed, a certificate of limited partnership must be filed, indicating the limited liability status of the limited partners. Second, there must be at least one general partner. The general partner can be a corporation. Third, the limited partners cannot be involved in the management of the business because such involvement would give the appearance of general partner status. Finally, limited partners cannot use their names in the name of the partnership, which would give the wrong impression to outside parties and create an estoppel type of relationship.

Under the RULPA, a limited partner who participates in the management of the firm in the same way the general partner does is liable only to those persons who are led to believe by the limited partner's conduct that the limited partner is a general partner. The RULPA has also provided a list of activities that can be engaged in by limited partners without losing their limited liability status. Those activities include:

1. Being employed by the general partnership as an employee or contractor
2. Consulting with or advising the general partner
3. Acting as a surety or guarantor for the limited partnership
4. Voting on amendments, dissolution, sale of property, or assumption of debt

If limited partners comply with the rules for limited liability, their liability is limited to the amount of their capital contribution. If they have pledged to pay a certain amount as capital over a period of time, they are liable for the full amount. For example, some real estate syndications that are limited partnerships allow the limited partners to make their investment in installment payments over two to four years. Limited partners in these arrangements are liable for the full amount pledged whenever an obligation to a creditor is not paid.

Tax Consequences

Limited partnerships are taxed the same way as general partnerships. The general and limited partners actually report the income and losses on their individual returns and pay the appropriate taxes. A limited partnership files an information return but does not itself pay any taxes.

One of the benefits of limited partnership status is the combination of limited liability with direct tax benefits. In this sense, a limited partnership is the best of both worlds. Because of this ideal situation, limited partnership interests are closely scrutinized by the IRS to determine whether they are, in reality, corporations as opposed to true limited partnerships. Some of the factors examined in determining whether an organization is a corporation or a limited partnership are (1) the transferability of the interests, (2) the assets of the general partners, and (3) the net worth of the general partners. From the perspective of the IRS, organization as a limited partnership is no assurance of treatment as such for tax purposes.

Management and Control

Profits and Distributions

A general partner has absolute authority to decide not only when distributions are made but if they will be made; the general partner, for example, might decide not to distribute funds but to put them back into the business.

Profits and losses are allocated on the basis of capital contributions. Under the RULPA, the agreement for sharing of profits and losses must be in writing.

Partner Authority

The authority of the general partner in a limited partnership is the same as the authority of the partners in a general partnership. These powers can be restricted by agreement. There are, however, some general activities the general partner cannot perform without the consent of the limited partners. These include:

1. Admitting a new general partner (also requires consent of other general partners)
2. Admitting a new limited partner unless the partnership agreement allows it
3. Extraordinary transactions, such as selling all the partnership assets

Limited partners can monitor the general partner's activity with the same rights provided to partners in general partnerships: the right to inspect the books and records and the right to an accounting.

Transferability of Interests

Although the assignment of limited partnership interests is not prohibited by the RULPA, a limited partnership agreement may provide for significant restraints on assignment. There are two reasons for transfer restrictions on limited partners' interests. First, limited partnership interests may have been sold without registration as exemptions to the federal securities law (see Chapter 22 for more details on securities registrations). If those exempt interests are readily transferable, the exemption could be lost. Second, for the limited partners to enjoy the tax benefits of limited partner status, the ease of transferability is a critical issue. The more easily an interest can be transferred, the more likely the limited partnership is to be treated (for tax purposes) as a corporation.

The assignment of a partnership interest does not terminate a limited partnership. The assignee is entitled to receive only the distributions and profits to which the partner is entitled. The assignee does not become a partner without the consent of the other partners. Under the RULPA, a limited partnership can agree that the assigning limited partner will have the authority to make the assignee a limited partner. The effect of the RULPA provision is to simplify transfers and allow limited partners to decide whether they want to transfer their interest or their limited partner status.

Dissolution and Termination of a Limited Partnership

A limited partnership can be dissolved in one of the following ways:

1. Expiration of the time period in the agreement or the occurrence of an event causing dissolution, as specified in the agreement

2. Unanimous written consent of all partners

3. Withdrawal of a general partner

4. Court order after application by one of the partners

Upon dissolution, a partnership can continue (assuming a general partner remains); but the partnership can also be terminated after dissolution. If termination occurs, all assets of the partnership are liquidated. The RULPA specifies that the money from the sale of the assets be used to pay partnership obligations in the following order of priority:

1. Creditors (including partners, but not with respect to distributions)

2. Partners and former partners, for distributions owed to them

3. Return of capital contributions

4. Remainder split according to distribution agreement

CORPORATIONS

Corporations have the following characteristics: unlimited duration, free transferability of interest, limited liability for shareholders/owners, continuity, and centralized management. Corporations are legal entities in and of themselves. Because they are treated as persons under the law, they can hold title to property, they can sue or be sued in the corporate name, and they are taxed separately. The latest U.S. economic census figures (1997) indicate that there are 1.6 million partnerships in the United States but 3.6 million corporations. Corporations earn nearly 90 percent of all business profits.

Types of Corporations

There are diverse types of corporations, each of which can be described by one or more adjectives. For example, there are **profit corporations** (those seeking to earn a return for investors) and **nonprofit corporations.** There are **domestic corporations** and **foreign corporations.** A corporation is a domestic corporation in the state in which it is incorporated and a foreign corporation in every other state. Further, corporations organized by government agencies that exist to achieve a social goal are called **government corporations. Professional corporations** are corporations that are organized by physicians, dentists, attorneys, and accountants; they exist by statute in most states. Professional corporation shareholders have no personal liability for any corporate debts, as in any other corporation, except for professional malpractice claims. The **corporate veil** or **shield** (explained later) will not give individuals personal immunity for professional negligence despite their general liability limitation through incorporation. **Close corporations** are the opposite of **publicly held corporations;** that is, they are corporations with very few shareholders. Close corporations and publicly held corporations are created in the same way, but most states then have a separate statute governing the operation of close corporations. Close corporation owners are generally given more discretion in their internal operations, and the degree of formality required for publicly held corporations is not required.

The **S corporation** (sometimes called subchapter S or sub S corporation) is formed no differently from any other corporation, but it must meet the IRS requirements for an S corporation and must file a special election form with the

IRS indicating it wishes to be treated as an S corporation. The benefit of an S corporation is that shareholders' income and losses are treated like those of partners, but the shareholders enjoy the protection of limited liability behind a corporate veil. The income earned and losses incurred by an S corporation are reported on the shareholders' individual returns, but the shareholders' personal assets are protected from creditors of the business. For tax purposes, the S corporation is like a partnership in the sense of the flow-through of profits and losses, and the shareholders avoid the double taxation of having the corporation pay tax on its earnings and their paying tax on the dividends distributed to them.

The term "C corporation" is often used in discussions of corporate formation. "C corporation" is a tax term meaning that the corporation has no pass-through benefits; the corporation pays tax on its income and individuals pay taxes on their dividends (see pg. 838).

> **BUSINESS PLANNING TIP**
>
> Under the Small Business Job Protection Act of 1996, S corporation requirements were modified. An S corporation must meet specific qualifications, including:
>
> - Being a domestic corporation
> - Having no more than seventy-five shareholders
> - Having no person other than an individual or certain trusts and estates, S corporations and certain exempt organizations including charitable organizations and qualified retirement trusts as shareholders
> - Having no nonresident aliens as shareholders
> - Having no more than one class of stock
> - Not being a member of an affiliated group
> - Not being a financial institution
> - Not being an insurance company
> - Not being a corporation to which IRC § 936 (dealing with Puerto Rico and possession tax credits) applies

The Law of Corporations

Examine Arizona's Corporation Laws:
http://www.azleg.state.az.us/ars/10/title10.htm

The **Model Business Corporation Act** (MBCA), as drafted and revised by the Corporate, Banking and Business Section of the American Bar Association, is the uniform law on corporations. The provisions of the MBCA are quite liberal and give management great latitude in operations. The MBCA is not adopted as widely as the UPA or the Uniform Commercial Code (UCC). Even those states adopting the MBCA have made significant changes in their adopted versions. As a result, each state's law on corporations is quite different. The following sections cover the revised MBCA rules, but each state may have its own variations.

Examine New York's Corporation Laws:
http://www.law.cornell.edu/ny/statutes/buscorp.htm

Formation

A corporation is a statutory entity. Formal public filing is required to form a corporation. The following procedures for corporate formation are those of the MBCA.

Where to Incorporate
The factors to be considered in determining in which state to incorporate are as follows:

1. The status of the state's corporation laws (Some states are oriented more toward management than to shareholders.)
2. State tax laws
3. The ability to attract employees to the state
4. Incentives states offer to attract the business (new freeways, office space, attractive urban renewal)

The Formation Document

All states require **articles of incorporation** to be filed in order to create a corporation. These articles give the structure and basic information about the corporation. Under the MBCA, the articles of incorporation must include the following information:

1. The name of the corporation
2. The names and addresses of all incorporators (In addition, each incorporator must sign the articles of incorporation.)
3. The share structure of the corporation: (a) common and preferred classes, (b) which shares vote, (c) rights of shareholders—preemptive rights
4. The statutory agent (the party who will be served with any lawsuits against the corporation)

Who Is Incorporating

The **incorporators** (required to be listed in the articles of incorporation) are the parties forming the corporation. Under the MBCA, only one incorporator is required, and that person may be a natural person, a corporation, a partnership, a limited partnership, or an association.

Incorporators are personally liable for any contracts entered into or actions taken during the pre-incorporation stage. Until the corporation exists, incorporators are acting as individuals. After incorporation, the corporation could agree to assume liability through a **novation** of the incorporators' acts.

For example, if an incorporator of a lumberyard entered into a contract for the purchase of lumber and the corporate board (after formation) agreed that the contract was a good one, the corporation could ratify it or enter into a novation to assume liability. In novation, the lumberyard agrees to substitute the corporation as the contracting party. In a **ratification,** the corporation assumes primary liability for payment, but the incorporator still remains liable. Incorporators generally are paid for their efforts in shares of the corporation's stock. They may also be the contributors of initial corporate assets and may be paid in shares for their contributions.

Postformation

After the paperwork of incorporating is complete, a corporation must begin its day-to-day operations with an **initial meeting.** At this meeting, the officers of the corporation are elected and **bylaws** are adopted to govern corporate procedures. The bylaws define the authority of each of the officers, prescribe procedures for announcing and conducting meetings (such as quorum numbers and voting numbers), and set the terms of officers and directors and who is eligible to serve in such offices. Articles of incorporation give an overview of a corporate entity; the bylaws constitute the operational rules.

Capital and Sources of Corporate Funds

A corporation has a variety of sources for funds. It may utilize short-term financing, which consists of loans from banks, or credit lines. The problems with short-term financing are higher interest rates and shorter payback periods. The other forms of financing used most frequently by corporations are debt and equity.

Debt Financing: The Bond Market

Long-term debt financing is available to corporations when they issue bonds. Bonds are, in effect, long-term promissory notes from a corporation to the bond buyers. The corporation pays the holders interest on the bonds until the maturity date, which is when the bonds are due or must be paid. The interest is fixed and is a fixed-payment responsibility regardless of the corporation's profitability. The benefits to debt financing are the tax deductibility of interest as an expense. Further, bondholders have the benefit of first rights in corporate assets in the event of insolvency. However, a corporation cannot maintain a sound financial policy or rating with debt financing only.

Equity Financing: Shareholders

Equity financing comes through the sale of stock in a corporation. It provides a means of raising capital up front with the exchange of proportionate corporate ownership and the promise of proportionate profits. Shareholders are given shares of stock in exchange for their money. To avoid personal liability, the shareholders must pay at least par value for their shares and must honor the terms of their subscription agreement (share purchase agreement). A shareholder who has not paid at least par value is said to hold "watered shares" and is liable to creditors for the amount not paid. For example, if a shareholder paid $500 for shares with a par value of $1,000, the shareholder would be personally liable for the $500 difference. Along with those shares of stock come certain promises of future performance from the corporation. The rights of shareholders depend upon the type of stock purchased. A discussion of the various types of stock follows.

Common Stock

Common stock is the typical stock in a corporation and is usually the most voluminous in terms of the number of shares. Common stock generally carries voting rights so that common shareholders have a voice in the election of directors, the amendment of the articles and bylaws, and other major corporate matters. Common stock generally does not have a fixed dividend rate and does not carry with it any right to have a dividend declared. Thus, common stock dividends are dependent on both profitability and decisions of the board of directors. If a corporation is dissolved, the common shareholders have a right to a proportionate share of the assets (after creditors and preferred stockholders have been paid).

Preferred Stock

Preferred stock is appropriately named because its owners enjoy preferred status over holders of a corporation's common stock. For example, preferred stockholders have priority in the payment of dividends. Some preferred dividends are even at a fixed rate, and some types of preferred stock guarantee the payment of a dividend so that if a dividend is not paid one year, the holder's right to be paid carries over until funds are available. This type of stock is **cumulative preferred stock.** Preferred shareholders also have priority over common shareholders in the event the corporation is dissolved and the assets distributed.

Liability Issues

Limited liability for shareholders is one of the advantages of corporate organization. However, there are times when individuals—such as shareholders, directors, and officers—can be personally liable for corporate obligations.

Shareholder Liability

Shareholders' personal liability is limited to the amount of their investment in the corporation. The personal assets of shareholders are not subject to the claims of corporate creditors. In some circumstances, however, a shareholder is liable for more than the amount of investment. For example, if a shareholder has not paid for her shares or has paid for them with overvalued property, creditors could turn to the shareholder's personal assets for satisfaction of her debt, but only to the extent of the amount due on the shares.

In other more serious circumstances, shareholders can be held liable for the full amount of corporate debts. A creditor who successfully pierces the corporate veil overcomes the shield of limited liability protecting shareholders from having to accept personal liability for corporate debts. The corporate veil can be pierced for several reasons. One is inadequate capitalization. The owners of a corporation are required to place as much capital at risk in the corporation as is necessary to cover reasonably anticipated expenses of the business. The purpose of this requirement is to ensure that someone does not use the corporation to avoid liability without actually transferring to the corporation some assets for the payment of corporate liabilities.

C O N S I D E R . . .

21.4   Max Rupe was the sole shareholder of Updike Oil Company, a corporation. There was no transfer of shares to Rupe. No records of any meetings or financial records existed. Updike had $56,328 in liabilities and $100 in capital stock. A creditor is seeking to pierce the corporate veil. Is success likely? [*U.S. National Bank of Omaha* v. *Rupe*, 296 N.W.2d 474 (Neb. 1980)]

Another theory a court can use to pierce the corporate veil is the **alter ego theory,** which means that the owners and managers of the corporation have not treated the corporation as a separate entity but have used the structure more as a personal resource. Personal and corporate assets and debts are mixed, there is no formality with regard to operations and meetings, and there are transfers of property without explanation or authorization.

The following case deals with an issue of piercing the corporate veil in a situation in which there is CERCLA (see Chapter 12) liability.

CASE 21.4

U.S. v. Best Foods, Inc.
524 U.S. 51 (1998)

Lifting the Veil Is Best for Cleanup, but Not Shareholders

FACTS

In 1957, Ott Chemical Co. manufactured chemicals at its plant near Muskegon, Michigan, and both intentionally and unintentionally dumped hazardous substances in the soil and

groundwater near the plant. Ott sold the plant to CPC International, Inc.

In 1965, CPC incorporated a wholly owned subsidiary (Ott II) to buy Ott's assets. Ott II then continued both the chemical production and dumping. Ott II's officers and directors had positions and duties at both CPC and Ott.

In 1972, CPC [now Best Foods] sold Ott II to Story Chemical, which operated the plant until its bankruptcy in 1977. Aerojet-General Corp. bought the plant from the bankruptcy trustee and manufactured chemicals there until 1986.

In 1989, the EPA filed suit to recover the costs of cleanup on the plant site and named CPC, Aerojet, and the officers of the now defunct Ott and Ott II.

The District Court held both CPC and Aerojet liable. After a divided panel of the Court of Appeals for the Sixth Circuit reversed in part, the court granted rehearing *en banc* and vacated the panel decision. This time, 7 judges to 6, the court again reversed the District Court in part. Best Foods appealed (Ott settled prior to the appeal).

JUDICIAL OPINION

SOUTER, Justice

The United States brought this action for the costs of cleaning up industrial waste generated by a chemical plant. The issue before us, under the Comprehensive Environmental Response, Compensation, and Liability Act of 1980 (CERCLA), is whether a parent corporation that actively participated in, and exercised control over, the operations of a subsidiary may, without more, be held liable as an operator of a polluting facility owned or operated by the subsidiary. We answer no, unless the corporate veil may be pierced. But a corporate parent that actively participated in, and exercised control over, the operations of the facility itself may be held directly liable in its own right as an operator of the facility.

The District Court said that operator liability may attach to a parent corporation both directly, when the parent itself operates the facility, and indirectly, when the corporate veil can be pierced under state law. The court explained that, while CERCLA imposes direct liability in situations in which the corporate veil cannot be pierced under traditional concepts of corporate law, "the statute and its legislative history do not suggest that CERCLA rejects entirely the crucial limits to liability that are inherent to corporate law."

"A parent's actual participation in and control over a subsidiary's functions and decision-making creates 'operator' liability under CERCLA; a parent's mere oversight of a subsidiary's business in a manner appropriate and consistent with the investment relationship between a parent and its wholly owned subsidiary does not."

Applying that test to the facts of this case, the court found it particularly telling that CPC selected Ott II's board of directors and populated its executive ranks with CPC officials, and that a CPC official, G.R.D. Williams, played a significant role in shaping Ott II's environmental compliance policy.

[W]here a parent corporation is sought to be held liable as an operator pursuant to 42 U.S.C. § 9607(a)(2) based upon the extent of its control of its subsidiary which owns the facility, the parent will be liable only when the requirements necessary to pierce the corporate veil [under state law] are met. In other words, . . . whether the parent will be liable as an operator depends upon whether the degree to which it controls its subsidiary and the extent and manner of its involvement with the facility, amount to the abuse of the corporate form that will warrant piercing the corporate veil and disregarding the separate corporate entities of the parent and subsidiary.

Applying Michigan veil-piercing law, the Court of Appeals decided that neither CPC nor Aerojet was liable for controlling the actions of its subsidiaries, since the parent and subsidiary corporations maintained separate personalities and the parents did not utilize the subsidiary corporate form to perpetrate fraud or subvert justice.

We granted certiorari to resolve a conflict among the Circuits over the extent to which parent corporations may be held liable under CERCLA for operating facilities ostensibly under the control of their subsidiaries.

It is a general principle of corporate law deeply "ingrained in our economic and legal systems" that a parent corporation (so-called because of control through ownership of another corporation's stock) is not liable for the acts of its subsidiary.

Although this respect for corporate distinctions when the subsidiary is a polluter has been severely criticized in the literature, nothing in CERCLA purports to reject this bedrock principle, and against this venerable common-law backdrop, the congressional silence is audible.

But there is an equally fundamental principle of corporate law, applicable to the parent-subsidiary relationship as well as generally, that the corporate veil may be pierced and the shareholder held liable for the corporation's conduct when, inter alia, the corporate form would otherwise be misused to accomplish certain wrongful purposes, most notably fraud, on the shareholder's behalf.

Nothing in CERCLA purports to rewrite this well-settled rule, either. If a subsidiary that operates,

(continued)

but does not own, a facility is so pervasively controlled by its parent for a sufficiently improper purpose to warrant veil piercing, the parent may be held derivatively liable for the subsidiary's acts as an operator.

The fact that a corporate subsidiary happens to own a polluting facility operated by its parent does nothing, then, to displace the rule that the parent "corporation is [itself] responsible for the wrongs committed by its agents in the course of its business." It is this direct liability that is properly seen as being at issue here.

Under the plain language of the statute, any person who operates a polluting facility is directly liable for the costs of cleaning up the pollution. This is so regardless of whether that person is the facility's owner, the owner's parent corporation or business partner, or even a saboteur who sneaks into the facility at night to discharge its poisons out of malice. If any such act of operating a corporate subsidiary's facility is done on behalf of a parent corporation, the existence of the parent-subsidiary relationship under state corporate law is simply irrelevant to the issue of direct liability.

This much is easy to say: the difficulty comes in defining actions sufficient to constitute direct parental "operation." Here of course we may again rue the uselessness of CERCLA's definition of a facility's "operator" as "any person . . . operating" the facility, which leaves us to do the best we can to give the term its "ordinary or natural meaning."

In a mechanical sense, to "operate" ordinarily means "[t]o control the functioning of; run: operate a sewing machine." And in the organizational sense more obviously intended by CERCLA, the word ordinarily means "[t]o conduct the affairs of; manage: operate a business." So, under CERCLA, an operator is simply someone who directs the workings of, manages, or conducts the affairs of a facility. To sharpen the definition for purposes of CERCLA's concern with environmental contamination, an operator must manage, direct, or conduct operations specifically related to pollution, that is, operations having to do with the leakage or disposal of hazardous waste, or decisions about compliance with environmental regulations.

With this understanding, we are satisfied that the Court of Appeals correctly rejected the District Court's analysis of direct liability. But we also think that the appeals court erred in limiting direct liability under the statute to a parent's sole or joint venture operation, so as to eliminate any possible finding that CPC is liable as an operator on the facts of this case.

In imposing direct liability on these grounds, the District Court failed to recognize that "it is entirely appropriate for directors of a parent corporation to serve as directors of its subsidiary, and that fact alone may not serve to expose the parent corporation to liability for its subsidiary's acts."

This recognition that the corporate personalities remain distinct has its corollary in the "well established principle [of corporate law] that directors and officers holding positions with a parent and its subsidiary can and do 'change hats' to represent the two corporations separately, despite their common ownership."

The Government would have to show that, despite the general presumption to the contrary, the officers and directors were acting in their capacities as CPC officers and directors, and not as Ott II officers and directors, when they committed those acts. The District Court made no such enquiry here, however, disregarding entirely this time-honored common-law rule.

In sum, the District Court's focus on the relationship between parent and subsidiary (rather than parent and facility), combined with its automatic attribution of the actions of dual officers and directors to the corporate parent, erroneously, even if unintentionally, treated CERCLA as though it displaced or fundamentally altered common-law standards of limited liability.

We accordingly agree with the Court of Appeals that a participation-and-control test looking to the parent's supervision over the subsidiary, especially one that assumes that dual officers always act on behalf of the parent, cannot be used to identify operation of a facility resulting in direct parental liability. Nonetheless, a return to the ordinary meaning of the word "operate" in the organizational sense will indicate why we think that the Sixth Circuit stopped short when it confined its examples of direct parental operation to exclusive or joint ventures, and declined to find at least the possibility of direct operation by CPC in this case.

Again norms of corporate behavior (undisturbed by any CERCLA provision) are crucial reference points. The critical question is whether, in degree and detail, actions directed to the facility by an agent of the parent alone are eccentric under accepted norms of parental oversight of a subsidiary's facility.

There is, in fact, some evidence that CPC engaged in just this type and degree of activity at the Muskegon plant. The District Court's opinion speaks of an agent of CPC alone who played a conspicuous part in dealing with the toxic risks emanating from the operation of the plant. G.R.D. Williams worked only for CPC; he was not an employee, officer, or director of Ott, and thus, his actions were of necessity taken only on behalf of CPC. The District Court found that "CPC became directly involved in environmental and regulatory matters through the work of . . . Williams, CPC's governmental and environmental affairs director. Williams . . . became heavily involved in environmental issues at Ott II." He "actively participated in and exerted control over a variety of Ott II environmental matters," and he "issued directives regarding Ott II's responses to regulatory inquiries."

We think that these findings are enough to raise an issue of CPC's operation of the facility through Williams's actions, though we would draw no ultimate conclusion from these findings at this point. Not only would we be deciding in the first instance an issue on which the trial and appellate courts did not focus, but the very fact that the District Court did not see the case as we do suggests that there may be still more to be known about Williams's activities.

Prudence thus counsels us to remand, on the theory of direct operation set out here, for reevaluation of Williams's role, and of the role of any other CPC agent who might be said to have had a part in operating the Muskegon facility.

The judgment of the Court of Appeals for the Sixth Circuit is vacated, and the case is remanded.

CASE QUESTIONS

1. Describe the corporate ownership history that surrounds the Muskegon facility.

2. Is there a special CERCLA rule for piercing the corporate veil?

3. What must be shown to hold a parent liable for the actions of the subsidiary?

4. Are joint directors of parent and corporate subsidiaries evidence of a need to pierce the corporate veil?

5. What does the court suggest shows there may be some evidence that the corporate veil can be pierced?

Corporate Tax Consequences

The Double-Taxation Cost of Limited Liability
Although corporations have the benefit of limited liability, they have the detriment of double taxation. This means that not only does the corporation pay taxes on its earnings but also the shareholders must report their dividend income on their separate returns and pay individual taxes on their dividend income. However, these shareholders pay taxes only if the dividends are paid. Unlike partnerships in which the partners pay taxes on earnings whether they are distributed or not, shareholders pay taxes on corporate earnings only when they are distributed to them.

Statutory Solutions to Double Taxation
There are ways to resolve the problem of the cost of double taxation. The S corporation, discussed on page 838, is one solution.

Corporate Management and Control: Directors and Officers

Election of Directors
A corporation might be owned by a million shareholders, but its operation will be controlled by the hands of a few, the **board of directors.** The shareholders elect these directors, who serve as the corporate policy makers. The directors also have responsibility for management of the corporation. To that end, the directors usually set up an **executive committee** composed of three board members to handle

Many companies have outside directors on their boards who are also paid as consultants to the company. For example, Dr. Henry A. Kissinger, the former secretary of state, has been a member of the American Express Board for a number of years. Dr. Kissinger receives a $64,000 annual retainer, a $30,000 pension, free life insurance, and the right to have the company make a $500,000 charitable gift at the time of his death as part of his director compensation. He also receives $350,000 a year in consulting fees from the company. W. R. Grace & Co. had five outside directors who also earned $1.5 million in consulting fees from the company.

ETHICAL ISSUES 21.1

Shareholder advocacy groups have proposed resolutions to reduce director compensation because such high payments mean they may not represent the interests of the shareholders.

The National Association of Corporate Directors has condemned the consultant-director dual role as a conflict of interest.

The American Express Board voted to halt the practice as a "bad idea" that "just confuses roles." Do you agree? Are there conflicts when directors also work for the corporation in exchange for large fees?

the more routine matters of running the corporation so that board meetings are not required as frequently.

Role of Directors

Directors are the strategic planning and policy makers for the corporation. They are also the outside perspective for the company. They can provide insight on current management practices (see the *Perot* case on p. 847). They also serve a watchdog role as with the now mandatory **audit committees** required of all stock exchange companies. Audit committees, made up of independent outside directors who have no contracts or former salary ties with the company, are responsible for assuring that the financial reports the management issues are accurate.

Institutional investors and other groups have been placing increasing pressure on boards for accountability. Some have developed standards for service on boards such as required stock ownership in the company, nominating committees to assure sufficient business background and knowledge, and term limits so that members do not become complacent. Some companies have procedures for the board to evaluate itself and its performance.

One area of director responsibility that receives ongoing attention is that of officers' compensation. Directors not only elect the officers of the corporation; they also decide the salaries for these officers and themselves. The issue of officer compensation has received congressional attention with the deductibility of officer compensation limited to $1 million annually and ongoing attention from shareholders in terms of limits on compensation. Shareholders continue to make proposals to limit executive compensation (see Chapter 22 for more information on such proposals) and exercise their rights of director removal if they feel the board is not responsive to their concerns about compensation.

Director Liability

Officers and directors are **fiduciaries** of the corporation, which means they are to act in the best interests of the corporation and not profit at the corporation's expense. They are subject to the **business judgment rule,** a standard of corporate behavior under which it is understood that officers and directors can make mis-

Re: The Best and Worst of Corporate Boards

Factors used: shareholder accountability, board quality, board independence, corporate performance

Best

1. Campbell Soup	Board conducts self-review and publishes results
2. General Electric	Outside directors own at least $450,000 in GE stock
3. IBM	Board hired outside CEO
4. Compaq Computer	Outside chairman, who reviews officer and director performance
5. Colgate Palmolive	Only one insider on the board

Worst

1. Archer Daniels Midland	Lack of independence on board
2. Champion International	Directors own little stock
3. H. J. Heinz	Board loaded with insiders; six directors over 70 years old
4. Rollins Environmental	All board members are insiders
5. Nationsbank	Lack of independence

Source: John A. Byrne, "Best and Worst Boards," *Business Week*, November 25, 1996, 83. Reprinted from November 25, 1996, issue of *Business Week* by special permission, copyright © 2002 by The McGraw-Hill Companies, Inc.

takes but they are required to show that their decisions were made after careful study and discussion. In those decisions, they may consult experts, such as attorneys, accountants, and financial analysts; but again, they need to show that these experts were well-chosen and reliable individuals.

The following case provides the answer for the chapter opening "Consider."

CASE 21.5

Grobow v. H. Ross Perot
539 A.2d 180 (Del. 1988)

Now Looky Here: H. Ross Perot as GM Gadfly

FACTS

In 1984, General Motors Corporation (GM) acquired 100 percent of Electronic Data Systems' (EDS) stock. Under the terms of the merger, H. Ross Perot, founder, chairman, and largest stockholder of EDS, exchanged his EDS stock for GM Class E stock. Perot became GM's largest shareholder, controlling 0.8 percent of GM voting stock. Perot was also elected to GM's Board of Directors.

Management differences developed, and Perot became increasingly vocal in his criticism of GM management. Saying he could no longer be a "com-

pany man," Perot said in public, "Until you nuke the old GM system, you'll never tap the full potential of your people," and "GM cannot become a world-class and cost-competitive company simply by throwing technology and money at its problems."

The Board decided to repurchase Perot's shares for $745 million if Perot would: (1) stop criticizing GM management (a penalty for default here was $7.5 million); (2) not purchase GM stock or engage in a proxy battle; and (3) not compete with EDS for three years or recruit EDS executives.

(continued)

Shareholders of GM (plaintiffs) filed derivative actions for breach of fiduciary duty by the directors for breach of loyalty and due care. The court of chancery dismissed the case, and the shareholders appealed.

JUDICIAL OPINION

HORSEY, Judge

As previously noted, the business judgment rule is but a presumption that directors making a business decision, not involving self-interest, act on an informed basis, in good faith and in the honest belief that their actions are in the corporations' best interest. Thus, good faith and the absence of self-dealing are threshold requirements for invoking the rule. *Unocal Corp.* v. *Mesa Petroleum Co.,* Del. Supr., 493 A.2d 946 (1985). Assuming the presumptions of director good faith and lack of self-dealing are not rebutted by well-pleaded facts, a shareholder derivative complainant must then allege further facts with particularity which, "taken as true, support a reasonable doubt that the challenged transaction was [in fact] the product of a valid exercise of business judgment."

Plaintiffs must plead particularized facts demonstrating either a financial interest or entrenchment on the part of the GM directors. Plaintiffs plead no facts demonstrating a financial interest on the part of GM's directors. The only averment permitting such an inference is the allegation that all GM's directors are paid for their services as directors. However, such allegations, without more, do not establish any financial interest.

Plaintiffs also do not plead any facts tending to show that the GM directors' positions were actually threatened by Perot, who owned only 0.8 percent of GM's voting stock, nor do plaintiffs allege that the repurchase was motivated and reasonably related to the directors' retention of their positions on the Board. Plaintiffs merely argue that Perot's public criticism of GM management could cause the directors embarrassment sufficient to lead to their removal from office. Such allegations are tenuous at best and are too speculative to raise a reasonable doubt of director disinterest. Speculation on motives for undertaking corporate action are wholly insufficient to establish a case of demand excusal.

Plaintiffs' remaining allegations bearing on the issue of entrenchment are: the rushed nature of the transaction during a period of GM financial difficulty; the giant premium paid; and the criticism (after the fact) of the repurchase by industry analysts and top GM management. Plaintiffs argue that these allegations are sufficient to raise a reasonable doubt of director disinterest. We cannot agree. Not one of the asserted grounds would support a reasonable belief of entrenchment based on director self-interest. The relevance of these averments goes largely to the issue of due care, next discussed. Such allegations are patently insufficient to raise a reasonable doubt as to the ability of the GM Board to act with disinterest. Thus, we find plaintiffs' entrenchment claim to be essentially conclusory and lacking in factual support sufficient to establish excusal based on director interest.

Having concluded that plaintiffs have failed to plead a claim of financial interest or entrenchment sufficient to excuse presuit demand, we examine the complaints as amended to determine whether they raise a reasonable doubt that the directors exercised proper business judgment in the transaction. By proper business judgment we mean both substantive due care (purchase terms), see *Saxe* v. *Brady,* Del. Ch., 40 Del. Ch. 474, 184 A.2d 602, 610 (1962), and procedural due care (an informed decision), see *Smith* v. *Van Gorkom,* Del. Supr., 488 A.2d 858, 872–73 (1985).

With regard to the nature of the transactions and the terms of repurchase, especially price, plaintiffs allege that the premium paid Perot constituted a prima facie waste of GM's assets. Plaintiffs argue that the transaction, on its face, was "so egregious as to be afforded no presumption of business judgment protection." In rejecting this contention, the Vice Chancellor reasoned that, apart from the hush-mail provision, the transaction must be viewed as any other repurchase by a corporation, at a premium over market, of its own stock held by a single dissident shareholder or shareholder group at odds with management, [which] have repeatedly been upheld as valid exercises of business judgment.

The law of Delaware is well established that, in the absence of evidence of fraud or unfairness, a corporation's repurchase of its capital stock at a premium over market from a dissident shareholder is entitled to the protection of the business judgment rule.

We have already determined that plaintiffs have not stated a claim of financial interest or entrenchment as the compelling motive for the repurchase, and it is equally clear that the complaints as amended do not allege a claim of fraud. They allege, at most, a claim of waste based on the assertion that GM's Board paid such a premium for the Perot holdings as to shock the conscience of the ordinary person.

Thus, the issue becomes whether the complaints state a claim of waste of assets, i.e., whether "what the corporation has received is so inadequate in value that no person of ordinary, sound business judgment would deem it worth that which the corporation has paid." By way of reinforcing their claim of waste, plaintiffs seize upon the hush-mail feature of the repurchase as being the motivating reason for the "giant premium" approved by the GM Board. Plaintiffs then argue that buying the silence of a dissident within management constitutes an invalid business purpose. Ergo, plaintiffs argue that a claim of waste of corporate assets evidencing lack of director due care has been well pleaded.

Plaintiffs' complaints as amended fail to plead with particularity any facts supporting a conclusion that the primary or motivating purpose of the Board's payment of a "giant premium" for the Perot holdings was to buy Perot's silence rather than simply to buy him out and remove him from GM's management team. To the contrary, plaintiffs themselves state in their complaints as amended several legitimate business purposes for the GM Board's decision to sever its relationship with Perot: (1) the Board's determination that it would be in GM's best interest to retain control over its wholly-owned subsidiary, EDS; and (2) the decision to rid itself of the principal cause of the growing internal policy dispute over EDS' management and direction.

In addition to regaining control over the management affairs of EDS, GM also secured, through the complex repurchase agreement, significant covenants from Perot, of which the hush-mail provision was but one of many features and multiple considerations of the repurchase. Quite aside from whatever consideration could be attributed to buying Perot's silence, GM's Board received for the $742.8 million paid: all the class E stock and contingent notes of Perot and his fellow EDS directors; Perot's covenant not to compete or hire EDS employees; his promise not to purchase GM stock or engage in proxy contests; Perot's agreement to stay out of and away from GM's and EDS' affairs, plus the liquidated damages provision should Perot breach his no-criticism covenant.

Plaintiffs' effort to quantify the size of the premium paid by GM is flawed, as we have already noted, by their inability to place a dollar value on the various promises made by Perot, particularly his covenant not to compete with EDS or to attempt to hire away EDS employees. Thus, viewing the transaction in its entirety, we must agree with the Court of Chancery that plaintiff's have failed to plead with particularity facts sufficient to create a reasonable doubt that the substantive terms of the repurchase fall within the protection of the business judgment rule.

Finally we turn to the other aspect of director due care, whether plaintiffs have pleaded facts which would support a reasonable belief that the GM Board acted with gross negligence, i.e., that it was uninformed in critical respects in negotiating the terms of the repurchase. On this remaining issue, plaintiffs assert that GM's Board failed to exercise due care and to reach an informed business judgment due to the absence of arms-length negotiations between the Board and Perot and the absence of "appropriate board deliberation."

Approval of a transaction by a majority of independent, disinterested directors almost always bolsters a presumption that the business judgment rule attaches to transactions approved by a board of directors that are later attacked on grounds of lack of due care. In such cases, a heavy burden falls on a plaintiff to avoid presuit demand.

Furthermore, plaintiffs recount that the repurchase proposal was first submitted to a Special Review Committee, consisting (presumably) of three outside directors and thereafter to the full Board. The complaints as amended, however, contain no allegations raising directly or by inference a reasonable doubt either that the Committee served a purposeful role in the review of the repurchase proposal or that the full Board reached an informed decision. On the contrary, it is clear from the record before us that the GM directors had been living with the internal dispute for months and had been considering a buy-out of Perot's interests for a number of weeks.

Apart from whether the Board of Directors may be subject to criticism for the premium paid Perot and his associates for the repurchase of their entire interest in GM, on the present record the repurchase of dissident Perot's interests can only be viewed legally as representing an exercise of business judgment by the General Motors Board with which a court may not interfere.

Affirmed.

CASE QUESTIONS

1. What must the shareholders prove to recover?

2. What is entrenchment?

3. Why is director independence important?

4. What does the court find regarding the payment of a premium to Perot?

5. How does the business judgment rule apply in the repurchase?

6. Do you think Mr. Perot was disruptive to running the company?

BUSINESS STRATEGY

Graef Crystal conducts an annual study of CEO pay packages with an analysis of 850 CEOs of publicly-traded companies. Crystal provides the data for the best CEO performers, in terms of stock and company performance, as well as the worst performers. This year's study includes the following conclusions:

The most over-compensated CEO in America is Linda Wachner, CEO of Warnaco Group. From 1991 to 1998, shares of Warnaco gave investors a total return of 10.4%, as compared to the 21% for the S & P 500. Yet during 1998, Wachner was compensated as follows:

$2.7 million	Salary
$6 million	Bonus
$6.5 million	Restricted stock
$73.5 million	Options
$75.6 million	Gain from exercised options

Other CEOs on the worst performer list include Sanford Weill and John Reed, the co-CEOs for Citigroup (the merger of Citibank and Travelers), who were each paid $176 million but there was a 2% drop of Citigroup's share price in 1998.

The "compensation heroes," as Crystal calls them, or those CEOs delivering the most for their salaries are:

Bernard Marcus and Arthur Blank—Home Depot, who each had pay of $3 million but who delivered an average annual return of 45%

Herb Kelleher—Southwest Airlines, who was paid only $674,000 despite the fact that Southwest's stock was up 38.4% last year

Crystal presents his report to the Council of Institutional Investors, a group of portfolio managers with over $1 trillion in assets. Member of this group do use the list as a starting point in making decisions as to where and when to invest their funds.

Michael S. Kesner, National Director of Compensation and Benefits Consulting for Arthur Andersen Company, notes:

With restructuring, cost-cutting, and consolidation the order of the day, the actual impact of, say, a $5 million CEO pay package on the bottom line of a $2 billion sales company is not clearly the issue. People are now saying, to paraphrase the sound advice of late Illinois Senator Everett Dirksen, "Hey, a percent of a billion here and a percent of a billion there adds up to real money." In light of wide-spread plant closings, layoffs, and long lines of unemployed workers seeking limited jobs, "pay for performance" has simply taken a backseat to what the general public considers "fair."

Warren Buffett, the chief executive officer of Berkshire Hathaway, disclosed that his salary of $100,000 remained the same in 1998 but that his fees for being a director fell about 11% to $176,600. Some of the salary and fees are taken in cash and some in equity securities.

Mr. Buffett does not use a compensation committee or consultant to determine the salaries of his officers. He alone makes the recommendations to the board on what he believes the officers should be paid. The proxy materials for Berkshire Hathaway do not include any information on how salaries are determined or whether they are competitive.

Berkshire Hathaway permits bonuses for officers but none have been paid in a number of years. The highest paid officer for Berkshire Hathaway earns $306,000 along with a $10,000 contribution to his pension plan.

The latest CEO compensation figures follow:

Name	Company	Compensation
Sanford Weill	Citigroup, Inc.	$224.4 million
John T. Chambers	Cisco Systems, Inc.	$157.3 million
Kenneth L. Lay	Enron Corp.	$140.4 million
L. Dennis Kozlowski	Tyco International	$125.3 million
John F. Welch	General Electric Co.	$122.5 million
Joseph P. Nacchio	Qwest Communications	$ 96.6 million
W. J. Sanders III	Advanced Micro Devices	$ 92.4 million

How can executive compensation have an impact on company performance as well as share performance? How do you think Milton Friedman [see Chapter 2] would react to controls on levels of compensation? How do you think he would react to this type of compensation program?

Source: Garry Strauss, "Study: Some CEO Salaries Don't Compete," *USA Today,* 28 September 1999, 3B.

C O N S I D E R . . .

21.5   William Shlensky was a minority shareholder of Chicago National League Ball Club, Inc. (the Cubs). In 1966, he brought suit against the directors of the Cubs for violation of the business judgment rule because at the time of the suit the Cubs did not play night games at Wrigley Field, their home field. All of the other nineteen teams in the major leagues had some night games with substantially all of their weekday and nonholiday games scheduled under the lights. Between 1961 and 1965, the Cubs had sustained operating losses. Mr. Shlensky filed a derivative suit (a suit on behalf of shareholders) against the Cubs' directors for negligence and mismanagement.

Mr. Shlensky's suit maintained that the Cubs would continue to lose money unless night games were played. The directors' response was that baseball was a "daytime" sport and that holding night games would have a "deteriorating effect upon the surrounding neighborhood."

Why does Mr. Shlensky believe the directors did not use good judgment? Is there a difference between negligence and differing business opinions? Does the business judgment rule allow directors to make mistakes? [*Shlensky* v. *Wrigley*, 237 N.W. 2d 776 (Ill. 1968)]

Officers and directors are also required to follow the **corporate opportunity doctrine,** under which officers and directors may not take an opportunity for themselves that the corporation might be interested in taking. For example, a director of a lumber company who discovers a deal on timberland would be required to present that opportunity to the corporation before she could take it. If the director does not first present the idea to the corporation, a constructive trust is put on the profits the director makes, and the corporation is the beneficiary of that trust. If, however, the director presents the opportunity and the corporation is unable or unwilling to take it, the director may go ahead with the opportunity without the problem of a constructive trust.

C O N S I D E R . . .

21.6   Former Governor J. Fife Symington of Arizona was, during the 1980s, a director of Southwest Savings & Loan, a federal thrift headquartered in Phoenix. Mr. Symington was also a developer who constructed two major commercial projects in Phoenix with Southwest Savings & Loan providing the loans for development. Southwest was a victim of the 1980s downturn and was taken over by the Resolution Trust Corporation (RTC). The RTC brought suit against Mr. Symington alleging he took advantage of his board position to obtain the loans. Mr. Symington said he was required to present the projects to the Southwest Board as part of the corporate opportunity doctrine and Southwest took the investment. Who is correct?

Officer Liability

Recent prosecutions have demonstrated an increased effort to hold corporate officers criminally responsible for the acts of the corporation. In environmental law, changes in the law and aggressive prosecutions have brought about convictions of officers, particularly concerning the disposal of hazardous waste. The issues of officer liability are covered in Chapters 9, 12, and 18.

Corporate Management and Control: Shareholders

Shareholder Rights: Annual Meetings

Shareholders have the opportunity to express their views at the annual meeting by electing directors who represent their interests. Annual meetings also give shareholders the opportunity to vote on critical corporate issues. Under the MBCA, the failure to hold an annual meeting does not result in dissolution or revocation of corporate status.

Shareholder Rights: Voting

At annual and special meetings, voting share shareholders have the right to vote. Shareholders may vote their own shares or delegate their votes in a variety of ways.

The Proxy The most common method of delegating voting authority is the **proxy,** with which shareholders can transfer their right to vote to someone else. This type of vote assignment is temporary. Under the MBCA, a proxy is good only for eleven months, which allows a shareholder to decide to give a different proxy before the next annual meeting. Many shareholder groups solicit proxies to obtain control. Those solicitations are subject to the federal securities laws, and certain disclosures are required (see Chapter 22).

Pooling Agreements Another method of grouping together shareholder votes is the **pooling agreement.** This is a contract among shareholders to vote their shares a certain way or for a certain director. One of the problems with pooling agreements is enforceability: If the agreements are breached, it is really too late to do anything about the breach because the corporation will take the action authorized by the votes or a particular director will take a seat.

Voting Trust One last form of shareholder cooperation is the **voting trust.** In this form of group voting, shareholders actually turn their shares over to a trustee and are then issued a trust certificate. The shareholders still have the right to dividends and could sell or pledge the certificate. However, the shares remain in the hands of the trustee, and the trustee votes those shares according to the terms of the trust agreement. The shareholders get their shares back only when the trust ends. Most states have specific requirements for the voting trust: A copy must be filed with the corporate offices, and some states have a maximum duration (such as ten years) for such trusts.

Shareholder Rights in Combinations

Because shareholders' interests are involved, corporations are not free to combine at will, or to merge or consolidate without shareholder input. All states have procedures for obtaining shareholder approval for business combinations.

The Procedure For all mergers, consolidations, and sales of assets (other than in the ordinary course of business), there must be shareholder approval. Further, that approval must be obtained in a manner prescribed by the MBCA.

- *Board resolution.* The process of obtaining shareholder approval begins with the board of directors: They must adopt and approve a resolution favoring the merger, consolidation, or asset sale.

- *Notice to shareholders.* Once the resolution is adopted, it must be sent to the shareholders along with a notice of a meeting for the purpose of taking action on the resolution. A notice is sent to each shareholder regardless of whether she is entitled to vote under the corporation's articles.
- *Shareholder approval.* The shareholders must then vote to approve the resolution at the announced meeting. In the cases of mergers and consolidations, all shareholders are entitled to vote whether they own voting or nonvoting shares because their interests are affected by the results. The number of votes needed to approve a merger under the MBCA is a majority. However, the articles of incorporation or the bylaws may require more, known as a super majority.

Shareholder approval is not required for a short-form merger, which is one between a subsidiary and a parent that owns at least 90 percent of the stock of the subsidiary. In the absence of these narrow requirements, the long-form merger provisions of resolution and voting must be followed.

Shareholder Rights: The Dissenting Shareholder

Not all shareholders vote in favor of a merger or a consolidation. Under the MBCA and most state statutes, these **dissenting shareholders** are entitled to their appraisal rights. **Appraisal rights** allow shareholders to demand the value of their shares. Under the MBCA, a dissenting shareholder must file a written objection to the merger or consolidation before the meeting to vote on either is held.

If the merger or consolidation is approved, the corporation must notify dissenting shareholders and offer them the fair value of the shares. Fair value is determined as of the *day before* the action is taken on the merger or consolidation, because the action taken will affect the value of the shares. If the dissenting shareholders do not believe the corporation's offer is fair, they can bring suit against the corporation for establishing fair value. However, if the value the corporation offered is found to be fair and the dissenting shareholders' rejection arbitrary, they will be required to pay the corporation's costs of the lawsuit.

Shareholders also enjoy some protections during merger activity that are offered under federal securities laws in terms of notice and disclosure (see Chapter 22).

Some corporations have experienced a **freeze-out,** which is a merger undertaken to get rid of the minority shareholders in a corporation. Although these minority shareholders have their dissenting rights, it is expensive to pursue a court action for a determination of fair value. The majority shareholders are thus able to buy out, at a low price, the minority shareholders, who are left without a remedy and usually with a loss. For this reason, many courts now impose on majority stockholders a fiduciary duty to the minority stockholders and will prevent a merger without a business purpose from freezing out minority shareholders. Courts, and some state laws (corporate constituency statutes), also require a showing that a merger or consolidation is fair to the minority shareholders. These general terms of "business purpose" and "fairness" are defined on a case-by-case basis.

Shareholder Rights: Inspection of Books and Records

The MBCA gives the shareholders the absolute right to examine shareholder lists. For other records (minutes, accounting), shareholders must give notice of their request. In addition to this mechanical requirement, some courts also require a

proper purpose, which means a shareholder has a legitimate interest in reviewing corporate progress, financial status, and fiduciary responsibilities. Improper purposes are those related to use of corporate records to advance the shareholders' moral, religious, or political ideas.

Shareholder Rights: Transfer of Shares

Stock shares can have **transfer restrictions,** which are valid so long as the following requirements are met:

1. The restrictions must be necessary. Valid circumstances include family-owned corporations, employee-owned corporations, and corporations that need restrictions to comply with SEC registration exemptions (see Chapter 22).

2. The restrictions must be reasonable. Requiring that the shares first be offered to the board before they can be sold is reasonable; requiring that the shares be offered to all the other shareholders first may be unreasonable if there are more than five to ten shareholders.

3. The restrictions and/or their existence must be conspicuously noted on the stock shares.

The Dissolution of a Corporation

A corporation can continue indefinitely unless its articles of incorporation limit its duration. Long before perpetuity, however, a corporation can be dissolved voluntarily or involuntarily.

Voluntary Dissolution

Voluntary dissolution occurs when the shareholders agree to dissolve the corporation. This type of dissolution occurs in smaller corporations when the shareholders no longer get along, the business does not do well, or one of the shareholders is ill or dies.

A voluntary dissolution begins with a resolution by the board of directors, which is then put before the shareholders at a special meeting called for that purpose. Under the MBCA, all shareholders (voting and nonvoting alike) vote on the issue of dissolution because all of them will be affected by it. Once the shareholders pass the resolution (a majority or two-thirds vote in most states), the assets of the corporation are liquidated, and debts and shareholders are paid in the order of their priorities. Each state also has filing and publication requirements for dissolution.

Involuntary Dissolution

An involuntary dissolution is forced by some state agency, usually the state-level attorney's office. A dissolution can be forced because of fraud or failure to follow state law regarding reporting requirements for corporations.

THE LIMITED LIABILITY COMPANY

Examine a state comparison chart, among other materials, for limited liability laws:
http://www.llcweb.com

The **limited liability company** (LLC), new to the United States and available in forty-eight states and the District of Columbia, has actually been in existence for many years in Europe (known as a GMBH) and South America (*limitada*). The LLC is more of an aggregate form of business organization than an entity such as a corporation. Owners of an LLC are called "members." An LLC provides limited lia-

Review "An Introduction to New Jersey's Limited Liability Company Act," by Lisa M. Fontoura:
http://www.cfg-lawfirm.com/articles/llc.html

bility (members lose only up to their capital contributions) and "flow-through" tax treatment like a partnership in that there is tax only at the member's level of income and not at the business level. An LLC is not a corporation or a partnership. It can be taxed as a partnership, with limited liability for all its owners, unlike a limited partnership, and all personal owners can participate in management without risking liability.

Formation

An LLC is formed through the filing of a document called the **articles of organization** that is filed with a centralized state agency. The name of the business formed must contain either "limited liability company," "L.L.C." or "LLC."

Sources of Funding

Members of an LLC make capital contributions in much the same way as partners make capital contributions.

Liability

Members of an LLC have limited liability; the most they can lose is their capital contributions. Debts belong to the LLC, and creditors' rights lie with the LLC's assets, not the personal assets of the members. However, many states require that the nature of the business organization appear on the business cards and stationery of the company so that members of the public are not misled about the nature of the business as well as the nature of the limited liability of the owners.

C O N S I D E R . . .

21.7   Larry Clark and David Lanham formed a limited liability company in Colorado called "Preferred Income Investors, LLC (PII). All of the necessary paperwork for the creation of an LLC had been filed with the secretary of state, as required by Colorado statute.

Larry Clark negotiated with a Westec representative about doing construction work for PII on a Taco Cabana restaurant the LLC was building. Clark gave the Westec rep his card, which had PII above Clark's name. Westec drew up a contract that was never signed by anyone from PII. However, Clark gave the oral authorization for the work and Westec completed it. PII did not have the assets to pay the bill for the work, and Westec sued to hold Clark liable for the contract. Clark said as an owner of a limited liability company he had no personal liability. Westec says it was never made aware that PII was an LLC and that it should be given that information in advance. Is Clark personally liable? [*Water, Waste, & Land, Inc., dba Westec v. Lanham*, 995 P.2d 997 (Colo. 1998)]

Tax Consequences

The LLC enjoys the so-called flow-through treatment: The LLC does not pay taxes; income and losses are passed through to the members to be reported on their individual returns. LLC agreements must be drafted carefully to enjoy flow-through status.

BUSINESS PLANNING TIP

Getting LLC Tax Status
If an LLC is not created according to both state
law and IRS guidelines, the tax benefits can be
lost. In December 1994, the IRS issued
guidelines on the four characteristics of an LLC
entitled to pass-through or flow-through status.
An LLC must not have more than two of the
following: limited liability for members,
continuity, free transferability of interests, and no
centralized management.

Management and Control

Members of an LLC adopt an operating agreement that specifies the
voting rights, withdrawal rights and issues, responsibilities of members, and how the LLC is to be managed. The members can agree to
manage collectively, delegate authority to one member, or hire an outsider to manage the business.

Transferability of Interest

A member's LLC interest is personal property and is transferable.
However, the transferee does not become a member without approval
by the majority of members. Members do not hold title to LLC property; the LLC owns the property, and each member has an interest in
the LLC that reflects the property's value. Further, the owners of the LLC should
structure their LLC and its operation in order to address their tax status issues.

Dissolution and Termination

Most LLC statutes provide that the LLC dissolves upon the withdrawal, death, or
expulsion of a member. Some states permit judicial dissolution, and all states permit voluntary dissolution upon unanimous (usually written) consent of the owners.

LLC agreements can dictate terms, timing, and results of dissolution, as well
as the rights of withdrawing partners.

LIMITED LIABILITY PARTNERSHIPS

A **limited liability partnership** (LLP) is a partnership with unique statutory protection for all its members.

Formation

Not all states have LLP statutes, but those that do have strict formal requirements
for the creation of an LLP. The failure to comply with these requirements results
in a general partnership with full personal liability for all the partners. The general requirements for LLP registration are filing (1) the name of the LLP (which
must include LLP or Reg LLP); (2) registered agent; (3) address; (4) number of
partners; and (5) description of the business.

Sources of Funding

As in partnerships and limited partnerships, LLP partners make capital contributions.

Liability

In most of the states with LLP statutes, partners are shielded from liability for the
negligence, wrongful acts, or misconduct of their partners. Other states provide
more extensive protection, such as limited liability even for debts entered into by
other partners. In order to attain this liability limitation, some states require, upon
registration, evidence of adequate liability insurance. In some states, professional
negligence by partners is not covered by the shield from liability.

Re: CEO Pay Worldwide

The average CEO compensation in the United States is $1.072 million, including basic compensation, bonus, perks, and long-term incentives such as stock options. About 30 percent of that compensation consists of long-term incentives. The United States has the highest CEO average salary. The United States is followed by Brazil ($701,000 with 50 percent in basic compensation and only 15 percent in long-term incentives). Hong Kong ($680,000 with about the same composition as Brazil), Britain ($645,000 with 2/3 in basic compensation), France ($520,000 with 3/5 in basic compensation), Canada ($498,000 with nearly 25 percent in bonus), Japan, Germany, and South Korea ($420,000, $398,000, and $150,000) are the bottom of the top nations and also have no long-term incentives in their CEOs' compensation packages.

Tax Consequences

All LLP income is a flow-through or pass-through to partners.

Management and Control

Partners can manage without risking personal liability exposure, because the LLP is identified as such and registered with the state.

Transferability

For tax and security regulation reasons, the transferability must be restricted and is generally governed by the same principles of transfer for limited partnerships.

Dissolution and Termination

Causes similar to those for the dissolution of limited partnerships and notification to the state are required.

INTERNATIONAL ISSUES IN BUSINESS STRUCTURE

Global trade has resulted in global business structures, with many companies discovering the benefits of **joint ventures.** A joint venture is a partnership of existing businesses for a limited time or a limited purpose. The existing businesses are then partners for that limited transaction or line of business. The Justice Department has relaxed antitrust merger rules to permit joint ventures so that U.S. firms can compete more effectively internationally. For example, Mobil and Exxon are involved in a joint oil exploration venture in the West Siberian Basin in Russia. The joint venture allows the combination of their experience and financing so that Russian negotiators can be persuaded to contract for the exploration rights.

In an attempt to break into the Japanese toy market, Toys "Я" Us, Inc., entered into a joint venture with McDonald's Co., Ltd., a Japanese toy company with 20 percent of the market. Nestlé and Coca-Cola have formed a joint venture to market ready-to-drink coffees and teas; Nestlé's expertise is in dry goods (instant coffee) and Coca-Cola is a beverage company, so each plans to take advantage of the other's established reputation.

BIOGRAPHY

PHAR-MOR AND MICHAEL MONUS

Michael Monus and David S. Shapira co-founded Phar-Mor, Inc., a discount drug store, in 1982. Mr. Shapira's family owned Giant Eagle, a private grocery store chain. Phar-Mor was based in Youngstown, Ohio, and, within 10 years, had grown to 310 stores and $3 billion in sales.

Mr. Monus ("Mickey") began the World Basketball League (WBL), a league for "short people"— 6'7" or less. He spent money lavishly on the teams, the coaches, the managers, and games. Mr. Monus was asked to serve as chairman of Youngstown State University's board of trustees.

Based on an anonymous tip that indicated $100,000 of Phar-Mor property had been transferred to the WBL, Phar-Mor began an investigation through Coopers & Lybrand, its outside auditor.

The investigation discovered that Mr. Monus had funneled about $10 million in Phar-Mor assets to the WBL. In addition, the auditors discovered that earnings had been overstated through a conspiracy of Mr. Monus, CFO, Patrick Finn, and two accounting employees. Phar-Mor president David Shapira announced that Phar-Mor would take a $350 million write-off that quarter. Further, Phar-Mor was forced to file a Chapter 11 bankruptcy. Sales at Phar-Mor declined 15 percent, and 55 stores were closed, with a proposal to close 31 more. Employees were fired, reducing the workforce from 24,500 to 19,800.

The FBI was brought in to investigate the case, and litigation is pending as to whether Coopers & Lybrand, Phar-Mor's auditor, has any responsibility for the financial improprieties.

Mr. Monus was convicted of 109 felony counts in May 1995, following his second trial. The first trial ended with a hung jury, and after an investigation for jury tampering, both a juror on Mr. Monus's first case and a friend of Mr. Monus's were charged with tampering.

In December 1995, Mr. Monus was sentenced to 20 years in prison, fined $1 million, and given 5 years probation. At his sentencing Monus offered the following:

In the 10 years I was at Phar-Mor, Phar-Mor grew to 300 stores in some 35 states and 20,000 employees. The important thing is not the numbers to me . . . but the employees—all those dedicated, loyal, and highly motivated people. I want them to know the sorrow and regret that I have. The sorrow and regret will live with me for the rest of my life.

Phar-Mor emerged from Chapter 11 in late 1995 under new ownership.

ISSUES

1. Why did others beside Mr. Monus participate in the scheme?

2. How did the "cooking of the books" escape the board, the audit committee, and the auditors?

3. Was Mr. Monus's sentence appropriate?

Source: Stephen D. Williger, "Phar-Mor: A Lesson in Fraud," *Wall Street Journal*, 28 March 1994, A14.

C O N S I D E R . . .

21.8 List ways a company could prevent itself from becoming a Phar-Mor. Be sure to discuss what employees, officers, and directors could do.

Business structures vary in other countries. In Germany, for example, a public company has both a board of directors and a shareholder advisory committee, which elects the board of directors. It is quite likely, however, that the shareholder advisory committee is composed of shareholders that are large institutional investors (such as banks) or representatives from labor unions.

SUMMARY

What are the various forms of business organization?

- Sole proprietorship—individual ownership and operation of a business

- Partnership—voluntary association of two or more persons as co-owners in a business for profit

- Corporation—an entity formed by statute that has the rights of a legal person along with limited liability for its shareholder owners

- Limited liability company—newer form of business organization in which liability is limited except for conduct that is illegal

- Limited liability partnership—newest form of business organization, in which partners' liability is limited

How is a partnership formed and operated?

- Uniform Partnership Act—law on partnerships adopted in forty-nine states

- Revised Uniform Partnership Act—update of partnership law

- Partnership by implication—creation of a partnership by parties' conduct

- Partnership by estoppel—partnership that arises by perception of third parties of its existence

- Dissolution—partner ceases to be associated with the partnership

- Limited partnership—partnership with two types of partners: general and limited

- General partner—full and personal liability partner

- Limited partner—partner whose personal liability is limited to capital contributions

- Uniform Limited Partnership Act—uniform law adopted in nearly every state

- Revised Uniform Limited Partnership Act— uniform law adopted in nearly every state

- Advances—partners' loans to partnership

How is a corporation formed and operated?

- Corporation—business organization that is a separate entity with limited liability and full transferability

- Domestic corporation—a corporation is domestic in the state in which its incorporation is filed

- Foreign corporation—category or label for corporation in all states except in state in which it is incorporated

- Professional corporation—entity with limited liability except for malpractice/negligence by its owner

- S corporation—IRS category of corporation with flow-through characteristics

- Model Business Corporation Act (MBCA)— uniform law adopted in approximately one-third of the states

- Articles of incorporation—document filed to organize a corporation

- Common stock—generally most voluminous type of corporate shares and usually voting

- Preferred stock—ownership interest with priority over common stock

- Corporate veil—liability shield for corporate owners

- Watered shares—failure to pay par value for shares

- Business judgment rule—standard of liability for directors

- Corporate opportunity doctrine—fiduciary responsibility of directors with respect to investments

- Board of directors—policy-setting body of corporations

- Proxy—right to vote for another

- Pooling agreement—shareholder contract to vote a certain way

- Voting trust—separation of legal and equitable title in shares to ensure voting of shares in one way

- Dissenting shareholder—shareholder who objects to merger

- Appraisal rights—value of shares immediately before merger that is paid to dissenting shareholder

How is a limited liability company formed?

- Articles of organization

- Flow-through of income

How is a limited liability partnership formed?

- Register with state

- Flow-through of income

- May need proof of liability insurance

QUESTIONS AND PROBLEMS

1. Gailey, Inc., incorporated in 1980, removed asbestos and mechanical insulation on contract jobs that required union labor. Richard Gaily had been the president, controlling shareholder, and director of Gailey, Inc., from its inception.

Universal Labs, Inc., was incorporated by Richard Gaily in March 1984 to analyze asbestos samples and air samples and to perform general laboratory work. Mr. Gailey was the sole shareholder of Universal Labs, Inc.

As president and director of Gailey, Inc., Mr. Gailey directed Gailey, Inc., to pay certain debts of Universal Labs. Subsequent to that, $14,500 was provided by Gailey, Inc., to Universal Labs to pay for the latter's start-up expenses and costs.

Gailey, Inc., filed a voluntary petition pursuant to Chapter 11 of the Bankruptcy Code on January 28, 1985. The case was converted to a Chapter 7 proceeding on September 30, 1985.

The trustee in bankruptcy filed suit alleging that Mr. Gaily usurped a corporate business opportunity belonging to Gaily, Inc., when he incorporated Universal Labs. Is the trustee correct? [*In re Gailey, Inc.,* 119 B.R. 504 (Bankr. W.D. Pa. 1990)]

2. Until his death in 1980, Cody Morton, husband of Dormilee Morton, operated a construction business from his home in Salem, Missouri. Upon Mr. Morton's intestate death, Mrs. Morton succeeded to her husband's ownership interest in the business, including ownership of supplies, material, and construction equipment. Steve Morton, their son, took over the operation and management of the construction company with Mrs. Morton contributing the capital assets of business, which consisted of the construction equipment.

From time to time, Mrs. Morton would sign bank notes and supporting documents granting security interests in the equipment, designating the borrower as "Dormilee Morton and Steven Morton d/b/a Morton Construction Company." In addition, she also provided funds for the operation of the business. The telephone for the business was situated in Mrs. Morton's home, where she also received the business's mail.

Between 1980 and 1984, Morton Construction Company employed laborers and other persons to construct commercial and residential buildings and was required to withhold federal income and Federal Insurance Contributions Act (FICA) taxes from wages paid to its employees. For the taxable quarters between 1980 and 1984, quarterly federal tax returns and an annual federal unemployment tax return for Morton Construction Company were filed with the IRS in the names of Dormilee Morton and Steven D. Morton, partners, by Steven D. Morton.

As a result of business conditions and difficulties, Morton Construction Company failed to make the required deposits of federal withholding and FICA taxes or otherwise pay the amounts of these taxes to the United States.

The IRS imposed assessments against Dormilee Morton, Steven Morton, and Morton Construction for $44,460.52. Tax liens were filed.

Dormilee Morton asserts that she should not be liable for taxes as she was not a general partner in the business but, at most, a limited partner. In support of this contention, she cites Steven Morton's notation on the appropriate tax forms that Morton Construction Company was a limited partnership and he was the general partner.

Is Mrs. Morton correct? Is she a limited partner? Is she personally liable for the wage taxes? [*United States* v. *Morton,* 682 F. Supp. 999 (E.D. Mo. 1988)]

3. Aztec Enterprises, Inc., was incorporated in Washington with a capital contribution of $500. Aztec's incorporator and sole stockholder was H. B. Hunting. Aztec operated a gravel-hauling business and was plagued with persistent working capital problems. Carl Olson, a frequent source of loans for Aztec, eventually acquired the firm. Mr. Olson, who had no corporate minutes or tax returns, personally paid Aztec's lease fees but did not pay when he had Aztec deliver gravel to his personal construction sites. Mr. Olson never had stock certificates issued to him. Despite annual gross sales of over $800,000, Aztec was unable to pay its debts. Truckweld Equipment Company, a creditor of Aztec, brought suit to pierce the corporate veil and recover its debt from Mr. Olson. Can it pierce the corporate veil? [*Truckweld Equipment Co.* v. *Olson,* 618 P.2d 1017 (Wash. 1980)]

4. Ranton Brouillette had a home he owned moved to a lot he owned with his brothers as partners. Because of a dispute, one of his brothers deliberately drove a bulldozer into the house and damaged it.
Mr. Brouillette's insurer says it is not required to pay because the house became partnership property and should be covered by the partnership's insurance. Who is right? [*Brouillette* v. *Phoenix Assur. Co.,* 340 So.2d 667 (La. 1976)]

5. Allan Jones sold a ski shop franchise to Edward Hamilton. Although Mr. Jones did not contribute equity to the business or share in the profits, he did give Mr. Hamilton advice and share his experience to help him get started. Most of Mr. Hamilton's capital came in the form of a loan from Union Bank. When Mr. Hamilton failed to pay, Union Bank sued Mr. Jones for payment under the theory that Mr. Jones was a partner by implication or estoppel. Was he? [*Union Bank* v. *Jones*, 411 A.2d 1338 (Vt. 1980)]

6. Heritage Hills (a land development firm) was organized on July 2, 1975, as a limited partnership, but the partnership agreement was never properly filed. Heritage Hills went bankrupt, and the bankruptcy trustee has sought to recover the debts owed by the partnership from the limited partners. Can he? [*Heritage Hills* v. *Zion's First Nat'l Bank*, 601 F.2d 1023 (9th Cir. 1979)]

7. In June 1985, Carolyn Boose sought the dental services of Dr. George Blakeslee, who proposed to fill two cavities in her teeth. As part of the procedure, he administered nitrous oxide to Ms. Boose. She was rendered semiconscious by the drug and while in this state Dr. Blakeslee lifted her shirt and fondled one of her breasts. He was subsequently charged with, and pled guilty to, the crime of indecent liberties.

Prior to the incident in question, Dr. Blakeslee had incorporated his dental practice as a professional services corporation. He was the corporation's sole shareholder, officer, and director. The corporation thereafter executed an employment agreement with Dr. Blakeslee, who signed the agreement both as an employee of the corporation and as its president.

At the time of the incident in question, Dr. Blakeslee and the corporation were together covered by an insurance policy with Standard Fire Insurance Company that provided general and professional liability coverage. The general liability portion of the policy provided coverage for bodily injury or property damage caused by an "occurrence" arising out of the use of the insured premises. The insurance contract defined "occurrence" as "an accident, including continuous or repeated exposure to conditions, which results in bodily injury or property damage *neither expected or intended by the insured*."

The professional liability portion of the policy limited coverage to damages for "injury . . . arising out of the rendering of or failure to render, during the policy period, professional services by the individual insured, or by any person for whom acts or omissions such insured is legally responsible. . . ."

In November 1985, Ms. Boose commenced an action against Dr. Blakeslee and the professional services corporation for the damages she allegedly sustained as a result of his conduct. Standard subsequently commenced a declaratory judgment action against Ms. Boose and Dr. Blakeslee in order to obtain a declaration of its rights and duties in connection with the lawsuit by Ms. Boose against Dr. Blakeslee and the corporation. All parties moved for summary judgment. The trial court granted judgment to Standard, concluding that it had no duty to defend or indemnify the insured (that is, Dr. Blakeslee and the corporation) against Ms. Boose's claim. Should the corporate veil be pierced to hold Dr. Blakeslee liable? [*Standard Fire Insurance Co.* v. *Blakeslee*, 771 P.2d 1172 (Wash. 1989)]

8. Master Chemical Company of Boston, Massachusetts, manufactured chemicals used primarily in the shoe industry. In 1982, when Master discovered that its underground storage tank filled with toluene was leaking, the two-thousand-gallon tank was emptied. In 1984, Master sold its plant and the tank was removed.

Goldberg-Zoino & Associates, Inc. (GZA), was hired to do the cleanup, and it hired MacDonald & Watson to do the excavation, transportation, and disposal of the toluene-contaminated soil in the area where the tank had been.

MacDonald & Watson had a permit for liquid waste disposal but none for solid waste disposal. MacDonald & Watson transported nine 25-yard dump-truck loads and one 20-yard load of toluene-contaminated soil to the disposal lot. The Justice Department brought criminal actions against MacDonald & Watson and three of its officers, including Eugene K. D'Allesandro, its president.

Can Mr. D'Allesandro be convicted? [*United States* v. *MacDonald & Watson Waste Oil Co.*, 933 F.2d 35 (1st Cir. 1991)]

9. Johnson & Johnson, Procter & Gamble, and Eastman Kodak have joined together to form a joint venture in order to develop security tags for their products in drug and grocery stores. Shoplifting thefts of drug store items are estimated to be $16 billion per year. The manufacturers point to Pampers, Tylenol, and Preparation H as the most frequently stolen items from stores.

The companies will jointly fund the development of security tags designed to set off alarms at store doors, much as the tags on clothing today.

What is the liability of the companies as joint venturers on this project?

10. A. W. Ham Jr. served on the board of directors for Golden Nugget, Inc., a Nevada corporation. In 1969, while Mr. Ham was a director and legal counsel for Golden Nugget, he obtained a leasehold interest with an option to purchase in the California Club. The California Club is at 101 Fremont Street, Las Vegas, Nevada, and is located next to a series of properties on which Golden Nugget operates its casinos. Mr. Ham leased the property from his former wife. Golden Nugget was looking for property to expand and had, in fact, been expanding onto other lots in the area. Was there a breach of a corporate opportunity? What if Mr. Ham offers to lease the property to Golden Nugget? [*Ham* v. *Golden Nugget, Inc.*, 589 P.2d 173 (Nev. 1979)]

RESEARCH PROBLEM

11. In Ethical Issues 21.1, the issue of conflicts of interest on the boards of W. R. Grace and American Express were raised. Go to these companies' Web sites (http://www.americanexpress.com and http://www.wrgrace.com) and evaluate how well these firms have performed over the past five years. Be sure to look at their boards of directors and their policies. Also, examine the performances of the companies listed under the best and worst boards in the "For the Manager's Desk" on p. 847. After studying these companies and their boards, develop a set of guidelines for selecting board members for a company.

BUSINESS STRATEGY APPLICATION

In this exercise, you have the opportunity to look at public documents that describe the corporate governance policies of Raytheon Corporation, a company that recently revamped all of its board policies. You will be able to see the issues these policies address.

You will then be able to develop for your company board policies and procedures that you believe reflect the best practices among those that have been provided to you.

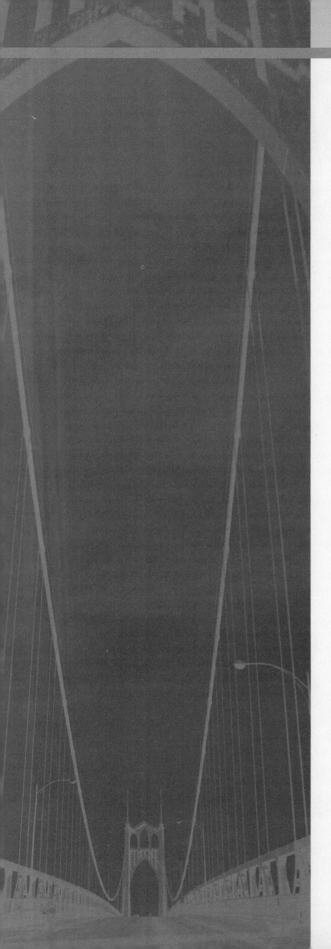

CHAPTER TWENTY-TWO

Securities Law

One of the methods for raising the capital needed for a corporation or partnership is to sell interests in them. Corporations sell shares, and partnerships sell limited partnership interests. Investors provide the capital these businesses need to operate. They give the businesses their money to work with and in return are given an interest in the business. The investors' hope is that the business will give them a profit on their investment (dividends) and that the value of their investment will grow as the business increases in value. The investment arrangement in theory is mutually beneficial. However, because people are so eager to have their money grow and because businesses need money, the interests of business and investors are so often at odds that there seems to be an inherent conflict of interest in the investment relationship. Because of this conflict, there are laws regulating investments at both state and federal levels. These laws are called securities laws, and they govern everything from the sale of securities to soliciting proxies from owners of securities. This chapter answers the questions: Why do we have securities laws and what is their history? What are the requirements that affect primary offerings of securities? How do securities laws regulate the secondary market? How do those laws protect shareholders in share and company acquisitions?

October. This is one of the peculiarly dangerous months to speculate stocks in. The others are July, January, September, April, November, May, March, June, December, August and February.

MARK TWAIN
Pudd'nhead Wilson

Wall Street has only two emotions: fear and greed.

BILL MCGOWAN
CEO of MCI

CONSIDER...

James Herman O'Hagan was a partner in the law firm of Dorsey & Whitney in Minneapolis, Minnesota. In July 1988, Grand Metropolitan PLC, a company based in London, retained Dorsey & Whitney as local counsel to represent it regarding a potential tender offer for common stock of Pillsbury Company.

O'Hagan did not work on the Grand Met matter, but on August 18, 1988, he began purchasing call options for Pillsbury stock. Each option gave him the right to purchase 100 shares of Pillsbury stock. By the end of September, O'Hagan owned more than 2,500 Pillsbury options. Also in September, O'Hagan purchased 5,000 shares of Pillsbury stock at $39 per share.

Grand Met announced its tender offer in October, and Pillsbury stock rose to $60 per share. O'Hagan sold his call options and made a profit of $4.3 million.

The SEC indicted O'Hagan on fifty-seven counts of illegal trading on inside information. He says he did nothing wrong. Who is right?

© AP/Wide World Photos

HISTORY OF SECURITIES LAW

Although most people think of the market crash of 1929 as the beginning of securities regulation, regulation actually began nearly twenty years earlier at the state level. Kansas had the first securities law in 1911, which regulated the initial sale of securities to members of the public. Some states followed the lead of Kansas, but until 1929 the field of securities was relatively free of regulation.

There was at that time a great deal of speculation in stocks. Investors traded "on margin," which means they borrowed money to invest in stock and when the stock went up in value, they sold it, paid off the loan, and still made money. On a Friday in 1929, however, stock prices dropped on all the exchanges and continued to drop. Investors defaulted on the margin loans, lenders foreclosed on their properties, and the entire country was thrown into a depression.

Review the Securities Act of 1933 and the Securities Exchange Act of 1934:
http://www.law.uc.edu/CCL

Because of the 1929 market crash, Congress perceived a problem with the investment market. As a result, the **Securities Act of 1933** and the **Securities Exchange Act of 1934** were passed, the former to regulate initial sales of stock by businesses and the latter to regulate the secondary trading of stock on the markets. These statutes and their accompanying regulations still govern the sale of securities today.

PRIMARY OFFERING REGULATION: THE 1933 SECURITIES ACT

A **primary offering**—an offering by an issuer, which could be its first, known as an initial public offering (IPO)—is a sale of securities by the business itself. The 1933 act regulates this initial sale of securities.

What Is a Security?

Because the 1933 act applies only to the sale of securities, the term *securities* requires definition. The language of the act itself is very broad and lists approximately twenty items that are considered securities, including notes; stock; bonds; debentures; warrants; subscriptions; voting-trust certificates; rights to oil, gas, and minerals; and limited partnership interests. Every investment contract that gives the owner evidence of indebtedness or business participation is a security.

In interpreting the application of the 1933 act, the courts have been very liberal. The landmark case on the definition of a security is *SEC v. W. J. Howey Co.,* 328 U.S. 293 (1946). In holding that the sale of interests in Florida citrus groves constituted the sale of securities, the U.S. Supreme Court defined a security as "a contract, transaction, or scheme whereby a person invests his money in a common enterprise and is led to expect profits solely from the efforts of a promoter or a third party." With this even broader definition than the actual 1933 act language, known as the *Howey* **test,** courts have been reluctant to impose restrictions on the definition of a security. In recent years, the only type of arrangement the U.S. Supreme Court has excluded from this definition is an employer pension plan in which employees are not required to make contributions. The exclusion of these plans from securities laws is probably based on the fact that there are other statutory protections afforded employees (see Chapter 19 and the discussion of the Employment Retirement Income Security Act).

C O N S I D E R . . .

22.1   Determine whether the following would be considered securities for purposes of the 1933 Securities Act:

1. General partnership interests
2. Limited partnership interests
3. Limited liability company interests
4. Limited liability partnership interests
5. Oil and gas leases

Regulating Primary Offerings: Registration

Visit the Securities and Exchange Commission:
http://www.sec.gov

The **Securities and Exchange Commission** (SEC) is the administrative agency responsible for regulating the sale of securities under both the 1933 and 1934 acts. The SEC is subject to all of the administrative rules covered in Chapter 6, for it is an administrative agency created in an enabling act of Congress, the 1934 Securities Exchange Act. The SEC can issue injunctions, institute criminal proceedings, enter into consent decrees, handle enforcement, and promulgate rules.

The rules promulgated by the SEC provide the requirements for the registration of securities, financial reporting, and stock exchange operations. The SEC has a complete staff of lawyers, accountants, financial analysts, and other experts to assist in both the review of informational filings and in the enforcement of the securities laws.

Regulating Primary Offerings: Exemptions

Unless an **exemption** applies, anyone selling securities must complete certain filing requirements before the securities can be sold legally. There are two types of exemptions: exempt securities and exempt transactions. These exemptions work only for the 1933 act.

Exempt Securities

Certain investments, called **exempt securities,** have been excluded specifically from coverage of the 1933 act. The following is a list of some of the exemptions:

1. Securities (bonds, etc.) issued by federal, state, county, or municipal governments for public purposes
2. Commercial paper (includes notes, checks, and drafts with a maturity date under nine months)
3. Banks, savings and loans, and religious and charitable organizations
4. Insurance policies
5. Annuities
6. Securities of common carriers (those regulated by the Interstate Commerce Commission)
7. Stock dividends and stock splits

Exempt Transactions

Exempt transactions are more complicated than exempt securities; more details are required to comply with the exempt transaction standards. The following subsections discuss these transaction exemptions, which are summarized in Exhibit 22.1.

The Intrastate Offering Exemption

This exemption exists because the Commerce Clause prohibits the federal government from regulating purely intrastate matters (see Chapter 5 for a full discussion of Commerce Clause issues). To qualify for the intrastate exemption, the investors (offerees) and issuer must all be residents of the same state. (If there is one out-of-state offeree, the exemption will not apply.) Further, the issuer must meet the following requirements:

1. Eighty (80) percent of its assets must be located in the state.
2. Eighty (80) percent of its income must be earned from operations within the state.
3. Eighty (80) percent of the proceeds from the sale must be used on operations within the state.

Under the SEC's Rule 147, there are restrictions on the transfer of exempt intrastate offerings, including a nine-month transfer restriction to state residents only.

Small-Offering Exemption: Regulation A

Examine registration form S-1:
http://www.law.uc.edu/CCL/ 33forms/index.html

Although it is not a true exemption, **Regulation A** is a shortcut method of registration. The lengthy, complicated processes of full registration are simplified in that only a short-form registration statement is filed. Regulation A applies to issues of $5 million or less during any twelve-month period.

The SEC groups or "integrates" registration. Three registrations of $2 million each would not qualify if issued within one twelve-month period. They would qualify, however, if issued over three years.

Small-Offering Exemption: Regulation D

Review Regulations A and D:
http://www.law.uc.edu/CCL/ 33ActRls/index.html

Regulation D is the product of the SEC's evaluation of the impact of its rules on the ability of small businesses to raise capital. It was designed to simplify and clarify existing exemptions, expand the availability of exemptions, and achieve uniformity between state and federal exemptions.

Regulation D creates a three-tiered exemption structure that consists of Rules 504, 505, and 506, which permits sales without registration. Sellers are, however, required to file a Form D informational statement about the sale. Rule 501 of Regulation D lists the definitions of various terms used in the three exemptions. For example, the term *accredited investor* includes any investor who at the time of the sale falls into any of the following categories:

1. Any bank
2. Any private business development company
3. Any director, executive officer, or general partner of the issuer
4. Any person who purchases at least $150,000 of the securities being offered
5. Natural persons whose net worth is greater than $1 million

EXHIBIT 22.1 1933 Securities Act Transaction Exemptions

NAME	SIZE LIMITATION	GENERAL SOLICITATION	OFFEREE/ BUYER LIMITATION	RESALE LIMITATION	DISCLOSURE	PUBLIC OFFERING	SEC FILING	TIME
Intrastate exemption, 15 U.S.C. §77(c)(a)(11)	No	No	Buyers must be residents of state of incorporation; triple 80 percent requirements	Yes, stock transfer restrictions Rule 147—9 months	No	Yes, in state	No	No restriction
Small-offering or small-issues exemption, 15 U.S.C. §77D, Regulation A	$5,000,000	Yes	Short-form registration required (offering circular)	No	Offering circular	Yes	Short-form	12-month period
Rule 504 Regulation D*	$1,000,000 or less (in 12-month period)	Yes	None, unlimited accredited and nonaccredited alike	Yes	No†	Yes	Notice of offering within 15 days of first sale	12-month period
Rule 505, Regulation D	Up to $5,000,000	No	No more than 35, excluding accredited investors	Yes—2 years†	Yes, to nonaccredited†	No	Notice of offering (15 days)	12-month period
Rule 506, Regulation D	No	No	Unlimited accredited and 35 nonaccredited investors; (nonaccredited must be sophisticated)	Yes, stock restrictions	Yes, to nonaccredited†	No	Notice of offering (15 days)	12-month period
Rule 144 (Private placement)								

*Only in certain circumstances ($500,000 if no blue sky registration)

†Must verify purchaser is buying for himself must have restrictions on shares.

6. Any natural person who had an individual income in excess of $200,000 in each of the two most recent years or joint income with that person's spouse in excess of $300,000 in each of those years and has a reasonable expectation of reaching the same income level in the current year

Rule 502 places a number of limitations on the means an issuer can use in offering securities. In order to qualify for these exemptions, securities cannot be sold through general advertising or through seminars initiated through advertising. Further, all of the securities sold must be subject to restrictions to prevent the immediate rollover of the securities involved in these exempt transactions.

The three tiers of Regulation D exemptions are as follows:

The **Rule 504** exemption applies to offerings of $1 million or less (within any twelve-month period). Sales of stock to directors, officers, and employees are not counted in the $1 million limitation. Recent changes permit the use of the Rule 504 exemption in offerings of up to $2 million, provided the offering is registered under a state **blue sky law.**

The **Rule 505** exemption covers sales of up to $5 million, provided there are no more than thirty-five nonaccredited investors. Issuers qualifying under this exemption cannot engage in public advertising. Also, if the issue is sold to both accredited and nonaccredited investors, the issuer must give all buyers a prospectus.

The **Rule 506** exemption has no dollar limitation, but the number and type of investors are limited. There can be any number of accredited investors, but the number of nonaccredited investors is limited to thirty-five, and these investors must be sophisticated (capable of evaluating the offering and its risk). There cannot be advertising under a 506 exemption, and there must be restrictions on the resale of the shares.

Corporate Reorganizations

If a firm is issuing new shares of stock under a Chapter 11 Bankruptcy reorganization supervised by a bankruptcy court, then registration is not necessary, provided there is court approval for the issue.

What Must Be Filed: Documents and Information for Registration

If none of the exemptions applies, the offeror of the securities must go through the registration process. The offeror (issuer) must file a **registration statement** and sample **prospectus** with the SEC. A prospectus here means the formal document the SEC requires all shareholders to have. However, for purposes of disclosure and misrepresentation issues, a prospectus is any ad or written materials the offeror provides or places.

For information on filing electronically, see:
http://www.abanet.org/
buslaw/efss/home.html

There is a filing fee based on the aggregate offering price of the sale. The SEC has twenty days to act on the filing, after which the registration statement automatically becomes effective. The SEC, however, always acts within that time period in some fashion. It need not actually approve or disapprove the offering within that time limit so long as a **comment** or **deficiency letter** is issued. A new registration, for a first-time offeror, generally takes about six months to get through the SEC. In 2000, the SEC reviewed 3,970 proposed stock offerings of which 1,350 were IPOs. The number of proposed offerings in 2000 was a 58 percent increase over 1999 filings.

The SEC's guide in reviewing the registration materials is the **full-disclosure standard.** The SEC does not pass on the merits of the offering or the soundness of the investment; rather, it simply requires that certain information be supplied. The information required in the registration statement is as follows:

1. A description of what is being offered, why it is offered, how the securities will fit into the business's existing capital structure, and how the proceeds will be used
2. An audited financial statement
3. A list of corporate assets
4. The nature of the issuer's business
5. A list of those in management and their shares of ownership in the firm
6. Other relevant and material information, such as pending lawsuits

The SEC does not verify the accuracy of the information, only that it is on file.

Before the registration statement is filed, the issuer is very much restricted in what can be done to sell the securities. And even after the registration is filed but is not yet effective, the issuer is restricted.

However, the issuer can run a **tombstone ad,** as shown in Exhibit 22.2, which simply announces that securities will be sold and who will have information—but clearly indicates that the ad is not an offer. Also, before the registration statement becomes effective, the issuer can send out a **red herring prospectus,** which has printed in red at the top that the registration is not yet effective. These red herrings are a way to get out information while waiting for SEC approval.

During this interval between filing and the effective date, there can be no sales and no general advertising. Activity is limited until the date the registration gets SEC approval and becomes effective. Exhibit 22.3 is a diagram of federal securities registration and exemptions.

The SEC permits firms to complete *shelf registrations.* Under this process, a firm completes all the registration requirements and is then free to issue the securities any time within a two-year period, generally when market conditions are most favorable. The company's quarterly and annual filings serve to update the shelf registration. This means of filing was permitted to facilitate the raising of capital by corporations.

Violations of the 1933 Act

Section 11 Violations
Section 11 of the 1933 act imposes civil and criminal liability on those who do not comply with the act's requirements regarding the submission of a registration statement. Section 11 is used when full disclosure has not been made in the registration statement or if any of the information in that registration statement is false. Section 11 is a statutory fraud section that applies to security registrations.

What Is Required for a Violation?
For an investor to recover civilly under Section 11, the following elements must be proved:

1. The investor purchased a security that was required to have a registration statement.
2. The registration statement contained a material misstatement or omission.

This announcement is neither an offer to sell nor a solicitation of offers to buy any of these securities. The offering is made only by the Prospectus, copies of which may be obtained in any State or jurisdiction in which this announcement is circulated only from such of the underwriters as may legally offer these securities in such State.

NEW ISSUE

January 22, 1999

$50,000,000

\<allaire\>

2,500,000 Shares
Common Stock

NASDAQ Symbol: "ALLR"

Price $20 Per Share

Prior to the offering there had been no public market for these securities. Allaire Corporation develops, markets and supports application development and server software for a wide range of Web development, from building static Web pages to developing high volume, interactive Web applications.

Credit Suisse First Boston

Dain Rauscher Wessels
a division of Dain Rauscher Incorporated
NationsBanc Montgomery Securities LLC

Hambrecht & Quist

Invemed Associates, Inc.

Needham & Company, Inc.

Charles Schwab & Co., Inc.

Tucker Anthony
Incorporated
C.E. Unterberg, Towbin

Wedbush Morgan Securities

CREDIT SUISSE | FIRST BOSTON

EXHIBIT 22.2 Sample of a Tombstone Ad

EXHIBIT 22.3
Federal Securities Registration and Exemptions

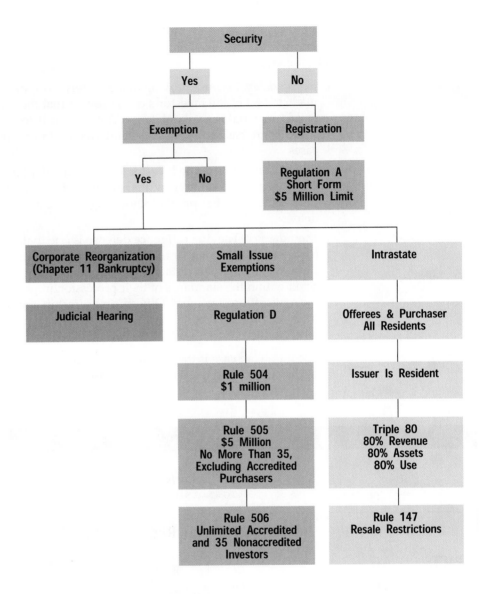

3. The investor need not show reliance unless the purchase was made over a year after the effective date.

4. The investor experienced a loss.

Who Is Liable?

Liability under Section 11 attaches to all individuals who signed the registration statement—each director and officer of the issuing corporation and every accountant, engineer, appraiser, attorney, geologist, or other expert whose input was used in the preparation of the statement. Underwriters are also included as potential defendants. Experts (such as accountants, engineers, appraisers, lawyers) are liable only for the information they provided. Directors and officers are jointly and severally liable under Section 11.

Defenses for Section 11 Violations

Several defenses are available to defendants. Proof of these defenses is the burden of the defendants.

1. *Immateriality.* Because proving that a **material misstatement** or omission was made is part of the investor's case, proving that the statement or omission was immaterial is a valid defense. The standards for what is or is not material are basically the same standards used in contract misrepresentation cases.

2. *Investor knowledge.* If the investor knew of the misstatement or omission and purchased the stock anyway, there is no Section 11 liability. Section 11 defendants can offer proof of knowledge of the investor to establish a defense.

3. *Due diligence.* The **due diligence** defense is one that allows defendants (nonissuers) to show that they were acting reasonably in preparing and signing the registration statement. The experts are required to show that they acted within the standards of their profession in preparing their portions of the registration statement. Officers and directors are required to show that they had no reason to suspect or had no knowledge of an omission or misstatement.

The following case is the leading case on Section 11 liability. It involves a variety of defendants and discusses the defense of due diligence.

CASE 22.1

Escott v. BarChris Constr. Corp.
283 F. Supp. 643 (S.D.N.Y. 1958)

Bowling for Fraud: Right Up Our Alley

FACTS

BarChris was a bowling alley company established in 1946. There was rapid growth in the bowling industry when automatic pin resetters went on the market in the mid-1950s. BarChris began a program of rapid expansion and in 1960 was responsible for the construction of over 3 percent of all bowling alleys in the United States. BarChris used two methods of financing the construction of these alleys, both of which substantially drained their cash flow.

In 1959 BarChris sold approximately one-half million shares of common stock. By 1960, its cash flow picture was still troublesome, and it sold debentures. The debenture issue was registered with the SEC, approved, and sold. In spite of the cash boost from the sale, BarChris was still experiencing financial difficulties and declared bankruptcy in October 1962. The debenture holders were not paid their interest; BarChris defaulted.

The purchasers of the BarChris debentures brought suit under Section 11 of the 1933 act. They claimed that the registration statement filed by BarChris contained false information and failed to disclose certain material information. Their suit, which centered around the audited financial statements prepared by a CPA firm, claimed that the statements were inaccurate and full of omissions. The following chart summarizes the problems with the financial statements submitted with the registration statements:

1. *1960 Earnings*
   (a) *Sales*
Per prospectus	$9,165,320
Correct figure	8,511,420
Overstatement	$ 653,900

   (b) *Net Operating Income*
Per prospectus	$1,742,801
Correct figure	1,496,196
Overstatement	$ 246,605

   (c) *Earnings per Share*
Per prospectus	$ .75
Correct figure	.65
Overstatement	$ .10

2. *1960 Balance Sheet*
   Current Assets
Per prospectus	$4,524,021
Correct figure	3,914,332
Overstatement	$ 609,689

3. *Contingent Liabilities as of December 31, 1960, on Alternative Method of Financing*
Per prospectus	$ 750,000
Correct figure	1,125,795
Understatement	$ 375,795
Capitol Lanes should have been shown as a direct liability	$ 325,000

4. *Contingent Liabilities as of April 30, 1961*
Per prospectus	$ 825,000
Correct figure	1,443,853
Understatement	$ 618,853
Capitol Lanes should have been shown as a direct liability	$ 314,166

5. *Earnings Figures for Quarter Ending March 31, 1961*
   (a) *Sales*
Per prospectus	$2,138,455
Correct figure	1,618,645
Overstatement	$ 519,810

   (b) *Gross Profit*
Per prospectus	$ 483,121
Correct figure	252,366
Overstatement	$ 230,755

6. Backlog as of March 31, 1961
Per prospectus	$6,905,000
Correct figure	2,415,000
Overstatement	$4,490,000

7. *Failure to Disclose Officers' Loans Outstanding and Unpaid on May 16, 1961* — $386,615

8. *Failure to Disclose Use of Proceeds in Manner Not Revealed in Prospectus: Approx.* — $1,160,000

9. *Failure to Disclose Customers' Delinquencies in May 1961 and BarChris's Potential Liability with Respect Thereto: Over* — $1,350,000

10. *Failure to Disclose the Fact that BarChris Was Already Engaged and Was About to Be More Heavily Engaged in the Operation of Bowling Alleys*

The federal district court reviewed all of the exhibits and statements included in the prospectus and dealt with each defendant individually in issuing its decisions. The defendants consisted of those officers and directors who signed the registration statement, the underwriters of the debenture offering, the auditors (Peat, Marwick, Mitchell & Co.), and BarChris's attorneys and directors.

JUDICIAL OPINION

McLEAN, District Judge

Russo. Russo was, to all intents and purposes, the chief executive officer of BarChris. He was a member of the executive committee. He was familiar with all aspects of the business. He was personally in charge of dealings with the factors. He acted on BarChris's behalf in making the financing agreement with Talcott and he handled the negotiations with Talcott in the spring of 1961. He talked with customers about their delinquencies.

Russo prepared the list of jobs which went into the backlog figure. He knew the status of those jobs.

It was Russo who arranged for the temporary increase in BarChris's cash in banks on December 31, 1960, a transaction which borders on the fraudulent. He was thoroughly aware of BarChris's stringent financial condition in May 1961. He had personally advanced large sums to BarChris of which $175,000 remained unpaid as of May 16.

In short, Russo knew all the relevant facts. He could not have believed that there were no untrue statements or material omissions in the prospectus. Russo has no due diligence defenses.

Vitolo and Pugliese. They were the founders of the business who stuck with it to the end. Vitolo was president and Pugliese was vice president. Despite their titles, their field of responsibility in the

(continued)

administration of BarChris's affairs during the period in question seems to have been less all-embracing than Russo's. Pugliese in particular appears to have limited his activities to supervising the actual construction work. Vitolo and Pugliese are each men of limited education. It is not hard to believe that for them the prospectus was difficult reading, if indeed they read it at all.

But whether it was or not is irrelevant. The liability of a director who signs a registration statement does not depend upon whether or not he read it or, if he did, whether or not he understood what he was reading.

And in any case, Vitolo and Pugliese were not as naive as they claim to be. They were members of BarChris's executive committee. At meetings of that committee BarChris's affairs were discussed at length. They must have known what was going on. Certainly they knew of the inadequacy of cash in 1961. They knew of their own large advances to the company which remained unpaid. They knew that they had agreed not to deposit their checks until the financing proceeds were received. They knew and intended that part of the proceeds were to be used to pay their own loans.

All in all, the position of Vitolo and Pugliese is not significantly different, for present purposes, from Russo's. They could not have believed that the registration statement was wholly true and that no material facts had been omitted. And in any case, there is nothing to show that they made any investigation of anything which they may not have known about or understood. They have not proved their due diligence defenses.

Kircher. Kircher was treasurer of BarChris and its chief financial officer. He is a certified public accountant and an intelligent man. He was thoroughly familiar with BarChris's financial affairs. He knew the terms of BarChris's agreements with Talcott. He knew of the customers' delinquency problems. He participated actively with Russo in May 1961 in the successful effort to hold Talcott off until the financing proceeds came in. He knew how the financing proceeds were to be applied and he saw to it that they were so applied. He arranged the officers' loans and he knew all the facts concerning them.

Moreover, as a member of the executive committee, Kircher was kept informed as to those branches of the business of which he did not have direct charge. He knew about the operation of alleys, present and prospective. In brief, Kircher knew all the relevant facts.

Knowing the facts, Kircher had reason to believe that the expertised portion of the prospectus, i.e., the 1960 figures, was in part incorrect. He could not shut his eyes to the facts and rely on Peat, Marwick for that portion.

As to the rest of the prospectus, knowing the facts, he did not have a reasonable ground to believe it to be true. On the contrary, he must have known that in part it was untrue. Under these circumstances, he was not entitled to sit back and place the blame on the lawyers for not advising him about it. Kircher has not proved his due diligence defenses.

Trilling. Trilling's position is somewhat different from Kircher's. He was BarChris's controller. He signed the registration statement in that capacity, although he was not a director.

Trilling entered BarChris's employ in October 1960. He was Kircher's subordinate. When Kircher asked him for information, he furnished it. On at least one occasion he got it wrong.

Trilling may well have been unaware of several of the inaccuracies in the prospectus. But he must have known of some of them. As a financial officer, he was familiar with BarChris's finances and with its books of account. He knew that part of the cash on deposit on December 31, 1960, had been procured temporarily by Russo for window dressing purposes. He should have known, although perhaps through carelessness he did not know at the time, that BarChris's contingent liability was greater than the prospectus stated. In the light of these facts, I cannot find that Trilling believed the entire prospectus to be true.

But even if he did, he still did not establish his due diligence defenses. He did not prove that as to the parts of the prospectus expertised by Peat, Marwick he had no reasonable ground to believe that it was untrue. He also failed to prove, as to the parts of the prospectus not expertised by Peat, Marwick, that he made a reasonable investigation which afforded him a reasonable ground to believe that it was true. As far as appears, he made no investigation. As a signer, he could not avoid responsibility by leaving it up to others to make it accurate. Trilling did not sustain the burden of proving his due diligence defenses.

Birnbaum. Birnbaum was a young lawyer, admitted to the bar in 1957, who, after brief periods of employment by two different law firms and an equally brief period of practicing in his own firm, was employed by BarChris as house counsel and assistant secretary in October 1960. Unfortunately for him, he became secretary and director of BarChris on April 17, 1961, after the first version of the registration statement had been filed with the Securities and Exchange Commission. He signed the later amendments, thereby becoming responsible for the accuracy of the prospectus in its final form.

It seems probable that Birnbaum did not know of many of the inaccuracies in the prospectus. He must, however, have appreciated some of them. In any case, he made no investigation and relied on the others to get it right. Unlike Trilling, he was entitled to rely upon Peat, Marwick for the 1960 figures, for as far as appears, he had no personal knowledge of the company's books of account or financial transactions. As a lawyer, he should have known his obligations under the statute. He should have known that he was required to make a reasonable investigation of the truth of all the statements in the unexpertised portion of the document which he signed. Having failed to make such an investigation, he did not have reasonable ground to believe that all these statements were true. Birnbaum has not established his due diligence defenses except as to the audited 1960 exhibits.

Auslander. Auslander was an "outside" director, i.e., one who was not an officer of BarChris. He was chairman of the board of Valley Stream National Bank in Valley Stream, Long Island. In February 1961 Vitolo asked him to become a director of BarChris. As an inducement, Vitolo said that when BarChris received the proceeds of a forthcoming issue of securities, it would deposit $1 million in Auslander's bank.

Auslander was elected a director on April 17, 1961. The registration statement in its original form had already been filed, of course without his signature. On May 10, 1961, he signed a signature page for the first amendment to the registration statement which was filed on May 11, 1961. This was a separate sheet without any document attached. Auslander did not know that it was a signature page for a registration statement. He vaguely understood that it was something "for the SEC."

Auslander attended a meeting of BarChris's directors on May 15, 1961. At that meeting he, along with the other directors, signed the signature sheet for the second amendment which constituted the registration statement in its final form. Again, this was only a separate sheet without any document attached.

Auslander never saw a copy of the registration statement in its final form. It is true that Auslander became a director on the eve of the financing. He had little opportunity to familiarize himself with the company's affairs.

Section 11 imposes liability in the first instance upon a director, no matter how new he is.

Peat, Marwick. Peat, Marwick's work was in general charge of a member of the firm, Cummings, and more immediately in charge of Peat, Marwick's manager, Logan. Most of the actual work was performed by a senior accountant, Berardi, who had junior assistants, one of whom was Kennedy.

Berardi was then about thirty years old. He was not yet a CPA. He had had no previous experience with the bowling industry. This was his first job as a senior accountant. He could hardly have been given a more difficult assignment.

After obtaining a little background information on BarChris by talking to Logan and reviewing Peat, Marwick's work papers on its 1959 audit, Berardi examined the results of test checks of BarChris's accounting procedures which one of the junior accountants had made, and he prepared an "internal control questionnaire" and an "audit program." Thereafter, for a few days subsequent to December 30, 1960, he inspected BarChris's inventories and examined certain alley construction. Finally, on January 13, 1961, he began his auditing work which he carried on substantially continuously until it was completed on February 24, 1961. Toward the close of the work, Logan reviewed it and made various comments and suggestions to Berardi.

It is unnecessary to recount everything that Berardi did in the course of the audit. We are concerned only with the evidence relating to what Berardi did or did not do with respect to those items found to have been incorrectly reported in the 1960 figures in the prospectus.

Accountants should not be held to a standard higher than that recognized in their profession. I do not do so here. Berardi's review did not come up to that standard. He did not take some of the steps which Peat, Marwick's written program prescribed. He did not spend an adequate amount of time on a task of this magnitude. Most important of all, he was too easily satisfied with glib answers to his inquiries.

This is not to say that he should have made a complete audit. But there were enough danger signals in the materials which he did examine to require some further investigation on his part. Generally accepted accounting standards required such further investigation under these circumstances. It is not always sufficient merely to ask questions.

CASE QUESTIONS

1. How much time transpired between the sale of the debentures and BarChris's bankruptcy?

2. Did BarChris disclose the amount of delinquent debts?

3. Who was sued under Section 11?

4. Were all of the misstatements or omissions material?

5. Who was held liable?

Penalties for Violations of Section 11

Violations of Section 11 carry maximum penalties of $10,000 and/or five years imprisonment. In addition, the SEC has the authority to bring suit seeking an injunction to stop sales that are based on false or omitted information in the registration statement. Those purchasers who are harmed by the false or omitted statements have a right of civil suit in federal district court for recovery of their losses and other damages.

The nature of the levels of damages and the certainty of recovery of awards led to large numbers of sizable class action suits under Section 11. In 1995, Congress passed, over a presidential veto, the Private Securities Litigation Reform Act of 1995, which is the first major change to the 1933 Securities Act since its enactment. This detailed act contains provisions that limit attorneys' fees to a reasonable percentage of the amount recovered or the agreed-upon settlement amount. The problem of "professional plaintiffs" was also addressed through a section that prevents a plaintiff from being named in more than five class action securities lawsuits in a three-year period.

Despite the intent of this 1995 statute, by 1998, additional congressional hearings established that although the federal restrictions on class actions were effective, class actions had simply shifted to state courts. In late 1998, Congress passed the Securities Litigation Uniform Standards Act to establish uniform requirements for bringing class actions in all courts (state or federal).

One final portion of 1995 reform of the act is the so-called "safe-harbor" protection. With certain precautions and qualifications, companies can now make forward-looking predictions for company performance in materials given to investors without the automatic liability that resulted formerly if future events were even addressed.

Section 12 Violations

Section 12 carries the same criminal penalties as Section 11 and covers the following offenses:

1. Selling securities without registration and without an exemption
2. Selling securities before the effective date of the registration statement
3. Selling securities using false information in the prospectus (In this case, prospectus includes not only the formal document but all ads, circulars, and so on used in the sale of securities.)

The SEC also has injunctive remedies here, and buyers also have the right of civil suit. The same defenses as those for Section 11 are applicable to Section 12.

THE SECURITIES EXCHANGE ACT OF 1934

The **Securities Exchange Act of 1934** regulates securities and their issuers once they are on the market. Securities sales, brokers, dealers, and exchanges are all regulated under the 1934 act. In addition, the act requires public disclosure of financial information for certain corporations. In effect, the 1934 act is responsible for the regulation of the securities marketplace. The SEC accomplishes its goal of regulating undesirable market practices in several ways, which are discussed in the following sections.

Securities Registration

Under the 1934 act, all securities traded on a national stock exchange must be registered. In addition, any issuer with over $10 million in assets and 500 or more shareholders must register its equity stock (not bonds) under the 1934 act if those shares are traded in interstate commerce. This registration is in addition to all the filing requirements for issuing discussed under the 1933 act.

Periodic Filing

Search the SEC's EDGAR (Electronic Data Gathering, Analysis, and Retrieval) database for corporate 10-Q, 10-K, and 8-K filings: http://www.sec.gov/ edgarhp.htm

In addition to the one-time registration required under the 1934 act, those same companies (national stock exchange companies or those with 500 or more shareholders and $10 million in assets) must comply with the periodic reporting requirements imposed by the SEC. Each quarter, these firms must file a **10-Q** form, which is basically a quarterly financial report. An annual report, the **10-K** form, must be filed by the company at the end of its fiscal year. Any unusual events—bankruptcies, spinoffs, takeovers, and other changes in company control—must be reported on the **8-K** form.

The Antifraud Provision

Review the Rules Promulgated under the Securities Exchange Act of 1934: http://www.law.uc.edu/CCL/ 34ActRls/index.html

In addition to regulating the reporting of information, the 1934 act regulates the propriety of sales in the marketplace. **Section 10(b)** and **Rule 10b-5** are the antifraud provisions of the 1934 act. These sections are statutory versions of common law fraud. If the idea of the free market is to work, all buyers and sellers must have access to the same information. To withhold information is to commit fraud and is a violation of 10(b). The language of Rule 10b-5 follows:

> *It shall be unlawful for any person, directly or indirectly, by use of any means or instrumentality of interstate commerce, or of the mails, or of any facility of any national securities exchange,*
> *(1) to employ any device, scheme, or artifice to defraud,*
> *(2) to make any untrue statement of a material fact or to omit to state a material fact necessary in order to make the statement made, in the light of the circumstances under which they were made, not misleading, or*
> *(3) to engage in any act, practice, or course of business which operates or would operate as a fraud or deceit upon any person, in connection with the purchase or sale of any security.*

Application of 10(b)

Of all the provisions of the 1934 act, Section 10(b) has the broadest application. It applies to all sales of securities: exempt, stock-exchange-listed, over-the-counter, public, private, small, or large. The only prerequisite for 10(b) application is that interstate commerce be involved in the sales transaction. As Chapter 5 indicates, it is not difficult to find an interstate commerce connection; for example, if the mails or phones were used in the transaction, 10(b) applies. The practical effect is that 10(b) applies to all sales of securities.

Proof of 10(b) Violation

The language of 10(b) does not really specify what constitutes an offense of misrepresentation. Determination of 10(b) violations has been left to the SEC and the

For information on material information disclosures, visit the SEC site:
http://www.sec.gov/rules/

courts, which have shown that violations of 10(b) can take a variety of forms. For example, if a corporation releases false information about dividends, company growth, or earnings, purchasers and sellers of the corporate stock would have a 10(b) action against corporate management and directors. If an owner of shares gives a buyer false or misleading information, the owner-seller is liable under 10(b). Market manipulations in which brokers buy and sell stock in wash or cover sales in an effort to create the appearance of activity are also covered under 10(b).

One of the most famous 10(b) cases is *SEC* v. *Texas Gulf Sulphur Co.*, 401 F.2d 833 (2d Cir. 1968). In that case, Texas Gulf Sulphur was involved in test-drilling operations in Canada. Early tests indicated that the company would make a substantial strike. Press releases did not indicate the richness of the strike. Corporate officers, geologists, and relatives bought stock before the richness of the find was finally disclosed, and the price of the stock soared. The court found that the overly pessimistic press release was misleading under 10(b) and held the purchasers liable.

Coverage of 10(b)

Anyone who has access to information not readily available to the public is covered under 10(b). Officers, directors, and large shareholders are included in this group. However, 10(b) also applies to people who get information from these corporate **insiders.** These people are called **tippees.** For example, relatives of officers and directors would be considered tippees if they were given nonpublic information. Who is covered under Section 10(b) has been a critical question during the past few years. The Supreme Court has made a distinction between true insiders and those who misappropriate information. The following case is the most recent U.S. Supreme Court ruling on 10(b) and misappropriation. The case answers the chapter opening "Consider."

CASE 22.2

United States v. *O'Hagan*
521 U.S. 657 (1997)

Pillsbury Dough Boy: The Lawyer/Insider Who Cashed In

FACTS

James Herman O'Hagan (respondent) was a partner in the law firm of Dorsey & Whitney in Minneapolis, Minnesota. In July 1988, Grand Metropolitan PLC (Grand Met), a company based in London, retained Dorsey & Whitney as local counsel to represent it regarding a potential tender offer for common stock of Pillsbury Company (based in Minneapolis).

O'Hagan did no work on the Grand Met matter, but on August 18, 1988, he began purchasing call options for Pillsbury stock. Each option gave him the right to purchase 100 shares of Pillsbury stock. By the end of September, O'Hagan owned more than 2,500 Pillsbury options. Also in September, O'Hagan purchased 5,000 shares of Pillsbury stock at $39 per share.

Grand Met announced its tender offer in October and Pillsbury stock rose to $60 per share. O'Hagan sold his call options and made a profit of $4.3 million.

The SEC indicted O'Hagan on 57 counts of illegal trading on inside information, including mail fraud, securities fraud, fraudulent trading, and money laundering. The SEC alleged that O'Hagan used his profits from the Pillsbury options to conceal his previous embezzlement and conversion of his clients' trust funds. O'Hagan was convicted by a jury on all 57 counts and sentenced to 41 months in prison. A divided Court of Appeals reversed the conviction, and the SEC appealed.

JUDICIAL OPINION

GINSBURG, Justice

We hold, in accord with several other Courts of Appeals, that criminal liability under § 10(b) may be predicated on the misappropriation theory.

Under the "traditional" or "classical theory" of insider trading liability, § 10(b) and Rule 10b-5 are violated when a corporate insider trades in the securities of his corporation on the basis of material, nonpublic information. Trading on such information qualifies as a "deceptive device" under § 10(b), we have affirmed, because "a relationship of trust and confidence [exists] between the shareholders of a corporation and those insiders who have obtained confidential information by reason of their position with that corporation." *Chiarella* v. *United States*, 445 U.S. 222, 228 (1980). That relationship, we recognized, "gives rise to a duty to disclose [or to abstain from trading] because of the 'necessity of preventing a corporate insider from . . . tak[ing] unfair advantage of . . . uninformed . . . stockholders.'" The classical theory applies not only to officers, directors, and other permanent insiders of a corporation, but also to attorneys, accountants, consultants, and others who temporarily become fiduciaries of a corporation. See *Dirks* v. *SEC*, 463 U.S. 646, 655, n. 14 (1983).

The "misappropriation theory" holds that a person commits fraud "in connection with" a securities transaction, and thereby violates § 10(b) and Rule 10b-5, when he misappropriates confidential information for securities trading purposes, in breach of a duty owed to the source of the information. Under this theory, a fiduciary's undisclosed, self-serving use of a principal's information to purchase or sell securities, in breach of a duty of loyalty and confidentiality, defrauds the principal of the exclusive use of that information. In lieu of premising liability on a fiduciary relationship between company insider and purchaser or seller of the company's stock, the misappropriation theory premises liability on a fiduciary-turned-trader's deception of those who entrusted him with access to confidential information.

The two theories are complementary, each addressing efforts to capitalize on nonpublic information through the purchase or sale of securities. The classical theory targets a corporate insider's breach of duty to shareholders with whom the insider transacts; the misappropriation theory outlaws trading on the basis of nonpublic information by a corporate "outsider" in breach of a duty owed not to a trading party, but to the source of the information. The misappropriation theory is thus designed to "protec[t] the integrity of the securities markets against abuses by 'outsiders' to a corporation who have access to confidential information that will affect th[e] corporation's security price when revealed, but who owe no fiduciary or other duty to that corporation's shareholders."

We agree with the Government that misappropriation, as just defined, satisfies § 10(b)'s requirement that chargeable conduct involve a "deceptive device or contrivance" used "in connection with" the purchase or sale of securities. We observe, first, that misappropriators, as the Government describes them, deal in deception. A fiduciary who "[pretends] loyalty to the principal while secretly converting the principal's information for personal gain" "dupes" or defrauds the principal.

Deception through nondisclosure is central to the theory of liability for which the Government seeks recognition.

Here, by contrast, Rule 10b-5's promulgation has not been challenged; we consider only the Government's charge that O'Hagan's alleged fraudulent conduct falls within the prohibitions of the rule and § 10(b). In this context, we acknowledge simply that, in defending the Government's interpretation of the rule and statute in this Court, the Government's lawyers have pressed a solid point too far, something lawyers, occasionally even judges, are wont to do.

The misappropriation theory comports with § 10(b)'s language, which requires deception "in connection with the purchase or sale of any security," not deception of an identifiable purchaser or seller. The theory is also well-tuned to an animating purpose of the Exchange Act: to insure honest securities markets and thereby promote investor confidence. Although informational disparity is inevitable in the securities markets, investors likely would hesitate to venture their capital in a market where trading based on misappropriated nonpublic information is unchecked by law. An investor's informational disadvantage vis-a-vis a misappropriator with material,

(continued)

nonpublic information stems from contrivance, not luck; it is a disadvantage that cannot be overcome with research or skill.

In sum, considering the inhibiting impact on market participation of trading on misappropriated information, and the congressional purposes underlying § 10(b), it makes scant sense to hold a lawyer like O'Hagan a § 10(b) violator if he works for a law firm representing the target of a tender offer, but not if he works for a law firm representing the bidder. The text of the statute requires no such result. The misappropriation at issue here was properly made the subject of a § 10(b) charge because it meets the statuary requirement that there be "deceptive" conduct "in connection with" securities transactions.

In sum, the misappropriation theory, as we have examined and explained it in this opinion, is both consistent with the statute and with our precedent. Vital to our decision that criminal liability may be sustained under the misappropriation theory, we emphasize, are two sturdy safeguards Congress has provided regarding scienter. To establish a criminal violation of Rule 10b-5, the Government must prove that a person "willfully" violated the provision. Furthermore, a defendant may not be imprisoned for violating Rule 10b-5 if he proves that he had no knowledge of the rule. O'Hagan's charge that the misappropriation theory is too indefinite to permit the imposition of criminal liability thus fails not only because the theory is limited to those who breach a recognized duty. In addition, the statute's "requirement of the presence of culpable intent as a necessary element of the offense does much to destroy any force in the argument that application of the [statute]" in circumstances such as O'Hagan's is unjust.

The Eighth Circuit erred in holding that the misappropriation theory is inconsistent with § 10(b). The Court of Appeals may address on remand O'Hagan's other challenges to his convictions under § 10(b) and Rule 10b-5.

Reversed.

CASE QUESTIONS

1. What did O'Hagan do with information obtained through his employment?

2. What does the court say the misappropriation theory is?

3. Did O'Hagan make money from nonpublic information?

4. Could others have done research and obtained the same information?

5. Will O'Hagan's conviction stand?

ETHICAL ISSUES 22.1

Dan Dorfman is a former *Wall Street Journal* reporter and respected commentator on the financial markets. He was a commentator for CNBC and has written commentaries for *USA Today* and *Money.*

During late 1995 and early 1996, financial press reports revealed that Douglas A. Kass and Dorfman were good friends; Kass is the chief of research and institutional trading at J. W. Charles Securities of Boca Raton, Florida. Dorfman has been a speaker at J. W. Charles's top-producer weekends. He was not paid a fee, but his hotel room and travel expenses for himself and his girlfriend were paid by J. W. Charles. Dorfman recommended several of J. W. Charles's securities in 1994, securities that performed poorly.

CNBC investigated the relationship of the friends and concluded that Dorfman had done nothing wrong, and they supported him and the integrity of his reporting.

Assume that Dorfman has done nothing illegal. Do you see any ethical breaches in his conduct? Did Dorfman create suspicions, even if they were unjustified?

Re: Pss't . . . Want to Make a Bundle? What's Ethical in Insider Trading?

Suppose you hear something that you think will make a stock move. When is it legal to take advantage of the information? The law on insider trading is confusing, even to the experts. See how well you know the subject.

1. The woman you live with, vice president of a large company, wants to take you out to celebrate. She's not supposed to tell anybody, but she lets you know that her company just landed a big government contract. Can you call your broker before the deal is announced?

   __Yes __No __Law unclear

2. You're in the theater lobby at intermission. You overhear a conversation between two men you know are top executives of a big company. "Our stock should really jump when we announce those earnings tomorrow," says one. Can you buy call options now?

   __Yes __No __Law unclear

3. A small textile company calls you in as a marketing consultant. Its president shows you samples of a new fabric that sheds dirt and never wears out. You're bowled over—but too busy to take on the account. Can you buy stock in the company?

   __Yes __No __Law unclear

4. You're a personnel executive at Mammoth Oil. You learn that the company has just hit a gusher. Can you buy before the news becomes public?

   __Yes __No __Law unclear

5. Your broker has an uncanny knack for picking takeover targets. Either he's very smart—or he's getting inside information. He just called to recommend Maximove, an obscure over-the-counter company. Should you buy?

   __Yes __No __Law unclear

6. You own stock in the company you work for, and you've been selling twenty-five shares each month to make payments on your Ferrari. You learn that the next quarterly report will show a huge, unexpected loss. Can you make your regular sale before the bad news hits?

   __Yes __No __Law unclear

7. You are a scientist at a research institute. Tomorrow you are going on television to release a study showing that a major fast-food chain's hamburgers cause baldness—and a Wall Street reaction is likely. Can you sell the chain's stock short now?

   __Yes __No __Law unclear

Here are the "correct" responses, compiled with the help of securities experts at Kirkpatrick & Lockhart and Gibson, Dunn & Crutcher:

1. **No.** A person who gets a tip from an insider can't trade if he knows the insider revealed the news improperly and if the insider gets some benefit from passing the tip. The SEC says that when there is a "private personal relationship," there is enough of a "personal benefit" to make the trade illegal.

2. **Yes.** The men probably didn't intend to give you the information, and they didn't get anything themselves for doing so. There is no securities fraud under these conditions.

3. **Law unclear.** There is no violation of the law unless there is some obligation to keep information confidential. A court might, however, say that the company president had a reasonable expectation that you would keep the discussion under your hat.

4. **No.** All employees are covered by the insider-trading rules. You can't take advantage of shareholders by trading because of significant information you pick up at work.

5. **Yes.** He and his source may be breaking the law. But as long as you don't know that—or don't have reason to know—you are safe.

6. **Law unclear.** This is a murky area, but some experts say it is illegal only if you make a trade motivated by inside information. The SEC would be likely to argue that simply trading while in possession of the information is enough to make the trade illegal.

7. **Law unclear.** It is not illegal simply to trade on information that will move markets. But prosecutors and the SEC have successfully alleged that someone who "misappropriates" his employer's information can be guilty of securities fraud.

If you answered all the questions correctly, you should be giving lectures on the subject. A score of three to six means you're as knowledgeable as most judges. Suppose you did worse. You clearly aren't inhibited by legal theory—and you may have piled up enough trading profits to mount a top-notch defense.

Source: "Pss't . . . Want to Make a Bundle?" *Business Week*, April 29, 1985, 85. Reprinted from April 29, 1985 issue of *Business Week* by special permission, copyright © 2002 by The McGraw-Hill Companies, Inc.

When Disclosure Must Be Made

Once information becomes public knowledge, insiders and tippees are free to buy and sell the shares affected. However, the time of "public knowledge" is not always easy to determine. In *SEC v. Texas Gulf Sulphur,* 401 F.2d 833 (2d Cir. 1968), some of the insiders and tippees waited to buy Texas Gulf Sulphur stock until after a press conference announcement had been made regarding a major mineral find. However, the information released at the press conference had not yet made its way out of the press conference room; there was not enough dissemination for it to be public knowledge. Those who bought by phone immediately following the announcement were found to be in violation of 10(b).

In 2000, the SEC promulgated a new rule that requires companies to release publicly any information they disclose to institutional investors and analysts. Known as the "fair-disclosure rule," material information about the company must be made available to everyone at the same time.

The rule was controversial during its promulgation as more than 6,000 investors sent in comments on the proposed rule and wrote in favor of the fair-disclosure standard. Many companies were already in compliance with the rule citing the Internet and its ease of communication. For example, many companies broadcast their conference calls to analysts at CCBN.com so that any investor could participate.

The application and enforcement of Section 10(b) have become two of the most significant issues affecting Wall Street. The complicated scenarios in insider trading are addressed in the Manager's Desk quiz from *Business Week,* on p. 883.

Visit the SEC Web site for the actual wording of the new rule:
http://www.sec.gov

Visit conference call Web sites:
http://www.bestcalls.com
http://broadcast.yahoo.com/home.html
http://www.on24.com

BUSINESS PLANNING TIP

Annual reports and 10Ks have become a critical part of disclosure for companies. Most companies disclose all environmental cleanup sites and note that it is impossible to predict future cleanup locations or costs. This disclosure is nearly universal for firms.

What Must Be Disclosed

Any material item must be disclosed. To determine whether an item is material, the question to be answered is, "Is this the type of information that would affect the buying or selling decision?" Examples of items that have been held to be material are

1. Pending takeovers
2. Drops in quarterly earnings
3. Pending declaration of a large dividend
4. Possible lawsuit on product line

The following Web sites highlight some of the issues of the Internet as a source of information about companies:
http://www.lfilmpro.com
http://www.vault.com
http://www.greedyassociates.com

One of the trends that has emerged in stock trading is the practice of "pump and dump." This practice uses the rapid communication of the Internet to disperse information about a company so that the market price is affected. Those who have pumped the stock then sell, or dump, their shares when their efforts on the Internet have caused a sufficient jump in the price.

For example, Mark S. Jakob was dealing in call options in Emulex stock in mid-August. His prediction that Emulex stock would take a dive was wrong, and the stock in fact increased in value. He had a loss of $100,000. In order to cover his losses, the 23-year-old sent an e-mail press release to an Internet wire service. The fake press release indicated that the CEO of Emulex would resign due to the fact that earnings had been overstated. The news release was then distributed to various Web sites.

The overall loss to shareholders in reaction to the negative news was $2.5 billion as the share price plummeted. However, Mr. Jakob made $240,000 on his trades in the stock.

Mr. Jakob was arrested for securities fraud and wire fraud.[1]

Re: Disclosing in Plain English

Corporations are renewing their commitment to plain English in communicating with their shareholders. The SEC is in the process of developing plain English rules for financial products sold by insurers. Plain English reduces sentence size and eliminates technical terms. For example, Texaco's 1996 annual report contained the following:

> *The increase in sales volumes included the impact of Texaco's aggressive strategy of marketing purchased crude oil, effectively utilizing the company's expansive trading and distribution network. Crude oil sales also reflected an increase in crude oil and NGL production volumes during 1996.*

The similar disclosure in 1998 was as follows:

> *Our sales revenues decreased in 1998 due to historically low commodity prices throughout our global markets. Crude oil, natural gas and refined product prices were all lower. Partly offsetting lower sales revenue due to declining prices were higher volumes.*

In 1997, CEO Peter Bijur's first sentence in the annual report contained 51 words. In 1998, with the mark of true plain English apparent, the first sentence has 15 words.

The federal government has been under an executive order to rewrite, by the end of 2002, all documents the public sees. Labels for over-the-counter drugs are to be rewritten in plain English by the end of 2005.

The benefits companies and agencies cite of plain English is less cost because employees require less training in complex forms and procedures. Customers are happier because they understand the information and the cost of customer complaint and question handling drops significantly because the volume is reduced dramatically.

The drawbacks include concerns from lawyers about substituting words that do not have a rich body of precedent behind them and possibly changing the true meaning of phrases, words and disclosures.

The handbooks for plain English are:

> William Strunk & E. B. White, *The Elements of Style*
> *The Complete Essays of Montaigne*
> Edward R. Tufte, *The Visual Display of Quantitative Information*

Simplify and Firehouse Communications are two companies offering services in changing reports for companies into plain English.

Source: David Leonhardt, "In Language You Can Understand," *New York Times*, 8 December 1999, C1, C16.

CONSIDER...

22.2 In August 1994, Mervyn Cooper, a psychotherapist, was providing marriage counseling to a Lockheed executive. The executive had been assigned to conduct the **due diligence** (review of the accuracy of the books and records) of Martin Marietta, a company with which Lockheed was going to merge.

At his August 22, 1994, session with Mr. Cooper, the executive revealed to him the pending, but nonpublic, merger. Following his session with the executive, Mr. Cooper contacted a friend, Kenneth Rottenberg, and told him about the pending merger. They agreed that Mr. Rottenberg would open a brokerage account, they would buy Lockheed call options and common stocks, and share in the profits.

When Mr. Rottenberg went to some brokerage offices to set up an account, he was warned by a broker there about the risks of call options. He told the broker that Lockheed would announce a major business combination shortly and that he would not lose his money.

Did Messrs. Rottenberg and Cooper violate Section 10(b)? What about the broker? [*SEC v. Mervyn Cooper and Kenneth E. Rottenberg*, No. 95-8535 (C.D. Cal. 1995)]

BIOGRAPHY

THE ETHICS OFFICER WHO WENT ASTRAY: MARISA BARIDIS

Marisa Baridis, 29, was the legal compliance officer at Morgan Stanley Dean Witter. Ms. Baridis was in charge of what is commonly referred to as the "Chinese wall" in brokerage houses. Her job was to be certain that sensitive information from the deal side of the house was not revealed to those on the side of the house who are trading clients' stock. Such information leakage would constitute insider trading.

Ms. Baridis did a fine job in her role as Morgan Stanley's compliance officer, but the information she sheltered did take a slight detour from her desk. Ms. Baridis sold the information on forthcoming client deals to brokers and college friends for between $2,000 and $10,000 per tip. For example, Ms. Baridis provided Jeffrey Streich, 31, a broker who specialized in speculative stock, with tips over a six-month period. Mr. Streich paid $2,500 for each tip Ms. Baridis gave to him. She also provided information to Mitchell Sher, 32, a vice president for a book distributor, who then used the information to trade in advance on the stock of companies such as Georgia-Pacific Corp. and Burlington Resources. Mr. Sher, who knew Ms. Baridis from their college days, also paid her for the tips.

Ms. Baridis provided tips to 10 people during her time at Morgan Stanley in exchange for cash payments. Mr. Sher indicated that he also took tips from Ms. Baridis when she worked for Smith Barney prior to transferring to Morgan Stanley.

Ms. Baridis's tip service ended when Mr. Streich turned state's evidence and agreed to wear a wire and be videotaped as he met Ms. Baridis for an exchange of cash and a tip. The video tape shows Mr. Streich handing Ms. Baridis $2,500 in one-hundred dollar bills. Just prior to making the transaction, Mr. Streich asked Ms. Baridis if she understood what she was doing. She responded, "I know it is like the illegalist thing you can do."

The SEC charged Ms. Baridis with violations of the insider trading laws. When her employers at Morgan Stanley read of her arrest, she was fired from her $70,000 per year job. Her father posted her $250,000 bond and she was forced to surrender her $4,000 per month apartment. She eventually entered a guilty plea and turned state's evidence in helping the SEC prosecute the 10 people to whom she had sold the information.

Source: "Remember Boesky? Many Gen X-ers Don't," *U.S. News & World Report,* November 22, 1999, p. 520.

One aspect of 10(b) that is overlooked because of focus on individual acts is the obligation of a corporation to offer candid and timely disclosures of corporate status and changes. A merger announcement should be made publicly if too many leaks are resulting in share activity. The disclosure of environmental liability in terms of possible Superfund site cleanup costs should also be made in a timely fashion.

The issue of earnings reports has been a significant one over the past three years as the SEC has investigated hundreds of cases of accounting fraud involving companies that "cooked the books." Other investigations do not necessarily involve fraud but, rather, the question of when earnings management crosses over into misrepresentation of the company's position. For example, America Online entered into a consent decree with the SEC, agreeing to pay a $3.5 million fine for overstatement of its earnings in 1995 and 1996. Although AOL did not admit any wrongdoing, the SEC questioned AOL's booking of advertising expenses in future years. The general accounting rule is that advertising can be booked as an expense and only rarely capitalized over time unless the company can show that it has determined an accurate formula showing that current advertising costs will bring in future revenues. AOL, using its model that the SEC disputed, was able to avoid booking as expenses over $385 million in advertising costs when it was struggling to survive during the 1995 and 1996 period. Its reported earnings would have been very different had it not capitalized the advertising costs.

However, there are disagreements about these kinds of expenses, because AOL clearly has demonstrated that its enormous advertising expenses during that time have resulted in increased customers and earnings with its share price in 2000 being thirty-eight times what it was during the 1995–96 period.

Standing to Sue under 10(b)

To be able to recover under Section 10(b), a party suing must have standing. **Standing** in these cases has been defined by the U.S. Supreme Court as the actual sale or purchase of stock in reliance upon the information or lack of information given. For example, persons who would have purchased stock had they known the truth could not recover for damages under 10(b). Likewise, they cannot recover damages because they would have sold their stock had they known the truth. There must be an actual sale or purchase for a plaintiff to satisfy the standing requirements of 10(b). In *Blue Chip Stamp* v. *Manor Drug Store*, 421 U.S. 723 (1975), the U.S. Supreme Court held that a pessimistic statement of income and potential was not a 10(b) violation because a potentially interested buyer who did not buy because of the pessimism did not have actual damages and, hence, no standing.

The U.S. Supreme Court has held that shareholders cannot immediately bring suit under 10(b) against their brokers if their brokerage contracts contain an arbitration provision. Standing now requires an exhaustion of arbitration methods [*Shearson/American Express, Inc.* v. *McMahon*, 482 U.S. 220 (1987)].

The Requirement of Scienter under 10(b)

A conviction under 10(b) cannot be based on negligence—that is, the failure to discover financial information. Because 10(b) is a criminal statute, there must be some intent to defraud or knowledge of wrongdoing, or *scienter* on the part of the violator. Convictions are only for knowing the financial information but failing to disclose it.

In *Ernst & Ernst* v. *Hochfelder*, 425 U.S. 185 (1978), the Supreme Court held that an accounting firm that had negligently performed an audit of a business based on a fraud could not be held liable under 10(b) because, although the accounting firm made a mistake, it had no intent to defraud.

In the month preceding the drop in the NASDAQ, many insiders at the so-called "dot-com" companies sold their stock and avoided the losses a 17 percent drop in NASDAQ has caused.[2] Insider sales of stocks on the NASDAQ typically average $1 billion to $3 billion per month, but the average jumped to $12 billion per month from November 1999 to February 2000.

Some analysts are noting that the sell-offs by insiders may have prompted the drop in the market. Examples of the trading include:

- Drugstore.com founder Jed Smith sold 150,000 of his 950,000 shares at a price of $23 per share. The price now is $9.88.

- MicroStrategy CEO Michael Saylor sold $80 million in his company's shares. The price of MicroStrategy shares dropped 62 percent within a few weeks of his sales.

- Beyond.com CEO Mark Breier (now ex-CEO) sold 80,000 shares of his company for $440,000 after he quit as CEO.

- Former surgeon general, C. Everett Koop, sold $3 million in shares of his drkoop.com at about $9 per share in February. The spokesperson for drkoop.com indicated the insiders there were "diversifying their portfolios."

Could these transactions be labeled as insider trading? What would you need to know about them to determine whether they were trading on inside information?

Penalties for 10(b) Violations

Review the Insider Trading and Securities Fraud Enforcement Act of 1988: http://www.law.uc.edu/CCL/ 34Act/sec21A.html

Under the **Insider Trading and Securities Fraud Enforcement Act of 1988,** an amendment to the 1934 act, violations of Section 10(b) can carry a fine of up to $100,000 and up to ten years in prison. Corporate officers face fines of up to the greater of either $1 million or three times the amount of profit gained or loss avoided as a result of the violation by the company or any employee under the officers' control. In addition, the officers can be required to return profits made on the inside information. These penalties are imposed only if an officer knew of the acts leading to the violation or acted with reckless disregard for such action. In addition, there is civil liability because those harmed by the insider trading are permitted to bring suit. The 1988 amendments also provided the SEC with additional funds and staff for investigation and enforcement. The amendments impose stricter regulations on brokers and dealers and permit the SEC to bring court actions to impose civil penalties on all violators. Finally, Congress authorized the SEC to pay bounties of up to 10 percent of the amount recovered to informants who report violations.

Insider Trading and Short-Swing Profits

In addition to the application of Section 10(b) and Rule 10b-5 to trading on inside information, the 1934 act also has a form of a strict liability statute for insider trading. Officers, directors, and 10 percent or more shareholders have greater access to inside information. They are involved in setting a corporation's policy and directions in dividend decisions, in product decisions, and in expansion decisions. They will always have access to information that is not yet available to the public. **Section 16** of the 1934 act is a *per se* liability section designed to deal with stock trading by corporate insiders, who are defined as officers, directors, and 10 percent shareholders of those companies required to be registered under the 1934 act.

Under 16(a), officers, directors, and 10 percent shareholders (10 percent of any class of stock) are required to file reports declaring their holdings. In addition, they must file updated reports within twenty days after any change in ownership (purchase, sale, or transfer).

Under 16(b), officers, directors, and 10 percent shareholders are required to give to the corporation any **short-swing profits**—that is, profits earned on the sale and purchase or purchase and sale of stock during any six-month period. For example, suppose Director Cadigan of a New York Stock Exchange company engaged in the following transactions:

April 11, 2001—Ms. Cadigan buys 200 shares of her corporation's stock at $50 each.

JOSEPH JETT: THE ROGUE TRADER

Joseph Jett fulfilled all requirements for a Harvard MBA in 1987, but he did not receive his degree because he still owed a balance on his tuition bill that he did not pay until 1994. After completing his Harvard course work, Mr. Jett was hired by CS First Boston. He was dismissed from that job and hired by Morgan Stanley. At Morgan Stanley, he became a victim of downsizing, was laid off, but was then hired by Kidder Peabody & Company as a trader in 1991. Based on his initial performance, which was somewhat negative, Kidder had doubts as to whether he should have been hired.

A former trader said, "I don't think he knew the market. He made mistakes a rookie would make." However, despite the doubts of colleagues, Mr. Jett's profit record was climbing. Several colleagues who tracked his trades found they were unprofitable, and his continual increases were not in sync with the fluctuations in the government bond market, the area in which Mr. Jett traded. Some co-workers raised concerns with supervisors and one spoke with Mr. Jett himself. They were fired quite rapidly after asking questions. Mr. Jett was promoted to managing director of Kidder's bond trading desk. The bond portion of Kidder's operation was 20 percent of its fixed income division.

Mr. Jett performed so well in his trades in 1993 that he earned a $9 million bonus. By April 1994, however, Kidder announced that their star trader had created $350 million in phony pretax profits. Mr. Jett had engaged in two years of phantom trading. General Electric, Kidder's parent, reduced its first-quarter earnings for 1994 by $210 million. Jett was fired in April 1994.

The SEC began an investigation of Kidder, Peabody and Mr. Jett. Kidder's board refused to advance to Mr. Jett funds for the federal investigation, saying that evidence of "bad faith" on Mr. Jett's part had been established. Mr. Jett's assets were frozen, but he did manage to pay his Harvard bill after the story of his lack of a degree was publicized. Of the 36-year-old Mr. Jett, CEO of GE Jack Welch said, "It's a pity that this ever happened. He could have made $2 or $3 million honestly."

By the end of 1995, Mr. Jett was under investigation by the U.S. attorney, the SEC, and the New York Stock Exchange.

Kidder fired Edward Cerullo, Mr. Jett's boss and the head of Kidder's fixed income area; Mr. Melvin Mullin, who hired Mr. Jett, was also fired. The CEO of Kidder, Michael Carpenter, resigned under pressure; and David Bernstein, Mr. Cerullo's assistant, was demoted. A report issued by Gary Lynch, former director of enforcement at the SEC, concluded that Mr. Jett acted on his own. Mr. Jett maintains Mr. Cerullo told him to make the trades. Mr. Lynch stated in his report, "The obvious motive for this effort was to achieve a degree of recognition and compensation that had previously eluded Jett in his professional career."

In October 1994, GE sold Kidder to Paine Webber at a $500 million loss. Half of Kidder's employees were laid off after Paine Webber took over the firm.

In February 1996, the SEC announced that in view of the inexplicable earnings increases, Mr. Jett's supervisors were lax in their oversight. Civil charges were filed against Jett and his supervisors. Mr. Cerullo settled the charges for a fine of $50,000 and a one-year suspension from brokering. Mr. Mullin and Mr. Jett litigated their charges. Following his hearing, the SEC charged Mr. Jett with lying by making up bogus diary entries. Mr. Jett maintains his innocence and filed a $25 million libel suit against Kidder, but the papers were never served and the lawsuit lapsed. Mr. Jett has released his book, attributing his difficulties to race issues.

ISSUES

1. List all the people affected by Mr. Jett's activities.

2. Describe his moral fiber.

3. Did Mr. Jett's supervisors not want to know the truth? Consider this rap song made up by Kidder employees:

Big Boss and Joe went skiing in the snow:
He said, Joe, what you're doing, don't wanna know;
But, keep on doing it, doing it though,
'Cause I am the Main Man at Kidder P Blow.
. . . Then one month Kidder P took a double blow;
Joe's profits were phony, the man said so;
And the Fed jacked rates so the economy'd slow;
April was the cruelest month at Kidder P Blow.
. . . GE aimed all the blame at Ed Cerullo
He was the man who'd let the boys go.
To Joe and the V-Man he never said no.
'Twas the worst of times at Kidder P Blow.

April 30, 2001—Ms. Cadigan sells 200 shares at $30 each.
May 15, 2001—Ms. Cadigan buys 200 shares at $20 each.

The SEC will match the highest sale with the lowest purchase. Director Cadigan has a profit of $10 per share even though she has a net loss. This profit must be returned to the corporation. It is irrelevant whether the officer, director, or 10 percent shareholder actually used inside information: The presumption under 16(b) for short-swing trades is that the officer, director, or 10 percent shareholder had access to inside information.

In a recent rule change, corporate officers can now exercise stock options and sell shares immediately. The requirement of a six-month waiting period between the option exercise and sale is eliminated.

Regulating Voting Information

There was once a time when shareholders could give their proxies to the company just by endorsing the backs of their dividend checks; proxies then were obtained easily and without much disclosure. The 1934 act changed the way proxies were solicited. With the same philosophy used for registration, the SEC required full disclosure to be the goal of all **proxy solicitations.** To achieve that goal, the SEC now requires prior filing and adequate representation of shareholder interests.

The Proxy Statement

Under Section 14 of the 1934 act, all companies required to register under the act must file their proxy materials with the SEC at least ten days before those materials are to be sent. Proxy materials include the proxy statement and all other solicitation materials that will be sent to shareholders. The proxy statement required by the SEC must contain the following details:

1. Who is soliciting the proxy
2. How the materials will be sent
3. Who is paying for the costs of soliciting
4. How much has been spent to date on the solicitation
5. How much is expected to be spent on the solicitation
6. Why the proxy is being solicited—annual meeting elections, special meeting on a merger, and so on

Exhibit 22.4 is a sample proxy.

Shareholder Proposals

Because the purpose of Section 14 is full disclosure, the representation of views other than those of corporate management is important in proxy solicitations. Shareholders can submit proposals to be included in proxy solicitation materials. If the company does not oppose what is being proposed, the proposition is included as part of the proxy materials. If management is opposed, the proposing shareholder has the right of a 200-word statement on the proposal in the materials. These proposals are not permitted along with their 200-word statements unless they propose conduct that is legal and related to business operations, as opposed to social, moral, religious, and political views. During the Vietnam era, many shareholders wanted to include proposals in proxy materials for companies

P

ARIZONA PUBLIC SERVICE COMPANY
P.O. Box 53999
Phoenix, Arizona 85072-3999

PROXY CARD

R

THIS PROXY IS SOLICITED ON BEHALF OF THE BOARD OF DIRECTORS FOR THE ANNUAL MEETING ON MAY 21, 1996.

O

The undersigned hereby appoints O. Mark DeMichele and Nancy C. Loftin, and each of them, proxies for the undersigned, each with full power of substitution, to attend the annual meeting of shareholders of Arizona Public Service Company to be held May 21, 1996, at 10:00a.m., Phoenix time, and at any adjournment thereof, and to vote as specified in this Proxy all the shares of stock of the company which the undersigned would be entitled to vote if personally present.

X

Voting with respect to the election of directors and the proposals may be indicated on the reverse of this card. Nominees for director are: O. Mark Demichele, Martha O. Hesse, Marianne Moody Jennings, Robert G. Matlock, Jaron B. Norberg, John R. Norton III, William J. Post, Donald M. Riley,

Y

Henry B. Sargent, Wilma W. Schwada, Richard Snell, Dianne C. Walker, Ben F. Williams Jr., and Thomas G. Woods, Jr.

**Your vote is important! Please sign, date, and mail promptly
in the enclosed postage-paid envelope.**

This proxy, when properly executed, will be voted in the manner directed herein. If no direction is made, it will be voted FOR the election of directors and FOR the proposals.

The board of Directors recommends a vote FOR the election of directors.	The board of Directors recommends a vote FOR the proposal to amend Article Sixth of the Company's Articles of Incorporation.	The board of Directors recommends a vote FOR the proposal to amend Article Fifth of the Company's Articles of Incorporation.
1. Election of Directors (see other side)	2. Proposal to amend Article Sixth of the Company's Articles of Incorporation.	3. Proposal to amend article Fifth of the Company's Articles of Incorporation.
FOR* ☐ **WITHHELD** ☐ *For all nominees, except withhold vote for the following: _____	**FOR** ☐ **AGAINST** ☐ **ABSTAIN** ☐	**FOR** ☐ **AGAINST** ☐ **ABSTAIN** ☐

4. In their discretion, the proxies are to vote upon such other business as may properly come before the meeting.

_____   _____
Signature   date

_____   _____
Signature   date

Please sign as your name(s) appear to the left. Joint owners should both sign.
Fiduciaries, attorneys, corporate officers, etc., should state their capacities.

EXHIBIT 22.4 Sample Proxy

Source: Reprinted with permission of the Arizona Public Service Company.

Iroquois Brands, Ltd., is a food company that imports French foie gras, a pâté made from the enlarged livers of force-fed geese. There is a French practice in raising the geese of funneling corn down the geese's throats and gagging them with rubber bands to keep them from regurgitating. A shareholder wishes to include a proposal in the proxy materials that proposes that the company study the practice as an unethical business practice (cruelty to animals). Should the proposal be included? Does Section 14 require that it be included? [*Lovenheim* v. *Iroquois Brands, Ltd.*, 618 F. Supp. 554 (D.C. 1985)]

that were war suppliers. Their proposals centered around the political opposition to the war and not the business practices of the company.

C O N S I D E R . . .

22.3 A shareholder for Cracker Barrel Cheese has submitted for SEC approval a proposal that would require the company not to discriminate against employees who are homosexuals. Should the SEC allow the proposal?

Remedies for Violations of Section 14

If proxies are solicited without following the Section 14 guidelines, the proxies are invalid. They must then be resolicited, and if the meeting has been held in which the invalid proxies were used, the action taken at the meeting can be set aside.

Shareholder Rights in Takeovers, Mergers, and Consolidations

The Definitions

Mergers A **merger** is a combination of two or more corporations, after which only one corporation continues to exist. If Hubbard Company and Inez Corporation decide to merge, then the newly merged corporation must be either Hubbard Company or Inez Corporation. One of the corporations ceases to exist, and the two continue under one name. If Hubbard and Inez decide to merge into Inez Corporation, then Inez will own all of Hubbard's assets and will assume all of Hubbard's liabilities. There are three types of mergers: horizontal, vertical, and conglomerate.

Consolidations In a **consolidation,** two or more companies combine into one new company and none of the old companies continues to exist. Instead of Hubbard Company and Inez Corporation becoming Inez Corporation, under a consolidation Hubbard and Inez become Jasmine Corporation. Each company involved in the consolidation gives all its rights and liabilities to the new company, which holds all assets of the consolidating companies and assumes all their liabilities.

Tender Offers A **tender offer** is not a business combination; it is a method for achieving a business combination. An offer that is publicly advertised to shareholders for the purchase of their stock is a tender offer. The offering price for the stock is usually higher than the market price of the shares, which makes the tender offer attractive to the shareholders.

Re: Shareholder Proposals

The **Corporate Social Issues Reporter** *has provided a tally of the types of shareholder proposals included in the proxies for publicly held companies during the 1999 annual meeting season. The tally is as follows:*

Environmental measures	*33*
Environmental standards compliance (Such as CERES environmental principles)	*10*
Board diversity	*7*

The average shareholder support for the measures was 15% of all voting shares. None of the proposals was passed at the shareholder meetings. At Cypress Semiconductor, 42% of the shareholders voted in favor of increasing board diversity. However, there were several companies where shareholders dropped proposals after management agreed to comply with the demands in the proposal. For example, Paychex agreed to seek out more women and minorities for its board and the Calvert Group dropped its diversity proxy proposal. McDonald's agreed to ban workplace discrimination based on sexual orientation.

In 1998, Unocal pulled out of Afghanistan following a shareholder proposal relating to human rights issues there. The proposal was withdrawn because Unocal had withdrawn from doing business there.

The *National Law Journal* reports shareholder activism is on the increase. In 1971, a proposal by GM shareholders, including the Episcopal Church, to halt GM business in South Africa, barely got 2% of the votes cast at the annual meeting. However, some activists have been successful in recent years with their shareholder proposals. For example:

- A Home Depot shareholder proposal to phase out sales of lumber from old forests passed and is in effect;
- A GE shareholder proposal for the company to clean up the Housatonic River in Massachusetts also passed and the company spent nearly $250 million doing so; and
- RJR split its food division from its tobacco division in response to shareholder activism.

The shareholder proposals for 2000 focused on opposition to genetically engineered food and Northern Ireland employment policies. Generic types of shareholder proposals include staggered terms for directors, independent board members, human rights issues and diversity in boards and the company.*

Shareholders are more organized, but so also are corporate secretaries in handling the proposals and shareholders.

Visit the Web site of the national corporate secretaries' organization:

http://www.ascs.org

Also, visit the Web site of one of the country's most active institutional shareholders:

http://www.calpers-governance.org

Source: Richard H. Koppes, "Future Governance and Activism Trends," National Law Journal, 3 July 2000, B1, B14.

*A full report on resolutions filed for the past five years can be obtained in THE CORPORATE EXAMINER, Interfaith Center on Corporate Responsibility, 475 Riverside Dr., Room 550, NY, NY 10115 212-870-2293

Originally the tender offer was used as a means for a corporation to reacquire its shares. However, it has become a tool of business combinations of every sort, sometimes friendly and sometimes hostile.

Takeovers **Takeovers** are accomplished through the use of tender offers and can be either friendly or hostile. A **friendly takeover** is one the management of a firm favors, whereas a **hostile takeover** is one the management of a firm opposes. Restrictions on the use of tender offers and procedures for accomplishing a takeover are discussed later in the chapter.

Acquisitions The acquisition of another firm's assets is either a means of expanding or a way of eliminating a creditor; **asset acquisition,** however, is different from the other business combinations. Because the corporate structure does not change, shareholder approval is not required for an asset acquisition. However, asset acquisitions are subject to the constraints of the Clayton Act.

1934 Act Regulation of Takeovers

In all of these business combinations (except asset acquisitions), someone is buying enough stock to own a company. That much buying and selling has long had the attention of the SEC. The Williams amendment to the Securities Exchange Act of 1934 regulates these offers to buy stock or tender offers, and the **Williams Act** was passed in 1968 to apply to all offers to buy more than 5 percent of a corporation's securities.

Filing Requirements under the Williams Act Any offeror subject to the Williams Act is required to file a tender offer statement with both the SEC and the target company. The offeror must also send or publish for shareholders of the target company all the information and details about the offer. If the target company is opposing the takeover (that is, if it is hostile), the target must also file its materials with the SEC.

A registration statement for a tender offer must include the name of the offeror, its source of funding for the offer, its plans for the company if its attempted takeover is successful, and the number of shares now owned.

Shareholders have seven days after a tender offer to withdraw their shares. This seven-day period is to prevent shareholders from being forced into a "now-or-never" transaction. The actual purchase of the shares cannot take place until at least fifteen days after the tender offer began. If the offeror changes the tender offer terms, shareholders must be notified; and if a better price is offered, all shareholders must be given ten days to tender their shares at that price (even those who have already tendered their shares at the lower price).

Williams Act Penalties for Violations The Williams amendments provide for both civil and criminal penalties for violations of the act's procedures. The penalties are based on the same type of language used for 10(b) violations. Criminal and

ETHICAL ISSUES 22.3

Joseph Horne Company, a department store in Pennsylvania, entered into an agreement to have Dillard's (a national retail chain) take it over. Dillard's performed its due diligence—the process of getting internal access to computers and records to verify financial statements. During due diligence, Dillard's assumed responsibility for ordering and shipping merchandise. Employees in Horne's management were told that they would no longer have jobs, and nearly 500 employees left Horne. Horne's Christmas merchandise was delayed and was often wrong, and the merger fell through. Horne says that Dillard's went too far. Dillard's says that due diligence is part of a takeover, that Horne's financial statements were inaccurate, and that Horne could have stopped the ordering and shipping at any time. One of the officers at Horne's bank says a Dillard's official told him that Dillard's would just wait until the company was in Chapter 11 bankruptcy and pick it up cheaply. Evaluate the ethics of both parties.

civil penalties are imposed for "fraudulent, deceptive or manipulative" practices used in making a tender offer. There are also penalties for omissions or misstatements of material facts in the tender offer materials.

Proposed Changes As the number of takeover bids has increased, concern over the adequacy of regulation has also increased. Both Congress and the SEC have proposed changes to tighten regulation of tender offers. For example, some proposals would require the tender offeror to disclose its financial situation and plans for the acquired company.

Special Protections for the Hostile Takeover In a noncontested takeover, the target company (within ten days after the date the tender offer commenced) must declare to its shareholders one of the following:

1. That it recommends acceptance or rejection of the offer

2. That it has no opinion and remains neutral

3. That it is unable to take a position

The target company must also justify its position.

In those cases in which the target company does not want to be taken over, both the target company and the offeror develop strategies for stopping the other. Some of the tactics used by a target company to fight takeovers are

1. Persuading shareholders that the tender offer is not in their best interests

2. Filing legal suits or complaints on the grounds that the takeover violates provisions of the antitrust laws

3. Matching the buy-out with a target company offer

4. Soliciting a "white knight" merger or a merger from a friendly party

State Laws Affecting Tender Offers

For an example of a state law governing takeovers, review:
www.indiana.gov/legislative/code/title23

Today over forty states have passed laws regarding takeovers. Initially these laws were Williams Act provisions at the state level. However, upon review of these types of statutes, the U.S. Supreme Court held that they were a violation of the Supremacy Clause (see Chapter 5) in that Congress had preempted the field by establishing a full regulatory scheme for takeovers under the Williams Act [*Edgar* v.

MITE Corp., 457 U.S. 624 (1982)]. Following the *MITE* case, the states have developed a new type of antitakeover statute that permits shareholders to have some say in whether a corporation should be taken over. This new breed of state law focuses on corporate governance and not securities regulation, and hence it avoids the preemption issues raised by the earlier statutes. However, these statutes are still subject to judicial review.

The Future for State Antitakeover Statutes

State antitakeover statutes are often classified into three generations. The first generation was the Illinois statute invalidated in *MITE* as preempted by the Williams Act. The second-generation statute is the Indiana statute upheld as valid in *CTS Corp. v. Dynamics Corp. of Am.*, 481 U.S. 69 (1987), as part of corporate governance regulation. There is now a third generation of antitakeover statutes, in which bidders are required to wait three years before taking over a company unless the board of the target company agrees to such a takeover. These statutes were enacted after the *CTS* decision and further extend the control of shareholders and the entrenchment of existing management. The effect is to make a takeover very unattractive because of the delay. Wisconsin's three-year, third-generation statute was upheld by the Seventh Circuit Court of Appeals in *Amanda Acquisition Corp. v. Universal Foods Corp.*, 877 F.2d 496 (7th Cir. 1989), and the U.S. Supreme Court denied *certiorari* for the review, giving an implicit validation to these more restrictive state statutes. The Court noted in its review of the Wisconsin statute:

Review Wisconsin's takeover statute (Chapter 180, Business Corporations): **www.legis.state.wis.us** *Click on Partnerships and Corporations*

> *If our views of the wisdom of state law mattered, Wisconsin's takeover statute would not survive. Like our colleagues who decided MITE and CTS, we believe that antitakeover legislation injures shareholders. . . . Skepticism about the wisdom of a state's law does not lead to the conclusion that the law is beyond the state's power. We have not been elected custodians of investors' wealth. States need not treat investors' welfare as their summum bonum. Perhaps they choose to protect managers' welfare instead. . . . Unless a federal statute or the Constitution bars the way, Wisconsin's choice must be respected.*

Since the time of the Wisconsin statute's passage and its declared judicial validity, other states have passed even more protective legislation for companies within their state borders. These statutes, for example, permit corporations to prevent 100 percent acquisition of their stock unless the takeover is done over a three-year period. Other statutes permit corporations to dilute the interest of an offeror by issuing new shares to existing shareholders once a takeover begins.

Proxy Regulations and Tender Offers

Once some shares are acquired, a firm poised for a takeover wages a proxy battle, which means it solicits proxies in order to be able to command the number of votes needed to gain control of the board. Even though these proxy solicitations originate outside the company, the proxy statement and solicitation materials must be filed with the SEC.

Failure to file these materials makes the proxies invalid, and any action taken at a meeting using the proxies can be set aside. Mergers voted on with invalid proxies can be "unwound." Either the SEC or shareholders are entitled to bring an action to prevent the use or undo the use of invalid proxies. If a shareholder successfully brings an action seeking a remedy for a violation of the SEC proxy solicitation rules outlined in Section 14, the offeror must fully reimburse the shareholder for all costs of the court action.

Proxies obtained using misleading information or by not disclosing material information are also invalid. Again, either the SEC or individual shareholders can bring suit to stop the use of these proxies or to set aside action taken with them.

Proxy contests are expensive. Who pays for their costs? If management wins, they can be reimbursed for reasonable costs. However, some courts limit this reimbursement right to battles waged over corporate policy and not over personality conflicts. If the new group wins, they can vote to reimburse for reasonable expenses, but many states require shareholders to ratify such reimbursement.

THE FOREIGN CORRUPT PRACTICES ACT

In the early 1970s, the nation, Congress, and other officials learned that U.S. companies doing business in other countries were bribing foreign officials for various reasons. Furthermore, these bribes were not disclosed anywhere and in fact were secret payments concealed by internal accounting procedures. As a result, the **Foreign Corrupt Practices Act** (FCPA) was passed in 1977 as an amendment to the 1934 Securities Exchange Act. See Chapter 9 for more details. While the FCPA is part of the 1934 act, it carries greater penalties of $1 million and/or ten years for officers and others who authorized or performed the conduct in violation of this antibribery statute and up to $2.5 million fines for the corporation.

STATE SECURITIES LAWS

Today all states have their own securities laws. In addition to federal laws, all issuers are required to follow state **blue sky laws** in all states in which their securities are sold. There are two types of state securities laws for registration purposes. There are those that follow the SEC standards for full disclosure: A filing is required, and so long as all the required information is there, the offering will be approved for public sale. Other states follow a **merit review** standard: The regulatory agency responsible for securities enforcement can actually examine a filed offering for its merits as to adequate capitalization, excessive stock ownership by the promoters, and penny-stock problems. These agencies apply a general standard that the offering must be "fair, just, and equitable." This general standard gives them great latitude in deciding which issues will be approved.

Many companies do not register their offerings in states where there is merit review. They sell in the other states to avoid the problems of being denied registration.

As on the federal level, all states have their own exemptions from registration. Most SEC exemptions also work at the state level, the only requirement being that the issuer file a notice of sale with the state agency.

In addition to regulating securities offerings, these state agencies also control the licensing of brokers and agents of securities within the state. The licensing process consists of an application and a background check conducted by the agency to identify possible criminal problems.

Exhibit 22.5 provides a summary of securities regulation under state and federal law.

INTERNATIONAL ISSUES IN SECURITIES LAWS

The following policy statement from the State Department summarizes the nature of international capital markets today: "The United States Government is committed to an international system which provides for a high degree of freedom in

EXHIBIT 22.5 State and Federal Securities Law

1933 ACT	1934 ACT	BLUE SKY
S1—Registration statement Financial information Officers/directors Prospectus 20-day effective date, deficiency letter	*Application* 750 or more shareholders with $5 million or more in assets or listed on national exchange	State securities registration Merit vs. disclosure standards Federally exempt securities may still need to register at state level
Section 11—Filing false registration statement Liability: Anyone named in prospectus or offering expert materials for it Material, false statement; privity not required unless longer than one year Defenses; due diligence; buyer's knowledge	Sec. 10b—insider trading/fraud *10K* Annual reports *10Q* Quarterly report *Foreign Corrupt Practices Act* Financial reports Internal controls Applies to 1933 and 1934 act registrants	
Section 12—Failure to file; selling before effective date; False prospectus Materials; false statement; privity required Defenses; due diligence; buyer's knowledge	*Section 14* Proxy registration Compensation disclosure *Section 16A* Officers, directors, 10% shareholders Sales registration	
Penalties $100,000 and/or five years (criminal/civil suit)	*Section 16B* Short-swing profit Tender offer regulations (Williams Act) *Penalties* $100,000 and/or ten years	

Visit stock exchanges around the world:
http://www.streeteye.com/ toplevel/tables/exch.html

the movement of trade and investment flows." There is free flow of money across borders, and although the United States does restrict foreign investments in atomic energy, air transport, hydroelectric power, and fishing, there is much international investment in U.S. projects.

The United States has ten stock exchanges; Germany, eight; France, seven; and Switzerland, seven; the United Kingdom, Japan, Canada, the Netherlands, Belgium, Luxembourg, Norway, Kuwait, Australia, and many other countries have at least one stock exchange each.

A directive from the European Union has developed uniform requirements for disclosure in primary offering. Often called a "listing of particulars" instead of a "prospectus," uniform information is given to shareholders prior to their purchases. One difficulty that must be resolved is that accounting practices outside the United States are not uniform. Often these practices create different financial pictures for investors.

Insider trading has been prosecuted vigorously in the United States for the past thirty years. European enforcement has been limited. For example, in 1988, the French government began investigating suspicious trades in Societe Generale SA stock. The case is still under investigation and no charges have been brought.

Most financial experts agree that insider trading in Europe is pervasive and there are few convictions and very light, if any, sentences and fines.[4] From 1995–2000, in the stock markets of Britain, Germany, France, Italy, and Switzerland, there were only nineteen criminal convictions. The total for just Manhattan in the United States for the same time period was forty-six convictions. Britain had only three convictions in that time, and France had none. Britain has the largest financial market in Europe.

In addition to the lack of convictions, there is little regulatory structure for investigation and prosecution. The following chart compares the size of securities regulatory agencies in various countries.

COUNTRY	STAFF	LISTED COMPANIES	COMPANIES/ STAFF
Denmark	20	242	12
U.K.	200	2,399	12
Luxembourg	5	53	11
Ireland	10	78	8
Switzerland	30	232	8
Germany	130	741	6
Sweden	50	258	5
Netherlands	43	214	5
Finland	27	129	5
Greece	65	246	4
France	219	784	4
Austria	30	96	3
Spain	92	481	3
Belgium	80	156	2
Portugal	112	135	1
Italy	403	239	1
Europe	1,616	6,483	5
U.S.	2,807	6,850	2

Source: Data is from the Organization for Economic Cooperation & Development (OECD).

The United States is the only country with proxy disclosure requirements. Although Japan regulates solicitations, Germany requires only advance notice of meetings.

SUMMARY

Why do we have securities laws, and what is their history?

- Securities Act of 1933—federal law regulating initial sales of securities

- Securities Act of 1934—federal law regulating securities and companies in the secondary market

What are the requirements that affect primary offerings?

- Primary offering—sale of securities by the business in which interests are offered

- Security—investment in a common enterprise with profits to come from efforts of others

- *Howey* test—Supreme Court definition of security
- SEC—federal agency responsible for enforcing federal securities laws
- Exemption—security not required to be registered
- Exempt transaction—offering not required to be registered
- Regulation D—small offering exemption rules
- Accredited investor—investor who meets threshhold standards for assets and income
- Rules 504, 505, 506—portion of Regulation D affording exemptions for variously structured offerings
- Registration statement—disclosure statement filed by the offeror with the SEC
- Prospectus—formal document explaining offering or any ad or written materials describing offering
- Comment letter—request by SEC for more information
- Deficiency letter—request by SEC for more information
- Full disclosure standard—review for information, not a review on the merits
- Tombstone ad—ad announcing offering that can be run prior to effective date of registration statement
- Red herring prospectus—redlined prospectus that can be given to potential purchasers prior to effective date of registration statement
- Shelf registrations—SEC approval process that allows approval and then waiting period for market conditions
- Material misstatement—false information that would affect the decision to buy or sell
- Section 11—portion of 1933 act that provides for liability for false statements or omissions in registration statements
- Due diligence—defense of good faith and full effort to Section 11 charges
- Section 12—portion of 1933 act that provides for liability for selling without registration or exemption before effective date or with a false prospectus

How do securities laws regulate the secondary market?

- 10-Q—periodic reporting forms required of 1934 act companies
- 10-K—periodic reporting forms required of 1934 act companies
- 8-K—periodic reporting forms required of 1934 act companies
- Section 10(b)—antifraud provision of Securities Exchange Act
- Rule 10b-5—SEC regulation on antifraud provision of Securities Exchange Act
- Insider—person with access to nonpublic information about company
- Tippee—person who gains nonpublic information from an insider
- Fair Disclosure Rule—SEC Regulation on disclosure to analysts
- Insider Trading and Securities Fraud Enforcement Act of 1988—federal law increasing penalties for insider trading violations
- Section 16—portion of 1934 act regulating short-swing profits by officers, directors, or 10 percent shareholders
- Short-swing profits—gain on sale and purchase or purchase and sale of securities
- Proxy solicitations—formal paperwork requesting authority to vote on behalf of another
- Blue sky laws—state securities registration regulations
- Merit review—regulation of merits of an offering as opposed to disclosure

How do securities laws protect shareholders in share and company acquisitions?

- Mergers, consolidations, tender offers, and asset acquisitions are regulated
- Williams Act regulates tender offers
- States have antitakeover statutes

QUESTIONS AND PROBLEMS

1. The Farmer's Cooperative of Arkansas (Co-Op) was an agricultural cooperative that had approximately 23,000 members. In order to raise money to support its general business operations, the Co-Op sold promissory notes payable on demand by the holder. The notes were uncollateralized and uninsured and paid a variable rate of interest that was adjusted to make it higher than the rate paid by local financial institutions. The notes were offered to members and nonmembers and were marketed as an "investment program." Advertisements for the notes, which appeared in the Co-Op newsletter, read in part: "YOUR CO-OP has more than $11,000,000 in assets to stand behind your investments. The Investment is not Federal [sic] insured but it is . . . Safe."

Despite the assurance, the Co-Op filed for bankruptcy in 1984. At the time of the bankruptcy filing, over 1,600 people held notes worth a total of $10 million.

After the bankruptcy filing, a class of note holders filed suit against Arthur Young & Co., alleging that Young had failed to follow generally accepted accounting principles in its audit, specifically with respect to the valuation of the Co-Op's major asset, a gasahol plant. The note holders claimed that if Young had properly treated the plant in its audited financials, they would not have purchased the notes. The petitioners were awarded $6.1 million in damages by the federal district court. Are the notes securities? [*Reves* v. *Ernst & Young*, 494 U.S. 56 (1990)]

2. Time, Inc., acquired all stock of Warner Communications, Inc., at $70 a share in 1989. Time, which became Time Warner, Inc., was saddled with over $10 billion in debt as a result of the purchase.

The company embarked on a highly publicized campaign to find an international "strategic partner" who would infuse billions of dollars of capital into the company and who would help the company realize its dream of becoming a dominant worldwide entertainment conglomerate. Ultimately, Time Warner formed only two strategic partnerships, each on a much smaller scale than had been hoped for. Faced with a multibillion dollar balloon payment on the debt, the company was forced to seek an alternative method of raising capital—a new stock offering that substantially diluted the rights of the existing shareholders. The company first proposed a variable price offering on June 6, 1991. This proposal was rejected by the SEC, but it approved a second proposal announced on July 12, 1991. Announcement of the two offering proposals caused a substantial decline in the price of Time Warner stock. From June 5 to June 12, the share price fell from $117 to $94. By July 12, the price had fallen to $89.75.

A group of shareholders that purchased Time Warner stock between December 12, 1990, and June 7, 1991, brought suit under Section 10(b) alleging that Time Warner made materially misleading statements and misrepresented the status of its strategic partnership discussions.

Did Time Warner violate Section 10(b)? [*Time Warner, Inc.* v. *Ross*, 9 F.3d 259 (3d Cir. 1993)]

3. Marshall Field & Co., a Delaware corporation with its principal office in Chicago, has operated retail department stores since 1852 and is the eighth largest department store chain in the United States, with thirty-one stores. CHH (Carter Hawley Hale), a California corporation that owned Neiman-Marcus, attempted several times to merge or take over Field's. During this time, Field's also received merger offers from Federated Department Stores and Dayton-Hudson. Still another retailer—Gamble-Skogmo—offered to acquire a 20 percent block of Field's stock to prevent a takeover. Field's turned down all offers. CHH finally offered a last-effort deal that Field's refused. CHH then began an unfriendly takeover.

In its information to shareholders, Field's suggested that independence was best, growth would continue, and stock prices would increase. These statements were doubtful, but shareholders rejected the takeover offer. CHH withdrew, and Field's stock declined dramatically. A Field's shareholder has sued for misrepresentation. Can he win? [*Panter* v. *Marshall Field & Co.*, 646 F.2d 271 (7th Cir. 1981)]

4. On March 24, 1977, Anschutz Corporation purchased from Kay Corporation a 50 percent interest in Metal Traders, Inc. (MTI). MTI trades in metal ores and concentrates, and it operates a Bolivian antimony mine. In its financial statement, Kay showed that MTI had just declared a $2 million cash dividend. It did not disclose that, to declare the dividend, it had to use a substantial portion of an unsecured line of credit, making it unlikely that MTI could continue its operations. When MTI went bankrupt, Anschutz filed suit under Section 11 of the 1933 act. Will Anschutz win? [*Anschutz Corp.* v. *Kay Corp.*, 507 F. Supp. 72 (S.D.N.Y. 1981)]

5. Beginning in March 1981, R. Foster Winans was a *Wall Street Journal* reporter and one of the writers of the "Heard on the Street" column (the "Heard" column), a widely read and influential column in the *Journal.*

David Carpenter worked as a news clerk at the *Journal* from December 1981 through May 1983. Kenneth Felis, who was a stockbroker at the brokerage house of Kidder Peabody, had been brought to that firm by another Kidder Peabody stockbroker, Peter Brant, Felis's longtime friend who later became the government's key witness in this case.

Since February 2, 1981, it was the practice of Dow Jones, the parent company of the *Wall Street Journal,* to distribute to all new employees "The Insider Story," a forty-page manual with seven pages devoted to the company's conflicts-of-interest policy. Mr. Winans and Mr. Carpenter knew that company policy deemed all news material gleaned by an employee during the course of employment to be company property and that company policy required employees to treat nonpublic information learned on the job as confidential.

Notwithstanding company policy, Mr. Winans participated in a scheme with Mr. Brant and later Mr. Felis and Mr. Carpenter in which he agreed to provide the two stockbrokers (Messrs. Brant and Felis) with securities-related information that was scheduled to appear in "Heard" columns; based on this advance information, the two brokers would buy or sell the subject securities. Mr. Carpenter, who was involved in a private, personal, nonbusiness relationship with Mr. Winans, served primarily as a messenger for the conspirators. Trading accounts were established in the names of Kenneth Felis, David Carpenter, R. Foster Winans, Peter Brant, David Clark, Western Hemisphere, and Stephen Spratt. During 1983 and early 1984, these defendants made prepublication trades on the basis of their advance knowledge of approximately twenty-seven *Wall Street Journal* "Heard" columns, although not all of those columns were written by Mr. Winans. Generally, he would inform Mr. Brant of an article's subject the day before its scheduled publication, usually by calls from a pay phone and often using a fictitious name. The net profits from the scheme approached $690,000. Was this scheme a 10(b) violation? [*United States* v. *Carpenter,* 791 F.2d 1024 (2d Cir. 1986); *affirmed, Carpenter* v. *United States,* 484 U.S. 19 (1987)]

6. Raymond Dirks was an officer in a Wall Street brokerage house. He was told by Ronald Secrist, a former officer of the Equity Funding of America Company, that Equity Funding had significantly overstated its assets by writing phony insurance policies. Mr. Secrist urged Mr. Dirks to investigate and expose the fraudulent practices. Mr. Dirks checked with Equity Funding management and received denials from them, but he received affirmations from employees.

Mr. Dirks discussed the issue with clients, and they "dumped" nearly $6 million in Equity Funding stock, but Mr. Dirks and his firm did not trade the stock. The price of the stock fell from $26 to $15 during Mr. Dirks's investigation. He contacted the *Wall Street Journal* bureau chief about the problem, but the bureau chief declined to get involved.

The SEC charged Mr. Dirks with violations of 10b-5 for his assistance to his clients. Did he violate 10b-5? [*Dirks* v. *SEC,* 463 U.S. 646 (1983)]

7. Vincent Chiarella was employed as a printer in a financial printing firm that handled the printing for takeover bids. Although the firm names were left out of the financial materials and inserted at the last moment, Mr. Chiarella was able to deduce who was being taken over and by whom from other information in the reports being printed. Using this information, Mr. Chiarella was able to dabble in the stock market over a fourteen-month period for a net gain of $30,000. After an SEC investigation, he signed a consent decree that required him to return all of his profits to the sellers he purchased from during that fourteen-month period. He was then indicted for violation of 10(b) of the 1934 act and the SEC's Rule 10b-5. Did Chiarella violate 10b-5? [*Chiarella* v. *United States,* 445 U.S. 222 (1980)]

8. The president's letter in Rockwood Computer Corporation's annual report stated that most of its inventory consisted of its old computer series. The letter suggested that its new series would cost more money for all users. However, the letter did not disclose, although evidence had indicated, that the new system might be less expensive for those who needed greater performance and capacity. Walter Beissinger (who sold his shares based on the information) brought suit under 10(b). Rockwood claims the statements were based on opinions of sales and were not statements of fact. Who should win? [*Beissinger* v. *Rockwood Computer Corp.,* 529 F. Supp. 770 (E.D. Pa. 1981)]

9. William H. Sullivan Jr. gained control of the New England Patriots Football Club (Patriots) by forming a separate corporation (New Patriots) and merging it with the old one. Plaintiffs are a class of stockholders who voted to accept New Patriots' offer of $15 a share for their common stock in the Patriots' corporation. They now claim that they were induced to accept this offer by a misleading proxy statement drafted under the direction of Mr. Sullivan, who owned a controlling share in the voting stock of the Patriots at the time of the merger. The proxy statement, plaintiffs claim, contained various misrepresentations designed to paint a gloomy picture of the financial position and prospects of the Patriots, so that the shareholders undervalued their stock. They seek to rescind the merger or to receive a higher price per share for the stock they sold. Does the court have the authority to rescind under Section 14? [*Pavlidis* v. *New England Patriots Football Club,* 737 F.2d 1227 (1st Cir. 1984)]

10. The National Bank of Yugoslavia placed $71 million with Drexel Burnham Lambert, Inc., for short-term

investment just months before Drexel's bankruptcy. In effect, the bank made a time deposit. Would the bank be able to proceed under a theory of securities laws violations? Would these time deposits be considered securities? [*National Bank of Yugoslavia* v. *Drexel Burnham Lambert, Inc.,* 768 F.Supp. 1010 (S.D.N.Y 1991)]

RESEARCH PROBLEM

More than a Book Offering

11. Simon & Simon, Inc. (SSI) is a Fortune 500 company primarily involved in publishing magazines and fiction and nonfiction popular press. Like other publishing firms, SSI has been interested in expansion through the acquisition of publishing firms or companies with a multimedia focus. Its shares are listed on the New York Stock Exchange.

SSI has been approached by University Press (UP), a small but successful publishing house with a focus on academic and research-oriented books that would like to sell its assets (physical as well as titles [copyrights]) to SSI. UP is a national company that markets largely through direct mailings and whose stock is sold on the over-the-counter market. SSI has its own bookstores in malls, downtown city centers, and a few strip malls. It releases approximately thirty major fiction titles (excluding its romance novel line)

and twenty major nonfiction titles each year. Other releases include children's books, cookbooks, "how to" books, coffee table (art) books, and several college and test-preparation guides. These types of releases total 100 a year. UP releases twenty-five new books each year, but it is in the unique position of having some of its titles continue selling long after the usual six-month hard-cover life of popular press books.

UP's board authorized its CEO to approach SSI. SSI's board heard the proposal for the first time yesterday. SSI's CEO told them, "We should act quickly. The price is right." Another board member asked, "Aren't there some legal issues here? Can we act this quickly?"

Prepare a memorandum for the SSI board and also for the UP board outlining all the legal issues, including corporate, antitrust, and securities issues.

NOTES

1. Alex Berenson, "Man Charged in Stock Fraud Based on Fake News," *New York Times,* 1 September 2000, C1, C2.

2. Del Jones, "Net Execs Sold Stock before Big Drop," *USA Today,* 6 April 2000, B1.

3. Constance L. Hays, "A PepsiCo Shareholder Meeting and a Very Unhappy Shareholder," *New York Times,* 22 April 2000, B1, B4.

4. Anita Raghavan, Silvia Ascarelli, and David Woodruff, "Insider Trading in Europe Is Virtually Risk-Free," *Wall Street Journal,* 17 August 2000, C1.

BUSINESS STRATEGY APPLICATION

In this exercise, you have the opportunity to look at the proxy statement for a Fortune 500 multinational company, Raytheon, Inc., along with excerpts from other companies' proxies, specifically their shareholder proposals. From these documents you have the

chance to discover what kinds of things investors and shareholders are concerned about as well as an opportunity to see the requirements for proxy statements and disclosures.

The United States Constitution

We the People of the United States, in Order to form a more perfect Union, establish Justice, insure domestic Tranquility, provide for the common defence, promote the general Welfare, and secure the Blessings of Liberty to ourselves and our Posterity, do ordain and establish this Constitution for the United States of America.

Article I

Section 1

All legislative Powers herein granted shall be vested in a Congress of the United States, which shall consist of a Senate and House of Representatives.

Section 2

The House of Representatives shall be composed of Members chosen every second Year by the People of the several States, and the Electors in each State shall have the Qualifications requisite for Electors of the most numerous Branch of the State Legislature.

No Person shall be a Representative who shall not have attained to the Age of twenty five Years, and been seven Years a Citizen of the United States, and who shall not, when elected, be an Inhabitant of that State in which he shall be chosen.

Representatives and direct Taxes shall be apportioned among the several States which may be included within this Union, according to their respective Numbers, which shall be determined by adding to the whole Number of free Persons, including those bound to Service for a Term of Years, and excluding Indians not taxed, three fifths of all other Persons. The actual Enumeration shall be made within three Years after the first Meeting of the Congress of the United States, and within every subsequent Term of ten Years, in which Manner as they shall by Law direct. The Number of Representatives shall not exceed one for every thirty Thousand, but each State shall have at Least one Representative; and until such enumeration shall be made, the State of New Hampshire shall be entitled to choose three, Massachusetts eight, Rhode Island and Providence Plantations one, Connecticut five, New York six, New Jersey four, Pennsylvania eight, Delaware one, Maryland six, Virginia ten, North Carolina five, South Carolina five, and Georgia three.

When vacancies happen in the Representation from any State, the Executive Authority thereof shall issue Writs of Election to fill such Vacancies.

The House of Representatives shall chuse their Speaker and other Officers; and shall have the sole Power of Impeachment.

Section 3

The Senate of the United States shall be composed of two Senators from each State, chosen by the Legislature thereof, for six Years; and each Senator shall have one Vote.

Immediately after they shall be assembled in Consequence of the first Election, they shall be divided as equally as may be into three Classes. The Seats of the Senators of the first Class shall be vacated at the Expiration of the second Year, of the second Class at the Expiration of the fourth Year, and of the third Class at the Expiration of the sixth Year, so that one third may be chosen every second Year; and if Vacancies happen by Resignation, or otherwise, during the Recess of the Legislature of any State, the Executive thereof may make temporary Appointments until the next Meeting of the Legislature, which shall then fill such Vacancies.

No Person shall be a Senator who shall not have attained to the Age of thirty Years, and been nine Years a Citizen of the United States, and who shall not, when elected, be an Inhabitant of that State for which he shall be chosen.

The Vice President of the United States shall be President of the Senate, but shall have no Vote, unless they be equally divided.

The Senate shall chuse their other Officers, and also a President pro tempore, in the Absence of the Vice President, or when he shall exercise the Office of President of the United States.

The Senate shall have the sole Power to try all Impeachments. When sitting for that Purpose, they shall be on Oath or Affirmation. When the President of the United States is tried the Chief Justice shall preside: And no Person shall be convicted without the Concurrence of two thirds of the Members present.

Judgment in Cases of Impeachment shall not extend further than to removal from Office, and disqualification to hold and enjoy any Office of honor, Trust or Profit under the United States: but the Party convicted shall nevertheless be liable and subject to Indictment, Trial, Judgment and Punishment, according to Law.

Section 4

The Times, Places and Manner of holding Elections for Senators and Representatives, shall be prescribed in each State by the Legislature thereof; but the Congress may at any time by Law make or alter such Regulations, except as to the Places of chusing Senators.

The Congress shall assemble at Least once in every Year, and such Meeting shall be on the first Monday in December, unless they shall by Law appoint a different Day.

Section 5

Each House shall be the Judge of the Elections, Returns and Qualifications of its own Members, and a Majority of each shall constitute a Quorum to do Business; but a smaller Number may adjourn from day to day, and may be authorized to compel the Attendance of absent Members, in such Manner, and under such Penalties as each House may provide.

Each House may determine the Rules in its Proceedings, punish its Members for disorderly Behaviour, and, with the Concurrence of two thirds, expel a Member.

Each House shall keep a Journal of its Proceedings, and from time to time publish the same, excepting such Parts as may in their Judgment require Secrecy; and the Yeas and Nays of the Members of either House on any question shall, at the Desire of one fifth of those Present, be entered on the Journal.

Neither House, during the Session of Congress, shall, without the Consent of the other, adjourn for more than three days, nor to any other Place than that in which the two Houses shall be sitting.

Section 6

The Senators and Representatives shall receive a Compensation for their Services, to be ascertained by Law, and paid out of the Treasury of the United States. They shall in all Cases, except Treason, Felony and Breach of the Peace, be privileged from Arrest during their Attendance at the Session of their respective Houses, and in going to and returning from the same; and for any Speech or Debate in either House, they shall not be questioned in any other Place.

No Senator or Representative shall, during the Time for which he was elected, be appointed to any civil Office under the Authority of the United States, which shall have been created, or the Emoluments whereof shall have been encreased during such time; and no Person holding any Office under the United States, shall be a Member of either House during his Continuance in Office.

Section 7

All Bills for raising Revenue shall originate in the House of Representatives; but the Senate may propose or concur with amendments as on other Bills.

Every Bill which shall have passed the House of Representatives and the Senate, shall, before it become a Law, be presented to the President of the United States; If he approve he shall sign it, but if not he shall return it, with his Objections to that House in which it shall have originated, who shall enter the Objections at large on their Journal, and proceed to reconsider it. If after such Reconsideration two thirds of that House shall agree to pass the Bill, it shall be sent, together with the Objections, to the other House, by which it shall likewise be reconsidered, and if approved by two thirds of that House, it shall become a Law. But in all such Cases the Votes of both Houses shall be determined by Yeas and Nays, and the names of the Persons voting for and against the Bill shall be entered on the Journal of each House respectively. If any Bill shall not be returned by the President within ten Days (Sundays excepted) after it shall have been presented to him, the Same shall be a Law, in like Manner as if he had signed it, unless the Congress by their Adjournment prevent its Return, in which Case it shall not be a Law.

Every Order, Resolution, or Vote to which the Concurrence of the Senate and House of Representatives may be necessary (except on a question of Adjournment) shall be presented to the President of the United States; and before the Same shall take Effect, shall be approved by him, or being disapproved by him, shall be repassed by two thirds of the Senate and House of Representatives, according to the Rules and Limitations prescribed in the Case of a Bill.

Section 8

The Congress shall have Power To lay and collect Taxes, Duties, Imposts and Excises, to pay the Debts and provide for the common Defense and general Welfare of the United States; but all Duties, Imposts and Excises shall be uniform throughout the United States;

To borrow Money on the credit of the United States;

To regulate Commerce with foreign Nations, and among the several States, and with the Indian Tribes;

To establish an uniform Rule of Naturalization, and uniform Laws on the subject of Bankruptcies throughout the United States;

To coin Money, regulate the Value thereof, and of foreign Coin, and fix the Standard of Weights and Measures;

To provide for the Punishment of counterfeiting the Securities and current Coin of the United States;

To establish Post Offices and post Roads;

To promote the Progress of Science and useful Arts, by securing for limited Times to Authors and Inventors the exclusive Right to their respective Writings and Discoveries;

To constitute Tribunals inferior to the supreme Court;

To define and punish Piracies and Felonies committed on the high Seas, and Offenses against the Law of Nations;

To declare War, grant Letters of Marque and Reprisal, and make Rules concerning Captures on Land and Water;

To raise and support Armies, but no Appropriation of Money to that Use shall be for a longer Term than two Years;

To provide and maintain a Navy;

To make Rules for the Government and Regulation of the land and naval Forces;

To provide for calling forth the Militia to execute the Laws of the Union, suppress Insurrections and repel Invasions;

To provide for organizing, arming, and disciplining, the Militia, and for governing such Part of them as may be employed in the Service of the United States, reserving to the States respectively, the Appointment of the Officers, and the Authority of training the Militia according to the discipline prescribed by Congress;

To exercise exclusive Legislation in all Cases whatsoever, over such District (not exceeding ten Miles square) as may, by Cession of particular States, and the Acceptance of Congress, become the Seat of the Government of the United States, and to exercise like Authority over all Places purchased by the Consent of the Legislature of the State in which the Same shall be, for the Erection of Forts, Magazines, Arsenals, dock-Yards, and other needful Buildings;—And

To make all Laws which shall be necessary and proper for carrying into Execution the foregoing Powers, and all other Powers vested by this Constitution in the Government of the United States, or in any Department or Officer thereof.

Section 9

The Migration or Importation of such Persons as any of the States now existing shall think proper to admit, shall not be prohibited by the Congress prior to the Year one thousand eight hundred and eight, but a Tax or duty may be imposed on such Importation, not exceeding ten dollars for each Person.

The Privilege of the Writ of Habeas Corpus shall not be suspended, unless when in Cases of Rebellion or Invasion the public Safety may require it.

No Bill of Attainder or ex post facto Law shall be passed.

No Capitation, or other direct, Tax shall be laid, unless in Proportion to the Census or Enumeration herein before directed to be taken.

No Tax or Duty shall be laid on Articles exported from any State.

No Preference shall be given to any Regulation of Commerce or Revenue to the Ports of one State over those of another; nor shall Vessels bound to, or from, one State, be obliged to enter, clear or pay Duties in another.

No Money shall be drawn from the Treasury, but in Consequence of Appropriations made by Law; and a regular Statement and Account of the Receipts and Expenditures of all public Money shall be published from time to time.

No Title of Nobility shall be granted by the United States: And no Person holding any Office of Profit or Trust under them, shall, without the Consent of the Congress, accept of any present, Emolument, Office, or Title, of any kind whatever, from any King, Prince or foreign State.

Section 10

No State shall enter into any Treaty, Alliance, or Confederation; grant Letters of Marque and Reprisal; coin Money; emit Bills of Credit; make any Thing but gold and silver Coin a Tender in Payment of Debts; pass any Bill of Attainder, ex post facto Law or law impairing the Obligation of Contracts, or grant any Title of Nobility.

No State shall, without the Consent of the Congress, lay any Imposts or Duties on Imports or Exports, except what may be absolutely necessary for executing its inspection Laws: and the net Produce of all Duties and Imposts, laid by any State on Imports or Exports, shall be for the Use of the Treasury of the United States; and all such Laws shall be subject to the Revision and Control of the Congress.

No State shall, without the Consent of Congress, lay any Duty on Tonnage, keep Troops, or Ships of War in time of Peace, enter into any Agreement or Compact with another State, or with a foreign Power, or engage in War, unless actually invaded, or in such imminent Danger as will not admit of delay.

Article II

Section I

The executive Power shall be vested in a President of the United States of America. He shall hold his Office during the Term of four Years, and, together with the Vice President, chosen for the same Term, be elected, as follows:

Each State shall appoint, in such Manner as the Legislature thereof may direct, a Number of Electors, equal to the whole Number of Senators and Representatives to which the State may be entitled in the Congress: but no Senator or Representative, or Person holding an Office of Trust or Profit under the United States, shall be appointed an Elector.

The Electors shall meet in their respective States, and vote by Ballot for two Persons, of whom one at least shall not be an Inhabitant of the same State with themselves. And they shall make a List of all the Persons voted for, and of the Number of Votes for each; which List they shall sign and certify, and transmit sealed to the Seat of the Government of the United States, directed to the President of the Senate. The President of the Senate shall, in the Presence of the Senate and House of Representatives, open all the Certificates, and the Votes shall then be counted. The Person having the greatest Number of Votes shall be the President, if such Number be a Majority of the whole Number of Electors appointed; and if there be more than one who have such Majority, and have an equal Number of Votes, then the House of Representatives shall immediately chuse by Ballot one of them for President; and if no Person have a Majority, then from the five highest on the List the said House shall in like Manner chuse the President. But in chusing the President, the Votes shall be taken by States, the Representation from each State having one Vote; a quorum for this Purpose shall consist of a Member or Members from two thirds of the States, and a Majority of all the States shall be necessary to a Choice. In every Case, after the Choice of the President, the Person having the greatest Number of Votes of the Electors shall be the Vice President. But if there should remain two or more who have equal Votes, the Senate shall chuse from them by Ballot the Vice President.

The Congress may determine the Time of chusing the Electors, and the Day on which they shall give their Votes; which Day shall be the same throughout the United States.

No Person except a natural born Citizen, or a Citizen of the United States, at the time of the Adoption of this Constitution, shall be eligible to the Office of President; neither shall any Person be eligible to that Office who shall not have attained to the Age of thirty-five Years, and been fourteen years a Resident within the United States.

In Case of the Removal of the President from Office, or of his Death, Resignation, or Inability to discharge the Powers and Duties of the said Office, the Same shall devolve on the Vice President, and the Congress may by Law provide for the Case of Removal, Death, Resignation, or Inability, both of the President and Vice President, declaring what Officer shall then act as President, and such Officer shall act accordingly, until the Disability be removed, or a President shall be elected.

The President shall, at stated Times, receive for his Services, a Compensation, which shall neither be encreased nor diminished during the Period for which he shall have been elected, and he shall not receive within that Period any other Emolument from the United States, or any of them.

Before he enter on the Execution of his Office, he shall take the following Oath or Affirmation:— "I do solemnly swear (or affirm) that I will faithfully execute the Office of President of the United States, and will to the best of my Ability, preserve, protect, and defend the Constitution of the United States."

Section 2

The President shall be Commander in Chief of the Army and Navy of the United States, and of the Militia of the several States, when called into the actual Service of the United States; he may require the Opinion, in writing, of the principal Officer in each of the executive Departments, upon any Subject relating to the Duties of their respective Offices, and he shall have Power to grant Reprieves and Pardons for Offenses against the United States, except in Cases of Impeachment.

He shall have Power, by and with the Advice and Consent of the Senate, to make Treaties, provided two thirds of the Senators present concur;

and he shall nominate, and by and with the Advice and Consent of the Senate, shall appoint Ambassadors, other public Ministers and Consuls, Judges of the supreme Court, and all other Officers of the United States, whose Appointments are not herein otherwise provided for, and which shall be established by Law: but the Congress may by Law vest the Appointment of such inferior Officers, as they think proper, in the President alone, in the Courts of Law, or in the Heads of Departments.

The President shall have Power to fill up all Vacancies that may happen during the Recess of the Senate, by granting Commissions which shall expire at the End of their next Session.

Section 3

He shall from time to time give to the Congress Information of the State of the Union, and recommend to their Consideration such Measures as he shall judge necessary and expedient; he may, on extraordinary Occasions, convene both Houses, or either of them, and in Case of Disagreement between them, with Respect to the Time of Adjournment, he may adjourn them to such Time as he shall think proper; he shall receive Ambassadors and other public Ministers; he shall take Care that the Laws be faithfully executed, and shall Commission all the Officers of the United States.

Section 4

The President, Vice President and all Civil Officers of the United States, shall be removed from Office on Impeachment for, and Conviction of, Treason, Bribery, or other high Crimes and Misdemeanors.

Article III

Section 1

The judicial Power of the United States, shall be vested in one supreme Court, and in such inferior Courts as the Congress may from time to time ordain and establish. The Judges, both of the supreme and inferior Courts, shall hold their Offices during good Behaviour, and shall, at stated Times, receive for their Services, a Compensation, which shall not be diminished during their Continuance in Office.

Section 2

The judicial Power shall extend to all Cases, in Law and Equity, arising under this Constitution, the Laws of the United States, and Treaties made, or which shall be made, under their Authority;—to all Cases affecting Ambassadors, other public Ministers and Consuls;—to all Cases of admiralty and maritime Jurisdiction;—to Controversies to which the United States shall be a Party;—to Controversies between two or more States;—between a State and Citizens of another State;—between Citizens of different States,—between Citizens of the same State claiming Lands under Grants of different States, and between a State, or the Citizens thereof, and foreign States, Citizens or Subjects.

In all Cases affecting Ambassadors, other public Ministers and Consuls, and those in which a State shall be Party, the Supreme Court shall have original Jurisdiction. In all the other Cases before mentioned, the supreme Court shall have appellate Jurisdiction, both as to Law and Fact, with such Exceptions, and under such Regulations as the Congress shall make.

The Trial of all Crimes, except in Cases of Impeachment, shall be by Jury; and such Trial shall be held in the State where the said Crimes shall have been committed; but when not committed within any State, the Trial shall be at such Place or Places as the Congress may by Law have directed.

Section 3

Treason against the United States, shall consist only in levying War against them, or in adhering to their Enemies, giving them Aid and Comfort. No Person shall be convicted of Treason unless on the Testimony of two Witnesses to the same overt Act, or on Confession in open Court.

The Congress shall have Power to declare the Punishment of Treason, but no Attainder of Treason shall work Corruption of Blood, or Forfeiture except during the Life of the Person attainted.

Article IV

Section 1

Full Faith and Credit shall be given in each State to the public Arts, Records, and judicial Proceedings of every other State. And the Congress may by general Laws prescribe the Manner in which such Acts, Records and Proceedings shall be proved, and the Effect thereof.

Section 2

The Citizens of each State shall be entitled to all Privileges and Immunities of Citizens in the several States.

A Person charged in any State with Treason, Felony, or other Crime, who shall flee from Justice, and be found in another State, shall on Demand of the executive Authority of the State from which he fled, be delivered up, to be removed to the State having Jurisdiction of the Crime.

No Person held to Service or Labour in one State, under the Laws thereof, escaping into another, shall, in Consequence of any Law or Regulation therein, be discharged from such Service or Labour, but shall be delivered up on Claim of the Party to whom such Service or Labour may be due.

Section 3

New States may be admitted by the Congress into this Union; but no new State shall be formed or erected within the Jurisdiction of any other State; nor any State be formed by the Junction of two or more States, or Parts of States, without the Consent of the Legislatures of the States concerned as well as of the Congress.

The Congress shall have Power to dispose of and make all needful Rules and Regulations respecting the Territory or other Property belonging to the United States; and nothing in this Constitution shall be so construed as to Prejudice any Claims of the United States, or of any particular State.

Section 4

The United States shall guarantee to every State in this Union a Republican Form of Government, and shall protect each of them against Invasion; and on Application of the Legislature, or of the Executive (when the Legislature cannot be convened) against domestic Violence.

Article V

The Congress, whenever two thirds of both Houses shall deem it necessary, shall propose Amendments to this Constitution, or, on the Application of the Legislatures of two thirds of the several States, shall call a Convention for proposing Amendments, which, in either Case, shall be valid to all Intents and Purposes, as Part of this Constitution, when ratified by the Legislatures of three fourths of the several States, or by Conventions in three fourths thereof, as the one or the other Mode of Ratification may be proposed by the Congress; Provided that no Amendment which may be made prior to the Year One thousand eight hundred and eight shall in any Manner affect the first and fourth Clauses in the Ninth Section of the first Article; and that no State, without its Consent, shall be deprived of its equal Suffrage in the Senate.

Article VI

All Debts contracted and Engagements entered into, before the Adoption of this Constitution, shall be as valid against the United States under this Constitution, as under the Confederation.

This Constitution, and the Laws of the United States which shall be made in Pursuance thereof; and all Treaties made, or which shall be made, under the Authority of the United States, shall be the supreme Law of the Land; and the judges in every State shall be bound thereby, any Thing in the Constitution or Laws of any State to the Contrary notwithstanding.

The Senators and Representatives before mentioned, and the Members of the several State Legislatures, and all executive and judicial Officers, both of the United States and of the several States, shall be bound by Oath or Affirmation, to support this Constitution; but no religious Test shall ever be required as a Qualification to any Office or public Trust under the United States.

Article VII

The Ratification of the Conventions of nine States, shall be sufficient for the Establishment of this Constitution between the States so ratifying the Same.

Amendment I (1791)

Congress shall make no law respecting an establishment of religion, or prohibiting the free exercise thereof; or abridging the freedom of speech, or of the press; or the right of the people peaceably to assemble, and to petition the Government for a redress of grievances.

Amendment II (1791)

A well regulated Militia, being necessary to the security of a free State, the right of the people to keep and bear Arms, shall not be infringed.

Amendment III (1791)

No Soldier shall, in time of peace be quartered in any house, without the consent of the Owner, nor in time of war, but in a manner to be prescribed by law.

Amendment IV (1791)

The right of the people to be secure in their persons, houses, papers, and effects, against unreasonable searches and seizures, shall not be violated, and no Warrants shall issue, but upon probable cause, supported by Oath or affirmation, and particularly describing the place to be searched, and the persons or things to be seized.

Amendment V (1791)

No person shall be held to answer for a capital or otherwise infamous crime, unless on a presentment or indictment of a Grand Jury, except in cases arising in the land or naval forces, or in the Militia, when in actual service in time of War or public danger; nor shall any person be subject for the same offense to be twice put in jeopardy of life or limb; nor shall be compelled in any criminal case to be a witness against himself, nor be deprived of life, liberty, or property, without due process of law; nor shall private property be taken for public use, with out just compensation.

Amendment VI (1791)

In all criminal prosecutions, the accused shall enjoy the right to a speedy and public trial, by an impartial jury of the State and district wherein the crime shall have been committed, which district shall have been previously ascertained by law, and to be informed of the nature and cause of the accusation; to be confronted with the witnesses against him; to have compulsory process for obtaining Witnesses in his favor, and to have the Assistance of Counsel for his defense.

Amendment VII (1791)

In Suits at common law, where the value in controversy shall exceed twenty dollars, the right of trial by jury shall be preserved, and no fact tried by a jury, shall be otherwise reexamined in any Court of the United States, than according to the rules of the common law.

Amendment VIII (1791)

Excessive bail shall not be required nor excessive fines imposed, nor cruel and unusual punishments inflicted.

Amendment IX (1791)

The enumeration in the Constitution, of certain rights, shall not be construed to deny or disparage others retained by the people.

Amendment X (1791)

The powers not delegated to the United States by the Constitution, nor prohibited by it to the States, are reserved to the States respectively, or to the people.

Amendment XI (1798)

The Judicial power of the United States shall not be construed to extend to any suit in law or equity, commenced or prosecuted against one of the United States by Citizens of another State, or by Citizens or Subjects of any Foreign State.

Amendment XII (1804)

The Electors shall meet in their respective states and vote by ballot for President and Vice President, one of whom, at least, shall not be an inhabitant of the same state with themselves; they shall name in their ballots the person voted for as President, and in distinct ballots the person voted for as Vice-President, and they shall make distinct lists of all persons voted for as President, and of all persons voted for as Vice-President, and of the number of votes for each, which lists they shall sign and certify, and transmit sealed to the seat of the government of the United States, directed to the President of the Senate;—The President of the Senate shall, in the presence of the Senate and House of Representatives, open all the certificates and the votes shall then be counted;—The person having the greatest number of votes for President, shall be the President, if such number be a majority of the whole number of Electors appointed; and if no person have such majority, then from the persons having the highest numbers not exceeding three on the list of those voted for as President, the House of Representatives shall choose immediately, by ballot, the President. But in choosing the President, the votes shall be taken by states, the representation from each state having one vote; a quorum for this purpose shall consist of a member or members from two-thirds of the states, and a majority of all the states shall be necessary to a choice. And if the House of Representatives shall not choose a President whenever the right of choice shall devolve upon them, before the fourth day of March next following, then the Vice-President shall act as President, as in the case of the death or other constitutional disability of the President—The person having the greatest number of votes as Vice-President, shall be the Vice-President, if such number be a majority of the whole number of Electors appointed, and if no person have a majority, then from the two highest numbers on the list, the Senate shall choose the Vice-President; a quorum for the purpose shall consist of two-thirds of the whole numbers of Senators, and a majority of the whole number shall be necessary to a choice. But no person constitutionally ineligible to the office of President shall be eligible to that of Vice President of the United States.

Amendment XIII (1865)

Section 1
Neither slavery nor involuntary servitude, except as a punishment for crime whereof the party shall have been duly convicted, shall exist within the United States, or any place subject to their jurisdiction.

Section 2
Congress shall have power to enforce this article by appropriate legislation.

Amendment XIV (1868)

Section 1
All persons born or naturalized in the United States and subject to the jurisdiction thereof, are citizens of the United States and of the State wherein they reside. No State shall make or enforce any law which shall abridge the privileges or immunities of citizens of the United States; nor shall any State deprive any person of life, liberty, or property, without due process of law; nor deny to any person within its jurisdiction the equal protection of the laws.

Section 2
Representatives shall be apportioned among the several States according to their respective numbers, counting the whole number of persons in each State, excluding Indians not taxed. But when the right to vote at any election for the choice of electors for President and Vice President of the United States, Representatives in Congress, the Executive and Judicial officers of a State, or the members of the Legislature thereof, is denied to any of the male inhabitants of such State, being twenty-one years of age, and citizens of the United States, or in any way abridged, except for participation in rebellion, or other crime, the basis of representation therein shall be reduced in the proportion which the number of such male citizens shall bear to the whole number of male citizens twenty-one years of age in such State.

Section 3
No person shall be a Senator or Representative in Congress, or elector of President and Vice President, or hold any office, civil or military, under the United States, or under any State, who, having previously taken an oath, as a member of Congress, or as an officer of the United States, or as a member of any State legislature, or as an executive or judicial officer of any State, to support the Constitution of the United States, shall have engaged in insurrection or rebellion against the same, or given aid or comfort to the enemies thereof. But Congress may by a vote of two-thirds of each House, remove such disability.

Section 4
The validity of the public debt of the United States, authorized by law, including debts incurred for payment of pensions and bounties for services in suppressing insurrection or rebellion, shall not be questioned. But neither the United States nor any State shall assume or pay any debt or obligation incurred in aid of insurrection or rebellion against the United States, or any claim for the loss or emancipation of any slave; but all such debts, obligations and claims shall be held illegal and void.

Section 5
The Congress shall have power to enforce, by appropriate legislation, the provisions of this article.

Amendment XV (1870)

Section 1
The right of citizens of the United States to vote shall not be denied or abridged by the United States or by any State on account of race, color, or previous condition of servitude.

Section 2
The Congress shall have power to enforce this article by appropriate legislation.

Amendment XVI (1913)

The Congress shall have power to lay and collect taxes on incomes, from whatever source derived, without apportionment among the several States, and without regard to any census or enumeration.

Amendment XVII (1913)

The Senate of the United States shall be composed of two Senators from each State, elected by the people thereof, for six years; and each Senator shall have one vote. The electors in each State shall have the qualifications requisite for electors of the most numerous branch of the State legislatures.

When vacancies happen in the representation of any State in the Senate, the executive authority of such State shall issue writs of election to fill such vacancies: *Provided,* That the legislature of any State may empower the executive thereof to make temporary appointments until the people fill the vacancies by election as the legislature may direct.

This amendment shall not be so construed as to affect the election or term of any Senator chosen before it becomes valid as part of the Constitution.

Amendment XVIII (1919)

Section 1
After one year from the ratification of this article the manufacture, sale, or transportation of intoxicating liquors within, the importation thereof into, or the exportation thereof from the United States and all territory subject to the jurisdiction thereof for beverage purposes is hereby prohibited.

Section 2
The Congress and the several States shall have concurrent power to enforce this article by appropriate legislation.

Section 3
This article shall be inoperative unless it shall have been ratified as an amendment to the Constitution by the legislatures of the several States, as provided in the Constitution, within seven years from the date of the submission hereof to the States by the Congress.

Amendment XIX (1920)

The right of citizens of the United States to vote shall not be denied or abridged by the United States or by any State on account of sex.

Congress shall have power to enforce this article by appropriate legislation.

Amendment XX (1933)

Section 1
The terms of the President and Vice President shall end at noon on the 20th day of January, and the terms of Senators and Representatives at noon on the 3d day of January, of the years in which such terms would have ended if this article had not been ratified; and the terms of their successors shall then begin.

Section 2
The Congress shall assemble at least once in every year, and such meeting shall begin at noon on the 3d day of January, unless they shall by law appoint a different day.

Section 3
If, at the time fixed for the beginning of the term of the President, the President elect shall have died, the Vice President elect shall be come President. If a President shall not have been chosen before the time fixed for the beginning of his term, or if the President elect shall have failed to qualify, then the Vice President elect shall act as President until a President shall have qualified; and the Congress may by law provide for the case wherein neither a President elect nor a Vice President elect shall have qualified, declaring who shall then act as President, or the manner in which one who is to act shall be selected, and such person shall act accordingly until a President or Vice President shall have qualified.

Section 4
The Congress may by law provide for the case of the death of any of the persons from whom the House of Representatives may choose a President whenever the right of choice shall have devolved upon them, and for the case of the death of any of the persons from whom the Senate may choose a Vice President whenever the right of choice shall have devolved upon them.

Section 5
Sections 1 and 2 shall take effect on the 15th day of October following the ratification of this article.

Section 6
This article shall be inoperative unless it shall have been ratified as an amendment to the Constitution by the legislatures of three fourths of the several States within seven years from the date of its submission.

Amendment XXI (1933)

Section 1
The eighteenth article of amendment to the Constitution of the United States is hereby repealed.

Section 2
The transportation or importation into any State, Territory, or possession of the United States for delivery or use therein of intoxicating liquors, in violation of the laws thereof, is hereby prohibited.

Section 3
This article shall be inoperative unless it shall have been ratified as an amendment to the Constitution

by conventions in the several States, as provided in the Constitution, within seven years from the date of the submission hereof to the States by the Congress.

Amendment XXII (1951)

Section 1

No person shall be elected to the office of the President more than twice, and no person, who has held the office of President, or acted as President, for more than two years of a term to which some other person was elected President shall be elected to the Office of the President more than once. But this Article shall not apply to any person holding the office of President when this Article was proposed by the Congress, and shall not prevent any person who may be holding the office of President, or acting as President, during the term within which this Article becomes operative from holding the Office of President or acting as President during the remainder of such term.

Section 2

This article shall be inoperative unless it shall have been ratified as an amendment to the Constitution by the legislatures of three fourths of the several States within seven years from the date of its submission to the States by the Congress.

Amendment XXIII (1961)

Section 1

The District constituting the seat of Government of the United States shall appoint in such manner as the Congress may direct:

A number of electors of President and Vice President equal to the whole number of Senators and Representatives in Congress to which the District would be entitled if it were a State, but in no event more than the least populous State; they shall be in addition to those appointed by the States, but they shall be considered, for the purposes of the election of President and Vice President, to be electors appointed by a State; and they shall meet in the District and perform such duties as provided by the twelfth article of amendment.

Section 2

The Congress shall have power to enforce this article by appropriate legislation.

Amendment XXIV (1964)

Section 1

The right of citizens of the United States to vote in any primary or other election for President or Vice President, for electors for President or Vice President, or for Senator or Representative in Congress, shall not be denied or abridged by the United States or any State by reason of failure to pay any poll tax or other tax.

Section 2

The Congress shall have power to enforce this article by appropriate legislation.

Amendment XXV (1967)

Section 1

In case of the removal of the President from office or of his death or resignation, the Vice President shall become President.

Section 2

Whenever there is a vacancy in the office of the Vice President, the President shall nominate a Vice President who shall take office upon confirmation by a majority vote of both Houses of Congress.

Section 3

Whenever the President transmits to the President pro tempore of the Senate and the Speaker of the House of Representatives his written declaration that he is unable to discharge the powers and duties of his office, and until he transmits to them a written declaration to the contrary, such powers and duties shall be discharged by the Vice President as Acting President.

Section 4

Whenever the Vice President and a majority of either the principal officers of the executive departments or of such other body as Congress may by law provide, transmit to the President pro tempore of the Senate and the Speaker of the House of Representatives their written declaration that the President is unable to discharge the powers and duties of his office, the Vice President shall immediately assume the powers and duties of the office as Acting President.

Thereafter, when the President transmits to the President pro tempore of the Senate and the Speaker of the House of Representatives his written declaration that no inability exists, he shall resume the powers and duties of his Office unless the Vice President and a majority of either the principal officers of the executive department or of such other body as Congress may by law provide, transmit within four days to the President pro tempore of the Senate and the Speaker of the House of Representatives their written declaration that the President is unable to discharge the powers and duties of his office. Thereupon Congress shall decide the issue, assembling within forty-eight hours for that purpose if not in session. If the Congress, within twenty-one days after receipt of the latter written declaration, or, if Congress is not in session, within twenty-one days after Congress is required to assemble, determines by two-thirds vote of both Houses that the President is unable to discharge the powers and duties of his office, the Vice President shall continue to discharge the same as Acting President; otherwise, the President shall resume the powers and duties of his office.

Amendment XXVI (1971)

Section 1
The right of citizens of the United States, who are eighteen years of age or older, to vote shall not be denied or abridged by the United States or by any State on account of age.

Section 2
The Congress shall have power to enforce this article by appropriate legislation.

Amendment XXVII (1992)

No law varying the compensation for services of the Senators and Representatives shall take effect until an election of representatives shall have intervened.

The Freedom of Information Act (FOIA) (Excerpts)

Section 552. Public Information; Agency Rules, Opinions, Orders, Records, and Proceedings (the Freedom of Information Act)

(a) Each agency shall make available to the public information as follows:

(1) Each agency shall separately state and currently publish in the Federal Register for the guidance of the public—

(A) descriptions of its central and field organization and the established places at which, the employees (and in the case of a uniformed service, the members) from whom, and the methods whereby, the public may obtain information, make submittals or requests, or obtain decisions;

(B) statements of the general course and method by which its functions are channeled and determined, including the nature and requirements of all formal and informal procedures available;

(C) rules of procedure, descriptions of forms available or the places at which forms may be obtained, and instructions as to the scope and contents of all papers, reports, or examinations;

(D) substantive rules of general applicability adopted as authorized by law, and statements of general policy or interpretations of general applicability formulated and adopted by the agency; and

(E) each amendment, revision, or repeal of the foregoing.

Section 552b. Open Meetings ("Sunshine Law")

(a) For purposes of this section—

(1) the term "agency" means any agency, as defined in section 552 (e) of this title, headed by a collegial body composed of two or more individual members, a majority of whom are appointed to such position by the President with the advice and consent of the Senate, and any subdivision thereof authorized to act on behalf of the agency;

(2) the term "meeting" means the deliberations of at least the number of individual agency members required to take action on behalf of the agency where such deliberations determine or result in the joint conduct or disposition of official agency business, but does not include deliberations required or permitted by subsection (d) or (e); and

(3) the term "member" means an individual who belongs to a collegial body heading an agency.

(b) Members shall not jointly conduct or dispose of agency business other than in accordance with this section.

Section 553. Rule Making

(c) After notice required by this section, the agency shall give interested persons an opportunity to participate in the rule making through submission of written data, views, or arguments with or without opportunity for oral presentation. After consideration of the relevant matter presented, the agency shall incorporate in the rules adopted a concise general statement of their basis and purpose. When rules are required by statute to be made on the record after opportunity for an agency hearing, sections 556 and 557 of this title apply instead of this subsection.

(d) The required publication or service of a substantive rule shall be made not less than 30 days before its effective date, except—

(1) a substantive rule which grants or recognizes an exemption or relieves a restriction;

(2) interpretive rules and statements of policy; or

(3) as otherwise provided by the agency for good cause found and published with the rule.

(e) Each agency shall give an interested person the right to petition for the issuance, amendment, or repeal of a rule.

Section 603. Initial Regulatory Flexibility Analysis

(a) Whenever an agency is required by section 553 of this title, or any other law, to publish general notice of proposed rulemaking for any proposed rule, the agency shall prepare and make available for public comment an initial regulatory flexibility analysis. Such analysis shall describe the impact of the proposed rule on small entities. The initial regulatory flexibility analysis or a summary shall be published in the Federal Register at the time of the publication of general notice of proposed rulemaking for the rule. The agency shall transmit a copy of the initial regulatory flexibility analysis to the Chief Counsel for Advocacy of the Small Business Administration.

(b) Each initial regulatory flexibility analysis required under this section shall contain—

(1) a description of the reasons why action by the agency is being considered;

(2) a succinct statement of the objectives of, and legal basis for, the proposed rule;

(3) a description of and, where feasible, an estimate of the number of small entities to which the proposed rule will apply;

(4) a description of the projected reporting, recordkeeping and other compliance requirements of the proposed rule, including an estimate of the classes of small entities which will be subject to the requirement and the type of professional skills necessary for preparation of the report or record;

(5) an identification, to the extent practicable, of all relevant Federal rules which may duplicate, overlap or conflict with the proposed rule.

(c) Each initial regulatory flexibility analysis shall also contain a description of any significant alternatives to the proposed rule which accomplish the stated objectives of applicable statutes and which minimize any significant economic impact of the proposed rule on small entities. Consistent with the stated objectives of applicable statutes, the analysis shall discuss significant alternatives such as—

(1) the establishment of differing compliance or reporting requirements or timetables that take into account the resources available to small entities;

(2) the clarification, consolidation, or simplification of compliance and reporting requirements under the rule for such small entities;

(3) the use of performance rather than design standards; and

(4) the exemption from coverage of the rule, or any part thereof, for such small entities.

Title VII of the Civil Rights Act (Employment Provisions) (Excerpts)

Section 703. Unlawful Employment Practices

Employer Practices

(a) It shall be an unlawful employment practice for an employer—

(1) to fail or refuse to hire or to discharge any individual, or otherwise to discriminate against any individual with respect to his compensation, terms, conditions, or privileges of employment, because of such individual's race, color, religion, sex, or national origin; or

(2) to limit, segregate, or classify his employees or applicants for employment in any way which would deprive or tend to deprive any individual of employment opportunities or otherwise adversely affect his status as an employee, because of such individual's race, color, religion, sex, or national origin.

Employment Agency Practices

(b) It shall be an unlawful employment practice for an employment agency to fail or refuse to refer for employment, or otherwise to discriminate against, any individual because of his race, color, religion, sex, or national origin, or to classify or refer for employment any individual on the basis of his race, color, religion, sex, or national origin.

Labor Organization Practices

(c) It shall be an unlawful employment practice for a labor organization—

(1) to exclude or to expel from its membership, or otherwise to discriminate against, any individual because of his race, color, religion, sex, or national origin;

(2) to limit, segregate, or classify its membership or applicants for membership, or to classify or fail or refuse to refer to employment any individual, in any way which would deprive or tend to deprive any individual of employment opportunities, or would limit such employment opportunities or otherwise adversely affect his status as an employee or as an applicant for employment, because of such individual's race, color, religion, sex, or national origin; or

(3) to cause or attempt to cause an employer to discriminate against an individual in violation of this section.

Training Programs

(d) It shall be an unlawful employment practice for any employer, labor organization, or joint labor-management committee, controlling apprenticeship or other training or retraining, including on-the-job training programs to discriminate against any individual because of his race, color, religion, sex, or national origin in admission to, or employment in, any program established to provide apprenticeship or other training.

Businesses or Enterprises with Personnel Qualified on Basis of Religion, Sex, or National Origin; Educational Institutions with Personnel of Particular Religion

(e) Notwithstanding any other provision of this subchapter, (1) it shall not be an unlawful employment practice for an employer to hire and employ employees, for an employment agency to classify or refer for employment any individual, for a labor organization to classify its membership or to classify or refer for employment any individual, or for an employer, labor organization, or joint labor-management committee controlling apprenticeship or other training or retraining programs to admit or employ any individual in any such program, on the basis of his religion, sex, or national origin in those certain instances where religion, sex, or national origin is a bona fide occupational qualification reasonably necessary to the normal operation of that particular business or enterprise, and (2) it shall not be an unlawful employment practice for a school, college, university, or other educational institution or institution of learning to hire and employ employees of a particular religion if such school, college, university, or other educational institution or institution of learning is, in whole or in substantial part, owned, supported, controlled, or managed by a particular religion or by a particular religious corporation, association, or society, or if the curriculum of such school, college, university, or other educational institution or institution of learning is directed toward the propagation of a particular religion.

Seniority or Merit System; Quantity or Quality of Production, Ability Tests; Compensation Based on Sex and Authorized by Minimum Wage Provisions

(h) Notwithstanding any other provisions of this subchapter, it shall not be an unlawful employment practice for an employer to apply different standards of compensation, or different terms, conditions, or privileges of employment pursuant to a bona fide seniority or merit system, or a system which measures earnings by quantity or quality of production or to employees who work in different locations, provided that such differences are not the result of an intention to discriminate because of race, color, religion, sex, or national origin, nor shall it be an unlawful employment practice for an employer to give and to act upon the results of any professionally developed ability test provided that such test, its administration or action upon the results is not designed, intended or used to discriminate because of race, color, religion, sex, or national origin. It shall not be an unlawful employment practice under this subchapter for any employer to differentiate upon the basis of sex in determining the amount of the wages or compensation paid or to be paid to employees of such employer if such differentiation is authorized by the provisions of section 206(d) of Title 29.

Section 704. Other Unlawful Employment Practices

Discrimination for Making Charges, Testifying, Assisting, or Participating in Enforcement Proceedings

(a) It shall be an unlawful employment practice for an employer to discriminate against any of his employees or applicants for employment, for an employment agency, or joint labor-management committee controlling apprenticeship or other training or retraining, including on-the-job training programs to discriminate against any individual, or for a labor organization to discriminate against any member thereof or applicant for membership, because he has opposed any practice, made an unlawful employment practice by this subchapter, or because he has made a charge, testified, assisted, or participated in any manner in an investigation, proceeding, or hearing under this subchapter.

Printing or Publication of Notices or Advertisements Indicating Prohibited Preference, Limitation, Specification, or Discrimination; Occupational Qualification Exception

(b) It shall be an unlawful employment practice for an employer, labor organization, employment agency, or joint labor-management committee controlling apprenticeship or other training or retraining, including on-the-job training programs, to print or publish or cause to be printed or published any notice or advertisement relating to employment by such an employer or membership in or any classification or referral for employment by such a labor organization, or relating to any classification or referral for employment by such an employment agency, or relating to admission to, or employment in, any program established to provide apprenticeship or other training by such a joint labor-management committee, indicating any preference, limitation, specification, or discrimination, based on race, color, religion, sex, or national origin, except that such a notice or advertisement may indicate a preference, limitation, specification, or discrimination based on religion, sex, or national origin when religion, sex, or national origin is a bona fide occupational qualification for employment.

The Civil Rights Act (Excerpts)

§ 1981. Equal rights under the law

(a) All persons within the jurisdiction of the United States shall have the same right in every State and Territory to make and enforce contracts, to sue, be parties, give evidence, and to the full and equal benefit of all laws and proceedings for the security of persons and property as is enjoyed by white citizens, and shall be subject to like punishment, pains, penalties, taxes, licenses, and exactions of every kind, and to no other.

(b) For purposes of this section, the term "make and enforce contracts" includes the making, performance, modification, and termination of contracts, and the enjoyment of all benefits, privileges, terms, and conditions of the contractual relationship.

(c) The rights protected by this section are protected against impairment by nongovernmental discrimination and impairment under color of State law.

§ 1981a. Damages in cases of intentional discrimination in employment

(a) Right of recovery. (1) Civil rights. In an action brought by a complaining party under section 706 or 717 of the Civil Rights Act of 1964 (42 U.S.C. § 2000e-5 [or 2000e-16]) against a respondent who engaged in unlawful intentional discrimination (not an employment practice that is unlawful because of its disparate impact) prohibited under section 703, 704, or 717 of the Act (42 U.S.C. § 2000e-2 or 2000e-3 [or 2000e-16]), and provided that the complaining party cannot recover under section 1977 of the Revised Statutes (42 U.S.C. § 1981), the complaining party may recover compensatory and punitive damages as allowed in subsection (b), in addition to any relief authorized by section 706(g) of the Civil Rights Act of 1964 [42 USCS § 2000e-5(g)], from the respondent.

The Americans with Disabilities Act (Excerpts)

Title I—Employment

Sec. 101. Definitions.
As used in this title: . . .

(8) Qualified individual with a disability.—The term "qualified individual with a disability" means an individual with a disability who, with or without reasonable accommodation, can perform the essential functions of the employment position that such individual holds or desires. For the purposes of this title, consideration shall be given to the employer's judgment as to what functions of a job are essential, and if an employer has prepared a written description before advertising or interviewing applicants for the job, this description shall be considered evidence of the essential functions of the job.

(9) Reasonable accommodation.—The term "reasonable accommodation" may include—
  (A) making existing facilities used by employees readily accessible to and usable by individuals with disabilities; and
  (B) job restructuring, part-time or modified work schedules, reassignment to a vacant position, acquisition or modification of equipment or devices, appropriate adjustment or modifications of examinations, training materials or policies, the provision of qualified readers or interpreters, and other similar accommodations for individuals with disabilities.

(10) Undue Hardship.—
(A) In general.—The term "undue hardship" means an action requiring significant difficulty or expense, when considered in light of the factors set forth in subparagraph (B).

(B) Factors to be considered.—In determining whether an accommodation would impose an undue hardship on a covered entity, factors to be considered include—
  (i) the nature and cost of accommodation needed under this Act;
  (ii) the overall financial resources of the facility or facilities involved in the provision of the reasonable accommodation; the number of persons employed at such facility; the effect on expenses and resources, or the impact otherwise of such accommodation upon the operation of the facility;
  (iii) the overall financial resources of the covered entity; the overall size of the business of a covered entity with respect to the number of its employees; the number, type, and location of its facilities; and
  (iv) the type of operation or operations of the covered entity, including the composition, structure, and functions of the workforce of such entity; the geographic separateness, administrative, or fiscal relationship of the facility or facilities in question to the covered entity.

Sec. 102. Discrimination.
(a) General Rule.—No covered entity shall discriminate against a qualified individual with a disability because of the disability of such individual in regard to job application procedures, the hiring, advancement, or discharge of employees, employee compensation, job training, and other terms, conditions, and privileges of employment.

(b) Construction.—As used in subsection (a), the term "discriminate" includes—

(1) limiting, segregating, or classifying a job applicant or employee in a way that adversely affects the opportunities or status of such applicant or employee because of the disability of such applicant or employee;

(2) participating in a contractual or other arrangement or relationship that has the effect of subjecting a covered entity's qualified applicant or employee with a disability to the discrimination prohibited by this title (such relationship includes a relationship with an employment or referral agency, labor union, an organization providing fringe benefits to an employee of the covered entity, or an organization providing training and apprenticeship programs);

(3) utilizing standards, criteria, or methods of administration—

(A) that have the effect of discrimination on the basis of disability; or

(B) that perpetuate the discrimination of others who are subject to common administrative control;

(4) excluding or otherwise denying equal jobs or benefits to a qualified individual because of the known disability of an individual with whom the qualified individual is known to have a relationship or association;

(5) (A) not making reasonable accommodations to the known physical or mental limitations of an otherwise qualified individual with a disability who is an applicant or employee, unless such covered entity can demonstrate that the accommodation would impose an undue hardship on the operation of the business of such covered entity; or

(B) denying employment opportunities to a job applicant or employee who is an otherwise qualified individual with a disability, if such denial is based on the need of such covered entity to make reasonable accommodation to the physical or mental impairments of the employee or applicant;

(6) using qualification standards, employment tests or other selection criteria that screen out or tend to screen out an individual with a disability or a class of individuals with disabilities unless the standard, test or other selection criteria, as used by the covered entity, is shown to be job-related for the position in question and is consistent with business necessity; and

(7) failing to select and administer tests concerning employment in the most effective manner to ensure that, when such test is administered to a job applicant or employee who has a disability that impairs sensory, manual, or speaking skills, such test results accurately reflect the skills, aptitude, or whatever other factor of such applicant or employee that such test purports to measure, rather than reflecting the impaired sensory, manual, or speaking skills of such employee or applicant (except where such skills are the factors that the test purports to measure). . . .

Sec. 104. Illegal Use of Drugs and Alcohol. . . .

(b) Rules of Construction.—Nothing in subsection (a) shall be construed to exclude as a qualified individual with a disability an individual who—

(1) has successfully completed a supervised drug rehabilitation program and is no longer engaging in the illegal use of drugs, or has otherwise been rehabilitated successfully and is no longer engaging in such use;

(2) is participating in a supervised rehabilitation program and is no longer engaging in such use; or

(3) is erroneously regarded as engaging in such use, but is not engaging in such use; except that it shall not be a violation of this Act for a covered entity to adopt or administer reasonable policies or procedures, including but not limited to drug testing, designed to ensure that an individual described in paragraph (1) or (2) is no longer engaging in the illegal use of drugs. . . .

The Family and Medical Leave Act (Excerpts)

29 U.S.C. § 2601 *et seq.*

§ 2601. Findings and purposes

(a) Findings

Congress finds that—

(1) the number of single-parent households and two-parent households in which the single parent or both parents work is increasing significantly;

(2) it is important for the development of children and the family unit that fathers and mothers be able to participate in early childrearing and the care of family members who have serious health conditions;

(3) the lack of employment policies to accommodate working parents can force individuals to choose between job security and parenting;

(4) there is inadequate job security for employees who have serious health conditions that prevent them from working for temporary periods;

(5) due to the nature of the roles of men and women in our society, the primary responsibility for family caretaking often falls on women, and such responsibility affects the working lives of women more than it affects the working lives of men; and

(6) employment standards that apply to one gender only have serious potential for encouraging employers to discriminate against employees and applicants for employment who are of that gender.

(b) Purposes

It is the purpose of this Act—

(1) to balance the demands of the workplace with the needs of families, to promote the stability and economic security of families, and to promote national interests in preserving family integrity;

(2) to entitle employees to take reasonable leave for medical reasons, for the birth or adoption of a child, and for the care of a child, spouse, or parent who has a serious health condition;

(3) to accomplish the purposes described in paragraphs (1) and (2) in a manner that accommodates the legitimate interests of employers;

(4) to accomplish the purposes described in paragraphs (1) and (2) in a manner that, consistent with the Equal Protection Clause of the Fourteenth Amendment, minimizes the potential for employment discrimination on the basis of sex by ensuring generally that leave is available for eligible medical reasons (including maternity-related disability) and for compelling family reasons, on a gender-neutral basis; and

(5) to promote the goal of equal employment opportunity for women and men, pursuant to such clause.

§ 2611. Definitions

(2) Eligible employee

(A) In general
The term "eligible employee" means an employee who has been employed—

(i) for at least 12 months by the employer with respect to whom leave is requested under section 2612 of this title; and

(ii) for at least 1,250 hours of service with such employer during the previous 12-month period.

(B) Exclusions
The term "eligible employee" does not include—

(i) any Federal officer or employee covered under subchapter V of chapter 63 of Title 5; or

(ii) any employee of an employer who is employed at a worksite at which such employer employs less than 50 employees if the total number of employees employed by that employer within 75 miles of that worksite is less than 50.

§ 2612. Leave requirement

(a) In general

(1) Entitlement to leave

Subject to section 2613 of this title, an eligible employee shall be entitled to a total of 12 workweeks of leave during any 12-month period for one or more of the following:

(A) Because of the birth of a son or daughter of the employee and in order to care for such son or daughter.

(B) Because of the placement of a son or daughter with the employee for adoption or foster care.

(C) In order to care for the spouse, or a son, daughter, or parent, of the employee, if such spouse, son, daughter, or parent has a serious health condition.

(D) Because of a serious health condition that makes the employee unable to perform the functions of the position of such employee.

(2) Expiration of entitlement

The entitlement to leave under subparagraphs (A) and (B) of paragraph (1) for a birth or placement of a son or daughter shall expire at the end of the 12-month period beginning on the date of such birth or placement.

(b) Leave taken intermittently or on a reduced leave schedule

(1) In general

Leave under subparagraph (A) or (B) of subsection (a)(1) of this section shall not be taken by an employee intermittently or on a reduced leave schedule unless the employee and the employer of the employee agree otherwise. Subject to paragraph (2), subsection (e)(2) of this section, and section 2613(b)(5) of this title, leave under subparagraph (C) or (D) of subsection (a)(1) of this section may be taken intermittently or on a reduced leave schedule when medically necessary. The taking of leave intermittently or on a reduced leave schedule pursuant to this paragraph shall not result in a reduction in the total amount of leave to which the employee is entitled under subsection (a) of this section beyond the amount of leave actually taken.

(2) Alternative position

If an employee requests intermittent leave, or leave on a reduced leave schedule, under subparagraph (C) or (D) of subsection (a)(1) of this section, that is foreseeable based on planned medical treatment, the employer may require such employee to transfer temporarily to an available alternative position offered by the employer for which the employee is qualified and that—

(A) has equivalent pay and benefits; and

(B) better accommodates recurring periods of leave than the regular employment position of the employee.

(c) Unpaid leave permitted

Except as provided in subsection (d) of this section, leave granted under subsection (a) of this section may consist of unpaid leave. Where an employee is otherwise exempt under regulations issued by the Secretary pursuant to section 2613(a)(1) of this title, the compliance of an employer with this subchapter by providing unpaid leave shall not affect the exempt status of the employee under such section.

(d) Relationship to paid leave

(1) Unpaid leave

If an employer provides paid leave for fewer than 12 workweeks, the additional weeks of leave necessary to attain the 12 workweeks of leave required under this subchapter may be provided without compensation.

(2) Substitution of paid leave

(A) In general

An eligible employee may elect, or an employer may require the employee, to substitute any of the accrued paid vacation leave, personal leave, or family leave of the employee for leave provided under subparagraph (A), (B), or (C) of subsection (a)(1) of this section for any part of the 12-week period of such leave under such subsection.

(B) Serious health condition

An eligible employee may elect, or an employer may require the employee, to substitute any of the accrued paid vacation leave, personal leave, or medical or sick leave of the employee for leave provided under subparagraph (C) or (D) of subsection (a)(1) of this section for any part of the 12-week period of such leave under such subsection, except that nothing in this subchapter shall require an employer to provide paid sick leave or paid medical leave in any situation in which such employer would not normally provide any such paid leave.

§ 2614. Employment and benefits protection

(a) Restoration to position
(1) In general

Except as provided in subsection (b) of this section, any eligible employee who takes leave under section 2612 of this title for the intended purpose of the leave shall be entitled, on return from such leave—

(A) to be restored by the employer to the position of employment held by the employee when the leave commenced; or

(B) to be restored to an equivalent position with equivalent employment benefits, pay, and other terms and conditions of employment.

(2) Loss of benefits

The taking of leave under section 2612 of this title shall not result in the loss of any employment benefit accrued prior to the date on which the leave commenced.

(3) Limitations

Nothing to this section shall be construed to entitle any restored employee to—

(A) the accrual of any seniority or employment benefits during any period of leave; or

(B) any right, benefit, or position of employment other than any right, benefit, or position to which the employee would have been entitled had the employee not taken the leave.

§ 2617. Enforcement

(a) Civil action by employees
(1) Liability

Any employer who violates section 2615 of this title shall be liable to any eligible employee affected—

(A) for damages equal to—

(i) the amount of—

(I) any wages, salary, employment benefits, or other compensation denied or lost to such employee by reason of the violation; or

(II) in a case in which wages, salary, employment benefits, or other compensation have not been denied or lost to the employee, any actual monetary losses sustained by the employee as a direct result of the violation, such as the cost of providing care, up to a sum equal to 12 weeks of wages or salary for the employee;

(ii) the interest on the amount described in clause (I) calculated at the prevailing rate; and

(iii) an additional amount as liquidated damages equal to the sum of the amount described in clause (I) and the interest described in clause (ii), except that if an employer who has violated section 2615 of this title proves to the satisfaction of the court that the act or omission which violated section 2615 of this title was in good faith and that the employer had reasonable grounds for believing that the act or omission was not a violation of section 2615 of this title, such court may, in the discretion of the court, reduce the amount of the liability to the amount and interest determined under clauses (i) and (ii), respectively; and

(B) for such equitable relief as may be appropriate, including employment reinstatement, and promotion.

The Uniform Commercial Code (Excerpts)*

ARTICLE I GENERAL PROVISIONS
Part 1 Short Title, Construction, Application and Subject Matter of the Act

Section I—203. Obligation of Good Faith

Every contract or duty within this Act imposes an obligation of good faith in its performance or enforcement.

Section 1—205. Course of Dealing and Usage of Trade

(1) A course of dealing is a sequence of previous conduct between the parties to a particular transaction which is fairly to be regarded as establishing a common basis of understanding for interpreting their expressions and other conduct.

(2) A usage of trade is any practice or method of dealing having such regularity of observance in a place, vocation or trade as to justify an expectation that it will be observed with respect to the transaction in question. The existence and scope of such a usage are to be proved as facts. If it is established that such a usage is embodied in a written trade code or similar writing the interpretation of the writing is for the court.

(3) A course of dealing between parties and any usage of trade in the vocation or trade in which they are engaged or of which they are or should be aware give particular meaning to and supplement or qualify terms of an agreement.

(4) The express terms of an agreement and an applicable course of dealing or usage of trade shall be construed wherever reasonable as consistent with each other; but when such construction is unreasonable express terms control both course of dealing and usage of trade and course of dealing controls usage of trade.

(5) An applicable usage of trade in the place where any part of performance is to occur shall be used in interpreting the agreement as to that part of the performance.

(6) Evidence of a relevant usage of trade offered by one party is not admissible unless and until he has given the other party such notice as the court finds sufficient to prevent unfair surprise to the latter.

Section 1—206. Statute of Frauds for Kinds of Personal Property Not Otherwise Covered

(1) Except in the cases described in subsection (2) of this section a contract for the sale of personal property is not enforceable by way of action or defense beyond five thousand dollars in amount or value of remedy unless there is some writing which indicates that a contract for sale has been made between the parties at a defined or stated price, reasonably identifies the subject matter, and is signed by the party against whom enforcement is sought or by his authorized agent.

(2) Subsection (1) of this section does not apply to contracts for the sale of goods (Section 2—201) nor of securities (Section 8—319) nor to security agreements (Section 9—203).

ARTICLE II SALES
Part 1 Short Title, General Construction and Subject Matter

Section 2—102. Scope; Certain Security and Other Transactions Excluded from this Article

Unless the context otherwise requires, this Article applies to transactions in goods; it does not apply to any transaction which although in the form of an unconditional contract to sell or present sale is intended to operate only as a security transaction nor does this Article impair or repeal any statute regulating sales to consumers, farmers or other specified classes of buyers.

Part 2 Form, Formation and Readjustment of Contract

Section 2—201. Formal Requirements; Statute of Frauds

(1) Except as otherwise provided in this section a contract for the sale of goods for the price of $500 or more is not enforceable by way of action or defense unless there is some writing sufficient to indicate that a contract for sale has been made between the parties and signed by the party against whom enforcement is sought or by his authorized agent or broker. A writing is not insufficient because it omits or incorrectly states a term agreed upon but the contract is not enforceable under this paragraph beyond the quantity of goods shown in such writing.

(2) Between merchants if within a reasonable time a writing in confirmation of the contract and sufficient against the sender is received and the party receiving it has reason to know its contents, it satisfies the requirements of subsection (1) against such party unless written notice of objection to its contents is given within 10 days after it is received.

(3) A contract which does not satisfy the requirements of subsection (1) but which is valid in other respects is enforceable

(a) if the goods are to be specially manufactured for the buyer and are not suitable for sale to others in the ordinary course of the seller's business and the seller, before notice of repudiation is received and under circumstances which reasonably indicate that the goods are for the buyer, has made either a substantial beginning of their manufacture or commitments for their procurement; or

(b) if the party against whom enforcement is sought admits in his pleading, testimony or otherwise in court that a contract for sale was made, but the contract is not enforceable under the provision beyond the quantity of goods admitted; or

(c) with respect to goods for which payment has been made and accepted or which have been received and accepted (Sec. 2—606).

Section 2—202. Final Written Expression: Parol or Extrinsic Evidence

Terms with respect to which the confirmatory memoranda of the parties agree or which are otherwise set forth in a writing intended by the parties as a final expression of their agreement with respect to such terms as are included therein may not be contradicted by evidence of any prior agreement or of a contemporaneous oral agreement but may be explained or supplemented

(a) by course of dealing or usage of trade (Section 1—205) or by course of performance (Section 2—208); and

(b) by evidence of consistent additional terms unless the court finds the writing to have been intended also as a complete and exclusive statement of the terms of the agreement.

Section 2—204. Formation in General

(1) A contract for sale of goods may be made in any manner sufficient to show agreement, including conduct by both parties which recognizes the existence of such a contract.

(2) An agreement sufficient to constitute a contract for sale may be found even though the moment of its making is undetermined.

(3) Even though one or more terms are left open a contract for sale does not fail for indefiniteness if the parties have intended to make a contract and there is a reasonably certain basis for giving an appropriate remedy.

Section 2—205. Firm Offers

An offer by a merchant to buy or sell goods in a signed writing which by its terms gives assurance that it will be held open is not revocable, for lack of consideration, during the time stated or if no time is stated for a reasonable time, but in no event may such period of irrevocability exceed three months; but any such term of assurance on a form supplied by the offeree must be separately signed by the offeror.

Section 2—206. Offer and Acceptance in Formation of Contract

(1) Unless otherwise unambiguously indicated by the language or circumstances

(a) an offer to make a contract shall be construed as inviting acceptance in any manner and by any medium reasonable in the circumstances;

(b) an order or other offer to buy goods for prompt or current shipment shall be construed as inviting acceptance either by a prompt promise to ship or by the prompt or current shipment of conforming or non-conforming goods, but such a shipment of non-conforming goods does not constitute an acceptance if the seller seasonably notifies the buyer that the shipment is offered only as an accommodation to the buyer.

(2) Where the beginning of a requested performance is a reasonable mode of acceptance an offeror who is not notified of acceptance within a reasonable time may treat the offer as having lapsed before acceptance.

Section 2—207. Additional Terms in Acceptance or Confirmation

(1) A definite and seasonable expression of acceptance or a written confirmation which is sent within a reasonable time operates as an acceptance even though it states terms additional to or different from those offered or agreed upon, unless acceptance is expressly made conditional on assent to the additional or different terms.

(2) The additional terms are to be construed as proposals for addition to the contract. Between merchants such terms become part of the contract unless:

(a) the offer expressly limits acceptance to the terms of the offer;

(b) they materially alter it; or

(c) notification of objection to them has already been given or is given within a reasonable time after notice of them is received.

(3) Conduct by both parties which recognizes the existence of a contract is sufficient to establish a contract for sale although the writings of the parties do not otherwise establish a contract. In such case the terms of the particular contract consist of those terms on which the writings of the parties agree, together with any supplementary terms incorporated under any other provisions of this Act.

Section 2—208. Course of Performance or Practical Construction

(1) Where the contract for sale involves repeated occasions for performance by either party with knowledge of the nature of the performance and opportunity for objection to it by the other, any course of performance accepted or acquiesced in without objection shall be relevant to determine the meaning of the agreement.

(2) The express terms of the agreement and any such course of performance, as well as any course of dealing and usage of trade, shall be construed whenever reasonable as consistent with each other; but when such construction is unreasonable, express terms shall control course of performance and course of performance shall control both course of dealing and usage of trade (Section 1—205).

(3) Subject to the provisions of the next section on modification and waiver, such course of performance shall be relevant to show a waiver or modification of any term inconsistent with such course of performance.

Part 3 General Obligation and Construction of Contract

Section 2—302. Unconscionable Contract or Clause

(1) If the court as a matter of law finds the contract or any clause of the contract to have been unconscionable at the time it was made the court may refuse to enforce the contract or it may enforce the remainder of the contract without the unconscionable clause, or it may so limit the application of any unconscionable clause as to avoid any unconscionable result.

(2) When it is claimed or appears to the court that the contract or any clause thereof may be unconscionable the parties shall be afforded a reasonable opportunity to present evidence as to its commercial setting, purpose and effect to aid the court in making the determination.

*Section 2—312. Warranty of Title and Against
Infringement; Buyer's Obligation Against
Infringement*

(1) Subject to subsection (2) there is in a contract
for sale a warranty by the seller that

   (a) the title conveyed shall be good, and its
transfer rightful; and

   (b) the goods shall be delivered free from any
security interest or other lien or encumbrance of
which the buyer at the time of contracting has no
knowledge.

   (2) A warranty under subsection (1) will be
excluded or modified only by specific language or
by circumstances which give the buyer reason to
know that the person selling does not claim title in
himself or that he is purporting to sell only such
right or title as he or a third person may have.

   (3) Unless otherwise agreed a seller who is a
merchant regularly dealing in goods of the kind
warrants that the goods shall be delivered free of
the rightful claim of any third person by way of
infringement or the like but a buyer who furnishes
specifications to the seller must hold the seller
harmless against any such claim which arises out
of compliance with the specifications.

*Section 2—313. Express Warranties by
Affirmation, Promise, Description, Sample*

(1) Express warranties by the seller are created as
follows:

   (a) Any affirmation of fact or promise made by
the seller to the buyer which relates to the goods
and becomes part of the basis of the bargain creates an express warranty that the goods shall conform to the affirmation or promise.

   (b) Any description of the goods which is made
part of the basis of the bargain creates an express
warranty that the goods shall conform to the
description.

   (c) Any sample or model which is made part of
the basis of the bargain creates an express warranty that the whole of the goods shall conform to
the sample or model.

   (2) It is not necessary to the creation of an
express warranty that the seller use formal words
such as "warrant" or "guarantee" or that he have
a specific intention to make a warranty, but an
affirmation merely of the value of the goods or a
statement purporting to be merely the seller's

opinion or commendation of the goods does not
create a warranty.

*Section 2—314. Implied Warranty:
Merchantability; Usage of Trade*

(1) Unless excluded or modified (Section 2—316),
a warranty that the goods shall be merchantable is
implied in a contract for their sale if the seller is a
merchant with respect to goods of that kind.
Under this section the serving for value of food or
drink to be consumed either on the premises or
elsewhere is a sale.

   (2) Goods to be merchantable must be at least
such as

   (a) pass without objection in the trade under
the contract description; and

   (b) in the case of fungible goods, are of fair
average quality within the description; and

   (c) are fit for the ordinary purposes for which
such goods are used; and

   (d) run, within the variations permitted by the
agreement, of even kind, quality and quantity
within each unit and among all units involved;
and

   (e) are adequately contained, packaged, and
labeled as the agreement may require; and

   (f) conform to the promises or affirmation of
fact made on the container or label if any.

   (3) Unless excluded or modified (Section 2—
316) other implied warranties may arise from
course of dealing or usage of trade.

*Section 2—315. Implied Warranty: Fitness
for Particular Purpose*

Where the seller at the time of contracting has reason to know any particular purpose for which the
goods are required and that the buyer is relying on
the seller's skill or judgment to select or furnish
suitable goods, there is unless excluded or modified under the next section an implied warranty
that the goods shall be fit for such purpose.

*Section 2—316. Exclusion or Modification
of Warranties*

(1) Words or conduct relevant to the creation of an
express warranty and words or conduct tending to
negate or limit warranty shall be construed wherever reasonable as consistent with each other; but
subject to the provisions of this Article on parol or

extrinsic evidence (Section 2—202) negation or limitation is inoperative to the extent that such construction is unreasonable.

(2) Subject to subsection (3), to exclude or modify the implied warranty of merchantability or any part of it the language must mention merchantability and in case of a writing must be conspicuous, and to exclude or modify any implied warranty of fitness the exclusion must be by a writing and conspicuous. Language to exclude all implied warranties of fitness is sufficient if it states, for example, that "There are no warranties which extend beyond the description of the face hereof."

(3) Notwithstanding subsection (2)

(a) unless the circumstances indicate otherwise, all implied warranties are excluded by expressions like "as is," "with all faults" or other language which in common understanding calls the buyer's attention to the exclusion of warranties and makes plain that there is no implied warranty; and

(b) when the buyer before entering into the contract has examined the goods or the sample or model as fully as he desired or has refused to examine the goods there is no implied warranty with regard to defects which an examination ought in the circumstances to have revealed to him; and

(c) an implied warranty can also be excluded or modified by course of dealing or course of performance or usage of trade.

(4) Remedies for breach of warranty can be limited in accordance with the provisions of this Article on liquidation or limitation of damages and on contractual modification of remedy (Sections 2—718 and 2—719).

Section 2—318. Third Party Beneficiaries of Warranties Express or Implied

Note: If this Act is introduced in the Congress of the United States this section should be omitted. (States to select one alternative.)

Alternative A

A seller's warranty whether express or implied extends to any natural person who is in the family or household of his buyer or who is a guest in his home if it is reasonable to expect that such person may use, consume or be affected by the goods and who is injured in person by breach of the warranty. A seller may not exclude or limit the operation of this section.

Alternative B

A seller's warranty whether express or implied extends to any natural person who may reasonably be expected to use, consume or be affected by the goods and who is injured in person by breach of the warranty. A seller may not exclude or limit the operation of this section.

Alternative C

A seller's warranty whether express or implied extends to any person who may reasonably be expected to use, consume or be affected by the goods and who is injured by breach of the warranty. A seller may not exclude or limit the operation of this section with respect to injury to the person of an individual to whom the warranty extends. As amended 1966.

Section 2—615. Excuse by Failure of Presupposed Conditions

Except so far as a seller may have assumed a greater obligation and subject to the preceding section on substituted performance:

(a) Delay in delivery or non-delivery in whole or in part by a seller who complies with paragraphs (b) and (c) is not a breach of his duty under a contract for sale if performance as agreed has been made impracticable by the occurrence of a contingency the nonoccurrence of which was a basic assumption on which the contract was made or by compliance in good faith with any applicable foreign or domestic governmental regulation or order whether or not it later proves to be invalid.

(b) Where the causes mentioned in paragraph (a) affect only a part of the seller's capacity to perform, he must allocate production and deliveries among his customers but may at his option include regular customers not then under contract as well as his own requirements for further manufacture. He may so allocate in any manner which is fair and reasonable.

(c) The seller must notify the buyer seasonably that there will be delay or non-delivery and, when allocation is required under paragraph (b), of the estimated quota thus made available for the buyer.

The Securities Act of 1933 and the Securities Exchange Act of 1934 (Excerpts)

Securities Act of 1933

Civil Liabilities on Account of False Registration Statement

SECTION 11. (a) In case any part of the registration statement, when such part became effective, contained an untrue statement of a material fact or omitted to state a material fact required to be stated therein or necessary to make the statements therein not misleading, any person acquiring such security (unless it is proved that at the time of such acquisition he knew of such untruth or omission) may, either at law or in equity, in any court of competent jurisdiction, sue—

(1) every person who signed the registration statement;

(2) every person who was a director of (or person performing similar functions) or partner in, the issuer at the time of the filing of the part of the registration statement with respect to which his liability is asserted;

(3) every person who, with his consent, is named in the registration statement as being or about to become a director, person performing similar functions, or partner;

(4) every accountant, engineer, or appraiser, or any person whose profession gives authority to a statement made by him, who has with his consent been named as having prepared or certified any part of the registration statement, or as having prepared or certified any report or valuation which is used in connection with the registration statement, with respect to the statement in such registration statement, report, or valuation, which purports to have been prepared or certified by him;

(5) every underwriter with respect to such security.

If such person acquired the security after the issuer has made generally available to its security holders an earning statement covering a period of at least twelve months beginning after the effective date of the registration statement, then the right of recovery under this subsection shall be conditioned on proof that such person acquired the security relying upon such untrue statement in the registration statement or relying upon the registration statement and not knowing of such omission, but such reliance may be established without proof of the reading of the registration statement by such person.

(b) Notwithstanding the provisions of subsection (a) no person, other than the issuer, shall be liable as provided therein who shall sustain the burden of proof—

(1) that before the effective date of the part of the registration statement with respect to which his liability is asserted (A) he had resigned from or had taken such steps as are permitted by law to resign from, or ceased or refused to act in, every office, capacity, or relationship in which he was described in the registration statement as acting or agreeing to act, and (B) he had advised the Commission and the issuer in writing that he had taken such action and that he would not be responsible for such part of the registration statement; or

(2) that if such part of the registration statement became effective without his knowledge, upon becoming aware of such fact he forthwith acted and advised the Commission, in accordance

with paragraph (1), and, in addition, gave reasonable public notice that such part of the registration statement had become effective without his knowledge; or

(3) that (A) as regards any part of the registration statement not purporting to be made on the authority of an expert, and not purporting to be a copy of or extract from a report or valuation of an expert, and not purporting to be made on the authority of a public or official document or statement, he had, after reasonable investigation, reasonable ground to believe and did believe, at the time such part of the registration statement became effective, that the statements therein were true and that there was no omission to state a material fact required to be stated therein or necessary to make the statements therein not misleading; and (B) as regards any part of the registration statement purporting to be made upon his authority as an expert or purporting to be a copy of or extract from a report or valuation of himself as an expert, (i) he had, after reasonable investigation, reasonable ground to believe and did believe, at the time such part of the registration statement became effective, that the statements therein were true and that there was no omission to state a material fact required to be stated therein or necessary to make the statements therein not misleading, or (ii) such part of the registration statement did not fairly represent his statement as an expert or was not a fair copy of or extract from his report or valuation as an expert; and (C) as regards any part of the registration statement purporting to be made on the authority of an expert (other than himself) or purporting to be a copy of or extract from a report or valuation of an expert (other than himself), he had no reasonable ground to believe and did not believe, at the time such part of the registration statement became effective, that the statements therein were untrue or that there was an omission to state a material fact required to be stated therein or necessary to make the statements therein not misleading, or that such part of the registration statement did not fairly represent the statement of the expert or was not a fair copy of or extract from the report or valuation of the expert; and (D) as regards any part of the registration statement purporting to be a statement made by an official person or purporting to be a copy of or extract from a public official document, he had no

reasonable ground to believe and did not believe, at the time such part of the registration statement became effective, that the statements therein were untrue, or that there was an omission to state a material fact required to be stated therein or necessary to make the statements therein not misleading, or that such part of the registration statement did not fairly represent the statement made by the official person or was not a fair copy of or extract from the public official document.

(c) In determining, for the purpose of paragraph (3) of subsection (b) of this section, what constitutes reasonable investigation and reasonable ground for belief, the standard of reasonableness shall be that required of a prudent man in the management of his own property.

Civil Liabilities Arising in Connection with Prospectuses and Communications

SECTION 12. Any person who—(1) offers or sells a security in violation of section 5, or

(2) offers or sells a security (whether or not exempted by the provisions of section 3, other than paragraph (2) of subsection (a) thereof), by the use of any means or instruments of transportation or communication in interstate commerce or of the mails, by means of a prospectus or oral communication, which includes an untrue statement of a material fact or omits to state a material fact necessary in order to make the statements, in the light of the circumstances under which they were made, not misleading (the purchaser not knowing of such untruth or omission), and who shall not sustain the burden of proof that he did not know, and in the exercise of reasonable care could not have known, of such untruth or omission, shall be liable to the person purchasing such security from him, who may sue either at law or in equity in any court of competent jurisdiction, to recover the consideration paid for such security with interest thereon, less the amount of any income received thereon, upon the tender of such security, or for damages if he no longer owns the security.

Penalties

SECTION 24. Any person who willfully violates any of the provisions of this title, or the rules and regulations promulgated by the Commission under authority thereof, or any person who willfully, in a registration statement filed under this title, makes any untrue statement of a material fact or omits to state any material fact required to be stated therein or necessary to make the statements therein not misleading, shall upon conviction be fined not more than $10,000 or imprisoned not more than five years, or both.

Securities Exchange Act of 1934

Regulation of the Use of Manipulative and Deceptive Devices

SECTION 10. It shall be unlawful for any person, directly or indirectly, by the use of any means or instrumentality of interstate commerce or of the mails, or of any facility of any national securities exchange—

(a) To effect a short sale, or to use or employ any stop-loss order in connection with the purchase or sale, of any security registered on a national securities exchange, in contravention of such rules and regulations as the Commission may prescribe as necessary or appropriate in the public interest or for the protection of investors.

(b) To use or employ, in connection with the purchase or sale of any security registered on a national securities exchange or any security not so registered, any manipulative or deceptive device or contrivance in contravention of such rules and regulations as the Commission may prescribe as necessary or appropriate in the public interest or for the protection of investors.

Proxies

SECTION 14. (a) It shall be unlawful for any person, by the use of the mails or by any means or instrumentality of interstate commerce or of any facility of a national securities exchange or otherwise, in contravention of such rules and regulations as the Commission may prescribe as necessary or appropriate in the public interest or for the protection of investors, to solicit or to permit the use of his name to solicit any proxy or consent or authorization in respect of any security (other than an exempted security) registered pursuant to section 12 of 78(*l*) this title.

Directors, Officers, and Principal Stockholders

SECTION 16. (a) Every person who is directly or indirectly the beneficial owner of more than 10 per centum of any class of any equity security (other than an exempted security) which is registered pursuant to section 12 of this title, or who is a director or an officer of the issuer of such security, shall file, at the time of the registration of such security on a national securities exchange or by the effective date of a registration statement filed pursuant to section 12 (g) of this title, or within ten days after he becomes such beneficial owner, director, or officer, a statement with the Commission (and, if such security is registered on a national securities exchange, also with the exchange) of the amount of all equity securities of such issuer of which he is the beneficial owner, and within ten days after the close of each calendar month thereafter, if there has been a change in such ownership during such month, shall file with the Commission (and if such security is registered on a national securities exchange, shall also file with the exchange) a statement indicating his ownership at the close of the calendar month and such changes in his ownership as have occurred during such calendar month.

(b) For the purpose of preventing the unfair use of information which may have been obtained by such beneficial owner, director, or officer by reason of his relationship to the issuer, any profit realized by him from any purchase and sale, or any sale and purchase, of any equity security of such issuer (other than an exempted security) within any period of less than six months, unless such security was acquired in good faith in connection with a debt previously contracted, shall inure to and be recoverable by the issuer, irrespective of any intention on the part of such beneficial owner, director, or officer in entering into such transaction of holding the security purchased or of not repurchasing the security sold for a period exceeding six months. Suit to recover such profit may be instituted at law or in equity in any court of competent jurisdiction by the issuer, or by the owner of any security of the issuer in the name and in behalf of the issuer if the issuer shall fail or refuse to bring such suit within sixty days after request or shall fail diligently to prosecute the same thereafter; but no such suit shall be brought more than two years after the date such profit was realized. This subsection shall not be construed to cover any transaction where such beneficial owner was not such both at the time of the purchase and sale, or the sale and purchase, of the security involved, or any transaction or transactions which the Commission by rules and regulations may exempt as not comprehended within the purpose of this subsection.

(c) It shall be unlawful for any such beneficial owner, director, or officer, directly or indirectly, to sell any equity security of such issuer (other than an exempted security), if the person selling the security or his principal (1) does not own the security sold, or (2) if owning the security, does not deliver it against such sale within twenty days thereafter, or does not within five days after such sale deposit it in the mails or other usual channels of transportation; but no person shall be deemed to have violated this subsection if he proves that notwithstanding the exercise of good faith he was unable to make such delivery or deposit within such time, or that to do so would cause undue inconvenience or expense.

(d) Wherever communicating, or purchasing or selling a security while in possession of, material non-public information would violate, or result in liability to any purchaser or seller of the security under any provision of this title, or any rule or regulation thereunder, such conduct in connection with a purchase or sale of a put, call, straddle, option, or privilege with respect to such security or with respect to a group or index of securities including such security, shall also violate and result in comparable liability to any purchaser or seller of that security under such provision, rule, or regulation.

Liability for Misleading Statements

SECTION 18. (a) Any person who shall make or cause to be made any statement in any application, report, or document filed pursuant to this title or any rule or regulation thereunder or any undertaking contained in a registration statement as provided in subsection (d) of section 15 of this title, which statement was at the time and in the light of the circumstances under which it was made false or misleading with respect to any material fact, shall be liable to any person (not knowing that such statement was false or misleading) who, in reliance upon such statement, shall have purchased or sold a security at a price which was affected by such statement, for damages caused by such reliance, unless the person sued shall prove that he acted in good faith and had no knowledge that such statement was false or misleading. A person seeking to enforce such liability may sue at law or in equity in any court of competent jurisdiction. In any such suit the court may, in its discretion, require an undertaking for the payment of the costs of such suit, and assess reasonable costs, including reasonable attorneys' fees, against either party litigant.

(b) Every person who becomes liable to make payment under this section may recover contribution as in cases of contract from any person who, if joined in the original suit, would have been liable to make the same payment.

(c) No action shall be maintained to enforce any liability created under this section unless brought within one year after the discovery of the facts constituting the cause of action and within three years after such cause of action accrued.

The Copyright Act (as Amended) (Excerpts)

Section 102. Subject matter of copyright: In general

(a) Copyright protection subsists, in accordance with this title, in original works of authorship fixed in any tangible medium of expression, now known or later developed, from which they can be perceived, reproduced, or otherwise communicated, either directly or with the aid of a machine or device. Works of authorship include the following categories:

(1) literary works;

(2) musical works, including any accompanying words;

(3) dramatic works, including any accompanying music;

(4) pantomimes and choreographic works;

(5) pictorial, graphic, and sculptural works;

(6) motion pictures and other audiovisual works;

(7) sound recordings; and

(8) architectural works.

(b) In no case does copyright protection for an original work of authorship extend to any idea, procedure, process, system, method of operation, concept, principle, or discovery, regardless of the form in which it is described, explained, illustrated, or embodied in such work.

Section 106. Exclusive rights in copyrighted works

Subject to sections 107 through 120, the owner of copyright under this title has the exclusive rights to do and to authorize any of the following:

(1) to reproduce the copyrighted work in copies or phonorecords;

(2) to prepare derivative works based upon the copyrighted work;

(3) to distribute copies or phonorecords of the copyrighted work to the public by sale or other transfer of ownership, or by rental, lease, or lending;

(4) in the case of literary, musical, dramatic, and choreographic works, pantomimes, and motion pictures and other audiovisual works, to perform the copyrighted work publicly; and

(5) in the case of literary, musical, dramatic, and choreographic works, pantomimes, and pictorial, graphic, or sculptural works, including the individual images of a motion picture or other audiovisual work, to display the copyrighted work publicly.

Section 107. Limitations on exclusive rights: Fair use

Notwithstanding the provisions of sections 106 and 106A, the fair use of a copyrighted work, including such use by reproduction in copies or phonorecords or by any other means specified by that section, for purposes such as criticism, comment, news reporting, teaching (including multiple copies for classroom use), scholarship, or research, is not an infringement of copyright. In determining whether the use made of a work in any particular case is a fair use the factors to be considered shall include—

(1) the purpose and character of the use, including whether such use is of a commercial nature or is for nonprofit educational purposes;

(2) the nature of the copyrighted work;

(3) the amount and substantiality of the portion used in relation to the copyrighted work as a whole; and

(4) the effect of the use upon the potential market for or value of the copyrighted work.

Section 406. Copyright registration in general

(a) Registration Permissive.—At any time during the subsistence of copyright in any published or unpublished work, the owner of copyright or of any exclusive right in the work may obtain registration of the copyright claim by delivering to the Copyright Office the deposit specified by this section, together with the application and fee specified by sections 409 and 708. Such registration is not a condition of copyright protection.

Section 591. Infringement of copyright

(a) Anyone who violates any of the exclusive rights of the copyright owner as provided by sections 106 through 118 or of the author as provided in section 106A(a), or who imports copies or phonorecords into the United States in violation of section 602, is an infringer of the copyright or right of the author, as the case may be. For purposes of this chapter (other than section 506), any reference to copyright shall be deemed to include the rights conferred by section 106(a). As used in this subsection the term "anyone" includes any State, any instrumentality of a State, and any officer or employee of a State or instrumentality of a State acting in his or her official capacity. Any State, and any such instrumentality, officer, or employee,

shall be subject to the provisions of this title in the same manner and to the same extent as any nongovernmental entity.

(b) The legal or beneficial owner of an exclusive right under a copyright is entitled, subject to the requirements of section 411, to institute an action for any infringement of that particular right committed while he or she is the owner of it. The court may require such owner to serve written notice of the action with a copy of the complaint upon any person shown, by the records of the Copyright Office or otherwise, to have or claim an interest in the copyright, and shall require that such notice be served upon any person whose interest is likely to be affected by a decision in the case. The court may require the joinder, and shall permit the intervention, of any person having or claiming an interest in the copyright.

Remedies for Infringement: Damages and Profits

Section 504.

(a) In General. Except as otherwise provided by this title, an infringer of copyright is liable for either—

1. the copyright owner's actual damages and any additional profits of the infringer, as provided by subsection (b); or

2. statutory damages, as provided by subsection (c).

(b) Actual Damages and Profits.—The copyright owner is entitled to recover the actual damages suffered by him or her as a result of the infringement, and any profits of the infringer that are attributable to the infringement and are not taken into account in computing the actual damages. In establishing the infringer's profits, the copyright owner is required to present proof only of the infringer's gross revenue, and the infringer is required to prove his or her deductible expenses and the elements of profit attributable to factors other than the copyrighted work.

(c) Statutory Damages—(1) Except as provided by clause (2) of this subsection, the copyright owner may elect, at any time before final judgment is rendered, to recover, instead of actual damages and profits, an award of statutory damages for all infringements involved in the action, with respect to any one work, for which any one infringer is liable individually, or for which any two or more infringers are liable jointly and severally, in a sum of not less than $500 or more than $20,000 as the court considers just. For the purposes of this subsection, all the parts of a compilation or derivative work constitute one work.

(2) In a case where the copyright owner sustains the burden of proving, and the court finds, that infringement was committed willfully, the court in its discretion may increase the award of statutory damages to a sum of not more than $100,000. In a case where the infringer sustains the burden of proving, and the court finds, that such infringer was not aware and had no reason to believe that his or her acts constituted an infringement of copyright, the court in its discretion may reduce the award of statutory damages to a sum of not less than $200. The court shall remit statutory damages in any case where an infringer believed and had reasonable grounds for believing that his or her use of the copyrighted work was a fair use

under section 107, if the infringer was: (i) an employee or agent of a nonprofit educational institution, library, or archives acting within the scope of his or her employment who, or such institution, library, or archives itself, which infringed by reproducing the work in copies or phonorecords; or (ii) a public broadcasting entity which or a person who, as a regular part of the nonprofit activities of a public broadcasting entity (as defined in subsection (g) of section 118) infringed by performing a published nondramatic literary work or by reproducing a transmission program embodying a performance of such a work.

Section 506. Criminal offenses

(a) Criminal infringement—Any person who infringes a copyright willfully and for purposes of commercial advantage or private financial gain shall be punished as provided in section 2319 of title 18.

The Foreign Corrupt Practices Act (Excerpts)

Section 78dd-2. Prohibited foreign trade practices by domestic concerns

(a) Prohibition. It shall be unlawful for any domestic concern, other than an issuer which is subject to section 78dd-1 of this title, or for any officer, director, employee, or agent of such domestic concern or any stockholder thereof acting on behalf of such domestic concern, to make use of the mails or any means or instrumentality of interstate commerce corruptly in furtherance of an offer, payment, promise to pay, or authorization of the payment of any money, or offer, gift, promise to give, or authorization of the giving of anything of value to—

(1) any foreign official for purposes of—

(A) (i) influencing any act or decision of such foreign official in his official capacity, or (ii) inducing such foreign official to do or omit to do any act in violation of the lawful duty of such official, or

(B) inducing such foreign official to use his influence with a foreign government or instrumentality thereof to affect or influence any act or decision of such government or instrumentality, in order to assist such domestic concern in obtaining or retaining business for or with, or directing business to, any person;

(2) any foreign political party or official thereof or any candidate for foreign political office for purposes of—

(A) (i) influencing any act or decision of such party, official, or candidate in its or his official capacity, or (ii) inducing such party, official, or candidate to do or omit to do an act in violation of the lawful duty of such party, official, or candidate,

(B) inducing such party, official, or candidate to use its or his influence with a foreign government or instrumentality thereof to affect or influence any act or decision of such government or instrumentality, in order to assist such domestic concern in obtaining or retaining business for or with, or directing business to, any person; or

(3) any person, while knowing that all or a portion of such money or thing of value will be offered, given, or promised, directly or indirectly, to any foreign official, to any foreign political party or official thereof, or to any candidate for foreign political office, for purposes of—

(A) (i) influencing any act or decision of such foreign official, political party, party official, or candidate in his or in its official capacity, or (ii) inducing such foreign official, political party, party official, or candidate to do or omit to do any act in violation of the lawful duty of such foreign official, political party, party official, or candidate, or

(B) inducing such foreign official, political party, party official, or candidate to use his or its influence with a foreign government or instrumentality thereof to affect or influence any act or decision of such government or instrumentality, in order to assist such domestic concern in obtaining or retaining business for or with, or directing business to, any person.

(b) Exceptions for routine governmental action. Subsection (a) of this section shall not apply to any facilitating or expediting payment to a foreign official, political party, or party official the purpose of which is to expedite or to secure the performance of a routine governmental action by a foreign official, political party, or party official.

(c) Affirmative defenses. It shall be an affirmative defense to actions under subsection (a) of this section that—

(1) the payment, gift, offer, or promise of anything of value that was made, was lawful under the written laws and regulations of the foreign official's, political party's, party official's, or candidate's country; or

(2) the payment, gift, offer, or promise of anything of value that was made, was a reasonable and bona fide expenditure, such as travel and lodging expenses, incurred by or on behalf of a foreign official, party, party official, or candidate and was directly related to—

(A) the promotion, demonstration, or explanation of products or services; or

(B) the execution or performance of a contract with a foreign government or agency thereof.

(g) Penalties. (1) (A) Any domestic concern that violates subsection (a) of this section shall be fined not more than $2,000,000.

(B) Any domestic concern that violates subsection (a) of this section shall be subject to a civil penalty of not more than $10,000 imposed in an action brought by the Attorney General.

(2) (A) Any officer or director of a domestic concern, or stockholder acting on behalf of such domestic concern, who willfully violates subsection (a) of this section shall be fined not more than $100,000, or imprisoned not more than 5 years, or both.

(B) Any employee or agent of a domestic concern who is a United States citizen, national, or resident or is otherwise subject to the jurisdiction of the United States (other than an officer, director, or stockholder acting on behalf of such domestic concern), and who willfully violates subsection (a) of this section, shall be fined not more than $100,000, or imprisoned not more than 5 years, or both.

(C) Any officer, director, employee, or agent of a domestic concern, or stockholder acting on behalf of such domestic concern, who violates subsection (a) of this section shall be subject to a civil penalty of not more than $10,000 imposed in an action brought by the Attorney General.

(3) Whenever a fine is imposed under paragraph (2) upon any officer, director, employee, agent, or stockholder of a domestic concern, such fine may not be paid, directly or indirectly, by such domestic concern.

(h) Definitions. For purposes of this section:

(1) The term "domestic concern" means—

(A) any individual who is a citizen, national, or resident of the United States; and

(B) any corporation, partnership, association, joint-stock company, business trust, unincorporated organization, or sole proprietorship which has its principal place of business in the United States, or which is organized under the laws of a State of the United States or a territory, possession, or commonwealth of the United States.

(2) The term "foreign official" means any officer or employee of a foreign government or any department, agency, or instrumentality thereof, or any person acting in an official capacity for or on behalf of any such government or department, agency, or instrumentality.

(3) (A) A person's state of mind is "knowing" with respect to conduct, a circumstance, or a result if—

(i) such person is aware that such a person is engaging in such conduct, that such circumstance exists, or that such result is substantially certain to occur; or

(ii) such person has a firm belief that such circumstance exists or that such result is substantially certain to occur.

(B) When knowledge of the existence of a particular circumstance is required for an offense, such knowledge is established if a person is aware of a high probability of the existence of such circumstance, unless the person actually believes that such circumstance does not exist.

(4) (A) For purposes of paragraph (1), the term "routine governmental action" means only an action which is ordinarily and commonly performed by a foreign official in—

(i) obtaining permits, licenses, or other official documents to qualify a person to do business in a foreign country;

(ii) processing governmental papers, such as visas and work orders;

(iii) providing police protection, mail pick-up and delivery, or scheduling inspections associated with contract performance or inspections related to transit of goods across country;

　　(iv) providing phone service, power and water supply, loading and unloading cargo, or protecting perishable products of commodities from deterioration; or

　　(v) actions of a similar nature.

　　(B) The term "routine governmental action" does not include any decision by a foreign official whether, or on what terms, to award new business to or to continue business with a particular party, or any action taken by a foreign official involved in the decision-making process to encourage a decision to award new business to or continue business with a particular party.

　　(5) The term "interstate commerce" means trade, commerce, transportation, or communication among the several States, or between any foreign country and any State or between any State and any place or ship outside thereof, and such term includes the intrastate use of—

　　(A) a telephone or other interstate means of communication, or

　　(B) any other interstate instrumentality.

APPENDIX K

Restatement of Torts (Excerpts)

Section 402A. Special Liability of Seller of Product for Physical Harm to User or Consumer

(1) One who sells any product in a defective condition unreasonably dangerous to the user or consumer or to his property is subject to liability for physical harm thereby caused to the ultimate user or consumer, or to his property, if

　　(a) the seller is engaged in the business of selling such a product, and

　　(b) it is expected to and does reach the user or consumer without substantial change in the condition in which it is sold.

　　(2) The rule stated in Subsection (1) applies although

　　(a) the seller has exercised all possible care in the preparation and sale of his product, and

　　(b) the user or consumer has not bought the product from or entered into any contractual relation with the seller.

Section 402B. Misrepresentation by Seller of Chattels to Consumer

One engaged in the business of selling chattels who by advertising, labels, or otherwise, makes to the public a misrepresentation of a material fact concerning the character or quality of a chattel sold by him is subject to liability for physical harm to a consumer of the chattel caused by justifiable reliance upon the misrepresentation, even though

　　(a) it is not made fraudulently or negligently, and

　　(b) the consumer has not bought the chattel from or entered into any contractual relation with the seller.

The Federal Trade Commission Act (Excerpts)

Section 5. Unfair Methods of Competition Unlawful; Prevention by Commission—Declaration of Unlawfulness; Power to Prohibit Unfair Practices

(a) (1) Unfair methods of competition in or affecting commerce, and unfair or deceptive acts or practices in or affecting commerce, are declared unlawful.

Penalty for Violation of Order; Injunctions and Other Appropriate Equitable Relief

(1) Any person, partnership, or corporation who violates an order of the Commission after it has become final, and while such order is in effect, shall forfeit and pay to the United States a civil penalty of not more than $10,000 for each violation, which shall accrue to the United States and may be recovered in a civil action brought by the Attorney General of the United States. Each separate violation of such an order shall be a separate offense, except that in the case of a violation through continuing failure to obey or neglect to obey a final order of the Commission, each day of continuance of such failure or neglect shall be deemed a separate offense. In such actions, the United States district courts are empowered to grant mandatory injunctions and such other and further equitable relief as they deem appropriate in the enforcement of such final orders of the Commission.

Section 7. Acquisition by One Corporation of Stock of Another

No corporation engaged in commerce shall acquire, directly or indirectly, the whole or any part of the stock; or other share capital and no corporation subject to the jurisdiction of the Federal Trade Commission shall acquire the whole or any part of the assets of another corporation in any section of the country, the effect of such acquisition may be substantially to lessen competition, or to tend to create a monopoly.

No corporation shall acquire, directly or indirectly, the whole or any part of the stock or other share capital and no corporation subject to the jurisdiction of the Federal Trade Commission shall acquire the whole or any part of the assets of one or more corporations engaged in commerce, where in any line of commerce in any section of the country, the effect of such acquisition, of such stocks or assets, or of the use of such stock by the voting or granting of proxies or otherwise, may be substantially to lessen competition, or to tend to create a monopoly.

The Clayton Act (Excerpts)

Section 8. Interlocking Directorates and Officers

No private banker or director, officer, or employee of any member bank of the Federal Reserve System or any branch thereof shall be at the same time a director, officer, or employee of any other bank, banking association, savings bank, or trust company organized under the National Bank Act or organized under the laws of any State or of the District of Columbia, or any branch thereof, except that the Board of Governors of the Federal Reserve System may by regulation permit such service as a director, officer, or employee of not more than one other such institution or branch thereof; . . .

The Sherman Act (Excerpts)

Section 1. Trusts, etc., in Restraint of Trade Illegal; Penalty

Every contract, combination in the form of trust or otherwise, or conspiracy, in restraint of trade or commerce among the several States, or with foreign nations, is declared to be illegal. Every person who shall make any contract or engage in any combination or conspiracy hereby declared to be illegal shall be deemed guilty of a felony, and, on conviction thereof, shall be punished by fine not exceeding one million dollars if a corporation, or, if any other person, one hundred thousand dollars or by imprisonment not exceeding three years, or by both said punishments, in the discretion of the court.

Section 2. Monopolization; Penalty

Every person who shall monopolize, or attempt to monopolize, or combine or conspire with any other person or persons, to monopolize any part of the trade or commerce among the several States, or with foreign nations, shall be deemed guilty of a felony, and, on conviction thereof, shall be punished by fine not exceeding $10,000,000 if a corporation, or, if any other person, $350,000 or by imprisonment not exceeding three years, or by both said punishments, in the discretion of the court.

The Robinson-Patman Act (Excerpts)

Section 2. Discrimination in Price, Services, or Facilities—Price; Selection of Customers

(a) It shall be unlawful for any person engaged in commerce, in the course of such commerce, either directly or indirectly, to discriminate in price between different purchasers of commodities of like grade and quality, where either or any of the purchases involved in such discrimination are in commerce, where such commodities are sold for use, consumption, or resale within the United States or any Territory thereof or the District of Columbia or any insular possession or other place under the jurisdiction of the United States, and where the effect of such discrimination may be substantially to lessen competition or tend to create a monopoly in any line of commerce, or to injure, destroy, or prevent competition with any person who either grants or knowingly receives the benefit of such discrimination, or with customers of either of them; Provided, That nothing herein contained shall prevent differentials which make only due allowance for differences in the cost of manufacture, sale, or delivery resulting from the differing methods or quantities in which such commodities are to such purchasers sold or delivered: Provided, however, That the Federal Trade Commission may, after due investigation and hearing to all interested parties, fix and establish quantity limits, and revise the same as it finds necessary, as to particular commodities or classes of commodities, where it finds that available purchasers in greater quantities are so few as to render differentials on account thereof unjustly discriminatory or promotive of monopoly in any line of commerce; and the foregoing shall then not be construed to permit differentials based on differences in quantities greater than those so fixed and established: And provided further, That nothing herein contained shall prevent persons engaged in selling goods, wares, or merchandise in commerce from selecting their own customers in bona fide transactions and not in restraint of trade: And provided further, That nothing herein contained shall prevent price changes from time to time where in response to changing conditions affecting the market for or the marketability of the goods concerned, such as but not limited to actual or imminent deterioration of perishable goods, obsolescence of seasonal goods, distress sales under court process, or sales in good faith in discontinuance of business in the goods concerned.

Section 3. Discrimination in Rebates, Discounts, or Advertising Service Charges; Underselling in Particular Localities; Penalties

It shall be unlawful for any person engaged in commerce, in the course of such commerce, to be a party to, or assist in, any transaction of sale, or contract to sell, which discriminates to his knowledge against competitors of the purchaser, in that, any discount, rebate, allowance, or advertising service charge is granted to the purchaser over and above any discount, rebate, allowance, or advertising service charge available at the time of such transaction to said competitors in respect of a sale of goods of like grade, quality, and quantity; to sell, or contract to sell, goods in any part of the United States at prices lower than those exacted by said person elsewhere in the United States for the purpose of destroying competition, or eliminating a competitor in such part of the United States; or,

to sell, or contract to sell, goods at unreasonably low prices for the purpose of destroying competition or eliminating a competitor.

Any person violating any of the provisions of this section shall, upon conviction thereof, be fined not more than $5,000 or imprisoned not more than one year, or both.

The Fair Labor Standards Act (Excerpts)

Unfair Labor Practices

Section 8

(a) It shall be an unfair labor practice for an employer—

(1) to interfere with, restrain, or coerce employees in the exercise of the rights guaranteed in section 7;

(2) to dominate or interfere with the formation or administration of any labor organization or contribute financial or other support to it: *Provided,* That subject to rules and regulations made and published by the Board pursuant to section 6, an employer shall not be prohibited from permitting employees to confer with him during work hours without loss of time or pay;

(3) by discrimination in regard to hire or tenure of employment of any term or condition of employment to encourage or discourage membership in any labor organization:

(4) to discharge or otherwise discriminate against an employee because he has filed charges or given testimony under this Act;

(5) to refuse to bargain collectively with the representatives of his employees, subject to the provisions of section 9(a).

(b) It shall be an unfair labor practice for a labor organization or its agents—

(1) to restrain or coerce (A) employees in the exercise of the rights guaranteed in section 7: *Provided,* That this paragraph shall not impair the right of a labor organization to prescribe its own rules with respect to the acquisition or retention of membership therein; or (B) an employer in the selection of his representatives for the purpose of collective bargaining or the adjustment of grievances;

(2) to cause or attempt to cause an employer to discriminate against an employee in violation of subsection (a) (3) or to discriminate against an employee with respect to whom membership in such organization has been denied or terminated on some ground other than his failure to tender the periodic dues and the initiation fees uniformly required as a condition of acquiring or retaining membership;

(3) to refuse to bargain collectively with an employer, provided it is the representative of his employees subject to the provisions of section 9(a);

(4) (i) to engage in, or to induce or encourage any individual employed by any person engaged in commerce or in an industry affecting commerce to engage in, a strike or a refusal in the course of his employment to use, manufacture, process, transport, or otherwise handle or work on any goods, articles, materials, or commodities or to perform any services; or (ii) to threaten, coerce, or restrain any person engaged in commerce or in an industry affecting commerce, . . .

(5) to require of employees covered by an agreement authorized under subsection (a) (3) the payment, as a condition precedent to becoming a member of such organization, of a fee in an amount which the Board finds excessive or discriminatory under all the circumstances. In making such a finding, the Board shall consider, among other relevant factors, the practices and customs of labor organizations in the particular industry, and the wages currently paid to the employees affected;

(6) to cause or attempt to cause an employer to pay or deliver or agree to pay or deliver money or other thing of value, in the nature of an exaction, for services which are not performed or not to be performed; and

(7) to picket or cause to be picketed, or threaten to picket or cause to be picketed, any employer where an object thereof is forcing or requiring an employer to recognize or bargain with a labor organization as the representative of his employees, or forcing or requiring the employees of an employer to accept or select such labor organization as their collective bargaining representative, unless such labor organization is currently certified as the representative of such employees.

Glossary

A

absolute privilege A defense to defamation; a protection given to legislators and courtroom participants for statements made relating to the proceedings; encourages people to come forward and speak without fear of liability.

acceptance Offeree's positive response to offeror's proposed contract.

accord and satisfaction An agreement (accord) to pay a certain amount, the payment of which constitutes full payment (satisfaction) of that debt.

accredited investor For purposes of Regulation D, an investor with certain financial stability who is not counted in number of purchaser limitations for Rules 505 and 506.

acid rain Environmental phenomenon caused when acid from coal smoke enters the atmosphere and then appears in precipitation in large areas, sometimes quite far from the coal-burning area.

act of state doctrine In international law, a theory that each country's governmental actions are autonomous and not subject to judicial review by the courts in other countries.

actual notice Private or individual notice sent directly to affected parties; this type of notice is effective only if the party actually receives it, as compared to constructive notice, for which publication is sufficient.

actus reus Latin term for the criminal act or conduct required for proof of a crime.

administrative agency Governmental unit created by the legislative body for the purposes of administering and enforcing the laws.

administrative law judge (ALJ) Special category of judicial official who presides over agency enforcement hearings.

Administrative Procedures Act (APA) Basic federal law governing the creation, operation, and reporting of federal administrative agencies.

advances In partnerships, loans by the partners to the partnership; makes the partner a creditor of the partnership.

adverse possession Acquisition of land title through use for the required statutory period.

affirm Action taken by an appellate court on an appealed case; the effect is that the court upholds the lower court's decision.

affirmative action Label given to employment processes and programs designed to help underrepresented groups obtain jobs and promotion.

Age Discrimination in Employment Act of 1967 Federal law that prohibits job discrimination on the basis of age; prohibits the consideration of age in an employment decision.

agency by estoppel Theory for creation of an agency relationship that holds the principal liable because the principal has allowed the agent to represent him or her as his or her principal.

agent One who acts on behalf of another and at his or her direction.

Air Pollution Control Act (1955) The first federal legislation to deal with air pollution.

Air Quality Act (1967) Federal law that designated HEW to oversee state plans for controlling pollution.

air rights Ownership rights of surface owner to air above land surface.

alter ego theory Theory used for disregarding the corporate protection of limited liability for shareholders; results when individuals treat the corporation's properties and accounts as their own and fail to follow corporate formalities.

American Competitive and Workforce Investment Act of 1998 Federal law that permits greater numbers of immigrants who are highly skilled.

American Competitiveness in the Twenty-First Century Act of 2000 Federal law that extended additional quotas for highly skilled immigrants.

Americans with Disabilities Act A 1991 federal law that prohibits discrimination in the workplace against persons with disabilities and requires employers to make reasonable accommodations for employees with disabilities who are otherwise qualified to perform a job.

answer Pleading filed by the defendant in a lawsuit; contains the defendant's version of the basis of the suit, counterclaims, and denials.

apparent authority Authority of an agent to act on behalf of a principal that results from the appearance of the agent's authority to third parties.

appellant The name on appeal for the party who appeals a lower court's decision.

appellate Adjective that describes courts and processes above the trial level; management of the appeals after trial court procedures.

appellate brief Lawyer's summation of issues of law and/or error for appellate court to consider.

appellate court A court of appeals or a court of review; a court whose function is to review the decision and actions of a trial court; does not hear witnesses; only reviews the transcript and studies the arguments and briefs of the parties.

appellee The name on appeal for the party who won a lower court's decision—that is, the party who does not appeal the lower court decision.

appraisal rights Rights of dissenting shareholders after a merger or takeover to be paid the value of their shares before the takeover or merger.

appropriation In international law, the taking of private property by a government; also known as expropriation; in torts, use of the name, likeness, or image of another for commercial purposes.

APR Annual percentage rate; a financing term representing the annual debt cost and a required disclosure under Regulation Z.

arbitrary and capricious Standard for challenging administrative agency rules; used to show decisions or rules were not based on sufficient facts.

arbitration Alternative form of dispute resolution in which parties submit evidence to a third party who is a member of the American Arbitration Association and who makes a decision after listening to the case.

area standards picketing Picketing that notifies the public that an employer's standards are lower than other firms in the area.

arraignment Hearing in criminal procedure held after an indictment or information is returned; trial date is set and plea is entered.

articles of incorporation Organizational papers of a corporation; list the company's structure, capitalization, board structure, and so on.

articles of limited partnership Contract governing the rights and relations of limited partners.

articles of partnership Organizational papers of a partnership; often called the partnership agreement; list rights of partners, profit/loss arrangements, and so on.

Asbestos Hazard Emergency Response Act (AHERA) Federal environmental legislation that requires removal of asbestos from public schools and other facilities where exposure is particularly dangerous (where young children are present).

asset acquisition Form of takeover in which another firm buys all the assets of a firm and gains control through control of the firm's property.

assignment In contract law, the transfer of the benefits under a contract to a third party; the third party has a right to benefits but is subject to any contract defenses.

assumption of risk Defense in negligence cases that prevents an injured party from recovering if it can be established that the injured party realized the risk and engaged in the conduct anyway.

attorney-client privilege Protection of client's disclosures to his or her attorney; attorney cannot disclose information client offers (with some exceptions, such as the client telling the attorney he is going to commit a crime); the confession of a crime already committed cannot be disclosed by the lawyer.

audit committee Committee of the board responsible for oversight of company financial statements.

authorization cards Cards signed by employees and required to establish the 30 percent support necessary to hold an election for a union as exclusive bargaining agent for the collective bargaining unit.

B

bailee Party who has temporary possession of the property of another.

bailment Temporary transfer of possession of personal property.

bailor Party who owns property and surrenders possession.

bait and switch Term given to advertising technique in which a low-price product is advertised and then the customer is told that the product is unavailable or is talked into a higher-priced product; prohibited by the FTC.

bargain and sale deed A special warranty deed.

bargained for exchange The mutual exchange of detriment as the consideration element in a contract.

basis of the bargain Information the buyer relies on in making the decision to make a purchase.

battle of the forms Term used to describe the problem of merchants using their purchase orders and invoices with conflicting terms as their contractual understanding; problem is remedied by § 2-207 of the UCC.

Berne Convention Implementation Act of 1988 Federal law that changed U.S. copyright law to comply with international agreement at Berne Convention.

best available treatment (BAT) An environmental law, the most advanced and effective technology for preventing pollution; a higher standard than the best conventional treatment.

best conventional treatment (BCT) Requirement imposed by EPA on point source pollution that requires the firms to use the best existing treatments for water pollution.

BFOQ Bona fide occupational qualification; a justification for discrimination on the basis of sex if it can be established that gender is a requirement for a job; also applies to discrimination on the basis of religion, national origin, and so on.

bilateral contract Contract in which both parties make promises to perform.

bilateral treaty In international law, a treaty between two nations.

bill of lading Receipt for goods issued by a carrier; used as a means of transferring title in exchange for payment or a draw on a line of credit.

Bill of Rights Portion of the U.S. Constitution that consists of the first ten amendments and includes such rights as freedom of speech, right to privacy, the protections afforded in criminal procedures under the Fourth Amendment search and seizure, and the Fifth Amendment protections against self-incrimination.

bill of sale Informal document or contract that serves to prove and transfer title to tangible personal property.

blacklisting Tactic used by employers to prevent employees involved with unions from getting work elsewhere; an exchange of employees' names to prevent unionism.

blue sky laws State laws regulating the sale of securities.

board of directors Policy-setting governing group of a corporation.

brief Document prepared by lawyers on the appeal of a case to provide the appellate court with a summary of the case and the issues involved.

bubble concept Tactic employed by the EPA in determining levels of air pollution that determines appropriate levels of release by assuming that all the pollution in an area comes from one source.

burden of proof The responsibility of the party for proving the facts needed to recover in a lawsuit.

business ethics *See* **ethics.**

business judgment rule Duty of care imposed upon members of corporate boards that requires adequate review of issues and information, devotion of adequate time to deliberations, and hiring of outside consultants as necessary for making decisions; the standard does not require foolproof judgment, only reasonable care in making the judgment.

business-to-business (B2B) transactions Direct contracts between manufacturers and customers; no middle-man transactions between producers and retailers; also refers to the practice of intertwining of customer operational records with those of the supplier for direct communication and ordering.

"but for" test In negligence, the standard used for determining whether the defendant's negligence caused the plaintiff's injury; "but for" the fact that the defendant was negligent, the plaintiff would not have been injured.

bylaws Operating rules of a corporation and its board; usually describe the officers and their roles and authority, along with meeting procedures and notices.

C

capacity Legal term for the ability to enter legally into a contract; for example, age capacity (minors do not have capacity).

causation In negligence, an element that requires the plaintiff to show that the defendant's lack of care caused the plaintiff's injury.

caveat emptor Latin term for "Let the buyer beware"; summarizes an attitude that once prevailed in contract law of a lack of protection for a buyer of defective goods.

celebrity endorsements Public figures advertising products on the basis of their personal use.

Celler-Kefauver Act Act that amended Section 7 of the Clayton Act and closed the loophole of merger through asset acquisition by regulating asset acquisitions.

certification Process of authorizing a union to represent exclusively a group of workers.

certiorari Latin term meaning "to become informed." A court agrees to hear a case when it grants *certiorari*.

charge Complaint to NLRB brought by a private party.

charitable subscription A promise to make payment to a charitable organization; a pledge; it is enforceable even though the charity gives nothing in exchange.

chattel mortgage Lien on personal property.

checks and balances Term describing our tripartite system of government, in which each branch has some check mechanism to control abuses of powers by the other branches.

Child Pornography Prevention Act Federal law that prohibited the transmission of child pornography over the Internet; struck down as unconstitutional infringement of right to free speech.

citation Name given to abbreviated description of a court case or statute; for example, 355 F. Supp. 291.

cite *See* **citation.**

civil law Laws affecting the private rights of individuals.

Civil Rights Act of 1866 and 1870 Initial act of Congress to help curb discrimination in employment; little was done with it once it was passed.

Civil Rights Act of 1964 Cornerstone of the antidiscrimination statutes; the original statute passed to prevent discrimination in housing, education, and employment.

class action suit In civil law, a suit by a group of plaintiffs with the same claims; generally used in antitrust and securities lawsuits.

Clayton Act One of the major antitrust laws; governs the control of business through mergers, acquisitions, and interlocking directorates.

Clean Air Act The first effective anti-air-pollution act and the cornerstone of air pollution legislation.

Clean Air Act Amendments of 1990 First major changes to federal environmental laws on air pollution since 1977; impose additional requirements on industrial emissions controls, auto emissions, and other types of chemical emissions that affect the ozone layer.

Clean Water Act The first effective anti-water-pollution act and the cornerstone of water pollution legislation.

close corporation A type of corporation created by statute that allows limited liability with direct tax benefits.

closed-end transaction Term used in Regulation Z to describe credit transactions with definite times for and amounts of repayment that are not ongoing; for example, retail installment contracts.

closed shop A place of employment restricting hirees to union members only.

closing argument The summary attorneys give to the jury before it deliberates and after all the evidence has been presented.

code of ethics A set of rules adopted by a company to establish acceptable behavior standards for its employees.

Code of Federal Regulations (C.F.R.) Series of volumes carrying the enactments of all federal agencies.

collateral Property subject to a lien, security interest, or chattel mortgage.

collective bargaining agreement Contract between management and labor represented by one union for a collective bargaining unit.

collective bargaining unit NLRB term for a group of employees represented by one bargaining agent and agreement; can be a plant, a national group, or a subpart of a plant.

comment letter SEC response to registration filing; requires additional information or clarification on proposed offering.

Commerce Clause Provision in the U.S. Constitution controlling the regulation of intrastate, interstate, and foreign commerce and delineating authority for such regulation.

commercial impracticability Contract defense for nonperformance under the UCC that excuses a party when performance has become impossible or will involve much more than what was anticipated in the contract negotiations.

commercial speech The speech of business in the form of advertising, political endorsements, or comments on social issues.

common law Originally, the law of England made uniform after William the Conqueror; today, the nonstatutory law and the law found in judicial precedent.

common stock Type of shares in a corporation; the voting shares of the corporation and generally the bulk of ownership.

community-right-to-know substance Under federal environmental laws, a toxin used by a business or an operation that must be publicly disclosed; EPA filing is required.

comparative negligence In negligence, a defense that allocates responsibility for an accident between the plaintiff and defendant when both were negligent and determines liability accordingly.

compensatory damages Damages to put nonbreaching party in the same position he or she would have been in had the breach not occurred.

complaint The first pleading in a lawsuit; the document that outlines the plaintiff's allegations against the defendant and specifies the remedies sought; with respect to federal agencies, can also be a formal change of rules or statutory violations by a company or individual.

Comprehensive Environmental Response Compensation and Liability Act (CERCLA) Federal law that authorized federal funds to clean up hazardous waste disposal.

Computer Software Copyright Act of 1980 Provides copyright protection for software.

concerted activities Organized economic weapons of union.

condition precedent In contracts, an event or action that must take place before a contract is required to be performed; for example, qualifying for financing is a condition precedent for a lender's performance on a mortgage loan.

conditions Events that must occur before contract performance is due.

conditions concurrent (conditions contemporaneous) In contracts, the conditions that must occur simultaneously for contract performance to be required; for example, in an escrow closing in real property, an agent collects title, insurance, funds, and other documents and sees that all the exchanges under the contract occur at the same time; the parties perform their part of the agreement at the same time.

confidential relationship A relationship of trust and reliance; necessary to establish the defense to undue influence.

confiscation In international law, the taking of private property by a government.

conglomerate merger A merger between two firms in different lines of business.

congressional enabling act Legislation that creates a new agency for enforcement of legislation or assigns enforcement of a new law to an existing agency; establishes the authority of the agency and scope of enforcement responsibilities.

consent decree For administrative agencies, a type of plea bargain; a settlement document for an administrative agency's charges.

consequential damages Damages resulting from a contract breach, such as penalties or lost profits.

consideration In contracts, what each party gives to the other as his or her part of the contract performance.

consolidation A form of merger in which two firms unite and become known by a new name.

constitution Document that contains the basic rights in a society and the structure of its government; cannot be changed without the approval of the society's members.

constructive notice Notice given in a public place or published notice, as opposed to actual notice.

Consumer Credit Protection Act Act that provides disclosure requirements for lenders and protections for debtors; more commonly referred to as the Truth-in-Lending Act.

consumer debt Debt entered into for the purpose of purchasing goods or services for personal or household use.

Consumer Leasing Act Act that provides for disclosure protection for consumers who are leasing goods.

Consumer Product Safety Commission Federal agency that establishes safety standards for consumer goods.

Contentious jurisdiction Consensual jurisdiction of a court that is consented to when the parties have a dispute; for example, U.N. courts.

contract Binding agreement between two parties for the exchange of goods, real estate, or services.

contract defense Situation, term, or event that makes an otherwise valid contract invalid.

contract interference Tort involving a third party's actions resulting in a valid contract being lost or invalidated; an unfair method of competition.

contributory negligence Negligence defense that results when the injured party acted in a negligent way and contributed to his or her own injuries.

Convention on Combating Bribery of Foreign Public Officials in International Business Transactions Treaty agreed to by OECD nations by which all agreed to make bribery of public officials a criminal act so as to curb corruption in business.

conventional pollutant EPA classification of water pollutant that must be treated prior to its release into waterways.

cooling-off period Under the Taft-Hartley Act, a provision that can be invoked by the president to require laborers threatening to strike in an industry that affects the health and safety of the nation to continue to work during a negotiation period.

copyright Under federal law, a right given to protect the exclusive use of books, music, and other creative works.

corporate opportunity A business proposition or investment opportunity that a corporation would have an interest in pursuing; precludes directors from taking a profit opportunity when the corporation would have an interest.

corporate political speech *See* **political speech.**

corporate veil The personal liability shield; the corporate protection that entitles shareholders, directors, and officers to limited liability; can be pierced for improper conduct of business or fraud.

corporation Business entity created by statute that provides limited liability for its owners.

corrective advertising Potential FTC remedy required when ads run by a firm have been deceptive; requires company to run ads explaining previous ads or run a new statement in future ads.

Council on Environmental Quality (CEQ) Agency under Executive Branch created in 1966 to formulate environmental policy and make recommendations for legislation.

counterclaim Pleading in a lawsuit in which the defendant makes allegations against the plaintiff in his or her response to the plaintiff's complaint.

counteroffer Response by offeree to offer or when offeree changes terms of offer.

county courts Lesser trial courts that hear smaller disputes and misdemeanor cases; like justice of the peace courts in many states.

course of dealing Pattern of a relationship between two parties who have contracted previously.

Court of Justice of European Communities The court of dispute settlement for the nations of the European Community.

covenants not to compete Promises to protect employers and buyers from loss of goodwill through employee or seller competition.

crime A wrong against society that carries penalties of imprisonment and/or fines.

criminal fraud A crime in which the victim is defrauded by an intentional act of the perpetrator.

criminal law As opposed to civil law, the law on wrongs against society.

cross-elasticity Economic term describing the willingness of customers to substitute various goods; for example, waxed paper for plastic wrap.

cross-examination Questioning by opposing parties of a witness in court; that is, defendant cross-examines plaintiff's witnesses and plaintiff cross-examines defendant's witnesses.

cumulative preferred stock Type of ownership in a corporation that gives the stock owners preference in the distribution of dividends and also guarantees earnings each year; in the event those earnings are not paid, they are carried over or accumulate until they can be paid.

customer and territorial restrictions Manufacturer's restrictions on retail sales locations and customers.

D

deed Transfers title to real property.

deed of trust Alternative form of creditor security in land purchases.

defamation Tort of making untrue statements about another that cause damage to his or her reputation or character.

default Judgment entered when the defendant fails to file an answer in a lawsuit.

defendant The party who is alleged to have committed a wrong in a civil lawsuit; the charged party in a criminal prosecution.

deficiency letter *See* **comment letter.**

del credere **agency** Agent who sells principal's goods to a buyer on credit and agrees to pay the principal if the buyer does not pay for the goods.

delegation Transfer of obligations under a contract; generally accompanied by assignment of benefits.

de minimis Latin term meaning small or minimal.

de novo Latin term for starting over or anew; a trial *de novo* is a special form of appeal of a trial decision that allows the case to be retried in a different forum.

deposition Form of discovery in which witnesses or parties can be questioned under oath in recorded testimony outside the courtroom.

derivative Type of investment that derives its earnings from a contractual agreement based on other obligations.

derivative suit Lawsuit brought on behalf of another through the other's rights; e.g., a shareholder suing to enforce corporation's rights.

dicta In a judicial opinion, the explanation for the decision; not the actual rule of law but the reasoning for the ruling.

Digital Millennium Copyright Act 1998 amendment to federal copyright laws that includes use of computer technology to copy music and other copyrighted materials as infringement.

digital signature Authorization for a contract provided via electronic means.

direct examination Term that describes a party's questioning of his or her own witness.

directed verdict Verdict entered by judge upon motion of a party after the presentation of either side's case; can be entered if the plaintiff has not met his or her burden of proof or if the defendant fails to rebut the plaintiff's case.

disclaimer A provision in a contract that eliminates liability such as a warranty disclaimer or a disclaimer of tort liability.

discovery Process occurring before a trial that involves each side's investigation of the case, the evidence, and the witnesses; consists of depositions, interrogatories, requests for admissions and productions, and so on.

disparagement Form of unfair competition in which a business, its trademark, or its name is maligned; business defamation.

disparate impact Theory for establishing discrimination; involves using statistical analysis to demonstrate that a particular practice or an employer's hiring practices have a greater impact on protected classes.

disparate treatment In discrimination law, the application of different rules or standards to people of different races, genders, or national origins.

dissenting opinion In an appellate court's review of a case, an opinion written by a judge who disagrees with the decision of the majority of the court.

dissenting shareholder Shareholder who has objected to a merger or consolidation and votes against it; is entitled to receive the value of his or her shares before the merger or consolidation.

dissolution In partnerships, occurs when one partner ceases to be associated with the business; in corporations, the termination of the corporate existence.

diversity of citizenship A term referring to a requirement for federal court jurisdiction that plaintiff and defendant must be citizens of different states.

documents of title Formal legal document that serves to prove and transfer title to tangible personal property.

domain registration Public filing for ownership of the name for a Web site.

domestic corporation A term used to describe a corporation in the state in which it is incorporated.

double jeopardy In criminal law, a constitutional prohibition against being tried twice for the same crime.

due diligence Under the Securities Act of 1933, a defense for filing a false registration statement that requires proof that the individuals involved did all they could to uncover the truth and could not have discovered the false statements despite their "due diligence."

due process Constitutional protection ensuring notice and a fair trial or hearing in all judicial proceedings.

duress In contract law, a defense that permits nonperformance of a contract if the party can show that physical or mental force was used to obtain the agreement to enter into the contract.

E

easement Right or privilege in the land of another.

EEOC complaint Complaint against an employer filed by either an employee or the EEOC; initiates an investigation by the EEOC.

effluent guidelines In environmental law, the standards for release of nonnatural substances into natural waters.

8-K form A filing required by the SEC under the 1934 Securities Act; an 8-K is filed by a registered company within ten days of a significant or material event affecting the company (for example, a dividend being suspended).

Electronic Communications Privacy Act of 1986 (ECPA) Federal statute that prohibits the interception of and/or eavesdropping on live conversations; designed to prevent listening device use on phone conversations, the act has reemerged with the Internet to be used against those who intercept or "eavesdrop" on e-mail.

Electronic Digital Interchange (EDI) Precursor to the Internet and B2B transactions that permitted direct ordering and replenishment between manufacturers and their customers.

Electronic Signatures in Global and National Commerce Act (called E-sign) A federal law that recognizes digital signatures as authentic for purposes of contract formation; e-sign puts electronic signatures on equal footing with paper contracts.

elements The requirements for proof of a crime.

embezzlement Name for the crime of an employee stealing funds, property, or services from his or her employer.

eminent domain In constitutional law, the taking of private property by a government entity for a public purpose, with compensation paid to the owner.

emissions offset policy EPA procedure for approval of new facilities in nonattainment areas.

employment at will Doctrine that gives the employer the right to fire an employee at any time with or without cause; the doctrine and its protection for employers have been eroded by judicial decisions over recent years.

Employment Retirement Income Security Act of 1974 (ERISA) Congressional act establishing requirements for disclosure and other procedures with relation to employees' retirement plans.

enabling act Act of a legislative body establishing an administrative agency and providing it with guidelines and authority for the enforcement of the law.

en banc French term for the full bench; refers to an appellate hearing in which the full court, as opposed to a panel of three judges, hears a case on review.

Endangered Species Act (ESA) Federal environmental law that requires federal agencies to disclose the impact of proposed projects on species listed as protected under the act.

enlightened self-interest Theory of corporate social responsibility under which managers believe that by serving society they best serve their shareholders.

environmental impact statement (EIS) Report required to be filed when a federal agency is taking action that will affect land, water, or air; an analysis of the effect of a project on the environment.

Environmental Protection Agency (EPA) The main federal agency responsible for the enforcement of all the federal environmental laws.

Equal Credit Opportunity Act (ECOA) Federal law that prohibits discrimination on the basis of race, sex, national origin, marital status, or ethnicity in the decision to extend credit.

Equal Employment Opportunity Act of 1972 Congressional act that established the EEOC and provided strong enforcement powers for Title VII provisions.

Equal Employment Opportunity Commission (EEOC) Federal agency responsible for the enforcement of Title VII and other federal antidiscrimination laws.

Equal Pay Act of 1963 Act prohibiting wage discrimination on the basis of age, race, sex, ethnicity, and so on.

equal protection Constitutional right of all citizens to be treated in the same manner and afforded the same rights under law regardless of sex, race, color, or national origin.

equitable remedy A remedy other than money damages, such as specific performance, injunction, and so on.

equity That portion of the law that originated to afford remedies when money damages were not appropriate; currently, remedies of law and equity have merged and courts can award either or both.

estoppel Doctrine of reliance; prevents parties from backing out of an obligation they have created; for example, a partner by estoppel has allowed others to use his or her name in connection with a partnership and is estopped from denying liability to third parties who have relied on that representation.

ethics Moral behavior constraints.

European Court of Human Rights A noncommercial court dealing with disputes over the treatment of a country's citizens.

exclusionary conduct Monopolistic behavior that attempts to prevent market entry and exclude competition.

exclusive dealing Antitrust term for contract arrangements in which the seller sells to only one buyer in an area.

exclusive distributorship *See* **sole outlet.**

exculpatory clause Clause that attempts to hold a party harmless in the event of damage or injury to another's property.

executed contracts Contracts in which performance has been completed.

executive branch That portion of the federal government that consists of the president and the administrative agencies; often referred to as the enforcement branch.

executive committee A working board of directors' committee that usually includes company officers and makes day-to-day decisions in between regular board meetings; manages ongoing operations.

executive order Law of the executive branch; sets policies for administrative workers and contracts.

executory contracts Contracts that have been entered into but not yet performed.

exempt securities Securities not required to be registered with the SEC under the 1933 Act.

exempt transactions Under the 1933 Securities Act, sales of securities not required to be registered, such as shares issued under a Chapter 11 bankruptcy court reorganization.

exemptions Under the Securities Act of 1933, the securities and transactions that need not be registered with the SEC.

exhausting administrative remedies Requirement that all procedures internal to an administrative body be exhausted before an individual pursues a remedy in court.

ex parte **contacts** Latin term for contacts with a judicial figure or hearing officer outside the presence of the opposing side.

express authority In agency law, the authority given either in writing or orally to the agent for his or her conduct.

express contract Contract agreed to orally or in writing.

express warranty Expressed promise by seller as to the quality, abilities, or performance of a product.

expropriation The taking of private property by a government for government use, also known as appropriation.

F

failing-company doctrine Under the Clayton Act, a justification for a generally illegal merger on the basis that the firm being merged is in financial difficulty and would not survive alone.

Fair Credit Billing Act Federal law governing credit card bills and requiring monthly statements, disclosure of dispute rights, and so on.

Fair Credit Card Disclosure Act of 1988 Amendment to TILA that requires disclosure of terms in credit card solicitations.

Fair Credit Reporting Act Federal law governing the disclosure of credit information to consumers and the content of those credit reports.

Fair Debt Collections Practices Act Federal law controlling the methods debt collectors may use in collecting consumer debts and also requiring disclosures to consumers when the debt collection process begins.

Fair Labor Standards Act (FLSA) Federal law on minimum wages, maximum hours, overtime, and compensatory time.

fair trade contracts Agreements requiring retailers not to sell products below a certain price; permitted in some states.

fair use One of the exceptions to copyright protection; permits limited use of copyright material; for example, an excerpt from a poem.

false imprisonment The intentional tort of retaining someone against his or her will.

Family and Medical Leave Act Federal law that permits unpaid leave up to 12 weeks with a job guarantee upon return; allowed for birth or adoption of child or illness of parent, spouse, or child.

featherbedding Union unfair labor practice of requiring payment for work not actually performed; for example, requiring payment for a minimum number of bricks even though the job does not involve that many bricks.

federal circuits Geographic groupings of the federal district courts for purposes of appellate jurisdiction.

Federal Consumer Product Warranty Law of 1975 The Magnuson-Moss Act; governs the definitions of limited and full warranties; requires disclosure of warranty terms.

federal district court The trial court of the federal system.

Federal Environmental Pesticide Control Act Federal law that requires registration of all pesticides with the EPA.

federal implementation plan (FIP) Under the Clean Air Act, requirements established by the EPA (in the absence of state action) regarding the control of emissions by plants and autos.

Federal Insurance Contributions Act (FICA) Federal law that requires the joint contribution by employers and employees of the funds used for the social security system.

Federal Privacy Act Federal law that prohibits exchange of information about individuals among agencies without request and notification, unless for law enforcement purposes.

Federal Register A daily federal publication that reports the day-to-day actions of administrative agencies.

Federal Register Act Federal law that establishes all the publications and reporting mechanisms for federal administrative law, such as the *Federal Register* and the *Code of Federal Regulations.*

Federal Register System Part of the federal government responsible for the publication of government notices and rules.

Federal Reporter Series of volumes reporting the decisions of the U.S. Court of Appeals.

Federal Supplement Series of volumes reporting the decisions of the federal district courts.

Federal Trade Commission (FTC) Federal agency responsible for regulation of unfair and deceptive trade practices, including deceptive advertisements.

Federal Trade Commission Act Federal law establishing the FTC and its regulatory role.

Federal Trademark Dilution Act Federal law that permits litigation to halt the use of a trademark that results in the loss of unique appeal for its owner.

Federal Water Pollution Control Act of 1972 Federal law that set goals of swimmable and fishable waters by 1983 and zero pollution discharge by 1985.

Federal Water Pollution Control Administration (FWPCA) Separate federal agency established to monitor water quality standards.

fee simple Highest degree of land ownership; full rights of mortgage and transferability.

fiduciary Position of trust and confidence.

Fifth Amendment Portion of the Bill of Rights of the U.S. Constitution providing protection against self-incrimination and ensuring due process.

finance charges For credit cards, the interest paid each month on outstanding balances.

financing statement Publicly filed document reflecting security interest.

First Amendment Portion of the Bill of Rights of the U.S. Constitution providing protection for freedom of speech and religious freedom.

fixtures Property that was once personal in nature that is affixed real property and becomes a part of it.

FOIA request Request to a government agency for information retained in that agency's files.

force majeure Clause in a contract that excuses performance in the event of war, embargo, or other generally unforeseeable event.

foreclosure Process of creditor acquiring mortgaged land for resale.

foreign corporation A corporation in any state except the state in which it is incorporated.

Foreign Corrupt Practices Act (FCPA) Federal law prohibiting bribes in foreign countries and requiring the maintenance of internal controls on accounting for firms registered under the 1934 Securities Exchange Act.

formal rulemaking Process for developing rules in an administrative agency; involves hearings and public comment period.

Fourteenth Amendment Provision of the U.S. Constitution that provides for equal protection and due process.

Fourth Amendment Part of the Bill of Rights of the U.S. Constitution that provides protection and assurance of privacy; the search and seizure amendment.

fraud Term for deception or intentional misrepresentation in contract negotiation.

Freedom of Information Act (FOIA) Federal law that permits access to information held by federal administrative agencies.

freeze-out Merger undertaken with the objective of eliminating minority shareholders.

friendly takeover A takeover of one firm by another firm when the target firm solicits or agrees to the takeover.

frolic or detour In agency law, set of rules used to determine when an agent is in the scope of employment; a frolic is a major deviation from duty and eliminates the principal's liability; a detour is a slight deviation such as lunch for a salesperson who makes calls all day.

FTC Improvements Act of 1980 Federal act that provided change in the role of the FTC and placed some limitations on its authority after the FTC's attempt to regulate children's television advertising.

full disclosure standard SEC standard for registration; materiality disclosure requirements; not a merit standard.

G

garnishment Judicial process of taking funds or wages for satisfaction of a judgment.

general partner Partner in a general or limited partnership whose personal assets are subject to partnership creditors in the event of nonpayment of partnership debts.

general warranty deed Deed that transfers title with highest guarantees of title.

geographic market Relevant geographic location for a firm's market; used as a basis for determining monopoly power and market share.

good-faith bargaining Mutual obligation of employer and union to meet at reasonable times, confer in good faith on employment issues, and execute a written agreement.

government corporation Corporation created by a government agency to achieve a social goal.

Government in the Sunshine Act Federal law that requires advance notice and open meetings of agency heads.

grand jury Special group of jurors established as a review board for potential criminal prosecutions; generally established for a year to eighteen months.

gratuitous agency Agency relationship in which the agent has the authority to act for the principal but will not be compensated.

gray market Market in which trade name goods are sold through unauthorized dealers or without authorization from the owner of the trade name.

group bids Takeover offer by more than one offeror acting in concert.

group boycotts A practice, prohibited by federal antitrust laws, in which several firms agree not to sell or buy from one or several other firms.

H

Hart-Scott-Rodino Antitrust Improvements Act 1976 Act that gave the Justice Department greater investigative authority in antitrust violations and established premerger notification requirements.

Hazardous Substance Response Trust Fund Fund set up by CERCLA for waste site cleanup that is funded by the responsible company.

hearing examiner or officer Quasi-judicial figure for agency hearings.

hearsay Testimony about the statements of another; often inadmissible evidence in a trial.

Home Equity Loan Consumer Protection Act of 1988 Amendment to TILA that requires disclosures in home equity loan documents, including the possibility of foreclosure, and allows three-day rescission period for home equity loans.

home solicitation sales Sales originated in the home of the buyer.

horizontal merger A merger between two competitors.

horizontal restraint of trade Anticompetitive activity among competitors; for example, price fixing among competitors.

hostile takeover A takeover not solicited or approved by the target's management.

hot cargo agreements Union economic weapon in which others agree not to handle the products of the struck employer.

***Howey* test** U.S. Supreme Court definition of a security; investment in a common enterprise with profits to come from the efforts of others.

hung jury Term used to describe a jury unable to come to a verdict.

hybrid rulemaking Process by which agency promulgates rules with some hearings but relies mostly on public comments.

I

Immigration Act of 1990 Federal law that requires I-9 form for every employee who is an immigrant.

Immigration and Naturalization Act (INA) Original federal act governing employer obligations on employing immigrants.

Immigration Reform and Control Act of 1986 (IRCA) Federal law imposing additional requirements on employers for lawful employment of immigrants.

implied authority Authority of an agent that exists because of business custom in the principal's operation and in industry.

implied contract A contract that arises from circumstances and is not expressed by the parties.

implied warranty of fitness for a particular purpose Warranty given by seller to buyer that promises goods will meet the buyer's specified needs.

implied warranty of merchantability Under the Uniform Commercial Code, Article 2, Sales, a warranty that the goods are of average quality, that is given in every sale of goods by a merchant.

implied-in-fact contract A contract deemed to exist because of the way the parties have interacted, e.g., accepting treatment at a doctor's office.

implied-in-law contract *See* **quasi contract.**

impossibility Contract defense that excuses performance when there is no objective way to complete the contract.

in personam **jurisdiction** Jurisdiction over the person; type of jurisdiction court must have to require a party to appear before it.

in rem **jurisdiction** Jurisdiction over the thing; a method whereby a court obtains jurisdiction by having property or money located within its geographic jurisdiction.

inadequate capitalization In corporation law, the lack of sufficient funds to cover the anticipated debts and obligations of a corporation.

incidental damages Damages suffered by the nonbreaching party to a contract as a result of the breach; for example, late performance fees on a buyer's contract because the seller failed to deliver on time.

incorporators Individuals who sign the incorporation papers for a newly formed corporation.

independent contractor Person who works for another but is not controlled in his or her day-to-day conduct.

indictment Formal criminal charges issued by the grand jury.

infant A minor; a person below the age of majority, in most states below the age of 18.

informal rulemaking Process by which an agency promulgates rules without formal public hearings.

information Formal criminal charges issued by a judge after a preliminary hearing.

infringement The use of a copyright, patent, trademark or trade name without permission.

inherence Theory of corporate social responsibility under which managers serve shareholders only.

inherently dangerous activities In agency law, those activities that carry a high risk and for which the party hiring an independent contractor cannot disclaim liability; for example, dynamiting a building to demolish it.

initial appearance In criminal procedure, the first appearance of the accused before a judicial figure; must take place shortly after arrest.

initial meeting First meeting of a corporation's organizers after the state provides certification that the corporation exists.

injunction Equitable remedy in which courts order or enjoin a particular activity.

insider A corporate officer or director or other executive with access to corporate information not available to the public.

Insider Trading and Securities Fraud Enforcement Act of 1988 Act increasing 1934 act penalties for insider trading.

instructions Explanation of the law applicable in a case given to jury at the end of the evidence and arguments.

intangible property Intellectual property, such as patents, copyrights.

intentional infliction of emotional distress Intentional tort in which the defendant engages in outrageous conduct that is psychologically damaging to the plaintiff.

intentional torts Civil wrongs against individuals that are committed with a requisite state of mind and intent to harm; includes defamation, false imprisonment, battery, assault, and intentional infliction of emotional distress.

Inter-American Court of Human Rights In international law, the court for resolution of noncommercial issues or the violation of human rights by a particular nation in North or South America.

interbrand competition Competition among like products; for example, competition between Pepsi and Coke.

interlocking directorates In antitrust law, the presence of the same directors on the boards of various companies that occupy positions in the same chain of distribution or are competitors; concern is the concentration of power.

International Chamber of Commerce Voluntary body with uniform rules on commerce and contracts.

International Court of Justice Voluntary court in the international system of law; nonbinding decisions.

Internet Corporation for Assigned Names and Numbers (ICANN) Organization that registers domain names for purposes of protection of those names as intellectual property.

interrogatories Method of discovery in which parties send written questions to each other, with responses required to be given under oath.

intervenors Interested parties who are permitted to participate in agency hearings even though they are not parties to the case.

intrabrand competition Competition among products made by the same manufacturer; for example, competition between Coke and Diet Coke.

invisible hand Theory of corporate social responsibility under which managers believe they serve society but do so in the best way by being accountable to shareholders.

J

joint venture A partnership for one activity or business venture.

judge Elected or appointed government official responsible for supervising trials, hearing appeals, and ruling on motions.

judgment The final decision of a court; formal entry of the decision or verdict.

judgment NOV Judgment *non obstante veredicto;* a judgment notwithstanding the verdict; a judgment issued by the judge after the jury has rendered a verdict; a trial court's reversal of a jury's decision on the grounds that the verdict was against the weight of the evidence.

judgment on the pleadings A dismissal of a suit by a court for the failure of the plaintiff to state a case in the complaint.

judicial branch The one (of three) branches of the federal government that consists of all levels of federal courts.

judicial review Review by appellate court of decisions and actions of a lower court to determine whether reversible errors in procedure or law were made.

junk bond Method for financing takeovers in which buyers have as their security the assets of the target firm; such security is only as good as the takeover is successful.

jurisdiction The concept of authority of a court to settle disputes.

jurisprudence The philosophy of law.

jury instructions Explanation to the jury of the law applicable in the case.

just compensation Principle in eminent domain that requires the government entity taking private property to pay the owner a fair amount.

justice of the peace courts Lower courts generally handling traffic citations and other lesser civil matters.

K

knock-off goods Goods manufactured by someone other than the trademark or trade name holder without authorization and not according to the standards of the owner.

L

Labor Management Cooperation Act Federal law providing funding for the study of alternative solutions to labor disputes.

Labor-Management Relations Act The Taft-Hartley Act; governs management conduct in its relationships with unions.

Landrum-Griffin Act Labor-Management Reporting and Disclosure Act; legislation passed to regulate unions and their governance.

Lanham Act Federal law dealing with trademark and trade name protection.

Lawyer's Edition Private publisher's series of volumes reporting U.S. Supreme Court decisions; contains summaries of the cases and the briefs of counsel.

lease Temporary possession and use of real property, or right of use and possession of personal property.

legal remedy At common law a legal remedy consisted of money damages vs. equitable remedies of injunctions and specific performance; different courts afforded different remedies in common law England but the distinction has disappeared today, and all courts have authority to award legal and equitable remedies.

legislative branch One of the three branches of government; at the federal level, consists of the Congress (the Senate and the House of Representatives) and is the branch responsible for making laws.

letter of credit Generally used in international transactions, an assurance by a bank of the seller's right to draw on a line of credit established for the buyer.

libel Written defamation; defamation in a newspaper or magazine or, in some states, on television.

license Right of access; generally oral; personal right that is not transferrable.

lien An interest in property used to secure repayment of a debt; entitles creditor to foreclosure rights in the event the debt is not repaid; creditor's right in property to secure debt.

life estate Right to use and occupy property for life.

like grade or quality Under Robinson-Patman Act, this means that there are no differences in the physical product.

limited jurisdiction Specialty courts that have only limited authority over certain types of cases with distinct subject matter; probate courts have limited jurisdiction over probate matters only.

limited liability company (LLC) A business entity with limited liability but management participation permitted by all; statutory creature.

limited liability partnership (LLP) Partnership in which *all* partners have limited liability; statutory creature with strict formation requirements.

limited partner Partner in a limited partnership who has no personal liability and can only lose his or her investment in the partnership; must be formed according to statutory requirements; cannot use name in partnership name and cannot participate in the firm's management.

limited partnership Type of partnership in which some partners have unlimited liability (general partners) and other partners have only their investments at risk in the business (limited partners); must follow statutory procedures to create properly a limited partnership.

limited partnership agreement Contract governing the rights and relations of limited partners.

line of commerce Area of business; determination used by the Justice Department in evaluating mergers.

lingering apparent authority Type of authority an agent has when the principal fails to announce that the agent is no longer associated with him or her.

liquidated damages Damages agreed to in advance and provided for in the contract; usually appropriate when it is difficult to know how much the damages will be.

lockout Economic weapon of employer in which employees are not permitted to work; shop is closed down to avoid a strike.

long arm statutes Statutes in each state that allow the state courts to bring in defendants from outside the state so long as they have some "minimum contact" with the state.

M

Madrid Agreement In international law, 1891 multilateral treaty for protection of trademarks that permits registration and protection through a centralized registrar in Geneva.

mailbox rule Timing rule in contract acceptances that provides that acceptance is effective upon mailing if properly done.

mandatory bargaining terms In collective bargaining, the terms both sides are required to discuss such as wages, hours, and so on.

market power The ability of a firm to control prices and product demand.

master-servant relationship Type of agency relationship in which the principal directly controls the agent; for example, principal controls hours and supervises work directly.

material fact (or misstatement) A statement of fact that would influence an individual's decision to buy or sell.

maximum achievable control technology (MACT) Under the 1990 Clean Air Act, the standard required for factories in controlling air emissions; replaced the old, less-stringent standard of best available technology (BAT).

mediation Alternative dispute resolution mechanism in which a third party is brought in to find a common ground between two disputing parties.

meeting the competition Defense to price discrimination that allows the defense of price reduction when competition in the area dictates that price.

mens rea Mental intent or state of mind necessary for the commission of a crime.

merchant's confirmation memoranda Memos between merchants, signed by one of them, that will satisfy the statute of frauds requirements and create an enforceable contract against both parties.

merchant's firm offer Under § 2-205 of the UCC, an offer required to be held open if made in writing by a merchant, even though no consideration is given.

merger Process of combining firms so that one firm becomes a part of the other and only one firm's name is retained.

merit review Process at the state level of reviewing securities registrations for their merit, as opposed to the federal review for full disclosure.

mineral rights Ownership rights to materials beneath the land surface.

minimum contacts Standard used for determining *in personam* jurisdiction over residents outside the state of the court of litigation; nonresident defendants must have some contact with the state to justify a court taking jurisdiction.

minimum wage Part of the FLSA that requires all employees to be paid a minimum wage.

mini-trial Alternative dispute resolution method in which the officers of two firms in a dispute listen to the key evidence in a case to see if a settlement can be determined.

minor An infant; an individual under the age of majority; generally someone under the age of 18.

Miranda **warnings** Statement required to be given to individuals when taken into custody to alert them to their right to remain silent, the fact that statements can be used against them, their right to an attorney, and the right to an appointed attorney if they cannot afford one.

misappropriation Intentional tort of using someone's name, likeness, voice, or image without permission.

misrepresentation In contract formation, misstatements of materials facts.

misuse In product liability, a defense based on the plaintiff's failure to follow instructions or use of a product for improper purposes.

Model Business Corporation Act (MBCA) Uniform law on corporations.

modify An option for an appellate court in its review of a lower court case; it is an action that is something less than reversing a decision but something more than simply affirming it. For example, an appellate court could agree with the verdict but modify the judgment amount or the remedy.

monopolizing Controlling a product or geographic market.

monopoly power The ability to control prices and exclude competition.

moral relativism Ethical theory holding that there is no absolute right and wrong and that right and wrong vary according to circumstances, often referred to as "situational ethics."

moral standards Ethical standards, as opposed to legal standards.

mortgage Lien on real property.

motion A party's request to the court for action.

motion for judgment on the pleadings A motion made to dismiss a suit for failure by the plaintiff to establish a cause of action in the pleadings.

motion for summary judgment A motion made for final disposition of a case in which there is no dispute of facts and only a dispute of law and its application.

motion to dismiss A motion made after the presentation of the plaintiff's case or the defendant's case for failure to establish a *prima facie* case (in the case of the plaintiff) or failure to rebut the presumption (in the case of the defendant).

multilateral treaty A treaty agreed to by several nations.

N

National Environmental Policy Act (NEPA) The federal legislation on environmental impact statements.

National Labor Relations Act (Wagner Act 1935) First universal federal legislation that gave employees the right to organize and choose representatives for collective bargaining.

National Labor Relations Board (NLRB) Federal agency charged with supervising union elections and handling unfair labor practice complaints.

National Pollution Discharge Elimination System (NPDES) A system established by the EPA that requires those who discharge pollutants to obtain a permit, the granting of which is based on limits and pretreatments.

nationalization The taking of private property by a government for governmental use.

natural law Law or principles of behavior that exist without being written; supreme laws that cannot be circumvented.

necessaries With regard to minors, items for which minors can be held responsible.

negligence Tort of accidental wrong committed by oversight or failure to take precautions or corrective action.

nexus Connection; a term used in constitutional analysis of the authority to tax; there must be a sufficient connection between the business and the taxing state.

NLRB National Labor Relations Board.

Noerr-Pennington **doctrine** An exception to the antitrust laws that allows business to lobby against competitors before legislative and administrative bodies, even though the effect may be anticompetitive.

Noise Control Act Federal statute controlling noise levels and requiring product labels.

Nolo contendere A "no contest" plea; the charges are neither denied nor admitted.

nonattainment area In federal air pollution regulation, an area unable to meet federal clean air goals and guidelines.

nonconventional pollutant EPA classification of pollutant that requires the highest level of treatment prior to release into waterways.

nonprofit corporations Those corporations performing a function that covers cost but does not provide a return on investment.

Norris-LaGuardia Act The anti-injunction act; one of the first federal labor acts passed to prevent courts from issuing injunctions to stop labor strikes except in dangerous or emergency situations.

novation Process of reworking a contract to substitute parties or terms, so that the old contract is abandoned and the new contract becomes the only valid contract.

nuisance Civil wrong of creating a situation (noise, dust, smell) that interferes with others' ability to enjoy the use of their properties.

O

Occupational Safety and Health Act Worker safety statute passed by Congress in 1970 that established OSHA and directs the development of safety standards in the workplace as well as systems for record keeping and compliance.

offer Indication of present intent to contract; the first step in making a contract.

offeree In contract negotiations, the person to whom the offer is made.

offeror In contract negotiations, the person who makes the offer.

Oil Pollution Act (OPA) Federal law providing penalties for oil spills and authorizing federal cleanup when private companies' cleanup efforts fail; also authorizes federal government to collect for costs of cleanup when firm or firms responsible for the spill fail to do so.

omnibus hearing In criminal procedure, a hearing held before trial to determine the admissibility of evidence.

open-end credit transaction Under Regulation Z, credit transactions without a definite beginning and ending balance; for example, credit cards.

open meeting law Law (at either state or federal level) requiring that notice be given of meetings of agency heads and that they be open to the public.

opening statement In a trial, each side's overview of the case and the evidence that will be presented.

opposition proceedings In non-U.S. countries, the patent process that allows third parties to appear and object to a patent application.

option A contract for time on an offer; an agreement to hold an offer open for a period of time in exchange for consideration.

oral argument Upon appeal of a case, the attorneys' presentation of their points on appeal to the panel of appellate judges.

ordinances Laws at the city, town, or country level.

ordinary and reasonably prudent person In negligence, standard used for determining the level of care required in any given situation.

Organization for Economic Cooperation and Development (OECD) International organization of countries committed to developing trade, initially through the elimination of corruption.

original jurisdiction Jurisdiction of trial courts; jurisdiction of courts where a case begins.

OSHA Occupational Safety and Health Administration; federal agency responsible for the enforcement of federal health and safety standards in business and industry.

overtime pay Pay rate required for work beyond the maximum forty-hour work week.

P

palming off Unfair trade practice of passing off mock goods as the goods of another.

Pan American Convention A 1929 treaty offering trademark protection to member countries.

parol **evidence** Extrinsic evidence regarding a contract.

partnership Voluntary association of two or more persons, co-owners in a business for profit.

partnership by estoppel *See* **estoppel.**

partnership by implication A partnership that exists because of the conduct of the parties rather than by agreement.

party autonomy The right of parties to determine privately their choice of law.

patent Government license or protection for a process, product, or service.

pattern or practice of discrimination In employment discrimination, a theory for establishing discrimination based on a pattern of dealing with minorities, women, and certain ethnic groups.

per curiam A judicial opinion of the full court with no judge or justice claiming authorship.

peremptory challenge Right to strike jurors with or without cause; lawyer's discretionary tool in selecting a jury; number of peremptory challenges is usually limited.

periodic tenancy Lease that runs from period to period, such as month to month.

per se "On its face"; "without further proof."

petition Often the first document in a case.

petitioner Party filing a petition; or in the case of an appeal, the party filing the appeal of a lower court decision.

picketing Economic weapon of labor unions; right to demonstrate in front of employer's place of business to display grievances publicly.

plain view exception Under the Fourth Amendment, an exception to the warrant requirement that applies when what is seen is in the "plain view" of the law enforcement official.

plaintiff Party filing suit, who is alleging a wrong committed by the defendant.

plea bargain A negotiated settlement of a criminal case prior to trial.

pleadings The complaint, answer, and counterclaim filed in a lawsuit.

point and click The process of using the Internet and a computer to form a contract—pointing to a box that indicates affirmation and clicking the mouse.

point sources In environmental law, direct discharges of effluents.

police power Constitutional term describing the authority given to the states to regulate the health, safety, and welfare of their citizens.

political speech Term given to speech of businesses related to political candidates or issues; given First Amendment protection.

pooling agreement Agreement among shareholders to vote their stock a certain way.

positive law Codified law; law created and enforced by governmental entities.

precautionary principle A principle used to guide regulations in the area of the environment and product liability; the principle mandates regulation as a prevention measure even when data are not clear as to whether harm results from product or practice (in environmental context).

precedent Prior judicial decisions; the law as it exists; *see also* **stare decisis.**

predatory pricing Discount pricing below cost for a short period of time in an attempt to drive new competition out of the market.

preemption Constitutional term from the Supremacy Clause, which provides that the federal government preempts state law where such preemption was intended or where the federal regulation is so pervasive that it prevents state regulation.

preferred stock Nonvoting shares of a corporation entitling its holders to dividend preference above the common shareholders.

Pregnancy Discrimination Act Federal law prohibiting discrimination in hiring or promotion decisions on the basis of pregnancy or plans for pregnancy.

preliminary hearing In criminal procedure, the hearing in which the prosecution establishes there is sufficient evidence to bind the defendant over for trial.

pretrial conference Meeting among lawyers and court to narrow issues, stipulate to evidence, and determine method of jury selection.

prevention of significant deterioration (PSD) **areas** Clean air areas given special protection by the EPA regarding the maintenance of air quality.

price discrimination Charging a different price for different customers on a basis other than different marginal costs.

price fixing Agreement among horizontal competitors to charge a uniform price.

prima facie **case** A case establishing all the necessary elements; without rebuttal evidence from the defendant, entitles the plaintiff to a verdict.

primary boycott Boycott by an employee or union against the employer.

primary offering In securities, the initial offering of the security for sale.

principal The employer or master in the principal-agent relationship.

private law The law of contracts and the intrabusiness laws such as personnel rules.

privity Direct contractual relationship.

probable cause Sufficient cause or grounds for the issuance of a search warrant.

probate courts Specialized courts set up to handle the probate of wills and estates and, generally, issues of guardianships and conservatorships.

procedural due process Constitutional protection that gives litigants in civil cases and defendants in criminal cases the right to notice in all steps in the process and the right of participation.

procedural laws Laws that provide the means for enforcing rights.

process servers Individuals licensed by a state to deliver summonses and subpoenas to individuals.

product liability Generic term used to describe the various contract and tort theories for holding parties liable for defective products.

product market Relevant product market for a firm; used as a basis for determining monopoly power.

professional corporation A statutory entity that permits professionals such as lawyers and doctors to incorporate and enjoy limited personal liability on all debts except for those arising from malpractice.

profit corporations Those corporations seeking to earn a return for their investors.

promissory estoppel A promise that causes another to act in reliance upon it; if the reliance is substantial, the promise is enforceable.

promulgation The process of passing administrative agency rules.

proper purpose A shareholder's legitimate interest in accessing a corporation's books and records.

prospectus A formal document describing the nature of securities and the company offering them; an ad or other description of securities.

proxy Right (given in written form) to vote another's shares.

proxy solicitation The process of seeking voting rights from shareholders.

public comment period In administrative rulemaking, the period during which any member of the public can comment on the rule, its content, and potential efficacy.

public law Law passed by some governmental agency.

publicly held corporation A corporation owned by shareholders outside the officers and employees of the firm.

puffing Offering opinion about the quality of goods and products; not a basis for misrepresentation; not a material statement of fact.

pump and dump Practice of buying a stock, touting it to many who then buy it, and then selling the stock at an inflated price; not a new practice, but it is easier and faster over the Internet.

Q

qualified privilege A defense to defamation available to the media that permits retraction and no liability so long as the information is not printed or given with malice or with reckless disregard for whether it is true.

quasi contract A theory used to prevent unjust enrichment when no contract is formed; the court acts as if a contract had been formed and awards damages accordingly.

quitclaim deed Transfer of title with no warranties.

quotas Affirmative action plans that dictate a specific number of minority or female applicants be accepted for jobs, graduate school, and so on. Outlawed by U.S. Supreme Court; can only have affirmative action goals, not specific quotas.

R

Railway Labor Act The first federal labor legislation that controlled strikes by transportation employees.

ratification A principal's recognition of a contract entered into by an unauthorized agent.

recording Public filing of land documents.

red herring prospectus A prospectus issued in advance of the effective date of a securities registration statement; permissible to release these before the registration statement is effective so long as a disclaimer that it is not an offer to sell securities is noted in red on the prospectus.

re-direct examination Plaintiff's questioning of his or her own witness after defendant's cross-examination is complete; or vice versa when defendant's witness is involved.

regional reporter Series of volumes reporting the appeals and supreme court decisions of state courts; grouped by geographic region; for example, Pacific Reporter for the western states.

registration statement Requirement under the Securities Act of 1933; a filing with the SEC that discloses all the necessary information about a securities offering and the offeror.

Regulation A Short form offering regulation under 1933 Securities Act.

Regulation D A regulation of the SEC governing the small offering exemptions under the 1933 act.

Regulation Z The Federal Reserve Board's regulation for the Truth-in-Lending Act; specifies disclosure requirements and offers examples of required forms.

Regulatory Flexibility Act Reform act for federal agency rules promulgation; requires publication of proposed rules in trade magazines so that industries and individuals affected can properly respond during the public comment period.

Rehabilitation Act of 1973 Federal law prohibiting discrimination by federal contractors on the basis of a handicapping condition.

relevant market Term used to describe the market studied to determine whether a particular seller has a monopoly.

reliance In misrepresentation, the element that establishes that the buyer placed some importance on the statement.

remainderman Interest in a third party following the death of the life tenant in a life estate.

remand Term used to describe the action an appellate court takes when a case is sent down to a lower court for a retrial or other proceeding on the basis of the appellate court decision.

rent-a-judge Means of alternative dispute resolution in which the parties hire a former judge and a private hearing room and have the judge determine liability.

repatriation Reaffiliating as a citizen of a country after having renounced that citizenship through expatriation.

request for admissions Discovery tool in which one side asks the other to admit certain facts as proven in a case.

request for production Discovery tool in which one side asks the other side to produce documents relevant to the case.

requirements contract Contract in which the buyer agrees to buy all requirements for his or her business from one seller.

resale price maintenance Practice of manufacturer attempting to control the price at which a product is sold at retail level.

rescission Process of rescinding a contract.

Resource Conservation and Recovery Act Federal law governing the transportation of hazardous materials; requires a permit for such transportation; also encourages environmental cleanup.

Resource Recovery Act Federal law that gave aid to state and local governments with recycling programs.

respondeat superior "Let the master answer"; doctrine holds principal responsible for torts of agent in scope of employment.

respondent On appeal of a case, the party who is not appealing; in a petition for a divorce, the party against whom the petition is filed.

restatement A summary of existing common law on a particular topic; for example, *Restatement of Contracts*.

Restatement of Agency A summary of the majority view of the states of the law of agency followed by courts in resolving agency issues and disputes.

Restatement of Contracts, Second General summary of the nature of common law contracts in the United States.

Restatement § 402A Portion of the *Restatement of Torts* that deals with product liability.

reverse Action of an appellate court in changing the decision of a lower court because a reversible error has been made.

reversible error Mistake made in lower court proceedings that is ruled as improper by an appellate court and that requires a reversal of the case and possible retrial.

Revised Uniform Limited Partnership Act (RULPA) New version of the Uniform Limited Partnership Act that includes changes in the rights of limited partners and distributions on liquidation.

Revised Uniform Partnership Act (RUPA) Newest uniform revision of law on limited partnerships.

revocation In contract law, the retraction by the offeror of an outstanding offer.

RICO Racketeer Influenced and Corrupt Organizations Act; federal statute regulating enterprises involved in gambling and other businesses that tend to attract organized crime figures.

right-to-sue letter Letter issued by the EEOC to a complainant after all necessary administrative steps have been taken in the case; permits the complainant to pursue court action.

right-to-work laws State laws providing employees with the right to work even though they are not union members.

Rivers and Harbors Act of 1899 A federal law revitalized during the 1960s and 1970s (prior to the enactment of specific federal legislation controlling emissions) to control water pollution.

Robinson-Patman Act Federal law that prohibits price discrimination.

rule of reason Standard for evaluation of antitrust activity that allows the court to consider various factors and does not require an automatic finding of a violation of antitrust laws.

Rule 10b-5 SEC antifraud rule.

Rules 504, 505, and 506 *See* **Regulation D;** the rules governing small offering exemptions under the Securities Act of 1933.

Runaway shop Employer economic weapon in which work is transferred to another plant to avoid the impact of a strike.

S

Safe Drinking Water Act 1986 Federal law that sets standards for drinking water systems and requires states to enforce them.

scheduled injuries Under workers' compensation systems, listed injury for which certain payments are to be made to the injured worker.

scienter Mental intent; under 10(b) of the 1934 Securities Exchange Act, a requirement of intent to defraud as opposed to a standard of negligence.

scope of employment Phrase used to describe the liability limits of the principal for the agent; an act must be committed within this scope for the imposition of liability on the principal.

search warrant Judicially authorized document allowing the search of individuals' or businesses' premises.

secondary boycott Union economic weapon in which others are asked not to deal with the struck employer.

Section 10(b) Antifraud provision of the 1934 Securities Act.

securities Investments in a common enterprise with profits to come largely from the efforts of others.

Securities Act of 1933 The federal law governing the initial issuance and sale of securities to the public.

Securities and Exchange Commission (SEC) Federal agency responsible for enforcement of federal securities laws.

Securities Exchange Act of 1934 The federal law governing secondary sales of securities, the markets, and the firms dealing with securities.

security agreement Contract that creates a security interest.

security interest Lien in personal property; created under Article IX of the UCC.

self-incrimination Protection provided under the Fifth Amendment of not being required to be a witness against oneself.

separation of powers Principle of U.S. Constitution that divides authority for various governmental functions among the three branches of government.

sexual harassment Unlawful suggestions, contact, or other advances in the workplace; prohibited under federal law.

Sherman Act Original federal antitrust law; prohibits monopolization and horizontal trade restraints, such as price-fixing and boycotts.

shopkeeper's privilege A defense to the tort of false imprisonment for store owners; allows reasonable detention of shoppers upon reasonable suspicion of shoplifting.

short-swing profits Profits made by corporate insiders during a period of less than six months between purchase and sale.

SIPS State implementation plans; state plans for attaining federal air quality standards.

Sixth Amendment Amendment to U.S. Constitution that guarantees the right to a jury trial in criminal cases.

slander Tort of oral defamation.

slander of title Slander of business.

slowdown Economic weapon that interrupts the employer's business but falls short of a stoppage or strike.

small claims court Specialized court designed to allow the hearing of claims of limited monetary amounts without the complexities of litigation and without attorneys.

small company doctrine Exemption from merger prohibitions that permits two smaller firms to merge in order to compete better against other, larger firms in the market.

social responsibility Theory of corporate social responsibility under which managers serve society by being accountable to society, not shareholders.

Social Security Act Federal legislation that provides for the benefits of social security and the payment mechanisms through FICA deductions.

sole outlet Manufacturer's only designated seller in a particular area.

sole proprietorship Method of business ownership; one person owns business, receives all profits, and is personally liable for all debts.

Solid Waste Disposal Act Federal law that provided money to state and local governments for research in solid waste disposal.

Sonny Bono Copyright Term Extension Act (CTEA) Federal law that amends copyright law to extend period of protection for copyrighted works.

sovereign immunity Doctrine that provides that courts in one country are that country's law and cannot be reversed by decisions of courts in other countries; e.g., a U.S. court cannot reverse a finding of not guilty by a court in Germany.

special warranty deed Deed that offers title protection only for grantor's period of ownership.

specific performance Equitable remedy in which party asks for performance of the contract as damages.

standing Right to bring suit; party who has experienced damages.

stare decisis Latin term for "Let the decision stand"; the doctrine of following or distinguishing case precedent.

state codes State laws passed by legislatures.

statute of frauds Generic term referring to statutes requiring certain contracts to be in writing.

statute of limitations Generic term referring to various state statutes controlling the time periods in which suits must be brought by plaintiffs; time varies according to the nature of the suit; for example, contract statutes of limitations are generally four years.

statutory law Law codified and written; passed by some governmental entity.

stipulated means In contracts, a method of acceptance specified or stipulated in the offer; if followed by the offeree, the mailbox rule applies for the timing of the acceptance.

stock restrictions Restrictions on the transfer of stock in a corporation; must be noted on the shares to be valid.

strict liability Degree of liability for conduct; an absolute standard of liability.

strict tort liability Standard established under the *Restatement of Torts* that holds product manufacturers and sellers liable for injuries resulting from their products regardless of whether they knew of the danger that caused the injury.

strike Economic weapon of employees; refusal to work for a given period of time.

Subchapter S corporation or S corporation A form of corporation for tax purposes that permits the direct flow-through of income and losses to the shareholders.

subject matter jurisdiction The right of a court to hear disputes involving certain areas of law and/or amounts.

subliminal persuasion A method of advertising using subtle and undetected means to persuade consumers to make purchases.

submarket In antitrust law, a segment of a market examined for purposes of determining either the impact on competition of a merger or the market strength of a competitor (for example, tennis court shoes as a submarket of the tennis shoe market).

substantial evidence test Basis for challenging the actions of an administrative agency on the grounds that the rule promulgated was not based on enough evidence.

substantial performance Contract defense for performing a contract slightly differently from what was agreed upon; justification for substitute but equal performance; generally applicable in construction contracts.

substantive due process Constitutional protection that requires laws to apply equally to all and not to deny property or rights without prior notice.

substantive laws Laws that give rights and responsibilities to individuals.

summary judgment Method for terminating a case at the trial court level when there are no issues of fact and only a decision on the application of law needs to be made.

summons Court document issued to the defendant in a lawsuit that explains the requirement of filing an answer and the time period in which it must be done.

Sunset Law Law that places an ending date on an administrative agency; if not renewed, an agency terminates at sunset on a particular date; the sun sets on the agency.

Superfund Federal fund used to clean up toxic waste disposal areas.

Superfund Amendment and Reauthorization Act Federal legislation extending CERCLA's authority and the liability of property owners and waste handlers for the cleanup of polluted lands.

superior skill, foresight, and industry Defense to monopolization based on "building a better mousetrap" and customers flocking to your door.

Supremacy Clause Constitutional provision allowing federal laws to preempt state laws where Congress intended or where the regulation is pervasive.

Supreme Court Reporter Series of volumes reporting the decisions of the U.S. Supreme Court.

Surface Mining & Reclamation Act of 1977 Federal law that requires restoration of surface coal mining land.

T

Taft-Hartley Act Labor Management Relations Act; federal law governing management in union relations.

takeover Process of one firm taking over another firm.

target firm The firm to be taken over in a takeover.

tender offer Offer to more than 10 percent of the shareholders of a firm for the purchase of their shares; generally part of a takeover effort.

10-K form Annual report filed with the SEC; required of all 1934 Act firms.

10-Q form Quarterly report filed with the SEC; required of all 1934 Act firms.

theft Crime of taking property away from another permanently.

three-day cooling-off period Under Regulation Z, the period a buyer has to change his or her mind about a transaction initiated in the home.

tippee Party who is privy to inside information about a corporation or its securities and uses the information to trade securities profitably.

title insurance Insurance purchased for buyer's benefit; insures the land title from recorded defects.

Title VII Portion of the Civil Rights Act of 1964 prohibiting employment discrimination.

tombstone ad Ad run in newspapers announcing an upcoming securities offering; permissible after the registration statement is filed but not yet effective; must indicate it is not an offer for sale.

tort Private intentional or negligent wrong against an individual.

tortious interference with contracts Conduct by one party that results in another's breaching his or her contract with a third person (applies also to corporation).

toxic pollutant EPA classification of pollutant that requires the highest level of treatment prior to release.

Toxic Substances Control Act Federal statute governing the control of the release of toxic substances into the environment.

trade dress The look, color, and decorative design of a business.

trade fixtures Personal property used in a trade or business that is attached to real property but is considered personal property.

trade libel Libel of a business.

trade name Name of a firm or product; entitled to federal protection for exclusive use.

trade restraints Obstacles to free and open competition.

trade secret A protected method for doing business or an item crucial to a business's success (such as a customer list).

trademark The symbol of a firm; entitled to federal protection for exclusive use.

traffic court Lesser trial court, in which traffic cases and violations of other city ordinances are tried.

transfer restrictions Limitations on the resale of shares of a corporation.

treaty In international law, an agreement between two or more nations.

treble damages In antitrust law and securities law, a civil remedy that permits successful claimants to recover three times the amount of their actual damages.

trial Process in a court of presenting evidence for a determination of guilt, innocence, or liability.

trial court First stop in the judicial system when a suit is filed; the court where the case is presented and witnesses testify.

trial *de novo* Latin for "trial again" or "trial anew."

trusteeship National union's action of taking control of a local union's treasury (through a trustee) and suspending all democratic union processes.

Truth-in-Lending Act (TILA) The Consumer Credit Protection Act; affords disclosure protection for consumer debt.

tying Anticompetitive behavior requiring the purchase of another product in order to get the product actually needed.

U

ultra vires Action taken beyond the scope of authority; with federal agencies, action taken that is beyond the congressional authority given in the enabling statute.

unauthorized appropriation The use of someone's name, likeness, or voice without permission for commercial advantage.

unconscionable term Used to describe contracts that are grossly unfair to one side in the contract; a defense to an otherwise valid contract.

underwriter In securities transactions, the brokerage house offering the shares in a company to the public.

undue influence Contract defense based on one party taking advantage of a relationship of trust and confidence.

unemployment compensation Funds paid to individuals who are without a job while they attempt to find new employment; a federal program administered by the states.

unenforceable contract A contract that cannot be enforced because of a procedural error.

unfair labor practice An economic weapon used by an employer or employee that is prohibited under the federal labor laws.

Uniform Commercial Code (UCC) Uniform law adopted in 49 states governing sales contracts for goods, commercial paper, security interests, documents of title, and securities transfers.

Uniform Domain Name Dispute Resolution Policy (UDRP) Policy of ICANN that provides the means, timing, and rules for resolving disputes over domain names.

Uniform Electronic Transactions Act (UETA) Uniform law for states that provides the rule for formation of electronic contracts.

uniform laws Series of laws drafted by groups of businesspeople, law professors, and lawyers; adopted and codified by states to help attain a more uniform commercial environment for transactions.

Uniform Partnership Act (UPA) Uniform law adopted in 49 states governing the creation, operation, and termination of general partnerships.

unilateral contract Contract in which one party promises to perform in exchange for the performance of the other party.

unincorporated association A group of individuals that acts as an entity but has no legal existence.

union shop A plant or business controlled by a union.

United Nations Convention on Contracts for the International Sale of Goods (CISG) U.N. version of Article II on sales of goods for international transactions.

United States Code (U.S.C.) Statutory volumes of congressional enactments.

United States Reports Official U.S. government reporter for Supreme Court decisions.

universal treaty A treaty accepted and recognized by all countries; for example, the Warsaw Convention on an travel.

UPA Uniform Partnership Act.

U.S. Constitution The cornerstone of the federal government's structure and the basis of private citizens' rights and protections.

U.S. Court of Appeals The appellate court of the federal system; hears appeals from lower federal courts.

U.S. Government Manual Book published by the U.S. government that includes descriptions and organizational charts for all federal agencies.

U.S. Supreme Court The highest appellate court in the federal system and also the highest appellate court for state appeals.

usury Charging interest above the statutory maximum.

V

venue Geographic location of a trial.

verdict The outcome or decision in a trial.

vertical merger Merger between a manufacturer and a retailer; a merger between two companies in the chain of vertical distribution.

vertical trade restraint Trade restraints among firms in the distribution system.

void contract In contracts, a contract that neither side is required to perform; for example, an illegal contract is void.

voidable contract In contracts, a contract one side can choose not to perform; for example, a minor can choose not to perform his or her contract.

voir dire Process of questioning jurors to screen for bias and determine whether a lawyer wishes to exercise his or her peremptory challenge.

voting trust Arrangement among shareholders to gain uniform voting and some power by signing over voting rights on shares to a trustee; shareholders still get dividends, but trustee votes the shares; must be in writing and recorded with the corporation.

W

Wagner Act National Labor Relations Act; federal law governing the rights of unions and establishing the NLRB.

warrant Court document authorizing an arrest or a search.

warranty A promise of performance or guarantee of quality on a good or service.

warranty deed Highest level of title protection in real property transfer; greatest number of warranties.

warranty of merchantability Warranty given in all sales by merchants that provides that goods are of average quality, are packaged properly, and will perform normally.

Warsaw Convention Agreement among various nations on the liability of air carriers for injuries, accidents, loss of luggage, and so on; an international agreement.

Water Pollution Control Act of 1948 First federal law directed at water pollution; authorized the surgeon general to study the problem.

Water Quality Act (1965) First federal law to set water quality standards.

watered shares Shares for which par value was not paid; shareholder is liable for the difference between what was paid and the par value per share.

Wheeler-Lea Act Amendment to the FTC Act that permits prosecution under Section 5 if a consumer is injured, even though there is no injury to a competitor.

whistle-blowing Act of an employee of a company disclosing to a regulatory agency or the press any violations of laws by his or her employer.

white-collar crime Crimes committed in business administration and/or professional capacity; the so-called "paperwork" crimes.

Williams Act Federal law governing the tender offer process.

work product An attorney's thoughts, research, and strategy in a case, nondiscoverable.

Worker Adjustment and Retraining Notification Act of 1988 Federal plant-closing law requiring advance notice of plant closures and layoffs.

workers' compensation State system of providing for payment for workers injured on the job to avoid having liability suits by employees against employers.

working requirements Non-U.S. countries' patent requirement that the process or product be placed on the market within a certain time after the patent is granted, or the patent protection is lost.

writ of certiorari Order of the U.S. Supreme Court for hearing a case; *see **certiorari**.*

Y

yellow-dog contract Agreement by employee with employer whereby employee will not join a union.

Z

Zero-based budgeting Process of agency budgeting in which the budget starts with a figure of zero rather than at the level of the previous year's budget; effect is to require an agency to justify its functions and expenditures for each budget period.

Table of Cases

Table of Products, People, and Companies

Index

CONSIDER...

E-COMMERCE AND THE LAW